The NatWest Student Book '98

The Essential Guide for Applicants to UK Universities and Colleges

KLAUS BOEHM & JENNY LEES-SPALDING

TROTMAN

This edition published by Trotman and Company Ltd
12 Hill Rise, Richmond, Surrey TW10 6UA

Nineteenth edition 1997

ISBN 0-85660-398-8

A CIP catalogue record for this book is available from the British Library

Typeset by Florencetype Ltd,
Stoodleigh, Devon

Printed and bound in Great Britain by
Clays Ltd, St Ives plc

CONTENTS

ACKNOWLEDGEMENTS

We are very grateful for the help we have received from the named contributors and the administrators of over 280 universities and colleges and of course UCAS, SCONUL and the HEFCE. In particular we would like to thank: John Sander (Student Employment Officer at Sussex University), Dr Derek Pollard, George Kiloh, Mrs Gwyn Edwards and the sixth form at Alleyn's School, Kate Millett and sixth formers at Tasker Milward School, Heather Chambers and students at Esher College.

The book would not be possible without the tremendous help we get from our student correspondents, especially those who provide so much valuable information on the ways of coping with student hardship. Many thanks to all of them.

Our special thanks to readers who have make suggestions for future editions. More please – do write to us.

Klaus Boehm & Jenny Lees-Spalding
Trotman
12 Hill Rise
Richmond
Surrey TW10 6UA   February 1997

ABOUT THE EDITORS

Klaus Boehm specialises in reference books, with a number of publishing houses. He has developed a wide range of titles including the *Dictionary of the History of Science*, *British Archives*, *The Royal and Ancient Golfer's Handbook*, *The Macmillan Nautical Almanac* and the prize-winning *The European Community* ('best single source on Europe').

Jenny Lees-Spalding was for many years academic registrar at London Guildhall University (then City Poly), working with students on first degree courses. She left to develop reference books with Klaus Boehm. She is also involved with an undergraduate programme based at City University.

Their joint titles include *Independent Careers* (a guide to becoming your own boss); and *The Equitable Schools Book*, the discriminating parents' guide to independent secondary schools ('the Wisden of the fee-paying circuit').

All their books share a common philosophy. Readers are intelligent people who make their own choices; reference books make a good starting point for preliminary investigations and developing a strategy but are no substitute for primary sources. Their books also have a European dimension, recognised by a commendation by the European Information Association.

Get a degree?
Get a job?
Get busy!

Get reading!!

Right now, you're facing some of the most important decisions you'll ever make - but with Ford, we make sure that whether you decide to go on to higher education or embark on your career now, you're opening doors rather than closing them.

That's because we offer opportunities to suit you whatever your decision - if you go to university, you could enrol on our sponsorship programme, or you might opt instead to join Ford now. Either way, you won't be giving up the chance to study for further qualifications.

ENGINEERING & SYSTEMS SPONSORSHIP

For school leavers who plan to read either an Engineering or a Systems/Information Technology degree at one of a number of approved higher education institutions.

MANAGEMENT ACCOUNTANCY TRAINEE SCHEME

You will study part-time towards full membership of the Chartered Institute of Management Accountants.

For specific details of the entry requirements for each scheme, call us on 01268 401166 or write for an information pack to the Recruitment Department, GB-15/4B-A12, Ford Motor Company Limited, Research & Engineering Centre, Laindon, Basildon, Essex SS15 6EE.

Please note that applications must be received by 28th February 1998 for the Sponsorship Schemes and 30th April 1998 for the Accountancy Scheme.

Unfortunately we are not able to consider applications from candidates who require a work permit for the UK.

These opportunities are open to both young men and women regardless of ethnic origin in line with Ford's equal opportunities policy.

FOREWORD

'Time for a change' – Student finance from here into the 21st century

Yes, it's all about to change. Student grants, student loans and the whole dog's breakfast of university finance are all due for a radical shake-up.

There's a broad consensus – even amongst vice-chancellors, the National Union of Students and the teaching unions – that higher education can only be funded with a contribution from those who benefit from it – that means YOU!

Not the bad news you might think. There are some advantages because the amount of cash on offer to you today, from maintenance grants and student loans, is far too paltry for most students to live on. At the moment, this amounts to some £3,440 which the NUS estimates will leave you with a shortfall of a good £1500 a year. And the fact is that only a third of students get the full means-tested maintenance grant (about one quarter get nothing at all). There is much student hardship. Definitely time for a change.

Most of the research for this edition was completed well before the general election. The Dearing Committee was still considering the whole issue of student finance. Both the Tory government and the Labour opposition were waiting for Dearing to recommend a fresh approach.

But today, as the new edition of *The Student Book* goes to press, we all know that we have a brand new Labour government. Although we can only guess at the timescale, the Labour party's approach to student finance is likely to be introduced while you are at university. Your prospects of receiving enough cash to see you through your course are brighter – and your chances of repaying the loan only after you can demonstrably afford to do so are a good deal better.

So what is a new Labour government likely to do?

Its approach is based on the belief that access to higher education should not depend on your ability to pay for it.

Labour judges the current loan arrangements inefficient, inequitable and a barrier to access to higher education. This is particularly because repayment is in the years immediately after graduation – when you may find real difficulty in getting a first job, setting up your first home and making ends meet.

The new government will favour a long-term mortgage approach, rather in line with the Australian system where your repayment is related to your ability to pay it and it is made through an established, efficient arrangement eg National Insurance. At the same time, they recognise the need to protect students on longer courses like medicine and architecture.

That's something to look forward to but it won't help you budget now.

Cash for Courses

You will have to budget on what's available today.

If you are starting a course in 1998 (or 1999 after a gap year), you are lumbered with the existing student grants and loans. And worse, several universities have already warned that they may charge you top-up fees – ie fees in excess of what your LEA will pay for you. When you have a budget, you will almost certainly find a large gap between what you can rely on getting and what you will inevitably spend during your course – often as large as £8000.

Then you will have to start being resourceful. You may find you can borrow from parents and/or banks. The majority of students (90%) now have a job at some point at university, very many during term time. You will find information on getting jobs locally, and perhaps the help given by the university, in *Where to Study;* basic budgeting information and detail on how to get the money is in *Cash for Courses*.

It's worth getting the sums right, so that your time as a student is not blighted by being broke – or at least not all the time.

Klaus Boehm and Jenny Lees-Spalding
Friday 2 May 1997

SPONSOR'S INTRODUCTION

Helping you make the most of being a student

Starting at college or university can be an exciting time, but deciding where to go can be a bit bewildering. To make it easier, NatWest is pleased to bring you this year's Student Book, which will help you choose the best place to study **and** make the most of your time when you're there.

Being a student means you probably have to make the most of a fairly small budget. Juggling your finances between having a good time and paying your rent can be a hard task. So it's important to choose a bank which understands and can help smooth the way. Which is why you should talk to NatWest, we can take the hassle out of managing your money and leave you with more time to enjoy yourself.

We're closer when you need us . . .

NatWest has more student branches on or near campus than any other bank. Plus, you'll have access to over 15,000 cash machines all over the country. Which means that we'll be close at hand when you need us.

. . . and students are one of our specialist subjects

We also have special Student Banking Teams at selected NatWest branches. They work with students all year round and can suggest ways to manage on a tight budget or provide useful advice when it's needed. So whenever you need help to make your money go further, you'll know exactly who to turn to.

We also have student advisers at other student branches, all over the country, so wherever you're going to study, we'll be there to help.

Why not find out more?

Finding out more about how NatWest can help you enjoy your student life is probably one of the simplest things you'll do this year.

So if you're going to be studying next year, or even the year after, why not call **0800 200 400**, Monday to Friday 8am–8pm, Saturdays 9am–6pm, or pop into a branch today and speak to a member of staff? They'll be delighted to give you more details on the NatWest Student Account.

In order to maintain and improve our services we may monitor and record your phone calls with us.

HOW TO GO ABOUT IT

BEFORE YOU APPLY

APPLY IN HASTE, REPENT AT LEISURE

To start off with, you'll need to be clear about your personal strategy so that your decisions match your own aims in life. Apply in haste, repent at leisure.

Are you looking for a degree as a means to an end – like a professional qualification – or as an end in itself? Is getting a degree worth all the hassle – your time, your effort and, most importantly, your money and the debt that you will almost inevitably take away with you on graduation? And if it is, do you want to take a year off before you start? Lots of big questions.

A degree as a means to an end

If you see your degree simply as the key to a specific career or professional qualification, start from the end and work backwards. If you are aiming at a profession, then you'll need to know which degrees will qualify you or whether you can choose from a range of degree courses and pick up the professional qualifications afterwards. Don't assume that you must always take the relevant degree: you've obviously got to go to a medical school to be a doctor but many accountancy firms, for example, positively prefer your degree to be in something different and for you to learn the accountancy afterwards. So you must be clear. You usually qualify quicker if you take the specialist degree; but if you are not sure, the longer route has advantages (eg you may be more marketable with a BSc than a BEd if you decide teaching is not for you).

Each profession has its own requirements; get the facts from the professional societies themselves. Listed under *Professional Qualifications* in *What's What in Higher Education*, they are very good at providing you with what you need and helpful on the telephone.

A degree as an end in itself

Happily there are still lots of students studying subjects for their own sake – often those who are more confident of finding their place in the job market after doing well on their degree course. If you are so inclined, don't let anyone dissuade you. But you may have to top it up later with occupational training or a professional qualification – regard your degree as a passport not a qualification for the job itself.

Do I want to go to university at all?

Prolonging your education is no prescription for success. If you are being rushed into applying for a 1998 start, keep cool.

You will find yourself under pressure to apply from all directions – from parents, school teachers and the fact that that's what all your mates are doing. A third of 18-year olds now go on to higher education – about 90% of any sixth form. Can you afford to stand out from the crowd?

Well, you can keep your options open – you can apply now for deferred entry; or apply for a place which you can turn down if you change your mind; or simply postpone your decision until after your A-levels. Don't let your agonising get in the way of your A-levels – ultimately it's having the best possible grades which matter, whether you apply now or leave it for a few years.

And if you come back to education later, you won't be alone. About 30% of first degree students are now over 21 when they start the course; if you are well organised, it might mean you have more money in the bank than the average 18-year old too. And if you make your first million before you're 25, you may skip university altogether.

Is a degree worth your money?

You'll have to decide that for yourself. There are no useful general answers.

You could start by looking at it as a business decision. There are real costs to be weighed against (uncertain) future benefits: you will be investing your time, energy and cash for the next three years in return for, you hope, greater employability and higher salary in the longer term, in addition to less tangible benefits such as friends, culture, independent learning, broader horizons ... But degree courses are no longer cost-free. Do the sums work out for you?

This will depend partly on the time frame you are prepared to consider. A six or seven year horizon is probably the longest that makes sense – you usually have to repay your student loan in five.

And much will depend on your job prospects. You could qualify as a doctor and still not find a job. Alternatively you could move straight into a job with only your A-levels behind you.

Think about the advantages to you of, say, starting as a trainee in a supermarket next year, as compared to starting as a graduate trainee in the same supermarket in the year 2001. What would the costs and benefits of a degree course look like?

But of course there are other things to take into account – there is more to life than money. A university education can help you discover and nurture interests that will be with you for the rest of your life – cultural, sporting, political, social, not to mention what you study for the next three years and the friends you make.

So try writing down your own estimated costs and benefits – here are some suggested items:

- **Costs**   Lost income (even if you have a grant, you have no full time job); day to day expenses (over and above your grant); cost of money (interest on overdrafts and loans); length of course (the number of years determines the total cost).
- **Benefits**   Your own chance of getting a job or a better job; higher income (graduates have tended to earn more than non-graduates); lifestyle (independence, time to try new things ...).
- **Net Balance** Weigh them up and come up with an answer for you.

Taking a year off

Taking time off between school and university can be a good thing in terms of your personal development, work experience and future job prospects and it is certainly worth looking at the possibilities – even if you are in a hurry to complete your degree and find a job. In practice, however, it's often the parents who are keen for their children to get on with their education (looking forward to the day when you're not a drain on their cash no doubt), so it's worth having some well thought-out plans when you put the proposition to them.

Many universities favour a year off and most will accept applications in 1997 for entry in 1999. Or you can apply next year, after you know your A-level grades (and so target your UCAS choices more accurately), but you would have to plan your gap year around any possible interviews.

A gap year is only any use, of course, if you are use it positively – not just mooching around the house or working a couple of hours a day in the local launderette. If you can use it to rake in some cash to help fund your studies, so much the better.

A two year planning horizon is recommended by people experienced in the field so, if possible, start planning in the first year of your A-level course. If money isn't the crucial consideration, you need to decide whether to go for real work experience or travel – or combine the two. One advantage of travel, if you have not lived away from home before, is that it forces you to live on a budget which is a vital experience for the modern student. There are plenty of ways of filling the year and organisations offering structured approaches; but unless you get your application in early you'll find the schemes get overbooked. Try looking at any of the following publications:

> *The Gap Year Guidebook*, Peridot Press, 2 Bleinheim Crescent, London W11 1NN
>
> *Opportunities in the Gap Year*, ISCO, 12a-18a Princess Way, Camberley, Surrey GU15 3SP
>
> *A Year Between*, Central Bureau for Educational Visits and Exchanges, 10 Spring Gardens, London SW1A 2BN
>
> *Voluntary Work and Young People*, National Youth Agency, 23 Albion Street, Leicester LE1 6GD
>
> *The International Directory of Voluntary Work*, 9 Park End Street, Oxford OX1 1HJ

Or you can approach some of the following organisations:

> Gap Activity Projects (GAP), 44 Queen's Road, Reading RG1 4BB
>
> Project Trust, The Hebridean Centre, Ballyhough, Isle of Coll, Argyll, Scotland PA78 6TE
>
> Raleigh International, Raleigh House, 27 Parson's Green Lane, London SW6 4HZ
>
> Schools Partnership Worldwide, 17 Dean's Yard, London SW1P 3PB
>
> Community Service Volunteers, 237 Pentonville Road, London N1 9NJ
>
> Kibbutz Representatives, 1a Accommodation Road, London NW11 8ED
>
> British Trust Conservation Volunteers, 36 St Mary's Street, Wallingford, Oxfordshire OX10 0EU
>
> British Institute in Florence, Palazzo Lanfredini, Lungarno Guicciardini 9, 50125 Florence, Italy

IF I WANT A DEGREE – WHAT NEXT?

Find out as much as you can for yourself.

The Student Book

Once you've decided that you want a degree, you'll need to get a strategy and make your own shortlist. Nobody can do that for you as well as you can do it for yourself. There is a mind-boggling mass of information to work through and the best place to start is *The Student Book*. It's aim is to get you started, whatever your own interests and academic position. You can start with any of the following sections:

How to go about it – how to apply, how to get the money, how to survive your first year, and what's what in higher education.

Where to Study – over 280 university and college profiles

Shortlisting – helps you begin shortlisting, whether you start with a place and want to know which universities are there, or start with a subject and want to know where it is taught, or want to know which are the top departments or universities.

Browse through *The Student Book*, then list the prospectuses worth getting.

Basic reference worth getting

Five free sources are worth getting hold of for yourself if you are considering their subject matter.

Charter for Higher Education (Freepost EDO 3138, London E15 2BR)

A Mature Student's Guide to Higher Education (UCAS, Fulton House, Jessop Avenue, Cheltenham, Glos GL50 3SH)

Student Grants and Loans (DFEE, Publications Centre, PO Box 6927, London E3 3NZ; tel 0171 510 0150, fax 0171 510 0196. Also available from your local education authority or school)

UCAS Handbook (UCAS, Fulton House, Jessop Avenue, Cheltenham, Glos GL50 3SH)

The European Choice: A Guide to Opportunities for Higher Education in Europe (DFEE, Publications Centre, PO Box 6927, London E3 3NZ; tel 0171 510 0150, fax 0171 510 0196).

Library reference books worth consulting

These are basic reference books. You can refer to them in your school, careers or local library.

Commonwealth Universities Yearbook (Association of Commonwealth Universities)

University and College Entrance: The Official Guide (Association of Commonwealth Universities for the Committee of Vice-Chancellors and Principals)

Entrance Guide to Higher Education in Scotland (COSHEP Committee of Scottish Higher Education Principals)

Degree Course Offers (Trotman)

Designated Courses (Department for Education and Employment)

GNVQs and Higher Education – Entry Conditions (GATE)

Guide to Courses and Careers in Art, Craft and Design (National Society for Education in Art and Design)

Design Courses in Britain (Design Council)

A Guide to Art & Design Courses: On Course for 1998 (Trotman)

The UK Guide to Erasmus (ISCO Publications, 12a-18a Princess Way, Camberley, Surrey GU15 3SP).

Prospectuses

Get hold of them; don't wait for your school to receive them from any of the central distribution systems. Prospectuses are your best primary source on universities and colleges. And they are improving. Some are still little better than glossy sales literature in which real facts are scarce – an astonishing number still lack even a contents page, an index or list of subjects offered. Some are beautiful, especially for those of the more ambitious art schools. But increasingly they are well constructed documents which tell you a good deal of what you want to know. Beware glossy photographs: a beautiful sylvan scene might not be the whole view; a turn of 180° may reveal the abattoir. Many prospectuses oversimplify and, while usually accurate in detail, may sin by omission. They usually contain hard information on courses, degrees, accommodation (or lack of it) and facilities. Some are full of disclaimers saying they may not be able to deliver what's described anyway ('This prospectus is provided for illustration purposes only'). Read your prospectuses several times – to make comparisons between them and for the detail (though they date quickly). Read between the lines. Try to identify the ethos. See what the prospectus says the strengths are (eg sport, religion); they may or may not match yours. They may have a video too.

Constituent colleges of universities (eg Cambridge, London, Oxford) have individual prospectuses. Departments/faculties often produce their own guides which list staff and research interests. You might be able to gauge the nature, direction and tone of a department from them. Many prospectuses and departmental guides now indicate the A-level grades or UCAS points which they are looking for.

Alternative prospectuses

Some students unions (SUs) produce alternative prospectuses to give a 'truer' picture for potential applicants of what the place is actually like – a few have an alternative prospectus video. They can be bitchy, selectively informative and moderately amusing; on the whole they're good and useful. Well worth a look, particularly if you're applying for accommodation, want to know the political leaning of the SU, or the idiosyncrasies of the more obvious student cliques. Many SUs are pleased to talk directly to sixth formers who take the trouble to contact them (see the profiles in *Where to Study* for contact points).

Open days

Most universities, colleges and departments hold open days for prospective students. These give you the opportunity to see the campus and town as well as any facilities that are particularly relevant to your choice of course (computer centre, studios etc). You may be able to reduce the cost of travel by trying to bunch the open days you attend.

If your school doesn't have details of open day dates, contact the university direct to find out if and when they take place. Sometimes the information is in the prospectus. Open days may only be available to those who have been offered a place. If open days are offered – go. Don't even think of spending three years of your life at a place you haven't visited.

Students with children: extra checks

Studying with a young child has its special problems and you need to address them before you apply. Katie Vincent writes:

'If you have a young child, it's really important that you find out about nursery facilities *before* you fill in your UCAS form. Once you have made your choices you will be stuck with them. Ring each of your possible choices and speak to the head of the nursery. Ask about waiting lists, minimum age and how you book a place. If your child is under two, don't apply for your own course until you have confirmed your nursery arrangements (many college nurseries will not accept children under two). And don't forget to budget for nursery costs. If your child is over five, find out about local schools and how to get into them. If you are planning to move out of your present locality you'll need to sort out accommodation possibilities early. Halls of residence do not usually accept children but some universities and colleges have family accommodation; keep bugging them and you might get into it.'

Many of the profiles in *Where to Study* describe the nursery arrangements and some college education departments have a nursery of their own for teaching purposes. Unlike most students, single parents may claim housing benefit (and council tax benefit); find out from your local DSS office or The National Council for One Parent Families (255 Kentish Town Road, London NW5 2LX, Tel 0171 267 1361).

Students with disabilities: extra checks

Like everyone else, you need to decide what you want to study and why, find out where it's taught and think about where you would like to live. But you also need to know if the institutions have the facilities and support services that you need. They should have – there are probably over 8,000 students with disabilites at British universities. A few have state of the art facilities like libraries for the partially blind.

Check on the facilities before you make your final shortlist. Skill (National Bureau for Students with Disabilities; 336 Brixton Road, London SW9 7AA; 0171 274 0565) recommends that you make direct contact with individual universities and colleges so you can discuss your needs, both for studying and daily living. You can then find out if you think that is the right place for you and also how they may be able to help you. Most universities and colleges have an special adviser or co-ordinator who you can talk to. You will probably be able to arrange a fact-finding visit if that would be helpful. Many establishments can now provide or help organise specialist support services, eg readers, note-takers, transcription, and many have specialist accommodation that they can make available to students throughout their course. Provision does vary, so always make individual enquiries. Make contact early, they may be able to improve their facilities in some way before you get there.

ENTRANCE REQUIREMENTS

You'll need to know about entrance requirements in general and, much more tricky, the requirements of the particular courses that interest you.

The present normal **minimum** for a first degree course (other than art & design) are: 5 subjects at GCSE to a minimum of grade C, of which 2 are passed at A-level; or 4 subjects at GCSE to a minimum of grade C, with 3 passed at A-level. (For the oldies, O-level passes and CSE grade 1 passes are accepted in place of GCSE.) Most universities will only accept AS-levels in place of a third A-level. Other qualifications such as Advanced GNVQs, Scottish Certificate of Sixth Year Studies, International Baccalaureate (IB) and many overseas qualifications are also accepted. Scottish Highers are the minimum for many Scottish universities but not usually elsewhere. If you have qualifications which do not appear in the prospectus, check directly before you apply. A recognised qualification in English language, such as GCSE or the JMB test, is normally required. In addition there may be special course or faculty requirements.

Remember that in practice most universities and colleges have higher requirements than these and they change annually. Conditional offers may be expressed by UCAS either specifically in terms of grades you must actually get, or the number of points your AS/A-level results must add up to on the following scale:

Grade	UCAS Points	
	AS-level	A-level
A	5	10
B	4	8
C	3	6
D	2	4
E	1	2

Scottish Highers are rated by UCAS on the scale A=6 B=4 C=2 but some Scottish institutions apply their own points ratings. The position should, however, be quite plain in any written offers. Neither the International Baccalaureate (IB) nor GNVQs score in the UCAS points system.

Entrance requirements may be waived or modified for mature students, usually defined as aged 21 and over. You will need to prove your willingness and ability to learn and some universities and colleges actively encourage mature student applications; others are little interested.

There are a number of access and foundation courses, which help you return to study or pick up eg science basics before a science degree. These may be accepted by some universities and colleges instead of the published entrance requirements. Art foundation courses are a special case: you may need to take an art foundation course, even if you have A-levels, in order to be accepted on to some art and design degree courses (check individual prospectuses).

MAKING A SHORTLIST

You can't apply to them all, so you need to make a shortlist. There are lots of things you need to consider. It's very personal and time-consuming. Our section on *Shortlisting* helps you start finding the universities and colleges located in your favourite city, the ones that teach your favourite subject and which are the top places. Here are some pointers:

University/College

SIZE AND PLACE
You need to find a congenial place to spend the next few years of your life. Do you want to be near home or are you anxious to put several hundred miles between you and your parents? Do you want a large, busy university with ten thousand students or a small cosy place where you'll know everyone?

RESEARCH

The quantity and quality of research going on in a university is a good measure of its standing. If you're really good, you will get into and thrive in the top places. If you're not, you are probably wasting a valuable UCAS choice if you apply there. It's all part of the game of accurately assessing yourself and your chances. To identify the top 50 institutions and the top departments in each subject, look at our *Research Quality Search Index*.

EMPLOYABILITY

Many employers are fairly conservative and still prefer graduates from Oxbridge or the universities well known in their field (eg Imperial for physics, LSE for economics) – or just the ones they have heard of. Despite claims to the contrary, all degrees are not equal in employment terms; those with some work experience as part of the course often have the most employable graduates. Ask about the employment record when you go for an open day and don't be fobbed off by waffle.

Subject and course

POPULARITY

Some subjects are highly competitive; in others they are crying out for students. Bear this in mind although don't, of course, apply for something you can't do. It's well known that law and veterinary science are two of the most difficult subjects to get into, but do you know that over 100,000 people apply for business studies? Conversely, if you have the minimum A-levels – or a science access course – you can walk into physical science degrees all over the country; and there are lots of incentives to attract people to engineering courses, particularly if you missed out on the right A-levels.

GETTING IN

Courses much in demand will be able to ask for higher than average grades; for others you only need the minimum requirements. So don't waste applications applying to courses which consistently ask for grades hopelessly higher than you are likely to get. Conversely, beware of courses which ask for the minimum grades if you are a high-flier. Many prospectuses give the offers made last year; look at Brian Heap's *Degree Course Offers* in your school/college library.

SUITABILITY

There are well researched tests to assess your suitability for a subject (eg Centigrade, contact Cambridge Occupational Analysts Ltd, Sparham, Norwich NR9 5AQ). Some universities make a real effort to help you sample subjects at first degree level before you apply, eg London University runs a sixth form summer school.

EMPLOYABILITY

There are lots of vocational degrees, which is fine if you *know* you want to stay in that area after graduation. Some other degrees may give partial exemption from professional qualifications or lead towards a range of jobs in a general way. For the remainder, you will have to ask about the employment record of specific courses.

What does matter is that you get a good degree; people with firsts really do earn more. And getting a good degree is partly dependent on selecting a subject that will grab you for the full duration of the degree course. So, if you **want** to read history or Akkadian, go for it – and worry about employers' demands later.

Costs

Don't forget costs. Can you afford it?

First and foremost, what are your chances of university accommodation, which is usually (but not always) cheaper? Can you afford the local rents (living in Bradford is cheaper than London; living at home probably cheaper than anywhere)? What is the distance from home in terms of travel costs at the beginning and end of term? Do the courses attract a mandatory grant? Are you locked into the costs for 3 or for 4 years? Is the university contemplating top-up fees? And what financial safety nets are provided if you get it all wrong?

A sign of the times is that some university prospectuses warn you to make sure that you have the money to pay all your expenses, not just their fees. But they offer to help you estimate them too.

GET A STRATEGY

Get a strategy which dovetails into the sort of A-level grades you can reasonably expect to get. You'll soon be sick to death of prospectuses, teachers, careers services, relatives and friendly advice – but listen to everything you're told and then ignore two-thirds of it. You parents may have a view (and you will probably remain financially dependent on them, so you should at least listen). But the choice of where to study and what to study is yours and yours alone. Avoid tunnel vision and don't be frightened of trying something you haven't done before. Don't be indoctrinated – you know your strengths and weaknesses better than anyone. Remember, you're choosing where to spend the next 3–4 years and laying the foundations for the rest of your life. So you need a personal strategy – now.

HOW TO APPLY

WHERE TO APPLY

You apply for a first degree course in one of two ways: through UCAS or direct. Each of our university and college profiles in *Where To Study* tells you which method to use.

UCAS processes applications for nearly all full-time degree courses at universities and colleges of higher education – including most studio-based art and design courses. UCAS is a sort of post office to which you make a single application; UCAS makes sure this is sent to the admissions staff at all of the institutions you have specified and makes sure they reply to you. UCAS plays no part at all in the selection process: the universities and colleges decide whether to admit you and on what terms.

There is only a handful of places to which you apply direct. Apart from the Open University, these institutions are mostly specialist colleges in eg music, drama or agriculture and some Scottish art colleges. There is no limit to the number of applications you make to them.

YOUR UCAS APPLICATION

In theory applying through the UCAS scheme is pretty simple – UCAS provides an orderly procedure and timetable for you to make up to six course applications by completing just one application form and letting UCAS do the rest. Not too difficult you might think.

Once you've ploughed through the 672 pages of the *UCAS Handbook* and the eight pages of notes that accompany the UCAS form – 106 notes in all (plus boxes containing scores more), set in a tiny typeface – you may have changed your mind.

Start with the *UCAS Handbook*. You can make up to six choices on the form, and for each you have to enter at least three separate codes – one for the name of the university or college, another for its number, and another for the course code, before noting the shortened course title in its officially abbreviated form – not in English but a fourth code. And if your chosen university has several campuses, there may be a campus code too. Don't try tackling all this without the university/college prospectuses to hand.

For those with ambitions in art and design, life is even more complicated with two overlapping systems and timetables.

How does it all end? UCAS gives you each university/college's decision as it is made. So you could have up to six offers of places. Don't refuse any until you have heard from them all, because the conditions attached to offers may be very different. Then you accept only two places – one first choice and one as a fall back (they give you a month to decide). If later, in August, you find your A-level results are not up to scratch UCAS will try to help you find a place through clearing.

That's the UCAS structure in general – got it? If so, here's a step by step approach to the nitty gritty and – most important – your application calendar for a 1998 start.

WANT TO HELP WITH THE NEXT EDITION? SEE PAGE 66

UCAS – THE NITTY GRITTY

UCAS, the Universities and Colleges Admissions Service to give it its full name, operates the central admissions scheme on behalf of all UK universities (except the Open University) and most colleges of higher education. You apply to UCAS for most full time first degree courses, including studio-based art and design courses (and HNDs). Its address is UCAS, PO Box 67, Cheltenham, Glos GL50 3SF, and it has a helpline (01242 227788; for the hard of hearing 01242 225857).

Applicants fill in a single application form (see *Filling in Forms*) and name a maximum of six courses, usually at different places. UCAS forwards copies of the applicant's form to the named universities/colleges and they send their decisions to the applicant through UCAS. Before long you may be able to apply via the internet and you can already use it to contact some universities and colleges.

Try to get your application in early – well before the deadline – or you may find you miss out. For entry in autumn 1998 applications must be with UCAS by 15 December 1997 (or 15 October 1997 if one of your choices is Oxford or Cambridge; there are other differences too so look them up in *Where to Study*).

First, you need the UCAS application form and *UCAS Handbook* (you must have this because you need the institution and course codes to fill in the form). You will either get these from your school/college, or from your local careers office or UCAS if you have left school. The *UCAS Handbook* will cost you £5 if you are outside the UK. Consult prospectuses; choose up to six courses, which may include different courses at the same institution, a mixture of degrees at different institutions, and more than one subject. The choice is yours. But if your choices are for medical or dental courses you are advised to use your last one or two choices for a different subject.

- Fill in the form (black ink only and be meticulous about reference codes);
- Complete and stamp the UCAS acknowledgement card;
- Buy a postal order for the application fee (amount not known at the time of going to press, but for 1997 entry it was £12, £4 to apply for only one course). Check with your school/college: at some you pay the school and they make a single payment themselves;
- Give form and fee to a referee (usually your headteacher); ask your referee to forward form, fee and confidential statement to UCAS.

You will be sent your acknowledgement card (expect delays at Christmas if you apply in December). Then, once your application and choices have been recorded on the UCAS computer, you will be sent an acknowledgement letter, giving an application number and a list of the institutions to which the form has been forwarded. You should check these details carefully. You cannot alter your application form once it has reached UCAS.

If UCAS receives your application by 15 December 1997 your chosen universities/colleges should normally have decided whether to offer you a place by 30 April 1998. If you have not heard by the first week of May, contact UCAS. After May, you will be restricted as to the number of conditional offers you may hold.

If you are taking A-levels in 1998, UCAS will receive your A-level results direct from your A-level board in August. If you have met the conditions of your offer, it is yours by right if you want it. UCAS will confirm your place within 10 working days; if you have not heard by day 11, check direct with the university. If your results are lower than those specified in the offer you may still be given the place but that decision lies entirely at the discretion of the university.

If you are unsuccessful in all six choices, there is the summer scramble known as clearing when you might still find a place as the universities and colleges try to fill all remaining vacancies. Universities have no real idea how many conditional offers to make, so there are some good courses on offer during clearing and up to 20% of places are filled then. You will automatically be sent information on clearing if you are eligible. There is nothing to prevent you from getting in touch with any university or college direct and you might get a verbal offer which will later be confirmed through UCAS. Go for it! If your A-level results are a lot better than you (and probably your academic referees) anticipated, you may be tempted to trade up to an altogether better place than the offer you hold. UCAS prohibits this – you are meant to withdraw and apply next year. However it does go on, and universities have been known to poach.

You can make a late application to UCAS (ie after 15 December) but the universities and colleges are under no obligation to consider your application – there may be no more vacancies. If you apply after 30 June, your application goes straight into clearing.

ART & DESIGN COURSES

For studio-based art and design courses, there are two application systems: for some courses you apply through Route A, for others through Route B, both through UCAS but working to different timetables. You can choose up to six courses and use either or both routes, but only choose four through Route B. (You can also mix art and non-art courses.)

Applications through Route A are made by filling in a UCAS form which is processed in the usual way. You are recommended to apply by mid-November to allow portfolio inspection. If you want to add Route B choices, there is a box on the form you should tick.

Through Route B, you can make up to four applications between January and March 1998. You send in your UCAS form (if you have already used this for Route A, UCAS will tell you how to add Route B choices), together with another form indicating your interview preference. When you receive any offers will depend on when you are interviewed.

DIRECT APPLICATIONS

Some colleges do not use UCAS, principally specialist institutions (eg some architecture, music, osteopathy colleges) or those offering part-time courses. You apply direct; check the profiles in *Where to Study*. It's all the more important to get hold of the prospectuses immediately, otherwise you may miss vital dates – closing dates for applications, dates for auditions, interviews, submission of portfolios etc. You can apply to as many of these colleges as you want, and also use your UCAS choices.

HOW TO START? *SEE SHORTLISTING*, PAGE 535

APPLICANT'S CALENDAR FOR A 1998 START

1997

June–September
Absolute must: get a strategy. Prepare your own shortlist. Write for prospectuses and spend your summer having a good read. Reduce your UCAS shortlist to six applications. There is no applications limit for the handful of colleges outside the clearing system (write direct for their application forms). Get hold of the *UCAS Handbook* and application form. Draft your personal statement (your sales pitch).

From 1 September
Your application form can be accepted by UCAS from 1 September. Find out where to apply for grants – normally your LEA (local education authority) in England and Wales. Write for grant forms, complete them and apply for a grant as soon as possible.

October
Send applications direct to any colleges not in UCAS.

15 October
If you are applying to Oxbridge, this is the last date for your application to reach both the university and UCAS. Remember your educational referee will need the form well beforehand. (Interviews are usually between September and December.)

November
Aim to get your completed application form to UCAS. (This is especially important if you are applying for Route A art and design courses which require sight of your portfolio.)

15 December
Last date for applications to reach UCAS. Remember your educational referee will need the form well before that. If you send in your form this late it can take up to six weeks to process; send it earlier if at all possible.

1998

January–March
Send in Route B art & design applications.

February/March/April
Most interviews, if necessary, are held and offers of places made.

1 April
Route B art & design, first choice interviews start.

30 April
You should have heard from all your UCAS choices by this date (except some art & design courses).

15 May
Route B art & design: 2nd choice interview starts.

May
You can now only hold one conditional offer firmly through UCAS, with a further offer as an insurance.

12 June
Route B art & design: third and final choice interviews start.

30 June
Normally the final deadline for submitting grant applications; each LEA has its own date. Late applications are accepted but the grant may be paid late, so get yours in early. Any late UCAS applications sent in after this go straight into clearing.

July
Route B art & design: pool for applicants with no offers.
Mid-August
A-level results! This is the time to be around, not on holiday, unless you are 100% confident. If you have met the conditions of any offer, UCAS will confirm your place rapidly – anyway within ten working days (if you have not heard by then, check direct with the university or college).

If you have passed, but not met the conditions of your offer, UCAS will place you in clearing automatically.

If you have a place it is important now to do some checking: do you have accommodation; is your grant fixed up; will your parents pay their contribution in full?
Late August/September
UCAS clearing: if you do not have a place, you will be sent information about clearing. Ring round the universities and colleges – they now fill vacancies, sometimes accepting lower grades than before. You can also get help from your school or your LEA careers office. Information on unfilled places is widely available, including the national press and various databases (ECCTIS, Prestel, etc).
September/October
Keep on ringing, there might still be places, even after the beginning of term.

FILLING IN FORMS

The university's selling document is the prospectus; yours is your completed application form(s). Sell yourself (but don't flannel – remember you may be interviewed by someone with your form in hand). This is your chance to influence the admissions tutors and if you fail to do yourself justice, the chances are they may reject you without giving you a second chance. Forget your reservations about the archaic school reward system (eg prefects) and write down any laurels you've earned. Remember selectors are looking for good grades and motivation, promise for the future, wide (but not necessarily straight) interests and positions of responsibility. In short they want to know whether you are likely to benefit from their degree course. But getting a place is even more of a lottery than marriage – so keep at it.

Take a photocopy of the form and fill it out in rough first. Read all the instructions for completing the form and follow them exactly (UCAS complains that each year 25% of forms have to be returned for correction). **Print in block capitals using a black biro** or use a wordprocessor. Keep it as neat as you can. **Remember**: mess up an application form and you mess up your chances. Sign and date it. If you think you need help, ask your teacher, tutor or careers officer. It is a good idea to ask someone sensible (parent, teacher or friend) to read over the rough version and make suggestions and comments, particularly on the Personal Statement, and to check for any spelling mistakes etc. Remember to tick the appropriate place on the form if you are applying for deferred entry.

The information you are usually asked for is this:

Personal details
Fairly straightforward unless you are a British expatriate or overseas student. You may be disconcerted to be asked by UCAS to reveal your ethnic origin and occupational background but UCAS states this information cannot be used for selection purposes because the universities and colleges only see it afterwards.
Address
Also fairly straightforward unless your address for correspondence is different from your

home address. If this is so, remember correspondence will continue until September next year. So make sure your correspondence address lasts this long or arrange for mail to be forwarded *efficiently*.

Who's going to pay your fees?

If you expect to get a grant the answer in England and Wales is your LEA (see *LEA)*.

Choice of course

Browse through *The Student Book*. Then make a shortlist of about ten universities and colleges, read their prospectuses and **get it right for you**. For UCAS choices, reduce this list to six and fill in using the correct codes. Check the *UCAS Handbook*; you are advised to list no more than five medical/dental courses for example.

Secondary education

Straightforward, put in date order.

Examinations for which results are known

Put down everything, even failures/low grades. You must tell the whole story and it needn't seem all bad, eg coming back from a failure or disappointing result indicates persistence, motivation and determination. Remember: one poor performance earlier in your school/college career won't count against you.

Examinations to be taken

Again, put in everything.

Employment

If you are applying from school and have worked part-time, you can include it here. Otherwise, most casual jobs would be better included in your personal statement.

Personal statement

This is the most difficult section but use the space positively. It is essential that you draft it out in rough first. This is the only chance you've got to sell yourself, so give relevant and precise information. Include everything which gives you some depth – don't put down (say) reading as an interest; you're expected to read, so be specific. Then you can answer actual questions if you get an interview. The admissions tutors will read dozens – maybe hundreds – so make it interesting so you stand out from the crowd. If you have a career in mind, say so (shows motivation) but don't lose sleep if you don't know. Again, make sure it is neat and easy to read (and the writing isn't too small – the admissions tutor receives a reduced photocopy). It can take a lot of time to get this section written – if possible try to draft it over the summer holidays. You may find it helpful to work in pairs or groups to decide what to cover.

REFERENCES

All applications must be supported by an educational reference. A lot of importance is attached to it in selection procedures, so get the best you can. Your headteacher or sixth form tutor is expected to write your reference if you are still at school or college. Don't go out of your way to flatter them but show interest, motivation, persistence and, above all, that you're teachable. References are often held to be confidential, but some teachers/tutors discuss them with students first. Anyway badger whoever writes your reference to write a full and fair one.

If you have not yet taken your A-levels you'll need accurate A-level predictions, not artificially inflated ones. Time is of the essence. Find out how long your referee needs to write it, their diaries are usually more clogged than yours. Make sure you give them enough time to write it and send it in ON TIME. Messing up your references is one of the easier ways of messing up your application.

INTERVIEWS

If you are called for an interview, find out if it is part of the selection procedure rather than a visiting or open day. If it is part of the selection procedure then prepare for the interview by predicting questions like: why are you applying here? Why have you chosen this particular degree? Ask your teacher/tutor to give you a mock interview and show you one of the better video guides to interview technique. When at the interview, show you have the personal qualities for a degree such as enjoying learning, reading, writing essays, doing lab work, wanting to argue and talk about new ideas, and being eager to find out things for yourself.

Don't forget an interview is a structured conversation, so avoid answering in monosyllables and be positive (avoid answering 'No', when you could answer 'Not precisely but I have . . .'). If you have more than one interviewer reply to the one who asks the questions and then bring the others in. Don't mumble, don't chew gum, don't pick your nose. Relax yourself as much as possible and wear what you feel most comfortable in. Wait to be told to sit down, and don't smoke. Try to repress all distracting mannerisms. Prepare questions for the interviewer at the end. Above all don't be cowed: you're interviewing them too.

HOW YOU ARE CHOSEN

Being chosen implies some kind of rationality. Well, there isn't much. In most cases, admissions staff only know your predicted grades. The actual results may or may not match these predictions – for you or the other applicants – so admissions staff are playing a futures market rather than dealing with real academic achievement. Each university has a target number of new student places which it wants to meet precisely, if possible, with teachable students. So (in general) they adopt one (or both) of two ways of going about it. Either they make a large number of conditional offers so the A-level exam results do the choosing; or put more reliance on interviews and references, so lower offers can be made with more assurance on final student numbers. The university's predicament is to get acceptable candidates on to its courses while leaving not a single place unfilled. Their predicament could be your opportunity.

After the A-level results are known, some universities and colleges top up their targets with people they would have rejected earlier in the year. Don't lose heart if you haven't got a place at this stage; keep badgering, even after the beginning of the autumn term. Selectors usually try very hard to be fair. But they might as well use a pin.

OFFERS

You may be offered a place in one of two ways – **unconditionally** or **conditionally**. Unconditional offers are what they say – you're in! Conditional (or provisional) offers are dependent upon your getting, for example, specified A (or AS) level grades or points, and maybe extra GCSEs. If they ask you for specified A-level grades, they will mean it (so you can't compensate for a poor grade in one subject by doing better than required in another). But there's no telling what they'll actually accept in August until the results are published and they can see what everyone has got.

The offers they made last year are often published in prospectuses and catalogued annually by Brian Heap in *Degree Course Offers* (Trotman). Use it with discretion: these are, after all, last year's offers and they may change before you apply. The permutations involved in the offer/acceptance bargaining are mind-boggling, but it's all supply and demand; if one course asks for 2 As and a B, it **may** be a better course than one asking for 3 Ds – but all you really know is that it's more popular. If they **really** want you, you may get in on 2 Es. Conversely some universities are rumoured to sulk if you have applied to Oxbridge and show this by raising their offers to Oxbridge levels which they wouldn't dream of asking from anyone else, which is simply unjust.

After May you will be restricted to two offers through UCAS. If you have more, you need to make your best guess as to what you will achieve in A-levels in the **future** in the light of your **current** offers. It is useful to have some sort of a multi-dimensional checklist in your head, or preferably on paper. If you are the sort of person who thinks better on paper than on your feet, why not try a do-it-yourself POP (Personal Offers Planner). Use the proforma and tailor it to your own personal needs.

When the crunch comes, choose the college and course you want. The rejected ones won't approve, but it's your life.

Personal Offers Planner (POP)

Make up a POP when you are **beginning** to develop a strategy. Keep it until August so that if you don't get the grades or points you need, you can get cracking with clearing and telephoning universities and colleges.

What you think you'll get

A or AS level subject	Expected grade	Points*
1.	....	....
2.	....	....
3.	....	....
4.	....	....
5.	....	....
Total points		....

What your offers say you must get

Subject	Offer 1	Offer 2	Offer 3	Offer 4	Offer 5	Offer 6
1.	....	....	....	....	....	....
2.	....	....	....	....	....	....
3.	....	....	....	....	....	....
4.	....	....	....	....	....	....
5.	....	....	....	....	....	....
Total points	....	....	....	....	....	....

* (A-level grades convert to points as follows: A = 10, B = 8, C = 6, D = 4 and E = 2. AS level grades convert: A = 5, B = 4, C = 3, D = 2 and E = 1.)

MATURE STUDENTS

Mature students are on the increase. More than one in three students now entering higher education is over 21. If you are qualified for a degree course, you should have no problem. If you are not but you can persuade admissions tutors that you can benefit from the course and will be successful, you can still be accepted. For some you may have to take an exam; for others you will be interviewed. There are courses which can help you back to study – access courses or foundation years of degree courses. For advice and further information, approach LEA careers advisers or try any ECCTIS Access Point.

If you have taken a course before – even if you did not complete it – you may be exempted from part of a degree. This is called 'advanced standing'. If you think you may qualify, make sure you say so on your form and expect to be asked for syllabuses, transcripts etc. In some cases you can also get credit for work experience and in-service training courses too. If you want advice, you can contact CATS (Credit Accumulation and Transfer Scheme, Open University Validation Services, 344–354 Gray's Inn Road, London WC1X 8BP; tel 0171 278 4411; fax 0171 833 1012). It is better to write but telephone advice is available.

DISABLED STUDENTS

Once you are satisfied you have a shortlist of universities and colleges where your support needs can be met, fill in your UCAS application form. You should indicate the nature of your disability and your needs in Sections 2 and 8 (all applicants fill in the box in Section 2, which is for monitoring purposes). This should allow the admissions staff to gain a basic understanding of your disability and needs and prevent your being asked inappropriate questions. If you attend an interview or open day and have any special requirements (eg communicators or parking facilities), make sure you let the college know in advance so it can be arranged.

Skill publishes *Higher Education and Disability: A guide to higher education for people with disabilities* (Skill: National Bureau for Students with Disabilities, 336 Brixton Road, London SW9 7AA; Tel 0171 274 0565).

IF YOU DON'T QUITE MAKE IT – ACTION LIST

If you don't get the grades you have been asked for, start by checking whether you can get on to the course anyway. If everyone else has made the grade, it'll be full and course tutors will be inflexible; if hardly anybody did, they may be prepared to take you. Speak to the course tutors – don't just assume they don't want you – you may be lucky. Then:

Keep shopping around
UCAS will automatically send you details of clearing in August/September if your conditional offer is not confirmed. This gives you another chance to get a place, even if it is not at one of the colleges you originally chose.

Keep up with last-minute information available

- get in touch with your school/college
- look in the national press – some list vacancies
- look in local press for advertisements
- listen to local radio services
- use one of the electronic databases – ECCTIS, Prestel and Campus 2000 – which are constantly updated
- ring universities and colleges direct – many have specially staffed units and open days.

Clearing is intended as a nice orderly filling of the last slots. In practice it can be mayhem (computer breakdowns, postal strikes or just life). Many colleges, desperate to meet targets precisely, take telephone applications (which are real) in preference to applications through clearing (which might not materialise). Some even by-pass the system and actively recruit by phone for hard-to-fill courses.

This leaves you in an impossible situation: do you run up a huge phone bill and maybe strike lucky? Or do you wait your turn through clearing and not make it? It's up to you. Remember, you are not alone. 10%–20% places are still up for grabs at the start of clearing. It is sensible to be flexible about where you study but more rigid about what you study. Good luck!

WHAT IF YOU COME COMPLETELY UNSTUCK?

Tough but not the end of the world. You can think about the following options:

- resit at your school or local FE college or at a sixth form college (get a list from the Conference for Independent Further Education, c/o Buckhall Farm, Bull Lane, Bethersden, Nr Ashford, Kent; tel 01233 820797), or do something different at your local FE college
- apply for a BTEC Higher Diploma (HND) if you have one A-level. If you choose somewhere with a diploma and a degree course in your subject you **might** be able to transfer later
- try for an Open University degree
- forget all about it and do something else. There's always the chance you can come back to it later, when you're older and wiser (when you are over 21, the minimum entrance requirements can sometimes be waived, so long as you can persuade admissions tutors you will benefit).

WHEN YOU DO HAVE A PLACE

When you have a place, you will have to adjust to it all becoming a reality at last. This means there will be dozens of things to do, but don't panic.

- start by confirming your place
- make sure of your accommodation

- tell your LEA, so your grant can be processed; Check whether your parents really are going to pay their parental contribution (and when!)
- arrange money for the start of term (even if you expect a full grant, it almost certainly won't have arrived when you do)
- get some passport photos (essential for first week of term)
- read the joining instructions you'll be sent
- find your exam certificates (results slips will only be acceptable for the most recent exams)
- get an exemption certificate so you don't have to pay prescription charges
- buy supplies of stationery, suitable clothes etc.
- don't let the gigantic reading list you're sent put you into a cold panic
- sort out travel arrangements and make sure you're there when required.

CAN'T FIND WHAT YOU'RE LOOKING FOR? USE THE INDEX!

CASH FOR COURSES: HOW TO GET IT

HOW TO GET THE MONEY

You don't get the money from one single source, at least the vast majority don't. You get most of it from two or three sources: student grants, student loans and your parents. For the remainder, you work or borrow even more.

If you are leaving school and going to university, you have a right to:

- A **student grant** (see below), which at the moment covers your tuition fees but watch out for top-up fees. It can also provides you with some money to live on, the precise amount depends on the income of your parents (page 28).
- A **student loan** (page 29), which you pay back after you finish your course.

So, for 1997/98, this adds up to the following:

What you get to live on	Grant plus parents	Loan	Total
Studying in London	£2,160	£2,085	£4,245
Studying out of London	£1,755	£1,685	£3,440
Living at home (wherever that is)	£1,435	£1,290	£2,725

You are very unlikely to be able to live on this. So you will almost certainly need to get more money to survive. This is why most students **borrow** (page 30); the majority work in the holidays and, increasingly, have jobs in term time as well – *Earn As You Learn* (page 30). You will have to work out what you can/will do.

For some students, this will not be enough and there are safety nets, called **hardship funds** (page 30) – not much money usually and only for students in dire financial straits, so don't rely on them. For the lucky few, there are some other sources of income: charities, company educational trusts, sponsorships, scholarships, career development loans and very few qualify for social security benefits (see page 31).

There are special cases: students from overseas and expats (page 32), mature students (page 33), disabled students (page 33) and self-financing students (page 33).

Money will almost certainly be tight. You need to be clear about banking (page 36) to cope with the peaks and troughs. Make sure you are good at budgeting (page 34) so you control the money you have got.

Student grants

Most students get an LEA grant. It does not come automatically – you apply for it before your course starts; for the second and subsequent years, you just complete income forms. The grant will pay all your tuition fees (except at a few independent colleges and if top-up fees become a reality); it will also give you some money to live on. Not much money, mind. For 1997/98 you could expect the following, though it's means tested on your parents income:

£2,160 if you are studying in London
£1,755 if you are studying elsewhere
£1,435 if you live at home.

The contribution to be paid (to you) by your parents is deducted and the remainder paid to you in termly instalments – usually a cheque which you pick up from the university at the start of each term. You will get more if the course lasts more than 30 weeks a year, you go abroad to a higher cost country or you have various other, specified, costs (dependents, disabilities etc). The system is well explained in the DFEE booklet *Student Grants and Loans* sent to you by the LEA with your grant application form and you can ring the DFEE on 01325 392822. A braille version is available from the RNIB (PO Box 173, Peterborough, PE2 6WS; tel 0345 023153).

Applying

In England and Wales you apply to the local education authority where you usually live (look up your local authority in the phone book – if you have both a district and county authority in your area, try the county). In Scotland you apply to the Scottish Education Department (Gyleview House, 3 Redheughs Rigg, Southgyle, Edinburgh EH12 9HH); in Northern Ireland to your local Education and Library Board.

You should apply early – normally between January and June but check the deadline for your own LEA. Don't wait until you have an offer of a place. If you miss their deadline it can lead to delays. Even if you get your forms in on time, you'll be lucky if your grant cheque is there at the start of term (recently, one university had received no first-year students' grant cheques at all from over 60 LEAs at the start of term). Your LEA could be one of the hard cases, so make sure you take enough money to tide you over for a few weeks, or can get some from your bank; you'll need to eat as well as settle in.

If your case is not straightforward, always confirm any conversations you have with your LEA in writing, or conduct dialogue by letters. LEAs do tend to say one thing and then several months later write something quite different; give only the information they ask for and get advice.

Some students on training courses in professions supplementary to medicine (eg OT, physiotherapy, radiography, orthoptics) have a separate system of NHS bursaries. These are broadly similar to LEA grants but administered by the Department of Health, through your college. Ask the college or the DoH (Student Grants Unit, North Fylde Central Office, Norcross, Blackpool, Lancashire FY5 3TA; tel 01253 856123).

Eligibility

You have a right to a student grant (it is called a mandatory grant) if you fulfil the following conditions. You are ordinarily resident in the UK (and have been so for at least three years); you are studying on a degree course or equivalent (DFEE decide which ones qualify – they are called 'designated courses'); and you have not done a course of this kind before. If this is not your first course, your grant may still be mandatory but the rules are complicated and very specific. You need to be careful and take advice early.

If you do not qualify for a mandatory grant, you are in the hands of your local authority – and the best of luck! They may still give you a grant, called a discretionary grant, but they are few and far between. And the amount is discretionary too – some don't even cover the tuition fees. Each local authority behaves differently; and they will treat you differently whether you're doing a non-designated course such as a film course, foundation art or professional law course or you are an HND student transferring to the second year of a degree course or repeating a year. Expect to go through some arbitrary tests and assessment (eg many LEAs audition drama students). If you are turned down, there is always an appeals procedure – however long-winded – which usually involves elected councillors who can legitimately be lobbied. Appeal and lobby!

NUS Information Service Sheets (on grants, loans, welfare benefits etc for students) are useful and available from NUS, 461 Holloway Road, London N7 6LJ, with a large sae.

Parents

The grant is means tested, so the more your parents earn, the more they are supposed to give you and the less grant you get (see our *Grants Rough and Ready Reckoner*). Parents have to be earning very little to be exempt from making a contribution; only 27% students get the full amount from the LEA. Conversely, some 26% of students get no grant to live on at all; parents are expected to provide the lot.

Your LEA will tell your parents how much they are to contribute, but it's not a legally binding requirement. Something like 40% of students fail to receive their full parental contribution. Certain deductions (eg pension contributions, but not income tax) can be made from parents' joint (or single) income, which then leaves something called the 'residual income'. The greater the residual income, the greater their contribution is expected to be – so, as the residual income goes up, your grant goes down. Your grant is based on your parents' income in the previous year – though if their circumstances change, you can ask for it to be reassessed (the Students Charter says this should only take 3 weeks). Many parents have real difficulty in paying.

Your parents are not expected to contribute if you are over 25, you have been self-supporting for three years or married for two. Get in touch with your students' union (SU) if you are in difficulties. The NUS also provides helpful information.

Grants rough and ready reckoner

What you get to live on for a 30-week academic year

Parents' residual income	Parents' contribution to you	Your grant if in London	Your grant if outside London	Your grant if living at home
£16,440	£0	£2,160	£1,755	£1,435
£16,450	£45	£2,115	£1,710	£1,390
£20,000	£318	£1,842	£1,437	£1,117
£23,000	£611	£1,549	£1,144	£824
£27,000	£1,045	£1,115	£ 710	£390
£31,000	£1,482	£678	£ 273	Nothing
£34,000	£1,882	£278	Nothing	Nothing
£37,000	£2,282	Nothing	Nothing	Nothing
£53,000	£4,415	No maintenance grant, even if there are two students in your family		

Student loans

Student loans come only from the Student Loans Company (at present). You apply once you have started your course – get the application form from your university or college. Unlike the grant, it is not means tested and you have to pay it back after you finish your course.

You are eligible if you are a home student on a full-time designated course of at least one year. The definitions are broader than for grants – so you may qualify even though you've been refused a grant. You can decide each year whether to apply for a loan for that year and sign up any time up until 31 July .

The maximum amount you can borrow is fixed annually by the government; it depends where you live while you are a student and on what year of the course you want a loan (you get less in your final year – no long vacation). You can apply for less than the maximum but, if you do, you cannot then apply for difference; you cannot apply later for earlier years of the course. For 1997/98 you can borrow any amount up to the following:

Student loans	Maximum loan	
	Full year in 1997/98	Final year in 1997/98
Students studying in London	£2,085	£1,520
Students studying elsewhere	£1,685	£1,230
Students who live at home (wherever that is)	£1,290	£ 945

The money is paid direct into your bank/building society account in one, two or three instalments (most students take the year's loan in one); if you get it all early in the year, you can stick it in the building society until you need it. Don't drink it, the summer can be hard.

To apply, go to the office at your university or college which deals with loans (ask when you enrol). Check what to take with you – generally your birth certificate, the letter from your LEA offering a grant and evidence of your bank/building society account details. The office will check your eligibility and give you an application form to send to the Student Loans Company. You will be sent a loan agreement to sign and return, and then you should get the money. Easy – so what about paying it back?

There is an interest charge. The amount you borrow is indexed to inflation. This means the amount you repay will have the same value in real terms as the sum you borrowed, but you are not asked to pay more. So while it's not free of interest like some bank loans, it's probably cheaper than other interest-bearing loans. Whether it seems high or low naturally depends on the relative movement of the commercial interest rates and the rate of inflation: student loans seem cheap when interest rates are high; they seem relatively high when commercial rates are low. You start repaying in the April after you finish the course, normally over five years. In some cases deferral is possible but you must arrange it with the Student Loans Company or you could end up in court.

The Student Loans Company gives written quotations on request and runs a free helpline for questions – 0800 405 0100. There have been complaints from universities and colleges that the helpline is constantly engaged and that written quotations take a very long time, so write well in advance of any urgent need for the loan. If you have a complaint, there is an ombudsman: the Student Loans Ombudsman, c/o The Student Loans Company.

Borrowing

A fact of student life these days. Consider the costs carefully. One business-like approach is to take the cheapest loan first.

1. **Free overdraft.** Most banks offer overdrafts, maybe up to £1,000, interest free.
2. **Student loan.** Interest at inflation rate only.
3. **Agreed overdraft.** Variable interest rate, bank base rate plus.
4. **Credit cards.** Ferocious interest rates.

You could also try a career development loan if you are eligible.

Earn as you learn

Working in the vacations

You can work in the vacations to supplement your income – most students do. The profiles of the universities and colleges in *Where To Study* give some of the local possibilities. Or you can return home and find a job there. You can use the summer for going further afield – start by looking at the *Directory of Summer Jobs in Britain* or the *Directory of Summer Jobs Abroad*, both published by Vacation Work (9 Park End Street, Oxford OX1 1HJ; tel 01865 241978; fax 01865 790885). They also have many other specialist guides (send sae for list).

Term time work

Increasingly students are having to earn money during term time too. Some universities don't allow it, others are more flexible or just pragmatic. But you need to be careful if you bend the rules – no good pleading time spent on a garage forecourt as a reason for failing to produce your next essay.

Browse through our university and college profiles in *Where to Study* to get a feel for the current position. Many universities permit term time work up to an explicit number of hours per week. As a rough guide, assume 10–12 hours per week is about the limit before your studying suffers. So, if you can earn £3.50–£4.50 an hour, you could aim to top up your term time income by about £35–£55 a week or more.

Many universities employ students on campus where they can, in libraries, bars, catering etc. And some have employment exchanges to help you find work on and off campus, regular part-time work or casual work when you need it. If you think you are going to need work in term time, suss it early or you may find the best jobs gone.

Hardship funds – including access funds

The government hands out some £30 million a year to universities and colleges, so they can distribute it to individual home students who have serious financial problems. These are called access funds and are intended to help students who would otherwise find it difficult to complete their course. Universities and colleges have their own criteria, see our profiles in *Where to Study*: some use the money to reduce fees for self-financing students or help with childcare, travel costs etc. So you may qualify for help in one college and be ineligible in another. (You are not usually eligible for access money unless you have already applied for a loan.)

Colleges often have their own hardship funds for students with short-term problems or whose financial circumstances change part way through their course, particularly those who are not eligible for access funds. But there's not much around for first years.

Other sources of income

Charities

There are lots of impoverished students chasing the little money handed out by educational charities, so don't pin your hopes on getting much.

You could waste a great deal of time chasing charities where your problem does not fall within their remit. A good shortcut is to start by getting advice from EGAS (Educational Grants Advisory Service, c/o Family Welfare Association, 501-505 Kingsland Road, Dalston, London E8 4AU). Telephone their student enquiry service on 0171 923 3513, to obtain an enquiry form. You'll have to complete this before EGAS can help. It normally takes about four weeks to get a response, so it pays to get your form in early and make sure it is completed accurately first time.

Company educational trusts

Many large companies have these. Find out if the companies where your parents work make grants to sons and daughters of their employees/staff.

Sponsorship

Sponsorships are offered by some employers in industry, government and professional partnerships. They are much sought after because they can solve two student problems at a stroke – financing yourself through university and getting a job when you graduate. The army even offers a gap year sponsorship. You're normally responsible for gaining your own admission on to a degree course.

Sponsorships are becoming fewer and competition for them is fierce, so you need to get cracking early. The best shortcut is the standard annual catalogue – *Sponsorship* for short – in your careers library (it is published by COIC, PO Box 348, Bristol BS99 7FE). Its full title is *Sponsorships offered to students by employers and professional bodies for first degrees, BTEC higher awards or comparable courses beginning in 1998)*. Several sponsorships are advertised in the UCAS handbook and the press too. But firms are showing signs of disillusion; some are offering sponsorship for the final year only; you apply in your second year. And your grant will be reduced by the amount of the bursary – or even killed completely.

Scholarships

This is a complex area. Many universities and colleges offer scholarships of some sort, either at entry or at the end of the first year; check prospectuses. There are also some specialist scholarships (eg in arts and sport). If you go for a scholarship, remember it can affect the amount of your grant.

Career Development Loans

Career Development Loans (CDLs) are designed to cover course fees, books, materials and living costs for up to 24 months. You may be eligible if you are 18+ and want to do a job-related course but cannot get a student grant. There is a maximum of £8,000 – up to 80% of your costs. CDLs are administered by some banks on behalf of the DFEE. You can get free booklets giving details of eligibility, an application form and lists of bank branches which you can apply to, from the DFEE on 0800 585 505.

Social security benefits

Don't rely on them. Almost no students are now entitled to benefits; disabled students, single parents, couples with dependent children and part-time students are the only exceptions. Try telephoning 0800 666 555 for information, or visit your local DSS office. The DSS also issues a leaflet FB23 called *Young People's Guide to Social Security*. Local authorities can award housing benefit and council tax benefit too.

Special cases

Students from overseas

Overseas students are not normally entitled to UK grants, but many countries have their own system of funding their students, administered by the embassy or high commission. If you are still overseas, you could try contacting the British Council locally or, if there isn't one, the British High Commission or Embassy. If you are already in the UK, the British Council Information Centre (10 Medlock Street, Manchester M15 4AA) runs an information service in Manchester and London which shares the same telephone number – 0161 957 7755 (or fax 0161 957 7762; email e-stuart.marshall@britcoun.org.uk). Or try UKCOSA (Council for International Education), 9 St Albans Place, London N1 0NX (tel 0171 226 3762; fax 0171 226 3373; email e-ukcosa@mailbox.ulcc.ac.uk); it also runs a student enquiry line 1pm–4pm, Monday to Friday on 0171 354 5210. There are some special concessions for refugees; ask the World University Service, 14 Dufferin Street, London EC1Y 8PD (0171 426 5800; fax 0171 251 1314; email retas@wusuk.org.uk). Most colleges and universities have special overseas advisers and many of the staff make a special effort to be sympathetic towards your problems, so talk to them.

If you are a student from outside the EU, you are expected to pay the full cost of your course so you will be charged higher tuition fees. You can look these up in our profiles in *Where to Study* – for 1996/97 they were £5,000–£7,000 a year for a course based in the classroom; some £7,000–£9,000 if it's based in a lab or studio and £14,000–£16,000 for clinical courses. The definitions are complicated but you will be classified as overseas **unless** you: have been ordinarily resident in the UK for 3 years (excluding any time spent here primarily for the purpose of education); are an EU national, resident in the EU for the last 3 years; are a UK citizen who has been abroad temporarily for the past 3 years, for the purpose of employment (yours, your spouse's or parents'); or are a refugee, new immigrant or EEA migrant worker. These definitions are open to a range of interpretations and you need to check your status with each university and college that offers you a place. If in doubt, consult the British Council. (Being classified as a home student for fees purposes does not necessarily make you eligible for an LEA grant.)

If you are an EU citizen, and resident in the EU, you pay the same fees as home students. Or you may not pay fees at all – if you would have qualified for a mandatory grant had you been British, you apply to your LEA (normally where you will be studying) for them to pay the fees. Some European students who are classified as 'migrant workers' may get an student grant – check with your LEA.

Expats

If you are British, living outside the EEA, the chances of getting government financial assistance are pretty slim. Worse still, you could be in some danger of being classed as an overseas student which means your fees will be a great deal higher. It's worth being crystal clear about your own residential status early on.

The fact that you are British is nowhere near enough. You need also to have been 'ordinarily resident' in the British Isles (possibly the EEA) for three years preceding the course; time spent at a UK boarding school isn't likely to help. The rules are complicated and somewhat different for deciding your status for payment of fees and your eligibility for grants/loans; and they are interpreted differently by the various universities, colleges and LEAs.

The onus is on you to satisfy the various authorities that you are 'ordinarily resident'. Each case is considered on its merits and there are no specific exemptions for particular groups like HM Forces or civil servants. To check out your own status, refer to the brief guide *Student Grants and Loans*, or the DFEE fact sheets – there's one for EU expats too

– all available from your LEA or the Department for Education and Employment, Sanctuary Buildings, Great Smith Street, London SW1P 3BT.

You can get help making your case, or advice if you haven't got one, from UKCOSA (Council for International Education) 9 St Albans Place, London N1 ONX (tel 0171 226 3762, fax 0171 226 3373; email e-ukcosa@mailbox.ulcc.ac.uk). It also runs a student enquiry line 1pm–4pm, Monday to Friday on 0171 354 5210. British universities and colleges are pretty on the ball about defining your status; contact the ones you are interested in early on – see *Where to Study*.

If you live in another EEA country, you should at least get your fees paid but your parents will normally need to have returned to the UK if you're to get a student grant.

Mature students

If you are over 26, you are not assessed on your parents' earnings and your grant covers 52 weeks of the year, rather than 30. If you are supporting a family you may be able to claim extra amounts but mature students are more likely to end their course in debt than younger undergraduates.

Disabled students

If you are a student with disabilities, you may find you need to buy specialist equipment to enable you to study or you may incur other extra costs related to your disability. If you get a mandatory grant, you can also apply for three extra disabled students' allowances, means tested like your grant. One is for general expenses (up to £1,275 per year in 1996/97); another for helpers eg interpreters, notetakers, readers, mobility helpers (up to £5,100 per year); and the third for specialist equipment eg computers, radio microphones, closed circuit televisions (up to £3,840 over the whole course). You might be able to claim for any extra travelling costs due to your disability. You apply for the disabled students' allowances directly to your LEA awards section. You may have to complete an application form or write in giving details of what you wish to claim for; and they may ask for a letter from your college to vouch for your needs.

Some students with disabilities are still able to claim income support or housing benefit (not on college accommodation). The position is complicated, so find out if you may be able to qualify from your local benefits agency office, the college welfare office or from **Skill**. Both income support and housing benefit are means tested, so your grant and any other income will be taken into account.

You can get a range of information sheets about financial assistance for students with disabilities in higher education from Skill: National Bureau for Students with Disabilities, 336 Brixton Road, London SW9 7AA (tel 0171 274 0565).

Self-financing students

If you are not eligible for a grant and do not have sponsorship or some other source of funding, you need to do your sums very carefully.

Fees for self-financing students are difficult to understand; some universities charge you more than they would charge an LEA, some less. In our profiles in *Where to Study*, we give the fees paid by self-financing home students in 1996/97. For classroom-based courses they were £750–£2,500; for lab/studio-based and pre-clinical courses £750–£5,500. So it's worth shopping around – and hoping that top-up fees come in after you have graduated.

GET HOLD OF THE PROSPECTUSES

HOW TO MANAGE YOUR MONEY

Budgeting

Money will be tight. Your grant and student loans are hardly likely to cover your costs over the three years (or more) of a first degree course. The average student debt is now thought to be about £2,000 in addition to student loans, and our guess is that students will now complete their course with debts in the region of £8,000.

That figure tends to focus minds.

To get a clear idea of your likely financial position, you'll need an income and expenditure budget for each year of the course, including any period spent overseas. You should expect the costs to go up through your course: in the second year most students move out of university accommodation (so costs go up); and in the final year you will need to devote more time to your studies (more fast food, no time to work).

Here is a crib to get you started. You can then add up your three or four annual budgets, get a glimpse of your financial position at the end of the course and see whether you need to add to your income to get there – get vac work, apply for an overdraft or whatever.

To stop your expenditure completely running away with you usually requires a much more detailed exercise. You'll need to estimate your weekly expenditure and check how closely your actual expenditure corresponds to your estimates.

Estimated expenditure table

	Yearly expenditure (52 weeks)	Academic year (30 weeks)	Weekly expenditure
Rent	£2340	£1350	£45
Food	£910	£525	£17.50
Electricity/gas	£286	£165	£5.50
Water	£78	£45	£1.50
Insurance (excl. bike, computer, etc)	£52	£30	£1
Travel – essential	£520	£300	£10
Books and equipment	£780	£450	£15
Laundry	£104	£60	£2
Entertainment and leisure	£780	£450	£15
TOTAL	£5850	£3375	£112.50

(*Source:* Student Employment Office, University of Sussex)

Annual income and expenditure budget

Income (for an academic year)		Expenditure (for an academic year)	
Cash in bank and savings	£	Tuition fees*	£ ....
Grant	£	Exam fees*	£ ....
Loan (don't underestimate)	£	Rent	£ ....
Parental contribution (actual)	£	Gas/electricity	£ ....
		Telephone	£ ....
Vacation earnings (net of tax and NI)	£	TV licence	£ ....
Term-time earnings (net of tax and NI)	£	Insurance (personal belongings)	£ ....
		Council tax (if any)	£ ....
Any special benefits (DSA/single parents)	£	Food/drink	£ ....
Any other source of income eg scholarships, charitable funding etc	£	Car/motor bike/bike	£ ....
		Rail card or bus pass	£ ....
		Fares	£ ....
		Field courses	£ ....
		Vacation expenses	£ ....
		Books	£ ....
		Stationery	£ ....
		Equipment	£ ....
		Clothes	£ ....
		Laundry	£ ....
		Leisure (fags, flicks, societies, contraceptives etc)	£ ....
		Other, eg childcare	£ ....
		Interest on overdraft/ credit cards	£ ....
TOTAL INCOME	£	TOTAL EXPENDITURE	£ ....
		BALANCE	£ ....

*If you are on an LEA grant these are normally paid for you, but check; and beware of top-up fees.

A weekly expenditure breakdown is also a great help as a basic building block from which to cost your own plans. This *Estimated Expenditure Table* is based on the experience of real students and suggests how to estimate your costs over three different time frames – a week, three terms and a calendar year – depending on what you do in the vacations.

Banking

You'll definitely need a student-friendly bank or building society which offers student banking packages. These provide a range of privileges not available to ordinary mortals – like free banking and free overdrafts.

But you don't get student packages automatically – you have to ask for them, even if you already have a bank account. Take a look at the sort of goodies on offer in our table, *Student Banking* 1996/97. Get the bumf and apply for a student account before you go.

Why? For starters, you'll need somewhere to bank your grant cheque when it finally arrives, and your student loan will be paid into your account direct. You don't want to find yourself with a grant cheque locked into your newly opened bank account because you don't have a cheque book or cash card yet.

Take a four or five year view of your banking arrangements – from the time your first grant cheque fails to arrive at the beginning of your first term, to the time you graduate with or without having a job to go to. Between those dates, you will probably face a succession of cash crises and need a bank overdraft to see you through. How else, for instance, do you pay a deposit in July to reserve your accommodation for the following autumn? Always keep the bank informed of an impending crisis and it may try to get you through it.

There are two basic choices: bank direct, 24 hours a day by phone; or bank through a branch – in which case it is probably a good idea to choose a bank with branches on or near your campus and at home. Basic bank equipment is a cheque book, a cash card and a monthly bank statement which tells you where you are. You might find a credit card useful, but beware of the ferocious interest rates. The rest is a service – authorised overdraft, commission-free travellers cheques, or discounted student insurance.

WANT TO HELP WITH THE NEXT EDITION? SEE PAGE 66

STUDENT BANKING 1996/97

Banking packages from year 1 until after graduation – but they change each August, so check

Bank	Interest free overdrafts	Interest paid on your credit balances	Charges on agreed overdrafts	Repayment period	Graduate packages	Other student services	Student advisers	More info
Abbey National (Free banking)	No, but very low interest charged on students accounts	Yes	1.5%	No set policy	None yet	Same as other customers	No	Banking Marketing Abbey National plc Abbey House 201 Grafton Gate East Central Milton Keynes MK9 1AN
Bank of Scotland (Free banking if within agreed overdraft)	£600	Yes	Authorised overdrafts over £600, 5% over base rate. Unauthorised overdrafts, 20% over base rate.	Subject to negotiation	Yes, for 1 year interest free £600 overdraft free banking; preferential interest rates; discounts on insurance etc	Commission-free travel facilities; discounts on travel insurance; student insurance	No	Product Development Bank of Scotland Uberior House 61 Grassmarket Edinburgh EH1 2JF
Barclays (Free banking)	Year 1, up to £1000 Year 2, up to £1250 Year 3+, up to £1500	Yes	Above interest free limit, 1% over base rate; unauthorised borrowing 12% over base rate.	Agreed on individual basis. Interest free facility available until 31 Dec after end of studies	Yes, including graduate loan, graduate overdraft and graduate managers	Commission-free travellers cheques, foreign currency, Student insurance; student Barclaycard	Yes	Students and Graduates Team Barclays Bank PLC PO Box 120, Longwood Close, Westwood Business Park Coventry CV4 8JN
Halifax (Free banking)	£1000 during course	Yes	6.2%	Convert to graduate package	Extension of student facilities for 1 year after course	Commission-free travellers cheques; student contents insurance.	No	Halifax Building Society Freepost, Trinity Road Halifax, West Yorkshire HX1 2BR

Bank	Interest free overdrafts	Interest paid on your credit balances	Charges on agreed overdrafts	Repayment period	Graduate packages	Other student services	Student advisers	More info
Lloyds (Free banking)	£500 Year 1 £750 Year 2 £1000 Year 3 £1250 Year 4 £1500 Year 5+	Yes	Monthly rate 0.6%; APR 7.4%	31 Dec after graduation or switch to graduate package	£700 interest-free overdraft in first year, £350 in second. Up to £5000 graduate loan, repayable over 5 years	Payment card Commission-free travellers cheques, foreign currency. Student insurance scheme	Yes	Lloyds Bank Plc Customer Relations PO Box 112 Canons House Bristol BS99 7LB
Midland (Free banking)	£750 Year 1 £1000 Year 2 £1250 Year 3 £1500 Year 4+	Yes	1% over base rate	Subject to negotiation	£1250 interest-free overdraft; fee-free overdraft for 2 years; preferential rate graduate loan up to £10,000; free banking, cards etc	Commission-free travellers cheques and foreign currency; student insurance; fee-free credit card	Yes	Marketing Department Midland Bank plc 10 Lower Thames Street London EC3R 6AE
NatWest (Free banking)	£1000 years 1–3 £1500 year 4 £2000 year 5+	Yes 2% gross	9% nominal	Subject to negotiation.	Free banking; preferential overdrafts (9%); continuation of interest free overdraft terms for existing customers for 6 months after graduation; commission-free purchase of travellers cheques and foreign currency; Graduate Loans; free Visa and Mastercard – all for 2 years after graduation	Free Mastercard and Visa card; eurocheque card; student budget planner; student insurance; commission free purchase of travellers cheques and foreign currency	Yes	National Westminster Bank PLC 41 Lothbury London EC2P 2BP
Royal Bank of Scotland (Free banking when in credit)	£500; £750 in final year	Yes	Base rate plus 3%–6% (manager's discretion)	Usually 1 June after graduation, depending on circumstances	Graduate loans	Commission-free travellers cheques and foreign currency; free Eurocheque card; 24 hour direct banking.	No	The Royal Bank of Scotland Plc Freepost Edinburgh EH2 0DG (no stamp required)
TSB (Free banking)	£500 Year 1 £600 Year 2 £700 Year 3 onwards	Yes	Authorised over-drafts above free limit 6.2%; unauthorised overdrafts 29.8%	End Sept the year following graduation	Student overdraft continues for year after graduation	£100 debit card; £250 Trustcard; commission-free travellers cheques and foreign currency	No	TSB Bank Plc Customer Care Victoria House Victoria Square Birmingham B1 1BZ

HOW TO SURVIVE YOUR FIRST YEAR

ACCOMMODATION

This is your major living cost.

Our university and college profiles in *Where to Study* tell you:

- what the college/university offers
- how much (roughly) it costs
- how many weeks you pay for each year. Crucial.

It matters how long you pay for: sometimes you only pay during term time; some contracts are for, say, 36 weeks of the academic year; some for a full 52 weeks. Term time only is fine if you've got a home to go to in the vacations. Academic year only (September through to June) is best if you want a base for most of the year and plan to travel in the summer. If you want to leave your junk there until next year, or want to occupy the same accommodation again you may have to pay a retainer (or bond or deposit) over the vacation. All-year contracts are a must for some, especially if you've got a family. But you are often given no choice; so if you want the place, you have to take it on for a full year which can be a huge financial burden.

The amount of college/uni accommodation is astonishingly variable. At the extremes: some have none and Oxbridge houses the vast majority of undergraduates in college or college-owned accommodation. Elsewhere, a very few universities and colleges are aiming to accommodate all their students; quite a number aim to house at least first year students. Much new accommodation is of conference standard, with ensuite bathrooms etc, to generate income for the university in the vacations. The advantage is more money for building and better accommodation; the downside is students are likely to be charged more.

Most universities and colleges guarantee to find first years somewhere to live even if the college cannot provide it. This may involve you in completing another form and sending it to the college accommodation officer by a specified date. Some students report that their university application worked like clockwork until their 'guaranteed accommodation' failed to materialise – sometimes even not there on arrival when it had been promised. Make sure the university has your accommodation form well before the closing date and make sure you are not fobbed off.

Most student accommodation costs a lot. Some SUs report students paying over 100% of their grant on rent. If you are lucky enough to have a choice, go for living in college. The standard of accommodation is variable but it's easier to make friends, you have more clout with the landlord, it's closer to college and (in theory at least) cheaper.

If college accommodation is beyond the pale or non-existent, look outside. Your first assumption should be that the best accommodation has already been nabbed. But get along there and sort out something before the start of term. You'll be at a long-term disadvantage if the course starts while you're still tramping the streets in search of a bed. There are particular problems where there is a shortage of cheap rented accommodation (leafy suburbs) or where there are other sources of tenants (eg holiday areas, where term starts before the holiday makers go home). Self-catering accommodation is usually cheaper, so long as you know how to feed yourself cheaply. The accommodation office should be able to give you a list of likely pads and, if you're lucky, a list of things to check when you're viewing. If you meet dozens of other hopefuls sent by the accommodation office everywhere, go to the local agencies.

Remember to consider any travel costs when looking at the rent – no point in something dirt cheap if it costs a fortune getting to lectures. Also, remember to ask about retainers during vacations; increasingly, you pay rent for the full year. Some private rented accommodation is pretty dire and, to help you avoid the experiences suffered by our correspondents, here's a rough list of horrors to check out:

- Electricity/gas/water safety – sockets, pipes, wiring and appliances – do they look safe and regularly serviced? Particularly look at gas water heaters and fires – landlords now have to have gas appliances serviced annually and provide you with proof of this. (If you are concerned about a gas appliance, the Health and Safety Executive runs an advice line which will put you in touch with your local office – 0800 300 363.)
- Fire safety – smoke alarms, exits, windows and doors.
- Damp – any sign of it, ventilation.
- Vermin and pests – signs, smells etc.
- TV licence – has it been paid? If not it's down to you in law.

Your LEA will assume that you will live at home if you are studying close by, and so give you less grant. Even so, living at home will almost certainly leave you better off, but you may miss out on some of the social facilities and be less involved in college life. You will need to get the support of your college to move away from home for 'educational reasons' – talk to the college office that deals with grants. You should definitely do this if you don't have proper facilities to study at home – a room of your own as a start.

Some mortgage companies have special packages for students if you can afford to buy a flat or house – maybe with two or three others. You need to know you can get on with your co-owners for the duration of the course and can cope with variable interest rates. You may need a parent to act as guarantor, or your parents may find buying you a house the most cost-effective way of handing out their parental contribution.

If all else fails, you may still be able to join the student squatters (except in Scotland). Whilst still legal, the law needs watching and you'll need to react quickly to landlords, particularly in going to court. The *Squatters' Handbook* is up-to-date on the developments in the law, and is available for £1 (+39p p+p) from the Advisory Service for Squatters (ASS), 2 St Paul's Road, London N1 2QN (0171 359 8814, 2–6pm, Monday to Friday). The ASS will help if you get in trouble in a squat, although you must act fast as you often only get two days before you are slung out.

You will, with luck, end up with at least a bed of your own, light, heat and somewhere to work. Cooking, washing and laundry facilities will invariably be shared. Find out if you need to take sheets, towels, saucepans, plates, cutlery, glasses . . . Plus whatever you need – garlic press, lemon squeezer, chip pan, cork-screw, water filter, favourite duvet. Don't take valuables unless you can't live without them, your digs are really secure and you are well insured.

AIDS – ACQUIRED IMMUNITY DEFICIENCY SYNDROME

AIDS has become the concern of everyone. The great majority of cases have occurred in the high risk groups: male homosexuals, intravenous drug abusers and haemophiliacs. However, AIDS is now beginning to spread among heterosexuals and none of us can afford to be complacent.

As well as the clinical cases of AIDS, there are many thousands of people who are carrying HIV-1 (Human Immunosuppressive Virus) who may not develop the disease for up to ten years. During all this time they may infect others. There is at present no effective cure for AIDS and a vaccine protecting against it may take many years to develop. To complicate matters there is a variant virus, HIV-2, which is found mainly in Africa or in people who have been there and this is thought to be more transmissible by heterosexual intercourse.

For all these reasons we need to think more carefully about our sexual behaviour. Sticking to one sexual partner obviously helps. When there is any element of risk, with gay or bisexual men or intravenous drug abusers, it is safer to use a condom or sheath which acts as a physical barrier to the transmission of the AIDS virus.

AIDS victims suffer from many disadvantages on top of their inevitably fatal disease. They cannot get life insurance or mortgages and may be ostracised or persecuted by prejudiced people. Much of this prejudice is based on fear and ignorance. AIDS cannot be transmitted by normal social contact nor by sharing food, swimming pools or lavatory seats.

If you suspect that you may have been in contact with AIDS you should discuss this with your student health service or seek counselling at a sexually transmitted diseases (STD) clinic. Blood tests for HIV-1 antibodies can be arranged, anonymously if necessary. If you lose weight for no obvious reason, develop persistent swollen lymph glands or suffer from frequent unexplained infections, you will need to consult your student health service. Usually the cause will turn out not to be AIDS.

For advice ring AIDS Helpline on 0171 242 1010, at the Terence Higgins Trust, or send a large sae for leaflets from AIDS Helpline, The Terence Higgins Trust, 52-54 Grays Inn Road, London WC1X 8JU (tel 0171 831 0330; fax 0171 816 4551). Information on HIV and AIDS is issued by the Health Education Authority and is available from your local health centre or direct from the Health Education Authority, Customer Services Dept., Marston Book Services Ltd, PO Box 269, Abingdon, Oxon OX14 4YN (tel 01235 465565; fax 01235 465556).

Dr Peter Andersen, Student Health Physician
University College London

ARRIVAL

Everyone experiences culture shock when they arrive at university or college – overseas students especially. Whatever the environment – red brick or ivory tower – it's new and it's unnerving. Don't worry, you'll get used to it. Make sure you register in the right place at the right time (see *Registration*). At least then you should get your grant and be able to apply for your loan. Find out what you have to do and when, and make yourself out a timetable. It's embarrassing to be late, or lost. Once that's over, submerge yourself in the first week's entertainment – usually a Freshers Fair, endless discos, wine and cheese parties and bar promotion nights. Don't waste money by joining ludicrous societies. Induction meetings will bore you to death, but you'll see the faces in power and you might sit next to someone interesting.

BOOKS

In the first week of term, if not before, you will be presented with an exhaustive reading list. Don't go to the bookshop and buy everything you're expected to – you'll never be able to afford it and they should all be in the library. Second-hand textbooks are often for sale for a fraction of the price – look on student union and departmental notice boards. If these are beyond your means, try borrowing or splitting the cost with others on your course, or being inventive in your use of the library. It is possible (just) never to buy a book, but most students buy a number – make sure they're essentials and not just your tutor's latest failed publication.

CHANGING COURSES

Once you've started, changing courses can be difficult. The dodges are known – get on an undersubscribed course and then switch. Practices vary from university to university but most places are sympathetic. The usual procedure is first to see tutors and then seek whatever permission is necessary. Watch out you do not lose your grant.

Transferring from one university to another can be more difficult and an agreed procedure doesn't exist. You can get advice from CATS (Credit Accumulation and Transfer Scheme, Open University Validation Services, 344–354 Gray's Inn Road, London WC1X 8BP; tel 0171 278 4411; fax 0171 833 1012). Different colleges, and different courses within them, will take different approaches to giving credit for earlier study. Check first before doing anything.

If you are on a grant, you should be able to transfer it to a new course – but only if you get the timing right (the transfer must be approved by the universities concerned before a notional date which is 4 months after the end of your first year) and if there's no extension of time involved (eg moving from the end of the first year of one course to the beginning of the second year of a new course of the same length, without taking time off between). But in either case, you can only transfer your grant if your course transfer is with the approval of **both** course organisers (or both institutions). So make sure you talk to everyone concerned before taking the plunge.

DISABLED STUDENTS

Many disabled students have studied successfully for a degree and have enjoyed the time they spent doing so. Sometimes this has involved a great deal of organisation and some problems along the way, but most people say it has been well worth it. Sometimes disabled students do meet difficulties and barriers, possibly as a result of the physical environment, the attitude of staff or maybe financial difficulties, but not all barriers are insuperable and many can be overcome.

Being well prepared is obviously an advantage, but you will not know exactly what your needs are until you have attended the course for a while. Make full use of any help and support available from the adviser for students with disabilities, welfare officer, student services officer or your personal tutor. There may be other resources such as the library or student union who can offer support too. Make sure you claim all the disabled students' allowances to which you are entitled. There may also be support agencies outside the university or college which may be able to help you, eg RNIB (Royal National Institute for the Blind), Access Centres (for computer assessments, advice) or the Dyslexia Institute. More information from Skill: National Bureau for Students with Disabilities, 336 Brixton Road, London SW9 7AA; tel 0171 274 0565; fax 0171 737 7477.

DISTRESS

Many SUs run their own 'nitelines' for students in distress, often in collaboration with the Samaritans – a national organisation. If you find yourself wanting to talk to someone immediately – try the university 'niteline' (if there is one) or telephone the Samaritans on their new central number, 0345 909090. It automatically connects you to an available line and you only pay for a local call.

DROPPING OUT

There are hundreds of reasons why students drop out – increasingly it's shortage of money. But they may succumb to family pressure to do something else; fall ill or in love; or just not like the course, the subject or the place they've chosen. Maybe they decide they didn't want to do a degree course at all. Men are more likely to drop out of a first year course than women. If you're thinking of dropping out, make sure you talk to tutors and student advisers before you take irrevocable steps. Watch out that you don't jeopardise your future grant possibilities.

If you hate your course and you're incurring frightening debts, the game's probably not worth the candle. Some students leave finding they've incurred substantial debts and with nothing to show for them. From a purely financial standpoint, if you are going to drop out, do it as early as possible and certainly during your first year (you may be able to transfer your grant then). The fifth term is probably the last term of a nine term degree course when you can cut your losses without an overwhelming level of debt. After that, financially speaking, you are better staying on and getting your degree.

Measuring drop-out rates is a statistical minefield, not unlike measuring truancy rates in schools. Publishing league tables of either is a nonsense. If you want to know about the patterns at the universities and colleges you are interested in, talk to the institutions themselves.

DRUGS

Many students will be tempted to experiment with drugs which alter their state of mind. Those that are legal, such as alcohol, nicotine and caffeine, will be sold in most student unions. Tobacco, particularly in the form of cigarettes, causes a great deal of long-term illness and increases the risk of circulatory side effects in those taking the contraceptive pill. Abuse of alcohol causes ill health and leads to loss of social inhibitions, sometimes with disastrous results, such as violence and unwanted pregnancies. Long-term alcohol abuse often leads to poor concentration and study difficulties. However, the temperate use of alcohol, particularly wine, can be the source of much civilised pleasure.

Experimenting with illegal drugs can be a very dangerous occupation – apart from the possibility of fines or imprisonment. Heroin, cocaine, amphetamines, barbiturates, LSD and marijuana are all illegal. New drugs of dependency keep cropping up. In recent years, ecstasy (which is an amphetamine derivative) and crack (which is a refined form of cocaine) have been commonly used. Heroin is the most dangerous, particularly if it is taken intravenously. Dependency develops very rapidly and soon takes over the addict's life. Those who are hooked may have to find £80 a day to feed their habit. This can lead to dealing in heroin, prostitution and other crimes. The intravenous route also leads to the possibility of developing blood infections, Hepatitis B and AIDS.

One aspect of drug dependency is often forgotten. Addicts are at the mercy of their suppliers who may cut or contaminate what they sell. With LSD, for example, there is no way of knowing what dose is being taken. An overdose may cause very frightening 'bad trips' and lead to psychotic episodes.

Marijuana, although illegal, is in a rather different category. It is relatively harmless and does not often lead to antisocial behaviour. However, there is a risk of causing fetal abnormalities during pregnancy. In Holland it has been legalised without any great increase in its use.

If you feel under pressure to experiment with any illegal drug, the best advice is 'don't'.

Students who get into trouble with the police for taking or supplying drugs can get advice from the Release Helpline (tel 0171 603 8654) or write to Release, 388 Old Street, London EC1V 9LT; fax 0171729 2599. If you are worried about a drug problem and want to stop, contact Narcotics Anonymous (Helpline 0171 730 0009, open 10-10, 7 days a week, or write to UK Service Office, PO Box 1980, London N19 3LS).

Dr Peter Andersen, Student Health Physician
University College London

EARN AS YOU LEARN

It is generally estimated that over 90% of students work at some point during their course. A large number work only in the vacations, however a sizeable and increasing percentage find themselves working part-time during term time. It is highly unlikely that you will go through university without choosing to work at some point.

Students' motivations for working are varied. Most do so out of financial necessity, especially those who work during term time. This necessity can take many forms. It is possible to survive on the basic grant and student loan, and some do. However, if a lack of funds means that you cannot afford textbooks or to take up at least some of the vast array of extracurricular opportunities, then working to top up your grant may be a sensible option.

Many students who could cope financially choose to work for other reasons. Responses to a recent survey carried out in a southern university included comments such as: '. . . it helps me to organise my time . . .'; '. . . I enjoy the freedom of having contact with the real world . . .'; '. . . the experience I am getting now will help when I come to look for a job on graduation'; '. . . working helps me to keep a perspective on why I chose to come to university and motivates me to keep studying'. So working needn't be seen only as a 'necessary evil'. The majority of employers who take on graduates like them to have had some previous work experience.

Set against all this are the implications for your academic pursuits. If you find yourself struggling to keep up with your coursework or make it to 9am lectures, then taking on a part-time job in term time is probably not a sensible option.

Term time work
Views within universities on students working in term time vary greatly. Some forbid it absolutely, others are more flexible. A number of pragmatic institutions have developed their own employment offices to help students find jobs and minimise the hassle associated with working.

Most universities which allow work set an explicit limit on the number of hours that you can work each week – a rough guide would be 10–15 hours. Most universities and students' unions employ students on campus where they can, in libraries, bars, administration, catering etc. There is more information in *Where to Study* and this should give you a feel for the current position.

Wages vary across the country and according to what type of work you undertake. The best paid opportunities are certainly in specialist jobs such as translation or tuition which can pay up to £20 an hour. At the other extreme bar work, cleaning and retailing jobs may pay is little as £3 a hour. The average is £3.50–£4.50 a hour; most students earn between £30–£100 a week. So even at the bottom of this scale, you can earn around £1000 a year if you work throughout term time; but it is probably sensible to give yourself some free weeks, especially around exam time.

Vacation work

You can work in the vacations without the concern that it may be affecting your studies. It is in the vacations that virtually all students try to find some kind of job to pay off the overdraft, fund a holiday or gain work experience. Most students return home where living costs are lower but some remain in their university town and others travel further afield with popular schemes such as Bunac (which offers jobs in summer camps in the USA).

Wages in vacations are much more variable and very much depend upon what you choose to do – some organisations will offer a reduced wage and some form of payment in kind. Don't underestimate the value of real training and work experience.

How do I find a job?

As a result of the large number of students looking for employment, competition can be fierce but almost everyone finds something that suits them. The key to finding the 'right job' for you is to be one step ahead of the crowd and prepare early – both for term time and vacation work.

Use all the resources at your disposal – if you are fortunate enough to have an employment office, find out where it is early on and start using it. All universities have careers offices and they will have information on local companies as well as useful hints on application forms, interviews etc.

Check out the opportunities on campus as quickly as possible: these are often the most student-friendly jobs and go quickly. There is often a waiting list for jobs in the union bar by the end of the first day of term!

Use the local paper and keep an eye out for advertisements in shop windows whilst you're walking around town.

Don't be afraid to ask around and approach potential employers on spec. Your careers or employment office will be able to offer assistance on how to do this.

Network – there may be opportunities to help out within your department or in a friend or relative's business. Again, don't be afraid to ask around and let people know that you are available to work.

What can I do to improve my chances of finding a 'good' job?

Without a doubt the single most useful thing that you can do to improve your earning potential is learn to type – the faster the better. This has the added advantage of helping you to prepare your academic work and will probably stand you in good stead when you graduate.

Other fairly common options are to obtain a lifeguard or sporting qualification, care work experience, improved IT skills or to exploit a strong academic subject. If you are good at languages, could you find translation work for local firms? If you are a mathematician, could you coach GCSE candidates?

John Sander, Student Employment Officer
Sussex University

EATING DISORDERS

Eating disorders are much in the news. Students are not immune to them and are sometimes particularly vulnerable. The disorders include obesity (the commonest), anorexia nervosa and bulimia, which are covered below. A useful guide to whether people are over- or under-weight is the Body Mass Index. This is calculated by dividing your weight in kilos by the square of your height in metres. There is no absolutely correct level of BMI for any individual. The average range is from 20–25. It should not be below 18 and if you are over 30 you are reckoned to be obese, medically speaking.

Anorexia nervosa

Anorexia nervosa has been described as 'the relentless pursuit of thinness' and this is its main characteristic. It ends in starvation and death for up to 10% of its sufferers. There is a morbid fear of over-eating and becoming too fat. It usually begins in teenage girls after menstruation has begun. They may have been through a puppy fat stage and been subjected to strong social pressures to conform to the ideal thin figure. Food and eating are often areas of tension within their families who may also be over protective. Anorexic girls see it as a way of controlling their bodies and it becomes a type of addictive behaviour. Girls who suffer from anorexia are emotionally and sexually immature but are often high achievers.

To begin with there is a voluntary restriction of food intake without loss of appetite. In addition to avoiding food, anorexics may induce vomiting, abuse laxatives and take excessive exercise. The condition has become more frequent in the past twenty years. It is uncommon in boys and men. There is evidence that it is commoner in the higher social groups.

Treatment is difficult. The more extreme cases, where weight falls below 35 kilos, have to be admitted to hospital. A regime of rewards for good behaviour, that is eating more, is instituted and in most cases the sufferer is offered some form of psychotherapy. They need to rethink their body images; most anorexics perceive themselves as fat although they are painfully thin. They need to overcome their emotional and sexual inhibitions and to come to terms with their families. They have to resist the images and attitudes in society which revere thin women.

Unfortunately specialised units for treating disorders are scarce and have long waiting lists. Students are usually in a more fortunate situation. Most universities offer help through their student health and counselling services, which have a great deal of experience in eating disorders. Women's support groups also have a place.

Bulimia

Women who suffer from bulimia are usually of normal weight or overweight. They resort to frequent bingeing of high calorie foods followed by self-induced vomiting. Bulimia usually develops in young women from 18 to 30. A study in a family planning clinic showed that 20% of women seen binged occasionally while 2% had full-blown bulimia.

Bulimics may also abuse laxatives and indulge in excessive exercise. The effects of bulimia come on insidiously. The enamel of their teeth may become eroded by the stomach acid in the mouth resulting from vomiting. They may develop fluid retention, irregular periods and finally the depletion of potassium in their blood may result in disorders of the rhythm of their hearts. Binge eating is often a response to stress and isolation. Students who find themselves alone for long periods may binge secretly.

Most bulimics get better. The first step is to share their 'shameful secret' with friends who may help them to eat more normally. Then they should contact their student health services for further help. They can keep a food and vomiting diary which points out the extent to which they are eating abnormally. They should also refrain from weighing themselves frequently as the normal daily variation in weight can be several pounds. The aim is to eat as normally as possible and to enjoy food.

Dr Peter Andersen, Student Health Physician
University College London

HARDSHIP FUNDS

Student hardship is now a universal problem and you should not be too proud to get your hands on your share of any hardship funds going. Hardship funds are one of the most genuinely useful ways universities and colleges can tackle individual cases. Many have their own hardship funds, in addition to government access funds, which often allow small loans to tide you over if your grant is late or if your money from overseas is delayed by exchange control. Some more substantial funds allow reductions in tuition fees if you are not getting a grant, or small cash handouts if you can prove hardship. In order to qualify for money from access funds, you must be a home student and normally need to have applied for a student loan. Other hardship funds may not be so restricted. Ask your tutor or your university or SU welfare staff if you're in difficulties. Some SUs have small hardship funds too.

HEALTH

Most universities and colleges have their own student health services linked to the National Health Service. It is advisable for new students to register with them as NHS patients in the first week of term. Your medical records from your family doctor at home will then follow you in weeks or sometimes months. When you are at home during vacations you can still see your family doctor as a temporary resident.

All the information you give to doctors, nurses and counsellors remains confidential and will not be passed on to the college authorities without your specific consent. If you prefer to have your medical problems dealt with outside your place of study, you are free to register with any NHS general practitioner near where you are living.

The staff in student health services are experienced in dealing with your particular needs. They will be able to offer advice on contraception, unwanted pregnancies, study difficulties and eating problems such as anorexia nervosa. They will discuss with you how to avoid sexually transmitted diseases including AIDS, and drug and alcohol problems. Information on healthy nutrition and keeping fit is available. Some centres also have attached dentists, opticians and physiotherapists.

Most health services will also have facilities for dealing with psychological problems. They employ counsellors, psychiatrists and psychotherapists who may normally be in short supply in the NHS as a whole. Again, it must be emphasised that these services are confidential.

Many colleges have special arrangements for physically disabled or chronically ill students, but it is important to inform them in advance of any difficulties you may have. Some groups of students, eg medics and dental students, need special immunisation cover for their clinical work.

Remember that the health centre staff are just as interested in preventing illness as in treating it, so feel free to consult them before health problems develop.

Dr Peter Andersen, Student Health Physician
University College London

HELP WITH NHS COSTS

The NHS awards no special status to students. From the age of 19 you will no longer be exempt from paying NHS charges for prescriptions, dental treatment, sight tests, glasses etc as you were at school. Like most other young adults you are expected to pay unless you can demonstrate that your income is sufficiently low to qualify for the NHS Low Income Scheme, and that your capital is almost non-existent (unless you are exempt eg because you are pregnant). Most students should have little difficulty in qualifying.

But many pay because they have not obtained the appropriate form (AG1). You should be able to get this from your student health centre, or from GPs, dentists, opticians, a DSS office or direct from the DSS Health Benefits Division (Sandyford House, Newcastle upon Tyne, NE2 1DB). Ask for their leaflet *Help with NHS Costs* while you are about it.

HOMOSEXUALS

If you are homosexual, and it's estimated 5–10% of the population are, then the campus provides a better-than-average environment to come to terms with your own sexuality. Student trendiness promotes the cultivation of gay acquaintances: 'Some of my best friends . . .' Trendy tolerance is easy but public hostility is undoubtedly to be found, especially in the light of AIDS statistics. It's worth remembering that landlords may not welcome overt homosexuals. You can get help and advice from your college homosexual society; most universities have one, maybe a LGBS. There you can meet other gays and, if you like, get into gay politics. Otherwise contact Campaign for Homosexual Equality (CHE, PO Box 342, London WC1X 0DU; tel 0402 326151).

For homosexual students, London is reckoned to be the best bet for its variety of gay social life. Gritty macho areas like the North-east and strong church-going areas like North Wales and Northern Ireland are not advised.

INSURANCE

Best advice is not to take expensive items with you – they might get nicked. It's worth getting anything you do take insured, whether you live in university accommodation or not. You can use Students' Possessions Insurance from Endsleigh Insurance Services (20 The Promenade, Cheltenham GL50 1BR; tel 01242 582563). SU or welfare services should be able to advise you on policies for musical instruments, computers, bikes etc. The most important thing is to get your insurance sorted out immediately so you are covered as quickly as possible. And the more broke you are, the more important it is to be insured in case you are cleared out.

There are occasional tales of unauthorised life insurance salesmen visiting halls and student flats. You are strongly advised not to sign anything and to inform the appropriate authorities. You'll also be sent unsolicited mail – ignore it. As a student, any personal insurance policy you're offered is likely to be a waste of time and money.

LEARNING

It will be different to school. Teachers at degree level treat you as an adult. Having taken the trouble to get there, it is assumed that you enjoy your subject, are committed to it and want to find out more about it. If so, all well and good. But you may find the pattern of work very different from what you're used to. No spoonfeeding; you do it yourself. Before you go, you will probably be sent a booklist. You may not be advised which books to read, use your own judgement. You'll be given a timetable for lectures and tutorials, seminars and practicals. Some lectures and seminars aren't compulsory, but most tutorials and practicals are. It's quite easy not to attend lectures, but it's your loss if you don't.

You will be expected to do a lot of written work and use a wide range of sources. Try to plan your time well, rushed work isn't usually good work. You might have to read your essay, for example, or lead a seminar discussion with other students. Don't be put off by this. Criticism, painful as it can be, sharpens understanding. Don't be put off by more sophisticated students, they are not necessarily brighter. And bright students can be haunted by the fear of failing and need time to adjust to new expectations. Use your own sense and go your own way. See D Rowntree, *Learn How to Study* (Macdonald) or R A Carman and W R Adams, *Study Skills* (Wiley). Sometimes there are courses for students who seem to lack study skills but if you know you need help, try and get it while you're still at school or college. Have a look at Harry Maddox, *How to Study* (Macmillan). Remember, you will have to handle much more information than you did for A-level.

Many universities and colleges have hugely increased their student numbers recently so you may find overflowing lectures, a shortage of books, overstretched specialist teaching space and inadequate contact with tutors. You'll just have to get good at working the system to make sure you don't lose out.

LIBRARIES

Universities spend far less in real terms on books and periodicals than they used to and some spend even less than others. On average, they spend £86.60 per full time equivalent student – but the range is between £40 and £260. You can look up the spending under Library in *Where to Study*. In addition, some libraries have sophisticated on-line facilities so that much extra information is available through national databases, CD-Rom etc.

As libraries will loom large in your student life, suss out your college library very early on and make sure you know how to use it. Check opening times and days; some libraries are closed completely at weekends, others are open 24 hours a day. If your library is under pressure, you'll have to work out ways of reaching recommended books early. Some are deliberately set up as study centres, with lots of seating and computer terminals. Most are central, warm and welcoming, providing a haven for students living off campus.

The university library will probably use a different classification system from the one you were used to at school or college. Most libraries have reader/user information services and will gladly explain how the library works; if there's a published guide, get hold of it. Also ask other students about it – a useful topic of conversation at ghastly induction meetings.

LIVING AT HOME

More students are living at home, mainly because it's cheaper. But it has its difficulties, most obviously because it may be a lot more difficult to take part fully in student life, less obviously because it may make participation in academic studies more isolated and late night use of libraries etc impossible. If you are going to live at home, make sure you have established the ground rules from the start: you are a student on a degree course, not a superannuated sixth former. Different considerations obviously apply to mature students with family constraints. If you attend a college which has large numbers of students living at home, it will be a lot easier to fit in.

For LEAs, it is a lot cheaper if you chose to be home based rather than live in the university/college or other accommodation. If you want to move away from home and your LEA has assessed you on a living at home basis, talk to the office at your university or college which deals with grants. You may be able to get the LEA's assessment changed if the college supports your moving away from home on 'educational grounds' (if you don't have proper facilities to study, such as a room of your own, for example). There is a special reduced grant and loan for students in London who it is believed could conveniently live at home but live elsewhere.

If your grant is discretionary, you are in the hands of your LEA. If the course you want to do is offered locally, they may refuse to pay for you to study elsewhere (eg art foundation course).

LIVING AWAY FROM HOME

For many students, starting at university means living away from home for the first time. If you are one of them, you may find your first few weeks difficult in two quite different ways – coping with the practicalities of day-to-day living and adjusting to the emotional problems of sudden independence.

Emotional problems

Homesickness may be inevitable (it's said to affect some 60% of students, though only some 12% suffer to the point they can't cope). For most it should gradually pass as you adapt to your surroundings. Making friends is important as you won't have parents, siblings or friends back home to rely on. Remember everyone's in the same boat. Don't rush into ephemeral friendships but equally don't avoid human contact for fear of getting hurt. Lasting friendships will form but not in the first five minutes. If you find it hard to cope don't be frightened to use welfare services, or Niteline (run by the SU at most universities), or the Samaritans, for advice and support. They'll be more use (and cheaper) than a bottle of Scotch.

Practicalities

Napoleon knew that armies march on their stomach – no food, no action – and much the same logic applies to student life. You need to be on top of the nitty gritty of everyday living to study and socialise effectively, otherwise your university career could be dominated by personal logistics – travelling, eating, sleeping and keeping clean, not to mention dealing with dentists, plumbers and bank managers.

It's not simply a matter of dosh – pleading poverty may sound fine at home but no good in the SU bar if you can't lay your hands on your grant money. And while it may be cool to be scruffily dressed, if you can't use a washing machine your clothes will probably smell. So, if you are one of the many who are not yet 100% confident of every aspect of living away from home, you could try testing out one or two of the following practical routines.

Money (see also *Cash for Courses*)

Banking: open a bank or building society account if you haven't already got one. (Look at more than one student deal before opening an account.) Make sure you really know how to deposit a cheque or cash; how to get money out (particularly from hole in the wall machines); and you can get and understand a bank statement.

Borrowing money: only go to established institutional lenders, including The Student Loans Company.

Budgeting: try an income/expenditure budget and monitor your actual expenditure against it. You'll find budgeting easier if you've done it before – eg if you've managed a personal clothes allowance, or been travelling on a fixed budget.

Transport

Bus/train/underground: if you're not used to public transport, can you get to grips with the timetable and buying a ticket? A return fare is cheaper than two singles; you may need a young persons rail card or student coach card to travel, so buy it in advance; find out about off-peak travel, all day tickets etc.

Minicab: have you ever ordered a minicab, and got them to tell you the approximate fare in advance? Before you get into the car ask the driver which company he is from to check it was the one you called.

Taxi: Have you ever had to hail a taxi in the street – getting it to see you and stop, giving your destination and paying when you arrive? In London, you pay the taxi driver after getting out (ie through the front window); in most other cities you pay before (ie through the partition).

Foot, bike or blades: Have you had to find your way round an unknown town using a map? Rollerblades (and helmet) are less likely to be stolen than a bike.

Staying in touch

Most students expect to have access to a telephone. If you can't cope with the communal phone which nobody answers, you could get a mobile (you get free local calls with some).

Both BT and Mercury offer chargecards which allow you to phone home at your parents' expense. If you are sharing a flat, you can bar the phone from outgoing calls so you still get in-coming calls but no bills. You can also arrange (currently only through Mercury) for a number of people on a single telephone number to have their own personal bill.

Many universities allow you access to e-mail. Do you know how to use it? Do you know the e-mail addresses of your nearest and dearest?

We assume nobody writes letters any more.

Computers

If you can afford it, get a notebook/laptop or a cheap word processor so you can type up essays; better still if it is compatible with the university/college system.

Health

Chemist: do you know how to get a free NHS prescription? Have you ever bought your own personal hygiene, sanitary, contraceptive items? You have to register in advance to be exempt from prescription charges (see *Help with NHS Costs*).

Dentists and doctors: sign onto an NHS practice. The college/uni will have its own health centre or will advise on good practices.

Shopping

Supermarkets: Have you done your own household shopping? Do you know where to find what you want and what it costs? Make a list before you go, buy own brands, look for the loss leaders and special offers.

Eating in

Buying food: find your nearest market and cheap supermarket. Food prices are often reduced just before closing time.

Storing food: Use a refrigerator if there is one. Food is often edible after the sell-by date; not after the eat-by date.

Cooking: Get in some practice at cooking before you go – and try eating what you have cooked! Get hold of a student cookbook which has cheap recipes and money-saving ideas.

Eating and drinking out

Menus: are you used to reading them, ordering what you have chosen, and paying? Watch for extras like cover charges which will be added to your bill.

Pubs: are you an old hand, and able to get the barman to take notice of your existence? Try finding out what's on offer (guest beers etc).

Laundry

Washing machines: have you ever used the family washing machine? If not, try now. Try using half the recommended amount of washing powder; take your own powder to the launderette.

Dryers: Have you ever used one? A clothes drying rack is cheaper.

Ironing: try at home – or rethink your wardrobe. An iron is usually provided in your accommodation; if not, get a travelling iron.

Libraries

Local library: Well-worth joining for additional books and resources.

MONEY MANAGEMENT

Expect to be broke; anybody can see that the trivial sums the government expects you to live on are inadequate. Unless you're well heeled, you will almost certainly have to borrow more than your maximum student loan to stay afloat. It is not uncommon to end up with debts of £2,000+ over and above the student loan. So manage what money you have to keep debts at a minimum.

The more forward-thinking colleges and universities believe that prevention is better than cure and run seminars on how to manage your money. Almost all try to apply a cure when things do go wrong – advice and, if you are lucky, money through hardship funds (though they are not adequate). Best advice is to tell the college about impending financial catastrophe before it occurs. Here are a few money management considerations:

- Cheap accommodation that is expensive to reach is no help: budget for rent plus fares.
- Buying a second hand bike is usually cheaper than a year's bus fares.
- You will spend a fortune replacing your belongings if they are nicked and you're not insured.
- Most banks offer interest free overdrafts up to £1000+. This is (obviously) the cheapest way to borrow, when you get to that stage.

- If you agree an overdraft with your bank manager, beyond the interest free limit, it should be cheaper for you than for ordinary mortals. Credit cards are an outrageously expensive way to borrow.
- A student loan costs you (later) an interest rate which is the same as inflation. This is about as cheap as borrowed money comes once you start paying interest.
- The astute student will apply early for a student loan and put it in the building society while living off the grant and interest free overdraft. There it will make a small amount of money – particularly for those who remember to arrange for it to be paid gross – until the grant and interest free overdraft are exhausted.
- If you find yourself overwhelmed you'll not be alone. Go and see the student adviser at your college/university or in the SU. Some run special programmes on money management which can offer practical suggestions. Don't consider dropping out without talking to those who may be able to help. Beware of leaving because of financial problems and ending up with the worst of all worlds – a few thousand pounds of debts and no degree to help you earn enough to pay it back.

However well you manage your money once you have got it, there's still one more problem: how to manage before your grant cheque turns up. There'll be a delay of a week or two if you are lucky, a month or more if you're not. You'll probably need to make bridging arrangements before you start term.

OVERCROWDING

Until recently, government policy has been to increase the number of students and to reduce the amount it costs the government. You'll be astonished to learn that this has not been without its problems; staff are now being trained to cope with larger classes and mountains of marking.

Many of the more established universities with other sources of money (rich alumni, research money) have not been so much affected. Some universities have increased their student numbers fairly steadily but some have grown very fast and are bursting at the seams (one or two colleges doubled their student numbers in two years). So beware of overcrowded lectures, little personal tuition, insufficient study space, too few copies of standard texts, cramped student bars ...

OVERSEAS STUDENTS' SURVIVAL

The first few weeks at college can be disorientating for anybody. But students from overseas may have the additional problems of coping with a different language and culture (especially if you haven't already spent much time in the UK).

Many universities and colleges have special orientation programmes and societies for overseas students which offer counselling, help and support (as well as social events). You may not necessarily want to surround yourself with compatriots while you have the opportunity to meet the locals but it can be helpful to know that others share your specific worries/problems. The NUS produces good literature on everything from fees to what to do if the immigration authorities refuse to let you into the country (absolutely must keep your visa up to date if you need one). It also has a list of useful addresses (National Union of Students, 461 Holloway Road, London N7 6HT; tel 0171 272 8900; fax 0171 263 5713; email nusuk@nus.org.uk). You can also get useful advice and information and a contact at most colleges from UKCOSA (Council for International Education, 9–17 St Albans Place, London N1 0NX; tel 0171 226 3762; fax 0171 226 3373; email ukcosa@mailbox.ulcc.ac.uk). The British Council Information Centre (Medlock Street, Manchester M15 4AA; tel 0161 957 7755; fax 0161 957 7762; email stuart.marshall@britcoun.org.uk) runs an information service in Manchester and London, which share the same telephone number. You can telephone or visit (though check their office opening hours); the London address is 10 Spring Gardens, SW1A 2BN. Two useful books – *Studying and Living in Britain* (published annually for the British Council) and *How To Study and Live in Britain* – are both published by Northcote House Publishers.

PARENTS

Establish the groundrules before you go – parental contribution (when and how it's to be paid), frequency of correspondence, phone calls, visits home etc. You are now an adult with a separate life to lead. Preserve your independence but don't distance yourself too much, or it will make contact difficult and Christmas impossible. Pride and/or concern will mean they'll want to come and see how you're getting on. Warn them what to expect. Don't let them just turn up – it will be at the most inconvenient moment. Fix an exact time and date when your more disreputable friends are out of the way.

POVERTY: COPING WITH IT

The amount that students have to live on – whether it's from grants or loans – has failed to keep up with inflation over recent years so the romanticised image of student life on a shoe-string is now a harsh reality for many. However, your allowance for the term may seem like riches beyond measure when you get your first cheque; it isn't, so be careful you don't blow it all in one glorious fortnight only to spend the rest of term trying to avoid your bank manager or working part-time.

The government assumes that your student grant, including parental contribution, and the loan will keep body and soul together until the long vacation, at which point you are expected to earn your own keep until the next academic year. This assumption causes particular difficulties if you haven't got a home to go to in the holidays; and it may pay you to keep the accommodation at college for the full calendar year, and work locally if work at home is scarce.

Students have tried living without their student loans. It's now almost impossible to do so and many have regretted it by the time the next academic year comes round. If you don't want a loan, make sure you really can manage without it. If you do want a loan, apply early and let it earn you some interest before you spend it.

Wherever it comes from (grant, parent, loan, job) you will want your money to go as far as possible. The *Pauper Notes* in each profile in *Where to Study* will help by listing some of the cheapest local amenities. In general, college accommodation is the best value although it is sometimes possible to find very cheap flat shares if you have the time and energy to hunt (and if you are lucky). Food, drink and entertainment are usually cheapest at the SU but keep an eye open for local alternatives (Chinese and Indian restaurants, student discounts at theatres, cinemas etc).

But don't be put off. Although you won't have a lot of spare cash, neither will anybody else; try not to skimp on food. Most students enjoy themselves in spite of their lack of money. After all, the best things in life are free ... they say.

PREGNANCY (UNWANTED)

Some years ago a woman student came to me and the consultation went something like this:

'Doctor, my period is late.'
'Are your periods usually regular?'
'Yes.'
'Have you got a boyfriend?'
'Yes.'
'Could you possibly be pregnant?'
'Of course not doctor.'
'Have you been having sexual intercourse with your boyfriend?'
'Well, not exactly.'
'Did you take any precautions?'
'No.'
'Why not?'
'I don't believe in sex before marriage.'

The student was pregnant.

This story illustrates many students' ambivalent attitude towards sex and contraception. In our service we have about five thousand young women students. On average we see one unwanted pregnancy a week. Probably there are others who go to outside agencies. This pregnancy rate is considerably below the national average for teenagers, which was 69 per 1000 in 1990, but still represents a lot of unnecessary suffering.

Most pregnant students opt for abortions after careful counselling. A few decide to keep their babies. They have to overcome great difficulties with accommodation and financial support. Their studies inevitably suffer.

All student health services offer comprehensive advice and services for contraception. These will cover barrier methods – male and female condoms and diaphragms for women – oral contraceptives, injectable contraceptives, and intra-uterine devices.

Most will choose the combined contraceptive pill as the most effective and safe. For healthy young women who are not smokers the balance of benefits and risks from taking the pill is tilted slightly in favour of the long-term benefits. However, it is worth remembering that although the pill is an excellent contraceptive it does not offer any protection against AIDS. The condom does.

Student health services are happy to talk about sexual problems or anticipated sexual problems to individual students or couples.

Dr Peter Andersen, Student Health Physician
University College London

Racial discrimination is still a sad fact of student life and can be perpetuated by staff or students. That aside, students from ethnic minorities are likely to find that they are confronted with less racial prejudice from whites at a university or college than in many other walks of life – although they may be surprised at the prejudice displayed by other student minorities. The Student Charter is meant to guarantee that there will be no racial discrimination from the staff.

Most universities now have well-organised Black, Jewish and Irish student groups, as well as societies representing overseas students and different national and religious minorities. Many of these groups are extremely active in the social and political life of the college and are a very good place to meet other students of a similar background. The existence of these groups, and national organisations such as the Anti-Racist Alliance and the Union of Jewish Students, has ensured that there is a constant challenge to racism wherever it appears on campus.

The desire to oppose racism wherever it occurs sometimes expresses itself in debates about whether people who are members of declared racist or fascist organisations (or groups with a declared religious purpose which masks a fundamentally racist mission) should have the right to organise or speak at a university. Since the government introduced a law safeguarding free speech on campus, students have found a variety of other means of showing their opposition to speakers who represent racist, fascist or quasi-religious groups.

The black civil rights leader, Martin Luther King, once said, 'If you are not part of the solution you are part of the problem'. Student unions go to great efforts to involve students in campaigns against racism, and anti-racism 'Weeks of action' and international cultural evenings are now common features in a Student Union calendar. Contact SU officers or your tutor if you have a problem on account of your race – on or off the campus.

READING DIFFICULTIES

If you have difficulties with reading, first have your eyes tested. Then get hold of M and E de Leeuw, *Read Better, Read Faster* (Penguin) or T Buzan, *Speed Reading* (David & Charles). Your local FE college may run helpful short courses. If you are dyslexic there are special units at certain colleges and in extreme cases you may be able to dictate essays and exam papers.

REGISTRATION

Put up with registration and enrolment – it only happens once a year and the first year is worst. Expect queues (take books, crosswords or try busking). Make sure you take everything they ask for or it will be even more boring. If they ask for the original certificates they will mean it, so get duplicates in advance if you've lost them (most accept the slips you were sent by your exam board only for the most recent exams). Take your GCSE certificates along too, if they ask you to bring *all* your certificates. Take a pen and don't lose your papers. If you've got problems with eg your grant, tell registration staff. It's a hellish time for everyone – staff and students – so we advise patience and getting your act together before you reach the head of the queue. You'll find it useful to take four or five recent passport photographs for ID, membership cards etc.

SAFETY AND SECURITY

Safety is becoming more of an issue, particularly (but not only) for women. Try and make sure you can get to and from your lectures/parties etc safely – ie that your lodgings are close to public transport, surrounding footpaths are well lit and you know which local routes are safe and which not. Many universities are very conscious of the problem and run late night buses for women students only, issue personal alarms and security leaflets and are introducing security systems and 24-hour portering services. If these aren't available at your university or college – well, start badgering.

Security is also a real problem. Universities and colleges are growing more vulnerable to intruders because their mission often includes wide access to the local community. There is a corresponding growth of ID cards of some sort to admit you to buildings, the library, computer facilities, the refectory or the SU.

SECTS

Students are easy targets for religious sects and a few are banned from campuses. If you are bothered by them, complain to the SU and tutors.

SELF-CATERING CHECKLIST

If you are in self-catering accommodation here are some points you may find useful:

- Find out what cooking facilities are available (oven, rings, grill, microwave, gas or electricity?)
  How many others share them?
  Are there restrictions as to when they can be used?
  Make sure you know how to operate them properly.
- What about cooking utensils, pots, pans, cutlery, crockery etc?
  Make yourself a list of things you know you will need and check how many of them are provided. A basic list could start with:

kettle	at least 1 saucepan	jug
frying pan	chopping board/surface	dishtowels
sharp knife	wooden spoon/spatula	cups and glasses
bread knife	ovenproof dish or bowl	tin opener
plates and bowls	cutlery	

then add whatever else you expect to use: fish slice, lemon squeezer, garlic press, potato peeler, cheese grater, sieve, bottle opener and cork screw.

- What food storage space is available? It can make a big difference if there is somewhere for you to store supplies (without fear of having them stolen) rather than having to dash to the shops every day. This is particularly noticeable during the summer if you don't have access to a fridge.

- Many students find it better to share cooking and food buying. This usually works quite well until somebody gets waylaid in the pub when it's their turn to cook. If you decide to take it in turns to cook (which will reduce considerably the time you spend cooking and shopping) it pays to be organised about it, especially where money is involved. Set up a kitty or an accounts book where everyone writes down how much they spend on communal food etc. It'll also save aggro later if you work out exactly what is communal and what isn't: milk, coffee, cleaning stuff etc. If possible keep some sort of emergency supplies so that you won't starve if your cook gets a last minute invitation on the way home.

- If you haven't done much cooking before, or even if you have and want some quick, inexpensive recipes then try some of these books:

> *The Student Cook Book* (Collins and Brown)
> *The Student Vegetarian Cook Book* (Collins and Brown)
> *The Student Pasta Cook Book* (Collins and Brown)
> *Peckish but Poor* by Cas Clarke (Headline)
> *Grub on a Grant* by Cas Clarke (Headline)
> *The Students' Cookbook* by Jenny Baker (Faber)
> *Cooking for One* by Catherine Kirkpatrick (Hamlyn)
> *Cooking in a Bedsitter* by Katherine Whitehorn (Penguin)
> *Frugal Food* by Delia Smith (Coronet)
> *Not Just a Load of Old Lentils* by Rose Elliott (Fontana)

Many supermarkets have series of recipe books that cater for all sorts of tastes and pockets.

SEX

Many students spend much of their time thinking about sex, but relatively little time actually doing it. Nevertheless, liberal attitudes towards sex still prevail on campus; and concern about AIDS is reflected in the sales of condoms. For students living in close proximity to each other, often for the first time free from parental control, the opportunity to experiment with sex can be irresistible.

SEXUAL HARASSMENT

It probably happens everywhere to a greater or lesser extent. But the stories are most consistent and extreme in the old male preserves. If you do have trouble – from staff or fellow students – make sure you tell someone; there's usually a staff code. Most SUs have an officer responsible for women's issues – that should be a good start.

If you are raped, telephone the local Rape Crisis Centre (in telephone book) or the London Rape Crisis Centre (tel 0171 837 1600). Men too get raped and there's a male rape centre in London called Survivors (call 0171 833 3737).

SEXUALLY TRANSMITTED DISEASES (STDS)

STDs have always been a risk associated with sexual relationships. In 1913 about 10% of the British population had syphilis. By 1985 there were fewer than 3,000 cases of syphilis treated in STD clinics but the annual incidence of gonorrhoea was still over 50,000. Between the end of the last war and some ten years ago, the spread of STDs was contained by early diagnosis, effective treatment and contact tracing achieved by the STD clinics. In the past few years the AIDS epidemic has overshadowed the other STDs but they are still a threat.

Syphilis was in several ways an earlier model of AIDS. It could be caught by sexual intercourse, it could lie dormant for years, it was often fatal and until the advent of antibiotics it was largely untreatable. There was a period in the 1960s and '70s when all STDs were thought to be treatable, which coincided with the introduction of the contraceptive pill and the breakdown of sexual taboos. However, the arrival of genital herpes on the scene changed all that.

The commonest STDs now are non-specific urethritis caused by chlamydial infection, gonorrhoea and monilial vulvo-vaginitis (thrush). The first two can unfortunately infect women without producing symptoms and are a risk to their future fertility. Human wart virus is also transmissible, from men to women and may be a causative factor in cervical cancer. You can greatly reduce the chances of catching any STD including AIDS if you avoid promiscuity and use condoms.

If you develop an unusual vaginal discharge, any genital sore or ulcer or unexplained lower abdominal pain, it is essential to consult your student health service or an STD clinic, also known as departments of genito-urinary medicine (GU clinics). These departments offer free advice, investigations and treatment and you can refer yourself directly without going through your GP.

Dr Peter Andersen, Student Health Physician
University College London

STAFF-STUDENT SEX

It happens. Both male and female students can be at risk, heterosexually or homosexually. It can be very ego-boosting (but not much more) to be 'courted' by an older, and apparently wiser, person. At its worst it is simply sexual harassment.

An affair with a tutor can lead to awkwardness, and more importantly from your point of view, it can increase pressure on you. And it can be very tacky if your tutor is your examiner. Permanent relationships have, very occasionally, been known but tread warily. Some universities and colleges are introducing codes of conduct to regulate staff-student sexual conduct. Others now require staff to report their sexual relationships with students (rather like the House of Commons Register of Members' Interests, but more entertaining). If a member of staff is making unwelcome advances to you, talk to your student counsellor (unless he/she is the offending party) or your SU.

STUDENT CONCESSIONS

Many shopkeepers will give you a discount on proof of student status, usually a NUS or ISIC card. You can also get many newspapers and journals cheap. Lists of local retailers offering discounts are available from your SU office, so use them. To get travel discounts you need an International Student Identity Card (ISIC) and to book your travel through a student travel office. The ISIC is an internationally accepted proof of student status and is available to full-time students of any age for the price of £5.50 (by post) and a passport size photo. It is valid from September to December of the following year and you will get free copies of the travel guide, *World Travel Handbook*. You must have an application form; get this from your local SU or student travel office or from ISIC Mail Order (Bleaklow House, Howard Town Mills, Glossop, Derbyshire SK13 8HT; tel 01457 868003; fax 01457 869361). You have to produce proof you are a full time student – either a student card or a letter from your college authorities confirming your status.

STUDENTS' UNIONS

Almost all universities and colleges have their own SU (sometimes called guild or association), which is normally affiliated to the NUS. Whatever the slant of the union (left, right or apolitical), it is run by students for students – more or less. It's usually responsible for entertainments (bands, discos, bars) and for funding clubs and societies. There is likely to be a union shop, which may be the cheapest place to buy stationery etc, Niteline for personal problems, a bar and maybe other eating and drinking spots. They also often run some form of welfare service which can be useful for advice and information on accommodation, work (in the SU and outside) and money matters. (Most university and college authorities are unenthusiastic about taking over all these services.)

How much you get involved in union activities and politics is up to you, but life could be very dull without them. Don't necessarily be put off by a college's reputation for radical or conservative student politics, but keep your eye on whether its SU engages in political censorship or racist or anti-middle-class activity. Things can change and your involvement could help to change them. Our profiles of universities and colleges sometimes give SU sixth form enquiry points, so you can check out what it's like in colleges that interest you in *Where to Study*.

STUDYING

Do it! If you don't know how, or want to improve on it, try reading *Study for Survival and Success* by Sander Meredeen (Paul Chapman Publishing). Many colleges run formal short courses at the beginning of the first term to help you develop study skills.

WANT TO HELP WITH THE NEXT EDITION? SEE PAGE 66

TERM TIME WORK

Working your way through college is still usually seen here as an American tradition but it has crept into British campus life by stealth and is now quite widespread. (See also *Earn as you Learn*.)

The position varies from university to university. Some still prohibit term time work outright, others are flexible or turn a blind eye. Many universities employ students where they can, so do their SU's; and, increasingly, they help students find work off campus. Some have set up employment agencies, to help students find regular part-time work or occasional jobs.

For your survival, check the rules and make sure you know where to draw the line between surviving financially and getting a degree. Don't rely on pleading fatigue to excuse your examination performance – a sickness certificate is one thing, claims of work fatigue (even if true) are quite another to most examiners.

Many universities permit term time work up to an explicit number of hours per week so that academic work is protected. There are only 24 hours in the day to distribute between studying, socialising and working for cash – not to mention sleep – and there is evidence that term time work lowers students' academic achievement. As a rough guide you can assume that 10 hours per week is about the limit before your studying suffers.

Like everything else, the good jobs go early. So if you know you will need to augment your income, look for work early on. Work in bars, restaurants, shops and offices is available in most areas; where students are employed on campus, it is normally in bars, catering, cleaning, libraries and maintenance. The pay can be paltry – at £2–£3 per hour, you need to know that it's worth it. You can earn more if you can type (at least 30 words/minute). Significantly, some universities pay more than the local rates, some less.

But it's not all negative. Some science students report that working mindlessly (stacking shelves, petrol station forecourt etc) is a good way of relieving the pressures of their highly intensive course; others go for more challenging work to enhance their CV; a few even end up being offered a worthwhile permanent job.

TIME MANAGEMENT

If you go to university or college direct from school, you may find that managing your time is a real problem. Your timetable may seem undemanding in comparison to school: you probably won't have to be anywhere in particular for a lot of the time. This can lead to much time wasting. Grip it from the start. A well known time management technique is to analyse your diary in detail for a whole week, which means recording what you do hour by hour. The results can be illuminating. Remember it's your own time you are wasting, nobody else's.

TOWN AND GOWN

Relationships between town and gown still matter. If they're harmonious, it means you'll feel welcome in the streets, shops and pubs, and late night travel won't be any more of a threat than elsewhere. If antagonistic, life is much harder, particularly if your accommodation is out of the main student area. You can be made to feel so uncomfortable that you stick within your college or campus rather than chance mixing with the locals – particularly where youth unemployment is high. And if your accommodation is an isolated bed-sit the locals can make life impossible. *You* may feel that you're an impecunious student; the local unemployed may see you as privileged, state subsidised, middle class. If you are worried about the position at any of the colleges, it could be worth contacting the SU. Many of them offer enquiry points for sixth formers – see *Where to Study*.

TRAVEL – LOCAL

Local travel can be horrendous at some universities and colleges but at others there is no need to travel at all. Check what travel is required before applying – otherwise you may find you are spending nearly as much time, energy and money as the average local commuter. You can get some idea from *Where to Study* and prospectuses.

Once you're living on your own money, you'll find you can walk much further than you ever thought possible; and, unless your nerve has completely failed you, a pushbike or pair of roller blades can be useful, if not essential. Hitching may be possible, depending on the area but it's not recommended for women alone, particularly after dark (some SUs run night-time minibuses for women). Buses are often cheaper than trains and both can be cheaper than the tube in London – but it will depend on your journey. Try to plan your local travel so that it does not eat all your money.

TRAVEL – NATIONAL

Travel further afield needs researching. You can start by looking for local opportunities on the college 'ride boards', advertising lifts to home, to London, to sporting events and cultural occasions. But to cut your travel costs usually means investing in one of the special cards offered by National Express Coaches and British Rail.

Cutting your coach costs: National Express Coaches offers a Student Coach Card for £8 which gives you 30% off adult fares for one year in UK and reductions on some Eurolines fares. Regulations do change so check that you are getting what meets your own travel requirements. To get one take a passport sized photograph to any National Express or Caledonian Express agent; you can find your nearest by telephoning National Express Coaches on 0990 808 080.

Cutting your rail costs: Start by buying a Young Persons Railcard for £16. It gives you a large but varying discount (usually 34%) on standard class fares, including savers, super-savers and cheap day returns. You need to check for full details at your local station as there may be certain ticket, route and time restrictions applicable. Keep an eye out for any discounts or special offers, particularly at the beginning of the academic year. Take two passport sized photographs with you and proof of your age if you are under 25, or that you are a student if you are 26 or over. Young Persons' Railcards are sold at railway stations with a ticket office, at rail appointed travel agencies and at student travel offices. Details from your nearest mainline station.

VACS

You'll never have holidays this long again until you retire, so make the most of them. It's probably essential to use them to inject some life into your bank balance as well. You can start by looking at some of the excellent books published by Vacation Work Publications (9 Park End Street, Oxford OX1 1HJ; tel 01865 241978, fax 01865 790885). The most popular are the *Directory of Summer Jobs in Britain* and the *Directory of Summer Jobs Abroad* but they also have an impressive list of specific regional and country titles. You can use a vacation job as a way of demonstrating work experience to bolster your CV.

If you are into travel, start with your student travel office, which sells the products of the 10 or so main student travel operators and has heaps of good advice on student/youth travel. If there isn't one on your campus, contact Student Travel Centre, Tours and Travel (STCTT, 24 Rupert Street, London W1V 7FN; tel 0171 434 1306; fax 0171 734 3836) or Campus Travel (headquarters at London Student Travel, 52 Grosvenor Gardens, London SW1W 0AG; European telephone enquiries 0171 730 3402; worldwide enquiries 0171 730 8111; fax 0171 730 6893; and on 26 student campuses).

No student pays the full scheduled air fare. There are all the usual methods of getting cheaper flights – bucket shops, ads, charter flights, standby fares, and advance booking (APEX and ABC). In addition, there are lots of student specials. The most obvious are youth fares and student charters. Youth fares allow a range of reductions (up to 25%) off the standard economy fare to European countries and some others. Some have to be bought from a student travel office, so ask there first. They are good value on long-haul and European flights, giving you full-fare service at student prices. Student charter flights operate in each vacation to Europe, Israel and the USA. You can get on them with a valid International Student Identity Card (ISIC) – check your student travel office.

Or, if you are under 26, you can travel cheaply by train with a 'Euroyouth' BIJ ticket. BIJ (Billets International Jeunesse) gives you a discount (the amount depends on the country) on second-class train tickets (including the Channel crossing) to destinations in Europe and Morocco. You can stop-over and you don't need to come back the same way as you go. You can buy a ticket from any British Rail station or your student travel office (or some other Eurotrain/British Rail/Sealink agents). If you want to hit the fleshpots of a number of European cities, you may prefer an Interail card. This will currently set you back some £279 for the whole of Europe (less if you choose a specific zone or have a Young Persons Rail Card). It is valid for two calendar months and entitles you to unlimited travel on national rail networks in 22 countries on the continent, as well as reductions on some hovercraft and ferry services. For advice on worldwide train travel try the International Rail Centre at Victoria station.

There are some coach routes to Europe which are cheap. Get a brochure from Eurolines (4 Cardiff Road, Luton, Bedfordshire LU1 1PP; tel 01582 404511; fax 01582 400694).

Other thoughts: if you are interested in working in an American summer camp, contact Camp America (37a Queen's Gate, London SW7 5HR; tel 0171 581 7373) or BUNAC (British Universities North America Club, 16 Bowling Green Lane, London EC1R 0BD; tel 0171 251 3472) which also arranges other working holidays in North America.

Work on a kibbutz can be arranged through Kibbutz Representatives (1a Accommodation Road, London NW11 8ED; tel 0181 458 9235) or Project 67 (10 Hatton Garden, London EC1N 8AH; tel 0171 831 7626).

And if you just want to bum around, you'll find cheap accommodation in youth hostels – contact the Youth Hostel Association (Trevelyan House, 8 St Stephen's Hill, St Albans, Hertfordshire, AL1 2DY; tel 01727 855215), in Scotland the Scottish Youth Hostels Association (7 Glebe Crescent, Stirling SK8 2JA; tel 01786 451181) or in Northern Ireland, YHANI (Youth Hostels Association of Northern Ireland, 22 Donegal Road, Belfast BT12 5JN; tel 01232 324733).

VICTIMISATION

If you think you are being victimised for reasons of politics, race, religion or sex you should contact your SU or try one of the following:

Campaign for Homosexual Equality (CHE)
PO Box 342, London WC1X 0DU; tel 0402 326151; fax 0181 743 6252
Catholic Students Council
96 Bradford Street, Birmingham B12 0PB; tel 0121 772 0522; fax 0121 773 6023
Commission for Racial Equality
Elliot House, 10–12 Allington Street, London SW1E 5EH; tel 0171 828 7022; fax 0171 630 7605; web http://www.open.gov.uk/cre/crehome.htm
Equal Opportunities Commission
Overseas House, Quay Street, Manchester M3 3HN; tel 0161 833 9244; fax 0161 835 1657
Liberty (National Council for Civil Liberties)
21 Tabard Street, London SE1 4LA; tel 0171 403 3888
National Organisation of Labour Students
John Smith House, 150 Walworth Road, London SE17 1JL; tel 0171 701 1234
National Union of Students
Nelson Mandela House, 461 Holloway Road, London N7 6LJ; tel 0171 561 6500; fax 0171 263 5713; email nusuk@nus.org.uk
Union of Jewish Students
Hillel House, 1/2 Endsleigh Street, London WC1H 0DS; tel 0171 380 0111; fax 0171 383 0390; email ujs@brijnet.org.uk
Youth Section Conservative Central Office
32 Smith Square, London SW1P 3HH; tel 0171 222 9000; fax 0171 222 1135; web http://www.conservative-party.org.uk

WELFARE

Universities and colleges generally are supportive. They normally provide specialist help for a range of problems. The NUS publishes an excellent *Welfare Manual* – intended for student advisers but you may be able to consult a copy in your library or SU office or contact NUS (461 Holloway Road, London N7 6LJ; tel 0171 561 6500; fax 0171 263 5713; email nusuk@nus.org.uk).

Students are not entitled to welfare benefits just because they are students: if you are for example disabled or a single parent, you will be entitled to some benefits. Ask your local DSS offices or Citizens Advice Bureaux or see the *Young People's Guide to Social Security* issued by the DSS. Those on low incomes are entitled to exemption from NHS charges (see *Help with NHS Costs*).

HOW TO START? *SEE SHORTLISTING*, PAGE 535

WHAT IF YOU DON'T SURVIVE YOUR FIRST YEAR

Work out what went wrong.

- If you're not up to higher education, look for a job. If you fancy eventually becoming your own boss, buy *Independent Careers* (Bloomsbury).
- If it was the wrong course, the wrong college, or the wrong place, try changing (fast, to keep your grant).
- If the reasons are personal or financial, try giving it a break. You **may** be able to return later, transfer credit to another institution or continue part-time somewhere else.

WHAT YOU CALL THEM/WHAT YOU DON'T

(ie formal address for academics). Below are the terms for **formal** address in speech and writing – what you call academics informally is up to you.

Status	Speech	Writing
Vice-Chancellor	Vice-Chancellor	Dear Vice-Chancellor
Principal	Principal	Dear Principal
Director	Director	Dear Director
Master (applies to some women as well)	Master	Dear Master
Warden	Warden	Dear Warden
Professor (even if knighted)	Professor Bloggs	Dear Professor Bloggs
Readers/Senior Lecturers/ Lecturers/Tutors	Dr/Mr/Ms/Mrs Bloggs	Dear Dr/Mr/Ms/Mrs Bloggs

Do not use Dear Sir, Dear Madam, or Dear Sir/Madam, when writing to tutors.

WHEN YOU'VE GOT STUCK IN

When you've settled in, and before you forget *The Student Book* completely, how about writing to us? We'd particularly like to know of anything you wish you'd known about before you applied or when you got there, and any money saving tips.

Please write to Klaus Boehm and Jenny Lees-Spalding,
The Student Book, c/o Trotman, 12 Hill Rise, Richmond, Surrey TW10 6UA.

If you're lucky, you might even get an acknowledgment – but no promises!

WHAT'S WHAT IN HIGHER EDUCATION

ABBREVIATIONS

Higher education is not only jargon-laden but studded with abbreviations and acronyms. Here are a few useful ones:

A-levels – GCE Advanced Level

ADAR – Art and Design Admissions Registry

APEL – Assessment of Prior Experiential Learning

APL – Assessment of Prior Learning

AS-levels – Advanced Supplementary levels

BA – Bachelor of Arts

BArch – Bachelor of Architecture

BBA – Bachelor of Business Administration

BEd – Bachelor of Education

BFI – British Film Institute

BN – Bachelor of Nursing

BPA – Bachelor of Performing Arts

BPharm – Bachelor of Pharmacy

BSc – Bachelor of Science

BSocSci – Bachelor of Social Science

BTEC – Business and Technology Education Council

BUSA – British Universities Sports Association

C&G – City & Guilds

CATS – Credit Accumulation and Transfer Scheme

CDS – Conference of Drama Schools

CE – Continuing Education

CEF – Clearing Entry Form (UCAS)

CIFE – Conference for Independent Further Education

COIC – Careers and Occupational Information Centre

COMETT – Community Programme in Education and Training for Technology

DFEE – Department for Education and Employment

DSA – Disabled Student Allowance

EC – European Community

ECCTIS – Educational Counselling and Credit Transfer Information Service

ECTS – European Credit Transfer System

EEA – European Economic Area

EGA – Educational Guidance for Adults

ERASMUS – European Community Action Scheme for the Mobility of University Students

EU – European Union

FE – Further Education

FORCE – Formation Continuée en Europe

FT – full time (of students and staff)

FTE – full-time equivalent (eg student)

GCE – General Certificate of Education

GCSE – General Certificate of Secondary Education

GATE – GNVQ and Access To Higher Education

GNVQ – General National Vocational Qualifications

GTTR – Graduate Teacher Training Register

HE – Higher Education

HEFC – Higher Education Funding Council

HEIST – Higher Education Information Service Unit

HEQC – Higher Education Quality Council

HNC – Higher National Certificate

HND – Higher National Diploma

IB – International Baccalaureate

ICP – Inter-University Co-operation Programme

IRT – Institution with RECognised Teachers (University of London)

ISIC – International Student Identity Card

IT – Information Technology

ITT – Initial Teacher Training

JCR – Junior Common Room

LEA – Local Education Authority

LGBS – Lesbian, Gay, Bisexual Society

LINGUA – Community Action Programmes to Promote Foreign Languages Competence in the European Community

LLB – Bachelor of Laws

MA – Master of Arts

MBA – Master of Business Administration
MChem – Master of Chemistry
MEng – Master of Engineering
MMath – Master of Mathematics
MPhys – Master of Physics
MRes – Master of Research
MSci – Master of Science
NCDT – National Council for Drama Training
NUS – National Union of Students
NVQ – National Vocational Qualification
ONC – Ordinary National Certificate
OND – Ordinary National Diploma
PAMs – Professions Allied to Medicine
PSHE – Public Sector Higher Education
PT – part-time (of students or staff)
QTS – Qualified Teacher Status
RSA – Royal Society of Arts
SA – Students' Association
SCE – Scottish Certificate of Education
SCR – Senior Common Room
SED – Scottish Education Department
SLC – Student Loans Company
SRC – Students' Representative Council
STEP – Sixth Term Examination Papers (entrance exam for Cambridge University)
SU – Students' Union
SWAS – Social Work Admissions System
TEMPUS – Trans-European co-operation scheme for higher education
UCAS – Universities and Colleges Admissions Service
UKCOSA – The Council for International Education
ULU – University of London Union
WUS – World University Service

ACCESS COURSES

Widening access means opening up higher education to non-standard students, particularly mature students. Access courses are designed to prepare you for a degree course if you are not already qualified – particularly in science and engineering. Some are excellent, some are suspect. Check what extra qualifications (if any) you need for your chosen degree course before you embark on an access course. Many access courses are run at local FE colleges, in which case you may be able to go locally. A useful book is *Access to Higher Education Courses Directory* available from ECCTIS.

Unlike students on the foundation year of degree courses, students on access courses are not eligible for a mandatory grant (but they may receive one of the fast disappearing discretionary grants). Some colleges are dropping access courses in favour of franchised degree courses with a foundation year. This may put you in a better position for a grant but check.

ACCESS FUNDS

Access Funds are provided by the government but distributed by universities and colleges at their own discretion, to home students in financial hardship. They are intended to support students after they have exhausted the possibilities of a student loan. Our university and college profiles sketch what's available at each institution and any stated priorities for deciding whom to help. Many institutions have their own hardship funds as well.

ADVANCED GNVQ

Advanced GNVQs are vocational qualifications, equivalent to 2 GCE A-levels, and sometimes called vocational A-levels. They are in broad occupational areas such as health and social care (which could lead to a degree course in eg nursing, social work, occupational therapy, teacher training) or manufacturing (which can lead to a degree course in engineering).

They are accepted by many universities although you may be asked to pass with a merit or distinction and perhaps also to take additional GNVQ units or a contrasting A-level (an A-level in a similar subject doesn't add much). Universities are more likely to accept a GNVQ if it is relevant to the degree course (they're more open minded about A-levels), so your choice of course is more restricted. But the success of GNVQ applicants is, on the whole, better than UCAS applicants in general. You can check out the detailed approach of most universities to GNVQs (and whether they require any additional qualifications) in *GNVQ and Higher Education – Entry Conditions (GATE)*.

AGRICULTURE

Agriculture is taught both as a first degree and for other vocational qualifications. Some agricultural colleges only teach for vocational qualifications and in general tend to be concerned more with training and less with the scientific aspects of the subject; they are not included in *The Student Book*. Many degree courses are offered by universities and colleges in much the same way as in any other science – you can look them up in the *Subject and Places Index*. And six distinguished agricultural colleges are rooted in both the scientific and the vocational traditions (Harper Adams; Royal Agricultural College; Scottish Agricultural College; Seale Hayne, part of Plymouth University; Welsh Institute of Rural Studies; Writtle College – look them up in *Where to Study*.)

A-LEVEL AND AS-LEVEL GRADES

Grades A–E at A-level and AS-level are accepted as passes; these are often turned into points by UCAS.

GRADE	UCAS Points	
	AS-level	A-level
A	5	10
B	4	8
C	3	6
D	2	4
E	1	2

If you have a conditional offer, you may well be asked to gain specific grades or a cumulative minimum number of points. A-level grades are not regarded as reliable pointers to future academic development but do help universities sort out students for places. Your job is to get your A-level grades. If you want to know the grades accepted for a particular course last year, look in Brian Heap's, *Degree Course Offers* (published by Trotman), or in many prospectuses. Most admissions tutors will normally accept two AS-levels in place of a third A-level but not in place of the first two. But there may be additional course requirements, so check.

AMERICAN COLLEGES

You can get an American degree without leaving the country because many US universities and colleges have a UK campus which admits British students. Their academic standards are very variable, so British students may find it difficult to get British employers and professional bodies to accept their degree as necessarily equal to a British degree. Some of the American colleges represented in the UK are excellent and of international standing.

ART & DESIGN

Degrees in art and design are offered at some (but not all) colleges of art and at a number of universities — see the *Subject and Places Index*. Some art colleges are now departments of universities; some have merged to form a group of art colleges such as the London Institute; others remain independent. They may offer their own degrees, those of the parent group (eg London Institute) or those of a university. There are hundreds of first degree and postgraduate courses in art and design. There are descriptions of them in *A Guide to Art & Design: On Course for 1998*.

Over 200 colleges offer foundation courses, which is one route to a degree; they are listed in *Art & Design Courses 1998* (Trotman, 12 Hill Rise, Richmond, Surrey TW10 6UA). Most students take a foundation course at their local art college (you are unlikely to get a grant unless you do). Anyway a large foundation course at a London college can be daunting for 16-year olds.

BOGUS DEGREES

A number of bogus degrees are offered by post, mostly postgraduate degrees. Sometimes the degree is for sale, sometimes a thesis is required. There is seldom any course of instruction. No college in *The Student Book* offers or accepts them. Under the Education Reform Act 1988, it is a criminal offence to award or seek to offer a UK degree if you do not have express authority to award it, and the Department for Education and Employment provides lists of authorised bodies. If in doubt contact the DFEE. There is no such constraint on offering UK certificates or diplomas, or bogus degrees from overseas, so beware.

CAMPUS

The meaning of the word is changing. It originally came from the US, meaning a purpose built university in its own grounds, and still validly describe many universities built in the 60s, eg Sussex and Lancaster. In contrast, Oxford and Cambridge which have colleges and faculties spread around town are not campus universities. But many UK universities and colleges now use the word campus to label each teaching site – anything up to half a dozen, maybe spread over half a county.

CATS

This is a national scheme operated by the Open University to help students transfer credit (see *Credit Transfer*). CATS stands for Credit Accumulation and Transfer Scheme (CATS, Open University Validation Services, 344–354 Gray's Inn Road, London WC1X 8BP; tel 0171 278 4411, fax 0171 833 1012). It should be able to help you if you:

- want to carry credit to a degree course, perhaps on the grounds that you have already taken part of a course or have work experience that duplicates part of the course;
- want to study for a degree at more than one college, perhaps because nowhere teaches the combination of studies you seek – eg Arabic and Hebrew;
- want to alternate periods of study with other activities – eg raising a family or earning your living.

You can make use of CATS in two different ways – either purely for obtaining advice before you apply for a degree course or by registering directly with CATS so that you become a CATS student and can then study at a number of places. A number of companies' in-house training schemes (eg IBM, W H Smith, Wimpey) and professional bodies' qualifications (eg IPM, CIMA) can count for credit too.

COLLEGE

This is a portmanteau word. It can mean many things from a school (eg Eton College), a crammer (Garret Tutorial College, Hackney), a distinguished seat of learning (University College London), to a professional institution (The Royal College of Surgeons). In post-school education, some colleges teach first degrees, but most do not.

The colleges in *The Student Book* are all in what is termed higher education and fall into several categories:

- specialist colleges, sometimes enormously distinguished and internationally known, which offer either degrees awarded by a university or their own qualifications – eg Royal College of Art, Jews' College, Royal Agricultural College or Welsh College of Music and Drama.
- colleges that are part of a university but you are admitted to the college – either on the Oxbridge model, where there is some university-wide teaching; or the very

independent colleges of the federal universities such as London and Wales (some would wish to be universities in their own right).

- higher education colleges. These are not universities although the majority have a link with a university and an increasing number have renamed themselves (eg Chester) University College. They run a variety of post A-level and other courses and degree students may be in the minority. Some award their own degrees (eg Cheltenham & Gloucester College); others offer degrees awarded by a university (eg Nene College). In this case, there is some sort of relationship with the university, increasingly becoming more formal and transparent and ultimately involving incorporation into the university as a satellite college (eg Chichester University College).

COMMUNITY SERVICE VOLUNTEERS

CSV is a national volunteer agency which involves young people in full-time community work in a wide range of projects throughout the UK, normally away from home. Volunteers are currently working with adults and children with learning difficulties or physical disabilities, with the homeless, the elderly, children whose families have broken up, young offenders, immigrants who want to learn English, battered wives and children on adventure playgrounds and play schemes. You don't need experience or qualifications to become a CSV – just the enthusiasm to commit yourself to the community and to improving the quality of other people's lives. No offer of service is refused: provided you can give between 4 and 12 months' full-time and are over 16, CSV will find a project for you. As a volunteer, you'd receive full board and lodging plus £23.50 per week spending money and travelling expenses. If you think you might be interested in becoming a CSV, try the freephone number 0800 374991 or write for information and an application form to CSV (237 Pentonville Road, London N1 9NJ; tel 0171 278 6601, fax 0171 837 9621).

COMPACTS

In British educational jargon, compacts are agreements between schools, universities and employers to provide alternative ways of getting into higher education and ultimately into employment. Students are admitted to higher education from school by meeting specific educational targets – usually agreed portfolios and vocational qualifications.

CONTINUING EDUCATION

Another educational term which means what its users want it to mean. Essentially CE means that you can't expect your education to end when you get your first degree. You can expect periods of re-education and re-training during your working life and that includes updating your knowledge of the subject you read for your degree. This contrasts with studying for a higher degree which is intended to take you deeper into your subject.

CORRESPONDENCE COURSES

These are essentially part-time courses by postal tuition. There have been some suspect courses and the responsible correspondence colleges have established a voluntary accreditation scheme. You can get a list of accredited colleges from the Open & Distance Learning Quality Council (27 Marylebone Road, London NW1 5JS; tel 0171 935 5391, fax 0171 935 2540). For advice on UK degrees available by correspondence, contact the DFEE (Department for Education and Employment).

COUNCIL TAX

Students are largely exempt. If you are lucky enough to live in college, in a hall of residence, a student hostel or a flat/cottage/house where all the adult residents are students, you are entirely exempt. If you live anywhere else, the position is more complicated. If two (non-student) adults already live there, the council tax is payable in full. If only one person lives there, you can apply for a 25% student discount.

CREDIT TRANSFER

If you change your course, or leave higher education altogether and return to it after a break, you may be able to transfer the credit for the work you did in your earlier course to your new one and so complete your new course faster. The jargon for this is credit transfer. You can carry a credit from one university to another, or from one course to another within the same college. You will need the help (and maybe the approval) of the course tutor from your first course so make sure you keep him/her informed. Also, if you are on a grant, watch out you don't lose it when you change course.

Some transfers are easier than others – from a HND to a linked degree course in the same place will probably be automatic. But you wouldn't, of course, expect to carry any credit to a physics degree on the basis of previous study in the social sciences.

The overlap in subject matter is not necessarily simple for admissions tutors to assess and there is often a noticeable reluctance even to try. Indeed, there can be widely differing approaches between the different courses in a single university. Some modular courses can, and do, admit a large number of students with credit. If you want to find out whether your previous work will count for credit, ask when you apply. If that doesn't work, ask CATS.

If your university is part of the Erasmus Scheme, you can study somewhere else in the EU for credit. Erasmus runs a credit transfer system (ECTS) – enquire direct to your university or college.

DEGREE COURSE STRUCTURES

There are different types of degree courses in terms of structure (single, multi-disciplinary) and approach (theoretical, vocational). As the courses become more flexible, the labels become harder to define but here are a few:

Single subject degrees
One subject is studied for the length of the course, although a wide variety of topics may be covered and the first year may be broad;

Joint honours
Two subjects are taken equally (you don't do twice as much work);

Combined (multidisciplinary or interdisciplinary)
Components from any number of subjects can be put together;

Modular (or unit based)
Students structure their own degrees from a range of units or modules. Increasingly, you may be able to add study of a language to any of these.

Theoretical
A specialist study without immediate applications;

Vocational
The degree is directly linked to work applications;

Sandwich
Part of the course is spent in a work placement.

Each university and college has its own language about its degrees so check thoroughly that it will provide what you expect. Check how the degree is assessed (eg examination, continuous assessment, project work). This can vary depending on the course.

Commonly a degree course lasts three years. But there are now a few accelerated courses lasting two years (typically 45 weeks a year); and many last four or more years – particularly if you spend a year abroad or in a work placement, if you get an additional qualification (eg QTS) as part of the course or if you are studying medicine or veterinary science. Degree courses may take more time if there is a foundation year, or if you start off with an access course.

DEGREES

First degrees are the main concern of *The Student Book*. Despite claims to the contrary, their value varies enormously – academically, economically and socially – and this variance reflects not only the quality of teaching but employers' perceptions of it. Never believe that all degrees are equal.

Most degrees are now honours degrees which are differentiated by classes (first, upper second, lower second and third). Again, don't believe that a first class degree from one university necessarily equals a first from another; whatever they say, it does not. Ordinary degrees (sometimes called a pass degree) may be awarded if a student fails to achieve honours standard although some courses (eg at the Open University) lead only to an ordinary degree.

Most first degrees lead to the award of bachelor status – usually BA, BSc, BEd or LLB (and some modern mouthfuls, BSocSci, BPhysChem). But then it becomes confusing. Some first degrees lead to masters, notably in Scotland (where many first degrees lead to an MA) and some 4-year science degrees go straight to eg MEng, MMath. Conversely, not all bachelor degrees are first degrees, eg BPhil is a higher degree, but these are usually masters or doctorates (MA, MSc, PhD), again with many variants. Don't get worried by the letters – where and what you study matter more.

Universities give their own degrees to their own students, as do a handful of colleges and institutes of higher education. A number of universities also offer their own degrees in affiliated colleges and maybe in some other colleges. Degrees from foreign universities (eg American universities) are offered in the UK but *The Student Book* does not cover them. But some students at UK universities, who spend a period abroad, may gain a foreign qualification in addition to their British degree.

DFEE

The Department for Education and Employment (Sanctuary Buildings, Great Smith Street, Westminster, London SW1P 3BT; tel 0171 925 5000) is the central government department responsible for education in England and Wales. Its publication office is at another address: DFEE, Publications Centre, PO Box 6927, London E3 3NZ (tel 0171 510 0150, fax 0171 510 0196). Most matters concerning grants are dealt with by your LEA. For Northern Ireland the equivalent central department is the Northern Ireland Department of Education (Rathgael House, Balloo Road, Bangor, County Down BT19 7PR; tel 01247 279000), and for Scotland the Scottish Education Department (Gyleview House, 3 Redheugh Rigg, Edinburgh EH12 9HH; tel 0131 556 8400).

DIPLOMA IN HIGHER EDUCATION (DIPHE)

In theory, the two year DipHE course is equivalent to the first two years of a degree course. This could be of interest to mature students not wishing to commit themselves to 3 years' study. Some colleges allow you to transfer from a DipHE course to a degree course; others haven't heard of them so check before you start.

DRAMA TRAINING

Drama courses preparing students for work in the professional theatre and the film, TV and radio industries are offered at a variety of universities and colleges. While some are degree courses, others often do not involve a large measure of academic work and take less than three years to complete.

So a lot of drama courses do not qualify you for a mandatory student grant. Your LEA may give you a discretionary grant, in which case it decides for itself how much to give you. But you can easily find yourself not only funding your living costs but also having to find the tuition fees (which are much higher than university fees).

To be in with a chance, choose a course approved by the National Council for Drama Training (NCDT). It publishes a list of its accredited acting and stage management courses and the addresses and telephone numbers of the schools which teach them (they may not accredit all the courses at each school). Write to The National Council for Drama Training (5 Tavistock Place, London WC1H 9SS, tel 0171 387 3650) enclosing a sae for your copy.

The NCDT list includes accredited courses at: ALRA (Academy of Live & Recorded Arts); Arts Educational Schools; Birmingham School of Speech & Drama; Bristol Old Vic Theatre School; Central School of Speech & Drama; Drama Centre London; Drama Studio London; Guildford School of Acting; Guildhall School of Music & Drama; London Academy of Music & Dramatic Art; London Academy of Performing Arts; Manchester Metropolitan University School of Theatre; Mountview Theatre School; Oxford School of Drama; Queen Margaret College; Rose Bruford College of Speech & Drama; RADA (Royal Academy of Dramatic Art); Royal Scottish Academy of Music & Drama; Webber Douglas Academy of Dramatic Art; Welsh College of Music & Drama.

What are the drama colleges like? You can look up some which teach first degree level or equivalent in *Where to Study*. For those that we do not profile, your best starting point is the prospectus and guide to accredited courses, published by the Conference of Drama Schools (c/o the Central School for Speech and Drama, 64 Eton Avenue, London NW3 3HY; send a C5 envelope and 38p stamp. For general enquiries telephone 0181 299 4516).

ECCTIS 2000

ECCTIS stores information on some 100,000 British and Irish courses, including access courses. It includes entry requirements and course content. It also catalogues credit transfers and credits for previous experience so you could find it useful whether you are still at school, you are a mature applicant, or if you are already doing a course and want to change to another.

You can only get your teeth into this mind-boggling mass of detail through an ECCTIS access point. These are rapidly being installed in schools and libraries and are already available in most careers offices (also British Council offices). Locate your nearest access point by contacting ECCTIS (Oriel House, Oriel Road, Cheltenham, Gloucestershire GL50 1XP).

ERASMUS/LINGUA

There are two EU initiatives for students – the Erasmus programme (the European Community Action Scheme for the Mobility of University Students, which is part of a programme called Socrates) and Lingua (which is the language-learning programme and works in the same way as Erasmus).

If you want to study in Europe under Erasmus or Lingua, you should make sure that your university or college is a participant before you apply (all UK universities and many HE colleges have some involvement). You may also get help with the extra costs involved (extra fees, higher living costs or costs incurred in local teaching practice), in which case your course must be approved as well. ECTS – the European Credit Transfer System – is a project within Erasmus which may help you with credit recognition and transfers. Many Erasmus students end up with two qualifications for the same course – one from their host university in addition to their UK degree.

UK students are taking a very active part in Erasmus schemes. All UK first degree courses involved in the Erasmus/Lingua programme are listed in *The UK Guide to Socrates-Erasmus* (ISCO Publications, tel 01276 21188). Ask your university or college about specific opportunities, your own eligibility, Erasmus/Lingua schemes and grants. For general information (only) contact: UK Erasmus Students Grants Council (The University, Canterbury, Kent CT2 7PD; tel 01227 762712, fax 01227 762711; e-mail erasmus@ukc.ac.uk).

EUROPE

The British graduates best equipped to work in Europe are those who can speak languages and, better still, understand the local environment, culture and networks in the different European countries. Whatever subject you study, you should be able to make your degree course help you prosper in Europe – by adding on European studies, languages or exchanges.

There is as varied an assortment of exchanges as you can imagine. They range from individual exchanges to course-based exchanges; some are effectively time out of your degree, some an integral part of the course; on some you may get minimal or no credit for your work done abroad, on others the work can count towards your degree (you may even collect an additional qualification in your host country). It's worth making sure they are well run. There's little point in going to Europe if, once you get there, your life is dogged by loneliness, you are living in a British ghetto, never meet local students and are locked out of overcrowded lectures – all of which can happen. Some colleges and universities have been in Europe for a long time and are canny at making sure you get a worthwhile educational experience and an adequate roof over your head; others have cashed in on the bandwagon and have a lot to learn.

EXTERNAL DEGREES

British external degrees are offered to students who study away from the university, usually in their own time. Despite the massive expansion of full-time higher education and the success of the Open University, there is still a real demand, particularly from overseas.

The majority of external students are studying for the wide range of London University degrees – BA, BD, BSc(Econ), BMus, LLB; also masters degrees and research degrees eg MPhil, PhD. No formal tuition is provided but there is a range of learning materials, short courses, informal tutorial assessments and reading lists from which students may pick and choose. Undergraduate programmes are a minimum of three years but external students usually take longer and registration is valid for eight years. External students set their own pace and can sit their London University exams in most countries in the world.

FILM AND TV EDUCATION

Film education, which almost always includes television, is usually treated as a mix of academic study and practical training. Precisely what that mix is on particular courses, and where they are available, is listed in *Media Courses UK*, published by the British Film Institute. You can buy it for £8.99 from Plymbridge Distributors Ltd (Estover Road, Plymouth PL6 7PZ; tel 01752 202301, fax 01752 202331).

Many universities and colleges profiled in *Where to Study* teach film and TV studies, often within more general media courses. Look them up in the *Subject and Places Index*.

FOUNDATION COURSES – ART & DESIGN

Art and design foundation courses are intended to help you identify the area in which you want to specialise on a degree course and – very importantly – to build up your personal portfolio to help you get onto one. Most students on degree courses have taken a foundation course even if they already have A-levels; only a few will take you with A-levels only. Some universities which do, have four year degree courses with an integral foundation year. This has a financial advantage (as part of a degree course you get a grant and loan, unlike foundation courses where grants are discretionary). But the disadvantage is that you are more or less committed to that institution for four years, whereas from a foundation course you can move on to the university or college that best suits your chosen area of specialisation.

There is a wide range of foundation subjects on offer – over 70, animation to zoological illustration – in over 200 courses. Most lead to a BTEC Diploma. They are taught at colleges (and a handful of universities) in most sizeable towns; you will find a list in *Art & Design Courses 1998*, the UCAS Art and Design Studies Handbook. Your LEA will probably only pay for local courses, particularly if you are under 19.

FRANCHISING

Like KFC or shoe franchises. The degree course you buy is specified and monitored by the franchise university but is taught (at least for the first year or two) in another college. These are often FE colleges so you may be able to at least start a degree in your own neighbourhood.

HEFC

Stands for Higher Education Funding Council. There are three of them, for England, Scotland and Wales. They provide the central funding for universities and higher education colleges in their area and assess the quality of research and teaching. In Northern Ireland, this is done by the Department of Education for Northern Ireland.

LANGUAGES

Even if you don't choose a degree course specialising in modern languages, you'll probably be able to pick up some of the languages your school didn't get round to teaching you. Each university and college has its own approach and you'll have to check what's available directly but a good starting point is the profiles in *Where to Study* followed by a detailed search of individual prospectuses.

Language options for non-linguists, free access to language centres and language-for-all programmes are becoming much more common – even the staff are taking up the new opportunities.

LEA

LEA stands for Local Education Authority. If you live in England and Wales, it is your LEA that pays your university or college fees and gives you your grant, so you need to know how to identify it.

If you don't know which yours is, look in the phone book; your LEA is part of your local authority (if you have both county and district councils in your area, go for the county). British expatriates and EU students apply to the one in which the university or college is located. The LEA will advise if you are in doubt about which LEA is yours.

In Scotland and Northern Ireland things are different. In Scotland, apply for a grant to the Scottish Education Department (Awards Branch, Gyleview House, 3 Redheugh Rigg, Southgyle, Edinburgh EH12 9HH); in Northern Ireland to your local Education and Library Board.

LEAGUE TABLES

Higher education league tables are here to stay. Government loves them. Newspapers love them. They create their own news.

Information on the quality of research and of teaching is published and is obviously useful (see *Quality*). But league tables, typically, rank universities, colleges, faculties and departments by one or more narrow (not necessarily academic) measure – graduate employment, cost per student, student union facilities and so on. One recent table ranked universities by the response time of their switchboards – very little use to you. Like school league tables, the rankings are often technically suspect and statistically crude.

LINGUA

See Erasmus.

LOCAL ROUTES

Some first degree courses can be taken locally, either completely or in part. Sometimes you can study for a year or two at your local FE college and do your final year or two at the university or college that awards the degree. There are very many permutations and possibilities. Enquire at your local FE college.

LONDON

With over 60 universities and colleges and a colossal student population, London is clearly a magnet for students. But there can be difficulties. Unless you're one of the lucky ones in student accommodation, you can become socially isolated. London's newer universities tend to be splintered over a number of sites, and it's up to you to be in the right place at the right time, both socially and academically. If you don't know your way around or have never been to London before, then you'll have to learn fast. Nobody is going to lead you round by the hand.

Then there is cost. Privately owned accommodation will be expensive and may be difficult to find. Expect to travel some distance for work and play – and to pay for it. Opportunities for entertainment are great but not cheap; use the SU facilities which are invaluable socially and probably your best bet financially.

Don't write London off just because of its costs: keep a balance. Your grant (and loan) are marginally higher; and London has some of the most distinguished university institutions and specialist colleges in the country, many of international standing. It's second to none on the British cultural scene and cool capital of the world. If you don't fancy a big city – well that's another matter.

MATURE STUDENTS

For grants purposes, mature students are those over 26 on 1 September in the year they wish to start their degree. You will no longer get any extra money but your parents income is irrelevant to your grant – as it is if you have worked for three years before the age of 26.

Over a third of students in higher education are now mature in the sense of being over 21. Some universities are more flexible about entrance requirements for mature students than others. Oxford and Cambridge both have colleges specially for mature students and they also form 90% of the student population at Birkbeck College in London.

UCAS publishes *A Mature Student's Guide to Higher Education* (free). There is a useful Mature Students' Union but the president, and so the union's address, changes each year. Write to the NUS (executive member responsible for mature students) to find the current president. Student unions at universities and colleges have different approaches to mature students; some have a mature student officer or section.

MILITARY AND NAVAL EDUCATION

You can combine military education with a first degree course – a vast variety of courses at a number of excellent universities. You will also be at some financial advantage over students funded by grants and loans alone. Start by checking out the military and naval establishments: look up Dartmouth, Sandhurst and Shrivenham in *Where to Study*.

MODULAR DEGREES

Also called course unit schemes, the information taught is parcelled up into discrete pieces called modules or course units. In principle these are building blocks rather like those in some A-level courses, but covering many more subjects. At some universities and colleges all degree work is included within a single modular structure; at others a modular scheme may cover a broad area like science and engineering.

Modular degrees are popular with students who want to choose their own pathway through the available study options. They allow students to study unconventional combinations of subjects, or add some computing or a language – while still finishing with a degree that makes sense to employers. Professional societies obviously specify pathways which they will accept for their own professional qualifications and the same will apply if you want a named degree (eg BSc in Physics). But providing you keep an eye on these external considerations, the flexibility of a modular degree structure allows you to follow your own interests as they develop during your degree course.

NORTHERN IRELAND

Northern Ireland has two universities, Belfast and Ulster. Grants regulations are the same as for the rest of the UK although you apply to your local Education and Library Board. Students are affiliated to both the UK and the Eire NUS.

NUS

The National Union of Students is the central organisation for UK students (NUS, Nelson Mandela House, 461 Holloway Road, London N7 6LJ; tel 0171 561 6500, fax 0171 263 5713; e-mail nusuk@nus.org.uk) . You may or may not agree with its politics but student pathways changes rapidly – locally and nationally. NUS is a federation of students' unions. If your SU is affiliated you will automatically become a member unless you opt out. You have the legal right to opt out of membership of your own SU but you may then find that you are unable to use all the union facilities; check the position locally. Information services and student concessions provided by NUS are invaluable.

OPEN UNIVERSITY

Founded nearly 30 years ago for part-time, mature students to study at home, it developed ground-breaking schemes for distance learning. It awards its own degrees, validates degrees in some other colleges and runs the national credit transfer scheme (CATS). The OU is a good alternative if you don't want to commit yourself to a full-time degree course or find it more satisfactory to study at home. (See Open University in *Where to Study*.)

OXBRIDGE

There is no such thing as Oxbridge. There are two quite separate (and large) universities, Oxford and Cambridge, each comprising about 30 colleges. You are admitted to a college, not to the university, and it's worth checking out which college you think you would be comfortable in, and whether they admit students to read the course you want. In *Where to Study* we profile each undergraduate college as well as the universities themselves.

If you think you might apply don't let yourself be put off by the 'Eton and Oxford' reputation or the prejudice of school teachers; they are two of only a handful of British universities that are truly of international standing and they are actively looking for bright students, particularly from comprehensive schools.

Both universities pre-date most others by several centuries. They have long and astonishingly prestigious histories and are still a primary training ground for cabinet ministers, headmasters, captains of industry etc as well as top comedians, media personalities and more ordinary mortals. There are several ways in which they are still different: for example you need to apply earlier and almost all applicants are interviewed. Unless you are applying for an organ scholarship, you cannot apply to both in the same year. In their collegiate system, some of your teaching will be in college, but much will be university-based – as are the examinations.

Some schools have long traditions of sending people to Oxbridge. If yours doesn't, that's fine, but you will have to do some research to discover what others will learn from their teachers. Find out which colleges are really good in your chosen subject and then decide whether you, too, are *really* good: if so, choose those colleges (as first choice, if you want them to look at you); any doubts, pick some completely different colleges. Don't be seduced by the buildings and the lawns. You may find the smaller, newer colleges less daunting than the big, grander ones. Find current students when you go up and visit and talk to them.

Women have been accepted in the universities since early this century – first in women's colleges and some 20 years ago the men's colleges began to accept women students. That may seem a long time ago to you but it's a relatively recent blip in the history of many colleges and most have at least one tame misogynist (is he in your subject?). It's hard to tell whether a college is truly co-ed or just a male bastion with some pix of female students in the prospectus – but you could start by looking at the number of male and female members of staff. All but a handful of the women's colleges are also now mixed.

Oxford and Cambridge universities (and many but not all their colleges) are relatively rich. There are obvious student benefits from being at a well-endowed college: many colleges give travel bursaries (for vacation travel) and some give book grants to all students. Student hardship is less evident at Oxbridge than at many universities; the colleges have a great deal of accommodation and most are sufficiently rich to ensure that virtually no students have to drop out because of financial problems.

PERFORMANCE ARTS

Performance arts courses (as distinct from performing arts courses) are not vocational training courses for would-be professional actors, singers and dancers but practical and theoretical courses taught in a non-vocational context. Put another way, they are degree courses providing an education in the understanding of the arts, not training. Performance arts courses are offered by a variety of universities and colleges in this book – see our *Subject and Places Index*.

CAN'T FIND WHAT YOU'RE LOOKING FOR? USE THE INDEX!

PROFESSIONAL QUALIFICATIONS

Degrees in themselves do not normally license you to practise a profession; you will also need a professional qualification. You can find out what qualifications you'll need to practise and how you get them from the professional societies themselves. You should also be able to find out how long it takes to qualify, how to survive financially while you do so and whether your own degree will give you any exemptions.

Accountants
(*Certified*): Student Recruitment, The Association of Chartered Certified Accountants (ACCA), 29 Lincoln's Inn Fields, London WC2A 3EE (tel 0171 396 5800; fax 0171 396 5858; email student.recruitment@acca.co.uk; web http://www.acca.co.uk);
(*Chartered*): Student Recruitment and Promotion Department, Institute of Chartered Accountants in England and Wales, Chartered Accountants' Hall, PO Box 433, Moorgate Place, London EC2P 2BJ (tel 0171 920 8677; fax 0171 920 8603; web http://www.icoew.co.uk /menus/careers/baca.htm); *(Scotland):* Careers and Student Publications Manager, Institute of Chartered Accountants of Scotland, 27 Queen Street, Edinburgh EH2 1LA (tel 0131 225 5673; fax 0131 247 4872; email icasaticas.org.uk);
(*Cost and Management*): Registry, Chartered Institute of Management Accountants (CIMA), 63 Portland Place, London W1N 4AB (tel 0171 917 9251; fax 0171 580 8956; email mw-registry@cima.org.uk);
(*Public Finance*): Student Marketing Officer, Chartered Institute of Public Finance and Accountancy (CIPFA), 3 Robert Street, London WC2N 6BH (tel 0171 543 5600)

Acoustics
Assistant Secretary, Institute of Acoustics, 5 Holywell Hill, St Albans, Herts AL1 1EU (tel 01727 848195; fax 01727 850553; email acoustics@clus1.ulcc.ac.uk)

Actuaries
Careers Committee Secretary, Institute of Actuaries, Napier House, 4 Worcester Street, Oxford OX1 2AW (tel 01865 794144; fax 01865 794164; email 100316.3313@compuserve.com; web http://actuaries.org.uk)

Advocates
(*Scotland*): Clerk of Faculty, Faculty of Advocates, Advocates Library, Parliament House, Edinburgh EH1 1RF (tel 0131 226 5071; fax 0131 225 3642)

Air Force
RAF, Freepost 4335, Bristol BS1 3YX (tel 0345 300 100)

Air Pilots & Navigators
The Clerk, The Guild of Air Pilots and Air Navigators, Cobham House, 291 Grays Inn Road, London WC1X 8QF (tel 0171 837 3323; fax 0171 833 3190)

Architects
The Library Information Unit, Royal Institute of British Architects (RIBA), 66 Portland Place, London W1N 4AD (tel 0171 580 5533; fax 0171 631 1802). (*Scotland*): Records Co-ordinator, Royal Incorporation of Architects in Scotland, 15 Rutland Square, Edinburgh EH1 2BE (tel 0131 229 7545; fax 0131 228 2188)

Army
See Sandhurst in *Where to Study*.

Barristers
(*England and Wales*): Education and Training Department, The General Council of the Bar, 2–3 Cursitor Street, London EC4A 1NF (tel 0171 440 4000; fax 0171 440 4002)
(*Northern Ireland*): The Secretary, Council of Legal Education (Northern Ireland), Institute of Professional Legal Studies, Queen's University, Belfast BT7 1NN (tel 01232 245133)

Chiropodists
The Secretary, Society of Chiropodists and Podiatrists, 53 Welbeck Street, London W1M 7HE (tel 0171 486 3381; fax 0171 935 6359)

Dentists
Communications Manager, General Dental Council, 37 Wimpole Street, London W1M 8DQ (tel 0171 486 2171; fax 0171 224 3294)

Dieticians
Education & Training Officer, British Dietetic Association, 7th Floor, Elizabeth House, 22 Suffolk Street, Queensway, Birmingham B1 1LS (tel 0121 643 5483; fax 0121 633 4399)

Doctors
Education Section, General Medical Council, 178 Great Portland Street, London W1N 6JE (tel 0171 580 7642; fax 0171 915 3599)

Engineers
Education & Training Department, The Engineering Council, 10 Maltravers Street, London WC2R 3ER (tel 0171 240 7891; fax 0171 240 7517; email pswindlehurst@engc.org.uk)

Health Visiting
See Nurses.

Mathematics
Deputy Secretary, The Institute of Mathematics and its Applications, Catherine Richards House, 16 Nelson Street, Southend-on-Sea, Essex SS1 1EF (tel 01702 354020; fax 01702 354111; email post@ima.org.uk; web http://www.ima.org.uk)

Navy, Merchant
Merchant Navy Training Board, Carthusian Court, 12 Carthusian Street, London EC1M 6EB (tel 0171 417 8400)

Navy, Royal
See Dartmouth in *Where to Study*.

Nurses, Midwives and Health Visitors
(*England and Wales*): ENB Careers, English National Board for Nursing, Midwifery and Health Visiting, PO Box 2EN, London W1A 2EN (tel 0171 391 6200/6205; fax 0171 391 6207; email enb.careers@easynet.co.uk)
(*Northern Ireland*): Recruitment Officer, National Board for Nursing, Midwifery and Health Visiting for Northern Ireland, Centre House, 79 Chichester Street, Belfast BT1 4JE (tel 01232 238152; fax 01232 333298)
(*Scotland*): Careers Manager, National Board for Nursing, Midwifery and Health Visiting for Scotland, 22 Queen Street, Edinburgh EH2 1NT (0131 225 2096; fax 0131 226 2492).

Occupational Therapists
Education Department, College of Occupational Therapists, 6–8 Marshalsea Road, London SE1 1HL (tel 0171 357 6480; fax 0171 207 9612)

Opticians
Registrar, General Optical Council, 41 Harley Street, London W1N 2DJ (tel 0171 580 3898; fax 0171 436 3525; email optical@globalnet.co.uk)

Optometrists
Careers Department, The College of Optometrists, 10 Knaresborough Place, London SW5 0TG (tel 0171 373 7765; fax 0171 373 1143; email careers@bcoptom.demon.co.uk)

Orthoptists
Honorary Secretary, British Orthoptic Society, Tavistock House North, Tavistock Square, London WC1H 9HX (tel 0171 387 7992; fax 0171 383 2584)

Pharmacists
Careers Education Division, The Royal Pharmaceutical Society of Great Britain, 1 Lambeth High Street, London SE1 7JN (tel 0171 820 3363; fax 0171 735 7629)

Physiotherapists
Careers Advisor, The Chartered Society of Physiotherapy, 14 Bedford Row, London WC1R 4ED (tel 0171 306 6666; fax 0171 306 6611; email kinsellad@csphysio.org.uk)

Podiatrists
The Secretary, Society of Chiropodists and Podiatrists, 53 Welbeck Street, London W1M 7HE (tel 0171 486 3381; fax 0171 935 6359)

Radiographers
Professional Support Officer, College of Radiographers, 2 Carriage Row, 183 Eversholt Street, London NW1 1BU (tel 0171 391 4500; fax 0171 391 4504)

Social Workers
Information Service, Central Council for Education and Training in Social Work (CCETSW), Derbyshire House, St Chad's Street, London WC1H 8AD (tel 0171 278 2455; fax 0171 278 2934)

Solicitors
(*England and Wales*): Information Services (Legal Education), The Law Society, Ipsley Court, Berrington Close, Redditch, Worcs B98 0TD (tel 01527 504400/504455; fax 01527 500018; web http://www.lawsociety.org.uk)
(*Northern Ireland*): The Secretary, Council of Legal Education (Northern Ireland), Institute of Professional Legal Studies, Queen's University, Belfast BT7 1NN (tel 01232 245133)
(*Scotland*): Deputy Secretary Education & Training, The Law Society of Scotland, Law Society's Hall, 26 Drumsheugh Gardens, Edinburgh EH3 7YR (tel 0131 226 7411; fax 0131 225 2934)

Speech Therapists
Careers Department, Royal College of Speech and Language Therapists, 7 Bath Place, Rivington Street, London EC2A 3DR (tel 0171 613 3855; fax 0171 613 3854)

Surveyors
Education Officer, The Royal Institution of Chartered Surveyors, Surveyor Court, Westwood Way, Coventry CV4 8JE (tel 0171 222 7000 or 01203 694757; fax 0171 334 3800; email careers@rics.co.uk)

Teachers
Communications Centre, Teacher Training Agency, PO Box 3210, Chelmsford, Essex CM1 3WA (tel 01245 454454; fax 01245 261668; email teaching@ttainfo.demon.co.uk)

Town Planners
Public Affairs Officer, Royal Town Planning Institute, 26 Portland Place, London W1N 4BE (tel 0171 636 9107; fax 0171 323 1582; email d-rose@policy.rtpi.co.uk)

Toxicologists
British Toxicology Society Secretariat, Institute of Biology, 20–22 Queensberry Place, London SW7 2DZ (tel 0171 581 8333; fax 0171 823 9409)

Transport
Education Officer, The Chartered Institute of Transport, 80 Portland Place, London W1N 4DP (tel 0171 467 9425; fax 0171 467 9440; email gen@citrans.hiway.co.uk)

Veterinary Surgeons
Education Department, The Royal College of Veterinary Surgeons, Belgravia House, 62–64 Horseferry Road, London SW1P 2AF (tel 0171 222 2001; fax 0171 222 2004; email admin@rcvs.org.uk)

QUALITY

The quality of UK university and college teaching and research is assessed officially – by peer groups – under broad subject areas. These do not necessarily match with university departments or faculties, still less the content of every first degree course. Teaching is analysed under some 61 subjects, research under 69, and this compares with about 500 subjects listed in our own *Subject and Places Index* and well over 100,000 degree courses on offer.

So if you want to know more about the underlying quality of the universities and colleges you are interested in, you can gain useful insights from these assessments; and if you want a more direct assessment of a course, you could be lucky and find that too.

Quality – Research
Quality and quantity of research varies widely between universities and between departments, although much of it is world-class. In our *Research Quality Search Index*, we present the Student Book Top 50 Institutions. Also the top departments in almost all subjects. The intention is to help you make your shortlist: you may want to study in a leading research-led university; alternatively you may want to avoid it like the plague.

Research assessment exercises are undertaken for all universities and colleges at the same time. The results of the most recent one can be found in *1996 Research Assessment Exercise: The Outcome*, available at £15 from HEFCE (Northavon House, Coldharbour Lane, Bristol BS16 1QD; tel 0117 931 7438; fax 0117 931 7463). For those with access to the internet, results can also be found on the HEFCE website, http://back.niss.ac.uk/education/hefce/rae96/

Quality – Teaching
The quality of education is assessed on a rolling programme. In England and Northern Ireland 23 subjects have been assessed, covering over half the student population (the position in Wales and Scotland is rather different).

The results are published in 23 subject overviews which evaluate the quality of the learning experience in the overall teaching of that subject, and a total of 750 subject reports on individual universities and colleges. Some of them are more up-to-date than others and some poor reports may have lead to rapid action.

There are obviously too many reports to summarise here. But subject overviews, and the individual reports of those universities and colleges in England and Northern Ireland which teach the subject, are available in:

anthropology
applied social work
architecture
business and management
   studies
chemical engineering
chemistry
computer studies
English
environmental studies

French
geography
geology
German and related
   languages
history
Iberian languages and
   studies
Italian
law

linguistics
mechanical
   engineering
music
Russian and East
   European languages
   and studies
social policy and
   administration
sociology

Each report costs £2, available from Stuart Grantham, Quality Assessment Publications, Northavon House, Coldharbour Lane, Bristol BS16 1QD (tel 0117 931 7447; fax 0117 931 7446; email s.grantham@hefc.ac.uk). If you have access to the internet, you can search by subject or institution on the HEFCE website on http://back.niss.ac.uk/education/hefce/qar/

SANDWICH COURSES

These are ways of alternating periods of academic study with periods of professional/industrial training out at work. There are thick and thin sandwiches, depending on the time spent out; the prospectus should tell you what is on offer. Sandwich courses give good work experience and help your employability later. Some universities are having difficulty finding sufficient places for their students, particularly those with work placements in Europe.

SCOTLAND

Scotland currently has thirteen universities: Aberdeen, Abertay Dundee, Dundee, Edinburgh, Glasgow, Glasgow Caledonian, Heriot-Watt, Napier, Paisley, Robert Gordon, St Andrews, Stirling and Strathclyde. It also has many distinguished institutions of higher education specialising in agriculture, textiles, technology and the arts, including the Royal Scottish Academy of Music and Drama (see *Geographical Search Index*). All are now represented by a single body, COSHEP (Committee of Scottish Higher Education Principals, St Andrew's House, 141 West Nile Street, Glasgow G1 2RN), which publishes the *Entrance Guide to Higher Education in Scotland* (from John Smith & Son, 57 St Vincent Street, Glasgow G2 5TB).

In contrast to England, there has been a tradition of Scottish students going straight on to a Scottish degree course after taking Highers aged 17 (and taking four years for an honours course). But many universities in Scotland now require A-levels or the Certificate of Sixth Year Studies.

SEMESTERS

This means half a year (although some universities and colleges have three semesters a year). An increasing number of universities divide the academic year into two semesters. Meanwhile there are a lot of teething troubles and complaints as two semesters are imposed on a three term curriculum.

SKILL: NATIONAL BUREAU FOR STUDENTS WITH DISABILITIES

Skill is a national charity that works to develop opportunities for people with disabilities and learning difficulties in all types of education and training over the age of 16. Amongst other activities, it runs an information service for individual students, their families, friends or people who work with them. A range of free information sheets is available as well as priced publications. You can write to the Information Officer, or telephone 2pm–5pm Monday–Friday or, if necessary, visit the office by appointment. (Skill: National Bureau for Students with Disabilities, 336 Brixton Road, London SW9 7AA; tel 0171 274 0565).

SOCRATES

Socrates is the European Union education action programme, covering school and higher education, language-learning, open distance learning, adult education, and exchanges. Only its higher education programme (Erasmus) and its language promotion programme (Lingua) are of direct interest to undergraduates (see *Erasmus*).

STUDENTS CHARTER

There is a Charter for Higher Education which you can get free by writing to Charters, Freepost EDO 3138, London E15 2BR.

Under this, applicants for places in higher education should receive clear and accurate information about institutions, courses, entry requirements, quality, residential accommodation, facilities for the disabled and financial help available. Their applications should be handled fairly and efficiently. When you get there you should get prompt payment of grants, loans and access funds, and receive equal treatment regardless of sex or race. Some universities now also have their own charters, often presented in their prospectuses.

STUDY ABROAD

There are many opportunities to study abroad as part of a degree courses – in Europe, North America or further afield. Each course has its own arrangements. Check prospectuses before you apply.

TEACHER EDUCATION

If you want to teach in a state maintained school you must have Qualified Teacher Status (QTS). There are two routes involving a first degree course. Either you take a degree in the subject you wish to teach, followed by a Postgraduate Certificate in Education (PGCE). Or you take an education degree, traditionally a BEd but increasingly a BA(QTS) or BSc(QTS).

For an education degree, you apply through UCAS in the usual way. You can find out where these are offered in the *Subjects and Places Index*. Applications for a PGCE are handled by GTTR (PO Box 239, Cheltenham, Gloucestershire GL50 3SL). To find out about professional requirements and the profession itself contact the Teacher Training Agency (Communications Centre, PO Box 3210, Chelmsford, Essex CM1 3WA; tel 01245 454454).

TRANSCRIPTS

In addition to your degree, a growing number of universities issue transcripts. This logs your achievements in the different elements of your degree – the marks for each paper/module/unit. Transcripts are useful evidence of what you have done – either to back up your claims to specialist studies or to explain away your final class of degree.

UCAS

The Universities and Colleges Admissions Service, PO Box 67, Cheltenham, Glos GL50 3SF. It has an Applicants Enquiry Service (tel 01242 227788). UCAS operates the central admissions scheme for universities and colleges of higher education (but you apply direct to the Open University). You apply through UCAS for all full-time and sandwich first degree courses, including studio-based art courses, and some non-degree courses such as Dips HE and HNDs.

GET HOLD OF THE PROSPECTUSES

UNIVERSITIES

Some universities have been around for 700 years, some for less than a decade; some have 6,000 students, some 16,000 (London University has 43,000); some are very concentrated, some federal – so it's hardly surprising that they are a pretty mixed bunch. Don't assume that they are much of a muchness or that employers consider them all equal. They are not (see *Quality*). They have in common the right to award their own degrees. They are usually large (10,000 plus), teach across a range of subjects to first degree level and have research students as well. Some of the newer universities also offer non-degree courses. Since the polytechnics became universities in 1992, there are often two universities in the same town, such as Sheffield University and Sheffield Hallam University.

The federal universities of Wales and London have very independent, constituent colleges. Many of these are world-class institutions and larger than some universities.

VOCATIONAL QUALIFICATIONS

Apart from the established professional qualifications, there is a relatively new framework for vocational qualifications. There are two kinds: General National Vocational Qualifications (GNVQs) are broad-based vocational alternatives to GCSE or A-level, increasingly taught at schools and FE colleges; and National Vocational Qualifications (NVQs), which specifically qualify you for a particular job(s). Sounds confusing? It is. Would you have allowed these two entirely different qualifications to have almost the same name?

For university entrance, you can forget about NVQs. But GNVQs are accepted by admissions tutors (see *Advanced GNVQs*).

WALES

Wales has two universities: University of Wales and Glamorgan University. Wales University is a federal university; you can find it, and its constituent colleges, in *Where to Study*. There are also two independent colleges with associated college status to the university, and the Welsh College of Music and Drama (see *Geographical Search Index*). All courses in Wales are taught in English but some are available in Welsh as well at some colleges.

WANT TO HELP WITH THE NEXT EDITION? SEE PAGE 66

WHERE TO STUDY

Profiles of some 280 universities and colleges. The top of each profile provides key information from the relevant administration and the prospectus. The remainder (*What It's Like* and *Pauper Notes*) shows you what it's like being there and how to survive on a shoestring; this almost always comes from students. You should not necessarily expect a complete match between the two sections.

UNIVERSITIES AND COLLEGES PROFILED ARE:

Aberdeen University
Abertay Dundee
  University
Aberystwyth University
ALRA
Anglia Polytechnic
  University
Architectural Association
Aston University
Bangor University
Bath College
Bath University
Belfast University
Birkbeck College
Birmingham Conservatoire
Birmingham University
Bolton Institute
Bournemouth University
Bradford & Ilkley
Bradford University
Bretton Hall
Brighton University
Bristol Old Vic
Bristol University
Bristol UWE
British Institute in Paris

British School of
  Osteopathy
Brunel University
Buckingham University
Buckinghamshire College
Buckland University
  College
Camberwell College of Arts
Camborne School of Mines
Cambridge University
  Christ's
  Churchill
  Clare
  Corpus Christi
  Downing
  Emmanuel
  Fitzwilliam
  Girton
  Gonville & Caius
  Hughes Hall
  Jesus
  King's
  Lucy Cavendish
  Magdalene
  New Hall
  Newnham

Pembroke
Peterhouse
Queens'
Robinson
St Catharine's
St Edmund's
St John's
Selwyn
Sidney Sussex
Trinity
Trinity Hall
Wolfson
Canterbury Christ Church
  College
Cardiff Institute
Cardiff University
Central England
  University
Central Lancashire
  University
Central Saint Martins
Central School of Speech
  and Drama
Charing Cross and
  Westminster
Chelsea College of Art

Cheltenham & Gloucester
  College
Chester University College
Chichester University
  College
City University
Colchester Institute
Courtauld Institute
Coventry University
Cranfield University
Dartington College of Arts
Dartmouth
De Montfort University
Derby University
Dundee University
Durham University
East Anglia (UEA)
East London University
Edge Hill University
  College
Edinburgh College of Art
Edinburgh University
Essex University
European Business School
Exeter University
Falmouth College of Arts
Farnborough College
Glamorgan University
Glasgow Caledonian
  University
Glasgow College of
  Building
Glasgow School of Art
Glasgow University
Goldsmiths College
Greenwich University
Guildford School of Acting
Guildhall
Harper Adams
Heriot-Watt University
Hertfordshire University
Heythrop College
Holborn College
Homerton College
Huddersfield University
Hull University
Humberside University
Imperial College
Institute of Archaeology
Institute of Education
Jews' College

Keele University
Kent Institute
Kent University
King Alfred's College
King's College London
King's College School of
  Medicine & Dentistry
Kingston University
Laban Centre
Lampeter University
Lancaster University
Leeds Metropolitan
  University
Leeds University
Leicester University
Lincoln University
Liverpool Hope University
  College
Liverpool John Moores
  University
Liverpool University
London Bible College
London Business School
London College of Fashion
London College of Music
London College of Printing
London Contemporary
  Dance School
London Guildhall University
London Institute
London International Film
  School
London University
Loughborough College of
  Art
Loughborough University
LSE
LSU Southampton
Luton University
Manchester Business
  School
Manchester Metropolitan
  University
Manchester University
Middlesex University
Moray House
Myerscough College
Napier University
National Extension College
National Film & TV School
Nene College

Newcastle University
Newport College
North East Wales Institute
North London University
Northern School of
  Contemporary Dance
Northumbria University
Norwich School of Art
Nottingham Trent
  University
Nottingham University
Oak Hill College
Open University
Oxford Brookes University
Oxford University
  Balliol
  Brasenose
  Christ Church
  Corpus Christi
  Exeter
  Harris Manchester
  Hertford
  Jesus
  Keble
  Lady Margaret Hall
  Lincoln
  Magdalen
  Mansfield
  Merton
  New College
  Oriel
  Pembroke
  Queen's
  Regent's Park
  St Anne's
  St Catherine's
  St Edmund Hall
  St Hilda's
  St Hugh's
  St John's
  St Peter's
  Somerville
  Trinity
  University College
  Wadham
  Worcester
Paisley University
Plymouth University
Portsmouth University
Prince of Wales's Institute
Queen Margaret College

Queen Mary & Westfield
RADA
Ravensbourne College
Reading University
Ripon & York St John
Robert Gordon University
Roehampton Institute
Rose Bruford College
Royal Academy of Music
Royal Academy Schools
Royal Agricultural College
Royal College of Art
Royal College of Music
Royal Free
Royal Holloway
Royal Northern College of
  Music
Royal Scottish Academy
Royal Veterinary College
St Andrews University
St Bartholomew's & Royal
  London
St George's
St Mark & St John
S Martin's University
  College
St Mary's University
  College

St Mary's Hospital
Salford University
Sandhurst
School of Pharmacy
Scottish Agricultural
  College
Scottish College of Textiles
Sheffield Hallam University
Sheffield University
Shrivenham
Silsoe College
Slade
SOAS
South Bank University
Southampton Institute
Southampton University
Spurgeon's College
SSEES
Staffordshire University
Stirling University
Strathclyde University
Sunderland University
Surrey Institute
Surrey University
Sussex University
Swansea Institute
Swansea University
Teesside University

Thames Valley University
Trinity & All Saints
Trinity College Carmarthen
Trinity College of Music
Ulster University
UMDS
UMIST
University College London
Wales College of Medicine
Wales University
Warrington University
  College
Warwick University
Welsh College of Music
  and Drama
Welsh Institute of Rural
  Studies
West Herts College
Westminster College
Westminster University
Wimbledon School of
  Art
Winchester School of Art
Wolverhampton University
Worcester College
Writtle College
Wye College
York University

WANT TO HELP WITH THE NEXT EDITION? SEE PAGE 66

ABERDEEN UNIVERSITY

University of Aberdeen, Regent Walk, Aberdeen AB24 3FX
(Tel 01224 272000) Map 1

STUDENT ENQUIRIES: Student recruitment services (Tel 01224
272090/1, Fax 01224 272576. E-mail schlia@admin.abdu.ac.uk)
APPLICATION: UCAS

Broad study areas: Arts, sciences, engineering, medicine, law,
theology, social sciences. (Subject details are in the *Subjects
and Places Index.*)

Founded: King's College 1495, Marischal College 1593; merging to one university in 1860.
Main undergraduate awards: MA, BSc, BD, BTh, LTh, LLB, BLE, MB ChB, BMedBiol, BEng,
MEng, BScEng. **Awarding body:** Aberdeen University. **Site:** 2 sites (King's College in Old
Aberdeen and medical sciences at Foresterhill). **Special features:** New Institute of Medical
Sciences, plus initiatives in ethnology and cultural studies. **Academic features:** Access
courses and summer school. Courses in all biosciences including tropical environmental
science, Celtic civilisation, petroleum geology, cultural history, safety engineering, land use
and marine resource management, countryside and environmental management, social
research. **Europe:** 12% first degree students take a language as part of course and 6%
spend 6 months abroad. Languages may be incorporated into many degrees; formal tuition
available for all first degree students (in French, German, Spanish, Celtic and Russian) at
various levels and access to self-tuition facilities in all European languages and many
others. Courses in law with French/European/German law, involve a period of study abroad
to obtain a diploma. Erasmus networks link with 300 institutions across Europe, plus 5
formal scholarship exchanges (Lausanne, Rennes, Zurich, Geneva and Kiel), open to non-
language students. **Library:** 5 library buildings, over 1,050,000 volumes, inter-library loan
service, short loan collections for course books in heaviest demand; informal classes on
use of library. Annual expenditure on library materials, £125 per FTE student (plus departmental purchases). **Specialist collections:** Jacobite material, transport and photographic
collections, pre-1800 British and European works, first editions of early science and medical
volumes. Almost 250,000 maps, many historical. **Other learning facilities:** Interactive video;
satellite TV for language teaching; extensive IT provision and computing facilities. **Welfare:**
3 doctors, dentist, health centre, chaplaincy; counselling service. **Special categories:** Every
3 years students elect Rector to represent them on university governing body. **Careers:**
Information and advice service; regular vacancy bulletins. **Amenities:** Union building with
snackbar, café, sewing room, launderette, 3 bars, music room with record library, supermarket; also large refectory with many facilities; SRC babysitting agency, late buses,
vacation employment office, university symphony orchestra, choral society and chapel
choir. **Sporting facilities:** Swimming pool; two extensive sports fields including running
tracks; rowing on River Dee; Cairngorms and Grampians (mountain hut) within easy reach
for climbing, walking and skiing.

Accommodation: In 1995/96, 49% of first degree students in university accommodation,
100% of first years (guaranteed for those who require it). 4,094 places available: 1,358 half-
board places at £64–£74 per week, term time only; 2,746 self-catering at £37–£50 per week,

mainly all year rental. Students usually live in privately owned accommodation for 2 years: rents £30–£45 per week for self-catering, £40–£55 B&B, £55–£70 for half-board, £60–£75 HB and weekend meals. 30% first degree students live at home. **Term time work:** University policy allows term time work for full-time first degree students (30% believed to work); limit of 12 hours per week. Term (and vac) work on campus in catering, bars, library and (in vacs) as porters, gardeners, groundsmen; also SRC Job Finder agency helps finding work off campus. **Hardship funds:** Total available in 1995/96: £237,322 government access and other funds; average £239 awarded, 994 students helped.

Duration of first degree courses: 3 years ordinary/designated, 4 years honours and divinity; 5 years MB ChB, MChem, MEng. **Total first degree students 1995/96:** 8,927. **Overseas students:** 773. **Male/female ratio:** 1:1. **Teaching staff:** 507 full-time, 116 part-time (plus research staff). **Total full-time students 1995/96:** 10,596. **Postgraduate students:** 1,669. **First degree tuition fees:** Home students, paying their own fees in 1996/97, paid £750 (classroom), £1,600 (lab), £2,800 (clinical); Overseas students £6,180 (classroom), £8,160 (lab), £15,000 (clinical).

WHAT IT'S LIKE   Aberdeen, the silver or granite city and oil capital of Britain, is in NE Scotland with good access by rail and plane; university is over 500 years old. Based on medieval burgh with attractive landscaped campus. Main campus 10 minutes from halls and 5 minutes bus from city centre, where union building is. Spanking new second site for Institute of Medical Sciences at Foresterhill, approx 20 minutes walk from main campus. About one-third housed in single study bedrooms and self-catering flats for 6 (same sex only). Hall place guaranteed for 1st year students. Private accommodation supply fluctuates; very expensive. Student/admin relations good. SRC effective; offers free legal, financial and welfare advice and supports 150 societies. Separate athletics association (supports sporting societies) and SU (beer, entertainment etc). Some continuous assessment, more on the way. Failure and drop-out rate both below average. Changing courses is quite easy, as in Scotland you're admitted to a faculty, not a department. Most students are Scottish, but lots of English, Welsh, Irish and overseas. Less private school people than average. Some recognition given to Scottish Gaelic.

PAUPER NOTES   **Accommodation:** Not much cheap accommodation although lots of hall places. **Drink:** Real ale at various outlets and, of course, excellent range of whiskies almost everywhere. Regular cheap nights at the union. **Eats:** Indian/Chinese/Italian very good, but not cheap. Lemon Tree good for vegan/vegetarian food and live entertainment. **Ents:** Several rock venues, including Union. Active folk scene, theatre, concert hall, arts centre, world cinema season (excellent value), alternative music festival. **Sports:** Facilities on campus (many free), for almost every sport imaginable. **Hardship funds:** University-arranged access funds available; worth applying. Other student/uni-arranged hardship funds and SRC applying for lottery money for further funds. **Travel:** Scottish students can still claim travel awards, expensive to travel south by train. Student Council runs lifts board. **Work:** A fair amount available and the Students' Council runs a popular babysitting agency; new Joblink helps students find part-time work (under 15 hours/week).

MORE INFO?   Get students' Freshers' Magazine. Enquiries to SRC 01224 272965.

BUZZ-WORDS   Fit like (how are you?); Nae baad (I'm fine, thank you); Quine (girl/lady); Loon (boy/man); Ken fit a meen? (do you know what I mean?).

ALUMNI (EDITORS' PICK)   Sandy Gall (ITV newscaster), Iain Cuthbertson (actor), Douglas Henderson, James Naughtie, Dr G Hadley (Convenor, Grampian Regional Council), David McLean MP, Alistair Darling, Sir Denys Henderson (ICI), Earl of Strathmore, Ian Crighton Smith, Catherine Gavin, Nikki Campbell (TV presenter), Kenneth McKeller, Gigi Callender, Dominic Addington, Evelyn Glennie (percussionist), Alasdair 'Shifty' MacFarlane and Richard Baker (local comedians).

ABERTAY DUNDEE UNIVERSITY

University of Abertay Dundee, Bell Street, Dundee DD1 1HG
(Tel 01382 308080, Fax 01382 308877) Map 1

STUDENT ENQUIRIES: Information and Recruitment Division
APPLICATIONS: UCAS.

Broad study areas: Business, building and surveying, applied science and technology, nursing, social sciences, languages. (Subject details are in the *Subjects and Places Index.*)

Founded: 1888, became Dundee Institute of Technology 1988; university charter in 1994. **Main undergraduate awards:** BA, BSc, BEng. **Awarding body:** Abertay Dundee University. **Site:** City centre; all buildings within ¼ mile of each other. **Access:** Close to bus station. City has good road and rail connections. **Academic features:** All courses include IT and have strong vocational bias; small classes. **Special features:** Good staff links with commerce and industry. **Europe:** 20% first degree students take a language as part of course. Year abroad for European business management/law courses. Language tuition and shorter period abroad an option on other degrees. **Library:** 100,000 volumes, 15,500 journals and periodicals, 400 study places, tied book system, audio-visual material. Annual expenditure on library materials, £77.50 per FTE student. Purpose-built library to open 1997. **Specialist collections:** Annual reports of 3,000–4,000 companies. **Other learning facilities:** Self-access language centre; computer centre with VAX system, for use by all students. **Welfare:** Counselling and advice, medical and health, accommodation, chaplaincy. All students have personal tutor. **Careers:** Information, advice and placement service. **Amenities:** SU building with bars, games rooms, laundry, etc. **Sporting facilities:** Indoor facilities at SU; access to many city facilities.

Accommodation: In 1995/96, 20% of all students in university accommodation, 50% of first years. 600 self-catering places available at £35–£45 per week, Sept–June. Students live in privately owned accommodation for 2 years: rents £35–£45 per week for self-catering or B&B, £50–£70 for half-board. **Hardship funds:** Access funds and other trust funds. Bursaries available for engineering and science-related courses.

Duration of first degree courses: 4 years; others: 5 years (sandwich degrees), 1 year less for unclassified degrees. **Total first degree students 1995/96:** 2,800. **Overseas students:** 180. **Mature students:** 620. **Male/female ratio:** 2:1. **Teaching staff:** 230 full-time, 150 part-time. **Total full-time students 1995/96:** 3,800. **Postgraduate students:** 282. **First degree tuition fees:** Home students, paying their own fees in 1996/97, paid £750 (classroom), £1,600 (lab); Overseas students: £4,600 (classroom), £5,600 (lab).

WHAT IT'S LIKE   Smallest uni in Britain offering vocational degree and HND courses. In centre of town so dead close to everything you could want. Accommodation is all around Dundee; college accommodation is in city centre, or 2–4 miles outside. Private accommodation is fairly easy to get and relatively inexpensive. All college accommodation has laundry facilities, mostly self-catering but halls of residence places are available. Overnight guests not allowed in college accommodation without prior permission. SA has large building nearby with a variety of facilities including two bars, games room (snooker, fully equipped leisure centre, table tennis and video machines), well-stocked shop and an excellent food service. Loadsa clubs and societies from role-playing to parachuting. Student welfare excellent and all counselling confidential. Students come from all over (lots of Irish). City looks a bit dingy but everyone is friendly with racism, homophobia and sexism being actively wiped out. In a nutshell it's a fine place to study.

PAUPER NOTES **Accommodation:** Good uni accommodation office. **Drink:** SA dead cheap – beaten only by a few local dumps charging £1 a pint but with unsavoury company. **Eats:** SA cheapest and best vegetarian locally; some places offer good breakfast deals. **Ents:** SA cheap and friendly; shows include comedians, hypnotists, bands, top DJs etc. Big screen cinema, pool tables, video games etc. **Sports:** SA provides all sports in association with district council: very cheap. **Hardship funds:** SA has fund for the needy. **Travel:** Dundee has cheap bus tickets to other Scottish towns. On main routes for easy hitching. **Work:** Available in SA; local ads in student newspaper; careers service has vacancies too.

MORE INFO? Ring SA on 01382 227477

ABERYSTWYTH UNIVERSITY

University of Wales, Old College, King Street, Aberystwyth, SY23 2AX (Tel 01970 622021, Fax 01970 627410) Map 3

STUDENT ENQUIRIES: Registrar
APPLICATIONS: UCAS

Broad study areas: Humanities, social sciences, law, library studies, business, sciences, agriculture, fine and performing arts. (Subject details are in the *Subjects and Places Index*).

Founded: 1872, receiving charter in 1889. Joined with Bangor and Cardiff in 1893 to form Wales University. Merged with College of Librarianship (1988), Welsh Agricultural College (1995). **Main undergraduate awards:** BA, BSc, BScEcon, LLB, BEng, MEng. **Awarding body:** Wales University. **Site:** Old College on sea front; Penglais 400 acre campus overlooking Cardigan Bay; Llanbadarn campus and accommodation within walking distance of Penglais. **Access:** Nearly all students live within walking distance of main teaching buildings. **Structural features:** Part of Wales University. **Academic features:** Industrial year scheme; range of degrees relating to the environment. Courses include: genetics and biochemistry; business studies and Welsh; life sciences with a foundation year; information and library studies by distance learning. Flexible degree schemes, students do not have to commit themselves until the end of their first or second year. **Special features:** Entrance scholarships worth £1,800 open to all candidates able to sit exams in UK; biennial school on Dylan Thomas with internationally known experts on the poet. **Europe:** Most students have access to language tuition as part of their course. Many formal exchange links with universities/colleges across the EU (and Austria) – open to all undergraduates. **Library:** 650,000 volumes, 3,000 periodicals; main library on Penglais site with over 500,000 volumes and 500 reader places; departmental collections. Annual expenditure on library materials, £107.32 per FTE student. Access to National Library of Wales (copyright). **Specialist collections:** 600 books printed pre-1701; private press books; first editions collection (Matthew Arnold, Swinburne and Shelley), Catherine Lewis Gallery of prints and watercolours and 1747 edition of Shakespeare annotated by Samuel Johnson. **Other learning facilities:** Computer unit, microprocessor development laboratory, language laboratories. **Welfare:** College medical centre, college chapel (available for baptisms and marriages), SU welfare service, learning support unit, mature students' counsellor; also a childcare co-ordinator, college nursery, after-school club, half term and holiday schemes. **Careers:** Information and advice (also available to those who do not complete their courses). Year in employment and 12-week summer placement schemes available through Graduate Recruitment Opportunities in Wales (GROW). **Amenities:** SU houses nightclub venue, bar, travel shop, food outlets, bank, shop, etc. Over 120 societies. **Sporting facilities:** Over 50 acres of playing fields on town outskirts; Cader Range and Snowdonia within easy reach. Outstanding sports hall with wide range of indoor sports and heated indoor swimming pool; all-weather pitch. Many sports teams.

Accommodation: In 1995/96, 50% of all students in college accommodation, 100% first years. 3,354 places available (up to 2,000 for first years): 2,065 self-catering places (1,130 for first years) at £33–£43 per week for single room, term time or longer; 332 places with en suite facilities (220 for first years) at £48–£51 per week, term time only; 1,289 places (870 for first years) half-board at £56.35 per week or 'pay-as-you-eat' at £48, term time only. Shared rooms cost less. Students live in privately owned accommodation for 1 year, usually second: rents £38–£45 per week self-catering (plus fuel); £48–£55 for B&B. Less than 1% first degree students live at home. **Term time work:** Part-time work restricted to 15 hours per week during term. Term (and vac) work on campus in bars and library (plus office work in vac); some help finding summer jobs off campus. **Hardship funds:** Total available in 1995/96: £143,000 government access funds (average £300 awarded); £3,000 own funds (average award £200) plus £7,500 other funds. Special help: for mature students, those with disabilities or childcare costs or whose financial circumstances worsen suddenly; own funds also available for overseas students. Some £22,000 assigned to students prior to starting their course, typically £600 pa to 40 new students annually – available to students on 4-year conversion courses and all students on academic merit.

Duration of first degree courses: 3 years; 4 years (modern languages). **Total first degree students 1995/96:** 4,818. **Overseas students:** 766. **Mature students:** 18%. **Male/female ratio:** 1:1. **Teaching staff:** 343 full-time, 33 part-time. **Total full-time students 1995/96:** 5,981. **Postgraduate students:** 1,234. **First degree tuition fees:** Home students, paying their own fees in 1996/97, paid £850; Overseas students, £6,050 (classroom), £8,020 (lab/studio).

WHAT IT'S LIKE   Founded in 1872 at a time of growing Welsh national consciousness, UW Aberystwyth is a close-knit university of some 6,500 students. Most students are taught at the Penglais campus, built in the 1960s with a superb view of Aberystwyth town and Cardigan Bay; while some are taught at the small but beautifully sited campus at Llanbadarn, which also houses other colleges. Most students come from outside Wales. The town itself is 50% Welsh speaking; some 10% of Aberystwyth students have Welsh as their first language and there are plenty of courses for those who want to learn Welsh. Lots of mature students (34%) and students from overseas (11%). Student accommodation is provided for half the student population, including all first years; some self-catering and some pay-as-you-eat. Launderette facilities are available. The college encourages students to take an industrial year out. Central library opens 9am-10pm. Aberystwyth is about halfway down the West Wales coast. Travel by rail or road is slow, but the scenery for miles around is beautiful. Most students stay in Aber over the weekends, and there are plenty of weekend ents and activities. The SU offers a wide entertainments package, 4 bars, 2 shops, travel bureau, insurance centre, 90 clubs and societies, a well-developed welfare service and opportunities for social, political and cultural activities. Sport is thriving with leagues in most sports. Students compete at local, Welsh and UK levels. Aber Rag is one of the world's biggest student charity appeals – it's great fun going on Rag trips collecting money anywhere in the UK! The town has a cinema, an arts centre, over 50 pubs and a weekly market. The local radio station has student volunteers and a student show. It is easy to meet other students. Family planning clinic offers advice on pregnancy and STDs. Hospital has an AIDS counsellor. Nightline, Lesbian and Gay Line are student-run confidential advice services.

PAUPER NOTES   **Accommodation:** Variety of halls with different catering systems. New student village. A few married quarters available. **Drink:** Two plush union bars serving good, cheap beer: Whitbread, Carlsberg/Tetley. Good town pubs: The Mill, Rummers, Inn on the Pier, etc. **Eats:** Good facilities. The Joint coffee bar, Munchies takeaway and sandwich bar. **Sports:** Everything available for £15 pa. Large campus sports centre, astro-pitch and pool. **Ents:** Regular live bands, discos, comedians etc; variety of musical clubs and societies. Student discounts at Aberystwyth Arts Centre based on campus. **Hardship fund:** Interest-free loans and donations for extreme cases. **Travel:** Travel shop on campus offering discounted student travel. **Work:** Many students take part-time work, mainly in hotels, pubs and restaurants and SU. University service finds 12 week summer placements with graduate employers.

ALUMNI (EDITORS' PICK)   Lord Cledwyn, Arthur Emyr, Most Rev. George Noakes (Archbishop of Wales), Berwin Price, Angela Tooby, Prince Charles.

ALRA

Academy of Live and Recorded Arts, Royal Victoria Building,
Trinity Road, London SW18 3SX
(Tel 0181 870 6475, Fax 0181 875 0789) Map 5

STUDENT ENQUIRIES: The Administrator
APPLICATION: Direct

Broad study areas include: Theatre, television, film. (Subject details are in the *Subjects and Places Index*.)

Founded: 1979. **Site:** In listed (Grade I) Victorian building on Wandsworth Common. **Access:** BR Clapham Junction or Wandsworth Common; bus to central London. **Academic features:** Actor's course (NCDT accredited) and courses in stage management, theatre, television, film and radio techniques. Modern approach and a concern for the individual student; academy is personally supervised by its founder Sorrel Carson. Modern and classical theatre, television and film (special emphasis); also improvisation, movement, ballet, tap, stagecraft, mime, historical dance, singing, Alexander technique, stage fighting. **Special features:** Guest speakers and directors from professional theatre and related fields, including Janet Suzman, Roger Rees, Kate O'Mara, Prunella Scales, Diana Rigg, Tim Piggot-Smith. **Other learning facilities:** Three fully-equipped theatres; television and broadcasting studios; dance hall; rehearsal studios; stage management workshop; design office; wardrobe and dressing rooms. **Careers:** Information and advice given; graduation audition showcase for agents, directors, producers and casting agents. **Welfare:** Student welfare officers. Information pack given to new students regarding housing, public libraries, doctors and health centres, banks etc. Year tutors supervise welfare and progress. **Amenities:** Royal Victoria Building has café, bar and restaurant. **Sports:** Good local sports facilities.

Accommodation: No college accommodation. Students given active help in finding self-catering accommodation locally – prices £40–£60 per week. **Hardship funds:** Assisted places to talented students not on grants; plus Sorrel Carson scholarships for 4 specially talented applicants.

Duration of courses: 3 years; **others:** 1 year (stage management and postgraduate courses). **Total first degree students 1995/96:** 150. **Overseas students:** Approx 5%. **Male/female ratio:** 1:1. **Teaching staff:** 15 full-time, 33 part-time. **Total full-time students 1995/96:** 168. **Postgraduate students:** 15. **Tuition fees 1996/97:** £7,500–£9,100 (plus VAT).

WHAT IT'S LIKE   'Acting is reacting' – never a truer word was spoken. This simple but effective slogan is the philosophy on which ALRA is built. The Academy looks for the potential within each individual and develops it into a totally sensitive, emotionally responsive and well-trained instrument. The entry audition does not consist of audition pieces but allows each potential student to show their acting ability through a day of workshops – including voice, improvisation, movement and some TV work. It is situated in the magnificent Royal Victoria Patriotic Building and is fully equipped with studios, dance halls, TV studio, café and three theatres. Comprehensive training is provided in all areas including voice, dance, TV and radio, stage combat, mask and mime, singing and stage technique to name but a few. It prepares you for the harsh reality of the acting profession. As a student you work with guest directors and tutors, most of whom are working actors bringing their experience and working knowledge; this adds vitality and energy to your training. Project work includes Shakespeare, Greek, Restoration, American and English drama. Playwrights vary each term, from Chekhov to Berkoff. From day one you are made to feel welcome, with a year tutor who will help you as best they can with any academic or personal problems you may have. You become a member of a large team, all working together to achieve the same goal.

PAUPER NOTES   **Accommodation:** Local help given. **Hardship funds:** Scholarships and assisted places available. **Work:** Lots of work locally in bars, restaurants, etc. Most find part-time work in order to survive.

CAN'T FIND WHAT YOU'RE LOOKING FOR? USE THE INDEX!

ANGLIA POLYTECHNIC UNIVERSITY

Anglia Polytechnic University
- Cambridge Campus, East Road, Cambridge CB1 1PT
  (Tel 01223 363271)
- Central Campus, Chelmsford, Essex CM1 1LL
  (Tel 01245 493131)

Map 4

STUDENT ENQUIRIES: Student Administration (Admissions) at Cambridge address. APPLICATIONS:UCAS

Broad study areas: Art & design, business, education, humanities, science, computing, professions allied to medicine. (Subject details are in the *Subjects and Places Index*.)

Founded: 1989, ex Essex Institute and Cambridgeshire College of Arts and Technology; university status 1992. **Main undergraduate awards:** LLB, BEd, BSc, BA. **Awarding body:** Anglia Polytechnic University. **Site:** 2 sites in Chelmsford town centre, 100 yards apart; single sites in Cambridge, Brentwood and Danbury (post-graduates). **Access:** Good train connections with London from all sites. **Academic features:** All courses available on modular, credit accumulation basis. Open course scheme allows individual negotiated pathways and accreditation of prior learning. **Europe:** All first degree students can take up to 3 language modules as part of their degree. European dimension on some courses (eg European business administration); specialist language programmes being developed in eg law and technology. Formal exchange links with 5 European universities/colleges, in France, Germany and Netherlands (mostly business studies and technology) as well as links for language students. **Library:** Library at all sites (new library at Chelmsford); 260,000 volumes, 650 periodicals, 800+ study places. Annual expenditure on library materials, £70 per FTE student. **Other learning facilities:** Computer centre; CAD/CAM centre; language centres; learning resource centre. **Specialist collections:** Law, education and management, music, French Resistance archive. **Welfare:** Counselling, medical and health education services. **Careers:** Information, advice and placement and access funds. **Amenities:** SU bookshop on all main sites, SU buildings with bars. Mumford Theatre at Cambridge. Nursery (3-5 year-olds) on all sites except Danbury.

Accommodation: In 1995/96, 24% students in university accommodation; single first year students guaranteed hall place in Chelmsford. 1,611 self-catering places available (605 for first years); £35–£49 per week in Chelmsford, £42–£55 (incl bills) in Cambridge, for 40 weeks/year. 300 extra places planned for Cambridge. Students live in privately owned accommodation for minimum of 1 year: rents in Chelmsford £40 plus bills for self-catering, £40–£45 B&B, £60–£65 for half board; in Cambridge £45 plus bills for self-catering, £45–£50 B&B, £70–£76 for half board. **Term time work:** University policy to allow term time work for full-time first degree students; no limit to hours worked. Term (and vac) work on campus in SU, offices etc. Student employment offices (on main campuses) help in finding work off-campus. **Hardship funds:** Total available in 1995/96: £125,900 plus interest, government access fund; £500 other funds. Special help given from access funds to mature students, those with dependants, disabled and final year students; own funds used for those in extreme hardship for whatever reason.

Duration of first degree courses: 3 and 4 years. **Total first degree students 1995/96:** 7,727 (full time). **BEd students:** 605. **Overseas students:** 193. **Mature students:** 52%. **Male/female ratio:** 9:11. **Teaching staff:** 444 full-time, 145 part-time. **Total full-time students 1995/96:** 8,083. **Postgraduate students:** 1,109. **First degree tuition fees:** Home students, paying their own fees in 1996/97, paid £750 (classroom), £1,600 (lab/studio); Overseas students £5,100 (classroom), £5,400 (lab/studio).

WHAT IT'S LIKE (Cambridge)   Enjoys a sometimes uneasy, sometimes mutually beneficial relationship with Cambridge University, the more prestigious university. Many students use their rather more luxurious facilities, while many of theirs prefer Anglia's more relaxed and informal environment. Competition between colleges reaches a peak in sport with successful leagues in football, rugby, rowing, hockey and cricket. Academic reputation good, particularly for humanities/social studies. Well-developed and dynamic SU ensures that student services, entertainments and welfare issues are not neglected. Accommodation improving with new halls of residence. Uni is addressing the problem of overcrowding. Wide variety of students doing degree, HND and day release. The opportunities are there for anyone with initiative to get on and pursue almost any field of endeavour or activity they choose.

PAUPER NOTES   **Accommodation:** Some cheap digs through housing associations. **Drink:** SU bar best value, local brews – Abbot Ale, Bakers Arms, The Tram Depot. **Eats:** SU Bateman Café, the Corn Exchange, Tatties, Peppercorns. Veg: Arjuna, King's Pantry. **Ents:** Bands, discos, comedy, large theatre on campus. Large summer ball. **Sports:** No sports facilities on campus (though sports teams are active and successful). Kelsey Kerridge sports hall and Parkside swimming pool (reduced rates to students at certain times). **Hardship funds:** Access fund – £600 max; bursaries, £200–£300. **Travel:** STA Travel, Campus Travel, good hitching after long walk to starting points. **Work:** University has own employment agency; also work in town (catering, pubs, shops, farms, factories).

ALUMNI (EDITORS' PICK)   Sacha Count (own lingerie firm), John Swinfield (presenter of ITV programme, Enterprise), Adam Ant, Fluck and Law ('Spitting Image').

WHAT IT'S LIKE (Essex)   Sites at Chelmsford and Brentwood. Chelmsford: big town, small campus but friendly. Most entertainment is college-based. Main courses are business studies, law, building studies, computer studies and nursing. Brentwood: quiet, mostly mature students, close to London. Teaching generally good. Small so atmosphere tends to be very friendly with everyone knowing each other. Students get involved in societies and college activities and most people enjoy their time here.

PAUPER NOTES   **Accommodation:** Halls of residence plentiful in Chelmsford. Accommodation generally quite expensive everywhere. **Drink:** Chelmsford Placcy (SU bar) cheapest in town; small but friendly bar in Brentwood. **Eats:** Small refectory at Chelmsford, good bar food; loads of pizza places and Indians. **Ents:** Cinema, bowling and theatre in Chelmsford. **Sports:** Excellent leisure centre in Chelmsford – cheap tickets available from university sports department. Good college facilities on Brentwood site. **Hardship funds:** Student services fund. **Travel:** Expensive bus fares and taxis. Brentwood – difficult to get to BR station from college. **Work:** Part-time work available term time and vacation in Chelmsford and Brentwood.

ALUMNI (EDITORS' PICK)   Jerry Hayes (MP), Mike Smith, Tom Sharpe.

ARCHITECTURAL ASSOCIATION

Architectural Association School of Architecture,
34–36 Bedford Square, London WC1B 3ES
(Tel 0171 636 0974, Fax 0171 414 0782) Map 6

STUDENT ENQUIRIES: Registrar's Office
APPLICATION: Direct

Broad study area: Architecture.

Founded: 1847. **Main awards:** Exemption from RIBA Parts 1 and 2, AA Diploma. **Awarding body:** RIBA, AA. **Site:** Central London. **Access:** Tottenham Court Road underground station. **Special features:** International character of school reflected by teaching staff offering a wide range of design options and teaching styles. Students recognised as individuals and expected to demonstrate a high level of self-motivation to benefit from rich and varied programme which includes seminars and tutorials with professional consultants and members of allied disciplines. **Academic features:** 1-year foundation course offered to develop creative skills in intensive programme of studio work. 5-year RIBA recognised course in architecture has emphasis on developing personal creativity with strong self-directed tutorials. **Europe:** No languages taught; study trips may visit Europe. **Library:** 24,000 books, 75,000 slides, 50 study places. Annual expenditure on library materials, £73 per FTE student. **Specialist collections:** Yerbury slide collection (3,000 slides on buildings of 1920s and 1930s). **Welfare:** Pastoral care and individual counselling available. **Careers:** Information and advice from practical training adviser. **Amenities:** International exhibition gallery, specialist bookshop, brasserie, bar, darkroom, video studios, etching, workshop, computer facilities.

Accommodation: No college accommodation. Most students live in self-catering shared accommodation at £50–£70 per week. **Hardship funds:** Vary from year to year.

Duration of courses: 5 years other: 1 year. **Total AA diploma students 1995/96:** approx 260. **Overseas students:** 80%. **Mature students:** 20%. **Male/female ratio:** 3:2. **Teaching staff (part-time):** 120. **Total full-time students 1995/96:** 380. **Tuition fees 1996/97:** £9,100 (home and overseas).

WHAT IT'S LIKE   The oldest, largest and many consider the best architectural school in the country, it's a private school with an affiliated professional association. Features a 5-year programme for RIBA Parts I and II and AA Diploma, plus a range of postgraduate courses and a foundation course. Choice of units ranging from conceptual to rigorously architectonic – all experimental and none aims to advocate any house style. Pass from year to year based on your final oral presentation of unit work and successful fulfilment of 3 other submissions (general studies, media studies and technical studies). No traditional structure, as nothing is strictly compulsory during the year, but high standards are expected. Students given a great deal of independence which requires more resilience to maintain one's own standards without being spoon-fed; sometimes a mild shock to those arriving from A-level. An intense, sometimes competitive atmosphere prevails, diluted

in the evenings as students and tutors collect themselves at the elegent school bar. The school year consists of very intense work alongside exhibitions, lectures, workshops and other events specially co-ordinated to complement study; some quite provocative and diverse. A variety of student exhibitions throughout the year; end of year projects review in July – the highlight of the London architectural calendar, consuming all three Georgian buildings; a place to see and be seen. School not cheap. Students sometimes drop out for financial reasons or take a year out. But heavy workload often means course can't be completed on time anyway – not a place to rush through. No general student political affil-iation or tendency. International mix of students, cosmopolitan environment, a variety of influences and dialogues. Several superb evening lecture series, with speakers from all over the world in many disciplines. Well-stocked bookshop includes in-house publications and a slide library. Newly re-fitted workshop for working with metal and wood, CAD studio, darkroom, etching and print studios. If you really love the cutting edge of architecture, and you can't wait to express your commitment and fascination without being stifled, then apply.
PAUPER NOTES   **Accommodation:** As varied as London itself – students seem to prefer old factory buildings/loft spaces in Hackney and City. Very good accommodation service at beginning of term. Co-ordinators can advise house/flat shares. Watch school notice-boards. **Drink:** Own bar, no time for anything else! **Eats:** Wagamama, Streatham Street – good cheap food, great architecture. Pollo Restaurant on Old Compton Street, Bar Italia on Frith Street. AA has its own lunchtime restaurant/bar. **Ents:** Christmas party and Carnival. Students' standby at West End theatres and galleries (reduced rates). **Sports:** none at AA; ULU and YMCA facilities nearby. Local Camden facilities open to students. **Hardship funds:** Loans from AA. **Travel:** Travel scholarships from AA, other institutes (architectural). STA Travel. **Work:** Working within school part-time. Part-time in practices possible during term time.
MORE INFO?   Enquiries to AASF co-ordinator on 0171 636 0974 ext 212.
INFORMAL NAME   AA.
ALUMNI (EDITORS' PICK)   Richard Rogers (architect for Lloyd's Building/Pompidou Centre), Mark Fisher (designer of Pink Floyd concerts), Ron Arad (furniture designer), Zaha Hadid (architect), Eileen Gray (architect, designer), Janet Street Porter (notorious), Nigel Coates, Nick Grimshaw, Michael and Patti Hopkins.

ASTON UNIVERSITY

Aston University, Aston Triangle, Birmingham B4 7ET
(Tel 0121 359 3611, Fax 0121 333 6350) Map 3

STUDENT ENQUIRIES: Registry
APPLICATIONS: UCAS

Broad study areas: Management, modern languages and European studies, engineering and applied sciences, life and health sciences. (Subject details are in the *Subjects and Places Index*.)

Founded: 1895. A Central Technical School 1927, College of Technology 1951, College of

Advanced Technology 1956; University Charter 1966. **Main undergraduate awards:** BSc, BEng, MEng, MPharm. **Awarding body:** Aston University. **Site:** Single, modern, green 40-acre campus, in centre of Birmingham. **Access:** 10 minutes walk from city centre, extensive local transport. **Structural features:** All departments in new or recently modernised locations; excellent and extensive computing facilities. **Academic features:** All courses have strong vocational element; 70% students are on sandwich courses. Combined honours programme allows wide combinations of subjects. Engineering faculty offers BEng and MEng; large business school and vision science department. **Special features:** Close links with industry and business. **Europe:** Languages may be taken as part of many first degree courses; 24% students spend 6-12 months abroad. Strong European focus in many degrees eg international business and modern languages, computer science/engineering with European studies. **Library:** 215,000 monographs, 115,000 bound periodicals, 1,460 current periodicals; 400 business and 500 medical CD-Rom periodicals; computerised catalogues, circulation and information services, on-line access to databases throughout the world; audio-visual laboratory, 800 reader places (91 with IT facilities). Annual expenditure on library materials, £125 per FTE student. **Other learning facilities:** Multi-media language suite; CAD laboratories; extensive computing facilites. **Welfare:** Health centre, dental surgery, opticians, student advice service, chaplaincy, money advice centre, careers service and accommodation office all on campus; also welfare officer, counsellors, personal tutors. Special category: Married students' flats; accommodation for physically handicapped students; nursery facilities. **Amenities:** Students' Guild has bars, dance hall and games room. Also print shop, secondhand book and stationery shop, travel agents, banks, hairdresser, post office. City facilities close by. **Sporting facilities:** Two well-equippped sports halls, swimming pool and all-weather pitch on campus. Sports ground, 20 minutes away, has 19 pitches, tennis and squash courts, cricket square and pavilion (with bar and cafe).

Accommodation: In 1995/96, 60% of all students in university accommodation, 100% of first years. 2,500 places available on main campus or university village plus additional residences owned by Guild of Students: 175 full board places at £46.65 per week, Sept–June; 1,810 self-catering places at £21.85–£31.85 per week, Sept–June; and 66 married students studio flats at £45 per week, all-year rental. Most students live in privately owned accommodation for 1 year: rents £25–£35 per week for self-catering, £40 for B&B. **Term time work:** University policy on term time work for full-time first degree students being considered (24% believed to work). Term (and vac) work on campus in bars, restaurants, travel agency and summer catering; university helps finding vac work off campus. **Hardship funds:** Total available in 1995/96: £74,603 government access funds, 123 students helped; £8,500 own funds, 22 students helped; plus £2,500 funds for overseas students (short-term help only). Special help: single parents with childcare needs, self-financing students, mature students, those subject to financial difficulties for reasons beyond their control; own funds generally available only for short-term unforeseen difficulties, priority for final year students.

Duration of first degree courses: BSc, 3 years (full-time), 4 years (sandwich); BEng/MEng, 3–5 years (full-time and sandwich). **Total first degree students 1995/96:** 3,980. **Male/female ratio:** 5:4. **Overseas students:** 242. **Mature students:** 515. **Teaching staff:** 250. **Total full-time students 1995/96:** 4,373. **Postgraduate students:** 1,024 (393 full-time). **First degree tuition fees:** Home students, paying their own fees in 1996/97, paid £750 (classroom), £1,600 (lab/studio); Overseas students, £6,030 (classroom), £7,990 (lab/studio).

WHAT IT'S LIKE Easily accessible by coach, car or train. Small, compact campus; very friendly. Accommodation on campus in single-sex, self- and full-catering flats. University

Village, 4 miles away, has hall for first and final years and more self-catering flats. Both sites have launderettes. SU-managed housing scheme for 200 students (some specifically for couples), 10 minutes' walk from campus. Good city bus service, many all night routes. Close to city centre facilities. SU active (about 70 societies, 40 sports clubs). Varied ents including one of the best student light shows in the country. Library open until 10 pm week-days, 5 pm Saturday, open Sunday in term 3. Campus health centre with full-time counsellor; understanding attitude towards contraception. Courses increasingly modular usually with one year placements. Good graduate employment record. High entry grades but felt worth it by those that make it.

PAUPER NOTES   **Accommodation:** Reasonable university accommodation. **Drink:** SU has the best prices in town, regular promotions. Campus pubs also very popular with students. **Eats:** SU offers variety, reasonable prices, veggie food; 3 catering outlets during day. Wide choice in town. **Ents:** SU provides discos, bands, cabaret. **Sports:** 2 sports centres on campus plus swimming pool. University sports ground few miles out of town. **Hardship funds:** Only for the most deserving cases (mixture of grants and loans). **Travel:** University offers travel scholarships; Campus Travel in SU offers student discounts etc. **Work:** Extremely hard to come by; campus pubs offer bar jobs. Welfare advertises jobs – mainly bar and shop work, some tele-sales.

MORE INFO?   Get Students' Alternative Prospectus. Enquiries to Schools Liaison Officer (0121 359 6531 ext 4062).

BANGOR UNIVERSITY

The University of Wales, Bangor, North Wales LL57 2DG
(Tel 01248 351151, Fax 01248 370451) Map 2

STUDENT ENQUIRIES: Academic Registrar
APPLICATIONS: UCAS

Broad study areas: Arts, social sciences, science, engineering, agriculture and forestry, health. (Subject details are in the *Subjects and Places Index.*)

Founded: 1884; founding college of Wales University. **Main undergraduate awards:** BA, BD, BEd, BMus, BN, BSc, BEng. **Awarding body:** Wales University. **Site:** Town centre. **Access:** 2 hrs travelling distance from M56, which links with M6. A55 is coastal expressway and A5 the scenic route through N Wales. Regular fast trains to and from London, Birmingham, Manchester. **Structural features:** Part of Wales University. **Largest fields of study:** Biological sciences, electronic engineering science, ocean science, accounting, banking, economics, psychology, agriculture and forestry. **Special features:** Sponsorship available with major financial services firms for degrees in banking, insurance and finance and with industrial companies for BEng/MEng. National Coaching Centre established (one of only two in UK universities). **Academic features:** School of Welsh Medium Studies; number of courses taught in Welsh. **Europe:** 11% first degree students take a language as part of course; 8% spend 6 months or more abroad. All arts undergraduates may take a language at Part 1;

French, German and Spanish available to science students. Degrees involving a year abroad include European financial management (a year at European university), chemistry with European industrial placement. Socrates exchange links with 100 universities across EFTA and EU, available to students in a wide range of subjects. **Library:** 8 library/computing buildings including ocean sciences library. 500,000 volumes in total, 2,200 periodicals, 900 study places, short loan scheme for texts in heavy demand. Annual expenditure on library materials, £99.66 per FTE student. **Other learning facilities:** Ocean-going research vessel, college farms, botanic garden, field station, natural history museum, computer building, multi-media language centre; support systems for deaf and visually-impaired students. **Welfare:** Comprehensive health service through local GPs; professional student counsellor, college chaplains, college counsellors, students' union welfare office. **Special categories:** Nursery run by psychology department, playgroup, SU Niteline. **Careers:** Information, advice and placement. **Amenities:** Professional theatre, concert halls, museum, art gallery. **Sporting facilities:** Sports centre, 50 acres of playing fields, unparalleled opportunities for outdoor activities in Snowdonia.

Accommodation: In 1995/96, 39% of all students in college accommodation, 78% first years. 2,300 places available (1,247 for first years): 897 part-board places (559 for first years) at £56–£59 per week, term time only and 880 self-catering places (688 for first years) at £34–£43 per week, for 38 weeks; 170 self-catering places, all year rental. Students live in privately owned accommodation for 2 years: rents £35–£45 per week for self-catering. **Term time work:** No university policy on term time work and no work provided on campus. **Hardship funds:** Total available in 1995/96: £126,795 government access funds, approx 687 awards made; also small endowments allowing 3–4 emergency payments each year. Special help: all on individual merit but priority to mature students, those with dependants and students with special needs. About 20 local scholarships are available (around £500 average).

Duration of first degree courses: 3 years; 4 years (languages, wide-entry, MEng, MChem and MMath). **Total first degree students 1995/96:** 4,578. **Overseas students:** 1,085 (+ 411 EU). **Mature students:** 1,844. **Male/female ratio:** 1:1. **Teaching staff:** 447 full-time, 23 part-time. **Total full-time students 1995/96:** 6,845. **Postgraduate students:** 769. **First degree tuition fees:** Home students, paying their own fees in 1996/97, paid £750 (classroom), £1,600 (lab/studio). Overseas students £5,870 (classroom), £7,720 (lab/studio).

WHAT IT'S LIKE Small, friendly coastal city, easily accessible by train, bus and car. Imposing 19th century main building on hill overlooking town centre, where other departmental buildings are also situated. Central SU and all halls/departments within ten minutes walk, except ocean sciences (3 miles over Menai Bridge on Anglesey, but regular bus service, easy hitch or cycle journey), and new site following merger with the Normal College 1 mile away. College accommodation for a third of students, with first years taking priority. Most is in halls (mixed, self-catered, Welsh speaking), including new, modern en-suite accommodation for 850 students. Launderettes on all hall sites and in SU; cooking facilities passable even in catered halls. Good quality private accommodation, but look early. Wide variety of food shops and restaurants (good prices). Good mix of ages (29% mature students) and nationalities from Europe and further afield; all regions of Britain well represented. Very friendly atmosphere. Academically strong in all areas; great strength in environmental sciences, music, Welsh, psychology, accounting and banking. New multimedia language centre. Extensive specialised libraries for arts, science and health studies. SU welfare office offers representation, personal support and advice on a wide variety of problems. Student-run Nightline and full time counsellor – all entirely confidential. SU runs food outlets (extensive range) and bars (inexpensive drink and regular promotions) in the

main venues which run massive entertainments (recent appearances from Dreadzone, Super Furry Animals, The Bigger the God and also Juice, the largest dance night in North Wales). Also in SU are travel office, shop, restaurant, bookshop, bank, showers, laundry, snooker room, games room, television lounge and meeting rooms. Community action organisation in SU to socialise and work with/for the local community. SU clubs and societies cater for range of cultural, social, religious, and political needs – some serious, some fun – there's one for everyone and if there isn't, they'll help you form one! The Athletic Union, with 44 clubs, provides activities from the conventional hockey/football, to Ki Aikido, live role-playing and Gaelic football. Well placed for water sports and mountaineering so outdoor pursuits clubs popular and active. Stage crew, entertainment, LGB etc; not overtly political but opportunities for students to become involved active in all areas of interest or concern. Lively student newspaper, Seren (in English), Y Ddraenen (Welsh) with news, reviews, music and photography. Active bi-lingual policy in SU – all publications and general meetings in Welsh and English – but free Welsh lessons for those who wish to learn.
Matthew Robins

PAUPER NOTES   **Accommodation:** Readily available (look early for the best ones); private accommodation (bedsits, shared flats/houses), about £38 a week in Bangor, £30 outside. College accommodation priority to 1st and 3rd years. **Drink:** SU bars cheapest. Extensive range of beers. **Eats:** SU Freddies and Glan (omnivorous/veggie/vegan); also Mrs P's Tea Bar. Herbs Restaurant – wide range of salads and health foods. Various British, Italian, Greek, Indian, Chinese eats. **Ents:** SU is major North Wales venue; big gigs, dance nights, lots of pubs, one local nightclub. SU card gives discount at theatre and cinema. **Sports:** College centre (due to be refurbished) has squash, weights, multigym, climbing wall, large multipurpose hall, with student reductions. Local pool with diving facilities. Normal site for martial arts clubs etc. Treborth athletics track, cricket, football, rugby. Ffridd site – womens rugby, football and sports hall. **Hardship Funds:** College access funds available. SU can give short term loans, in exceptional circumstances. **Travel:** Travel office in SU, with many discount schemes. Overseas scholarships eg Canada/US/EU. Cheap boats to and from Dublin (popular student pastime!). Intercity London-Bangor 3½ hrs; also National Express coaches. Local bus service reliable. SU runs minibus lift service after evening events. **Work:** University Job Mart, helps students find part-time work. Uni and SU employ students in bars and catering outlets. Most types of casual work, including specialist and vac work, especially in outdoor pursuits.

MORE INFO?   Enquiries to SU President (01248 353709). Handbooks and guides available from SU.

ALUMNI   Dr Robert Edwards (pioneer of test-tube babies), Roger Whittaker (singer, songwriter), Dr David Rees (Director of National Inst for Medical Research), Ann Clwyd (MP), Robert Einion Holland (Chief General Manager, Pearl Assurance), Lord Dafydd Elis Thomas (Chairman, Welsh Language Board), John Sessions (poet and impressionist), Frances Barber (actress).

HOW TO START? *SEE SHORTLISTING*, PAGE 535

BATH COLLEGE

Bath College of Higher Education
- Newton Park, Bath BA2 9BN
  (Tel 01225 873701, Fax 01225 874123)
- Sion Hill Place, Lansdown, Bath BA1 5SJ
  (Tel 01225 425264, Fax 01225 445228)

Map 3

STUDENT ENQUIRIES: Prospectus Officer at Newton Park
APPLICATIONS: UCAS

Broad study areas: Art & design, education, applied and environmental sciences, humanities, music, social sciences. (Subject details are in the *Subjects and Places Index.*)

Founded: 1983 ex Bath College of Higher Education and Bath Academy of Art. **Main undergraduate awards:** BA, BSc, BA/BSc (QTS). **Awarding body:** Bath College. **Site:** Newton Park and Sion Hill, about 4 and 1½ miles respectively from Bath city centre. **Access:** Rail, road (M4/A4), local buses. **Europe:** 15% first degree students take a language as part of course, including students in music and graphic design; international degree in English and education studies with TEFL involve 6 months a year in Rotterdam. Links with over 20 European institutions. **Library:** 1 library at each site; 150,000 volumes, 5,500 AV resources in total, 600 periodicals, 260 study places. Annual expenditure on library materials, £57 per FTE student. **Other learning facilities:** Computer systems (PCs and Macintosh), CD-Rom, JANET, Internet; slide library. **Welfare:** Welfare officer, accommocation officer. **Careers:** Information and advice; placement.

Accommodation: In 1995/96, 25% of all students in college accommodation, 90% of first years. 600 self-catering places available, £35–£41 per week, for 40 weeks. Students live in privately owned accommodation for 2–3 years: £39–£45 per week for self-catering, £60–£70 half-board with weekend meals. **Term time work:** College policy to allow term time work for full-time first degree students, so long as it does not interfere with college commitments (c 70% believed to work). Students can apply for term (and vac) work on campus in library, offices, domestic service, catering, maintenance. **Hardship funds:** Total available in 1995/96: £59,774, government access funds, 525 students helped; first years given limited help, £100 max unless exceptional circumstances.

Duration of first degree courses: 3 years; BA/BSc (QTS) 4 years. **Total first degree students 1995/96:** 1,996. **Total BA/BSc (QTS) students:** 481. **Overseas students:** 160. **Mature students:** 750. **Male/female ratio:** 2:5. **Teaching staff:** 115 full-time, 25 associate staff. **Total full-time students 1995/96:** 2,303. **Postgraduate students:** 180 f-t, 560 p-t. **First degree tuition fees:** Home students, paying their own fees in 1996/97, paid £750 (classroom), £1,600 (lab/studio); Overseas students £5,400-£6,100.

WHAT IT'S LIKE   It's divided between two sites: Sion Hill, 15 minutes walk from town; and Newton Park, 4 miles towards Bristol. There is a regular bus service from Bath to the college. Halls are for first years, all self-catering. They are split into courts at Newton Park and houses at Sion Hill, where rooms are in a Georgian crescent, and each has a kitchen shared with other students. Each site has a canteen open for lunch, coffee and snacks in the morning and afternoon. Bars on each site are subsidised. SU very active, holding events each week and liaising with university. At Newton Park there is a sports hall and college teams hold matches, home or away, each week. There is a strong student presence in Bath with students from university and college of further education all sharing same pubs and clubs. Lots of very individual pubs. In accordance with an old by-law in Bath, many of the clubs are underground such as The Swamp, Moles and The Hub, where you have to be a member. BCHE students have concession nights at all decent clubs. There are several markets throughout the week eg Great Western antique market, an indoor market and, on Saturdays, a large flea market on Walcot Street. The college is on the bus route to Bristol, so you have the amenities of both a large town and city.

PAUPER NOTES   **Accommodation:** Expensive and difficult to find. **Drink:** Good real ales, BX, Buttcombe, Eldridge Pope. Excellent pubs with atmosphere: Salamander, The Bell, The Curfew, The Hat and Feather, The Boater; cheap at SU bars. **Eats:** From veggie burgers to à la carte, eating places for all walks of life, eating habits and more importantly pockets. Schwartz Burgers, The Paragon, The Tapas Bar. **Ents:** Venues for all tastes. Moles nightclub, The Hub, good student cinema deals at Robins; gigs at the Uni and BCHE; much jazz, rock, pop and classics – Bristol 9 miles away. **Sports:** College teams play on a regular basis, also Bath leisure centre, with pool, squash and tennis. **Hardship funds:** Access fund. **Work:** Often neccessary; lots of part-time jobs in bars. 25% get paid term-time work; 60% local vacation work.

MORE INFO?   Enquiries to the Student Union (01225 872603)

INFORMAL NAME   BCHE

ALUMNI   Anita Roddick (Body Shop), Mary Berry (cook), Sue Cuff (TV), Howard Hodgkin, Martin Potts (painters), Nicholas Pope, Veronica Ryan, Nigel Rolfe, Peter Randall-Page (sculptors).

BATH UNIVERSITY

The University of Bath, Claverton Down, Bath BA2 7AY
(Tel 01225 826826, Fax 01225 826366) Map 3

STUDENT ENQUIRIES: Director of Admissions
APPLICATIONS: UCAS

Broad study areas: Engineering, science, languages, architecture, management, economics, sociology. (Subject details are in the *Subjects and Places Index*.)

Founded: 1894, as Merchant Venturers' Technical College; full university status 1966. **Main undergraduate awards:** BA, BArch, BPharm, BSc, BEng, MEng. **Awarding body:** Bath University. **Site:** Campus 1 mile from Bath city centre. **Access:** Local buses. **Europe:** 20% first degree students take a language as part of course and 10% spend 6 months or more abroad. Language option on most courses. Erasmus links with large number of European universities/colleges in many subjects. **Library:** 200,000 volumes, 3,000 periodicals, 1,200 study places, course books on short loan. 350 PCs open 24 hours. Annual expenditure on library materials, £87 per FTE student. **Welfare:** Counsellor, doctors, psychiatrist, chaplain, dentist. Special categories: Some accommodation for married students, some facilities for disabled, nursery (15 places, £6.25 a day). **Amenities:** Bookshop, banks, general shop (SU), chapel, supermarket, travel agency, post office, newsagent and hairdresser. **Sporting facilities:** Include a sports hall, swimming pools (1 Olympic), running track, Astro-turf floodlit pitches. All playing fields on campus. **Employment::** Strong tradition in engineering and pharmacy.

Accommodation: In 1995/96, 35% of all students in university accommodation, 100% of first years. 1,920 self-catering places available (1,360 for first years), £38–£47 per week, for term time or longer. Students live in privately owned accommodation for 2 years, rents £40–£50 per week for self-catering. 2% first degree students live at home. **Term time work:** No university policy on term time work for full-time first degree students (20% believed to work). Vacation work only on campus in bars, offices, library, registry, conferences office; university helps find work off campus only for sandwich placements. **Hardship funds:** Total available in 1995/96: £181,000 government access funds, 450 students helped; £10,000 own funds, 16 students helped; some weighting in favour of students with dependants, single-parent families, etc.

Duration of first degree courses: 3 years; 4 years (sandwich, MEng). **Total first degree students 1995/96:** 4,656. **Overseas students:** 261. **Mature students:** 476. **Male/female ratio:** 3:2. **Teaching staff:** 379 full-time, 10 part-time. **Total students 1995/96:** 6,606. **Postgraduate students:** 828 (+1,292 part-time). **First degree tuition fees:** Home students, paying their own fees in 1996/97, paid £1,600; Overseas students £6,080 (classroom), £8,040 (lab).

WHAT IT'S LIKE   650 feet above city of Bath. Exposed and windy; unattractive modern buildings are concentrated on central pedestrian area but set in lots of open space giving a good, roomy feel. City's beauty easily makes up for any shortcomings. Facilities on campus include medical centre, launderettes, 4 banks and a building society (all with cash points). Residences all self-catering; quiet low-rise blocks. Refectories with health food counters and SU coffee bar with veggy and fast food. Academic concentration on science, technology, especially sandwich courses, hence strong links with industry. Employment prospects are excellent. Varying proportion of continuous assessments; training course for new lecturers. Library open 24 hours a day with adequate reading space. Good links with town; majority of students live in town, so lots of opportunity to join in local life. Good student town. Small city but Bath has 3 cinemas, a theatre, 8 nightclubs, fairly good book-shops and excellent pubs. SU facilities include shop, travel bureau and coffee bar. Student-run bar/venue with largest capacity in Bath. Active SU with about 160 clubs; high standard in teams and competitions. Good SU welfare and advice provision.

PAUPER NOTES   **Accommodation:** All first years live on campus; places for disabled students. City accommodation often expensive, about £45 per week and sometimes hard to find; help given by university accommodation office. **Drink:** Plenty of pubs, lots of real ale pubs and student pubs. Local brews: Smiles, Salisbury, Bishop's Tipple; Scrumpy paradise. **Eats:** A range of food on campus, good selection of restaurants in town including vegetarian and wholefoods, Harvest and Huckleberry's, kebabs, curries and fish and chips, pizzas and burgers; Thai, Lebanese, Japanese and (excellent) Indian, the Rajpoot. **Ents:** Events held almost every night in the Venue; discos, live music, Sunday cinema. Extensive freshers week, discount card for shops, cinemas, restaurants. **Sports:** Swimming pools and excellent facilities for squash and tennis on campus (including new swim-ming pool and tennis courts), Astroturf and 8 lane athletics track free to students; many teams and clubs from snooker to hot-air ballooning. Sports centre in town more expensive. Sports scholarships available. **Hardship funds:** University access fund; money advice centre, excellent welfare and academic advice from SU. **Travel:** Many hitch from town to campus; buses frequent and reasonable. Good rail and coach links: London 75 mins by train, Bristol 15 mins. SU travel shop on campus for discounts. **Work:** Some tourism, p-t shop work; standard availability. About 30% students work evenings/Saturdays in term time. Large tourist industry means summer and Xmas work available. Job Centre advertises in SU and student employment centre on campus.

MORE INFO?   Get students' Alternative Prospectus from SU – ring 01225 826612 ext 5063. ALUMNI   John Kiddey (TV reporter), Martin Hedges (world champion canoeist), Chris Martin, David Trick, Gareth Adams and John Sleightholme (England rugby players), Dr Fox (Capital Radio DJ), Don Foster MP.

BELFAST UNIVERSITY

Queen's University of Belfast, University Road, Belfast BT7 1NN, Northern Ireland (Tel 01232 245133, Fax 01232 247895; e-mail S Wisener @ qub.ac.uk) Map 1

STUDENT ENQUIRIES: **Admissions Officer**
APPLICATIONS: **UCAS**

Broad study areas: Agriculture, arts, education, engineering, law, medicine and dentistry, science, theology, architecture, accounting, social sciences. (Subject details are in the *Subjects and Places Index*.)

Founded: 1845. **Main undergraduate awards:** BA, BAgr, BD, BDS, BEd, BEng, BMedSc, BMus, BSc, BSSc, BTh, LLB, MB, BCh, BAO, MEng, MSci. **Awarding body:** Queen's University of Belfast. **Site:** Main site about 1 mile from city centre; medical site about 1 mile from main site. **Access:** Most live within 1 mile of main site. **Europe:** 7% first degree students take a language as part of their course and some spend a period abroad. Language teaching for non-specialists in 13 languages, at various levels (1,000+ students enrolled each year). Compulsory period of study at a partner university in a range of courses; European mobility programmes enable selected students to spend 3–9 months overseas. Some students may interrupt their course to work in Europe. **Library:** Main library (central site), and libraries for science, medicine and agriculture and food science. Around 1 million books in main libraries, plus 80,000 in departmental libraries. Annual expenditure on library materials, £92.71 per FTE student. **Other learning facilities:** Include marine biology station, astronomical observatory, conservation laboratory, phytotron, palaeoecology centre, field centre, electron microscope unit, microprocessor laboratory, NI technology centre, computer centres (open access), non-specialist language teaching. **Amenities:** SU building with supermarket, secondhand bookshop, bars, discos, laundrette, bank, insurance company, travel agency; cinema on campus, bookshop; Officers' Training Corps, Air Squadron. **Careers:** Information and advice service. **Welfare:** Health service, student counselling service, student support officer. **Sporting facilities:** Excellent playing fields and physical education centre.

Accommodation: In 1995/96, 20% of all students in university accommodation, 55% of first years. 1,900 places available (1,340 for first years who are given priority): 900 catered places (2 meals per day), £54 per week (single), £46 (double); 1,000 self-catering places, £31–£41 per week. Rents in privately owned accommodation, £28–£36 per week, self-catering; £40–£50 half-board. 40% first degree students live at home. **Term time work:** University policy to allow term time work for full-time first degree students (45% believed to work). Term (and vac) work on campus in SU, catering, library and PE centre; vacancy list for work off campus and SU liaison with employers. **Hardship funds:** Special help to: students in private accommodation with high rents (possibly including those in university accommodation); single parents, mature students with dependants and those with disabilities; own funds usually for non-UK students, suffering unforeseen hardship.

Duration of first degree courses: 3 or 4 years; 5 years for BDS, MB, BCh, BAO. **Total first degree students 1995/96:** 8,755 f-t; 1,156 p-t. **Total BEd students:** 1,283. **Overseas students:** 967 (f-t), 53 (p-t). **Mature students:** 991. **Male/female ratio:** 11:9. **Teaching and research staff:** 1,035 full-time, 56 part-time. **Total full-time students 1995/96:** 10,371. **Postgraduate students:** 3,357. **First degree tuition fees:** Home students, paying their own fees in 1996/97, paid £750; Overseas students, £5,000 (classroom), £6,500 (lab/studio), £8,000 (preclinical), £14,750 (clinical).

WHAT IT'S LIKE   Politically contentious city, student body has always held itself apart from the troubles. Many students live at home. For many it's an extension of school and school friends (most NI schools are single-sex and denominational although this is slowly changing). Academic standards high. Fair proportion of graduates go overseas for jobs, most remain at home. University area one of the most beautiful in Belfast, bordering posh Malone Road. Facilities good: 2 diners, coffee lounge, 2 bars renovated and 2 large venues with licensed bars. Crèche facilities. SU active. Accommodation improving, though many students live in poor privately rented accommodation. Public transport until 11 pm. University area is centre of night life. Major pop acts play in Belfast; regular discos and gigs in SU and town. Renaissance of pubs and eating places; also 4 major cinema complexes (including one 10-screen) showing national releases and Queen's Film Theatre has excellent alternative films. Annual festival, second only to Edinburgh in size and diversity. Main drug is alcohol. Police over-stretched but active in student area.

PAUPER NOTES   **Drink:** Lots of good bars in university area. SU cheap; Speakeasy and Bunatee SU bars – specials all year round. **Eats:** Pizza, kebabs, KFC and burger joints abound. Spice of Life vegetarian. Most pubs do lunches. **Ents:** SU main venue for bands and discos. **Sports:** Excellent facilities on campus including pool, gym, indoor football court; leisure centres, ice rink and ten-pin bowling. Sports shop in SU. **Hardship funds:** Bursar's loans and access funds. **Travel:** Cheap travel on railways. Hitching not practical for obvious reasons. 15% off bus fare with SU card. **Work:** Bar work, cloakrooms, bouncers, shop staff, library assistants – pay about £3 per hour. Approx 40% do some kind of p-t work (fewer during exams). SU employs some 140 students part-time. 20% work locally during vacation, although many find work at home.

MORE INFO?   Ring SU Welfare Officer (Siobhan Fearon) or Education Office (Cormac Bakewell) on 01232 324803.

ALUMNI   Trevor Ringland, Nigel Carr and Philip Matthews (all rugby players), Brian Mawhinney MP, Seamus Heaney (poet), Bernadette McAlliskey (née Devlin), Kenneth Branagh (actor), Lord Tombs (former Chairman of Rolls-Royce), Brian Moore (writer).

BIRKBECK COLLEGE

Birkbeck College, University of London, Malet Street,
London WC1E 7HX (Tel 0171 631 6000,
Fax 0171 631 6270) Map 6

STUDENT ENQUIRIES: Registry
APPLICATIONS: Direct

Broad study areas: Arts, economics, law, natural sciences, social sciences. (Subject details are in the *Subjects and Places Index*).

Founded: 1823. **Main undergraduate awards:** BA, BSc, BSc(Econ), LLB. **Awarding body:** London University. **Site:** In London University's central precinct in Bloomsbury. **Access:** Easily reached by underground (near Russell Square, Goodge Street, Warren Street and Euston stations) and close bus routes. **Structural features:** Part of London University. **Special features:** Provides degree level teaching and research facilities for students 'engaged in earning their livelihood during the day' – so is primarily part-time. Provision to change to full-time study in the final year (with permission from college). **Europe:** 11% first degree students take a language as part of course; available to all humanities students (most take at least one). No formal arrangements for periods abroad but French, Spanish and geology departments have European links. **Library:** 250,000 books; 1,000 periodicals. Annual expenditure on library materials, £76.31 per FTE student. Late opening hours designed to provide good study conditions for part-time students. Students also use main London University library next door in Senate House. **Other learning facilities:** Self-access centre for language and literature: self-tuition courses available in a number of languages, with language laboratory and computer-assisted packages; expanding collection of recordings in major European languages, sound-recording studio and tape facilities; intensive taught course in English for academic purposes and study skills. **Computing facilities:** Access via terminals and micros to both college and university machines; advisory service; college central computing service produces range of technical bulletins and regular newsletter.

Duration of first degree courses: 4 years part-time; 3 years for some advanced students. **Total first degree students 1995/96:** 3,409. **Mature students:** 90%. **Male/female ratio:** 1:1. **Teaching staff:** 200 full-time, 20 part-time. **Total full-time students 1995/96:** 437 (mostly postgraduate). **Postgraduate students:** 2,246. **First degree tuition fees:** Part-time students paying their own fees in 1996/97, paid £576–£1,080.

WHAT IT'S LIKE   Unique college catering primarily for those in full-time employment who choose to gain a London University degree through evening study. Most classes are held between 6 and 9 pm; wide age range but mainly 20s and 30s. Students without formal qualifications are often accepted. Degrees take 4 instead of 3 years and students may transfer to full-time study after 2 years. (Postgraduate and research degrees also possible through part or full-time study.) Services for both full-time and part-time students: union office, library and snack bar are open in the evenings as well as daytime; also dining club, serving hot meals from 5 pm weekdays. SU magazine welcomes student contributions.

Other facilities include a nursery, lively bar, a freshers fair, and over 30 other SU funded clubs and societies, covering a wide range of interests. Birkbeck students highly motiv-ated, and some manage to put time into union activities, clubs, and societies on top of work, study and family life. ULU (University of London Union) nearby, housing major sports and social facilities; so are Senate House Library and Dillons university bookshop. Located in the heart of academic London, it is well served by public transport and nearby shops, entertainment, and places of interest abound.

PAUPER NOTES   **Drink:** SU bar. **Eats:** College snack bars. ULU next door. **Ents:** Free live music/cabaret each week. **Sports:** All facilities at ULU. Football and volleyball teams. **Hardship funds:** Some college assistance possible. **Travel:** ULU Travel is next door. **Work:** Ask SU for help – some casual work.

ALUMNI   Baroness McFarlane of Llandaff (Manchester University), Dame Elizabeth Estève-Coll (Vice Chancellor, East Anglia University), Frank Sidebottom (cabaret singer), Sidney Webb (founder of LSE and other things), Helen Sharman (first British astronaunt), Laurie Taylor (sociologist and journalist).

BIRMINGHAM CONSERVATOIRE

Birmingham Conservatoire, Paradise Place, Birmingham B3 3HG (Tel 0121 331 5901/2, Fax 0121 331 5906) Map 3

STUDENT ENQUIRIES: The Registrar
APPLICATIONS: Direct

Broad study areas: Music: performance, composition, world music, community music. (Subject details are in the *Subjects and Places Index.*)

Founded: 1886 as part of Birmingham and Midland Institute; music faculty of Central England University since 1992. **Main awards:** BMus, MA, PGDip, DPS. **Awarding body:** Central England University. **Site:** City centre. **Access:** 10 minutes' walk from railway station. **Structural features:** Part of Central England University. **Academic features:** Initial full-time honours degree course (BMus) on modular structure; first study performance or compo-sition with range of options including ethnic music, music administration, jazz, improvisation, conducting, music technology and recording teaching skills and school studies. Also MA, PGDip, Diploma in Professional Studies. Good record of professional placements. **Special features:** Workshops and master classes with internationally renowned musicians. Purpose-built complex includes Adrian Boult Hall; also administrative headquarters of City of Birmingham Symphony Orchestra; many CBSO principals teach at Conservatoire. **Europe:** Exchange links with European universities/colleges being developed. **Library:** 41,000 volumes, 30 periodicals, 32 carrels. **Specialist collections:** Dodd Bows. **Welfare:** Medical facilities at Cambrian Hall nearby. **Careers:** Information and advice.

Accommodation: See Central England University. **Term time work:** Conservatoire policy to allow students part-time work. Term (and vac) work available on campus as eg cleaners, porters, concert stewards. **Hardship funds:** See Central England University. Own hardship funds of approx £3,000 (average of £50 awarded). Entrance scholarships awarded on audition results.

Duration of first degree courses: 4 years. **Total first degree students 1995/96:** 365. **Overseas students:** 21. **Mature students:** 4. **Male/female ratio:** 1:1. **Teaching staff:** 20 full-time, 170 part-time. **Total full-time students 1995/96:** 395. **Postgraduate students:** 75. **First degree tuition fees:** Home students, paying their own fees in 1996/97, paid £1,600; Overseas students £8,000.

WHAT IT'S LIKE   Ideally situated, in modern purpose-built city centre development. Easy access to relatively cheap transport (no parking at college) and main arts centres including town hall, symphony hall and repertory theatre. Recent developments (new library, canteen, keyboard lab and further practice rooms) together with concert hall, listening room and computers make the college well equipped. Ample opportunities for dedicated musicians with emphasis on professional discipline within a lively and friendly atmosphere. Courses combine a high level of practical and academic standard with centrality on the first study; modern teaching methods used in all areas. Established orchestras, choirs, bands and chamber music and students encouraged to develop own activities with staff guidance. Ethnomusicology and community music being developed – both courses and work experience. Staff/student relationships excellent. Growing emphasis on student welfare with active on-site student body and SU office offering help and advice in all areas. Hardship funds are available in some cases. Places in halls of residence for most first years (Cambrian Hall most accessible, four minutes walk) – other accommodation also available. Birmingham social life ranges from cheap student pubs to international clubs, reasonable restaurants, sports facilities and good shops. Some work available, including gigs and stewarding, although often competitive. Very few students fail to complete the course and most leave Birmingham having enjoyed their time there.

PAUPER NOTES   Accommodation: Uni housing list can be expensive. Halls good and some very close. **Drink:** The Shakespeare (M&B), Prince of Wales (Ansells), The Grapevine, The Wellington, Atkinsons (local ale). **Eats:** Lots of reasonable restaurants and sandwich bars. College canteen reasonably priced. **Ents:** Rock and classical concerts with regular big names. City centre excellent for a good night out. Everyone catered for. **Sports:** SU card and uni identity card get reductions at most sports centres and shops. **Hardship funds:** Limited funds available. **Travel:** Travel can be expensive so best to live close. **Work:** Some Xmas shows offer work plus chance to gain experience; pub work in term-time; stewarding at the symphony hall. Can use musical talents to earn money, eg gigs or teaching but very competitive.

MORE INFO?   Ring SU on 0121 753 1726.

ALUMNI   Ernest Elemont (violinist), Peter Aston, Paul Beard, Brian Ferneyhough, Jean Rigby, Nicholas Wood, orchestral musicians, singers in major opera companies, professors of music, music advisers, directors of music companies.

GET HOLD OF THE PROSPECTUSES

BIRMINGHAM UNIVERSITY

The University of Birmingham, Edgbaston, Birmingham B15 2TT (Tel 0121 414 3344, Fax 0121 414 3971) Map 3

STUDENT ENQUIRIES: Director of Admissions
APPLICATIONS: UCAS

Broad study areas: Arts, business, social science, education, engineering, law, medicine and dentistry, science. (Subject details are in the *Subjects and Places Index*.)

Founded: 1828, as Birmingham School of Medicine and Surgery, and 1875 Mason College; granted charter in 1900. **Main undergraduate awards:** BA, BCom, BDS, BEng, MEng, BMedSc, BMus, BNurs, MMath, MNatSc, MPhys, BSc, LLB, MBChB. **Awarding body:** Birmingham University. **Site:** At Edgbaston, 2½ miles from city centre. **Access:** Just off A38; buses between university and city centre; trains between University Station (on campus) and New Street Station, in city centre. **Special features:** Barber Institute of Fine Arts and Music. **Europe:** Languages possible, as subsidiary or option, on a number of degrees; 4% spend 6 months or more abroad. Languages unit will train any student. Formal exchange links with over 120 European universities/colleges. **Library:** Main library with over 2,000,000 volumes plus ten subject libraries. Annual expenditure on library materials, £138 per FTE student. **Other learning facilities:** Computer services, television services. **Welfare:** Student welfare officer and adviser to overseas students. University health centre, counselling service, Guild of Students welfare service; medical and dental service both obtainable by telephone. Day nursery on main campus. **Careers:** Information and advice centre (including video-tape presentations of various careers). **Amenities:** Union building controlled by Guild of Students with hall, bars, etc; bookshop, banks, supermarket, travel agent, opticians and hairdressers on site. **Sporting facilities:** Multi-activity centre with swimming pool, gymnasia, etc; seventy acres of playing fields including all-weather pitches and running track; Raymond Priestley centre for rock climbing, sailing, and sub-aqua diving adjacent to Coniston Water in Lake District.

Accommodation: In 1995/96, 40% of all students in university accommodation, 98% first years. 6,024 places available (3,907 for first years): 2,397 half-board places (1,825 for first years) from £62.10 per week shared to £79 for single, ensuite, term time only; 3,627 self-catering places (2,082 for first years) at £32–£51.76 per week, Sept-June (and 835 postgraduate). Students live in privately owned accommodation for 2 years: rents £28–£38 per week for self-catering, £37–£45 for half-board. 3% first degree students live at home. **Term time work:** No university policy on term time work for full-time first degree students. Term work available on campus. **Hardship funds:** Total available in 1995/96: £296,967 government access funds (awarded as partial postgraduate scholarships and remainder as hardships payments, average award £330); £162,500 own funds (average award £1,480) plus £5,000 other funds. **Special categories:** hardship payments to single parents, those with dependants and mature students with families; other funds available for academically able students without sufficient funding and overseas students in the faculty of education and continuing studies.

Duration of first degree courses: 3 years; 4 years including language courses, MEng, MMath, MNatSc, MPhys, BCom, BNurs; 5 years MBChB and BDS. **Total first degree students 1995/96:** 12,374. **Overseas students:** 860. **Mature students:** 1,329. **Male/female ratio:** 1:1. **Teaching staff:** 978 full-time (plus 188 clinical), 144 part-time (plus 48 clinical). **Total full-time students 1995/96:** 15,668. **Postgraduate students:** 3,221 f-t, 2,251 p-t. **First degree tuition fees:** Home students, paying their own fees in 1996/97, paid £750 (classroom), £1,600 (lab/studio), £2,800 (clinical); Overseas students £5,770 (classroom), £7,655 (lab/studio), £14,090 (clinical).

WHAT IT'S LIKE   City of Birmingham ideally located in the centre of Britain, easily accessible by road, rail and air. University campus is 3 miles from the centre in Edgbaston, not far from the cricket ground. Excellent reputation academically and some of the best facilities in the country, including large sports centre with swimming pool, synthetic pitches, numerous squash courts, 2 sports halls etc. There are 34 schools in university so mixture is wide and varied. The Guild of Students (SU), housed in one of UK's largest union buildings, provides 3 bars, 6 catering outlets, 5 nightclubs, substantial welfare facilities and comprehensive academic representation. Over 150 societies offering everything from mountaineering to science fiction. Guild also funds extremely successful athletic union, recognised as one of the best in the country. Birmingham as a city is rapidly establishing itself as a cultural centre. Wide range of venues caters for all sorts of musical tastes, from the Symphony Hall to Ronnie Scott's Jazz Club. Rumoured to be more trees in Birmingham than in Paris and more canals than Venice. One of the most varied and exciting cities in Britain and an ideal choice to maximise your time at university.

PAUPER NOTES   **Accommodation:** Wide range of both catered and self-catering accommodation on campus. Plenty of rented accommodation within two miles. **Drink:** The Guild; pubs in Selly Oak; local beers are not up to much – the best real ale is at the Guild, especially its Irish bar, Fingals (also has weekly guest beers). **Eats:** Wide choice and reasonable prices at the Guild. Bristol Road (Selly Oak), famous for its dozens of curry houses, ridiculously cheap and tasty. **Ents:** Jazz, rock, indie, rave, classical, etc all catered for at the Guild and within Birmingham. Stratford is easy driving distance; many theatres and cinemas in Birmingham. **Sports:** University facilities excellent, including the swimming pool. Edgbaston cricket ground within walking distance; Birmingham also has first-class football teams. **Hardship funds:** The Guild and university provide some. **Travel:** Easy access to roads and rail. BR station on campus. Plenty of cycle paths around city and getting better. Tickets available for most kinds of transport from the Guild. **Work:** Nearly 500 jobs within the Guild itself, eg bars, security, cleaning, marketing; also local bars and restaurants. Vac work in halls of residence due to conference trade and plenty of temping agencies.

MORE INFO?   Alternative Prospectus from Student Admissions Service (0121 472 1841 ext 2267); general information from President (ext 2250).

INFORMAL NAME   BUGS (Birmingham University Guild of Students)

ALUMNI   Sir Alex Jarratt (Jarratt Report), Victoria Wood (comedienne/writer), Sir Austin Pierce (British Aerospace), Desmond Morris (writer/broadcaster), Sir Peter Walters (BP), Ross Whitley, The Hon J J Bossano (Chief Minister, Gibraltar), Dr D M Mutasa (Speaker of Parliament, Zimbabwe).

WANT TO HELP WITH THE NEXT EDITION? SEE PAGE 66

BOLTON INSTITUTE

Bolton Institute of Higher Education, Deane Road, Bolton
BL3 5AB (Tel 01204 528851, Fax 01204 399074; Freephone
0800 262117; e-mail enquiries @ bolton.ac.uk) Map 2

STUDENT ENQUIRIES: Marketing Officer
APPLICATIONS: UCAS

Broad study areas: Textiles, engineering, business, education, computing, life sciences, arts. (Subject details are in the *Subjects and Places Index*).

Founded: 1982, ex Bolton Institute of Technology and Bolton College of Education (Technical). **Main undergraduate awards:** BA, BEd, BEng, BSc. **Awarding body:** Bolton Institute (Manchester University for in-service teacher education and research degrees). **Site:** 3 campuses in Bolton town centre. **Access:** Easily reached by road and rail. 10 miles north of Manchester. **Europe:** 1% first degree students have the option to take a language and spend a period abroad as part of course. Exchange links with France and Portugal for business studies and civil engineering students. **Library:** 130,000 books and related materials together with microfilms, microfiches, audiocassettes and tape slide presentations. Annual expenditure on library materials, £56.64 per FTE student. **Other learning facilities:** Access to Prestel. On-line access to major bibliographic machine readable databases, e-mail and the internet. **Welfare:** Specialist staff in counselling, welfare and special needs; also international officer and multi-faith service. **Careers:** Professional careers advisors offering guidance, counselling and information. **Amenities:** SU with numerous clubs and societies, travel shop. **Sporting facilities:** Sports hall, playing fields, squash court.

Accommodation: 1995/96, 700 self-catering places in halls, at £1,580 for 40 weeks (Sept-June). Private sector rent from £30 per week, excluding fuel charges. **Term time work:** University policy to allow term time work for full-time first degree students. Term (and vac) work on campus in SU bar and shop. **Hardship funds:** Total available in 1995/96: £82,000 government access funds, 615 cases supported; £21,500 own funds, 146 cases supported. Special help: from access funds for child and dependant care, rent support and hardship cases; own funds also available to offset part-time fees (students on benefit), hardship cases and interest-free loans where a grant is delayed.

Duration of first degree courses: 2–5 years full-time/sandwich. **Total first degree students 1995/96:** 4,674. **Total BEd students:** 24. **Overseas students:** 467. **Mature students:** 2,800. **Male/female ratio:** 4:3. **Teaching staff:** 250 (full-time and part-time). **Total full-time students 1995/96:** 2,804. **Postgraduate students:** 770. **First degree tuition fees:** Home students, paying their own fees in 1996/97 paid £1,600 (classroom or lab/studio).

WHAT IT'S LIKE   It's spread over three campuses in Bolton, one of the largest towns in the country. Massive range of students – full and part-time, traditional, mature, overseas. Huge range of courses. Expects university status during 1997. SU in new building (offices, clubs and societies and welfare advice centre). New bar and venue sells good, cheap food throughout the day; late licence at weekends. Shops at two sites. SU politically

and socially active and involved with NUS campaigns and local events; produces monthly mag, Inspire, to keep everyone up to date with news, views and events. BIHE has 2 large halls of residence – perfect for first years, as meeting people there is a doddle. Both have washing machine rooms and one has a common room. But rent is higher than average Bolton student house, where you pay about £35 per room. Living is fairly cheap and there is literally a pub on every corner. Both the Institute and the town have sports facilities and there is a big leisure centre just down the road from Deane Campus. Only drawbacks: limited parking and lack of crèche. Fairly easy to find casual work in Bolton, in SU bar or shop or locally in restaurants, bars, shops, telesales department. Hardly any problems between students and locals. Usually a circuit of selected pubs commonly frequented by students (SU bar comes top, of course) and these change according to taste.
Claire Livingstone

PAUPER NOTES   **Accommodation:** Private sector accommodation difficult; no married quarters. Approx 800 places in college accommodation. **Drink:** Loads of pubs. Greenhall Whitley, Witches, Pendles. **Eats:** Excellent SU pizza franchise, jacket spuds and sandwiches. Refectory food is average and expensive. Reasonable veggy choice. **Ents:** Good on campus. Live bands (middle market), regular film nights, alternative discos, heavy etc. Apart from pubs, local ents are negligible. **Sports:** On campus sports hall, squash courts. Local sports centres, gyms, swimming pools. **Work:** Bar work for hard-up students, also college shop.
BUZZ-WORDS   BIHE – Bolton Institute of Higher Education.

BOURNEMOUTH UNIVERSITY

Bournemouth University, Talbot Campus, Fern Barrow, Poole, Dorset BH12 5BB (Tel 01202 524111, Fax 01202 513293, Internet www.bournemouth.ac.uk) Map 3

STUDENT ENQUIRIES: Registrar
APPLICATIONS: UCAS

Broad study areas: Marketing, advertising and public relations; product design and manufacture; applied computing and electronics; conservation sciences; finance and law; business, tourism, catering; health and community services; management systems; media production. (Subject details are in the *Subjects and Places Index*.)

Founded: Founded as Dorset Institute in 1976 (then Bournemouth Poly), ex Bournemouth College of Technology and Weymouth College of Education; university status in 1992. **Main undergraduate awards:** BA, BSc, BEng, LLB. **Awarding body:** Bournemouth University. **Site:** 2 sites (and three associate centres in Poole, Yeovil and the Isle of Wight). **Access:** Buses. **Academic features:** Placement year in 24 degree programmes. **Europe:** 14% first degree students learn a language as part of their course and 21% spend 6 months or more abroad. Language study available to all students as an extra subject; an integral part of eg tourism, electronic systems design and exchanges in a range of subjects. Links with over 50 European universities/colleges. **Library:** Libraries on each site; total of 160,000 titles, 2,000 periodicals, 1,200 study places, restricted loan collection. Annual expenditure on library materials, £73.82 per FTE student. **Welfare:** Doctors, nurse, dentist, counsellors, psychologist, chaplains, accommodation staff, family planning advisers, SU welfare officer. **Careers:** Information, advice and placement. **Amenities:** Large SU entertainment facilities with nightclub and bistro, and two smaller refreshment areas. Nursery with 30 places. **Sporting facilities:** Good resort amenities, especially for sailing and other water sports; all-weather pitches and good sports hall on Talbot campus, with 2 squash courts, weights room, wall-climbing facilities and large gymnasium. Mini-gym on Bournemouth campus.

Accommodation: In 1995/96, 2% of all students in university accommodation, 10% of first years. 248 self-catering places available at Talbot campus (200 for first years) at £47 per week, Sept–June; 155 places in hall of residence at Bournemouth campus, at £50 per week. 1,900 places in 130 hotels, for groups of 6–60 new students as (pseudo) halls of residence, at £7.25–£10 per day (prices controlled by the Accommodation Officer). Privately owned accommodation: rents £35+ per week for self-catering, £55 half-board. **Term time work:** University policy to allow term time work for full-time first degree students. Term-time work on campus in bars, library, help with open day tours; careers centre co-ordinates work off campus. **Hardship funds:** Total available in 1995/96: £158,579 government access funds, 800 students supported. Special help: students with child care needs, mature students and those with high travel and housing costs.

Duration of first degree courses: 3–4 years (full time); 4 years (sandwich); 4–5 years (extended programme). **Total first degree students 1995/96:** 7,600. **Male/female ratio:** 1:1. **Teaching staff:** 380. **Total full-time students 1995/96:** 8,500. **Postgraduate students:** 1,330. **First degree tuition fees:** Home students, paying their own fees in 1996/97, paid £750 (classroom), £1,600 (lab/studio); Overseas students £6,250.

WHAT IT'S LIKE   Regarded as a leading vocational university, it focuses on niche market courses and is proud of its high level of graduate employment. There are a number of sites around town. Main campus holds the majority of students and houses 250 in the Student Village, similar to Brookside Close. Hurn House in the town houses another 150 and there are plans for a new accommodation block for 500. Most first year students live in hostels and then move into rented accommodation. Students' Union focuses on student needs, providing advice, representation and, of course, entertainments; also a good opportunity to become involved in various clubs and societies (about 40) and with student media. The Old Firestation in town has recently been renovated for use as the union's nightclub with a 2 am dance licence – unlike most clubs in Bournemouth. New union bar on main campus; union's radio station, Nerve FM is being relaunched.

PAUPER NOTES   **Accommodation:** Housing for 400 – about to be doubled. **Drink:** SU bar cheapest in town with regular promotions. **Eats:** Refectory not cheap. SU provides a range of inexpensive meals with vegetarian options. **Ents:** Variety of clubs in town. SU club, the Old Firestation, has regular weekly events including free bands on Wednesdays. **Sports:** Main hall, squash courts, gym and all-weather courts on campus. Playing fields and swimming pool nearby. Range of university sporting clubs. **Hardship funds:** Small fund operated under strict rules; normally used for rent. **Travel:** On-campus travel office offering cheap service. **Work:** Part-time work in catering and bars, on and off campus.

MORE INFO?   Enquiries to Paula Redshaw, SU Vice-President Communications (01202 523755).

BRADFORD & ILKLEY

Bradford & Ilkley Community College, Great Horton Road,
Bradford BD7 1AY (Tel 01274 753026, Fax 01274 741060)
Map 2

STUDENT ENQUIRIES: Admissions Officer
APPLICATIONS: UCAS

Broad study areas: Art & design, community studies, leisure and recreation studies, education, social studies. (Subject details are in the *Subjects and Places Index.*)

Founded: 1982 ex Bradford College and Ilkley College. **Main undergraduate awards:** BA, BEd. **Awarding body:** Bradford University. **Site:** Bradford and Ilkley. **Academic features:** Open and distance learning facilities available. **Europe:** Number of first degree students taking a language or spending time abroad not known. **Library:** 256,921 volumes; 1,105 journals. Annual expenditure on library materials, £28.4 per FTE student. **Specialist collections:** Slide collection of over 60,000 journal reprints. **Welfare:** Student service centre (including counsellors and nursing staff). **Special categories:** Learning support (disabilites) tutor and day nurseries. **Careers:** Advisory service. **Amenities:** SU building with several bars. **Sporting facilities:** Shared with Bradford University.

Accommodation: In 1995/96, 438 self-catering places available (334 Bradford, 164 Ilkley), at £36 per week (£26 shared). **Hardship funds:** Total available in 1995/96: £92,188 government access funds, 329 students supported; £10,000 own funds, 34 students supports; plus £8,830 repayable loans, 137 cases supported. Special help: those with children, emergency situations/changes of circumstances and towards completion of qualification; own funds also available in emergency situations in form of interest-free loans, and child care allowance scheme targeted at part-time students.

Duration of first degree courses: 3 years; others: 4 years. **Total first degree students 1995/96:** 2,902 full-time, 3,731 part-time. **Overseas students:** 2%. **Mature students:** 56%. **Male/female ratio:** 1:2. **Teaching staff:** 558 full-time, 400 part-time. **Total full-time students 1995/96:** 4,388. **Postgraduate students:** 95 full-time, 221 part-time. **First degree tuition fees:** Home students, paying their own fees in 1996/97, paid £750 (classroom), £1,600 (studio); Overseas students £6,100.

WHAT IT'S LIKE   Deceptively large college (approx 36,000 students) spread over 50 sites. Non-elitist community college with high proportion of overseas, mature and especially local students, many on minimum grant. Active and campaigning SU, recently located in new union building on college campus. Students represented on all college committees with direct and uncompromising stance. Book early for accommodation – self-catered halls of residence for 270 and new block of 60 (expensive but very tasty). Exciting, diverse and very affordable social scene. Local community has friendly and easy-going attitude to strangers but like in any big city, be aware of personal safety.

PAUPER NOTES   **Accommodation:** Many cheap properties available but beware of standards. **Drinks:** Union building has cheap drinks and promos and, no question, is best in town. Several large student-orientated pubs in easy reach of campus. **Eats:** Food from five continents with student discounts at prices you can afford. **Ents:** SU has regular club night and events throughout the week. Bradford Film Theatre and Pictureville for ultimate independent cinema releases, new and old. **Sports:** Full range of sports facilities, mostly shared with university. **Hardship funds:** Limited funds for the very desperate via college student services. **Travel:** Cheap buses, trains and taxis. **Work:** Hard to get and hang on to.

ALUMNI   David Hockney; New Model Army; Berhard Ingham; Terry Rooney MP; Michael Jack MP; Terrorvision.

BRADFORD UNIVERSITY

University of Bradford, Bradford, West Yorkshire BD7 1DP
(Tel 01274 733466, Fax 01274 305340) Map 2

STUDENT ENQUIRIES: Schools Liaison Office
APPLICATIONS: UCAS

Broad study areas: Engineering, languages, health sciences, professions supplementary to medicine, science, social science. (Subject details are in the *Subjects and Places Index*.)

Founded: 1966. **Main undergraduate awards:** BA, BEng, MEng, MPharm, BSc. **Awarding body:** Bradford University. **Site:** Main campus close to city centre, management centre in parkland 2 miles away. **Academic features:** A positive attitude towards non-standard and mature applicants; wide range of qualifications and/or experience accepted for entry. Engineering courses with foundation year for applicants with non-standard qualifications. Many courses have a practical orientation and 55% of students are on sandwich degree courses. Distinctive courses include chemistry with pharmaceutical and forensic science, environmental management and technology, information systems and multimedia technology, medical engineering, peace studies. **Special features:** Recently absorbed Bradford and Airedale College of Health into new health faculty. Fellowships in music, theatre and visual arts ensure a very active student arts scene. **Europe:** 14% first degree students take a language as part of course and spend 6 months or more abroad. Language courses available for all students (including Japanese and Urdu), either as part of their course or on an extra-curricular basis. Formal exchange links with 12 European universities/colleges. **Library:** 3 sites: 530,000 volumes, 2,500 current periodicals, 1,000 study places. Annual expenditure on library materials, £110 per FTE student. **Other learning facilities:** Personal computer connections to large campus network (access to eg e-mail, university library, information services); network access points in most offices, work areas and study bedrooms in halls; some study bedrooms have telephones for voice and data communication. **Welfare:** Counselling service, overseas student advisers, health service. 49-place day nursery. SU welfare office. **Careers:** Information and advice service (with overseas section); annual recruitment fairs. **Amenities:** Communal building with 3 bar areas, dance floor, disco bar; SU travel office and shop; bank and bookshop on campus; studio theatre, music centre, art gallery, campus radio, darkroom. **Sporting facilities:** Indoor sports centre, plus solarium, sauna, fitness suite, sports shop and 25-metre pool; sports grounds 3 miles away; additional squash courts and artificial turf areas at halls of residence.

Accommodation: In 1996/97, 31% of all students in university accommodation, 100% of first years who cannot live at home. 2,189 places available (1,650 for first years): 402 half-board places (375 for first years) at £59.90 per week, term time only; and 1,791 self-catering places (1,175 for first years) at £35.15–£53.50 (en suite) per week, term time or Sept–June. Most students live in privately owned accommodation for 2 years, rents typically £25–£30 per week self-catering. **Hardship funds:** Total available in 1995/96: £164,000 government access funds; £28,000 own funds (average award £200). Special help: students incurring childcare costs; mature students; self-financing students; own funds also available for overseas students experiencing financial difficulties which have arisen through no fault of their own since embarking on a course. A limited number of partial-fee bursaries are normally awarded to self-financing students: £5,000 for undergrads, £28,000 postgrads, 40 students benefit.

Duration of first degree courses: 3 years; 4 years (some sandwich courses and those with foundation year); 5 years (sandwich). **Total first degree students 1995/96:** 5,981. **Overseas students:** 716. **Male/female ratio:** 3:2. **Teaching staff:** 460 full-time, 375 part-time. **Total full-time students 1995/96:** 6,769. **Postgraduate students:** 788. **First degree tuition fees:** Home students, paying their own fees in 1996/97, paid £858; Overseas students £6,090 (classroom), £7,950 (lab/studio).

WHAT IT'S LIKE   Small, friendly campus university, five minutes' walk from city centre. 6,000 students, 600 of whom are based at the management centre, 2 miles from main campus, on main bus routes. Technological university awarded charter in 1966 (formerly Bradford College of Technology). Academic strengths – engineering, modern languages, business studies but also some humanities such as women's studies, peace studies. Most courses include placement, either industrial or educational, many abroad. Private accommodation averages £27pw, mostly in large, Victorian terraced houses within 1 mile of campus. SU offers 4 bars on campus, shop, travel agency, print shop, welfare service, wide range of clubs and societies and athletics clubs. Bradford, formerly Victorian textile capital, now extremely cosmopolitan and friendly – a great place to be a student. Cheap entertainment and food (cheapest and best curries in the country – try them or be forever socially inadequate!). Products of 20 different real ale breweries can be sampled in the city. Students friendly and down-to-earth; no failed Oxbridge complex here. Despite reputation as cheapest university city in the country, students rumoured to have largest per capita overdrafts (after London) – must be enjoying themselves.

PAUPER NOTES   **Accommodation:** Places in halls for all first years. Housing in city cheap and local. Most non-hall accommodation is in 4/8 bedroom houses. Cheap but prices are rising – you get what you pay for and standard is poor. **Drink:** SU bars cheaper than local pubs – watch for promos. Bradford still relatively cheap drinking town with many pubs specialising in real ales. Best beers are Tetleys, Websters, Theakstons and Youngers. **Eats:** The best curry houses in Britain. Great value Indian, Pakistani, Chinese, Greek, Arabian, Italian all close to campus. Burger, fish & chip and pizza places in town – many with student discounts. **Ents:** Gigs, films, discos, comedians every week on campus. Many student discounts – famous Alhambra Theatre in city, Theatre-in-Mill and 3-screen cinema on campus, National Museum of Film Photography & Television nearby. **Sports:** Cheap sports centre on campus (swimming 60p). New astroturf pitches very near campus. Playing fields 3 miles away on direct bus route. **Hardship funds:** Funds run by Union and University. Excellent welfare department. **Travel:** Transport interchange and motorways. Campus Travel provides great cheap student deals. **Work:** Some temporary work available in bars/security/care work/factories – £2.20–£3.50 per hour. Some is late night – problems combining with early morning lectures.

MORE INFO? Enquiries to Communications Officer, SU (01274 383300).

ALUMNI Dr Barry Seal MEP, Roland Boyes MP, Ian Bruce MP, David Hinchcliffe MP, Alice Mahon MP, Ann Taylor MP, Tony O'Reilly (chairman of Heinz International), John Hegley (poet), Ifem Onura (Huddersfield Town FC).

BRETTON HALL

Bretton Hall, West Bretton, Wakefield, West Yorks WF4 4LG
(Tel 01924 830261, Fax 01924 830521,
e-mail bretton@mailhost.bretton.ac.uk) Map 2

STUDENT ENQUIRIES: Admissions Co-ordinator or Registrar
APPLICATIONS: UCAS

Broad study areas: Education, performing arts, theatre design, English. (Subject details are in the *Subjects and Places Index*.)

Founded: 1949. **Main undergraduate awards:** BA, BA(QTS). **Awarding body:** Leeds University. **Site:** 18th-century buildings with modern developments in 500-acre rural setting. **Access:** 1 mile from M1; public transport from Wakefield, Barnsley. **Structural features:** A college of Leeds University. **Academic features:** Practically based BA degrees with associated specialisms in primary and early years; professional and industrial links in design and performance courses. **Special features:** Visiting artists, writers and performance companies. **Europe:** Language as elective modules in many courses. Exchange programmes in fashion and education. **Library:** 90,000 volumes, 400 periodicals, 65 study places, reference or short term loan. Videos and microfiche reader facilities. **Other learning facilities:** Media resources centre. Off-site performance and textile design theatres and studios. **Welfare:** Doctor, chaplain, counsellors, sick bay (staffed). **Amenities:** Bookshop and art gallery on campus, playing fields.

Accommodation: In 1995/96, 30% of all students in college accommodation, 100% of first years. All single rooms: self-catering £30.50–£60 per week; half-board places £65 per week. **Term time work:** College policy to allow part-time work for first degree students (within reason); 50% believed to work. Term (and vac) work available on campus in bars, library, entertainment, technical assistance. **Hardship funds:** Total available in 1995/96: £35,195 government access funds; support for 166 cases. Special help: single parents, self-financing students, changes of personal circumstances, final year students.

Duration of first degree courses: 3 years; 4 years BA(QTS). **Total first degree students 1995/96:** 1,260; **BA(QTS) students:** 470. **Overseas students:** 24. **Mature students:** 162. **Male/female ratio:** 1:3. **Teaching staff:** 88 full-time, 55 part-time. **Total full-time students 1995/96:** 2,011. **Postgraduate students:** 271. **First degree tuition fees:** Home students, paying their own fees in 1996/97, paid £1,660 (classroom), £2,770 (lab/studio); Overseas students £5,000 plus £340 university fee.

WHAT IT'S LIKE   Based around an 18th-century mansion, set in 260 acres of beautiful landscaped parkland, which includes the Yorkshire Sculpture Park, country park, two lakes and a lot of squirrels. Easy access from M1. 168 students on campus – catered, individual rooms, mixed hostels. Major housing area 10 miles away in Normanton – 3 students per self-catering maisonette. Most students in private accommodation in local villages and towns. A lot of mature students, some overseas. Small college, friendly relations with staff/students. Developing SU – students here tend not to be politically active. Large number of students with cars – useful because of isolated position. Number of societies gradually increasing – very easy to set up, with lots of SU and college backing. Good local markets in Barnsley, Wakefield and Huddersfield. Two excellent multiscreen cinemas about 10 miles away. Campus is best meeting place as accommodation is so scattered. Only arts courses available. Course loads vary – BA(QTS) quite tough but good. Much small group teaching (seminars, workshops and tutorials). Continuous assessment – few exams. Lots of practical experience. Intake from all over UK – mostly state schools. Typical student – arty. Typical lecturer – arty! High BA(QTS) employment rate; BA rate difficult to say – arts jobs more difficult to get, many go on into postgraduate courses eg PGCE.

PAUPER NOTES   **Accommodation:** Very hard to find but prices off-campus not too expensive. **Drink:** West Bretton one of only 3 dry villages in England! SU bar saves the world, with good selection of subsidised beers etc. Whitbreads, Youngers, Clarkes, Taunton cider. **Eats:** Vegetarian food usually best bet in canteen. SU bar sells hot snacks. Good curry houses in Wakefield. Local real Italian pizzeria which will deliver to campus. **Ents:** Regular events, plus outside trips to Leeds, Sheffield etc. Increasing number of nightclubs in surrounding area have student nights; cheap entry and good music. **Sports:** All students entitled to free Passport to Leisure for Wakefield MDC's sport/leisure facilities. Good local swimming pool, small and cheap. Sport at Bretton depends on involvement of students. **Hardship funds:** Access fund available plus short-term loans from college. **Travel:** Student season tickets available for local buses and trains. **Work:** Even more difficult to get term/vac work; none available on campus. Possible to get bar/shop jobs part-time, transport permitting. About 10% get work.

MORE INFO?   Enquiries to 01924 830282.

ALUMNI   Anne Collins (opera singer), Colin Welland (actor/playwright, author), David Rappaport (founder of Hull Truck), Nicholas Parsons (TV personality), John Godber (playwright), Ken Robinson (TIE/Arts in Education), Moira Stewart (newsreader).

BRIGHTON UNIVERSITY

University of Brighton, Lewes Road, Brighton, East Sussex BN2 4AT (Tel 01273 600900, Fax 01273 642825) Map 4

STUDENT ENQUIRIES: Academic Registry Enquiries
APPLICATIONS: UCAS

Broad study areas include: Art & design, humanities, education, engineering, business management, health, information technology. (Subject details are in the *Subjects and Places Index.*)

Founded: As Brighton Polytechnic, ex-Brighton Colleges of Technology, Art and Education and East Sussex College of HE; university status 1992. **Main undergraduate awards:** BA, BEd, BSc, BEng, MEng. **Awarding body:** Brighton University. **Site:** 3 major sites in Brighton, one at Eastbourne. **Access:** Bus and train services provide regular inter-site travel. **Europe:** 20% first degree students take a language as part of course and 5% spend 6 months or more abroad. Language tuition available to all students. Formal exchange links, most open to non-language specialists, with 15 EU universities/colleges. **Library:** 7 libraries, over 500,000 volumes, 3,250 periodicals, 20,000 videotapes, 820 study places. Annual expenditure on library materials, £53.01 per FTE student. **Other learning facilities:** Media units for film and video, including darkroom and graphic design studio. 2,000 computer terminals/micros linked to each other and to JANET. Specialist staff to advise. **Welfare:** Welfare and accommodation officers, doctor, personal counsellor and chaplain on each site. **Careers:** Careers counsellor and information rooms on all sites. **Amenities:** Bars; bookshops at Moulsecoomb and Falmer sites. **Sporting facilities:** Swimming pool at Eastbourne campus; recreation facilities, including extensive playing fields in Brighton and Eastbourne, 6 gymnasia, dance studios.

Accommodation: In 1995/96, 1,100 places in halls of residence, 500 in university-leased flats. Students live in privately owned accommodation for at least 2 years: rents £40–£43 per week for self-catering (+ bills). 1% first degree students live at home. **Term time work:** University policy to allow term time work for full-time first degree students (37% believed to work). Some term work available on campus; also university careers centre workshop for term and vac work. **Hardship funds:** Total available in 1995/96: £253,222 government access funds, 1,408 students helped, average £190 awarded; £10,000 own welfare funds, 183 helped, range £10–£150, plus fee waiver system. £30,000 available for international students prior to starting courses.

Duration of first degree courses: 3 years; others: 4 years (teacher training and sandwich). **Total first degree students 1995/96:** 8,714. **Total BEd students:** 974. **Overseas students:** 676. **Mature students:** 1,012. **Male/female ratio:** 1:1. **Teaching staff:** 640 full-time, 40 part-time. **Total full-time students 1995/96:** 10,122. **Postgraduate students:** 1,838. **First degree tuition fees:** Home students, paying their own fees in 1996/97, paid £948 (classroom), £1,890 (lab/studio); Overseas students £5,940 (classroom), £6,900 (lab/studio).

WHAT IT'S LIKE   Brighton is a cosmopolitan town with a lot going for it. Too often called 'London by the sea' (and nearly as expensive as London), it offers an extraordinarily diverse spectrum of socialising opportunities. Array of clubs, shops, restaurants, parks, cinemas, pubs and of course the beach – pebbles though it may be. Two glorious piers, although only one is attached to the land! A lively town, Brighton has the rough with the smooth, including typical levels of unemployment and homelessness and a small degree of racism and violence. The bonus of an overall breeze of liberty and freedom (could it be the sea air?) often results in students staying in the area after graduation. With two universities and a technical college, Brighton is very much a young town (20,000 students make up around 10% of the population) although Brighton University has a large number of mature students, who blend in well with student life. The university is based on four main campuses. The largest number of students (some 4,000) are at the main campus at Moulsecoomb; three buildings close together, two miles from the town centre. This houses accountancy, computing, pharmacy, engineering and architecture. The JCR at Cockcroft is a busy place (MTV blaring, games being played and pizza eaten). It also houses the majority of SU offices and staff, including the welfare unit, sports office and shop. The university nursery is her (SU offers a subsidy to a limited number of single parents). Grand Parade, right in the h of Brighton, just across the road from the infamous, and exotically out of place, P (the Taj Mahal of the south or farmhouse in drag). This is home to humanities students and most art-based students. An energetic part of the university, it also has two galleries and a theatre with some of the best and cheapest shows in town. Falmer has a family atmosphere; four miles out, in the picturesque South Downs and directly across the road from Sussex Uni. It holds the SU half-term playscheme and the Daisychain nursery is close. Playing fields and gyms provide venues for a lot of university sports; the SU bar has a relaxed atmosphere and is fast becoming the centre for students living in Falmer halls as well as non-residential students. Difficult for physically disabled students, particularly those in wheelchairs. Eastbourne is 26 miles away, based on various sites within walking distance of each other and the town centre. Relatively small scale sites result in a friendly atmosphere, with centre of SU activity (SU bar, shop and office) and a day nursery at the Bishopsbourne building. SU provides access to wide range of services, including sports, clubs and societies, entertainments (including nightclub), food and drink, welfare and campaigns, bars, nightclubs, the newspaper (Babble) and a Southern African scholarship. Brighton is a truly amazing place, and needs visiting if nothing else. Try it – you'll love it! **PAUPER NOTES** **Accommodation:** Finding accommodation has turned into an art form over the last few years; average rent in Brighton is about £35 for a hell hole, £40–£45 for a reasonably nice place (slightly less in Eastbourne). Properties should be seen early as they disappear faster than Take That did. Student services also run a head leasing scheme to keep a check on landlords. University halls of residence for 1,500+ students dotted around Falmer, Eastbourne, Phoenix (at Grand Parade) and Moulsecoomb, both catering and self-catering. Be warned – these rooms are small, but the community atmosphere can often make up for it. New luxury rooms being built at Falmer. **Drink:** Countless pubs and cool bars. **Eats:** Dead Parrott and Cockcroft café cheap but cool. **Ents:** Joint ents with Sussex Uni; comedy. **Sports:** New sports centre being built at Falmer. **Hardship funds:** Uni operated access fund. **Travel:** All sites can be reached by train or bus (saver tickets and YP railcards are advised, especially the UniZone train tickets). Parking is a nightmare, in town and at university. Hitching popular, especially at Falmer. **Work:** Not easy in Brighton. 43% have regular part-time jobs; 96% work in some vacations which can be beneficial if it is linked to the course or just to give a change. Some hotel/bar work but pay not brilliant (and 3 nights/week makes 9am lectures a trial). Jobs available locally in the summer if you're quick off the mark; University careers workshop helps.

BRISTOL OLD VIC

Bristol Old Vic Theatre School, 2 Downside Road, Clifton, Bristol BS8 2XF (Tel 0117 973 3535, Fax 0117 923 9371) Map 3

STUDENT ENQUIRIES: Admissions
APPLICATIONS: Direct

Broad study areas: Acting and theatre arts and technique. (Subject details are in the *Subjects and Places Index*.)

Founded: 1946. **Site:** Main Clifton site with other venues around the city. **Access:** Adjacent Dart bus stop. **Academic features:** Vocational training for theatre and related media.

Structural features: Close ties and working arrangements with the Bristol Old Vic Company, BBC Radio, HTV, and both local universities. **Special features:** Visiting specialists in all fields of the profession. All permanent staff have wide professional experience. **Library:** No formal library, though the school stocks many play sets, individual texts and music. The central and reference libraries and Bristol University theatre collection are open to certain student use. **Other learning facilities:** Lighting, sound, video, prop making, carpentry, stage design and wardrobe facilities. **Welfare:** Access to Bristol University student health service. **Careers:** Information and advice given. No guarantee of placement. **Sporting facilities:** Lcal facilities only.

Accommodation: No college accommodation. Private accommodation in nearby areas; apply to Accommodation Officer to help find digs 3 weeks before commencement. Allow £2,500+ per academic year. **Hardship funds:** No special hardship funds. Advice about grant-making trusts available. 70% of students are self-financing.

Duration of courses: 3 years; others: 2 and 1 years. **Male/female ratio:** 3:2. **Teaching staff:** 19 full-time, 12 part-time. **Total full-time students 1995/96:** 117. **Tuition fees 1996/97:** £6,900.

WHAT IT'S LIKE Training ground for all aspects of theatre/drama, including dance, mime, directing, stage combat, stage lighting, stage design and management, wardrobe, sound and lighting. Small institution with enormous amount of energy. Life can be emotionally and physically exhausting, yet rewarding and worthwhile. Treats students as professionals, allowing them a glimpse of the biz: rigorous discipline; sometimes not enough room for error/human fallibility. Teaching is classically orientated; little radical input on the curriculum although this is gradually changing. Sometimes frustrations outweighed by rewards. Training realistic and totally practical. Building is small but facilities are improving; the atmosphere is friendly, but intense – usual working day is 8.30 am – 7 pm. Commitment to possibility of a hard, penniless, unglamorous career in theatre has to be total, otherwise you will not endure the course.

PAUPER NOTES **Accommodation:** No college accommodation. **Drink:** Beaufort Arms, Renatos, King's Arms. **Eats:** Snacks on premises. **Ents:** Theatre Royal and New Vic, Watershed, Arnolfini. **Sports:** All Bristol Uni SU facilities available. **Hardship funds:** The Madeleine Farrell Fund, the Nat Brenner Fund. **Work:** Front of house work at the Bristol Old Vic, bar/restaurant work, hotel security, supermarket staff. Very difficult with long working day – weekends best.

MORE INFO? Enquiries 0117 973 3535.

ALUMNI Brian Blessed, Samantha Bond, Simon Cadell, Christopher Cazenove, Stephanie Cole, Annette Crosbie, Daniel Day Lewis, Jeremy Irons, Jane Lapotaire, Tim Pigott-Smith, Miranda Richardson, Patricia Routledge, Greta Scacchi, Patrick Stewart, Gene Wilder.

CAN'T FIND WHAT YOU'RE LOOKING FOR? USE THE INDEX!

BRISTOL UNIVERSITY

University of Bristol, Senate House, Tyndall Avenue, Bristol
BS8 1TH (Tel 0117 928 9000, Fax 0117 925 1424) Map 3

STUDENT ENQUIRIES: The Registrar
APPLICATIONS: UCAS

Broad study areas: Arts, sciences, medicine, engineering, law, social sciences. (Subject details are in the *Subjects and Places Index*.)

Founded: 1876, charter granted 1909. **Main undergraduate awards:** BA, BDS, BEng, MEng, BSc, MSci, BVSc, LLB, MBChB. **Awarding body:** Bristol University. **Site:** University precinct ¼ mile from city centre. **Access:** Walking, good bus services. **Academic features:** Courses in biochemistry, chemistry, microbiology and pharmacology include year in industry. Course in deaf studies. The language centre markets its expertise to industry, providing linguistic teaching and support, such as translation for business. **Europe:** 11% first degree students take a language as part of course and 12% spend 6 months or more abroad. Student exchanges to 130 European universities/colleges through Socrates/Erasmus; links with 70+ European universities through Santander and Coimbra groups (academic, cultural and socio-economic ties). Founder member of Medical Schools' European Credit Transfer Scheme (allows medical students to spend 1-3 terms abroad which counts to final degree). **Library:** Main library (arts and social sciences and headquarters) and 13 branch libraries. 1,250,000 volumes, 6,100 periodicals, 2,250 study places. Late night opening in main library and law library (term time). Short loan collections for heavily used course books. Annual expenditure on library materials, £112 per FTE student. On-line public access terminals in all libraries give access to information about books, periodicals and CD-Roms. Strong emphasis on reader service and guided tours provided for new students. **Specialist collections:** Sir Allen Lane's Penguin collection of autographed works, Wiglesworth ornithological collection, Exley mathematics library, medical library collections, manuscript and early printed rare books, original notebooks and sketch books of Isambard Kingdom Brunel, complete collection of election manifestos since 1892. **Other learning facilities:** Open learning centre (to develop computing and personal development skills); many computer rooms in university precinct (some open 24 hours/day) and in most halls of residence; access to word processing, e-mail, WorldWide Web, larger multi-user systems etc. **Welfare:** Health centre, chaplains, day nursery, counselling service, adviser to overseas students. New initiative to provide access for deaf students. **Amenities:** Three theatres, Van Dyck Gallery, university bookshop. Active SU with bars, restaurants, recreational facilities. **Sporting facilities:** Indoor swimming pool, fitness training facilities, squash courts, playing fields incorporating multi-use floodlit synthetic hockey/soccer pitch, tennis courts and grass pitches for rugby, soccer and cricket.

Accommodation: In 1995/96, 37% of all students in university accommodation, 88% of first years. 3,903 places available (2,698 for first years, 314 of which in shared rooms): 1,907 half-board places (1,621 for first years) from £66 per week, single room, term time only; 1,996 self-catering places (1,061 for first years) from £32, single room, Oct–June. Most students live in privately owned accommodation except in first year: £43–£50 per week for self-catering and £70–£80 full board. 5% first degree students live at home. **Term time work:** University policy to allow term time work for full-time first degree students; limit of 10–12 hours per week. Term (and vac) work available on campus in bars, offices, library; also student employment office helps find work off campus. **Hardship funds:** Total available in 1995/96: £352,347 government access funds, 1,050 students helped. Eligibility restricted to students on full LEA grants; supplementary awards for child care, commuting or disability costs; Students' Union fund of £4,500 for overseas students with child care needs.

Duration of first degree courses: 3 years; 4 years (MEng, MSci and degrees involving languages, study abroad or industrial experience); 5 years (MBChB, BDS and BVSc). **Total first degree students 1995/96:** 8,925. **BEd students:** 45. **Overseas students:** 609. **Mature students:** 1,078. **Male/female ratio:** 10:9. **Teaching staff:** 890 full-time. **Total full-time students 1995/96:** 10,833. **Postgraduate students:** 1,908. **First degree tuition fees:** Home students, paying their own fees in 1996/97, paid £750 (likely to match LEA fee from 1997); Overseas students £6,470 (classroom), £8,509 (lab/studio), £15,767 (clinical).

WHAT IT'S LIKE   It's a very beautiful city with the university located close to both city centre and rural escape. It's quite lively with arts and cultural events – music, films, poetry at Watershed and Arnolfini exhibition centres. Clifton/Redland still student areas, increasing number moving to live further away as university grows. Bristol University sprawls considerably – one of the first things to strike you. Departments embedded in the city; some in elegant Georgian squares, others in grey, square blocks called modern architecture. But never judge a book ... most departments have excellent facilities and reputations, which keep student morale high and compensate those that are upset Oxbridge rejected them! Some first years in lodgings; most in university accommodation, some well away from the departments. Many of the first-years' halls are 2 miles away, but the union runs an evening shuttle service. Some 2nd and 3rd years stay in hall but most find private accommodation, which can be expensive (£40–£50/week). Much of the student-sprawl is brought together by the SU – one of the largest SU buildings in Britain, so 10,000 students trek there to meet up. SU relatively wealthy too, so lots of money spent on hundreds of societies and entertainments. Good societies include ballooning, ballroom dancing and debating. The swimming-pool, bars, restaurant and burger-bar might appeal. Union has the second largest venue for bands in Bristol. Like London, Bristol has developed a number of centres rather than just one. Clifton is studentland, Broadmead is a shopping centre, St Paul's has a great annual festival. Look out for the Tropic club and Lakota. West country real ale and scrumpy are pub specialities. The general sprawl and vastness of Bristol mean that typical students are hard to define. The traditional student is aged 18–19, from grammar or private school and usually had a year out in India or similar exotic climes. But be wary of stereotypes, the university is ultimately cosmopolitan. Courses vary – some heavily dependent on exams, others lots of assessed course work. All are moving towards a modularised framework. Very good reputation with most students showing keen and active interest in achieving good results.

PAUPER NOTES   **Accommodation:** House/flat shares £40–£50 pw in Clifton, Cotham, Redland or Hotwells. Normally have to pay for 52 weeks. **Drink:** Epi (Union) bar or hall bars. Smiles bitter is popular local brew, sold widely but especially at The Highbury Vaults. Cider in Coronation Tap. Kings Street/Clifton popular but expensive. **Eats:** Union restaurant and burger bar, Cafe Zuma. Good take-aways. **Ents:** Lots of national bands, comedians etc in SU; local/student bands in pubs (eg Bristol Bridge, Kings Arms). **Sports:** University sports centre at Woodland House (too small though); pool attached to Union; 46 sports clubs. Sports grounds 1 mile from halls, 4 miles from SU. **Hardship funds:** Access funds (£20–£200). **Travel:** University scholarship schemes. Easy access for hitching to London. **Work:** Student employment officer at SU helps find work.

MORE INFO?   Get students' Alternative Prospectus. Enquiries to Matt Salter (0117 973 5035 ext 155).
ALUMNI   Sue Lawley (BBC), Susan Engels (actress, RSC), Frances Horovitz (poet), Hugh Cornwell (lead singer with The Stranglers), Paul Boateng MP, David Hunt MP, Alistair Stewart (newsreader).

BRISTOL UWE

University of the West of England Bristol, Frenchay Campus, Coldharbour Lane, Bristol BS16 1QY (Tel 0117 965 6261, Fax 0117 976 3804) Map 3

STUDENT ENQUIRIES: Head of Admissions and Student Recruitment. APPLICATIONS: UCAS

Broad study areas: Art & design, computing, business, social science, humanities, education, engineering, languages, law, health, science, built environment. (Subject details are in the *Subjects and Places Index*.)

Founded: As Bristol Polytechnic, ex Bristol Technical College, College of Commerce and West of England College of Art and Redland and St Matthias colleges of education, Avon & Gloucestershire College of Health; university status 1992. **Main undergraduate awards:** BA, BA(QTS), BSc, BEng, BTP. **Awarding body:** Bristol UWE. **Site:** 5 main campuses. **Access:** Buses from Bristol city centre to all campuses. **Europe:** 12% first degree students take a language as part of course and 4% spend 6 months or more abroad. Language modules available on a range of degrees; all students have access to self-tuition facilities. Formal exchange links with many European universities/colleges, in a range of subjects. **Library:** 4 libraries, total of 370,000 books, 2,700 periodicals, 1,200 study places, electronic information retrieval facilities available. Annual expenditure on library materials, £70.86 per FTE student. **Welfare:** Student health service, welfare and counselling services, two nurseries (student discount). **Careers:** Information, recruitment fairs, careers and `milk round' programme. **Amenities:** Bookshops on 4 campuses, chaplaincy centre, student union shops, bank, centre for performing arts. SU has supermarket, bars, TV and games room, advisory services and large number of sports clubs and societies. **Sporting facilities:** Artificial pitch (hockey and football), two gymnasia, recreation centre containing four squash courts, weight training/fitness room, sunbed, playing fields (soccer and cricket).

Accommodation: In 1995/96, 16% of all students in university accommodation, 30% first years. 2,060 self-catering places available (1,320 for first years), £34–£42 per week, for 40 or 46 weeks. Plans to increase head tenancy scheme and build another hall of residence. Students live in privately owned accommodation for 2+ years: rents £35–£40 per week for self-catering, £35–£42 for B&B, £43–£55 for half-board. Demand high for the first term of the year. **Term time work:** No university policy on term time work for full-time first degree students (some 50% believed to work). Work available in SU; also vacancy noticeboard in careers/SU office. **Hardship funds:** Total available in 1995/96: £340,000 government access funds; £9,000 own funds (loan fund) plus £50,000 other funds (nursery fees remission). Special help for student parents.

Duration of first degree courses: 3 years; BA(QTS) and sandwich, 4 years. **Total first degree students 1995/96:** 13,256. **Total BA(QTS) students:** 909. **Overseas students:** 216. **Male/female ratio:** 10:9. **Teaching staff:** 900 full-time. **Total full-time students 1995/96:** 15,153. **Postgraduate students:** 3,134. **First degree tuition fees:** Home students, paying their own fees in 1996/97, paid £750 (classroom), £1,600 (lab); Overseas students £5,979.

WHAT IT'S LIKE   Five sites across the city and satellite sites at Bath, Swindon and Gloucester. Main site, Frenchay Campus, is 6 miles from the city centre, nestling between the M4 and M32 for good access. Serviced by a bus service – regular in the day, less so at night. Cramped car parking on site although sports courts being turned into more parking. Three bars, ents venue and SU offices. 10,000+ students makes it either impersonal or bustling with excitement. St Matthias (or St Matts) is main site for humanities and psychology in quiet residential suburb of Fishponds; beautiful site of a converted abbey. Very Oxbridge! A long journey from city centre; regular daily bus service but inadequate parking; best union bar. Health and social care are at Glenside Campus, just down the road from St Matts. Attractive, converted site, with best uni accommodation but few social provisions. SU runs ents in social club. Inadequate bus service, iffy parking. Bower Ashton is next to beautiful Ashton Court estate, providing art, media and design students with great visual inspiration. In need of refurbishing but has good spirit. SU bar and few ents events. Rather difficult to get to; bus service a problem. Redland Campus houses education in fashionable residential area between Gloucester Road and Whiteladies Road (aka Clifton); has a good bar. Bristol is an attractive and active city for students. Relationship between students and locals is good and plenty to do (arts, exhibitions, pubs, film, restaurants, live music etc). SU is active with offices and committees on all sites. SU runs clubs and societies, SCA, Bacus magazine, entertainments and nursery. Politically independent but active on local and national campaigns. Owns the retro night club in town, the Tube Club, and bars at all main sites. Plenty to see and do.

PAUPER NOTES   **Accommodation:** With 2 universities in Bristol, housing is becoming increasingly difficult and costly; prices will shock students other than Londoners (£160–£190 a month). **Drink:** Lots of good places to drink (over 400 pubs in Bristol central region). Popular student pubs: The Bristol Flyer, The Hobgoblin on Gloucester Road; Cadbury House in Montpelier; The Steam Tavern, The Dog and Duck in Clifton. **Eats:** SU good range of food especially at Frenchay (Pizza Tower) and St Matts. Refectory prices fairly high. Gloucester Road is curry heaven; Whiteladies Road is bistro haven! Good choice of South American restaurants in central Bristol. **Ents:** Union nightclub in city centre and regular campus events. Sin! at Frenchay every Friday – popular sounds and late bar. Comedy night weekly at Jesters Comedy Club (sponsored by SU). Termly Freshers, Snow and May balls and Sutra dance party. **Sports:** Many different clubs. Campus sports facilities very poor. **Hardship funds:** Hardship loan fund maximum £100, summer hardship fund minimum approx £200; dual control by uni and SU. **Travel:** STA Travel Shop at Frenchay. **Work:** Usual bar, security, catering, shop work plus Playscheme. Union rate £4/hour. Plenty of work in town.

ALUMNI   Jack Russell (England wicket keeper), Mark Knopfler (Dire Straits guitarist), Kyran Bracken (England rugby).

HOW TO START? *SEE SHORTLISTING*, PAGE 535

BRITISH INSTITUTE IN PARIS

British Institute in Paris, University of London, 11 rue de
Constantine, 75340 Paris Cedex 07 (Tel 00 331 45 55 71 99)

STUDENT ENQUIRIES:
In Paris: Secretary to French Department
(Fax 00 331 45 50 31 55)
In England: The London Secretary, British Institute in Paris,
Senate House, Malet Street, London WC1E 7HU
(Tel 0171 636 8000, ext 3920; Fax 0171 580 8486)
APPLICATIONS: UCAS or direct to Paris or London offices.

Broad study areas: French studies, professional translation
studies. (Subject details are in the *Subjects and Places Index.*)

Founded: 1894, as private organisation, becoming Senate Institute of London University in
1969. **Site:** Central Paris. **Access:** Bus routes 63, 83, 93, 94, 69, 28, 49 and on RER route B
and on metro routes, Saint-Denis – Genevilliers and Balard-Créteil. **Structural features:** Part
of London University. **Academic features:** Degree course in French studies (3 years, entirely
in Paris); also courses leading to certificate and diploma in French and English translation;
certificate of proficiency in French in contemporary French studies and in French for business. 1-year course in French language and literature and in political science, history or
plastic arts for joint honours undergraduates taught partly at the Institute and partly at the
Institut d'Etudes Politiques or the Universities of Paris I and IV. MA courses in French and
English translation, in contemporary French studies, and in contemporary French theatre.
Distance education offered in translation and proficiency in contemporary French. The
certificate in French and English translation and of proficiency in French can be prepared
fully by correspondence. **Special features:** Institute has dual purpose: French department
for English-speaking students (age 18+) to study French language, literature and history;
English department for French students to study English language and literature. Many
British universities give financial support, though London University is responsible for
Institute as a whole. French language courses are at 5 levels: Preliminary, Elementary (first
year degree or third year remedial), Advanced 1, 2 and 3 (degree level, majoring in French
at third year level). French is language of instruction; minimum period one term. Also 3
intensive courses at Easter for finalists. Institute is recognised centre for London and
Cambridge examinations. Publishes an academic journal, Franco-British Studies. **Library:**
British Institute French Translation Library, Cultural Centre English/Translation Library (both
lending and reference). Annual expenditure on library materials, £80 per FTE student. **Other
learning facilities:** Tape and video-tape library, computer-assisted learning, film resources.
Welfare: Best to take out health insurance before you go. French social security benefits
and Mutuelle (ie supplementary health scheme) available for full-time students. **Amenities:**
Student club and cafeteria, access to all sports and leisure facilites of the universities of
Paris.

Accommodation: Institute is non-residential, but accommodation secretary has address
register. Some places for students at Cités Universitaires in the Paris area (apply by late
May); good rooms, hostel and paying-guest accommodation for early birds. **Term time work:**
Institute's policy to allow term time work for full-time first degree students; limit of 10 hours

per week (30% believed to work). Term (and vac) work available in Institute cafeteria, exam invigilation, clerical work; help provided in finding work placements elsewhere. **Hardship funds:** Working scholarships available (full fees in exchange for light duties 2 hours a day). Access funds available to top up accommodation and food expenses.

Duration of courses: 3 years (degree), 1-2 years (certificate/diploma/MA courses). **Total first degree level students 1995/96:** 286. **Overseas students:** 36. **Mature students:** 15. **Male/female ratio:** 1:4. **Teaching staff:** 5 full-time, 12 part-time. **Total full-time students 1995/96:** 111 (full year), 100 (part year). **Postgraduate students:** 33. **Tuition fees:** Home students, paying their own fees in 1996/97, paid F13,650; Overseas students, F15,000; Degree course: £1,450.

WHAT IT'S LIKE   The atmosphere is reassuringly friendly and a tremendous help to new arrivals – well organised staff/student introductory meeting gives an overall view of studies, a sketch of what Paris has to offer and an idea of where to go to find it. The course options are designed to make the most of cultural life in Paris and they do it brilliantly: theatre, cinema and art options in particular provide a window on French society for English students living in the country for the first time. Obligatory courses ensure a high standard of grammar and written French is achieved. Facilities can be cramped: the library is small but carries a wide range of up to date newspapers and periodicals (a great saving as they are expensive in France). Municipal libraries are easy to join and excellent but university libraries are often full. You can usually find a computer for essay writing in the Institute computer room plus help for the computer illiterate. The canteen is a convivial meeting place, decent size and a good atmosphere. There is also a university restaurant just across the Seine for good meals at reasonable prices. The large Institute film collection can be seen in the video room; the notice board is excellent for finding rooms, conversation exchanges and part-time jobs. Can be an invisible barrier between the French and English departments; students tend to keep to their own nationality groups. Contacts with French people can be made by joining associations, volunteering for charity work and doing conversation exchanges; the possibilities are endless with some effort. Overall, the Institute is an ideal base for the English student in Paris for the first time. Help, advice and a warm atmosphere help ease new arrivals quickly into life in the capital and the standard and variety of courses on offer cannot be too highly praised.

PAUPER NOTES   **Accommodation:** Lots of garrets and rooms with French families available; only for very early birds. Some small reasonable flats to share. Best to be found on very useful American Church noticeboards, Quai d'Orsay. But beware that landlords can be rogues and are often unwilling to return deposits ('caution', as it is known there). **Drink:** Chartier restaurant and Café de la Paix, rue Montmartre, for drinks. French wine so prevalent that the Institute's Club serves English beer as a nostalgia jerker. **Eats:** French university restaurants excellent dietetically, and fairly cheap (15 francs a meal). Also cheap M&S dishes! For self-caterers, food and drink is so cheap. Try 'Ed, l'épicier' supermarket. **Ents:** Plenty of student reductions for plays in the small playhouses; BI organises theatre visits (group rates) each term. Cheap bowling (!) in the Mouffetard. There are choral groups and orchestras, who welcome foreigners. **Sports:** Paris University facilities available; otherwise be prepared to pay capital city prices for gym clubs, swimming clubs etc, of which every arrondissement has its own: football clubs, rugby clubs, skiing clubs, hiking clubs, etc; to find addresses and telephone numbers go to the local arrondissement's Mairie. Forest Hill tennis clubs are cheapest for students, though perhaps not cheap. Those interested in playing rugby, contact commercial clubs like France-Soir/Figaro Club. There are good walking areas within 15 minutes of centre, and swimming is plentiful. **Hardship funds:** For students who attend all lessons at BI and who prove lack of funds, there are generous meal/rent allowances. **Work:** Noticeboards in the Institute and the American Church have plenty of ads – notably babysitting (ask for 40F/hr). Also, Institute bar, library etc, for deserving paupers. Some students work 'au pair' and study part-time or as 'assistants' in schools and take special assistants' course.

ALUMNI   Michael Sadler (dramatist); Sir Christopher Mallaby (HM Ambassador to Paris); Charles de Gaulle.

BRITISH SCHOOL OF OSTEOPATHY

The British School of Osteopathy, 1–4 Suffolk Street, London
SW1Y 4HG (Tel 0171 930 9254, Fax 0171 839 1098)
Map 6

STUDENT ENQUIRIES: Admissions
APPLICATIONS: Direct

Broad study area: Osteopathy.

Founded: 1917. **Main undergraduate award:** BSc. **Awarding body:** Open University. **Site:** Single site in central London (just off Trafalgar Square). **Access:** Underground and mainline stations within easy reach; also on various bus routes. **Academic features:** Course is student-centred with a focus on problem-solving in a clinical context. **Structural features:** Links with medical schools and universities for specialist areas of the teaching course and research activities. **Europe:** No language tuition or formal exchanges. **Library:** 9,000 volumes, 110 periodicals, 70 study places. **Specialist collections:** Collections of rare books on osteopathy. **Other learning facilities:** Well-equipped human performance laboratory and anatomy resource room; computer-aided interactive anatomy, Internet. **Welfare:** Full-time counsellors. Elected SU welfare officer; student welfare committee of staff and students. **Amenities:** SU active in organising social functions with similar institutions. **Sporting facilities:** Squash court and weights room on site. Student sports clubs make arrangements externally for playing facilities with other institutions, eg local medical schools.

Accommodation: No college accommodation but arrangements with other institutions for small number of students. Most students live in privately owned accommodation. School holds list of places with local families. 60% first degree students live at home. **Term time work:** School does not advise term time work but many believed to work. Term (and vac) work available in school bar, reprographics and office. **Hardship funds:** Bursary fund and student welfare funds for severe hardship available for students in years 2–4. Students on an LEA grant will have 15% tuition fees paid.

Duration: of standard pathway, 4 years; extended pathway, 5 years. **Total first degree students:** 350. **Mature students:** 60%. **Overseas students:** 35. **Male/female ratio:** 2:3. **Teaching staff:** 3 full-time, 130 part-time. **Postgraduate students:** Being developed. **Tuition fees 1996/97:** £5,600, home and overseas (LEA award covers 15% of fees).

WHAT IT'S LIKE   It's the largest alternative medicine training centre in Europe, housed in a large corner building (traditional architecture) just off Trafalgar Square. Inside it's a maze of staircases and corridors leading to lecture theatres, treatment rooms, offices and a library containing the largest collection of osteopathic medical literature. Access easy: close to Piccadilly Circus and Charing Cross tube stations; many buses stop in Trafalgar Square; Charing Cross BR station nearby. Strong railings for locking bicycles to, but cycling in London has its special dangers. SU affiliated to NUS, concentrates on welfare, social activity, sport and staff relations. Course involves much physical contact between students while learning and practising osteopathic technique. BSO students become remarkably relaxed about stripping off to their underwear in front of each other. But this does not mean that training at the BSO is akin to a four-year orgy. What it does mean is that sex, sexuality and intimacy become demystified. Part-time counsellor provides confidential support; four years of a heavy course, often with financial problems too, can wear down even the most resilient. BSO is located in centre of country's largest entertainment complex: everything is on offer. National Gallery and St Martin's in the Fields, with its lunchtime concerts, 30 seconds' walk; Coliseum about a minute away; Theatre Royal Haymarket just around the corner; countless cinemas nearby. Pubs, wine-bars, restaurants and nightclubs too numerous to be counted, but pretty pricey. Workload phenomenal. Course much the same as at medical school (one year less to do it in!) but training holistic, ie health and illness are looked at in terms of the patient rather than the disease; there is slightly less emphasis on biochemistry and pharmacology than at medical school, since osteopathy is a drug-free system of medicine. Anatomy vitally important: students learn the entire body at a level of detail doctors only approach during postgraduate surgical training. Much of the course is osteopathic technique: clinical training starts with observation in first year and gradually increases, under supervision, until fourth year students see patients all the way through from taking their case histories to providing final treatment. Work assessed by combination of written exams, viva voces, essays and Objective Structured Practical Examinations (OSPEs). There is inevitably some attrition, mostly first year. About a third to a half of all students are 18–22 year-olds, mostly straight from sixth form; another third to a half are between 25–35, many of them graduates; the remainder are in their late 30s, even into their 40s, doing what they have always wanted to do before it is too late! An independent college, there is a substantial discrepancy between a grant for fees and what is charged. You'll be left with a shortfall of over £5,000 to fund yourself.

PAUPER NOTES   **Accommodation:** None although some available in nurses accommodation. College and SU help find it. **Drink:** SU has cheapest drinks in central London. Fullers is main beer. **Eats:** Large canteen in basement. Very good value. **Ents:** Lots of SU social events. **Sports:** Squash court, gym, weight-training room, all on campus. Off campus access to any sport you can think of if enough people interested. Riding and hang-gliding very popular. **Hardship funds:** Osteopathic Education Foundation help some students from 2nd year. **Work:** A heavyweight course and students do clinical work during the so-called holidays. Good time-management and masses of energy enable people to earn some money.

MORE INFO?   Enquiries to any SU member (0171 930 6093).

INFORMAL NAME   BSO.

GET HOLD OF THE PROSPECTUSES

BRUNEL UNIVERSITY

Brunel University, Uxbridge, Middlesex UB8 3PH
(Tel 01895 274000, Fax 01895 203096) Map 5

STUDENT ENQUIRIES: Admissions Office (applications etc) or
Student Recruitment Office (course information, open days etc)
APPLICATIONS: UCAS

Broad study areas: Pure and applied sciences, engineering, technology and computing, social sciences, humanities, education, mathematics, business and management, preforming and fine arts, sport, health. (Subject details are in the *Subjects and Places Index*.)

Founded: 1966; merged with West London Institute 1995. **Main undergraduate awards:** BSc, BA, BEng, LLB. **Awarding body:** Brunel University. **Site:** 4 self-contained campuses to the west of London: main campus (near Uxbridge), Runnymede (near Egham), Twickenham (on Thames at Richmond Lock) and Osterley (Isleworth). **Access:** Uxbridge or Osterley underground; West Drayton, Egham or St Margaret's main line stations; M4, M25 and M40. **Academic features:** Many degree courses available as 4 year (thick or thin) sandwich or 3 year full-time and emphasise relevance and practical application. Modular structure allows students to add eg languages, management, computer science, or to take joint honours in a range of disciplines. Student exchanges in many departments with Europe and USA. Foundation courses in science and engineering for applicants without science A-levels. Broad-based courses in natural sciences and in engineering science and technology. Optional 1-year extensions to BEng courses for MEng/Diploma in engineering management. **Special features:** Music and sport bursaries. Associate student scheme for mature part-time returners. **Research centres:** 24 centres including innovation and the culture of technology; health economics, bioengineering; youth work; law (criminal, consumer, computer, the family); power systems. **Europe:** Students can take language modules as assessed part of degree; many opt for extra-curricular courses. Some formal exchange links. **Library:** 580,000 volumes, 3,000 periodicals, 2,500 items of AV and microfilm material. Annual expenditure on library materials, £88.78 per FTE student plus significant additional electronic information. **Other learning facilities:** Computer centres, audiovisual centre, EFL/language centre, experimental techniques centre, metrology centre. **Welfare:** Medical centre, chaplaincy, counsellors, nursery, welfare unit. **Careers:** Information and advice services. **Amenities:** Bookshop, bank, supermarket, travel shop, student newspaper, radio station, nursery, refectory, coffee and snack bars, university art gallery, art and music classes, student music bursaries. **Sporting facilities:** Sports centres, squash courts, climbing wall, playing fields, all-weather playing surface; floodlit training facilities; dry ski slope in Uxbridge, boat house on Thames. Rowing, sailing, canoeing. Coaching, classes, biomechanics lab, sports injury clinic etc. Centre of excellence for weightlifting, basketball. Students' sports bursaries.

Accommodation: *Uxbridge and Runnymede:* In 1995/96, 41% of all students in university accommodation, 76% first years (remainder chose to make own arrangements). 2,450 self-catering places available, at £35–£47 per week, for 37 or 50 weeks. Aim is to house all first and some final year students in university owned/leased accommodation. *Osterley and Twickenham:* 10% of all students in university accommodation, 25% first years. 344 places in halls (priority to first years living furthest from campus) at £48.50–£54.50 per week including 5 meals. 10% first years live at home. All campuses: Rents in privately owned accommodation £45–£55 per week for self-catering, £55–£65 for B&B. **Term time work:** University policy to allow term time work for full-time first degree students. Some term (and vac) work available on campus in SU bars and clerical support in admin. **Hardship funds:** Total available in 1995/96: £215,478 government access funds, used to help 799 students.

Duration of first degree courses: 3 or 4 years (up to 6 years part-time). **Total first degree students 1995/96:** 9,125. **Overseas students:** 251. **Mature students:** 3,383. **Male/female ratio:** 2:1. **Teaching staff:** 501 full-time. **Total full-time students 1995/96:** 9,626. **Postgraduate students:** 3,112 (2,232 p/t). **First degree tuition fees:** Home students, paying their own fees in 1996/97, paid £750 (classroom), £1600 (lab/studio); Overseas students, £6,180 (classroom), £8,195 (lab/studio).

WHAT IT'S LIKE   *Uxbridge and Runnymede*   It's an expanding university on the outer reaches of West London, ideally situated on the Metropolitan and Piccadilly tube lines but far away from any tourists. The only university in the country to operate the thin-sandwich degree system for the majority of its courses: four years, including two periods of work experience. This helps to explain why graduates have one of the best employment records in the country. For greater flexibility, some traditional three-year courses have recently been introduced. Two sites: Uxbridge, noted for its '60s concrete architecture; and Runnymede near Egham in Surrey, where the St Trinian's films were made. The SU has excellent facilities: six bars, two band/disco venues, well-resourced information and advice centre, three catering outlets, nursery and a communications unit which produces the student newspaper. The backbone of the SU is some 100 sporting clubs and social/cultural societies. If you want anonymity at university, Brunel may not be the place for you; however, if you enjoy being part of a community atmosphere, it may be just what you are looking for.

PAUPER NOTES   *Uxbridge and Runnymede*   **Accommodation:** Cheapest on campus (some ensuite rooms). Most off-campus accommodation in Hayes, West Drayton and Southall. **Drink:** Range of brands at competitive prices. SU bars stock mainly Scottish & Newcastle products, some Courage and Whitbread. **Eats:** Pub food at Pinn Inn, main meals at Gallery Diner, sandwiches and snacks at Sandwich Bar – all on campus. Good variety of international dishes. **Ents:** Nightclub venues – Thumpers and The Academy. Ents includes regular bands, Now Dance!, Hot Spots live comedy, theme nights and cabaret. **Sports:** Sports centre on campus, newly refurbished Astro turf ground. Swimming pool in Uxbridge. **Hardship funds:** Short-term welfare loans from SU. **Travel:** Agents on campus. Lift-share system also in operation. **Work:** Employment is available in the SU, university and local area. Work placements are available throughout the country.

WHAT IT'S LIKE   *Osterley and Twickenham*   Two sites approx 1 mile apart. River Thames flows past the Gordon House campus; Lancaster House campus on Great West Road (easy access Heathrow and London) but noise caused by aircraft can be problem, especially during summer term. Five halls of residence house approx 300 students – mainly first years. Rented accommodation outside halls quite expensive and scarce, especially in Richmond and Twickenham areas. Hounslow is cheaper, so consequently favoured by students. Library facilities are good considering the available resources. Despite excellent reputation for sports studies and high-class sports teams, lack of actual pitches for football, rugby and hockey quite startling. Entertainment regularly organised by SU with the May Ball the highlight of everyone's social calendar. SU considers itself there for the welfare and well-being of its student membership. With London/West End being so close (via Hounslow and Richmond stations) there are plenty of distractions from academic side of student life. Loads of pubs, wine bars, restaurants, theatres, cinemas and horse and dog tracks provide scope for frittering away grant cheques. Staff-student relationships generally very amicable but, of course, there have been exceptions over the years. It's not a bad place to get a degree.

PAUPER NOTES *Osterley and Twickenham* **Accommodation:** Very difficult to find cheap accommodation in Richmond and Twickenham environs; some less expensive digs in Hounslow area. Alms house run by local charity, £16–£24 per week. **Drink:** Fullers Brewery is just up the road in Chiswick. ESB (Extra Special Bitter) is not the weakest tipple! Town Wharf – draught pils, good value for money. **Eats:** College catering facilities expensive but range of food good. Richmond has wide range of tastes and price. The Shack, Linkfield Rd, best cooked breakfast around. Minars Tandoori Restaurant, Hounslow, reasonable price, excellent food, including vegetarian. **Ents:** Bear Cat Cabaret Club, Turks Head Pub, St Margarets Road (off campus). Watermans Art Centre has cinema, bands, workshops etc. **Sports:** Two swimming pools close to campus/sports hall on Lancaster House campus. Isleworth pool – free with leisure card at off-peak times. Large leisure centre at Brentford plus smaller one in Old Isleworth near the GH campus. **Hardship funds:** Access welfare fund. Small short-term loans. **Travel:** 2 travel scholarships of £500. **Work:** 40% students have term-time work. Some campus work; stewarding, bar work, security. Complaints that work has bad effect on academic studies. 30% work in vacations but increasingly difficult to find.

MORE INFO? Ring Jeremy Church (01895 462200).

ALUMNI (EDITORS' PICK) M Naylor, Kathy Cook, P Stimpson, Brian Hooper, Alan Pascoe, Dave Otley, Phil Bainbridge.

BUCKINGHAM UNIVERSITY

The University of Buckingham, Hunter Street, Buckingham
MK18 1EG (Tel 01280 814080, Fax 01280 824081) Map 4

STUDENT ENQUIRIES: Admissions Office
APPLICATIONS: UCAS

Broad study areas: Business, law, computer science, humanities, social sciences. (Subject details are in the *Subjects and Places Index*.)

Founded: 1974 as an independent university. **Main undergraduate awards:** BA, BSc, LLB. **Awarding body:** Buckingham University. **Site:** 3 sites near Buckingham town centre. **Access:** Buses from Aylesbury and Milton Keynes (both have main line railway stations). **Academic features:** Degree courses in business economics. **Special features:** Britain's only independent university receives no direct government financial support. 2-year degree courses, and a range of cross-disciplinary supporting courses. Academic year is 4 terms long and runs January–December. Law course entry also available in July. Applications welcomed from mature students. **Europe:** 67% first degree students take a language as a minor or free choice course. 4% spend 6 months or more abroad. Formal exchange links with 7 European universities/colleges (in France, Germany and Spain); some graduates can transfer to MBA at Strasbourg or Tubingen, and complete in 1 year. **Library:** 2 libraries; 85,000 volumes in total, 495 periodicals, computerised catalogue, 220 study places, short loan collection. **Other learning facilities:** Audio-lingual language labs; satellite TV viewing room for live broadcasts in 6 European languages; video facilities; library of audio and video recorded materials in over 12 languages. Computer labs with IBM-compatible microcomputers, peripherals connected to Orion minicomputer. Support available for students with disabilities, particularly dyslexia. **Welfare:** University medical officer, advisory system, counsellor, adviser to women students. **Careers:** Information and advice service, full-time careers adviser. **Amenities:** Student social centre; concert hall. Oxford 23 miles, Milton Keynes 12 miles away. **Sporting facilities:** Access to sports and recreational facilities.

Accommodation: In 1995, 60% of all students in university accommodation, guaranteed for first years. 450 self-catering places available, £60+ per week in term time (£30 pw in vacations). Students live in privately owned accommodation for 1 year: £60–£70 per week self-catering. **Hardship funds:** In 1995, 100 students helped with tuition fees, 50 with living expenses. Other funds available for hardship during the course; 29 students helped in 1995. Financial help primarily aimed at helping students with tuition fees.

Duration of first degree courses: 2 years (8 terms); **others:** 9 terms; 3 years. **Total first degree students 1996:** 814. **Overseas students:** 706. **Mature students:** 382. **Male/female ratio:** 5:4. **Teaching staff:** 83 full-time, 30 part-time. **Total full-time students 1995:** 925. **Postgraduate students:** 149. **First degree tuition fees 1996:** Home and overseas: £9,744 (LEA grant reduces this by £2,224 in 1997).

WHAT IT'S LIKE Buckingham is the ideal university town, blending great antiquity with a beautiful rural setting, a safe environment and a central location within easy reach of commercial and artistic centres. Historic Warwick, London and Stratford-upon-Avon are all about an hour from Buckingham. The university provides opportunities for students from all over the world; one big plus is the compact 2 year degree course which helps many a student to save time. Frequent dinner and discos organised by the fifty different cultural societies. Annual university/town barbecue and fireworks party in November; other fun events include Rag week (August) and Graduation Ball (in February). University sports club holds frequent competitions. Britain's only private university and now with a new business school. All staff are student-friendly; small tutorials mean more attention. Baroness Thatcher is University Chancellor. Buckingham has something to offer every student and the rural setting helps to study better.

PAUPER NOTES **Accommodation:** Private accommodation not hard to find; many students prefer these to halls. **Drink:** University bar popular, as are pubs: Villiers, Grand Junction, The Mitre. **Eats:** Ethnic food and take-aways in town. **Ents:** Good entertainment in Milton Keynes and Oxford. Discos and ethnic nights on campus. **Sports:** Sports centre, all-weather tennis courts, multi-gym, snooker room, fencing, martial arts on campus; number of sports clubs. Also swimming pools, squash and badminton courts. **Hardship funds:** Some funds available. **Work:** In SU shops, computer rooms, local supermarkets, pubs and restaurants.

BUCKINGHAMSHIRE COLLEGE

The Buckinghamshire College, Queen Alexandra Road,
High Wycombe, Bucks HP11 2JZ Map 4
(Tel 01494 522141, Fax 01494 471585)

STUDENT ENQUIRIES: Admissions Registrar
APPLICATIONS: UCAS

Broad study areas: Business and leisure management, timber and construction, design including furniture design, social sciences. (Subject details are in the *Subjects and Places Index*).

Founded: 1893, ex High Wycombe College of Technology and Art and Newland Park College of Education. **Main undergraduate awards:** BA, BSc. **Awarding body:** Brunel University. **Site:** 3 sites: 2 in High Wycombe (one near town centre; Wellesbourne on outskirts) and Newland Park, 12 miles away near Chalfont St Giles. **Access:** All sites served by excellent roads and railways; about 40 mins from London. **Structural features:** A college of Brunel University. **Academic features:** Degree in European business studies includes a semester in Europe, international business admin a year in USA. Courses in forest products technology; 3-dimensional design. **Europe:** 60% first degree students take a language as part of course and 50% spend 6 months or more abroad. Formal exchange links, many open to non-language specialists, with 12 European universities/colleges. **Library:** 3 libraries, 120,000 volumes, multimedia services, 700 periodicals, 350 study places. Annual expenditure on library materials, £41.54 per FTE student. **Welfare:** Doctor, dentist, FPA, solicitor, chaplain, counsellor. **Careers:** Information, workshops, vocational counselling and placement service. **Amenities:** SU bars and theatre. **Sporting facilities:** Gymnasium and playing fields.

Accommodation: In 1995/96, 30% of all students in college accommodation, 50% of first years. 970 places available: 190 full board places (150 for first years) £47.88–£53.88 per week, 780 self-catering places at £42–£43 per week, all term time only. Students live in privately owned accommodation for 2+ years: rents £35–£45 per week for self-catering, £35–£50 B&B, £50–£65 for half-board. Accommodation office has lists of available accommodation. 30% first degree students live at home. **Term time work:** College's policy to allow term time work for full-time first degree students (45% believed to work). Term (and vac) work available on campus in SU bars, offices and casual summer work eg decorating; also student advisory service helps find work outside college. **Hardship funds:** Total available in 1995/96: £93,000 government access funds, 420 helped, average £200 awarded; £30,000 own funds, 52 students helped. Special help: overseas students, those with children, self-financing, mature students – higher priority to final/penultimate year; own funds also available for those outside scope of access fund guidelines. Some money assigned before the start of the course to non-standard entry students.

Duration of first degree courses: 3 years (full-time), 4 years (sandwich). **Total first degree students 1995/96:** 2,227. **Overseas students:** 396. **Male/female ratio:** 3:2. **Teaching staff:** 300+ full-time. **Total full-time students 1995/96:** 5,262. **Postgraduate students:** 982. **First degree tuition fees:** Home students, paying their own fees in 1996/97, paid £750 (classroom), £1,600 (lab/studio); Overseas students, £5,500.

WHAT IT'S LIKE   Undergraduates are on three sites: High Wycombe, Wellesbourne and Newland Park. Newland Park fairly isolated near Chalfont St Giles village. Life mainly campus-based in pleasant rural setting. Buildings mainly 1960s, grouped around Georgian mansion. Most students live on campus (new halls of residence); own social facilities building with two bars and entertainments hall. Wellesbourne is smallest campus with one faculty; brand new bar, The Final Whistle. Very close to town centre, where main High Wycombe campus is. This campus has a 900 capacity SU-owned nightclub and bar, The Venue, providing cheap beer and entertainment nightly. Main halls of residence within 2 minutes. Fairly attractive town centre – pubs, sports centre, shopping centres, cinema. All three sites are connected by public bus service. Established SU supports number of clubs and societies, including strong athletic union. Services offered to students include help for overseas students, accommodation advice and student counsellors. Students come from all over the country.

PAUPER NOTES   **Accommodation:** Off-campus expensive, some reasonable, others dire. College accommodation reasonable – no married quarters. **Drink:** Student bars cheap – pubs not, but some offer students' drinks promotions. **Eats:** Food at student bars (early morning till late at night). High Wycombe refectory has greater choice but expensive; lots of places to eat close by. Good variety near Newland Park if you have transport. **Ents:** The Venue is the place to be in High Wycombe in the evenings; Range of ents at Newland Park to suit all tastes. Nothing exciting off campus. **Sports:** Well equipped gyms on all three sites. Local sports centres with good offers for students. **Hardship funds:** College has emergency loan fund. **Travel:** London only 25 mins by road; direct rail link to London (Marylebone). **Work:** Many bar jobs on campus (only students employed). Jobs also available through local agencies.

ALUMNI   Howard Jones, Martin Grierson.

BUCKLAND UNIVERSITY COLLEGE

Buckland University College, Ewert Place, Oxford OX2 7YT
(Tel 01865 311113, Fax 01865 316655) Map 3

STUDENT ENQUIRIES: Academic Registrar
APPLICATIONS: Direct

Broad study areas: Law, management.

Founded: 1963. **Main undergraduate award:** BSc, LLB. **Awarding body:** London University. **Site:** Oxford, a mile north of city centre. **Access:** Fast London-Oxford coach and rail links; local buses. **Europe:** No first degree students take a language or spend time abroad. **Library:** 30 study places; special short-term loan scheme; library open 9–6. Annual expenditure on library materials, £90 per FTE student. **Welfare:** College welfare officer. **Careers:** Information and advice service. **Amenities:** Common rooms; leisure centres and sports facilities nearby, cultural and social amenities of Oxford.

Accommodation: No college accommodation. Buckland inspects and allocates accommodation to all students, some for exclusive use of its students: £45–£60 per week for self-catering; £60–£90 B&B and half-board; £90–£120 all found. **Term time work:** College policy to allow term time work for full-time first degree students (15% believed to work); limit of 12 hours per week. No work available in college. **Hardship funds:** Total available in 1995/96: £2,000 own funds, given annually as scholarship to student making most outstanding contribution to life of college.

Duration of first degree courses: 3 years. **Total first degree students 1995/96:** 50. **Overseas students:** 15. **Mature students:** 9. **Male/female ratio:** 1:1. **Teaching staff:** 2 full-time 12 part-time. **Total full-time students 1995/96:** 64. **Postgraduate students:** 15. **First degree tuition fees:** Home students in 1996/97 paid £1,850 (LEA grant covers about 50% of fee); Overseas students £2,450.

WHAT IT'S LIKE   An independent specialist law school providing courses for the London University LLB by full and part-time study. Specialist academic and professional staff are drawn from university teachers and those practising in the legal profession. All courses are taught through a combination of lecture sessions and seminars. Mock trials, moots and debates form part of the learning process and visits are arranged to the Old Bailey, Royal Courts of Justice and other relevant locations. Sports programme is organised at a local leisure centre including squash, tennis, 5-a-side football, basketball and badminton. The Student Committee organises term-time parties locally and end of term parties have been held at Planet Hollywood and the Hard Rock Cafe in London. The college is in Summertown, a five minute bus ride from Oxford city centre. Accommodation is available within easy walking distance of college. BUC offers the benefits of a larger institution on a more personal scale.
PAUPER NOTES   **Accommodation:** College links with inexpensive hostels, especially for overseas students; some accommodation in college's houses. **Work:** Some still find vacation work in Oxford.
INFORMAL NAME   BUC.

CAMBERWELL COLLEGE OF ARTS

Camberwell College of Arts, Peckham Road, London SE5 8UF (Tel 0171 514 6300, Fax 0171 514 6310) Map 5

STUDENT ENQUIRIES: **College Administrator**
APPLICATIONS: **UCAS**

Broad study areas: Art & design, history of art, conservation, metalwork, ceramics, graphic design. (Subject details are in the *Subjects and Places Index*.)

Founded: 1898. **Main undergraduate award:** BA. **Awarding body:** London Institute. **Site:** 2 main buildings and an annexe. **Access:** Waterloo, Peckham Rye, Elephant & Castle stations, then bus; bus from Oval, Vauxhall or Victoria station. **Structural features:** Constituent college of the London Institute. **Library:** 40,000 volumes, 85 periodicals, 40 study places. Annual expenditure on library materials, £40 per FTE student. **Other learning facilities:** Word processing, video viewing, photographic and computer facilities, media resources unit. **Welfare:** Easy access to all London Institute's facilities, own student information officer. **Careers:** Information and advice service. Weekly job-hunting workshops. **Amenities:** College shop, bar, student union facilities.

Accommodation: Limited places in the London Institute's 2 halls of residence. Approx cost: £70–£90 per week, including heating. Institute's accommodation service helps find privately rented accomodation: rent approx £50 per week, excluding bills and meals. **Term time work:** College policy to allow term time work for full-time first degree students. Term (and vac) work available in college in SU bar, library work and during exhibition period; also careers service circulates lists of jobs outside college. **Hardship funds:** Access funds available.

Duration of first degree courses: 3 years. **Total first degree students 1995/96:** 855. **Overseas students:** 60 **Mature students:** 160. **Male/female ratio:** 2:3. **Teaching staff:** 36 full-time, 200 part-time. **Total full-time students 1995/96:** 1,120. **Postgraduate students:** 85. **First degree tuition fees:** Home students, paying their own fees in 1996/97, paid £1,600; Overseas students £5,950.

WHAT IT'S LIKE   Built on 3 sites. The main one on Peckham Road is an ugly sixties monstrosity tacked, rather uncomfortably, onto a beautiful Victorian, purpose-built art school. The other two sites are a prefab sculpture annexe and an old grammar school. The diversity of the architecture is outdone only by the diversity of the students. Courses range from art history to paper conservation. SU provides opportunities for meeting in a crowded, smoky atmosphere to exchange drunken conversations over loud music in friendly and inexpensive bar. Regular termly bashes with bands, cabarets etc. The number of clubs is growing by the minute. Accommodation in London is expensive and difficult to find but it is probably easier to find somewhere to live near Camberwell than other London art schools. Being in the capital means almost every type of entertainment is available (at a price). All the courses require hard work, application and self-motivation. Support facilities, such as the library and media resources departments, are stretched. Not much space; studios are very cramped. Most of the staff are highly respected practitioners in their field. PAUPER NOTES   **Accommodation:** Institute halls in Tooting (B&B) and Battersea (full board). Some flats available through college; rented accommodation expensive but available. **Drink:** SU bar cheap but shuts at 8pm. Most students then go to The Kerfield or Hermit's Cave (both Camberwell Green). **Eats:** College canteen. Seymour's Sandwich Shop (scrummy sanis, fresh homemade soup, always vegetarian); Tadim's Turkish Bakery (lots of calorific pastries, biscuits and cakes); Camberwell Carrot (claims to be only organic, vegan and vege cafe in south London; not too pricey, fresh food daily, delicious breads and cakes). **Ents:** SU provides entertainment and Camberwell is very close to the centre of London. **Sports:** New sports centre 5 mins away in Peckham. 2 mins swimming pool. SU football team. **Hardship funds:** Some access funds. **Travel:** Some college trips abroad: possibility of exchange trips to America. **Work:** Part-time work not difficult to find in London if you don't mind what you do. Jobs in SU bar; can get paid for helping at SU events (from go-go dancing to DJ-ing).

WANT TO HELP WITH THE NEXT EDITION? SEE PAGE 66

CAMBORNE SCHOOL OF MINES

Camborne School of Mines, Trevensen, Pool, Redruth, Cornwall
TR15 3SE (Tel 01209 714866, Fax 01209 716977) Map 3

STUDENT ENQUIRIES: The Registry
APPLICATIONS: UCAS

Broad study areas: Geology, surveying and resource management, mining and minerals engineering, environmental science and technology. (Subject details are in the *Subjects and Places Index.*)

Founded: 1859; part of Exeter University since 1993. **Main undergraduate award:** BEng. **Awarding body:** Exeter University. **Site:** Outskirts of Camborne, Cornwall. **Special features:** Experimental mine. Pilot minerals separation plant. Occasional lectures from visiting industrial consultants. **Europe:** 30% of first degree students take a language as part of course. Field work in France, Portugal and Spain to enhance practical and language skills. Formal exchange links with European universities/colleges. **Library:** 8,000 volumes, 168 periodicals, 40 study places, course books kept in closed access. Annual expenditure on library materials, £75 per FTE student. **Specialist collections:** Rare early mining publications. **Welfare:** Personal tutors; professional counsellor. **Careers:** Exeter University careers service has office on-site. **Amenities:** Carn Brea leisure centre and purpose-built student club with squash court, bar, TV and billiards room.

Accommodation: In 1995/96, 12% of students in college accommodation, 20% of first years. 50 self-catering places available (26 for first years): £40 per week. Additional hostel accommodation being developed. Many students live in privately owned accommodation for whole course: rents £40–£50 per week for self-catering, £50–£60 for half-board and weekend meals. Accommodation officer advises. 8% first degree students live at home. **Term time work:** No school policy to allow term time work for full-time first degree students (15% believed to work). Some help given finding vac work in the mining industry. **Hardship funds:** Government access funds available, around 20 students helped. Each case considered on merit.

Duration of first degree courses: 3 years. **Total first degree students 1995/96:** 263. **Overseas students:** 15. **Mature students:** 20. **Male/female ratio:** 8:1. **Teaching staff:** 26 full-time, 8 part-time. **Total full-time students 1995/96:** 340. **Postgraduate students:** 43. **First degree tuition fees:** Home students, paying their own fees in 1996/97, paid £1,600; Overseas students £7,770.

WHAT IT'S LIKE   There are not many places of higher education where the President of the SU is on first name terms with all students and academic staff. CSM is more of a community than a gathering or crowd of students. But enough students to offer a wide range of activities and societies. As mining, mineral surveying, geological engineers or environmental scientists, students are generally involved with outdoor activities and CSM students spend much of their spare time involved in sports. There are teams for all major sports along with other minority sports such as surfing (only 4 miles from best surf beach in Europe), rock-climbing (the school has its own climbing wall), scuba-diving, gliding etc. Situated in a major tourism area CSM offers the chance to study in an area of outstanding natural beauty that also has a thriving night-life: less than 3 miles away from both the grandeur of the Cornish coastline and entertainment at the best nightclub in the south-west. Students social club is situated away from campus and has bar, squash courts and other less physical pursuits, as well as acting as headquarters for many a night out. CSM has retained much of its traditional activities and warm family atmosphere following the merger with Exeter University, and hopes to gain further from the larger SU body.

PAUPER NOTES **Accommodation:** College has cheap modern hostel and married quarters. Numerous low-priced holiday lets during termtime. **Drink:** Cheap bar in students' club with choice of ales; numerous friendly pubs within walking distance. **Eats:** Cheap on-campus food (9.30–3.0 pm); vegetarians well catered for. **Ents:** Modern, well-equipped students' club with regular ents. Good local nightclubs; cinema in Redruth. **Sports:** College rugby, soccer, hockey, squash, cricket, badminton etc. Caving and climbing clubs. Water sports and large leisure centre both nearby. **Hardship funds:** Some access funds. **Travel:** Regular international exchanges with other mining institutions worldwide. Nearby mainline station and direct intercity coach links. **Work:** About 5–10% get paid work during term-time; difficult to find. Industrial vacation work in relevant subjects abroad available. Local mining operations. Excellent vacation opportunities – mostly Australia/South Africa, often leading to full-time employment.

MORE INFO? Enquiries to SU President (01209 714866).

INFORMAL NAME CSM.

BUZZ-WORDS Emmet (person from east of Tamar river).

CAMBRIDGE UNIVERSITY

University of Cambridge, Cambridge, CB2 1TN
(Registry Tel 01223 332200, Fax 01223 66383) Map 4

STUDENT ENQUIRIES: Cambridge Intercollegiate Applications Office, Kellet Lodge, Tennis Court Road, Cambridge CB2 1QJ, Tel 01223 333308 or The Tutor for Admissions of any Cambridge college.
APPLICATIONS: UCAS and to the university/college (see below)

Broad study areas: Arts, social sciences, science, technology, medicine. (Subject details are in the *Subjects and Places Index*.)

The University and Colleges: Each college is a self-governing community which elects its own fellows, admits its own undergraduates and provides academic, sporting and social facilities. Most colleges admit undergraduates to read all the subjects at Cambridge although some acquire a reputation in a particular subject. For most undergraduates the college is the focal point of their Cambridge life.

THE COLLEGES

There are 29 undergraduate colleges:

Men and Women:
Christ's
Churchill
Clare
Corpus Christi
Downing
Emmanuel
Fitzwilliam
Girton
Gonville & Caius
Homerton (separate profile
  which you can find
  under 'H')

Hughes Hall
  (mature only)
Jesus
King's
Magdalene
Pembroke
Peterhouse
Queens'
Robinson
St Catharine's
St Edmund's
  (mature only)
St John's

Selwyn
Sidney Sussex
Trinity
Trinity Hall
Wolfson
  (mature only)

Women only:
Lucy Cavendish
  (mature only)
New Hall
Newnham

HOW TO APPLY TO CAMBRIDGE UNIVERSITY

Entry is on the basis of A-levels already taken or to be taken, sometimes in conjunction with S-papers or Sixth Term Examination Papers (STEP). It is possible to apply either to a college of preference or by submitting an open application not naming any college of preference (for details refer to the *University of Cambridge Undergraduate Prospectus*). In either case a preliminary application form should be submitted as early as possible, and by 15 OCTOBER at the latest. You have also to submit a completed UCAS form naming Cambridge as one of your university choices: THIS MUST REACH UCAS BY 15 OCTOBER. You may not apply to Oxford as well as Cambridge in the same year unless you are a candidate for an organ award. The prospectus and form may be obtained from your school, or from the Admissions Tutor of any Cambridge college, or from the Cambridge Inter-collegiate Applications Office.

Europe: 7% first degree students take a language as part of their course and spend 6 months or more abroad. All students have access to private study facilities in the Language Centre and may take language courses in addition to their degree work (subject to approval from the faculty and the college). No formal exchange links with European universities/colleges at university level.

Accommodation: In 1995/96, 85% of all students in college accommodation, 100% first years. Provision and price varies between the colleges: average approx £50 per week self-catering. Around 50% second years live in privately owned accommodation: rents £30–£50 per week for self-catering, plus bills. Hardly any students live at home as you have to live within six miles of Great St Mary's church. **Term time work:** University policy does not allow term time work for full-time first degree students. **Hardship funds:** Total available in 1995/96: £383,461 government access funds, 538 students helped (349 u/gs); colleges have own hardship funds; numerous university and college scholarships and studentships are available, particularly for self-financing students (but more for postgraduate than under-graduate).

Duration of first degree courses: 3 or 4 years. **Total first degree students:** 10,822. **BEd students:** 328. **Overseas students:** 660 plus 308 EU. **Mature students:** 426. **Male/female ratio:** 3:2. **Teaching staff:** 2,800. **Postgraduates:** 4,562. **Total full-time students:** 15,384. **First degree tuition fees:** Home students, paying their own fees in 1996/97, paid £750 (classroom), £1,600 (lab), £2,800 (clinical); Overseas students £5,886 (classroom), £7,722 (lab), £14,283 (clinical); college fees of £2,500-£3,000 are paid in addition to university tuition fees.

WHAT IT'S LIKE   Cambridge is a very diverse university and, although it is pretty and old, the student stereotypes of Living Soap and Porterhouse Blue cohabit fairly successfully. The university is varied enough to accommodate all types, and most will find their niche. Cambridge is a collegiate university, so your application is to an individual college. Much of student life revolves around college – eating, most sports clubs, facilities, and a fair amount of teaching. The colleges are different, and it is worth looking at a few, but don't agonize too much over your choice. The main points to consider are whether a college is single sex; its size; its location; its wealth; whether it is old or new; percentages of independent/state school students; and male/female balance. Work-load is on the heavy side, but normally quite manageable. Despite positive moves in a number of subjects, assessment is still predominently by exams. Combined degrees are rare, but changing course is relatively easy depending on the course. Drop-out rate is lowest in the country. Over 300 university-wide societies and clubs, catering for everything from martial arts to politics via drama, music, hillwalking and philosophy. Cambridge lacks a central focus for big events – there is no central SU building for gigs etc. College life is sometimes claustrophobic, but basically friendly and supportive. Cambridge town centre is picturesque and dominated by the university. Geared entirely towards students and tourists – some have trouble keeping the latter out of their rooms. Lively for a not over-sized town, though character changes out of term. Excellent market and good number of good pubs. Venues like the Boat Race and various jazz clubs attract good names from the small to mid-sized gigs circuit. Most tours get to either the Corn Exchange or the Junction. London is one hour by train.

PAUPER NOTES   **Accommodation:** Most students live in college or college hostels. Students living out tend to congregate in the Chesterton Road or Mill Road areas. **Drink:** College bars are popular, cheap and numerous. Good pubs include the Maypole, King Street pubs, The Mill and the more expensive Eagle. Out of town try the Wrestlers on the Newmarket Road, or the Rupert Brooke in nearby Granchester. **Eats:** College food varies from the survivable up to the quite good. Most cater for vegetarians. Good late night kebabs – Gardenia on Rose Crescent or the 'death van' on Market Square (or try Mill Road). Plenty of standard restaurant chains in town – pizza and curry well represented. **Ents:** University venues numerous and increasingly sophisticated but generally too small for big names, though the Corn Exchange and the Junction see most tours (Blur, the Chippendales etc). Arts Cinema is excellent. **Sports:** Most colleges have own sports facilities – 20 boathouses in Cambridge and as many rugby pitches. University-wide teams numerous and good. **Hardship funds:** Funds, including access funds, available on university-wide basis eg Newton Bursary fund. Colleges are able to give assistance in certain cases. **Travel:** Most colleges have funds – ask your tutor. **Work:** Term-time work not permitted by university regulations unless tutorial permission is given; under 5% do work (mainly in pubs and shops – average £3 per hour). The relatively long holidays give opportunity for vacation work. Around Cambridge this includes fruit-packing, teaching in language schools and tutorial colleges, punting tourists in summer, college kitchens.

MORE INFO?   Get Alternative Prospectus from Cambridge University Students' Union, Tel 01223 356454.

CAMBRIDGE-SPEAK   Buttery (college bar); gyps/bedders (men/women who clean up for you and make beds); sets (sets of rooms, bedroom(s) and sitting room); JCR (Junior Common Room); supervision (tutorial); Fellows (teaching staff of a college); Hall (college dining room and sometimes refers to evening meal in college, often formal); Courts (quads in college).

ALUMNI (EDITORS' PICK)   Milton, Charles Darwin, Dame Frances Dove, Marlowe, Coleridge, Ethel Sargant (research botanist), Rupert Brooke, Keynes, Pepys, Erasmus, Wilberforce, Newton, Byron, Constance Herschell (chemist), John Cleese, the Spies, Mary Archer, Pitt the Younger, Margaret Drabble, A A Milne, Miriam Margolies, Joan Bakewell, Rajiv Gandhi, Lord Mountbatten, Bertrand Russell, EM Forster, Sylvia Plath, Griff Rhys Jones, Graham Greene, Emma Thompson, Fry and Laurie, Clive James, Germaine Greer, Shirley Williams, David Attenborough, Diane Abbot, Brian Redhead, Carol Vorderman, Baroness Seear, David Baddiel, Jeremy Paxman, Sandi Toksvig, Ian McKellen, Baroness Warnock, Phillipa Pearce.

CHRIST'S

Christ's College, Cambridge CB2 3BU
(Tel 01223 334953, Fax 01223 334967)

Founded: 1439; women undergraduates first admitted 1978. **Admission:** Pre A-level, by matriculation or conditional offers; some places offered on A-level results, school reports and interview. **Scholarships:** Unlimited number of scholarships (£100) mainly awarded on results of university examinations (approx 100 awarded for 1996/97). **Europe:** 30 students learn a language or spend time abroad. **Travel grants:** Approx 100 available each year (from £60 to £1,000). **Library:** Modern college working library; old library with antiquarian collection; separate law library. **Eating arrangements:** Choice of formal or informal meals. Fixed charge of £74 per term for meals, plus breakfast (£1.20), lunch (£1.60), dinner (£2.25). **Gate/guest hours:** None. **Other college facilities:** Theatre, concert hall, auditorium, playing fields, boathouse, squash courts, and modern public rooms. Medieval dining hall. Chapel.

Accommodation: In 1995/96, 100% of all students in college accommodation: £39 per week average, plus meals to choice at cost, term time only. No first degree students live at home. **Term time work:** College policy not to allow term time work. **Hardship funds:** Own funds, £35,000, 50% of students helped according to need. £60,000 available for overseas students prior to course, approx 10 helped.

Undergraduates: 230 men, 149 women. **Postgraduates:** 61 men 39 women. **College fees for 1996/97:** LEA grants cover college fees; undergraduates not on grants pay £2,650 in addition to university fees.

WHAT IT'S LIKE   A medium-sized college with both traditional Cambridge college buildings and more controversial 1960s architecture (New Court at the back of college a prime example). The most central college, within 5 minutes of 2 cinemas, banks, nightclubs and 14 pubs. 379 undergraduates, with a broad mix of subjects and approx equal state and public school backgrounds. Overseas students in each year from all over the world; not many mature students. Friendly and sociable place with an enthusiastic student executive despite the usual apathy. One of the best colleges academically but don't take its reputation too seriously. First and third years live in college, with second years often in college-owned hostels. Rooms vary from adequate and purely functional to almost penthouse style; and from the new King Street development to Milton's old room. Kitchens provided to give an alternative to cheap but mundane Upper Hall food. Formal hall is available every night except Saturday and makes a pleasant change. Two college bars: the Buttery (popular and friendly but only open until 8.30 except at weekends) and the Late Night Bar in New Court (small but cosy and quite lively). Party room, JCR, TV room, theatre, library, music practice rooms and squash courts are all available for students. Ents are excellent. Sports clubs (and associated drinking societies) are active and all shapes and sizes are catered for. Very successful teams in rowing, rugby and football. Christ's arguably best film society in Cambridge and drama is alive and kicking. Music socs of all types can be found here: choral, classical, contemporary etc. Student exec is always ready to support new clubs in college.

PAUPER NOTES   **Accommodation:** College provides accommodation for everyone at reasonable prices, but rents rising. **Drink:** Cheaper in college than in pubs – good selection of drinks in Buttery. The Bun Shop and Cambridge Arms are popular haunts after Buttery closes and for Sunday lunch. **Eats:** Cheap food in college, filling if you're hungry. Pizza Hut, Burger King, Mr Chips, Gardenia's and many more close by. **Ents:** Major ents twice termly and parties in Party Room most weekends. Drama, films, concerts etc all strong. Cindy's is close for tacky, crowded, cheap student nights (weekly). Route 66 has variety of music. Corn Exchange and Junction have occasional big names and a selection of jazz and blues bands. **Sports:** Free squash courts in college. Extensive sports grounds 10 minutes' cycle ride away. Boathouse nearby and well equipped. Pool, table football, table tennis etc in college. **Hardship funds:** Readily available from tutors: help with accommodation costs, books etc for those on full grants; scholarships and book grants reward academic performance. **Travel:** Travel grants easy to obtain, varying from £50 to several hundred pounds. **Work:** Hardly anyone works in term time – not encouraged by the college. Vacation work available in college (conferences etc) for the few who don't go home for vacations.

MORE INFO?   Write to CCSU President at the college.

ALUMNI (EDITORS' PICK)   General Smuts, John Milton, Charles Darwin, Lord Mountbatten, C P Snow, David Mellor, Richard Whiteley (Countdown).

CHURCHILL

**Churchill College, Cambridge CB3 0DS
(Tel 01223 336202, Fax 01223 336180)**

Founded:1960; women undergraduates first admitted 1972. **Admission:** Conditional offers: usually AAA (no S-level or STEP) for sciences; usually AAB (no S papers) for arts. Virtually all candidates interviewed. Undergraduates not admitted for education, land economy, theology. **Academic features:** Word-processing and computing courses; modern language courses for non-linguists. Churchill Archive Centre: 20th-century British history. **Europe:** 4% students learn a language as part of their course and spend 6 months or more abroad. Formal exchange links in Paris for some science and engineering students. **Travel grants:** Small long vacation travel fund. **Library:** 2 undergraduate libraries open 24 hours a day. Books in greatest demand lent for limited period only. **Eating arrangements:** Self-service breakfast, lunch and dinner; formal dinner. Vegetarian available. **Gate/guest hours:** None.

Other college facilities: Buttery, bar, theatre; extensive playing fields and tennis and squash courts within college grounds; multi-gym; boathouse (rowing); 22 PC workstations and 10 Apple Macs for student use, ethernet connections in 150 student rooms; music recital and practice rooms, visual arts studio. Late night taxi service to provide safe travel back to college at college expense.

Accommodation: In 1995/96, 100% of all students in college accommodation (modern bedsitting rooms or sets), although 4th year of new 4-year degrees may not be accommodated. 400 places available (133 for first years): £202–£440 for 10-week term (most around £320) plus meals at subsidised prices. No first degree students live at home. **Term time work:** No college policy to allow term time work (2% believed to work). Some vacation work available in college; and help with finding vac work out of college. **Hardship funds:** Own funds in 1995/96, £6,500 used to help 12 students encountering financial hardship.

Undergraduates: 304 men, 117 women. **Postgraduates:** 146 men, 71 women. **Teaching staff:** Men: 63 fellows, 15 research fellows. Women: 8 fellows, 4 research fellows. **College fees for 1996/97:** LEA grants cover college fees; undergraduates not on grants pay £2,637 in addition to university fees.

WHAT IT'S LIKE   Renowned as one of the more liberal Cambridge colleges, Churchill has a relaxed and friendly atmosphere. Students are admitted from all areas of the country; overseas students well represented and high proportion of state school students. A medium sized college so easy to fit in without getting lost in the crowd. Strong science bias but arts still alive and kicking. Founded in 1962, the modern architecture ensures that rooms are light and airy with up-to-date facilities; college attitude to students helpful and friendly – very few rules, no visiting restrictions. Dining hall serves a wide range of reasonable food (including salads and sandwiches). Kitchen between every ten or so students with adequate cooking facilites and outgoing phone. Large on-site playing fields, tennis and squash courts and a multi-gym. Easy to get involved; sports teams include football, hockey, rugby, cricket, and many more; most teams have a women's equivalent. Superb music facilities including a recital room and several practice rooms. Large air-conditioned lecture theatre-cum-cinema shows 3–5 films a week. Bar is large but can get quite crowded; free disco every Thursday night. Active SU provides Sky TV, games room and a shop. Excellent library open 24 hours caters well for most subjects; librarian very willing to fill any gaps. 4 computer rooms; computers frequently updated. Free language courses (French, German and Chinese); computing courses now available. Although over a mile from the town centre, not as isolated as many would have you believe; free taxi service back from town after dark. The guaranteed accommodation and the fact that everything is on site make up for the distance from town. Lively and sociable, Churchill makes for a very enjoyable three years.

PAUPER NOTES   **Accommodation:** All undergraduates on-site for full 3 years; flats and college-owned houses for married students. **Drink:** College bar big and popular. The Cow and Calf is local pub. **Eats:** College food vastly improved; two veggie options. Chips ad infinitum (well almost). Lots of cheap curry houses and kebab emporia in town. **Ents:** Excellent lively and very friendly bar, with free weekly disco (the Pav). 3–5 films a week. The annual Spring Ball (in February!) one of the best value in Cambridge. Numerous cocktail parties in college. Lots of ents at all the other colleges. College magazine (Winston). **Sports:** Good multigym in college. Good well-kept college pitches. Tennis, squash courts, boat club, rugby, football, hockey, American football, artificial nets. Reasonably sporty college (with the emphasis on taking part and on the post-match drinks). Chess, aerobics, canoeing, mountaineering, badminton, sailing – you name it! **Hardship funds:** Yes, but you need to be in dire straits. **Travel:** Generous travel grants, both for study and for recreation. (Only once in three years, on submission of a report.) Easy to hitch – close to M11. Rail station 4 miles, bus station 2 miles. **Work:** During term-time actively discouraged. Vac work available in college particularly over summer. But work load too great to give you much time to earn vac money whatever your subject.

ALUMNI (EDITORS' PICK)   No famous alumni as yet, but fellows are exceptionally distinguished (have been 12 Nobel prize winners).

CLARE

Clare College, Cambridge CB2 1TL
(Tel 01223 333246)

Founded: 1326; women undergraduates first admitted 1972. **Admission:** Most candidates apply during fourth term in sixth form; normally A-levels plus STEP for sciences, and A-levels alone for arts. **Scholarships:** Organ scholarship (£250 pa) every other year; an average of 7 choral and 2 instrumental exhibitions (£100 pa). **Europe:** 10% first degree students take a language as part of course and spend 6 months or more abroad. Formal exchange links (Heidelberg and Paris) open generally but some preference to linguists. **Travel grants:** Funds available at college's discretion; 3 major Parkin Grants, college travel grants, and 8 Thirkill Grants for those who have played a prominent part in college life; Mellon Fellowship for third year undergraduates who spend 2 years at Yale. **Library:** Forbes Mellon Library new building. 25,000 volumes, collection of past examination papers, law reading room. **Eating arrangements:** Self-service buttery, formal dinner in hall Mondays-Thursdays. Ticket system. **Gate/guest hours:** Porter lets college members in all night; guests not booked in overnight expected to leave by 2 am. **Other college facilities:** Music and record libraries, music room and practice rooms, computing and word-processing facilities and link to university mainframe, picture guild, pianos, harpsichord, meeting rooms, darkroom, studio and pottery room (with wheel and kiln); squash courts near college, outstanding playing fields (about 1½ miles away), rowing, punts available in summertime.

Accommodation: In 1995/96, 100% of all students in college accommodation in mixture of sets, bedsitters and hostels: £29–£32 per week, plus meals to choice, term-time only (2-room set plus all meals, £1,700 pa). No first degree students live at home. **Term time work:** No college policy to allow term time work. Vacation work available in college in library, portering, helping with conferences; ads displayed for work outside college. **Hardship funds:** Some own funds, figures not available.

Undergraduates: 230 men, 210 women. **Postgraduates:** 108 men, 61 women. **Teaching staff:** Men: 63 fellows, 3 research fellows Women: 9 fellows, 2 research fellow. **College fees for 1996/97:** LEA grants cover college fees; undergraduates not on grants pay £2,640 in addition to university fees.

WHAT IT'S LIKE   Undoubtedly one of the most beautiful colleges, complete with seventeenth century court, bridge and gardens bordering the Cam. Well placed, being very central but slightly off the Kings Parade tourist route. Lectures and shops are all within a comfortable walk/cycle. All undergraduates have the option to live in; most rooms are bedsits or sets but there are a few houses and flats. Coin-operated washing machines and driers.

Rooms are allocated by random ballot. The first year rooms are some of the best in Cambridge. Cooking facilities on the whole border on the inadequate, partly because college encourages communal eating in Buttery or Hall. Relations between the college and the students are fairly healthy. The Union of Clare Students is one of the most active in Cambridge, providing facilities, social events and representation at all levels of college life. There is an active Green Group and also a women's group which organises excellent self-defence classes, arranges for the provision of rape alarms and runs various social events. The ratio of men to women is approaching a healthy 50:50 which makes the college take women's issues seriously and the atmosphere less male dominated than a lot of Cambridge. There are around 30 college societies, in addition to all the university-wide societies. A very strong musical tradition with an excellent choir and regular recitals and concerts as well as great jazz and blues nights. Ents in Clare Cellars cater for a wide range of music tastes. Sport is equally popular; caters for everyone so, if you've never played, don't worry. The work load is heavy (as at all Cambridge college). Weekly supervisions can be intimidating but challenging and often exceptionally rewarding. A higher proportion of students from state schools than most colleges and actively committed to equal opportunities. For many subjects, a year out is recommended before coming up. Go to one of their open days to see the college for yourself.

PAUPER NOTES   **Accommodation:** Varies in quality – generally good and relatively very cheap. **Drink:** Expensive in town pubs; college bars cheaper. **Eats:** College canteen operates on credit basis – settle up at end of term. Generally pleasant, fairly cheap: vegetarian choices always available, vegans can be catered for. Plenty of pub food in town, reasonable restaurants. **Ents:** Some of best music in Cambridge esp jazz; Clare's underground cellars an excellent venue if a little sweaty. Lots of live music in pubs, particularly The Boat Race. Theatre cheap and accessible, many film screenings in and out of colleges. **Sports:** Good college/university facilitites, most free. Town facilities cheap with leisure card. **Hardship funds:** Good university-administered access funds and Clare's own available for the few in real difficulty. If you had to work then you'd surely qualify. Very few, if any, drop out on purely financial grounds. **Travel funds:** Worth asking what's available – you may be pleasantly suprised. Trips usually need to have some academic interest. **Travel:** None other than a bike necessary in Cambridge. **Work:** Paid term-time: generally not even considered, no time. Small percentage find paid vacation work locally. College doesn't recommend Christmas or Easter vac work.

ALUMNI (EDITORS' PICK)   David Attenborough (naturalist and broadcaster), Paul Mellon (philanthropist), Harvey & one of his Wallbangers, Richard Stilgoe (entertainer), James Watson (Nobel Laureate – DNA), Chris Kelly (broadcaster), Hugh Latimer (martyr), Cecil Sharp (folk songs), Siegfried Sassoon (poet), Peter Lilley MP, Matthew Parris (journalist), Norman Ramsey (Nobel Laureate).

CORPUS CHRISTI

Corpus Christi College, Cambridge CB2 1RH
(Tel 01223 338056)

Founded: 1352; women undergraduates first admitted 1983. **Admission:** Primarily based on public examination results, school report and interview. **Scholarships:** Awarded to those already in residence on the basis of academic performance. **Library:** Butler Library (working undergraduate library); Parker Library (medieval manuscripts and early books). **Travel**

grants: Considerable sums annually. **Eating arrangements:** All meals provided in hall and/or bar. **Gate/guest hours:** Entry after 11pm by key. **Other college facilities:** Extensive sports grounds; 7-acre garden with open-air swimming pool; river boathouse.

Accommodation: In 1995/96, 99% of all students in college accommodation (sets and single rooms): £200–£455 per term (mostly around £320) plus meals. No first degree students live at home. **Term time work:** No college policy to allow term time work. Some bar work in college and domestic work in vacs.

Undergraduates: 158 men, 100 women. **Postgraduates:** 81 men, 75 women. **Teaching staff:** Men: 41 fellows, 4 research fellows, 22 lecturers, 18 life fellows, 18 honorary fellows; Women: 7 fellows, 7 lecturers. **College fees for 1996/97:** LEA grants cover college fees; undergraduates not on grants pay £2,709 in addition to university fees.

WHAT IT'S LIKE   Located in the middle of Cambridge, and fighting for the title of Cambridge's smallest college; both in terms of space and numbers. The buildings comprise Old Court, one of the prettiest in the city, and the gothic New Court. Undergraduates guaranteed accommodation for length of course; all has been recently upgraded and the farthest hostel is only a third of a mile away. The rooms vary from the old and luxurious, to a very few that can be classed as pretty small. A hefty fixed kitchen charge has to be paid, whether you eat in hall or not; but the college food is good, with usually two vegetarian options, and lavish guest nights. Cheaper snacks are also available at lunchtime. The bar is one of the most popular in Cambridge and, as well as drinks, it offers occasional events and special entertainments. Free sports facilities are fifteen minutes away; squash, tennis, rugby and football pitches, and an open air pool. A particularly strong college for drama and music and all are encouraged to participate in plays, orchestra and informal concerts and recitals. The college has recently built its own theatre, as part of a new accommodation and arts facility. College library is small, but nearly all departmental libraries are close by. Undergraduates are discouraged from keeping cars. Corpus is usually near the top of the academic leagues, but pressure within college is minimal, although Cambridge has fairly high workloads generally. Most people can expect to receive some supervision within college, but to go out for others. College deals sympathetically with money problems, and has awards and prizes available. Minimal guest restrictions. The JCR is active in student politics, and the committee is easy to contact and talk to. The college is aiming to increase the proportion of women students. The college's central location puts it next to lots of pubs, and the biggest venue in Cambridge, the Corn Exchange. *Sacha Deshmukh* PAUPER NOTES   **Accommodation:** 4 college hostels; everyone guaranteed accommodation. Some rooms c £19 per week. **Drink:** Good bar and several nearby pubs. **Eats:** College food relatively expensive but good quality. Vegetarian choices. **Ents:** Good drama and music; a variety of active orchestras. **Sports:** Good college facilities; everyone encouraged to join in regardless of abilities. **Travel:** College awards travel grants, in particular the Lazard award for research in France. **Work:** Hard to get, though some available in the vac. Work available in college bar.

MORE INFO?   Write to Harriet Hughes, JCR President, at the college.

ALUMNI (EDITORS' PICK)   Christopher Marlowe, Christopher Isherwood, Sir Frederick Lawton (Lord Justice of Appeal), Lord Sieff of Brimpton (Marks & Spencer), Sir Eric Faulkner (Lloyds Bank), Mark Elder, Joe Farman (discoverer of hole in ozone layer), Christopher Booker (journalist/writer), E P Thompson (historian/nuclear disarmer).

DOWNING

Downing College, Cambridge CB2 1DQ
(Tel 01223 334800)

Founded: 1800; women undergraduates first admitted 1978. **Admission:** All offers based on school reference, interviews and A-levels or equivalent. **Scholarships:** Scholarships on performance in university exams. Organ scholarship, choral and instrumental awards every year. Substantial awards available for Downing graduates intending to train for the legal and medical professions. **Largest fields of study:** Natural sciences, law, engineering, medicine but applications welcome in all subjects. **Europe:** 7% first degree students take a language as part of course and spend 6 months or more abroad. No formal exchange links with European universities/colleges. **Travel grants:** Endowed trust funds. **Library:** Well-stocked college library. **Eating arrangements:** Undergraduates may take all meals in hall. Limited facilities provided for self-catering. **Gate/guest hours:** Gates always open. Guests not booked in overnight must leave by 1.45 am. **Other college facilities:** Coffee and reading room, auditorium, bar; 2 tennis courts and 2 squash courts in college precincts; sports ground 10 min cycle ride away; boathouse.

Accommodation: In 1995/96, 92% of all students in college accommodation: average rent £30–£50 per week, term time only. No first degree students live at home. **Term time work:** College policy does not allow term time work outside college; work available in college in library and as computer assistants. **Hardship funds:** Some funds available.

Undergraduates: 258 men, 136 women. **Postgraduates:** 125 men, 60 women. **Teaching staff:** Men: 33 fellows, 2 research fellows Women: 4 fellows, 2 research fellow. **College fees for 1996/97:** LEA grants cover college fees; undergraduates not on grants pay £2,769 in addition to university fees.

WHAT IT'S LIKE   Just off the main tourist trail through Cambridge, next door to the major science sites, and a short walk from the arts faculties. Members of Downing enthuse about the sense of space which its leafy site provides, with an outstanding range of classical style buildings. A major investment programme recently completed: a new library, accommodation block, and luxurious common room. Most undergraduates can live in good rooms on site for the duration of their course. College is strong academically in all areas, with a traditional reputation for law, medicine and natural sciences. Modern computer facilities are available. Its sporting reputation lives on, with recent victories in both men's and women's university rowing, football and rugby. The emphasis is on fun participation and there is a down-to-earth approach which keeps the friendly atmosphere and strong sense of team-spirit. Largely non-political, the JCR is very high-profile but concentrates on student welfare. A good relationship with the college authorities and representation on all relevant governing committees. The student-run bar (one of the cheapest in Cambridge) is in itself something of a tourist attraction within Cambridge, especially at the end of term. Successful May week events (guest sets by top DJs); weekly ents with a variety of styles from aspiring student DJs (Indie to Rare Groove and Breakbeat). Most desired pursuits are covered by a club or society; the music and drama societies are especially active, along with the choir, which has toured all over the world. Members of Downing get involved in a wide range of activities throughout the university, from Footlights Comedy, through drama, films and photography, to every kind of sport. But with a membership of just under 400, many people still choose to finish the evening with their friends in the late-night bar.

PAUPER NOTES **Accommodation:** Many rooms recently refurbished, some en-suite; prices in line with rest of university. **Drink:** College bar cheap and good; new range of alcoholic fruit juices and cocktails and Greene King, IPA & Abbot, hand-pulled. College wine reasonable, under £3 a bottle. Surrounded by pubs; Alma Brewery nearby for scrumpy. **Eats:** (In college) middling to good, wide choice and generous portions; vegetarian, excellent salads, baked potatoes, rolls and sandwiches; credit system. Out of college, many jacket potato, pizza (student discount), Indian and other restaurants. **Ents:** Annual June Event extremely popular university-wide. Parties, sweaty bops; bands in Corn Exchange; pub crawls. Many productions and revues in college and throughout Cambridge; good range of cheap films (college film soc, two cinemas close by). **Sports:** College sports ground some distance (but paddock in college for practices); short cycle ride to boathouse. Netball, tennis, squash courts and multi-gym within college. Uni sports centre, gym and weights free; swimming pool nearby. **Hardship funds:** Funds available; application to impartial Vice Master who considers individual cases. **Travel:** Travel grants available; some standard links with USA. **Work:** Very few get paid term-time work (other than college bar and supervising in college library), largely because of studies – there isn't the time for it. Paid vacation work tends to be nearer students' homes and restricted to summer; very few stay in college over the summer.

MORE INFO? Ring JCR President, 01223 334825.

ALUMNI (EDITORS' PICK) Sir Graham Smith (Astronomer Royal), John Cleese, F R Leavis, Lord Goodman, Prof Lord John Butterfield, Brian Redhead, Michael Winner, Mark Cox, Michael Atherton, Dr Alan Howard, Sir Peter Hall, Trevor Nunn, Thandie Newton (actress).

EMMANUEL

**Emmanuel College, Cambridge CB2 3AP
(Tel 01223 334200, Fax 01223 334426)**

Founded: 1584; women undergraduates first admitted 1979. **Admission:** Conditional offers generally 3 A grades at A-level or higher (or IB or Scottish equivalents); S or STEP papers also often required for science. Post A-level applications welcomed. **Europe:** 12% first degree students take a language as part of course and 3% spend 6 months or more abroad. **Library:** Large college library; Sancroft Library (old books) and Watson Collection (illustrated books). **Eating arrangements:** No compulsory eating arrangements. **Gate/guest hours:** No gate hours but guests must leave by 2 am (unless registered as overnight guests). **Other college facilities:** Grand piano, harpsichord and organ; 2 squash courts, table tennis room, tennis courts and open-air swimming pool in college precincts; playing fields and boat house; new Queen's Building with theatre and concert facilities.

Accommodation: In 1995/96, 100% of all students in college accommodation (first and third years in college – old or modern rooms; second years in college or college hostels): average rent £398 per term. For an average room and 3 meals daily, approx £3,008 pa. No first degree students live at home. **Term time work:** College policy not to allow term time work apart from 2 college bar managers. **Hardship funds:** Funds available to undergraduate and graduate students.

Undergraduates: 257 men, 176 women. **Postgraduates:** 96 men, 84 women. **Teaching staff:** Men: 40 fellows, 9 research fellows, 1 lecturer Women: 3 fellows, 5 research fellows.

College fees for 1996/97: LEA grants cover college fees; undergraduates not on grants pay £2,655 in addition to university fees.

WHAT IT'S LIKE   Known principally for its ducks, but also for being friendly and unpretentious. Emma has a strong college identity, due in part to the best student-run bar in Cambridge (recently refurbished). Students are drawn from a large range of backgrounds – almost 40% are women and applications from state schools are actively encouraged. Though one of the richer Cambridge colleges, this will not affect your rent bill. However, it is reflected in full undergraduate housing for three years, a commitment to tutorial teaching and an increasing provision for hardship funds. The college SU is politically and socially very active and there are a lot of well-financed clubs. It is not hard to enjoy Emma, its grounds and students.

PAUPER NOTES   **Accommodation:** All 1st and 3rd and most 2nd years in college accommodation (although self-catering facilities poor). Living out very expensive and rare. **Drink:** Beer from £1.10–£1.30 a pint in college bar. **Eats:** Compulsory fixed termly charge a bone of contention. Quality varies. Many places nearby in town. **Ents:** Ents every second week free, 2 good venues in town. Drama Society. Weekly films in new theatre, £1.50. **Sports:** Good free sportsground 15 min away by bike. Closest college to sports hall and swimming pool. **Hardship funds:** Extensive funds available via tutorial system (useful to have a good tutor). **Travel:** No travel grants. Travelling in Cambridge easy. No cars allowed. **Work:** Not encouraged during term except in college bar or library. Some services/office vacancies in vacations.

INFORMAL NAME   Emma.

ALUMNI (EDITORS' PICK)   Michael Frayn, Eldon Griffiths MP, Professor Sir Fred Hoyle, Tom King MP, Cecil Parkinson MP, Sir George Porter, Griff Rhys Jones, Graeme Garden.

FITZWILLIAM

Fitzwilliam College, Cambridge CB3 0DG
(Tel 01223 332000)

Founded: 1869; women undergraduates first admitted 1978. **Admission:** By results in public exams: conditional and unconditional offers on basis of interview and school report only. **Scholarships:** Scholarships awarded on university examinations. **Europe:** 9% first degree students taking a language as part of course spend 6 months or more abroad. No formal exchange links; modern linguists (and some law students) study at a European university. **Travel grants:** Contributions to travel costs made from Sir John Stratton Travel Fund and other college sources. **Library:** College library (open 24 hours). **Eating arrangements:** Breakfast and lunch in hall, choice of self-service and formal dinner. Small amenities charge but most meals paid for as required. Some overnight accommodation is available for guests if certain conditions satisfied. **Other college facilities:** Bar, laundry, guest rooms, music room, squash courts, playing fields near college, boathouse on river, photographic darkroom, weights room.

Accommodation: In 1995/96, 85% of all students in college accommodation, 100% of first and third years; students pay £264–£460 per term. Some students live for 1 year in privately owned accommodation, £40–£50 per week. **Hardship funds:** Small amounts (£50–£250) through the Tutors Fund and University's Bell, Abbott, and Barnes Funds and Newton Trust Bursaries.

Undergraduates: 273 men, 161 women. **Postgraduates:** 148 men, 29 women. **Teaching staff:** Men: 45 fellows, 2 research fellows, 3 lecturers. Women: 6 fellows, 3 lecturers, 2 research fellow. **College fees for 1996/97:** LEA grants cover college fees; undergraduates not on grants pay £2,784 in addition to university fees.

WHAT IT'S LIKE   It's not only Fitzwilliam's red-brick exterior that distinguishes it from the traditional Cambridge college – the diverse student intake helps too. Students from state schools make up 70% of the undergraduate population. The atmosphere is down-to-earth and friendly and there is a strong sense of community, perhaps due to the college's location slightly out of town. It is, however, still only a five-minute cycle ride into the centre, and the rest of the colleges are close enough to be able to enjoy what the university as a whole has to offer. On the social front, it is known for the biggest and best student events in town, augmented by a Christmas Ball. Clubs and societies range from martial arts to aerobics; music is well catered for with the West Cambridge Symphony Orchestra complementing the choir, the swing band, and numerous other less formal groups. Sport is extremely well provided for, with opportunities for all; three squash courts in college and the sports ground is five minutes away. Represents strongly in all the major sports, but the emphasis is on activity as relaxation with many social teams and minority sports such as volleyball, netball and basketball on offer. Accommodation is guaranteed in college for the first and final years, with roughly half of second years also living in. Corridors are divided into eight rooms, with adequate bathroom and kitchen facilities (two ring burners, some microwaves but no ovens). Current third-year rooms are palatial and trendily done out in black and red pine (each with a telephone) but correspondingly more expensive than Old Court; new Wilson Building also high standard and some rooms even ensuite. An active JCR involves itself with a wide range of issues, and an excellent welfare system provides each student with a tutor (there to help and listen in any situation, confidentially) as well as access to a women's tutor and a chaplain. Though fairly apathetic politically, attitudes in general are healthy and egalitarian. Few restrictions on visitors or overnight guests. Contraceptive, drinks and games machines can be found in the central block. All students have access to computing facilities – 486 PCs and Apple Macs. An award-winning chapel (opened in 1990) available for use by the students. Bar has two full-time bar staff and is one of the best in the university. Professional-standard cinema planned, to be run by students.

PAUPER NOTES   **Accommodation:** Few married quarters, rooms for all (if desired) with and without basins. **Drink:** College bar cheaper than pubs. **Eats:** Cafeteria good; subsidised by fixed charge. Varying standard but always a vegetarian option and salad bar. **Ents:** 2 excellent large events per term. Films, concerts; careers evenings; superhalls; Christmas revue. **Sports:** All free – athletics, basketball, badminton, chess, croquet, darts, football, hockey, rugby, martial arts, mountaineering, netball, squash, softball, tennis, volleyball. **Hardship funds:** On individual basis. **Travel:** Number of college and university awards. **Work:** No term-time employment by university regulations (bent for fundraising); some holiday jobs in college or part-time in area.

MORE INFO?   Enquiries to JCR President 01223 332088.

INFORMAL NAME   Fitz.

ALUMNI (EDITORS' PICK)   Lord St John of Fawsley, Norman Lamont, Dr A Szent-Gyorgi (Nobel prizewinner), Derek Pringle, Phil Edmonds (cricketers), Christopher Martin Jenkins (cricket commentator), President Sharma of India, Nick Clarke (Radio 4 newscaster), Dr David English (President of Methodist Conference).

GIRTON

Girton College, Cambridge CB3 0JG
(Tel 01223 338999)

Founded: 1869; men undergraduates first admitted 1979. **Academic features:** Mathematics tripos course to take account of candidates with single subject mathematics. 4 year courses in physics and in engineering. Member of group to encourage ethnic minority applications (GEEMA) and a special entry scheme for disadvantaged applicants. **Admission:** Conditional offers on A-level with some matriculation offers. Post A-level and candidates for deferred entry welcomed. **Largest fields of study:** Biological and physical sciences; engineering. **Scholarships:** Scholarships and exhibitions awarded on results of tripos examinations; organ scholarships, choral and instrumental awards. **Europe:** 8% first degree students take a language and spend a year abroad as part of their course (modern and medieval languages students). Formal exchange link with Utrecht University (for modern language students). **Travel grants:** Some available. **Library:** College library (80,000 volumes). **Eating arrangements:** No compulsory meals. Lunch arrangements with Clare, Downing and Pembroke colleges. Formal dinner in hall once a week. **Guest/gate hours:** College members must be back in college by 6 am (if without overnight exeats); guests after 10.30 pm only if accompanied by college member. **Other college facilities:** Playing fields, croquet lawns, swimming pool, cricket, soccer and rugger pitches, boathouse, tennis courts, squash court.

Accommodation: In 1996/97, 100% of students in college accommodation: £370 per term (incl heat) plus £75 kitchen fixed charge. No first degree students live at home. **Term time work:** College policy not to allow term time work. **Hardship funds:** The Buss Fund for undergraduates; The Pillman Fund for research and graduates; bursaries for overseas students.

Undergraduates: 253 men, 250 women. **Postgraduates:** 102 men, 68 women. **Teaching staff:** Men: 24 fellows, 7 research fellows, 24 lecturers, 4 professional fellows, 2 supernumerary fellows, 3 bye-fellows, 3 life fellows, 6 honorary fellows Women: 18 fellows, 4 research fellows, 17 lecturers, 3 professional fellows, 2 bye-fellows, 15 life fellows, 19 honorary fellows. **College fees for 1996/97:** LEA grants cover college fees; undergraduates not on grants pay £2,688 in addition to university fees.

WHAT IT'S LIKE   Set in pleasant, extensive grounds about 2½ miles from city centre; most find bikes essential. Friendly and relaxed atmosphere. College finds accommodation for all. Wolfson Court housing 100, is more modern and includes a new law library, reading room and computer room complex. Several college houses available, most next to college. Fixed rent for all rooms (inc college houses), regardless of size. Food quite cheap and quite good; several choices, including salads and vegetarian meals (vegan on request). No Saturday or Sunday evening meal. Self-catering facilities on each corridor and coin-operated washing machines. Good, extensive library with convenient opening hours. College societies range from subject-related to music, drama and film club; well-equipped darkroom available. Sports available on site – facilities, mostly good, for hockey, lacrosse, tennis, netball, rugby, soccer, squash, cricket, croquet. Also heated indoor swimming pool (water polo), multigym and successful rowing club. Lively bar in atmospheric college cellars with pool table, darts board, table football etc. Busy most times and cheap. Serves Abbott and Ruddles; unique barman. Party rooms, TV room; JCR hires out discotheque and organises annual event, garden party and band nights and discos. Academic standards average, but improving. Fairly easy to change subjects. Workloads realistic and despite traditional atmosphere of degrees, interesting and unpressurised. Part one (first two years) engineering and natural sciences have a heavy workload (be prepared). Friendly and relaxed atmosphere; good relations between senior and junior college members. Very mixed intake; male/female ratio nearly equal; strong overseas contingent; varied educational and home backgrounds; down-to-earth and unpretentious. No restrictions on entry into college but after midnight entrance is by front gate only (gate locked at 2 am but porter always on duty) or with security key. Key can also be used as a charge-up card: students can assign money to their key (maximum £30) for use in the canteen. All rooms, facilities, library, bar etc contained within one building. Frequent buses but not always running to timetable: approx cost 70p. JCR bikes available for students. Free taxi from town midnight Friday and Saturday nights.

PAUPER NOTES **Accommodation:** Accommodation for all undergraduates. No married quarters but houses available (rooms same rent as room in college) very near to college. **Drink:** Guinness, Ruddles, Newquay – good selection of bottled and tap beers. College bars (have to know people in other colleges to drink in their college bars) and Girton village pub. **Eats:** Best eating places in town, some on Castle Hill, thatched pub in Madingley 2 miles away serves cheap food. College meals about £1.20–£1.50, vegetarian available. **Ents:** Local bands in college bars – some more famous play in Corn Exchange (fairly expensive); film, bop, band or other ents (eg bingo, generation game) each week in college. **Sports:** Very good facilities – swimming pool on cool side. New astro-turf cricket nets. Univ sports advertised at societies fair, realistic prices. **Hardship funds:** Access funds. Pay bill in installments if negotiated (rare). **Travel:** Bikes essential. Bus frequent but not always regular. Taxi to town £4. Travel grants available for summer vacation. **Work:** Some work in college kitchens – otherwise not officially allowed during term time – temping possible in holidays.

ALUMNI (EDITORS' PICK) Arianna Stassinopoulos (writer and broadcaster), Angela Tilby (writer and TV producer), HM Queen Margarethe of Denmark, Prof Rosalyn Higgins (professor of international law, University College, London), Mrs Doris Wheatley (chairman and managing director, Cambridge Communications Ltd), Prof Dorothy Wedderburn, Joan Robinson (economics), Baroness Warnock, Professor Gillian Beer, Mrs Juliet d'A Campbell – current Mistress (Ambassador to Luxembourg), Sandi Toksvig (comedian).

GONVILLE & CAIUS

Gonville & Caius College, Cambridge CB2 1TA
(Tel 01223 332447, Fax 01223 332456, e-mail: admissions
@cai.cam.ac.uk). See also: http://www.cai.cam.ac.uk

Founded: 1348; women undergraduates first admitted 1979. **Admission:** On basis of A-level results already obtained; increasingly high proportion of places also offered to pre A-level candidates conditional on certain grades in A-level examinations. Candidates usually asked to offer 1 or 2 subjects at S-level or STEP if they wish to study maths or medicine. **Academic features:** Caius has more medical students than other colleges, and teaching fellows in every pre-clinical medical subject. Particularly strong in law and history. French and German lector in addition to modern languages teaching fellows. **Scholarships:** Unlimited scholarships and exhibitions on university examinations. **Europe:** Approx 40 students learning a language or spending time abroad. **Travel grants:** Numerous minor travel grants plus Paton-Taylor travelling scholarship for projects of an academic nature; awards from Leonard Gluckstein Memorial Fund for travel associated with historical or archaeological studies; grants from Handson Bequest for medical projects. **Library:** College library contains collection of modern books; also largest surviving medieval collection in university and various collections bequeathed by Fellows. **Eating arrangements:** Self-service breakfast and lunch; undergraduates encouraged to dine in hall as often as possible and there is minimum dining requirement. **Gate/guest hours:** No restrictions. **Other college facilities:** College boathouse and boatman; cricket pitch; sports ground and pavilion; auditorium; 2 computer centres and 3 out-stations.

Accommodation: 100% of students in college accommodation, average rent £37 per week inclusive. No first degree students live at home. **Term time work:** No college policy to allow term time work. Occasional vac work available in college library. **Hardship funds:** College bursaries, worth up to £500 and no limit to number that may be awarded (50 approx in 1995/96). Additional hardship funds available if required: sums up to £3,000 awarded in one or two cases in recent years. Overseas students eligible for overseas bursaries for maintenance or to cover fees, maximum around £3,000. No real reason any student at this college should suffer hardship.

Undergraduates: 201 men, 176 women. **Postgraduates:** 159 men, 88 women. **College fees for 1996/97:** LEA grants cover college fees; undergraduates not on grants pay £2,649 in addition to university fees.

WHAT IT'S LIKE   The main college buildings (the Old Courts) are in the centre of town, beautifully situated next to the Senate House. The buildings are attractive and ornate – pretty flower beds! Most first years live in Harvey Court (1960s halls, admired by architects), 10 minutes walk away on the Backs and next to the arts faculties and university library. 2nd years live out in college houses, allocated by ballot; ballot order is reversed to choose 3rd year rooms in the Old Courts. Gate hours not unrestricted – porters' lodge closes at 2 am but access is possible afterwards (if somewhat grudgingly given). Washing machines/irons etc are readily available (if rather antiquated) and 2–5 people share a 'gyp-room' (kitchen) which contains a fridge and cooking rings. Officially only minor cooking is allowed, as it is compulsory to eat in hall 45 times a term. All staircases are mixed. Approx 5–10% students are from overseas (more in the MCR) and special efforts made to ensure their integration into college life. Little ostentatious wealth among students – few leave without an overdraft. Relations between the administration and students are friendly and each student has a personal tutor. College SU is active and well regarded: affiliated to CUSU and NUS, it concentrates more on welfare issues than party politics. Like other Cambridge colleges, the character changes with each new intake of students but generally thought of as a tolerant and relaxed atmosphere. College bar okay; courts tend to be very sociable. Everyone knows everyone else because of the compulsory dinner system which brings the college together once a day. Some find it insular – but many current Caians are involved on a university level in various activities, including sports, rag, CUSU and all political spheres (CUCA through the Greens to Uni-left). Strong subjects are history and medicine; economics, engineering and law are also well represented. It is very easy to change subject for Part II (eg law to English, economics to SPS). Workloads vary hugely between individuals and between courses: arts subjects require self-reliance (1–2 supervisions a week, few lectures); natural sciences and medicine are much more structured. The standard of teaching is excellent, though courses are fairly theoretical and can be stuffy and restricting. College library is open 24 hours a day. Hockey is the sport at which Caius excels, and rowing is very popular, but most other sports are played at a more laid-back level. If your interest is not represented among the 40+ clubs and societies in college, it is easy to start up a new one (eg women's rugby and mixed netball recently). Debating, music, drama and rag are all thriving. The majority of students are from London/home counties: college is keen to attract more state school entrants but currently large majority independent and grammar schools. Drop-out rate approx 1 a year (from 150). Lively women's group – women prominent in college, although under 40% of student body.

PAUPER NOTES **Accommodation:** Balloted accommodation, 85% excellent (some 2nd year houses poor); reasonable rents. Married quarters. All students housed in college-owned property. Modern 1st year halls; 2nd year houses; 3rd year Old Courts. **Drink:** Bitter £1.40 pint in college bar (shuts at 10.30pm). **Eats:** College caters for all diets although dinners not great; good vegetarian restaurants and health food shops in town. **Ents:** Frequent (cheap) college bops and other events; renowned rag bops (beer £1 a pint). Thriving drama society; regular (classical) concerts, plays. Arts cinema in town is excellent; also 2 mainstream cinemas. **Sports:** Excellent sports ground with clubhouse (best in Cambridge – drinks can be bought on credit) and squash/tennis courts. Good standard. **Hardship funds:** College recognises the financial stress on students; has ever-increasing grants and bursaries and is lenient about paying bills. **Travel:** William Wade Travel Grants of £200+ each for approximately 15-20 people. Approx £6 return to London (coach). **Work:** In vacation, students not allowed to stay in accommodation (except for academic reasons); most find work closer to home.

INFORMAL NAME Caius (pronounced Keys).

MORE INFO? Ring GCSU External Officer, Emma Foulds, on 01223 332400.

ALUMNI (EDITORS' PICK) Titus Oates, David Frost, Captain Wilson, Venn (of venn diagrams), Harold Abrahams, Sir Nevill Mott (Nobel Laureate, physics), Kenneth Clarke MP, Mark Bailey (England rugby player).

HUGHES HALL

Hughes Hall, Cambridge CB1 2EW
(Tel 01223 334893, Fax 01223 311179)

Founded: 1885. **Admission:** Primarily a graduate college but also admits some mature (over 21) and affiliated students. Applicants must offer evidence of recent study and ability to work at a high standard and may be required to take a written test at interview. Undergraduates not admitted to medicine, science or modern languages. **Scholarships:** Small bursaries available. **Library:** Reading room and computing facilities. **Eating arrangements:** Cafeteria system for all meals except 2 formal dinners a week (optional). **Gate/guest hours:** None; all students have keys. **Other college facilities:** Library, sitting rooms, bar, television room, computer room. College has 2 boats and informal links with other colleges for field games and squash.

Accommodation: All undergraduates can be accommodated. Study bedrooms for 200 students; several college houses nearby; average room £47 per week. **Hardship funds:** Small fund available.

Undergraduates: 5 men, 4 women. **Postgraduates:** 144 men, 113 women. **Teaching staff:** Men: 25 fellows, 9 research fellows. Women: 9 fellows, 3 research fellows. **College fees for 1996/97:** LEA grants cover college fees; undergraduates not on grants pay £2,613 in addition to university fees.

JESUS

Jesus College, Cambridge CB5 8BL
(Tel 01223 357626, Fax 01223 339313)

Founded: 1496; women undergraduates first admitted 1979. **Admission:** By conditional offer (STEP for maths only). Post A-level candidates admitted on basis of A-levels, school reports and interviews. **Scholarships:** Foundation scholarships and exhibitions on performance in university examinations. **Europe:** 20–25% students learn a language as part of their course and 10% spend 6 months or more abroad. **Travel grants:** Available on application in Lent term. **Library:** New quincentenary library, over 30,000 volumes. **Eating arrangements:** Self-service with alternative formal Hall dinner. Each undergraduate pays kitchen fixed charge (£92.50) plus cost of meals taken. **Gate/guest hours:** Free access until 2 am. Overnight guests have to be signed in. **Other college facilities:** New computer centre, bar, common room, shop, party room, TV room, stereo-reproduction room, multi-gym, billiards room, launderette, sports fields within the college grounds, boat house.

Accommodation: 100% of students in college accommodation: range £216–£501 per term (average £345). No first degree students live at home. **Term time work:** College policy not to allow term time work. **Hardship funds:** Named funds plus college loans.

Undergraduates: 287 men, 215 women. **Postgraduates:** 93 men, 60 women. **Teaching staff:** Men: 43 fellows, 5 research fellows, 2 lectors. Women: 7 fellows, 2 research fellows, 1 lector. **College fees for 1996/97:** LEA grants cover college fees; undergraduates not on grants pay £2,673 in addition to university fees.

WHAT IT'S LIKE   Friendly, medium-sized college just off the tourist track (an advantage in summer). Only 3 minutes' walk to city centre with full range of shopping facilities. College is one of the few in Cambridge that has all its sports grounds and facilities on site giving an atmosphere of openness as well as producing a strong sporting tradition; participation is possible at all levels, including very active women's teams. Students are well-integrated from all social backgrounds and very active in university activities. Flourishing college music society and drama. 98% of students housed by the college. Rooms tend to be warm and well-furnished though not the cheapest around; about 85% have washbasins. There are a number of 3-room sets available for 3rd years; second years and some third live in college houses – literally opposite the college. Students can have a painting in their room for a year from the college art collection. Food is quite good with Formal Hall (3-course waitress served meal to which gowns must be worn) rated as one of the best in Cambridge and only £2.80. Student bar is both lively and popular; a pint of bitter is £1.50. Also a full-sized snooker table, reading room and TV room. New library and computing centre. Jesus positively encourages applications from state sector and across the board in terms of subjects; no strict quotas in operation. English and history are particular strengths, but overall well placed in the academic stakes. One of the more friendly Fellowships, always approachable and willing to listen to students and their problems.
PAUPER NOTES   **Drink:** Cheap bitter, good brands. **Sports:** Sport free on college site. **Hardship funds:** Very generous system of college grants and loans. **Travel:** Travel scholarships available.
MORE INFO?   Enquiries to President JCR (01223 339447).
ALUMNI (EDITORS' PICK) Alastair Cooke, John Biffen MP, Jacob Bronowski, Raymond Williams, Sam Brittan, Sir Peter Gadsden, Sir David Trench, S T Coleridge, Archbishop Cranmer, Sterne, Malthus, Prince Edward.

KING'S

King's College, Cambridge CB2 1ST
(Tel 01223 331100)

Founded: 1441; women undergraduates first admitted 1972. **Admission:** Great majority by conditional pre A-level offers; some places offered to post A-level applicants with high exam grades. Undergraduates not admitted for veterinary science. Encourages applicants from all backgrounds and kinds of school and, by interviewing every candidate, attempts to assess potential rather than examination performance. **Scholarships:** Choral scholarships and organ studentships awarded at entrance; academic scholarships also awarded on university examinations. **Europe:** 9% first degree students take a language as part of course and spend 6 months or more abroad. No formal exchange links with European universities/colleges. **Travel grants:** Many undergraduates awarded travel grants (about £150), usually for second year summer vacation. **Library:** 110,000 volumes; extensive music section. Record library. **Eating arrangements:** Self-service cafeteria. Standing charge covers kitchen overheads, individual meals are paid for. **Gate/guest hours:** None. **Other college facilities:** 2 bars, launderette, darkroom, arts centre, computer room, film projection room, picture loan collection, croquet garden, punts, sports grounds. No compulsory gowns or formal meals.

Accommodation: Almost all students in college accommodation (around 2% live out by choice): £252–£299 per term room only (mostly study bedrooms, some sets). No first degree students live at home. **Term time work:** College policy not to allow term time work. **Hardship funds:** General funds, as well as funds to help mature students, those with children or in non-college accommodation, 250 students helped 1995/96. Some funds available for research students prior to course.

Undergraduates: 233 men, 146 women. **Postgraduates:** 160 men, 100 women. **Teaching staff:** Men: 47 fellows, 14 research fellows, 2 lecturers. Women: 6 fellows, 6 research fellows, 3 lecturers. **College fees for 1996/97:** LEA grants cover college fees; undergraduates not on grants pay £2,613 in addition to university fees.

WHAT IT'S LIKE   King's effectively has the best of both worlds – from outside it presents the best known and most impressive exterior in Cambridge; within it's informal and relaxed. In nearly every field, social, academic, artistic – even sport at a pinch – it can hold its own (at least) with the rest of the university. It is King's breakdown of Cambridge cliché that makes it stand out – here students, staff and fellows do actually achieve some sense of community. High ratios for women, state school, mature and graduate intake, resulting in a mature and well-balanced student body: it actively welcomes and encourages applicants from all backgrounds. Minority subjects are a speciality. The student activism of the '60s and '70s that led to the tag of Red King's has left its legacy – the college offers a unique degree of student representation and involvement. The college is home to most shades of opinion and is seen as a tolerant place to be. Student hardship is taken seriously; a very sympathetic finance tutor runs workshops during freshers week (though not just for freshers) with help and advice. The college is relatively affluent and can bail people out. It also welcomes the disabled – a set of rooms specially converted for wheelchair access. It's a nice place but be prepared to work hard!
PAUPER NOTES   **Accommodation:** All undergraduates can live in. College accommodation ranges from not bad to pricey-but-good (bedroom plus sitting room for many final

years). **Drink:** College bar the only financial relief for the real drinker. **Eats:** Adequate choice in canteen, less good for vegetarians. Town tends to be either McDonalds or expensive, with lots of restaurants and one kebab shop. **Ents:** Good for films and student plays both on and off campus; music generally agreed to be naff. **Sports:** College facilities improving. **Hardship funds:** Lots and lots of lovely lolly. **Travel:** Town is compact so little need for transport. Travel abroad can be funded by college. **Work:** Lots of badly paid tourist industry work in summer, also colleges themselves are quite good. 5% or less get paid work during term (shop/pub work); many students get vacation work in their home area.
ALUMNI (EDITORS' PICK) Sir Robert Walpole, Rupert Brooke, J M Keynes, E M Forster, The King's Singers, Michael Mates MP, Salman Rushdie, Alan Turing.

LUCY CAVENDISH

Lucy Cavendish College, Lady Margaret Road, Cambridge CB3 0BU (Tel 01223 332190)

Founded: 1965 as a women's college. **Admission:** Women only. Normally 2 A-levels or equivalent recognised qualifications (incl Open University credits) and evidence of recent academic achievement. Access courses are reviewed individually. College written entrance papers and interviews. College admits mature (21 and over) women undergraduates with equal number of graduates. Supervisions in college and at other colleges by men and women. **Largest fields of study:** English, law, history, archaeology, anthropology, veterinary medicine. **Scholarships:** Supplementary awards (details available from college). **Europe:** Links with European universities/colleges through the university. **Travel grants:** Limited number of small grants. **Library:** College library (15,000 books, currently expanding). **Eating arrangements:** Lunches every day; evening meal 3 times a week. Cooking facilities for residents. **Other college facilities:** Computer facilities. Fine gardens. Exercise room.

Accommodation: 100% students offered college accommodation (most with en-suite facilities): £54 per week, plus food and fuel. **Term time work:** No college policy to allow term time work. Vac work only available in college in bar, library, waitressing, cleaning etc. **Hardship funds:** Own funds available plus some supplementary funding from charitable foundations. All candidates given details of awards for which eligible.

Undergraduates: 76 women. **Postgraduates:** 79 women. **Teaching staff:** Women: 25 fellows, 9 research fellows, 10 lecturers. **College fees for 1996/97:** LEA grants cover college fees; undergraduates not on grants pay £2,715 in addition to university fees.

WHAT IT'S LIKE   It's a unique Cambridge college in that it caters exclusively for mature female undergraduates and postgraduates. The age for entry is 21 though in practice most students are 25–55. Staff are used to coping with the particular problems of mature students and are very supportive. It has an excellent atmosphere and, being small, it is possible to know everyone. It consists of 4 old houses, one of which contains the library, and four purpose-built new buildings, one with a dining room and bar. The majority of students live in, accommodation being either study bedrooms in the older houses, shared flats in Oldham Hall, or single ensuite study bedrooms in the new buildings. It is a short walk or bicycle ride to centre of Cambridge. Lectures and teaching take place around the university, at faculty buildings and in other colleges. In all respects it is a full university college and all

the facilities of Cambridge are available for students. The workload is intense but most mature students take their work seriously and, despite family and other commitments, do well in their degrees. Food is excellent – there is always a vegetarian option and plenty of salads. Lunch available every day, with one formal and one informal dinner a week; supper is available on another 2 evenings. The Students' Association of the college is social, rather than political, and organises parties, weekly aerobic and yoga classes and links with other mature students in the university. As a small college there are few facilities for team sports but many students row, play hockey, lacrosse etc in other college teams. For many students the second chance Lucy Cavendish offers revolutionises their lives and many go on to careers in law, teaching, medicine and management in industry. PAUPER NOTES **Accommodation:** Very nice study bedrooms about £43/week including heating; some married or family accommodation. **Eats:** College food some of best in the university; vegetarian option. **Ents:** Cambridge and other colleges full of entertainment. **Sports:** Lucy Cavendish joins other colleges for most sport. **Hardship funds:** College bursaries help. **Work:** About 20% find vacation work; not usually any conflict with required vacation study.
INFORMAL NAME Lucy.

MAGDALENE

Magdalene College, Cambridge CB3 0AG
(Tel 01223 332100 (switchboard), 01223 332135 (admissions),
Fax 01223 462589)

Re-founded: 1542; women undergraduates first admitted 1988. **Admission:** Conditional offers of a fairly high standard, only very rarely involving one STEP or S-paper grade. All candidates interviewed. Further mathematics A-level not required for mathematics or engineering. **Specialist subjects:** Natural sciences, engineering, law, architecture. **Scholarships:** Choral and music awards every year, organ scholarship every second year. Generous scholarships and bursaries available in all subjects: scholarships awarded to those gaining first in tripos; at least one full-cost research scholarship each year, plus some bursaries for overseas students. **Europe:** 5% first degree students take a language as part of course and spend 6 months or more abroad. No formal exchange links with European universities/colleges. **Travel grants:** Available (including research) in all subjects. **Library:** Over 25,000 volumes; also Wigglesworth Law Library, Pepys library (including the diaries) and Old Library. **Eating arrangements:** Meals at cost (dinner £2.45), both formal and self-service facilities. **Gate/guest hours:** Gates shut 2-6 am. **Other college facilities:** Bar, film society; 2 grand pianos, harpsichord and organs; launderettes; photographic darkroom; boathouse, squash court, fives court, gym, table tennis room, 25 acres of playing fields nearby (shared); 3 computer terminals.

Accommodation: All students in college accommodation: 420 rooms in halls of residence at £30.60–£38.60 per week. No first degree students live at home. **Term time work:** No college policy to allow term time work. Vac work available (housekeeping, clerk of works). **Hardship funds:** Various special funds of moderate value exist.

Undergraduates: 201 men, 114 women. **Postgraduates:** 83 men, 42 women. **Teaching staff:** Men: 31 fellows, 7 research fellows, 18 lecturers, 1 bye-fellow. Women: 4 fellows, 2 research fellows, 1 bye-fellow. **College fees for 1996/97:** LEA grants cover college fees; undergraduates not on grants pay £2,769 in addition to university fees.

WHAT IT'S LIKE   With the longest river frontage of any college it is an extremely attractive place to read for a degree. A mixed college of about 430, it is no longer a bastion of the male public schools and now enjoys a broad cross-section of students. Sports facilities continue to be of a high quality. Rugby is traditionally strong, rowing is encouraged and good and athletics are now very strong. On the arts side, drama, journalism and music are fully catered for. Law is a particularly strength, along with engineering and architecture. The college bar is very popular and formal hall has a deservedly good reputation being candlelit, cheap and available seven nights a week. Every student is housed in above average rooms, due to large investment in property and renovation work, not least the splendid Quayside.

PAUPER NOTES   **Accommodation:** Room quality varies greatly from the very plush to store-box; all are comfortable. Due to its male heritage, there is a dearth of cooking facilities. Washing machine provision has improved and there is a laundry service. Married quarters for those merely contemplating marriage. **Drink:** Excellent bar. The Pickerel is the Magdalene pub. **Eats:** Hall is good value. Beware however of the fixed kitchen charge paid on the bill by everyone however often (or not) they eat in college. **Ents:** Limited in college; unlimited out of college. Cheap ents from barn dance to club nights. Multi-screen cinema in town. **Sports:** Facilities – excellent and free at college/university level for major field sports; free playing fields, squash, swimming and most others. **Hardship funds:** College is poor (by local standards) but helps out readily. **Travel:** Good scholarships – especially the Power Scholarship to Michigan and the Mandela Scholarship for South African students. Funds for individual travel are increasing with more endowment becoming available. **Work:** No term-time work allowed officially. During vac college employs staff to help.

ALUMNI (EDITORS' PICK)   Lord Ezra, Lord Justice Cumming-Bruce, Professor J Boardman, Sir Michael Redgrave, Lord Ramsay, Nick Estcourt, Gavin Hastings, Anthony Jay, Bamber Gascoigne, Samuel Pepys, I A Richards, Charles Kingsley, Lord Pilkington, Jonathan Ridgeon, William Burt, Viscount Melia, Lord Derby, Prince Szudek (of Poland), Rob Wainwright.

NEW HALL

New Hall, Huntingdon Road, Cambridge CB3 0DF
(Tel 01223 351721, Fax 01223 352941)

Founded: 1954, as a women's college. **Special features:** One of the newer Cambridge colleges and intends to continue to admit only women. Major collection of contemporary women's art. **Admission:** Women only. Most candidates admitted on conditional offer largely based on A-level, IB, CSYS or equivalent only, although maths candidates asked to take STEP or S-level. Low offers sometimes made to particularly strong candidates. Post A-level candidates admitted on school record and interview. Mature candidates assessed on individual basis. **Largest fields of study:** English, modern & medieval languages, natural sciences. **Scholarships:** Given to students in residence. **Europe:** 10% first degree students take a language and spend 6 months or more abroad as part of course. No formal exchange links but participates in European exchange schemes. Students may study a language (for certificate or diploma); language options in English and History tripos; engineering students encouraged to learn a language. **Travel grants:** Awarded annually. **Academic facilities:** Library, computer facilities with links to university computer. **Eating arrangements:** Cafeteria system (pay as you eat), formal meals and self-catering, including vegetarian (special arrangements for particular requirements). **Gate/guest hours:** None. **Other college facilities:** 2 lecture rooms with projector, party room, bar, art studio, sewing room, darkroom, video room, squash court, tennis courts and croquet lawn; sports ground shared with Fitzwilliam and Churchill.

Accommodation: College accommodation available for all students: £33.50–£38.80 per week (£25.10 shared) with kitchen facilities or normal Hall. No first degree students live at home. **Term time work:** No college policy to allow term time work (under 1% believed to work). Vacation work available in college kitchen, housekeeping etc; college supportive in finding vac work out of college. **Hardship funds:** Funds available for special help to those with children, self-financing, low-income backgrounds, overseas students.

Undergraduates: 325 women. **Postgraduates:** 59 women. **Teaching staff:** Men: 17 Fellows, 10 lecturers, 1 appointed supervisor, 6 external directors of studies Women: 25 Fellows, 14 lecturers, 4 appointed supervisors, 4 external director of studies. **College fees for 1996/97:** LEA grants cover college fees; undergraduates not on grants pay £2,763 in addition to university fees.

WHAT IT'S LIKE   All-women's colleges are fast becoming a rarity; but New Hall is a thriving college. There are numerous societies, including many successful sports clubs, and many students belong to university societies and sports teams. There is an effective welfare system and student/Fellow relationships are good. A dynamic and enthusiastic ents committee provides regular events in college. It manages to avoid the insularity of many other Cambridge colleges; intercollegiate relationships are excellent ensuring many opportunities for socialising outside college. Students are fortunate in having 24 hour facilities including library, laundry, computer rooms (and centrally located chocolate and icecream machines!). Cafeteria food is varied and wholesome and there are kitchens throughout the college if you prefer to cook for yourself. Accommodation provided for all students; new buildings offer high quality, ensuite accommodation. The college offers all tripos subjects and will arrange supervisors from outside college who are specialists in particular subjects.

PAUPER NOTES   **Accommodation:** College or hostel accommodation for all students. **Drink:** College bar very cheap; happy hour once a week. **Eats:** Cafeteria system (meal costs £1–£1.50 average). Excellent vegetarian selection. Formal hall with waitress service on Tuesday evening (plus 2 Fridays a term). No breakfast provided. 24-hour garage right opposite college. Large selection of restaurants in town. **Ents:** Discos/events regularly; developing reputation for large-scale events. Bar being revamped. **Sports:** Squash court, 2 tennis courts, large boat club. Most sports represented by college teams. **Hardship funds:** Available. **Travel:** Travel grants and vacation study grants available. **Work:** Not allowed during term. 5-10% get local vacation work, 50% get holiday work elsewhere.

MORE INFO?   Write to JCR President.

ALUMNI (EDITORS' PICK)   Tilda Swinton (film star), Joanna MacGregor (concert pianist), Sonia Ruseler (TV news presenter), Sue Perkins (comedienne).

CAN'T FIND WHAT YOU'RE LOOKING FOR? USE THE INDEX!

NEWNHAM

Newnham College, Cambridge CB3 9DF (Tel 01223
335700, Fax 01223 357898, http://www.newn.cam.ac.uk)

Founded: 1871, as a women's college. **Admission:** Women only. Mainly on A-level grades and interviews, with little use of S-papers or STEP. **Scholarships:** Scholarships and prizes awarded on results of university exams. **Academic features:** All university subjects offered. **Europe:** 15% first degree students take a language as part of course and 10% spend 6 months or more abroad. Formal exchange links with large number of universities/colleges. **Library:** 85,000 volumes, large antiquarian collection, networked to database search facilities. **Travel and book grants:** Generous funds available. **Eating arrangements:** Modern dining room for cafeteria service, and hall for formal dinners. All meals paid for in cash or debit to college bill. Guests welcomed. Good self-catering facilities. **Gate/guest hours:** No restrictions. **Other college facilities:** Two large computer centres (fully equipped and networked); bar, undergraduate kitchens; washing machines; music room with piano and harpsichord; practice rooms with pianos; multi-gym, playing fields and tennis courts in large college grounds; nearby squash court; punt hire scheme in summer.

Accommodation: College accommodation available on site for all undergraduates: £470 for 10-week term includes heating, kitchen facilities and element towards subsidised food. **Term time work:** College policy to allow term time work (5% or less believed to work); limited to 3–6 hours per week, depending on type of work. Term (and vac) work available in college in bar, waitressing, library and with admissions interviews; help in getting work outside college only if relevant to course eg engineering. **Hardship funds:** Funds including travel and book grants (£14,000 in 1995/96) and hardship funds (some £2,000+). Many are specific bequests eg Isaac Newton Trust for those on full maintenance grants; from 1996, college will provide room bursaries and 15 extra college bursaries of £250 each; others for engineering, maths, mature students, students from India etc.

Undergraduates: 414 women. **Postgraduates:** 128 women. **Teaching staff:** Women: 45 fellows. Men and women: 18 college lecturers and directors of studies, 10 research fellows, 4 special supervisors. **College fees for 1996/97:** LEA grants cover college fees; undergraduates not on grants pay £2,757 in addition to university fees.

WHAT IT'S LIKE   Established in 1871 specifically for the education of women, it successfully combines the tradition of Cambridge with a modern and forward way of thinking. The ivy-clad red brick Victorian buildings surround some of the largest and arguably most beautiful gardens in Cambridge. A setting conducive to both work and play. Academically very strong; as the fight against women's under-achievement in Cambridge continues, Newnham is proud to be in the top half of the college league table. This strength stretches across all the disciplines but most notably in biological sciences, English and law. Similarly thriving are the wide range of leisure activities. Sports are consistently of a high standard and with the (unusual) advantage of playing fields and tennis/netball courts on-site. Boathouse shared with Jesus. Raleigh Music Society co-ordinates orchestral and choral ensembles of varying sizes for popular performances throughout the year. And theatrical interest is catered for by the Anonymous Players, who are very active in Cambridge. Other college societies include art, astronomy, photography, journalism, women's group, environment group, computing ... College actively promotes opportunities for all, proved by the equal state/independent school mix and high overseas student intake. Grants, funds and bursaries

are widely available for expenses such as travel and books and the college is generous to students with financial difficulties. The college library is one of the largest in Cambridge and the with a second computer room, the computer facilities are plentiful and high quality. The buttery serves a wide variety of good food, with vegetarian and salad bar options every meal. Self-catering is always an option as the kitchens (one for every 8–10 students) are all well equipped. Laundry facilities are also very good. No college bedders, so greater privacy. Security standards are high though rules are lenient; gate hours do not exist and guests are always allowed. Newnhamites socialise both in and out of college. The new bar is the centre for college ents and weekly formal halls attract many visitors. Diversity of Newnham and Newnhamites ensures that all students are able to find their niche.
Laura Pugsley

PAUPER NOTES **Accommodation:** Live in all 3 years, but possible to live out. **Drink:** Cheap college bars (especially Newnham). Many town pubs – The Bath, The Anchor, The Fountain, The Granta. **Eats:** Sweeney Todd's, The India House, both close. In town, The Bun Shop (great paella), Tatties, Nadia's (best cakes). **Ents:** Diverse and inexpensive college ents – John's and Queens' film societies are best. Nightclubs – Route 66, 5th Avenue. Anything and everything is here. **Sports:** At Newnham – free multi-gym; hockey/football/lacrosse pitch, netball/tennis courts, shared squash courts. Kelsey Kerridge sports hall and swimming pool. **Hardship funds:** Lots – college and university. Access grants; books, vacation grants. **Travel:** Many travel grants available from college and university. **Work:** Catering department and college bar for work in term time. Catering dept, housekeeping, library in vacation.

MORE INFO? Get University Alternative Prospectus.

ALUMNI (EDITORS' PICK) Baroness Seer, Baroness David, Julia Neuberger, Frances Gumley, Sarah Rowland Jones, Dorothy Hodgkin, Margaret Drabble, AS Byatt, Germaine Greer, Sylvia Plath, Joan Bakewell, Susie Menkes, Miriam Margolis, Katharine Whitehorn, Shirley Williams, Emma Thompson, Ann Mallalieu, Mary Archer, Anne Campbell MP.

PEMBROKE

Pembroke College, Cambridge CB2 1RF
(Tel 01223 338100)

Founded: 1347. Women undergraduates first admitted 1984. **Admission:** Applications for admission on A-level or equivalent results or by conditional offer. **Scholarships:** College and Foundation scholarships, exhibitions and prizes awarded for merit in university examinations. **Europe:** 15% first degree students take a language as part of course and 8% spend 6 months or more abroad. No formal exchange links with European universities/colleges. **Travel grants:** Grants towards cost of vacation travel for suitable projects, and to graduate students for research visits. **Library:** Reading and borrowing facilities in all degree subjects. Word processing and computing rooms, linked to CU data network and Internet. **Eating arrangements:** Self-service breakfast, lunch and evening meal. Formal dinner. Fixed charge (1996/97) of £261 pa; in addition meals are paid for as taken (eg dinner £3.25). **Gate/guest hours:** Gates closed 2 till 6 am, but access for keyholders. Overnight guests permitted by prior arrangement; other guests leave by 2 am. **Other college facilities:** Sports (cricket, hockey, rowing, rugby, soccer, squash, netball, tennis, table tennis), music (rehearsal rooms, pianos, organ, instrumental awards scheme), drama room, photographic darkroom, junior parlour, bar, party cellar, extensive gardens.

Accommodation: All students in college or nearby college hostels, some 2-roomed sets but mainly single study bedrooms, centrally heated with wash basins (many rooms have telephone and computer sockets): rents £285–£570 per term (average £365). No first degree students live at home. **Term time work:** College policy not to allow term time work. **Hardship funds:** Some assistance may be given from trust funds.

Undergraduates: 234 men, 153 women. **Postgraduates:** 120 men, 68 women. **Teaching staff:** Men: 43 fellows, 10 research fellows Women: 7 fellows, 3 research fellows. **College fees for 1996/97:** LEA grants cover college fees; undergraduates not on grants pay £2,760 in addition to university fees.

WHAT IT'S LIKE   Medieval courtyard, architecture pleasant and homely, beautiful gardens; very central and well located for most subjects. College accommodation for all 1st years. In total 45% live in college and new building (1997) will add rooms for 90 students; others live in nearby college-owned hostels. Standard variable but on the whole good; rents vary from very low to high for the very good rooms. Friendly porters, bedders and housekeeping staff. No provision for married students. Food available on a cafeteria basis; breakfast good, lunch and supper dull though an alternative waitress-service dinner (formal Hall) each night is better. Cooking facilities are limited. JP (Junior Parlour – College SU) active socially rather than politically. Relations with college authorities and teaching staff very friendly; joint JP/college committee, numerous fellow/student contacts both academic and social. Progressive admissions tutors, who welcome applications from all backgrounds/ethnic groups; 10% from overseas. Undergraduates are outgoing, very friendly and going places. Bike necessary but it will be pinched. Fine college library, bar, soundproof music rooms, video room, party rooms, computer rooms, college catered private functions and a large sports ground. Sport is strong, especially rowing, cricket and rugby. Opportunities are also plentiful in the arts, notably drama and music. Strong subjects: natural science, English, economics, engineering, SPS, anthropology – a nice mix. Changing subject fairly easy. A happy, friendly community, easy going in every way.

PAUPER NOTES   **Accommodation:** Everyone in relatively cheap college rooms or college hostels. **Drink:** Excellent cheap bar with very friendly barman. Well sited for many local pubs – Mill, Anchor, Eagle. **Eats:** Sainsbury's nearby and local market (good for fruit). Cheap restaurants nearby (McDonalds, Pizza Hut). Cafeteria known as trough (enough said but food improving). Reciprocal arrangements with other colleges, particularly Girton where food excellent and cheaper. **Ents:** Regular college bops, karaoke and Event (cheaper version of a May Ball and, they say, more fun); free video room for hire. Regular cheap films and ents at other nearby colleges. Much cheap and often good student theatre and close to Arts Theatre. Weekly university-wide student night at local nightclub. Strong connections with Footlights comedy. **Sports:** Wide range of facilities – own boathouse; football/rugby/cricket grounds, squash and tennis courts; multigym in new building and university gym free. **Hardship funds:** Isaac Newton Trust awards to those on full grant; other hardship funds and many bursaries. Access funds well organised. Financial pressures as anywhere else but many safety valves, fair rents, etc. **Travel:** Number of travel awards – easy to get one. **Work:** Pembroke library supervision, £1/hour to sit and study; various jobs in vacations.

MORE INFO?   Enquiries to JP President (leave message) on 01223 338110 or e-mail jp@pem.cam.ac.uk.

ALUMNI (EDITORS' PICK)   R Porter, Peter May, Ted Hughes, Tom Sharpe, Christopher Hogwood, Clive James, Peter Cook, Eric Idle, Bill Oddie, Tim Brooke-Taylor, Ray Dolby, R A Butler, David Monroe, William Pitt, Thomas Gray, Edmund Spenser, Sir Robert Sainsbury, Lord Prior, Lord Chief Justice Taylor.

PETERHOUSE

Peterhouse, Cambridge CB2 1RD (Tel 01223 338200)
Admissions Tutor (01223 338273)
Admissions Secretary (01223 338223)

Founded: 1284; women undergraduates first admitted 1985. **Admission:** Flexible admissions policy. Realistic level of offers, with low ratio of offers to places. All candidates interviewed: mode of admission tailored to individual cases. No undergraduates admitted for geography, land economy or veterinary medicine. **Largest fields of study:** History, natural sciences, engineering. **Scholarships:** Examination, prizes, scholarships and exhibitions (£50 to £150) for performance in tripos; annual organ scholarship (£250); music awards (£50 plus tuition); further named college examination prizes in many subjects. **Europe:** 3% first degree students take a language as part of course and 2% spend 6 months or more abroad. Participates in the university exchange with the universities of Poitiers and Utrecht. **Travel grants:** Approx 30 pa travel grants awarded (average value £200). **Library:** Approx 40,000 volumes. **Eating arrangements:** All meals provided in hall (breakfast £1.14 or £1.69, lunch £1.85, dinner £2.30). **Gate/guest hours:** Gates close at 2 am, when guests, other than overnight guests, required to leave; gate keys issued for out-of-hours use. **Other college facilities:** Bar, croquet lawns, squash court, multi-gym, computer room, punts, washing machines, playing fields, boathouse. New library, theatre and concert hall.

Accommodation: All students in college-owned accommodation (first and third years in college, second years next door): £314 per term average (range £151–£476). No first degree students live at home. **Term time work:** No college policy to allow term time work (1% believed to work). Some term time work available in college as library assistants. **Hardship funds:** Fund administered by tutors. Help given to any student suffering financial hardship.

Undergraduates: 185 men, 66 women. **Postgraduates:** 63 men, 25 women. **Teaching staff:** Men: 31 fellows, 8 research fellows, 3 bye-fellows. Women: 3 fellows, 2 research fellows. **College fees for 1996/97:** LEA grants cover college fees; undergraduates not on grants pay £2,607 in addition to university fees.

WHAT IT'S LIKE   Peterhouse has a lively and friendly student community. The oldest and smallest Cambridge college and, as such, provides an excellent launch-pad to university life. Peterhouse students do not conform to the most common Oxbridge stereotypes. The college authorities do not believe in positive discrimination assuring the diversity of the student body. If they think you are bright enough they'll offer you a place, regardless of your ethnic, social or religious background. No pretensions (or desires) to be at the intellectual cutting edge of Cambridge, and languishes in glorious anonymity in the middle of the academic table. However, Peterhouse students perform consistently well in certain subject areas, most notably history and law. Accommodation is of a reasonable standard and undergraduates are provided with rooms for all three years at relatively inexpensive rents. All meals take place in the college's thirteenth-century hall. Food varies from being curious to identifiable, but standards are improving, particularly for vegetarians. Basic JCR services include a small but fun bar, a common room with television, video and daily newspapers, a pool room and a launderette. A new computer room offers state-of-the-art word processing equipment for student use. A recently acquired college punt has proved very popular. Own boat club and is steadily improving its stature in college rowing. Sports ground shared with Clare College which boasts two football pitches, a rugby pitch and an all-weather tennis court. There is a well-equipped multi-gym in college. Above all else, Peterhouse is a happy and tolerant college where it is far from difficult to get involved and make a mark. Apathy (be it political or social) can sometimes be a problem, but the college is very much on the up. Comfortable and unpretentious, Peterhouse is a great place to spend your university career.

PAUPER NOTES   **Accommodation:** Some shared same-sex sets and married quarters for graduates only. **Drink:** College bar is loud and cheap. Ace local pubs The Cross Keys and The Mill. **Eats:** Cambridge is expensive but there are some cheap spots – Curry Centre and The Little Rose. **Ents:** Film society, bops, bands, bar and pool room. Occasional plays in college theatre. **Sports:** Kelsey Kerridge Sports Hall is a cheap supplement to college facilities. **Hardship funds:** Access funds are available and widely advertised. **Travel:** Excellent travel grants, usually around £200 but can be £300. **Work:** Vacation grants for work in college over the holidays.

QUEENS'

Queens' College, Cambridge CB3 9ET
(Tel 01223 335540, Fax 01223 335522)

Founded: 1446; women undergraduates first admitted 1980. **Admission:** Entry in all subjects is via conditional offers based on A-levels. For mathematics, medicine and natural sciences, S-levels or STEP may be used according to candidate's choice. All candidates interviewed. Several open days each year for prospective candidates. **Scholarships:** Not awarded on entrance but on subsequent university examinations. Bursaries available for eligible students. **Travel grants:** Awards made from college expedition fund and other funds as well as grants to individuals. **Europe:** 16 students learn a language and spend time abroad. **Library:** Undergraduate library with copies of all course books; full borrowing facilities both in term and over vacation. Law library. Computer suite with micro-computers and access to university main frame and Internet. **Eating arrangements:** Self-service for all meals; formal dinner also available. **Gate/guest hours:** Very relaxed. **Other college facilities:** Bar, 220-seat theatre, squash courts, table tennis, croquet, punts, organ, piano, harpsichord, record library, dark room, launderette, rooms for TV, college nursery; boathouse and playing fields nearby.

Accommodation: All students in college accommodation (sets and bedsits, medieval and modern): £330 per term average (range £290–£385). No first degree students live at home. **Term time work:** College policy does not normally allow term time work (3% believed to work). Term (and vac) work available in college in bars and library. **Hardship funds:** Several funds to help those who suffer financial difficulty.

Undergraduates: 292 men, 170 women. **Postgraduates:** 171 men, 90 women. **Teaching staff:** Men: 38 fellows (2 research fellows, 36 lecturers). Women: 6 fellows, (1 research fellow, 5 lecturers). **College fees for 1996/97:** LEA grants cover college fees; undergraduates not on grants pay £2,727 in addition to university fees.

WHAT IT'S LIKE   It's a centrally located college containing over 450 undergraduates and 250 graduates from a good mixture of backgrounds. For Oxbridge it has a high proportion of state school entrants, female students (2:1 male:female) and overseas students.

Academically the college performs consistently well (usually featuring in the top 3), but the students are bright rather than self-consciously intellectual. The strength of the college lies in its balance between work and the more social side of college life. There is a down-to-earth, friendly atmosphere; a well-established contact scheme introduces freshers to other members of college. This includes third years and graduates as well as second years. The college is socially very active with numerous clubs and societies. There is always plenty happening around college; the college theatrical and musical societies are amongst the most renowned in Cambridge. The sports clubs do very well and most sports are represented. The facilities are second to none: newly built multi-purpose hall has created one of the best theatre, cinema and disco locations in Cambridge. Also on site are three music rooms, an excellent multigym, 3 squash courts and a badminton court. The college straddles the River Cam and is famous for the misnamed Mathematical Bridge. The banks of the river provide an excellent site for work, play or simple relaxation. Punting (college has its own punts) is also plenty of fun. Accommodation is offered on site to all undergraduates for a minimum of 3 years. This provides for a friendly atmosphere, good relations between the years, and also helps the finances. Accommodation tends to be either beautiful or have good facilities, though not usually both. Rooms are on the whole large but self-catering is discouraged and difficult (though by no means impossible); this is to try and encourage eating together, again adding to the friendly atmostphere. The best way to judge the atmosphere of the college is to attend an open day. If possible come and have a look around and see for yourself why this is now the most popular college in Cambridge.
PAUPER NOTES **Accommodation:** Accommodation for all students, rents still fairly reasonable. No married quarters; mixed sharing allowed in sets with 2 bedrooms. College crèche. **Drink:** Local brews: Greene King, Tolly Cobbold. Bar relatively cheap – pubs in town varied. **Eats:** Town: wide variety from Pizza Hut to high-class dining clubs. Erainas, great Greek restaurant, good for large parties, cheap; India House, excellent curry just round the corner; Gardenia's late night 'munchies' haven, heavenly chips, kebabs and much more. College: standard high – increasingly varied options, caters for vegetarians – attempts some more ethnic options. **Ents:** The most happening college – 2 discos most weekends, plus live bands, plays, concerts and busy bar. Also 2 films per week in college cinema. Town: 2 large clubs and the gig venues – Corn Exchange and The Junction. Tuesday night at 5th Avenue night club, £2 for students, run by CUSU. **Sports:** Cheap/good sports centre 10 min walk. On college site: squash, badminton, multi-gym, table tennis – sports ground 1½ miles. All major sports (even Tiddlywinks – European championships held in old hall!); strengths – rugby, football, rowing, squash and basketball. Open-air swimming pool nearby. **Hardship funds:** College very accommodating – quiet word to tutor goes a long way. College Appeal resulting in more hardship funds. **Travel:** STA Travel in town very cheap; college gives limited grants and travel scholarships each year. **Work:** Term-time: not allowed unless in college bar; some bar work/guided punting in summer – work during May Balls. A few work locally. Are financial pressures but probably less than elsewhere – and college would probably find funds.
MORE INFO? Enquiries to JCR President, Kate Grange (01223 335567).
ALUMNI (EDITORS' PICK) Archbishop of Sydney, Stephen Fry, Erasmus, Graham Swift, T H White, Mike Foales (first Briton in space).

HOW TO START? *SEE SHORTLISTING*, PAGE 535

ROBINSON

Robinson College, Cambridge CB3 9AN
(Tel 01223 339143, Fax 01223 464806)

Founded: 1977 as first college for men and women (undergraduates admitted from 1979). **Admission:** Offers made on basis of interview and A-levels or equivalent, tailored to individual candidates. Some matriculation offers. No particular entry route preferred; STEP not generally required. **Scholarships:** Awarded on examination results. Scholarships to Hong Kong and Thailand; organ and choral scholarships; named subject prizes and scholarships. **Europe:** 10% first degree students take a language as part of course and 6% spend 6 months or more abroad. Formal exchange programme with universities in France, Netherlands, Germany and Israel. **Library:** Extensive college library and separate law library. **Eating arrangements:** Both cafeteria and formal hall; residents required to pay fixed kitchen charge. **Gate/guest hours:** No gate hours; guest rooms available. **Other college facilities:** Cafeteria, computer room, access to university network available in most rooms, bar, music rooms, party room, dark room, TV room, theatre, auditorium; Frobenius organ, harpsichord, joint sports ground with Queens'; boathouse shared with Downing, squash and tennis courts, extensive gardens.

Accommodation: All students can be accommodated in college accommodation: £1,140 per year average (range £639–£1,467). No first degree students live at home. **Term time work:** No college policy to allow term time work (very few do work). Vac work available in college in housekeeping, catering and in departments. **Hardship funds:** Financial assistance fund and bursaries available and book and travel grants.

Undergraduates: 245 men, 141 women. **Postgraduates:** 92 men, 38 women. **Teaching staff:** Men: 39 fellows, 4 research fellows Women: 11 fellows, 4 research fellows. **College fees for 1996/97:** LEA grants cover college fees; undergraduates not on grants pay £2,742 in addition to university fees.

WHAT IT'S LIKE   Robinson sees itself as something much needed to bring Cambridge into the 20th century. Its youth, relative to its more illustrious neighbours, is no disadvantage and its students have a growing reputation in the university. Unlike most new colleges, it has genuinely attractive buildings in large landscaped gardens of exceptional beauty. As a result everyone lives and works together on one site (unlike other sprawling colleges), giving it a friendly and close-knit atmosphere. The college supplements its income by acting as a conference centre out of term. This means that students also benefit by living in comfortable, centrally-heated rooms most with ensuite bathrooms. Other facilities are, frankly, superb. The bar is big, friendly and funky with long opening hours. The cafeteria offers a good choice and is affordable. Twice weekly Hall is also exceptional and self-catering is made easy by convenient, fully-fitted kitchens (about six people to each kitchen). Conferences also mean that an embarrassingly long list of facilities are available (theatre, 2 auditoriums, record library, darkroom, gym and JCR). Students tend to be more out-going and active than the Cambridge norm. Students' Association happily distributes funds for almost any interest and has full financial control of its affairs (again unusual in Cambridge). Most notable is thriving ents scene, ranging from high-quality drama and live music to sophisticated club-nights, which shames the usual school-disco Cambridge night life. Robinson is lively, groovy and comfortable.
PAUPER NOTES   **Accommodation:** Outstanding mid-range pricing policy for rents, majority ensuite. All years accommodated by college. **Drink:** Bar excellent, but pricey relative

to most student bars – open at lunchtimes as well as evenings. **Eats:** Good variety, not cheap (but always a nutritious economy meal offered). Hall (twice weekly) brilliant; good bar food too; vegetarian food improving fast. **Ents:** Packed programme in drama and ents eg discos, bops (cheap), films (popular); great reputation. **Sports:** Boathouse, sports ground, squash and tennis courts, gym, croquet lawn. All facilities are free. **Hardship funds:** Well provided for but problems growing fast. Generous book grants. Financial tutor available. **Travel:** Good college grants for academic-related travel, less good for other travel; many benefit from university grants. **Work:** No termly work allowed; college employs many students each vac, good wage and free accommodation.

MORE INFO?   Ring James Gordon-MacIntosh (01223 249021).

ST CATHARINE'S

St Catharine's College, Cambridge CB2 1RL
(Tel 01223 338300)

Founded: 1473; women undergraduates first admitted 1979. **Admission:** Conditional offers on A-level results, and rarely also on S-level or STEP examinations. **Europe:** 8% first degree students take a language as part of course and spend 6 months or more abroad. Formal exchange links with Heidelberg (open to all undergraduates). **Travel grants:** Various grants available. **Library:** 2 college libraries. **Eating arrangements:** All meals available in college dining hall. No compulsory meals. **Gate/guest hours:** Keys issued on payment of deposit; guest rooms for limited periods. **Other college facilities:** Large new 3 manual organ, music practice room with grand piano; sports field with pavilion, squash, badminton, and tennis courts; boathouse; computer facilities; graduate common room.

Accommodation: All students in college accommodation: £230–£451 per term. No first degree students live at home. **Term time work:** No college policy to allow term time work. **Hardship funds:** Various funds available.

Undergraduates: 269 men, 153 women. **Postgraduates:** 98 men, 42 women. **Teaching staff:** Men: 40 fellows, 13 research fellows Women: 4 fellows. **College fees for 1996/97:** LEA grants cover college fees; undergraduates not on grants pay £2,691 in addition to university fees.

WHAT IT'S LIKE   It's not the biggest, the smallest, the prettiest or the wealthiest but, as superlatives go, St Catharine's (Catz) is considered by many to be the friendliest college in Cambridge. And it's true. It lies smack bang in the middle of Cambridge, within easy walking distance of university departments, pubs and shops. Students are drawn from a wide range of social, geographical and educational backgrounds and there is a healthy balance between the sexes, making for a genuine community spirit within the college. All first and third years live in college rooms which vary from big and old to small and modern – many of the latter with private bathrooms. All second years live in college-owned flats about 10 minutes' walk from the main site. Students successfully juggle work commitments with other pursuits – sport is especially popular and provides a chance to have a laugh and make friends as well as keep fit. There is a very popular wine society, while the Catz-based Shirley Society is the oldest literary group in Cambridge (recent speakers include Jeremy Paxman and Stephen Fry). Social life centres upon the bar, which is one of the biggest in Cambridge and attracts a lot of students from other colleges. In short, Catz is incredibly relaxed and easy to enjoy. If you are bewildered by the sheer number of colleges and are looking for somewhere unpretentious and unintimidating, then look no further: you have found it.

PAUPER NOTES   Accommodation: All live in college rooms or flats. **Drink:** A number of good pubs (The Mill being the closest) but tend to be quite expensive – college bars cheaper. **Eats:** College: good choice including vegetarian options, average quality; formal hall is good value. Town: good sandwich shops, fast food outlets; restaurants fairly expensive. **Ents:** Very good for films and plays, not so good for nightclubs; college ents committees arrange regular bops. New nightclub, Punhnahs, and The Junction is good. **Sports:** Superb college facilities 10 mins walk (include rugby, football, tennis, cricket, squash and new astroturf hockey pitch – only a swimming pool is missing). Very strong in university sports. Good discounts on city facilities with Cityleisure Card (£1); otherwise expensive. **Hardship funds:** Students have to be very definitely in need. **Travel:** Most students get summer travel bursaries but there's not much cash to go round. **Work:** Very few students get paid work during term – officially not allowed. College has work during (summer) conference season; many seasonal jobs in Cambridge tourist industry.

MORE INFO?   Write to Alison Merifield, at the college.

ALUMNI (EDITORS' PICK) Howard Brenton (controversial playwright), Sir Ian McKellen, Steve Punt (Mary Whitehouse Experience), Jeremy Paxman, Allan Green, Richard Dodds.

ST EDMUND'S

**St Edmund's College, Cambridge CB3 0BN
(Tel 01223 336250)**

Founded: 1896; in 1965 became a graduate college and gained approved foundation status in 1975. **Admission:** Primarily a graduate college but also admits some mature and affiliated undergraduates (21 and over) for any subject. **College facilities:** Micro-computing facilities (terminal to university mainframe); bar; football pitch, tennis courts, croquet lawn, boat club.

Accommodation: In 1995/96, 50% of all students in college accommodation: £36–£48 per week. 6 apartments for married students with children. Students may live in privately owned accommodation: rents £45–£55 per week for self-catering, £40–£60 for B&B, £45–£55 half-board. **Term time work:** No policy on term time work. Very small amount of term (and vac) work available in college library and computing facility.

Undergraduates: 50 (men and women). **Postgraduates**: 170 (men and women). **Teaching staff:** Men: 24 fellows, 5 research fellows, 12 lecturers, 2 professors, 4 senior research fellows, 4 university executive fellows. Women: 3 fellows, 2 research fellows, 1 university executive fellow. **College fees for 1996/97:** LEA grants cover college fees; undergraduates not on grants pay £2,724 in addition to university fees (postgraduates £1,683).

ST JOHN'S

St John's College, Cambridge CB2 1TP
(Tel 01223 338600)

Founded: 1511; women undergraduates first admitted 1981. **Admission:** Candidates are welcome to apply for conditional offers (which may include STEP or S-grades for science subjects) or on the basis of A-levels already taken. **Scholarships:** Scholarships awarded to members of the college on the basis of examinations. Scholars receive generous book grants and other privileges. **Europe:** 40 students learn a language and spend time abroad. **Travel and other grants:** Travel grants available to all undergraduates for course-related travel. All receive book grants and financial help with extra-curricular expenses. **Library:** New college library (plus early 17th century Old Library) with over 100,000 volumes, ranging from medieval manuscripts to modern university textbooks; full set of Law Reports; skeletons for medical students. **Eating arrangements:** Self-service buttery dining room; formal dinner also available 6 evenings a week. **Gate/guest hours:** College members may come and go as they wish; certain regulations regarding overnight guests. **Other college facilities:** Bar, college orchestra, 2 choirs and musical society, theatre in School of Pythagoras; badminton court, multi-gym, disco cellar; music practice rooms, art studio, drawing office and large auditorium; film society; 26-acre playing fields near college; modern squash courts, table tennis and billiards rooms, pool for college punts. Computer room (30 workstations, scanners, laser printers, CD-Rom) with data links to university network.

Accommodation: All students in college accommodation: £408.32–£466.18 per term (£347.51 each if sharing a set of rooms). No first degree students live at home. **Term time work:** No college policy to allow term time work.

Undergraduates: 357 men, 186 women. **Postgraduates:** 199 men, 73 women. **Teaching staff:** Men: 51 fellows, 9 research fellows Women: 9 fellows, 6 research fellows, 1 lector. **College fees for 1996/97:** LEA grants cover college fees; undergraduates not on grants pay £2,577 in addition to university fees.

WHAT IT'S LIKE   There are two main reasons why students want to live in St John's. It is a big and varied college, and it has fantastic resources to help you do whatever you want to do while a student. John's has over 500 undergraduates, from all countries, schools and backgrounds, and the college structure means that you can meet all those people in different groups, years or courses effortlessly. The large graduate presence and the proximity to town increases the range of people (and conversation) that you will come into contact with here. Workwise, St John's has a strong (and prestigious) academic tradition. The annual exam-assessed courses, run by the university not the college, are academic and tough, but rewarding. It is easy to switch between courses, and many people do. Multimillion pound library, with individual workstations and a good range of books including all of the recommended texts. Also two computer rooms containing c.30 computers, numerous software, laser printers, and CD-Rom, as well as being connected to the central computer network and e-mail (some of the accommodation also connected). Sports of all description and all levels (from the fitness-freak to the mal-coordinated couch potato) are catered for with 3 male and 2 female football teams, 3 rugby teams, cricket, netball, basketball, tennis etc. The Lady Margaret Boat Club runs numerous college boats for rowers from novice to boat race standard. The emphasis for all sports is a healthy, fun and social one. Whatever else you enjoy, you should find your niche here. The Music Society is active, staging weekly recitals plus orchestral concerts and a mixed voice choir. Facilities include individual practice rooms, a grand piano and two concert venues. The chapel choir is reckoned by many to be the finest in Cambridge and performs concerts as well as singing in chapel. The film society runs two (recent) films a week in the 250-seater purpose-built Palmerston Room and the Lady Margaret Players has its own theatre. The other societies range from chess to photographic (with darkroom) to vegetarian, and if none of them take your fancy then you can start your own! However there are also those who just want to have a good time and enjoy being a student. The bar is the social focus for the whole of the college, and has very friendly bar staff. St John's has a reputation for excellent, value-for-money (read cheap) entertainments from bands to hypnotists and once a year St John's also holds a May Ball (black tie, expensive and lavish) and a June Event (any dress, cheapo version of the above).

All of the students are housed in college-owned accommodation, which is of a very high standard, often in very old and impressive buildings. The reasonable rents include heating, electricity and water. The rooms range from single person bedsits with shared kitchens and bathrooms between four to shared palatial flats which have to be seen to be believed! The food is good too in comparison with other colleges, and there is always a vegetarian option. The college resources are most prominent in the good financial incentives to come to St John's. There are numerous grants and awards available, ranging from travel grants, extra-curricular activities' grants, and hardship grants to the book grant (half of all books expenditure can be reclaimed – within limits!). There are even added resources for those who get 1st class results. All in all, situated in the middle of a beautiful green town with amazing history and architecture, and a friendly and relaxed atmosphere, St John's is the best place to make your time as an undergraduate whatever you want it to be. *Sam Keayes*

PAUPER NOTES **Accommodation:** College – average price, great architecture, fantastic standard, available for all 3–6 years. **Drink:** College bar – good atmosphere and fairly cheap. **Eats:** Cheap and cheerful buttery or subsidized and stately formal hall – both with veg option. **Ents:** 2 ents rooms and a huge film society means you can always have a cheap night out. **Sports:** College fields, pavilion, hardcourts, squash courts, multigym, snooker room etc; provides for all sports except swimming which is off-campus. **Hardship funds:** Plentiful and accessible – tailored to suit individual circumstances. **Travel:** Many travel grants (up to £450) – more for geographers/academic work plus £150 extra-curricular grant for everyone. **Work:** Not really available or encouraged during term-time. Plenty of bar/shop work for vacs.

ALUMNI (EDITORS' PICK) Jonathan Miller, J Michael Brearley, Piers Paul Read, William Wordsworth, Trevor Bailey, Douglas Adams, Rob Andrew, Derek Jacobi.

SELWYN

Selwyn College, Cambridge CB3 9DQ
(Tel 01223 335846)

Founded: 1882; women undergraduates first admitted 1976. **Admission:** By conditional pre A-level offer after interview; some places offered on A-levels, school reports and interviews. All applicants resident in the UK are invited for interview. **Scholarships:** Organ scholarships awarded 2 years out of 3; annual choral and instrumental exhibitions; book prizes, scholarships and exhibitions awarded to firsts and other outstanding performances in university examinations. **Largest fields of study:** Engineering, history, modern languages, natural sciences. **Europe:** 25% students study a language as part of their course; 10% spend a period abroad. College has foreign national teachers in French, Italian and German. **Travel grants:** Available. **Library:** College library (35,000 books), with law and history reading rooms; 2 computer rooms. **Eating arrangements:** Breakfast, lunch and dinner taken in hall; informal self-service and formal dinner. **Gate/guest hours:** College gates closed between 2 and 6 am; late keys obtainable. Undergraduates permitted to put up a guest in their own rooms. **Other college facilities:** Bar, shop, 3 rooms for private functions, drama facilities; music practice rooms; photographic dark room; shared sports ground with King's College. Choral evensong 3 times weekly.

Accommodation: All students in college accommodation: most charged £960 per year (range £610–£1,330). No first degree students live at home. **Term time work:** College policy to strongly discourage term time work (negligible number do). University careers service helps finding vac jobs. **Hardship funds:** Chadwick Fund, Keasbey awards.

Undergraduates: 202 men, 151 women. **Postgraduates:** 84 men, 34 women. **Teaching staff:** Men: 54 fellows, 4 research fellows, 33 lecturers Women: 5 fellows, 2 research fellows, 2 lecturers. **College fees for 1996/97:** LEA grants cover college fees; undergraduates not on grants pay £2,757 in addition to university fees.

WHAT IT'S LIKE   It's next to the Sidgwick (arts) site and the University Library, well off the tourist routes. Buildings are a mixture, neo-gothic to 1960s. Bravery, brashness and broccoli is the stuff of which men and women of Selwyn are made. Most introspective, and least overtly intellectual of Cambridge colleges; life lived at high speed. With term lasting a mere eight weeks, the lecturers' determination to cram as much information into students' skulls is only matched by the same students' desire to put such cerebral pursuits firmly in their place and spend their time on the more important things of life. Most reach a suitable balance, thus satisfying both the expectations of their tutors and the demands of, for example, the determined and successful Boat Club. What else? Musical menageries, variously attended societies, pointless parties, pseudo-intellectuals, committed Christians, strange slang, friendly Fellows, the cheapest (and best) Ball in town, a magazine named after the national bird of New Zealand. All this, and a library with a goldfish bowl extension that is almost impossible to get into. Truly a place with plenty of character, and a lot of fun.

PAUPER NOTES   **Accommodation:** College houses all undergraduates in good-quality rooms. £90 kitchen fixed charge. **Drink:** Selwyn bar good atmosphere – cheaper than pubs but not subsidised. Good local breweries inc Greene King, Abbot, Tolly Cobbold. **Eats:** College canteen has good range of dishes, including vegetarian, vegan (on request) and kosher (on request and expensive). Most meals cost £1.20–£1.70. **Ents:** College – cheap and regular eg 4 per term: discos, bands, cocktail parties etc. Univ – sparse but improving. Ents tend to be college based and run. **Sports:** College – lively, good participation. Good place to learn to row. Excellent facilities – ¾ mile from college. Univ and town sports centres both 1½ miles. **Hardship funds:** Two hardship funds. Students apply via their tutor. **Travel:** College very generous with scholarships for vac travel. **Work:** College authorities don't object. Work in pubs/restaurants easy to find.

MORE INFO?   Enquiries to First Year Representative (01223 335846).

ALUMNI (EDITORS' PICK)   Malcolm Muggeridge, E R Nixon, Lord Rayner, D Trelford, D Lumsden, Simon Hughes MP, Rt Hon John Selwyn Gummer, Huw Davies, Rob Newman, Clive Anderson, Hugh Laurie.

SIDNEY SUSSEX

Sidney Sussex College, Cambridge CB2 3HU
(Tel 01223 338800)

Founded: 1596; women undergraduates first admitted 1976. **Admission:** Places are given on the basis of performance in public examinations. **Scholarships:** Unlimited number of scholarships, exhibitions and prizes awarded on performance in university examinations; Evan Lewis-Thomas Law Studentships for law graduates to prepare for practice as barristers and solicitors. **Europe:** 10% study a language and spend a period abroad as part of their course. Informal exchange links with European universities being established. **Travel grants:** Available. **Library:** Modern, open 24 hours. **Eating arrangements:** All meals may be taken in hall; also self-catering facilities. **Gate/guest hours:** Until 2 am; keys available for late admission. **Other college facilities:** Music practice room with piano, grand piano and harpsichord, new organ; sports field and pavilion shared with Christ's College; modern boathouse shared with Corpus Christi, Girton and Wolfson; squash and tennis courts; two common rooms, two bars.

Accommodation: 99% of students in college accommodation: £60 per week average, full board. **Hardship funds:** Own funds, £10,000+ per year, average sum awarded £100; plus £10,000 other funds, average sum awarded £200. Special help to self-financing students and those with children; other funds for students on full grants and those who need to travel as part of course.

Undergraduates: 184 men, 137 women. **Postgraduates:** 80 men, 37 women. **Teaching staff:** *Men:* 31 fellows, 6 research fellows. *Women:* 7 fellows, 2 research fellows, 1 lektorin. **College fees for 1996/97:** LEA grants cover college fees; undergraduates not on grants pay £2,757 in addition to university fees.

WHAT IT'S LIKE   Small (310+ undergraduates), co-residential college with pleasant architecture/gardens and central location. Accommodation is cheaper than average in the university but is good quality and guaranteed to all undergraduates for three years, either in college or in nearby house/hostel. All staircases have washing and catering facilities, though these vary enormously from staircase to staircase. Hall serves three self-service meals a day (except Sundays) and optional formal supper; culinary standard is also variable, but receptive to student suggestions; reasonable choice provided (including vegetarian and choice of salads). Laundry room. Wide and popular range of extra-curricular activities in which anyone, no matter what standard, can participate. Student-run bar doubles as a venue for fortnightly bops; sports facilities include playing-fields and tennis courts (a mile away), a boathouse and squash court; a successful drama society, plus chapel choir and orchestra. Academically, a gifted Fellowship, reasonable library (open 24 hours/day) and good tripos results, especially in geography, engineering, and medicine. Reasonable relations with fellows – students enjoy full representation on governing body and other college committees. Socially, very easy-going with few of the cliques found in other colleges; probably the friendliest college. A very fair admissions policy means no one should be discouraged from applying. College keen to obtain as many applicants as possible. SU President available to talk informally about college life and Cambridge in general. Open days from Easter for sixth-formers. Thriving SU promotes student welfare and provides some focus for limited political debate and activity. Less political apathy than at other colleges.

PAUPER NOTES   **Accommodation:** Guaranteed for all undergraduates for three years, married accommodation available. Some graduate rooms available. **Drink:** College bar very cheap. Lots of pubs nearby (Maypole is good one) because college is centrally located. Carlsberg-Tetley beers good. **Eats:** Not very good value – very touristy. Not many take-aways. Nadia's Patisserie, good sandwiches (open Sundays). **Ents:** University theatre (ADC) nearby, weekly productions. Arts Cinema across the road – excellent variety. Bops organised by different colleges and advertised throughout. No good nightclubs. **Sports:** Cambridge town sports centre relatively expensive. No great skill required to play sport at college level. Wide variety of sports available – emphasis on fun. **Hardship funds:** Fund of £7,500 a year, administered by tutors. **Travel:** For vacation travel small amount (about £100) available quite easily for second years. £300 for 'deserving cases'. **Work:** Very few students get paid work during term. Would be difficult to find suitable work, given lack of time. Few people get local vacation work.
MORE INFO?   Enquiries to President SSCSU (01223 338860).
ALUMNI (EDITORS' PICK)   John Patten, David Thomson, C T R Wilson, C F Powell, David Owen, Oliver Cromwell, Asa Briggs.

TRINITY

**Trinity College, Cambridge CB2 1TQ
(Tel 01223 338400)**

Founded: 1546; women undergraduates first admitted 1977. **Admission:** Pre A-level candidates considered for conditional offers which may include S-level papers or STEP. Post A-level candidates considered on their record. Most candidates will be interviewed. **Largest fields of study:** Natural sciences, medical sciences, mathematics, economics, English, engineering, law, modern languages, history. **Scholarships:** Scholarships awarded on university examinations; organ scholarship (£250 pa) offered in alternate years, 6 choral exhibitions (£100 pa) annually; numerous college prizes. **Europe:** 10% first degree students take a language as part of course and 7% spend 6 months or more abroad. No formal exchange links with European universities/colleges. **Travel grants:** Grants for projects and research; small grants for vacation travel. **Library:** Magnificent Wren Library with over 50,000 volumes plus a reading room; separate law reading room. **Eating arrangements:** Breakfast, lunch and dinner available in hall on cafeteria system, plus formal dinner. Fixed annual price of £247.20 plus cash payment for individual meals. Small kitchens on all staircases. **Gate/guest hours:** Great Gate locked at 2 am but college members may enter or leave at any time. **Other college facilities:** 3 large common rooms, 2 student computer rooms, bar, games and party rooms, buttery, 2 launderettes, record lending library, music practice rooms, small theatre; 3 sports grounds, squash, tennis and badminton courts; boathouse with excellent modern facilities.

Accommodation: All students in college accommodation: most charged £950 pa (range £750–£1,500), including heating. No first degree students live at home. **Term time work:** No college policy to allow term time work.

Undergraduates: 454 men, 205 women. **Postgraduates:** 228 men, 82 women. **Teaching staff:** *Men:* 61 fellows, 26 research fellows, 18 professorial fellows. *Women:* 4 fellows, 1 professorial fellow. **College fees for 1996/97:** LEA grants cover college fees; undergraduates not on grants pay £2,550 in addition to university fees.

WHAT IT'S LIKE   It just takes one look at Great Court for many people to make up their minds about Trinity – a spacious, luxurious icon of wealth and antiquity. However, such people are usually among the hordes of picture-snapping tourists. Whilst it is true that the college is architecturally stunning, that tells you nothing about what it is like actually being a student there. In a college of such size, it is impossible to generalise about people. There are students from the length and breadth of the country and from all types of school; there are more men than women at the moment (but changing); and a high proportion (10%) of overseas students (a uniquely enriching feature). Conveniently situated in the centre (for Sainsbury's and the pubs) and within 10 minutes walk from most of the faculties. Whole range of college accommodation – standard hall of residence rooms, to mock oak-beamed Tudor rooms in Great Court, to yuppie-style flats at Burrells' Field with cable TV, telephone and Internet link. All accommodation is a short walk from the main college (the first college to allow mixed sharing in the second and third years). In terms of finance, can be extremely generous; numerous funds, grants, bursaries and prizes. There are modern, and extensive computer facilities (2 computer rooms, PowerPCs and Pentiums). The library is well stocked (300,000+ books and CDs) with CD-Rom access. The Wren library contains original manuscripts from Isaac Newton and AA Milne's original notes about Winnie the Pooh should you need them! The College Bar is quaint, often packed but woefully inadequate for the size of the college. The drinks are cheap though and the witticisms of the barstaff make it worth the inevitable wait for your drink. Club nights constrained by the lack of a decent suitable room but there are Trinity's legendary cheap cocktails and they still seem to attract people from all over the university. Exciting plans to relocate the bar to a larger integrated student complex, though date uncertain. There are four common rooms for student use, and two lecture theatres. Plenty of university-wide societies hold their meetings there though college population itself seems rather apathetic. There are Women's and Green groups along with the students' union – TCSU – for those who wish to get involved in student politics. Over 24 societies (aerobics, international affairs, tiddlywinks); plenty of music rooms, excellent choir and Dryden society regularly puts on high quality drama (and scope for funding for new societies). As to sport; men's football and cricket teams currently riding high, and recent successes in rowing (men and women). Students do get involved in various traditions (such as the Great Court Run) but with the tongue placed firmly in the cheek. A large college may not suit everyone but it means that there is a high chance of meeting like-minded people and you can get involved in a huge variety of activities. Trinity gives you the opportunity to pick and choose. It really is what you make of it. If that does not appeal to you, then there is always the prospect of being taught by world experts in beautiful surroundings and with excellent facilities.   *Faisal Islam*

PAUPER NOTES   **Accommodation:** All undergraduates guaranteed a college room for whole course. **Drink:** Cheap college bar that is often packed – 90p for SU pint, £1.20 for Theakston's Old Peculier. **Eats:** Reasonable food in hall, cheap – £1.90 for a 3-course meal, filling but bland; always a vegetarian option. **Ents:** SU ents popular and populous too! Massive range of clubs and societies all operating on site. **Sports:** College sports facilities excellent and no shortage of willing participants. Superbly equipped boathouse, multigym, football, rugby and hockey pitches, squash, tennis and badminton courts all within 5 minutes walk. **Hardship funds:** Good college hardship funds; tutors sympathetic to substantiated claims. **Travel:** Many travel bursaries/project funds for all sorts of vacation activities. **Work:** Vacations work locally declining (college happy to allow rooms to be used over vac if needed). Work during term prohibited though some still manage it.

TRINITY HALL

Trinity Hall, Cambridge CB2 1TJ
(Tel 01223 332500, Fax 01223 332537)

Admissions Office (Tel 01223 332535,
Internet http://www.trinhall.cam.ac.uk/admissions/)

Founded: 1350; women undergraduates first admitted 1977. **Largest fields of study:** Natural sciences, law, engineering, modern languages. **Scholarships:** Scholarships and exhibitions awarded on the results of university examinations taken while in residence; numerous college prizes. **Europe:** 10% students study a language and spend a period of time abroad as part of their course. No formal exchange links with European universities/colleges. **Travel grants:** Elmore travel exhibition annually on result of modern and medieval languages tripos; grants from Benn and Gregson funds for vacation travel of educational or adventurous nature. **Library:** New library and separate law library; also historic library (chained books). **Eating arrangements:** All meals available in hall; paid for by computer card. Super Hall (special dinner) on Thursdays. **Gate/guest hours:** Gate closed at 2 am; all undergraduates on central site may have gate key. **Other college facilities:** Bar, music room with piano and harpsichord; washing machines and driers; boathouse; squash and tennis courts; playing fields. All student rooms in College are connected to the Internet.

Accommodation: All students guaranteed college accommodation for 3 years (not guaranteed for fourth year of 4-year courses): £28–£46 per week including heat; plus meals available in cafeteria and charged to end of term bill. No first degree students live at home. **Term time work:** College policy not to allow term time work for first degree students (term time work in college only in exceptional circumstances). University careers service helps find vac work. **Hardship funds:** Own funds £6,500, 32 students helped (but more could be made available if particular need); mainly for those on or near full grant – all cases considered individually on merit. Various scholarships and travel funds also available according to need. Current college appeal will increase money available for bursaries and hardship funds.

Undergraduates: 196 men, 133 women. **Postgraduates:** 154 men, 68 women. **Teaching staff:** *Men*: 31 fellows, 4 research fellows *Women*: 4 fellows, 2 research fellows. **College fees for 1996/97:** LEA grants cover college fees; undergraduates not on grants pay £2,706 in addition to university fees.

WHAT IT'S LIKE   Small college in pleasant setting on the Backs. Very central, yet relatively quiet. Friendly atmosphere; relations between staff and students relaxed (very helpful porters). Amenities include a modern JCR complex of common room, computer facilities, versatile lecture theatre, music room – all adjoining the small but popular bar. Accommodation varies considerably: all 1st years and some 3rd years live in college, everyone else on two other college sites close by (although some 4th years have to find own accommodation). Variable self-catering facilities are available on every site. College food is tolerable: cafeteria every day, as well as the occasional formal halls and super halls (usually good value). Most sports catered for; playing fields, tennis and squash courts are 10 mins from college. Football and rowing are big college sports for both sexes but many other sports also regularly put out teams. Several active societies: outstanding in music and drama. Apolitical yet active JCR co-ordinates many of the college activities and provides internal services, as well as representing students on the governing body. College actively seeks a wide range of applicants. Male/female ratio currently 3:2, relaxed attitude to co-residence. Academically high, main subjects natural sciences, law, engineering though most mainstream subjects catered for. Size and good internal facilities make the college self-contained, perhaps even a little insular at times.

PAUPER NOTES   **Accommodation:** Can get rooms from £260–£400 a term. OK, so long as you aren't married or have kids. One set for disabled student. **Drink:** No cheap places in Cambridge. College bar is reasonable but goes for quality, not cheapness (though cheaper than town), Bop's exceptional value. **Eats:** Canteen cheap but subsidised by kitchen charge £200 pa. **Ents:** Excellent college ents: active discos and plays. Town good for film buffs, and increasingly better music (Junction, Corn Exchange). **Sports:** A mecca for sports (apparently). Main sports (rowing, hockey, football, rugby) are free at college level. **Rag:** Very active, something for everyone – bungee jumping to slave auction. **Hardship funds:** Money available; growing awareness of students' financial problems. **Travel:** Poor connections except to London; hitching not bad. No need for public transport during term – everywhere is walkable or cyclable. Travel bursaries available. **Work:** No time for it in term time and it is officially forbidden. Not much in Cambridge, but being an undergraduate does help with getting summer work. Vacation residence is expensive.

MORE INFO?   Enquiries to JCR President 01223 332534.

ALUMNI (EDITORS' PICK)   Robert Runcie, Geoffrey Howe, Norman Fowler, Samuel Silkin, A Nunn May, Rev David Sheppard, A H Mars-Jones, Lord Simon of Glaisdale, J B Priestley, Tony Slattery.

WOLFSON

Wolfson College, Cambridge CB3 9BB
(Tel 01223 335900)

Founded: 1965. **Admission:** Primarily graduate college but mature undergraduates over 21 admitted (some are affiliated students, who already have a first degree, reading for BA in 2 years). **Travel grants:** College travel fund. **Library:** 13,000 books, 44 periodicals, many study places. **Eating arrangements:** Meals in hall. Vending machines, cafeteria in club room. **Other college facilities:** Tennis court, multi-gym, boat house.

Accommodation: 90% in college accommodation. 1% live at home. **Term time work:** No college policy to allow part time work for undergraduates. Some term time work available in college as bartender and porter. **Hardship funds:** College hardship fund.

Undergraduates: 68 men, 22 women. **Postgraduates:** 300 men, 150 women. **College fees for 1996/97:** LEA grants cover college fees; undergraduates not on grants pay £2,649 in addition to university fees.

WHAT IT'S LIKE   It's cosmopolitan, relaxed, unpretentious and friendly. Students are over 21, doing every imaginable degree (mostly postgraduate), from every corner of the world. Lawyers and vets, particularly strong. Food OK. Plenty of college accommodation. Close to modern languages and humanities faculties.

PAUPER NOTES   **Accommodation:** Married and family flats available. Undergrads live in for all three years; average cost £40 pw. **Drink:** Cheap college bar: Flowers £1 a pint. **Eats:** Food good, vegetarians catered for. Twice weekly formal halls popular. **Ents:** All college events free. Weekly disco and band nights. **Sports:** Excellent gym and tennis court on site. Most sports supported. **Hardship funds:** Some from college; many more available via university. **Travel:** Travel exhibitions available. College good for contacts as it's highly international. **Work:** In college bar, porter's lodge or around town.

ALUMNI (EDITORS' PICK)   C Bowman (singer/entertainer, well known in Ireland), Steve Richards (Channel 4 Garden Club presenter), Mathew Fisher (Procul Harum).

CANTERBURY CHRIST CHURCH COLLEGE

Canterbury Christ Church College, Canterbury, Kent CT1 1QU
(Tel 01227 767700, Fax 01227 470442) Map 4

STUDENT ENQUIRIES: Admissions Office
APPLICATIONS: UCAS

Broad study areas: Teacher training, nursing and professions allied to medicine, humanities, performing arts, media. (Subject details are in the *Subjects and Places Index*.)

Founded: 1962; merged with Canterbury School of Radiography and various schools of nursing since 1988. **Main undergraduate awards:** BA, BA(QTS), BSc. **Awarding body:** Kent University. **Site:** Campus 10-min walk from city centre; art department in city centre. **Europe:** 15% first degree students learn a language as part of their course (built into eg business studies, tourism studies); language tuition available to all students. **Special features:** College has its own radio station. Mature students with one A-level or from an access course accepted. **Largest fields of study:** Teacher education and health-related studies. **Library:** 200,000 volumes, 800 periodicals, 328 study places. Annual expenditure on library materials, £45 per FTE student. **Welfare:** Doctor, nurse, sick bay, chaplain, counsellor, nursery facilities nearby. **Careers:** Information and advice. **Amenities:** Student building. **Sporting facilities:** Tennis courts, gymnasium and fitness centre.

Accommodation: In 1995/96, 15% of all students in college accommodation, 37% first years; others in head-leased properties, managed by college. 3,182 places available (1,200 for first years): 186 full-board places (all first years) £66 per week term time only; 486 self-catering places (all first years), £40–£51 per week; 255 head-leased places (not for first years) at £40–£50 per week, Sept-July; and 2,000 private lodgings (528 first years) at £45 per week, usually all year. Privately owned, college managed, accommodation: £40–£50 per week self-catering. **Term time work:** Small number of first degree students believed to work; term work available on campus in library, bars etc. **Hardship funds:** Total available in 1995/96: £81,875 government access funds, 331 students helped.

Duration of first degree courses: 3 years. **Total first degree students 1995/96:** 3,000; **Total BA(QTS) students:** 808. **Male/female ratio:** 1:4. **Teaching staff:** 273 full-time, 36 part-time. **Total full-time students 1995/96:** 4,000. **Postgraduate students:** 700. **First degree tuition fees:** Home students, paying their own fees in 1996/97, paid up to £825 plus validation fee of £350; Overseas students £5,100.

WHAT IT'S LIKE   Despite its expanding campus, increase in student numbers and diversification of courses, C4 manages to maintain its friendly and personal atmosphere. Located within 5 minutes walk of the city centre and overlooked by the cathedral, it is a cosmopolitan college with an active international programmes office integrating students from all over the world. Originally a teacher training college, it now runs BA/BSc courses including media, industry, tourism, nursing and occupational therapy; also a good history department. All first years under 21 are housed in college halls; remainder in college-owned, head-leased houses. Canterbury has a large student population so accommodation is expensive (£40–£55 per week) and hard to find. This historic city wasn't designed with traffic in mind; parking is difficult and the rush hour lasts all day. The SU building is the centre of most student activity and social life; purpose built 10 years ago, it contains a large bar area, 2 smaller bars (one non-smoking), disco/band/event area (with large video projector) and 2 TV lounges with satellite facilities. SU has many flourishing clubs and societies, all run by students for students, including campus radio and TV stations. Diverse events programme, renowned in Canterbury (live bands, comedy nights, discos, club nights and cabarets), although space limited in the union building. Canterbury is in an ideal location – easy access to London, the continent and many small seaside towns. Although it is busy, it is ideal for those who enjoy life away from the hustle and bustle of large inner cities.

PAUPER NOTES   **Accommodation:** Some; plans for more. No married quarters; few squats. **Drink:** Variety of pubs, some of most crowded in England. **Eats:** Large selection on and off campus. Huge range of different foods in city; many restaurants offer student discounts. **Ents:** Union has 5 events a week including discos, films, bands, stand up and alternative events; regularly takes over local club. 4 formal balls a year, culminating in all-night extravaganza, the Summer Ball. **Sports:** New sports ground. Many thriving sports clubs, including highly successful swimming, badminton and women's rugby teams. **Travel:** Hitching opportunities to London and the continent. **Work:** Mainly in pubs, restaurants, supermarkets and offices; some work in SU bar. Seasonal fruit picking and teaching English in language schools popular in the summer. Many students in small city means limited work.

MORE INFO?   Enquiries to SU President (01227 782417).

INFORMAL NAME   Christ Church; C4.

GET HOLD OF THE PROSPECTUSES

CARDIFF INSTITUTE

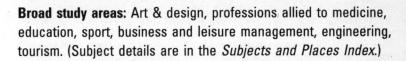

University of Wales Institute Cardiff, PO Box 377, Western Avenue, Llandaff, Cardiff CF5 2SG
(Tel 01222 506070, Fax 01222 506911) Map 3

STUDENT ENQUIRIES: Information Office
APPLICATIONS: UCAS

Broad study areas: Art & design, professions allied to medicine, education, sport, business and leisure management, engineering, tourism. (Subject details are in the *Subjects and Places Index*.)

Founded: 1976 as South Glamorgan Institute, ex four colleges (art, education, technology, food technology and commerce); part of Wales University in 1995. **Main undergraduate awards:** BA, BSc, BEng. **Awarding body:** Wales University. **Site:** 4 campuses within easy travelling distance of each other and the city centre. **Europe:** First degree students encouraged to take a language as part of course and opportunities for them to spend time abroad. Formal exchange links with a number of EU universities/colleges, open to non-language students. **Library:** 4 libraries, total of 210,000 volumes, 1,000 periodicals, 430 study places; reference and short-term collections; access through library computer to British Library and Library of Congress (London). **Special collections:** Permanent collection of prints and books on the work of the designer Erte. Extensive collection of slides. **Welfare:** Doctors, nurses, chaplains, professional welfare and accommodation officer. **Careers:** Careers advisory officer. **Sporting facilities:** Sports halls, gymnasia, swimming pool, athletic track (international standard), rugby and football pitches, etc; Wales Sports Centre for the Disabled; access to all sporting facilities of Cardiff University and to Welsh Institute of Sport. **Employment:** Art and design, manufacturing industry, hospitals and environmental health, hotels, sports, tourism, arts administration, teaching, social work.

Accommodation: In 1995/96, nearly 800 places available (full board, part board or self-catering): from £41 per week (self-catering) to £65 per week (full board). Accommodation service helps find private rented accommodation. 20% first degree students live at home. **Term time work:** College's policy to allow term time work for full-time first degree students; limit of 12 hours per week max (70% believed to work). No work on campus. **Hardship funds:** Government access fund.

Duration of first degree courses: 3 years; **others:** 4 years. **Total first degree students 1995/96:** 4,396. **Total education students:** 691. **Overseas (non EU) students:** 85. **Mature students:** 520. **Male/female ratio:** 1:2. **Teaching staff:** 374. **Total full-time students 1995/96:** 5,350. **Postgraduate students:** 535. **First degree tuition fees:** Home students, paying their own fees in 1996/97, paid £750 (classroom), £1,600 (lab/studio); Overseas students £5,250.

WHAT IT'S LIKE   It's on 4 sites. Accommodation at reasonable cost for reasonable quality (and warm), with good access to all college centres. 2 halls of residence with good community atmosphere, lots of trust, team spirit and fun! Travel cheap and accessible (taxi and bus) and SU minibuses (eg from all sites to gigs) but nowhere is too far on a bike. Entertainment very strong. Serious drinking and eating. Great atmosphere; very friendly and easy going. Constant bombardment from SU with dances, games, shows, bands, discos.

Lots of drinks promotions with prizes and freebies, also theme nights, bands and club nights. Local pubs good, so is the beer (price and quality); Claude Hotel is best, constantly provides for bands, sponsorship for SU clubs, freebies, fancy dress and parties (all because of liaison with SU). Clubs are quite expensive but good to visit in groups. Beaches, hills, nature paths, rugby, football, skating, swimming, all strong in Cardiff and vicinity. Castles, museums, cinemas – you name it! A student orientated city, with citizens of all nationalities. Good relationship between students and locals. SU sports facilities excellent: swimming pool, physiotherapy service, squash courts, gymnasiums, sports hall, multigym, hockey pitches, football, cricket and first-class rugby pitches. Plenty of clubs and societies provide sporting opportunities for men and women. Students from all over Britain (40% from Cardiff) and from all backgrounds (90% from state schools). FE courses as well as HE which range right across the board from PE to fine art. Regular exchange programme all over the world.

PAUPER NOTES   **Accommodation:** All first years can live in halls. Plenty of good accommodation with understanding landlords if you look hard. **Drink:** Claude Hotel, Tut'n'Shive, Philharmonic. Brains Beers good, and SA (Skull Attack) very strong; for mega blitz try Hurlimans Lager at Roath Park. 42nd Street, Brain's concession to yuppie market. **Eats:** Campus food varies – Colchester Avenue and Eldorado theme bar at Llandaff both good. Peppermill Diner, Jumpin Jacks, El Paso Mexican good restaurants. Roath and Canton areas good for vegetarians and ethnic. **Ents:** Cardiff offers all facilities of large city. Chapter and Sherman theatres good for students with specialist film seasons. Nightclubs, cinemas etc. **Sports:** Plentiful on campus and in city eg National Sports Centre. Various leisure centres, swimming pools, golf club etc. **Travel:** Accessible and easy for hitching; 10% student discount on trains; good bus service. **Work:** Lots of catering/waitering work in pubs and restaurants, youth club coaching, casual work at Cardiff International Arena, ice rink and supermarkets.

INFORMAL NAME   UWIC

ALUMNI (EDITORS' PICK) Gareth Edwards, Rhodri Lewis, Stuart Baxter, Sian Williams, Sally Hodge, Nigel Cousins, Richie Collins, John Bevan, Anne Diamond, Jill Dando, Michael Buerk, David Bryant, Sean McGaughie (Pontypool rugby star), Tony Copsey (Llanelli rugby star), Lisa 'ab fab sweetie' Jones.

CARDIFF UNIVERSITY

University of Wales, Cardiff, PO Box 921, Cardiff CF1 3XQ
(Tel 01222 874839, Fax 01222 874457) Map 3

STUDENT ENQUIRIES: Undergraduate Registry
(Admissions Office), Tel 01222 8744404, Fax 01222 874130;
Prospectus requests, 01222 874899
APPLICATIONS: UCAS

Broad study areas: Business, law, life and physical sciences, engineering, architecture, transport, maritime studies, humanities and social studies. (Subject details are in the *Subjects and Places Index.*)

Founded: 1883, joined Aberystwyth and Bangor to form Wales University in 1893. Merged in 1988 with UWIST (founded 1866). **Main undergraduate awards:** BA, BD, BMus, BSc, BEng, BScEcon, LLB, BPharm, BArch. **Awarding body:** Wales University. **Site:** Close to Cardiff city centre. **Academic features:** 4-year integrated sandwich courses, 5-year two-tier courses in architecture and town planning. **Europe:** 7% first degree students take a language as part of their course, 2% spend 6 months or more abroad. Language tuition available for all students. Formal exchange links with European universities/colleges; also 51 Erasmus schemes, 41 involving non-language specialists. **Library:** 10 libraries; almost 1 million books and 9,000 different journal titles, 2,000 study places. Annual expenditure on library materials, £99.85 per FTE student. **Specialist collections:** Salisbury Library of Celtic and Welsh material. European Documentation and Information Centre. Also special collections in law, architecture and company information. **Other learning facilities:** Computing service (2,000 PCs, 300 Macs and Unix systems), open to all students with many on-line information sources. SuperJANET (one of only 12 centres in UK) and Internet connect computers to other computers and databases in UK and abroad. **Welfare:** Students' advisory, counselling and health services; dyslexia resource centre; international office to assist overseas students. Anglican, Catholic, Baptist, Methodist and United Reformed, Greek Orthodox and Jewish chaplains. Special categories: Residential facilities for students with families and those with disabilites; day care centre. **Careers:** Information, advice and placement. **Amenities:** Large purpose-built SU with bars, nightclub, 7 restaurants/fast food outlets, TV and reading rooms, snooker and pool room, general shop, travel shop, launderette, banking and insurances services; university bookshop on campus; Wales University Air Squadron; Officer Training Corps. **Sporting facilities:** Multi-purpose indoor/outdoor sports centre, squash and fitness centre and playing fields complex.

Accommodation: In 1995/96, 40% of all students in university accommodation, 100% of first years. 4,700 places available (3,300 for first years): 530 half-board places (all for first years) at £53 per week, term time only; and 4,170 self-catering places (2,770 for first years) at £30–£46 per week, Sept–June. Students live in privately owned accommodation for 2 years: rents £40–£45 per week, self-catering. **Term time work:** University offers part-time work through Unistaff scheme; up to 15 hours work a week in term time (and also in vacations) in university bars, refectories, offices, libraries, labs, sports centre; also university agency supplies student workers to local shops and offices; directory of local casual work. **Hardship funds:** Total expended in 1995/96: £290,898 government access funds, 950 students helped; plus £8,357 other funds, 26 cases supported. Special help: final-year students encountering unexpected hardship, including final year Commonwealth students and female students whose health is affected during course.

Duration of first degree courses: 3 years; **others:** 4 years, 5 years. **Total first degree students 1995/96:** 9,983 (plus medical and dental students); **Overseas students:** 786 (u/g) and 632 (p/g). **Male/female ratio:** 1:1. **Teaching staff:** 772 full-time, 40 part-time. **Total full-time students 1995/96:** 13,052. **Postgraduate students:** 2,190 (full-time). **First degree tuition fees:** Home students, paying their own fees in 1996/97, paid £750 (classroom), £834 (lab); Overseas: £5,880 (classroom), £7,740 (lab).

WHAT IT'S LIKE   University buildings, spread throughout the city centre, are a mixture of beautiful old architecture and not quite as beautiful new. The SU enjoys a central position directly opposite the main college building. Its huge night club has 1700 capacity and a 1500 capacity concert venue. Bands such as Oasis, Pulp, Black Grape, Kula Shaka, The Orb, Orbital and The Prodigy have all headlined at the Union recently, and the latest dance night Lust For Life made it to the top ten UK club nights (the only SU to do so). Union boasts over 60 sports clubs and 120 societies from rugby to lacrosse and from debating to live role playing. Student paper, Gair Rhydd, was runner up in the 1996 Guardian Media Awards and recently launched X-Press Radio and Wales first FM student radio station. Cardiff itself enjoys all the benefits of a capital city but is compact enough to save on bus fares as almost everywhere of interest is within walking distance. The National Stadium, Cardiff Arms Park, remains a Mecca for rugby fans the world over and there are plenty of parks and gardens for a Sunday afternoon stroll. The city, university and union all have a tremendous sense of identity – a mixture of Welsh heritage, the student lifestyle and pride in being a part of the fastest growing capital city in Europe.

PAUPER NOTES   **Accommodation:** Halls of residence relatively inexpensive. Private sector, £35–£40 per week average; can be difficult to find in Sept–October. **Drink:** SU consistently cheap, beer from £1.30/pint and regular drink promotions. Local brewery, Brains (near monopoly on the town); most popular brews are its smooth, dark and SA (known as Skull Attack) worth a go. **Eats:** Cardiff is city of 1000 curry houses; fierce competition results in seriously low prices. Variety of eating places staggering, from greasy spoons to Cajon and Creole, plethora of Italians to Harry Ramsden's. **Ents:** Plenty happening in SU with big name bands. Also watch first division rugby, top ice hockey team, go bowling, cinema, 3 excellent theatres, concert venues (pubs for 150 to 6000 capacity CIA); Cardiff Arms Park and banks like Bon Jovi, U2 and REM; student discounts on everything but the biggest bands. **Sports:** Gyms and sports centres range from free SU/university facilities to excellent but more expensive David Lloyd fitness centre. Swimming pools, velodrome and an ice rink. **Hardship funds:** Small access funds; one-off payments available to students in desperate need. SU offers debt counselling. **Travel:** Discounted travel from STA Travel (in partnership with SU). **Work:** Bar and catering work from uni and SU; local agencies worth a try in vacations. Prospects good if you try early.

INFORMAL NAME   Cardiff Uni

ALUMNI (EDITORS' PICK)   Neil Kinnock MP, Glenys Kinnock MEP, Tim Sebastian, Sian Phillips, Philip Madoc, Bernice Rubens, Vincent Kane, Sian Lloyd.

CENTRAL ENGLAND UNIVERSITY

University of Central England in Birmingham, Perry Barr, Birmingham B42 2SU (Tel 0121 331 5000, Fax 0121 331 6358) Map 3

STUDENT ENQUIRIES: Recruitment Unit, Registry
APPLICATIONS: UCAS

Broad study areas: Built environment, engineering, art & design, business, computing, education, law, health, social sciences, music. (Subject details are in the *Subjects and Places Index*.)

Founded: 1971 as Birmingham Poly, from a number of colleges of art, commerce, education, music and PE; university status in 1992. **Main undergraduate awards:** BA, BSc, BEng, MEng, LLB. **Awarding body:** Central England University. **Site:** Split on seven sites. **Access:**

Buses and trains from Birmingham city centre. **Academic features:** Current study on the needs of women engineers. Courses in criminal justice and policing, and automotive engineering. **Europe:** Less than 1% first degree students take a language as part of course; available on some engineering courses, and options in eg business studies, hotel & catering. Formal exchange links with universities/colleges 4 EU countries. **Library:** Main library containing 300,000 volumes, 1,200 journals, 800 study places, course books on reference; also 7 specialist libraries. Extensive information on other media eg CD-Rom, slides, videotape. **Specialist collections:** Rare books collection; collection of children's books; large collection of sheet music; Marion Richardson archive. **Other learning facilities:** Information services department (IBM 9370 system, 3 Prime 50 series mini computers plus workstations with access to institutional, national and international networks). **Welfare:** Student advice centre at Perry Barr, women's officer, 3 chaplains, counsellor, nurses. **Careers:** Information, advice and placement. **Amenities:** Bookshop, general shop, bank, insurance broker, 2 nurseries.

Accommodation: In 1995/96, 8% of all students in university accommodation, 17% of first years. 877 self-catering places available, all for first years, £37–£45 per week. Students live in privately owned accommodation for 2+ years: £27–£37 per week self-catering, £40–£60 half-board, £55–£80 half-board and weekend meals. 65% first degree students live at home. **Term time work:** No university policy to allow term time work for full-time first degree students. No work available on campus; course related work placements only. **Hardship funds:** Total available in 1995/96: £196,906 government access funds, 501 students helped; £15,000 own funds, 40 helped. Special help to: self-financing students for eg fees, those from low income backgrounds, those with child care costs, special needs, unexpected financial commitments etc; own funds for those not eligible for Access funds.

Duration of first degree courses: 3 years **other:** 4 years. **Total first degree students 1995/96:** 9,861; **BEd/QTS students:** 612. **Overseas students:** 490. **Mature students:** 824. **Male/female ratio:** 1:1. **Teaching staff:** 539 full-time, 82 part-time. **Total full-time students 1995/96:** 10,713. **Postgraduate students:** 2,304. **First degree tuition fees:** Home students, paying their own fees in 1996/97, paid £750 (classroom), £1,600 (lab/studio); Overseas students £6,000.

WHAT IT'S LIKE   An amalgam of modern/old buildings split over seven sites; the largest being Perry Barr, then Gosta Green (graphics), Westbourne Road (teacher training and nursing), Conservatoire (music school), Bourneville (arts), Margaret Street (fine arts), and the jewellery school. Halls places limited but improving. Most students share houses. SU runs magazine, 2 shops, bank, student advice centre, Endsleigh and all sports and societies (full-time sports officer and 40 teams in a range of sports). 2 successful SU bars – one at Perry Barr (north of the city), one at Westbourne Road (south). Entertainments cater for diversity of students. Large student population – many part-time/mature. Access to sites good although problems with car parking. Many good courses – business, music and graphics especially. Birmingham is a student city (40,000 students in total) – many cheap student nights in clubs, also some discounts on theatres, cinemas. Lots of cheap shops and a square mile of markets in the centre, selling everything you can imagine.
PAUPER NOTES   **Accommodation:** Hall places limited (ditto places with access for disabled). Accommodation available in all areas of city. University housing scheme, restrictive contracts. Large numbers live at home. **Drink:** SU bars cheapest in area; many real ale pubs, Black Country Beers. Lots of student nights (one for every night of the week). **Eats:** B'ham renowned for its curry and Balti houses. **Ents:** Varied and cheap ents. Many local events, bands etc. Student discounts at nightclubs, theatres, cinemas (Sunday night at city centre cinema). **Sports:** No facilities on campus, but ongoing campaign. SU hires

good pitches/halls from city. **Hardship funds:** University provides emergency cover (min) from government access funds. **Travel:** Cheap buses and trains in city, B'ham is easy to get to and from. **Work:** Most take jobs in term-time – pubs, clubs etc – easy to find; pay OK.
ALUMNI (EDITORS' PICK)   Alfred Bestall (the creator of Rupert Bear), Judy Simpson, Kathy Cook (Olympic athletes), Betty Jackson (fashion designer), Larry (cartoonist), Zoe Ball (children's TV presenter).

CENTRAL LANCASHIRE UNIVERSITY

University of Central Lancashire, Preston PR1 2HE
(Tel 01772 201201, Fax 01772 892946) Map 2

STUDENT ENQUIRIES: Admissions Office
APPLICATIONS: UCAS

Broad study areas: Business; cultural, legal and social studies; sciences and environment; art, design and technology; health. (Subject details are in the *Subjects and Places Index*.)

Founded: 1973 as Preston, then Lancashire, Poly; university status in 1992. **Main undergraduate awards:** BA, BSc, BEng. **Awarding body:** Central Lancashire University. **Site:** Town centre campus in Preston. **Access:** Road and rail. **Academic features:** Courses include fashion promotion, employee relations, financial services, horticultural technology. Modular credit accumulation and transfer scheme throughout. Exchange programmes in USA, China and Europe. **Europe:** 10% first degree students take a language and spend 3 months or more abroad as part of course. Language training is available for all students (a variety of levels, examined or not). Formal exchange links with 100+ European universities/colleges and opportunities for work placements overseas. **Library:** 400,000 volumes in total, 1,700 periodicals, 3,500 journals, 1,200 study places; restricted loan collection; slide library, video and audio cassettes. Annual expenditure on library materials, £47.43 per FTE student. **Specialist collections:** Preston Incorporated Law Society Library; collection of illustrated books and local history. **Welfare:** 5 counsellors and 3 accommodation officers, health centre, FPA, legal advice, multi-faith centre, pre-school centre; separate advisers for overseas students, those with special needs and racial equality. **Careers:** Information officer; advice and placement service. **Amenities:** Arts centre, sports centre with human performance laboratory, observatories, bookshop, students' union with shops and bank, conference facilities, catering service. Shopping centres, cinemas and theatre in town.

Accommodation: In 1995/96, 20% of all students in university accommodation, 60% of first years. 1,850 self-catering places available (1,700 for first years): £874 pa (shared room in university house); £1,690–£1,920 (single room in halls), Sept to July. Students live in privately owned accommodation for 2+ years: £30–£35 per week self-catering (+fuel), £26–£55 (5 or 7 day self-catering or full board). **Term time work:** University's policy to allow term time work for full-time first degree students (30% believed to work); no work on campus. **Hardship funds:** Total available in 1995/96: £220,000 government access funds, 683 students helped. Special help: students with excessive travel or accommodation costs, childcare costs, self-financing students, those with special needs or ineligible for student loan. £13,010 own funds, 75 helped. Small local trust fund also available for part-time students.

Duration of first degree courses: 3 years; **others:** 4 years (sandwich). **Total first degree students 1995/96:** 9,503 (full-time/sandwich), 4,801 (part-time). **Overseas students:** 183. **Mature students:** 9,000. **Male/female ratio:** 1:1. **Teaching staff:** 580 full-time, 56 part-time. **Total full-time students 1995/96:** 10,000. **Postgraduate students:** 294 (full-time); 1,149 (part-time). **First degree tuition fees:** Home students, paying their own fees in 1996/97, paid £750; Overseas students £5,979.

WHAT IT'S LIKE   Preston has undergone a large re-development that has made it quite a busy town. It has maintained its friendly atmosphere without letting its abundance of rain dampen the spirit. University has also expanded, library been extended and the accommodation increased dramatically over the last few years. The union building houses 3 bars, numerous food outlets, 3 shops (including inexpensive doc martins), admin offices, plus 1,100 capacity venue.

PAUPER NOTES **Accommodation:** University expensive – private sector slightly better. **Drink:** SU bars reasonable, good selection – cheap bitter/lager. Lots of local pubs: Robinsons, Theakstons, Thwaites and Matty Brown. SU is the best pub and is surrounded by friendly pubs. **Eats:** SU offers a good range of burgers and meals – few vegetarian restaurants, many Indian, few Chinese. Roobarb for vegetarian near university library. Lots of reasonably priced places to eat. **Ents:** SU good; Guild Hall, Charter Theatre, 8-screen Warner and 10-screen UCI. **Sports:** No university playing fields but uses local authority facilities. **Hardship funds:** Access funds; none from SU. **Travel:** Good for hitching (M6/M61); main line rail; bus. **Work:** Difficult but work available in pubs, warehouses, restaurants, etc. SU employs a large number of students.

BUZZ-WORD   Love – get used to being called Love.

ALUMNI (EDITORS' PICK)   Joe Lydon (rugby league international).

CENTRAL SAINT MARTINS

Central Saint Martins College of Art and Design,
Southampton Row, London WC1B 4AP
(Tel 0171 514 7000, Fax 0171 514 7024) Map 6

STUDENT ENQUIRIES: **Information Office**
APPLICATIONS: **UCAS (Route B)**

Broad study areas: Art & design. (Subject details are in the *Subjects and Places Index.*)

Founded: 1989, ex Central School of Art & Design and St Martin's School of Art. **Structural features:** Part of the London Institute. **Main undergraduate award:** BA. **Awarding body:** London Institute. **Site:** 5 sites in Soho, Covent Garden, Holborn and Clerkenwell. **Europe:**

15% of first degree students learn a language as part of their course and 33% spend 6 months or more abroad. Language support for first degree students. Formal exchange links with France through Artaccord; and with 14 European universities/colleges through Erasmus. **Library:** Libraries on main sites; 80,000 volumes, 250 periodicals, 126 study places, slide libraries, 100,000 transparencies. **Welfare:** London Institute student services. **Careers:** London Institute careers service. **Amenities:** Shop selling course materials; common room, canteen and coffee bar; dances, films etc organised by SU; TV and cine equipment; reprographic centre, computer room, language centre.

Accommodation: See *London Institute*. **Term time work**: College's policy to allow term time work for full-time first degree students. Occasional term time work on campus during exhibitions and private views; also college has placement contacts for work outside college. **Hardship funds:** Access fund.

Duration of first degree courses: 3 years; 4 years sandwich, 5 years part-time. **Total first degree students 1995/96:** 1,850. **Male/female ratio:** 1:2. **Teaching staff:** 78 full-time, 67 visiting lecturers. **Total full-time students 1995/96:** 2,400. **Postgraduate students:** 485. **First degree tuition fees:** Home students, paying their own fees in 1996/97, paid £1,600; Overseas students £5,950

WHAT IT'S LIKE   Based on 5 main sites in the heart of London, it's an art and design college which is both ancient and modern – true of the buildings and the staff alike. Students are a mix of ages, backgrounds and interests, reflected in a diversity of personal styles. A large increase of students from Asia and the Far East. Good staff/student ratio and the quality of teaching varies within each department; constant strain on the limited resources available. Students have to pay for the majority of the materials they use, so it's expensive to study art or design at degree level. There's a bar at Southampton row (currently shared with Westminster University law students); student DJs play on Friday nights and there's a general CSM party/gathering/happening. The London Institute SU also runs major one-off parties in massive venues (eg Ministry of Sound, Heaven, Hanover Grand) as well as ents such as DJ competitions, video and film nights, games and cocktail nights; also sports weekly such as aerobics, circuit training and football.

PAUPER NOTES   **Accommodation:** Limited access to halls of residence. London Institute has accommodation officer. **Drink:** Westminster University bar, shared with CSM, pubs and bars in surrounding central London. **Eats:** Rosie's Restaurant at Southampton Row site; Esmerelda's cafe at Charing Cross. Surrounded by sandwich shops and greasy-spoons. Food For Thought at Neals Yard has vegetarian deals for students after 2 pm. **Ents:** Cheap and cheerful college ents. Prince Charles (£1.50) and MGM (£1.75) cinemas with SU card. Film club shows cheap and unusual films every Tuesday. **Sports:** Aerobics, football, yoga, circuit training; student membership to various sports and leisure centres. **Hardship funds:** Access funds; limited in-house funds. **Travel:** London Transport expensive; get a bike. **Work:** SU has original jobs; work available in bar and coffee bars and at college ents.

ALUMNI (EDITORS' PICK)   Zandra Rhodes, Ralph Koltai (set designer for National Theatre), John Napier (set designer for RSC), Rachel Wilson (printmaker), Lionel Bart (composer/playwright), Robyn Denny (fashion designer), Linda Kitson (Falklands war artist), Bruce Oldfield (fashion designer), Rifat Ozbech (fashion). Hussein Chalyan (fashion), Alexander Queen (fashion designer).

CENTRAL SCHOOL OF SPEECH AND DRAMA

The Central School of Speech and Drama, Embassy Theatre, 64 Eton Avenue, London NW3 3HY
(Tel 0171 722 8183, Fax 0171 722 4132) Map 5

STUDENT ENQUIRIES: Admissions Officer
APPLICATIONS: UCAS; acting (direct).

Broad study areas: Drama, performing arts, art and design, speech therapy, education. (Subject details are in the *Subjects and Places Index*.)

Founded: 1906. **Main undergraduate awards:** BA, BSc. **Awarding body:** Open University. **Site:** Swiss Cottage (main site) and Camden. **Access:** Swiss Cottage station (main site), King's Cross (Camden); buses. **Academic features:** Unique provision of academic study and professional/practical training in related fields of art, design and the performing arts, education and therapy. Many well-known guest directors and tutors from the theatre, teaching, speech therapy and related professions. Also offers DipHE, with possible transfer to theatre studies course. **Europe:** Language tuition not currently available. **Library:** 24,000 volumes, 30 study places; computerised subject searching (CD-Rom and on-line). Free information sheets and bibliographies. Students have access to the British Library via inter-library loans. Annual expenditure on library materials, £70 per FTE student. **Other learning facilities:** Media resources unit, providing support and training in a range of media including video, sound, photography and computing. **Welfare:** Student counselling and advisory service. Ecumenical chaplaincy. **Amenities:** Fully equipped proscenium theatre (seating 274); 4 modern studios and range of design studios and workshop facilities, a lecture theatre and a speech and language therapy clinic.

Accommodation: No school accommodation. College helps to find lodgings 30 minutes of school: £50–£70 per week, self-catering. **Term time work:** School policy not to allow term time work without advance permission. Term (and vac) work occasionally available in school as ushers, in catering and cleaning. **Hardship funds:** 1995/96, total available £20,990 government access funds, some 39 students helped (average £538); £30,000 own funds for loans.

Duration of first degree courses: 3 years; BSc clinical communication 4 years. **Total first degree students 1995/96:** 475; **Overseas students:** 18. **Mature students:** 85. **Male/female ratio:** 1:3. **Teaching staff:** 36 full-time, 150 part-time (including visiting lecturers). **Total full-time students 1995/96:** 600. **Postgraduate students:** 86 on post-experience courses. **First degree tuition fees:** Home students, paying their own fees in 1996/97, paid £3,425 (except acting £4,200); Overseas students £6,550.

WHAT IT'S LIKE   The school has two sites linked by both bus and tube (average journey time 15 minutes). The main site at Swiss Cottage is centred around the late-Victorian Embassy Theatre, conveniently next to the underground station; the other at St Pancras, King's Cross, offers excellent facilities to students following courses in art, directing, puppetry and various production-related courses. The college is small, creating a friendly and sociable atmosphere. Recent building programme has provided a new library, computer room, bar and student space; the emphasis is on expansion and improvement of quality. The SU actively participates in a wide variety of entertainments and campaigns. Both sites have ideal access to Primrose Hill, Regent's Park (where the football team plays on Sundays), the West End and most of Central London. The student population includes a cosmopolitan mix of students. Drop out rate is low, workload tends to be heavy and changing courses virtually unknown.   *Simon Vyvyan*

PAUPER NOTES   Accommodation: No halls; union housing officer helps. 10–15% live at home. NW3 expensive; many prefer the cheaper areas in NW6/NW10. **Drink:** Swiss Cottage (nearby pub) and college bar. Several excellent pubs in Hampstead, 15 mins away. **Eats:** College canteen. Reasonably priced meals in local community centre cafe. Various take-aways; usual fast food places. **Ents:** CSSD students go free to all performances in Embassy Theatre and studios. SU holds regular functions. Local cinema, Hampstead Theatre and the whole of London. **Sports:** Football pitch opposite college; swimming, badminton, weights etc at Swiss Cottage sports centre; tennis courts 15 mins walk. **Hardship funds:** Some loans available; assisted places (increasing); access fund. **Travel:** Some departments reimburse travel if course-related eg teaching practice. **Work:** Cleaning jobs, bar and waiter work, ushering on campus are most common. Hard to fit in as classes from 9–6 and a lot of courses call for long rehearsals. Youth work to bulb picking in vacations.

INFORMAL NAME   CSSD or Central.

MORE INFO?   Ring Simon Vyvyan (0171 483 0144).

ALUMNI (EDITORS' PICK)   Laurence Olivier, Peggy Ashcroft, Vanessa Redgrave, Judi Dench, Dawn French, Jennifer Saunders, Deborah Warner, Jim Cartwright, Bruce Robinson, Josette Simon, Amanda Donohoe, Lindsay Duncan, Michael Elphick, Jeremy Brett, Cameron Macintosh.

CHARING CROSS AND WESTMINSTER

Charing Cross and Westminster Medical School,
(University of London), The Reynolds Building, St Dunstan's
Road, London W6 8RP (Tel 0181 846 1234) Map 5

STUDENT ENQUIRIES: **Admissions Officer**
(Tel 0181 846 7202, Fax 0181 846 7222)
APPLICATIONS: **UCAS**

Broad study area: Medicine.

Founded: 1818 and 1834. **Structural features:** Part of London University; merging with Imperial College in 1997. **Main undergraduate awards:** MB BS, BSc. **Awarding body:** London University. **Site:** Fulham and Chelsea. **Access:** Hammersmith and Baron's Court underground stations; South Kensington underground station. **Europe:** No students take a language or spend time abroad as part of course. **Special features:** Introduction of a fibre-optic remote teaching system which enables clinical students on different hospital sites to receive lectures by cable simultaneously and to communicate between sites. **Library:** On both sites: 42,000 volumes, 300 periodicals; 250 study places; videos; inter-active CD-Rom and electronic databases. **Welfare:** FPA, couselling service, psychiatrist, chaplain. **Careers:** Advice and limited placement service. **Amenities:** All resources of London University. **Sporting facilities:** International size swimming-pool, squash courts and gymnasium at Charing Cross site. Sports grounds in Surrey.

Accommodation: In 1995/96, 20% of all students in school accommodation, all first years can be. 240 self-catering places available (160 for first years): £46–£56 per week. Students live in privately owned accommodation for 3–4 years: rents £65–£80 per week for self-catering. 11% first degree students live at home. **Term time work**: School's policy to allow term time work for full-time first degree students (so long as it does not interfere with studies). Term (and vac) work available on campus in library, bar, clerical work. **Hardship funds:** Total available in 1995/96: £41,422 government access funds, 66 students helped.

Duration of first degree courses: 5 years (MB, BS); 1 year (intercalated BSc). **Total first degree students 1995/96:** 905. **Overseas students:** 37. **Mature students:** approx 78. **Male/female ratio:** 1:1. **Teaching staff:** approx 160 full-time, 200 part-time. **Total full-time students 1995/96:** 947. **Postgraduate students:** 42 full-time; 134 part-time. **First degree tuition fees:** Home students, paying their own fees in 1996/97, paid £850 for certain categories, otherwise £1,600 (pre-clinical), £2,800 (clinical); Overseas students £8,500 (pre-clinical), £15,700 (clinical).

WHAT IT'S LIKE   Incredibly friendly and welcoming medical school, primarily based at Charing Cross Hospital (in Hammersmith), and at the Chelsea and Westminster (the newest teaching hospital in Europe). Both are linked with associated teaching hospitals via a fibre optic TV network, so clinical students can be taught and interact with tutors miles away. SU and preclinical lectures are at Charing Cross Hospital. SU very active and organises student bops, a secondhand bookshop and probably the cheapest bar in London. Merger with Imperial and St Mary's is imminent and course will be progressively integrated. Best London medical school rugby team – won United Hospitals Cup (oldest rugby cup in the world) three times in last four years. Success in football, hockey and netball is just as outstanding. Many very well supported clubs including orchestra, Light Operatic Society, water polo, choir, squash, CU, Islamic society and mountaineering. Facilities include library, TV and snooker room, cafeteria, weights room and a Dillons bookshop. Hospital also has a swimming pool, gym and squash courts, available at reduced student rates. Rag Week sees the invasion of London and everyone gives up work for a week, to be abducted to Wales or pay for friends to be covered in foam. In the Easter holidays, students travel throughout the south of England raising money and gaining hangovers on the legendary Fun Bus. The infamous Speculum is a yearly round-up of gossip and scandal published by students and aimed to shock. Friendly halls of residence at Pimlico and Notting Hill Gate for all first years if they want. Afterwards most students live as close to Hammersmith as possible in rented accommodation. No offers are made without interview, large numbers of graduates considered and students wishing to intercalate are encouraged. It really is about working hard and playing even harder.   *Isobel Fitzgerald O'Connor*
PAUPER NOTES   **Accommodation:** Hard-to-let council accommodation, nurses home, friends' parents who are persuaded to buy houses locally. **Drink:** SU bar cheap: all spirits 95p, so is pint of XXXX/Tetleys, £1.15 for Lowenbrau. Local pubs expensive. **Eats:** Stockpot (King's Road), Broadway Café, local curry houses – good value; also hospital canteen and refectory. **Ents:** Riverside Studios (TFI Friday), local cinemas (student discounts), Lyric,

Hammersmith (student standbys). **Sports:** Hospital sports club (student discounts); local council facilities cheap with Lifestyle card. **Hardship funds:** Access funds (priority to 4th year students and those with real financial hardship); scholarships for BSc study. **Travel:** Scholarships for electives. Free bus between 2 main hospitals. **Work:** Difficult as courses require long hours. Good jobs in Hammersmith, large department stores, temp jobs at Olympia an Earls court, nursing, bar and library work at medical school. Also a lot are paid to re-write GP notes.

INFORMAL NAME   CXWMS or The Cross

ALUMNI (EDITORS' PICK)   Professor Harold Ellis (world-famous general surgeon), Thomas Huxley (pioneering scientist), Dr Livingstone (explorer), Sir Anthony Dawson (Queen's physician), Dame Josephine Barnes (early woman obstetrics consultant), Niall Campbell (Sky TV psychiatrist).

CHELSEA COLLEGE OF ART

Chelsea College of Art and Design
- **Manresa Road, London SW3 6LS**
  (Tel 0171 514 7750, Fax 0171 514 7777) Map 6
- **40 Lime Grove, London W12**
  (Tel 0171 514 7750, Fax 0171 514 7838)

STUDENT ENQUIRIES: **Manresa Road for fine art**
(Tel 0171 514 7750, ext 7759); Lime Grove for design
(Tel 0171 514 7750, ext 7820 for textiles and public art and
design, ext 7883 for interiors)
APPLICATIONS: **UCAS**

Broad study areas: Art & design. (Subject details are in the *Subjects and Places Index.*)

Founded: 1891, later incorporating art departments of Regent Street Polytechnic and Hammersmith College of Arts and Crafts. **Structural features:** Part of the London Institute. **Main undergraduate award:** BA. **Awarding body:** London Institute. **Site:** 4 sites in Chelsea/Fulham/Shepherd's Bush. **Access:** Tube (South Kensington/Sloane Square); buses along King's Road for Chelsea/Fulham. Tube (Shepherd's Bush/Goldhawk Road) for Shepherd's Bush. **Largest fields of study:** Painting, sculpture, combined media, design (textiles, interiors, public art). **Europe:** No students take languages or spend time abroad as part of their course. **Library:** 3 libraries at Manresa Road, South Park and Lime Grove buildings; 70,000 volumes, 200 periodicals, 30 study places. Annual expenditure on library materials, £73 per FTE student. **Specialist collections:** Fine art at Manresa Road. **Welfare:** Student services officer. **Careers:** Information and advice. **Amenities:** Shops for students' materials on all sites. **Employment:** Strong tradition of freelance work in fine art, industrial employment in design.

Accommodation: In 1995/96, 10% of all students in college accommodation, 20% of first years: full-board at £65–£75 per week. Students live in privately owned accommodation for

2+ years. 12% first degree students live at home. **Term time work**: College's policy to allow term time work for full-time first degree students; 20% believed to work. No work available in college. **Hardship fund:** Government access funds; no college funds.

Duration of first degree courses: 2–3 years; **other:** part-time or mixed mode 4–5 years. **Total first degree students 1995/96:** 688. **Overseas students:** 60. **Mature students:** 55. **Male/female ratio:** 2:3. **Teaching staff:** 41 full-time, 120 part-time. **Total full-time students 1995/96:** 1,164. **Postgraduate students:** 48. **First degree tuition fees:** Home students, paying their own fees in 1996/97, paid £1,600; Overseas students £5,950.

WHAT IT'S LIKE   It's a small college, spread over 4 sites: Manresa Road (behind Chelsea Fire Station), Hugon Road (just off the Wandsworth Bridge Road), Bagley's Lane (near Chelsea Harbour) and Lime Grove (shared with Hammersmith & West London College). This means it lacks strong single identity despite efforts of staff and SU. Different courses at different sites, so make sure you look round the site you're applying to. Chelsea site, housing fine art courses, has the best facilities (most events take place here) and the academic reputation to match. Beware, students are expected to motivate themselves and tutors with famous names can prove elusive. If you do the foundation course at Bagley's Lane you'll probably have a great time, and get a place on a higher course but you may have to create your own social life. Hugon Road site is a converted school, with the atmosphere to match; the interior design/decoration students share uneasily with over a hundred BTEC students and it's a long walk from the tube. Being in central London, Chelsea has a problem with accommodation. There are 400 places in 2 halls of residence; however, competition for these places with all the other thousands of London Institute students is stiff. Important to start looking early, it may take a few months to find adequate accommodation, years to find sought after housing co-op or council housing. Typical student is middle class (though that's changing), easy going, pretentious but friendly and clad in shabby chic. Student shops (open from a couple of hours a week to half-day every few days) and along with every other service are run for profit. Chelsea concentrates its meagre resources on the libraries. There are financial difficulties in studying at Chelsea but millionaires are certainly encouraged to apply! Chelsea's results are excellent due to the quality staff and the excellent quality of students it has been able to attract.

PAUPER NOTES   **Accommodation:** £50–£70 for anywhere vaguely close; very limited halls. **Drink:** London Institute SU bars cheapest beer. **Eats:** Canteens reasonable if you're into school dinners, however not cheap – can lack ambience! **Ents:** Parties at eg Heaven, Ministry of Sound, Videodrome all run by London Institute SU. **Sports:** Gym, football, discounts at local leisure centre. **Hardship funds:** Access fund, minimal to non-existent – understanding bank manager and careful budgeting essential. **Travel:** No student fares but travelcards; bus often cheaper, and better for most Chelsea sites. Cycling dangerous, wet and cold in winter. **Work:** Many people get Saturday jobs in town – big department stores.

MORE INFO?   Get students' Alternative Prospectus.
Enquiries to Students Union (0171 371 9532).

ALUMNI (EDITORS' PICK)   Alexei Sayle, Graham Gough, Simon Edmonson (painter), Sarah Jane Hoare (stylist with Harpers & Queen), Henry Moore, Vincent Price, Patrick Caulfield, John Berger, Dirk Bogarde; Anish Kapoor (Turner prize winner) and Peter Doig (runner up); Helen Chadwick, Gavin Tirk, Richard Deacon, Kerry Stewart (artists).

CHELTENHAM & GLOUCESTER COLLEGE

Cheltenham & Gloucester College of Higher Education,
PO Box 220, The Park, Cheltenham, Gloucestershire GL50 2QF
(Tel 01242 532700) Map 3

STUDENT ENQUIRIES: Schools Liaison Officer
(Tel 01242 532825, Fax 01242 256759)

APPLICATIONS: UCAS

Broad study areas: Arts, fashion and media; business & management; computing multimedia; environmental studies, leisure and tourism; hotel and catering managment; landscape architecture; sport exercise sciences; teacher education. (Subject details are in the *Subjects and Places Index*.)

Founded: 1990, from merger of College of St Paul and St Mary with part of GlosCAT. **Main undergraduate awards:** BA, BEd, BSc. **Awarding body:** Cheltenham & Gloucester College. **Site:** Three campuses in Cheltenham. **Access:** Train, coach, M5 motorway, Birmingham and Bristol airports. **Special features:** Voluntary C of E foundation. **Academic features:** Modular structure for all undergraduate courses. Links with industry and commerce. **Europe:** 5% first degree students take a language as part of course; some also spend 6 months or more abroad. Formal exchange links with a number of European universities/colleges, all open to non-language specialists. **Library:** 500,000 volumes, 1,900 periodical titles. Annual expenditure on library materials, £52 per FTE student. **Specialist collections:** Early children's books; college archives from 1847; Dymock poets archive; history of sport collection, slide collection of fine art and fashion. **Other learning facilities:** Film and TV, dance and drama studios; language laboratories; access to a number of CD-Roms, electronic on-line databases and the Internet. **Welfare:** Counsellors; medical officer and nursing staff; academic counsellors; personal tutors; chaplains. **Careers:** Information and advisory service. **Sporting facilities:** 40 acres playing fields, swimming pool, sports hall, physiology and biomechanics laboratories.

Accommodation: In 1995/96, 55% first years in college accommodation. 727 places available (715 for first years): 512 half-board places at £66–£72 per week (34 week contracts) and 203 self-catering places at £52 per week (40 week contracts). Some students live in privately owned accommodation for their whole course: rents £42–£45 per week for self-catering, £45–£50 B&B, £60–£65 for half-board. **Term time work:** College's policy to allow term time work for full-time first degree students; 60–70% believed to work. Term (and vac) work available on campus in SU bar, acccommodation services, catering, registry, libraries. **Hardship funds:** Total available in 1995/96: £118,132 government access funds, 500 students helped.

Duration of first degree courses: 3 years; 4 years (with work placement). **Total first degree students 1995/96:** 4,700. **BEd students:** 730. **Overseas students:** 50. **Mature students:** 2,463.

Male/female ratio: 1:2. **Teaching staff:** 274 full-time. **Total full-time students:** 5,400.
Postgraduate students: 279. **First degree tuition fees:** Home students, paying their own fees
in 1996/97, paid £2,750; Overseas: £5,200 (classroom), £6,500 (lab/studio).

WHAT IT'S LIKE   A fast growing and dynamic institution, hoping to gain university status.
Now caters for 5,000 full-time students and 2,000 part-time students. Three separate sites
are spread over Cheltenham; undergoing great change, with new buildings for academic
and accommodation space. Excellent academic record for teacher training, business
courses and art-based programmes. Also opportunities to study abroad for a term on many
courses. The modular scheme provides greater choice and power for the student. On-site
accommodation for approximately 500 students, both catered and self-catering. About 40%
of students are local and increasing numbers are living at home. SU, in new multi-million
pound building, runs 3 bars, 2 shops, a welfare advice centre, over 30 sports clubs, around
20 societies and regular entertainment. Clubs regularly successful in national competitions,
ie British Colleges and BSSA Champions – badminton, cricket, women's hockey, swimming,
women's rugby, water-polo, and tennis. Recreation centre, National Hunt Racecourse in
Cheltenham and ski centre in Gloucester. Good areas for shopping and leisure activity close
to the main sites with pleasant Cotswold countryside surrounding both towns.
PAUPER NOTES   **Accommodation:** Halls of residence (new ones are nice but expensive); 1st years priority. Shortfall made up from individual flats to terrace housing. Average
rents £40 per week. **Drink:** Multitude of pubs and wine bars. Expensive in comparison to
SU bars. **Eats:** Impressive variety (price and nationality): Cantonese, Greek, French. **Ents:**
SU events of good value, eg hypnotists, comedians, discos, bands, and 5 formals. Town
entertainments include nightclubs, fringe theatre, Everyman theatre, literature and music
festivals, town hall events, art galleries and museums. **Sports:** Excellent facilities including
swimming pool. **Hardship funds:** Access funds. **Travel:** Bike almost essential in Cheltenham.
Buses relatively efficient, making car ownership unnecessary. **Work:** Quite easy to find:
bar, restaurant, shop work and clerical jobs.
ALUMNI (EDITORS' PICK)   Omar Arteh, Samuel Baldeh, David Bryant, P H Newby,
Sarah Potter, Graham Brookhouse, Don Hale, Chris Broad.

CHESTER UNIVERSITY COLLEGE

University College Chester, Cheyney Road, Chester CH1 4BJ
(Tel 01244 375444, Fax 01244 373379) Map 2

STUDENT ENQUIRIES: The Registry
APPLICATIONS: UCAS (except nursing etc)

Broad study areas: Education, sciences, PE, humanities, nursing
and midwifery, theology. (Subject details are in the *Subjects and
Places Index.*)

Founded: 1839 by Church of England. **Main undergraduate awards:** BA, BSc, BEd. **Awarding
body:** Liverpool University. **Site:** 30-acre campus within walking distance of Chester centre.

Access: 15 mins from M56, 45 mins from M6, buses from town centre to site. **Academic features:** All BA/BSc students have a work-based learning component up to one semester; employment-related enterprise modules in first-year course. Staff and student exchanges with universities and colleges in New York, Canada, Finland, Greece, Russia and Spain. **Largest fields of study:** Teacher training, PE. **Europe:** 12% first degree students take a language as part of their course and 1% spend a semester in another European country. Languages for beginners available (1 term); BA/BSc students can take a language as first year or minor subject. **Library:** Recently extended: 120,000 volumes, 550 periodicals, 250 study places. Annual expenditure on library materials, £100 per FTE student. **Other learning facilities:** Human performance laboratory; satellite remote-sensing suite; CCTV studio and media centre; integrated live arts (art, design and technology building). **Welfare:** Chaplaincy; student counsellor, student services centre on campus; personal tutorial system. **Careers:** Full-time careers service; work-based learning for all undergraduates. **Amenities:** 25-metre pool, squash courts, sauna/solarium and astrograss floodlit all-weather pitch. **Employment:** Teaching profession, commerce, media, personnel.

Accommodation: In 1995/96, 32% of all students in college accommodation, 65% first years. 480 places available (282 for first years): 360 full-board places (294 for first years) from £59–£63 per week and 183 self-catering places at £30–£40 per week, all term time only. Students live in privately owned accommodation for 2+ years: rent £30–£40 per week self-catering. 35% first degree students live at home. **Term time work:** College's policy to allow term time work for full-time first degree students; 40% believed to work. Term (and vac) work available on campus in library, bar, schools liaison/representatives. **Hardship funds:** Total available in 1995/96: £50,305 government access funds, 91 students helped.

Duration of first degree courses: 3 or 4 years. **Total first degree students 1995/96:** 2,258; **BEd students:** 773. **Male/female ratio:** 1:3. **Teaching staff:** 128 full-time, 15 part-time. **Total full-time students 1995/96:** 2,389 (2,399 part-time). **Postgraduate students:** 131. **First degree tuition fees:** Home students, paying their own fees in 1996/97, paid £750 (classroom), £1,600 (lab); Overseas students £6,542 (classroom), £8,544 (lab).

WHAT IT'S LIKE   Founded in 1839, situated on a 30-acre site ten minutes' walk from the town centre. All facilities are on the one campus and include library and media centre, health centre just off campus (with confidential counselling, pregnancy and contraception advice), bookshop, union shop, launderette and newly renovated SU bar. Sports facilities include 2 squash courts, 2 gymnasia, swimming pool, sauna and solarium, 6 tennis courts, all-weather pitch and various grass pitches. Also Northgate Arena, five minutes' walk away. Sports teams are all above average as PE is a major subject. Nine halls of residence, many single study bedrooms; the dining halls cater for all tastes. Student village on campus, with 84 final year students in self-catering houses and several college-owned houses a few minutes' walk away (more each year); most others live in nearby Garden Lane area – accommodation at varying standards and prices. Because the majority of students live so close to college there is a great community atmosphere. College has a cosmopolitan feel with regular intakes of Hong Kong students and an exchange programme with the State University of New York. Typical students: either arty, with a big folder; psychological, with a small folder; or sporty, with no folder. Generally non-political SU runs clubs and societies and has elected reps on all major college committees. Entertainment-wise, there are weekly bops and twice-weekly college nightclub nights as well as visiting bands, novelty acts and theme nights with quiz nights and karaoke in the bar. English, psychology, PE and primary education are the most popular courses all leading to a combined studies degree from Liverpool University.

PAUPER NOTES **Accommodation:** If it's cheap it usually lo... modation on campus shared. **Drink:** College bar. Cheap bitter... Clavertons, Bouverie Arms; loads of pubs, mainly Greenhalls, a... easily be found. **Eats:** Bombay Palace. Wide variety of burgers, pizz... restaurants. Check out Uneeque pizzas on Garden Lane. **Ents:** Nomin... ents, discount at theatres, cinemas, etc. **Sports:** Campus swimming poo... courts. **Travel:** National Express coach cards, ISIC and railcards av... ...U. **Hardship funds:** Access funds. **Work:** Bar and restaurant work in city centre. ...tudents who look for jobs get them – around 25% overall; few (10%) stay over summer but they generally get jobs.

ALUMNI (EDITORS' PICK) John Carlton (rugby international), Carol Lewis (assistant governor, HM Borstal), Walter Winterbottom (director of Sports Council), Richard Palmer (Secretary British Olympic Committee), The Venerable Francis William Harvey (Archdeacon of London), Lynn Davies (British long jump record-holder), George Courtney (top British football referee).

CHICHESTER UNIVERSITY COLLEGE

Chichester University College,
- **Bognor Regis Campus, Upper Bognor Road,
  Bognor Regis, West Sussex PO21 1HR**
  (Tel 01243 816000, Fax 01243 816081)
- **Bishop Otter Campus, College Lane, Chichester,
  West Sussex PO19 4PE**
  (Tel 01243 816000, Fax 01243 816080) Map 4

STUDENT ENQUIRIES: Admissions Office (Bognor) or General enquiries (Bishop Otter)
APPLICATIONS: UCAS

Broad study areas: Education, performance arts, social studies and humanities, health studies, sports science, art, environmental science and mathematics. (Subject details are in the *Subjects and Places Index*.)

Founded: 1977 as West Sussex Institute, ex Bishop Otter College Chichester (1839) and Bognor Regis College (1947). **Structural features:** Accredited college of Southampton University. **Main undergraduate awards:** BA, BA(QTS), BSc. **Awarding body:** Southampton University. **Site:** 2 sites (Chichester and Bognor Regis). **Access:** Both sites within walking distance of respective town centres. **Europe:** No languages taught. Erasmus exchanges to a range of European countries for students in eg dance, maths and sports studies. **Library:** Library on each site. 200,000 volumes in total, 850 periodicals, 120 study places; short loan collections. Major new learning resources centre. Annual expenditure on library materials, £55.70 per FTE student. **Specialist collections:** Bishop Otter College collection

...ury British art, Gerard Young local history collection, art slides, official educa-
...documents, 19th century British parliamentary papers, Historical Association pamphlets, music scores, specialist theological collection. **Other learning facilities:** 2 PC networks, 100 work stations; video edit suites, mobile video production unit; photographic centre. **Welfare:** Accommodation officers, health centre, doctors, counsellors, chaplain, welfare officer for international students. Special provision: Limited nursery facilities and half-term play scheme. **Careers:** Information and advice, both individually and as part of course. **Amenities:** SU with many societies, travel and insurance bureaux. Chapel, art gallery, art collection. **Sporting facilities:** Sports halls and pitches.

Accommodation: In 1995/96, 20% of students in college accommodation (priority for first years). Approx 450 half board places, £59 per week (includes heat and 2 meals per day), term time only; additional places available in 1997. Students live in privately owned accommodation for other years: £35–£40 per week self-catering; £40–£45 B&B; £60–£70 half board and weekend meals. **Term time work:** College policy to allow term time work for first degree students (30% believed to work). Term (and vac) work available on campus in SU bar and contract catering. **Hardship funds:** Total available in 1995/96: £60,000 government access funds (£150 average award); £7,000 own funds for short-term loans (£120 average award). Special help to single parent students and for travel expenses; also for students whose grants arrive late.

Duration of first degree courses: 3 years; 4 years BA(QTS). **Total first degree students 1995/96:** 2,350; **BA(QTS) students:** 866. **Overseas students:** 100. **Mature students:** 37% (57% on BA(QTS)). **Male/female ratio:** 1:3. **Teaching staff:** 97 full-time, 17 part-time. **Total full-time students 1995/96:** 2,500 (1,300 part-time). **Postgraduate students:** 340. **First degree tuition fees:** Home students, paying their own fees in 1996/97, paid £825; Overseas students £6,110.

WHAT IT'S LIKE It's made up of two colleges, Bognor Regis and Bishop Otter (Chichester). Redevelopment means that the majority of first years will be on campus; all other students live in accommodation in either town (Bognor is cheaper). Inter-site transport is provided. Both colleges have a friendly atmosphere for both study and socialising. Mixture of education students, BA/BSc and postgraduate; some international students. Campus parking is a problem with permits at a premium (campus residents not eligible). Ideally placed on the south coast so excellent for water sports enthusiasts. Many clubs and societies provided by the SU for a wider range of sporting and cultural activities. A small friendly college which offers a good alternative to the larger establishments around the country.

PAUPER NOTES **Accommodation:** Most first years in hall (some ensuite rooms in Chichester; often shared rooms in Bognor). **Drink:** SU bar on each site for cheap drinks; nice pubs in both towns, very cheap in Bognor. Ballards Brewery and Gales HSB excellent local beers. **Eats:** Several good eating places in town, especially Chichester. **Ents:** Ents at colleges with bands performing regularly, films and plays throughout the year. Chichester excellent for theatre lovers, weak for other night life activities. Bognor has a couple of night clubs. **Sports:** College sport excellent; both towns have a leisure centre. Chichester has access to swimming pool. **Hardship funds:** Little available but support systems improving. **Travel:** Cycling easiest and cheapest means of travel. Hitching difficult. **Work:** SU bar work, shop and security on campus; same plus factories in town (£2.75–£3.75 per hour). Some students work locally in vacations – Butlins, bars, farm work.

MORE INFO? Ring SU (01243 816390).

CITY UNIVERSITY

City University, Northampton Square, London EC1V 0HB
(Tel 0171 477 8000, Fax 0171 477 8559) Map 6

STUDENT ENQUIRIES: Undergraduate Admissions Office
APPLICATIONS: UCAS

Broad study areas: Engineering, computing, mathematics, actuarial science and statistics, nursing & health sciences, social sciences, journalism, media studies, business & management, law, music. (Subject details are in the *Subjects and Places Index.*)

Founded: 1894 as Northampton Institute; university status in 1966. **Main undergraduate awards:** BA, BSc, BEng, LLB, BMus, MEng. **Awarding body:** City University. **Site:** Islington, close to City of London. **Access:** Angel or Barbican underground stations. **Europe:** Language tuition available on all courses. **Academic features:** Courses include optional 1-year professional placement; major individual project in final year. All courses offer introduction to IT and development of communication skills; many lead to exemptions from professional exams. **Library:** Extended library with 280,000 volumes, 1,800 periodicals, 615 study places; 4 branch libraries at Barbican and nursing/radiography centres. Annual expenditure on library materials, £73 per FTE student. **Other learning facilities:** Computing services including Internet access, 400 Unix workstations/PCs and 22 Novell/Unix servers. **Specialist collections:** Anderson Music Library, Erna Auerbach Collection, London Society Library, Walter Fincham Optics Collection. **Welfare:** University health centre, counselling service and chaplaincy; all students have a personal tutor. **Careers:** Information, advice and placement service. **Amenities:** Bookshop on site, new SU recreational facilities, including bars, shops and concert venues. **Sporting facilities:** Saddlers sports centre (good indoor sports, fitness centre and sauna); swimming pool; squash courts; playing fields in south London.

Accommodation: In 1995/96, 25% of all undergraduates in university accommodation, guaranteed for first years (if they meet criteria). 982 places available (500+ for first years): 320 catered places (240+ for first years) at £81 per week, term time only, and 366 self-catering places (280 for first years) at £69–£71, Sept–June; plus 296 self-catering places, mostly postgraduate. Students live in privately owned accommodation for 1+ years: rents £60–£75 per week for self-catering; good range and supply locally. **Term time work:** No university policy on part time work for students. **Hardship funds:** Total available in 1995/96: £172,087 government access funds, 666 students helped. Special help: students living in private accommodation.

Duration of first degree courses: 3–4 years; **others:** 4–5 years. **Total first degree students 1995/96:** 4,257. **Overseas students:** 15%. **Mature students:** 35%. **Male/female ratio:** 6:4. **Teaching and research staff:** 593. **Total full-time students 1995/96:** 6,837. **Postgraduate students:** 4,281. **First degree tuition fees:** Home students, paying their own fees in 1996/97, paid £750 (classroom), £1,600 (lab); Overseas students £5,900 (classroom), £7,100–£8,500 (lab).

WHAT IT'S LIKE In the triangle formed by Angel, Old St and Barbican tubes – each 5–10 minutes walk away. Halls and academic sites within the triangle. Not a campus, but most activity takes place in main building (1960s brick and concrete; accessible by numerous buses). First and final year students who want to, live in halls; others rent flats/houses in north or east London. Overnight guests allowed in halls for two nights in any one week – but no one ever checks. Welfare advice available from SU, university health centre or Barts Hospital clinic (very close, very busy). Active SU runs a community action project and a crèche for working/student parents in the half term holidays. Discos/bands on Fridays, films on Tuesdays and other ents during the week. Islington's pubs are a walk away and the West End is accessible. Top subjects are banking and finance, business, engineering, computing, optics and social sciences. High proportion of students are sponsored. Most students are here either due to a desire to see London Town or because of sponsorship.

PAUPER NOTES **Accommodation:** All 1st and 3rd years in hall. Block of flats close to the university. Rents high. **Drink:** 2 union bars (approx 20% off a pint) and bars in halls of residence. **Eats:** Really good food in union bars. Best to shop at the markets (Chapel & Whitecross Streets). Good veg curry house – as much lunch as you can eat for £4+. Campus food missable. **Ents:** Discount during freshers' week; all other City ents free with ents card. Venue has club atmosphere + appropriate music. **Sports:** University sports centre very nearby and cheap for students; swimming pool in main building; sports ground (not close but coach transport arranged by SU). **Hardship funds:** Union will haggle with finance office/banks on students' behalf – good relationship with both. **Travel:** Travelling bursaries awarded by ex-student club (The N'ions). London fares high – get a bike or be prepared for the costs. **Work:** Work for union in bars or ents, or for university in halls of residence kitchens.

ALUMNI (EDITORS' PICK) Charles Farnecombe (conductor), John Alvey, Michael Fish.

COLCHESTER INSTITUTE

Colchester Institute, Sheepen Road, Colchester,
Essex CO3 3LL (Tel 01206 718000, Fax 01206 763041) Map 4

STUDENT ENQUIRIES: Enquiries Office
APPLICATIONS: UCAS

Broad study areas: Music, business, hospitality and catering, occupational therapy, design, environment, leisure, humanities. (Subject details are in the *Subjects and Places Index*.)

Founded: 1976 ex North East Essex Technical College, Colchester School of Art and St Osyth's College, Clacton. **Main undergraduate awards:** BA, BSc. **Awarding body:** Anglia Polytechnic University. **Site:** Campuses at Colchester, Clacton and Witham. **Access:** Each campus near town centre and railway station. **Special features:** Ensemble in residence, master classes. Strong links with industry; international work placements. **Structural features:** Links with Britten-Pears School at Snape and joint courses with Essex University. **Europe:** Language tuition part of all first degree courses and available to all full-time students. Some work placements available in Europe. **Library:** Libraries at all 3 sites; c.127,000 items including audio-visual materials; CD-Rom; 500+ periodicals, 270 study places. Annual expenditure on library materials, £19.25 per FTE student. **Welfare:** Qualified nurses, medical room, student counsellor. Special categories: Residential facilities for disabled students. **Careers:** Information and advice. **Amenities:** SU shop, refectories, bar at Clacton; 3 restaurants at hotel school. **Sporting facilities:** Gymnasia, judo, fencing, etc; tennis, playing fields, weight training room. **Employment:** Music performance/teaching; management; environmental health; design consultancies; research; marketing.

Accommodation: In 1996/97, 208 half-board places in college accommodation at Clacton: £418–£532 a term (single), £308–£392 a term (shared); 14 self-catering at Colchester at £45 per week. Students in privately owned accommodation pay £35–£50 per week, self-catering; £55–£70 full board. 20% first degree students live at home. **Term time work**: Institute's policy to allow term time work for full-time first degree students; 30% believed to work. Term (and vac) work available on campus in bars and SU. **Hardship funds:** In 1995/96, £41,364 government access funds, over 134 students helped. Special help: self-financing students, child care costs for those suffering financial hardship.

Duration of first degree courses: 3 years; others 2 years. **Total first degree students 1995/96:** 670. **Overseas students:** 9. **Mature students:** 160. **Male/female ratio:** 4:5. **Teaching staff:** 280 full-time, 200 part-time. **Total full-time students 1995/96:** 3,900. **First degree tuition fees:** Home students, paying their own fees in 1996/97, paid £1,330–£1,475; Overseas students £5,480–£5,850.

WHAT IT'S LIKE   Mainly on 2 sites – Colchester (Sheepen Road) and Clacton – but also recently acquired School of Occupational Therapy in Witham. Sheepen Road site built in late '50s and early '60s, with newer additions (library, buildings for art & design and hair & beauty therapy and new resource centre). It houses the nationally respected schools of music and art & design; it caters for day students only, from GCSE resits to BA courses. There are excellent welfare facilities and a relaxed, informal atmosphere; a daytime student social area provides video games, pool tables etc. Refectory and snack facilities are good. Clacton site is on the sea front – part of the old Grand Hotel, famous for once having Edward VII as a guest. It is smaller but has residential facilities including a bar (for residents only). Full sports facilities near both sites. A well-developed SU has exec on both campuses. There are disabled facilities; mature students are welcome and have made their mark at Sheepen Road.

PAUPER NOTES   **Accommodation:** Residential accommodation at Clacton for some courses; only a token amount at Sheepen Road but accommodation officer for house-shares and digs. **Drink:** Student pubs (Hole in the Wall, The Cups, Kings Arms, Oliver Twist, Playhouse) are plentiful in Colchester. Clacton has own bar. **Eats:** Lots of good, cheap restaurants around (Clowns, Rumpoles, Tilly's) plus the usual high street fast-food fodder. Both sites have training restaurants (very cheap and good). **Ents:** Colchester is (despite what Blur say) a good place for going out. Essex University (2 miles from town centre), Colchester Arts Centre, Hippodrome nightclub, Mercury Theatre, 6-screen Odeon, Minories Art Gallery, 7 museums. SU runs social events (bands etc), trips to London (shows, concerts etc). **Sports:** Good leisure centre at Colchester, with gym, swimming pool, ten-pin bowling etc. Sports and leisure centre at Clacton, swimming pool 3 minutes from site.

Hardship funds: Access fund, but don't rely on it as hundreds apply. **Travel:** Inter-site transport available and free. Many courses organise trips abroad eg catering students have placements in Europe and USA, art & design often organise trips to Europe. **Work:** Lots available in bars and restaurants.
ALUMNI (EDITORS' PICK)   Graham Coxon (Blur's guitarist), Martin Litton (jazz pianist), Farnaby Brass Quartet, Ebony Wind Quartet.

COURTAULD INSTITUTE

Courtauld Institute of Art, University of London, Somerset House, Strand, London WC2R 0RN (0171 872 2777) Map 6

STUDENT ENQUIRIES: Secretary to the Registrar
(Tel 0171 873 2645, Fax 0171 873 2410)
APPLICATIONS: UCAS

Broad study area: History of art. (Subject details are in the *Subjects and Places Index.*)

Founded: 1931. **Structural features:** Part of London University. **Main undergraduate award:** BA. **Awarding body:** London University. **Academic features:** Postgraduate courses in the history of art, history of architecture, conservation, art museum studies and the history of dress. **Site:** Central London. **Europe:** All first degree students take a language as part of course but none spend time abroad. **Library:** Over 115,000 volumes, 220+ current periodicals, approx 200 study places; a slide library with over 250,000 b/w and coloured slides. Annual expenditure on library materials, £198 per FTE student. **Specialist collections:** Witt Library (photographs and reproductions of paintings, drawings and graphics), Conway Library (photographs of sculpture and architecture). Courtauld Institute Galleries (French Impressionist and Post-Impressionist paintings, Flemish and Italian Old Master paintings and drawings, Turner watercolours). **Welfare:** London University facilities and in-house welfare officer. **Careers:** University information and advice service. **Amenities:** SU is affiliated to ULU and students can make use of their gymnasium, swimming pool, squash courts, etc.

Accommodation: Students can live in London University halls of residence. Apply to university accommodation office (Malet Street, London WC1E 7HU). Some students live in privately owned accommodation for 2 years: rents £45–£70 per week for self-catering. 3% first degree students live at home. **Term time work:** Institute's policy to allow term time work for full-time first degree students (50% believed to work); limit of 10 hours per week. Term (and vac) work available on campus in library and assistance with open days. **Hardship funds:** Some funds available: average £200 awarded. Travel scholarships also available.

Duration of first degree courses: 3 years. **Total first degree students 1995/96:** 112. **Overseas students:** 3. **Mature students:** 15. **Male/female ratio:** 1:2. **Teaching staff:** 22 full-time, 3 part-time. **Total full-time students 1995/96:** 336. **Postgraduate students:** 223 f-t; 80 p-t. **First degree tuition fees:** Home students, paying their own fees in 1996/97, paid £750; Overseas students £6,550.

WHAT IT'S LIKE Situated in Somerset House, one of the most
in London, on the Strand and close to the Thames. Spacious, good fac.
Courtauld's world famous art collection. Very good library facilities – beautiful
(great to work in) and the Witt and Conway libraries for pictorial reference. Good
rooms; own fully modernised lecture theatre. Students have large comfortable c n
room space and a smart refectory selling cheap food. Small, friendly atmosphere. Large
cross-section of students; the 'finishing school' reputation is long gone. High standards
academically; all tutors expect complete dedication. Social life revolves around frequent
parties and Christmas and summer balls. Added to this is the more informal social life
whereby, when the college closes, anyone left in the building is encouraged to go to the
pub. Much use is made of King's College Union, next door. Theatre outings arranged. The
college magazine and life drawing club are among the activities organized by the Student
Union. The Courtauld has no accommodation and refers its students to the intercollegiate
halls. As members of London University, students can make use of all ULU sporting facilities at Malet Street. It's within walking distance of London's galleries and libraries and, of
course, the West End and all the entertainments London has to offer.
PAUPER NOTES **Accommodation:** Intercollegiate halls. **Drink:** King's College bar next
door. **Eats:** Cheap refectory. **Ents:** Parties in college. **Sport:** ULU facilities. **Hardship funds:**
Emergency hardship loans. **Travel:** Institute has travel scholarships. **Work:** Several jobs in
libraries and galleries for those that need them.
INFORMAL NAME CIA
ALUMNI (EDITORS' PICK) Giles Waterfield, Neil McGregor, Alan Bowness, Anthony
Blunt, Anita Brookner, Vincent Price, James Sainsbury.

COVENTRY UNIVERSITY

Coventry University, Priory Street, Coventry CV1 5FB
(Tel 01203 631313, Fax 01203 838793) Map 3

STUDENT ENQUIRIES: **Registry Services Manager**
APPLICATIONS: **UCAS**

Broad study areas: Art & design, built environment, business,
engineering, health and social sciences, international studies
and law, mathematical and information sciences, natural and
environmental sciences. (Subject details are in the *Subjects and
Places Index.*)

Founded: 1970 as Coventry Poly ex Lanchester College of Technology, Coventry College of
Art and Design, and Rugby College of Engineering Technology; university status in 1992.
Main undergraduate awards: BA, BSc, BEng, MEng, LLB. **Awarding body:** Coventry
University. **Site:** Coventry city centre; large modern campus. **Access:** 5 miles M6/M1 inter-
section; 30 mins Birmingham by train, 75 mins London Euston; adjacent to National Express
coach station. **Academic features:** All courses modular. Credit transfer possible. **Europe:**
25% first degree students take a language as part of course (available to all) and 10%

spend 6 months or more abroad. Several courses have European routes with year abroad eg applied biology, building. 125 formal exchange links across Europe, including some open to non-language specialists. **Library:** Main library plus art and design library; 300,000 volumes in total; 4,000 periodicals, 1,155 study places; short loan collection of 8,000 course books and articles. Annual expenditure on library materials, £100 per FTE student. **Welfare:** Doctor, FPA, multi-faith chaplaincy; international office; educational guidance, student counselling service. Special categories: Residential facilities for disabled students. **Careers:** Information and advice service. **Amenities:** Two SU buildings, shopping area and travel bureau; nursery. **Sporting facilities:** 37-acre playing field, sports centre; Coventry swimming pool (Olympic standard) and city sports centre adjoin campus.

Accommodation: In 1995/96, 26% of all students in university accommodation, 70% of first years. 2,550 places available, mainly for first years: 547 half-board places at £63.50 per week and 2,003 self-catering places at £43.50 per week (incl fuel), Sept–June. Students live in privately owned accommodation for 2+ years: rents £25–£35 per week for self-catering, £48 for B&B, £60 for half-board. Coventry is well-off for student accommodation. **Hardship funds:** Total available in 1995/96: £193,000 government access funds, 190 students helped; £6,000 own welfare fund, 459 students helped plus £20,000 fee remission funds, 20 students helped.

Duration of first degree courses: 3 years; **others:** 4 years (sandwich). **Total first degree students 1995/96:** 13,751. **Overseas students:** 525. **Male/female ratio:** 3:2. **Teaching staff:** 594 full-time, 56 part-time. **Total full-time students 1995/96:** 10,593. **Postgraduate students:** 724. **First degree tuition fees:** Home students, paying their own fees in 1996/97, paid £750 (classroom), £1,600 (lab/studio); Overseas: £6,300 (if paid in full by 31 October).

WHAT IT'S LIKE   Convenient for city centre and adjacent to cathedral. Easy to get to – M1, M6, very near bus station and about 15 mins walk to train station. University accommodation is expensive, mostly for first year students and priority to overseas and particular courses, eg occupational therapy. Priory Hall is pricey but includes food for weekdays; poor cooking facilities. Laundry facilities recently renewed but still inadequate. Some vegetarian food available (but little vegan). Most students live in private rented accommodation; still fairly cheap on national scale. Large number of part-time students and mature students. Nursery excellent but inadequate; SU runs half-term play schemes for 5–11 year-olds. Library opens longer near exam time but number of books inadequate due to increasing student numbers. New SU is good socially and good ents. 5 bars with catering facilities; venue with 2000 capacity. Over 120 societies. Good campaigning. Excellent welfare bureau. Women's priority transport provided every night. Coventry city not particularly safe at night. Increasingly becoming a student town with plenty of pubs where students are welcome. Good transport links with Birmingham for concerts, theatre etc. Close to Warwick University and Warwick Arts Centre. Many courses have national representation; several are specialist eg horse studies; many are now modular. Reasonable teaching facilities. Students have good relationships with administration and lecturers. Generally good standard of education and good social life.

PAUPER NOTES   **Accommodation:** Priory Hall, expensive with pay-as-you-eat system; Caradoc Hall, 4 miles out, dangerous area but popular; 50-odd university houses in various states of repair, from swimming pools to subsidence; new student village being built (though rent high and area dodgy). **Drinks:** SU cheapest and best – 3 bars, all with different catering outlets from baps to full meals. Warwick Uni only 3 miles away. Pubs mostly M&B, also Whitbread and Ansells. **Eats:** Many excellent Balti houses. Sir Colin Campbell, Hope & Anchor, good, cheap for lunch. Vegetarian – The Wedge. **Ents:** New ents venue (Planet);

5 bars on 4 floors. Two cinemas, theatre in town. Multi-screen cinema, bowling alley etc 2 miles away. **Sports:** SU runs comprehensive keep-fit programme – very popular. Refurbished gym. **Travel:** Freewheelers organisation offering safe lifts; good bus service, women's priority transport. **Work:** SU employment and university runs employment bureau; some 25% get paid term-time work. Most students return home for vacation work; little locally.
ALUMNI (EDITORS' PICK)   John Kettley (TV weatherman), Steve Ogrizovic (Coventry City FC goalkeeper), Alan Smith (Arsenal footballer), Peter Hadfield (founder of Two Tone), Jerry Dammers (The Specials).

CRANFIELD UNIVERSITY

Cranfield University, Cranfield, Bedford MK43 0AL
(Tel 01234 754171, Fax 01234 752462) Map 4

STUDENT ENQUIRIES: Academic Registrar.
APPLICATIONS: Direct

Broad study areas: Aeronautical engineering, biotechnology, business studies, marine technology, mechanical and production engineering, manufacturing, metallurgy and materials science. (Subject details are in the *Subjects and Places Index*.)

Founded: 1946; Royal Charter in 1969. **Structural features:** A largely postgraduate university; first degrees are offered at *Shrivenham* and *Silsoe* – look them up separately. **Main awards:** MBA, MSc, PhD. **Awarding body:** Cranfield University. **Site:** Single campus at Cranfield (other sites at Silsoe and Shrivenham). **Access:** M1; BR station at Milton Keynes. **Europe:** Many 'double degree' programmes with institutions in France, Belgium, Germany, Greece and Spain. Major European management school. **Library:** 800 periodicals and access to CD-Rom databases. Annual expenditure on library materials, £300 per FTE student. **Other learning facilities:** Wind tunnel, airfield, extensive networked computer facilities. **Careers:** Information, advice and counselling service. **Welfare:** Welfare office and medical centre. **Special facilities:** Married and family accommodation, play groups, crèches. **Amenities:** Many and varied student societies and student association. **Sporting facilities:** Gym, sports hall, multi-gym and playing fields.

Accommodation: In 1995/96, 600 places available in university accommodation: 360 half-board places from £51–£67 per week and 242 self-catering rooms at £136–£155 per month, year rental. Flats/houses for couples: £177 per month (2-bed, unheated) to £250 per month (3-bed, heated). **Hardship funds:** Total available in 1995/96: £110,500 government access funds, 120 students helped who experienced financial hardship.

Staff: Academic/research: 650. **Postgraduate students:** 1,500. **Overseas students:** 30%. **First degree tuition fees:** Home students, paying their own fees in 1996/97, paid £2,490 (MSc, MPhil, PhD) £12,500 (MBA); Overseas students £10,000–£14,700.

WHAT IT'S LIKE   One of the three campuses of Cranfield University. Cranfield began as a college of aeronautics in 1946 before gaining its Royal charter as a university in 1969. This campus specialises in postgraduate work; based on an old RAF airfield, it is just off the Milton Keynes junction of the M1, and within easy reach of Bedford, where a number of students choose to live. With an average student age of 25, and 50% overseas student population, its claim as Britain's unique university is justified. Accommodation is made up of full-board halls of residence, self-catering shared houses and flats, and houses that are let to married students. The courses are very tough, as you would expect from postgraduate work, and the norm is a 9–5 workload. As such, when it comes to letting off steam, it is to the 30–40 clubs and societies that students tend to turn. These societies, supported by the Cranfield Students' Association, cover a wider range of activities and interests including many of the different cultural groups to be found on campus. Other entertainment is based around occasional Students' Association events, the SA bar (the Cuckoo's Nest) and the myriad of local village pubs. The SA is a small organisation, run from an office at the heart of the campus. As well as the usual union services, it has a shop selling cheap standard stationery items and crested goods and offers a variety of office services. Cranfield is different and may not be to everyone's liking; however, its courses and unique atmosphere make it somewhere to consider.

PAUPER NOTES   **Accommodation:** Good lists available from housing office; married/family accommodation on campus. **Drink:** New SA bar has cheapest drinks on campus including the cheapest pint of Old Peculiar you are likely to find. Leathern Bottel, in Cranfield. **Eats:** Halls provide food; The Swan (Cranfield Village) has curry night. **Ents:** Regular events in CSA. Milton Keynes and Bedford nearby; discounts with NUS card. **Sports:** Limited on-campus facilities; swimming pool in Milton Keynes or Bedford. **Hardship:** Limited funds available. **Travel:** Double degree offered with university in France. **Work:** 48-week year, so no long vac! Variety of bar and other casual employment through CSA; library reshelving work; chambermaid. Rates £2.75–£3.50.

DARTINGTON COLLEGE OF ARTS

Dartington College of Arts, Totnes, Devon TQ9 6EJ
(Tel 01803 862224, Fax 01803 863569) Map 3

STUDENT ENQUIRIES: Registry
APPLICATIONS: UCAS

Broad study areas: Music, performance writing, theatre, visual performance, arts management. (Subject details are in the *Subjects and Places Index*.)

Founded: 1961. **Main undergraduate award:** BA. **Awarding body:** Plymouth University. **Site:** In beautiful grounds on River Dart. **Access:** Road and rail access to Plymouth and Exeter (within half hour), Totnes 2 miles. **Academic features:** Modular programme in performance arts. **Special features:** Close relationship with the Dartington Hall Trust, a unique establishment concerned with industry, education, arts and community development in a rural area. **Europe:** Formal exchange links with 5 EU universities/colleges. Research into integration of theatre, music and visual arts within European higher education. **Library:** 46,000 items (books, scores, sound recordings, slides, films, CD-Rom). Annual expenditure on library materials, £200 per FTE student. **Other learning facilities:** Specialist performance technology centre, studios, workshops and practice rooms. **Welfare:** Health centre, part-time nurse; counselling service; welfare officer. **Amenities:** Refectory, bar, laundrette; extensive grounds. Dartmouth and Torbay within easy reach.

Accommodation: In 1995/96, accommodation on site for all first years who request it. Partial self-catering and self-catering places at £37–£40 per week, term time only. Students live in privately owned accommodation for 2 years: £40–£45 per week. **Hardship funds:** Total available in 1995/96: £13,877 government access funds, 93 students helped. Special help: single parents, mature students with families, final year students.
Duration of first degree courses: 3 years. **Total first degree students 1995/96:** 459. **Overseas students:** 4. **Mature students:** 230. **Male/female ratio:** 2:3. **Teaching staff:** 16 full-time, 117 part-time (including visiting staff). **Total full-time students 1995/96:** 459. **First degree tuition fees:** Home students, paying their own fees in 1996/97, paid £1,600; Overseas students £5,500.

WHAT IT'S LIKE   Beautiful, isolated campus, 30-minute walk from Totnes. 13th-century hall surrounded by courtyard and Elizabethan gardens. Small campus, intimate and comforting but claustrophobic at times. Provision for disabled students improving on a difficult campus – on the side of a hill. A small college, not a lot of money put into SU but still provides a variety of events from cabaret, folk nights and music in the bar to regular live bands. Easy reach of Torbay, Plymouth, Exeter and Dartmoor, though local bus service infrequent. Totnes has great secondhand market every Friday and main line railway station; town and college mix well. Good pubs, not many eateries but standard is quite high and choice varied, and every type of therapy you can think of. Staff/student relationships are good within college's friendly atmosphere. Positively encourages applications from mature students. Library hours good (except at weekends); provision of texts/recorded material very good. College nurse each morning and two GP surgeries per week. Counsellor on site for confidential and personal problems; also a welfare officer in the SU. Accommodation off campus improving. Rented flats and houses are the norm but rooms in family houses are also available. Good college accommodation officer. No accommodation for married students (with or without children) and no crèche. Rural, so own transport a definite advantage. High-class visiting lecturers ensure that courses relate to current thinking in all subject areas. Workload can be high at times. Students from a wide variety of social and educational backgrounds. Good visual and sound studios. More male than female lecturers but this deficiency is under constant appraisal. Easy-going college with no racism or calculated sexism. Some students do leave early in first term but stick it out. Failure rate is low. It's great – you'll love it.
PAUPER NOTES   **Accommodation:** 3 residential blocks for 68 students, self-catering (fridge, toaster, kettle, microwave and cooking ring); single rooms with wash basins; kitchenette and 2 baths for every 12 students. Self-catering accommodation for 80 students at Foxhole (20 minute walk); all rooms with wash basins. First years have priority for on-site accommodation. **Drink:** Student club sells variety of beers and lagers but is not as cheap as most SU bars. Pub also on campus but more expensive. Totnes pubs are well used both by students and locals. **Eats:** Cafeteria on campus subsidised but only open at lunchtime. Usual moans about prices and standard of food; fresh fruit and salads available at a price. Wide variety of vegan/vegetarian eating in Totnes. Also Chinese, fish and chips, pizza. Good

value in local pubs. **Ents:** Visiting theatre companies, dance, concerts of all kinds, art exhibitions run by Dartington Arts Society. SU organises bands, discos, cabaret, gang shows, etc. Lots of home-grown entertainment. No cinema in town but arts society has good cinema on campus. **Travel:** Travel scholarships available. No student fares for local travel. Hitching is easy – but take care. **Sports:** Squash courts, outdoor pool and tennis in summer term. Indoor swimming pool and gym in Totnes. Plenty of countryside to jog in or river walks. **Hardship funds:** Not bad, meeting every term. **Work:** About 5% work. Work scarce. Some on campus (bar); not much in Totnes (two supermarkets worth a try).
MORE INFO?   Ring SU President on 01803 863984.
INFORMAL NAME   DCA
ALUMNI (EDITORS' PICK)   Josie Lawrence.

DARTMOUTH

Britannia Royal Naval College, Dartmouth, Devon Map 3

STUDENT ENQUIRIES: Captain A N Du Port,
The Officer Enquiry Section, Room 128, Victory Building,
HM Naval Base, Portsmouth, Hampshire PO1 3LS.

Broad study areas: Naval studies, strategic studies, international studies, navigation, computing.

Founded: Training on River Dart since 1863. College buildings completed in 1905. **Site:** Beautiful hillside setting overlooking the Dart estuary. **Access:** Nearest British Rail stations at Paignton and Totnes. **Entry conditions:** Candidates must be at least 17 years old and under 22, 23 or 26 (dependent on the type of entry). Many graduate entrants. Before entry candidates must pass Admiralty Interview Board and medical examination. **Entry dates:** Main entries in September, January and May. **Special features:** All naval officers start their careers at Dartmouth, as do many officers of foreign navies. The time spent at Dartmouth depends upon course taken. After period of general naval training, students go on to specialist training either at sea, at Dartmouth, at other naval establishments or at civilian universities. **Welfare:** Excellent, including full medical and dental facilities. **Amenities:** Full range of sporting and recreational facilities, including gymnasium, swimming pool, sports grounds with hard hockey pitch; over 100 boats and yachts and a beagle pack.

Accommodation: Single or shared cabins for all students.

Duration of courses: up to 4 terms. **Male/female ratio:** 10:1 **Total full-time students 1996/97:** approx 400.

WHAT IT'S LIKE   Dartmouth is the Royal Naval Officers' new-entry training establishment and so, to gain admission, you first have to join the Royal Navy. Day-to-day life at BRNC is very different from that of a normal university as the students are here as officers to learn how to be leaders in the Royal Navy as well as to acquire the academic knowledge that will equip them for their future careers. The officer population is male and female and includes a number from overseas. Daily routine is full, varied and demanding, geared to producing a healthy body and an agile mind. Teaching staff comprises full-time civilian lecturers and serving naval personnel and the academic courses cover a wide range of subjects from international affairs to celestial navigation. Most officers are accommodated in either single or double rooms and full board is provided. Visitors are welcome but no provision made for their overnight accommodation (abundance of small hotels and guest houses in the holiday town of Dartmouth). College is poorly served by public transport and although the town is an easy walk away, those wishing to venture further afield will find their own transport a necessity. Wide range of cultural, recreational and sporting activities which include music, drama, sailing, rugby, riding, cricket and squash to name but a few.

ALUMNI (EDITORS' PICK) HRH Duke of Edinburgh, HRH the Prince of Wales, HRH the Duke of York.

DE MONTFORT UNIVERSITY

De Montfort University, The Gateway, Leicester LE1 9BH
(Tel 0116 255 1551, Fax 0116 257 7515) Map 2

STUDENT ENQUIRIES: Academic Registrar
APPLICATIONS: UCAS

Broad study areas: Arts and humanities, agriculture and horticulture, applied sciences, built environment, design, education, engineering, law, health and community, business, computing. (Subject details are in the *Subjects and Places Index*.)

Founded: 1969 as Leicester Poly; university status in 1992. **Structural features:** Four centres, DMU Leicester, DMU Bedford, DMU Lincoln and DMU Milton Keynes. Students study at one centre for the duration of their course. **Main undergraduate awards:** BA, BSc, BEd, BEng. **Awarding body:** De Montfort University. **Site:** Split on 6 sites; 2 near Leicester city centre, one in Bedford, one in Milton Keynes, and two in Lincolnshire. **Access:** Easy access by rail and road. **Academic features:** Modular courses available in most disciplines. First year of wide range of courses available at franchise centres around the country. Policy of encouraging mature students. **Europe:** 20% first degree students learn a language as part of their course, 1% spend time abroad. Languages available on many courses. Formal exchange links with European universities/colleges in EU and Scandanavia, available to wide range of students. **Libraries:** On both Leicester sites; 400,000 volumes in total, 2,500 periodicals, 995 study places; collection of audio-visual material, electronic information resource provision. Bedford site: 110,000 volumes, 880 periodicals, 190 study places. Annual expenditure on library materials, £70.90 per FTE student. **Other learning facilities:** Excellent computing facilities. **Specialist collections:** Victoria & Albert slide collection at Leicester; Hockcliffe collection of children's literature at Bedford. **Careers:** Information, advice and placement service. **Welfare:** Counselling, student health service, chaplaincy, legal information service. **Amenities:** Bookshop, exhibition hall, SU, health centre, purpose-built campus at Milton Keynes; day nursery at Bedford. **Sporting facilities:** Excellent sporting facilities at Bedford, good elsewhere. **Employment:** Strong links with textile and fashion, and engineering industries.

Accommodation: In 1995/96, 10% of all Leicester students in university-controlled accommodation, 41% of first years (priority to overseas students and those with special circumstances); 25% of Bedford students, 70% of first years. 1,300 places available: self-catering £41.20 per week (city centre) and £32.50 (suburban halls); full-board (B&B and evening meal) £49.85 per week, Sept–June (retainer paid over Christmas vac); some shared rooms at lower rents. Students live in privately owned accommodation for 2+ years: £30–£35 per week self-catering, £28–£40 B&B, £45–£55 full-board. Good supply of rented accommodation in Leicester; university helps, publishes regular housing lists etc. 25% of first degree students live at home. **Term time work:** University policy to allow term time work for first degree students (45% believed to work); limit of 12 hours per week. No work available on campus. **Hardship funds:** Total available in 1995/96: £300,686 government access funds, 710 students helped. Special help: to those with high costs eg childcare costs, health/disability costs or high travel/accommodation costs. Over 100 self-supporting students helped.

Duration of first degree courses: 3 years; **others:** 4 years sandwich, 5 years extended. **Total first degree students 1995/96:** 10,679. **Overseas students:** 550. **Mature students:** 4,520. **Male/female ratio:** 1:1. **Teaching staff:** 1,150 full-time, 380 part-time. **Total full-time students 1995/96:** 18,330. **Postgraduate students:** 1,292. **First degree tuition fees:** Home students, paying their own fees in 1996/97, paid £750 (classroom), £1,600 (lab/studio); Overseas students £5,600 (classroom), £6,300 (lab/studio).

WHAT IT'S LIKE   *Leicester*   Leicester's a great place. City campus not attractive but Scraptoft picturesque. Only patch of grass at City recently covered up with enormous engineering building (environmentally friendly – solar panels etc). Canal next to union; some nice walks and cycle paths; also Castle Gardens site. Campus can be a bit depressing at first glance; actually much nicer than you first think. Accommodation generally good, but not enough. Lots of terraced houses (Tudor Road is longest row of terraces in Britain); average rent £30/wk. Narborough Road is a complete student community: shops, chippies, pubs, launderettes etc, all open at unsociable hours. Alternatively, big student community up near the other uni – London Road area. Highfields can be dodgy, but parts of it great – very multicultural. Victoria Park/Queens Road area is lovely but a bit far (unless you've got a bike). Library open 9am to 9pm and at weekends. SU has stationery, travel and copy shop. Not as political as you might first think; AGM and CGMs attract a handful of students while the rest eat lunch and wonder what all the noise is about. Politically active people should go elsewhere, unless they fancy a challenge! Socially excellent – John Peel's favourite student venue! – attracts some big names. Arena has state-of-the-art PA and when it's full it's a great venue – big stage, upper viewing area around dancefloor, and an enormous bar adjacent to stage; smaller gigs in the Toxic Club. Big bands (tickets £8–£10); specialised discos Wed–Sat nights including Pandora's Box (techno and dance), the Big Cheese ('70s and '80s dance). Quite a few students have cars, but a hassle to park anywhere in Leicester, especially on campus! (When Leicester's football team is playing at home don't even think about it – you won't find a space within a 5 mile radius of Filbert St.) Student counselling service; health service with sickbay (friendly, helpful and pride themselves on confidentiality); interdenominational chaplaincy.

In town centre, Silver Arcade has loads of arty and interesting shops (good for second-hand clothes and jewellery). Shopping centre has amazing market with loads of fruit and

veg, secondhand/new clothes too; and food so cheap – come 5 o'clock, they're giving the stuff away! Also exotic fruit and veg and a great fish, meat and cheese market; again, silly prices. Blossom's (veggie), Bread and Roses, Que Pasa and Rum Runner (Mexican and good fun) and, of course, the SU, are good places to eat. Also some good Indian restaurants and kebab shops. Favourite student pubs and clubs are: The Princess Charlotte (live gigs every night, big names and free soup Sunday lunchtime); Pump and Tap (live music most nights, free food Sundays, nice atmosphere); closest pub to the 'Narby', The Magazine (great decor, nice beer, live music upstairs and a big beer yard, free condoms on bar). Several gay/mixed pubs. Eight clubs (some studenty, one for lesbians, gays and bi-sexuals, some ravey, some less so). Phoenix Arts theatre is popular; nice café, and a full timetable of events, films, etc. Haymarket good but a bit pricey and Haymarket studio has some interesting stuff for students rather than the bigger productions. Good relations with local community (but careful at night in the centre). Some complaints about noise from student residents. Generally, a great place to live, particularly first time away from home, with all the benefits of a cosmopolitan city – not in the least intimidating or threatening. Lots of green bits – parks etc. and everything is within easy reach. Leicester people are generally very friendly. Not a million miles from some nice countryside if you're that way inclined.
PAUPER NOTES **Accommodation:** Good – hundreds of terraced houses. New halls at Leicester city but still not enough for all first years. **Drink:** SU good and cheap. Good local pubs cater specifically for students. **Eats:** SU food good and cheap, as are takeouts in Narborough Road. Couple of local pubs do vegetarian and vegan food. **Ents:** Princess Charlotte 5 mins from SU on low key/indie/thrash/rock circuit. **Sports:** Uni sports centre – keep fit, step-aerobics etc and a gym. **Hardship funds:** Small funds; uni hardship/access fund. **Travel:** Good local bus service. Midland Fox operates cheap student season tickets; SU travel shop. **Work:** Loads of pubs. Work in the SU – waiting list can be anything from 1 to 6 months. Pay is standard, ie £3/hr or less.
MORE INFO? Enquiries to SU, 0116 255 5576.
BUZZ-WORDS DMU (De Montfort University), Narby (abbreviation of Narborough Road – the student area of the city), Scrappy (Scraptoft campus).
ALUMNI (EDITORS' PICK) Charles Dance, Gary Lineker.

WHAT IT'S LIKE *Bedford* Spiralling towers and crumbling edifices of Bedford symbolise its history and tradition. Excellent standing nationally in producing secondary teachers of outstanding calibre and questioning graduates. Good sporting reputation. BA/BSc courses with modular programme incorporates teaching innovations upheld by dedicated teaching staff. Adequate facilities are well maintained. Student accommodation refurbished to a good standard. Main student block set in beautiful surroundings of Victorian terrace housing with picturesque gardens (listed buildings). Social life well supported by two recently renovated bars with convivial atmosphere; varied entertainment calendar; 700-capacity complex. Balls always sell out and are always massively enjoyed. Good variety of events, recently included hypnotism, comedy, karaoke, cabaret and all manner of music (hardcore to ambient jazz). Many societies – dance, black society, Irish, women's, Catholic, Green ... Those at DMU Bedford don't mind working, but do like to have a good time.
PAUPER NOTES **Accommodation:** Halls cheap considering proximity to London. Accommodation register for students living out. **Drink:** 2 college bars. Many excellent country pubs. **Eats:** Multi-racial town with varied eating establishments. **Sports:** Very good facilities (swimming pool needs upgrading). Local squash and golf at reduced rate. Sports clubs run by students with expert staff coaching if wanted. High standard in teams. **Ents:** Varied with both local and big bands eg Amazulu, Geno Washington, Voice of the Beehive, Real Thing, KWS, Bad Manners. **Hardship funds:** Access and college funds; financial advice services. **Work:** Pubs, swimming pools, sports centres, coaching, taxis (if over 24). Over

campus (bar and shop work, stewards). SU job link service. 20% usually ...ping etc in vacation.

Ring Phil Damant on 01234 211688

...DITORS' PICK) Mandy Pickles and Glenn Prebble (England U21 hockey), Lisa ... (Olympic rhythmic gym), Sally Bunyard (Olympic basketball), Sian Williams (England women's football), Kerry Bason (GB mountain bike team), Kelly Buckley (England squash).

DERBY UNIVERSITY

University of Derby, Kedleston Road, Derby DE22 1GB
(Tel 01332 622222, Fax 01332 294861) Map 2

STUDENT ENQUIRIES: Student Office
APPLICATIONS: UCAS

Broad study areas: Art & design, education, engineering, science, social science, professions allied to medicine. (Subject details are in the *Subjects and Places Index*.)

Founded: 1851, as a training college; 1983 became Derbyshire College of HE; university status in 1992. **Main undergraduate awards:** BA, BEd, BSc. **Awarding body:** Derby University. **Site:** Split on 5 sites. **Access:** Buses from Derby city centre. **Academic features:** Modular degree with 50 options; degrees in psychology, occupational therapy, accountancy and environmental monitoring. Biological imaging degree. **Special features:** Artist-in-residence. **Europe:** 6% first degree students take a language as part of course and 3% spend 6 months or more abroad. Formal exchange links with some 5 EU universities/colleges. **Library:** Main libraries at Kedleston Road and Mickleover sites; 315,000 volumes, 1,900 periodicals, 500 study places. Annual expenditure on library materials, £62.72 per FTE student. **Other learning facilities:** Computer centre and media services centre. **Welfare:** Head of student services, assistant deans, wardens and college nurse, doctor, chaplaincy, student counsellors. **Careers:** Information and advisory service. **Amenities:** SU shop, chemist, travel agency, insurance services, bank, hairdressers, bars, bookshops at main campus. **Sporting facilities:** Gymnasia, heated indoor swimming pool at Mickleover site, rugby/football pitches, running track.

Accommodation: 30% students in university accommodation, 70% of first years. 2,500 places in halls and registered lodgings (priority given to first year students): £38–£50 per week self-catering halls, £30 per week lodgings. **Hardship funds:** Chancellory administers access and a hardship fund.

Duration of first degree courses: 3 years; others: 4 years (sandwich). **Total first degree students 1995/96:** 9,000; **BEd students:** 1,000. **Overseas students:** 300. **Mature students:** 6,000. **Male/female ratio:** 5:6. **Teaching staff:** 400 full-time, 300 part-time. **Total full-time students:** 8,500. **Postgraduate students:** 500. **First degree tuition fees:** Home students, paying their own fees in 1996/97, paid £1,300 (classroom), £2,770 (lab/studio); Overseas students £4,850.

WHAT IT'S LIKE   It's concentrated on 7 sites in Derby, a small city with a friendly atmosphere. Main site is Kedleston Road, on a hill with magnificent views of the countryside from upper floors; Mickleover site is the base for drama, education and social science. All sites are on main bus routes from town centre; Green Lane, actually in town centre. College accommodation varies from purpose-built blocks (Laverstone Court and Lonsdale Hall) to converted Victorian residences along Uttoxeter New Road. 50% of students live in private rented accommodation. Varied student body: large proportion of mature students and many overseas from countries as far apart as Ghana and Malaysia as well as America and Europe. Library on 3 sites. Gymnasium and a multi-gym for weight training at Kedleston Road. A recreation room at Kedleston Road plus a venue hall with 1,000 capacity for bands, conferences etc. There are two bars and an SU block at Mickleover where many events are held. SU particularly effective at representing student point of view on university committees and co-ordinating many effective campaigns. It also runs over 50 clubs and societies – mountaineering and caving, students against bloodsports, football, rugby, biology and Asian. Student discounts available at Derby Playhouse, Showcase cinema, sports and record shops. Wide range of pubs to choose from in town centre and plenty of country pubs (mostly Bass, Ind Coope, Marstons or Wards). Nationally renowned art and design faculty and photography courses. Students friendly, not that politically active; everyone seems to get on very well. Community spirit has been maintained during expansion. People find it easy to settle in and have a very enjoyable time.

PAUPER NOTES   **Accommodation:** Prices going up due to expansion of college and Toyota car plant. Cheap accommodation in Normanton area. **Drink:** SU bar cheapest drinks in town. Ye Olde Dolphin Inn (oldest pub in Derby), The Spa Inn (Abbey Street) serves Burton ale; Wherehouse on Friar Gate (one of students' favourites). **Eats:** College restaurant reasonable. Best takeaway Tomadore on Babington Lane (pizzas and chilli burgers a speciality), Ronos on Abbey Street. Many good Indian restaurants (often student discount). Abbey Street kebab shops best. Good health food shops. **Ents:** SU has theme discos, bands (eg Carter, Courdroy, USM, Chumbawumba), comedy acts, hypnotist, weekly sports night. Annual favourites are Freshers Ball and Adult Night. In town many bands at the Assembly Rooms and Wherehouse (gives student discounts); 2 cinema multiples, 2 theatres. **Sports:** On campus – 2 gyms and multigym, swimming pool (Mickleover site), football, rugby and hockey pitches. **Hardship funds:** Temporary loans from student services; emergencies, see SU. **Travel:** Intersite buses. Good local buses. Centre of country so easy for all transport networks. Railcards, coachcards and ISIC from SU office. **Work:** Reasonable supply of work, much of it in the university. Some 20% get work in summer – bars, stores etc.

MORE INFO?   Ring Student Union on 01332 348846.

INFORMAL NAME   Derby Uni

BUZZ-WORDS   UDSU (University of Derby Students Union); UNR (Uttoxeter New Road); G/L (Green Lane); K/R or Keddy (Kedleston Road).

ALUMNI (EDITORS' PICK)   Barry Evans (Leicester/England – rugby), John Blakemore (photographer/lecturer), Berni Yates (fashion designer), Russell Harty.

WANT TO HELP WITH THE NEXT EDITION? SEE PAGE 66

DUNDEE UNIVERSITY

University of Dundee, Dundee DD1 4HN
(Tel 01382 344160, Fax 01382 221554) Map 1

STUDENT ENQUIRIES: Student Recruitment Service
APPLICATIONS: UCAS

Broad study areas: Medicine & dentistry, law & accountancy, arts & social sciences, art & design, science & engineering, architecture & town planning, management & consumer studies. (Subject details are in the *Subjects and Places Index*.)

Founded: 1882; independent university status in 1967. **Main undergraduate awards:** BA, BAcc, BArch, BDes, BDS, BEng, BFin, BMSc, BSc, LLB, MA, MB ChB. **Awarding body:** Dundee University. **Site:** Near city centre; teaching hospital in suburbs. **Access:** Rail and bus stations in walking distance; motorway links and direct rail and bus services to other parts of UK. **Academic features:** Students able to switch between arts & social sciences and science & engineering subjects respectively before entering the second year. Opportunity to acquire IT skills available to all students. **Europe:** 2% of first degree students take a language as part of course and 1% spend 6 months or more abroad. All students have access to language centre. Formal exchange links with a number of universities/colleges in Western Europe, open to a range of students. **Library:** Main library with approx 500,000 volumes; medical, law, art and departmental libraries; archives department; inter-library loan scheme. Annual expenditure on library materials, £140 per FTE student. **Other learning facilities:** IT services, media service; micro centre; Tay estuary research centre; language centre. **Welfare:** Student advisory and counselling services; health service offers routine medical examinations by local GP. **Careers:** Information and advice service. **Amenities:** SU building with swimming pool, shop, bars, restaurant, bookshop, coin laundry; chaplaincy centre; civic repertory theatre adjoining campus. **Sporting facilities:** Large indoor sports complex; university sports grounds and water sports centre; more than 20 golf courses including St Andrews and Carnoustie within half an hour's drive; skiing, climbing and hill walking in surrounding countryside.

Accommodation: In 1995/96, 30% of all students in university accommodation, 65% of first years (all those that require it). 2,358 places available: 750 half-board places, £59 per week, term time only; 1,540 self-catering places at £32–£46 per week, Sept–June or longer; plus 68 flats for students with families. Dundee has buoyant private sector housing at reasonable costs. 15% first degree students live at home. **Term time work:** University's policy not to encourage term time work for full-time first degree students but realises it is inevitable in the current climate (20% believed to work); advisory limit of 20 hours per week. Term (and vac) work available on campus in SU and residences. **Hardship funds:** Total available in 1995/96: £150,000 government access funds, 403 students helped; £10,000 own funds, 39 students helped. Special help: students with children, self-financing students, and others in severe financial hardship; other funds available for those of Scots birth or extraction studying medicine, dentistry, science or engineering.

Duration of first degree courses: 4 years; **others:** 5 years (architecture, dentistry, medicine). **Total first degree students 1995/96:** 7,274. **Overseas students:** 6%. **Mature students:**

21%. **Male/female ratio:** 1:1. **Teaching staff:** 768 full-time, 70 part-time, 405 honorary (mainly in medicine and dentistry). **Total full-time students 1995/96:** 7,982. **Postgraduate students:** 708. **First degree tuition fees:** Home students, paying their own fees in 1996/97, paid £750 (classroom), £1,600 (lab/studio), £2,800 (clinical); Overseas students £5,500–£5,800 (classroom-based courses, including architecture), £7,600–£9,500 (lab/studio), £14,900 (clinical).

WHAT IT'S LIKE Campus a mixture of modern, 18th and 19th-century buildings, 2 mins from city centre (but no through traffic allowed). All facilities on campus, except medical faculty on a separate campus 3 miles away. Ninewells Hospital is the largest teaching hospital in Europe. Plentiful accommodation of reasonable standard. Excellent relationship between university and students – community atmosphere, close liaison with city. Students from all over the country and high proportion of mature students. Large library, recently extended and open till midnight. Also excellent sports centre on campus; new lift for disabled students. SU is centre of students' social life; politically apathetic with low turn out at elections. Four bars – one new, another refurbished – and games room with many pool tables and up-to-the-minute video games. Excellent debating union. Limited car parking spaces for students. Most courses are very flexible; transfers are easy at beginning of each year. Many field trips, several abroad. Work load really what you make it; drop out rate is low. Work assessment varies from course to course – all include exams but large move towards continuous assessment and anonymous marking. Exemptions possible for exams in first year. Open learning service offers free tuition in foreign languages. Complete student support network: student counsellors, full-time student advisor, careers service, health service, plus SU-run welfare team. Free dental treatment provided in campus dental hospital. Over 90 active societies – many sports orientated (rugby team is notorious). City geared towards students who form about 5% of population. Many pubs, two theatres, 3 cinemas (one devoted to showing alternative films). Easy to meet other students. Neither trendy nor pretentious; extremely friendly and lots of fun.

PAUPER NOTES **Accommodation:** Two new luxury halls of residence. Cheapest private flats found by word of mouth. **Drink:** Unions definitely cheapest and often have new drinks promos. Excellent Heavy throughout city. Most pubs do special promos from time to time – watch noticeboards. **Eats:** Union pizza parlour, Liar bar sells snacks, also cheap coffee bar and vending machnies. Good local restaurants and pub grub. **Ents:** Varied SU ents programme. Dundee rep theatre; cinemas – 2 mainstream and 1 art house. **Sports:** Sports centre on campus (being extended); multi-gym recently upgraded. Swimming pool in Association; leisure centre 10 mins from campus. **Hardship funds:** Summer hardship fund, access fund, Laeg Trust. **Travel:** No travel scholarships. Cheap fares available through Campus Travel in SU. **Work:** SU bars, library, security, or local work in pubs, DJs, painting, decorating, advertising etc. SU noticeboard for term and summer vac. Other work difficult. Approx 20–30% work in term time and increasing; under 5% locally in vacations.

MORE INFO? Get students' Alternative Prospectus. Enquiries to Maryanne McIntyre (01382 21841).

ALUMNI (EDITORS' PICK) David Leslie (ex-Scottish rugby captain), George Robertson MP, Selina Scott.

WHAT IT'S LIKE *Duncan of Jordanstone* Now the architecture and art & design faculty of Dundee University – the university's biggest faculty with 1,600 students (and steadily increasing). The college consists of two large buildings linked by a couple of bridges. It is surrounded by university buildings, 5 minutes walk from the city centre. The fine art, graphics and printed textiles courses have a very high standing and the television and video imaging courses are unique in Britain. There is a small union, open every day, with a club night on Fridays and a fundraising party on Wednesdays. The refectory food is not good; students frequent the university union and sports centre, a few yards away. The main university union has plans to improve the college union, including the refectory. Accommodation isn't too bad compared to other Scottish cities. Halls are available, although most students prefer to rent privately. Although small, Dundee has a large student population, most of whom have a good time.

DURHAM UNIVERSITY

University of Durham, Old Shire Hall, Durham DH1 3HP
(Tel 0191 374 2000, Fax 0191 374 7250) Map 2

STUDENT ENQUIRIES: Academic Registrar
APPLICATIONS: UCAS

Broad study areas: Arts, sciences (including biomedical sciences), social sciences, humanities, engineering, law, music, oriental languages, education. (Subject details are in the *Subjects and Places Index.*)

Founded: 1832. **Main undergraduate awards:** BA, BSc, LLB, MSci, MEng, MMath. **Awarding body:** Durham University. **Site:** Durham city centre and south of river; base in Stockton-on-Tees. **Special features:** University consists of 12 colleges and 2 societies, largely self-governing, although teaching is organised centrally. New college at Stockton-on-Tees, providing teaching and accommodation. **Europe:** 12% first degree students take a language as part of course and spend 6 months or more abroad. All students can use language centre in their free time. Formal exchange links with increasing number of universities/colleges and Erasmus exchanges for variety of students. **Library:** Main library has over 800,000 volumes, plus departmental and college libraries. Annual expenditure on library materials, £132.88 per FTE student. **Welfare:** Student health centre; sick-bay facilities in each college; specialised service for students with hearing and other disabilities. **Careers:** Advisory service. **Amenities:** Wide range of facilities in colleges and centrally (bar, book-shop, minibus) at Dunelm House, modern SU building; small theatre; museum of oriental art. **Sporting facilities:** Sports hall; 60 acres of playing fields.

Accommodation: In 1995/96, 70% of all students in university accommodation, 95% first years: full-board at £650 per term. Many students live in privately owned accommodation for 1+ years: rents £30–£50 per week for self-catering, £50–£60 for half-board, up to £70 with weekend meals. **Hardship funds:** Information not available.

Duration of first degree courses: 3 years; **others:** 4 years. **Total first degree students 1995/96:** 7,692; **BA(Ed) students:** 389. **Overseas students:** 132. **Mature students:** 850. **Male/female**

ratio: 1:1. **Teaching staff:** 800 full-time. **Total full-time students 1995/96:** 7,607. **Postgraduate students:** 1,995. **First degree tuition fees:** Home students, paying their own fees in 1996/97, paid £750 (classroom), £1,600 (lab); Overseas students £5,980 (classroom), £7,925 (lab).

WHAT IT'S LIKE Frequently referred to as 'the oasis of the north', it's a quiet, picturesque city, boasting both a castle and an awe-inspiring cathedral. Durham is a collegiate university, although teaching is based departmentally. The college is the main focus of a student's life. Colleges vary greatly: the Castle and those known as 'the Bailey Colleges' are old, formal and have an (unfair) reputation for attracting a more toffee-nosed clientele. The 'Hill' colleges are 1960s monstrosities but tend to be a lot more open and friendly. Hild and Bede maintain aloof neutrality between Hill and Bailey colleges. All colleges have their own dining halls, library and study areas; most people live in for two years, sometimes three. Teaching is either within the department, at the Elvet Riverside lecture theatres or at the science site. Somewhat bizarrely (given the well-known fact that scientists don't read books), the science site is also the home of the newly-extended library. The SU suffers socially from the collegiate system but is still a focal point for a variety of student societies, the charities' organisation, DUCK and Palatinate ('Durham's Independent Student Newspaper' as the slogan goes). It also houses the welfare department and is adjacent to the well-stocked careers centre. Sport plays an important role in university life (although it's possible to avoid it altogether). University standards are high but inter-collegiate rivalry is largely friendly and college teams cater for all standards. There are university and college events and the city has three night clubs and a small cinema. Should the tranquillity of Durham prove too stifling, Newcastle is only 20 minutes away by train and offers a wide range of gigs, clubs, theatres and concerts. *Jane Marriott*

PAUPER NOTES **Accommodation:** Most college accommodation okay, some ensuite. Good SU accommodation office for those living out. **Drink:** All colleges have bars: Castle's surroundings undoubtedly best; Hatfield's bar more like a transport cafe. Prices reasonable in college and SU bars. Local pubs good but more pricey: Market Tavern, Shakespeare and Court Inn are popular student hang-outs. **Eats:** Food varies in colleges – and vegetarians a rarity in some. In town, there are good Indian and Chinese restaurants, plethora of pizza places and more up-market and continental Pierre Victoire and Stones. Cafe culture abundant – Regatta tea rooms popular with rowers, Vennels with banoffi pie is hang-out for arty types. **Ents:** Regular college events, some SU ones. Active theatre and comedy groups. **Sports:** Graham Sports Centre (university); college sports clubs. **Travel:** STA travel bureau. Some college grants and Shell bursaries for travel. **Work:** Not much around; the lucky ones get work in a college bar.

BUZZ-WORDS Dunelm (SU building), Hill/Bailey (location of college and implied rivalry between the two).

ALUMNI (EDITORS' PICK) Judith Hann (presenter, Tomorrow's World), Harold Evans (ex-editor of *The Times*), Will Carling (England rugby captain), Nasser Hussain (England test cricketer), Hunter Davies (writer), Jonathan Edwards (world triple jump record holder).

CAN'T FIND WHAT YOU'RE LOOKING FOR? USE THE INDEX!

EAST ANGLIA (UEA)

University of East Anglia, Norwich, Norfolk NR4 7TJ
(Tel 01603 456161, Fax 01603 458553) Map 4

STUDENT ENQUIRIES: Admissions Office (Tel 01603 592216)
APPLICATIONS: UCAS

Broad study areas: Physical and natural sciences; mathematics; computing and information systems; professions allied to medicine; education; economic and social studies; English, American and European studies; law; world art studies and music.
(Subject details are in the *Subjects and Places Index*.)

Founded: 1963. **Main undergraduate awards:** BA, LLB, BSc, BEng. **Awarding body:** UEA. **Site:** 2 miles from centre of Norwich. **Access:** Frequent bus service. **Special features:** Excellent links with contemporary writers: Malcolm Bradbury, Rose Tremain, Angela Carter, Ian McEwan and Kazuo Ishiguro have taught or studied at UEA. Togther with associated institutes (John Innes, Food Research, British Sugar Technical Centre and MAFF Food Science Laboratory) forms largest concentration of research scientists working on plant and food science in Europe. Also climatic research unit. **Academic features:** Most degree courses combine study of several related disciplines, and include continuous assessment. **Europe:** 14% first degree students take a language as part of course and 3% spend 6 months or more abroad. Also participates in many European research projects, from IT to greenhouse warming. **Library:** Over 650,000 volumes, including books, volumes of periodicals, music scores and material in microform. 1,000 reading places, 100 study carrels; restricted loan collection of books in heavy demand, computerised catalogue system. Annual expenditure on library materials, £105 per FTE student. **Other learning facilities:** Computing centre, James Platt language learning centre, audio-visual centre. **Welfare:** Medical centre on campus with sick bay and dental service; student counselling service; chaplaincy. Special categories: Nursery on campus, plus some accommodation for married students. **Careers:** Information and advice service. **Amenities:** Union House has common rooms, printing rooms, television studios. Bookshop, newsagent, supermarket, post office, travel agent, banks, launderette, bars, cafeterias, coffee shop and restaurants on site; Sainsbury Centre for Visual Arts (19th- and 20th-century European paintings and sculpture; ethnographic collection); university art collection (20th century). **Sporting facilities:** Indoor and outdoor sports facilities, including 40 acres playing fields, astroturf pitches and eight-lane athletics track; some 40 sports clubs.

Accommodation: In 1995/96, 45% of all students in university accommodation, 96% of first years (guaranteed if apply before a specific date and live more than 12 miles away). 1,500 self-catering places available: £47.70–£51.65 per week, Sept–June or longer. Students live in privately owned accommodation for 1–2 years: average rents £35–£40 per week. **Term time work:** University policy to allow term time work for first degree students. Term (and vac) work available on campus in bars, catering, offices etc; also careers centre advertises external vacancies. **Hardship funds:** Total available in 1995/96: £189,167 government access funds, average £245 awarded; own hardship fund of £60,000 plus other funds made

12 grants totalling £3,550 and 1,180 loans of £177,562; £30,900 nursery fund, 45 student parents using UEA nursery with means tested charges.

Duration of first degree courses: 3 years; **others:** 4 years (courses involving study abroad). **Total first degree students 1995/96:** 6,892. **Overseas students:** 555. **Male/female ratio:** 1:1. **Teaching staff:** 460 full-time. **Total full-time students 1995/96:** 8,761. **Postgraduate students:** 1,869. **First degree tuition fees:** Home students, paying their own fees in 1996/97, paid £750 (classroom), £1,600 (lab/studio); Overseas students £6,000 (classroom), £6,980–£7,960 (lab/studio).

WHAT IT'S LIKE   UEA started up in the mid-sixties is and still growing. New courses in occupational therapy and physiotherapy bring more new students and a continuing building programme is improving the already impressive facilities. Approximately 2 miles from centre of historic Norwich; easy access to the countryside and city. Although relatively small, Norwich offers a massive range of entertainments, so much so that many graduates stay in the city to live after their degrees. On campus the Union of Students provides for all students' welfare and academic needs, running many shops, bars, clubs and societies including sports clubs, as well as an award-winning TV station, newspaper and radio station. It also has a major concert venue which is renowned for attracting big names each term. With so much on offer three years at UEA need not be spent solely in study. The university has an excellent record of academic achievement and has produced experts in fields as diverse as landscape archaeology and development studies. A high degree of inter-disciplinary study allows students to tailor their degrees to suit their personal interests. Also by accepting students from a wide variety of academic backgrounds, instead of accepting the standard three A-levels, UEA is as stimulating socially as it is academically. All in all UEA allows for personal as well as academic advancement and is an excellent place to study for a degree. Come here – nowhere else will do!

PAUPER NOTES   **Accommodation:** Accommodation mostly single rooms, some ensuite. Prices reasonable in private sector (£30 p/w in city). **Drink:** Cheapest pint at the union bar (£1 a pint, lager and bitter); good pubs include The Belle Vue, Fugitive and Firkin (for real ales brewed on premises), Adam and Eve (for when Mummy and Daddy visit). **Eats:** Tree House for veggies and vegans; thousands of cheap Indian; some Chinese, Mexican and Italian restaurants; usual high street junk food outlets. **Ents:** Union provides best large venue in East Anglia, LCR which attracts huge bands; city venue the Waterfront (rave, jazz, dance, alternative). Cinema City for art films and cheap matinees (no multiples at present but promises). **Sports:** Athletics and hockey centre next to campus; good sports centre and a huge range of sports clubs. Not so hot on swimming pools. **Hardship funds:** Access funds and some other funds. Help from SU advice unit. **Travel:** 2 hours to London by car, 2½ by train. SU runs excellent travel shop. **Work:** Various work on and off campus. SU runs employment agency, Employability.

MORE INFO?   Apply for Student Handbook. Enquiries to 01603 503711.

INFORMAL NAME   UEA.

ALUMNI (EDITORS' PICK)   Jonathan Powell (BBC), Selina Scott (TV presenter), Jenny Abramsky (Radio 4), Ian McEwan, Kazuo Ishiguro, Ruth Rendell (authors), Noelle Walsh (Editor, *Good Housekeeping*), Vanessa Evans (Editor, *Country Homes & Interiors*), Tim Bentinck & David Vann (actors), Andy Ripley (rugby player), Sandbrook (International Institute for the Environment & Development), Dennis Callopy (MD, E6 Music Group), Clive Sinclair.

EAST LONDON UNIVERSITY

University of East London, Barking Campus, University of
East London, Longbridge Road, Dagenham, Essex RM8 2AS
(Tel 0181 590 7000, Fax 0181 519 3740 or 590 7799) Map 5

STUDENT ENQUIRIES: Department of Student Administration
APPLICATIONS: UCAS

Broad study areas: Design, built environment, business, health, sciences, technology, social sciences. (Subject details are in the *Subjects and Places Index.*)

Founded: 1970 as East London Poly; university status in 1992. **Main undergraduate awards:** BA, BSc, BEng, LLB. **Awarding body:** University of East London. **Site:** 5 sites, divided into 2 campuses (Barking and Stratford). **Access:** Close to BR stations, underground and bus routes. **Academic features:** Broad based programmes allow students to sudy 2 or 3 subjects eg design and environmental studies. **Europe:** All students have access to language tuition at various levels; languages encouraged for combined studies and engineering students. Formal exchange links with a number of European universities/colleges. **Library:** Five libraries with subject bias; over 300,000 books in total, 1,000 study places. Annual expenditure on library materials, £54.98 per FTE student. **Specialist collections:** Charles Myers Library of industrial psychology. **Welfare:** Professional welfare officers, with access to external agencies, eg charities and aid centres; also doctor, FPA, chaplain. Nurseries at both campuses. **Careers:** Information, advice and placement service. **Amenities:** SU officers and premises on each campus, music centre at Barking campus. **Sporting facilities:** Swimming pool, 2 gymnasia, squash court, tennis courts, fitness centre, playing fields.

Accommodation: In 1995/96, 1,275 places available: 508 self-catering places at Barking , £51 per week, Sept–June; 542 self-catering at Stratford, £35.50–£49.50 per week; 225 self-catering places at West Ham, £34–£36 per week; plus 150 half-board places in Romford YMCA, £76.06 per week. Priority at Barking is given to first year students; some places suitable for students with physical disabilities. Rents for privately-owned accommodation; £35–£45 per week for self-catering (excl bills), £50 for B&B, £65–£70 full-board. 66% first degree students live at home. **Term time work:** University's policy to allow term time work for full-time first degree students. Term time work available on campus in SU bars and shops; also university advertises local Job Centre vacancies. **Hardship funds:** Total available in 1995/96: £295,100 government access funds, 1,324 students helped; £10,000 own funds, 35 students helped. Special help: with tuition fees and additional course costs; those with high accommodation or travel costs, with dependants, or exceptional unforeseen circumstances. Own funds for final year students facing unexpected hardship.

Duration of first degree courses: 3 years; **others:** 4 years sandwich; 4 or 5 years part-time. **Total first degree students 1995/96:** 9,477. **Overseas students:** 785. **Mature students:** 62%. **Male/female ratio:** 1:1. **Teaching staff:** 495 full-time, 137 part-time. **Total number of students:** 12,089. **Postgraduate students:** 1,809. **First degree tuition fees:** Home students, paying their own fees in 1996/97, paid £750 (classroom), £1,600 (lab/studio); Overseas: £5,800.

WHAT IT'S LIKE University has 7 sites, stretching 8 miles across East London from Barking to Stratford. Unwanted local buildings house the school of architecture (Holbrook) and fine art department (Greengate); former is in a one-time children's school still with minature toilets, latter in Castle Grey Skull building complete with gargoyles. The business school however has rather plush and purpose-built lecture rooms with all mod cons. Barking is an active site accommodating courses such as cultural studies, law and land surveying. UEL is renowned for its open access policy and vocational courses – there's something for everyone, and they're always developing new courses. It is at the gateway to central London entertainments and there is a huge range of ents in the Union bars, where cheap beer flows in a safe/harassment free environment. The union also supports student led clubs and societies for those wanting to get active: climbing mountains to debating with the Tory club!

PAUPER NOTES **Accommodation:** Plenty of private housing to rent in East London; prices rising. Uni accommodation at Barking and Stratford – both pricey for what you get. **Drinks:** 2 SU bars (Barking and Maryland) – cheap beer. **Eats:** Greengate House has a union coffee bar with wholesome cheap nosh. Food outlets at all sites with diversity of cultural foods. **Ents:** SU Barking bar: various entertainments. SU Maryland bar – comedy, quiz, film, indie, rave and acid jazz nights. **Sports:** Barking facilities reasonable; nothing at Stratford. **Hardship funds:** Access funds; hardship funds. Financial advice from SU and student services. **Travel:** Railcards, ISIC cards and National Express. **Work:** SU shop and bar. Local supermarket, fast food outlets and telephone research/sales work popular.

ALUMNI (EDITORS' PICK) Garry Bushell (TV editor of *The Sun*), Mark Frith (freelance journalist with *Smash Hits*), Dame Vera Lynn, Trevor Brooking.

EDGE HILL UNIVERSITY COLLEGE

Edge Hill University College, St Helen's Road, Ormskirk, Lancashire L39 4QP (Tel 01695 575171, Fax 01695 579997) Map 2

STUDENT ENQUIRIES: Admissions Office (01695 584274)
APPLICATIONS: UCAS

Broad study areas: Education, arts, business, environmental sciences, maths, English, health, social sciences. (Subject details are in the *Subjects and Places Index*.)

Founded: 1885. **Main undergraduate awards:** BA, BSc, BA/BSc(QTS). **Awarding body:** Lancaster University. **Site:** Semi-rural campus at main Ormskirk site. Other sites at Chorley and Aintree. **Access:** Easy reach of main motorway and rail links; Liverpool and Southport 20 minutes away. **Academic features:** Modular BA/BSc scheme. **Special features:** Linked to a network of colleges in the north west through Open College of the North West and the Merseyside Open College Forum. **Europe:** 3% first degree students take a language as part of their course; opportunities for those taking French to study abroad. **Library:** 250,000 books, audio-visual and reference materials; short loan collections. Annual expenditure on library materials, £65.43 per FTE student. **Other learning facilities:** TV studio, language laboratories, multimedia, satellite and CD-Rom facilities, 400 computer workstations. **Welfare:** Welfare rights officer, counsellors, accommodation officers, health centre, childcare facilities. **Careers:** Information, advice and placement. **Amenities:** SU building with cafe, restaurant, fast food outlet; bookshop on campus. Majority of buildings adapted for wheelchair access. **Sporting facilities:** Good facilities including a double gym and heated swimming pool.

Accommodation: In 1995/96, 100% of first years in college accommodation. 800 places available: 400 half-board places at £54 per week and 400 self-catering places at £31–£42.50 per week (some ensuite). Students live in privately rented accommodation for 1–2 years: average £35 per week for self-catering, £40 for B&B, £50–£55 for half board. **Hardship funds:** Total available in 1995/96: £65,033 government access funds, 211 students helped.

Duration of first degree courses: 3 years; others: BA/BSc(QTS) 4 years. **Total first degree students 1995/96:** 5,400; **BA/BSc(QTS) students:** 1,025. **Overseas students:** 100. **Mature students:** 3,060. **Male/female ratio:** 2:7. **Teaching staff:** 231 full-time, 19 part-time. **Total full-time students 1995/96:** 4,100 **Postgraduate students:** 1,180. **First degree tuition fees:** Home students, paying their own fees in 1996/97, paid £1,050.

WHAT IT'S LIKE Campus with attractive buildings, ranging from 1930s to modern smoked glass and steel. 45 acres of playing fields and beautiful gardens. A very relaxing and attractive place to study, just outside Ormskirk (a small ancient market town). Within easy reach of Southport (7 miles) and Liverpool (15 miles). Both provide excellent nightlife (clubs, cinemas, theatres, restaurants, etc) and good shopping facilities. Ormskirk has a cheap and popular market on Thursdays and Saturdays and a small indoor market. Campus life very easy-going. Students generally settle in very quickly and the drop-out rate is low. College rooms are comfortable, warm and generally well-furnished. Meals in refectory and cooking facilities available in halls. SU finances societies and provides welfare, academic and general support. Societies very active, especially the athletic union, drama, Christian union, rock, film, media. Also there is an active community work scheme and a child care facility on campus. Students seem happy with courses. Nearly 40% on QTS courses. Good staff/student relations – each student allocated a personal tutor.
PAUPER NOTES **Accommodation:** Most non-resident students live in Ormskirk and Southport. 85% first years in halls (17 mixed, 3 single sex). **Drink:** College club on campus, cheapest place in town. Favourite haunts – Buck 'I'th' Vine and The Cricketers (numerous happy hours). Town has 16 pubs ranging from wine bars to scruffy and cosy – something for everyone. **Eats:** Good value lunchtime snack – cafe, restaurant and fast food diner on campus. Good restaurants and takeouts in town and food in several pubs. **Ents:** Events every night: bands, quizzes and discos with top club DJs. Club trips twice weekly. Student discounts at local cinemas. **Sports:** Sports complex include all-weather pitches. **Hardship funds:** Access fund. **Travel:** Bus to Southport; train to Liverpool and Preston. **Work:** Limited term-time work in Ormskirk.
ALUMNI (EDITORS' PICK) Ann McCormack (commercial planner, Metal Box Co), Jonathan Pryce (actor), Russell Slad (football manager).

HOW TO START? *SEE SHORTLISTING*, PAGE 535

EDINBURGH COLLEGE OF ART

Edinburgh College of Art, Lauriston Place, Edinburgh EH3 9DF
(Tel 0131 221 6000, Fax 0131 221 6001) Map 1

STUDENT ENQUIRIES: Registration Office
APPLICATIONS: UCAS; direct for art and design.

Broad study areas: Architecture, design and applied arts, fine art, town planning and housing studies. (Subject details are in the *Subjects and Places Index.*)

Founded: 1907. **Structural features:** an associate college of Heriot-Watt University. **Main undergraduate awards:** BA, BArch, MA. **Awarding body:** Heriot-Watt University; Edinburgh University. **Academic features:** Courses in visual communication, tapestry, sculpture and printmaking. **Site:** Edinburgh city centre. **Europe:** No students learn a language. Extensive exchange opportunities across Europe and elsewhere. **Library:** 92,500 volumes, 110,000 slides; 483 periodicals, 140 study places. **Other learning facilities:** Computer facilities. **Welfare:** Counselling and welfare services available. **Amenities:** College shop, student common room, snack bar, music room and photographic dark room.

Accommodation: 43 places in self-catering flats. Further information on halls of residence available from accommodation and welfare officer. **Hardship funds:** Some discretionary funds.

Duration of first degree courses: 4 years; others: 5 years. **Total first degree students 1995/96:** 1,340. **Overseas students:** 100. **Mature students:** 22%. **Male/female ratio:** 7:9. **Teaching staff:** 115 full-time, 50 part-time. **Total full-time students 1995/96:** 1,595. **Postgraduate students:** 340. **First degree tuition fees:** Home students, paying their own fees in 1996/97, paid £1,600; Overseas students £7,300.

WHAT IT'S LIKE Right in the middle of town, with a brilliant view of Edinburgh Castle, the art college is near just about everything in Edinburgh – art galleries, theatres, cinemas, shops, libraries, pubs, restaurants and Wonderland toyshop. The main building is a fascinating piece of Victorian architecture, dominated inside by the sculpture court – the main exhibition space. Associated with Heriot-Watt University, it still retains its own governing body and is independently funded. It has also retained its own identity rather than being swallowed up by the larger institution. The college consists of two faculties – environmental and art & design, both very highly thought of. SU is very active within the college; its office is busy but friendly and there's always has someone on hand for welfare, accommodation or legal advice. SU now runs the central Apple Mac facility for students; also photocopying and telephone facilities; darkroom available for black and white processing and printing (in and out of college hours), and a much-used music room. The SU also runs Albertina's snack bar, offering the cheapest chip buttie in town and the Wee Red Bar, at weekends, is a legendary club venue. There are numerous societies active within the college including the women's group, lesbian and gay society, Christian Union, Archie (architects), Slag (landscape architects), Scoop (sculpture co-operative), film, entertainments and painting.

PAUPER NOTES   **Accommodation:** Cowgate flats, central and cheap; usually allocated to students leaving home for the first time and to overseas students. ECA students can apply for Heriot-Watt leased flats. Excellent college accommodation service. **Drink:** Edinburgh has a huge range of pubs, lots licensed until late. SU runs clubs in Wee Red Bar – sometimes four or five times a week. **Eats:** Albertina's, the student union café, has to be the cheapest place to eat in Edinburgh. Lots of local pubs do lunchtime special deals for students; plenty of good cheapish restaurants in town. **Ents:** Many different clubs in Edinburgh cater for all different tastes. Numerous cinemas and theatres nearby as well as cabaret and live band venues. **Sports:** Heriot-Watt University sports facilities at Riccarton (7 miles out) rarely used by ECA students; numerous Edinburgh sports facilities, especially swimming pools. **Hardship funds:** Most students eligible for access funds. College can give £75 emergency loans. **Travel:** Travel scolarships given on merit. Various travel award schemes plus some organised outings and trips abroad. **Work:** If you're determined to find work during term-time, it's possible (50% do some); expect about £3 an hour. Part-time bar work popular. Vacation work can be found (majority find it necessary) especially during Festival in summer; some find work at home.

ALUMNI (EDITORS' PICK)   John Bellamy, John Houston, Gwen Hardy and Elizabeth Blackadder (painters); Sean Connery, Suzie Wighton (primary health care worker Palestinian camps), Ron Brown and Roy Williamson ('The Corries'), Albert Mallard (comic).

EDINBURGH UNIVERSITY

The University of Edinburgh, Old College, South Bridge,
Edinburgh EH8 9YL
(Tel 0131 650 1000, Fax 0131 668 4565) Map 1

STUDENT ENQUIRIES: Schools Liaison Service (0131 650 4360)
APPLICATIONS: UCAS

Broad study areas: Humanities, divinity, law, medicine & veterinary medicine, music, science and engineering, social sciences. (Subject details are in the *Subjects and Places Index*.)

Founded: 1583. **Main undergraduate awards:** BA, BCom, BD, BEng, BMus, BSc, BV&MS, LLB, MA, MBChB, MEng, MChem, MChemPhys, MPhys. **Awarding body:** Edinburgh University. **Site:** Edinburgh city centre (arts, law, music, social sciences, veterinary medicine and medicine); science and engineering 2 miles south at King's Buildings campus; divinity at New College in city centre. **Access:** Waverley BR station and central bus station (St Andrew Square) nearby; airport 8 miles. **Academic features:** Wide range of courses in Scottish studies and Scots language; environmental geoscience; courses in physics with music or meteorology. **Europe:** 10% first degree students take a language as part of their course and 1% spend 6 months or more abroad. Languages available on graduating or non-graduating basis; many degree courses allow students to add a language in first or second year. Formal exchange links with over 50 European universities/colleges, most open to non-language specialists. Member of Coimbra Group and UNICA (capital cities network). **Library:** Main library in very large library building, also various faculty libraries. Over

2 million volumes and pamphlets, long and short loan services. Annual expenditure on library materials, £117.89 per FTE student. **Other learning facilities:** On-line computing network and associated facilities. **Specialist collections:** Reid music library, Erskine medical library, European Institute library, New College (divinity) library, and specialist law, science and veterinary libraries; Russell collection of early keyboard instruments; also historic collection of wind instruments; Talbot Rice Gallery with permanent Torrie Collection of painting and sculpture and visiting exhibitions. **Careers:** Advice and placement. **Amenities:** SA bars and shops, over 140 clubs, sports centre, playing fields and Firbush Point field centre on Loch Tayside for climbing and water sports.

Accommodation: In 1995/96, 29% of all students in university accommodation, 100% non-home based first years. 5,800 places available (3,650 for first years): 1,700 full-board places (1,650 for first years) at £67 per week (£74–£77 ensuite), term time only; 3,600 self-catering places (1,900 for first years) at £42, Sept–June or longer. 400 more places in owned or leased accommodation by 1997. Students live in privately owned accommodation for 1–2 years: rents £40–£45 per week for self-catering or B&B. 17% first degree students live at home. **Term time work:** University's policy to allow term time work for full-time first degree students (25–33% believed to work); limit of 15 hours per week max. Term (and vac) work available on campus; also university student employment service. **Hardship funds:** Total available in 1995/96: £343,870 government access funds, average £300 awarded; £250,000 own funds. Special help: those with children, mature students, self-financing undergraduates; help for overseas students limited. Some £90,000 assigned to self-financing students before starting course.

Duration of first degree courses: 4 years (hons), 3 years (general); **others:** 5 years (medicine, veterinary medicine, fine art, MEng, MPhys, MChem, MChemPhys). **Total first degree students 1995/96:** 12,871. **Overseas students:** 2,213. **Mature students:** 1,301. **Male/female ratio:** 11:10. **Teaching staff:** 2,586 full-time, 178 part-time. **Total full-time students 1995/96:** 15,084. **Postgraduate students:** 2,213. **First degree tuition fees:** Home students, paying their own fees in 1996/97, paid £750 (classroom), £1,600 (lab/studio), £2,800 (clinical); Overseas students £6,210 (classroom), £8,160 (lab/studio), £14,840 (clinical).

WHAT IT'S LIKE   Edinburgh is a very special place: no other city centre resembles it, with its main street exposed on one side to reveal the famous castle overlooking Princes Street Gardens. The university itself is almost entirely located in the centre, apart from the main science campus (King's Buildings), which is well connected by bus to the centre, and part of the veterinary faculty which is quite far out. The university boasts 2 student unions: EUSA (Edinburgh University Students' Association) is by far the larger – the biggest students' association in the country – and provides most of the welfare services, including 5 student union houses. It does this so effectively that most students believe that the services are actually provided by the university, and not the students. EUSA also incorporates the Students' Representative Council, which undertakes most of the representational work for the students. There is a special union for postgraduates and mature students. An extremely wide range of academic courses and generally easy to change course if one finds that things don't work out quite as the prospectus implied they might. Welfare, counselling and advice on AIDS, contraception, pregnancy, etc is supplied by 3 main outlets: the University's Student Counselling Service; student-run telephone Nightline and walk-in information centre; and the much-used EUSA Advice Place which has a base on each of the two main campuses. As one might expect from the Festival City, Edinburgh is very well provided with all forms of entertainment. It is exceptionally well-endowed with theatres, museums, cinemas and galleries and the wide range of pubs, with Scotland's civilised licensing hours, proves a winner with most students. Common meeting-places for students are in the union houses; popular Friday Night at Teviot Row (biggest disco light rig in Scotland) and weekly Roadrunner at Potterrow.

PAUPER NOTES **Accommodation:** All first year students guaranteed some form of university accommodation and have priority for halls of residence. Large number of furnished flats/houses owned or approved by student accommodation service. Some accommodation for married students. **Drink:** Union bars – cheap drink, even cheaper with frequent promotions and a happy hour at every club night. **Eats:** In unions by day. At night the best eats are at Pierre Lapin (vegetarian French), Kings Balti (Indian) and Maxies Bistro. **Ents:** All unions have clubs at night; Potterrow is venue to a lot of Indie bands. Filmsoc shows 130 films a year for £14 membership. Excellent freshers' week. **Sports:** Sports Union boasts huge range of facilities and clubs. Free sports facilities at King's Buildings House, and the Commonwealth Pool. **Hardship funds:** University has small short-term loans and crisis funds for students in desperate long-term financial need. **Travel:** Many exchange schemes. Many discounts through Edinburgh Travel Centre (run by EUSA). **Work:** Limited number of on-campus jobs, shrinking number off-campus; 20–25% get paid work during term-time (many in bar jobs). Approx 70% get employment for at least part of summer vac, with tourist industry and Festival. New employment service helps finding part-time jobs; minimum wage of £2.60/hour, maximum 15 hours/week in term-time.

BUZZ-WORDS EUSA 'yoo-sah' (Edinburgh University Students' Association); Pollock (main halls of residence); KB (King's Buildings ie science campus).

MORE INFO? Ring EUSA office on 0131 650 2656.

ALUMNI (EDITORS' PICK) David Hume (philosopher), Charles Darwin, James Africanus Horton (first African graduate from a British University), Sally Magnusson (TV journalist), Peter Roget (of Thesaurus), Sir David Steele, Sir Walter Scott, Sir James Barrie, R L Stevenson, Sir Arthur Conan Doyle, Malcolm Rifkind, David Livingstone, Gordon Brown.

ESSEX UNIVERSITY

University of Essex, Wivenhoe Park, Colchester CO4 3SQ (Tel 01206 873333, Fax 01206 873423, e-mail admit@essex.ac.uk) Map 4

STUDENT ENQUIRIES: Admissions Officer
APPLICATIONS: UCAS

Broad study areas: Comparative humanities, arts, social sciences, law, mathematical sciences, computer science, physical and life sciences, electronic engineering. (Subject details are in the *Subjects and Places Index*.)

Founded: 1962, Royal Charter received 1965. **Main undergraduate awards:** BA, BSc, LLB, BEng, MChem, MEng, MMaS, MPhys. **Awarding body:** Essex University. **Site:** 2 miles east of Colchester. **Access:** Bus service from Colchester station and from town centre. **Academic features:** New degrees in audio systems engineering, philosophy and artificial intelligence, freshwater and marine biology, English and a foreign language. **Europe:** 9% first degree students take a language as part of course and 3% spend 6 months or more abroad. Formal exchange links with some 55 European universities/colleges across Europe, open to students in a variety of subjects. **Library:** 690,000 volumes, 3,200 periodicals, 1,000 study places; 3-hour loan system for course books. Annual expenditure on library materials, £144.58 per FTE student. **Specialist collections:** Latin American and Russian collections. **Welfare:** Doctors, FPA, chaplain, student counsellors, welfare rights advice. Some residential facilities for married and disabled students; 98 nursery/playgroup places. **Careers:** Information, advice and placement service. **Amenities:** Bookshop, general shop, banks and post office; 217-seat theatre, exhibitions gallery; SU building with shop, bar, travel centre, print room, newsletter etc; film society; University Radio Essex; art studio. **Sporting facilities:** Sports hall, weights room, aerobics studio, fitness room, indoor climbing wall, fitness testing lab, gymnasium, squash courts; floodlit all-weather playing area and tennis courts; wide range of sports including water sports association with club house and dinghies.

Accommodation: In 1995/96, 54% of all students in university accommodation, 100% of first years. 2,460 places available (1,500 for first years): all self-catering, at £33–£52 per week, Sept–June. Students live in privately owned accommodation for 1–2 years: £30–£45 per week self-catering, £40 B&B. 16% of first degree students live at home. **Term time work:** University policy to allow term time work for first degree students. Term (and vac) work available on campus in SU bars and entertainment; university vac work available in domestic, catering, language teaching; also SU advertises other local vacancies. **Hardship funds:** Total available in 1995/96: £100,099 government access funds, approx 205 students helped on individual basis. Own fund (no fixed amount) also provides short-term loans and loans to overseas students for private accommodation. Individual advice available on alternative sources of funding. 4 overseas scholarships also available.

Duration of first degree courses: 3 years; **others:** 4 years (eg languages, environmental and industrial chemistry, information management systems). **Total first degree students 1995/96:** 4,143. **Overseas students:** 515. **Mature u/g students:** 1,463. **Male/female ratio:** 1:1. **Teaching staff:** 327 full-time. **Total full-time students 1995/96:** 5,571. **Postgraduate students:** 1,428. **First degree tuition fees:** Home students, paying their own fees in 1996/97, paid £1,430 (classroom), £3,060 (lab/studio); Overseas students £6,130 (classroom), £8,125 (lab/studio).

WHAT IT'S LIKE It's a campus university, built in large park about 2 miles from Colchester – compact, with friendly atmosphere. The main features of concrete skyline are 6 residential towers; each divided into 14–16 flats with 13–16 people sharing kitchen; some mixed, double and married flats. Also flats (for 4 people) in new houses on campus. Single first years guaranteed campus accommodation. Accommodation on campus is supplemented by 600 rooms in purpose-built flats on estate down the road; university owns property in Colchester and operates contract housing scheme. Otherwise look privately – distances 1 to 9 miles from university. Bus sporadic, especially to main BR station. SU runs: live groups and discos, own radio station, newspaper plus sporting, cultural, practical and political societies, as well as student help and advice. Colchester garrison town 55 miles from London; relations with town okay. Wivenhoe, couple miles away, trendy ex-fishing village, now thriving port. Some reasonable pubs if prepared to look for them. Winter can be cold and windy with North Sea winds prevailing. Relations between students and university administration fairly good. Result of degree depends on continuous assessment and more traditional annual sit-down exams. Easy to change course. Almost all first-year courses unspecialised leaving open as many options as possible for final degree. Students mixed; some yuppies; few yearning for old, radical days of Essex students.

PAUPER NOTES **Accommodation:** Cheap accommodation difficult. **Drink:** SU bar biggest and cheapest in East Anglia; many good pubs in Wivenhoe (Sociology-on-Sea) and surrounding area. Many good local real ales – Greene King, Adnams. **Eats:** SU food good and cheap. Veggie food catered for. **Shops:** Second-hand bookshop and SU shop (alternative food) on campus. SU travel agent; proliferation of charity shops. **Ents:** Very good SU film soc. Good uni theatre. Fairly good ents, but not many student campus bands. **Sports:** No swimming pool on campus but astroturf and cheap facilities. **Hardship fund:** Both university and SU have limited funds. **Travel:** Most travel scholarships abolished. Good SU travel shop. **Work:** Still some summer work on campus and jobs off campus in term. 5–10% find some term-time work; 30% vacation.

MORE INFO? Ring SU on 01206 863211.

ALUMNI (EDITORS' PICK) Brian Hanrahan, Virginia Bottomley MP, President Oscar Arias of Costa Rica (Nobel Peace Prize 1987), Peter Joslin (Chief Constable of Warwickshire), Gwyn Jones (Welsh Development Agency), Rudolfo Neri Vela (Mexico's only astronaut).

EUROPEAN BUSINESS SCHOOL, LONDON

European Business School London, Regent's College, Inner Circle, Regent's Park, London NW1 4NS (Tel 0171 487 7507, Fax 0171 487 7425) Map 6

STUDENT ENQUIRIES: External Relations Manager
APPLICATIONS: UCAS or direct

Broad study areas: Business studies with modern languages. (Subject details are in the *Subjects and Places Index*.)

Founded: 1967. **Structural features:** Part of an international network with links in France, Germany, Italy, Spain, Russia, Japan and USA. **Main undergraduate award:** BA. **Awarding body:** Open University. **Site:** Single 11-acre campus in the heart of Regent's Park (shared with Regent's College and School of Psychotherapy & Counselling). **Access:** 5 minutes' walk from Baker Street underground and buses. **Academic features:** Integrated language and business course, including study abroad and work experience (including in USA), courses in leadership, public speaking, computer skills and management techniques. **Special features:** January and September start dates. 48 weeks in-company training in at least 3 countries and 5 companies. 1-year foundation year before degree course for those who need it. **Europe:** All students take at least one language and spend up to two 6-month periods in two different countries. **Library:** 25,000 volumes, 1,000 periodicals, 120 study places. Annual expenditure on library materials, £69 per FTE student. **Specialist collections:** Royal Institute of Public Administration, Overseas Development Institute, College of Homeopathy and Institute of Linguists libraries. **Other learning facilities:** IBM and Apple computer laboratories; CALL and language laboratories. **Careers:** Information, advice and placement service. **Employment:** Managerial positions throughout the world: 21% in financial services & banking, 13% in marketing & advertising, 28% in manufacturing,

6% consultancy, 4% in pharmaceutical/cosmetics, 3% in leisure industry, 8% postgraduate, 3% property, 6% media, 6% retail & textiles, 3% travel & transport; all those seeking work employed within 6 months. **Welfare:** Personal tutors. **Amenities:** Music practice room, art gallery, bar. **Sporting facilities:** Tennis courts, weights room, multi-gym, dance studio. Students can join University of London Union and use their sports facilities.

Accommodation: In 1995/96, 20% of all students in college accommodation (10% first years). 220 places available: full-board at £120–£180 per week, term time only. 5% first degree students live at home. **Hardship funds:** Scholarships and bursaries available.

Duration of first degree courses: 4 years **other:** 3½ years. **Total first degree students 1996/97:** 660. **Overseas students:** 80%. **Male/female ratio:** 3:2. **Teaching staff:** 50 full-time, 30 part-time. **Total full-time students 1995/96:** 630. **First degree tuition fees:** £7,200 (home and overseas).

WHAT IT'S LIKE   Situated in the heart of London and surrounded by nearly 500 acres of beautiful royal park. The campus has a dynamic and cosmopolitan atmosphere with first-class facilities including large common room, bar, tennis courts, refectory, library. Students come from 75 countries and all speak at least 2 languages (40% speak 4). The pace of work is very demanding and there is a strong emphasis on developing personal skills for leadership and teamwork, as well as on work experience. Most students spend the summer break working in the UK or overseas to build up their experience and make themselves more attractive to future employers.
PAUPER NOTES   **Accommodation:** Expensive, single, double and triple rooms. **Drink:** College bar – nice, panelled and reasonable prices. **Eats:** College refectory – good food, great variety, nice surroundings, reasonable prices. Also restaurant and a coffee/lunch bar on campus. **Ents:** Student centre organises trips, theatre, etc. **Sports:** On campus tennis courts (2 grass, 1 hard), fitness centre, basketball court. Football pitches in Regent's Park. **Work:** About 5% work part time in term (most get sufficient funding from parents). Vacation work required for course; approx 25% get paid.
INFORMAL NAME   EBS
MORE INFO?   Ring Lucy Kennedy on 0171 487 7454.

EXETER UNIVERSITY

University of Exeter, Northcote House, The Queen's Drive, Exeter EX4 4QJ (Tel 01392 263263, Fax 01392 263108) Map 3

STUDENT ENQUIRIES: Admissions Office
APPLICATIONS: UCAS

Broad study areas: Literary, cultural and language studies; education; sciences, pure and applied, physical and natural; social studies; engineering; law; information technology; music; drama. (Subject details are in the *Subjects and Places Index*.)

Founded: 1885 as a college of art, becoming a university college in 1922; university status in 1955. Camborne School of Mines joined in 1993 (you can look it up separately). **Main undergraduate awards:** BA, BEd, BSc, BEng, LLB, LLB (Eur), BA(Ed), BSc(Ed), BMus, MEng, MPhys, MChem, MMath, MStat. **Awarding body:** University of Exeter. **Site:** 2 modern campuses in Exeter: Streatham Campus, a 245-acre garden site 1 mile from city centre; St Luke's Campus (School of Education), 1½ miles away and ½ mile from city centre. **Access:** Minibus connects 2 sites; bus from city centre. **Structural features:** Camborne School of Mines, in Cornwall, is part of engineering faculty. **Academic features:** Modular degree programme allows students in arts, law and social studies to design their own programme from beginning of second year, around 1 or 2 fields of study. Suitably qualified entrants may apply for entry direct to second year. Fine art can be combined with English, French or Italian in conjunction with Plymouth University's faculty of art and design, located in Exeter; also Italian with design. **Europe:** Most departments offer degree programmes which include a period of study in Europe and lead to the award of a degree with European Study; other students may take additional language modules. **Library:** 1,000,000 volumes and journals; separate faculty libraries, especially law and education. Annual expenditure on library materials, £110 per FTE student. **Specialist collections:** Rare editions, examples of early printing. University also runs Cathedral Library (distinguished collections of Anglo Saxon and medieval works) and the Devon and Exeter Institution Library (West Country material). Bill Douglas and Peter Jewell Collection (history of cinema and popular culture). **Welfare:** Health centres; counselling service; family centre on Streatham Campus, run jointly with Guild of Students; chaplaincy; welfare advice centres (Guild of Students). **Amenities:** Shops, bank etc on campus; Guild buildings with licensed bars, launderettes, etc; Northcott Theatre (with its own professional company, also provides for amateur productions). **Sporting facilities:** Sports hall on Streatham Campus, offering wide range of facilities, open-air pool during the summer, plus all-weather pitches, tennis courts, playing fields, athletics track; indoor heated swimming pool and gymnasia at St Luke's.

Accommodation: In 1995/96, 47% of all students in university accommodation; guaranteed for all first years. 4,163 places available: 1,968 full-board places at £77.35 per week (£85.26 for ensuite), term time only; and 1,918 self-catering places at £40.95 per week (£59.57 for ensuite), October–July (some excluding Easter vac); 277 places in university-owned houses close to campus; also 16 family flats. Most students live in privately owned accommodation for 2 years, £40–£50 per week self-catering. **Term time work:** No university policy to allow part time work. Term (and vac) work available on campus in halls of residence on regular basis, plus casual work in bars, refectories, stewarding, office work, cleaning and waitressing; also Guild of Students Jobscheme, links with local Jobcentre and employment agencies. **Hardship funds:** Total available in 1995/96: £257,154 government access funds, average £285 awarded, 916 students helped. Special help for mature students with dependants and those with serious domestic difficulties.

Duration of first degree courses: 3 years; 4 years for eg undergraduate masters degrees and those with education, European study or languages. **Total first degree students 1995/96:** 6,587; **Education students:** 926; **International students:** 183. **Mature students:** 825. **Male/female ratio:** 1:1. **Teaching staff:** 793 full-time, 89 part-time. **Total full-time students 1995/96:** 7,903. **Postgraduate students:** 2,287. **First degree tuition fees:** Home students, paying their own fees in 1996/97, paid £750 (classroom), £1,600 (lab/studio); Overseas students £6,210 (classroom), £7,770 (lab/studio).

WHAT IT'S LIKE   Main site, Streatham, is set in beautiful grounds close to city centre with two guild buildings incorporating bars, coffee bar, stationery, travel and print shops.

It also has an outdoor swimming pool, sports complex and theatre. St Luke's, the education school, is about a mile away and also close to town. Luke's has excellent sports facilities, including a covered pool, plus coffee bar, bar and shops. NatWest bank on both sites, other banks close to hand in the city. Nearly all first years in hall: some purpose-built but comfortable; others more attractive converted 19th-century houses. Campus self-catering flats vary from luxurious with ensuite facilities, to cheap, cheerful and convenient but cramped. Very limited car-parking. Guild of Students is apolitical to reflect members varied social and cultural background; provides excellent ents programme and a variety of well-used welfare services. Superb sporting reputation and over 100 clubs and societies. Course structure varies from traditional to modular, many students have the opportunity to spend a year abroad. Exams (mainly unseen) spread over two years but some dissertations. Personal tutor system could be improved. Library facilities generally good although can be overcrowded. High academic standard; drop-out and failure rates relatively low. Climate good; beautiful countryside and beaches close at hand.

PAUPER NOTES **Accommodation:** Plentiful on campus, halls expensive but good facilities. Several student areas in town, many live in the country. **Drink:** Guild bars, Ram and Ewe, still best bet; Ram has regular guest bitters. Other old favourites includes The Red Cow, Black Horse and Cider Gate Bar. **Eats:** Best restaurants include Harpoon Louies for fish and steak; Crockers for posher meals; On the Waterfront for dustbin-lid pizzas; Herbies, incredibly cheap vegetarian. **Ents:** Ents programme includes big name bands and twice-weekly campus disco. Cheap arts events and good student theatre. **Sports:** Two pools; cheap equipment hire; campus gym, weights and dance studio. **Hardship fund:** Access fund (apply early). £50 loans available from Guild as last resort. **Travel:** Some travel scholarships. Good road and rail links. Guild travel shop on campus. Good hitching (success in Rag Hitches in past). Efficient Guild minibus service within Exeter. **Work:** Guild Job Scheme helps students find work on and off campus (about 5% do); mainly bar, waiting, telesales and retail, otherwise fairly scarce. Few work locally during vac, 50+% find work at home.

ALUMNI (EDITORS' PICK) Richard Hill, Mike Slemen (England Rugby players), Paul Jackson (BBC comedy producer), Tony Speller and Boner Wells (Tory MPs), Paul Downton, Richard Ellison (England cricketers).

FALMOUTH COLLEGE OF ARTS

Falmouth College of Arts, Woodlane, Falmouth, Cornwall TR11 4RA (Tel 01326 211077, Fax 01326 211205) Map 3

STUDENT ENQUIRIES: Admissions Office
APPLICATIONS: UCAS

Broad study areas: Art, design, communication. (Subject details are in the *Subjects and Places Index*.)

Founded: 1902 as private venture; taken over by local authority in 1938; incorporated 1989. **Main undergraduate award:** BA. **Awarding body:** Plymouth University. **Site:** Near Falmouth town centre, 5 minutes from sea. **Academic features:** Programmes include graphic communication, advertising, illustration, fine art, broadcasting and journalism studies, visual culture, photographic communication and ceramics. Unitised programmes of study. **Europe:** Languages not part of course but optional classes; 3% spend 3 months or more abroad. Formal exchange links with institutions in western Europe; industrial placement in Europe. **Library:** 30,000 books, 200 journals. **Careers:** Advice service. **Amenities:** SU arranges social and sports activities; excellent sailing; on-site shop and crèche. **Welfare:** Welfare and accommodation staff, counselling service.

Accommodation: List of approved lodgings sent to students; rents £35–55 per week. Under 5% of first degree students live at home. **Term time work:** College policy to allow term time work (15% believed to work). No work available on campus.

Duration of first degree courses: 3 years. **Total first degree students 1995/96:** 644. **Overseas students:** 27. **Male/female ratio:** 1:1. **Teaching staff:** 50 full-time, 30 part-time. **Total full-time students 1995/96:** 1,065. **Postgraduate students:** 100. **First degree tuition fees:** Home students, paying their own fees in 1996/97, paid £750 (classroom), £1,600 (studio); Overseas students £5,995.

WHAT IT'S LIKE   Set in the picturesque south western peninsula of Cornwall, the college is far removed from the usual hustle and bustle of much of the country. Falmouth is about 70 miles from Plymouth and can feel pretty isolated at times, especially during the wet, dull days of winter. Now affiliated to Plymouth University. Many foreign students, particularly from Scandinavia and Far East. There is no college accommodation, although some planned for 1998. Most students live in private rented properties – more sought after as the college expands and worth looking as early as possible. There are many opportunities to get involved with the SU. Many societies and clubs, from a full array of sports to some more interesting and unusual ones. Despite the lack of venues the SU is active on the social scene and runs a full programme of entertainment throughout the year. College has its own bar (not run by the union) which offers the cheapest drinks in town. Students hoping to find part-time work in Falmouth might be disappointed although some is available (mainly bar and shop work); it improves in the tourist season, from about Easter onwards. There are opportunities for students to stay down over the summer vacation as the season lasts well into September.

PAUPER NOTES   **Accommodation:** Average rents £35–£45 per week, exclusive. **Drink:** Jacobs Ladder, The Pirate Inn, Quayside Inn; some local pubs have drinks promotions. **Eats:** Fast food canteen in refectory/student centre. **Ents:** SU runs a variety of ents. **Sport:** Everything available from cliff-jumping to horse-riding. **Hardship:** Access funds; small SU loans. **Work:** Scarce apart from tourist season, mainly bar work and waiting: rates £3–£3.75 per hour.

MORE INFO?   Enquiries to Student Union, tel 01326 319443, fax 01326 319763, e-mail su@falmouth.ac.uk.

ALUMNI (EDITORS' PICK)   Fergus Walsh (BBC Radio 4 correspondent), Juliet Morris (BBC TV presenter), Martyn Perks (designer).

FARNBOROUGH COLLEGE

Farnborough College of Technology, Boundary Road,
Farnborough, Hampshire GU14 6SB
(Tel 01252 515511, Fax 01252 549682) Map 4

STUDENT ENQUIRIES: Information Office (01252 391391)
APPLICATIONS: UCAS

Broad study areas: Aerospace engineering, business, computing, media, leisure studies, environmental management. (Subject details are in the *Subjects and Places Index.*)

Founded: 1957, originally as training wing of former Royal Aircraft Establishment. **Main undergraduate awards:** BA, BSc, BEng. **Awarding body:** Surrey and Portsmouth universities. **Site:** Two sites, Farnborough and Aldershot (all degree courses at Farnborough). **Access:** Easy reach of London; Farnborough campus on A325, close to junctions 4 and 4A on M3; short walk to railway station. Good local bus service. **Academic features:** Wide range of courses (A-levels, vocational and professional courses, first degrees, masters degrees). Degree courses in computer-aided engineering, environmental management for business. **Special features:** Maintains close links with industry, commerce and local community. **Europe:** A few students spend 6 months or more abroad; no formal exchange links with European universities/colleges at present. **Library:** 60,000 books, 340 periodicals, CD-Rom information network, 320 study places. Dialog and JANET offered on line. Annual expenditure on library materials, £45 per FTE student. **Other learning facilities:** Computer facilities, language and science laboratories, engineering workshops, 3 wind tunnels, fitness suites, TV and radio stations. **Careers:** Information, advice and placement service. **Welfare:** Counselling service, occupational health unit, accommodation officer, learning support unit. Kindergarten on weekdays throughout the year. **Amenities:** SU arranges live bands, discos, theatre, films, charity and fund-raising events. **Sporting facilities:** Good health and fitness suite. Local recreation centre has indoor sports facilities (10 minutes walk).

Accommodation: In 1995/96, 204 places available in student village (all for first years): 94 half-board places at £58–£61 per week; 110 self-catering at £25–£46 per week. Students live in privately owned accommodation for 2 years: £35–£50 per week for self-catering, £55–£70 B&B. Advice and help from college accommodation officer. **Term time work:** College's policy to allow term time work for full-time first degree students (c 80% believed to work). Term (and vac) work available on campus eg cleaning, admin during summer vac; also college recruitment officer helps students get work off campus. **Hardship funds:** Total available in 1995/96: £45,000 government access funds; £2,500 own funds for loans.

Duration of first degree courses: 3 or 4 years. **Total first degree students 1995/96:** 285 **Overseas students:** 4. **Mature students:** 140. **Male/female ratio:** 6:5. **Teaching staff:** 240 fulltime, 300 part-time. **Total full-time students 1995/96:** 3,015. **Postgraduate students:** 150. **First degree tuition fees:** Home students, paying their own fees in 1996/97, paid £750 (classroom), £1,660 (lab/studio); Overseas students £3,000 (classroom), £5,979 (lab/studio).

ALUMNI (EDITORS' PICK) Verity Larby-Walker and Peter Hull (1992 and 1996 Olympics), Beverley Kinch (long jump and 100 metres), Steve Benton (national cyclist), Vicki Elcoate (Deputy Director of Council for National Parks).

GLAMORGAN UNIVERSITY

University of Glamorgan, Pontypridd, Mid Glamorgan
CF37 1DL (Tel 01443 480480, Fax 01443 482008) Map 3

STUDENT ENQUIRIES: Admissions Officer
APPLICATIONS: UCAS

Broad study areas: Business and accounting, built environment, science, humanities and social sciences, engineering, law, computing, sports science, maths. (Subject details are in the *Subjects and Places Index.*)

Founded: 1913, college first founded; Wales Poly, gained university status 1992. **Main undergraduate awards:** BA, BSc, BEng, MEng, LLB. **Awarding body:** University of Glamorgan. **Site:** Two site campus in Treforest, Pontypridd; law school 1 mile away. **Access:** Good road and rail links. **Academic features:** Many courses are modular, so students can design own study programme. **Europe:** 12% first degree students take a language as part of course, 45% have the option; languages including Welsh, available to all students. 12% spend 6 months or more abroad (60% have the option). Active collaboration with large number of institutions in most European countries. European business studies introduced into a number of courses. **Library:** Over 150,000 volumes, 1,000 serial publications, 730 study places. Annual expenditure on library materials, £46.78 per FTE student. **Specialist collections:** Welsh writing in English. **Other learning facilities:** Computer centre, media services. **Welfare:** Health centre; 3 student advisers; 2 counsellors; 1 full-time, 2 part-time chaplains; 1 CSV for special needs; playcentre. **Careers:** Information, advice and placement. **Amenities:** SU with bars, cafes, shop, travel centre, launderette, welfare advice etc. **Sporting facilities:** Floodlit sports fields, tennis courts; recreation centre with squash/badminton courts, multi-gym, trimnasium, conditioning room, sauna, solarium, climbing wall.

Accommodation: In 1995/96, 1,317 places in hall (75% for first years): £36–£40 per week self-catering (£46 ensuite), £54 per week part-catered, £65 per week fully catered, Sept–June. Most students live in privately owned accommodation: £35–£40 per week for self-catering, £30–£55 for B&B, £35–£60 for half-board. **Term time work:** No university policy on part-time work for students. Term work available on campus in SU. **Hardship funds:** Total available in 1995/96: £149,320 government access funds, 234 students helped; special help to self-funding students, single parents, special needs students, mature students.

Duration of first degree courses: 3 and 4 years. **Total first degree students 1995/96:** 7,687. **Overseas students:** 1,000. **Mature students:** 4,500. **Male/female ratio:** 6:4. **Teaching staff: full-time:** 550. **Total full-time/sandwich students 1995/96:** 10,103. **Postgraduate students:** 1,800. **First degree tuition fees:** Home students, paying their own fees in 1996/97, paid £852; Overseas students £5,600 (classroom), £6,000 (lab/studio).

WHAT IT'S LIKE   It's situated in the valleys on the outskirts of Pontypridd, a busy market town between Merthyr Tydfil and Cardiff. With its own valley line train station just off campus, Treforest is easily accessible. The main campus is situated on a hillside and commands extensive views of the valley and hills opposite. An excellent halls of residence development means that approximately 1,300 students can find accommodation on campus (about half with ensuite facilities) on either full or self-catered terms. Many students live in private rented accommodation in the local area. Renowned for its mixture of students from Wales and around the world, the diverse ages and backgrounds create a friendly and interesting culture. The library is open late (11.45pm) during the week; also open at weekends and in vacations. SU has two buildings on campus, providing focal points for activities. The main union building houses the George Knox pub, Smiths Café Bar (open 11 to 11 serving food and a variety of drinks), and Shafts Nightclub. Other union facilities include Suds launderette, a general store, travel centre, insurance office, many active clubs and societies and a welfare advice service.

PAUPER NOTES **Accommodation:** Full range, including some self-catering on campus. **Drink:** Union George Knox bar and Smiths Cafe Bar are cheapest. Plenty of good local pubs within 10 mins walk of campus. **Eats:** Smiths, at the union, offers a variety of hot and cold fast foods (snacks and fresh sandwiches to full breakfasts and evening meals). Not as much choice locally, some pub grub; plenty of good restaurants in Cardiff. **Ents:** Shafts (union club) open nightly with live bands, discos, cabaret and films. Cardiff has several nightclubs, cinemas and theatres. Municipal Hall in Pontypridd is a theatre/cinema, with good student deals. **Sports:** On-campus sports centre offers a range of facilities. 4 local swimming pools. **Hardship fund:** Union hardship loans (limited) when you hit rock bottom. University access funds. **Travel:** Good train service to Treforest and Pontypridd from Cardiff. Local buses stop at campus halls and near university entrance. Good union travel shop.

MORE INFO? Get union guide or more information by ringing 01443 408227.

GLASGOW CALEDONIAN UNIVERSITY

Glasgow Caledonian University, City Campus,
Cowcaddens Road, Glasgow G4 0BA
(Tel 0141 331 3000, Fax 0141 331 3005) Map 1

STUDENT ENQUIRIES: Academic Registrar/Schools and Colleges Liaison Officer. APPLICATIONS: UCAS

Broad study areas: Business, health, science and technology. (Subject details are in the *Subjects and Places Index*.)

Founded: 1875 Queen's College, merged with Glasgow College, founded 1971); university status in 1992. **Main undergraduate awards:** BA, BSc, BEng. **Awarding body:** Glasgow Caledonian University. **Site:** City centre, West End. **Access:** Bus, underground, rail. **Academic features:** Optometry degree (unique in Scotland); BEng sandwich with electronic and manufacturing options. Degrees in chemistry with IT and instrumentation; risk management. **Europe:** 85% first degree students take a language as part of course and 6% spend 6 months or more abroad. Formal exchange links established in most European countries. **Library:** 222,286 volumes, 1,200 periodicals, 1,110 study places; study copies held. Annual expenditure on library materials, £65.17 per FTE student. **Other learning facilities:**

Computers, learning resources unit. **Welfare:** Student counsellors, financial advisers, chaplaincy team, nurse, doctor. **Careers:** Information, advice, guidance interviews, psychometric testing, workshops, placement and temporary employment service (most programmes are vocational). **Sporting facilities:** Sports hall, multigym.

Accommodation: In 1995/96, 5% of all students in university accommodation, 32% of first years (priority given to those from some distance, with special needs or from overseas). 730 places available: £34–£55 per week (depending on meals, single or shared), Sept–June. Some students live in privately owned accommodation for their whole course, from £40 per week for self-catering. Most first degree students live at home. **Term time work:** University policy to allow term time work for first degree students (25% believed to work). Term (and vac) work available on campus in sports hall and careers service; also careers service helps find outside work. **Hardship funds:** Total available in 1995/96: £214,000 government access funds, 1,194 students helped; £100,000 childcare funds, plus £50,000 loans fund. Special help: students whose income is less than full grant; students with children, self-financing students; students who experience delays with grants.

Duration of first degree courses: 3 to 5 years. **Total first degree students 1995/96:** 8,801. **Overseas students:** 526. **Mature students:** c.1,800. **Male/female ratio:** 3:4. **Teaching staff:** 555 full-time. **Total full-time students 1995/96:** 9,752. **Postgraduate students:** 1,714. **First degree tuition fees:** Home students, paying their own fees in 1996/97, paid £750 (classroom), £950 (lab/studio); Overseas students £6,060.

WHAT IT'S LIKE   It incorporates three campuses, and major building since it became a university is creating new financial services centre, sports hall and 400 bed accommodation. The refectory has been upgraded and extended, many lecture halls refurbished and there is a new SU bar and disco, a 550-capacity venue. All improving dramatically, with many new facilities and opportunities to meet the increasing student numbers. City campus (early 70s) borders the city centre with easy access to buses, trains and underground. Close to shopping precinct with cinemas, theatres, pubs and discos. Students Association provides a lively union with cheap entertainments, booze and food. Also produces a magazine, has a welfare centre and three sabbaticals who represent students on college committees, etc. Runs many clubs, societies and sports clubs, from political to sub-aqua. Union shop sells confectionery, cigarettes and stationery at reasonable prices. Little accommodation but getting better (new halls of residence at city campus); being in the city there are many good flats and bedsits within easy travelling distance.
PAUPER NOTES   **Accommodation:** West End of city and south side popular. Red Road flats and Cobbington Place with Glasgow District Council, David Naismith Building with YMCA. **Drink:** Union for good cheap spirits and beers – Whitbread, Scottish & Newcastle (£1.15 a pint). New bar at Park Campus. **Eats:** Wide range of food at cheap prices at union diner. **Ents:** Discos and bands weekly (eg Ministry of Sound, the Damned); ents card £20. Video screens at City and Park campuses for sports events etc. **Sports:** Easy transport to sports facilities off campus. Sports club goes on day/weekend trips. Games hall and weights room on campus – new sports centre. **Hardship funds:** Short-term loans and access fund, and fund for direct emergencies. **Travel:** Transcard system for buses, trains and underground – all stopping near college. **Work:** Possible although not guaranteed.
ALUMNI (EDITORS' PICK)   Alan Christie (ex-NUS chairman, British Youth Council), Pat Nevin (Chelsea FC and Scotland), Colin Calder (Radio Producer with BBC), Claire English (TV presenter), Peter Lawwell (Celtic FC).

GLASGOW COLLEGE OF BUILDING

Glasgow College of Building & Printing,
60 North Hanover Street, Glasgow G1 2BP
(Tel 0141 332 9969, Fax 0141 332 5170) Map 1

STUDENT ENQUIRIES: Academic Registrar
APPLICATIONS: Direct

Broad study areas: Building, construction, surveying. (Subject details are in the *Subjects and Places Index*.)

Founded: 1972 ex College of Building (founded 1927) and College of Printing. **Main undergraduate award:** BSc. **Awarding body:** Glasgow Caledonian University. **Europe:** No students take a language or spend time abroad as part of their course. Exchange scheme with Budapest. **Library:** 20,000 volumes, 190 periodicals, 150 study places, CD-Rom. **Other learning facilities:** 11 computing rooms. Television studio, recording studio and editing suites. **Careers:** Information and advice service. **Welfare:** Childcare support scheme, counsellor. **Amenities:** Shop. **Sporting facilities:** Gymnasium, conditioning and fitness area.

Accommodation: No college accommodation; students have access to Glasgow Caledonian University accommodation service. 75% first degree students live at home. **Term time work:** College's policy to allow term time work for full-time first degree students (80% believed to work). No work available on campus. **Hardship funds:** Total available in 1995/96: £40,000 government access funds.

Duration of first degree courses: 4 years; **others:** 3 years. **Total first degree students 1995/96:** 200. **Overseas students:** 30. **Mature students:** 75. **Male/female ratio:** 6:1. **Teaching staff:** 158 full-time. **Total full-time students 1995/96:** 1,950. **Postgraduate students:** 20. **First degree tuition fees:** Home students, paying their own fees in 1996/97, paid £740; Overseas students £4,750.

WHAT IT'S LIKE   It's a 14-storey glass-fronted tower block overlooking George Square. Well-placed for transport and faculties. Parking at college impossible. No halls of residence but SRC compiles an accommodation register at start of academic year. 3% overseas students; over 1,500 full-time students, 3,200 part-time. Wide range of students due to variety of courses and employment rate is high. Most students straight from schools in west, north and central Scotland; many stay at home with parents and aspire to job, family, car etc. Ratio of male to female in full-time courses is 2:1, on part-time courses, 7:1. Active students' association with photocopier, common room, welfare office and pool tables.

PAUPER NOTES   **Accommodation:** Shared in local authority flats or private sector if lucky. **Drink:** Cheapest at other SUs, plenty of trendy pubs nearby but the less trendy the pub, the cheaper the prices. **Eats:** Canteen average, some vegetarian. Fast food readily available nearby. **Ents:** Plenty of discos/clubs around city centre. Local theatre and cinema. **Sports:** Underused facilities in college PE department. **Travel:** Travel services at Strathclyde Univ Union. **Work:** High unemployment and skint student population makes work hard to find and you'll get paid next to nothing.

MORE INFO?   Enquiries to Students Association (0141 331 1355).

INFORMAL NAME   GCBP.

GLASGOW SCHOOL OF ART

Glasgow School of Art, 167 Renfrew Street, Glasgow
G3 6RQ (Tel 0141 353 4500, Fax 0141 353 4528) Map 1

STUDENT ENQUIRIES: Registrar's Office
APPLICATIONS: Direct

Broad study areas: Fine art, architecture, design.
(Subject details are in the *Subjects and Places Index*.)

Founded: 1840. **Main undergraduate awards:** BA, BArch. **Awarding body:** Glasgow University. **Site:** Glasgow city centre. **Europe:** No students take a language or spend time abroad. **Library:** 50,000 volumes, 257 periodicals, 150 study places, 60,000 slides, 200 video cassettes. **Welfare:** Full-time welfare officer. **Careers:** Information and advice service. **Amenities:** Active student union, activities committee organises a comprehensive programme of exhibitions, annual fashion show and social functions including dances, gigs and clubs.

Accommodation: In 1995/96, 9% of all students in school accommodation. 120 self-catering places in 4–6 bedroomed flats. Most students live in privately owned accommodation: £45–£49 per week, self-catering. **Term time work:** College policy to allow part time work for first degree students. No work available on campus. **Hardship funds:** Total available in 1995/96: £36,162 government access funds, minimum £100 awarded. Special help: mature students, those with children, final year students.

Duration of first degree courses: 4 years. **Total first degree students 1995/96:** 1,400. **Male/female ratio:** 1:2. **Overseas students:** 40. **Mature students:** 26%. **Teaching staff:** 85 full-time, 35 part-time. **Total full-time students:** 1,400. **Postgraduate students:** 70. **First degree tuition fees:** Home students, paying their own fees in 1996/97, paid £900; Overseas students £6,250.

WHAT IT'S LIKE Centrally located for major shops, cinemas, theatres and nightclubs. School itself has regular film shows (courtesy of the Mackintosh Film Society), twice weekly discos with regular clubs on Friday nights, 'Knucklehead' and 'Divine' on Saturday nights. Also highly successful annual fashion show and activities week (lectures, workshops, recitals, gigs, talent show). Clubs and societies, partly funded by the SU, range from karate to juggling to chess. Own student pub, where most activities take place, the Vic Café Bar which is open 6 days a week and offers a full range of food and drink. As well as fine art and design, the college includes the Mackintosh Architecture School, and industrial and interior design courses. Students pay for all materials for all courses plus a materials fee to the school. Welfare services and counselling are available. Limited self-catering hostel accommodation.
PAUPER NOTES **Accommodation:** Expensive; cheap rented accommodation usually limited to bare essentials. Art school hostel. **Drink:** SU Vic Café bar. Local bars eg Brunswick Cellars, Nico's, Uisgebeatha (pronounced Ischkibar) and Halt Bar (live bands). **Eats:** SU Vic Café bar has good food; also Charlie Reid Day Centre. Sauchiehall Street (various Chinese, Indian, Turkish, Thai, traditional cafés, most offer veg food). **Ents:** Art School Union, GFT (student rate) cinema, RSAMD (regular theatre), 13th Note (for up and coming bands).

Sports: Kelvin Hall Sports Centre, swimming pool (Woodside Baths); local community centre for Tai Kuido, yoga, dance. **Hardship funds:** Available on first come, first served basis. SU helps find sources of alternative income. **Travel:** Many student discount schemes. **Work:** Difficult to find, mainly waiting/bar work/odd jobs (about £2.50–£3/hr); word of mouth or student newspaper, Artemis.

ALUMNI (EDITORS' PICK) Steven Campbell, Peter Howson, Adrian Wyzsenski, Ken Curry, Robbie Coltrane, John Byrne, Pam Hogg.

GLASGOW UNIVERSITY

University of Glasgow, Glasgow G12 8QQ
(Tel 0141 339 8855, Fax 0141 330 4045,
Web site http://www.gla.ac.uk/) Map 1

STUDENT ENQUIRIES: Registrar's Office
APPLICATIONS: UCAS

Broad study areas: Arts and social sciences, divinity, engineering, law and financial studies, medicine, science, veterinary medicine. (Subject details are in the *Subjects and Places Index*.)

Founded: 1451. **Main undergraduate awards:** BA, BAcc, BArch, BD, BDS, BEd, BMus, BN, BSc, BEng, MEng, LLB, MA, MB ChB, MSci, BVMS, BTechEd, BTheol, BTechnol. **Awarding body:** Glasgow University. **Site:** Compact central campus. **Access:** Within easy reach of bus, rail and underground stations. **Europe:** 20% first degree students take a language as part of course and 5% spend 6 months or more abroad. Most first degree students have access to language tuition. A wide range of exchanges with universities/colleges across the EU for students in many subject areas. **Library:** Main and departmental libraries with around 1.5 million volumes; separate reading room with all first year texts. Annual expenditure on library materials, £103.31 per FTE student. **Specialist collections:** Extensive and valuable collection of books and manuscripts. Also Hunterian Museum (anatomical and surgical drawings, instruments etc); Hunterian Art Gallery (old masters, Whistlers, Chardins, Charles Rennie Mackintosh House), ethnographic and Roman collections. **Other learning facilities:** Computer centre, language laboratories. **Welfare:** Student health centre (works in co-operation with students' own local doctor). Student counselling service, special needs adviser and academic advisers for all students. **Careers:** Advice (including summer vacation jobs) and placement service. **Amenities:** SRC shops, travel bureau, bank, insurance bureau, printing and photocopying facilities; 2 student unions with lounges, bars, TV rooms; mature student association. **Sporting facilities:** Physical education building offering wide range of indoor sports, 25m swimming pool, 3 activity halls, cardiovascular and muscle-conditioning suites and sauna. Athletic grounds with bar and pavilion about 2 miles from campus. Access to international sports facilities in Kelvin Hall sports arena.

Accommodation: In 1995/96, 65% of all students who require it in university accommodation, 99% of first years. 4,000 places available (2,800 for first years): half-board (with weekend meals) at £62 per week term time only, and self-catering places at £36.50–£40 per week, Sept–June. Students live in privately owned accommodation for 2 years: rents £42–£47 per week for self-catering, £55–£65 for B&B, £65–£75 for half-board. 40% first degree students live at home. **Term time work**: No university policy on part time work in term time (30% of students believed to work). Term (and vac) work available on campus in registry, assisting at matriculation, schools liaison; also SRC operates a JobShop. **Hardship funds:** Total available £379,932 government access funds, 1,326 students helped; £74,161 own funds, 363 students helped, plus £13,000 other funds (29 students helped). Special help: students who would have met requirements for housing benefit, those with additional costs arising from disability, or with child-minding costs; other funds also available for students of medicine, science or technology, students from Glasgow or the west of Scotland, final year Commonwealth students.

Duration of first degree courses: 4 years (hons); **others:** 3 years and 5 years. **Total first degree students (full-time) 1995/96:** 13,108. **Overseas students:** 1,178. **Mature students:** 23%. **Male/female ratio:** 1:1. **Teaching staff:** 1,233 full-time. **Total full-time students 1995/96:** 15,713. **Postgraduate students:** 1,977 (full-time), 1,324 (part-time). **First degree tuition fees:** Home students, paying their own fees in 1996/97, paid £750 (classroom), £1,393 (lab/studio), £2,293 (clinical); Overseas students £6,400 (classroom), £8,370 (lab/studio), £11,500–£15,160 (clinical).

WHAT IT'S LIKE   It comes as a surprise to many freshers that Glasgow University has two independent student unions; the first major decision is not what course to study, but which union to join. Glasgow University Union (GUU) is the bigger, and many say the better of the two. Within this grade II listed building at the foot of University Avenue, the best and cheapest watering holes on campus can be found in the form of the renowned Beer Bar or Beerie and, in the basement, Deep 6 (recently refurbished) – the newest bar in Glasgow and the cheapest prices in town. On further inspection, 5 other bars can be found as well as libraries, dining room, smoke room, buffet (excellent filled rolls), billiards hall (10 full size tables), pool hall, disco, bedrooms and, last but by no means least, the debates chamber where big bands have been known to play and (as its name suggests) debates are held. The Union is one of the top debating unions in the world. The Queen Margaret Union (QM) is situated on the other side of the hill from the GUU. Here members of either union can enjoy several facilities, but being on a smaller scale than the GUU, choice is limited. Athletic club's excellent Stevenson Building contains Olympic swimming pool and many indoor sports, as well as assisting university's teams and sporting clubs. All students automatically join one of the unions and athletic club on matriculation. Glasgow makes no concessions to trendy innovations but gives security of ancient Scottish university education, with wide-ranging chances in corporate life. Cultural and educational opportunities set in Gothic grandeur of varsity buildings refute slum-bound image of Glasgow; the city (especially West End), where university situated, is very attractive.

PAUPER NOTES   **Accommodation:** 15 bedrooms at cheap rates in union for overnight stays. Large percentage live at home. **Drink:** GUU beer bar and basement bar cheapest on campus with excellent promotions. **Eats:** GUU catering – fresh filled rolls, vegetarian dishes, halal meat and normal meat-catering also in Beer Bar. **Ents:** Theatre Royal, Glasgow Film Theatre and Citizens Theatre all offer student discounts. GUU has its own nightclub, the Hive (cheap and popular). **Sports:** Kelvin Hall and Stevenson Building. **Travel:** Scholarships on offer include McGill, Georgetown and Freiburg universities. **Work:** Work not well paid and difficult working hours. Shops and lots of bar work in summer.

ALUMNI (EDITORS' PICK)   Ian McGregor, Teddy Taylor (MP, Conservative), John Smith (MP, former leader of the Labour Party), William Boyd (author), Pat Kane ('Hue and Cry'), Donald Dewar.

GOLDSMITHS COLLEGE

Goldsmiths College, University of London, New Cross,
London SE14 6NW (Tel 0171 919 7171, Fax 0171 919 7113,
Web page www.gold.ac.uk/) Map 5

STUDENT ENQUIRIES: Registry Admissions Office
(Tel 0171 919 7000, Fax 0171 919 7500, e-mail admissions
@gold.ac.uk). APPLICATIONS: UCAS

Broad study areas: Humanities, social sciences, visual and performing arts, design, media and communications, education, mathematical and computing studies. (Subject details are in the *Subjects and Places Index.*)

Founded: 1891. Became a school of London University in 1988. **Main undergraduate awards:** BA, BA(Ed), BMus, BSc. **Awarding body:** London University. **Site:** Campus in south-east London. **Access:** New Cross Gate (BR) or New Cross stations (BR and underground) and buses. **Academic features:** Access to extensive evening study programme for all students. Many degree courses available part-time; many in combined subjects. **Europe:** 10% first degree students take a language as part of course and spend 6 months or more abroad. Languages available as options for students on many degrees. Formal exchange links with some 15 EU universities/colleges. **Library:** Purpose-built central library; over 200,000 volumes, 1,500 periodicals, audio visual collections with facilities, Prestel, computer-based literature search, 424 study places. Annual expenditure on library materials, £53.31 per FTE student. **Other learning facilities:** Language laboratories, computer-enhanced learning facilities, satellite reception, audio and video cassettes. **Welfare:** Doctors, counsellors, solicitor (via SU), chaplains, nursery (20 places). **Careers:** Careers advisers; London University appointments board. **Amenities:** College bookshop, refectory and bar; audio visual facilities, theatre; SU building with launderette, coffee bar etc. **Sporting facilities:** Sports grounds and playing fields near Sidcup (30 minutes); tennis courts, gymnasia and practice field on site; swimming pool nearby.

Accommodation: In 1995/96, 28% of students in college accommodation, 70% of first years. 1,100 places available (690 for first years): 200 half-board places at £60 per week and 900 self-catering places at £40–£50 per week, term time only. Students live in privately owned accommodation for 1 year minimum: rents £45–£50 per week for self-catering, £60 B&B, c£80 for half-board. 27% first degree full-time students live at home. **Term time work:** College helps find work outside campus with weekly job opportunities bulletin and noticeboard of local vacancies. **Hardship funds:** Total available in 1995/96: £129,259 government access funds, over 1,000 students helped; small amount of own funds. Special help: students over 50 years old and in need, students with no source of funding.

Duration of first degree courses: 3 years; **others:** 4 years including design, education and those involving languages, work experience and extension degrees. **Total first degree students 1995/96:** 4,601. **Overseas students:** 11%. **Mature students:** 49%. **Male/female ratio:** 1:2. **Teaching staff:** 300 full-time. **Total full-time students 1995/96:** 4,500. **Postgraduate students:** 1,500. **First degree tuition fees:** Home students, paying their own fees in 1996/97, paid £880; Overseas students £6,440 (classroom), £8,190 (lab/studio).

WHAT IT'S LIKE Famous for turning out diverse characters such as cow-pickling Damien Hurst, Mary Quant and the rather unusual Julian Clary. The beautiful building, which would look more in place alongside the grand Naval College in nearby Greenwich, is a bit of a gem in New Cross. But although the area lacks aesthetic beauty, it is a prime location for some of the trendy places in south east London, with swish little cafes and restaurants, and easy access to Central London – 10 minutes to London Bridge, 20 to Charing Cross, and well served by buses even late at night. Very good reputation for drama, music, visual art, communications and sociology – makes for a very diverse and interesting, though terminally trendy, student population. The *Evening Standard* called it 'the Oxbridge of the art world'. Most first years guaranteed a hall place. These range from utilitarian (but you can fall out of bed into your lecture) to sophisticated house and garden a bus ride away. It's very accessible so students find private accommodation in Greenwich, Camberwell, Brixton or Central London (if funds allow!). Teaching is at New Cross, though some students venture into other London colleges for lectures. SU provides 'Panhandle' food outlet, launderette, welfare services, clubs and societies (most popular athletics union, African diaspora, various funk/house music clubs, cultural societies, lesbian and gay); also two bars (including Sports Bar which shows Sky Sport in comfy carpeted slob zone), sports and entertainments. Football team is successful, rugby is popular, as is aerobics and women's basketball. Nearby are: Greenwich with its park, historic ships and buildings, pubs and market; Blackheath with its wide open space (where Cornish rebels fought in 1493 with 'such valour and stoutness') and striking architecture; Lewisham, for its shops; Brockley, for virtually nothing; and New Cross, for Goldsmiths and economically feasible Chinese and Indian takeaways, and one of the best Thai restaurants in London. All sorts of off-beat characters; the place where the school geek is trendy. Large numbers of overseas and mature students make for an even more interesting mix. On the whole, a good place to study for those city lovers who hate isolated, tight campus universities – it is down to earth, trendy and unusual.

PAUPER NOTES **Accommodation:** First years almost guaranteed hall place. Outside it is cheap for London but not always beautiful. Many live at home. **Drink:** Union bar the cheapest (£1/pint promotions) and open late some nights. Local pubs reasonable and some open late. **Eats:** Main canteen fine but pricey. SU Panhandle cheaper. Immediate area has number of reasonable cafés – greasy spoons to health food caffs. **Ents:** Union has good ents programme. If that isn't enough there are c200 clubs in London! **Sports:** Active athletics union. Sports ground ½ mile away. Practice field and gym at college; also ULU facilities (bit of a trek). **Hardship funds:** SU has limited fund for loans and helps explore other sources of money. **Travel:** Tube, train and bus. **Work:** SU offers part-time jobs and has a job shop. Loads of pubs employ students and plenty of local agencies.

MORE INFO? Enquiries to SU (0181 692 1406).

ALUMNI (EDITORS' PICK) Vic Charles (world karate champion), Linton Kwesi Johnson (poet and musician), Mary Quant (fashion designer), Merlyn Rees MP, Colin Welland, Jack Brymer, Graham Sutherland, Malcolm McLaren, John Cale (Velvet Underground), Tom Keating (artist), Derek Hatton (politician), Julian Clary, Damien Hirst (artist), Julia Carling, John Illsley (Dire Straits).

GET HOLD OF THE PROSPECTUSES

GREENWICH UNIVERSITY

University of Greenwich, Wellington Street, London
SE18 6PF   (Tel 0181 316 8590, Fax 0181 316 8239) Map 5

STUDENT ENQUIRIES: Course Enquiries Officer
APPLICATIONS: UCAS

Broad study areas: Business, built environment, education, engineering, health, humanities, social sciences, sciences, mathematics, computing, law. (Subject details are in the *Subjects and Places Index*.)

Founded: 1970 as Thames Poly, ex Woolwich Poly, Hammersmith College of Building and Art, Dartford College of Education, Avery Hill College, Garnett College and Thames College of Healthcare; university status in 1992. **Main undergraduate awards:** BA, BSc, BEd, BEng, LLB. **Awarding body:** Greenwich University. **Site:** 8 sites (Chatham, Dartford, Deptford, Eltham, Jewry Street, Kings Hill, Roehampton and Woolwich). **Special features:** Mature students may be admitted without normal entry requirements. Considerable transferability between courses allowed. **Europe:** 6% first degree students take a language as part of course and spend 6 months or more abroad. European study available with a wide variety of subjects. Language labs open to all students. Exchange programmes with many European universities (also with USA). **Library:** 12 libraries; 450,000 volumes, 2,000 periodicals, 1,000 study places; short loan for course texts; photocopying; on-line information services. Annual expenditure on library materials, £56.72 per FTE student. **Other learning facilities:** Computer centre, microcomputer facilities on all sites. **Welfare:** 6 counsellors, 2 advisers, nursing officer and nurses, medical officers and consultant psychiatrist, Anglican and RC chaplains. **Careers:** Information, advice and placement. **Amenities:** Students' union, stationery and bookshop; dance and drama hall; crèche at Woolwich and Avery Hill. **Sporting facilities:** Multi-gyms, heated indoor swimming pool, playing fields, tennis, netball, squash courts, fitness rooms.

Accommodation: In 1995/96, 20% of all students in university accommodation, 100% first years who require it (guaranteed). 2,600 places available (2,000 for first years): 700 half-board places (670 for first years), £53–£65 per week semester time only, and 1,800 self-catering places (1,280 for first years) at £38–£58.50 per week, Sept–July. University-managed accommodation offered for entire course. Privately owned accommodation rents: £35–£50 per week for self-catering, £45–£55 B&B, £50–£65 for half-board. **Hardship funds:** Government access funds.

Duration of first degree courses: 3 years (full-time), 4 years (sandwich). **Total first degree students 1995/96:** 13,987. **BEd students:** 1,076. **Overseas students:** 562. **Male/female ratio:** 4:3. **Teaching staff:** 520. **Total full-time students 1995/96:** 11,499. **Postgraduate students:** 3,104. **First degree tuition fees:** Home students, paying their own fees in 1996/97, paid £750; Overseas students £6,000.

WHAT IT'S LIKE   Spread over 8 sites, the uni stretches from Roehampton (in the south west of London) through Wapping (just east of the City of London), to Dartford in Kent and as far as Chatham (in the Medway tunnel). Each site specialises in different types of courses – Wapping: accountancy, Chatham: geology & earth sciences, Deptford: environmental, Woolwich: arts & sciences, Avery Hill: teacher training, and Dartford: architecture & surveying. Uni accommodation is reasonable (all rooms are single) and accommodation is guaranteed for all first years. Uni and highly active SU strictly enforce policies of equality of opportunity, which give rise to a pleasant, friendly, cosmopolitan community. Fortnightly newspaper *The Sarky Cutt.* Staff/student relationship is good. 49% of students are mature. Greenwich is a lively, fun and safe place to study, live and meet interesting people from a large cross-section of the community.

PAUPER NOTES **Accommodation:** Accommodation fairly expensive; uni accommodation office helps. Student squats in Wickham Lane; no married quarters. **Drink:** SU bars are only places to be. SU bar at Eltham – cheap, fun and friendly. **Eats:** Refectories on all sites; 10% discount with SU card at Cuisine of India; some reasonably priced restaurants around. **Ents:** Bands and cabaret at SU regularly. SU film society shows a film each week. **Sports:** Excellent sporting facilities incl squash courts, tennis courts, swimming pool, football, hockey, lacrosse and rugby pitches. **Work:** Some SU bar, registry, lab work – loads of part-time off-campus work available. Jobshop for work on and off campus. SU pays £3.50/hour.

ALUMNI (EDITORS' PICK) Hale & Pace (TV comedians), Brian Jacks (Olympic judo medallist), Ann Packer (Olympic athletics medallist), Rachel Heyhoe-Flint (cricketer), Prof Ian McAllister (Prof of Politics, Univ of New South Wales).

GUILDFORD SCHOOL OF ACTING (GSA)

GSA Guildford School of Acting, Millmead Terrace, Guildford, Surrey GU2 5AT (Tel 01483 60701, Fax 01483 35431) Map 4

STUDENT ENQUIRIES: Admissions officer
APPLICATIONS: Direct

Broad study areas: Drama, stage management. (Subject details are in the *Subjects and Places Index.*)

Founded: 1964. **Main undegraduate award:** BA. **Awarding body:** Surrey University. **Site:** Several sites in centre of Guildford. **Access:** Easy access on A3 or main line train. **Academic features:** Vocational training in drama and stage management. **Europe:** No languages or exchange links. **Library:** 6,000 volumes, 25 periodicals, 16 study places. **Special collection:** Theatre collection including plays, music (vocal scores). **Welfare:** Lectures on health and welfare; counsellor. **Careers:** Careers service gives information and advice. **Amenities:** Entertainment through SU. No sports facilities.

Accommodation: No school accommodation. Private accommodation: £40–£60 self-catering , £50–£80 B&B, £40–£60 half-board (+ weekend meals), £90 B&B + evening meal (eg YMCA). **Term time work:** School's policy to allow term time work for full-time first degree students (majority believed to work). Term (and vac) work available in school eg cleaning, stage management and office duties. **Hardship funds:** No government access funds. In 1995/96, £77,000 own funds, 40 students helped. Individual students receive help from trust funds etc.

Duration of first degree course: 3 years. **Total first degree students 1995/96:** 95. **Mature students:** 18. **Male/female ratio:** 4:5. **Teaching staff:** 18 full-time, 70 part-time. **Total full-time students 1995/96:** 210. **Postgraduate students:** 0. **First degree tuition fees:** In 1996/97, home and overseas students paid £6,450 (acting), £6,700 (musical theatre).
ALUMNI (EDITORS' PICK)   Michael Ball, Celia Imrie, Brenda Blethyn, Gaby Roslin, Owen Teale.

GUILDHALL

Guildhall School of Music & Drama, Silk Street, Barbican, London EC2Y 8DT (0171 628 2571; Fax 0171 256 9438) Map 6

STUDENT ENQUIRIES: Academic Registrar
APPLICATIONS: Direct

Broad study areas: Acting, drama and theatre arts, music.
(Subject details are in the *Subjects and Places Index*.)

Founded: 1880, degree status granted 1945. **Main undergraduate award:** BA, BMus.
Awarding body: City University (acting, stage management, technical theatre) and Kent University (music); Guildhall School of Music & Drama. **Site:** Barbican, central London.
Access: Moorgate underground station. **Special features:** All teachers active in their professions outside the School. The Takacs Quartet, quartet-in-residence. **Library:** Over 60,000 volumes, 50 periodicals, 44 study places; listening facilities. Audio visual room with 17 study carrels, special resources room with computer facilities and multimedia/electronic music workstations; separate drama library and study area. **Specialist collections:** Alkan Society Collection, Appleby Collection (guitar music), Harris Collection (opera vocal scores), Merrett Collection (double bass), Rosenweig Jewish Collection, Worshipful Company of Musicians Westrup Collection. **Other learning facilities:** Professional 16-track recording studio. **Welfare:** Welfare services department, doctor, nurse, counsellor, chaplain. **Careers:** Advice from Principal and senior members of staff. **Amenities:** Music hall, theatre (orchestra pit of 80), lecture recital room, John Hosier Practice Annexe (46 practice studios), theatre-training gymnasium, Barbican Centre. **Employment:** Music specialists in schools, actors and stage managers.

Accommodation: In 1995/96, 25% students in School hall of residence (Sundial Court); 180 places available. Students live in privately owned accommodation for 2+ years (Assistant Manager of Sundial Court helps): private lodgings, hostel and self-catering accommodation and flats, from £55 per week. **Hardship funds:** Limited funds available: approx 150 students helped from bursary fund. Money may be assigned prior to starting course at principal's discretion and according to need.

Duration of first degree courses: 4 years (BMus); **others** 3 years. **Total first degree students 1995/96:** 462. **Male/female ratio:** 1:1. **Teaching staff:** 12 full-time, 514 part-time. **Total full-time students 1995/96:** 679. **Postgraduate students:** 217. **First degree tuition fees:** Home students, paying their own fees in 1996/97, paid £3,414; Overseas students £6,900.

WHAT IT'S LIKE   Modern building of deep red brick and grey stone/concrete in the bowels of the Barbican Centre (with the LSO and RSC, so free/reduced tickets and rehearsal passes). Also practice bunker near Barbican tube station, with 46 rooms of varying shapes and sizes. New halls of residence; some students live at Barbican YMCA, which provides all meals and cuts out travelling expenses. Other accommodation includes Henry Wood House in Camberwell (shared with other music colleges) – cheaper but further out and self-catering. Otherwise look through papers, agencies, adverts or word of mouth and consult School welfare officer's accommodation list. Relations between admin and students generally good. Teaching staff, on the whole, are excellent personally and professionally – most are working with top orchestras, opera and theatre companies, so know the problems which students face. Courses cover all aspects of the performing arts – music, drama, stage management and scene painting. Not much collaboration between courses, except for timetabled musicals/operas etc. Relatively easy to change courses/teachers; motives, personality clashes and ability all play a part. Exams are mainly sit-down, but trend towards continuous assessment. Drop-out rate is virtually nil; general attitude is happy, and social activity is on the increase. 12% of students come from outside Europe (3–4% from Europe). School library is open till 7.15pm Mon-Thurs; also access to University of London library at Senate House and the magnificent Barbican Library. No sports facilities on-site but thriving football team and pool team. Access to sports centre and swimming pool at City University nearby. School snack bar open 8.30 am – 4.30 pm; lunchtime refectory in Lauderdale Tower (a 5-minute walk through the Barbican). Discos, jazz nights and other events held in main college Music Hall. SU helpful and efficient, strictly non-political. Publishes a regular newsletter. Societies include theatre, contemporary music, early music, Christian Union, Overseas Students Association etc.

PAUPER NOTES   **Accommodation:** Large numbers live at home. Majority in shared houses in Walthamstow, Hackney, Leyton or Stratford. **Drink:** SU bar. Molly Blooms has most friendly service. **Eats:** Canteen at Lauderdale Tower 5 minutes' walk from school. **Ents:** Cheap tickets for concerts, operas, shows, plays, etc through SU. **Sports:** Swimming pool and sports facilities at City University. **Hardship funds:** Many scholarships available. **Travel:** Cycling is popular. **Work:** Most students work: some private teaching; busking; outside engagements (mostly City Livery Company dinners); depping in West End shows; gigs. Stewarding work: occasionally in college; regular at Barbican Centre, Coliseum, Southbank.

ALUMNI (EDITORS' PICK) Sir Geraint Evans, Fred Astaire, James Galway, Claire Bloom, Dudley Moore, Jacqueline du Pré, Peter Skellern, Max Jaffa, Mollie Sugden, Julia MacKenzie, Benjamin Luxon.

WANT TO HELP WITH THE NEXT EDITION? SEE PAGE 66

HARPER ADAMS

Harper Adams, Newport, Shropshire TF10 8NB
(Tel 01952 820280, Fax 01952 814783) Map 3

STUDENT ENQUIRIES: Admissions Secretary
APPLICATIONS: UCAS (or direct if early).

Broad study areas: Agriculture, agricultural engineering, agricultural marketing, land management, environmental protection. (Subject details are in the *Subjects and Places Index*.)

Founded: 1901. **Main undergraduate award:** BSc. **Awarding body:** Open University. **Site:** Single campus for all teaching, living accommodation and recreation. College farm surrounds the campus. **Access:** M54 from the south; M6 and A519 from the north. **Academic features:** A modular system for most courses, allowing a range of options. All degree courses are sandwich courses; teaching links with appropriate universities. **Europe:** 8% first degree students take a language as part of their course and 5% spend 6 months or more abroad. Language options available on agri-food marketing and business studies degrees. Formal exchange links with colleges in many EU countries and in Bulgaria. **Library:** 38,000 volumes, 800 periodicals. Links with university libraries on joint courses. **Other learning facilities:** Covered soil working area, specialised laboratories, glasshouse complex, mixed commercial farm, purpose-built computer centre. **Welfare:** Regular surgeries held at college. **Careers:** Information, advice and placement service. **Amenities:** 2 common rooms, SU bars, bookshop, cafeteria, stage and auditorium, hall for dances etc. **Sporting facilities:** Squash and tennis courts, swimming pool, sports hall, sports fields – all on campus.

Accommodation: In 1995/96, 45% of all students in college accommodation, 100% of new students. 546 places available (180 ensuite): 511 full-board places from £53–£79 per week and 35 self-catering places at £36 plus bills, term time only. Students live in privately owned accommodation for 2 years: rents £25–£40 per week for self-catering, £35–£43 B&B, £30–£40 for half-board. Some college houses for mature students with families. 1% first degree students live at home. **Term time work:** No college policy to allow term time work for full-time first degree students. Help in finding industrial placements only; vac jobs on farms posted. **Hardship funds:** Total available in 1995/96: £17,000 government access funds, 40 students helped. Special help: mature students, self-financing, those with children; 50% available to students prior to starting course.

Duration of first degree courses: 4 years sandwich. **Total first degree students 1995/96:** 891. **Overseas students:** 26. **Mature students:** 150. **Male/female ratio:** 7:3. **Full-time students 1995/96:** 1,585. **Postgraduate students:** 32. **First degree tuition fees:** Home students, paying their own fees in 1996/97, paid £1,600; Overseas students £5,500.

WHAT IT'S LIKE   It's the biggest agricultural college in England and largest provider of students to the land-based industries. Shortly expects to be able to award its own degree. Life's hard and fast and you're here to work hard and play hard. Always something to do with usual agric antics. Good sport – rugby, football, hockey, netball, shooting, basketball,

robics, Gaelic football, snooker, squash, badminton, archery, golf. All teams
gue. Worst rivals, Cirencester. Best rivals, Seale Hayne. Very large student bar.
it means you get out of it what you put in – and never, ever lose your sense of

PAUPER NOTES **Accommodation:** Victorian, New Cambrian and up-to-date hostels (2 with ensuite bathrooms). **Drink:** Bar (48 pumps). Local pubs (also good for food). **Eats:** Cafeteria and canteen on campus. Curry houses, chip shops, Chinese, kebab house in town. **Ents:** Social fund £20 per semester. All bands free, at least 1 a week. **Sports:** Playing fields, tennis courts, climbing wall, sports hall, swimming pool on campus. National Sports Hall at Lilleshall nearby. **Work:** Available locally.

INFORMAL NAME HAAC; Harper.

ALUMNI (EDITORS' PICK) Barbara Woodhouse.

HERIOT-WATT UNIVERSITY

Heriot-Watt University, Riccarton, Edinburgh EH14 4AS
(Tel 0131 449 5111, Fax 0131 449 5153) Map 1

STUDENT ENQUIRIES: Admissions Officer/Education Liaison
Officer. APPLICATIONS: UCAS

Broad study areas: Accountancy and economics, engineering, building and architecture, science, textiles, languages. (Subject details are in the *Subjects and Places Index*.)

Founded: 1821, granted charter in 1966. **Main undergraduate awards:** BA, BArch, BEd, BEng, BSc, MEng. **Awarding body:** Heriot-Watt University. **Site:** Modern campus at Riccarton, 8 miles from central Edinburgh. **Access:** Bus from central Edinburgh. **Structural features:** Faculties of environmental studies and art & design are joint with Edinburgh College of Art; faculty of textiles joint with Scottish College of Textiles; education joint with Moray House; all can be looked up separately. **Academic features:** Most courses on modular system. Combined studies degrees offer scope for choice and flexibility. Unusual specialist degrees eg brewing & distilling, interpreting and translating. **Europe:** 5% first degree students (plus language specialists) take a language as part of course and 3% spend 6 months or more abroad. A language can be studied jointly with eg civil engineering or accountancy; language tuition available to all students. Large number of formal exchange links in EU, some allowing students to acquire an additional qualification from partner institution. Some industrial placements abroad. **Library:** 150,000 volumes, 2,500 periodicals; on-line information system. Annual expenditure on library materials, £97.46 per FTE student. **Other learning facilities:** Television centre, computer centre, computer-based learning. **Welfare:** GP and dental services. Counsellor, tutor/mentors, university chaplains, nursery. **Careers:** Information and advice service; close links with employers. **Amenities:** New purpose-built SU at Riccarton. **Sporting facilities:** Excellent sports centre on Riccarton campus.

Accommodation: In 1995/96, 40% of all students in university accommodation, 100% of first years from outside Edinburgh who require it (guaranteed). 1,500 places available: over

300 half-board places at £62.50–£71.50 per week; 861 self-catering at £31–£38.50 (£47–£48.25 ensuite); plus 200 places in flats on campus, 100 off campus. Students live in privately owned accommodation for 2 years, rents £150–£200 per month. 12% first degree students live at home. **Term time work**: No university policy on part time work. Vacation work only available on campus in catering and residences. **Hardship funds**: Government access funds.

Duration of first degree courses: 4 years; 3 years for some ordinary degrees; 5 years for some MEng. **Total first degree students 1995/96**: 4,000. **Overseas students**: 700. **Mature students**: 1,300. **Male/female ratio 1995/96**: 6:5. **Teaching staff**: c750 full-time, c100 part-time. **Total students 1995/96**: 5,000 (full & part-time). **Postgraduate students**: 2,000 (full & part-time). **First degree tuition fees**: Home students, paying their own fees in 1996/97, paid £750 (classroom), £1,600 (lab/studio); Overseas students £6,400 (classroom), £8,400 lab/studio).

WHAT IT'S LIKE   A single campus built on an old estate, but with striking features and plans for some student friendly changes. Travel from Edinburgh city centre by bus or train. Accommodation good and all first years are offered a place on campus; full board and self-catering flats and self-catering halls, two with ensuite facilities and extra laundries. Central laundry with front load machines and driers. All blocks are mixed with no visiting restrictions. University leases flats of various sizes from private landlords; mostly reasonable. Campus can be quiet at weekends, but has advantage of being close to one of the most exciting cities in Europe. Overseas students, predominantly from Malaysia and Norway, with many European exchanges included. Many of the mature students are from overseas; most home students are school leavers. Main sport facilities on campus, open 7 days a week, is well used by students, staff and local community. Other facilities on campus include shop (7 days a week) travel shop, bank, bookshop and hairdressers. Library (also 7 days) is well used. Renowned as a technological institution; courses predominantly science and engineering but others include highly thought of business courses etc. Strong workload and specialised vocational courses. Possible to transfer (easiest in first or second year) to general degree provides good safety net for those who made the wrong choice or wish to keep their horizons broad. Courses are modular; assessment by exam and project work. There is much scope for further study and research. Union building on campus offers drop-in advice and support centre, bars, catering and a club. Entertainments range from live bands, comedy network, drinks promotions to regular club nights. Many active student societies range from politics and debates, to kite flying and brewery, holding events such as beer festivals, sports competitions, pub crawls and cover a wide range of interest. Edinburgh is a good student city. Many pubs, cinemas and theatres offer student deals, and reciprocal agreements allow students to use other unions. City's famed international festival in summer and best New Year's celebrations (Hogmanay) which tend to last about a week! Heriot-Watt provides the pleasant combination of city night life and a peaceful campus environment.

PAUPER NOTES   **Accommodation**: Careful reading of adverts in papers may yield bargains. **Drink**: Union provides cheapest pint around; other good pubs offer local brews. **Eats**: Residences' food is fair. Union cheap meals and snacks. Student deals in some pubs. **Ents**: Many local pubs offer free bands midweek. Several 'alternative' theatres and cinemas. Good variety on club scene. **Sports**: Several good sports centres in city including ice rinks, swimming pools (incl Commonwealth Pool and Leith Waterworld) and all-round complexes. **Hardship funds**: Access funds. Students' Association can make small loans (usually up to £75). **Work**: Much bar work. Vacation jobs harder to come by but many departments help with course-related jobs.

HERTFORDSHIRE UNIVERSITY

University of Hertfordshire, College Lane, Hatfield, Herts AL10 9AB (Tel 01707 284000, Fax 01707 284738) Map 4

STUDENT ENQUIRIES: Higher Education Liaison
(Tel 01707 284458), or appropriate Admissions Office
APPLICATIONS: UCAS

Broad study areas: Art & design, business, engineering, nursing, law, humanities, sciences, education. (Subject details are in the *Subjects and Places Index.*)

Founded: 1952; Hatfield Poly until university status in 1992. **Main undergraduate awards:** BA, BEd, BEng, MEng, MPhys, BSc, LLB. **Awarding body:** Hertfordshire University. **Site:** Three campuses, all some 20 miles north of London. **Access:** Hatfield campus at Junction 3, A1(M); Wall Hall campus near M1; Hertford campus near A10. All fairly near railway stations with regular fast services to London; local buses between campuses and nearby towns. University's bus company operates between campuses and throughout Hertfordshire. **Academic features:** High proportion of sandwich courses; most courses on modular structure. Some 50% students are over 25. **Europe:** Language tuition offered on wide range of courses in eg engineering, environmental studies and humanities. University policy that all students should have possibility of a European dimension to their studies. Formal exchange links with 40 universities/colleges across Europe. **Library:** 250,000 volumes over 3 campuses. CD-Rom and database facilities. Annual expenditure on library materials, £88.93 per FTE student. **Other learning facilities:** Field centre, observatory, computer centres, audio/visual aids service. **Welfare:** Student services provide specialist help, in addition to personal tutorial system. General medical and nursing facilities, professional counsellors, chaplaincy, day nursery, financial and legal advisory services. Residential facilities for disabled and families. **Careers:** Advisory and placement service; recruitment fair. **Amenities:** SU buildings; music and drama centres. **Sporting facilities:** Wide range of sports. Sports halls, swimming pools.

Accommodation: In 1995/96, 55% of all students in university accommodation, 65% of first years. 2,945 places available (2,000 for first years), all self-catering at £40–£50 per week, Sept–June. Students typically live in privately owned accommodation (in university head-tenancy schemes) for 2 years: rents £40 per week for self-catering, £50–£60 for half-board and weekend meals. 20% first degree students live at home. **Term time work:** University's policy to allow term time work for full-time first degree students (80% believed to work). Term (and vac) work available on campus in bars, offices, sports coaches, grounds staff, library, catering etc (wherever possible own students employed); also SU Job Centre helps find work outside university. **Hardship funds:** Total available in 1995/96: £275,081 government access funds. Special help: single parents, low-income families, plus students in severe hardship due to exceptional circumstances (demand for funds always exceeds supply).

Duration of first degree courses: 3 years (full-time; accelerated computer science sandwich); **others:** 4 years (sandwich), 2 years (accelerated LLB). **Total first degree students 1995/96:** 15,528; **Total BEd students:** 568; **Overseas students:** 700. **Mature students:** 50%. **Male/female ratio:** 1:1. **Teaching staff:** 730. **Total full-time students 1995/96:** 13,050. **Post-**

graduate students: 2,050. **First degree tuition fees:** Home students, paying their own fees in 1996/97, paid £700–£900 (classroom), £900–£1,600 (lab/studio); Overseas students £5,750 (classroom), £5,950 (lab/studio).

WHAT IT'S LIKE   Surprisingly large, it's grown enormously and now occupies 500 acres of Hertfordshire countryside with sites in Hatfield, Hertford, St Albans, Bayfordbury and Watford. Very accessible to London night life or for weekend trips. Campuses within easy reach of railway stations with frequent services to London (25 minutes) and easily reached by road network. University's own bus company offers economical transport between campuses, stations, local towns, markets and superstores. Each campus has own distinct character. Lots of money has been spent on refurbishing and upgrading buildings and new accommodation. Hatfield (engineering, information sciences, natural sciences, health and human sciences) is spacious, open, green site with modern hi-tech buildings. Hertford's focal point is 17th-century mansion set in 100 acres of parkland, home to the business school. Watford campus (humanities and education) has impressive parkland location with 18th-century 'castle', landscaped gardens and sculpture park. University observatory and field station located in grounds of Bayfordbury House with large lake, woodland and farmland. St Albans is a city centre campus, home to law students. All campus libraries and computer centres open for at least 12 hours every weekday and computer centre at Hatfield open until late at night for private study. Good accommodation in student village and halls of residence. Students guaranteed at least one year in university accommodation. Over 30 university sports clubs; sports facilities for most indoor and outdoor activities, either on campus or at local centres. SU with 90+ clubs and societies lively and active on campus; excellent entertainment programme.

PAUPER NOTES   **Accommodation:** On campus good. Head tenancy scheme extensive throughout area. **Drink:** All SU bars have good range of real ales; most students drink on campus. Otherwise expensive; Philanthropist & Firkin (St Albans) or White Horse (Hertford) for excellent trad beers. **Eats:** Cheap food in SU. Hatfield improving. Many small eating houses throughout area but no defined student quarters. **Ents:** Excellent SU ents. UCI 9-screen cinema close to Hatfield campus, cheap prices for students. **Sports:** On campus, good sports centre though few artificial pitches. Off campus, Gosling Stadium, Welwyn Garden City. **Hardship fund:** Limited access fund. University and SU support students with acute problems. **Travel:** University bus service between halls and campus. Very good access to London. SU travel office at Hatfield. **Work:** Most students on work-linked degrees. New employment bureau in SU to help students find part-time work; bar, catering, security and shop work (average £3.50/hour).

HEYTHROP COLLEGE

Heythrop College, University of London, Kensington Square, London W8 5HQ (Tel 0171 795 6600, Fax 0171 795 4200) Map 6

STUDENT ENQUIRIES: Academic Registrar
APPLICATIONS: UCAS

Broad study areas: Biblical studies, theology, philosophy.

(Subject details are in the *Subjects and Places Index*.)

Founded: In 17th century Liège as a Jesuit college. Later providing a residential seminary for Jesuits and other students in Oxfordshire until transfer to London premises in 1970. **Structural features:** Part of London University (since 1970). **Main undergraduate awards:** BA, BD. **Awarding body:** London University. **Site:** Attractive central London site. Collegiate scheduled buildings in Kensington Square. **Access:** Kensington High Street underground station. **Europe:** No students take a language or spend time abroad as part of their course, although there are postgraduate exchanges with a number of universities in Europe. **Library:** 250,000 items (many 17th century), 150 study places. Annual expenditure on library materials, £175 per FTE student. **Welfare:** Students use the facility of the university health service. **Amenities:** Refectory, college choir; proximity to theatres, cinemas, museums, galleries. **Sporting facilities:** Tennis courts; football and cricket teams. **Employment:** Christian ministry, teaching, social work, media, police force etc.

Accommodation: No college halls of residence; students are accommodated in London University intercollegiate halls. 20% of first degree students live at home. **Term time work:** No policy to allow part time work (but 50% believed to work). Term work available in college library. **Hardship funds:** Total available in 1995/96: £3,300 government access funds, average £150 awarded; other funds dependent on donations, average award £250.

Duration of first degree courses: 3 years. **Total first degree students 1995/96:** 114. **Overseas students:** 14. **Mature students:** 63. **Male/female ratio:** 3:2. **Teaching staff:** 25 full-time, 8 part-time. **Total full-time students 1995/96:** 200. **Postgraduate students:** 86 f-t, 145 p-t. **First degree tuition fees:** Home students, paying their own fees in 1996/97, paid £1,748; Overseas students £3,090.

WHAT IT'S LIKE   It's the second smallest college in London University and specialises in theology and philosophy. Now takes more young students, giving a more vibrant atmosphere. Some students are members of religious orders, studying towards some sort of church ministry; others with no religious background studying philosophy pure. The college comprises many different types and backgrounds and, together with the close-knit atmosphere, means it's not the average arty-student type place. Very friendly; most social life revolves around SU. Library probably the best in the country for theology and also well stocked for philosophy. 2 JCRs incorporating tea and coffee facilities, drinks machines, microwave, TV and stereo. Student book and stationery shop (both operating on minimum profit basis). There's an excellent shared refectory. Heythrop is remarkable for its one-to-one tutorial system, giving priority to the individual. Lecturers are specialist and skilled. An unusual mix of age groups, nationalities and outlooks on life. Close friendships are readily formed. Lots of societies, all actively supported.

PAUPER NOTES   **Accommodation:** Inter-collegiate halls of residence give preference to first years. Number of chaplaincies. **Drink:** ULU cheap with promotions. 2 well-patronised local pubs. Try Bar Royale in Camden on a Friday night. **Eats:** ULU. If you don't mind abuse try Mr Wu's in Chinatown, £3 a menu. **Ents:** Student discounts to theatres, galleries, clubs and cinemas (eg Prince Charles in Leicester Square £1.50). **Sports:** ULU good. Bloomsbury centre good deal at £50 pa. **Hardship funds:** Discretionary college fund. **Travel:** Excellent but expensive; travelcards save money. **Work:** Reasonable amount of work if you're not fussy – in library, department stores (w/e), ULU.

CAN'T FIND WHAT YOU'RE LOOKING FOR? USE THE INDEX!

HOLBORN COLLEGE

Holborn College, 200 Greyhound Road, London W14 9RY
(Tel 0171 385 3377, Fax 0171 381 3377,
E-mail hlt@holborncollege.ac.uk) Map 5

STUDENT ENQUIRIES: Admissions Officer
APPLICATIONS: Direct or UCAS

Broad study area: Law.

Founded: 1969, as an independent college to provide courses for London University LLB (external students) and for English Bar examinations. **Main undergraduate award:** LLB. **Awarding body:** London University; Wolverhampton University. **Site:** West Kensington. **Access:** Baron's Court, West Kensington, West Brompton underground; buses. **Academic features:** Full-time, part-time, distance learning and intensive revision courses available for most study programmes. LLB and LLM in collaboration with Wolverhampton University plus London University degree programme for external students and vocational courses. **Library:** Own reference library and reading rooms. **Other learning facilities:** IT facilities. Publishes own textbooks and course materials. **Careers:** Information and advice. **Amenities:** Bookshop (textbooks, stationery), canteen, library, sports facilities, students' common rooms. Extra-curricular academic and social activities.

Accommodation: No college accommodation. Information available from college on privately owned accommodation and hostels: rents £60–£90 per week for self-catering, £65–£100 for B&B, £110–£175 for studio flat. 30% first degree students live at home. **Term time work**: College's policy to allow term time work for full-time first degree students (25% believed to work); limit of 15 hours a week. Term (and vac) work available in college in library, postroom and administration; also helps finding vac work. **Hardship fund:** Limited help available in genuine cases.

Duration of first degree courses: 3 years. **Total first degree students 1995/96:** 850. **Overseas students:** 500. **Mature students:** 60. **Male/female ratio:** 1:1. **Teaching staff:** c43 full-time, c50 part-time. **Total full-time students 1995/96:** 975. **Postgraduate students:** 100. **First degree tuition fees:** In 1996/97, fees were £2,000–£4,500 (home and overseas); an LEA grant may cover £890 of the fee.

WHAT IT'S LIKE   It's not in Holborn, it's in Fulham, west London. Housed in attractive redbrick building with excellent facilities; main block houses a canteen, students' common room, bookshop, academic and welfare offices in addition to teaching rooms; also library, landscaped courtyards and multi-purpose recreation area. Over 1,000 full- and part-time students with a good international mix (many others following distance learning pro-grammes worldwide). Being relatively small, students get to know each other easily and the atmosphere is friendly. College has developed its own specialist teaching materials and publishes some 200 titles including textbooks, casebooks, revision workbooks and suggested solutions, which are supplied to students within the tuition fees. Syllabuses are covered by a mix of lectures, seminars, written assignments and mock examina-tions. Teaching staff reflect a healthy mix of practitioners and academics. Extracurricular activities include mooting, mock trials, guest lectures and court visits. Staff are friendly, eager to help and have good relationship with students.

PAUPER NOTES   **Accommodation:** College helps find places in nearby student hostels, shared flats and rented rooms in area (not a problem). **Drink:** Good local pubs eg the Colton Arms and the Dove on the river, have local brews eg Fuller's London Pride. **Eats:** College restaurant provides cosmopolitan food at reasonable prices. Bargains in North End Road market nearby. Large number of cafés and restaurants in Fulham – all prices. **Ents:** College organises trips to theatre, concerts, weekends away, discos etc. Students' society organises special events eg annual Glitter Ball at Savoy, Dorchester or Grosvenor House and the cultural evening featuring international entertainment. Best casual night-club Crazy Larrys. **Sports:** All-weather pitch on campus. Use of International Students House (Regent's Park), Fulham swimming pools and Eternity Wharf sports centre (round the corner). Annual staff-student cricket match and five-a-side football. **Hardship funds:** Help available for genuine cases. **Travel:** Easy walk from Barons Court and West Kensington tubes, frequent buses. **Work:** College gives assistance and advice; few on-campus summer vacation jobs available. Some 25% work part-time during term and during vac – shop work etc.

MORE INFO?   Enquiries to Paul Little (0171 385 3377).

HOMERTON COLLEGE

Homerton College, Hills Road, Cambridge CB2 2PH
(Tel 01223 507111) Map 4

STUDENT ENQUIRIES: The Registry
APPLICATIONS: UCAS

Broad study area: Education.

Founded: 1695 in London and began teacher training 1850; moved to Cambridge in 1894. **Structural features:** An approved society of Cambridge University. **Main undergraduate awards:** BEd, BA. **Awarding body:** Cambridge University. **Site:** A single 30 acre site (with garden, playing fields and orchards) about one mile south of the city centre, and within easy reach of the railway station. **Access:** By rail, on the Liverpool Street-King's Lynn or Kings Cross-Cambridge line. By road, via the M11 or A14/A1. **Academic features:** BEd degree, including lower primary (4–8) or upper primary (7–11) age ranges. New BA in a specialist subject and educational studies (not incorporating QTS). **Special features:** Links with Kokebe College (Ethiopia), Vanderbilt Univ (USA) and the Faculty of Education of the University of Guyana. **Europe:** No students take a language or spend time abroad. **Library:** 100,000 volumes, 300 current periodicals. About 100 study places. **Other learning facilities:** Computing/resources centre. **Welfare:** College sick bay on site, with nursing sister. Own doctor holds regular surgeries. Full range of university medical and counselling services. **Careers:** Information, advice and placement service. **Amenities:** New education block and drama studio with theatre facilities. All the societies of Cambridge University. **Sporting**

facilities: Squash courts, playing fields for soccer and hockey, indoor facilities for badminton and gym.

Accommodation: In 1995/96, 33% of all students in college accommodation, 90% of first years (exceptions are some mature students). 290 places available (150 for first years): half-board places at approx £72 per week, term time only. Students live in privately owned accommodation for 3 years: £45–£55 per week for self-catering. **Hardship funds:** Total available in 1995/96: £24,630 government access funds, average 237 students helped.

Duration of first degree courses: BEd 4 years; BA 3 years. **Total first degree students 1995/96:** 656. **BEd students:** 626. **Overseas students:** 3. **Mature students:** 40. **Male/female ratio:** 1:10. **Teaching staff:** 51 full-time, 20 part-time. **Total full-time students 1995/96:** 955. **Postgraduate students:** 314. **First degree tuition fees:** Home students, paying their own fees in 1996/97, paid £750 (classroom), £1,600 (lab/studio); Overseas students £6,036.

WHAT IT'S LIKE   An independent college, which also has approved college status within Cambridge University. It is a ten minute cycle ride from the city centre (but banks within a five minute walk). Extensive building programme providing new library, drama studio and teaching rooms. The library is well-equipped for teaching resources, as well as books for main subject study; students can also use university faculty libraries. SU puts on regular events in lively college bar; also at least one major event a term, which attracts on average 500 people from other colleges in Cambridge. For those quieter nights in, there is an SU room (open 24 hours) with TV, video and stereo. Accommodation is provided for all first years in comfortable rooms, with bathrooms and kitchens on each corridor. Meal tickets, for all students living in college accommodation, used in the buttery (snacks) or dining hall – both a reasonable standard. The intake is 50/50 split between state and private education; 10:1 ratio of women to men on the BEd course but balance redressed by the postgraduate intake (Homerton has boasted a good reputation on on the university rugby team!). Students from the different courses mix well together. Most freshers settle in quickly, warming to the friendly atmosphere and helpful staff and students. BEd course been up-dated and improved and now there is a new BA in education (3-year, without qualified teacher status). Generally the work-load is reasonable, allowing for plenty of time to take part in college and university activities.

PAUPER NOTES   **Accommodation:** Some shared double rooms for non-first years. **Drink:** Homerton Bar – very cheap. **Eats:** Varied and cheap: cafeteria (incl veggie options) and buttery (open daily serving hot snack meals). Lots of local restaurants and take-aways. **Ents:** Film society, regular discos, May Ball, live bands. Bar has juke box, darts, pool, games. All university ents. **Sports:** All form of sports in college. **Hardship funds:** College fund. **Travel:** Erasmus scheme (France, Austria). **Work:** Vac work in Cambridge in great demand so majority work in home town. Term work as babysitters, bar work, music teaching, Saturday shop work.

MORE INFO?   Enquiries to Lucy Baines (01223 411217).

ALUMNI (EDITORS' PICK)   Julie Covington, Cherie Lunghi.

HOW TO START? *SEE SHORTLISTING*, PAGE 535

HUDDERSFIELD UNIVERSITY

University of Huddersfield, Queensgate, Huddersfield
HD1 3DH (Tel 01484 422288, Fax 01484 516151) Map 2

STUDENT ENQUIRIES: Assistant Registrar (Admissions)
APPLICATIONS: UCAS

Broad study areas: Applied sciences; accounting, law and business; computing and maths; design and technology; education; engineering; human and health sciences; music and humanities. (Subject details are in the *Subjects and Places Index*.)

Founded: 1841; Huddersfield Poly until gained university status in 1992. **Main undergraduate awards:** BA, BSc, BEng, LLB, BMus, BEd, MEng. **Awarding body:** Huddersfield University. **Site:** Main Queensgate campus in town centre; teacher training at Holly Bank, 2 miles away; midwifery and physiotherapy in Wakefield. **Access:** Queensgate campus within walking distance of bus and railway stations. **Academic features:** Most degree courses within CAT scheme. **Special features:** Hosts annual Huddersfield Festival of Contemporary Music. **Europe:** 15% first degree students take a language as part of course and 2% spend 6 months or more abroad. Formal exchange links with universities/colleges in Denmark and France. Languages available in a wide range of courses. **Library:** 300,000 volumes, 2,200 periodicals, 750 study places; multiple copies of recommended books, including copies for reference use only; media centre with CD-Rom and AV materials; separate libraries for music, education and health studies. Annual expenditure on library materials, £55.36 per FTE student. **Other learning facilities:** Wide range of networked computing facilities. **Welfare:** Counsellors, chaplain, overseas students' adviser, health centre, welfare officer, nursery. Residential facilities for disabled students. **Careers:** Information, advice and placement service. **Amenities:** SU with bar, films, night club, etc. **Sporting facilities:** University sports hall with fitness centre; playing fields and all-weather pitches. Municipal sports centre with Olympic standard facilities.

Accommodation: In 1995/96, 1,990 places available (mainly first years): 190 half-board places at £62 per week and 1,800 self-catering places at £30–£44 per week, Sept–July. Students live in privately owned accommodation for 2+ years: £30–£38 per week for self-catering, £35–£40 B&B, £50–£60 for half-board. **Hardship funds:** Government access funds. Special help: self-financing students, those with dependants and students with disabilities.

Duration of first degree courses: 3 years; **others:** 4 years (sandwich); 2 years BEd. **Total first degree students 1995/96:** 6,850 (full-time), 1,225 (part-time); **Total BEd students:** 120 (full-time), 255 (part-time). **Overseas students:** 350. **Male/female ratio 1995/96:** 1:1. **Teaching staff:** 440 full-time, 50 part-time. **Total full-time students 1995/96:** 9,130. **Postgraduate students:** 2,500. **First degree tuition fees:** Home students, paying their own fees in 1996/97, paid £750 (classroom), £1,600 (lab/studio); Overseas students £5,380 (classroom), £6,055 (lab/studio).

WHAT IT'S LIKE   The main campus is in the centre of Huddersfield (Hudds) close to the main shopping area and 10–15 minutes' walk from the bus and train stations. The Storthes Hall campus is 20 minutes' bus ride away (free buses every 25 mins). Seven major supermarkets, a range of independent and chain shops, and excellent markets – indoor/outdoor and secondhand. Student discounts at many shops, eg clothes, stationery, hairdressers. Halls of residence give wide range of quality from ensuite to under-resourced; but limited, only half the first years get a place. Some halls are on or close to campus, others a bus journey away. All except Holly Bank are self-catering. Private accommodation is improving in supply but not in quality. Most students live about 20 minutes' walk away but some much further. Limited sports facilities: sports hall on campus and playing fields an expedition away. Municipal facilities better and widely used via Kirklees Passport discount scheme. The SU supports sports clubs and societies (over 50). The SU is based in Milton Hall which has a coffee bar, shop, travel office and two bars; provides a variety of entertainment in its new nightclub venue. University refectory has snacks and 'school dinners' of limited quality. Campus has bookshop and shop. Library is overstretched but opens over weekends. Computing facilities are okay in most departments. Students come from all over the country and overseas, and most courses have a good mix of students from different backgrounds. Relationship with the community is improving. Large student population in town. Hudds is one of the largest towns in the UK; it's close to Leeds and Manchester, and overall has good facilities for students.

PAUPER NOTES   **Accommodation:** Mostly private sector – average cost £30 per week. Married accommodation limited. **Drink:** Beer prices £1–£1.60 per pint bitter. Range of student pubs across the road from the main campus. Mainly Bass and Courage houses. Some real ale (Electricians Arms and Rat & Ratchet). **Eats:** SU coffee bar in Milton Hall, Blue Rooms (vegetarian), numerous curry houses, take-away pizzas and kebabs. **Ents:** Union has a variety of different style discos. Most clubs have student nights, which vary in popularity. One cinema (mainstream) plus theatre. Annual Contemporary Music Festival. **Sports:** Good municipal sports centres, pools, etc. **Hardship funds:** SU welfare loan fund, very stringent and limited. **Travel:** M1 and M62 excellent hitching. Good public transport. SU travel office has cheap deals. **Work:** Some in pubs and union bars, otherwise limited; about 15% work during term time. Summer – forget it really; very little found.

MORE INFO?   Enquiries to SU, tel 01484 538156.

INFORMAL NAME   Hudds Univ.

HULL UNIVERSITY

University of Hull, Hull HU6 7RX
(Tel 01482 346311, Fax 01482 465936) Map 2

STUDENT ENQUIRIES: Admissions office or schools and colleges liaison service. APPLICATIONS: UCAS

Broad study areas: Sciences, engineering, accounting and finance, business, European languages, computing, social sciences, humanities, nursing, law, education, arts. (Subject details are in the *Subjects and Places Index*.)

Founded: 1927, charter granted 1954. **Main undergraduate awards:** BA, BEng, MEng, BMus, BSc, LLB, MMath, MPhys, MChem. **Awarding body:** Hull University. **Site:** Campus 3 miles north of city centre. **Access:** Easy access by bus and train. **Academic features:** Teaching year of two semesters, 15 weeks each. Modular degree structure. Franchised first year science/engineering degrees for students without relevant A-levels. **Europe:** 4% of first degree students take a language and spend time abroad. Exchange links with over 70 European universities/colleges, all open to non-language students. Language tuition available to all students, as part of their course or module. **Library:** 850,000 volumes, 5,800 periodicals, 1,750 study places, reserve collection of course books; separate map, chemistry, social science and law libraries. Annual expenditure on library materials, £96.18 per FTE student. **Other learning facilities:** Audio-visual and language centres, computer centre. **Specialist collections:** Philip Larkin collection, history of Labour and left-wing movements, 20th-century social and political archives, 20th-century poetry; distinguished art collection, specialising in British art 1890–1940; Thompson collection of Chinese ceramics. **Welfare:** Advice centre, counselling service, Nightline, chaplains. Nursery with 50 full-time and some part-time places (cost according to income). Facilities for disabled students. **Careers:** Information, advice and placement service. **Amenities:** Bookshop on campus; SU bars, shop, travel bureau, launderette, television rooms; Middleton Hall (auditorium of over 500). **Sporting facilities:** Indoor purpose-built sports and fitness centre and all playing fields, including floodlit all-weather surface, on campus.

Accommodation: In 1995/96, 61% of all students in university accommodation (including head-lease scheme), 100% of first years. Traditional halls, £68 per week full board; other halls £52 per week half board, £39 per week self-catering (all 31 week contracts); houses £33 per week plus fuel (37 weeks). Flats with ensuite facilities, £48 per week (50 weeks). 8% first year students live at home. **Term time work:** University allows term time work for full-time first degree students (25% believed to work). No jobs on campus at present but possibility of an SU jobshop. **Hardship funds:** Total available in 1995/96: £147,550 government access funds, 1,123 students helped. All causes of financial hardship are assessed; scholarships on academic merit for those unable to obtain funding.

Duration of first degree courses: 3 or 4 years. **Total first degree students 1995/96:** 6,639. **Overseas students:** 780. **Mature students:** 13%. **Male/female ratio:** 1:1. **Teaching staff:** 400 full-time, 70 part-time. **Total full-time students 1995/96:** 7,828. **Postgraduate students:** 1,189 (f/t). **First degree tuition fees:** Home students, paying their own fees in 1996/97, paid £750 (classroom), £1,600 (lab/studio); Overseas students £5,950 (classroom), £7,950 (lab/studio).

WHAT IT'S LIKE   It has always had a reputation for being a friendly place (something you can only experience for yourself) and it's expanding fast. All academic departments are on one campus about two miles out of the city centre. University accommodation is situated around this, and student houses (with ensuite bathrooms) back onto the central site. Halls of residence are three miles away in Cottingham (the biggest village in the country, more like a small town). The modern Lawns Halls are particularly popular, boasting their own balconies with each room. Being so flat, Hull is a cycling city and therefore you don't tend to notice the distance. Many 2nd and 3rd years leave university-owned accommodation and move into private accommodation. Places in shared houses are around £32/week – cheap but certainly not luxurious. Most social events centre around the well-equipped SU, which the vast majority of students use as their evening meeting place. The union ents committee puts on many bands throughout the term (some pop/chart material) and run lots of films. SU is also a centre for some 100 societies, and 55 sporting clubs as part of an active athletic union. SU manages the sports centre (with astroturf); health and

fitness centre which includes spa pool, saunas and sun beds. SU has an amazing welfare advisory service run by students. Unemployment has hit Hull hard; the city *is* recovering, capitalising on new industries and on links with Europe and many pubs and clubs seem to be thriving. Local venues eg Adelphi Club and the Blue Lamp provide a stream of lesser known acts which lead to a cheap, good night out. Theatre is extremely good in Hull, particularly Spring Street Theatre (home to Hull Truck Company of Bouncers and Up and Under fame) which puts on late night cabarets, comedy, music and drama. The Film Theatre at the City Library shows films not on general release and then there are two multiplex cinemas, an ice arena, Megabowl and Princes Quay (the biggest shopping centre built on water!). For a weekend escape you can try a 'Dutch dash' on North Sea ferries (duty free and liberal Amsterdam!) Hull is a very cheap place to live and the quality of teaching high. PAUPER NOTES **Accommodation:** Private: improving with increased number of houses available. University: reasonable, but nothing for married students or those with children. **Drink:** SU bar – very cheap. Schnapps bar in town, the Minerva (at the marina) brews own beer. **Eats:** SU (food hall with international dishes including veggie food). Italian and Mexican are popular; Ray's Place for an Indian. **Ents:** Fantastic band scene. Hull home of Kingmaker, Space Maid, Beautiful South and Moist. **Sports:** Excellently equipped sports centre on campus. Numerous centres in local areas. **Hardship funds:** VC's Hardship as well as Union loans. Access funds improved – smaller sums to more people. **Travel:** Expedition fund. Travel Centre in SU. **Work:** Not bad if you like pubs and hamburgers.
MORE INFO? Enquiries to SU (01482 466278).
ALUMNI (EDITORS' PICK) Sir Ron Dearing, Tony Galvin, Sarah Greene, Roy Hattersley MP, Chris Mullin, Roger McGough, Philip Larkin (was librarian), Ben Watt and Tracy Thorne (Everything but the Girl), John McCarthy, Jill Morrell, Kevin MacNamara MP.

HUMBERSIDE UNIVERSITY

Humberside University Campus, Cottingham Road,
Hull HU6 7RT (Tel 01482 440550, Fax 01482 471343;
E-mail: marketing @ humber.ac.uk) Map 2

STUDENT ENQUIRIES: Marketing department
APPLICATIONS: UCAS

Broad study areas: Accountancy, administration, art & design, architecture, business, computing, engineering and technology, languages, social sciences. (Subject details are in the *Subjects and Places Index*.)

Founded: 1861 as Hull School of Art. Became Humberside Polytechnic in 1976 and Humberside University in 1992. **Structural features:** Became Lincolnshire & Humberside University in 1996, following the opening of a new campus in Lincoln (look up *Lincoln* separately). Students study at either one campus or the other. **Main undergraduate awards:** BA, BSc, BEng. **Awarding body:** Lincolnshire & Humberside University. **Site:** 3 sites, in and around Hull city centre. **Academic features:** Applications encouraged from those without formal entrance requirements; degree course place guaranteed for students who pass a university-validated access course. Students on several business courses can spend a year in America, Australia or New Zealand. **Europe:** 25% first degree students take a language as part of course and 15% spend 6 months or more abroad. Languages are part of European degree programmes (including Finnish and Swedish). Formal exchange links with a number of European universities/colleges. **Library:** One on each Hull site; total of 200,000 volumes, 1,560 periodicals, 750 study places. Annual expenditure on library materials, £45.19 per FTE student. **Other learning facilities:** Computer centre with 800 student workstations, sound and TV studios, language laboratories, video editing facilities, high speed network. **Welfare:** Nurses, chaplains, revenue officer, counselling service, advice centre, international office. **Careers:** Information, advice and placement service. **Amenities:** SU with shops, snack bars, refectory, bars. **Sporting facilities:** Gym, health and fitness club.

Accommodation: In 1996/97, 85% of first years in university accommodation. 1,600 places available: 400 full-board places at £50–£60 per week, term time only; 1,200 self-catering places including head lease, etc at approx £35 per week, Sept–June. Students live in privately owned accommodation for 2+ years: £33–£40 per week for self-catering; private rented accommodation fairly abundant and competitively priced. 20% first degree students live at home. **Term time work**: University's policy to allow term time work for full-time first degree students (50% believed to work). Term (and vac) work available on campus in SU bars, admin and promotion work; also careers service has noticeboard for temp and casual jobs, including vacancy details from local Job Centre. **Hardship funds:** Total available in 1995/96: £157,728 government access funds, £110 average award. Own funds: Special help for eg concessionary fees for part-time courses for students on state benefits.

Duration of first degree courses: 3 years; **others:** 4 years (sandwich). **Total first degree students 1995/96:** 11,327. **Overseas students:** 1,467. **Mature students:** 6,458. **Male/female ratio:** 1:1. **Teaching staff:** 410 full-time, 43 part-time. **Total full-time students 1995/96:** 9,427. **Postgraduate students:** 606. **First degree tuition fees:** Home students, paying their own fees in 1996/97, paid £1,300 (classroom), £2,770 (lab/studio); Overseas students £5,000 (classroom), £5,400 (lab/studio).

WHAT IT'S LIKE   It's split on three sites, one in Hull city centre, two in the busiest student area. Excellent access by motorway, rail, ferry and air. Many foreign students and opportunities for study abroad. Few halls of residence, but plenty of head-leased properties managed by the university. Lots of student accommodation so housing not a problem. Hull has a large student population (20,000+) and local businesses try hard to attract students to drink, eat, shop etc. Many opportunities for bargains, discounts and general value for money. Academic staff are of a high standard, teaching well-respected courses; but with scarce resources, seminar groups are large and teaching accommodation inadequate. Much of the library stock has now been transferred to the Lincoln campus 50 miles away, making access to certain books and journals difficult. Students' Union under-funded but supports many clubs and societies, as well as running 2 bars, shops and cafes. SU is affiliated to the NUS but is politically dead; it works mainly for improved student welfare, academic services and to provide facilities on all sites. Main union building is on the Cottingham Road site; although small, it has a bar (capacity 500) and three shops including a bookshop. Sports facilities poor and small changing rooms far from facilities but sports teams remain competitive and successful.

PAUPER NOTES   **Accommodation:** From £30 per week; loads to choose from in Hull. **Drink:** Cheap at SU, capacity nights with nightclub licence. Scruffy Murphy's, Firkin and

Haworth are main student pubs but many to choose from. **Eats:** You name it, Hull's got it: chippies, Chinese, Malaysian, Lebanese, and French . . . all well priced. **Ents:** Different club for students every night, all offering excellent bar promos. Range from 70's, indie, dance and foam parties. Several cinemas, ice arena, go-karting, live gigs. **Sports:** Local gyms, sports clubs. **Hardship funds:** Limited funds from university.

ALUMNI (EDITORS' PICK) Ann Brown and Christine Ford (England Women's Basketball), Mary Parkinson (TV presenter), Eliot Morley MP.

IMPERIAL COLLEGE

Imperial College of Science, Technology and Medicine,
South Kensington, London SW7 2AZ
(Tel 0171 589 5111, Fax 0171 594 8004) Map 6

STUDENT ENQUIRIES: Assistant Registrar (Admissions)
APPLICATIONS: UCAS

Broad study areas: Science, engineering, medicine, environmental science. (Subject details are in the *Subjects and Places Index*.)

Founded: 1907. **Structural features:** Part of London University. The Imperial College School of Medicine is the result of amalgamating with the medical schools of St Mary's Hospital and Charing Cross & Westminster (you can look up them up separately). **Main undergraduate awards:** MEng, BEng, BSc, MSci, MB, BS. **Awarding body:** London University. **Site:** 16-acre site in South Kensington. Medical school sites in Paddington, Chelsea, Fulham. **Access:** South Kensington and Gloucester Road underground stations and buses for main site; medical school sites close to tube and buses. **Academic features:** MEng courses in electrical and electronic engineering with management and in mechanical engineering with a year abroad; MSci in geology with environmental applications and BSc in geology with mineral exploration. Humanities programme offering weekly lectures in associated studies and foreign language courses. **Special features:** Established 'to give the highest specialised instruction and to provide the fullest equipment for the most advanced training and research in various branches of science especially in its application to industry'. Applications from women are strongly encouraged. Musician-in-residence leads a variety of musical activities. Some 99 visiting professors. **Europe:** Increasing number of first degree students take a language as a formal part of course; all students have access to language laboratory facilities. Wide range of exchange schemes with prestigious technological institutions across Europe providing unergraduates with the opportunity to undertake project work for 3–12 months abroad. Strong commitment to year abroad courses (available in all departments). **Libraries:** Departmental libraries for research material and local services. Central library for course books and interdisciplinary material. 725,000 volumes, 4,000 periodicals, 1,600 places. Haldane collection covers humanities, general reading and music including CDs and tapes. Annual expenditure on library materials, £170 per FTE student. **Other learning facilities:** Computer centre on South Kensington campus; 240-acre college field station at Silwood Park (near Ascot). **Welfare:** Advisory committee; vacation training scheme; careers advisory service; student accommodation office; health centre, student counsellor, welfare adviser, Nightline, nursery, disabilities officer. **Amenities:** SU building with refectory, bar, bookshop, etc; wide range of societies. **Sporting facilities:** Sports centre on campus with indoor swimming pool; boathouse at Putney; 60-acre sports ground at Harlington; playing field at Teddington. **Employment:** Traditionally industry; but increasing number of graduates enter accountancy, banking, insurance etc, as well as general commercial areas.

Accommodation: Over 2,000 places on or near campus. First year students who accept an unconditional offer by 11 Sept are guaranteed a place in either Imperial or intercollegiate hall. **Term time work:** College policy to allow term time work; limit of 6–8 hours per week. Term (and vac) work available in college bars, offices, library. **Hardship funds:** Total available in 1995/96: £300,000 government access funds, average £300 awarded; £12,000 own funds (average award £250). Special help for mature students, those with child care responsibilities or disabilities, self-financing students; own funds also available for those experiencing unforeseen short-term need.

Duration of first degree courses: 3, 4 or 5 years (science and engineering); 5 years (medicine). **Total first degree students 1995/96:** 5,155. **First degree overseas students:** 977. **Male/female ratio:** 5:2. **Teaching staff:** 857. **Total full-time students 1995/96:** 7,461. **Postgraduate students:** 2,306.**First degree tuition fees:** Home students, paying their own fees in 1996/97, paid £750; Overseas students £7,750 (mathematics), £16,650 (clinical medicine), £9,800 (pre-clinical and all others).

WHAT IT'S LIKE It's in South Kensington near Hyde Park and the museums. All the benefits of central London and usual drawbacks of expense and accommodation. Halls across Exhibition Road; off Fulham Road (20 minutes' walk, most self-catering); and some houses in south Ealing. Few places also available at London University halls, a tube trip away. All first years offered places in IC residences, all undergraduates can spend at least one year in college accommodation. International reputation and very high academic standards. Courses fairly intensive, but lower than average failure rate. Men still greatly outnumber women and 1 in 3 students is a postgraduate. SU not affiliated to NUS, politically independent, tends to concentrate on college matters. It supports over 200 clubs from motorcycle to Amnesty International, as well as social clubs for most cultural and ethnic groups (32% of students from overseas). SU also runs bookstore, newsagents, cafés, bars, cinema, advice centre, gym and concert hall. Excellent student media led by weekly newspaper, *Felix*, radio station and television network. ULU facilities and events at Malet Street are open to IC students. 4 constituent colleges organise rag stunts, such as tiddly-winking down Oxford Street, and other social events. The medical school is the most popular medical school, with friendly atmosphere and strong traditions for revues and rugby. IC adage: 'Work hard, play hard' – balance often difficult but student life very much what you make of it.

PAUPER NOTES **Accommodation:** Never cheap; single room in college halls typically approx £52 pw but cheaper shared rooms available. Small chance of married quarters. **Drink:** College bar + 2 union bars – very cheap. Guest ales. Queens Arms – good atmosphere. **Eats:** Union runs Da Vinci's Café/Bar, burger bar, pizza bar, refectory (all cheap). Local area expensive except Indian and pasta bar in South Kensington. Best: veggie and Indians in Euston/Notting Hill etc. **Ents:** Weekly free discos, bands (c £3) and comedy nights. Cheap events on campus. Still many free gigs/exhibitions in London. Pub gigs good value. Union cinema. **Sports:** Campus sports centre very cheap for swimming, squash, weights. Sport generally cheap. Group transport to excellent college grounds at Heathrow and medical school grounds in Teddington. **Hardship funds:** Access fund arranged by College. **Travel:** Bike and A-Z London essential! Car parking only possible with disability/medical. STA branch on campus; expedition fund available. **Work:** Good temping prospects in vacation – on campus, cleaning residences, clerical and tutoring in London. Term-time work relatively easy to get but difficult to find the time with high course standards. SU setting up employment bureau.

MORE INFO?   Ring SU President (0171 594 8060).

INFORMAL NAME   IC.

ALUMNI (EDITORS' PICK)   H G Wells, Sir Lewis Casson, Sir Granville Bantock, Joan Ruddock MP, Sir John Egan, Francis Wilson, Brian May.

INSTITUTE OF ARCHAEOLOGY

Institute of Archaeology, University College London, 31–34 Gordon Square, London WC1H 0PY (Tel 0171 380 7495, Fax 0171 383 2572) Map 6

STUDENT ENQUIRIES: Admissions Secretary
APPLICATIONS: UCAS

Broad study area: Archaeology.

Founded: 1937. Part of University College London since 1986. **Main undergraduate awards:** BA, BSc. **Awarding body:** London University. **Site:** University precinct in Bloomsbury, central London. **Access:** Warren Street and Euston Square underground stations. **Europe:** No students take a modern language as compulsory part of their degree course. Variable number of students spend time on fieldwork abroad (no formal links). **Academic features:** Eight degree programmes offered. All staff are practising archaeologists or archaeological scientists. **Library:** Specialist archaeology library: 40,000 volumes (some in store), 1,000 periodicals, 60 study places; recommended books temporarily restricted for use of students. **Other learning facilities:** Access to computing facilities for all; science laboratories. **Specialist collections:** Petrie Museum of Egyptological material and Classical Archaeology Museum. **Welfare:** Institute health centre and counsellor. **Careers:** Institute careers guidance tutor; UCL and London University careers services. **Amenities:** Institute common room. Students have access to all SU facilities at UCL (including sporting).

Accommodation: No Institute accommodation; students apply to University College London; places for all first years. **Term time work:** No formal policy on part time work in term time. Some work on campus in eg SU and library. **Hardship funds:** See *University College London.*

Duration of first degree courses: 3 years. **Total first degree students 1995/96:** 290. **Overseas students:** 30 (+ 30 EU). **Mature students:** 130. **Male/female ratio:** 2:3. **Teaching staff:** 37 full-time, 7 part-time. **Total full-time students 1995/96:** 420. **Postgraduate students:** 130. **First degree tuition fees:** Home students, paying their own fees in 1996/97, paid £860; Overseas: £9,445.

WHAT IT'S LIKE   It's in a six-storey building facing onto Gordon Square, surrounded by UCL and London University buildings – convenient really. It has a common room in the basement – nearly all students and some of the lecturers will be found there. Food and drink served from 10 till 4.30 Mon-Fri. The Society of Archaeological Students (SAS) produces a magazine and organises parties every term (two in first term): generally very popular, both for staff and students. Staff are very helpful and interact socially with students. Wide range of optional courses in second and third years, and several in first year. Institute library is very useful but sometimes overstretched due to numbers using it. Various other libraries (eg UCL main and Senate House) are helpful. Where possible, courses run field trips. All first years go on a primitive technology weekend; mainly this is intended for everyone to get to know each other but it takes in some extremely useful archaeological ideas.

PAUPER NOTES   **Accommodation:** UCL and intercollegiate halls, various rates, self-catering obviously cheapest; flats etc. **Drink:** Union bars have cheapest beer, and most popular. **Eats:** Unions (esp UCLU) plus college refectories, McDonald's etc. **Ents:** Theatre and cheap films at the Bloomsbury Theatre. Union bars have themes most evenings. **Sports:** Institute football team. ULU and UCL for those who want to keep fit. **Travel:** Fieldwork grants for LEA-supported students, to help with the 70 days fieldwork requirement.

MORE INFO?   Get students' Alternative Prospectus.

ALUMNI (EDITORS' PICK)   James Coppice Norman, Nick Branch, Andrew Hobley.

INSTITUTE OF EDUCATION

Institute of Education, University of London,
20 Bedford Way, London WC1H 0AL
(Tel 0171 612 6104, Fax 0171 612 6097) Map 6

STUDENT ENQUIRIES: Information office, student programmes office. APPLICATIONS: GTTR for PGCE; direct for other courses

Broad study area: Education (largely postgraduate).

Founded: 1902, became Institute of Education in 1932. **Structural features:** A postgraduate school of London University. **Main awards:** BEd, PGCE, MA, MSc, MPhil, PhD, EdD. **Site:** Bloomsbury, central London. **Access:** Russell Square underground. **Academic features:** Postgraduate teacher training courses involving close partnership with local schools and colleges. Modular masters and advanced diploma courses in most educational specialisms, enabling students to accumulate credits over a period of time. Research degrees of MPhil and PhD; EdD course, involving taught and research components. BEd for serving teachers. **Library:** 300,000 volumes, 2,000 periodicals, 250 study places. Annual expenditure on library materials, £55.32 per FTE student. **Specialist collections:** Curriculum resources collection. **Welfare:** London University health service, chaplain, student adviser, nursery facilities. Facilities for married students. **Careers:** Information and advice. 90% of those on initial training course employed within 6 months. **Amenities:** Central London and London University. Dillons bookshop, 5 minutes walk.

Accommodation: Institute has an accommodation officer and students can use London University accommodation office. 230 places in halls; a number of self-contained flats available, average £78 per week. **Hardship funds:** Loans available for students in temporary financial difficulties.

Male/female ratio: 2:3. **Teaching staff:** 267 full-time. **Total full-time students 1995/96:** 1,587 (2,868 part-time). **Tuition fees:** Home students, paying their own fees in 1996/97, paid £1,600 (PGCE), £2,490 (diploma and higher degrees); Overseas students £6,470.

WHAT IT'S LIKE   Unlike most London University colleges, it's almost entirely postgraduate – a world centre for the study of education. Three broad categories of work: initial professional training; advanced courses for graduates; and research degrees (MPhil, PhD). It has a high reputation for research and, occasionally, this filters down to practical training. It is a fairly strange place to spend a year. Situated just off Russell Square, in a huge concrete and tinted glass monstrosity, it's near Euston and King's Cross BR stations. Nearby is Dillon's, also the undergraduate haunt of ULU. The SU Society is a fairly liberated union, popular with students from other colleges and dedicated to providing the best service for all students. It offers a variety of services in the minute space allowed – a bar, snack bar, lunch counter and shop. Good relationship with the Institute, and many joint ventures are undertaken, such as the South African Scholarship Scheme. A lot of activity centres around educational issues, such as anti-racist and anti-sexist education. SU has cheap bar, free discos on a Friday, and general non-threatening environment.

PAUPER   NOTES   **Accommodation:**   Flats,   self-catering   accommodation   and single/double rooms with food and heating included. **Drink:** Varies, but usually at least 2 real ales and 3 lagers in bar. **Eats:** Cheapish meals in snack bar/lunch counter. A good variety of vegetarian and salads. **Ents:** Regular discos and sometimes bands are invited – cheap or free entrances. **Sports:** Join ULU facilities. **Hardship funds:** Hardship fund administered by college. Nursery subsidy. **Travel:** Cheap fares available from STA (round corner). **Work:** Bar work, stewarding, kitchen work for special events.

JEWS' COLLEGE

Jews' College, Albert Road, Hendon, London NW4
(Tel 0181 203 6427, Fax 0181 208 6420) Map 5

STUDENT ENQUIRIES: Academic Registrar
APPLICATIONS: UCAS

Broad study areas: Jewish studies. (Subject details are in the *Subjects and Places Index.*)

Founded: 1855, to train rabbis, leaders and teachers for the Anglo-Jewish community and overseas. **Structural features:** An affiliated college of London University. **Main undergraduate award:** BA. **Awarding body:** London University. **Site:** Hendon (densely populated Jewish area) **Access:** Buses from central London. **Academic features:** College linked to London University for all degrees. **Special features:** Lecturers regularly visit from Bar-Ilan University, Israel. **Europe:** No students take a European language or spend time abroad as part of their course, although most students spend at least 1 year in Israel prior to their degree course. **Library:** Outstanding reference and information centre for all things Jewish; 80,000 volumes, 142 periodicals; priceless 15th- and 16th-century manuscripts. **Welfare:** Student counsellor; honorary medical officer available for consultation. Special arrangements for mature students. **Security:** Entrance door locked at all times. **Careers:** Direct links to United Synagogue for those wishing to pursue the ministry. **Amenities:** SU provides range of services.

Accommodation: Very limited college accommodation; students accommodated with local families or flats in the area: £40–£60 per week for self-catering, £45–£65 for B&B, £60–£75 for half-board. 10% of first degree students live at home. **Term time work:** College policy to allow term time work for first degree students (60% believed to work). Term (and vac) work available in college computer unit, library; college helps find outside work via teaching network/United Synagogue. **Hardship funds:** Grants and scholarships available in certain cases.

Duration of first degree courses: 3 years. **Total first degree students 1995/96:** 29. **Mature students:** 5. **Overseas students:** 0. **Male/female ratio:** 2:5. **Teaching staff:** 3 full-time, 10 part-time. **Total full-time students 1995/96:** 30. **Postgraduate students:** 65. **First degree tuition fees:** Home students, paying their own fees in 1996/97, paid £3,000 (fees for overseas students by negotiation).

WHAT IT'S LIKE   It's in north west London; a small (but growing), cosy college, with a warm, vibrant atmosphere. It's especially popular with students who have taken years out to attend Talmudic colleges or seminaries. Good student/staff relationships. Modern purpose-built campus boasts the most extensive Judaica library in Europe and is particularly strong in early rabbinic literature, Jewish history and Maimonidean studies. Numerous conference rooms and the London-based Institute of Jewish Education. SU offers programme of social and cultural events in conjunction with the Union of Jewish Students. Facilities include refectory, lounge and snooker tables. Degrees can lead to teaching, administrative, or ministerial posts within the community. Some use their degree as a basis for entrance into the professions. Location means most forms of entertainment are nearby. Prospective students are in for a busy and enjoyable time.

PAUPER NOTES   **Accommodation:** College helps find kosher accommodation locally. **Eats:** Discounts at some kosher restaurants. **Hardship funds:** Bursaries available for needy students. **Work:** Some vacation work etc available.

INFORMAL NAME: JC.

ALUMNI (EDITORS' PICK) Lord Jakobovits, Rabbi Dr Jonathan Sacks, Prof S Greenbaum (London University), Dr Stefan Reif (Director, Taylor Schechter Geniza Research Unit, Cambridge), Prof Alan Corre, Dov Zackheim, Rabbi Dr Cyril Harris (Chief Rabbi of South Africa).

HOW TO START? *SEE SHORTLISTING*, PAGE 535

KEELE UNIVERSITY

Keele University, Staffordshire ST5 5BG
(Tel 01782 621111, Fax 01782 632343) Map 2

STUDENT ENQUIRIES: Head of Admissions and Recruitment
APPLICATIONS: UCAS

Broad study areas: Arts, languages, social sciences, education, sciences, business, law. (Subject details are in the *Subjects and Places Index.*)

Founded: 1949, ex University College of North Staffordshire. **Main undergraduate awards:** BA, BSc, MSci. **Awarding body:** Keele University. **Site:** Campus 2 miles from Newcastle-under-Lyme. **Access:** M6, buses to campus from Stoke station. **Academic features:** 4-year course (foundation year + 3 years) with few course requirements. All courses modular. 330+ dual honours combinations available and concurrent Cert in Primary Ed possible. **Europe:** 16% first degree students take a language as part of course and 13% spend 5 months or more abroad. Formal exchange links with 50 universities/colleges in EFTA and EU, many open to non-language specialists. Languages (French and German) may be combined with other subjects; or as subsidiary courses (French, German and Spanish) open to all undergraduates. **Library:** 500,000 volumes, 1,500 periodicals, 800 study places, separate foundation year library. Annual expenditure on library materials, £109.97 per FTE student. **Specialist collections:** Turner mathematics collection, Wedgwood archives. **Welfare:** Doctors, dentist, FPA, counsellor, solicitor (SU), chaplains, financial adviser, counselling service; nursery. **Careers:** Information and appointments service. **Amenities:** Bookshop on campus; SU premises with launderettes, supermarket, newsagent and banks; variety of bars and restaurants. **Sporting facilities:** Multi-purpose sports centre with adjoining playing fields, tennis courts and athletics track; 7 squash courts, climbing wall and fitness centre gymnasium; sports shop.

Accommodation: In 1995/96, 80% of all students in university (or rent-controlled) accommodation, 100% of first years. 3,200 places available at £26–£42 per week (variety of letting periods). **Term time work:** University's policy to allow term time work for full-time first degree students. Term (and vac) work available on campus in bars, catering outlets etc; also SU job shop helps find work off campus.

Duration of first degree courses: 4 years (with foundation year), 3 years (without foundation year). **Total first degree students 1995/96:** 4,204. **Overseas students:** 363. **Mature students:** 338. **Male/female ratio:** 1:1. **Teaching staff:** 479 full-time, 16 part-time. **Total full-time students 1995/96:** 5,714. **Postgraduate students:** 1,920. **First degree tuition fees:** Home students, paying their own fees in 1996/97, paid £750 (classroom), £1,600 (lab/studio); Overseas students £6,025 (classroom), £7,900 (lab).

WHAT IT'S LIKE   Keele? This may be (and in most cases probably is) the first time you have heard of such a place, and no doubt friends and family will give a puzzled look when you mention it! However, your time at Keele will possibly be the most eye-opening, memorable and, above all, enjoyable days of your life. The campus is the largest in England (and very picturesque) and is in the heart of the Staffordshire potteries. It is not just the setting

...nat makes Keele special, but the fact that the majority of students live on campus makes for the strikingly friendly, community atmosphere – like nothing you will experience again. 70% full time students live on campus (priority given to freshers and finalists), either in 4-person flats, basic rooms or rooms with ensuite facilities. Courses are joint honours, including a subsidiary course in the first year, which makes for broader learning and diversity in study. The library opens 7 days a week until 10 pm, with a short loan library for books in high demand. SU has a ballroom (1,100 capacity) and nightclub (600 capacity); ents include 4 main discos each week, ranging from alternative/indie, '70s/'80s discos, club dance nights, gigs (big names such as Brand New Heavies, Pulp), comedy, club tours (Perfecto, Up Yer Ronson) and termly balls. The SU is apolitical, with a combination of highly motivated, enthusiastic and dedicated students, sabbaticals and full-time staff, whose love of Keele and determination to work for the students ensure that each and every one has a fantastic and unforgettable university experience.

PAUPER NOTES **Accommodation:** Most students on campus; university has good off-campus housing lists, and rents low (c. £35/week). **Drink:** 7 cheap SU bars, 4 halls bars, 1 university bar (slightly more expensive). Two pubs close to each campus entrance, The Golfers Arms (now owned by SU, with excellent food and beers). **Eats:** Bar meals and fast food in union, pizzas in the sports centre (delivery service available), and sandwiches and veggie food in Harvey Green's. Off campus: local places will deliver pizza, curries, etc. **Ents:** SU ents (discos, club dance nights, gigs, comedy, club tours and termly balls). Locally: New Vic Theatre, gigs at Victoria Hall, Stoke Beer Festival, gay clubs in Hanley, Time and Space and The Void for top club nights and The Place for excellent student dance nights. **Sports:** Excellent facilities on campus: huge sports centre, new multi-gym, tennis courts, flood-lit astro-turf, extensive playing fields. Local swimming pool in Newcastle (under-Lyme). **Hardship funds:** Limited loans from SU for those in exceptional financial trouble. **Travel:** Travel office in SU. Two bus routes on campus (last bus leaves Hanley at 11.50 pm but taxis are cheap and efficient). SU free minibus service from campus to home. Car parks for each hall plus a general union car park, registration is essential. **Work:** University (£2.98/hr) and union (£3.20/hr) offer employment in shops, catering, bars and security. Local work is relatively easy to find.

MORE INFO? Get the Blaggers Handbook or Alternative Prospectus. Enquiries to SU (01782 711411).

BUZZ-WORDS Potters (locals), Duck (what Potters call everyone), Hanley-Duck (Hanley).

ALUMNI (EDITORS' PICK) John Golding, David Pownall, Jack Straw MP, Gerry Northam, Sue Robbie, Alan Michael, Ian Taylor, Bernard Lloyd, Neil Baldwin.

KENT INSTITUTE

Kent Institute of Art and Design, Oakwood Park, Oakwood Road, Maidstone, Kent ME16 8AG (Tel 01622 757286) Map 4

STUDENT ENQUIRIES: **Marketing Officer**
APPLICATIONS: **UCAS**

Broad study areas: Art & design, architecture. (Subject details are in the *Subjects and Places Index*.)

Founded: 1987 by merger of Canterbury College of Art, Maidstone College of Art and Medway College of Design. **Main undergraduate award:** BA. **Awarding body:** Kent University. **Site:** Three separate campuses (Canterbury, Maidstone, Rochester), each shared with other educational establishments and close to a town or city centre. **Academic features:** International links; range of design specialisms; record of student awards and commissions; professional facilities (eg, computers, video studios, bronze foundry). **Europe:** Some students take a language and study abroad as part of degree course. Exchanges with Düsseldorf (architecture) and links with colleges in France, Germany, Russia and Sweden. **Library:** Three separate libraries, each c20,000 volumes. Annual expenditure on library materials, £48 per FTE student.

Accommodation: In 1995/96, 34% of all students in institute accommodation, 16% of first years. 742 places available (355 for first years): self-catering at £45 average per week, Sept–June. Students living in privately owned accommodation pay £38–£45 per week for self-catering, around £40 for B&B, £50–£55 for half-board and weekend meals. **Term time work:** Institute's policy to allow term time work for full-time first degree students (10% believed to work). Some term time work available on campus in bars. **Hardship funds:** Total available in 1995/96: £42,443 government access funds; £1,500 hardship loan fund.

Duration of first degree courses: 3 years; **other:** 5 years (part-time). **Total first degree students 1995/96:** 984. **Overseas students:** 234. **Mature students:** approx 150. **Male/female ratio:** 1:1. **Teaching staff:** 64 full-time, 200 part-time. **Total full-time students 1995/96:** 2,200. **Postgraduate students:** 50. **First degree tuition fees:** Home students, paying their own fees in 1996/97, paid £1,600; Overseas students £7,200.

WHAT IT'S LIKE *Maidstone* 60s building with some new additions, on the edge of town. Very good courses (graphic design, film and video, photography, illustration and foundation) and course facilities pretty good. Some 700 students, so everyone knows everyone; not much cliqueness. Active SU, affiliated to NUS. Regular college parties and gigs. Canteen and fully licensed bar. Some local bars available for parties. Slight, but not unusual, town-student rivalry. Cheap local market Tuesdays and Saturdays. Free use of huge local sports centre (Mote Park). Football and basketball teams at college (need more people). You need to be very self-motivated at this college.
PAUPER NOTES **Accommodation:** 200 places in new halls, £45 pw. Also students in privately rented accommodation, lodging with families or in college-owned houses. **Drink:** College bar (£1.40 a pint). In town Drakes, Davinchis club (student night Wednesdays), also trendy wine bars. **Eats:** Canteen okay but pricey. In town, Babs Kebabs, various pizzas, Mexican and Mongolian restaurants, good Chinese takeout. **Ents:** College parties, pool comp, bands etc. In town cinema, bars, bowling. Union bar (live bands each week), cheap with NUS card. **Sports:** Mote Park complex, swimming etc. College football and basketball teams. **Hardship fund:** College access fund. Welfare and accommodation officers very helpful. **Work:** Many part-time jobs in bars, restaurants, shops, and summer fruit picking.
MORE INFO? Enquiries to SU President (01622 679685).

WHAT IT'S LIKE *Canterbury* The city itself has a large student population and there are popular student pubs etc. The Institute has long-term leases (45 rooms in flats/houses), manages a head leasing scheme (175 rooms) and arranges accommodation in other privately owned student houses. Vast majority of students live in student houses within 20 minutes' walk of college. General art and design students on FE courses mostly live at home. International students in all departments from many countries of the world. Institute manages a bar and an excellent refectory (good food and quality service available

9am-11.30pm). SU assists with sports and social activities and a variety of clubs etc. Growing interest in football team, plus involvement in everything from rock climbing to aerobics, jazz dance or abseiling.

PAUPER NOTES **Accommodation:** Rents £40–£45 per week. **Drink:** College bar cheap. City Arms, Millers Arms, Simple Simons, Jolly Sailor, Bell & Crown and Imperial most popular pubs in Canterbury. **Eats:** Excellent value food, wide range, in college refectory. Many good restaurants in Canterbury – some cheap, some not. **Ents:** Gigs etc as regular events. Pool, video etc plus ents in bar. **Sports:** Institute sports facilities. **Hardship funds:** Limited loan fund of small amounts available through accommodation and welfare office. **Travel:** Some exchanges to Europe, Russia, Canada etc. **Work:** Some work helping at college gigs; restaurant, bar, shop and cleaning work available.

INFORMAL NAME   Canterbury Art College; KIAD.

ALUMNI (EDITORS' PICK)   Ian Dury.

KENT UNIVERSITY

University of Kent at Canterbury, Canterbury, Kent
CT2 7NZ (Tel 01227 764000, Fax 01227 452196) Map 4

STUDENT ENQUIRIES: Undergraduate Admissions Office
APPLICATIONS: UCAS

Broad study areas: Humanities, maths and statistics, natural sciences, law, social sciences, information technology. (Subject details are in the *Subjects and Places Index*.)

Founded: 1965. **Main undergraduate awards:** BA, BEng, BSc, LLB. **Awarding body:** University of Kent. **Site:** 300-acre campus, on outskirts of Canterbury. **Access:** Good road and rail links with London and Europe. **Academic features:** Wide range of courses: single subject, joint and multi-disciplinary and those wih a year abroad or working in industry. **Europe:** Many students study a language as part of degree; language study at different levels can be combined with almost every subject, with or without a year abroad. Formal Erasmus and other exchange links with many EU universities/colleges – open to students in a range of disciplines eg computer science, drama, economics, law, maths and social psychology. **Library:** Over 1 million books, periodicals, pamphlets, slides, microfilms and electronic media form. Annual expenditure on library materials, £115.80 per FTE student. **Special collections:** Early and rare materials, research collections and archives; close links with Cathedral library. **Welfare:** Personal tutorial system; health and counselling service; SU provides legal and financial advice; day nursery, chaplaincy, travel bureau. **Careers:** Careers advisory service. **Amenities:** Dillons bookshop on site; Gulbenkian Theatre; Cinema 3 (The Regional Film Theatre), own radio station. **Sporting facilities:** Sports centre provides facilities for over 30 different activities (including coaching to international standard).

Accommodation: Most first year students live in university-owned accommodation; all guaranteed one year on campus. Approx cost £38.15 per week self-catering, year long contracts; £46.48 per week B&B, term-time only. **Hardship funds:** Total available in 1995/96:

£122,330 government access funds, 346 students helped. Special help to students without grants (assigned prior to start of course).

Duration of first degree courses: 3 years; **others:** 4 years. **Total first degree students 1995/96:** 5,802. **Overseas students:** 14%. **Male/female ratio:** 1:1. **Teaching staff:** 427 full-time, 14 part-time. **Total full-time students 1995/96:** 7,081. **Postgraduate students:** 1,127. **First degree tuition fees:** Home students, paying their own fees in 1996/97, paid £750 (classroom), £1,600 (lab/studio); Overseas students £6,245 (classroom), £8,150 (lab/studio). £170 college fee added to all fees.

WHAT IT'S LIKE   Kent is a green, campus university overlooking the town. The surroundings are very pleasant, the view of the cathedral magnificent. The university is based on four colleges (Keynes, Rutherford, Darwin and Eliot) but is spreading out with self-catering accommodation forming a Brookside-like housing estate. Campus accommodation is in college rooms and self-catering houses; standard varies (excellent to reasonable) and few shared rooms. Most first years get a place on campus, although more accommodation is needed; in town it is expensive and the demand always outweighs availability so some students live in Whitstable and Herne Bay. The proportion of mature students is increasing (as is the number of postgraduates). A very large overseas student population – roughly 30%, not predominantly European – results in a varied, exciting mix (overseas cultural societies stage great ents). There is a high percentage of students from the Home Counties (due to its location). The SU is excellent – socially and politically very active and provides some of the cheapest social events in the country. It also has an excellent welfare department (and the university's is improving). Discrimination is a problem like anywhere but anti-sexist, -racist and -homophobic campaigns are very active and campus life overall is quite free from prejudice. Gay scene is small but friendly and enthusiastic. Canterbury is definitely a student town, although slight tensions between student and non-student scenes. Loads of pubs and restaurants, theatre, small cinema; art cinema on campus. 2 clubs/music venues, plus a brand new one; union organises popular club nights. All in all the university and town are relatively small which results in a friendly, community atmosphere.

PAUPER NOTES   **Accommodation:** Little that is cheap in Canterbury. **Drink:** Fremlins and Shepherd good local brews. Pubs: Black Griffin, Falstaff Tap, Three Compasses, Woody's. Union bar far the cheapest. **Eats:** Wide variety of cheap places, including ethnic (Mexican to Indian). **Ents:** Marlowe Theatre gets all major touring plays. Works and Penny Theatre popular club venues. **Sports:** Good sports centre on campus. In town, new sports centre and swimming pool. **Hardship funds:** Union welfare fund – limited budget. Access funds. **Travel:** Buses cheap, trains adequate. **Work:** Available if you are prepared to search and to work for peanuts; usually bar work in town.

MORE INFO?   Enquiries to Dom Wand, President SU (tel 01227 765224; e-mail dsw@ukc.ac.uk or union@ukc.ac.uk).

INFORMAL NAME UKC.

BUZZ-WORDS   LBG – Lesbian and Bisexual and Gay Group. K, R, E, D – the four colleges, Keynes, Rutherford, Eliot, Darwin (all references to rooms abbreviate the college names). PW – Park Wood ('Brookside' housing estate). JCC – Junior college Committee (college part of the SU).

ALUMNI (EDITORS' PICK)   Kazuo Ishiguro, Ted Harrison, Colin Lazzerini (founder of Loose Tubes), Paul Ross (TV presenter), Gavin Estler (news reporter).

GET HOLD OF THE PROSPECTUSES

KING ALFRED'S COLLEGE

King Alfred's College of HE, Sparkford Road, Winchester
SO22 4NR (Tel 01962 841515, Fax 01962 842280) Map 3

STUDENT ENQUIRIES: Admissions Officer
APPLICATIONS: UCAS

Broad study areas: Arts, education, business studies/computing, health studies, applied sciences, humanities. (Subject details are in the *Subjects and Places Index*.)

Founded: 1840, as diocesan training college for teachers. **Main undergraduate awards:** BA, BSc, BEd. **Awarding body:** Southampton University (but college applying for own degree-awarding powers). **Site:** Overlooking city of Winchester. **Academic features:** Exchange opportunities open to most first degree students; linked with universities in Europe, USA and Canada. **Library:** 120,000 volumes, 590 periodicals, 375 study places. Annual expenditure on library materials, £79.62 per FTE student. **Welfare:** College nurse, counsellors, chaplain (college chapel), childcare provision. Some residential facilities for married students. **Careers:** Information, advice and individual guidance service. **Amenities:** Theatre, television centre, learning resources centre, computer studies centre, library, art/design workshop, arts centre, human movement studio, sports hall, SU building with bar, laundry, bank, etc. **Sporting facilities:** Gymnasium, sports hall, squash courts, dance studio, playing fields. **Employment:** Industry, management, civil service, teaching, media, nursing.

Accommodation: 1,100 places in halls of residence anticipated (accommodation for first year students); £68 per week for single room, £63 shared (including £26 for catering), for 30 weeks; £51 self-catering (£54 en suite), 40 weeks. **Term time work**: College's policy to allow term time work for full-time first degree students. Term (and vac) work available on campus in catering, library, accommodation office, registry; also student services run a job shop to help find work off campus. **Hardship funds**: Not known.

Duration of first degree courses: 3 years; **others:** 4 years for primary education; 2 years BEd secondary design and technology. **Total first degree students 1995/96:** 2,819. **Total BEd students:** 964. **Overseas students:** 42. **Mature students:** 2,953. **Male/female ratio:** 2:7. **Teaching staff:** 155 full-time, 20 part-time. **Total full-time students 1995/96:** 3,218. **Postgraduate students:** 1,355. **First degree tuition fees:** Home students, paying their own fees in 1996/97, paid £750 (classroom), £1,600 (lab/studio); Overseas students £5,000 (classroom), £6,800 (lab/studio).

WHAT IT'S LIKE   It's attractively situated on a hillside 10 minutes' walk from Winchester city centre, with picturesque views, and both modern and traditional buildings. Approximately 1000 places in college accommodation and a large new development. Places for all first years (who apply in time) and some others. There is a student Nightline listening and information service. Social life centres around the SU, with discos, bands, quizzes, promotions, films and more. Winchester has a fine selection of pubs, a couple of clubs, and good shopping centre. Southampton is 12 miles away, 20 minutes by train; London just over an hour by train. Range of sports available through athletics union. Regular student

drama productions and visiting companies. Exchanges available with Canada, USA, Poland, Spain and Japan. Not hard to change courses during the first year. Workload reasonable to heavy, with continuous assessment. Good academic reputation. SU active both socially and politically; respected LGB society and SU provides welfare advice, social and sporting amenities, student radio station *The Voice*, magazine *Hard Times* and annual handbook. Crèche available for limited number of 3–5-year-olds. Students come mainly from the Midlands and the south. College is close-knit atmosphere, and drop-out rate still fairly low. PAUPER NOTES **Accommodation:** Expensive, similar rates to the London area, not easy to find. College accommodation includes meal card system. **Drink:** Union cheapest. Royal Oak, Exchange and Nash Tun very student friendly (discounts on food); Winchester pub prices, average to high. **Eats:** Good selection in town. **Ents:** Active ents committee. Film Soc, SU theatre productions, abundant theatre groups. Good range of active clubs and societies. **Sports:** Free campus sports, many sports clubs, discounts at town leisure centre and pool. **Hardship fund:** Heavily in demand. Occasional short-term loans. **Travel:** Security service minibus runs every night. **Work:** Usually plenty (pubs, shops, light industrial, student union), reasonable rates. Large number get paid part-time work; 70% get vacation work. MORE INFO? Write to Chris Hulse or Clare Tozer, SU (01962 827419).
INFORMAL NAME KAC, King Alf's.
BUZZ-WORDS JST (John Stripe Theatre); TP (teaching practice); The Dytche (recreation ground); Bar End (sports ground).

KING'S COLLEGE LONDON

King's College London, Strand, London WC2R 2LS
(Tel 0171 836 5454, Fax 0171 872 3400) Map 6

STUDENT ENQUIRIES: School Office which administers the course
APPLICATIONS: UCAS

You can look up *King's College School of Medicine and Dentistry* separately.

Broad study areas: Humanities; law; physical sciences; engineering; life, basic medical and health sciences; medicine and dentistry. (Subject details are in the *Subjects and Places Index*.)

Founded: 1829. **Structural features:** Part of London University. **Main undergraduate awards:** BA, BMus, BSc, MSci, BEng, MEng, LLB, BPharm, BSc with RGN, BA/BSc with PGCE. **Awarding body:** London University. **Site:** 4 sites, one each in Strand, Kensington, Chelsea and Waterloo. **Access:** Good underground and bus services to all campuses. **Special features:** Many modular courses offer a very wide range of subjects. **Europe:** 10% first degree students take a language as part of course and 6% spend 6 months or more abroad. Formal exchange links with a large number of universities/colleges; most open to all undergraduates. Single or combined courses in languages; also offered to students whatever their discipline (sometimes compulsory eg business management). LLB in English and French law (2 years at King's, 2 years at Sorbonne, Paris). **Library:** Over 800,000 books; over 2,500 periodicals, microfilms, tapes, videos, computer tapes, CDs and computers; short-term collections in most popular subjects. Annual expenditure on library materials, £85.48 per FTE student. **Specialist collections:** Enk (classics); Burrows (modern Greek and Byzantine studies); Box (Old Testament); Liddell Hart (military studies); Ford (science); Adam Archive. **Welfare:** Doctors, psychotherapists, chaplains, student advisers. **Careers:** Information, advice and placement service. **Amenities and sporting facilities:** All facilities of ULU (including swimming pool); sports ground, boat club and sailing club; modern gym, squash and tennis courts.

Accommodation: In 1995/96, 30% of eligible students in college accommodation, 95% first years who apply. 2,146 places available (1,520 for first years) including leased properties and intercollegiate halls: 1,220 self-catering places (915 for first years) at £35–£52 per week, 806 half/full board places at £74–£108 per week – some term time, most Sept–June or longer. Students live in privately owned accommodation for 1–2 years: £45–£60 per week for self-catering. 20% first degree students live at home. **Hardship funds:** Total available in 1995/96: £307,000 government access funds, 850 students helped; £35,000 own funds 50 students helped. Special help: those with considerable financial difficulties, those with dependants, mature students and those not eligible for grant.

Duration of first degree courses: 3 years; **others:** 4 years. **Total first degree students 1995/96:** 7,544. **Overseas students:** 656. **Mature students:** 21%. **Male/female ratio:** 1:1. **Total teaching staff:** 764 full-time, 85 part-time. **Total full-time students 1995/96:** 10,307. **Postgraduate students:** 2,773. **First degree tuition fees:** Home students, paying their own fees in 1996/97, paid £750 (classroom), £1,600 (lab/studio), £2,800 (clinical); Overseas students £7,250 (classroom), £9,000 (lab/studio), £16,750 (clinical).

WHAT IT'S LIKE   A multi-site institution right in the heart of London, King's is a vibrant go-ahead college of London University. Impressive academic standards are reached in a wide range of subjects with diverse course structures. A varied and high-quality ents programme centres mainly on the Strand campus and Tutu's – the student nightclub – with Shark! the popular Friday night. Strand and Cornwall House campuses are within walking distance of the major tourist attractions and theatreland. Chelsea campus provides the unique atmosphere of the King's Road, while Kensington is well situated between Notting Hill Gate and High Street Kensington. Each site has its own distinctive flavour. All in all KCL is an exciting and stimulating place to enjoy student life.

PAUPER NOTES   **Accommodation:** Halls – varied, all over London, some expensive. Student village at Hampstead and new hall on South Bank. Excellent head-leasing scheme run by college accommodation office. **Drink:** SU run Strand bar, The Waterfront, Tutu's and Kensington bar, Reggie's. College runs Chelsea bar. Each has promotional nights and real ale seasons and cheaper than pubs. **Eats:** SU has original and varied menu at Tutu's Café and Waterfront deli. College outlets at the Strand, Kensington, Chelsea and Hampstead. Restaurants everywhere. **Ents:** SU disco night on Fridays, Indie night on Saturdays. Lots of new bands. 53 societies. **Sports:** College sports ground at Berrylands, gym on South Bank and weights room at Kensington. Also good indoor sports facilities at the ULU. 25 sports clubs. **Hardship funds:** Access funds; Principal's Fund and the Overseas Students' Fund. **Travel:** Extensive exchange programme, scholarships, STA travel shop at the Strand. **Work:** SU casual work (bars, catering, shop and at ents); lots of bar jobs (about £3.30/hour); many opportunities in Covent Garden area. About 10% find term work; some in vac – being in London means there are lots of opportunities but an expensive place to spend time.

MORE INFO?   Enquiries to Duncan Rasor, SU President (0171 836 7132).
INFORMAL NAME   KCL/King's.
ALUMNI (EDITORS' PICK)   Archbishop Desmond Tutu, Sir Shridath Ramphal, Chapman Pincher, Lord Edmund-Davies, Susan Hill, Angela Rumbold, Arthur C Clarke, Pat Reid, John McGregor, Ivison Macadam (founder NUS), Rory Bremner, Archbishop Carey.

KING'S COLLEGE SCHOOL OF MEDICINE & DENTISTRY

King's College School of Medicine & Dentistry, Bessemer Road, London SE5 9PJ (Tel 0171 737 4000, Fax 0171 346 3693) Map 5

STUDENT ENQUIRIES: Medical Admissions Office (ext 4017) or Dental School Office (ext 2528). APPLICATIONS: UCAS

Broad study areas: Dentistry, medicine. (Subject details are in the *Subjects and Places Index.*)

Founded: 1831. **Structural features:** Part of King's College, London University. Merger with UMDS under discussion. **Main undergraduate awards:** BDS, MB BS. **Awarding body:** London University. **Site:** Camberwell Green/Denmark Hill area; main college in Strand. **Access:** British Rail from Victoria, Blackfriars or London Bridge to Denmark Hill station; underground to Brixton, Elephant & Castle, or Oval, and then bus; various buses from central London. **Academic features:** Basic medical and dental sciences taught in multi-faculty environment of King's College London. Medical students also admitted from Oxford and Cambridge universities for clinical studies only. One year foundation course in natural sciences for those lacking specific sciences background. **Special features:** Both medical and dental degree programmes integrate basic and applied science teaching with clinical contact. **Europe:** No students learn a language as part of their course but they may choose to spend time abroad as part of their elective period. **Library:** 30,000 books and bound journals, plus on-line computer information services; 65 study places at Denmark Hill. **Other learning facilities:** Use made of multi-media technology and computer-assisted learning packages. **Welfare:** Doctor, dentist, FPA, psychiatrist, counsellor, chaplain, independent financial adviser, hospital chapel. **Careers:** Information, advice and resident appointments service. **Amenities:** Own facilities at Denmark Hill, including a sports ground close by, as well as all the facilities of King's College and of London University.

Accommodation and hardship funds: See *King's College London.* **Term time work:** No restrictions placed on part time work although demands of courses make many jobs impossible. Some term (and vac) work available in bars on campus; also King's College scheme for providing work.

Duration of first degree courses: 5 years; 6 years including foundation course. **Total first degree students 1995/96:** 960. **Overseas students:** 40. **Male/female ratio:** 1:1. **Teaching staff:**

111 full-time, 30 part-time (clinical only). **Postgraduate students:** 198. **First degree tuition fees:** Home students, paying their own fees in 1996/97, paid £1,600 (foundation course, years 1 & 2), £2,800 (years 3–5); Overseas students £9,000 (foundation course, years 1 & 2), £16,750 (years 3–5).

WHAT IT'S LIKE   It's into the second year of a brand new medical curriculum. The old divide between pre-clinical and clinical has vanished and you now see the hospital and patients from day one! In the first two years your time is divided between the King's College Strand site and a new purpose built education centre at King's Hospital in Denmark Hill. Time at the Strand gives a flavour of London life and mixes you with students from all faculties and allows you to enjoy Covent Garden, Leicester Square and the West End. After 2 years (3 if you intercalate a BSc) all your time is spent at the hospital, learning at the bedside, at clinics, in theatre and in tutorials. In the final year, after taking most of the formal exams, students follow and assist a house officer as a kind of apprentice. Not all the course is at King's. 2 months are spent in district hospitals, which are popular as the teaching is more relaxed and the patients present with more usual things rather than some of the rarities of a large teaching hospital. One-off trips to the coroner's court and even Broadmoor, are also part of the course. The clinical students have their own students union, the Guild, which represents students to the college, improves library provision, equal opportunities etc and arranges many entertainments and dinners – any excuse (Post Path, Halfway, Fresher's, Dean's Birthday). The Guild occupies the top floor of the medical school at Denmark Hill, The Penthouse, where there is a Blackwell's Medical Bookshop, games room (with 20p pool tables), quiet room and disco room (scene of legendary Wed/Fri discos, popular with staff and students alike); also a bar with a roof-top beer garden and fountain (wow!). Also many clubs and societies. Own sports ground in nearby Dulwich Village; few London students can walk to their sports grounds.

PAUPER NOTES   **Accommodation:** At least 1 year in KCL halls (widely varying standard). Private accommodation at £50–£60 per week in Camberwell and East Dulwich. **Drink:** Student-run Penthouse bar – 5 draught bitters, 3 lagers, weekly guest ale; £1–£1.50 a pint. **Eats:** Med school/hospital refectories. Local Chinese, Indian, Thai, English – many with hospital discounts. **Ents:** Penthouse discos Wed/Fri. Thurs wide-screen film night. Outside hospital, Camberwell and Brixton nightspots fairly cheap eg Brixton Ritzy and The Fridge. **Sports:** Brixton Sports Club – all sports. Cheap membership gives reductions. Med school Griffin sports ground – tennis, netball, hockey, rugby, multigym, bowls and squash courts. **Hardship Funds:** Access fund. Earmarked funds for postgrads/FDS medics. **Travel:** 15-seater minibus. Few travel scholarships for elective students. **Work:** Bar work. Lucrative hospital guinea-pig research work especially if you are asthmatic!

MORE INFO?   The Guild, ww.kcl.ac.uk/kis/su/kcsmd/top.htm/

ALUMNI (EDITORS' PICK)   Richard S Snell (author of Snell's Anatomy, universally popular amongst medics), Dr Reita Faria (ex-Miss World, now practising doctor), J L Dawson (Surgeon to Royal Household), Sir R M Feroze (President, Royal College of Obstetricians and Gynaecologists), Graeme Garden (The Goodies).

WANT TO HELP WITH THE NEXT EDITION? SEE PAGE 66

KINGSTON UNIVERSITY

Kingston University, River House, Kingston upon Thames
KT1 1LQ (Tel 0181 547 2000, Fax 0181 547 7093)
Map 5

STUDENT ENQUIRIES: Admissions Office
APPLICATIONS: UCAS

Broad study areas: Accounting and business; architecture; art & design; built environment; computing and IT; health sciences; humanities; education; languages and law; science and engineering; social sciences. (Subject details are in the *Subjects and Places Index.*)

Founded: 1970 as Kingston Poly, ex Kingston Colleges of Technology and Art and Gipsy Hill College of Education; university status in 1992. **Main undergraduate awards:** BA, BEd, BSc, BEng, LLB, MEng. **Awarding body:** Kingston University. **Site:** 4 campuses: Penrhyn Road, Knights Park, Kingston Hill and Roehampton Vale – all in 3 mile radius and linked by free university bus service. **Access:** British Rail (Kingston or Surbiton stations), buses. **Academic features:** Courses include aerospace engineering, history of ideas, geographical information systems, landscape architecture, furniture design, resources & the environment. **Special features:** Links with Gateway School of Recording and Music; modern music rehearsal hall and recording studio. Extra-curricular visiting lecture programme. **Europe:** All students are able to study a language. Formal Erasmus links with a number of European universities/colleges in a range of different subjects. **Library:** On each campus, total of 350,000 books, 3,000 periodicals; 930 study places; short loan service for course books; slide library at Knights Park, music library at Kingston Hill. Annual expenditure on library materials, £61.52 per FTE student. **Other learning facilities:** Large academic computing facilities; 2 language labs. **Welfare:** Holistic health and counselling centre on each site (GPs, dentists, nurse-counsellors, pschotherapist, hypnotherapist, osteopath, chiropodist, aromomatherapists, reflexologists); ecumenical chaplain and contacts in all faiths. **Careers:** Information, advice and placement service. **Amenities:** Guild of Students' facilities on each campus; wide range of clubs and societies; bars, shops, travel shop, catering outlets, second-hand book shop. **Sporting facilities:** State of the art fitness centre and aerobics studio, gym, playing fields for all major sports, tennis courts; wide range of sporting activities and sports clubs.

Accommodation: In 1995/96, 2,261 students in university accommodation: self-catering places at £48–£56 per week, Sept–June. Also head tenancy schemes. Students live in privately owned accommodation for 2+ years: £45–£55 per week for lodgings, £60–£75 half-board. **Term time work:** University's policy to allow term time work for first degree students. Some term (and vac) work on campus; also help finding work off campus (university advertises JobCentre posts and has strong links with local employers); plenty of part time work in town centre. **Hardship funds:** Total available in 1995/96: £337,250 government access funds, 808 students helped; £51,558 own funds, 193 helped. Emergency loans for late grants and unforseen emergencies.

Duration of first degree courses: 3 years; **others:** 4 years (sandwich, language and undergraduate masters courses). **Total first degree students 1995/96:** 11,017; **total BEd students:** 545. **Overseas students (including EU):** 843. **Mature students:** 2,440. **Male:female ratio:** 1:1. **Teaching staff:** 542 full-time, 400 part-time. **Total full-time students 1995/96:** 9,892. **Postgraduate students:** 1,946. **First degree tuition fees:** Home students, paying their own fees in 1996/97, paid £750 (classroom), £1,600 (lab/studio); Overseas students £5,500 (classroom), £7,000 (lab/studio).

WHAT IT'S LIKE   Contrary to the appearance of the official prospectus, Kingston is not all romantic sunsets over the Thames and peaceful strolls down tree-lined boulevards. The truth? Well, here it is. Kingston town centre is a road planner's ultimate revenge, with traffic wardens to match. Too many cars, too many buses, and far too many students. But shopping facilities are excellent and so is public transport into central London (Waterloo 20 mins). Many excellent restaurants to suit all tastes and budgets; several popular student pubs although London prices make Guild bars the usual choice; three very average night clubs with student nights on Mondays and Wednesdays and a three-screen cinema. University is renowned for its fashion and engineering departments. Many sandwich and modular courses, work experience opportunities and field trips. Erasmus scheme means good relations with European academic institutions and strong languages; also linked to some American colleges. Changing course obviously depends on requirements and subscriptions but generally university is helpful. Overall academic standard is very good but food is dreadful (go to Guild snack bars instead: better quality and inexpensive). Kingston University Guild of Students (KUGOS) is very active, although not very radical; provides major Kingston venues and ents – weekly bands, discos, comedians, cabarets and films. There are 4 bars, 3 shops, over 80 social, cultural, sporting and political clubs; a confidential welfare service; campus banking and insurance; travel agency and many part-time jobs. Most active societies are rugby, law, sub-aqua, canoeing and mountaineering. Accommodation situation improved; two new halls of residence with 800 places, but expensive. Good rented accommodation is scarce and very expensive (approx £50 pw) and things getting harder. It's not all bad though: bus services are good and many students live in slightly cheaper surrounding areas of New Malden, Surbiton, Tolworth and Norbiton. No such thing as a typical Kingston student; most are from south or south-east and from private or grammar schools. There is every type here ranging from the hyper trendy art students at Knights Park to conscientious engineers at Canbury Park and finally to the Golf GTI brigade in the law department at Kingston Hill. Anything goes. Money is the bane of every student's life and Kingston is not a cheap place to live; however, if you do find somewhere to sleep and don't own a car, it's a great place to be. Most students end up staying in the area, so it can't be all bad!

PAUPER NOTES   **Accommodation:** Expensive. **Drink:** Guild bars average 30–35p per pint cheaper than pub prices. Popular student pubs include The Kingston Mill, The Ram and The Railway Tavern. **Eats:** Good Guild snacks available (pizzas, rolls, samosas etc). Good restaurants, Indian, Italian, Chinese, everywhere. **Ents:** Options cinema half price twilight shows around 6.00pm (3 films). Guild provides major Kingston venues – weekly bands, discos, films. **Sports:** Squash, tennis, golf clubs – cheaper through the Guild. University fitness centre, playing fields, tennis courts. **Hardship funds:** Small Guild loans. **Travel:** Guild travel office (STA). Hitching bad. **Work:** Many part time jobs in the Guild; in Kingston, work in pubs, shops, restaurants. About 50% work in term time – about 20–30% work locally in vac – most travel into London, or Gatwick and Heathrow.

MORE INFO?   Enquiries to SU 0181 549 9961.

ALUMNI (EDITORS' PICK)   Glenda Bailey (editor of Marie Claire).

LABAN CENTRE

Laban Centre for Movement and Dance, Laurie Grove,
New Cross, London SE14 6NH
(Tel 0181 692 4070, Fax 0181 694 8749) Map 5

STUDENT ENQUIRIES: Course information.
APPLICATIONS: Direct

Broad study area: Dance.

Founded: 1945 in Manchester. **Main undergraduate award:** BA. **Awarding body:** City University. **Site:** South East London. **Access:** New Cross or New Cross Gate stations (underground and BR from Charing Cross); various buses. **Academic features:** In addition to degree courses, offers a range of diploma and postgraduate (MA, PhD) courses eg dance theatre, dance movement therapy, teaching and notating dance, visual design for dance. **Special features:** Visiting artists as teachers and performers. Annual international summer school, junior year abroad scheme for US students. Access to buildings for the disabled. EFL taught. **Library:** Dance collection, related subjects, notation scores, periodicals, record collection, Peter Williams dance archive, 40–45 study places, access to City University library and IT facilities. Annual expenditure on library materials, £110 per FTE student. **Welfare:** Physiotherapist, counsellor, chaplains. **Careers:** Information and advice. **Amenities:** 13 purpose-built studios, sound studio, music rooms, modern studio theatre and wardrobe department. Fully equipped pilates studio for body training. In-house publications: *Dance Theatre Journal* and *International Working Papers*. **Employment:** Dance peformance, teaching, community art, dance animateurs, arts administration.

Accommodation: No college accommodation. Students live in privately owned accommodation for whole course: rents c.£50 per week for self-catering. Few first degree students live at home. **Term time work:** Centre's policy to allow term time work for full-time first degree students (99% believed to work); limit of 3 hours per day. Term (and vac) work occasionally available on campus. **Hardship funds:** Small interest-free loans available for short term.

Duration of first degree courses: 3 years. **Total first degree students 1995/96:** 190. **Overseas students:** 27%. **Male/female ratio:** 1:3. **Teaching staff:** 22 full-time, 25 part-time. **Total full-time students 1995/96:** 300. **Postgraduate students:** 100. **First degree tuition fees:** Home students, paying their own fees in 1996/97, paid £7,500 (LEA award may contribute to the fees).

WHAT IT'S LIKE   Housed in a converted church with purpose-built dance studios and pilates studio, near Goldsmiths campus. Students can use many Goldsmiths facilities, also workshops at Greenwich Dance Agency. BR and tube available for easy access to central London. (But don't travel alone at night; use common sense.) SU has no sabbatical officer, but is run by a committee of students. Active politically and socially, especially in the context of dance and its role in society. Challenging courses – ballet, Limon and Graham – and many choreographic opportunities. Heavy timetable – 8.45 am until 7.30 pm some days and weekends when necessary, plus written work especially for BA students.

Drop-out rate high. Student financial problems causing more to drop out; lots of students forced to work during term as well as vacations. Many overseas students. Range of courses and overall teaching standard is high. Relations between students and management is improving through active commitment on both sides. The Laban Centre is very liberal and supports groups of all kinds (eg religious, lesbian etc).

PAUPER NOTES Accommodation: Accommodation list available; SU can help. **Drink:** Goldsmiths' SU bar next door, many local pubs. Marquis of Granby, New Cross Inn, Rosemary Branch, Fox 'n' Firkin, Studio Bar, Gipsy Moth, Rose Inn. **Eats:** Goldsmiths' provide vegetarian food. Wholefood Café, Mary's Café, Coffee Shak, Escaped. Many Indian/Chinese/Italian restaurants (reasonably priced) nearby. **Ents:** Goldsmith SU very active with discos and bands quite regularly. Bonnie Bird theatre has dance companies regularly. Greenwich Cinema. The Venue (for bands). **Sports:** Ladywell Leisure Centre (half price admission with vantage card). Deptford swimming baths. **Hardship funds:** College loans fund (small amounts and not for long). **Travel:** Several bus routes, train/tube (New Cross, New Cross Gate). Lisa Ullman fund provides opportunity for dance students to travel abroad. **Work:** Local work in pubs, restaurants. Jobs in college, eg office work, cleaning, repairs, door duties.

MORE INFO? Get students' Alternative Prospectus. Enquiries to SU (0181 691 7840).

ALUMNI (EDITORS' PICK) The Cholmondeleys, David Massingham, Matthew Bourne; Lea Anderson, Jacob Marley (choreographers); Mark Murphy (V-tol dance company).

LAMPETER UNIVERSITY

University of Wales, Lampeter, Dyfed, SA48 7ED
(Tel 01570 422351, Fax 01570 423 423) Map 3

STUDENT ENQUIRIES: Recruitment Officer
APPLICATIONS: UCAS

Broad study areas: Humanities, divinity, management, women's studies. (Subject details are in the *Subjects and Places Index*.)

Founded: 1822. **Structural features:** Part of Wales University (since 1971). **Main undergraduate awards:** BA, BD. **Awarding body:** Wales University. **Site:** Lampeter town centre. **Academic features:** Modular structure; course options in eg church history, Islamic studies and anthropology. Information studies available to all first year students. **Europe:** 10% first degree students take a language as part of course and 5% spend 6 months or more abroad. Part-time French and German courses available. Formal exchange links with universities/colleges in Western Europe. **Library:** Main and Founders libraries; 200,000 volumes, 950 periodicals, 190 study places. Annual expenditure on library materials, £61.65 per FTE student. **Specialist collections:** Tracts collection; early Welsh periodicals; Bibles, prayer-books, hymnals, catechisms and ballads; mss collection including 15th-century Books of Hours. **Welfare:** Nurses, counsellor, chaplain; doctor close by. Residential facilities for disabled students; children's crèche. **Careers:** Information, advice and placement service. **Amenities:** Bookshop on campus; purpose-built SU. **Sporting facilities:** Sports hall; new multigym; playing fields less than 5 mins from campus; free use of town swimming pool; college sailing club at Aberaeron.

Accommodation: In 1995/96, 92% of first year students in university accommodation: 720 places available (435 for first years): 165 full-board places (all for first years) £63 per week and 215 (140 first years) at £38 + pay-as-you-eat, term time only; and 352 self-catering places (130 for first years) at £20–£42.50 per week, Oct-June or longer. Students live in privately owned accommodation for 1+ year: £30–£35 per week for self-catering (exclusive of bills). **Term time work:** University policy to allow term time work for first degree students (50% believed to work). Term work available on campus in SU bars; admin, clerical and computing in vac. **Hardship funds:** Total available in 1995/96: £24,000 government access funds, about 70 students helped.

Duration of first degree courses: 3 years; **others:** 4 years (philosophy, Welsh, modern languages). **Total first degree students 1995/96:** 1,600. **Male/female ratio:** 1:1. **Teaching staff:** 85 full-time, 30 part-time. **Total full-time students 1995/96:** 1,440. **Postgraduate students:** 150. **First degree tuition fees:** Home students, paying their own fees in 1996/97, paid £750 (classroom), £1600 (lab/studio); Overseas: £4,750 (package deal including accommodation £6,500).

WHAT IT'S LIKE   It's situated in beautiful rural west Wales with all the amenities necessary to have a good social and academic time. Accommodation good (if on the small side); all first years automatically qualify for a place on campus with the option of returning onto campus in the third year. There are no visiting restrictions and few other restrictions although some halls are classed as 'quiet'. Local rents are rising (£30–£40 so still relatively cheap) and students being pushed further away from campus. Student population mixed: high percentage of mature students; large number of Welsh students (many Welsh speaking); 15% are from overseas (Greece, America, France, Germany, Spain) with exchange schemes running with Canadian and Swedish universities. Lampeter's secluded position means that the entertainment tends to be centred on the Union building, much of it home-grown although regular visits from large named bands ensure a diverse ents diary. The Union itself is quite active but not at all party-political; many clubs and societies play an integral role in students' lives. Squash and tennis courts, multi-gym, sports hall and redgras hockey pitch on campus; sports pitches 5 minutes walk away.

PAUPER NOTES   **Accommodation:** Commercial housing market becoming crowded but cheap isolated dwellings often available out of town. Caravans also available. **Drinks:** Union bar, cheapest hostelry in town; new extention soon. 12 pubs in town so plenty of choice. **Eats:** SU Pooh's Corner caters for all manner of diets: vegetarian, vegan, meat eaters and cheap. **Ents:** Regular bands and comedy club. Two films a week, trips to Swansea cinema, lots of discos. **Sports:** No charge for sports hall on campus, squash courts, town swimming pool. **Hardship funds:** College access fund; Union provides small bridging loans when necessary. **Travel:** Isolated so reliance on local buses. Nearest rail stations Aberystwyth and Carmarthen. **Work:** SU employs around 60 students in bar, shop, catering, stewards and crew. Work sometimes available in town.

MORE INFO?   Ring SU President on 01570 422619

ALUMNI (EDITORS' PICK)   T E Lawrence (of Arabian fame), Sulak Sivaraska (Thai human rights campaigner), Sue Slipman (National Council for One Parent Families).

CAN'T FIND WHAT YOU'RE LOOKING FOR? USE THE INDEX!

LANCASTER UNIVERSITY

Lancaster University, University House, Lancaster LA1 4YW
(Tel 01524 65201, Fax 01524 846243) Map 2

STUDENT ENQUIRIES: Undergraduate Admissions Office
APPLICATIONS: UCAS

Broad study areas: Sciences, engineering, management, social sciences, humanities, education, creative arts. (Subject details are in the *Subjects and Places Index.*)

Founded: 1964. **Main undergraduate awards:** BA, BA(QTS), BBA, BMus, BSc, LLB, BEng, MChem, MEng, MMath, MPhys, MSci, MStat. **Awarding body:** Lancaster University. **Site:** Single campus at Bailrigg, south of Lancaster. **Access:** On main London-Glasgow line; A6 and M6 main roads. **Academic features:** Flexible course structure makes it easy to change course and allows specialisation. Flexible BSc combined science; undergraduate masters degrees in biological sciences, maths, statistics, physics and chemistry. Mature students welcomed. **Special features:** Medici String Quartet (artists-in-residence). Exchange programme in many subjects with US universities. **Europe:** 15% first degree students take a language as part of course and 8% spend 6 months or more abroad. Exchange programmes in many departments (particularly strong links with Copenhagen University and Copenhagen Business School). **Library:** About 1,000,000 items, over 3,000 periodicals, 820 reader places; short loan system for course books. Annual expenditure on library materials, £116.18 per FTE student. **Specialist collections:** Redlich collection (music); Quaker collection; library of Burnley Grammar School. **Other learning facilities:** Language resource centre, TV studio. **Welfare:** Collegiate advisers, doctors, dentists, psychiatrist, chaplains, professional student counsellors. Residential facilities for disabled and some married students; nursery (102 places). **Careers:** Information, placement and advice service. **Amenities:** Bookshop; varied and numerous eating places; various shops and banks on campus; Ruskin Centre; Peter Scott art gallery; Jack Hylton music rooms; Nuffield theatre. **Sporting facilities:** Wide range of sporting and recreational facilities (including swimming pool, sauna, solarium, and rock-climbing wall); outdoor centre in the Yorkshire Dales.

Accommodation: In 1995/96, 54% of all students in university accommodation, 90% of first years (all who want it). Approx 4,000 self-catering places (3,281 for first degree students) at £32–£47 per week, term time or longer. Students live in privately owned accommodation for 1+ years: £32–£40 per week for self-catering, plus bills. **Term time work:** No university policy on part time work. Term (and vac) work available in SU bars etc; also placements and vacation work advertised by SU and careers service. **Hardship funds:** Total available in 1995/96: £179,490 government access funds, 610 students helped; £32,000 own funds, 31 students helped; plus £50,000 other funds, 35 helped. Special help: mature students with family commitments, lone parents, students with special needs; other funds available for overseas students. Some funds available prior to starting course, mainly for postgraduates.

Duration of first degree courses: 3 years; **others:** 4 years (undergraduate masters, languages and sandwich courses); 5 years (sandwich MEng). **Total first degree students 1995/96:** 7,630. **Overseas students:** 1,508. **Mature students:** 28%. **Male/female ratio:** 1:1. **Total teaching staff:** 765. **Total full-time students 1995/96:** 8,756. **Postgraduate students:** 2,703 (inc part-time). **First degree tuition fees:** Home students, paying their own fees in 1996/97, paid £750 (classroom), £1,600 (lab/studio); Overseas students £6,100–£7,085 (classroom), £8,065 (lab/studio).

WHAT IT'S LIKE An attractive modern site in pleasant grounds 2 miles south of Lancaster. Very accessible – M6 and London-Scotland rail link and good access to other major cities. Excellent location for outdoor activity – particularly sea and Lake District. Reasonable accommodation for 1st and some 3rd year students, in 8 colleges on main campus. Each college has own bar, student-run JCR and tradition; keen rivalry between them produces very good atmosphere. Active and powerful SU campaigning and providing information including: strong advice centre (abortion loans, HIV and disabilities awareness campaigns, campus watch scheme); athletic union (over 30 clubs); non-sporting and cultural societies; very good SU shop; SU-run newspaper and radio station. Social events (Sugar House nightclub, on-campus, concerts, balls etc). Courses extremely flexible – three subjects in first year, nearly all with some continuous assessment. Chance to study abroad in 2nd year. Staff generally very helpful and friendly. High proportion of mature students. Friendly university; excellent atmosphere, international flavour.

PAUPER NOTES **Accommodation:** University headlease scheme; flats on campus. Married flats available. Graduate college on campus. **Drink:** 9 bars on campus, lots of local pubs; good choice, reasonable prices. **Eats:** Cheap chippy, pizza place and excellent burger bar on campus. Usual fast food, takeaways plus good international range of restaurants in town. **Ents:** Excellent off-campus student nightclub (Sugar House), good bands on and off campus; film club showing latest releases; theatre group excellent. **Sports:** Excellent sports centre on campus; swimming pool; good athletic union. **Hardship funds:** Limited funds available from university and from individual colleges. **Travel:** Good hitching scheme. Buses regular (1, 2 or 3-term passes). Women's safe transport; cycle path. Some travel scholarships from colleges. **Work:** Term-time, some in Sugar House and bars. In vacs, tourist and conference trade, catering department.

MORE INFO? Get Alternative Prospectus. Ring Lee Devlin 01524 65201 x 2206 or Education & Welfare Office x 2202.

BUZZ-WORDS JCR (Junior Common Room), SCR (Senior Common Room), LUSU (Lancaster University Students' Union).

ALUMNI (EDITORS' PICK) Eric Bolton (Senior Chief Inspector of Schools); Robert Fisk (award-winning correspondent of *The Times*); Simon Smith (RU England International); Gary Waller MP; Michael Handley, MEP; Green (Scritti Politi, rock band).

HOW TO START? *SEE SHORTLISTING*, PAGE 535

LEEDS METROPOLITAN UNIVERSITY

Leeds Metropolitan University, Calverley Street, Leeds LS1 3HE
(Tel 0113 283 3113, Fax 0113 283 3114) Map 2

STUDENT ENQUIRIES: Course Enquiries Office
APPLICATIONS: UCAS (SWAS for DipHE social work)

Broad study areas: Business, art and design, health sciences, social sciences, education, engineering, informatics. (Subject details are in the *Subjects and Places Index*.)

Founded: 1970 as Leeds Poly from amalgamation of various 19th colleges. University status in 1992. **Main undergraduate awards:** BA, BEd, BSc, BEng, LLB. **Awarding body:** Leeds Metropolitan University. **Site:** 2 campuses: Leeds City Campus in city centre and 100-acre Beckett Park Campus, 3 miles to the north. **Access:** Frequent buses link campuses. Good road, rail and air links. **Academic features:** Degree courses in consumer services management, European marketing and public relations; information systems for business. **Europe:** 15% first degree students take a language as part of course and 12% spend 6 months or more abroad. Study or work placement abroad offered on the majority of courses. Formal exchange links with over 100 universities/colleges in western Europe. **Library:** Central library, plus smaller campus and subject libraries; 500,000 volumes in total, 2,500 periodicals; extensive AV and IT-based resources; over 1,000 study places. Annual expenditure on library materials, £44.06 per FTE student. **Welfare:** 2 student health centres staffed by nurses; FPA; physiotherapy service; counsellors; budget adviser; students' union welfare officer; chaplains. Childcare advice available; Nightline service; international students advisory group. **Careers:** Information, advice and placement service; job shop. **Amenities:** Bank and shop on both campuses; SU building with bars and other recreational facilities. **Sporting facilities:** Specialist PE facilities, including swimming pool, dance studio, floodlit all-weather athletics track and field, regional gymnastics centre, tennis courts, health and fitness suite.

Accommodation: In 1995/96, 10% of all students in university accommodation, 33% first years (plans to house 50% first years by 1997). 1,250 first year places available: self-catering/half-board, £31.20–£52 per week, Sept–June. Some students live in privately owned accommodation for whole course: rents £30–£40 per week for self-catering in shared house, £45–£65 for B&B, £55–£75 for half-board, up to £85 with weekend meals. **Term time work:** University's policy to allow term time work for full-time first degree students (majority believed to work). Term (and vac) work available on campus, clerical work in eg admissions; also university Jobshop helps find work off campus. **Hardship funds:** Total available in 1995/96: £200,000 government access funds, average £300 awarded; £10,000 own funds, 30 students helped. Special help: self-financing students, mature students, students with children; own funds also available for overseas students.

Duration of first degree courses: 3 years full-time; 4 years sandwich **Total first degree students 1995/96:** 7,942 (full-time and sandwich); **BEd students:** 700. **Overseas students:** 295. **Mature students (full-time):** 5,940. **Male/female ratio:** 1:1. **Teaching staff:** 658 full-time,

475 part-time. **Total full-time and sandwich students 1995/96:** 10,666. **Postgraduate students:** 2,506. **First degree tuition fees:** Home students, paying their own fees in 1996/97, paid £750 (classroom), £1,600 (lab/studio); Overseas students £5,740 (classroom), £6,660 (lab/studio); plus registration fee.

WHAT IT'S LIKE   Leeds is not only the gateway to the north, but an expanding city full of young people. It has two universities, many shopping precincts, including the expensive Victorian arcade, a huge market, and an excellent football team. Many shops, cinemas and theatres offer good discounts to students. Leeds Metropolitan Uni is the largest HE institution in the north east with three main sites and a number of smaller ones. Many students live in Headingley, Burley and Hyde Park. Halls of residence include Beckett Park, Highfield, the plush Sugarwell Court and new Kirkstall Breweries halls with a bar. The SU provides three bars (capacities 600–1500), numerous cafés, two shops, sports and cultural clubs, discos, concerts, live comedy, bank facilities, a fully confidential student advice service and almost everything you need to survive student life apart from paying you to be there! Metro Uni students are usually distinguishable from the Uni 'up the road' because they look less like the stereotypical student. For every aspect of student life Leeds Metro Uni is the place to be.

PAUPER NOTES   **Accommodation:** Headingley and Hyde Park completely student orientated, hardly any normal people. **Drink:** SU cheaper than pubs with regular happy hours. Skyrack and Oak popular. The Faversham for the discerning clubber. **Eats:** Cheap hot and cold food on campus, with everything else nearby. **Ents:** Best bops in the north at city site. Regular free bands at Beckett Park site. Major bands and comedy at reduced rate in SU. Some of the best clubs in the north: Vague, Back 2 Basics, Up yer Ronson. **Sports:** Probably the best sports facilities in Yorkshire on campus. Swimming pools, weights room, regular aerobics, gym, most sports catered for. **Hardship funds:** Available if desperate. **Travel:** Usual discounts. **Work:** Job shop run by Uni. SU jobs (security, bar); off campus (supermarkets, restaurants, bars, clubs, pubs). Lots available.

ALUMNI (EDITORS' PICK)   Marc Almond (Soft Cell), Sir Henry Moore, Ron Pickering, Mick Hill, Bill Slater, Les Bettinson.

LEEDS UNIVERSITY

University of Leeds, Leeds LS2 9JT
(Tel 0113 243 1751, Fax 0113 233 3991) Map 2

STUDENT ENQUIRIES: Access and Recruitment Office
APPLICATIONS: UCAS

Broad study areas: Business and economics, science and engineering, medicine & dentistry, humanities, law, European languages. (Subject details are in the *Subjects and Places Index*.)

Founded: 1904. **Main undergraduate awards:** BA, BBcS, BChD, BEng, MEng, BSc, MBChB, LLB. **Awarding body:** Leeds University. **Site:** Main central site close to city centre. **Access:** Nearby bus and railway stations; bus, or within walking distance of halls of residence.

Academic features: Many degrees modularised and available part-time. **Europe:** 10% first degree students study a language, most of whom spend a period abroad. Language tuition generally available. Formal exchange links with 100+ universities/colleges across Europe plus 53 Erasmus exchanges involving 41 departments across all faculties. **Library:** Over 2,500,000 volumes including microfilm, 3,000 study places. Annual expenditure on library materials, £116 per FTE student. **Other learning facilities:** Computing service, language centre, media services. **Welfare:** Health centre, advisers for disabled students, day nursery, chaplaincies. **Careers:** Advice and placement service. **Amenities:** Union with bars, coffee lounges, discos, newspaper; 600-seat theatre. **Sporting facilities:** Two sports halls on campus; sports ground within 3 miles; outdoor huts in Lake District and Pennines; Olympic standard swimming pool and golf in Leeds.

Accommodation: In 1995/96, 34% of all students in university accommodation, 95% of first years (all who chose it). 6,513 places available (4,883 for first years): 850 full-board places (765 for first years) from £75 per week and 1,020 half-board places (918 for first years) from £63 per week, term time only; 4,627 self-catering places (3,200 for first years) at £30–£41 per week (£44–£46 ensuite), October–early July. 600 more places planned. Students live in privately owned accommodation for 1–2 years: £32–£46 per week for self-catering (other types of accommodation limited; also little inexpensive accommodation for couples, with or without children). **Hardship funds:** Total available in 1995/96: £345,024 government access funds, 840 students helped; £50,000 from charitable funds, average award £800. Special help: single parents, mature students, self-financing students and others who can demonstrate hardship; limited other funds available for overseas students facing hardship, in final year.

Duration of first degree courses: 3 or 4 years; **others:** 5 years. **Total first degree students 1995/96:** 15,649. **Overseas students:** 2,063. **Mature students:** 1,979. **Male/female ratio:** 7:6. **Teaching staff:** 1,330. **Total full-time students 1995/96:** 17,571. **Postgraduate students:** 4,477 (full-time). **First degree tuition fees:** Home students, paying their own fees in 1996/97, paid £880; Overseas students £6,080 (classroom), £8,070 (lab/studio), £7,080 (classroom and lab combined), £14,850 (clinical).

WHAT IT'S LIKE   One of Britain's largest universities with nearly 20,000 students. Vast range of courses cater for most tastes. Campus about 10 minutes' walk from city centre, avoiding isolation of some campus universities, yet retaining separate identity. University accommodation is in halls and flats which stretch from the campus to the north of the city, about 4 miles away. Most first years live in and then move out into private accommodation – mainly concentrated in the Hyde Park and Headingley area, 10 minutes' walk from the university. Very large SU supports 180 societies and 53 sports clubs (including sub aqua, hunt saboteurs, ballroom dancing and lacrosse) and provides a very wide range of services. SU boasts 4 bars (and must be Britain's biggest bitter outlet!), stationery shop, ABTA registered travel shop, launderette, opticians, hair salon, print room and exam paper sales, bookshop, card and ticket shop, fully equipped games room and a concert venue (which has put on acts such as Elastica, Pogues, Underworld, Corduroy PNEI, Transglobal Underground). Impressive welfare services with advice from 6 full-time staff. Leeds is a large city of ¾ million people, with a well-equipped city centre. For those of sporting bent, there's football at Elland Road, rugby league and cricket at Headingley and an international swimming pool. Reasonable choice of theatres and cinemas, both large and small, including the West Yorkshire Playhouse. A lively and diverse city, recommended to anyone.

PAUPER NOTES   **Accommodation:** First years guaranteed university accommodation. New married quarters. **Drink:** 4 bars in SU, cheap beer. Plenty of nearby friendly student orientated pubs, several good real ale pubs. **Eats:** Student 'meal deals' in uni refectory, good value. Many Indian and Italian restaurants, some very cheap. Six restaurants/take-outs opposite university. **Ents:** Regular gigs in the SU. Many clubs in town. Local bands include Back to Basics, Up yer Ronson, Vague, Orbit. Thriving dance scene. **Sports:** 53 sports clubs. Well-equipped sports centre on campus. International swimming pool just down the road. **Hardship funds:** Welfare loans available to everyone. Larger grants and loans available for worst cases. **Travel:** Some scholarships. Travel shop in the SU building. Leeds is on the M1 – excellent rail and coach links and easy hitching. **Work:** Part-time work in union bars, library and clerical posts. Bar and shop work available in town.

MORE INFO?   Get students' Alternative Prospectus. Enquiries to SU Education Secretary, (0113 231 4223).

ALUMNI (EDITORS' PICK)   Sir Geoffrey Allen FRS, Sir George Porter, Mark Knopfler (Dire Straits), Nicholas Witchel (BBC newsreader), Jack Straw MP, Andy Kershaw, Andrew Eldritch (of Sisters of Mercy), Marc Almond.

LEICESTER UNIVERSITY

University of Leicester, University Road, Leicester LE1 7RH
(Tel 0116 252 2522, Fax 0116 252 2200) Map 2

STUDENT ENQUIRIES: Admissions & Student Recruitment
Office (Tel 0116 252 5281/2674, Fax 0116 252 2447,
E-mail admissions:le.ac.uk, Web http://www.le.ac.uk/)
APPLICATIONS: UCAS (direct if occasional, part-time or with
study abroad)

Broad study areas: Arts, science and engineering, social sciences, law, medicine. (Subject details are in the *Subjects and Places Index*.)

Founded: 1919, receiving charter in 1957. **Main undergraduate awards:** BA, BSc, BEng, LLB, MBChB, MChem, MEng, MMath, MPhys. **Awarding body:** Leicester University. **Site:** 1 mile from Leicester city centre. **Access:** Railway station (15 minutes' walk); M1 and M69 motorways 5 miles from campus. **Academic features:** All courses except medicine are modular (basic teaching unit a 12-week 10-credit module). Some courses allow study in USA and elsewhere. **Special features:** Research centres focusing on football hooliganism, youth employment, public order, federalism. Genetic fingerprinting discovered here by Prof Sir Alec Jeffreys. Halls of residence set in Botanic Gardens. **Europe:** 14% first degree students take a language as part of course and 7% spend 6 months or more abroad. Languages built into a number of degree courses and available to all students. Formal exchange links with over 35 EU universities/colleges in a wide range of subjects. **Library:** Main library has 923,000 volumes, plus CD-Rom, microfilm, videos etc; multiple copies of prescribed textbooks on short loan. 1,085 study places. Also 3 subsidiary libraries. Annual expenditure on library materials, £98 per FTE student. **Specialist collections:** Robjohn's Collection of Bibles; works of Bunyan; English local history. **Other learning facilities:** Audio-visual services, computer centre, Apple Mac labs, language laboratory, university bookshop, Leicester University Press; student learning centre to develop study skills. **Welfare:** Doctors, student health education project (SHEP), welfare officers, financial advice for student budgeting, pastoral care in university accommodation, personal tutors, FPA, psychiatrist, counsellors, chaplains, student legal advice centre, Nightline telephone contact service. Nursery (independent) with favourable terms for student parents, playscheme at half terms; study support centre for students with special needs. **Careers:** Information and advice service. **Amenities:** Bookshop, travel centre, nightclub, disco, general shops and banks on site; Leicester University Theatre (links with Haymarket and Phoenix professional theatres in Leicester); Archduke Trio (resident chamber music group), 70 student societies. **Sporting facilities:** Excellent sports facilities including fine athletics tracks, astroturf pitches, fitness centre and two sports halls; 40+ sports clubs. **Employment:** 31% further study and training; 16% public sector; 24% industry and commerce.

Accommodation: In 1995/96, 60% of all students in university accommodation, 98% first years. 3,894 places available, 2,125 for first years: 1,841 half-board places (1,341 for first years) at £54.74–£73.64 per week, term time only; 2,053 self-catering places (850 for first years) at £34.79–£47.25 per week, Sept–June or longer. Privately owned accommodation: £35–£70 per week for self-catering (info available from SU). Small number of first degree students live at home. **Term time work:** University policy to allow term time work for first degree students. Term (and vac) work available on campus in bars, accommodation, clerical; SU Employment Centre helps find work on and off campus. **Hardship funds:** Total available in 1995/96: £210,000 government access funds, grants and loans, 640 students helped; £8,000 own funds, 125 helped (mainly short-term loans), plus £33,600 SU short term loans and other funds (456 students helped). Special help: students with special needs, those with dependants, mature students, self-financing students and those with field course requirements during long vac; own funds also available for international students (£5,000), short-term loans for others. International student scholarships available before the start of the course, £25,000, up to 15 students benefit.

Duration of first degree courses: 3 years; **others:** 4–5years; medicine 5 years. **Total first degree students 1995/96:** 6,770. **Overseas students:** 576. **Mature students:** 1,067. **Male/female ratio:** 1:1. **Teaching staff:** 603 full-time, 43 part-time. **Total full-time students 1995/96:** 8,516. **Postgraduate students:** 1,746. **First degree tuition fees:** Home students, paying their own fees in 1996/97, paid £750; Overseas students £6,030 (classroom), £8,040 (lab), £14,835 (clinical).

WHAT IT'S LIKE   University close to the city centre. Most first years given places in self-catering accommodation (near campus) or halls of residence (about 3 miles away in attractive area of Oadby). Halls are mixed and single sex (students choose) and a bus service and night-time SU minibus link them to campus. 3 years in university accommodation possible but SU-run property management scheme ensures private accommodation for those wanting to live out. The large number of postgraduate and overseas students have excellent SU support services. Half term play scheme and generous nursery subsidy for student parents. Campus constantly busy with union building and library open seven days a week. Restaurants and cafés all over campus cater for wide range of tastes. SU has 99 different societies; sports association over 40 active and friendly affiliated clubs. Excellent commercial services in SU building including large shop, travel agent and night club. Ents programme extremely full and varied with 3 main venues in SU plus big ones in town. Large number of international cultural events as well as discos, films, quizzes and top name bands. Plenty of scope to get involved with fortnightly union council meetings, campaigns and various committees. Politically moderate – no racist, sexist or homophobic behaviour allowed in building. Plenty of opportunities to make friends, meet partners; no restrictions on hours. Extensive information for all students on birth control, Aids;

confidential pregnancy testing and advice centre open most of week. Few students have cars – parking not allowed on campus, though each hall has car parking space. City is extremely busy, with all kinds of shops, pubs and clubs and a huge student population. Plenty of shops, cinemas, theatres offer student discount scheme. Biggest academic departments are medicine and law; large number of scientists, and thriving and varied arts and humanities courses. Work assessed by combination of course work and exams; more emphasis on continuous assessment since courses modularised. Relatively easy to change course. SU education and research office to help with any academic problems. Students come from all over the world and there is an excellent mixture of creeds, colours and social backgrounds. Typical student involved in at least 1 society or sports club – make lots of friends through that as well as hall or house. Work taken fairly seriously but everyone takes time to enjoy. Graduates go on to wide range of vocations and jobs plus huge range of postgraduate courses.

PAUPER NOTES **Accommodation:** Hall accommodation for c.1500 students. Self-catering flats for approx 1,500. Others live in private accommodation. SU runs flat-finding service and property management scheme. **Drink:** SU bars cheapest in city. Local breweries Hoskins, HOB (notable real ales), Everards (large Midlands brewery). **Eats:** SU refectory seats over 1,000 diners. Large central university restaurant plus numerous coffee bars around campus. Leicester notable for Indian food. Rise of Mexican, Cajun food restaurants in town – good atmosphere. **Ents:** New SU nightclub, The Venue, capacity 1,600; old club, The Asylum, still very popular. In-house ents weekly. **Sports:** 2 large university sports grounds, 3 miles from campus (1 adjacent to halls of residence); well-equipped sports hall on campus plus many training and fitness classes. **Hardship funds:** SU hardship fund and Vice-Chancellor's fund. Grants above £200 are rare. **Travel:** Regular bus service from halls to campus (3 miles). Leicester central, well connected for trains (London St Pancras 1¼ hrs). Good SU travel agent. **Work:** Union bar staff. Part-time work plentiful in Leicester. Union job agency and others in town centre are student friendly. About 50% work in term-time, usually in SU or through it; almost all students want to work over vac but hard to find.

MORE INFO?   President SU, 0116 2556282.

ALUMNI (EDITORS' PICK) Professor John Ashworth, Professor Laurie Taylor, Professor Alan Walters, Professor Malcolm Bradbury, David Puttnam, J H Plumb, C P Snow, Ron Pickering, Mike Nicholson, Sue Cook, John McVicker.

LINCOLN UNIVERSITY

Lincoln University Campus, Brayford Pool, Lincoln LN6 7TS (Tel 01522 882000, Fax 01522 882088; E-mail marketing @lincoln.ac.uk, Internet http:/www.lincoln.ac.uk) Map 2

STUDENT ENQUIRIES: Marketing department
APPLICATIONS: UCAS

Broad study areas: Communications and media, environment, food and nutrition, health, humanities, international relations, law, management, psychology, social policy, tourism. (Subject details are in the *Subjects and Places Index*.)

Founded: 1995 as the Lincoln Campus of Humberside University, becoming Lincolnshire & Humberside University in 1996. **Structural features:** Students study at either Lincoln or Humberside – no travel between them. (You can look up *Humberside* separately). **Main undergraduate awards:** BA, BSc. **Awarding body:** Lincolnshire & Humberside University. **Site:** Heart of historic city of Lincoln; additional site in Grimsby, relocating to Lincoln in 1999. **Academic features:** Students on a number of courses able to study in Europe or the US. Applications encouraged from those without formal entrance requirements. **Europe:** 25% first degree students take a language as part of course and 15% spend 6 months or more abroad. Formal exchange links with a number of 62 EU universities/colleges in a range of subjects. **Library:** 10,000 volumes (to increase year by year), 200 journals, 50 CD-Roms; inter-library loans from Humberside. **Other learning facilities:** 81 Pentium workstations with CD-Rom, language labs, IT labs, video editing suites, group study rooms (with large screen monitors); 200 personal study areas. **Welfare:** Advice and information centre includes careers, counselling, advice, chaplaincy, student revenue, accommodation. **Careers:** Information and advice service. **Amenities:** SU shop, snack bars, bars. **Sporting facilities:** Membership of nearby gym and other clubs.

Accommodation: In 1996/97, approx 300 self-catering places available, £40 per week (£44 ensuite), 42 week contract. **Term time work**: University's policy to allow term time work for full-time first degree students (50% believed to work). Term (and vac) work available on campus in SU bars, admin and promotion work; also careers service has noticeboard for temp and casual jobs, including vacancy details from local Job Centre. **Hardship funds:** Not yet known.

Duration of first degree courses: 3 years; **others:** 4 years (sandwich). **Total first degree students 1996/97:** 500 (will increase). **Overseas students**: 25%. **Teaching staff:** 59 (full-time and part-time). **First degree tuition fees:** Home students, paying their own fees in 1996/97, paid £1,300 (classroom), £2,770 (lab/studio); Overseas students £5,000 (classroom), £5,400 (lab/studio).

WHAT IT'S LIKE Brand new university campus, with easy access by road and rail (and set to be even easier when new link road built). It is a beautiful new building, currently housing 500 students who, although few in number, are enthusiastic. At present, campus has only a single academic building and the halls of residence. Lincoln itself is quickly adapting to the influx of students, but this will also take time. No Students Union office on campus yet, which can make life difficult, and union struggles without extra funding to provide the services students expect. So far, SU runs a small shop stocking a wide range of items; no SU recognised clubs or societies, although help is given wherever possible. While no university social and recreational facilities, students use local pubs, clubs and societies. An excellent opportunity to study and become an academic whiz-kid; socially and facility-wise, it leaves a lot to be desired at present but should improve when phase 2 is eventually finalised? But it's your chance to be there and help shape it.

PAUPER NOTES **Accommodation:** Very limited both in halls of residence and in the private sector. **Drink:** A few pubs beginning to compete for business. **Eats:** Loads of chippies; also Chinese, pizzas, kebabs, usual junk food. **Ents:** Kiss Nightclub (official student night on Thursdays, excellent bar promos and odd special event), Ritzy. Also cinemas and new retail park. **Sports:** Local clubs.

GET HOLD OF THE PROSPECTUSES

LIVERPOOL HOPE UNIVERSITY COLLEGE

Liverpool Hope University College, Hope Park, Liverpool
L16 9JD (Tel 0151 291 3000, Fax 0151 291 3100)
Map 2

STUDENT ENQUIRIES: Admissions Office
APPLICATIONS: UCAS

Broad study areas: Education, humanities, social sciences, creative & expressive arts, environmental & biological sciences. (Subject details are in the *Subjects and Places Index.*)

Founded: 1980. **Main undergraduate awards:** BA, BEd, BSc, BDesign. **Awarding body:** Liverpool University. **Site:** Single site on rural outskirts of Liverpool. **Access:** Bus to Liverpool city centre; M62 within one mile. **Academic features:** Degree courses in American studies, theology, design, European studies, health and physical recreation. **Europe:** 6% first degree students take French as part of course and spend 6 months or more abroad. All students can take a language as optional extra. Some formal exchange links in Europe. **Library:** New library; 210,000 volumes, separate reference/reading room for first degree students; learning resource centre. **Other learning facilities:** Computer laboratory for interactive learning. Primary resource centre and religious education centre. Students have use of Liverpool University library. **Welfare:** Doctor, 3 chaplains, counsellor, two chapels (C of E and RC). **Careers:** Information, advice, work experience and placements. **Amenities:** SU common rooms, general shop and bookshop on campus, banking, playgroup. **Sporting facilities:** Sports fields, gymnasia, squash and tennis courts, outdoor pursuits centre.

Accommodation: In 1995/96, 30% of all students in college accommodation, 55% of first years. 850 half-board places available (500 for first years), £55–£56.50 per week, term time only. Most students live in privately owned accommodation for 2+ years: £30–£40 per week for self-catering. 25% first degree students live at home. **Term time work:** College policy to allow term time work for full-time first degree students (25% believed to work). Term (and vac) work available on campus in SU bars and libraries. **Hardship funds:** Total available in 1995/96: £70,000 government access funds, 260 students helped; £2,000 own funds, 5 helped. Special help: mature students with dependants; own funds also available for students ineligible for access funds or student loans.

Duration of first degree courses: 3 years; **others:** 4 years (BEd; courses in American or European studies). **Total first degree students 1995/96:** 3,300. **BEd students:** 920. **Overseas students:** 120. **Mature students:** 1,200. **Male/female ratio:** 2:5. **Teaching staff:** 178 full-time, 33 part-time. **Total full-time students 1995/96:** 3,500. **Postgraduate students:** 930. **First degree tuition fees:** Home students, paying their own fees in 1996/97, paid £800 (classroom), £1,650 (lab/studio); Overseas students £6,500.

WHAT IT'S LIKE Main site in Childwall, a 20-minute bus ride from city centre. Easy access to M62 (1 mile) and Speke Airport (5 miles). Derwent House SU, the Derge, is the centre of college activity. It has two bars (very cheap — Heineken £1.10 a pint, vodka 75p per shot) and Reg's Bettabuys shop. Anyone coming to Liverpool Hope could easily graduate with degree in socialising! Half-term crèche available. Car parking limited. Practically all first years who require accommodation get it. Living in Liverpool is not too expensive. Sports clubs are very successful — football club reached national semis, rugby league top 2nd div SRL, excellent women's football team.

PAUPER NOTES **Accommodation:** Halls of residence. **Drink:** Derwent, SU building, 2 bars — 1 open lunchtime. **Eats:** Hot/cold food at reasonable cost at 2 servery/snack facilities; sandwich/salad bar in Derwent. Reg's Bettabuys (student shop) has range of eats at rock bottom prices. **Ents:** Derwent House — extensive ents: disco/bands 3–4 nights a week; Carter, Thomas Lang, Bad Manners, Comedy Club, Jo Brand have all appeared. Vibrant city nightlife: numerous pubs and clubs. **Sports:** Sports hall, gym, 2 squash courts, tennis courts, sports field. Numerous athletic clubs and non-sporting societies through SU. **Hardship funds:** Usual student hardship arrangements — access funds etc. **Travel:** Possible to European countries through Erasmus and Assistantships possible to USA through American studies. **Work:** Jobs few and far between.

MORE INFO? Enquiries to Students Union 0151 737 3663.

ALUMNI (EDITORS' PICK) David Alton MP, Willy Russell (playwright).

LIVERPOOL JOHN MOORES UNIVERSITY

Liverpool John Moores University, Roscoe Court,
4 Rodney Street, Liverpool L1 2TZ
(Tel 0151 231 5090/5091, Fax 0151 231 3194) Map 2

STUDENT ENQUIRIES: Recruitment Team
APPLICATIONS: UCAS

Broad study areas: Sciences, built environment, education, business, computing, design and visual arts, engineering, healthcare, law, social work, modern languages. (Subject details are in the *Subjects and Places Index*.)

Founded: 1970 as Liverpool Poly; university status in 1992. **Main undergraduate awards:** BA, BEd, BA/BSc(QTS), BSc, BEng, LLB, MEng. **Awarding body:** Liverpool John Moores University. **Site:** Various sites in Liverpool city centre and one in southern suburb. **Special features:** Links to 20+ local access courses through the Merseyside Open College Federation; positively welcomes, and long experience of supporting, mature students with non-standard qualifications or from access courses. **Academic features:** Integrated credit scheme offers range of subjects, single and joint honours, major/minor degree choice. **Europe:** 6% first degree students learn a language as part of their course and spend 6 months or more abroad. International business studies includes a range of languages. **Library:** On all sites; 550,000 volumes in total, 3,000 periodicals, 1,209 study places. Annual expenditure on library materials, £70 per FTE student. **Other learning facilities:** Learning resource centres, including library, multi-media, audio-visual centres. **Welfare:** Doctor, chaplain, counsellor, accommodation officer, nursery. **Careers:** Information, advice and placement service. **Amenities:** SU wine bar, book and stationery shop, bank, bars on 3 other sites.

Accommodation: In 1995/96, 36% of all students in university accommodation, majority of first years. 2,009 self-catering places available, all for first years: £29–£49 per week, Sept–May. Students live in privately owned accommodation for 2+ years: rents £30–£35 per week for self-catering, £40–£60 full-board. Liverpool Student Homes, run jointly with Liverpool University, co-ordinates private sector accommodation for students; often flats for 6–7 in Victorian houses. **Term time work**: University's policy to allow term time work for full-time first degree students (30% believed to work). Term (and vac) work available on campus in SU bars and offices (particularly during clearing); also Job Shop helps find work off campus and careers service notified of vacancies. **Hardship funds:** Total available in 1995/96: £271,000 government access funds, 950 students helped; £5,000 own hardship funds, plus £150,000 fee-remission funds, 280 helped.

Duration of first degree courses: 3 years (full-time); 4 years (sandwich) **other:** extended degree courses 4 years (full-time), 5 years (sandwich). **Total first degree students 1995/96:** 12,000. **BEd/QTS students:** 982. **Overseas students:** 600. **Mature students**: 40%. **Male/female ratio:** 7:6. **Teaching staff:** approx 825. **Total full-time students 1995/96:** 11,448. **First degree tuition fees:** Home students, paying their own fees in 1996/97, paid £750 (classroom), £1,600 (lab/studio); Overseas students £5,661 (classroom), £6,324 (lab/studio).

WHAT IT'S LIKE 2 main sites in the city centre plus education faculty 3 miles away. Accommodation varies from poor-but-cheap to excellent; over 1,700 places provided, including 2 new city centre halls. No visiting restrictions. Active SU, socially and politically balanced, supports more than 70 sporting, social and political clubs and societies; also magazine and award-winning radio station (Shout FM). SU runs 8 shops and 6 bars (cheap and plush), and the Haigh; puts on regular, quality ents (very popular, queues a regular feature) and runs the recreation department. Sport-for-all philosophy; national champions in several sports including Gaelic football and rugby league. Good staff/student relations. Wide range of subjects and easy to change course. Continuous assessment plus exams. Industry years and field trips on some courses/ Average facilities – new learning resource centre (but cramped); student services and careers service; comprehensive welfare advice from university and SU – strictly confidential. Good relationship with community. Wide range of theatres – from enormous Empire to tiny Unity. Art galleries and museums and a good shopping centre from the Albert Dock to the St John's Centre and Church Street. 2 large cinemas, including one 8-screen, and SU film nights. SU bars and good pubs in abundance. Excellent town clubs. High North-West intake (40% from Liverpool), mainly from state schools. Students from all over country; growing number from overseas. Ugly racism minimal. Easy to get attached to Liverpool – a vibrant, exciting city, despite what the media says, with a tremendous night life.

PAUPER NOTES **Accommodation:** Uni accommodation in city centre, mostly excellent standard. **Drink:** Haigh Building, Mediation, Baa Bar, Garlands, Flanagans. **Eats:** Venue and wine bar in the Haigh Building, various site canteens. All sorts of food in city; excellent Chinatown. **Ents:** Haigh Building, venue on campus. Royal Court, Neptune Theatre (off-the-wall comedy). **Sports:** Everton Sports Centre, Kirkby Sports Centre, Toxteth Sports Centre. SU gym (£20 membership or £2/session). **Hardship:** Uni access fund. **Travel:** Campus travel shop. Student discounts locally. **Work:** In city – bars to clothes shops (av £3.21/hr).

SU employs 150 students (bars, admin, café). Successful SU job shop (1,000 students registered); max 17½ hours a week.
INFORMAL NAME: JMU
ALUMNI (EDITORS' PICK) Debbie Greenwood, Martin Offiah, Julian Cope, Con McConville, Desmond Pitcher (chairman of North West Water).

LIVERPOOL UNIVERSITY

University of Liverpool, PO Box 147, Liverpool L69 3BX
(Tel 0151 794 2000, Fax 0151 708 6502) Map 2

STUDENT ENQUIRIES: SCILAS (Schools, Colleges, International Liaison and Admissions Service). APPLICATIONS: UCAS

Broad study areas: Arts, engineering, law, science, social and environmental studies, medicine & dentistry, veterinary science, professions allied to medicine. (Subject details are in the *Subjects and Places Index.*)

Founded: 1881. **Main undergraduate awards:** BA, BArch, BCom, BDS, BEng, BMus, BSc, BVSc, LLB, MBChB. **Awarding body:** Liverpool University. **Site:** 85 acres in city centre. **Europe:** 7% of students learn a language as part of their course and spend 6 months or more abroad. Language centre is open to all students. A number of degrees with European perspective in engineering, law and science, maths. Exchanges with universities across EFTA and EU, most open to non-language specialists. **Library:** 2 main libraries plus others in departments; 1,300,000 books, 5,000 periodicals; 1,100 study places. Annual expenditure on library materials, £74.25 per FTE student. **Specialist collections:** Spanish Civil War; science fiction, Merseyside poets. **Other learning facilities:** Computing service; botanic gardens; veterinary field station; marine laboratory on Isle of Man. **Careers:** Information, advice and limited placement service. **Welfare:** 2 student counsellors, student health service, chaplains. **Amenities:** 120 cultural/social clubs. Several theatres, concert hall, places of worship etc in city. **Sporting facilities:** Two sports centres on campus, one with swimming pool. Playing fields near halls of residence.

Accommodation: In 1995/96, 3,479 places available (2,627 for first years): 2,247 full-board places in halls of residence (all for first years), £63–£77 per week, term time only; 1,220 self-catering (280 for first years), £40–£46 per week, contracts of 39–52 weeks. All first years live in if accepted through main UCAS system, unless living at home. Students live in privately-rented accommodation for 2 years: rents £25–£45 per week; average is £33 for 42 weeks, with half rent paid for remaining 10 weeks. Over-supply of private accommodation. **Term time work:** No university policy allowing part time work for full time first degree students. **Hardship funds:** In 1995/96, £269,309 government access funds. Special help: students with children, self-financing or mature students.

Duration of first degree courses: 3 and 4 years; **others:** 5 years (medicine, dentistry, vet science). **Total first degree students 1995/96:** 10,369. **Overseas students:** 431. **Mature**

students: 1,957. **Male/female ratio:** 1:1. **Total full-time students 1995/96:** 12,179. **Postgraduate students:** 3,715. **Teaching staff:** 1,003. **First degree tuition fees:** Home students, paying their own fees in 1996/97, paid £750 (classroom), £1,600 (lab/studio), £2,800 (clinical); Overseas students £5,945 (classroom), £7,995 (lab/studio), £14,453 (clinical).

WHAT IT'S LIKE   Main university precinct is only a five minute walk from the city centre, which caters extremely well for its student population with loads of inexpensive eating places, pubs and clubs. Liverpool is an exciting, vibrant and friendly city with a rich cultural history. It is an inexpensive place to live and socialise in. The Guild of Students can be found right in the middle of the university campus on Mount Pleasant, opposite the Catholic Cathedral. It provides a range of services for every student – from over 100 clubs and societies, cafes, bars and shops and an advice centre (offering free, confidential and non-judgmental service to all students). Guild building programme recently led to improved facilities – better bars and shops as well as a brilliant night club venue (with a capacity for 2,500) which provides an extensive entertainments programme most nights of the week. Guild entertainments include films, comedy, concerts and a variety of discos catering for most music tastes.

PAUPER NOTES   **Accommodation:** New good quality self-catering accommodation; limited accommodation for married students. **Drink:** Guild's good for cheap drink (still £1 a pint), many Yorkshire beers. Some clubs sell midweek pint even cheaper. **Eats:** Vegetarian restaurants and food shops in town. Great cheap eating places near university do lunchtime student specials. Guild provides excellent range of food until late evening. Good food on rest of campus – but rarely open at awkward hours. **Ents:** Great ents – very cheap/free. Friday dance nights, midweek comedy, films/discos in Guild. **Sports:** Excellent university sports centre and swimming pool. **Hardship funds:** Limited Vice-chancellor's fund. **Travel:** Campus Travel in the Guild can sort out train/coach fares. **Work:** Vac work extremely hard to find; careers service helps. Little work in city (and poorly paid). Limited term work in Guild.

MORE INFO?   Get students' Alternative Prospectus. Enquiries to Schools Liaison Officer (0151 794 4141).

INFORMAL NAME   Liverpool Uni.

ALUMNI (EDITORS' PICK)   Hugh Jones (marathon runner), Judge O'Donoghue, Dr N Cossons (Director of Science Museum), Joan Rodgers (opera singer), Patricia Routledge (actress), Jon Snow (ITN reporter), Robert Kilroy-Silk (TV presenter), Steve Coppell (footballer), Dame Rose Heilbron (Lady High Court Judge), Phil Redmond (TV writer – Brookside), Lord Evans of Claughton, Ann Leuchars (TV newscaster), Maeve Sherlock (ex-NUS President).

LONDON BIBLE COLLEGE

London Bible College, Green Lane, Northwood, Middlesex HA6 2UW (Tel 01923 826061, Fax 01923 836530) Map 5

STUDENT ENQUIRIES: Registrar
APPLICATIONS: Direct

Broad study areas: Religious studies and theology.

(Subject details are in the *Subjects and Places Index*.)

Founded: 1943. **Main undergraduate award:** BA, BTh. **Awarding body:** Brunel University. **Site:** 9 acre site, north west of London. **Access:** Metropolitan line to Northwood; by road off A404 Rickmansworth Road. **Academic features:** Course in Christian life and Ministry, including possibility of placement in Brazil. Unusual subjects in theology degree (eg sociology of religion, missiology, linguistics, music and worship, children's ministry and pastoral theology); transfer possible between two degree routes. Also postgrad programmes, taught and research based. **Europe:** No students learn a language or spend time abroad. **Library:** 38,000 volumes, 180 periodicals, 100 study places. Annual expenditure on library materials, £100 per FTE student. **Welfare:** Doctor, counsellor. **Careers:** Information, advice and formal placement service. **Amenities:** Bookshop on college premises; games room, tennis courts, football pitch, gym, music rooms, kitchens, TV lounge (including Sky). **Employment:** Christian ministry, missionary work, RE teaching, youth and children's work.

Accommodation: In 1996/97, 30% of all students in college accommodation. 105 full-board places available: £2,610 per year, term time only. **Term time work:** College's policy to allow term time work for full-time first degree students; limit of approx 6 hours/week. Term (and vac) work sometimes available on campus in kitchen, waiting during conferences, maintenance. **Hardship funds:** Total available in 1995/96: £34,000 own funds, c 40 students helped. Special help: overseas students, self-financing students.

Duration of first degree courses: 3 years. **Total first degree students 1995/96:** 254. **Overseas students:** 50. **Mature students:** 227 (average age 31). **Male/female ratio:** 1:1. **Teaching staff:** 20 full-time, 4 part-time. **Total full-time students 1995/96:** 288. **Postgraduate students:** 69. **First degree tuition fees:** Students, paying their own fees in 1996/97, paid £3,105 (LEA may contribute £890 towards fee).

WHAT IT'S LIKE   An international, interdenominational, evangelical college community of 350 students from 34 countries all over the world; 25% students from overseas including Eastern Europe. Students' average age is 30, almost all with some work-experience. The residential suburb of Northwood is 30 mins from central London on the Metropolitan Line, and conveniently close to the M25. One-third live on campus in pleasant, spacious grounds; no accommodation for married students. On-site facilities include a launderette, football pitch, tennis courts, a well-stocked bookshop (some publishers' discounts), a student-run stationery shop, and a modern student centre with TV lounges (including Sky), kitchen, music rooms, table-tennis room, weightlifting equipment, a pool table and changing rooms. Good academic standard and excellent library facilities. High motivation and commitment characteristic of students; in addition to academic work all perform some practical Christian activity each week, either in a local church or in a college team – drama, open-air evangelism, schools work, producing videos, preaching, children's work etc. Some practical assignments during the vacations, especially in summer – sometimes overseas eg Southern Africa, Asia, Europe (E & W). Student-faculty relations are excellent; student reps sit on faculty and Governors' Board meetings. Practical training department gives guidance for future work; students enter a wide range of full-time Christian (or secular) employment, several each year go on to postgraduate studies. The college has a warm and friendly atmosphere, with mutual respect and encouragement. Groups of no more than 12 act as support groups and provide forum for social events. Confidential counselling available.

PAUPER NOTES   **Accommodation:** Not cheap area. Often local church members will rent rooms to LBC students at below the market rate. (College has a list of digs.) **Eats:** College meals very good; offers vegetarian food. Few cheap eating places in the area; non-resident students can sometimes get an evening meal in college free if a resident student is absent. **Ents:** Evening concerts by students several times a year. **Sports:** Soccer, rugger, cricket, volleyball teams; local squash courts and swimming pools have cheap afternoon slots which students can use. **Hardship funds:** College bursary funds to help with tuition fees (mostly for overseas students); students run a gift-fund to help day-to-day expenses if needed. **Travel:** Normal student discount. **Work:** Permission needed for term-time work. Small proportion (10%) get p-t jobs eg shop work, but little available locally; most students get vac work at home.

MORE INFO? Enquiries to Student President

INFORMAL NAME LBC.

ALUMNI (EDITORS' PICK) Os Guinness, Derek Tidball, Clive Calver, Terry Virgo.

LONDON BUSINESS SCHOOL

London Business School, Sussex Place, Regent's Park, London NW1 4SA (Tel 0171 262 5050, Fax 0171 724 7875) Map 6

STUDENT ENQUIRIES: Information Officer, MBA Programme
APPLICATIONS: Direct.

Broad study area *(Not at first degree):* Business administration. (Subject details are in the *Subjects and Places Index.*)

Founded: 1965. **Structural features:** Graduate school of London University. **Main awards:** MBA, MSc, PhD. **Awarding body:** London University. **Site:** Located at Regent's Park in an elegant Nash terrace overlooking the lake. **Access:** Tube (Baker Street). **Academic features:** Case teaching, group assignments, visiting speakers, student consultancy projects, assessed class participation. Significant number of professors from abroad. Lots of guest speakers. Research centres include economic forecasting, small business, finance, business strategy and central and eastern Europe. All MBA students graduate with a language other than English (languages include Japanese and Mandarin). 40% of MBA programme go on international exchange for a term with top exchange schools worldwide. **Library:** Corporate library includes comprehensive stock of annual reports and Extel cards – online data base facilities available. **Other facilities:** Computer labs; close-circuit TV centre. **Careers:** Information, advice and placement service. **Employment:** Merchant banking, finance, strategy consulting, manufacturing and service industries worldwide. **Welfare:** Lisson Grove Health Centre nearby. Students have personal faculty advisers. **Amenities:** Close to West End. **Sports:** On campus – gym and aerobics room; off campus – squash at Lord's cricket ground; soccer and other sports in the park.

Accommodation: Limited school accommodation. Many students have their own houses which they share with other MBA students. **Hardship funds:** London University access funds. Substantial scholarship programme.

Duration of courses: 21 months full-time; 30 months part-time; **others:** PhD 3 years plus. **Male/female ratio:** 4:1. **Teaching and research staff:** 110. **Total full-time students 1995/96:** c600 MBA. **Tuition fees:** MBA students in 1996/97 paid £10, 500.

WHAT IT'S LIKE   A Nash terrace overlooking Regent's Park lake – an elegant facade hiding very well-equipped lecture theatres and computer rooms; supposedly the best business library and IT facilites in Europe. On campus bedrooms small but functional. A well catered, subsidised restaurant and cafeteria, two bars and wine bar. LBS is fun but incredibly demanding – not for the faint hearted. Students typically put in 80-90 hour weeks during the first year; weekends and evenings off are rare! The top European business school; both students and faculty totally motivated and committed, with a strong career ethos among students. Probably the highest percentage of women (27%) among world's best business schools and very international (75% students come from 46 different countries). International focus in curriculum, as well as in various projects and overseas field visits. An international exchange programme allows students to spend a term in another top business school (in Europe, Asia, North and South America). Average graduating salary – £40,000 plus, although they will swear that is **not** why they are here! Average age of entrants is 28. An exclusive, multi-layer admissions procedure with tough entry requirements, including minimum of two years' professional experience (apply early; places are quickly filled). Low drop-out rate and few overall failures. Part-timers on MBA programme are usually sponsored and take three years to complete course. Great emphasis on high quality of teaching and research; most staff have experience in business schools abroad and consulting links with industry/commerce. Students are very vocal if they are not getting value for time or money and formal assessments by students of lecturers each term. Almost everyone is there to work hard – not for fun. Football, aerobics and squash are popular and there's a lot of jogging and boating around Regent's Park; gymnasium on site. Careers clubs (such as finance and consultancy) are well attended; students can mix freely with guest speakers, generally senior business figures (eg Michael Heseltine, Rick Greenbury). Students' association non-political, purely administrative and social. 3 or 4 large events per term, well attended, especially the unforgettable summer ball!
PAUPER NOTES   Clearing banks offer low interest loans to UK students which most take up. All students earn money for their project works and in summer vacations.
ALUMNI (EDITORS' PICK)   John Egan (CE, BAA), Iain Vallance (BT chairman), Matthew Carrington MP, Sir Ronald Dearing (chairman SEAC), Bernard Taylor (CEO Medeva), Sir Richard Greenbury (MD Marks & Spencer), David Currie, Richard Brealey, Gary Hamel.

LONDON COLLEGE OF FASHION

The London College of Fashion, 20 John Princes Street, London W1M 0BJ (Tel 0171 514 7400, Fax 0171 514 7484) Map 6

STUDENT ENQUIRIES: College Administrator
APPLICATIONS: UCAS or direct

Broad study areas: Fashion, textiles, fashion journalism, design technology. (Subject details are in the *Subjects and Places Index*.)

Founded: 1910; became part of London Institute 1986. **Main undergraduate award:** BA. **Awarding body:** London Institute. **Site:** 5 sites in Central London: 3 around Oxford Street, 2 in the City. **Access:** Oxford Circus and Bond Street underground stations for West End sites. Old Street and Liverpool Street stations for Barbican and City sites. **Academic features:** New degrees in womenswear, accessories, fashion management, costume and makeup for the performing arts. 3 year full-time and 4 year sandwich courses. **Special features:** Largest UK college covering whole of fashion industry including fashion design, clothing technology, fashion promotion and journalism. **Europe:** 100% first degree students take a language as part of course and 5% spend 6 months or more abroad. No formal exchange links with universities/colleges. **Library:** 40,000 books, 250 periodicals, 157 study places. Specialist fashion collection of unique interest. **Other learning facilities:** Textile lab, computer centres, all specialist fashion facilities. **Careers:** Information and advice service. **Welfare:** Student services, advice and counselling. **Special facilities:** Crèche available through London Institute (not on site). **Amenities and sporting facilities:** None on site.

Accommodation: Institute accommodation: £48–£56 per week for B&B and £79 full board, term time only. Accommodation officer helps find private accommodation: £40–£50 per week B&B plus some extras. **Term time work:** College's policy to allow term time work for full-time first degree students (50% believed to work). No work in college but careers service publicises part-time and vacation jobs. **Hardship funds:** Access funds, charities and specialist bursaries.

Duration of first degree course: 3 years; 4 years sandwich. **Total first degree students 1995/96:** 455. **Overseas students:** 181. **Mature students:** 0. **Male/female ratio:** 1:4. **Teaching staff:** 87 full-time, 49 part-time. **Total full-time students 1995/96:** 2,437. **Postgraduate students:** 28. **First degree tuition fees:** Home students, paying their own fees in 1996/97, paid £1,600; Overseas students £5,950.

LONDON COLLEGE OF MUSIC

London College of Music at Thames Valley University,
St Mary's Road, Ealing, London W5 5RF
(Tel 0181 231 2304, Fax 0181 231 2546) Map 5

STUDENT ENQUIRIES: Admissions Tutor
APPLICATIONS: Direct.

Broad study areas: Music. (Subject details are in the *Subjects and Places Index.*)

Founded: 1887; became part of Thames Valley University in 1991. **Main awards:** BMus, MMus, PgDip, PhD. **Awarding body:** Thames Valley University. **Site:** West London. **Access:** South Ealing and/or Ealing Broadway (BR and tube) station. **Special features:** Conservatoire within a university. Emphasis on range of relationships with music industry. **Academic features:** Range of undergraduate and postgraduate courses covering performance, composing, popular music, musicology. **Europe:** 20% students learn a language; French,

German and Italian available to all singing students and to other undergraduates if places available. No students spend time abroad. **Library:** c30,000 volumes, study places. Annual expenditure on library materials, £25 per FTE student. **Other learning facilities:** Recording studios and audio visual facilities. **Welfare:** Doctor. **Careers:** Information and advice service; specialist week.

Accommodation: See *Thames Valley University*. 20% first degree students live at home. **Term time work**: College's policy to allow term time work for full-time first degree students (75% believed to work); limit of 8 hours a week. Term (and vac) work available on campus in bars and stewarding in orientation week; TVU Temps Agency helps. **Hardship funds:** See *Thames Valley University*.

Duration of first degree courses: 3 years; **others:** 1or 2 years. **Total first degree students 1995/96:** 200. **Overseas students:** 50. **Male/female ratio:** 1:3. **Teaching staff:** 80 part-time. **Total full-time students 1995/96:** 350. **Postgraduate students:** 50. **First degree tuition fees:** Home students, paying their own fees in 1996/97, paid £1,650; Overseas students £5,047. ALUMNI (EDITORS' PICK)   David Caddick (musical director, Royal Shakespeare Co), Martin Ellerby (composer), Raphael Terroni (pianist), Edward Blakeman (flautist, Head of Woodwind, LCM, Radio 3 presenter), John Treleaven (international tenor), Rosalind Sutherland (singer), Andrew Simpson (composer).

LONDON COLLEGE OF PRINTING

London College of Printing and Distributive Trades,
Elephant & Castle, London SE1 6SB
(0171 514 6500, Fax 0171 514 6535) Map 6

STUDENT ENQUIRIES: Marketing Manager
APPLICATIONS: UCAS

Broad study areas: Printing, publishing, graphic and retail design, media and communication, retail management, business. (Subject details are in the *Subjects and Places Index*.)

Founded: 1990, ex London College of Printing (1895) and the College for the Distributive Trades. **Structural features:** Part of the London Institute. **Main undergraduate award:** BA. **Awarding body:** London Institute. **Site:** 3 sites: Elephant & Castle, Clerkenwell and Davies Street (near Oxford St). **Access:** All sites close to underground and buses. **Academic features:** Range of courses from access and one-year diplomas to undergraduate and postgraduate degrees in all specialist areas. Exceptional practical and vocational provision at all levels. **Europe:** Most courses offer language development. **Library:** 3 libraries of specialist material – books, periodicals, slides, audio and visual. Students also have access to libraries in the 4 other colleges of the London Institute. **Specialist collections:** History of the book. **Other learning facilities:** Language laboratories; state-of-the-art equipment in printing, DTP, multimedia, film, video and photography; computer suites; plus facilities of other London Institute colleges. **Welfare:** London Institute accommodation office, careers service, counsellors, specialist help and advice on funding, personal matters, legal help etc. **Careers:** Information and advice service. **Amenities:** Canteen, student bar. **Employment:** Design and printing; tourism; photography, film and television industries; teaching; journalism; publishing; retailing and retail design; business management; marketing, advertising and PR.

Accommodation: 115 places in hall (for students from outside London).

Duration of first degree courses: 3 years. **Total first degree students 1995/96:** 900. **Male/female ratio:** 3:2. **Teaching staff:** 270 full-time. **Total full-time students 1995/96:** 4,000. **Postgraduate students:** 308. **First degree tuition fees:** Home students, paying their own fees in 1996/97, paid £1,600; Overseas students £5,950.

WHAT IT'S LIKE   It has long been a leading graphic arts college and has emerged into teaching all-round media and communications; with the merger with the College of Distributive Trades, it provides business studies/management courses and has expanded into travel, tourism, fashion and furnishing. The schools of printing technology, graphic design, and business and management are housed at the Elephant and Castle. Media is sited at Back Hill, Clerkenwell, and the schools of retail studies and professional studies occupy the former British Council building in Davies Street. Student accommodation in London is scarce and very expensive but the London Institute runs two halls of residence; Furzedown Halls in Tooting and Ralph West in Battersea. There is also an accommodation service at the Institute which aims to help students find somewhere comfortable, safe and reasonably affordable to live. In general, a good college, not so good location; not the place to hang around after dark! Little around the site – dated shopping centre and some pubs. Good technical resources, CD-Roms, PCs, video recorders, library (not quiet, big social centre). Tutors and staff helpful and friendly.
PAUPER NOTES   **Accommodation:** Two halls of residence; accommodation service minibus for your accommodation search. **Drink:** SU bar (shuts early if not serving many students). Prince of Wales, Gibraltar are student pubs. **Eats:** Cafeteria at Elephant site; student reductions on food. Chips, beans etc and sandwiches (run out by lunchtime). **Ents:** LISU runs parties throughout term in London clubs on Mondays (not all that cheap). **Sports:** Swimming pool, multigym next door. **Hardship Funds:** Possible but scarce. **Travel:** No travel scholarships. **Work:** Tutors can sometimes help (good contacts). SU bar, shops, restaurants etc around London.
ALUMNI (EDITORS' PICK)   Trevor McDonald (newsreader), Neville Brody (designer *City Limits, The Face*), Dave King (Arts Council Designer).

LONDON CONTEMPORARY DANCE SCHOOL

London Contemporary Dance School, The Place, 17 Duke's Road, London WC1H 9AB (Tel 0171 387 0152, Fax 0171 383 4851) Map 6

STUDENT ENQUIRIES: School Office
APPLICATIONS: Direct.

Broad study areas: Dance.

Founded: 1966. **Main undergraduate award:** BA. **Awarding body:** Kent University. **Site:** The Place; a large building with its own theatre, off Euston Road. **Access:** King's Cross and Euston tube and BR stations, buses. **Special features:** Part of The Place, a national centre for contemporary dance, which also includes The Place Theatre, The Video Place and The Place Dance Services. Leading European centre for training professional dancers in contemporary dance and choreography. **Admission:** Candidates for degree course must pass the dance audition, although academic qualifications are not necessarily required. **Academic features:** Core of the degree course is professional training; parts are taught in liaison with other institutions including Central Saint Martins School of Art and Design and Guildhall School of Music and Drama. **Europe:** No students learn a language or spend time abroad. **Library:** Extensive collection of dance, arts, psychology and related studies in addition to a general collection. Annual expenditure on library materials, £70 per FTE student. **Welfare:** School osteopath visits weekly. Resident full-time student services officer. **Careers:** Personal contact service for jobs. **Amenities:** 9 dance studios, music studio, The Place Theatre for student workshop performances; restaurant, student common rooms.

Accommodation: Student services officer gives advice on accommodation. **Term time work:** School's policy to allow term time work for full-time first degree students (90% believed to work). Term (and vac) work available on campus in bars, cleaning, ushers. **Hardship funds:** For 2nd and 3rd year students only – competitive scholarship/endowment fund.

Duration of first degree courses: 3 years. **Total first degree students 1995/96:** 90. **Overseas students:** 55. **Mature students:** 23. **Male/female ratio:** 1:7. **Teaching staff:** 15 full-time, 6 part-time. **Total full-time students 1995/96:** 140. **Postgraduate students:** 12. **First degree tuition fees:** Students, paying their own fees in 1996/97, paid £7,900.

WHAT IT'S LIKE Large building in central London known as The Place, also the home of London Contemporary Dance Trust, The Place Theatre and the professional Richard Alston Dance Company. Euston and King's Cross tube and BR stations only a few minutes' walk away and good bus services. No halls of residence but there are many local hostels and usually fairly easy to find flats. Rent gets cheaper out of central London but travel is very expensive. As a private institution, fees are expensive and local authorities usually reluctant to give grants. Close, friendly atmosphere – very international (40% from overseas) and more women than men. Helpful student adviser/counsellor and each student is allocated to a tutorial group. School library open throughout college hours. SU small but active, providing social events and links between students and admin. Degree course consists of practical work with theoretical contexts of dance and is designed to train students in professional dance performance. Drop-out rate is 30%. Timetable is heavy (25–30 hours a week), starting early and often finishing late; social life is limited during the week as early nights are essential for survival. However, there is plenty of entertainment available in London for the weekends. Exchange programmes are available with various different dance centres across the world. Generally, employment for successful candidates good, but training very rigorous and suited to dedicated dancers wishing for professional careers, prepared to work extremely hard.

PAUPER NOTES **Accommodation:** No college accommodation; average rents locally about £50–£60 a week. **Eats:** Café for school and theatre on premises has delicious, cheap, healthy, home-made food; caters for vegetarians. Many local cafés. **Drink:** Local pub Mabels just across road; drink generally expensive in London. **Work:** Some available in theatre, theatre bar and in admin. Part-time work quite easy to find but can interfere with training.

INFORMAL NAME LCDS
ALUMNI (EDITORS' PICK) Richard Alston, Siobhain Davies, Robert North, Anthony Van Laast, Linda Gibbs, Ian Spink, Darshan Singh Bhuller, most performing members of Richard Alston Dance Company.

LONDON GUILDHALL UNIVERSITY

London Guildhall University, 31 Jewry Street, London EC3N 2EY (Tel 0171 320 1000, Fax 0171 320 3462) Map 6

STUDENT ENQUIRIES: Admissions Officer, 133 Whitechapel High Street, London E1 7QA
APPLICATIONS: UCAS

Broad study areas: Business, economics, law, human sciences, sociology, arts, design & manufacture. (Subject details are in the *Subjects and Places Index.*)

Founded: 1970 as City of London Poly ex City of London College, Sir John Cass College and King Edward VII Nautical College and London College of Furniture; university status 1992. **Main undergraduate awards:** BA, BSc. **Awarding body:** London Guildhall University. **Site:** 8 teaching sites in City, Aldgate and Whitechapel. **Access:** British Rail, London Docklands Railway, underground and bus services. **Special features:** 2 semesters a year. Flexible credit accumulation system (CAS) allows students to specialise from the beginning of their course, or delay final decisions until the end of year 1. Positive attitude to mature, local students and those with disabilities. **Academic features:** Courses in communications and audio-visual production studies, insurance and banking studies, furniture and interiors. **Europe:** 10% first degree students take a language as part of course and 1% spend 6 months or more abroad. 3 languages offered and may be incorporated in degrees in all faculties. Formal exchange links with 28 European universities/colleges – all open to non-language specialists. Dual qualification open to students in geography and law/economics. **Library:** 4 libraries; 260,000 volumes in total, 2,000 periodicals, 700 study places, slide collections (art), map collection. Annual expenditure on library materials, £54.25 per FTE student. **Special collection:** Fawcett Library (women's studies). **Other learning facilities:** Multimedia resources (CD-Rom, workstations, databases etc), computer centre; TV studio, language laboratories, GIS, specialist wood-working and machine tool laboratories. **Welfare:** Student counsellors; chaplain; full-time nurse and part-time doctor; access to solicitor. **Careers:** Information, advice and placement. **Amenities:** Refectories or snack bars on all teaching sites; SU building with bars, TV and games rooms, discos etc. **Sporting facilities:** Gymnasium, aerobics studio and multigym, outdoor sports ground.

Accommodation: In 1995/96, 25% of first-year students in university accommodation. 461 places available: 102 full-board places at £65 per week and 359 self-catering places at £52–£60 for 34 weeks. Many students live in privately owned accommodation for whole course: £50–£55 per week for self-catering. Over 50% first degree students live at home. **Term time work**: University's policy to allow term time work for full-time first degree students. Term (and vac) work available on campus in SU bars, registries, at one-off events. **Hardship funds**: Total available in 1995/96: £218,000 government access funds, awards of £200–£1,000. Help targeted at: self-funded students, those with childcare costs, other exceptional circumstances (eg medical costs). Funds also available as fee remission for part-time and overseas students.

Duration of first degree courses: 3 years; **others**: 4 years (sandwich and language). **Total first degree students 1995/96**: 7,220. **Overseas students**: 800. **Mature students**: 1,272. **Male/female ratio**: 1:1. **Teaching staff**: 390 full-time. **Total full-time students 1995/96**: 7,264. **Postgraduate students**: 1,042. **First degree tuition fees**: Home students, paying their own fees in 1996/97, paid £1,000; Overseas students £5,880.

WHAT IT'S LIKE   A university with a laid back and friendly atmosphere. One of the most diverse and non-traditional universities in the country: over 40% of students are from black and ethnic minorities, 50% are over 21, and 8 sites over the massive cultural and social divide of City and East End. The nature of the university changes from site to site, in an almost collegiate fashion, but all are brought together at the SU and halls. Obvious advantages include the enormous range of entertainments, from chirpy East End pubs to high profile clubs, gigs, theatres, historical sites (one refectory looks over the Tower of London), museums, markets (including Petticoat Lane), art galleries, and ethnic food (curry houses to traditional Jewish food including a 24-hour bagel shop). The down side is the cost: food, beer and accommodation is expensive, but bargains can be found, particularly further out. It's not particularly easy to find accommodation, especially if you're not realistic about what you can get for your money. Staff generally helpful, good teachers and reasonable workload. The very large, flexible modular system is popular and successful. The Moorgate site in the City, houses law and business courses which are highly regarded – as are politics, social policy and management and some of the arts courses. Because of the nature of the place, the SU has a major role in bringing everyone together and acts as a melting pot. The wide range of cultural and religious societies reflects the mix of students. SU (in new building) is politically active; welfare and educational advice centre and strong societies (such as lesbian, gay and bisexual society and Jewish society) ensure that students always have somewhere to turn. Venue bar and two smaller bars and several (healthy!) food bars means students are well looked after. Sporting facilities not great, but wide range of clubs (field sports, martial arts, outdoor pursuits and so on). Ents varied – retro, handbag, techno, acid jazz, alternative, comedy club and lots of general silliness for special events (Sex Party for World AIDS Day, space hopper racing for Rag).

PAUPER NOTES   **Accommodation:** Some uni accommodation. Private housing can be cheaper, but be prepared to live further out – Hackney, Stepney, Leyton popular. Lots live at home. **Drinks:** SU bars excellent. Regular promotions and good atmosphere. Bars, pubs and clubs everywhere, but expensive. **Eats:** University provides canteen style food, SU food good and varied with new eat-as-much-pasta-as-u-like etc. Lots of local cheap places, especially curry houses down Brick Lane and at Spitalfields. **Ents:** SU cheap and varied ents, social societies, gigs, outings, rag week etc. **Sports:** Two gyms and one sports ground (Chigwell, Essex). **Hardship funds:** Limited and targeted access fund, short term emergency loans from university and SU. **Travel:** Tubes, buses, night buses, Docklands Light Railway; Liverpool St, Fenchurch St and Moorgate for BR. **Work:** SU employs as many students as possible. Local jobs (shops, telesales etc); lots of temp work in City (£3–£4/hr; £8 if you're a wordprocessing whizz!). Possibility of SU job service.

INFORMAL NAME LGU.
ALUMNI (EDITOR'S PICK) Kate Hoey MP, Graham Allan MP, Jim Moir *alias* Vic Reeves (entertainer), Terry Marsh (boxer), Mark Thatcher.

LONDON INSTITUTE

The London Institute, 65 Davies Street, London W1Y 2DA
(Tel 0170 514 6000, Fax 0171 514 6131) Map 6

STUDENT ENQUIRIES: Communications and Marketing Office
APPLICATIONS: to the individual colleges through UCAS

Broad study areas: Art & design, fashion, media, printing. (Subject details for the constituent colleges in the *Subjects and Places Index*.)

Founded: 1986. **Structural features:** A single federated structure, bringing together five famous colleges of art, design and related technologies, each of which admits its own students. Each college has its own strong traditions and distinctive character; each has its own prospectus.
You can look each college up separately:

Camberwell College of Arts
Central Saint Martins College of Art and Design
Chelsea College of Art and Design
London College of Fashion
London College of Printing and Distributive Trades.

Site: 18 sites in Central London. **Special features:** Institute's Davies Street Gallery exhibits students' work from all five colleges. **Academic features:** Courses range from access and first diploma to PhD, all studio based. Institute students often progress from a foundation course at one of the colleges to a degree course at another, and can switch between subject areas as their interests develop. New language centre offers free tuition. Increasing number of students complete part of their course abroad. 2,000 of the many leading artists, designers, broadcasters, photographers and media professionals based in London act as visiting tutors. **Welfare:** Central student services with satellite offices in each college provides help with accommodation, support and counselling, personal and financial problems, day nursery facilities (crèche at Elephant & Castle) and careers. Also chaplaincy and help for students with disabilities. **Amenities:** Network of college shops (sell art and design materials etc). Institute SU provides range of social programmes and monthly newsletter, *Blue*. Access to sporting, social and cultural facilities of the capital.

Accommodation: 2 institute halls of residence in south London and more planned.
Total first degree students 1995/96: 4,777 **Male:female ratio:** 6:4 **Teaching staff:** 1,697 **Total number of students:** 15,585. **First degree tuition fees:** Home students, paying their own fees in 1996/97, paid £1,600; Overseas students £5,950.

WHAT IT'S LIKE   Being in the centre of London has particular advantages – the vast array of galleries, museums as well as the artists and designers working outwards from the centre. It's very international, with students from all over the world. There's an overseas students' induction programme to help ensure an easy transition to working in Britain. And for British students, who may find living and working in the capital a new and initially strange experience, there's a student induction programme too. London Institute Student Union provides range of social programmes, including running parties, and produces a monthly newsletter.

ALUMNI (EDITORS' PICK)   Elizabeth Frink, Mervyn Pake, Dirk Bogarde, Graham Sutherland, Frank Auerbach, Henry Moore, Bruce Oldfield, Humphrey Lyttleton, Gilbert & George, Nicola Bailey, Katherine Hamnett, Mel Calman.

LONDON INTERNATIONAL FILM SCHOOL

London International Film School, 24 Shelton Street, London
WC2H 9HP (Tel 0171 836 9642, Fax 0171 497 3718,
E-mail lifs@cityscape.co.uk, Web http://www.tecc.co.uk/
lifs/index.html) Map 6

STUDENT ENQUIRIES: The Administrator
APPLICATIONS: Direct

Broad study areas: Film studies. (Subject details are in the *Subjects and Places Index.*)

Founded: 1956 as London School of Film Technique. **Main awards:** Diploma, Certificate. **Awarding body:** LIFS. **Site:** A converted warehouse in Covent Garden. **Access:** Covent Garden tube station. **Academic features:** Writing drama for film scripts. Directing workshops. Practical sessions with actors. Extra-mural course in music for films. Courses begin each term. Time equally divided between practical film-making and formal tuition. **Special features:** Acceptance depends upon educational achievement and examples of relevant work, eg photography, previous films, video, film scripts, story boards; experience in film, TV or related areas taken into account. **Europe:** Opportunities exist to make films in Europe in the final term. **Library:** Technical books, periodicals, 17 study places. **Welfare:** National health services nearby. **Careers:** Graduates are automatically acceptable as members of BECTU, with access to vacancy registers covering film and TV. **Amenities:** Two viewing theatres, two fully equipped studios, video rehearsal studio, comprehensively equipped camera, sound and editing departments. Equipment includes 35 mm Panavision, 16 mm and 35 mm Arriflex cameras, Nagra sound recorders, Steenbeck editing tables, video camera and editing equipment. LIFS Film Society run by students. SU plays large part in school.

Accommodation: No school accommodation. Privately owned accommodation varies considerably. **Hardship funds:** None available.

Duration of courses: 2 years. **Total students (all full-time) 1995/96:** 125. **Overseas students:** 80. **Mature students:** 0. **Male/female ratio:** 4:1. **Teaching staff:** 27 full-time, 24 part-time. **First degree tuition fees:** Students, paying their own fees in 1996/97, paid £12,207.

WHAT IT'S LIKE   Great location – it's in the middle of the West End in Covent Garden, occupying a 19th century fruit warehouse. Access is easy by tube, being near Covent Garden, Leicester Square and Tottenham Court Road stations. An exciting international mix of students from Europe, Asia, Africa and the Americas as well as a number of UK students, often on LEA grants. The 2-year course is divided into 6 terms and students arrange themselves into groups that make a film each term Everyone takes courses in various areas of film making, so gaining a broad base of skills. Some students try to specialise by taking on the same role in their group films, while others prefer to try different jobs to broaden their experience – it's up to the individual. There are theory lectures that involve watching and discussing films but as the course progresses, students spend more time actually making their group's films or working on other students' films. This is a great strength of the school – many students leave having worked on 15–20 short films in the space of 2 years. The school has a high reputation for technical expertise and the diploma is recognised by BECTU (automatic membership for graduates who find work). Graduates have achieved leading positions in the film industry world wide. There are irregular visits by guest speakers who are actively involved in large scale features and invite guests from the film and television industry to the end of term screenings. A number of school documentaries have been screened on television and films are shown at the London Film Festival and other festivals all over the world. Students also participate in various student film competitions such as the Fuji Film Scholarship Awards (recently won twice). Facilities are not plush – spartan but functional. Plans to upgrade main cinema and coffee bar areas soon.
PAUPER NOTES   This is an expensive school in an expensive area. **Drink:** The Two Brewers, Seven Dials, Café Boheme, Bar Sol Ona, Freuds; various places around Covent Garden. **Eats:** Cheapest but not worst: LIFS coffee shop; various places around Covent Garden and Soho. **Ents:** Film society evening screenings; numerous cinemas and theatres around London.
INFORMAL NAME LIFS.
ALUMNI (EDITORS' PICK)   Arnold Wesker, Mark Forstater, George Cosmatos, John Irvin, Franc Roddam, Les Blair, Mike Leigh, Michael Mann, Mark Kasdan, Don Boyd, Bill Douglas, Horace Ove, Simon Lourish, Tak Fujomoto.

LONDON UNIVERSITY

University of London, Senate House, Malet Street, London WC1E 7HU (Tel 0171 636 8000, Fax 0171 636 5841)

STUDENT ENQUIRIES: To constituent colleges.
APPLICATIONS: To constituent colleges, mostly through UCAS; see individual profiles

Broad study areas: All the main subjects are taught in London University by one or more of its constituent colleges.

Founded: 1836 bringing together two existing London colleges, King's and University College.
Structural features: A federal university consisting of over 50 institutions in which teaching and research are carried out; students belong both to the college or institute at which they study and to the university. There is also an external programme through which students elsewhere can study for London University degrees. **Site:** University site in Bloomsbury, including 35 acres between British Museum and Euston Road, on which University College, Birkbeck, SOAS and Institute of Education are located. Almost all London University colleges are within a radius of 3 miles of the Bloomsbury site except for Royal Holloway in Surrey and Wye College in Kent. **Academic features:** Colleges, Institutes and London's unique external system offer over 900 undergraduate and 400 Master's degree courses as well as many Diploma and Certificate courses via Birkbeck College and the Centre for Extra-Mural Studies. London offers the biggest choice of courses in the UK. Many degrees on modular system. All the separate teaching institutions select their students themselves and you apply to them, not to the university. Look up their profiles:

Birkbeck College
British Institute in Paris
Charing Cross and Westminster Medical
    School
Courtauld Institute
Goldsmiths College
Heythrop College
Imperial College of Science, Technology
    and Medicine
Institute of Archaeology (part of University
    College)
Institute of Education
Jews' College
King's College School of Medicine and
    Dentistry (part of King's College)
King's College London
LSE (London School of Economics and
    Political Science)
Queen Mary & Westfield College
Royal Free Hospital School of Medicine

Royal Holloway
Royal Veterinary College
St Bartholomew's and Royal London
    School of Medicine & Dentistry (part of
    QMW)
St George's Hospital Medical School
St Mary's Hospital Medical School (part of
    Imperial College)
School of Pharmacy
Slade School of Fine Art (part of
    University College)
SOAS (School of Oriental and African
    Studies)
SSEES (School of Slavonic & East
    European Studies)
UMDS (United Medical and Dental
    Schools of Guy's and St Thomas's
    Hospitals)
University College London
Wye College

There are also many specialist postgraduate institutions.

Awarding body: London University. **External students:** The University will register and examine eligible students world-wide who are not registered at colleges of London University. First degrees in arts subjects, computing, divinity, economics, law, mathematics, music (examinations in UK only). Masters degrees with full distance learning materials include agriculture, economics, environment. Enquiries to the External Programme at Senate House. **Europe:** Most colleges of the university have well-equipped language courses and course unit structure allows incorporation of languages into degree courses, particularly in the early years. A number of degree courses involve a year abroad and several colleges offer European studies degrees. University is involved in over 100 Erasmus programmes, including almost all major European universities. Member of UNICA (universities in capital cities in Europe) which is considering the special problems of studying in a capital city. **Library:** 1,300,000 books and 5,500 current periodicals; particularly strong in the humanities. Many distinguished specialist collections. Colleges have their own libraries. **Students' union:** University union (ULU) is in Malet Street. Most colleges have their own unions. Athletic ground in Motspur Park, Surrey; university boathouse at Hartington Road, Chiswick; sailing clubhouse at Welsh Harp Reservoir, Brent. **Welfare:** Central Institutions Health Service for the Birkbeck College, Institute of Education, School of Pharmacy, SOAS and SSEES; other colleges make their own arrangements. **Other learning facilities:** Excellent university computer centre, one of two national facilities providing resources to university users all over the UK. Also its own specialist collections and galleries. **Summer schools:** London University runs annual summer schools to allow sixth formers to sample a subject and the university environment. Apply to Senate House for a summer school prospectus.

Accommodation and hardship funds: See individual college profiles.

Duration of first degree courses: 3 or 4 years; **others:** medicine/dentistry 5 years. **Total first degree students 1995/96:** 47,834 (full-time); 16,888 (part-time). **Overseas students:** 10,604. **Total full-time students 1995/96:** 94,036. **External students:** 24,500. **Postgraduate students:** 17,699 full-time; 11,615 part-time. **Tuition fees:** Each college sets own fee; see individual colleges.

WHAT IT'S LIKE   London University is possibly the most diverse university in the UK – with over 80,000 students, it's certainly the largest. You could be studying at a Senate Institute with 300 students or a large multi-faculty college with 12,000 students but you are at the same university. Because of this it is possible for everyone to find their place. There is the opportunity to participate fully in university life at the various colleges, but it is just as easy to lead your own separate life outside college – or do both. London contains opportunities for you to do anything you have never done before and now wish to do – but it is up to you to seek it out and get involved. If you live in London, you will have to get used to spending large amounts of your day travelling; even if you live close to the centre, specialist libraries, research centres etc may not be. London is also relatively expensive, although it is possible to live quite cheaply with a wide range of rented accommodation available. Student Unions make the expense easier to bear offering cheaper food and drink etc; each college and institute has its own and you can use the University of London Union (ULU) in Malet Street. It is easy to get lonely in London – but it is also easy to make friends with so many different activities going on. All the colleges have student sport clubs and societies and ULU has many federal ones; ULU also has a very good and comprehensive range of sports facilities. The opportunity for part-time work is also great in London with so many retail and service outlets. Whatever you are looking for from university, London offers it.

PAUPER NOTES   **Accommodation:** Inter-collegiate and college run halls available for most first years and some third years. Accommodation offices at both college and university level run head-lease schemes. Newspaper *Loot* published daily with all types and prices of rentals. Students live in all parts of London, from Mayfair to Brixton. **Drink:** Everywhere very expensive except for SU bars. Some cheaper pubs out of the centre. **Eats:** Every type of food you could possibly wish to try is served somewhere in London. Hunt around and meals for under a fiver are easy to come across eg Centrale W1 (Italian), China Rendezvous W1 (Chinese), Côte à Côte SW11 (French), Food for Thought WC2 (vegetarian). **Ents:** Cheapest ents at SUs. London has the best opportunities to see every film/play/exhibition released and most outlets have student concessionary rates. Even the West End shows offer reduced last minute tickets to students. **Sports:** Nearly all have grounds and boathouse etc; on site only at Royal Holloway, everyone else has about 30 mins journey. Some facilities on site at some colleges; the best and cheapest indoor facilities are at ULU (including a swimming pool). **Hardship funds:** Available from each college. **Travel:** No student discounts available on underground or buses although passes can be bought for up to a year which dramatically reduces the cost of travel. For travel awards etc see the individual colleges. **Work:** Most SUs offer paid work; also an enormous number of part-time jobs available. Often it is a case of going into premises and finding out as many do not advertise.

ALUMNI (EDITORS' PICK) Rt Rev George Carey, Archbishop of Canterbury (King's), Edwina Currie (LSE), Robert Mugabe, President of Zimbabwe (external system), David Owen (UMDS), Jonathon Ross (SSEES).

LOUGHBOROUGH COLLEGE OF ART

Loughborough College of Art and Design, Epinal Way, Loughborough, Leicestershire LE11 0QE
(Tel 01509 261515, Fax 01509 265515) Map 2

STUDENT ENQUIRIES: Admissions Officer
APPLICATIONS: UCAS

Broad study areas: Art & design. (Subject details are in the *Subjects and Places Index.*)

Founded: 1958. **Main undergraduate award:** BA. **Awarding body:** Loughborough University. **Academic features:** New degrees in drawing and illustration design. **Europe:** Students with language training can study at art and design institutions in Spain, France and Germany on Erasmus programme. **Library:** 50,000 volumes, 400 periodicals, 150 study places; extensive slide collection and video library. Annual expenditure on library materials, £29.25 per FTE student. **Other learning facilities:** Artists' books collection, IT facilities. **Welfare and Careers:** Students have access to Loughborough University counselling and careers services. **Sporting facilities:** Swimming pool, running track, sports hall, sports pitches, squash courts, etc.

Accommodation: In 1995/96, 25% of all students in college accommodation (priority for first and final years). 300 self-catering places available: £42.50 per week (£38.50 shared). Students live in privately owned accommodation for 2+ years: £20–£40 per week self-catering, £30–£50 half board. **Term time work:** College's policy to allow term time work for full-time first degree students. Term (and vac) work available on campus in library, caretaking, cleaning, some administration, labouring; plans for employment agency run by SU. **Hardship funds:** Total available in 1995/96: £17,283 government access funds, 77 students helped, £50–£600 awarded; £1,000 own funds, 2–3 students helped. Special help: those with dependants, self-financing etc; own funds also available for small travel bursaries.

Duration of first degree courses: 3 years. **Total first degree students 1995/96:** 633. **Overseas students:** 8. **Mature students:** 10%. **Male/female ratio:** 1:2. **Teaching staff:** 30 full-time, 48 part-time. **Total full-time students 1995/96:** 1,022. **First degree tuition fees:** Home students, paying their own fees in 1996/97, paid £1,600; Overseas students £5,800. Also registration fee £275.

WHAT IT'S LIKE   It shares a campus with the FE college and is across the road from Loughborough University and SU. Foundation courses on separate town centre site. Medium-sized market town, with markets every Thursday and Saturday, small shopping precinct and good high street stores, but no M&S! Centrally situated between Nottingham, Derby and Leicester. Joint SU (one of the largest) serves the university, FE college, college of art and design and RNIB vocational college. 6 bars (new Broadwalk Bar), 6 shops, night-club, nursery, travel agency, 3 banks, 4 catering outlets, opticians, dentist, hairdressers and other shops. Many students are local. Courses are strongly vocational for practising artists. 12 halls of residence for approximately 280 students – large houses pleasantly situated on main road into town, all mixed, all self-catering. Student representative council to represent the general and academic interests of students.
PAUPER NOTES   See Loughborough University.

LOUGHBOROUGH UNIVERSITY

Loughborough University, Loughborough, Leics LE11 3TU
(Tel 01509 263171, Fax 01509 223905) Map 2

STUDENT ENQUIRIES: Senior Assistant Registrar (Admissions)
APPLICATIONS: UCAS

Broad study areas: Engineering, science, physical education and sport science, social science and humanities. (Subject details are in the *Subjects and Places Index*.)

Founded: 1909; university status in 1966. **Main undergraduate awards:** BA, BSc, BEng, MChem, MEng. **Awarding body:** Loughborough University. **Site:** 216 acres about a mile from town centre. **Access:** 1 mile from M1; 1½ miles from railway station; 8 miles from East Midlands airport; bus service between town and campus. **Special features:** Excellent industry links: many staff with industrial experience; a number of specialist professors seconded from industry. Range of specialised centres and institutes including those in polymer technology and materials engineering; water engineering; computer-human interface research; landscape ecology; coaching and recreation management; consumer ergonomics; surface science and technology. **Europe:** 5% first degree students take a language as part of course and 1% spend 6 months or more abroad. 70% students have access to languages as part of their degree and plans for more. Formal exchange links with over 90 universities/colleges in all EU countries and in all disciplines. **Library:** Pilkington Library has 600,000 volumes, 400 study places. Annual expenditure on library materials, £106.05 per FTE student. **Other learning facilities:** Computing services. **Welfare:** Medical services, counsellors, advice centre, chaplains, wardens. **Careers:** Active careers service.

Amenities: Purpose-built SU building with bars, cafés, shops, travel office, banks, bookshop, dentist, optician, hairdresser, launderette; performance area for 2,000; day nursery/playgroup; student arts centre with darkroom, studio equipment, record and cassette library; associated music centre; drama studio with workshop; campus radio station. **Sporting facilities:** Sports halls, gymnasia, swimming pools, squash courts, floodlit all-weather areas and athletics stadium, tennis courts, fitness centre, dance studio, numerous playing pitches.

Accommodation: In 1995/96, 64% of first degree students in university accommodation. 5,041 places available (2,813 for first years): 3,523 full board (2,208 for first years) at £63.10 per week and 1,518 self-catering (989 for first years) at £33.62–£43.70 per week, depending on contract period. Students live in privately owned accommodation for 1+ years: rents £30–£40 per week for self-catering, £45–£50 B&B. 5% first degree students live at home. **Hardship funds:** Total available in 1995/96: £157,000 government access funds, 300 students helped; £9,000 own funds, 15 helped (also 70 given short-term emergency loans) plus £2,000 other funds, 5 students helped. Special help: students with special needs, disabled students, those with dependants, mature students or those experiencing unforeseen financial pressures particularly finalists. Funds also available for overseas and part-time students.

Duration of first degree courses: 3 or 4 years **others:** 4 or 5 years. **Total first degree students 1995/96:** 7,489. **Overseas students:** 1,022. **Mature students:** 19%. **Male/female ratio:** 2:1. **Teaching staff:** 527 full-time, 25 part-time. **Total full-time students 1995/96:** 10,215. **Postgraduate students:** 2,521. **First degree tuition fees:** Home students, paying their own fees in 1996/97, paid £750; Overseas: £5,740 (classroom), £7,510 (lab/studio).

WHAT IT'S LIKE   University has over 10,000 students of which some 20% are from overseas, 18% are mature. Engineering, sciences and PE are most popular subject areas, not so many arts-based courses. Workloads vary hugely; science courses require a lot of time in practicals. Many take years out in industry or abroad. Assessment equally distributed through course work, exams and practicals. Effective academic representation through system of course reps. Good facilities for students with disabilities. Accommodation excellent – over 5000 places. For those living out, there are small ghettos of student-inhabited streets; good atmosphere and generally centred on a pub! Area is flat so good for biking although approx 40% students own cars; town 10–15 minutes walk. SU has a membership from 4 constituent student bodies – university, art college, FE college and RNIB vocational college – over 14,000 members in all. It has confidential advice centre and nursery provision with subsidised places. Students meet easily; SU is centre of activity with 6 bars (including newly redeveloped Broadwalk Bar), food outlets, travel bureau and loads of ents: excellent cabaret, theme discos and free bands on the NME/MM circuits. Council represents student interests in all areas of life. Most active societies are Rag (raised £221,588 last year, another record year) and athletics union (50+ clubs – many very successful; athletic union champions for last 10 years). Everything is on campus – some freshers don't leave it for a whole year! Good community action group, active town/student relations. Lots of pubs, markets twice a week, theatres.
PAUPER NOTES **Accommodation:** In halls, though many 2nd year students choose to live out. Some married quarters. Rents in private sector c £33/week. **Drink:** 6 bars in SU building; drinks up to 20p cheaper. Regular drinks promotions, guest beers and lots of soft drinks. Loads of student pubs in town. Three Nuns and The Swan popular. **Eats:** Hall of residence food plentiful. SU fast food outlets Chinese, Mexican, donuts, pizzas etc, pleasant piazza coffee bar. Town has plethora of restaurants and takeaways, student discounts available, curry and Chinese houses very popular. One vegetarian restaurant and a number of

wholefood shops. Ashley Road filled with catering outlets. **Ents:** Excellen[t]
every Thursday at SU; regular films, discos and top cabaret acts, nightclub wit[h]
tive nights. Drama on campus as well as in adjacent cities. In town, 3 nightclubs (stu[d]
rates), six-screen cinema. **Sports:** Excellent facilities on campus – open to SU sports club
members. **Hardship funds:** Available; subsidised nursery places. **Travel:** ABTA travel bureau
in SU – variety of cheap tickets/holidays. **Work:** Casual jobs available in SU, as well as
shop/bar work in town. New SU employment agency.
ALUMNI (EDITORS' PICK)   Alastair Biggart (Channel Tunnel), Peter Bonfield (ICL), Rob
Dickens (British Phonographic Industry), Sebastian Coe, David Moorcroft, Christina Boxer,
Danny Nightingale and Steve Scutt, Sue Shoblon, Forbes Robinson, Steve Backley, Bob
Wilson.

LSE

London School of Economics & Political Science,
University of London, Houghton Street, London WC2A 1AE
(Tel 0171 955 7124/7125, Fax 0171 831 1684) Map 6

STUDENT ENQUIRIES: Assistant Registrar (Admissions)
APPLICATIONS: UCAS

Broad study areas: All social sciences. (Subject details are in
the *Subjects and Places Index*.)

Founded: 1895. **Structural features:** Part of London University since 1900. **Main undergraduate awards:** BA, BSc, LLB. **Awarding body:** London University. **Site:** Central London (just off Aldwych). **Access:** Aldwych, Holborn and Temple underground stations; buses. **Academic features:** Unique concentration on economic and social sciences, taught in 18 departments. **Special features:** Number of public lectures from leading figures from business, politics, academia. One-year courses for visiting overseas students. **Europe:** 3% first degree students take a language as part of course and 1% spend 6 months or more abroad. Limited range of Erasmus exchange links. Language studies centre provides tuition (English, French, Spanish, German and Russian) as part of some degrees or additional courses. **Library:** British Library of Political and Economic Science is a national collection in field of social science as well as School's working library; 881,000 volumes, 4,600 current periodicals. Annual expenditure on library materials, £138.57 per FTE student. Teaching library: 31,500 volumes, with additional copies of more important course books; short loan collections of periodicals. Shaw Library: collection of general literature. **Welfare:** Doctor, dentist, FPA, psychiatrist, nursing sister, chaplains, women's adviser, disabled students' adviser. Nursery with 24 places. **Careers:** Information and advice service. **Amenities:** SU with restaurant, bar, shop, legal advice centre, newspaper and magazine; facilities of London University union in Malet Street. **Sporting facilities:** Sports grounds at New Malden; circuit-room, squash court and gymnasium on site.

Accommodation: Accommodation guaranteed for new undergraduates from outside London (approx 75% postgraduates also accommodated). 2,016 LSE places available: 195 full-board places at £45–£77 per week, 1,092 at £39–£77 per week (with pay-as-you-eat canteen), term time or longer; 729 self-catering places at £45–£75, Sept–June. Privately owned accommodation: rents £45–£100 per week for self-catering, £55–£90 for B&B. **Term time work:** Part time work accepted as financial necessity for some students. Some work available in School library and environmental improvements. **Hardship funds:** Total available in 1995/96: £157,518 government access funds, average £733 awarded; £355,118 own funds, 308 students helped. Special help: students with health problems, disabilities, childcare problems; own funds also available to students facing unanticipated financial difficulties. In addition, some £850,000 for entrance awards, based on financial need and academic merit, assigned to self-financing students of any nationality prior to course (some 200 students helped).

Duration of first degree courses: 3 or 4 years. **Total first degree students 1995/96:** 2,763. **Overseas students:** 3,211. **Mature students:** 20%. **Male/female ratio:** 3:2. **Teaching staff:** 310 full-time, c200 part-time. **Total full-time students 1995/96:** 5,089. **Postgraduate students:** 2,834 (incl 795 part-time). **First degree tuition fees:** Home students, paying their own fees in 1996/97, paid £750 (classroom), £1,600 (labs); Overseas: £7,596.

WHAT IT'S LIKE   Not a typical British university. The London School of Economics and (oft un-acronymed) Political Science has a student population half of which are from overseas and a similar percentage are postgraduates, so the demography is vastly different from many other institutions. The buildings are centred around the pedestrianised Houghton Street and are not attractive by anyone's definition: some say the cramped maze of corridors give the place an *esprit du corps*. Academically the LSE is extremely strong and tops the ratings fairly consistently. Nearly all assessment is exam based, and there is rarely an opportunity to resit. Each student has a tutor, who is officially responsible for overseeing their welfare and education. For a few this works exceptionally well; for some less so. The SU is active and vociferous. The diversity of beliefs, backgrounds and culture of the student body leads to varied and ferocious debate. Many key figures are attracted to speak each year due to the international reputation. The social life is based around the SU bar, the numerous societies, SU politics, and that little place known as central London. Life is expensive in London, but on graduation many LSE students give up their left wing credentials and swap them for an American Express platinum card.

PAUPER NOTES   **Accommodation:** 3 halls of residence, self-catering apartments and houses; all first years from out of London guaranteed accommodation. 300 places in intercollegiate halls. Private accommodation expensive, so is the travel involved. **Drink:** Cheap places – SU bars, Three Tuns and the Underground. Hall bars. **Eats:** SU cafe – good vegetarian and vegan. LSE's Brunch Bowl, Pizzaburger, Robinson Room offer varied, reasonably-price range. **Ents:** LSE: packed Friday night discos (+ cheap beer), Chuckle Club for great comics every Saturday. Prince Charles cinema for cheap films. **Sports:** Gym, weights, squash and badminton courts on site. Sports grounds in New Malden. ULU's swimming pool and facilities. **Welfare:** SU advice and counselling service. **Hardship funds:** SU hardship fund and specialist funds eg 'Women's right to choose fund' and 'Disabled students'. School spends £1.5 million on scholarships, access funds etc. **Travel:** Some travel scholarships. STA branch on campus. **Work:** Some casual work in School and SU – whole of London casual market.

MORE INFO?   Get students' Alternative Prospectus and SU Handbook.

ALUMNI (EDITORS' PICK)   Worldwide: current or past, over 23 Presidents, Prime Ministers or Head of State; 41 Governors or Chairs of banks; 120 Ambassadors or Ministers; some 30 MPs. Also John F Kennedy, Mick Jagger, George Soros, John Moore, Lord Young, Maurice Saatchi, Lloyd Grossman, Ralph Dahrendorf, Roland Dumas, Paul Volker, Carlos (the Jackal), Kim Campbell, Virginia Bottomley, Clare Francis, Bernard Levin, Pierre Trudeau, Edwina Currie, Michael Meacher, Ron Moody, Nitin Desai (UN), R K Nalayanan, B K Nehru.

LSU SOUTHAMPTON

LSU College of Higher Education, The Avenue, Southampton
SO17 1BG (Tel 01703 228761, Fax 01703 230944) Map 3

STUDENT ENQUIRIES: Registry (01703 225333)
APPLICATIONS: UCAS

Broad study areas: Arts, education, humanities, languages, sciences, sport studies, theology. (Subject details are in the *Subjects and Places Index.*)

Founded: 1904, by La Sainte Union Sisters. **Structural features:** College of Southampton University. **Main undergraduate awards:** BA, BA/BSc(QTS), BSc, BTh. **Awarding body:** Southampton University. **Site:** Single campus in Southampton city centre. **Access:** 5 minutes from city centre; 1 hour from London by train; close to airport. **Academic features:** Flexible modular structure. **Special features:** Emphasis on community atmosphere. **Europe:** Staff and student exchanges in EU. **Library:** 115,000 volumes, 530 periodicals, 237 study places. Annual expenditure on library materials, £63 per FTE student. **Welfare:** Counsellor, pastoral care team, chaplaincy team, nursery; also SU welfare service. **Careers:** Information and advice. **Amenities:** SU coffee bar, staff/student social club, bookshop on campus. **Sporting facilities:** Heated indoor swimming pool, 2 gyms, weight and fitness facilities.

Accommodation: In 1995/96, 100% of first years in college accommodation. Some full board, some self-catering; rents from approx £49 per week, academic year long contracts. Students live in privately owned accommodation for 2 years: rents approx £50–£59.99 per week for self-catering, £60–£79.99 for full-board. 50% of first degree students live at home. **Term time work:** College policy to allow term time work for first degree students. Term (and vac) work available on campus in library, bars, cleaning, catering; also outside jobs advertised on noticeboards. **Hardship funds:** Total available in 1995/96: £55,000 government access funds, 180 students helped.

Duration of first degree courses: 3 years; others: 4 years for languages, BA/BSc(QTS). **Total first degree students 1995/96:** 1,700. **Total BEd/QTS students:** 886. **Mature students:** 50%. **Male/female ratio:** 1:4. **Teaching staff:** 95 full-time, 30 part-time. **Total full-time students 1995/96:** 1,900. **Postgraduate students:** 200. **First degree tuition fees:** Home students, paying their own fees in 1996/97, paid £1,520 (classroom), £3,145 (lab/studio); Overseas students £6,225 (classroom), £8,175 (lab/studio).

WHAT IT'S LIKE   Compact and very attractive, green campus, close to train and coach station. Accommodation has improved – two new buildings, one self-catering hall – priority given to first years. City centre campus means restricted car parking but public transport good. Courses are split roughly in three between QTS courses, BA combined studies, and thirdly podiatry, theology and other courses. Personal tutor system works well and builds excellent staff/student relationships. Catholic college, but open to students of all faiths or none. Professional counselling service on campus. Careers advice well co-ordinated. Library recently doubled in size, with a vastly improved service. Media resources centre offers cost price stationery. Liaison between university and institute improving especially over library and sports facilities and events. SU has welfare and women's officers. SU raises thousands of pounds for charity, runs recycling schemes and runs a bi-monthly magazine. SU clubs and societies growing each year – at present over 30 – easy to get involved or establish new clubs. At least one event a week run by union – varied and excellent value; good use made of outside venues throughout Southampton including the Guildhall. Staff/student social club bar, guests must be signed in. Southampton has large student population of over 25,000. Nightclubs, 3 theatres, cinemas and Guildhall have student discounts.

PAUPER NOTES   Accommodation: First years guaranteed hostel accommodation. **Drink:** 3 student only nightclubs, number of pubs close to college welcome students. **Eats:** SU coffee bar, good vegetarian food. Refectory, bar food at lunchtime. Good selection of restaurants in city. **Ents:** SU entertainment weekly, local pubs put on live bands. **Sports:** College gym and weights rooms, lots of sports teams; sports centre close by; county cricket ground and premiership football. **Hardship funds:** College access fund. SU support and advice. **Travel:** Southampton University travel centre; good bus and train services. **Work:** Plenty of bar work, waitressing/waitering, kitchen staff.

MORE INFO?   Enquiries to Jim Gardner, SU President (Tel 01703 226379/221513, Fax 01703 226379).

INFORMAL NAME   LSU.

LUTON UNIVERSITY

University of Luton, Park Square, Luton LU1 3JU (Tel 01582 34111, Fax 01582 743400) Map 4

STUDENT ENQUIRIES: Marketing unit (Tel 01582 489012)
APPLICATIONS: UCAS

Broad study areas: Design & technology, business & management, humanities, science, computing, health care & social study. (Subject details are in the *Subjects and Places Index*.)

Founded: 1957 as Luton College. University status in 1993. **Main udergraduate awards:** BSc, BA, LLB. **Awarding body:** Luton University. **Site:** Main campus in town centre; Putteridge Bury site (management) 4 miles from main campus. **Access:** 5 mins from M1, bus and railway stations and international airport. **Academic features:** Most courses part of a modular degree scheme. **Europe:** 15% first degree students take a language as part of course (including building and engineering students) and 7% spend 6 weeks abroad. Formal exchange links with EU universities/colleges – open to non-language specialists. **Library:** 140,000 volumes, 800 periodicals, 500 study places; microfilm and video facilities. Annual expenditure on library materials, £59.19 per FTE student. **Other learning facilities:** Computer services, approx 600 PCs for student use; communication services: TV, video and radio stations. **Welfare:** Personal tutor for each student, doctor, FPA, independent adviser, on-site nurse; student services give advice on eg welfare, housing, finance. **Careers:** Information and advice service; courses on interviewing etc. **Amenities:** Bookshop, closed circuit TV; theatre in Luton. **Sporting facilities:** Gymnasium, martial arts room, weight training room, playing fields. Regional sports centre, Olympic pool in town.

Accommodation: In 1995/96, 1,600 places, mostly for first years; cost £45–£48 per week. Students live in privately owned accommodation for 2+ years: average £37.50 per week, self-catering. 33% first degree students live at home. **Term time work**: University's policy to allow term time work for full-time first degree students. Term (and vac) work available on campus in SU bars, offices, library, recruitment fairs, admissions etc; also on-site employment agency. **Hardship funds:** In 1995/96, £150,000+ available. Special help for mature students, those with disabilities, local students, ethnic minorities, women returners, unemployed.

Duration of first degree courses: 3 years; **others:** 4 years (sandwich). **Total first degree students 1995/96:** 5,658. **Overseas students:** 500. **Mature students:** 7,185. **Male/female ratio:** 1:1. **Teaching staff:** 950 full-time, 800 part-time. **Total full-time students 1995/96:** 8,200. **Postgraduate students:** 860. **First degree tuition fees:** Home students, paying their own fees in 1996/97, paid £750 (classroom), £1,600 (lab/studio); Overseas: £4,700 (classroom), £5,100 lab/studio).

WHAT IT'S LIKE   It's got four campuses. Main campus at Park Square is in central Luton next to parish church and Arndale Shopping Centre, which boasts usual shops and good indoor market. Putteridge Bury campus (management centre) is 4 miles away, a magnificent neo-Elizabethan mansion set in very attractive grounds. Vocational courses are at the third campus, next to Dunstable town centre; and humanities and media at the fourth campus, 5 minutes' walk away. Main campus is about 2 minutes (by taxi) from coach and railway stations and about 10 minutes from Luton International Airport. For those wanting excitement and who have money to spend, London is only half an hour away by train. Student population is increasing fast and extensive building programme means there are now 1,600 places in halls throughout the town. A university head tenancy scheme provides shared housing for majority of students. Large numbers in the private sector – reasonably priced, students are their bread and butter and university housing more expensive. Socially SU is centre of all activities. Being cheapest place to drink in town, it is always packed out. Union building has underground nightclub and two bars where you can watch television and videos on a large screen and deafen yourself listening to the CD jukebox. Regular discos weekly and a number of live bands every term plus all the usual things that happen within a thriving SU! Clubs and societies have really taken off. In town, Cannon cinema receives all latest releases very quickly; arts cinema in town library shows unusual but brilliant films; another arts centre has regular live music, comics, exhibitions etc; the more popular nightclubs have student night every week. All usual fast food joints and pizza places scattered through town; excellent Chinese and Indian restaurants; odd Italian and French restaurants, usually hidden up some obscure side street. Contrary to popular belief, Luton is a fun place to study; typical student conscientious and hard-working but when necessary can go through a metamorphic change and become the ultimate party animal.

PAUPER NOTES   **Accommodation:** Average rent £35–£40 pw, plus bills. University rents on average £7 pw more expensive. **Drink:** SU bar cheapest. Pubs generally cater for students. **Eats:** Refectories on campus: Church Street fast food; Vicarage Street, good food but vegetarian provision not good. SU range of hot food on student budget. Plenty of chip shops, kebab, Chinese and Indian (veggie curry, Leagrave Road). **Ents:** SU nightclub cheapest and safest. Local nightclubs have student nights (very cheap). Cinema (student nights Mon-Thurs) and town library has good cheap plays and films. **Sports:** Local sports facilities backed by university contacts. 3 sports centres, baths, playing fields within 3 miles. **Hardship funds:** Access fund. **Travel:** Mostly walking; poor university transport; local transport good and student discount. Get a coach and rail card. Hitching fairly easy on M1. **Work:** Job shop advertises local and national vacancies. Term and vacation job opportunities.

ALUMNI (EDITORS' PICK)   Paul Young (pop singer), Sir David Plaistow (Chairman of Vickers).

MANCHESTER BUSINESS SCHOOL

Manchester Business School, Booth Street West, Manchester M15 6PB (Tel 0161 275 6311, Fax 0161 275 6489) Map 2

STUDENT ENQUIRIES: Admissions Officer, MBA Office
APPLICATIONS: Direct

Broad study areas (Not at first degree): Business, management. (Subject details are in the *Subjects and Places Index*.)

Founded: 1965. **Special features:** Postgraduate only; a faculty of Manchester University. **Main awards:** MBA, PhD, Diploma in Business Administration (DBA). **Awarding body:** Manchester University. **Site:** University area of Manchester Education Precinct, 1 mile from city centre. **Access:** Regular bus service from most parts of the city. **Academic features:** MBA course combines management theory and practice leading in the later stage to consultancy-type projects within organisations. Doctoral programme involves one year of taught courses followed by a research project leading to the thesis. **Europe:** Most students take a language as part of course. Formal exchange links with 6 EU universities/colleges. **Library:** 30,000 volumes, 800 journals, over 100 databases, newsclippings and annual report files. **Other learning facilities:** Advanced computing facilities; commercial information services. **Welfare:** Emergency doctor, psychiatrist, chaplain, solicitor. **Careers:** career development centre. **Amenities:** University sports centre nearby (swimming pool, sauna, squash, etc). **Employment:** International commerce, finance, consultancy, marketing, line management.

Accommodation: No school accommodation. Students live in privately owned accommodation for whole course: rents £40–£150 per week for self-catering.

Teaching staff: 45 full-time. **Total full-time students 1995/96:** 260. **Total part-time students 1995/96:** 120. **Doctoral students:** 70. **Male/female ratio:** 2:1. **Tuition fees:** Home students in 1996/97 paid £7,500; Overseas students £9,000.

WHAT IT'S LIKE   Emphasis on putting theory into practice; use of projects as major teaching tool, with less emphasis on more traditional exam and case study approach. Formal training in all the basic aspects of management, but the project dominates course.

Subject matter varies but working with groups of fellow students is always required. This can be rewarding or frustrating (sometimes both) and teaches you how to rely on other people in pressurised situations. Strong individualists who find it difficult to work in teams have a tough time. Students are all postgraduate; from a wide range of backgrounds with degrees ranging from medieval English literature to banking. Most have had significant work experience varying from being a diplomat in Peking to running a small business – 18 months with this body of students is a great source of learning. Student views given increasing consideration by new director. Courses require mental stamina and considerable personal commitment; the rewards in terms of personal achievement and learning within a group environment cannot be denied. Good chance of getting on the international exchange programme, to spend one term at a prestigious business school in the USA, Europe, Asia or Australasia. Excellent social scene developed around the multi-cultural makeup of the student body. Non-profit making MBS club arranges several sports and social events each term.

PAUPER NOTES **Accommodation:** Average MBA student spends £300 a month, including electricity. **Drink:** MBS club. **Eats:** Good choice of fairly cheap lunch in MBS canteen; vegetarian choices daily. On the Eighth Day for vegetarian. **Ents:** University Theatre, postgrad film society, Royal Exchange Theatre, Hallé Orchestra, Palace Theatre (Grand Opera and Ballet), Royal Northern College of Music, just across the road. **Sports:** MacDougall Centre (plus swimming pool) within walking distance. Special discount at up-market Y-Club (£2.50 to enter). Peak District close at hand, and sailing at nearby Tatton Mere. **Travel:** Campus Travel in Oxford Road has good deals. **Work:** Almost all take on summer jobs in UK or Europe. Salaries £400–£2000 (average £600 a week).

MORE INFO? Get students' Alternative Prospectus.

ALUMNI (EDITORS' PICK) Joe Matthews (managing director, Adamson-Butterley), Terence Riorden (managing director, Benrose Ltd), Andrew Slinn (general manager for Europe – Readicut International), Chris Kirkland (business development executive, Burmah Oil), Tim O'Brian (project manager, Norcros), James Ross (chief executive, Cable and Wireless), John Ward (president of Midland Montagu, America).

MANCHESTER METROPOLITAN UNIVERSITY

The Manchester Metropolitan University, All Saints, Manchester M15 6BH (Tel 0161 247 2000, Fax 0161 247 7383) Map 2

STUDENT ENQUIRIES: Academic Registrar
APPLICATIONS: UCAS (SWAS for social work programme)

Broad study areas: Art & design, education, sport science, clothing and food technology, hotel, catering and tourism management, social science, business, science, humanities, law, engineering. (Subject details are in the *Subjects and Places Index*.)

Founded: 1970 as Manchester Poly, incorporating various colleges of art, technology, commerce and education. University status in 1992. **Main undergraduate awards:** BA, BEd, BSc, BEng, LLB. **Awarding body:** Manchester Metropolitan University. **Site:** In or near city centre, except for Didsbury site (6 miles away), Hollings (3 miles), Elizabeth Gaskell (2 miles), Crewe and Alsager (40 miles south). **Access:** Regular bus service to Didsbury, Hollings and Elizabeth Gaskell sites. Good rail service between Crewe and Manchester. **Europe:** 20% first degree students take a language as part of course (2,000 students) and 11% spend 6 months or more abroad. Language an option on most courses. Exchange links with 49 universities in France, Germany and Spain (many open to non-language specialists; some providing an additional foreign qualification). **Library:** 8 libraries, total of 1 million volumes, 4,500 periodicals, 3,000 study places. Annual expenditure on library materials, £83 per FTE student. **Specialist collections:** Include book design, children's literature 1870–1930, local collections. **Other learning facilities:** Extensive computing facility. **Welfare:** Counsellors, chaplains, learning support advisers (learning skills and disability). Branch surgery at Didsbury and All Saints; local GPs at Alsager. Nursery shared with Manchester University. Legal advice from solicitors via SU. Some accommodation for disabled students. **Careers:** Information and advice. **Amenities:** Horniman Theatre, art galleries and studios. SU building including bar, restaurant, shop, launderette and games room. **Sporting facilities:** Sports facilities include gymnasia, sports halls, tennis and squash courts, weight training and swimming pools at Didsbury and Alsager. Playing fields at Carrington and at Crewe and Alsager; track and field athletics.

Accommodation: In 1995/96, 10% of all students in university accommodation, 20% of first years (higher proportion at Crewe and Alsager). 2,417 places available (2,070 for first years): 1,784 full-board places (1,604 for first years) at £61.50 per week, 633 self-catering places (544 first years) at £40.30 per week, term time only. 780 more places at All Saints campus by 1998. Most students live in privately owned accommodation for whole course: rents £35–£42 per week for self-catering, £37–£52 for B&B, £56–£59 half-board and weekend meals. **Hardship funds:** Total available in 1995/96: £501,134 government access funds, average £250 awarded. Special help: self-financing students, those with children, mature students.

Duration of first degree courses: 3 years; **others:** 4 years (sandwich); up to 7 years (part-time). **Total first degree students 1995/96:** 18,438. **BEd students:** 1,572. **Overseas students:** 618. **Mature students:** 17,185. **Male/female ratio:** 9:11. **Teaching staff:** 1,170 full-time, 569 part-time. **Total full-time students 1995/96:** 20,183. **Postgraduate students:** 5,499. **First degree tuition fees:** Home students, paying their own fees in 1996/97, paid £750 (classroom), £800 (lab/studio); Overseas students £5,600 (£6,000 if paid in 3 instalments).

WHAT IT'S LIKE   It's the largest non-collegiate university in Europe having over 20,000 students in the middle of the largest higher educational campus in western Europe. Martin Luther King Building on All Saints site, 5 mins from city centre, acts as central point for SU activity although facilities provided on 4 other sites over 6-mile radius. SU runs 6 bars, 3 catering outlets, 6 shops, launderette, bank, travel service, welfare service, student magazine, crèche facilities and social, entertainment events. Student welfare advice at SU and university helps with accommodation, finance, legal and course problems. Active athletic union provides fun in the bar and on the field; many societies have something for everyone – all found within the MLK Building. Manchester is an active and popular city which caters for most tastes; active gay scene. The university has many specialised and interesting courses.

PAUPER NOTES   **Accommodation:** Hall space limited but increasing. Private rented accommodation available but look early; prices appear to be decreasing. **Drink:** Dry 201, Flea & Firkin, Red Lion, Robinski's, Queen of Hearts, Jabez Clegg, Sshed, Manto, Canal Bar,

Joshua Brooks. **Eats:** Rusholme for Asian food, Chinatown, Greens, 8th Day, Café Alto, Corner House and Lime Tree Café. **Ents:** Weekly films, club nights, comedy and cabaret nights, bands, fashion show, all in main SU building. **Sports:** Carrington Sports Ground, All Saints Sports Centre, Didsbury gym and pool, Mable Tylecote gym. **Travel:** Buses frequent along Oxford Road corridor – save money with termly bus pass. **Work:** Bar work, security, catering at SU; supermarkets, waiting, club/bar work- reasonable pay.
ALUMNI (EDITORS' PICK)   L S Lowry (painter), Ossie Clark (fashion designer), Julie Walters (actress), Bryan Robson (footballer), Mick Hucknall (lead singer of Simply Red), Steve Coogan (comedian).

MANCHESTER UNIVERSITY

University of Manchester, Manchester M13 9PL
(Tel 0161 275 2000) Map 2

STUDENT ENQUIRIES: Schools & Colleges Liaison Office
APPLICATIONS: UCAS

Broad study areas: Science and engineering, social sciences, humanities, languages, law, medicine, dentistry, pharmacy, speech pathology and therapy. (Subject details are in the *Subjects and Places Index.*)

Founded: 1851, charter granted in 1903. **Main undergraduate awards:** BA, BSc, BEng, MEng, BSocSci, BDS, BEd, BNurs, LLB, MBChB, MusB. **Awarding body:** University of Manchester. **Site:** 1 mile south of city centre. **Access:** Bus. **Special features:** Jodrell Bank Radio Telescope; Nuffield radio astronomy laboratories at Jodrell Bank; University Theatre, Science Park, Manchester Museum, Whitworth Art Gallery. Lindsay String Quartet in residence. Joint Centre for European Studies. **Europe:** 14% of first degree students take a language as part of their course and spend a period abroad. **Library:** John Rylands University library, over 3 million volumes, 8,000 periodicals, 650 study places, course books on reference. Also over 1 million mss and 800,000 microform titles. Annual expenditure on library materials, £125.20 per FTE student. **Specialist collections:** Charters, early printed and rare books, manuscripts, military documents, archives (eg of *Manchester Guardian*). **Welfare:** Central academic advisory service, counsellors, student health service, SU welfare office, inter-denominational chapel, crèche. **Careers:** Information, advice and placement service. **Amenities:** SU bars, live music venue, second-hand bookshop, student market etc. **Sporting facilities:** Indoor sports centres, wide range of outdoor sport (Firs Athletic Ground, athletics union, boat house, yacht club, football pitches).

Accommodation: In 1995/96, 42% of all students in university accommodation, 100% first years (guaranteed for all who want it). 9,381 places available: 3,177 half-board places at £53–£74 per week, term time or longer; 5,635 self-catering places at £29–£51 per week, Sept–June; and 569 assorted, married, postgraduate etc at £32–£68 per week, all year. Students live in privately owned accommodation for 1–2 years on average: rents £28–£40 per week for self-catering, £36–£40 for B&B, £44–£48 for half-board, **Hardship funds:** Limited assistance is available in exceptional circumstances.

Duration of first degree courses: 3 years; **others:** 4 years (some arts and science courses and nursing); 5–6 years (medicine and dentistry). **Total first degree students 1995/96:** 16,504. **Overseas students:** 963. **Male/female ratio:** 1:1. **Full-time students 1995/96:** 16,848. **Postgraduate students:** 3,042 (full-time). **First degree tuition fees:** Home students, paying their own fees in 1996/97, paid £750 (classroom), £1,600 (lab/studio), £2,800 (clinical); Overseas: £5,890 (classroom), £7,810 (lab/studio), £14,380 (clinical).

WHAT IT'S LIKE   Screw up your eyes and Manchester in May could look like Venice in January – the university's central square shows more than passing resemblance to St Mark's Square for the romantically inclined (difference being that one is surrounded by water, the other suffused in drizzle). The university takes many of its characteristics from its mother city: it's gruff, grandly built, hard-working and friendly. 15,000-strong student body allows for huge range of tastes; somewhere in the mass of the university there is someone who shares your interests and desires, whatever they may be. Halls of residence, especially Whitworth Park, known as The Toblerones, good bet for first years trying to establish social niche. The university kicked off the social science revolution in the '60s. Before that, it had established firm reputation in classics, arts and sciences. Reputations all still well-founded.

PAUPER NOTES   **Accommodation:** Every kind available, including married quarters. **Drink:** SU bars (The Serpent, The Cellar) very cheap and lively. Jabez Clegg opposite is handy and old-style. Loads of cheap pubs and clubs. **Eats:** The Curry Half Mile, Rusholme – thousands of brilliant meals under £5. Lots of good vegetarian food (Veg Café, The 8th Day Café, The Fallen Angel); China Town. **Ents:** The Academy – hundreds of big names, top NW venue (1,900 capacity). Corner House for arty films, lots of mainstream cinemas. **Sports:** McDougall Centre, The Armitage Centre (uni run) very cheap. **Hardship funds:** Uni access funds – small amounts for large number of applicants. SU gives emergency money up to £75. **Travel:** Hitching good outside city centre. Buses very frequent; metrolink trams; bike lanes. **Work:** Some work in bars, shops and fast food places, on and off campus, but not enough jobs to go round.

ALUMNI (EDITORS' PICK)   Mark Carlisle MP, Sir Rhodes Boyson MP, Sir Maurice Oldfield (MI6), Robert Bolt (playwright), Anthony Burgess (novelist), Christabel Pankhurst (suffragette), Peter Maxwell Davies (composer), Sir Frank Worrall (sport), Lord Lever (politician), Alan Gowling (sport), John Tomlinson (music), Anna Ford (broadcaster), C A Lejeune (film critic), Rik Mayall (actor), Francis Thompson (poet), Ian McNaught Davis, Ben Elton.

MIDDLESEX UNIVERSITY

Middlesex University, White Hart Lane, London N17 8HR
(Tel 0181 362 5000, Fax 0181 362 6076) Map 5

STUDENT ENQUIRIES: Admissions Enquiries
APPLICATIONS: UCAS

Broad study areas: Art & design, business, education, performing arts, engineering, science, humanities, social science, health studies, nursing. (Subject details are in the *Subjects and Places Index.*)

Founded: 1973 as Middlesex Poly, incorporating various colleges of technology, education, speech & drama, Hornsey College of Art, London College of Dance. University status 1992. **Main undergraduate awards:** BA, BSc, BEng, MEng. **Awarding body:** Middlesex University. **Site:** 6 major campuses, 2 minor campuses and 4 hospital locations – all in north London; dance in Bedford. **Access:** All campuses served by tube, bus or BR. **Academic features:** Courses include: artificial intelligence, contemporary writing, ecology and ecotechnology, garden design, health studies and herbal medicine, jazz, music technology, race and culture. Special entry procedures for mature students including those without formal qualifications. **Specialist centres:** Research centres include: enterprise and economic development, flood hazard, microelectronics, urban pollution, criminology, tennis performance. **Europe:** Language skills available on every course. All disciplines can be studied partly at an institution abroad, sometimes with the opportunity to gain an additional overseas qualification. Many work placements can be in Europe. **Library:** 6 main libraries, plus 7 others; total of 450,000 volumes, 3,000 periodicals, 1,250 study places, 15,000 video tapes, course books for reference. Library at Trent Park with 7,000 records and tapes, 10,000 books on music. Art and design library at Cat Hill has 300,000 slides and illustrations. Annual expenditure on library materials, £48.07 per FTE student. **Other learning facilities:** 3 TV studios, 6 computer centres, 3 language centres. **Specialist collections:** Silver Studio Collection – complete archive of a London design studio 1880–1960; Sir J Richards library (design, fine art, planning and conservation). **Welfare:** Counsellors, advice staff, nurse in each of 6 health centres, special needs worker, 3 nurseries, half-term playschemes. Ecumenical chaplaincy. **Careers:** Careers advisers (seminars, employer presentations and practical workshops). **Amenities:** Bookshops at Bounds Green, Enfield, Hendon, Tottenham and Trent Park. **Sporting facilities:** Sports hall, astroturf pitch, indoor and outdoor tennis courts, squash courts, saunas, indoor and outdoor swimming pools, playing fields, health & fitness centre, gymnasia including multigym. Tennis performance centre.

Accommodation: In 1995/96, 15% of all students in university accommodation, approx 80% of first years who wish it. 2,411 self-catering places (58% with ensuite facilities) £46–£54 per week. Priority given to first years and overseas students. Privately rented accommodation, £45–£60 per week plus bills. 40% first degree students live at home. **Term time work:** University's policy to allow term time work for full-time first degree students (60% believed to work). Term (and vac) work available on campus in catering, library, offices etc; also careers service and adverts help find work off campus. **Hardship funds:** Total available in 1995/96: £480,500 government access funds, 748 students helped, average £651 awarded. Special consideration to single parents or students with dependents and students with special needs (45% of all funds).

Duration of first degree courses: 3 years, 4 years (sandwich, BEd, MEng and part-time courses), part-time 5–8 years. **Total first degree students 1995/96:** 13,594. **Overseas students:** 1,049. **Mature students:** 64%. **Male/female ratio:** 1:1. **Teaching staff:** 621 full-time, 194 part-time. **Total full-time students 1995/96:** 16,505. **Postgraduate students:** 2,998. **First degree tuition fees:** Home students, paying their own fees in 1996/97, paid £2,400; Overseas students £5,900–£7,000.

WHAT IT'S LIKE *Middlesex* Sites all over north London range in style from the traditionally picturesque parklands of Trent Park, to converted grammar schools, the prototype for the Pompidou Centre (at Bounds Green), modern new buildings and the old home of ballerina Anna Pavlova (Ivy House). Communication and travel between sites can be difficult to get used to but services are improving. Social life can suffer on some of the smaller or out of the way sites but the SU has increasing representation at these sites and things are slowly improving. Entertainments are provided up to 6 nights a week at a variety of campuses – discos (10–15 a week), live bands (occasionally), comedy, cabaret, jazz etc; also large freshers ball and 3-day summer festie at end of year. A new venue at Enfield set to be the premier venue in the area. Bars on 4 sites, each with a different atmosphere and competitive prices. Halls spread around various sites, including new buildings at Tottenham, Enfield and Hendon, range from traditional halls to self-contained flats (3–5 room) in halls building. Not much cheaper than private accommodation but are advantages, especially at Trent Park, of being on site and in a safe environment. Private accommodation can be expensive at London prices; best to share. Excellent sports facilities; SU organises competitive sport (table tennis team is nationally known). New state of the art sports centre at Hendon and good facilities on other major sites. Cat Hill art & design faculty and the performance arts and drama courses are among the best in the country. Renowned for unusual courses, often not available elsewhere, such as herbal medicine. Well respected business school at Hendon. A high percentage of mature students and large numbers from overseas; university now has units worldwide including Malaysia, Hong Kong, Latin America and parts of Europe.　*Ashley Jarvis*

PAUPER NOTES　**Accommodation:** Private accommodation hard to find but accommodation service helps; halls just cheaper. **Drink:** Cheap bars on 6 site. **Eats:** Food outlets at all sites. SU provides cheap food with good vege/vegan products. **Ents:** On a variety of sites throughout the week. College ents usually cheaper than London prices. **Sports:** Wide range of sports facilities available to all students (£15); £3 to join union team, small coaching charge. **Hardship funds:** Access funds; SU loans (£50); good university and union welfare advice. **Travel:** Cheap inter-campus bus in term. Free minibus service Trent Park to/from tube station. **Work:** Some temp work in SU (bars, shops, security). Vacancies on noticeboards. Usually lots of summer work in London.

ALUMNI (EDITORS' PICK)　Adam Ant (pop star), Ally Capellino (Alison Lloyd and Jonathan Platt), Wendy Dagworthy (fashion); Ray Davies (pop star – Kinks), Lynsey de Paul (pop star), Richard Torry; Gerald Hoffnung, Anish Kapoor (international artist), Richard Wilson (sculptor), Vivienne Westwood (fashion designer), Omar (singer), Nick Harvey MP.

WHAT IT'S LIKE　*London College of Dance*　It's quite small, at present only about 70 students, but that's how it's intended and leads to a friendly and intimate atmosphere. Though now part of Middlesex University it is situated in Bedford – not London as its name suggests. LCD is not a stage school as such, but the students on the dance degree course are taught to such a high standard that a dancing career is often possible. Good student/teacher ratio. Music staff particularly helpful and very talented and often compose pieces for students to use in teaching practice etc. Small number of mature students seem to fit in quite well. Very well equipped. Spacious mirrored studios with sprung floors, air-conditioning, piano and music system (though watch out for a hefty studio fee). The Bowen-West Community Theatre is a stone's throw away, for student performances and many other shows. Attractive setting in leafy square only ten minutes' walk from the hustle and bustle of the town centre. SU small, organises parties and represents students at meetings with staff. No facilities or bars but can use Bedford College bar and disco. Courses are good; workload is quite hard and there's continuous assessment. It's widely recognised that the college produces good teachers and the degree course is the only one of its kind in the country. Most students look upon dance as a form of bringing enjoyment to anyone, whatever age or ability, and strive to keep it a recognised, worthwhile art form. LCD involves a lot of hard work but it's also a lot of fun.

PAUPER NOTES　**Accommodation:** No halls of residence; plenty of outside accommodation at decent prices (but inspect it personally). **Drink:** Bedford College bar (reduced prices), good local pubs (including country ones if you have a car), one popular nightclub

and one popular but expensive disco pub. **Eats:** College meals; subsidised
of local choice, especially pizzas and Indian. Local pubs also have good
Ents: Bedford College disco; own Xmas/Hallowe'en parties. **Sports:** Use of Bed
sports facilities, public swimming pool, squash courts, leisure complex. **Hardship**
helps people in great difficulty. **Travel:** Usually by bike – but good bus services. S   us
for reduced coach travel. **Work:** Part-time jobs, including teaching dance.
INFORMAL NAME   LCD.

MORAY HOUSE

Moray House Institute of Education, Heriot-Watt University,
Holyrood Road, Edinburgh EH8 8AQ
(Tel 0131 556 8455, Fax 0131 557 3458) Map 1

STUDENT ENQUIRIES: **Registrar**
APPLICATIONS: **UCAS**

Broad study areas: Education, community education, physical education, leisure and sport studies, social work. (Subject details are in the *Subjects and Places Index*.)

Founded: 1835. Became Institute of Education of Heriot-Watt University in 1991. **Special features:** Moray House incorporates National Coaching Centre, and Scottish centres for sensory impairment, for international education and for physical education, movement and leisure. **Main undergraduate awards:** BA, BEd, BSc. **Awarding body:** Heriot-Watt University. **Site:** Holyrood Campus in Edinburgh; Cramond Campus (physical education, movement and leisure) 6 miles west of city centre. **Access:** Holyrood within walking distance of Waverley station; Cramond on a bus route. **Europe:** Some language training available for students going on exchanges. Formal exchange links with universities/colleges in France, Germany, Italy and Spain. **Library:** 135,000 books, 800 periodicals, 240 study places. Short loan collection of books in heaviest demand; microfilm and microfiche facilities, teaching practice collection, community studies collection, physical education library. Annual expenditure on library materials, £35 per FTE student. **Other learning facilities:** Outdoor centre in Invernesshire; resource centres for AV and computing; closed circuit television. **Careers:** Information and advice service provided by Heriot-Watt. **Welfare:** Medical officers, physiotherapist, welfare officer, accommodation officer, counsellor, chaplains for various religions. **Amenities:** Student unions on both campuses; variety of sports and other clubs. **Sporting facilities:** Gyms and games hall on both campuses. Swimming pool and playing fields at Cramond.

Accommodation: In 1995/96, 25% of all students in university accommodation, 100% of first years that wish it. 500 half-board places available, £55–£59 per week, term time only. Students live in privately owned accommodation for 2–3 years: £44 per week for self-catering (including fuel), £61 for half-board. **Term time work:** No policy on part time work for first degree students. Vac work on campus in residences. **Hardship funds:** Total available in 1995/96: £64,000 government access funds, 190 helped, £100–£750 awarded. Special help: single parents, those with child care expenses or above average accommodation costs.

Duration of first degree course: Standard 4 years, others 3 years. **Total first degree students 1995/96:** 1,359; **BEd students:** 971. **Overseas students:** 254. **Mature students:** 240. **Male/female ratio:** 1:3. **Teaching staff:** 145 full-time, 15 part-time. **Total full-time students 1995/96:** 1,877. **Postgraduate students:** 499. **First degree tuition fees:** Home students, paying their own fees in 1996/97, paid £800–£1,200; Overseas: £5,600–£5,995.

WHAT IT'S LIKE   It's on two contrasting campuses some 8 miles apart: Holyrood, period buildings, just off Edinburgh's Royal Mile and half-way between Edinburgh Castle and the Parliament; and Cramond, on the north-west outskirts of the town, a purpose-built college for PE, leisure management and movement. Halls of residence accommodate c300 students from a mixture of courses, countries and ages. Holyrood halls two miles from campus; Cramond hall on campus. Costs of breakfast and dinner are incorporated in the hall fees. Laundry on site, common room; plus ents committee. No visiting restrictions but after 10 pm overnight visitors should book a guest room. Rented accommodation for those preferring to live out not always easy to find but accommodation officer will help. Travel easy, good bus service into town. Edinburgh huge city, c40,000 students. Vast number of pubs, theatres, cinemas. Within the campuses many student societies. SU open most nights with variety of clubs, bands, discos, parties, etc. Students' Association busy political hive of activity internally and working externally with NUS. Staff/student relations good; happy atmosphere. Two counsellors in college handle all student problems. Work assessed differently within different courses: some by continuous assessment; some by examination. Academic links now established with university; all degrees now university status. Students come from all over Scotland and England, also from Sri Lanka, Malaysia and USA. Anti-racist and anti-sexist policies within college/SA. Employment prospects good: teachers, social workers, community education workers.

PAUPER NOTES   **Accommodation:** Institute halls at both campuses. **Drink:** SU bars on both campuses; also other institution's SUs. **Eats:** World's End and Holyrood Tavern student discount lunches, local take-away. **Ents:** Moray House SU – both campuses – bands, clubs, parties. Party Ceilidh Disco, FBI & Shaft – very popular union events. **Sports:** Cramond campus is sport and physical education centre; Holyrood campus, pool, gym, squash etc. **Hardship funds:** Access fund; loans. **Travel:** Excellent buses from Edinburgh to anywhere; likewise trains. **Work:** Both campuses – student wardens (free digs), SU bar (also in vacation); pub work.

INFORMAL NAME   Moray House.

ALUMNI (EDITORS' PICK)   Elaine C Smith, Danny Munro (Runrig and other members).

WANT TO HELP WITH THE NEXT EDITION? SEE PAGE 66

MYERSCOUGH COLLEGE

Myerscough College, Myerscough Hall, Bilsborrow, Preston
PR3 0RY (Tel 01995 640611, Fax 01995 640842) Map 2

STUDENT ENQUIRIES: Academic Registrar
APPLICATIONS: UCAS or direct.

Broad study areas: Aboriculture, agriculture, equine science and leisure. (Subject details are in the *Subjects and Places Index*.)

Founded: 1894. **Structural features:** an associate college of Central Lancashire University. **Main award:** BSc. **Awarding body:** Central Lancashire University. **Site:** Two campuses – main site (Myerscough) 6 miles north of Preston. **Access:** Easily accessible from M6 motorway/A6 Preston-Lancaster road. BR station at Preston. **Academic features:** Modular courses allowing a range of options. BSc horticultural management offered in conjunction with Central Lancashire University. **Special features:** Strong links with allied industries. **Europe:** No students take a language as part of their course but industrial placements are available throughout Europe. Formal links with Portugal. European studies built into some courses. **Library:** 30,000 volumes, 190 periodicals taken. **Other learning facilities:** 3 lowland farms/1 hill farm, embryo transfer unit, 2ha nursery, 0.3ha glass, 5ha landscaped grounds, 20ha sportsgrounds, 30ha woodland, conservation areas, comprehensive range of irrigation systems and constructions on own 9-hole golf course, specialised workshops, indoor/outdoor schools and equestrian unit, laboratories, computer centre, audio-visual suite. **Welfare:** Residential wardens; full-time student counsellor. **Amenities:** TV/common rooms, college bar, shop, stage and auditorium, active sports and social club. **Sporting facilities:** Tennis courts, football, rugby, cricket, hockey, bowling, golf, horse riding, badminton, basketball; leisure centre.

Accommodation: 331 places in college accommodation: £2,430 pa for single room plus food. Students live in privately owned accommodation for 1–2 years: £35 per week self-catering, plus bills. 20% of first degree students live at home. **Term time work:** College policy to allow term time work for first degree students (25% believed to work). College helps find industrial placements only.

Duration of first degree courses: 4 years. **Mature students:** 20%. **Male/female ratio:** 3:1. **Total full-time and sandwich students:** 882. **First degree tuition fees:** Home students, paying their own fees in 1996/97, paid £1,600.

WHAT IT'S LIKE   It's one of the oldest agricultural colleges in the country and recently celebrated its centenary under a new name, Myerscough College. It provides training and education for a wide range of land-based and rural leisure careers. Facilities and teaching resources are good. Courses have strong practical element and generally include a total of one year's industrial placement in Britain or abroad. Good student social life including discos, films, bands, live entertainment, plus lively night-life in nearby university town of Preston. Excellent shops, restaurants, cinemas. Good road/rail access; Lake District, Fylde coast, and all major NW cities nearby.

...IER UNIVERSITY

...er University, Edinburgh, Craiglockhart Campus,
2.. Colinton Road, Edinburgh EH14 1DJ
(Tel 0131 444 2266, Fax 0131 455 4666) Map 1

STUDENT ENQUIRIES: Information Office, Freepost, Edinburgh
EH14 0PA (Tel 0131 455 4330, Fax 0131 455 4666).
APPLICATIONS: UCAS (CATCH for nursing courses)

Broad study areas: Applied arts, engineering, science, business, nursing. (Subject details are in the *Subjects and Places Index*.)

Founded: 1964 as Napier Poly; university status in 1992. **Main undergraduate awards:** BA, BEng, BSc. **Awarding body:** Napier University. **Site:** 5 major sites with 6 annexes. **Academic features:** Most courses are sandwich, all are vocationally oriented. Modular system taught in semesters. Degree courses include interior design; applied physics with computing; quantity surveying (multi-mode attendance); publishing; hospitality management; electronic and communication engineering. **Special features:** Access courses in engineering, electronics, sciences, physics for those without formal entry qualifications. **Europe:** Number of students learning a language or spending time abroad, not known. All students offered language tuition. **Library:** 4 libraries; 250,000 volumes, 2,500 periodicals, 1,275 study places. Annual expenditure on library materials, £56.23 per FTE student. **Welfare:** Medical officers, nurse, student advisers, chaplains. **Careers:** Information, advice and placement service. **Amenities:** SU facilities at all main sites, sports dome, swimming pool.

Accommodation: In 1995/96, 21% of all students in university accommodation, 66% of first years. 168 self-catering places in hall of residence; £32 per week (shared), £42 (single), 35 week contract. 546 places in controlled flats/houses; £38–£48 per week, 42 weeks. Most students live in privately owned accommodation for whole course: average rents £44 per week for self-catering, £58 per week for half-board. 411 more places planned for 1997. **Hardship funds:** Total available in 1995/96: £168,611 government access funds, 1,200 students helped. Special help: mature/married students with children.

Duration of first degree courses: 3 or 4 years; **others:** 4 or 5 years. **Total first degree students 1995/96:** 7,544; **Mature students:** 29%; **Overseas students:** 2%. **Male/female ratio:** 2:1. **Teaching staff:** 600. **Total full-time students 1995/96:** 6,991. **Postgraduate students:** 1,170. **First degree tuition fees:** Home students, paying their own fees in 1996/97, paid £750 (classroom), £1,050 (lab/studio); Overseas students £5,720 (classroom), £6,325 (lab/studio)

WHAT IT'S LIKE It's spread over 10 sites throughout Edinburgh and beyond to the borders (new faculty of health studies) – a fact that, in itself, creates obvious communication problems. Napier Students' Association (NSA) has bars at main sites, each with its own atmosphere, also shops at 3 sites and a large venue for stage bands. Edinburgh is not short of pubs. Uni halls of residence house a tiny proportion of students, some in pretty poor shape. Academically, emphasis is on science, technology and commercial disciplines. Significant increase in short, high-turnover, money spinning courses, offered mainly by professional studies faculty. Uni now appears to be filled past capacity. It's not alone in expanding student intake without funding and facilities to match. Uni now making a priority of teaching standards and student resources. 250 new student flats just opened in the city centre, however demand outstrips supply.

PAUPER NOTES **Accommodation:** Edinburgh is expensive; accommodation hard to find. Uni flats and halls reasonably priced. **Drink:** NSA bar prices amongst cheapest in Edinburgh. Beamish Red excellent, Cidermaster not to be missed. Loads of pubs – any in The Grassmarket or Rose Street good, also Bennets Bar, the Malt Shovel, Berties and of course the famous Diggers (The Athletic Arms) which serves the best beer in town! **Eats:** Merky Bar (NSA bar at Merchiston), quality cheap food; traditional chippies, Kalpna (voted best vegetarian restaurant in Britain). Restaurants to suit every taste, Mexican to American, Spanish to Armenian. **Ents:** Tons of cinemas including a 12-screen UCI and a 6-screen Odeon; Filmhouse and Cameo independent cinemas. Many theatres from the Lyceum to the Bedlam Theatre. Edinburgh nightclubs, from mainstream Century 2000 to the more student orientated Shag and Shady Ladies. NSA ents – discos, ceilidhs etc – high quality, quantity and variety. **Sports:** University sports dome at Sighthill, many active sports clubs. Council run free low cost sports centres and swimming pools. **Hardship funds:** Access fund; NSA hardship loan fund. **Travel:** NSA sells ISIC, rail and NUS cards and student bargains. Edinburgh has good bus network and reasonable fares. **Work:** Not guaranteed or well paid, but are jobs to be had in pubs, hotels, bookshops, shops or even McDonald's! NSA Job Club and piloting an employment bureau (big take-up rate).

MORE INFO?   Get students' Alternative Prospectus. Enquiries to Students Union on 0131 229 8791.

BUZZ-WORDS   Merky Bar (Merchiston Union), Shitehill (Sighthill campus), The Prince (our beloved Principal).

ALUMNI (EDITORS' PICK)   Ian Buchanan (Edinburgh Councillor), Steve Jacks (Radio Forth DJ), Jane Franchie (BBC Scotland), Greg Kane (Hue & Cry), Gavin Hastings (Scottish rugby).

NATIONAL EXTENSION COLLEGE

National Extension College, 18 Brooklands Avenue, Cambridge CB2 2HN (Tel 01223 316644, Fax 01223 313586) Map 4

STUDENT ENQUIRIES: Head of Degree & Professional Services
APPLICATIONS: University of London External Programme (Senate House, Malet Street, London WC1 7HU; tel 0171 636 8000, extn 3150). Then apply to NEC.

Broad study areas: Law, economics, management, humanities, languages, divinity. (Subject details are in the *Subjects and Places Index*.)

Founded: 1963, ex University Correspondence College. **Main undergraduate awards:** BA, BD, LLB, BSc. **Awarding body:** London University (external). **Special features:** Home-based teaching by correspondence; students are from a wide range of ages and background.

Teaching is by NEC tutors; work schedules are individually worked out and assignments set by tutors. **Welfare:** Subject tutors are also personal tutors.

Duration of first degree courses: 3–8 years. **Total first degree students 1995/96:** 257. **Overseas students:** 126. **Mature students:** Most. **Male/female ratio:** 1:1. **Teaching staff:** 97 part-time. **First degree tuition fees:** Students in 1996/97 paid £135 plus registration fee £25 per assignment for home students; £27 for overseas.

WHAT IT'S LIKE   After passing A-level law, Fiona Mont is taking a London University law degree with NEC:

'I tried to do it on my own at first and found it very difficult. Having a tutor is much better – it's good to have someone checking that you're heading in the right direction. I'm hoping to become a solicitor and the Law Society recommended this as the best home study route to my degree. I might take the exam next year – which is quicker than if I'd gone to university. After the degree I'll need a year at Law School and then at least 18 months as an articled clerk. I expect to qualify finally in about 2002!'

When the Institute of Materials decided that Leopold Norris's degree in materials science was too academic to grant Chartered Engineer status, Leo decided to take his Engineering Council Part 2 with NEC to bridge the gap:

'I didn't have enough engineering or technological experience. So I chose papers which would give me a broader knowledge. There were no evening classes, and I have a busy time at work, so NEC was the obvious choice. I've just sat the exams, though, so I'm waiting to find out how I've done ...'

Peter Pike is taking a BA course in French:

'I've always been interested in French literature and often wanted to study it in more depth.' However, with a busy career as a commercial claims manager in the insurance industry, going to university was never an option. 'If I'd known about home study before I would have done it years ago. What is so good about the degree, though, is the range of papers you can choose from. It means I can do some German too.'

NATIONAL FILM & TV SCHOOL

National Film and Television School, Beaconsfield Studios, Station Road, Beaconsfield, Bucks HP9 1LG (Tel 01494 671234, Fax 01494 674042) Map 4

STUDENT ENQUIRIES: Admissions
APPLICATIONS: Direct

Broad study areas *(Not at first degree)*: Film and television studies, programme making and screen studies. (Subject details are in the *Subjects and Places Index*.)

Founded: 1970. **Main awards:** Associate of NFTS. **Awarding body:** National Film and Television School. **Site:** Beaconsfield. Intention is to move to the old Ealing Studios in London. **Access:** British Rail. **Special features:** Postgraduate, post-experience school. From 1997, the school year runs from January to December, based on 2 semesters. **Entrance:** 50–60 students admitted annually; average age 25 years. No formal entrance qualifications but applicants need to demonstrate knowledge of basic skills in practice and theory within their area of study. **Academic features:** Courses specialising in animation direction, cinematography, direction (documentary/fiction), editing, producing, screen design, sound, screenwriting and music. Range of prestigious resident and visiting tutors. **Europe:** Strong links with other film schools. Corporate membership of CILECT (Centre International des Ecoles de Cinema et Television); school is founding member of GEECT (European Association of Film and Television Schools); staff and student exchanges with other European schools. **Library:** 2,500+ volumes, 35 periodicals (entire collection film-oriented). **Careers:** Advice service. **Amenities:** Student membership of British Academy of Film and Television Art; Corporate membership of British Film Institute, and CILECT.

Accommodation: No school accommodation. **Hardship funds:** Own small fund.

Duration of postgraduate course(s): 2 or 3 years. **Male/female ratio:** 2:3. **Teaching staff:** 18 full-time. **Postgraduate students:** 169. **Tuition fees:** Home students, paying their own fees in 1997, paid £2,500; Overseas students £11,000.

WHAT IT'S LIKE   Fully equipped school, having taken over the British Lion studio in Beaconsfield. Provides practical hands-on film training for a small number of students in all the major disciplines of film making. Allows students to gain a considerable amount of useful experience, and to build up a show-reel of work to promote themselves in the profession and the industry. Under a new director, the school has been redefining its curriculum, reviewing its selection procedures and developing a short course programme. The essential means of learning are still practical hands-on film, video and TV production but this practical work is, more than ever before, complemented with a more structured course which offers screening and analysis of films, workshops, lectures and seminars. Beaconsfield is isolated. Most students live in London and commute out; the school offers a free bus service that takes students to Beaconsfield in the morning and back to London at the end of the day. Possibility of a move to Ealing sometime soon. A film course is only as good as the people who run it, whatever the structure. The few excellent tutors need their numbers boosting. Some are full-time; some part-time because they are working, which is good for contacts in the industry.

ALUMNI (EDITOR'S PICK)   **Directors:** Beeben Kichon, Peter Hewitt, Michael Coton Jones, Elaine Proctor, Michael Redford, Danny Cannon. **Documentary:** Molly Dineen, Nick Broomfield, Jane Bokove, Chris Cox. **Cinematographers:** Dianne Tammes, Oliver Stapleton, Gabriel Berenstein, Cinders Forshaw, Andrez Sekula. **Animators:** Nick Parks, David Anderson, Joanne Woodward, Mark Baker. **Writers:** Shawn Slovo, Alrick Riley, Nicholas Martin. **Music Composers:** Julian Wastall, Trevor Jones, Philip Appleby, Julian Nott. **Editors:** Ena Lind, Alex Mackie, David Freeman. **Sound:** Ronald Bailey, Danny Handbook, George Richards. **Producers:** Jennifer Howarth, Steve Morrison, Steve Bayly. **Art directors:** Laurence Dorman, Carmel Collins.

CAN'T FIND WHAT YOU'RE LOOKING FOR? USE THE INDEX!

NENE COLLEGE

Nene College of Higher Education, Park Campus, Boughton
Green Road, Northampton NN2 7AL (Tel 01604 735500,
Fax 01604 720636, E-mail rdo.apply@nene.ac.uk) Map 4

STUDENT ENQUIRIES: Central Registry
APPLICATIONS: UCAS

Broad study areas: Design and industry, education, humanities,
social science, business, nursing, professions allied to medicine.
(Subject details are in the *Subjects and Places Index*.)

Founded: 1975, ex colleges of education, art and technology. **Main undergraduate awards:**
BA, BA(QTS), BSc. **Awarding body:** Nene College. **Site:** 2 sites: Park Campus on northern
edge of Northampton; Avenue Campus, 1 mile from town centre. **Access:** Public transport
or car (1,000 parking spaces); 5 miles from M1 and good road, rail and air links. **Academic
features:** Combined and single honours degrees. European business studies with year
abroad. American intern programme and exchange on some degree courses. Unique international leather technology centre. **Europe:** 5% first degree students take a language as
part of course and spend 6 months or more abroad. Formal exchange links with 17 universities and business schools in Europe for European business students. **Library:** 2 libraries;
200,000 volumes, over 1,000 periodicals, 1,000 study places. Annual expenditure on library
materials, £54 per FTE student. **Other learning facilities:** Resource centres at both
campuses; IT centres; computers with extensive terminal network, e-mail and Internet;
media services; language labs at Park. **Welfare:** Doctor, dentist, FPA, solicitor, chaplain,
counsellors; system of personal tutors and student peer support. **Amenities:** SU buildings
and rooms, bookshop on both sites, banking facilities and cashpoint. **Sporting facilities:**
Sports hall, access to all-weather pitch, tennis courts, playing fields, dance studio.
Employment: Teaching; social and health services, chiropody, leather technology, industry
and commerce; public sector services; management training.

Accommodation: In 1995/96, 76% of first year students requiring it in college accommodation. 1,420 self-catering places available, £24.99–£48.51 per week, term time only (plus
retainer over Christmas and Easter). Students live in privately owned accommodation for
2+ years: rents £35–£40 per week self-catering, plus bills. 23% of first degree students live
at home. **Term time work:** College policy to allow term time work for first degree students
(45% believed to work). Term (and vac) work available in college bar, security, shop,
tour guides; plenty of local temporary work. **Hardship funds:** Total available in 1995/96:
£127,000 government access funds. **Special help:** single parents and mature students.
Limited scholarships.

Duration of first degree courses: 3 and 4 years. **Total first degree students 1995/96:** 6,490.
BA(QTS) students: 743. **Overseas students:** 110. **Mature students:** 32%. **Male/female ratio:**
2:3. **Teaching staff:** 400 full-time, 40 part-time. **Total full-time students 1995/96:** 7,456.
Postgraduate students: 762 (+65 research). **First degree tuition fees:** Home students, paying
their own fees in 1996/97, paid £1,266; Overseas students £6,080.

WHAT IT'S LIKE   It's on two campuses, with a population that includes a fairly large number of mature students. Crèche facilities are available. Halls have recently been refurbished and new halls built. Extended library facilities, including disabled computer link, on campus. Adequate sporting facilities with plans for development. Both campuses have their own SU offices, bars and canteens. Currently over 80 clubs and societies cater for all, from parachutists to film buffs. SU offers full welfare and support services and operates a hectic social scene for all tastes, with top names throughout the year. Good ties with NUS and very involved in campaigning on student issues. As Nene expands, so too does the Union. So get involved and have a whale of a time in Northampton.

PAUPER NOTES   Accommodation: New halls, ensuite rooms. Many first years in halls. **Drink:** Three SU bars offer cheap beers and spirits. In town various student nights in pubs. **Eats:** SU canteens (one at each site) superb value. Town has wide range of food – 'eat as much as you can' nights very popular! **Ents:** Expanding SU ents programme including 4 balls a year. Good transport to London and Birmingham for concerts, plays etc. **Sports:** Wide range. **Hardship fund:** SU hardship fund. College access fund. **Travel:** Very accessible by road, train and bus. **Work:** Fairly easy to get p-t work, but pay not great.

MORE INFO?   Get students' Alternative Prospectus. Enquiries to President SU (01604 735500 ext 2272).

ALUMNI (EDITORS' PICK)   David J. (Bauhaus), Daniel Ash (Love & Rockets), John (Neds Atomic Dustbin).

NEWCASTLE UNIVERSITY

University of Newcastle upon Tyne, 6 Kensington Terrace, Newcastle upon Tyne NE1 7RU (Tel 0191 222 6000, Fax 0191 222 6139) Map 2

STUDENT ENQUIRIES: Admissions Officer
APPLICATIONS: UCAS

Broad study areas: Agricultural and biological sciences, arts, speech, engineering, medicine, dentistry, science, humanities, social sciences, law. (Subject details are in the *Subjects and Places Index.*)

Founded: Early 19th century. Formerly the Newcastle Division of Durham University, its present title dates from 1963. **Main undergraduate awards:** BA, BSc, BEng, MEng, MPhys, MMath, MChem, LLB, MBBS, BDS. **Awarding body:** Newcastle University. **Site:** 45 acre site, close to city centre. **Academic features:** Combined arts and sciences degrees; 4-year engineering degrees for those without maths/science A-levels. **Europe:** 8% first degree students take a language as part of course and 5% spend 3 months or more abroad. Formal Erasmus links with a large number of European universities/colleges in a wide range of subjects. **Library:** 1,200,000 volumes, 5,500 periodicals, 700 study places. Annual expenditure on library materials, £154 per FTE student. **Specialist collections:** Archaeology (Gertrude Bell); history of medicine (Pybus); English literature (Robert White); Japanese science and technology (Robert Phillifent). **Other learning facilities:** Espin Observatory (largest telescope in north of England), Museum of Antiquities, Shefton Museum of Greek Art and Archaeology, Hatton Gallery, computing service, 2 farms, marine biological station, Moorbank Gardens. **Welfare:** Counselling service, union society welfare, student advice centre, chaplaincy. **Careers:** Careers advisory service, wide range of facilities including personal interviews, careers education programmes, talks, seminars, library and information service and employer contact. **Employment:** 1994 graduates – 49% direct into employment, 22% into professional training or further academic study, 9% unemployed, 10% unknown. **Amenities:** SU one of largest in UK with wide range of facilities including 13 food and drink outlets, shops, sporting and cultural facilities. Excellent local theatres, cinemas, bars, concert halls etc. **Sporting facilities:** Sports centres, 18-hole golf course, tennis courts, extensive outside sporting facilities, including all-weather pitch.

Accommodation: In 1995/96, 45% of all students in university accommodation, guaranteed place for first years. 5,000 places available: half-board at £57 per week, self-catering at £39 per week, Sept–June. Most students live in privately owned accommodation for 2 years: average £32 per week for self-catering. **Term time work:** No university policy on part time work. Some work available on campus and careers service helps finding vac work. **Hardship funds:** Total available in 1995/96: £189,526 government access funds, 603 students helped; £3,500 own funds, 38 students helped, including those eligible for access funds.

Duration of first degree courses: 3 and 4 years; **others:** 5 years town & country planning, dentistry, medicine. **Total first degree students 1995/96:** 9,483. **Overseas students:** 1,200. **Male/female ratio:** 11:9. **Teaching staff:** 1,852. **Total full-time students 1995/96:** 11,405. **Postgraduate students:** 1,922. **First degree tuition fees:** Home students, paying their own fees in 1996/97, paid £750 (classroom), £1,600 (lab/studio), £2,800 (clinical); Overseas students £6,060 (classroom), £8,040 (lab/studio), £14,810 (clinical).

WHAT IT'S LIKE   Attractive and lively city, close to beautiful Northumbrian countryside and coast, accessible by rail, coach and Metro. Excellent social life (recently nominated the world's best party city) with many good pubs and restaurants offering happy hours and/or student discounts. Good nightclubs eg Planet Earth, Ritzy's, Tuxedo Royale (a ship moored on the Tyne). Good for live music (eg SU and new 10,000 seat Arena), cinema (2 multiplex and the highly-rated Tyneside Cinema, showing more artistic films), theatre and sport (Newcastle United, Newcastle Rugby Club). Compact single campus close to city centre; SU impressive listed building, 7 bars, wide range of reasonably priced food, first class entertainment, bands, Friday night disco etc, wide range of social, political and sports clubs. Lively and popular freshers' week; excellent welfare service; award-winning student newspaper. Around 60% of students from private schools but still a good mix, with 20% mature students and 12% international (from over 100 countries); union active and well-used. SU provides advice on childcare and limited subsidy service (apply early). Many excellent courses (a 1995 survey showed that a majority felt Newcastle provided 'an excellent educational experience'), though recent change to semesters and modules had mixed reception. Medicine, dentistry, science, engineering, social sciences, education, agriculture highly rated. Good library recently expanded. Car parking can be difficult.

PAUPER NOTES   **Accommodation:** Private sector cheap and plentiful and mostly close to city centre, some as low as £25/week, though some areas should be treated with caution. University provides flats, halls and some houses with range of facilities and rents. **Drink:** Union cheapest in the city: 1 beer and 1 lager kept at £1/pint this year. 7 SU bars, some recently refurbished; good range of beers, frequent promotions. **Eats:** Cheap and wide range in SU; pizzas, hot meals, stotties, vegetarian. Newly refurbished women's cafe in union. Lots of places to eat out. **Ents:** Big name live bands in union (Pulp, Cream (The Club),

Therapy?); dance nights, DJs including Sasha and Paul Okenfold; Newcastle Arena (Blur, Morrisey); City Hall; Riverside for world music. Tyneside cinema and two 10-screen cinemas; Playhouse, Theatre Royal, Live Theatre and university's own studio theatre. **Sports:** Good sports facilities on campus plus local facilities eg swimming pool etc. Newcastle United (now also involved in ice-hockey and rugby); Gateshead Stadium for athletics; Newcastle Arena for ice-hockey and basketball. **Hardship funds:** Access Fund; emergency hardship fund in summer. **Work:** Average opportunities – about 30% work during term time.

MORE INFO? Get Students Handbook and Alternative Prospectus video (contact General Office, Students Union (0191 232 8402).

ALUMNI (EDITORS' PICK) Rowan Atkinson (comedian), Bryan Ferry (musician), Miriam Stoppard (TV doctor), Richard Hamilton (painter), Kate Adie (reporter).

NEWPORT COLLEGE

University of Wales College Newport, Caerleon Campus,
PO Box 179, Newport NP6 1YG (Tel 01633 430088,
Fax 01633 432006) Map 3

STUDENT ENQUIRIES: Information Centre
APPLICATIONS: UCAS

Broad study areas: Business, computing, electronic and electrical engineering, art & design, education, humanities. (Subject details are in the *Subjects and Places Index*.)

Founded: 1975 as Gwent College; became a university college of Wales University in 1996. **Main undergraduate awards:** BA, BA(QTS), BSc, BEng. **Awarding body:** Wales University. **Site:** 2 sites: 1 in residential area on edge of town; 1 in village 3 miles away. **Access:** Regular bus service from sites to main campus at Caerleon. **Europe:** All students can take a language as part of their course. Some opportunities for short periods of study in Europe. Some formal exchange links with universities/colleges in western Europe. **Library:** 120,000 volumes, 600 periodicals; 360 study places; CD-Rom. Annual expenditure on library materials, £43 per FTE student. **Specialist collections:** David Hurn collection (books and journals on documentary photography); Primrose Hockey collection (local history); collection of 30,000 slides on art and design. **Careers:** Information, advice and placement service. **Welfare:** Student health service (2 medical officers, 2 nurses), welfare service (3 welfare officers, access fund co-ordinator), 2 counsellors – all available on each site. Crèche during school holidays. **Amenities:** Shop on each campus; bar and recreational area on residential site at Caerleon. **Sporting facilities:** Tennis courts, gymnasia and games pitches at Caerleon campus.

Accommodation: College accommodates all first year students who request it (before a certain date). 687 self-catering places at £38.20 per week (£44.50 ensuite). Private sector rents: £31.50–£35 per week self-catering; £39.50–£50 B&B; £50–£65 half-board. **Term time**

work: College's policy to allow term time work for full-time first degree students (30% believed to work). Term (and vac) work available on campus as marketing, library and estates assistants, telephone operators. **Hardship funds:** Total available 1995/96: £56,262 government access fund (202 students helped); £1,000 own funds (130 students helped). Special help to single parents, mature students, and those with medical problems; own funds also available for short-term help.

Duration of first degree courses: 3 years; **others:** 4 years (sandwich BEng), 2 years (special BEd). **Total first degree students 1995/96:** 2,634; **BA(QTS) students:** 650, **Overseas students:** 230. **Mature students:** 1,937. **Male/female ratio:** 9:11. **Teaching staff:** 175 full-time, 19 part-time. **Total full-time students 1995/96:** 2,882. **Postgraduate students:** 819. **First degree tuition fees:** Home students, paying their own fees in 1996/97, paid £750 (classroom), £1,600 (lab/studio); Overseas students £5,944.

NORTH EAST WALES INSTITUTE (NEWI)

The North East Wales Institute of HE (NEWI), Plas Coch, Mold Road, Wrexham, Clwyd LL11 2AW (Tel 01978 290666, Fax 01978 290008) Map 2

STUDENT ENQUIRIES: Admissions Office (01978 293045)
APPLICATIONS: UCAS

Broad study areas: Art, education, health studies, environmental and natural sciences, computing, engineering, building, business. (Subject details are in the *Subjects and Places Index*.)

Founded: 1975 ex two technical colleges and a teacher training college. **Structural features:** Associate college of Wales University. **Main undergraduate awards:** BA, BA(QTS), BEd, BEng, BNursing, BSc. **Awarding body:** Wales University. **Site:** Plas Coch campus and North Wales School of Art and Design. **Europe:** Opportunities to learn a language (including Welsh) or spend time abroad. Some exchanges. **Library:** Library on each site with subject bias – approx 10,000 volumes, 500 periodicals, 350 study places. **Other learning facilities:** Resources laboratories, computer links (SuperJANET and Internet), reprographic services, media and edit suite. **Welfare:** Welfare officer, counsellors, nurses, doctor on call, chaplain. **Careers:** Information and advice service. **Amenities:** Bookshops and café, SU bar and shop; 890-seater concert venue. **Sporting facilities:** Playing fields, sports hall and gym on campus. Swimming pools and sports centres in Wrexham. North Wales excellent for water sports and outdoor pursuits.

Accommodation: In 1995/96, 617 self-catering places available, 2 miles from main campus. Students live in privately owned accommodation for 2+ years: rents £33–£49 per week for self-catering. **Hardship funds:** No information available.

Duration of first degree courses: 3 years; **others** 4 years for 2+2 and BEd/QTS. **Total first degree students 1995/96:** 1,296; **QTS students:** 496. **Overseas students:** 25. **Mature students:** 302. **Male/female ratio:** 10:9. **Total full-time students 1995/96:** 2,345. **Postgraduate students:** 394. **First degree tuition fees:** Home students, paying their own fees in 1996/97, paid £750 (classroom), £1,600 (lab/studio); Overseas: £5,850 (classroom).

WHAT IT'S LIKE   Two sites, reasonably close. College accommodation spread round the town, within walking distance but also bus services. Many students are local but others come from the length and breadth of the UK and significant numbers from overseas (Europe and Africa particularly) with a great diversity of age groups. NEWI accommodation offered to freshers, international and final year students (first come, first served). All NEWI accommodation is self-catering hostels (on and off campus). Usually comfortable, warm and not too expensive; facilities range from decent to downright inadequate but social gatherings frequently occur in the kitchens. New student village on Plas Coch site and hopes for more. Private sector, generally adequate. Courses increasingly modular; lectures are often small with a high level of student input; work load sporadic and time-consuming but not too mind blowing. Course work important in assessment but exams still dominate. Many vocational courses (eg education and youth/community work). New library; computer network gives access to e-mail and Internet, which compensates for any lack of books on shelves. College facilities improving although sports facilities still lacking (but local facilities and SU sports clubs improvise to ensure training). Student services provide confidential counselling and a friendly information service; also SU welfare service. Union/college liaison is good. Small but active union is apolitical, centred around students and their needs; variety of clubs and societies and easy to start your own. Wrexham has sporting facilities, good pubs and a cinema but a bit of a cultural desert – Chester and Mold nearest theatres. SU provides a variety of entertainments – discos (twice weekly) bands, hypnotists, famous comedians, as well as home-grown talent – always something going on. Size of union, and whole college, makes for a close-knit community where making friends is no worry. In fact many ex-students finding the pull of the bar just too much, feeling impelled to return once in awhile to meet old friends.

PAUPER NOTES   **Accommodation:** Private rented sector locally: cheap and sufficient but under increasing pressure. **Drinks:** SU bar, plenty of pubs, coffee shops, local brews Marston's Pedigree. **Eats:** Okay for junk food, eg burger joints and pizzas, chip shops, also Chinese and Indian restaurants. Excellent sandwich shops. **Ents:** Good, popular; discos twice a week in SU bar, live bands, theme nights, comedians, quizzes, etc. **Sports:** Good facilities in Wrexham. Olympic pool and diving boards; **Hardship funds:** Access fund – students must be over 19. SU can give £50 loans. **Travel:** Not good: once you're here you're stuck. **Work:** SU jobs in bar, door staff etc; also in library. Locally, unemployment high but bar jobs plentiful. Student job service for part-time jobs. Holiday work often available in some local factories and hostelries.

MORE INFO?   Enquiries to President, Student Union (01978 293225).

INFORMAL NAME   NEWI.

HOW TO START? *SEE SHORTLISTING*, PAGE 535

NORTH LONDON UNIVERSITY

University of North London, 166–220 Holloway Road,
London N7 8DB (0171 607 2789) Map 5

STUDENT ENQUIRIES: Course Enquiries Office
(tel 0171 753 5066/7or 607 5755), fax 0171 753 5075).
APPLICATIONS: UCAS

Broad study areas: Science, computing and engineering, business, environmental and social studies, humanities, education. (Subject details are in the *Subjects and Places Index.*)

Founded: 1971 as North London Poly, from two older institutions. University status 1992. **Main undergraduate awards:** BA, BEd, BEng, BSc, LLB. **Awarding body:** North London University. **Site:** Main campus on Holloway Road in Islington; environmental and social studies nearby at Highbury Fields. **Access:** Good rail, underground and bus connections. **Academic features:** Most courses modular. Flexible entry requirements and foundation year programmes; commitment to mature students; strong local community involvement. **Europe:** 16% first degree students take a language as part of course and spend 6 months or more abroad. Open languages for all students and staff; modular system allows languages in most courses. Exchange links throughout the whole of Europe covering a wide range of subjects. **Library:** 2 libraries; 300,000 volumes in total, 1,500 periodicals. Annual expenditure on library materials, £64 per FTE student. **Specialist collections:** European Documentation Centre, polymers, HG Wells. **Welfare:** Chaplain, advisers, counsellors and accommodation officer. **Special categories:** Disabled students co-ordinator, dyslexia support, childcare co-ordinator. **Careers:** Information, advice and placement service. **Amenities:** Student Centre with SU bars, shops, entertainment venue; on-site banking, cafeterias and bars. **Sporting facilities:** Dance studio, 2 gymnasia, weights room; sports centre nearby.

Accommodation: Accommodation guaranteed for all first years who live more than 25 miles from university. 836 places available: 454 single rooms (some half-board), 382 places in self-catering shared flats: rents £46 per week (shared room) to £61 (including meals), all year contracts. Students live in privately owned accommodation for 2 years: rents from £50 per week for self-catering. **Hardship funds:** Total available in 1995/96: £293,434 government access funds, 679 students helped; £6,500 own funds, 13 helped. Special help: single parents and students with child-minding costs, those excluded from loan scheme, self-financing students, those prevented from taking up employment through illness, disability etc. Own funds for students with dependents, on science based courses and continuing BEd.

Duration of first degree courses: 3 or 4 years (sandwich). **Total first degree students 1995/96:** 8,602 full time. **BEd students:** 490. **Male/female ratio:** 5:6. **Teaching staff:** 438 full-time, 84 part-time. **Total full-time students 1995/96:** 9,021. **Postgraduate students:** 1,615. **First degree tuition fees:** Home students, paying their own fees in 1996/97, paid £1,410 (classroom), £2,710 (lab/studio); Overseas students £5,950 (classroom), £6,200 (lab/studio). 5% prompt payment discount.

WHAT IT'S LIKE   UNL reflects life in London, a real melting pot of ages, cultures and experiences all bubbling together in Islington. Spread over five sites, within 15 minutes walk of each other, and with a new Student Union Centre, the university is building towards easing the overcrowding that can be seen at lunchtimes. Student services centre, located at the main site, is a one stop shop with expert help available on accommodation, finances, careers, childcare, counselling, sports clubs or personal disabilities. SU housed in a new entertainments centre; many active clubs and societies – based on and off campus. Learning centre is the home of the library (plus small library at Ladbroke House); it's generally well stocked but some course resources getting old. To help new students settle in, innovative team of 60 current students constantly on hand in freshers week to help with any problems. Buy an A-Z, learn the shortcuts and make the most of the different atmospheres at the different sites.   *Sarah Flynn*

PAUPER NOTES   **Accommodation:** Over 850 places in halls, around £50 a week. Private accommodation at least £60 pw. **Drink:** Good bars in student union centre at Ladbroke House. Local pubs include The Tappet (Holloway Road – a student favourite). Camden and Upper Street (Islington) a bus ride away. **Eats:** Crowded and overpriced on campus; plenty of local cafes and sandwich bars nearby. **Ents:** SU centre has events through the week to suit most tastes. London is your oyster; loads of student discounts available. **Sports:** Plenty of sports clubs. Discounts on Islington sports facilities with an Izzz card. **Hardship funds:** Available but must be a really deserving case. **Travel:** Buy an A-Z and walk! Loads of buses; travelcards are cheaper. **Work:** Student services' Job Shop helps with part time work. Some bar work. As in real life, not enough jobs to go round.

ALUMNI (EDITORS' PICK)   Jeremy Corbyn MP, Garth Crooks (Tottenham Hotspur), Malcolm Fraser, Claire Rayner, Neil Tennant (Pet Shop Boys).

NORTHERN SCHOOL OF CONTEMPORARY DANCE

Northern School of Contemporary Dance, 98 Chapeltown Road, Leeds LS7 4BH (Tel 0113 262 5359, Fax 0113 237 4585) Map 2

STUDENT ENQUIRIES: The Administrator
APPLICATIONS: Direct.

Broad study areas: Contemporary and classical dance, choreography. (Subject details are in the *Subjects and Places Index*.)

Founded: 1985. **Main award:** BPA (Dance). **Awarding body:** Leeds University. **Site:** Leeds (Chapeltown), close to city library/art gallery and universities. **Access:** Very accessible. **Academic features:** Courses include classical and contemporary dance, choreography and allied arts, performance, theory and practice of dance in education design. **Europe:** No students learn a language or spend time abroad. **Learning resources:** Own theatre, Dome Theatre. **Welfare:** Own physiotherapist in attendance; counselling on tutorial system. **Careers:** Information, advice and placement service available. **Amenities and sporting facilities:** City facilities only.

Accommodation: No school accommodation. Students live in privately owned accommodation: rent £20–£40 per week, self-catering. 10% first degree students live at home. **Term time work**: School's policy to allow term time work for full-time first degree students (98% believed to work). Term work available on campus theatre, front of house. **Hardship funds:** In 1995/96, total available £1,901 government access funds, £5,510 own and other funds; average amount awarded £20 per week; any student with less than £40 per week eligible to apply.

Duration of first degree courses: 3 years (full-time); **Total full-time students 1995/96:** 200. **Male/female ratio:** 2:3. **Teaching staff:** 10 full-time, 6 part-time. **First degree tuition fees:** Home students, paying their own fees in 1996/97, paid £1,160; Overseas students £5,900.

WHAT IT'S LIKE   It's quite different from other colleges offering similar qualifications and the students are far from 'normal'. Based in a beautiful green domed synagogue converted to a working theatre, tears, blood, sweat and laughter are shed from 8.30am to 6.00pm (plus any evening rehearsals). College takes pride in accommodating a hotch-potch of people – all ages, sexes, creeds and colours – creating a rare environment where you can be yourself and learn about others. Despite this diversity of people, backgrounds and ideals, everyone has a common denominator – commitment. You have to be committed to survive (4 classes a day; ballet, contemporary dance, jazz, body, music, lighting and design, creative arts, teaching practice, anatomy, choreography, performance, dance history, etc). It couldn't be more intense, which makes for the universal feeling of being completely knackered. Everyone is in the same boat so there is a very close-knit feeling in the college. Everyone knows everyone – close staff-pupil relationships too – so no-one is isolated but gossip is rife; and you can't hide much when standing in a 6 x 10 m studio in a leotard and tights all day every day. Can be insular but it is part of Leeds University, which provides a short but essential break from dancers and gives access to university libraries, SUs, etc. College SU is not politically or socially active but students are welcome to join in university activities. Technical progress is continually assessed and written assignments are set half-termly with exams at the end of the year. The graduation performance is the biggy; people come from all over to watch, admire and criticise, the most ruthless examination of all – the public eye. It's a vocational course and the academic demands are not great. However, it's terrifically demanding, mentally and physically, and although you don't need previous dance training, in your audition they look for someone with spirit, the will to dance, and perhaps a masochistic streak. Dance students are usually very short of money because grants are discretionary, and even if you're lucky enough to have one you don't get much; and there is no time or energy left to work in the evenings. But don't be frightened off, there's lots of fun. Leeds has a massive student population so there are loads of good pubs, clubs, theatre and cinema. A pint in the local recommended of an evening – to help you relax and *try* to be 'normal'.   *Charlotte Darbyshire*

PAUPER NOTES **Accommodation:** Student digs. **Drink:** Good mixture of pubs, cheap/good atmosphere. **Eats:** Cheap, informal – Indian, vegetarian. **Ents:** Cheap student nightclubs/plays/theatre/bars. **Sports:** No time for extra sports – occasional swim/sauna and gym workout. **Hardship funds:** Scarce. **Travel:** Student fares/hitching.

MORE INFO?   Enquiries to Students Union (0113 237 4101).

GET HOLD OF THE PROSPECTUSES

NORTHUMBRIA UNIVERSITY

University of Northumbria at Newcastle, Ellison Building,
Ellison Place, Newcastle upon Tyne NE1 8ST
(Tel 0191 232 6002) Map 2

STUDENT ENQUIRIES: Assistant Registrar (Tel 0191 227 4064)
APPLICATIONS: UCAS

Broad study areas: Art & design, business, social sciences, engineering and technology. (Subject details are in the *Subjects and Places Index.*)

Founded: 1969 as Newcastle Poly, university status 1992. **Main undergraduate awards:** BA, BA(QTS), BSc, BEng, LLB, MEng. **Awarding body:** Northumbria University. **Site:** 4 sites – Newcastle Campus in city centre; Coach Lane campus 3 miles away; Carlisle Campus, 50 miles away; Longhirst, Morpeth, 15 miles north of Newcastle. **Academic features:** Degree courses in media production, travel & tourism, history of modern art, design and film; business information technology, fashion promotion, communication engineering. **Special features:** National coaching centre. Specialist centres include microelectronics education, small businesses, Newcastle Fashion Centre. **Europe:** 15% first degree students take a language as part of course and 5% spend 6 months or more abroad. Language element in 20+ degree courses, either compulsory or optional; all students can use university's language lab to start a language at any time at any level. Formal exchange links with a number of EU universities/colleges. **Library:** Library at each site; total of 500,000 volumes, 3,750 periodicals, 1,100 study places, short loan only for recommended volumes. Annual expenditure on library materials, £71.88 per FTE student. **Specialist collections:** EC Documentation Centre. **Welfare:** Health services, welfare officer, student counsellor, accommodation service, chaplains, playgroup. Some places in hall for disabled students, 24 places in local authority flats for married students. **Careers:** Information, advice and placement service. **Amenities:** Large SU buildings (300-seat theatre, ballroom, second-hand book shop). **Sporting facilities:** Indoor sports on city campus, outdoor sports 2 miles away.

Accommodation: In 1996/97, 20% of all students in university accommodation, 55% first years (most non-local students that need it). 2,400 places at Newcastle Campus (2,000 for first years): 343 full-board places (285 for first years), £63 per week and 259 half-board places (215 for first years), £49.50 per week, term time only; 1,750 self-catering places (1,465 for first years) at £39–£41 per week, Sept–June or longer. Students live in privately owned accommodation for 2+ years: rents £27–£45 per week for self-catering, £44.50 for B&B (£62 with evening meal). Accommodation for all who need it at Carlisle and Longhirst campuses. **Term time work:** University's policy to allow term time work for full-time first degree students; no work on campus. **Hardship funds:** Total available in 1995/96: £235,000 government access funds, 860 full-time students helped; £80,000 own funds, 300 part-time students helped. Special help: single parents, married on low income with children, disabled, those with substantial travel costs, independent students and mature students with own homes.

Duration of first degree courses: 3 years (full-time); 4 years (sandwich), 3–6 years (part-time). **Total first degree students 1995/96:** 11,646; **QTS students:** 523. **Overseas students:** 698.

Mature students: approx 50%. **Male/female ratio:** 1:1. **Teaching staff:** approx 900 (full and part-time). **Total full-time students 1995/96:** 13,534. **Postgraduate students:** 790 full-time, 2,145 part-time. **First degree tuition fees:** Home students, paying their own fees in 1996/97, paid £750 (classroom), £1,600 (lab/studio); Overseas students £4,800 (classroom), £6,000 (lab/studio).

WHAT IT'S LIKE   Newcastle claims to be the best city in the UK and best party city in the world! Mostly modern campus spilling over into the town centre, close to excellent metro and bus services. Also some suburban sites at Coach Lane (including new campus being built), Carlisle and Longhirst. Halls split between sites and residential area, from fully catered to shared flats. Social life is good with one of the biggest SUs in the UK providing a wide range of clubs and societies, with facilities for some of the best club nights in the city. Newcastle has everything a big city has to offer – hundreds of pubs, clubs, cinemas and shops etc. A bus ride away from the Metro Centre (Europe's biggest shopping centre) and from Northumberland National Parks. Wide mix of students – many local, mature, part-time and overseas students makes for a cosmopolitan atmosphere. SU has fully equipped theatre, bars, dark-room, sports centre and student paper. Welfare help and advice from uni and at SU, including women's officer and contacts for sexual and racial harassment procedures. Assessment is mixture of continuous assessment and sit-down exams, depending on courses. Most courses changing to unitisation, so modular assessment and semesters. Authorities sympathetic to course change if students genuinely unhappy. Library good – biggest in region. SU tries to build and develop strong links with local community, to widen access to building and resources to groups in the city. Strong commitment to taking students out into the community. Also a great new student newspaper – well worth a read.

PAUPER NOTES   **Accommodation:** Helpful accommodation office with info on housing at all prices; landlord accreditation scheme (checks gas and general safety). **Drink:** Three bars on main site (serve Bass), one at Coach Lane – excellent drinks promotions throughout the year in SU. **Eats:** Variety of excellent, subsidised food at SU (2-course meal for £1.50); also veggie, vegan, kosher, sandwiches etc. **Ents:** Excellent range at SU popular club nights, touring bands and guest DJs. **Sports:** Wide variety of sports clubs plus Gateshead Stadium. **Hardship funds:** Hardship funds available. Helpful local banks. **Travel:** Busways – students' termly save card. **Work:** New employment office in SU with lots of term and vacation jobs. MORE INFO?   Enquiries to SU Deputy President, Justin Forrest (0191 227 4757).
ALUMNI (EDITORS' PICK)   Steve Cram, Paul Shriek (fashion designer), Rodney Bickerstaff, Karen Boyd (designer), Jeff Banks, Sting.

NORWICH SCHOOL OF ART

Norwich School of Art & Design, St George Street, Norwich
NR3 1BB (Tel 01603 610561, Fax 01603 615728) Map 4

STUDENT ENQUIRIES: Registrar
APPLICATIONS: UCAS

Broad study areas: Art & design, cultural and visual studies.
(Subject details are in the *Subjects and Places Index*.)

Founded: 1989, incorporating Norwich School of Art and Great Yarmouth College of Art and Design. **Main undergraduate award:** BA. **Awarding body:** Anglia Poly University. **Site:** 2 city centre sites. **Europe:** No students learn a language or spend time abroad as part of their course although language tuition available as supplementary subject to all students. Formal exchange links with various European universities/colleges. **Library:** 35,000 volumes, 120 periodicals, 60 study places; slide library: 145,000 slides. Annual expenditure on library materials, £33 per FTE student. **Welfare:** Student counselling service available. **Amenities:** Refectory, shop.

Accommodation: In 1995/96, 5% of all students in school accommodation, 14% of first years. 32 self-catering places available (all for first years) at £34.50–£39 per week, either term time only or Sept-July. Most students live in privately owned accommodation for whole course: rents £25–£50 per week for self-catering. **Term time work:** College's policy to allow term time work for full-time first degree students. Term (and vac) work available on campus in library and gallery supervision. **Hardship funds:** Total available in 1995/96: £23,278 government access funds, 126 students helped. Special help: eg those with dependants, self-financing students or those with medical expenses, course materials costs etc.

Duration of first degree courses: 3 years. **Total first degree students 1995/96:** 448. **Overseas students:** 14. **Male/female ratio:** 1:1. **Teaching staff:** 45 full-time, 100 part-time. **Total full-time students 1995/96:** 806. **First degree tuition fees:** Home students, paying their own fees in 1996/97, paid £1,600; Overseas students £5,979.

WHAT IT'S LIKE   Beautifully set in the city centre, overlooking the River Wensum, there are three sites within 500 yards of each other. Courses all challenging and diverse; good relationship between staff and students. There is a very good community and social life within the college (though virtually no sporting facilities). SU has its main hall and bar (with cheap drinks) in an attractive converted church; abundance of gigs, big name bands nearby at UEA. College accommodation very limited; students tend to live in private rented accommodation within a 15 minute walk of college. Great opportunities for second years to study in Europe and sometimes worldwide, for a term. Free welfare and counselling service available (fully confidential). Very easy access to London, 2 hours by train. Many discounts in theatres, cinemas, clothes shops and restaurants in city.   *Dan Ferguson*
PAUPER NOTES   **Accommodation:** College has hardly any; private accommodation mostly close. **Drink:** 365 pubs in Norwich. Main art school pub The Mischief. Trendy drinking spots: The Garden House, Hectors House, The Murderers. **Eats:** Often student discounts. Mexican, Greek, Italian, Chinese, Thai, veggie. Curry war (menus at half price). **Ents:** Film society at college; fringe film at Cinema City; reduced rates at Cannon and Odeon. Many clubs in Norwich; best night out Marvel at The Loft and Return to the Source at the Waterfront. **Sports:** UEA and community centres; gyms, swimming pools etc. **Hardship funds:** Limited access funds. **Work:** Many bar jobs and telephone work, standard pay.
INFORMAL NAME   NSAD.
MORE INFO?   Contact SU on 01603 766846

WANT TO HELP WITH THE NEXT EDITION? SEE PAGE 66

NOTTINGHAM TRENT UNIVERSITY

The Nottingham Trent University, City Centre Site,
Burton Street, Nottingham NG1 4BU
(Tel 0115 941 8418, Fax 0115 948 4266) Map 2

STUDENT ENQUIRIES: Registrar
APPLICATIONS: UCAS

Broad study areas: Art and design, education, business, engineering and computing, building and environmental studies, law, economics, social sciences, humanities, science and mathematics. (Subject details are in the *Subjects and Places Index*.)

Founded: University status in 1992 (previously Nottingham Poly, then Trent Poly). **Main undergraduate awards:** BEd, BA, BSc, BEng, LLB, MChem, MEng, MPhys. **Awarding body:** Nottingham Trent University. **Site:** 3 sites: city site, close to centre of Nottingham; 2 sites in Clifton, about 4 miles away. **Access:** City centre site near rail and coach stations; bus services from Clifton sites. Near M1 and East Midlands Airport. **Academic features:** MEng in computer aided engineering and manufacturing systems engineering with management. Part-time MBA. BA business and quality management. **Special features:** Credit accumulation and negotiated study programmes. **Europe:** 17% first degree students take a language as part of their course; 4% spend 6 months or more abroad. Open access to wide range of languages. **Library:** Main library on each site plus number of small reference libraries; 400,000 volumes in total, 2,500 periodicals, 1,250 study places. Annual expenditure on library materials, £52.01 per FTE student. **Other learning facilities:** Extensive computing facilities for all students; modern, open-access language laboratories; science and engineering laboratories. **Welfare:** Doctors, nurses, counsellors, chaplains, welfare officer. **Careers:** Information, advice and placement. **Amenities:** Shop, bar, bookshop, bank, travel bureau and playgroup at all sites; closed circuit television studio. **Sporting facilities:** Playing fields and athletic track at Clifton; health & fitness studios at City and Clifton.

Accommodation: In 1996/97, 2,780 university places: 2,412 self-catering, £48–£51 per week, 41 week contract; 368 catered, £64.32 per week, 32 week contract. 850 places in university-managed properties: £35–£44 per week, 41 week contract. Students living in privately rented accommodation pay £35–£40 self-catering, £60–£65 catered. **Hardship funds:** Fund available to alleviate cases of temporary financial hardship.

Duration of first degree courses: 3 or 4 years. **Total first degree students 1995/96:** 15,382; **BEd students:** 1,021. **Overseas students:** 1,094. **Mature students:** 10,236 (full and part-time). **Male/female ratio:** 3:2. **Teaching staff:** 960 full-time. **Total full-time students 1995/96:** 17,403. **Postgraduate students:** 3,098. **First degree tuition fees:** Home students, paying their own fees in 1996/97, paid £1,320 (classroom), £2,800 (lab/studio); Overseas students £5,650 (classroom), £5,950 (lab/studio).

WHAT IT'S LIKE   The city is famous. Robin Hood and his Merry Men waged war against the evil sheriff. That was history. Today the city is home to over 35,000 students, of which Nottingham Trent University has 22,000, split between 2 sites in the city and Clifton. The university has a total of 26 departments and a growing number of new degree courses to suit everyone. You'll soon learn that size is everything and an eclectic mix of students from all over the country, indeed the world, packed into the country's most central pulsing city makes for one sensational experience. The SU offers itself as the central venue for student life. It has it all – five bars, two fitness gyms, over 80 clubs and societies, two nurseries, niteline service, student advice centre, women's minibus, two student shops, *Platform* the weekly student newspaper, *Kick FM*, the turbo-charged radio station, TUBES the student employment bureau ... the list of services just goes on and on. Add to this an ents programme that makes other universities go green with envy and you can see that there is only one choice! Colourful, pulsating and relentless. Get out and sample some life, student style.   *Benjamin Morrison and Sue Williams*

PAUPER NOTES   **Accommodation:** 3,000 places in halls of residence – all modern and ensuite and within 3 mile radius of uni. **Drink:** 99p a pint in union bars. Nottingham boasts more pubs and clubs per square mile then anywhere else in UK. Good student pubs in town centre. **Eats:** Substance at city, Peggy-Sue's Rock and Roll Diner at Clifton. Loads of places in city; veggies are in for a treat. **Ents:** Gorgeous people and great night life. Nottingham attracts discerning clubbers, drinkers, rockers, party-goers from all over the country. Union – Shipwrecked – £1.50 treble. Loads of cinemas, theatres. **Sports:** Over 80 clubs and socs. National Water Centre, Trent Bridge (test cricket), 2 football clubs, ice skating, loads of sports halls. **Travel:** Ticket Express and STA situated on campus. **Work:** TUBES, union-managed bureau of employment bureau, finds students jobs in union eg bars, house services as well as in city.

NOTTINGHAM UNIVERSITY

The University of Nottingham, University Park, Nottingham NG7 2RD (Tel 0115 951 5151, Fax 0115 951 5795) Map 2

STUDENT ENQUIRIES: Schools & Colleges Liaison Office, Registrar's Department.
APPLICATIONS: UCAS

Broad study areas: Arts, humanities, law, social science, education, science, agricultural and food sciences, engineering, medicine, health sciences. (Subject details are in the *Subjects and Places Index*.)

Founded: 1881. **Main undergraduate awards:** BA, LLB, BSc, BEng, MEng, MMath, MPhys, MChem, BPharm, BM, BS, BN, MSci. **Awarding body:** Nottingham University. **Site:** Main campus at University Park (330-acre campus to west of city centre); agriculture and food sciences at Sutton Bonington, 10 miles south. **Access:** Buses from city centre and railway station; campus 4 miles from M1. Daytime shuttle coach between University Park and Sutton Bonington. **Academic features:** Modular degree course structure; teaching in

2 semesters. 4-year first degrees in mathematics, physics, chemistry. **Europe:** Increasing number of degrees combining languages with other subjects; all students may use the language centre. Many departments have established Erasmus and Socrates links. **Library:** Over 1,000,000 volumes and pamphlets, 5,000+ periodicals; short loan collection for books most in demand. Annual expenditure on library materials, £112.67 per FTE student. **Other learning facilities:** Cripps computing centre; university language centre, learning support unit, museum and arts centre. **Welfare:** Health service, chaplaincy, counselling service. **Careers:** Advisory service. **Amenities:** SU with shop, minibuses, travel agency, hair-dressers; campus bookshops; performing arts studio, theatre, 2 banks. **Sporting facilities:** Indoor sports centre, playing fields, 2,000-metre international rowing course nearby, swimming pool.

Accommodation: 3,000 full-board places (12 halls in University Park, 1 at Sutton Bonington), £1,920 a year, 30 weeks; plus 1,300 self-catering places in flats, £1,350 a year, 44 weeks. All first years applying before 6 August can be accommodated. **Term time work:** University allows term time work (recommended limit of 15 hours a week) and runs a Student Employment Service. **Hardship funds:** Access funds, emergency hardship fund, childcare support bursaries.

Duration of first degree courses: 3 years; **others:** 4 years; 5 years (medicine); 6 years (architecture). **Total first degree students 1995/96:** 9,440. **Overseas students:** 1,000. **Mature students:** 800. **Male/female ratio:** 6:5. **Teaching staff:** 896 full-time. **Total full-time students 1995/96:** 12,960. **Postgraduate students:** 1,700. **First degree tuition fees:** Home students, paying their own fees in 1996/97, paid £750 (classroom), £1,600 (lab/studio), £2,800 (clinical); Overseas students £6,360 (classroom), £8,400 (lab/studio), £15,384 (clinical).

WHAT IT'S LIKE   On an attractive campus but only a short bus ride from the city centre – the best of both worlds. On campus everything is within easy walking distance: 12 halls of residence providing facilities, such as meals and washing machines; campus libraries; the SU (known as UNU) with shop, travel centre, print shop and two bars. With over 150 clubs and societies, one of the largest rags (Karnival) and local community work groups in the country, participation in student life is vast. There is something for everyone and it is very easy to get involved. All first years can be accommodated in halls, providing Nottingham is their first choice, and so meeting people is very simple. The SU is active but not party political, with a large input from students. Nottingham is a very popular university and the high quality of the courses and teaching is part of the attraction.

PAUPER NOTES   **Accommodation:** Three main student areas: Beeston, Lenton and Dunkirk. Average £30–£37 a week. **Drink:** Cheap hall bars and Union bar. Happy Return, Grove, Three Wheatsheaves, The Bell Inn, Old Trip to Jerusalem are popular; nearer town gets expensive. **Eats:** University food counter. SU bar provides bar meals. Lots of cheapish Indian, Chinese near campus and student areas. **Ents:** Comedy and jazz nights in SU bar. Own theatre group (well-known at Edinburgh Fringe). **Sports:** Well-equipped free sports centre on-campus, large sports ground. **Hardship funds:** £50 loans; access funds – apply to university. **Travel:** Cheap bus travel offered for regular users; union provides free late night minibus. SU travel centre offers competitive fares. **Work:** Vacation work for university conference centre, local pork pie factory as well as the usual temping and bar work.

ALUMNI (EDITORS' PICK)   D H Lawrence, Brian Moore (England rugby international).

OAK HILL COLLEGE

Oak Hill College, Chase Side, Southgate, London N14 4PS
(Tel 0181 449 0467, Fax 0181 441 5996) Map 5

STUDENT ENQUIRIES: Admissions Officer
APPLICATIONS: Direct

Broad study areas: Theology and pastoral studies.
(Subject details are in the *Subjects and Places Index.*)

Founded: 1932. **Main undergraduate award:** BA. **Awarding body:** Middlesex University. **Site:** Cockfosters/Southgate area. **Access:** Underground to Southgate (Piccadilly line), then walk or bus (about 1 hr from Westminster). **Academic features:** Module in homiletics. Successful DipHE candidates can transfer to degree course. Number of mature students admitted without the formal qualifications. **Special features:** Some modules may be taken with Middlesex University and the American exchange programme. **Europe:** No students learn a language or spend time abroad. **Library:** 27,000 volumes, 182 periodicals, 30 study places; course books placed on temporary reference; tape library, video library. **Welfare:** Chaplain, personal tutor. **Special categories:** Houses for married couples plus families; crèche. **Careers:** Advice service. Vocational placement scheme. Church of England training college. **Sporting facilities:** All-weather tennis courts; football/rugby field on site; municipal squash courts and swimming pool near by; also cricket pitch.

Accommodation: In 1996/97, 95% students in college accommodation. 100 places available: 35 full-board places (single students in halls of residence) at £2,634 per annum, term time only; 65 self-catering places (married students renting houses) up to £4,500 pa. Few students live at home. **Term time work**: College's policy to allow term time work for full-time first degree students if absolutely necessary (2% believed to work). **Hardship funds:** Funds assigned to students prior to starting course for non-ordinands; £80,000 available.

Duration of first degree courses: 3 years. **Total first degree students 1995/96:** 53. **Overseas students:** 10%. **Mature students:** 95%. **Male/female ratio:** 7:1. **Teaching staff:** 11 full-time, 4 part-time. **Total full-time students 1995/96:** 74. **Postgraduate students:** 17. **First degree tuition fees:** Home and overseas students, paying their own fees in 1996/97, paid £2,978.

WHAT IT'S LIKE   First and foremost an Anglican training college and those students training for the ministry are supported by their diocese. It is housed in a compact, much extended former stately home in 60 acres of parkland and woods, two miles from Barnet in north London. Singles usually accommodated in rooms in main building; most married couples in college-owned houses and flats on campus or near by. Individual studies available. Food is good, as are cooking and washing facilities. While majority of students are training for Church of England ministry, some are from other denominations, some studying to test vocation. Expanding library; good bookshop. Relations with all staff on first-name basis. Student representation on all committees and involved in interviewing for new staff members. Prayer and worship an integral part of day when college meets together. All students in tutorial groups for pastoral care. Long-standing links with colleges in US (with which student exchanges can be arranged) and Africa (students fundraise for training college in Uganda). Two semesters per year, courses usually run for one; some can be taken at Middlesex University. College courses include: biblical studies, counselling, sociology, world religions, communication, Greek, Church history, doctrine, liturgy, preaching, philosophy, ethics. Assessment is continuous and/or by exam. Varied teaching styles: seminars, lectures, workshops, role play, videos, tutorials. Good placement scheme with churches within 15 miles. College missions, block placements, and courses in hospital chaplaincy and urban studies in vacations. London is easily accessible – trains take 45 minutes from local station a mile away. Families well catered for: green spaces and equipment for children to play, playgroup for children up to 2½ years, babysitting rota. Programme in evening for partners. Spouses welcome at all lectures.

PAUPER NOTES   **Accommodation:** Study bedrooms for singles, year-round leases in some cases. Houses for marrieds on and off campus. **Drink:** Good local pubs, especially in countryside few miles to north. **Eats:** College meals good (often seconds), include vegetarian and fresh fruit. **Ents:** TV and video room. Social committee events eg College Ball, panto, reviews. Classical music programme. Cinema in Barnet. **Sports:** On site: tennis, football, rugby, cricket, snooker, volleyball, croquet, table tennis. Near by: squash (courts booked by college), swimming (Southgate Leisure Centre one mile away), cricket, running club, fishing. All sports subsidised by college. **Hardship funds:** College bursary fund. In cases of real need the college community will almost invariably try to meet the need itself. **Travel:** Expenses reimbursed for Sunday and block placements. **Work:** Paid manual vacation-work available.

INFORMAL NAME   Oak Hill (former students known as Old Oaks).
ALUMNI (EDITORS' PICK)   Rt Rev George Carey (former tutor).

OPEN UNIVERSITY

Open University, Walton Hall, Milton Keynes MK7 6AA (Tel 01908 274066)

STUDENT ENQUIRIES: **Central Enquiry Service (01908 653231 – answering service out of office hours)**
APPLICATIONS: **Direct**

Broad study areas: Arts, environment, mathematics and computing, science, social science, technology. (Subject details are in the *Subjects and Places Index*.)

Founded: 1969. **Main undergraduate awards:** BA, BSc. **Awarding body:** Open University. **Admission:** No educational qualifications required but students should be 18 or over and resident in the European Union, Switzerland, Gibraltar or Slovenia. Early applications take precedence over later ones, so apply early. **Academic features:** Approx 130 courses, many multi- or inter-disciplinary. Degrees built up according to CATS: a minimum of 360 points for a degree; for an honours degree, 360 points with 120 points' worth of courses at honours level. Individual courses may be taken on one-off basis for vocational, updating or as refreshers. Community education study packs available in eg energy saving, consumer decisions. Wide range of courses provided for professionals in commerce, industry, education, and the caring services (including a certificate, diploma and Masters degree in management). Postgraduate study also possible (taught and research based, and PGCE). **Special features:** Students study at home using specially written course texts, set books, computing, radio and television broadcasts and other audio-visual materials. Also face-to-face tuition at regional study centres and, for some courses, home kits and annual residential schools. **Library:** For staff and full-time students only. **Careers:** Literature, *Career Development with the Open University* and a series of leaflets. **Amenities:** Network of more than 290 study centres. The Open University Students' Association, whose membership includes all currently registered students, provides support services in both education and welfare. **Hardship funds:** Funds for students experiencing financial hardship. Some LEAs may also help and give funds for residential school.

Duration of first degree courses: 4–5 years average, 5–6 years average for honours. **Total first degree students 1996:** 104,373. **Mature students:** Almost all. **Male/female ratio:** 1;1. **Teaching staff:** 815 full-time, approx 7,500 part-time. **Total full-time students 1995 (all postgrad):** 400. **Postgraduate students:** 11,800. **First degree tuition fees:** UK students in 1996 paid £320 for each 60 point course; £160 for each 30 point course (plus residential school fee of £199). Higher fees are charged for students resident outside the UK.

WHAT IT'S LIKE   A large-scale distance teaching organisation; studying with it is a unique experience. Student are recommended to spend 10–15 hours a week studying, but this varies greatly. The well-organised and self-disciplined do just that, others cram everything into a frantic weekend of study closeted away from family and friends. The OU provides students with units of written information and details of set books; these are supported with radio and television broadcasts. (Unfortunately, broadcasts are increasingly at unsocial transmission times but are available on video.) Most courses have tutorials of varying frequency: foundation course has many more than third and fourth level courses. Some courses (all foundation courses) also have summer schools held at universities throughout the country. The prospect of spending a week away from home with hundreds of strangers can be daunting, but everyone's in the same situation and most enjoy the intensive study and social life. Many OU students have problems with isolation. It's easy to feel that you are the only OU student in your area, though it's unlikely to be true. One source of support is the Open University Students' Association (OUSA) which exists to serve the needs of OU students through its welfare and services provisions; to promote the student voice by its representation and education function on OU boards and committees; and to campaign for lower fees and grants for fees for part-time students. Most study centres have an OUSA branch where students can meet like-minded people and derive inspiration and stimulation for further study. Studying with the OU is not cheap. Fees continue to rise but help is available for the unemployed and low-waged (apply to OU). There is also a fund administered by OUSA to help with the other study related costs (contact OUSA, PO Box 397, Walton Hall, Milton Keynes MK7 6BE). Being an OU student means being in charge of your own learning experiences. You can study what you want when you want, cross discipline areas and even take a year off. Study can be fitted into odd moments through the day or in the evening, weekend or holiday periods. But it's no easy option; it's difficult to cope with all the demands on your time and keep up with the deadlines. However, its very popularity indicates how worthwhile its students feel it to be – not only in the acquisition of a qualification, but in proving to yourself that you can do it.

OXFORD BROOKES UNIVERSITY

Oxford Brookes University, Gypsy Lane, Headington,
Oxford OX3 0BP (Tel 01865 741111, Fax 01865 483983)
Map 3

STUDENT ENQUIRIES: Registry
APPLICATIONS: UCAS

Broad study areas: Arts, publishing, languages, hotel management, business, education, social sciences, biological and earth sciences, architecture, health, computing, mathematics, engineering, built environment, planning. (Subject details are in the *Subjects and Places Index*.)

Founded: 1865 as a school of art, becoming Oxford Poly in 1970; university status 1992. **Main undergraduate awards:** BA, BA(QTS), BSc, BEng, LLB. **Awarding body:** Oxford Brookes University. **Site:** Gipsy Lane (1 mile from city centre), Wheatley (6 miles from city centre) and Headington Hill Hall (1 mile from city centre). **Access:** Free transport between sites. **Academic features:** Modular courses allow study on a full-time, part-time or mixed-mode basis. New courses in physiotherapy, automotive engineering, biological and environmental chemistry, leisure planning. Languages for business courses; foundation courses in art & design, engineering and science. Access courses at seven local centres give entry to university courses. **Europe:** 19% first degree students take a language as part of course and spend 6 months or more abroad. Formal exchange links with 198 universities/colleges throughout Europe. **Library:** 3 libraries, 320,000 volumes, 2,500 current journals, 835 study places (increasing). Annual expenditure on library materials, £71.41 per FTE student. **Other learning facilities:** Computer services: over 500 PC student workstations, e-mail and Internet access for all students, some available 24 hours/day, 7 days a week. Educational methods unit: TV, graphics and photography. Consultancy and training in teaching methods, course design and evaluation. **Welfare:** Counsellors, careers, accommodation, housing and chaplaincy staff, nurses, FPA, visiting GPs and specialist advisers for international students, mature students and students with disabilities. SU welfare advice centre. Nursery (48 places). **Amenities:** New SU with bars, entertainments venue, shops, banks. **Sporting facilities:** New sports centre with badminton courts, squash courts, dance studio, weights training room, climbing room; 12 tennis courts, playing fields, pitch-and-putt golf course.

Accommodation: In 1995/96, 70% of first year students who need it in university halls. 3,000 places available: 2,200 in halls, 550 in shared housing and 200 in lodgings. In halls: 450 half-board places at £70 per week and 1,750 self-catering places at £44 per week, most 42 weeks. Students usually live in privately rented accommodation after first year: rents approx £45 per week for self-catering, 52 week contracts. **Term time work**: University's policy to allow term time working (50% believed to work). Term (and vac) work available on campus in SU bars, ents and in registry, accommodation, catering; SU Job Shop helps find work on and off campus. **Hardship funds:** Total available in 1995/96: £259,000 government access funds, 614 students helped; £40,000 own funds, 130 helped. Own funds assist overseas and part-time students with unforeseen difficulties; some available for some part-time students or local students on benefit.

Duration of first degree courses: 3 years; **others:** 4 years. **Total first degree students 1995/96:** 8,776. **BA(QTS) students:** 305. **Overseas students:** 1,934. **Mature students:** 6,131. **Male/female ratio:** 1:1. **Teaching staff:** 454 full-time, 174 part-time. **Total full-time students 1995/96:** 7,945. **Postgraduate students:** 2,119. **First degree tuition fees:** Home students, paying their own fees in 1996/97, paid £1,059 (classroom), £2,910 (lab/studio); Overseas students £5,898.

WHAT IT'S LIKE   Based on two sites: main site at Headington, 1½ miles from city centre; business and education is at Wheatley, 5 miles away. Intersite transport is free and frequent, from 8 am to 11.15 pm. Regular bus service (24-hour bus link to London stops outside university). Halls of residence (two of which are new) are close to campus; offer full board and self-catering accommodation, all with laundry facilities. Over half first year students get a place in halls or uni houses. Students mixed: 50% are mature; lots of 18-year old public school leavers; many from the home counties and London but a few also from north of England and Scotland. Studies based on modular course system – which means exams every term but no finals; successful and popular although regulations can be complex. A few non-modular courses still available and well-respected. Top subjects: architecture, education, estate management, town planning, hotel and catering, business studies, law; others of high quality too. Many new and exciting courses, eg tourism, or retail management. Changing course possible but not advised; drop-out rate is low. Library average and open till 10 pm; labs well equipped and stay open late. Good sports facilities with brand new sports hall. Student services and SU have excellent advice services. SU organises lively, value for money ents – summer ball best for its price in Oxford. New SU with large venue, 4 union bars provide cheap drink in safe environment; most recent bar, Morals, very well designed. SU not political but active in getting students to join societies etc. Oxford is a student city, geared to students' needs but expensive (but good market). Parking is very difficult and few halls allow cars. Very good social life, easy to meet other students in halls, in town as well as via SU.

PAUPER NOTES   **Accommodation:** Halls usually cheapest. Most first years from 100+ miles in halls; increasing number of 2nd and 3rd years. Extensive private sector, average rent £42–£50 pw plus bills. **Drink:** SU cheapest. **Eats:** Campus food improved; reasonable but not much choice. Student discounts in most town restaurants. **Ents:** Reasonably priced SU events; over 50 clubs/societies including excellent drama soc (Edinburgh fringe). **Sports:** New university sports centre. Existing facilities cheap. **Hardship funds:** Available. **Travel:** Easy access to London (£6 return by coach), regular buses, trains and coaches to Gatwick and Heathrow. **Work:** SU employs good range of casual staff. Jobs in city and university, terms and holidays. Lots of students work part-time.

INFORMAL NAME   Brookes

MORE INFO?   Enquiries to President OBSU (01865 484781) or SU office on 01865 484750 (fax 01865 484799).

ALUMNI (EDITORS' PICK)   Adrian Reynard (Reynard Racing), Tim Rodber (England rugby).

CAN'T FIND WHAT YOU'RE LOOKING FOR? USE THE INDEX!

OXFORD UNIVERSITY

University of Oxford, Oxford OX1 2JD
(Registry Tel 01865 270000, Fax 01865 270708) Map 3

STUDENT ENQUIRIES:
(1) (University) Oxford Colleges Admissions Office,
University Offices, Wellington Square, Oxford OX1 2JD
(2) (Colleges) The Tutor for Admissions, ... College,
Oxford.
APPLICATIONS: UCAS and to the university (see below)

Broad study areas: Arts, humanities, physical and biological sciences, politics, economics, history, classics. (Subject details are in the *Subjects and Places Index.*)

THE UNIVERSITY AND THE COLLEGES

Oxford is not a campus university – university and college buildings are scattered throughout the town centre. It is a federation of 39 independent, self-contained and self-governing colleges, 30 of which admit first degree undergraduates. There are also 6 private halls, founded by different Christian denominations. The university provides the curricular framework within which college teaching takes place, as well as providing a wide range of resources for teaching and learning – libraries, labs, museums, computing facilities etc. It sets the exams and awards degrees. Each college selects its own students, houses them (for at least 2 out of 3 years), provides meals, common rooms, libraries, sports and social facilities and is responsible, through the tutorial system, for its students' academic work. The majority of colleges teach most, but not all, of the university courses; so you need to check that the course you want is available at the college you prefer. Your college will be the hub of your life.

THE COLLEGES

You can look up these colleges and private halls:

Women only:
St Hilda's

Men and women:
Balliol
Brasenose
Christ Church
Corpus Christi
Exeter
Harris Manchester
   (for mature students)
Hertford
Jesus

Keble
Lady Margaret Hall
Lincoln
Magdalen
Mansfield
Merton
New College
Oriel
Pembroke
Queen's
Regent's Park
   (permanent private
   hall)

St Anne's
St Catherine's
St Edmund Hall
St Hugh's
St John's
St Peter's
Somerville
Trinity
University College
Wadham
Worcester

There are five other permanent private halls – Blackfriars (principally members of the Dominican Order); Campion Hall (men only, principally members of the Society of Jesus); Greyfriars (principally members of the Franciscan Order); St Benet's Hall (men only, principally for Benedictines); Wycliffe Hall.

HOW TO APPLY TO OXFORD UNIVERSITY

You may choose a college of preference, or put in an open application to the university. Candidates will be allocated second and third choice colleges and if you are not accepted by any of these colleges, your application will then be available to all other colleges for consideration. It is not possible to apply to both Oxford and Cambridge in the same admissions year, unless you are a candidate for an organ award.

The key deadline is **15 October** for two forms:

The *Oxford Application Form* – You must return this to the Oxford Colleges Admissions Office (University Offices, Wellington Square, Oxford OX1 2JD) by 15 October, with the application fee of £10. Instructions for completing the form are given in the *Undergraduate Prospectus*; ask at your school or, if you have left school, write to the Secretary of the Oxford Colleges Admissions Office.

The *UCAS Form* – You must return this to UCAS before 15 October.

Europe: 9% first degree students take a language as part of course and spend 6 months or more abroad. University has links with a large number of European universities. Most undergraduate exchanges are for language specialists but opportunities in other subjects is increasing. Undergraduates have access to self-instruction courses, language laboratories and to classes in main European languages. 4-year law course includes 1 year at a university in France, Germany or Netherlands.

Accommodation: All colleges provide accommodation for first year undergraduates; most also house third year students and many provide accommodation for all undergraduates. Students have to live within six miles of the centre of the city, in approved lodgings, so living at home is extremely rare. **Term time work:** University policy not to allow term time work for first degree students. **Financial help for students:** Government access funds £372,771 in 1996/97. Variety of other funds available to help students (eg from particular countries/areas, studying particular subjects, or suffering financial hardship); awards generally made on the basis of academic merit or financial need. Most colleges also offer scholarships and have funds for students in financial difficulty. In virtually all cases, awards are made only to students already on their course, except for some overseas student awards.

Duration of first degree courses: 3 and 4 years. **Total first degree students 1995/96:** 10,823. **Overseas students:** 2,666. **Male/female ratio:** 3:2. **Teaching staff:** 1,500 full-time, 250 part-time. **Total full-time students 1995/96:** 15,236. **Postgraduate students:** 4,413. **First degree university tuition fees:** Home students, paying their own fees in 1996/97, paid £750 (classroom), £1,600 (lab/studio), £2,800 (clinical) although a reduction may be made. Overseas students £6,150 (classroom), £8,150 (lab/studio), £15,000 (clinical). College fees of up to £3,500 are paid *in addition* to university tuition fees.

WHAT IT'S LIKE   It's the oldest university in the English-speaking world, laden with tradition and with many beautiful buildings dating from every century since the 1200s. The university is made up of about 30 semi-autonomous colleges. Students live, eat, socialise and are taught there and the college identity is very strong. Most colleges guarantee students accommodation for at least two years, so students often live in rented accommodation for one year. All colleges except St Hilda's (women only) are mixed. Visiting restrictions are minimal if they exist at all. There is a low proportion of mature students (although Harris Manchester caters specifically for them) but a high percentage of overseas students, particularly graduates. Most high-street chains represented in town; lots of restaurants and cafes; less choice when it comes to clubs though the pubs are good. Oxford is easily accessible by train and two bus services to London (every 15 minutes, 24 hours a day). Reasonable city bus service, especially along Cowley which is a popular student area. Most people use bikes as it's small and car parking is extremely restricted. Every college has a JCR (Junior Common Room) for undergraduates and a MCR (Middle Common Room) for graduates – some more political than others and which are separate from the university-wide Student Union (OUSA). There are over 300 university societies and voluntary groups. Short academic year, with three terms of eight weeks. Courses are highly specialised with a heavy workload. Instruction largely by tutorials, with a tutor to student ratio of 1 to 3 at the most. No continuous assessment – entire degree hinges on one set of exams at end of the course. University libraries very well stocked but closed on weekends; college libraries vary. Public schools and the south are over-represented but there is an active Target Schools programme (run by OUSU), aimed at encouraging state school applicants. Employment prospects after graduation better than average but perhaps not as good as they were. There is no longer a typical Oxford student.

PAUPER NOTES   **Accommodation:** Private accommodation very expensive; second only to London in housing costs. Many students live out for at least one year. East Oxford is saturated with students. **Drink:** College bars much less expensive than town equivalents. **Eats:** Huge variety ranging from five star to kebab vans. College food varies in quality. Vegetarian food universally available. **Ents:** Continuous college discos. Many nightclubs, most with student nights. **Sport:** Very well provided for at college level; new university gym. **Hardship funds:** All colleges have them. Level of generosity varies; can be loans, grants, combinations. **Travel:** College travel grants often generous. **Work:** Students not allowed to work during term (though some do). Oxford has a huge student population so there is heavy competition for employment in vac.

MORE INFO?   Get Alternative Prospectus from The Student Union, 28 Little Clarendon Street, Oxford OX1 4AR (01865 270777) – cost £4.50 (inc p&p).

OXFORD-SPEAK   Lots: JCR (Junior Common Room – undergraduate or junior members of a college), ditto MCR (Middle – graduates) and SCR (Senior – fellows); subfusc (cap and gown), sets (set of bedroom(s) and sitting room), hall (college dining hall), battells (college bill), come up (to arrive at Oxford), go down (to leave), collections (mock exams), boatie (rower), doss (skive), Norrington Table (league table of colleges by finals results), PPE (philosophy, politics and economics course) Greats or *lit hum* (classics, ancient history & philosophy).

ALUMNI (EDITORS' PICK)   Oscar Wilde, Margaret Thatcher, Roy Jenkins, Harold Wilson, Michael Heseltine, Denis Healey, Benazir Bhutto, Roger Bannister, Rowan Atkinson, Dudley Moore, Willy Rushton, Melvyn Bragg, Sir Robin Day, Tony Benn, Kris Kristofferson, Bill Clinton, Barbara Castle.

HOW TO START? *SEE SHORTLISTING*, PAGE 535

BALLIOL

Balliol College, Oxford OX1 3BJ
(Tel 01865 277777)

Founded: 1263; women undergraduates first admitted 1979. **Admission:** No undergraduates admitted for archaeology and anthropology, earth sciences, joint schools with English, geography, human sciences or theology. **Scholarships:** None at entrance. Awards made at end of first year. **Europe:** 8% students study a language and spend a period abroad as part of the formal requirements of their courses. All undergraduates have access to language tuition at the university language laboratory. Formal exchange links in Paris and Munich. **Travel grants:** Grants for academic purposes awarded annually on tutors' recommendations. **Library:** Library aims to provide at least basic coverage in all main subjects. **Eating arrangements:** Undergraduates not required to take meals in college; average undergraduate spends approx £556 in hall. All meals in hall on cafeteria basis, JCR pantry for snacks and breakfast. **Gate/guest hours:** Gate locked at midnight. All students have keys. 2 guest rooms. **Other college facilities:** Nearby sports field and pavilion (with 2 squash courts).

Accommodation: All undergraduates offered rooms in college (usually bedsits) for their 1st year and either their 2nd or 3rd year and possibly both. More accommodation being built. Rent and establishment charge £1,050 for 25 weeks; average expenditure on laundry and electricity £140 for 25 weeks. Under 1% of first degree students live at home. **Term time work:** College policy to allow term time work (10% believed to work); limit of approx 6 hours per week. Term (and vac) work available in college – library invigilation and computer officer. **Hardship funds:** Hardship fund available.

Undergraduates: 276 men, 122 women. **Postgraduates:** 105 men, 42 women. **Teaching staff:** 55 fellows (46 men, 9 women), 21 lecturers (14 men, 7 women). **College fees 1996/97:** LEA grants cover college fees; undergraduates not on grants pay £3,037 in addition to university fees.

WHAT IT'S LIKE   Good academically and active in all other aspects. Co-residential, medium-sized, with two years living in (heavily subsidised) and sometimes three. There is a laundry room in college; few kitchens and poorly equipped. Separate middle common room, with superlative facilities and cosmopolitan atmosphere, five minutes away. Relaxed dining hall; JCR Pantry renowned for its very late and excellent breakfast service. Autonomous JCR with lively political debate and enjoyable social focus. Sports facilities are central and a weights room in college; many successful teams. Sunday night concerts free and famous in Oxford. Good library facilities (all-night law library). Active women's group, left caucus and academic societies, all with regular speaker meetings. Forward looking college with high academic standards and friendly atmosphere to suit all needs and purposes.

PAUPER NOTES   **Accommodation:** In college quite cheap; most live out for 1 year which is expensive (up to £50 pw or £65 in college annexe). **Drink:** Student-run bar, with excellent atmosphere. **Eats:** Hall and JCR Pantry cheap and quality improving; veggie choices available but plain. **Ents:** Non-elitist summer event, free weekly ents, variable bops, interesting Christmas panto. **Sports:** Very close by with football, hockey, squash, tennis, netball, rugby. Good weights in college. Darts, pool and video games in bar. **Hardship funds:** College loans/grants help those living out. Book grants. Grants, loans and short-term cash loans to all who need them. **Travel:** Grants, travel scholarships, 8 yearly awards to US, yearly internship with Mayor of Baltimore. **Work:** Not in term and little during holidays. Considerable vacation/project grants.

ALUMNI (EDITORS' PICK)   Adam Smith, Harold Macmillan, Ted Heath, Bryan Gould, Graham Greene, H H Asquith, the Huxleys, Gerard Manley Hopkins, Peter Snow, Anthony Powell, John Schlesinger, Denis Healey, Chris Patten, R H Tawney, Christopher Hill, King of Norway.

BRASENOSE

Brasenose College, Oxford OX1 4AJ
(Tel 01865 277510)

Founded: 1509; women undergraduates first admitted 1974. **Admission:** Standard Oxford arrangements. No undergraduates admitted to earth sciences; human sciences; metallurgy; modern history and English (joint school); oriental studies; theology. **Largest fields of study:** PPE, law, modern history. **Scholarships:** Awarded at the end of the first year. **Library:** About 40,000 volumes on open shelves and a further collection of about 12,000 older books; 90 periodical subscriptions; separate modern history and law reading rooms. **Eating arrangements:** Breakfast, lunch and dinner in hall; tea available in New Buttery. **Gate/guest hours:** Unrestricted. **Other college facilities:** Shop, bar, sports ground, pavilion, squash and tennis courts about 10 minutes' walk from college; boathouse.

Accommodation: In 1995/96, 90% of all undergraduates in college accommodation; all first, third and fourth years can live in and 50% second years (more in 1997). Full board at £82 per week on average, term time only (range £1,523–£2,373 pa); first years allocated mid-price rooms (other rooms allocated by ballot). No first degree students live at home. **Term time work:** No college policy to allow term time work. Vac work only available in college in the bursary, domestic help during summer conferences. **Hardship funds:** The college has limited discretionary fund for assistance in case of hardship.

Undergraduates: 220 men, 122 women. **Postgraduates:** 66 men, 44 women. **Teaching staff:** *Men:* 29 fellows, normally 2 research fellows, 19 lecturers. *Women:* 2 fellows, 10 lecturers. **College fees 1996/97:** LEA grants cover college fees; undergraduates not on grants pay £3,056 in addition to university fees.

WHAT IT'S LIKE   Positioned along one side of Radcliffe Square, beside the towering dome of the Camera, Brasenose is ideally situated. All main libraries (Bodleian, Radcliffe Camera and faculty libraries) are extremely convenient; very close to shops, pubs, cinemas and nightlife. Though not one of the most imposing or palatial Oxford college, the 16th-century Old Quad and adjoining, ironically named, miniature Deer Park are very picturesque. Small enough for a sense of community; large enough not to be claustrophobic. Some modern rooms but mainly old 'character' rooms which are being steadily renovated to very high standard (basins in all and ensuite bathrooms for finalists). Currently 1st and 3rd year undergraduates are guaranteed rooms and about half the 2nd years are in the college annexe – but more building is underway. Academically variable (usually lodged in the middle of the Norrington Table) after a brief spate of success. Widely known as the place for law and PPE; tutors and library facilities are excellent in these areas. College library is more comprehensive than it looks in most other subjects, and has extensive research stacks. Lawyers also have own specialist library, one of the largest in the university. JCR is generally moderate although all political views are present. Incorporates students from a variety of backgrounds, schools and regions and is moving towards equal numbers of men and women; SCR very committed to widening intake. General friendly attitude throughout the college; everyone seems to find somewhere to fit in. Reputation as a strong rugby, rowing and cricket college, but also strong in other sports (both male and female). Facilities are close by and very comprehensive, including two football pitches, a rugby and a hockey pitch, cricket field and nets, squash, tennis and netball courts, and excellent boathouse. Also beginning to build reputation for drama, with summer festival a regular feature. Facilities feature a college-run bar, recently enlarged and upgraded – bar staff very popular and reputedly best student bar in Oxford. Also in college is Gertie's, the tea bar, serving hot and cold food and drink just when you need it most. New purpose-built computer room for junior members which houses 8 modern computers at present. JCR has Sky TV and video, a pool table, Coke machine, hot drinks, snacks and various games machines (plus Monopoly and Trivial Pursuits). Runs societies as diverse as The Brasenose Players, Christian Union, Women's Group, Indolents (general sports club) and Wine Society, as well as its own wittily malicious student Noserag.

PAUPER NOTES Accommodation: Live in college (usually) 1st and 3rd years. Accommodation in college character rooms, attractive and well equipped. Frewin annexe good facilities, modern and warm. Accommodation for most 2nd years being built. Much cheaper than living out. Hardship fund for those not allocated rooms. Oxford very expensive; up to £50/week room, shared houses are normal. **Drink:** College bars; 4 central student pubs – Turf, Kings Arms (always full), White Horse (very small), the Bear. **Eats:** College, 3 large meals per day; good vegetarian options. Carfax chippy, Mehdi's Kebab Van. **Ents:** Free college ents: excellent sweaty bops and regular big screen events. Usual smash hit cinemas, plus the Phoenix, more arty. Lots of student drama. **Sports:** BNC sports facilities good and close to college, variety of courts and pitches. **Hardship funds:** Strictly means tested. Have to be absolutely broke, and preferably injured, to get one. Access fund. Vacation grants available. **Travel:** A few travel grants; £5 return on bus to London and good national coach services. **Work:** Term time work strongly discouraged by the college. Some college bar work available; always tight in town during term because of number of students. Lots more around during vacations.

INFORMAL NAME BNC (in writing); Nose (sporting supporters).

ALUMNI (EDITORS' PICK) Colin Cowdrey (cricketer), Michael Palin (Monty Python), William Golding (novelist), Robert Runcie (ex-Archbishop of Canterbury), Sir Arthur Evans, John Buchan, Lord Scarman, Stephen Dorrell MP, William Webb-Ellis (inventor of rugby).

CHRIST CHURCH

Christ Church, Oxford OX1 1DP
(Tel 01865 276151)

Founded: 1525; women undergraduates first admitted 1980. **Admission:** By interview. Undergraduates not admitted to computation; earth sciences (geology); human sciences as single honours; nor to the joint schools of classics/English, engineering/materials,

materials/economics/management, metallurgy/science of materials, maths/computation, modern history/English. **Largest fields of study:** PPE, modern history, law, English, modern languages, classics, geography, physics, mathematics, chemistry, engineering. **Scholarships:** Scholarships and other prizes awarded for meritorious work during residence. **Europe:** 16% first degree students take a language as part of course and spend 6 months or more abroad. No formal exchange links. **Travel grants:** Limited assistance provided to encourage travel by undergraduates, irrespective of subject of study. **Book grants:** Available for all undergraduates. **Library:** Over 100,000 volumes; collections of early printed books and manuscripts; large law library. **Eating arrangements:** All meals in hall. Breakfast and lunch available on cash payment. **Gate/guest hours:** Undergraduates have own keys. Guests not admitted before 9 am, and must have left by 2 am. **Other college facilities:** Music room, computer room, playing fields nearby, multigym, sports pavilion, squash courts, tennis courts, boat house. Picture gallery (famous collection of Old Masters). Because Christ Church is both a college and cathedral it has a strong musical tradition.

Accommodation: All students in college accommodation, shared sets or bedsits: half-board at £63.70 per week, term time only (heat, light and laundry charges according to use). No first degree students live at home. **Term time work:** College policy not to allow term time work. **Hardship funds:** Available from own funds and from trust funds.

Undergraduates: 254 men, 170 women. **Postgraduates:** 102 men, 45 women. **Teaching staff:** *Men:* 36 fellows, 4 research fellows, 31 lecturers. *Women:* 2 fellows, 2 research fellows, 4 lecturers. **College fees 1996/97:** LEA grants cover college fees; undergraduates not on grants pay £3,054 in addition to university fees.

WHAT IT'S LIKE   One of the most architecturally outstanding and famous colleges in the university, which leads to much tourism and also a great deal of college pride. Easy access being right in town centre, although maintains relative peace and quiet. Large main college site means all college accommodation close together, rather than scattered around the town. Accommodation excellent – mostly large and beautiful rooms in good state of repair. Almost no cooking facilities for undergraduates but food served in hall is adequate. Mixed college residency but no mixed room sets. Majority white, British students but some exceptions and a few overseas students, particularly graduates. Good relationship with college administrators – students have certain amount of say in college policies. No overnight guests allowed officially but this rule seldom enforced. Probably less than 10% students have cars, mainly because of very restricted parking facilities. Active JCR – mainly social rather than political; involved in charity work. JCR welfare rep offers counselling service within college, backed up by college nurse. University-wide counselling service good and confidential. Hardship grants readily available to those with financial difficulties. Active drama society in college, but focus on music (particularly the cathedral choir) and sport (active in many areas, especially rowing and rugby). Good sports facilities all within walking distance of college. Large student population means good social cross-section and therefore a tendency to be quite insular but nevertheless easy to meet students from other colleges through societies etc. College especially good for history and law – good law library open all night; college library excellent. Expected to cope with heavy workload but not enormous academic pressure. Prestigious college – high graduate employment rate (many go on to well paid jobs in the city etc), augmented by careers association run by ex-members. Relatively low drop-out rate – a few students per year, perhaps 2 or 3. Male/female ratio 3:2 but getting better.

PAUPER NOTES   **Accommodation:** Rooms in college excellent almost without exception. Single rooms to suite of 4 rooms per person and double rooms available in college.

Married flats available; 1st and 2nd years live in college, 3rd years in college accommodation on the Iffley Road. **Drink:** JCR prices two-thirds of town pubs. Half price cocktails at discos and other social events. Many popular pubs near, off licence outside college. **Eats:** Food cheap and of reasonable quality in hall; also breakfast, lunch and tea served daily in JCR. Good health-food shop very close; many reasonable restaurants in town. **Ents:** Discos and other entertainments regularly held. Amusement machines, pool table, Sky TV and dartboard in JCR. Also table football. College magazine. Good independent cinemas in town. **Sports:** Excellent sports facilities 15 minutes on foot from college; also own weights room, squash court and other free facilities. Strong traditions of success in most sports, particularly rowing and rugby. Health centre/swimming pool at Temple Cowley does cheap student package. **Hardship funds:** Grants available from college/university by negotiation, if suitably broke. Also residence grant money for study abroad. **Travel:** Generous travel grants liberally distributed. Good student fares eg coach Oxford-London. **Work:** As a rule students don't get paid work during term. Grants available to discourage holiday jobs. Some summer work available in Oxford.

MORE INFO?   Kate Heard, JCR President

ALUMNI (EDITORS' PICK)   Lord Hailsham, Sir William Walton OM, Sir Adrian Boult CH, Rt Hon Norman St John Stevas, Sir Antony Acland, Sir Robert Armstrong, Judge James Pickles, Peter JF Green, Peter Jay, Mark Girouard, Lewis Carroll, Gladstone, Sir Alec Douglas Home, Antony Eden, Sir Leon Brittan, Nigel Lawson, Hugh Cluarshie, Howard Goodall, Sir Robert Peel, W H Auden, ex-president Bhutto, Auberon Waugh, Anthony Howard.

CORPUS CHRISTI

Corpus Christi College, Oxford OX1 4JF
(Tel 01865 276700)

Founded: 1517; women undergraduates first admitted 1979. **Admission:** No special provisions or requirements differing from those applying to Oxford generally. Undergraduates not admitted to archaeology and anthropology, botany, geography, geology (earth sciences, human sciences), music (except for organ scholars), oriental studies, zoology, modern languages and related joint schools, theology. **Largest fields of study:** Classics, history and PPE. **Europe:** All members of the college can attend courses run by the university's language laboratories. **Travel grants:** Some available. **Library:** Old Library with unrestricted access but restricted borrowing hours. **Eating arrangements:** All meals available in college except for Saturday dinner and Sunday breakfast. **Gate/guest hours:** Keys available to all members. Some restrictions on frequency and duration of entertainment of guests in college. **Other college facilities:** Squash courts and playing fields; boathouse; music room, computer suite.

Accommodation: College accommodation available to all students; full board approx £70 per week, term time only. No first degree students live at home. **Term time work:** College policy not to allow term time work. **Hardship funds:** A maintenance support fund is available to all students should they need financial assistance.

Undergraduates: 136 men, 91 women. **Graduates:** 61 men, 37 women. **Teaching staff:** *Men:* 34 fellows, 17 lecturers. *Women:* 3 fellows, 2 research fellows, 4 lecturers. **College fees**

1996/97: LEA grants cover college fees; undergraduates not on grants pay £3,047 in addition to university fees.

WHAT IT'S LIKE   Its strength lies in its size: this is Oxford's smallest college. Good situation within the city. Atmosphere intimate and friendly and cosy beer cellar provides meeting place for all. JCR active and well supported. Fundamentally an academic college with propensity towards classics, but strong in PPE, English, history and medicine and gaining strength in sciences. (No tutors in zoological sciences.) Work load high in all subjects; library amongst best (open 24 hrs a day). Corpus is better-than-average sporting college for its size; facilities good – squash court, boathouse, tennis courts, playing fields and pavilion. Accommodation amongst Oxford's best, all undergraduates (and most graduates) able to live in. Food compares favourably with other colleges. Discipline tactful; poor work not tolerated. No aristocratic pretensions; public/state school ratio roughly equal and male/female ratio is approx 3:2. Tolerant college, if gossipy. Good social life and good ents. No particular political bias – most people are very open-minded.

PAUPER NOTES   **Accommodation:** Very good; one of few colleges where every student able to live in. Overseas students and finalists given priority in staying in college accommodation during vac. Married quarters – college houses. **Drink:** Oxford pubs expensive: college bars cheaper especially Corpus beer cellar. **Eats:** College food nutritional and cheap, veggie option. Kebab vans, chippy, fast food a whole array. Many good and cheapish Indian, Chinese, etc. **Ents:** Phoenix, PPP, Cannon cinemas, Oxford Playhouse. **Sports:** Men's rowing good, other sports variable. Nearest pool 2 miles away. **Hardship funds:** Special fund; book grants and vacation residence grants. **Travel:** Scholarships from college, university awards, good student travel centres. Good bus service to London and airports. **Work:** Can work on college maintenance staff; other temp work available in Oxford.

MORE INFO?   Enquiries to JCR President, 01865 276690 (or 276700 for messages).

ALUMNI (EDITORS' PICK)   Sir Isaiah Berlin, Lord Beloff, William Waldegrave MP, J L Austin, Sir Robert Ensor, R Brinkley, G W Most (classics), Baron Hailey, Lord Clyde, E C Robertson-Glasgow, K H Bailey, Lord Cameron of Lochbroom, Brian Sedgemore MP, Vikram Seth.

EXETER

Exeter College, Oxford OX1 3DP
(Tel 01865 279600)

Founded: 1314; women undergraduates first admitted 1979. **Admission:** Undergraduates admitted for all subjects apart from biology, botany, human sciences, geography, metallurgy, oriental studies, zoology. **Scholarships:** and exhibitions awarded for meritorious work during undergraduate courses. **Europe:** 8% first degree students take a language as part of course and spend 6 months or more abroad. No formal exchange links. Some visiting European students in residence. **Travel grants:** Generous provision made from endowed funds for both academic and general purposes. **Library:** Well stocked. **Eating arrangements:** Self-service breakfast and lunch and served dinner available in early 17th-century hall daily throughout term; cost is approx £4.50 per day if all meals are taken. Some self-catering facilities. **Gate/guest hours:** All members have late keys. No guests allowed between 2 and 8 am unless they have been booked in overnight. **Other college facilities:** Bar, sports clubs, playing field, boathouse and multi-gym. College chapel has fine choir made up of students and boys from Cathedral school.

Accommodation: All students accommodated in college for first year, and many offered a second year (usually for finals). College also has hostels available; generally able to house all who do not want privately rented accommodation. Most undergraduates charged £1,511–£1,707 pa. No first degree students live at home. **Term time work:** College policy not to allow term time work. **Hardship fund:** Well-endowed fund administered by the Rector and Tutors' Committee.

Undergraduates: 214 men, 121 women. **Postgraduates:** 116 men, 56 women. **Teaching staff:** *Men*: 29 fellows, 3 research fellows, 14 lecturers. *Women*: 8 fellows, 8 lecturers. **College fees 1996/97:** LEA grants cover college fees; undergraduates not on grants pay £3,089 in addition to university fees.

WHAT IT'S LIKE   Small and cosy; everyone knows everyone else. Central position gives good access to shops and facilities. Friendly, with thriving JCR and cheery bar staff. Facilities are being slowly improved, eg a new staircase and lecture room built (also new computers, washing machines, security cameras). Students complain about the food (but leads to student solidarity); dinner in 2 sittings, gowns worn for formal hall. Everyone has a late key. Cheap bar. Impressive fellows garden. Exeter has settled at around the top of the league tables, but non-academic pursuits are encouraged. JCR provides a wide range of facilities – newspapers, magazines, a drinks machine, pool table, televisions and video. Traditional links with West Country, but recently more people from Merseyside than from Devon. Healthy public/state school ratio and improving male/female ratio.

PAUPER NOTES   **Accommodation:** Not expensive for Oxford – but not cheap. University married quarters. All 1st and most 3rd years live in college itself. College owns flats (amazing), houses and hostels for students. **Drinks:** Very cheap college bar close to main student pub The King's Arms. **Eats:** Town has many good places. College food marginally improved, and cheap (chefs been on vegetarian courses.) Lots of cheap sandwich bars and late night kebab vans (open till 2am). **Ents:** Good local cinemas eg Phoenix. Regular college entertainments. Several student theatres and student discounts at main venues. Good clubs if you look hard enough for them. **Sports:** University sports centre close. College has own sports pitches including squash 10 mins by bike. **Hardship funds:** Hardship fund, plus many college funds. **Travel:** Easy to hitch to London and only £5 by bus. College travel grants generous and easy to get. **Work:** Work available behind college bar. Great demands for teaching English to foreign students in summer; also waiting jobs £3–£4/hour, but living in Oxford is expensive. Classicists forbidden to get summer jobs.

MORE INFO?   Contact JCR President 01865 279614.

ALUMNI (EDITORS' PICK)   J R Tolkien, Sir Michael Levy, Sir Roger Bannister, Robert Robinson, Tariq Ali, Richard Burton, Martin Amis, Alan Bennett, Nevil Coghill, Ned Sherrin, Russell Harty, William Morris, John Ford, Sir Charles Lyell, J A Froude, Edward Burne-Jones, Imogen Stubbs, Will Self.

GET HOLD OF THE PROSPECTUSES

HARRIS MANCHESTER

Harris Manchester College, Oxford OX1 3TD
(Tel 01865 271006)

Founded: 1786, moved to Oxford in 1889. Women undergraduates first admitted 1907.
Admission: Mature students (over 25) only. Undergraduates not admitted for most science courses. **Special features:** Became part of the University in 1990 as college for mature students (as Manchester College; changed name in 1996). **Largest field of study:** English.
Europe: 2% first degree students take a language as part of course. No formal exchange links. **Library:** 3 libraries: Tate (general); Carpenter (world religions); Old (books before 1800); 40,000 volumes, 30 periodicals, 40 study places. **Other college facilities:** Chaplain, JCR bar.

Accommodation: In 1995/96, 90% of all students in college accommodation, 100% of first years who wish to live in (no married accommodation available). 80 places available: full-board at £96 per week, term time only. Students may live in privately owned accommodation. **Term time work:** College policy to allow term time work, limit of 10 hours per week (10–15% believed to work). Term (and vac) work available in college in kitchen, library, cleaning, occasional office work; night portering in vacs. **Hardship funds:** £5,000 own funds available.

Undergraduates: 50 men, 40 women. **Postgraduates:** 10 men, 7 women. **Teaching staff:** *Men:* 4 fellows, 6 lecturers. *Women:* 5 fellows, 6 lecturers. **College fees for 1996/97:** LEA grants cover college fees; undergraduates not on grants pay £3,116 in addition to university fees.

WHAT IT'S LIKE   Make no mistake about it Manchester College – now renamed Harris Manchester – is on an accelerated ascendency in Oxford University life. An ideally situated college slap-bang in the middle of town, it has a small but vibrant and very friendly student community with an average age of 30. Student accommodation is generally good and available for the full three years if needed. Rooms are either c15th century or brand new. The new quad offers homes for Harris Manchester students as well as some All Souls Fellows. Food is amongst the best in any Oxford college. Academically it is experienced and tuned in to the varying demands of mature students in all their guises and backgrounds.
PAUPER NOTES   **Accommodation:** Available in college for all years but not cheap. **Drink:** JCR bar – Kings Arms – it's near enough and isn't The Turf. Lots of good places – look out for happy hours, £1 a pint nights etc. **Ents:** JCR functions throughout the year. Active drama group. Masses of ents in Oxford. **Sports:** Croquet, basketball, soccer, eights boat and sailing. Joins up with other colleges for other sports. **Hardship funds:** Difficult to get any extra help. **Work:** Bar work, cleaning and waiting are most common.
MORE INFO?   Contact Frank Stringer, JCR President
ALUMNI (EDITORS' PICK)   Josiah Wedgwood, John Datton, Sir Henry Tate.

HERTFORD

Hertford College, Oxford OX1 3BW
(Tel 01865 279400)

Founded: 1874; women undergraduates first admitted 1974. **Admission:** Places on the basis of an interview in December. Entry is competitive with the emphasis being on promise. **Academic features:** Law, geography, engineering, Japanese and all mainstream subjects. **Europe:** 10% first degree students take a language as part of course and spend 6 months or more abroad. Formal exchange links with the British Institute in Paris for modern linguists. **Library:** Undergraduate and antiquarian libraries. **Eating arrangements:** Swipe-card system charged at end of term. **Gate/guest hours:** All students issued with gate keys. **Other college facilities:** JCR complex, lecture theatre, sports ground, boathouse, orchestra, computer, bar, rowing, squash court, music practice room, multi-gym.

Accommodation: 195 places in college, 231 in college houses. Standard charge £1,346.47 for 25-week year (including laundry and heating); fixed kitchen charge to a maximum £124 (for those living in college). No first degree students live at home. **Term time work:** College policy not to allow term time work. **Hardship funds:** White, Boyd and Keasbey funds.

Undergraduates: 213 men, 152 women. **Postgraduates:** 108 men, 45 women. **Teaching staff:** *Men:* 27 fellows, 6 research fellows, 17 lecturers. *Women:* 10 fellows, 10 lecturers. **College fees 1996/97:** LEA grants cover college fees; undergraduates not on grants pay £3,222 in addition to university fees.

WHAT IT'S LIKE   The friendly college, where everyone can find their niche and enjoy themselves. Facilities are more than adequate for a small college, with popular television/video games/pool room and brand new student coffee bar. The college has excellent computer facilities and a fairly well stocked library. Room sizes vary but all are comfortable and the college prides itself on being able to provide accommodation for all undergraduates. Exceptionally well situated, just 2 minutes from town centre and 30 seconds from the Bodleian Library. Academically, the college has been consistently successful in the last 20 years; strong reputation for geography and law. Workload varies, but averages 2 essays and tutorials a week. Famously pleasant and unsnobbish atmosphere results from very wide range of regional and social backgrounds and the ever-popular and very friendly traditional student-run bar – one of the last remaining genuine, down-to-earth and exciting college bars in the university. Students generally develop a strong affinity to the college, demonstrated in consistent sporting success, particularly in football and hockey. Though generally politically laid back, students have a thriving JCR and close ties with graduates and fellows. Hertford students are closely connected with many university societies, while forming the backbone of student journalism and broadcasting. *Tom Fletcher*

PAUPER NOTES   **Accommodation:** All years guaranteed accommodation. Limited married quarters. **Drink:** College bar cheap and very popular. Other college bars frequented. Pubs in city centre. **Eats:** College cheap, food improving; vegetarian options for all meals. Huge variety in town. **Ents:** Regular college bops, video showings and entertainments. Students ents go on all the time in different colleges. **Sports:** Hertford sports ground 1½ miles from college. Squash courts, tennis courts (summer only). Football, hockey (men's and women's) traditionally strong. **Hardship funds:** Access funds on university scale.

Keasbey and Alumni grants for Hertford students. 2 college bursaries. **Travel:** A few college grants. **Work:** Not allowed in term; a few students do get casual work but not really enough time.
ALUMNI (EDITORS' PICK) Evelyn Waugh, John Donne, Gavin Maxwell, Thomas Hobbes, Jonathan Swift, Charles James Fox.

JESUS

Jesus College, Oxford OX1 3DW
(Tel 01865 279700)

Founded: 1571; women undergraduates first admitted 1974. **Admission:** Undergraduates not admitted to anthropology, archaeology, fine art, oriental studies. **Scholarships:** Various scholarships and grants: Sankey scholarships (expenses of being called to the Bar). **Europe:** 5% first degree students take a language as part of course and spend a year abroad. Formal exchange links with Trier, Germany. **Travel grants:** Charles Green studentships for classical or other studies abroad; Dodd Benefaction for vacation travel abroad. **Eating arrangements:** Continental/cooked breakfast, cafeteria lunch and dinner, and set dinner in hall. **Gate/guest hours:** 8 am to midnight. **Other college facilities:** Library, bar, music room, 3 squash courts, sports field, IT rooms.

Accommodation: All undergraduates guaranteed college accommodation for all of their course; some rooms in college, most in flats outside. Most undergraduates in college charged £1,075 pa including heat and light (range £927–£1,075). No first degree students live at home. **Term time work:** No college policy to allow term time work (small number believed to work); students may, with permission of tutor, work in college bar.

Undergraduates: 169 men, 136 women. **Postgraduates:** 106 men, 33 women. **Teaching staff:** *Men:* 28 fellows, 17 research fellows, 16 lecturers. *Women:* 4 fellows, 1 research fellow, 1 lecturer. **College fees 1996/97:** LEA grants cover college fees; undergraduates not on grants pay £3,060 in addition to university fees.

WHAT IT'S LIKE Founded by Queen Elizabeth in 1571, a compact, pretty college with 3 quads right in centre of Oxford. Handy for libraries, shops and entertainments but tends to attract tourists. Good library, sociable common room, OK food served at convenient cafeteria, laundry facilities and a popular bar. Accommodation is excellent and inexpensive. All first years live in as do some finalists. All second and third years live either in college or in modern self-catering college flats about 2 miles away. Welsh connections now folklore, if anything Irish people more prominent. No admissions discrimination; Jesus people tend to come from wide range of backgrounds and schools. Politically centre/left and pretty sound. Regular social events – easily the cheapest and most widely available in Oxford. Wide range of college societies and sporting clubs; drama and photographic societies recently formed and generously funded. Active Christian Union, chapel choir and other music groups. Sporting record rapidly improving, especially in football and rugby and in women's rowing and hockey. College squash and tennis courts and large sports ground. Excellent academic standards; academic pressure being increased year by year. Nearly all subjects taught in college. Work loads and timetables vary. Student/don relationships good. Gates close at midnight, but college members have keys; no visiting restrictions. Worst point: tends to be socially isolated. Most people know your news (or think they do) before you know it yourself. Best point: friendly, game for a laugh, unpretentious and cheap.

PAUPER NOTES   Accommodation: Very high standard, cheap college accommodation. **Drink:** Extremely popular bar. **Eats:** OK food. Very popular credit card system. All minority eaters catered for but quality ropey. **Ents:** Free weekly ent in bar or JCR – discos, bands, talent nights and game shows. Weekly video in JCR. Lots on in Oxford. **Sports:** All free. A multigym and ergometer recently acquired. Free pool table and bar games. **Hardship funds:** Student grants/loans etc, guaranteed for academic 'stars'; Jesus is one of the richest colleges and as such is able to cushion its students (particularly the most academic ones) from financial hardship. **Travel:** Gratuitous grant max £300. Most cycle in Oxford. **Work:** Jobs available in college bar (pretty well paid) or helping at open days.

MORE INFO?   Enquiries to JCR President 01865 279700.

ALUMNI (EDITORS' PICK)   T E Lawrence ('Lawrence of Arabia'), Lord Wilson of Rievaulx, James Burke, Magnus Magnusson, Paul Jones (Manfred Mann).

KEBLE

Keble College, Oxford OX1 3PG (01865 272727; admissions enquiries 01865 272708; E-mail admissions@keb.ox.ac.uk)

Founded: 1870; women undergraduates first admitted 1979. **Admission:** Conditional offer or on basis of grades achieved plus interview. International and other alternative qualifications welcomed. Undergraduates not admitted for music or oriental studies (except Japanese). **Scholarships:** Awards given for meritorious work during undergraduate course. Organ and choral awards; award of course fees and maintenance to one third world scholar at any time. **Europe:** 9% first degree students take a language as part of course and spend 6 months or more abroad. Exchange links arranged in some faculties. **Travel grants:** A number of study and travel grants are provided by Keble Association. Academic prizes and competitive bursaries (£8,000) for worthwhile vacation projects involving travel, 20 benefit. **Library:** Over 40,000 books, 24-hour opening; some textbooks available on lease basis. Terminal for university electronic catalogue (OLIS). **Eating arrangements:** Keble Hall (the longest in Oxford) accommodates everyone in one sitting. Breakfast, lunch and Sunday brunch, self-service; dinners, waitered service. **Gate/guest hours:** Wicket gate keys available for all students. Guest rooms available for overnight stay. **Other college facilities:** JCR, bar, music room, sports ground, boathouse, laundry, TV room, squash courts, weights room, darkroom, computer rooms.

Accommodation: In 1995/96, 65% of all students in college accommodation, (all live in for two years): £1,287–£1,520 pa, term time only (meals pay-as-you-eat). 93 new rooms for final year students at £2,129 per year. Small proportion of students choose to live in privately owned accommodation: rents £2,500 pa for self-catering. No first degree students live at home. **Term time work:** College policy not to allow term time work. **Hardship funds:** £2,500–£3,500 own funds, approx 15 students helped. Special help: those hit by unexpected hardship while on course; organ and choral scholars.

Undergraduates: 321 men, 141 women. **Postgraduates:** 145 men, 44 women. **Teaching staff:** *Men:* 36 fellows, 23 lecturers. *Women:* 3 fellows, 8 lecturers. **College fees 1996/97:**

LEA grants cover college fees; undergraduates not on grants pay £3,289 in addition to university fees.

WHAT IT'S LIKE   It's one of the largest Oxford colleges both in terms of student numbers and its imposing Victorian structure. All undergraduates guaranteed two years in college accommodation and a new on-site building allows 75% of third years to be in college. Accommodation good: all rooms have central heating and washbasin; hot showers and baths plentiful (many bedrooms ensuite). One problem is the absence of cooking facilities although new residential block for finalists has shared kitchens in flats. But three meals a day are provided seven days a week in hall; good value with vegetarian and vegan alternatives and a wide choice of food. JCR (small student union) has good facilities and provides the focus for lively activity and debate; officers provide internal and external representation and relations with the SCR are good. The wide-ranging social and geographical makeup of the students, and equal numbers from private/state schools, makes Keble a friendly and open college. The number of Keble women has increased recently and the JCR Women's Officer represents a powerful female perspective. Academic performance important and work pressure can be high. Extra-curricular activity does not seem to have been unduly hindered – the college sporting achievements remain very high; music and drama also flourish.

PAUPER NOTES   **Accommodation:** 2 or 3 years in college accommodation. **Drinks:** College bar plus good pubs; Lamb and Flag less than 2 minutes' walk from college. Good local beer: Morrells. **Eats:** St Giles Café (greasy spoon), numerous sandwich shops, G&D's icecream café, nearby Pizza Hut (student nights) and at least 3 well-used kebab vans. **Ents:** Plenty about; student nights vary. Numerous college drama productions within university; JCR ents, DTM's (tacky club), Park End club (disco). Excellent independent cinema. **Sports:** Everything and anything available at all levels, usually free. **Hardship fund:** SCR sympathetic to specific cases. College supports loan for those in extraordinary need. **Travel:** Travel scholarships available from college. Hitching not too difficult. Very cheap student bus fare to London (£6 return). **Work:** Pub work, local shops, language and other teaching available. Most find something esp during tourist season. Term-time work discouraged but available in college bar and university library.

MORE INFO?   Enquiries to Carrie Thompson (01865 272754).

ALUMNI (EDITORS' PICK)   Sir Peter Pears, Rev. Chad Varah (founder of Samaritans), Michael Croft, Imran Khan, Andreas Whittam Smith (founder of the *Independent*).

LADY MARGARET HALL

Lady Margaret Hall, Oxford OX2 6QA
(Tel 01865 274300)

Founded: 1878; men undergraduates first admitted 1977. **Admission:** For pre A-level candidates, interview with a view to a conditional offer; for post A-level candidates, interviews and sometimes short written tests. Undergraduates not admitted for geology, metallurgy, geography, or for oriental studies other than Hebrew. **Scholarships:** Awarded to undergraduates in residence on academic merit; organ scholarship; various college essay prizes. **Europe:** Only students in modern languages and joint courses learn a language and spend a period abroad as part of their course. No formal exchange links. **Travel grants:** Armorel

Holiday Gifts (total about £1,000 pa) to help needy undergraduates to have a good holiday. Maude Royden long vacation travelling exhibition (normally £200). Other grants in connection with academic work. **Library:** Open 24 hours; over 50,000 books on open shelves; law reading room; science reading room. **Eating arrangements:** All meals in hall. JCR kitchen/pantries on all floors. **Gate/guest hours:** Gate closed at midnight. All members of college issued with keys. Guest hours: 9 am to midnight (to 2 am at weekends). **Other college facilities:** Bar, music practice rooms, 2 grand pianos and several upright pianos, tennis courts, croquet lawn, boathouse. Squash court, shared facilities for other sports.

Accommodation: All but about 35 undergraduates are able to live in college; single study bedrooms (some third years have private bathrooms). Standard accommodation charge 1996/97 is £1,428 pa plus meals as taken. **Hardship funds:** Limited grants available for unexpected hardship during course.

Undergraduates: 188 men, 185 women. **Postgraduates:** 78 men, 55 women. **Teaching staff:** *Men:* 20 fellows, 1 research fellow, 9 lecturers, 7 professors and supernumerary fellows. *Women:* 14 fellows, 4 lecturers, 2 professors and supernumerary fellows. **College fees for 1996/97:** LEA grants cover college fees; undergraduates not on grants pay £ 3,214 in addition to university fees.

WHAT IT'S LIKE   Notably relaxed college with male/female ratio of 1:1. Beautiful, expansive gardens rolling down to the river where the college has its own punt house. 80% of students live in for 3 years; rooms are varied in shape and size but good basic standard with plenty of kitchens (legacy from its days as a women's college) and ensuite bathrooms in many rooms. Liberal atmosphere with good state/private school balance, an anti-discrimination statute and amiable tutor-student relations. Its distance (10 minutes' walk) from the town centre isn't a problem to socialising and working there; instead LMH benefits from a good college spirit, spacious feel and excellent on-site facilities. Results are better than average and its absence from the tourist trail in the summer is a virtue never to be overestimated.

PAUPER NOTES   **Accommodation:** Very good, many rooms recently refurbished. **Drink:** Cheap – recently rebuilt bar on-site. **Eats:** Good college food, reasonably priced – vegetarian options. **Ents:** Many cheap JCR events in refurbished venue (JCR has own PA and drum kit). **Sports:** Good but relaxed. Squash and tennis courts and 5-a-side football pitch on-site. **Hardship funds:** Principal's fund and JCR living-out fund. **Travel:** Holiday fund in memory of a former undergraduate for students who have recently been unable to afford a good holiday. **Work:** Some work in college over vac – helping with conferences and in library. 7% work during term-time. 61% worked an average of 8 weeks in vacation.

MORE INFO?   Enquiries to JCR President, 01865 274300.

ALUMNI (EDITORS' PICK)   Benazir Bhutto, Lady Antonia Fraser, Diana Quick, Gertrude Bell, Dame Veronica Wedgwood, Dame Josephine Barnes, Elizabeth Longford, Eglantine Jebb, Baroness Warnock, Matthew Taylor MP, Andrew Q Hands, Barbara Mills, Caryl Churchill.

CAN'T FIND WHAT YOU'RE LOOKING FOR? USE THE INDEX!

LINCOLN

Lincoln College, Oxford OX1 3DR
(Tel 01865 279800)

Founded: 1427; women undergraduates first admitted 1980. **Admission:** Uniform Oxford colleges' system. No undergraduates admitted for biology, botany, geography, geology/earth sciences, human sciences, metallurgy and science of materials, music (except for the organ scholar), oriental studies, zoology, theology. **Scholarships:** Various, for undergraduates and graduates once in residence; graduate entrance scholarships. **Europe:** 10% first degree students take a language as part of course and spend 6 months or more abroad. **Travel grants:** Up to £200 for undergraduates, £318 research grant for graduates; £202 for clinical medicals. **Library:** Aims to provide all essential texts for undergraduate disciplines and most of texts for graduate taught courses. **Eating arrangements:** Meals in hall; also snacks in bar, teas in JCR/MCR. **Gate/guest hours:** Gate closes at 7–8 pm during term, college members have keys. **Other college facilities:** Playing field, squash court, multi-gym; computing facilities; music practice rooms; bar.

Accommodation: In 1995/96, college provides accommodation for all undergraduates who require it; almost all students in college. 276 half-board places at approx £59 per week, term time only. Private sector rents £45–£50 for half-board. No first degree students live at home. **Term time work:** No college policy to allow term time work, but *some* work available in the Development Office. **Hardship funds:** Grants and interest-free loans for graduates and undergraduates in financial difficulties. Commemoration Fund, Keith Murray Fund.

Undergraduates: 170 men, 97 women. **Postgraduates:** 90 men, 62 women. **Teaching staff:** *Men:* 34 fellows, 5 research fellows, 30 lecturers. *Women:* 5 fellows, 6 lecturers. **College fees 1996/97:** LEA grants cover college fees; undergraduates not on grants pay £3,002 in addition to university fees.

WHAT IT'S LIKE   Lincoln is a small, centrally located college with a friendly atmosphere. It accommodates all undergraduates for all of their college life and claims to serve the best food in the university (veggie too). It is one of the oldest colleges with a striking library in the converted All Saints Church (open 7 nights a week) but the low-beamed, homely atmosphere of the bar holds more interest with the students. Content within their own environment, a diverse bunch of individuals participate in a multitude of activities on university, college and personal levels. Sports teams are enthusiastic and often successful. The emphasis is put on participation, and many teams achieve impressive results for a college of this size. The facilities are comprehensive and well looked after, with the main fields only a ten minute's bike ride away. Closer to home is the boat club, squash court and well-equipped multi-gym, with darts and pool (free) in the college. The non-sporting clubs and societies are wide ranging, from mountaineering to debating, acting to running children's camps. And, of course, wining and dining remains a common priority. The JCR is apolitical as a whole; meetings are well attended and supplied with free drink, making for an amusing atmosphere. It tries to be practical and conscientious, without being fanatical. Academically, Lincoln is good to strong, even though work is not a sole occupation for the majority of undergraduates. The pressure applied by tutors is not excessive, except in needy cases. The hardship fund is excellent, and the college is dedicated to keeping students on if they perform well; the drop-out rate is minimal. No large quads and only one dreaming spire to boast of but the knowledge (and appreciation) that small is indeed beautiful.

PAUPER NOTES **Accommodation:** College provides accommodation for all; one of the cheapest, and rooms range from excellent (incl self-catering houses) to fairly reasonable. **Drink:** College bar subsidised, with good selection including weekly guest beers. **Eats:** College food is excellent and popular; snacks available in college bar. Usual range of snack bars, fast-food in city centre. **Ents:** Lively for a small college: bops, videos, cabarets, boat parties, etc. **Sports:** Excellent multi-gym; good pavilion and playing fields. Increasingly successful sporting college, and it's all free, including boat club. **Hardship funds:** Excellent provision. Generous help given. **Travel:** Good – travel grants easily available for holidays of some intellectual value. **Work:** Some work (well paid) available in college in term and vacation.

ALUMNI (EDITORS' PICK) Sir Peter Parker, John Le Carré, Edward Thomas, John Wesley, Baron von Richthofen (The Red Baron).

MAGDALEN

Magdalen College, Oxford OX1 4AU
(Tel 01865 276000)

Founded: 1458; women undergraduates first admitted 1979. **Admission:** Entry by interview (pre or post A-level). Flexible subject quotas. Undergraduates not admitted to geography, geology and metallurgy. **Scholarships** and prizes awarded each year. Organ and choral awards. **Europe:** 9% first degree students take a language as part of course, most of whom spend 6 months or more abroad. Links with Leiden and Leuven for biochemistry and chemistry. **Travel grants:** Funds for a number of purposes. **Library:** Particularly strong in history, classics, PPE, law (new law library) and sciences; Old Library with fine collection of Renaissance and 18th-century volumes. **Eating arrangements:** Cafeteria system, with formal dinner available twice a week. Optional 'pay-as-you-dine' in hall (approx £4 a day for 3 meals). **Gate/guest hours:** Gate keys issued. **Other college facilities:** JCR shop, wine cellar and bar; 11 tennis courts (8 grass, 3 hard), 3 new squash courts, 15 college punts, very successful rowing club, sports ground in beautiful riverside setting, with probably best cricket square in Oxford. Free membership of JCR computing scheme (4 PCs, 3 Apple Macs, laser, inkjet and dot matrix printers; range of software on hard disks; university computer network and e-mail links). Choral foundation with very strong musical tradition.

Accommodation: All undergraduates entitled to spend first three years in college accommodation (350 live in): £40–£57 per week, term time only. Community kitchens for self-catering or 'pay-as-you-dine' in Hall. Private accommodation more expensive. 1% of first degree students live at home. **Term time work:** No college policy to allow term time work (5% believed to work). Vac work only available in bar, tour scheme and library; college helps find vac work with references and contacts. **Hardship funds:** Limited funds available according to need (in 1995/96 all applicants' needs were met).

Undergraduates: 240 men, 136 women. **Postgraduates:** 150 men, 76 women. **Teaching staff:** *Men:* 40 fellows, 4 research fellows, 15 lecturers, 12 professors. *Women:* 3 fellows, 2 research fellows, 5 lecturers, 1 professor. **College fees for 1996/97:** LEA grants cover college fees; undergraduates not on grants pay £3,087 in addition to university fees.

WHAT IT'S LIKE   Strikingly beautiful (Great Tower and Cloisters) with extensive grounds (Addison's Walk, Deer Park, Fellows Garden) which give a sense of space rare in Oxford. Common room and bar act as focus for college – probably most thriving bar in town but not cheap. Most people enjoy their freedom and independence. No image/routine is imposed upon you – you can be who you want in Magdalen. Most accommodation good – some rooms palatial though most 1st years housed in infamous Waynflete Building. Modernisation programme continuing including plumbing and central heating. New building scheme with aim of accommodating all students in college and providing a theatre, recital rooms, etc. Sports facilities are brilliant. 45% of students are women and increasing state school intake; many foreign postgraduates. Academically quite hot with pressure increasing but never to neurosis level. Arts often regarded as better than sciences but new Magdalen science park, so things may change. Music and drama societies are very active and the college choir has a worldwide reputation. Services in chapel daily and well attended.

PAUPER NOTES   **Accommodation:** Everyone offered 3 years' accommodation; room ballot system means you can choose room according to pocket (none really cheap). Married quarters not easily available at Magdalen. **Drink:** £1.10 a pint in college bar. **Eats:** Cheap food in hall. More expensive but better in spectacular college bar. **Ents:** Very active college ents incl trips to Amsterdam and Alton Towers; videos, hypnotists, discos and bands frequently. Good college and univ theatre and brilliant cinema arrangements. **Sports:** Excellent facilities; new squash court. **Hardship funds:** Offered by both college and the university (college fund expanded as students' financial situations worsen). **Travel:** Travel grants given by college are quite generous. Cheap travel shop for students on the High St. **Work:** Paid work and free accommodation in college often available during the vacations.

MORE INFO?   Enquiries to JCR President (01865 276011).

ALUMNI (EDITORS' PICK)   Sir Peter Medawar, Sir John Betjeman, Lord Denning, A J P Taylor, Dudley Moore, Oscar Wilde, Lord Joseph, Joseph Addison, Edward Gibbon, Sir Charles Sherrington, Sir Robert Robinson, Dr Charles Daubeny, Sir Christopher McMahon, C S Lewis, R G Collinwood, Sir Peter Strawson, Kenneth Baker, Lord Gibson.

MANCHESTER COLLEGE

See Harris Manchester College

MANSFIELD

Mansfield College, Oxford OX1 3TF
(Tel 01865 270999)

Founded: 1886; women undergraduates first admitted 1955. **Admission:** Submitted work and interview (pre- or post-A level candidates). Undergraduates not accepted for modern languages, biological sciences, chemistry, medicine. **Largest fields of study:** English, engineering, geography, history, law, maths, PPE, theology. **Scholarships:** Scholarships and exhibitions awarded at any stage of an undergraduate's course in recognition of high academic standards. Also a number of college prizes. **Travel grants:** 2 travel scholarships. **Library:** Spacious library. Strong in theology; other subjects have smaller but up-to-date collections. **Eating arrangements:** All meals available in hall, Monday–Saturday and evening meal on Sundays. Cooking facilities in all college houses and on some staircases. **Gate/guest hours:** Unrestricted. **Other college facilities:** Own boat club; shares Merton sports grounds. Croquet, table tennis, bar. Refrigerators on all staircases.

Accommodation: In 1995/96, 66% of students in college accommodation, all first years. 133 places available: 95 full-board places at £80.71 per week; 36 ensuite self-catering rooms at £49.98 per week, term time only; and 20 self-catering at £55, Sept–June. Some students live in privately owned accommodation for 1 year, £40–£55 per week for self-catering. **Hardship funds:** £1,500 own funds, average award £150.

Undergraduates: 123 men, 68 women. **Postgraduates:** 41 men, 23 women. **Teaching staff:** *Men:* 13 fellows, 1 research fellow, 6 lecturers. *Women:* 2 fellows, 1 research fellow, 6 lecturers. **College fees for 1996/97:** LEA grants cover college fees; undergraduates not on grants pay £3,411 in addition to university fees.

WHAT IT'S LIKE   It's often said to offer all Oxford's advantages without many of the pitfalls. A small college on a quiet and spacious site, yet close to city centre, libraries and science area. Brand new computer room giving lots of computers. College is working towards improving the female/male and state/independent school ratios, by visiting students' local schools and building links in the East End of London. Those who have found the college too small or who have wanted to extend their non-academic activities have gone on to be prominent in university societies, music, drama and the SU. JCR and MCR enjoy good relations and work closely with the college authorities.
PAUPER NOTES   **Accommodation:** Subsidised college accommodation for at least two years. Living-out grants for third year. **Drink:** New college bar run by JCR/SCR – prices kept as low as possible. **Eats:** Food (with veg options) provided on site and in bar; kitchens and vastly improved cooking facilities allow self-catering. **Ents:** Frequent college events – video nights/cabaret/discos/bands/karaoke. Active involvement in drama, journalism, politics, sport, rag. **Sports:** Good/extensive sports facilities shared with Merton College. **Hardship Funds:** College fund becoming more accessible for students with financial problems. **Travel:** A few travel scholarships awarded each year by college. **Work:** In bar on rota basis.
ALUMNI (EDITORS' PICK)   Rev Prof G B Caird (Dean Ireland's professor of the exegesis of holy scripture, Oxford University), Paul Crossley (pianist), C H Dodd (theologian, chairman of New English Bible translators), Michael White (music critic), Chris Cragg (*Financial Times*), M von Trott (would-be assassin of Hitler).

MERTON

Merton College, Oxford OX1 4JD
(Tel 01865 276310)

Founded: 1264; women undergraduates first admitted 1980. **Admission:** By interview and conditional offer. **Largest fields of study:** Chemistry, literae humaniores, mathematics, modern history, physics, PPE and law. **Scholarships:** Postmasterships and exhibitions awarded at end of first (and later) years for distinguished work. **Europe:** 20 students learn a language and spend time abroad. **Travel grants:** Various travel grants to 'subsidise well-thought-out plans for vacation travel'. **Library:** Fine Old Library (over 80,000 volumes; medieval manuscripts and chained early printed books). **Eating arrangements:** All meals available in hall. **Gate/guest hours:** Gate closed at midnight during term. Guests must leave college by midnight. **Other college facilities:** Music room and organ; nearby playing fields, sports pavilion, boathouse.

Accommodation: 100% of students offered college accommodation. 345 places available at £73 per week full board, term time (or longer if required). No first degree students live at home. **Term time work:** No regulations governing part time work but students expected to discuss it with tutor. Some vacation work in the library. **Hardship funds:** £20,000 own funds, average award £200. Special help: travel, study, book grants, hardship.

Undergraduates: 157 men, 100 women. **Postgraduates:** 103 men, 53 women. **Teaching staff:** *Men:* 36 fellows, 10 research fellows, 19 lecturers. *Women:* 6 fellows, 2 research fellows, 5 lecturers. **College fees for 1996/97:** LEA grants cover college fees; undergraduates not on grants pay £2,969 in addition to university fees.

WHAT IT'S LIKE   One of the oldest, most beautiful colleges in Oxford, Merton provides a quality atmosphere in which to live and study. Socially, Merton is relaxed, friendly and increasingly heterogenous. Traditionally poor ratios for educational background have greatly improved and there are now as many successful female applicants as male. JCR active in providing a varied, broad-based social calendar including bops, live bands, pantos and bar quizzes among other things. Also flourishing music and drama societies, well-supported choir and an annual, cheap Christmas Ball (unique in Oxford). Much participation in many sports, both at college level and, for a few stars, university level. Recent successes achieved in rowing, basketball, korfball, American football and badminton. Excellent library facilities, outstanding tutors and motivated students achieve considerable academic success and a relatively high proportion of undergraduates go on to read for a second degree. Merton's small size and easy-going student body mean it quickly becomes your home, providing a base from which to venture into whichever aspects of Oxford life you desire.
PAUPER NOTES   **Accommodation:** Good-quality, cheap accommodation for all under-graduates (important as private market expensive) – all within 10 minutes' walk of college. **Drink:** Bar is college social centre, relatively cheap drinks. **Eats:** Excellent food, heavily subsidised; includes vegetarian. **Ents:** Increasing and varied; well attended and usually free. **Sports:** Well endowed, including college sports pavilion and weights room. Widespread participation in range of sports. **Hardship funds:** College will help in extreme circumstances. **Travel:** Grants available. **Work:** Hardly any students have jobs during term time.
MORE INFO?   Enquiries to Kate Downey, JCR President, 01865 276310.

HOW TO START? *SEE SHORTLISTING,* PAGE 535

NEW COLLEGE

New College, Oxford OX1 3BN
(Tel 01865 279555)

Founded: 1379; women undergraduates first admitted 1979. **Admission:** Undergraduates admitted for all subjects except archaeology, anthropology, geology, geography, earth sciences, history/English. **Europe:** 12% first degree students take European language as part of course and spend 6 months or more abroad. No formal exchange links. **Study grants:** About 30 a year. **Library:** Over 70,000 volumes. **Eating arrangements:** All meals provided in hall. **Gate/guest hours:** Late keys available – new smart-card gate and library access system. **Other college facilities:** 8-acre sports ground 1km from college; college punts and boathouse.

Accommodation: In 1995/96, 85% of students in college accommodation, all first years. 350 places available £58.17 per week half-board, term time only; 48 new self-catering rooms. Some students live in privately owned accommodation for 1 year: approx £55 per week, self-catering. **Hardship funds:** 50 students helped by government access funds, via university; £5,000 own funds, 35 helped. Special help: those not living in college accommodation; those on maximum LEA grants.

Undergraduates: 236 men, 173 women. **Postgraduates:** 114 men, 72 women. **Teaching staff:** *Men:* 33 fellows, 6 research fellows, 14 lecturers. *Women:* 5 fellows, 3 research fellows, 5 lecturers. **College fees for 1996/97:** LEA grants cover college fees; undergraduates not on grants pay £3,075 in addition to university fees.

WHAT IT'S LIKE One of the oldest, largest and most beautiful colleges, its size helps create its friendly and tolerant atmosphere. New College is centrally located, with extensive grounds and excellent facilities. There's a diverse range of personalities from a variety of educational and social backgrounds. The active Target Schools scheme has increased the numbers from state schools and the college has one of the best male:female ratios in Oxford. Recent developments have made the college accessible to the disabled. The bar is arguably the best in Oxford, the ents renowned and the Commemoration Ball legendary! Wide student involvement in extra-curricular activities adds to the lively atmosphere. College drama is strong and the thriving Music Society stages an annual festival. The chapel choir is world-famous and there is an enthusiastic student orchestra. Sports facilities are good (plush new pavilion); rowers and rugby teams (both male and female) enjoying particular success. For the academically minded, New College offers superb teaching facilities and has a respectable though not intimidating academic record. Tutors rely more on individual interest than official sanctions so it's up to you how hard you work. Reading weeks are held in the college's Alpine chalet. Outstanding student welfare provision and the JCR has recently pushed for more hardship funds and better representation for minorities. Despite apathetic tendencies, the college is broadly left wing and students espouse a healthy mix of ideals and beliefs. In this united and supportive community atmosphere, it's easy to carve out your own niche, which is probably why most New College students swear they wouldn't want to be anywhere else. *Helen Evans*

PAUPER NOTES **Accommodation:** 1st and 2nd years guaranteed comfortable rooms in college (some palatial); rents average for Oxford. Most 3rd years live out (living out grant available). Limited married accommodation. **Drink:** Good, cheap college bar is popular; wide and changing variety of beers, darts and table football. **Eats:** 2 sittings of hall each night

(1 formal, 1 informal); food edible if repetitive, vegetarian good. Plenty of restaurants in Oxford. **Ents:** High profile college ents, including frequent bops, band nights and huge summer garden party. Sky TV and video in JCR. **Sports:** Excellent college sports ground very close; good boathouse and punts scheme. Swimming pool in town. **Hardship funds:** Provided by bursar or university wide fund; JCR can also give ad hoc loans. College committee for student hardship; JCR living out fund for finalists. **Travel:** Numerous travel grants for course-related vacation travel. **Work:** Officially not allowed in term; some bar and library work available in college. Most students work during long vac.

MORE INFO?   Enquiries to Helen Evans, JCR President, 01865 279578.

ALUMNI (EDITORS' PICK)   Nigel Rees, Tony Benn MP, Lord Longford, Len Murray, John Fowles, Hugh Gaitskell, Naomi Woolf, Kate Beckinsale, Hugh Grant.

ORIEL

Oriel College, Oxford OX1 4EW
(Tel 01865 276555)

Founded: 1326; women undergraduates first admitted 1985. **Admission:** Conditional/unconditional offer on the basis of extended interview. Full range of subjects available except human sciences, computation and fine arts. **Largest fields of study:** Modern history, PPE, modern languages, natural sciences. **Scholarships:** Scholarships or exhibitionerships available on the basis of work within the college. **Europe:** 13% students learn a language as part of their course, 2% spend 6 months or more abroad. Informal links with several European universities/colleges; link with Bonn for students of German. **Travel grants:** Small grants available. **Library:** 70,000 books; liberal hours. **Eating arrangements:** All meals available in college. **Gate/guest hours:** Free access 24 hours a day for college members. Liberal guest rules. **Other college facilities:** Facilities for all major sports; drama; music.

Accommodation: All undergraduates accommodated in college for two years, most for three; average charged £1,174 pa (range £1,040–£1,308); average £10.03 per day for room, six luncheons and seven dinners a week. No first degree students live at home. **Term time work:** College policy not to allow term time work. Vac work available in college eg painting of buildings, cleaning, library, furniture removal. **Hardship funds:** £10,000 own funds, 60 students helped.

Undergraduates: 186 men, 101 women. **Postgraduates:** 88 men, 53 women. **Teaching staff:** *Men:* 32 fellows, 24 lecturers. *Women:* 5 fellows, 2 research fellows, 7 lecturers. **College fees for 1996/97:** LEA grants cover college fees; undergraduates not on grants pay £3,215 in addition to university fees.

WHAT IT'S LIKE   Among the prettiest and oldest of Oxford colleges, located in the town centre, Oriel is renowned for its friendly, intimate atmosphere. The college can provide accommodation for all three years, with a choice of single or double rooms, flats for 3 or house for 4; good kitchen facilities and security. College hall for breakfast, lunch and dinner is reasonable standard and price; excellent termly guest and annual subject dinners. Very good library (open 24 hours), though the beer cellar is more a focal point for student activity.

Not only the venue for the termly bop but also contains a pool table, dartboard and video games machines. JCR shop sells cheap stationery, food etc. 2 launderettes and a tea bar every weekday (paid for on battels). TV room, JCR video which can be hired out, and Sky in beer cellar and JCR, with sports and movie channels. Good sporting reputation, especially for rowing. Has been Head of the River in Torpids and Eights more times than any other college in the past 20 years. Many college societies for all interests, with funding available from JCR, including philosophy, arts, literature and drinking societies. Drama society produces a play every summer which is presented in the college's First Quad. The JCR works to maintain and improve student rights and facilities. Oriel provides an atmosphere where students can work and play, pursue their interests and generally enrich their lives. Student make-up is cosmopolitan, and the atmosphere relaxed. Excellent support from fellow students and tutors, all of whom are always willing to listen and help with problems of any nature. Good prospects for career and graduate/research work. Oriel has arguably the strongest college identity in Oxford, and makes a happy home for students, not only for the duration of their course, but for life.

PAUPER NOTES   **Accommodation:** College accommodation reasonably priced; students accommodated for all three years. **Drink:** College bar cheaper than pubs in town. **Eats:** Provision for veggies and great choice of places in town. **Ents:** Good college ents eg bops, summer ceilidhs, video evenings. Cinemas, plays, concerts and live bands in bars, comedy shows aplenty. **Sports:** College sports ground with squash and tennis courts; weights room in college; boathouse by river. **Hardship funds:** University funding available; also grants from college and college trusts available to those in difficulty. **Travel:** Travel grants from college for academic purposes; student discount holidays and fares. **Work:** Bar shifts available; students employed by college during vacations in library, helping with summer conferences etc (£3.60/hr) and can stay in college at cheap rate.

MORE INFO?   Contact Scott Allen

ALUMNI (EDITORS' PICK)   Sir Walter Raleigh, Cecil Rhodes, Beau Brummel, A J P Taylor, Norman Willis, Cardinal Newman, Matthew Arnold, Alderman Sir Christopher Walford (ex Lord Mayor of London).

PEMBROKE

Pembroke College, Oxford OX1 1DW
(Tel 01865 276444)

Founded: 1624; women undergraduates first admitted 1979. **Admission:** On basis of interview, school reports and sometimes aptitude tests (for pre A-level candidates, acceptance is conditional on A-level grades). **Scholarships:** Awarded at the end of the first year, based on performance in public examination. **Europe:** 10% first degree students take a language as part of course and spend 6 months or more abroad. A few formal exchange links. **Travel grants:** Limited funds available for small number of grants. **Library:** Working collection of about 30,000 books covering all subjects taught; closes at 2 am. **Eating arrangements:** Breakfast and (pay-as-you-eat) lunch, plus dinner each evening (formal 6 nights a week) in hall. JCR pantry for hot/cold snacks, drinks etc. **Gate/guest hours:** No set hours. **Other college facilities:** Sports ground (1 mile from college), boathouse, bar, photographic darkroom, computer rooms.

Accommodation: In 1995/96, 72% of all undergraduates in college accommodation, all first years (and finalists who wish it). 263 places available: £6.34–£7.34 (plus electricity) per day, dependent on size of room, term time only. Self-catering facilities are available. No first degree students live at home. **Term time work:** College does not normally allow term time work (2% believed to work).

Undergraduates: 203 men, 149 women. **Postgraduates:** 94 men, 45 women. **Teaching staff:** *Men:* 34 fellows, 3 research fellows, 18 lecturers. *Women:* 4 fellows, 1 research fellow, 11 lecturers. **College fees for 1996/97:** LEA grants cover college fees; undergraduates not on grants pay £3,090 in addition to university fees.

WHAT IT'S LIKE The most important characteristic of Pembroke is its friendly, informal and tolerant atmosphere, largely due to its student body coming from a variety of backgrounds and countries. Student life within the college is dominated by a strong JCR which is one of the most represented bodies in Oxford. Whilst the JCR has managed to get rid of the once notorious Pembroke apathy, its meetings have remained extremely funny and are certainly unique in the university. College life also benefits from the various societies ranging from the intellectually challenging Johnson Society to the intellectually challenged drinking societies. Music and drama are well represented with some of the university's top thespians coming from Pembroke and members actively involved with both the National Youth Theatre and Orchestra. Whilst finding itself comfortably placed in the middle of the academic table, Pembroke is also known for its sporting success. The men's first eight was Head of the River in 1995 and the women rowers are among the strongest in Oxford. However, students who take sport less seriously are also catered for. Amenities are improving on the main college site and the excellent, recently built Sir Geoffrey Arthur Building overlooks the Isis. In the summer the lawns and stunning Chapel Quad come into their own with Pembroke's diligent gardener ensuring it is a strong contender for the Oxford in Bloom competition, which it frequently wins. Relations with the SCR have improved. Pembroke remains one of the most expensive colleges in Oxford. Overall there is little that compares with the unique Pembroke experience!

PAUPER NOTES **Accommodation:** All first years required to live in college; varying quality of rooms but extensive refurbishment programme. Most second years live in nearby rented accommodation. All finalists may live in the excellent Sir Geoffrey Arthur Building (GAB). **Drinks:** College bar very small; serves a range of alcoholic and non-alcoholic drinks. College is surrounded by variety of pubs. **Eats:** All meals can be taken in hall – some dinners formal, some informal. Microwave and fridge on most staircases in main college; kitchen on each staircase in GAB. **Ents:** Good Ents committee. Summer Ball (every 2 years) rivals anything in Oxford. **Sports:** Own sports field, boat-house etc. Rowing, rugby, darts and pool extremely strong (free pool table). **Hardship funds:** Large college fund; vacation grants available. Also university access funds. **Travel:** Central location so most of Oxford within walking distance. Bike recommended, but not essential; bike storage available. **Work:** Discouraged in term time; otherwise only with express approval of tutors.
MORE INFO? JCR President (01865 276427).

QUEEN'S

The Queen's College, Oxford OX1 4AW
(Tel 01865 279120)

Founded: 1341; women undergraduates first admitted 1979. **Admission:** By the procedures common to all Oxford colleges. Undergraduates not admitted for English, geography, metallurgy, fine arts. **Scholarships:** Various scholarships and exhibitions offered, to students on any course, for distinguished work; college bursaries for excellence in non-academic activities (sports, etc); choral, organ or instrumental awards offered for distinguished performance (not restricted to students reading music). **Europe:** 16% first degree students take a language as part of course and spend 6 months or more abroad. No formal exchange links. **Travel grants:** Some available. **Library:** Over 140,000 volumes, including good coverage of all undergraduate subjects. **Eating arrangements:** Breakfast available in hall, Florey Building and Iffley Road building; lunch and dinner in hall. Meals charged at cost. **Gate/guest hours:** Undergraduates can have their own keys. **Other college facilities:** Chapel with superb modern pipe organ and concert piano; convenient sports field; boathouse with several good eights; tennis courts; squash courts; beer cellar.

Accommodation: 100% of students in college accommodation. Rooms at £382.14 per term plus food at cost. No first degree students live at home. **Term time work:** College policy not to allow term time work.

Undergraduates: 186 men, 114 women. **Postgraduates:** 69 men, 40 women. **Teaching staff:** *Men:* 24 fellows, 6 research fellows, 19 lecturers. *Women:* 3 fellows, 3 research fellows, 8 lecturers. **College fees 1996/97**: LEA grants cover college fees; undergraduates not on grants pay £3,020 in addition to university fees.

WHAT IT'S LIKE   Probably one of the most flourishing of Oxford colleges, Queen's stands imposingly on the High Street; its cupola and quad designed by Hawksmoor who supervised the building at Blenheim Palace. Accommodation is now available to all students for three years, either in college itself or the two annexes (one of which has been recently renovated) which house the first years. Academically it still tends to do extremely well especially in modern languages, maths and law. It has regular success in sporting competitions and college societies include a popular drama society and an acclaimed choir. There is also a dark-room for students' use. Facilities are good although no self-catering for those living in. College food is more than adequate for most, being cheap, available every day and quite edible! The beer cellar is among the best in Oxford, and popular entertainments are organised ranging from discos and bands to day-trips to France. The JCR is active if mainly apolitical. Although still a northern college, it is no longer insular and it can be considered cosmopolitan and highly active.

PAUPER NOTES   **Accommodation:** College rents comparatively inexpensive. **Drink:** Beer cellar, wide variety at excellent prices and the main college focal point. Few feel the need to drink elsewhere but if you fancy a change there are several good pubs close by. **Eats:** Good selection of food at subsidised price. Breakfast and lunch are self-service, dinner set menu. **Ents:** Renowned in Oxford for the quality and variety of its JCR organised ents. Close to town centre with all the usual cinemas and theatres. **Sports:** Excellent football, rugby and cricket pitches conveniently situated by the river across from the college boathouse. Tennis and squash courts. **Travel:** Generous funding for those with course-related excuses. **Work:** Hardly anyone works in term time; most need to work in the long vac.

ALUMNI (EDITORS' PICK)   Henry V, Rowan Atkinson (comedian), Leopold Stokowski (conductor), Brian Walden (TV presenter), Gerald Kaufman (politician), Edmond Halley (astronomer).

REGENT'S PARK

Regent's Park College, Pusey Street, Oxford OX1 2LB
(Tel 01865 288120)

Founded: 1810; women undergraduates first admitted 1922 (ministerial) and 1978 (non-ministerial). **Admission:** By the procedures common to all Oxford colleges. Undergraduates not admitted for sciences. **Largest fields of study:** Theology, and arts subjects generally. **Scholarships:** Some available. **Europe:** 5% first degree students take a language as part of course and spend 6 months or more abroad. Special links with Bonn. **Travel grants:** Available. **Library:** 33,000 approx, 40 current periodicals, 25 study places and Angus Library of historic Baptist materials. **Eating arrangements:** Meals in hall. **Gate/guest hours:** All students given keys. **Other college facilities:** Kitchens on each level. Games room. TV room, JCR etc.

Accommodation: In 1995/96, 98% of students in college accommodation, at £1,512 pa. No first degree students live at home. **Term time work:** College policy not to allow term time work. **Hardship funds:** Some available.

Undergraduates: 37 men, 32 women. **Postgraduates:** 7 men, 2 women. **Teaching staff:** *Men:* 6 fellows, 1 research fellow, 9 lecturers. *Women:* 3 lecturers, 1 research fellow. **College fees for 1996/97:** LEA grants cover college fees; undergraduates not on grants pay £3,224 in addition to university fees.

WHAT IT'S LIKE   Close to the city centre, with a small but attractive quadrangle framed on three sides by 20th century neo-classical buildings and, on the fourth, by houses from the 18th century and earlier – including the oldest inhabited house in Oxford. Undergraduates able to live in college throughout their whole course, mainly in study bedrooms but an increasing number of student flats on main site. A small but very friendly and active college, students are involved in many clubs and societies inside and outside college. One or two social events (at least) weekly ranging from barn dances to discos to Sunday afternoon tea; a college play is performed each year and sports clubs (particularly rowing and football) are enthusiastically supported and very successful. Students have very large input in the running of college and their views are listened to and well respected by college authorities. Four or five students a year in training for the Baptist ministry, with a further 10 or 12 part-time students. With traditions based in theology and Baptist Ministry, college provides strong support for Christian community within college and encourages opportunities to question and grow in faith. However these views are not at all imposed. Good food provided throughout the week, with a formal hall on Friday evenings. Self-catering at weekends; well-equipped kitchens provided for student use. E-mail facilities.
PAUPER NOTES   **Accommodation:** Most live in at reasonable rates. College married quarters. **Drink:** Cheap bar, friendly atmosphere. **Eats:** Food good with vegetarian meals

available at both lunch and dinner. **Ents:** Regular and varied ents, 2 discos a term, annual ball. **Sports:** Sports well catered for: good football team and rowing crews. **Hardship funds:** Two – one for rent, one for general hardship. **Travel:** Travel grants available from college. **Work:** Disallowed during term. Most students get vac work but mostly in home area.

MORE INFO?   Ring Gavin Foster 01865 288150

ST ANNE'S

St Anne's College, Oxford OX2 6HS
(Tel 01865 274800)

Founded: 1878; men undergraduates first admitted 1979. **Admission:** College has tutorial fellows in all the main subjects. **Largest fields of study:** English, history, law, mathematics, modern languages, PPE. **Scholarships:** Scholarships and exhibitions awarded for good academic work and success in examinations. **Europe:** Most students learning a language spend a year abroad. **Travel grants:** Funds available to undergraduates during their course. **Library:** Large library, with many special collections. **Eating arrangements:** All meals available in hall but not compulsory; limited self-catering facilities in college houses. **Gate/guest hours:** No gate hours. Guests may stay overnight if signed in. **Other college facilities:** Extensive computer systems. Sports facilities shared with St John's, squash courts with St Antony's; boathouse on river.

Accommodation: In 1995/96, 82% of all undergraduates in college accommodation, 100% of first years. 368 rooms available at £66 per week (including £10.50 per week towards meals). Some second year students live in privately owned accommodation for 1 year: rents £50–£55 per week for self-catering. College has equalisation scheme; all students pay termly levy which is used to subsidise those living out. **Term time work:** Discouraged but available in college in bar and library. **Hardship funds:** Funds available for individual cases of hardship.

Undergraduates: 299 men, 189 women. **Postgraduates:** 74 men, 49 women. **Teaching staff:** *Men:* 25 fellows, 6 research fellows, 14 lecturers, 1 lector. *Women:* 13 fellows, 6 research fellows, 3 lecturers. **College fees for 1996/97:** LEA grants cover college fees; undergraduates not on grants pay £3,199 in addition to university fees.

WHAT IT'S LIKE   There is no typical 'Stans' student; a huge variety of backgrounds, hailing from towns all over the country and all over the world. The comparably large size of this college (approx 470) and its position just outside the busy town centre makes for a friendly and easy-going atmosphere, as does the well-stocked college bar and the student-run buttery. Stans students also are involved in numerous university-wide activities as well as running societies – drama, debating, musical, religious, film, photographic, etc – within the college. All college rooms are singles, 80% of students have college accommodation, which is mixed, and there are no gate or guest restrictions. Student/staff relations are very good and Stans library is one of the best in Oxford, open 0830–0200 hours during the week. Welfare arrangements are extremely efficient, freshers are encourage to come up early, when special social events are organised and a system of student sponsors helps freshers to settle in. College ents are generally good; frequent bops are well attended; bands play in the bar, films and videos are shown etc. Moreover Stans is close to numerous pubs, cafes, bars and restaurants. Sports facilities are shared with nearby St John's college and Stans has raised money to build a college boathouse.   *Sarah Mitchell*

PAUPER NOTES   **Accommodation:** 80% live in, only 2nd years live out. Expensive private accommodation subsidised by college equalisation scheme. **Drink:** College bar SCR run with students behind the bar and cheap. **Eats:** Vegetarian meals every night in college. Very cheap JCR buttery. **Ents:** One college social event/week on average. Subsidised, generally well organised and well attended; videos shown frequently, also films, cheap guest dinners, and bands in the bar. **Sports:** New multi-gym. Very popular college team sports. **Hardship funds:** Extant but not well publicised. **Travel:** Large availability of funds for travel abroad. **Work:** Students discouraged from term work except in college library, bar and buttery. Local pubs employ undergraduates. Good summer work in Oxford.
MORE INFO?   Enquiries to JCR Secretary 01865 274800.
ALUMNI (EDITORS' PICK)   Maria Aitken, Frances Cairncross, Baroness Young, Iris Murdoch, Libby Purves, Tina Brown, Elizabeth Turner, Joanna Richardson, Naomi Mitchison, Dame Cicely Saunders, Edwina Currie.

ST CATHERINE'S

St Catherine's College, Oxford OX1 3UJ
(Tel 01865 271700)

Founded: 1962; women undergraduates first admitted 1973. **Admission:** Undergraduates not admitted for classics, theology. **Scholarships:** Awarded for academic excellence at end of first year. **Europe:** Modern language students only (about 12 per year) spend a period abroad as part of their course. No formal exchange links. **Travel grants:** Limited number for use in long vacation. **Eating arrangements:** Hall, buttery, individual staircase facilities. **Gate/guest hours:** Unrestricted. **Other college facilities:** JCR has debating pit, bar, buttery, TV room and private dining room; Bernard Sunley Building with lecture and film theatre, outdoor and indoor theatres, music room (with harpsichord and grand piano), squash courts and 6 tennis courts, several college punts, shared playing fields nearby.

Accommodation: In 1995/96, 75% of all students in college accommodation, 100% first years. 356 self-catering rooms in college (135 for first years) at £51.10 per week, and 56 self-catering in college houses at £41.86, rentable all year. Students live in privately owned accommodation for 1 year. No first degree students live at home. **Term time work:** College policy to allow term time work with tutor's permission; limit of 6 hours per week. Term (and vac) work available in college in bar, library, offices, security, waiting. **Hardship funds:** Some funds and awards available.

Undergraduates: 290 men, 146 women. **Postgraduates:** 100 men, 51 women. **Teaching staff:** *Men:* 31 fellows, 13 research fellows, 38 lecturers. *Women:* 2 fellows, 1 research fellow, 10 lecturers. **College fees 1996/97:** LEA grants cover college fees; undergraduates not on grants pay £3,110 in addition to university fees.

WHAT IT'S LIKE   Whilst it is one of the newest undergraduate colleges in the university, Catz was founded as a way of enabling poor students to study at Oxford in the 19th century. Representing the very best of 1960s architecture, it is a set of long, low buildings, with lots of glass, and some very beautiful gardens. Catz moved to these buildings and its current site, about 5 minutes from the town centre, when it became a college in 1962. A new residential building in a similar style to the rest of the college has recently been completed. Since it is a newer college, a lot of the attitudes within Catz are more liberal than other colleges – for example, the latest opening bar! As the largest college, there is great diversity amongst Catz students with a high proportion of overseas and visiting students and a great sense of community. Students are guaranteed at least two years in college accommodation, and many can live in for three. The accommodation is good – rooms have masses of storage space, there are self-catering facilities, and bathrooms are excellent, some rooms being ensuite. The social life is very good – a very large and well-equipped JCR-bar complex, which is the centre of the social scene. There are ents every other week, and usually a major event (eg Catz Night, or the college barbeque – basically an excuse for lots of cheap alcohol) every term, at which the whole college lets its hair down. Dropout rates are low, and changing course, provided you are academically good, is fairly easy. Catz is prominent in virtually every university society, from sport to drama and music, and there are many active college societies. In-college facilities include a music house with a Steinway grand, squash and tennis courts, gym, sports field, dark room, punts, computer room, and a largish theatre.

PAUPER NOTES   **Accommodation:** College cheapest (£550 a term). Living out nearly London prices. **Drink:** Catz bar – excellent £1.25 a pint, cheap spirits. **Eats:** Hall – quite good food, 3 course evening meal £2.60 or less with tickets, lunch £1.40, breakfast £1.00. Vegetarian food good. Pete's Café – informal, cheaper alternative. Self-catering facilities on all staircases. **Ents:** Catz has good ents with discos, bands, etc – entry is free but restricted to JCR members and guests. Oxford theatrical productions are cheap and frequent. **Sports:** College squash, tennis and netball courts, weights room, punts, shared boathouse, sports field (1 mile away). **Hardship funds:** College discretionary awards in extreme cases – theoretically unlimited. **Travel:** Generous travel awards are made by college and JCR. **Work:** In hall, bar and library during term. Conference work and gardening in college during vacs (£170 per week plus board & lodging).

INFORMAL NAME   Catz.

ALUMNI (EDITORS' PICK)   A A Milne, John Birt, Simon Winchester, Peter Mandelson, Jeanette Winterson, Matthew Pinsent.

ST EDMUND HALL

St Edmund Hall, Oxford OX1 4AR
(Tel 01865 279000)

Founded: 1317; women undergraduates first admitted 1978. **Admission:** Pre A-level candidates may apply for conditional offer; post A-level candidates apply on basis of school record, A-level grades and interview. Undergraduates are not admitted for theology, classics, biology, zoology, human sciences, oriental studies. **Academic features:** Particular strengths in Eastern European studies (including tutors in Russian and Czech language) and material and earth sciences. College welcomes applicants for joint schools. **Special features:** The Ruskin Master of Drawing is a fellow of the college. **Scholarships and bursaries:** Awards after first year of study. Musical bursaries. Support for academic projects. Small grants for travel and for developing language abroad. **Europe:** 12% first degree students take a language as part of course and spend 6 months or more abroad (including those taking English law with French/German law). No formal exchange links. **Library:** In restored Early English church, some 50,000 volumes, microfilm/fiche reader, microscope; word processing facilities are available. **Eating arrangements:** Cafeteria style service, formal dinner every Sunday night; formal guest dinner three nights per term. **Gate/guest hours:** No restrictions. **Other college facilities:** Boathouse, tennis courts and hockey pitches, football in university park.

Accommodation: In 1995/96, 65% of all students in college accommodation, 100% of first years. First year undergraduates pay £80.50 per week for accommodation, breakfast, dinner and heating; meal arrangements vary for later years. Students live in privately owned accommodation for 1 year. No first degree students live at home. **Term time work:** College policy not to allow term time work. Some vacation work offered in college. **Hardship funds:** £10,000 own funds, 71 students helped in 1995/96.

Undergraduates: 274 men, 142 women. **Postgraduates:** 63 men, 36 women. **Teaching staff:** *Men:* 28 fellows, 12 research fellows, 17 lecturers. *Women:* 3 fellows, 10 lecturers, 1 lecteur, 1 lektorin. **College fees 1996/97:** LEA grants cover college fees; undergraduates not on grants pay £3,174 in addition to university fees.

WHAT IT'S LIKE   Teddy Hall, as it is affectionately known, is one of Oxford's friendliest colleges. There is a strong and loyal hall spirit, but this is not claustrophobic, and the small size of the college gives it an intimate and friendly atmosphere. Aularians are active both at college and university levels: sports teams are notoriously strong, and there are also excellent music, drama and journalism traditions. JCR meetings generally well-attended and remarkably free of party-political biases. Teddy Hall ents are renowned in the university and frequently draw students from other colleges. Located in the centre of Oxford, near shops, libraries and sports pitches, the college is a blend of old and new – the front quad is picturesque and medieval, and the library is in an eleventh century Norman church. The more modern back quad is visually less impressive but better equipped (washing facilities, kitchens etc). Whatever your interests and beliefs, you are almost certain to find your niche here.

PAUPER NOTES   **Accommodation:** 1st and 3rd years guaranteed accommodation in college and 2 annexes. Limited 2nd year rooms allocated by ballot – most live out. Flats for married students. **Drink:** Cheap, lively and friendly college bar. **Eats:** Food variable. Vegetarian option at all sittings. Compulsory number of breakfasts and dinners must be eaten if living in. Guest nights are excellent with fierce competition for limited tickets. **Ents:** Wolfson Hall in college, the largest student venue in Oxford, is used to its full potential; frequent discos and bands, cocktail evenings, weekly videos. **Sports:** All good especially athletics, rugby, football, netball and rowing. Excellent facilities. **Hardship funds:** Available upon consideration of individual circumstances. **Travel:** Limited grants available. **Work:** Many students get agency work in vacs (lots about); bar work in term time.

MORE INFO?   Enquiries to JCR President (01865 279048).

INFORMAL NAME   Teddy Hall.

ALUMNI (EDITORS' PICK)   Sir Robin Day, Terry Jones (Monty Python), Hugo MacNeill, Stuart Barnes, Sir Michael Rose.

WANT TO HELP WITH THE NEXT EDITION? SEE PAGE 66

ST HILDA'S

St Hilda's College, Oxford OX4 1DY
(Tel 01865 276884)

Founded: 1893 as a women's college. **Admission:** Women only; by conditional offer on the basis of interview and submission of school written work. **Largest fields of study:** English, modern languages, PPE, law, history, mathematics, biological sciences. **Europe:** 13% first degree students take a language as part of course and spend 6 months or more abroad. **Travel grants:** About £6,000 annually, including grants for undergraduates' travel abroad, for classics students and for historians' travel grants. **Library:** Good range of books for most honour schools. **Eating arrangements:** Maintenance fee includes meal tickets for a certain number of meals in hall; additional tickets can be bought as required (breakfast £1; main meal £2). **Gate/guest hours:** During week, open to all 9 am to 11 pm and to accompanied visitors until 2 am; overnight visitors must be signed in. **Other college facilities:** Music building, pianos and harpsichord, small chapel, tennis court, croquet lawn, netball court, punts, computers and printers (with access to university computing facilities), JCR bar, buttery, washing machines and spin driers, cooking facilities.

Accommodation: In 1995/96, 72% of all students in college accommodation, 100% of first years. 254 full-board places at £53.94 per week term time only. Students normally live in privately owned accommodation for 1 year. Virtually no first degree students live at home. **Term time work:** College policy to allow some paid term time work after consultation with tutors. Term (and vac) work in college library; in JCR bar in vacs. **Hardship funds:** £18,000 own support funds, average award £100.

Undergraduates: 391 women. **Postgraduates:** 61 women. **Teaching staff:** *Men:* 16 college lecturers. *Women:* 26 fellows, 7 research fellows, 12 lecturers. **College fees 1996/97:** LEA grants cover college fees; undergraduates not on grants pay £3,167 in addition to university fees.

WHAT IT'S LIKE   St Hilda's continues to cultivate a reputation for being relaxed, friendly and welcoming and full of active students who make a great contribution to university life. The last all-female Oxford college, the undergraduates are proud of their status and appreciate the supportive, community atmosphere. The college is open plan, lying over six acres of gardens alongside the River Cherwell; river, lawns and own punts conspire to make summer term extremely pleasant. As at all Oxford colleges, work is pressurised, but help and encouragement are always on hand from tutors and friends. The emphasis seems to be on co-operation rather than competition and your academic life can be as stimulating as you want it to be. Other students do their level best to relieve candidate and fresher stress (bear in mind when you come for interview). Accommodation is in single furnished rooms; a college room is guaranteed for first and final years and the rent includes 60 meal tickets per term. The food is excellent; good quality and value for money with snack and vegetarian options and a formal dinner once a week. A kitchen is always nearby if you prefer to cook for yourself and snacks-between-meals can be bought in the bar or buttery. Other amenities include a computer room, snooker table, snack machines, laundries, common rooms, TVs and video and tennis courts; also the Jacqueline Du Pré music building (probably the best student music facility in the university). The boat club is thriving with pro and fun crews and lots of parties. But if rowing isn't your scene – what about standing for a committee post, auditioning for Drama Cuppers or organising the Arts Festival? Hilda's women also have a high profile in university clubs and societies. The city centre is ten minutes away, but the college situation makes it a peaceful retreat from smog and noise. Head away from town and you are immediately in an area full of interesting shops and a variety of restaurants/fast food outlets, off-licence, a liberal smattering of pubs, supermarket and venue for bands/club nights. Come and go as you please; late or overnight guests welcome provided you sign them in, and yes, men are allowed! Plans include improvements to the already excellent library and accommodation. So there you have it; we rest our case!

PAUPER NOTES   **Accommodation:** Not the cheapest, but reasonable. **Drink:** College bar one of Oxford's cheapest; fine range of beers and spirits. **Eats:** Excellent value and quality in college; good healthy range and veggie alternative which often proves more popular than carnivore option. Organic food at cheap prices can be ordered weekly by individuals. **Ents:** Regular college ents – cheap! College drama, photography, choir, arts, debating, film society. **Sports:** College tennis courts, punts, boat club. Numerous societies eg rugby, squash, netball, hockey. **Hardship funds:** Many available at college's discretion; stringent assessment but applications encouraged. **Travel:** Travel grants quite easy to come by, £150 Europe, £100+ worldwide. **Work:** In term, library invigilation, bar shifts. In vac, college will employ students for conferences (kitchens, silver service etc); wages not brilliant, convenient if you need to be around college during vac.

MORE INFO?   Enquiries to Charlotte Walton (Schools Liaison Officer), or Tamsin Lishman (JCR President) 01865 276846.

ALUMNI (EDITORS' PICK)   Marjory-Anne Bromhead (economist at World Bank), Nicola Le Fanu (composer), Kate Millett (feminist writer), Beryl Smalley (historian), A Bullard (vice-president, Amcon Corp, USA), Dame Helen Gardner (critic), Barbara Pym (novelist), D K Broster, Jacqueline Du Pré (cellist), Catherine Heath (writer), Hermione Lee (broadcaster).

ST HUGH'S

St Hugh's College, Oxford OX2 6LE
(Tel 01865 274900)

Founded: 1886; men undergraduates first admitted 1987. **Admission:** College welcomes applications from all kinds of school. Undergraduates not admitted for human sciences or theology. **Scholarships:** Up to 26 scholarships (£200 plus free vacation lodgings) and exhibitions awarded annually to matriculated undergraduates; various essay prizes; organ scholarship and instrumental award. **Europe:** 10% first degree students (modern languages and joint courses) take a language as part of course and spend 6 months or more abroad. No formal exchange links. **Travel grants:** Limited amount of money available for students attending required courses. **Library:** Separate law and science reading rooms. **Gate/guest hours:** All undergraduates have keys. Visitors out by 2 am. Overnight guests at weekend by arrangement. **Other college facilities:** JCR bar, bar billiards, tennis, croquet, rowing, particularly large and pleasant garden, computer.

Accommodation: All undergraduates offered study bedroom for at least 3 years; 1996/97 charges, £1,470 per annum. No first degree students live at home. **Term time work:** College policy not to allow term time work. Work in college available only in vacs.

Undergraduates: 229 men, 177 women. **Postgraduates:** 91 men, 68 women. **Teaching staff:** *Men:* 33 fellows, 1 research fellow, 15 lecturers. *Women:* 12 fellows, 2 research fellows, 10 lecturers. **College fees 1996/97:** LEA grants cover college fees; undergraduates not on grants pay £3,202 in addition to university fees.

WHAT IT'S LIKE   Now establishing itself as one of Oxford's most energetic, egalitarian, and educationally exciting colleges. Set in 14 acres of landscaped grounds in north Oxford it provides a supportive environment in which to enjoy the university as a whole. Extensive modern facilities include computer rooms and music rooms. The atmosphere is relaxed, with both students and staff considerate and tolerant of each other, something essential in such a small community. Fifteen minutes walk from town, less if you're a cyclist. Can be a bit insular, but students very outgoing and some of the most active on a university level. Admissions are evenly split between the sexes as well as the state and private school sectors.

PAUPER NOTES   **Accommodation:** Everyone housed. Good quality. **Drink:** Recently redecorated college bar – extensive facilities, friendly atmosphere, good beer, but fairly expensive. **Eats:** Average, cheap food for all needs/diets in college, bar food in bar. Lots of places to eat out in Oxford. **Ents:** Excellent regular ents (music, live bands, jazz etc) in college, weekly videos and lots of active societies. **Sports:** Active football, rowing and rugby clubs. Tennis, croquet and multigym on site. Swimming pool nearby as are shared rugby/hockey/football/cricket grounds. Very active boat club. **Hardship funds:** Available in extreme cases. JCR hardship fund also available. **Travel:** Lots of small (£50–£300) grants available for summer trips. **Work:** Same as any other medium-sized city. Bar work plentiful, sometimes in college. Lots of vac work in college.

MORE INFO?   Enquiries to JCR President (01865 274425).

ALUMNI (EDITORS' PICK)   Barbara Castle, Jane Glover, Catherine Johnston, Emily Davison (early suffragette), Dame Peggy Ashcroft, Mary Renault, Kate Adie, Joanna Trollope.

ST JOHN'S

St John's College, Oxford OX1 3JP
(Tel 01865 277300)

Founded: 1555; women undergraduates first admitted 1979. **Admissions:** Undergraduates not admitted for geology, metallurgy. **Scholarships:** Awards offered on examination results annually; organ and choral scholarships annually. Special funds for visually impaired undergraduates. **Europe:** 12% first degree students take a language as part of course and spend 6 months or more abroad. Formal exchange links in Munich, Geneva and Pisa – open to all undergraduates. **Travel grants:** Awarded annually on tutors' recommendations. Book grants; instrumental awards. **Library:** 39,000 older books, and working library of 33,000 volumes, many rare books and manuscripts. **Eating arrangements:** Breakfast, lunch and early dinner self-service in hall, semi-formal dinner. Snacks available from college bar. **Gate/guest hours:** Late keys issued. **Other college facilities:** Sports ground a mile from the college, tennis court, pavilion; boathouse in Christ Church meadow.

Accommodation: All students in college accommodation. 485 places available (some Jacobean, some Victorian, some modern); self-catering at £36.82–£47.53 per week, term time only (graduates pay all year but are credited for days away from college). No first degree students live at home. **Term time work:** College policy to allow term time work (5% believed to work). Work in college for postgraduates only. **Hardship funds:** Some funding available for hardship grants and loans and for academic purposes; one Oxford Student Scholarship assigned before the start of the course, full academic and maintenance fees.

Undergraduates: 234 men, 133 women. **Postgraduates:** 113 men, 64 women. **Teaching staff:** *Men:* 32 fellows, 10 research fellows, 16 lecturers, 1 lecteur, 1 lektor. *Women:* 3 fellow, 5 research fellows, 16 lecturers. **College fees 1996/97:** LEA grants cover college fees; undergraduates not on grants pay £3,017 in addition to university fees.

WHAT IT'S LIKE   The rumours about the wealth of St John's are all true, and as a student the material advantages are obvious – accommodation for all undergraduates, good kitchen facilities, cheap food in hall, and facilities to rival any in Oxford (a well-stocked library, 2 excellent computer rooms, 2 squash courts and brand new weights room on site and so on). A new quad has just been built. As one of the larger colleges, the sporting facilities are good – a sports ground only a mile away with rugby, football and hockey pitches in addition to two tennis courts and a boathouse on the River Isis. But what sets St John's apart from the rest of Oxford is not the legendary work ethic, which is shared by Univ and Merton (and which comes from other students, rather than directly from tutors), but an apparently endless supply of ambition – almost everyone becomes involved in extra-curricular activities, and it seems that the desire to achieve highly in finals is matched by endeavour beyond the library. Such dynamism leads to enthusiastic JCR debates and active drama, music and sports societies, as well as a really lively college social life. Students work hard but also take advantage of excellent extra-curricular facilities. The result is a vibrant and exciting place to earn a degree.

PAUPER NOTES   **Accommodation:** College accommodation for all undergrads – cheap by Oxford standards (£5.26–£6.80 per day). Married flats 200 metres away. **Drink:** Sub-pub prices in college bar; the Lamb and Flag next door. **Eats:** Cheap food in hall (3-course dinner £1.90) + bar food. Veggie options. **Ents:** Within college great dinners, bops, karaoke, hypnotists, garden party, ball every 3 years. **Sports:** Croquet lawn and 2 squash courts within college, sportsground 1 mile away. **Hardship funds:** £100 book grant pa for everyone, undefined hardship fund. Rent rebate scheme (those on grant and loan receive up to £140 rebate). **Travel:** Travel grants available, c£150 for summer trips. **Work:** About 5% work in term-time (hard to fit in though as workload heavy). About 75% find some sort of work in vac, mostly at home rather than at Oxford.

ALUMNI (EDITORS' PICK)   Robert Graves, Philip Larkin, John Wain, Kingsley Amis, Tony Blair.

ST PETER'S

St Peter's College, Oxford OX1 2DL
(Tel 01865 278900)

Founded: 1929; women undergraduates first admitted 1979. **Admission:** Pre and post A-level candidates apply on the basis of A-level results (known or future), school record, and interview. College welcomes applications from older candidates, especially in PPE. Undergraduates not accepted for classics, PPP, experimental psychology, human sciences, oriental studies, metallurgy. **Scholarships:** Organ scholarship and two choral awards annually at entrance. Other awards (including instrumental award) for students in residence. **Europe:** Modern linguists only (some 8 per year) take a language as part of course and spend 9 months abroad. No formal exchange links. **Travel grants:** Grants are made annually to members of the college from the Christian Deelman Fund, a graduate travel fund and St Peter's Society. **Library:** Ample reading space, mainly undergraduate texts, with a few older and more specialist works. Separate law library. **Eating arrangements:** Breakfast normally residents only. Lunch and dinner, pay as you go (informal dinner at 6.15pm, formal at 7.15pm). **Gate/guest hours:** No restrictions except as to noise and good order. Gate locked at 11 pm but keys available. **Other college facilities:** Music room, usual athletics and other facilities, JCR.

Accommodation: In 1995/96, 62% of all students in college accommodation, 100% of first years. 287 places available (117 for first years): 165 full board at £88 per week, term time only; 88 self-catering places at £35–£45, Sept–June; 32 new rooms at £52–£55 per week. Most undergraduates are charged £1,552 pa (£2,200 with meals). Students live in privately owned accommodation for 1 year: rents £40–£60 per week, self-catering. No first degree students live at home. **Term time work:** No college policy to allow term time work (5% believed to work). Some vacation jobs in college in cleaning, secretarial, conference-hosting. **Hardship funds:** Variable funds, 14 students helped in 1995/96.

Undergraduates: 186 men, 128 women. **Postgraduates:** 90 men, 59 women. **College fees 1996/97:** LEA grants cover college fees; undergraduates not on grants pay £3,267 in addition to university fees.

WHAT IT'S LIKE   It's in the centre of Oxford, just off the major pedestrianised shopping area and at the heart of the town's many restaurants and sandwich bars. The college is a small collection of buildings that includes the ancient New Inn Hall, a new accommodation block (St George's Gate) and award-winning lodge Linton House. Unpretentious and friendly, a place where students enjoy a busy social life and pursue academic goals in an environment free of intimidation and undue stress. Tutors' demands and deadlines are fair and relationships between the governing body, the Master and the students are excellent. Cinemas and theatres are close, as are libraries (college library is open 22 hours a day) plus the town's top night clubs, cocktail bars and popular pubs. These supplement the hectic social calendar organised in college which includes black tie evenings, a ball, sweaty bops (discos), singalongs and student concerts. The undergraduate common room (JCR) regularly hosts local bands, karaoke and blind date nights, often as intercollegiate events. The bar believed to be one of the best in Oxford with good cheap beer and many theme nights. JCR has satellite TV, video, pool and football tables, photocopier, games machines and newspapers – national and student. Drama and music excellent standard – a number of productions staged each term in college. Tremendous number of sports available at all levels for men and women, including rowing, rugby, soccer, hockey, tennis, squash, badminton, athletics, netball, basketball, pool and darts. Many of top college teams extremely successful university-wide but plenty of opportunities to play casually and just for fun. College is encouraging women to apply and male/female ratio is improving all the time. The college women's adviser and student women's officer organise events, talks and self-defence classes. The college provides counselling through students and professionals which supplements the help available from university-wide groups, and a college nurse holds a daily surgery.

PAUPER NOTES   **Accommodation:** 1st year guaranteed live in, most live out in 2nd. **Drinks**: Close to many pubs and cheap bar at Union Society. **Eats:** Good college food at cheap prices; vegetarians well catered for. Lots of places to eat off-site. **Ents**: Cinemas and theatres a stone's throw away. **Hardship funds:** University access fund; academic and choral scholarships available. College hardship fund easily accessible. **Travel:** College travel grants and scholarships. **Work:** Term time work discouraged and is difficult to find (few have Saturday jobs). Most go home to work in the long vacations.

MORE INFO?   Enquiries to Andrew McGuffie, JCR President (01865 278912).

INFORMAL NAME   SPC.

ALUMNI (EDITORS' PICK)   Sir Rex Hunt, Rev W Awdry, Sir Paul Reeves, Peter Wright, Ken Loach, Sir Paul Condon.

SOMERVILLE

Somerville College, Oxford OX2 6HD
(Tel 01865 270600)

Founded: 1879; male undergraduates first admitted in 1994. **Admission:** Undergraduates not admitted for anthropology, geography, theology. **Scholarships:** Various scholarships and exhibitions, both open and closed (usually £200 and £150 pa respectively), awarded at any time in an undergraduate's career for work of especial merit; also Bousfield Scholarships, for candidates from GPDST schools, and Dorothy McCalman Scholarship (£100), for candidates who have earned their living for 3 years. **Europe:** 6% of students learn a language as part of their course and spend 6 months or more abroad. European students come as undergraduates, visiting students or on the Erasmus programme. **Travel grants:** Various grants and awards. **Library:** Over 100,000 volumes, with strong science, history, literature, languages and philosophy collections; also an ICL computer room, electronic calculators and microfiche reader. **Eating arrangements:** Cafeteria system in hall. Meals paid for on ticket system. **Gate/guest hours:** Undergraduates have keys. **Other college facilities:** JCR bar, tennis and croquet, 2 new boats, organ and several pianos. Small independent nursery for children of college members.

Accommodation: Most students live in college accommodation; 100% of first years and final years who choose it. 276 places available (120 for first years): full board at £64.92 per week, term time only. Annual average charge £1,623 (with 120 meal tickets). Some second year students live in privately owned accommodation. **Hardship funds:** Limited funds available for unexpected financial difficulties.

Undergraduates: 247 women, 116 men. **Postgraduates:** 50 women, 25 men. **Teaching staff:** *Men:* 9 fellows. *Women:* 21 fellows, 5 research fellows, 26 lecturers. **College fees 1996/97:** LEA grants cover college fees; undergraduates not on grants pay £3,172 in addition to university fees.

WHAT IT'S LIKE   Having been a women's college since 1879 (and proud of it), Somerville welcomed men for the first time in 1994. It retains a pro-women environment and has a friendly, tolerant and supportive atmosphere but also a reputation for the outward-looking social and political activism of the students. Although by no means one of the richer colleges, its main quad is spacious and quiet, and much used in the summer (lawn tennis court, croquet). The buildings range from Victorian to the rather ugly new constructions (but, as one perceptive student put it, if you live in one of these buildings, at least you don't have to look at them!) The library is one of the best and most beautiful in Oxford and accessible to students 24 hours a day – vital in your inevitable essay crises. The JCR provides various amenities: 2 laundries, various televisions, video, sewing machine, typewriter, photocopier and pool table. There is also an ICL computer room (24 hour access), music rooms and one of Oxford's few crèches. Accommodation in college is generally quite good; compulsory during your first year and guaranteed for your final year. However, most students live out during their second year which can be a real financial strain despite university, JCR and college financial aid. College food is reasonable and cheap; the JCR provides cooking facilities which, although limited, are better than most other places. Academic pressure depends on subject, but tutors and fellows are generally enthusiastic and sympathetic. Somerville is very close to the centre of town and maintains a thriving social life. Little Clarendon Street (or 'Little Trendy Street') is right next to college and boasts some of the best restaurants in Oxford as well as the infamous G&D's ice-cream parlour. In-college entertainments are invariably inundated by students from other colleges. Drama, music, theatre and sports activities are very well subscribed. The new men undergraduates are already making their mark in the male sports in the university, while the women's boat club is famous for dominating the river. The college has a relaxed and cosmopolitan environment which attracts students from a variety of backgrounds and has a particularly good state school/independent school ratio.

PAUPER NOTES **Accommodation:** All 1st and 3rd years guaranteed accommodation. College equalisation scheme where students in college help to fund those forced to live out. Adequate kitchen facilities and bathrooms. **Drink:** Cheap and often packed bar. Lots of nearby pubs – Eagle & Child, Lamb & Flag, Horse & Jockey. **Eats:** College food generally okay – cheapest and best to opt for vegetarian dishes. **Ents:** Excellent range and frequency; joint events often held with other colleges. Close to the Phoenix cinema and Jericho Tavern (behind college) often has live bands. **Sports:** Members active in many university teams; boat club being expanded. **Hardship funds:** Access funds, hardship funds, vacation residence funds open to all students; college sympathetic. Some scholarships. **Travel:** Generous travel grants; some for specific subjects. **Work:** Officially no work allowed. Unofficially vac jobs easy to find; term-time hard to keep up – restaurant/bar work most common, average rate £3–£5/hour.

MORE INFO?   Ring Rachel Isba, 01865 270593.

ALUMNI (EDITORS' PICK)   Indira Gandhi, Iris Murdoch, Vera Brittain, Ann Oakley, Joyce Gutteridge, Victoria Glendinning, Kate Mortimer, Dr Cicely Williams, Anne Scott James, Dame Kiri Te Kanawa, Winifred Holtby, Dorothy Sayers, Dorothy Hodgkin FRS, Shirley Williams, Esther Rantzen, Margaret Thatcher, Elspeth Barker.

TRINITY

Trinity College, Oxford OX1 3BH
(Tel 01865 279900)

Founded: 1555; women undergraduates first admitted 1979. **Admission:** Candidates admitted through any of the usual modes of entry. Undergraduates not admitted for geography, PPP, music, experimental psychology, human sciences, oriental studies, archaeology and anthropology, computation. **Scholarships:** College exhibitions based on academic achievement after first year; scholarships awarded for final year. Designated college for Jardine Scholars from Hong Kong, Japan and Bermuda, and Inlaks Scholars from India; also a scholarship for Canadian undergraduate following a science course. **Europe:** 11% first degree students take a language as part of course and spend 6 months or more abroad. No formal exchange links. **Travel grants:** Travelling bursaries including one for a finalist (£1,700); special fund for classical studies; college funds for academically approved projects. **Library:** Open 24 hours (keyholders at night). Combined arts, science and law library. **Eating arrangements:** All meals can be taken in hall. **Gate/guest hours:** Gate keys issued to college members. **Other college facilities:** Computer room, beer cellar, music society (organ, 2 pianos), squash court, boathouse, playing fields and pavilion; spacious lawns and gardens.

Accommodation: Almost all undergraduates (100% of first years) accommodated in college or in new student block about a mile away if they wish. Most charged £384 per term plus establishment charge (£63–£86 per term). No first degree students live at home. **Term time work:** No college policy to allow term time work. Term (and vac) work in college available in library, archives, gardens and kitchens; tutors give help and advice on vac jobs, through their own contacts. **Hardship funds:** Keasbey Grants, Abbott's and university hardship funds. Some college funds.

Undergraduates: 177 men, 102 women. **Postgraduates:** 58 men, 47 women. **Teaching staff:** *Men:* 21 fellows, 3 junior research fellows, 21 lecturers. *Women:* 5 fellows, 1 research fellow, 8 lecturers. **College fees 1996/97:** LEA grants cover college fees; undergraduates not on grants pay £3,068 in addition to university fees.

WHAT IT'S LIKE   Centrally located, architecturally attractive college in extensive gardens. Accommodation is of a very high standard owing to recent refurbishment and new buildings. Undergraduates housed for 3 years; all rooms have facilities. Fridges can be rented cheaply and there are now kitchens in all quads. Library is accessible 24 hours, seven days a week and the bar is shaking off its drab reputation and could now be called lively. Similarly, Trinity has shaken off cobwebs of apathy; while still fairly middle of the road it does have representation in a range of university activities: sport, drama, Union etc. Its all-round appeal makes this a wonderful college at which to spend a few years.

PAUPER NOTES   **Accommodation:** All guaranteed accommodation. Not all on-site but relatively cheap. **Drink:** Beer cellar cheap and relaxed; very close to best pubs (King's Arms, White Horse). **Eats:** College food good due to sympathetic chef. **Ents:** 4 musical events per term and unlimited non-music events (eg quizzes). **Sports:** Average facilities; bit far to go. Good ethos (participation and fun – ie we lose a lot). **Hardship funds:** Good possibilities. President is very sympathetic to student hardship. **Travel:** Ditto – though over-subscribed so not as much cash available. **Work:** Difficult (and frowned upon) in term time apart from in college library and bar (about 3 jobs); long vacs allow holiday work.

MORE INFO?   Write to president of JCR, e-mail trinacct@sable.ox.ac.uk.

ALUMNI (EDITORS' PICK)   Cardinal Newman, Jeremy Thorpe, Sir Terence Rattigan, Lord Clark ('Civilisation'), Anthony Crosland, Miles Kington, William Pitt the Elder, A V Dicey, W Anson (both great constitutional lawyers), R Hillary (author), Sir Hans Krebs (biochemist), R Porter (immunology) (both Nobel Laureates), Lord North, Sir Arthur Quiller-Couch, Sir Angus Ogilvy, Ross and Norris McWhirter, Marmaduke Hussey, Robin Leigh-Pemberton.

UNIVERSITY COLLEGE

University College, Oxford OX1 4BH
(Tel 01865 276602)

Founded: 1249; women undergraduates first admitted 1979. **Admission:** Undergraduates not admitted for biology, geography, theology, human science, or history and English; modern language combinations (but not all joint courses) must include Russian. College has one of largest numbers of science undergraduates in university; also specialises in Russian and psychology. **Scholarships:** Various scholarships and exhibitions, awarded after first year (except organ and choral scholarships). Book grants also available. **Travel grants:** A number awarded each year. **Library:** 2 libraries, 50,000 volumes, of which 35,000 on open shelves. 100 reader seats. **Other college facilities:** Computing room (MS-DOS machines and Apple Macs, some connected to university network); music practice room. Squash court and multigym. Sports ground a mile from college (including hard and grass tennis courts. Own boathouse.

Accommodation: College accommodation available to undergraduates in first 3 years if wanted. 330 places available at rent of £57.12 per week, term time (plus vacations if wanted). Annual room rent £1,447; token charge for meals in hall (approx £5 for 3 meals). No first degree students live at home. **Term time work:** College policy to allow term time work within college only (5–10% believed to work). Term (and vac) work available: waiting, cleaning, portering. **Hardship funds:** £30,000 own funds, 300 students helped; plus £5,000 other funds, awards £100–£150. Special help: own funds available for accommodation costs.

Undergraduates: 278 men, 135 women. **Postgraduates:** 93 men, 32 women. **Teaching staff:** *Men:* 30 fellows, 1 research fellow, 16 lecturers. *Women:* 3 fellows, 11 lecturers. **College fees 1996/97:** LEA grants cover college fees; undergraduates not on grants pay £3,073 in addition to university fees.

WHAT IT'S LIKE   Once known as the Pub on the High Street, Univ is often described as sound but low-profile, rather insular. In fact, it is as good a place as any in Oxford. Thoroughly down-to-earth, it is extremely cosmopolitan, with particularly close US and Australasian links. The work ethos is taken very seriously and pays off: ranked third in Oxford's academic league table in 1996. But this is not at the price of somewhat stuffy intellectualism and Univ is very much an all-rounder. Its beer cellar is one of the biggest and best stocked in the university though the hall food gets a bad press. Its drama and music societies are as ambitious as they are active and its sports teams consistently successful: rowing, rugby, football and hockey teams, for both sexes, are particularly high profile. The JCR (student body) is apolitical in the positive sense of avoiding factions, but committed to improving the living and working environment of the college. It prides itself on being tolerant in every respect, encouraging diversity and commitment. And then there's JCR Tea (3p a cup, 7p a sandwich) and legendary sweaty bops twice a term. What more could you ask for?   *J C Gray*

PAUPER NOTES   **Accommodation:** College accommodation available for 3 years; costly (as whole of Oxford) but on a par with most other colleges. **Drink:** Beer cellar excellent. Pubs quite popular eg Eastgate, Wheatsheaf (next door), Turf (town centre), The Cricketers (Iffley Road), Isis Tavern (on river). **Eats:** College food includes vegetarian option. **Ents:** College ents cheap and frequent. PPP Cinema – but very few bands in Oxford. Comedy at Apollo Theatre (eg Harry Enfield). **Sports:** Free college sports facilities including sports ground and boathouse; gym and squash court on site. **Hardship funds:** Some £30,000 allocated each year; Parker and Allington funds for dire circumstances. **Travel:** College travel grants, substantial summer bursaries and Keasby Bursary fund for student travel. **Work:** In college beer cellar; otherwise little term time work. Most go home to work in vacations; some work for college bursary/works dept.

MORE INFO?   Enquiries to JCR President 01865 276606.

ALUMNI (EDITORS' PICK)   V S Naipaul, Richard Ingrams, Shelley, Clement Attlee, Roger Utley, Bill Clinton, Andrew Morton, Peter Snow, Bob Hawke, Armando Ianucci.

WADHAM

Wadham College, Oxford OX1 3PN
(Tel 01865 277946)

Founded: 1613; women undergraduates first admitted 1974. **Admission:** General pattern of Oxford entrance. Particularly encourages state school and women applicants. Undergraduates not admitted for archaeology & anthropology, earth sciences, engineering & materials, fine art, theology, geography or metallurgy. **Scholarships:** Awarded for meritorious performance in university examinations and consistently excellent performance in tutorials. **Europe:** 14% first degree students take a language as part of course and spend 6 months or more abroad. No formal exchange links, except assistantships. **Travel grants:** Various travel grants. **Library:** Large, modern library with space for 135 readers. **Eating arrangements:** Self-service breakfast, lunch and dinner in hall or student refectory. **Gate/guest hours:** No restrictions. **Other college facilities:** Largest college theatre, gymnasium, computer room, JCR cafeteria and bar, launderette, organ and grand piano, squash court, weight-training room; sports ground 1½ miles from college.

Accommodation: All first and third year students and some second years can be accommodated in college (single and shared sets and bedsitters). £525 per term covers all accommodation charges and dinner (breakfast and lunch extra). No first degree students live at home. **Term time work:** College policy not to allow term time work. **Hardship funds:** Some assistance with research expenses for graduates. Loans or grants available according to circumstances.

Undergraduates: 255 men, 176 women. **Postgraduates:** 102 men, 36 women. **College fees 1996/97:** LEA grants cover college fees; undergraduates not on grants pay £3,133 in addition to university fees.

WHAT IT'S LIKE   Very large and reasonably diverse student community. Improving male:female ratio (more women than men admitted this year) and enlightened admissions policy. Everyone is made to feel welcome. Wadham claims to be 'an island of normality in a sea of intellectual and class snobbery'. Anachronistic JCR/MCR system abandoned in favour of unified SU, which is dynamic and politically active. Has a reputation for social and political consciousness, and environmental awareness and some of the best student ents in Oxford, offset by almost terminal laid-backness of some members. SCR can be sympathetic and tutors generally likeable. College facilities are good; sports ground 15 mins away, library open 24 hours, theatre, squash and badminton courts, weights room.

SU subsidised launderette, TV, video, vending/games machines, photocopier, magazine, newssheet and own PA system; SU shop stocks everything (condoms, washing powder, stationery ...). Accommodation ranges from old, quaint and airy to newer, goldfishbowl-like and warm, to brand new, disinfected and well-equipped (ie kitchens). All first years and finalists live in. Many second years live in a new building by the sports ground, while those who do live out get financial assistance from a rent equalisation scheme. Graduates go on to do everything/anything/nothing (recent batch of Wadham student journos now making names for themselves in national papers). Wadhamites are extremely active in journalism, environmentalism, politics, arts, sports ... they're everywhere, in every university society from tiddlywinks to Cherwell to Green Party Students – and sometimes even in the library. The gardens are breathtaking; the food less so.

PAUPER NOTES   **Accommodation:** Most students in cheap(ish) college accommodation; rent equalisation scheme means those living out pay the same. **Drink:** College surrounded by pubs. Wadham's new bar looks like railway carriage but very cheap and friendly. Other college bars a good bet for cheap pints. **Eats:** College lunch good value for pie/chips/beans (veg food better than meat). Surrounded by sandwich shops. Also St Giles Café (greasy, trucker atmosphere) a big favourite. Plenty of kebab/potato vans, burger bars, Indians, Chinese etc in town. **Ents:** Excellent in college – from bops to quizzes, Blind Date, cabaret, trips to seaside, live bands and some of Oxford's finest student DJs. Good cheap Indie venues; plenty low-cost student drama in Wadham theatre; free SU discos one of the best in university. Excellent alternative cinemas: Phoenix and Ultimate Picture Palace. **Sport:** Own sports ground 1½ mile, squash and badminton courts on site; most sports catered for. Public pools £1 a go. Sport good – teams vary from taking yourself very seriously to laughing a lot. Women's football extremely good laugh and good results. **Hardship funds:** Domestic bursar usually sympathetic to rent arrears sob-stories. College hardship fund but not adequate (have to take out student loan first). Can also apply to university. Debt is a serious problem – lots of counselling provided but no magic wand. **Travel:** Travel grants available. Oxford on arterial routes to almost anywhere – by rail/coach/motorways or hitching good. NUS cards get reductions on nearly all travel. Car a nuisance as parking non-existent and fines exorbitant. **Work:** University rules prohibit term time work but some (2%) have to. Most work in vacs: college manual labour, tour guides in summer, A-level tutoring, some pub work and waitressing.

MORE INFO?   Wadham Alternative Prospectus from SU President, 01865 277969. University Alternative Prospectus (from university SU, 01865 270777).

ALUMNI (EDITORS' PICK)   Christopher Wren, Michael Foot, Alan Coren, Melvyn Bragg, Sue Brown (first woman to cox Blues boat), Lyndsay Anderson, Patrick Marber.

WORCESTER

Worcester College, Oxford OX1 2HB
(Tel 01865 278300)

Founded: 1714; women undergraduates first admitted 1979. **Admission:** College welcomes both pre- and post-A-level candidates, and keen to have applications from schools with no previous connection. Undergraduates not admitted for archaeology & anthropology, biochemistry, human sciences, metallurgy and science of materials, economics and management. **Scholarships:** Scholarships and exhibitions are awarded for exceptionally good work. Two instrumental awards are available each year to any undergraduate. Book bursaries of £100 available to all undergraduates. **Europe:** 10% first degree students take a language as part of course and spend 6 months or more abroad. No formal exchange links. **Travel grants:** About £10,000 available annually for travel with some reasonable academic purpose. Additional travel grants for geologists. **Library:** Undergraduate library including individual reading cubicles. Separate law library and a number of valuable antiquarian collections. **Eating arrangements:** Bar lunches available; choice of self-service or formal dinner. **Gate/guest hours:** Undergraduates are issued with a security key. **Other college facilities:** Cellar bar, buttery, 26 acres of college grounds including gymnasium equipped with 9-station multigym, squash courts, 7 tennis courts, playing fields; boathouse.

Accommodation: First and second years accommodated in single study bedrooms in college; 50 rooms available for third years in nearby houses. Average room charge £1,150 pa (for 25 weeks); meals paid for as taken. No first degree students live at home. **Term time work:** College policy to allow term time work, limit of 4 hours per week (2% believed to work). Work available in college bar, hall (vac only), occasional admin and research work.

Undergraduates: 227 men, 114 women. **Postgraduates:** 73 men, 50 women. **Teaching staff:** *Men:* 26 fellows, 9 research fellows, 16 lecturers, 5 professorial fellows. *Women:* 4 fellows, 5 research fellows, 9 lecturers, 1 professorial fellow. **College fees 1996/97:** LEA grants cover college fees; undergraduates not on grants pay £3,124 in addition to university fees.

WHAT IT'S LIKE   Very friendly college, with beautiful quad and renowned gardens; lake and sports fields on site. Accommodation is either old, interesting and cold or new, warm and well equipped. Cooking facilities available in new Sainsbury Building and third-year block. Washing facilities good and cheap. Students live in for first two years and some for all three. Relations with SCR good. Renovated library open all night; separate law library. Buttery, complete with log fire and Trivial Pursuits, is important social centre. Food good; very popular cheap cellar bar. JCR apolitical but organises social events and negotiates actively. Restrictions on overnight guests largely ignored. Contraceptive and pregnancy advice from college doctor (plus woman doctor). Active drama group and music society. Annual summer show in gardens. High participation in sports (squash courts, new weights room). Top subjects: law, modern languages (which includes a year abroad); courses traditional. Subject changes possible but not encouraged; workload   substantial, not oppressive. Drop out rate low. Mixed from 1979 and women gradually increasing (almost 50:50 intake this year); women's group fairly active. Typical student (from University Alternative Prospectus) – 'The archetypal Worcester student is happy, well-adjusted, effortlessly brilliant, modest to the point of self-effacement, Byronic in his wasted talents, a sparkling conversationalist and wit, and a respectable table-football player.' People from all areas and backgrounds are welcome.
PAUPER NOTES   **Accommodation:** College accommodation generally affordable; living out very expensive. **Drink:** College bars generally good value. Worcester bar cheaper than most. Good local pubs. **Eats:** Food good value and generally good quality. Breakfast, lunch and choice of informal or formal evening meals available. Formal hall offers excellent food with service at the same price as informal hall in return for a jacket and gown. Very good local restaurants. **Ents:** Oxford does not have a major venue for big concerts, but minor pop and cult bands play here. Worcester ideally placed for cinemas and theatres. Social committee active – arranging discos in bar and various theme cocktail parties. **Sports:** Great sports facilities on site (football, rugby, cricket and hockey pitches, tennis, squash, basketball). Only Oxford college to have facilities on site. **Hardship funds:** Generally large

grants given to those who are truly needy rather than lots of small grants to many, also vacation grants for those who *have* to stay up late/come up early. £100 book bursary available for all students. Prizes (c.£20–£60) for good work. **Travel:** Cheap bus fares to London. Travel scholarships available for educationally-related trips. **Work:** Officially against regulations to work in term time and generally too little time to do so (although some work on occasional evening). Easier to find work in Oxford than in much of the country – waitering etc widely available for reasonable pay.

MORE INFO? Enquiries to Tom Young, JCR President 01865 278380.

ALUMNI (EDITORS' PICK) Sir Alistair Burnet, Thomas de Quincey, Richard Lovelace, John Sainsbury, Rupert Murdoch, Donald Carr, Richard Adams, Anna Markland, David Kirk (ex-captain of New Zealand rugby team), Lord Palumbo, many of the Sainsbury family.

PAISLEY UNIVERSITY

University of Paisley
- Paisley PA1 2E (Tel 0141 848 3000, Fax 0141 887 0812)
- Craigie Campus in Ayr, Beech Grove, Ayr KA8 0SR
  (Tel 01292 260321, Fax 01292 611705) Map 1

STUDENT ENQUIRIES: Corporate Communications (Paisley); Registry (Craigie).
APPLICATIONS: UCAS

Broad study areas: Engineering, science, technology, computing, education, business, social studies, media, surveying. (Subject details are in the *Subjects and Places Index.*)

Founded: 1897, Paisley College merged with teacher training college in Ayr in 1993; university status in 1992. **Main undergraduate awards:** BA, BAcc, BEd, BEng, BSc, BEng. **Awarding body:** Paisley University. **Site:** Main campus, Paisley town centre; Craigie campus close to centre of Ayr on west coast of Scotland (education, business, media, nursing). **Access:** 8 motorway (A77 for Craigie), rail and air. **Academic features:** Numerous visiting professors. Combined awards through CATS. Close links with number of FE colleges. Courses in business admin, media, radio upgrading HND to degree. **Europe:** Language options on many degrees; some students have spent a period abroad on practical sandwich placements. Economics and management exchange links with a number of EU universities/colleges. **Library:** Over 200,000 volumes, 1,400 periodicals, up to 607 study places (77 Craigie); short loan collection. Group reading room available. New library and resource centre at Paisley. Annual expenditure on library materials, £77.39 per FTE student. **Other learning facilities:** Extensive computing facilities. **Welfare:** 6 student advisory officers; safety officer, occupational health nurse; welfare adviser; nursery (at Paisley), chaplaincy. **Careers:** Personal careers counselling service and information centre; seminars for final year students; annual careers fair. **Amenities:** SU building with a variety of affiliated clubs and societies. New SU building 1998. **Sporting facilities:** New sports centre with all-weather pitches, football, rugby pitches, fitness suite, tennis and squash courts.

Accommodation: In 1995/96, 20% of all students in university accommodation; first year students from outside area given preference. 1,069 places available: 967 self-catering places (Paisley), at £24.20–£31.84 per week; and 102 (Craigie) at £54 per week, term time only. Privately owned accommodation rents: £30–£50 per week for self-catering, £50–£70 B&B, £60–£90 for half-board. Many students live at home (always been a feature in west of Scotland). **Term time work:** 60% of full time first degree students believed to work. Term (and vac) work available on campus as guides for open days, enrolment, induction etc; vacancies off campus advertised in careers service. **Hardship funds:** Total available in 1995/96: £124,000 government access funds, 1,100 students helped, average £210 awarded; £12,000 own fund, 240 students benefit. Help available with partial fees payment prior to starting course.

Duration of first degree courses: 3–4 years (full-time); 4–5 (sandwich); **others:** 4½ years (honours engineering). **Total first degree students 1995/96:** 7,140. **Overseas students:** 225. **Mature students:** 2,021. **Male/female ratio:** 1:1. **Teaching staff:** 384 full-time, 34 part-time. **Total full-time students 1995/96:** 5,843. **Postgraduate students:** 615. **First degree tuition fees:** Home students, paying their own fees in 1996/97, paid £750; Overseas students £5,250 (classroom); £6,750 (lab).

WHAT IT'S LIKE   Campus is in the centre of town, five minutes' walk from the train station; Craigie campus is some 40 miles away on the coast, a good 15 minutes from its local station (though there is a bus service). University has expanded fast recently. SU provides main source of entertainment. At Paisley it is in a building called The Buroo. Facilities include two bars, snack bar, video games, pool tables, large video screen and satellite TV. Wide variety of clubs and societies, including sports, politics, departmental, social and religious. University accommodation variable; many students forced into the private sector where quality and price are a matter of luck of the draw. Reasonable university student advisory service, includes careers, access fund and counselling and welfare. Overall, it is a fairly good place to go if you want to learn, have a good time and get a job at the end of it.

PAUPER NOTES **Accommodation:** Some university accommodation for couples/families. **Drink:** SU bar (the Buroo). **Eats:** The Buroo. **Ents:** Paisley Arts Centre, Town Hall, the Buroo. **Sports:** The Lagoon centre (council run); University Thornly Park Development. **Hardship Funds:** Uni access funds; SA hardship fund. **Travel:** Trains to Glasgow approximately every ten minutes. **Work:** Jobs in union as steward, DJ, entertainments crew; some off campus. Very seasonal but a lot of students fail to find a job in the summer.

MORE INFO?   Get students' Alternative Prospectus. Enquiries to President SA (0141 889 9940).

ALUMNI (EDITORS' PICK)   Gavin Hastings (Scottish/British Lions rugby football international); Douglas Druburgh (junior world curling champion).

CAN'T FIND WHAT YOU'RE LOOKING FOR? USE THE INDEX!

PLYMOUTH UNIVERSITY

University of Plymouth
- Drake Circus, Plymouth PL4 8AA
  (Tel 01752 600600, Fax 01752 232141)
- Exeter Faculty of Arts & Education, Earl Richards Road
  North, Exeter EX2 6AS (Tel 01392 475022)
- Exmouth Faculty of Arts & Education, Exmouth, EX8 2AT
  (Tel 01395 255309)
- Seale-Hayne Faculty of Agriculture, Food & Land Use,
  Newton Abbot TQ12 6NQ (Tel 01626 325800) Map 3

STUDENT ENQUIRIES: Admissions office at appropriate campus
APPLICATIONS: UCAS

Broad study areas: Art & design, education, human sciences, science, technology, business, agriculture, food and land use, humanities. (Subject details are in the *Subjects and Places Index*.)

Founded: 1970 as a Polytechnic, incorporating Rolle College of Education, Exeter College of Art and Seale-Hayne College of Agriculture; university status in 1992. **Main undergraduate awards:** BA, BSc, BEd, BEng, MEng, LLB, MMath. **Awarding body:** Plymouth University. **Site:** Main campus in Plymouth city centre, three faculty campuses located in Exeter (art), Exmouth (education) and outskirts of Newton Abbot (agriculture), each with its own accommodation, academic welfare support services and social amenities. **Access:** Road and rail links to all sites good. **Special features:** Extensive participation in European Space Agency satellite communication and broadcasting programme. **Academic features:** Modular degree scheme covering science, social science, arts and marine studies. Participation in international student exchange programme and European credit transfer system; many international links. First year modules offered at partner colleges in Devon, Cornwall and Somerset, so students in south-west can study nearer home. **Europe:** Languages can be studied as part of course. Formal exchange links with 70 universities/colleges across Europe. Courses across all faculties involve work and/or study abroad. **Library:** Specialist libraries on each Site: total of 400,000 volumes and AV materials, 3,000 journals. Desk top publishing, colour laser printer, binding and lettering equipment. Annual expenditure on library materials, £69.37 per FTE student. **Other learning facilities:** Data comms network across all four campuses including CD-Rom, national and international databases, e-mail. Short course, workshops and seminars on computing. Navigation simulator, computer-aided engineering facilities, diving school. **Welfare:** Counselling, chaplaincy, medical and other welfare services on each campus including legal advice, counselling. Nursery at Plymouth. **Careers:** Careers education programme; careers fair; information rooms and advice; computer-assisted guidance system. **Amenities:** Main SU building and offices on Plymouth site; SU bar on each campus; also shops, launderettes, cheap travel opportunities, visiting bands and Rag Week, sporting and musical activities. Student newspapers. **Sporting facilities:** Recreation facilities at all sites. Sports offered include archery, fencing, golf, rugby, hockey; water sports well catered for eg diving, sailing, water-skiing. Indoor activities include aerobics, badminton, karate, yoga.

Accommodation: In 1995/96, 14% of all students in university accommodation, 32% of first years. 1,591 places available, including 1,366 self-catering places for first years: from £30 per week, term time only. Many students live in privately owned accommodation for whole course: rents £35–£50 per week for self-catering, £55–£70 for catered lodgings. **Term time work:** Maximum of 10 hours per week paid work within the university. **Hardship funds:** Total available in 1995/96: £335,000 government access funds, 700 students helped; £10,000 own funds, 80 students helped. Special help: childcare, travel and high course costs; students estranged from parents; serious on-going hardship.

Duration of first degree courses: 3 years; **others:** 4 years (BEd/sandwich courses). **Total first degree students 1995/96:** 13,932. **BEd students:** 879. **Overseas students:** 1,207. **Mature students:** 6,620. **Male/female ratio:** 1:1. **Teaching staff:** 673 full-time. **Total full-time students 1995/96:** 15,794. **Postgraduate students:** 2,534. **First degree tuition fees:** Home students, paying their own fees in 1996/97, paid £750 (classroom), £1,150 (lab/studio); Overseas students £5,500 (classroom), £6,400 (lab/studio).

WHAT IT'S LIKE   *Plymouth*   Situated in the city centre, five minutes walk from both train and bus stations and the main shopping areas. Four halls of residence on campus, another 5 mins walk away. Only a third of first years housed in halls but plenty of other accommodation and a fairly good accommodation office on campus. Student services centre provides counselling, careers advice and a chaplaincy (can be overstretched). The marine recreation facilities are second to none and university owns a watersports centre on Plymouth waterfront. Other sports facilities are available, out of town but free buses on Wednesdays and Saturdays. Variety of good courses, particularly in the marine and business fields. Fairly good relationship between staff and students. Plymouth is an excellent city – Dartmoor, beaches and the sea all within easy reach. SU is rapidly expanding with a strong commercial arm providing two bars, a well-stocked shop, launderette, travel centre and games room. Full-time ents manager and ents improving all the time. Union's welfare, rights and advice unit highly regarded by both students and the university. Wide range of clubs and societies to join, watersports being some of the most popular. Good social life, SU band nights weekly, student-run nightclubs, good restaurants.
PAUPER NOTES   **Accommodation:** Fairly available; see SU noticeboards, *Western Evening Herald* (Thurs). **Drink:** Excellent range of ciders, local Dartmoor ales and Sutton ales from Thistle Pk Tavern. Union bar cheaper than town. Some clubs have promo nights weekly. **Eats:** Curries, excellent food on Barbican; Jade Garden (Chinese takeaway) brilliant. **Ents:** SU has weekly band nights. Good variety of nightclubs. Couple of cinemas and good theatres. **Sports:** Uni sports centre 4 miles from campus. Squash courts on campus. Excellent watersports facilities and centre. **Hardship funds:** Available. **Travel:** Good hitching from Marsh ills roundabout. Frequent trains and buses to London. Free women's minibus twice nightly and home from nightclubs. **Work:** Some in SU, local pubs; summer vac jobs difficult but not impossible to find – a few seasonal tourism jobs.
MORE INFO?   Get *UPSU Handbook.* Enquiries to any UPSU Executive Member (01752 663337).

WHAT IT'S LIKE   *Exmouth*   This is where the sun always shines and there are endless things to keep a happy-go-lucky fresher cheerful and entertained. Well perhaps that is a slight exaggeration, although the sun does shine sometimes. Not exactly Leeds or Sheffield in terms of night life (the owner of Sam's nightclub might disagree) but one of the friendliest places you've been to and you will enjoy every minute of your freshers fortnight. Exeter is only 20 minutes away. For budding sporty types, there's a range of active sports societies – something to suit all tastes, and if not, it's easy to start your own society with some mates. SU will always be there for you, whether it's personal traumas or just the best way to have a good time! Bar is on two levels and always lively with a friendly atmosphere. The university has a strong theatre arts department and the BEd course has a good reputation. Excellent student/staff relations – most staff are kind, friendly and helpful. University life is what you make of it, the more effort you make to have a good time and the more you put into it, the more you will get out of it.

PAUPER NOTES **Accommodation:** 50% first years in halls (£40 pw): converted Victorian houses (some with sea views) or purpose-built study blocks. Plenty of accommodation in town (£30–£40 pw) of fairly high standard. **Drink:** Excellent SU bar, 34 pubs, scrumpy, local real ales. **Eats:** Refectory on campus – respectable food. Loads of take-aways in town. **Ents:** Campus – regular ents in SU bar, and termly balls. Sky TV, occasional cabaret and comedian nights. In Exmouth: 3 screen cinema, night club, fun fayre, theatre. Exeter good for bands and clubs. **Sports:** Good pitches, gym and weights room on campus. Soccer, rugby and hockey very active. Watersports available. Good student deals in town. **Hardship funds:** Some available; SU for advice. **Travel:** Excellent for hitching to London, the North and Midlands. uses and trains to Exeter. **Work:** Lots work during term-time: mainly barwork, waitressing, supermarkets or in residential homes. Some summer work in pubs, clubs, holiday camps, teaching foreign students.

MORE INFO? Enquiries to SU President, 01395 264783.

ALUMNI (EDITORS' PICK) Anna Tait (art editor of Photographic Journal), Chris Cook, Steve Mattheson (artists), Pam St Clements ('Pat' in EastEnders).

PORTSMOUTH UNIVERSITY

University of Portsmouth, University House, Winston Churchill Avenue, Portsmouth PO1 2UP (Tel 01705 876543, Fax 01705 843082) Map 3

STUDENT ENQUIRIES: **Assistant Registrar (Admissions)**
APPLICATIONS: **UCAS**

Broad study areas: Business, science, engineering, languages, computer science, design, humanities, environmental studies, healthcare. (Subject details are in the *Subjects and Places Index.*)

Founded: 1869 as Portsmouth and Gosport School of Science and Art, becoming Portsmouth Poly in 1969. University status in 1992. **Main undergraduate awards:** BA, BSc, BEng, MMath, MEng, MPhys. **Awarding body:** Portsmouth University. **Site:** Main campus near town centre, Milton site 2½ miles away (business studies, economics, information science, education, management). **Access:** Free minibus or public transport to Milton site. **Academic features:** Many courses in business, science and engineering include BA foundation year. **Europe:** 20% first degree students take a language as part of course and 15% spend 6 months or more abroad. Students in engineering, science, business and social science can include a language as part of the degree; all students have access to languages on a supplementary basis. Formal exchange links with over 50 EU universities/colleges, many open to non-language specialists. Library is designated European Documentation Centre, automatically receiving all EU publications. **Library:** Central university library, and branch library; total of 600,000 volumes, 3,500 periodicals, 900 study places; short loan library. Annual expenditure on library materials, £63.58 per FTE student. **Welfare:** Student counsellors, 2 doctors and sick bay, psychiatrist, solicitor, 3 chaplains. Residential facilities for married students, 40-place nursery (£4.50 per half day, £45 per week full-time). **Careers:** Information, advice and placement service, 6 careers advisers. **Amenities:** SU shop, bank, bars, travel bureau; Royal Naval Unit, Army Officer Training Corps and University Air Squadron. **Sporting facilities:** Wide range of sports; excellent sailing and windsurfing on Solent.

Accommodation: In 1995/96, 11% of all students in university accommodation, 35% of first years. 1,892 places available (1,600 for first years): 778 half-board (some extra meals) at £58.45–£66.85 per week, term time only; and 1,114 self-catering places at £35.77–£47.25 per week, Sept–June. 700 more places planned. 12 places for students with disabilities and 7 for one-parent families. Most students live in privately owned accommodation for whole course: rents £35–£41 per week for self-catering; £45 for B&B, £60 for half-board. 11% of first degree students live at home. **Term time work**: University's policy to allow term time work for full-time first degree students (60% believed to work). Term (and vac) work available on campus in SU bars, offices, graduation ceremonies. **Hardship funds:** Total available in 1995/96: £350,647 government access funds, 861 students helped; £29,720 own funds, 405 helped with loans. Special help: child care costs, exceptional travel, compulsory field trips, self-financing students; own funds also available for part-time and overseas students.

Duration of first degree courses: 3 years or 4 years. **Total first degree students 1995/96:** 10,904. **BEd students:** 46. **Overseas students:** 1,148. **Mature students:** 1,927. **Male/female ratio:** 1:1. **Teaching staff:** 842 full-time, 274 part-time. **Total full-time students 1995/96:** 11,493. **Postgraduate students:** 1,722. **First degree tuition fees:** Home students, paying their own fees in 1996/97, paid £750; Overseas students £5,600 (classroom), £6,800 (lab/studio).

WHAT IT'S LIKE   Situated on two main sites around Portsmouth, varying from modern tower blocks to beautiful old listed buildings and ex-army barracks. There's plenty of private rented accommodation. Student social life is hectic with ents every night – discos, bands, theatre, folk and films. Over 150 clubs and societies offer everything from underwater hockey to instant liberalism to conkers; water sports especially popular. Commercial Road is good shopping centre and Kings Theatre offers new play every 2 weeks; also Theatre Royal, Hornpipe Theatre – community arts centre with student concessions. Surveying, engineering and science courses excellent, offering good sandwich courses. Cultural, literary and language studies homely with friendly atmosphere. Portsmouth a naval port and some pubs are services-orientated though most are full of friendly students. SU runs bars and provides some of best student services.

PAUPER NOTES   **Accommodation:** No squats; halls fairly cheap; 3 housing co-ops about half the price of private accommodation. Cheap emergency accommodation in one hall. **Drink:** SU inexpensive. Most pubs have a cheap night. Local brew, Friary Meux. **Eats:** SU and some pubs good value. **Ents:** SU nightclub, the Garage, for bands, discos and club nights. Lively nightlife on the seafront. Hornpipe – alternative plays, music, films. **Sports:** 46 different sports via SU. Transport to and from games arranged by SU. **Hardship funds:** Three hardship funds. **Travel:** SU travel shop offers discount for students. No travel funds. **Work:** Lots of summer work: ferries, fairground etc. Jobs in union (restaurant, bars, security); pub jobs in term time. On-site job shop helps.

PRINCE OF WALES'S INSTITUTE

The Prince of Wales's Institute of Architecture,
14 Gloucester Gate, Regent's Park, London NW1 4HG
(Tel 0171 916 7380, Fax 0171 916 7381) Map 5

STUDENT ENQUIRIES: The Registrar
APPLICATIONS: Direct (by 1st March).

Broad study areas *(Foundation year/postgraduate)*: Architecture, fine art, traditional art. (Subject details are in the *Subjects and Places Index.*)

Founded: 1992. **Main awards:** Foundation certificate, RIBA pt 2, MA, PhD. **Awarding bodies:** RIBA and Wales University. **Site:** On the edge of Regent's Park. **Access:** Camden Town (underground), Camden Road (BR), many buses. **Academic features:** Many student projects are 'live', undertaken in conjunction with planners, local councils and communities; students can design and build simple buildings. All staff practising artists/architects. Summer schools, foundation course and various postgraduate courses. **Structural features:** National and international connections with architectural schools, politicians, architects and the construction industry. **Europe:** No students take a language as part of course or spend time abroad. Developing exchanges with Eastern European countries. **Library:** 5,000 books; all main architecture and building journals. **Other learning facilities:** Well-equipped computer, metal and wood workshops; dark-room facilities. 70 sq ft personal studio space per student. **Careers:** Advice and placement service. **Welfare:** Free access to Marylebone Health Centre. **Amenities:** Canteen; facilities expanding. All galleries, museums, cinemas etc of London. **Sporting facilities:** None on-site. Local facilities in Regent's Park.

Accommodation: In 1995/96, 40% of all students in college accommodation in Hampstead: self-catering at £60 per week, term time only. **Term time work:** Institute policy to allow part time work but none available on site. **Hardship funds:** Bursaries available.

Duration of courses: foundation 1 year; diploma 2–3 years; BA/PhD 2 years min. **Total foundation students 1995/96:** 19. **Overseas students:** 31. **Mature students:** 50. **Male/female ratio:** 4:3. **Teaching staff:** 8 plus numerous visiting lecturers. **Total full-time students 1995/96:** 65. **Postgraduate students:** 49. **Tuition fees:** Home students, paying their own fees in 1996/97, paid £650 (£3,000 for postgraduate); Overseas students £4,500 (£6,000 postgraduate).

WHAT IT'S LIKE   Only been operating since 1992 so student culture is in its early period of formation. An exciting aspect of being a student at the Institute now is the ability to help establish and determine this culture for the future generations of students. Life is formed around the demanding curricula for each course – a typical day begins early and ends late. The long hours in the studio allow for the nurturing of relationships within each class, although this is contrasted with life outside the Institute. Small number of students live in King's College accommodation in Hampstead but majority in private accommodation. With so many students in the city, student interaction outside the Institute occurs infrequently. Highly diverse student body, with many cultures from throughout the world;

this rich mix of students colours all aspects of student life. Many students have come from study or practice other than architecture. The atmosphere is full of potential, but lacks definition and character, both in the sense of architectural education and socially. As more students pass through the Institute and develop its reputation internationally, the character and culture of student life will solidify.

PAUPER NOTES **Accommodation:** Few halls places; private accommodation expensive. **Eats:** Institute canteen. **Hardship funds:** Financial assistance offered. **Work:** Little time, so weekends only practical – some students work in term time.

QUEEN MARGARET COLLEGE

Queen Margaret College, Clerwood Terrace, Edinburgh EH12 8TS (Tel 0131 317 3000, Fax 0131 317 3256) Map 1

STUDENT ENQUIRIES: Admissions Office
APPLICATIONS: UCAS

Broad study areas: Food science, hospitality and tourism management, nursing, professions allied to medicine, theatre arts. (Subject details are in the *Subjects and Places Index*.)

Founded: 1875. **Main undergraduate awards:** BA, BSc. **Awarding body:** Queen Margaret College. **Site:** 2 main sites: 24-acre landscaped site 4 miles from city centre; new campus in Leith. **Europe:** Erasmus links in occupational therapy, physiotherapy and communications. **Library:** 90,000 volumes, 900 current periodicals, 400 study places; books in heavy demand held in reserve only. **Other learning facilities:** Computer workshops. **Welfare:** Doctor, student counsellor, accommodation officer. College guide for mature students. **Careers:** Information, advice and placement service, careers adviser. **Amenities:** Licensed bar; theatre; bank; college shop, bookshop run twice a week. **Sporting facilities:** Swimming pool, tennis courts, all-weather sports surface, squash court, multi-gym, games hall.

Accommodation: In 1995/96, 15% of all students in college accommodation, 44% first years. 507 places available: 148 half-board places at £61.70 per week and 284 self-catering at £37.79, term time only. Many students live in privately owned accommodation for whole course: rents £30–£45 per week for self-catering, £40–£45 B&B, £60–£65 for half-board. **Hardship funds:** Total available in 1995/96: £55,422 government access funds, 160 students helped.

Duration of first degree courses: 4 years; **others** 3 years (ordinary degrees). **Total first degree students 1995/96:** 2,400 **Overseas students:** 200. **Mature students:** 175. **Male/female ratio:** 1:4. **Teaching staff:** approx 170 full-time. **Total full-time students 1995/96:** 2,600. **Postgraduate students:** 20. **First degree tuition fees:** Home students, paying their own fees in 1996/97, paid £750; Overseas students £5,850.

WHAT IT'S LIKE   A modern, attractive and rapidly expanding college; three campuses across the city of Edinburgh. The main Corstorphine campus is 4 miles west of the city centre in beautifully landscaped grounds and is well-equipped (tennis and squash courts, swimming pool, multi-activity all-weather surface, library, 24 hour IT centre, gym, theatre, kitchens, food science labs, drama, media and TV studios, photography lab etc). Second campus at Leith, opened in 1994, is in a beautifully restored Grade 1 listed building. It caters for health care courses and has excellent facilities (including library, IT centre, cafe, student common room). Third campus is the Scottish Television Gateway Studios (opened in 1996), providing state-of-the-art facilities for drama students. Despite rapid expansion, the college maintains a friendly and sociable atmosphere. Fifth of students live in newly refurbished halls (now show-home standard!); laundry facilities and a small shop on campus. Many students choose to live in town after first year; large numbers of students in Edinburgh, so accommodation is expensive and sometimes difficult to find. The SA runs events most evenings such as karaoke, quizzes, comedy nights, cocktail nights, and the now infamous EH12 club on Wednesday nights. Guest DJs come from top UK clubs including Back to Basics and Cream. Courses are predominantly health care and many departments are known for their excellence eg occupational therapy and physiotherapy; more arts and management courses being introduced. Most courses are now modular; extremely low drop out rate. Majority of students are Scottish with a growing contingent of Scandinavians, especially Norwegians. High graduate employment rate in variety of fields; many courses also give a professional qualification.

PAUPER NOTES   **Accommodation:** Halls of various prices (self-catering and catered). **Drink:** SA bar. Lively and friendly atmosphere. **Eats:** SA sells food and snacks at budget prices. **Ents:** Union events most nights. **Sports:** Gym, squash and tennis courts and swimming pool at college. **Hardship funds:** College loan system for students with good reasons. Access fund. **Travel:** Edinburgh offers many student concessions on trains and buses. **Work:** Some jobs on campus but most students find work in pubs, shops and restaurants in city centre. Vacancies advertised in SA.

INFORMAL NAME   QMC.

QUEEN MARY AND WEST-FIELD

Queen Mary and Westfield College, University of London, Mile End Road, London E1 4NS (Tel 0171 975 5555, Fax 0171 975 5500) Map 5

STUDENT ENQUIRIES: Admissions Office
APPLICATIONS: UCAS

Broad study areas: Arts, medicine, dentistry, engineering, informatics and mathematical sciences, laws, natural sciences, social sciences. (Subject details are in the *Subjects and Places Index*.)

Founded: 1989, from 2 London University colleges: Westfield College (founded 1882) and Queen Mary College (1887). In 1995, merged with 2 medical colleges, St Bartholomew's and The London Hospital. **Structural features:** Part of London University. You can look up St Bartholomew's and Royal London separately. **Main undergraduate awards:** BA, BEng, MEng, BSc, MSci, LLB, MB, BS, BDS. **Awarding body:** London University. **Site:** Main campus on Mile End Road; clinical studies at Whitechapel, West Smithfield and Charterhouse Square sites. **Access:** Stepney Green or Mile End underground stations 5 minutes' walk. Docklands Light Railway Bow Road station and bus or 10 minutes' walk; buses. **Academic features:** Course-unit system allows students to make up tailor-made degree programme, with guidance (includes Georgian and Catalan). Unusual BSc course in basic medical sciences; students study alongside trainee doctors and dentists, to gain general scientific grounding. **Special features:** Large number of visiting professors. **Europe:** Many courses include language tuition, including science and engineering; language learning unit open to all students. Wide-ranging European studies options. Formal exchange links with 25 EU universities/colleges. Range of European Commission research and development programmes. **Library:** 600,000 volumes, 2,500 periodicals, intensive use collection on 3-hour loan only. 7 departmental libraries; European Documentation Centre. Annual expenditure on library materials, £125.40 per FTE student. **Other learning facilities:** Language laboratory; very good computer facilities, including help desk, computer shop and many short courses. **Welfare:** Health centre, chaplains, counsellors, nursery. **Careers:** Information, advice and placement service. **Amenities:** Bookshop, travel centre and bank on site; SU building with nightclub, snackbar, bars, Nightline. **Sporting facilities:** Multigym, squash courts on site; London University central facilities (including swimming pool) accessible; sports ground in Essex (on tube line).

Accommodation: In 1995/96, 27% of all students in university accommodation, 100% of first years (who qualify and apply). 1,972 places available (c.1,200 for first years): 300 full-board (150 for first years) at £66.80 per week and 700 B&B at £53, term time only; plus 972 self-catering places (100 for first years) at £55 per week, Sept–June. 170 additional places to be built on or adjacent to campus. Students live in privately owned accommodation for 1–2 years: rents £40–£60 per week for self-catering, £50–£65 for B&B, £55–£70 for half-board. Ample private accommodation within a 3 mile radius. **Hardship funds:** Total available in 1995/96: £261,000 government access funds, home students only; £10,000 own funds, overseas students only. Special help for students suffering exceptional financial hardship. Some departmental scholarships available.

Duration of first degree courses: 3 years; **others:** 4 years. **Total first degree students 1995/96:** 6,514. **Overseas students:** 934. **Mature students:** 19%. **Male/female ratio:** 7:5. **Teaching staff: full-time:** c500. **Total full-time students 1995/96:** 7,664. **Postgraduate students:** 1,666. **First degree tuition fees:** Home students, paying their own fees in 1996/97, paid £750 (classroom), £1,600 (lab/studio); Overseas students £6,900 (classroom), £8,600 (lab/studio).

WHAT IT'S LIKE   In the East End of London, a mile from the City and 5 minutes from Canary Wharf, the Mile End site has impressive 1880's architecture and is hard to miss. Medical school is based at Whitechapel and Charterhouse Square (Royal London and Barts sites). Easy access to centre of London, plenty of local culture. New self-catering halls overlooking Regents Canal and the main buildings at Mile End; other halls at South Woodford (20 minutes by tube plus half-hourly night buses). Plentiful self-catering/private rented accommodation. Large overseas community, well integrated. SU is active; runs various catering outlets (including griddle and pasta/pizza bar), newly refurbished bar, nightclub and nightly entertainments programme. Also welfare and counselling services – East

London Nightline run from QMWSU. Over 100 clubs and societies, squash court, multigym and sports hall on site; sports grounds at Theydon Bois (on Central line), Hale End and Chislehurst. Renowned for science, engineering and law but many top-quality smaller scale arts and social science departments. Course unit system provides flexibility. Language courses require a year spent abroad, usually very profitable experience. Work assessed by annual exams and coursework, with fixed level of passes required to proceed. Generally unpopular system of having to take a year out to retake – no September resits. Students of fairly mixed background, but noticeable tendency towards London-based students. Large numbers of American associate students. Strong equal opportunities policy.

PAUPER NOTES   **Accommodation:** Private rented plentiful. **Drink:** SU bar has wide range of drinks. Good East End pubs. Firkin pubs at Mile End and Hackney, selling the famous Dogbolter. **Eats:** Excellent local Indian cuisine. Cheap vegetarian wholefood at The Cherry Orchard (Bethnal Green) Cheap bagels and curry in Brick Lane. **Ents:** New SU nightclub (el venue) with licence until 2 am Thurs, Fri, Sat. Regular discos, weekly gigs of up and coming bands, plus cabaret, quizes, film nights, sports nights. Annual Valentine Ball. **Sports:** Gymnasium, multigym and squash courts on campus. Wide range of clubs and societies. Good local sports centres. **Hardship funds:** Some funds available. **Travel:** STA branch in SU. **Work:** Bar and stewarding work in SU. Student ambassador scheme.

INFORMAL NAME   QMW.

ALUMNI (EDITORS' PICK)   Peter Hain, Geoffrey Drain, Sir Roy Strong, Judge Alan Lipfriend, Rhys Williams, Dr Adam Neville, Lady Falkender, Ruth Prawer Jhabvala, Malcolm Bradbury, Andrea Newman, Simon Gray, Christopher Holmes, Mel Gingell, Patrick Moore, Dr Paul Dean, Sir Norman Lindop, Elizabeth Andrews, Bruce Dickinson (formerly of Iron Maiden).

RADA

Royal Academy of Dramatic Art, 62–64 Gower Street, London WC1E 6ED
(Tel 0171 636 7076, Fax 0171 323 3865) Map 6

STUDENT ENQUIRIES: Admissions
APPLICATIONS: Direct.

Broad study areas: Drama. (Subject details are in the *Subjects and Places Index*.)

Founded: 1904, by Sir Herbert eerbohm Tree; Royal Charter in 1920. **Main awards:** Diploma, Honours Diploma. **Awarding body:** RADA. **Site:** Gower St and Chenies St, in heart of London University area. **Access:** Central site, close to bus routes and several tube stations. **Academic features:** Acting course and stage management courses. **Library:** 17,000 volumes, 10 periodicals; video-tape library. Annual expenditure on library materials, £150 per FTE student. **Specialist collections:** G B Shaw collection. **Welfare:** Access to all essential services. **Careers:** Information, advice and placement service. **Amenities:** Three fully-equipped theatres, the Vanbrugh, the GS and Studio 14; broadcasting studio, scenery and property workshops, design office and wardrobe, common rooms, canteen, bar.

Accommodation: There is no Academy accommodation. **Hardship funds:** Bursary fund.

Duration of diploma courses: 9 terms (acting); **others:** 6 terms (stage management), 4 terms (specialist technical training). **Total diploma students 1995/96:** 145. **Overseas students:** 14. **Mature students:** 20. **Male/female ratio:** 1:1. **Teaching staff:** 18 full-time, 80 part-time. **Total full-time students 1995/96:** 145. **Tuition fees:** Students, paying their own fees in 1996/97, paid £7,440.

WHAT IT'S LIKE   Acting, stage management and technical courses all very demanding and the hours are long. But then RADA training is possibly the best in the world. Because of this, very large numbers apply each year; selection is by audition or interview. Links to the profession are good – guest designers and directors work on all final year productions. Agents and casting directors keep a watchful eye over final year acting students, while second year stage managers spend half a term on secondment, working with professionals. RADA life is not cheap; local authorities are unlikely to pay the fees. Martin Sutherland
PAUPER NOTES   **Accommodation:** No London accommodation is cheap; but is always plenty to choose from nearby. **Drink:** Bar on site; local actor and stage management bars. **Eats:** Canteen on site, cheap subsidised food. Access to West End eateries. **Ents:** In-house shows are free, also some other productions. Usual London nightlife. **Sports:** Local YCA etc. **Hardship funds:** Very limited.
ALUMNI (EDITORS' PICK) Alan Bates, Sir John Gielgud, Dame Flora Robson, Susannah York, Sir Richard Attenborough, Glenda Jackson, Joan Collins, Ben Cross, Robert Lindsay, Lisa Eichhorn, Jonathan Pryce, Juliet Stevenson, Kenneth Branagh, Anton Lesser, John Hurt, Richard Briers, Albert Finney, Anthony Hopkins, Sir Anthony Quayle.

RAVENSBOURNE COLLEGE

Ravensbourne College of Design and Communication,
Walden Road, Elmstead Woods, Chislehurst, Kent BR7 5SN
(Tel 0181 289 4900, Fax 0181 325 8320) Map 5

STUDENT ENQUIRIES: Admissions Officer
APPLICATIONS: UCAS

Broad study areas: Design, broadcasting, multimedia. (Subject details are in the *Subjects and Places Index*.)

Founded: 1962, incorporating Bromley and Beckenham colleges of art. **Main undergraduate award:** BA. **Awarding body:** Sussex University. **Site:** 18-acre main site, a mile from Chislehurst. **Access:** British Rail from Charing Cross to Elmstead Woods. **Europe:** No languages taught. 6 formal exchange links in EU. **Library:** 30,000 volumes in total, 180 periodicals; slide library. **Other learning facilities:** Desktop publishing and computer image generation laboratories. Broadcast studios equipped to industry standard. Internet and JANET. Quantel suite. **Careers:** Information and advice service. **Amenities:** All workshops necessary for art and design courses (plus process and dye labs, printing rooms, etc); SU bar; television studios/facilities. **Sporting facilities:** Links with local sports centres and health clubs.

Accommodation: In 1995/96, 18% of all students in college accommodation, 70% of first years. 92 self-catering places available (preference given to first years), £50 per week, term time only. Students live in privately owned accommodation for 2–3 years: rents £30–£55 per week for self-catering. **Hardship funds:** Total available in 1995/96: £23,000 government access funds, 92 students helped.

Duration of first degree courses: 3 years. **Total first degree students 1995/96:** 415. **Overseas students:** 44. **Male/female ratio:** 3:1. **Teaching staff:** 34 full-time, 60 part-time. **Total full-time students 1995/96:** 638. **First degree tuition fees:** Home students, paying their own fees in 1996/97, paid £1,600; Overseas students £6,000.

WHAT IT'S LIKE   The town is quiet, with few local pubs. The word nightlife wasn't around when Chislehurst was built, so students make their own: party, party! The college has a good atmosphere. SU bar is packed on event nights (Tuesdays and Thursdays). SU puts on bands (Indie to R&B, funk to house), all kinds of discos, barn dances, fancy dress extravaganzas and pub sing-along nights. The main attraction is the cheap beer, happy hours, and a friendly atmosphere; there's also a film club. Easy access to London, only 15 minutes by train. Bromley is close with pubs (not too bad) and leisure centre; nice, not too expensive. College very relaxed until degree shows approach. Good reputation in industry. Because of small number of students, there's a lot of inter-departmental co-operation and everyone gets to know one another. Counselling tutor on hand two days a week. SU small but with more than ¾ of college involved, it's active politically as well as socially. At Ravensbourne you get out what you put in!

PAUPER NOTES   **Accommodation:** Not all 1st years in college housing, so get to know one and crash out there. College accommodation list ever increasing for new students. **Drink:** SU bar excellent, cheapest around. Excellent atmosphere. Quite a few good local pubs, bit expensive compared to bar. **Eats:** Good, cheap food in canteen eg £1–£2 for a filling hot lunch; vegetarians well catered for. Chislehurst – not much use for students; few bars and cafés. Bromley best bet for fast food. **Ents:** SU event nights, cheap, sometimes free, entry. Film club. Not a lot outside college – only cinemas and pubs. **Sports:** No on-site sports. Excellent sports centre in Bromley, 10 mins by bus. **Hardship fund:** Access fund available once a year – only given to those who really need it. **Travel:** Good bus and trains – night buses from London. **Work:** Local shops.

INFORMAL NAME   RCDC.

ALUMNI (EDITORS' PICK)   Karen Franklin (Clothes Show); Maria Cornego (fashion designer).

HOW TO START? *SEE SHORTLISTING*, PAGE 535

READING UNIVERSITY

University of Reading, Whiteknights, Reading RG6 6AH
(Tel 0118 987 5123, Fax 0118 931 4404) Map 4

STUDENT ENQUIRIES: Sub-Dean of Faculty
APPLICATIONS: UCAS

Broad study areas: Arts, social sciences, law, pure and applied sciences, engineering, agriculture, food studies, surveying, education. (Subject details are in the *Subjects and Places Index*.)

Founded: 1892. **Main undergraduate awards:** BA, BSc, BEng, LLB, BA(BEd), MMath, MPhys, MChem, MEng. **Awarding body:** Reading University. **Site:** Whiteknights Campus, 300 acres 1½ miles from centre of Reading; also buildings at Bulmershe Court, a mile away. **Access:** Easy access to 4; frequent bus service from campus to town. Good trains and buses to London and elsewhere. **Europe:** 10% first degree students take a language as part of course and 9% spend 6 months or more abroad. Languages available in a wide range of courses. Formal exchange links with over 42 universities/colleges in all EU countries, most open to non-language specialists. **Library:** Main library with 700,000 volumes; extra copies of course books most in demand kept in reserve collection; various faculty libraries including education (300,000 volumes). Annual expenditure on library materials, £88 per FTE student. **Specialist collections:** Overstone Library (economics, literature and history); Stenton Library (history); Cole Library of early medicine and zoology; Finzi poetry collection. **Other learning facilities:** Computer centre; university museums (English rural life, Greek archaeology, and zoology), language laboratories (university-wide language programme). **Welfare:** Counselling, study adviser, overseas student adviser and health centre with doctors, dentists and psychiatrist; tutor system, mature student group, nightline, legal advice (through SU), chaplains. **Careers:** Advisory service. **Amenities:** Union building with bars, shops, travel and insurance services etc; many athletic and social clubs; boathouses on Thames; sailing and canoeing on Thames and nearby gravel pits; sports hall. Reading film theatre, bookshop, banks, playing fields on the campus, playgroup, nursery.

Accommodation: In 1995/96, 44% of all students in university accommodation, 90% of first years. 4,700 places available (3,300 for first years): 3,000 full-board places (2,000 first years) from £68 per week and 1,700 self-catering (1,100 first years) from £40, term time or longer. Students live in privately owned accommodation for 1–2 years: rents £35–£40 per week for self-catering, c£47 for B&B. Private accommodation plentiful in area. **Term time work**: University's policy to allow term time work for full-time first degree students (25% believed to work). Term (and vac) work occasionally available on campus. **Hardship funds:** Total available in 1995/96: £180,000 government access funds, 400 students helped; own funds as required, 50 students helped in 1995/96. Special help: those with children (esp single parents), self-financing and mature students; own funds also available to self-financing overseas students.

Duration of first degree courses: 3 years; 4 years (languages, art, food technology, typography, undergraduate masters and sandwich courses). **Total first degree students 1995/96:**

7,754. **Overseas students:** 1,324. **Mature students:** 24%. **Male/female ratio:** 1:1. **Teaching staff:** approx 700 full-time, 30 part-time. **Total full-time students 1994/94:** 9,720. **Postgraduate students:** 4,566. **First degree tuition fees:** Home students, paying their own fees in 1996/97, paid £750 (classroom), £1,600 (lab/studio); Overseas students £6,120 (classroom), £7,920 (lab/studio).

WHAT IT'S LIKE Situated on the edge of the town; mainly on the Whiteknights Park, an open, green campus. Reading is reasonably orientated towards students; its main virtue is its proximity to London and Oxford, but it has good shopping facilities and excellent rail, coach and motorway connections. Inter-site travel poor but at night the SU provides free transport between sites. Getting about during the rush hour is a problem. ore accommodation being built to house increased student numbers; conference-standard so more expensive. Most first years able to live in (guaranteed a place in hall if you put Reading as first choice). Overseas students get some priority over self-catering but not accommodation in general. Reading not cheap. SU has good facilities; not very political; good on welfare, excellent for sporting and non-sporting clubs (over 200 clubs/societies). It provides entertainments and services with cheap bars, shops and a very thorough student welfare service. JCRs are strong in halls. Most activities found on campus. SU central on campus, runs mini markets in SU; 4 bars; safety bus for evening transport. Disability awareness (good support network, accommodation priority, special arrangements for exams, flat campus though access to buildings variable). Courses vary: some very specialised eg land management, meteorology; others, increasingly, modular. Flexibility in first year to change subjects. Workload realistic. Life at university and Reading is largely what you make it.
PAUPER NOTES **Accommodation:** 14 halls of residence, student houses (self-catering limited but increasing). Student flats. Married quarters. **Drink:** All halls have a bar (cheaper than pubs, more expensive than union). SU has 3 bars at main site; one at Bulmershe. Various local pubs but expensive. **Eats:** Reasonable service offered by university. Union outlets serve cheap snacks, hot and cold plus vegetarian. Usual takeaways and some restaurants in town. **Ents:** Comprehensive and varied ents programme – some live music, weekly discos and free bar band nights in SU. Film theatre on campus (2 films/week). **Sports:** Sports centre on campus. Cheap sports sales in SU. Some swimming pools give NUS discount. 100+ sports clubs (football good). **Hardship fund:** Access fund. Help from SU welfare office to find money from trusts. **Travel:** Easy to hitch to and from. Excellent travel office gives student fares. Good communications but very busy at peak times. **Work:** Work in SU bar, catering and security. Some part-time jobs available, temping during the summer.
BUZZ-WORDS The Ath Pav (The Athletic Pavilion where SU sports clubs have a drink after matches).
ALUMNI (EDITORS' PICK) Andy Mackay (composer and performer, Roxy Music), Baroness Pike (chairman, Broadcasting Complaints Commission), Sir Richard Trehane (ex-ilk Marketing Board), Steve Vines (Observer labour editor), Gillian Freeman (novelist and biographer), Phil Vesty (Olympic walker), Richard Livsey (Liberal MP for Brecon), Clive Ponting (former civil servant), Elspeth Huxley (writer), Sir Noel Stockdale (chairman ASDA/FI group), Susanne Charlton (BBC weatherperson), Jennie Orpwood (disabled Olympic swimmer).

GET HOLD OF THE PROSPECTUSES

RIPON & YORK ST JOHN

University College of Ripon & York St John, The College,
Lord Mayor's Walk, York YO3 7EX
(Tel 01904 656771, Fax 01904 612512) Map 2

STUDENT ENQUIRIES: Assistant Registrar Admissions
APPLICATIONS: UCAS

Broad study areas: Education, humanities, occupational therapy, performing arts, social sciences. (Subject details are in the *Subjects and Places Index.*)

Founded: 1975, from amalgamation of St John's College York and The College Ripon. **Main undergraduate awards:** BA, BSc, BA/BSc (QTS), BHSc. **Awarding body:** Leeds University. **Site:** Two campuses, 25 miles apart, close to centres of Ripon and York. **Access:** Good road and rail links: A1, M1, M62. Regular inter-site campus buses. **Special features:** Modular degrees on semester pattern. Exchange schemes with North America and Canada. **Europe:** 8% first degree students take a language as part of course and spend 6 months or more abroad. Formal exchange links with 16 European universities/colleges. **Library:** Library on each site; 175,000 volumes, 600+ periodicals, 400 study places, course books for reference and loan, on-line searches. Annual expenditure on library materials, £51 per FTE student. **Specialist collections:** 19th-century children's books. Local studies collection. **Other learning facilities:** New learning resource area; religious education centre, AV materials, slide and record library; CCTV unit and video equipment, dance studios, computing facilities on both campuses. **Welfare:** Doctors, dentists, 2 chaplains. Chapel on each campus. **Careers:** Information, advice and placement. **Amenities:** SU both sites – bars, coffee bars, shops. **Sporting facilities:** Gymnasia, Olympic standard pool, squash courts, dry-slope skiing, extensive playing fields.

Accommodation: In 1995/96, 34% of all students were in college accommodation (71% of first years). 1,199 places available: 789 full board in hall (399 at York, 390 at Ripon), £62–£67 per week; 410 self-catering places in college houses/flats in York; lodgings at both sites. **Term time work:** College's policy to allow term time work for full-time first degree students. No term time work available on campus but some summer work during clearing; college job club helps find vac work . **Hardship funds:** Total available in 1995/96: £48,465 government access funds, 143 students helped; £950 other funds, 6 students helped.

Duration of first degree courses: 3 years; **others:** 4 years BA/BSc(QTS). **Total first degree students 1995/96:** 3,100. **BA/BSc(QTS) students:** 758. **Male/female ratio:** 1:3. **Teaching staff:** 142 full-time. **Total full-time students 1995/96:** 3,215. **Postgraduate students:** 135. **First degree tuition fees:** Home students, paying their own fees in 1996/97, paid £1,885 (classroom), £2,770 (lab/studio). Overseas students £5,120 (classroom), £7,490 (lab/studio).

WHAT IT'S LIKE   As the name suggests, it is based partly in York, partly in Ripon. Main campus in York, just outside city walls has clear view of the Minster; 5 sites around the city – 3 residential. Ripon campus 25 miles away is much quieter, set in spacious grounds;

good community relations. Minibus service links the two campuses 4 times daily. All new students accommodated in halls (21-meal package included in residence fees and kitchen areas provided). College also rents other houses and has built new self-catering flats and houses (The Grange) for over 400 students. York rents rising. ore women than men (more pronounced at Ripon). Mature students steadily increasing, and there is 15 place crèche on York site. Exchange programmes to both Europe and America every year; gives an international flavour to campus. Well-developed SU provides variety of clubs and societies, entertainments, welfare services, two shops, two bars, part and full-time staff. Focal point for social life, some political activity, much apathy. Professional counselling network on both campuses, run by staff and students. College as a whole has a very friendly atmosphere. York has much to offer: top tourist city with 365 pubs, clubs, restaurants, two theatres, arts centre, a 12-screen cinema, market, art gallery, bowling alley, monuments, museums. London is 2 hrs by train. Limited car parking but car not really necessary. Ripon is very different: a quiet market town with pubs, market, restaurants; no train station but regular buses to Harrogate. Well-regarded courses, mostly modular; low drop-out rate. Attracts students from all over Britain, most from comprehensives or colleges of FE. Overall picture is one of healthy academic development with much social interaction.

PAUPER NOTES **Accommodation:** College housing for all new students; outside accommodation provided by college and housing agencies. **Drink:** SU only cheap place. Yorkshire home of good beer. **Eats:** *York* – anything at any price; *Ripon* – Valentino's cheap Italian, Indian, Dominic's nice but pricey. Special discount in over 50 places in Ripon and York arranged by SU. **Ents:** *York* – Theatre Royal, cinema, Fibbes (live music), May Horse, Gillygate (sponsors sports teams). **Sports:** *York* – on campus pool, squash courts, 2 gymnasia 5 minutes walk. *Ripon* – on-site gym, pool in city. Harrogate for further facilities. **Hardship funds:** Access fund, childcare fund (very limited but well used), number of funds to help those in trouble (eg abortion fund). **Travel:** *York* – main line InterCity, 2 hrs to London. *Ripon* – bus to Harrogate and Leeds. **Work:** Campus vacation work and much local work in Ripon and York (pubs and clubs).

ALUMNI (EDITORS' PICK)   Jeff Squires, Geoff Cooke.

ROBERT GORDON UNIVERSITY

The Robert Gordon University, Schoolhill, Aberdeen AB10 1FR (Tel 01224 262000, Fax 01224 262133) Map 1

STUDENT ENQUIRIES: Admissions Office
APPLICATIONS: UCAS

Broad study areas: Architecture, art & design, business, computing, surveying, engineering, applied sciences, food and consumer studies, applied social studies, information studies and librarianship, professions allied to medicine. (Subject details are in the *Subjects and Places Index.*)

Founded: 1750, Robert Gordon Institute became a university in 1992. **Main undergraduate awards:** BA, BSc, BEng. **Awarding body:** Robert Gordon University. **Site:** 8 sites in or near city centre. **Special features:** Semester system. 1 year exchange programmes with Oregon State University and Illinois Institute of Technology. **Europe:** 7% first degree students learn a language as part of their course and 4% spend 6 months or more abroad. Languages incorporated into a number of degrees. Number of formal EU exchange links, all open to non-specialists. **Library:** 160,000 volumes in total, 1,400 periodicals, 620 study places. Annual expenditure on library materials, £104 per FTE student. **Welfare:** Accommodation officer, student counsellors, careers officers, English lanaguage tutor, chaplaincy, medical advisory service, nursery. **Careers:** Information and advice service. **Amenities:** SA with bars, games room, shop, laundrette. **Sporting facilities:** Facilities available at Kepplestone.

Accommodation: In 1995/96, 25% of all students in university accommodation, 80% of first years. 1,600 places available (1,100+ for first years): 130 full-board places (all first years) at £52.57 per week and 1,300 self-catering (970 first years) at £37–£58 per week, Sept–May; 150 places in direct leased flats, university managed, £40–£60 per week, year-long contracts. Privately owned accommodation: rents £40–£60 per week for self-catering or B&B, £50–£65 for half-board. 45% of first degree students live at home. **Term time work:** University's policy to allow term time work for full-time first degree students (high percentage believed to work). Term (and vac) work available on campus as janitors, porters, ground staff. **Hardship funds:** Total available in 1995/96: £139,076 government access funds, 364 students helped; £48,675 own funds, 1,050 helped. Special help: students with high accommodation costs, mature students with child care costs, final year, self-financing, personal or medical costs etc.

Duration of first degree courses: 3 years (ordinary), 4 years (honours); **others:** sandwich courses 5 years for honours. **Total first degree students 1995/96:** 5,271. **Overseas students:** 305. **Mature students:** 20%. **Male/female ratio:** 1:1. **Teaching staff:** 320 full-time. **Total full-time students 1995/96:** 6,300. **Postgraduate students:** 481. **First degree tuition fees:** Home students, paying their own fees in 1996/97, paid £750 (classroom), £1,350 (lab/studio); Overseas students £5,000 (classroom), £6,500–£9,750 (lab/studio).

WHAT IT'S LIKE   It's spread over six sites throughout the city. Large student population locally and RGU students mix easily with those from Aberdeen University, ACFE and Northern College. Courses range from fine art to mechanical and offshore engineering with a highly practical slant on most, particularly attractive to employers. Relatively easy to change from ordinary degrees to honours and vice versa. Assessment varies from course to course but exams play a large part, along with lab work, practical etc. SA building has a bar/disco (The Asylum), and a lounge bar/snack bar (Theos), TV room, pool room, laundry, canteen, cable TV and has over 30 clubs and societies, ranging from hockey to fencing to Chinese boxing to boardgames. SA campaigns on many student issues as well as discussing them with the governors. Produces *Cogno*, the monthly student newspaper. Students from all over UK, with quite large overseas contingent. Atmosphere hardworking, but lively, and employment prospects are good.
PAUPER NOTES   **Accommodation:** Some short-life hard-to-let flats available. **Drink:** RGU Union, Prince of Wales (real ale), Ma Cameron's, Caledon Bar (for architecture and art students). **Eats:** RGU, Littlejohns, La Lombarda (Italian). **Ents:** Aberdeen Exhibition and Conference Centre for more famous bands, and Capitol and Music Hall for smaller but well known. SA ents, Odeon/Cannon cinemas, HM Theatre (occasional student discounts), lively student clubs, Ritzy on a Monday night, the Pelican Club. **Sports:** SA clubs and societies, RGU swimming pool; Aberdeen Leisure Centre (Wednesday afternoons). **Hardship funds:**

Several university-run funds. **Travel:** BR railcard. CampusTravel on site. **Work:** Usual part time jobs in bars, tutoring, babysitting and local shops.
MORE INFO? Enquiries to SA President (01224 262262).

ROEHAMPTON INSTITUTE

Roehampton Institute London, Roehampton Lane, London
SW15 5PU (Tel 0181 392 3000, Fax 0181 392 3131) Map 5

STUDENT ENQUIRIES: Admissions Officer
APPLICATIONS: UCAS

Broad study areas: Arts and humanities, education, science, social sciences. (Subject details are in the *Subjects and Places Index.*)

Founded: 1975, incorporating Digby Stuart (1874), Froebel Institute (1892), Southlands (1872) and Whitelands Colleges (1841). **Structural features:** An institute of Surrey University. **Main undergraduate awards:** BA, BA(QTS), BSc, BMus. **Awarding body:** Surrey University. **Site:** 2 sites in Putney/Roehampton area: 3 colleges in Roehampton Lane (Digby Stuart, Froebel and Sutherland); Whitlands on West Hill in Putney. **Access:** Bus, train and underground. **Academic features:** Most degrees are combinations of 2 subjects (over 600 possible combinations). **Europe:** 5% first degree students take a language as part of course and 8% spend 6 months or more abroad. Language tuition available to all students. 14 formal EU exchange links, for language students only. **Library:** Library at each site; 350,000 volumes in total, 1,500 periodicals, 500 study places. Annual expenditure on library materials, £84.33 per FTE student. **Specialist collections:** Early childhood and children's literature archives. **Welfare:** Welfare officer, doctor, medical centre, counsellors, chaplains, dyslexia support unit. **Careers:** Counsellor on site. **Amenities:** SU building at each site, recreation officer. **Sporting facilities:** Facilities in and near colleges for wide variety of sports.

Accommodation: In 1995/96, 23% of all students in institute accommodation, 75% of first years. 1,065 places available at either £70 per week (including fuel and 12 meals a week) or £57–£60 per week (self-catering), term time only. Students live in privately owned accommodation for 2 years, average £55 per week, self-catering. **Term time work:** Institute's policy to allow term time work for full-time first degree students. Term (and vac) work available on campus in bars, catering, office, library, conferences etc (students employed wherever possible); also SU employment service helps find work outside the institute. **Hardship funds:** Total available in 1995/96: £171,300 government access funds, 744 students helped; also £10,000 own funds.

Duration of first degree courses: 3 years; 4 years (BA(QTS) and BA with languages); 5 years BA(QTS) with languages. **Total first degree students 1995/96:** 4,800 full time, 300 part time. **BA(QTS) students:** 1,100. **Overseas students:** 250. **Mature students:** 37%. **Male/female ratio:** 1:3. **Teaching staff:** 300. **Total full-time students 1995/96:** 5,250. **Postgraduate students:**

1,000. **First degree tuition fees:** Home students, paying their own fees in 1996/97, paid £750 (classroom), £1,600 (lab/studio); Overseas students £5,373 (classroom), £7,122 (lab/studio); plus £340 once-only validation fee.

WHAT IT'S LIKE   Made up from four colleges in south west London: Whitelands, Froebel, Digby Stuart and Southlands. Whitelands is at West Hill, south east of Putney; the other three are all along Roehampton Lane, about 2 miles away. Each has a unique identity, creating its own friendly atmosphere, while at the same time, students can benefit from being part of a larger institution. Three colleges have religious affiliations but allow their students to choose whether or not to be involved. Teaching takes place in all four colleges (a free bus service). Institute accommodation for most first years and those third years that want it; good accommodation office helps other students. Geographically it's well placed to get the best from one of the biggest cities in the world (only 20 minutes from the centre), but far enough away not to be affected by the rat race of central London. Wimbledon, Putney, Kingston and Richmond are all close by for shopping, working or socialising. SU is very active and provides plenty of entertainment, welfare and activities that cater for all: weekly discos, bar games and events across the Institute. The sports and societies are well established: range of activities with the football and rugby teams being particularly successful. Institute has a range of student services, including counselling, accommodation and finance advice and a health centre.

PAUPER NOTES   **Accommodation:** Institute accommodation for most 1st and some 3rd years. **Drink:** 4 bars; prices pretty low for London. **Eats:** Not bad in residence; vegetarians catered for. Lots of places to eat outside, and some deliver free. **Ents:** Local cinemas, clubs, theatres; and all of London. **Hardship fund:** Some available. **Sports:** Well-established field sports. Amateur sport encouraged. **Travel:** BR (arnes Station). Good buses. Hitching not recommended. **Work:** Jobs in the bar; work available in Putney and Richmond. SU runs agency for part-time jobs.

ALUMNI (EDITORS' PICK)   Ashley Ward (English athletics international), Vivien Leigh.

ROSE BRUFORD COLLEGE

Rose Bruford College, Lamorbey Park, Sidcup, Kent
DA15 9DF (Tel 0181 300 3024, Fax 0181 308 0542,
E-mail admiss@bruford.ac.uk) Map 5

STUDENT ENQUIRIES: Admissions office
APPLICATIONS: UCAS

Broad study areas: Drama, theatre arts, music technology, theatre design. (Subject details are in the *Subjects and Places Index*.)

Founded: By Rose Bruford in 1950. **Main undergraduate award:** BA. **Awarding body:** Manchester University. **Site:** 2 sites: Lamorbey Park (Sidcup, Kent), and Greenwich (London). **Access:** Sidcup site 25 min by train from London, 15 mins from Greenwich; easy access from A20/20 or A2/2. Greenwich site near trains, buses, underground. **Academic**

features: Courses on a wide range of aspects of theatre – acting, actor-musicianship, directing, design, stage management, lighting design etc. Degrees accredited by National Council for Drama Training. **Special features:** Visiting students from Portugal and Texas; links with the Central Academy of Drama, Bejing. **Europe:** No students learn a language. Formal links in Portugal. **Library:** 30,000 books, 12,000 slides, 100 periodicals, 30 reading places. **Other learning facilities:** Audiovisual and photocopying facilities; tuition in library use and research methods; Internet and JANET connections. **Welfare:** Welfare officer on site; local doctors and dentists. **Careers:** Agents, theatre managers and related employers invited to college productions. Professional placements. **Amenities:** Barn theatre, new 450-seat theatre in the round. Extensive grounds at Sidcup; canteen and common room at both sites.

Accommodation: Halls of residence at both sites. Privately owned accommodation £50–£60 per week for self-catering. Approx 2% students live at home. **Hardship funds:** Total available in 1995/96: £8,000 government access funds, average £300 awarded. Some bursaries available.

Duration of first degree courses: 3 years. **Total first degree students 1995/96:** 480. **Overseas students:** 48. **Male/female ratio:** 1:2. **Teaching staff:** 16 full-time, and large number of visiting tutors. **Total full-time students 1995/96:** 355. **First degree tuition fees:** Home and overseas students, paying their own fees in 1996/97, paid £7,000.

WHAT IT'S LIKE Set over two sites in south east London, the college offers a wide range of degree courses spanning all aspects of theatrical work. Sidcup site is set in an attractive park that is good to work in; Greenwich campus houses large rehearsal spaces and workshops for other forms of work. Most students are timetabled for at least 30 hours a week, which increases for those involved in college productions. These take place either in the Barn Theatre in Sidcup or at Greenwich. One London season a year: college hires a West End venue to showcase the students' work. College tries to recreate the atmosphere of a full working theatre so many hours are spent on practical work. Alongside this there is an academic side to the course so most students leave with a thorough understanding of the industry they are entering. Course is very draining but there is a good sense of unity and usually the 'buzz' outweighs the tiredness. The SU exists to help students through problems and to try and create a good social life for everyone, which culminates in an annual Summer Ball. As the college is small, union reps have to contend with a full time course and organising the union. This does mean that the union is disadvantaged but it manages to get along. Three years at Rose Bruford are hectic but happy and the unsociable hours and heavy workload prepare students fully for a career in the world of theatre.
PAUPER NOTES **Accommodation:** Most students rent houses or lodge with local families. **Drink:** Ye Olde Black Horse (Sidcup), The Spotted Cow (Hither Green), The Duke (Creek Road site). **Eats:** Canteens on both sites; McDonald's etc nearby. **Ents:** Close to central London for all types of ents; college shows every term. **Sports:** Good local facilities nearby. **Hardship funds:** College trust funds. **Travel:** College refunds course travel expenses. **Work:** Working during term time is difficult with the long hours. Holiday jobs essential.
INFORMAL NAME RBC, Bruford's, Bru's.
ALUMNI (EDITORS' PICK) Freddie Jones, Pam St Clement, Tom Baker, Nerys Hughes, Angharad Rees, Barbara Kellerman, Gary Oldman, Emma Wray, Janet Dibley, Jon Iles, Diane Louise Jordan, Cathy Shippton, Barry Kilerby (Mr Blobby).

ROYAL ACADEMY OF MUSIC

Royal Academy of Music, Marylebone Road, London
NW1 5HT (Tel 0171 873 7373, Fax 0171 873 7374) Map 6

STUDENT ENQUIRIES: Academic Registrar
APPLICATIONS: Direct

Broad study areas: Music.

Founded: 1822. **Main awards:** BMus(Perf), Diploma of Advanced Studies, MMus. **Awarding bodies:** Royal Academy of Music and London University. **Site:** Central London. **Access:** Baker Street or Regent's Park underground stations. **Special features:** Many distinguished visiting musicians eg Alberni Quartet. Six international chairs – Bruno Giuranna (viola studies), Christopher Hogwood (historical performance), Sir Colin Davis (conducting and orchestral studies), Empire Brass (brass studies), Richard Rodney Bennett (composition and contemporary music), Robert Tear (vocal studies). International composer festivals. **Academic features:** Joint vocal faculty with Royal College of Music. **Europe:** Language tuition available for all undergraduates; required for opera and singing students. Formal exchange links with conservatoires in Europe (as well as USA and Australia). Member of a consortium of 18 leading European conservatoires established to set up a permanent exchange programme. **Library:** approx 175,000 items in total, 40 periodicals and approx 10,000 books. **Specialist collections:** Sir Henry Wood, Sullivan Archive and Otto Klemperer collections of orchestral scores. **Welfare:** Student services; counsellor. **Careers:** Information and advice. **Amenities:** Local music shop within a few yards; refurbished concert hall, opera theatre; 5 organs; RAM Magazine; canteen, students' club (licensed); social facilities.

Accommodation: Access to London University halls of residence. 1% of first degree students live at home. **Term time work:** College policy to allow term time work for first degree students (30% believed to work). Term work available in college bars, offices, library, security and fire stewarding; adverts for jobs elsewhere on noticeboards. **Hardship funds:** Substantial awards and funds available, particularly for postgraduate students.

Duration of first degree and equivalent courses: 4 years. **Total first degree students 1995/96:** 280. **Overseas students:** 24. **Mature students:** 25. **Male/female ratio:** 9:11. **Teaching staff:** 7 full-time, 103 part-time. **Total full-time students 1995/96:** 518. **Postgraduate students:** 177. **First degree tuition fees:** Home students, paying their own fees in 1996/97, paid £1,600 (£3,400–£3,600 for other courses); Overseas: £9,100 (£8,800–£10,500 for other courses).

WHAT IT'S LIKE   Housed in a classic sandstone Victorian building along Marylebone Road, the Academy has an extremely vibrant atmosphere. It's in the heart of London; all students live out – mainly in shared flats/houses around north London, which can make for a bit of a journey into college. All undergrads enter the BMus performance course – it's very demanding but assures a good degree and high level of performance after 4 years. Practice the order of the day (every day!) for students looking to make the grade as professional musicians. Excellent tuition from some of the finest members of the profession. Very exciting programme of concerts and masterclasses. No average type of student – except the one with a genuine love of, and energy for, music. Many overseas/postgrad students. The RAM has an ever-developing social life in college: freshers' week; regular jazz nights, parties, karaoke … Most students also enjoy a good social life outside college. Definitely the place to be if you hope to become a performing musician.

PAUPER NOTES Accommodation: RAM accommodation officer very helpful – plans for new hall of residence in pipeline. **Drink:** RAM bar reasonably priced – and 7 pubs within 100 yards. **Eats:** Excellent food at reasonable prices at RAM restaurant. Good snacks etc locally. **Ents:** Free jazz nights; film soc; termly Ball. Very close to West End; many excellent student offers on concerts etc throughout London. **Sports:** Football team (plays against other music colleges, local banks etc); excellent ULU facilities close by. **Hardship fund:** Admin always willing to listen. Various forms of assistance. **Travel:** Erasmus scheme and award system for summer schools. **Work:** Many gigs and teaching jobs (make sure people know of your existence). Bar work and concert stewarding at RAM, £3/hr (concert work through RAM's own concert secretary). It is expensive to be a music student in London so many students need paid work.

INFORMAL NAME RAM.

MORE INFO? Enquiries to SU president (0171 837 7337).

ROYAL ACADEMY SCHOOLS

Royal Academy of Arts, Piccadilly, London W1V 0DS
(Tel 0171 439 7438, Fax 0171 434 0837) Map 6

STUDENT ENQUIRIES: Secretary
APPLICATIONS: Direct

Broad study areas *(not at first degree level)*: Painting, sculpture.

Founded: 1768. **Structural features:** A post-graduate institution. **Main award:** Postgraduate diploma. **Awarding body:** Royal Academy Schools. **Site:** Piccadilly. **Access:** Green Park and Piccadilly underground stations; various buses. **Academic features:** All courses are of 3 years' duration, with annual examinations; the majority of teaching is done by visiting tutors. **Library:** 15,000 volumes, various periodicals. **Specialist collections:** Old master drawings/prints. **Welfare:** Chaplain. **Careers:** Advice service. **Amenities:** Shop, canteen

Accommodation: Schools' secretary will advise. **Funding:** Scholarships and bursaries (state and private) available.

Duration of courses: 3 years. **Total full-time students 1995/96:** 60, all postgraduate. **Tuition fees:** Home and overseas students, paying their own fees in 1996/97, paid £6,400.

WHAT IT'S LIKE In the West End, behind the Academy Gallery and next to the Museum of Mankind (entrance via Burlington Gardens). It's the only full-time 3-year, postgraduate course in the country; an independent college, not state-run. Schools are focused on painting and sculpture (intake of approximately 15 painters, 3–4 sculptors a year), printmaking a related study. Students encouraged to follow their own creative star. For first year painters there is an introductory study period where the importance of drawing is emphasised. Each student has a personal working space. Wide variety of artist teachers; each student has two personal tutors and a limited choice on majority vote to invite staff of their choosing. Being in central London, very good access to all the large galleries and many independent galleries such as those in Cork Street are a few moments away; possibilities for seeing all kinds of art work are vast. Free entrance to RA exhibitions. A small bar in the canteen and parties can be arranged. The Royal Academy Schools are basically a set of studio spaces with regular tutoring, but being a small institution it does not operate in the same way that other colleges do. As a result, students are not hampered by the machinations of a larger college or university and there is more room for student influence in the running of the school. Visiting hours are 1pm–2pm or 4–4.30pm.

PAUPER NOTES   **Drink:** Subsidised real ale at college bar. **Eats:** Canteen very cheap by London standards. Plenty of cheap alternatives in area. **Ents:** Free admission to all RA exhibitions. **Grants:** DFEE money available for RA Schools fees and maintenance. **Hardship funds:** Available to those without DFEE grants. **Travel:** Travel scholarships to selected students. Occasional visits to far-away lands.

ROYAL AGRICULTURAL COLLEGE

Royal Agricultural College, Cirencester GL7 6JS
(Tel 01285 652531, Fax 01285 650219) Map 3

STUDENT ENQUIRIES: Admissions Secretary
APPLICATIONS: UCAS or direct

Broad study areas: Agriculture, rural land and estate management, equine business management, international agribusiness management. (Subject details are in the *Subjects and Places Index*.)

Founded: 1845. **Main undergraduate award:** BSc. **Awarding body:** Royal Agricultural College. **Site:** 30-acre campus, 1 mile from Cirencester. **Academic features:** New international degree including 1 year's study in New Zealand or Canada. Combination of technical and business teaching. Some courses lead to membership of Royal Institution of Chartered Surveyors (Rural Practice Division). **Europe:** 34% first degree students take a language as part of course (compulsory on international courses and equine business management course); 14% take evening language courses, open to all. 10% spend 6 months or more elsewhere in Europe, many others go worldwide. Formal exchange links with many EU universities/colleges. **Library:** 26,500 volumes, 600 periodicals, 160 study places, reference works, statistical publications, 500 videos. Annual expenditure on library materials, £82 per FTE student. **Other learning facilities:** Own farm of 770 hectares; Centre for Agriculture and Rural Skills. **Welfare:** Doctor, counselling service, student welfare officer, chaplain, personal tutors. **Careers:** Careers adviser; information, advice and placement. **Employment:** Farm, plantation, nursery and estate managment; land agency; leisure management; conservation; rural investment and advisory services; food industry; retailing, marketing and journalism. **Amenities:** Common rooms, bar, snack bar, student union shop.

Sporting facilities: Sports pitches including floodlit all-weather hockey and tennis, facilities for squash, rowing, water sports and field sports, gym.

Accommodation: In 1995/96, 40% of all students in college accommodation, 90% of first years. 260 full-board places at £70–£110 per week, term time only. Students live in privately owned accommodation for 2 years: rents £30–£45 per week for self-catering, £50–£55 for B&B, £70–£80 half-board. 1% of first degree students live at home. **Term time work:** College's policy to allow term time work for full-time first degree students (10% believed to work). Term (and vac) work available on campus in bar, waiting at dinners and farm work (vac only); some other vac jobs displayed on noticeboards. **Hardship funds:** Total available in 1995/96: £70,000, 80% of which awarded prior to course commencement. 38 college and industry-funded scholarships (up to £2,000) awarded annually.

Duration of first degree courses: 3 years or 4 years (sandwich). **Total first degree students 1995/96:** 453. **Overseas students:** 44. **Mature students:** 32. **Male/female ratio:** 2:1. **Teaching staff:** 47 full-time, 5 part-time. **Total full-time students 1995/96:** 645. **Postgraduate students:** 73. **First degree tuition fees:** In 1996/97, the fees for both home and overseas students were £4,338–£6,006 (an LEA award contributes £890 towards the fees)

WHAT IT'S LIKE   On the outskirts of Cirencester in the Cotswolds, it's a very compact campus set in private grounds. Staff are approachable and most have wide industrial and professional experience. College farms 770 hectares on a commercial basis which is used to demonstrate modern farming practice. Students, the largest percentage of whom have been privately educated, come from all over British Isles, the Commonwealth and other overseas countries. Significant mature student population. College helps find holiday work and jobs for graduates. Legendary social scene with the May Ball a highlight. Self-discipline a help when it comes to coping with the excellent social life (provided by the SU) and keeping abreast with academic workload. Locally, there are pubs that tolerate students and then there are non-student pubs. The college does not involve itself in politics. Exceptional former student network and life membership of the former student association (RACA).

PAUPER NOTES   **Accommodation:** Single study bedrooms in college (refurbished). Digs, cottages, flats in Ciren area. **Drink:** Good college pubs: The Crown, The Tunnel, The Nelson and Walter Mitty's. College bar not subsidised but good meeting place. **Eats:** College food reasonably priced and good (£2.30 for 3-course meal). Good local places: Harry Hare's, Tatyan's, The Catherine Wheel, The Polo Canteen, The Wild Duck, Greasy Joe's. **Ents:** College hosts 5 formal balls during year; 'Bout-do' dances every Friday and other regular events. Students frequent Oxford, Bristol, Cheltenham and London regularly, hence most have car. **Sports:** Most sports catered for on campus, including floodlit all-weather pitch and a multi-gym, as well as locally. Very active rugby club and beagle pack. **Travel:** Bursaries available. **Work:** Term time is very difficult to find but some manage it. Paid vacation work popular for work experience especially lambing and harvesting jobs.

MORE INFO?   Enquiries to SU Chairman (01285 652531, ext 2219).

INFORMAL NAME   RAC; Cirencester; The Royal; Ciren.

ROYAL COLLEGE OF ART

Royal College of Art (RCA), Kensington Gore, London SW7
2EU (Tel 0171 584 5020, Fax 0171 584 8217) Map 6

STUDENT ENQUIRIES: Registrar (Admissions)
APPLICATIONS: Direct

Broad study areas *(postgraduate only)*: Art, design and communication.

Founded: 1837; Royal Charter in 1967. **Structural features:** A postgraduate college. **Main awards:** MA, MPhil, PhD. **Awarding body:** Royal College of Art. **Site:** Opposite Hyde Park, beside the Albert Hall. **Application:** Entry for Masters courses by competitive examination; usually about 350 places a year. Candidates, normally aged over 21 with a first degree, send in portfolios of recent work. Applications for asters and PhD by end January. **Academic features:** International reputation for work in areas from painting and sculpture to industrial design eg vehicle design and goldsmithing to communications media (film, photography and graphics). Project or thesis work, following individual student proposals, forms an essential part of degree work. PhD work may be carried out in any discipline provided resources exist; minimum period of study is 2 full-time equivalent years. **Europe:** College encourages student exchanges and all students have access to language tuition. **Bursaries:** Application for state bursaries from English and Welsh candidates through RCA (but award is not automatic). Scottish candidates apply to Scottish Education Department and Northern Irish candidates apply to Ministry of Education, Northern Ireland. (For addresses see *How to go about it*.). Home students only are eligible for UK state bursaries. **Special facilities:** 4 major galleries, seminar rooms, 2 lecture theatres.

Accommodation: No college accommodation. **Term time work:** College policy to allow term time work. Some available in college: cloakroom and selling catalogues at degree shows; bar work, help with mailings etc. **Hardship funds:** Some money available.

Duration of Master's degree course(s): 2 years. **Male/female ratio:** 1:1. **Teaching staff:** 198 full-time, 92 part-time. **Total postgraduate degree students 1995/96:** approx 800. **Tuition fees:** Home students, paying their own fees in 1996/97, paid £3,143; Overseas: £11,975.

WHAT IT'S LIKE   The only exclusively postgraduate college in Britain offering both art and design education. It is a prestigious educational institution enjoying a growing international reputation for quality. But the reality is far from glamorous: the majority of courses last for only two years so there is a lot of hard work, stress and financial hardship. Certainly the most exciting part of being an RCA student is the opportunity to meet other postgraduates and professionals from a great variety of art and design disciplines. While money, space and resources are getting tighter, at present the college is quite well funded. There is a student fund for those suffering hardship due to unforeseen circumstances, and an access fund which helps UK students with costs of accommodation and travel. It is important to realise that these will prove to be two of the most expensive years of your career. But the experience is undoubtedly worth the hardship and worry. The RCA is an exciting place to study, a place where the people are truly inspiring.

PAUPER NOTES   Accommodation: Difficult to find and expensive. No college halls, but accommodation and welfare office very helpful in finding homes with dependable land-lords and affordable rents. **Drink:** Art Bar and RCAfé – SU run so prices reasonable. **Eats:** College canteen meals and snacks, food neither great nor cheap. RCAfé has great cappuc-cinos and sandwiches. **Ents:** The Art Bar runs regular events, including jazz nights, weekly discos and big parties (Christmas, Valentine). **Sports:** Few facilities but use of Imperial College facilities. SU runs football at attersea and basketball at Imperial.
INFORMAL NAME   RCA.
ALUMNI (EDITORS' PICK) David Hockney, Peter Blake, Ian Dury, The Chapman Brothers, Henry Moore, Barbara Hepworth, Bridget Riley, Ridley Scott, Zandra Rhodes, Helen Chadwick, Edward Burra.

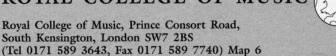

ROYAL COLLEGE OF MUSIC

Royal College of Music, Prince Consort Road,
South Kensington, London SW7 2BS
(Tel 0171 589 3643, Fax 0171 589 7740) Map 6

STUDENT ENQUIRIES: Assistant Registrar (Admissions)
APPLICATIONS: Direct

Broad study areas: Music.

Founded: 1883, by Prince of Wales (later Edward VII). **Main awards:** BMus, PgDip, MMus, DMus. **Awarding body:** Royal College of Music. **Site:** South Kensington. **Access:** South Kensington and Gloucester Road underground stations; various buses. **Academic features:** BMus with strong performance orientation. BSc physics with music, taught jointly with Imperial College. Range of postgraduate courses in performance and composition. Prizes available. **Special features:** Many visiting musicians including John Williams, George Benjamin, Evelyn Glennie, Eileen Croxford, John Lill, Mstislav Rostropovich, Dorothy DeLay (violin) and William Pleeth (cello); many master classes. College has formal relationships with many musical organisations, including exchanges in Europe, North America and Australia. **Europe:** Singers study application of French, Italian, German, Russian, Spanish. **Library:** Reference and loan collections; over 250,000 volumes, including rare early printed material and manuscripts. **Specialist collections:** Portraits of musicians. Instrument Museum. **Other learning facilities:** Extensive reference library, multimedia computing, recording studios and research facilities. **Welfare:** Welfare officer, doctor, dentist, FPA, psychiatrist, Alexander Technique, chaplain. **Careers:** Information and advice. **Amenities:** Britten Theatre, large concert hall. Nearby music shop gives 10% discount to RCM students; facilities of London University (including Imperial College swimming pool and gym).

Accommodation: In 1996/97, 45% of students in college accommodation, self-catering with practising facilities, average £60 per week; some half-board accommodation for women available nearby. Other students live in privately owned accommodation: rents £50–£70 per week for self-catering. London rents are expensive; students need to ensure no objections to practising instruments. 5% of first degree students live at home. **Term time work:** College encourages term time work for full-time first degree students – considered an important part of professional development as performers (80% believed to work). Term (and vac) work available on campus in stewarding, orchestral stage work, admin; full-time external engagements office helps find work outside college. **Hardship funds:** Total available in 1995/96: £32,000 government access funds, 180 students helped; £450,000 own funds, 120 helped. Special help: those in demonstrable need; own funds also available for those of special ability and/or meeting specific terms of bequests — some funds assigned prior to starting course.

Duration of first degree courses: 4 years. **Total first degree students 1995/96:** 380. **Overseas students:** 140. **Male/female ratio:** 3:4. **Teaching staff:** 13 full-time, 200 part-time. **Total full-time students 1995/96:** 550. **Postgraduate students:** 150. **First degree tuition fees:** Home students, paying their own fees in 1996/97, paid £1,600; Overseas students £7,900–£10,500.

WHAT IT'S LIKE For an enjoyable and productive student life, the RCM is the best music college in the country. The professors are amongst the finest teachers in the UK and the facilities are first-rate, especially the Britten Theatre. Active Students' Association ensures that life doesn't become monotonous, arranging parties, concerts, football matches and other social events. Highlights of the social calendar are Rag Week (a week of mayhem in aid of charity) and the Summer Ball. The RCM attracts students from all over the country as well as about 30% from abroad (around 50 countries represented), making for a truly cosmopolitan atmosphere. The RCM continues to produce the high standard of musical education it always has; you would be hard pushed to find a student who was not proud to be here.

PAUPER NOTES **Accommodation:** New hall of residence, offers good value accommodation with extensive practice facilities. **Drink:** Students' Bar can be a home from home, serving all manner of drinks at great prices. **Eats:** RCM canteen convenient. Better value across the road at Imperial College. **Ents:** Numerous parties and other events, plus proximity to the West End etc. **Sports:** Football team. Imperial College Sports Centre close and good value. **Hardship funds:** Scholarships and exhibitions. Access fund gives out thousands of pounds a term to the needy. RCM Society offers interest-free loans of up to £1,500 for the purchase of instruments. **Work:** Appointments Office and Development Fund offer external engagements to students.

ALUMNI (EDITORS' PICK) Holst, Britten, Tippett, R Vaughan Williams, Andrew Lloyd-Webber, Oliver Knussen, Rick Wakeman, Colin Davis, Peter Pears, Janet Baker, Barry Douglas, Julian Bream, James Galway, Gwyneth Jones, Joan Sutherland, John Lill, Elizabeth Maconchy, Neville Marriner, Sarah Walker, David Willcocks.

ROYAL FREE

Royal Free Hospital School of Medicine, University of London, Rowland Hill Street, London NW3 2PF (Tel 0171 794 0500, Fax 0171 794 3505) Map 5

STUDENT ENQUIRIES: Registrar
APPLICATIONS: UCAS

Broad study areas: Medicine.

Founded: 1874. **Structural features:** Part of London University; merging in 1998 with University College. **Main undergraduate awards:** BSc, MBBS. **Awarding body:** London University. **Site:** Hampstead. **Access:** Belsize Park underground and Hampstead Heath R stations. **Special features:** BSc course open to those who have successfully completed first 2 years of MBBS course; integration of clinical and pre-clinical teaching. **Library:** 27,000 volumes, 400 periodicals, 230 study places; reference copies of course books. **Centres of excellence:** Liver diseases, gastroenterology, neurological science, haematology, immunology. **Welfare:** Doctor, dentist, FPA, psychiatrist, chaplain, hospital chapel. **Amenities:** SU bar. **Sporting facilities:** Squash courts on site, athletics ground at Enfield.

Accommodation: In 1995/96, 20% of all students in school accommodation, 71% of first years. 79 self-catering places available (60 for first years): 30 double rooms at £50 per week, term time only; 19 single at £60 per week, year contracts. Students live in privately owned accommodation for 4 years: rents £50–£75 per week for self-catering. 10% first degree students live at home. **Term time work:** School's policy to allow term time work for full-time first degree students so long as academic work does not suffer. Term (and vac) work available on campus in student bar, library, registry (vac only); occasional locum attachments only for clinical students (attend for 48 weeks/year). **Hardship funds:** Total available in 1995/96: £33,700 government access funds, 81 students helped; negligible other funds.

Duration of first degree courses: 5 years; **other:** 6 years (intercalated BSc). **Total first degree students 1995/96:** 574. **Overseas students:** 28. **Male/female ratio:** 1:1. **Teaching staff:** 115 full-time, 28 part-time. **Total full-time students 1995/96:** 630. **Postgraduate students:** 172. **First degree tuition fees:** Home students, paying their own fees in 1996/97, paid £1,000; Overseas students £8,750 (pre-clinical), £15,450 (clinical).

WHAT IT'S LIKE   Currently all subjects are taught at Royal Free Hospital in Hampstead. But it will soon merge with University College Medical School when pre-clinical will based in Bloomsbury and clinical divided between Royal Free, University College and the Whittington Hospital (in Highgate). Pre-clinical students live in London University halls in Bloomsbury; 100 hall places in West Hampstead reserved for first years and finalists. Flats/houses available in Hampstead at a price. Active SU with full range of clubs and societies. Student facilities on site include 2 squash courts, 300-seat theatre, SU bar and disco, new Junior Common Room, computer room (access to the Internet). Very well stocked library opens late and at weekends. Automatic membership of hospital recreation centre and ULU with use of all facilities. Annual freshers and rag week, regular live bands and entertainment on site. Personal tutor and fully confidential counselling. Continuous assessment throughout course; most students intercalate for a BSc degree. Good balance between work and relaxation. One of the friendliest medical schools with a full ethnic and religious mix. Very close to Belsize Park tube station for easy access to central London (theatres, shops, museums etc). Chance to meet many other students – not just medics – and experience life in one of the nicest parts of London – Hampstead Heath is within easy walking distance.

PAUPER NOTES   **Accommodation:** Halls of residence; hospital-owned clinical house. Some cheap properties on short-term lease. **Drink:** Cheap bar owned by medical school. Good local brew Highgate Mild. Annual Camden Beer Festival. **Eats:** Pizzas, kebabs, fish and chips, cheap Mexican and four curry houses all within 2 minutes. Local trendy Hampstead restaurants. **Ents:** Good cinemas locally; Hampstead Theatre; 2 comedy clubs, Dingwalls in Camden Town and Camden Palais. **Sports:** Squash courts and recreation centre (gym and pool) on site. Sports ground at Enfield. Rowing at ULU boathouse, Chiswick. Swiss

Cottage Sports Centre – 2 swimming pools – cheap for students. **Hardship funds:** Some special grants/bursaries for hard-up students; apply to registry. Access funds. Students don't drop out for financial reasons (medical students generally have good relations with major banks). **Travel:** Annual trip to Belize. **Work:** Auxiliary nursing, portering, lab work available in summer vacation. Term-time work available but almost impossible to fit in with academic studies. Most pre-clinical students go home to work in vacations.
INFORMAL NAME   The Free.
MORE INFO?   Enquiries to SU president (0171 794 0500 x 4332).
ALUMNI (EDITORS' PICK)   Dr Hillary Jones (TV-am).

ROYAL HOLLOWAY

Royal Holloway, University of London, Egham Hill,
Egham, Surrey TW20 0EX (Tel 01784 434455,
Fax 01784 437520) Map 4

STUDENT ENQUIRIES: Schools & International Liaison Officer
APPLICATIONS: UCAS

Broad study areas: Humanities, modern languages, social sciences, performing arts, sciences, management. (Subject details are in the *Subjects and Places Index*.)

Founded: In 1985 from the merger of 2 London University colleges: Bedford College (founded 1849) and Royal Holloway (1886). both were originally women's colleges, but have admitted men since the 1960s. **Structural features:** Part of London University. **Main undergraduate awards:** BA, BMus, BSc, MSci. **Awarding body:** London University. **Site:** 120-acre parkland campus; Founder's building, in style of Château of Chambord, and many new buildings. **Access:** Egham station (Waterloo-Reading line); buses. Close to Heathrow airport, M3, M4 and M25. **Europe:** 18% first degree students take a language as part of course and 20% spend 6 months or more abroad. Course unit system allows a language to be added to many degrees and most undergraduates have access to languages. Formal exchange links with universities throughout Europe, many open to non-language specialists. **Library:** 2 main libraries; several departmental collections; 500,000 volumes in total, 1,700 periodicals, 630 study places; restricted loan collections. Annual expenditure on library materials, £100+ per FTE student. **Other learning facilities:** 300 computer workstations for student use in computer centre and academic departments. Extra-curricular college certificates in computer applications or communication skills available by modular study. **Welfare:** Dean of students, wardens, counsellor to students, doctors, FPA, psychiatrist, chaplains, inter-denominational chapel, SU welfare service, nightline. **Careers:** Information, advice and placement. **Amenities:** Purpose-built SU building; theatre; orchestra and choirs. **Sporting facilities:** Wide variety of sports; playing fields and tennis courts on site.

Accommodation: In 1995/96, 50% of all first degree students in college accommodation, 100% of first years. 2,600 places available (1,650 for first years): 1,800 'girovend' (room, heat, light plus contribution to catering overheads; subsidised meals then available) at

£42–£62 per week, term time only; and 600 self-catering places at £50–£53, Sept–June. 250 more places expected for 1997. Students live in privately owned accommodation for 1–2 years: rents £40–£55 per week for self-catering, £45–£55 B&B, £50–£60 for half-board. 5% first degree students live at home. **Term time work**: University's policy to allow term time work for full-time first degree students, to limit of 15 hours per week (55% believed to work). Term (and vac) work available on campus in bars, catering, portering etc, particularly in SU; careers office has some info on (mainly vac) work off campus. **Hardship funds:** Total available in 1995/96: £130,000 government access funds; small general hardship fund plus a large number of college, departmental and faculty prizes; competitive entrance scholarships also available prior to starting course for overseas students and for scientists of high academic ability.

Duration of first degree courses: 3 years; 4 years if involving a language. **Total first degree students 1995/96:** 4,621. **Overseas students:** 420. **Mature students:** 870. **Male/female ratio:** 11:9. **Teaching staff:** 330 full-time, 38 part-time. **Total full-time students 1995/96:** 5,012. **Postgraduate students:** 601. **First degree tuition fees:** Home students, paying their own fees in 1996/97, paid £1,600; Overseas students £6,860 (classroom), £8,250 (lab/studio).

WHAT IT'S LIKE   London University's country campus – near Windsor and 30 minutes from central London. It's based in the truly amazing, Victorian purpose-built Founder's Building. An established centre of academic excellence. Sciences, maths/arts and SU buildings relatively new; also residences (every study bedroom has a shower/toilet ensuite). SU active, mostly social rather than political. Over 100 clubs and societies ranging from political to social, religious to sporting. It also provides a varied and enjoyable ents programme most days in the week; top bands, alternative comedians. SU operates four bars around campus, good prices. Sports teams have very strong record.

PAUPER NOTES   **Accommodation:** College accommodation good. Local area expensive. Married residence 50 yards from campus. **Drink:** Best place for cheapies – union bars. Stumble Inn on campus has nice pub atmosphere and cheap prices. **Eats:** SU coffee bar – cheap and varied. Girovend credit card food system on campus; vegetarian on menu. Local places – Windsor, Staines. **Ents:** New cabaret venue open on campus. Drama dept does lots of plays. Very active ents. Lot of fringe theatre, 3 cinema groups, bands and alternative comedy every week. **Sports:** Campus playing field and small gym. Egham Sports Centre good but expensive, Staines nearest swimming. **Hardship funds:** BA few are available. **Travel:** French and ski societies do good cheapies. **Work:** College employs students during vacs, plenty of bar work etc during term with SU and local area.

MORE INFO?   Get Students' Alternative Prospectus. Enquiries to General Secretary, SU (01784 435035).

ALUMNI (EDITORS' PICK)   Ivy Compton-Burnett, Richmal Crompton, Felicity Lott, Janet Fookes MP, David Bellamy, Kathleen Lonsdale, Jean Rook, Marie Patterson, George Eliot.

CAN'T FIND WHAT YOU'RE LOOKING FOR? USE THE INDEX!

ROYAL NORTHERN COLLEGE OF MUSIC

Royal Northern College of Music, 124 Oxford Road, Manchester M13 9RD (Tel 0161 273 6283, Fax 0161 273 7611) Map 2

STUDENT ENQUIRIES: Secretary for Admissions
APPLICATIONS: Direct

Broad study areas: Music, performing arts. (Subject details are in the *Subjects and Places Index*.)

Founded: 1973 from Northern School of Music and Royal anchester College of Music. **Main awards:** BMus, BA, PPRNCM, PGDip, MMus. **Awarding body:** Manchester University. **Site:** Fine modern buildings 1 mile south of city centre. **Access:** uses from city centre. **Academic features:** All undergraduate courses are 4 years (2 years broad musical education, 2 years specialisation); college runs a joint course with Manchester University. **Europe:** 20% first degree students (all singing students) take a language as part of course; some language classes may be open to other students. No students spend time abroad as a course requirement. Formal exchange links with conservatoires in Paris, Lyon, Copenhagen, Frankfurt, Prague and Belgrade, open to all students. Annual orchestral tours, especially to France. **Library:** Extensive reference and lending sections of books and performing material. Vast record collection with playback facilities for records, tapes, CDs and videos. Annual expenditure on library materials, £70 per FTE student. **Specialist collections:** Henry Watson Collection of Musical Instruments; Library of Jascha Horenstein; Adolf Brodsky archive; original manuscripts of Alan Rawsthorne, and a unique collection of Scandinavian music. **Other learning facilities:** Electronic studio, keyboard laboratory, professionally-staffed recording studio. **Welfare:** Chaplain, counsellors, instrument purchase loan scheme. **Careers:** Advisory service. **Amenities:** Opera theatre, concert hall, recital room; Junior Common Room; roof garden; refectory with bar. Full programme of public events takes place throughout the academic year. **Sporting facilities:** Tennis, football and cricket at hall of residence.

Accommodation: In 1995/96, 31% of all students in college accommodation, 66% of first years. 180 places available: 148 full-board places at £67 per week and 32 self-catering at £46 per week, term time only. Most students live in privately owned accommodation for 3 years: rents £30–£55 per week for self-catering, £50–£60 for B&B. 5% of first degree students live at home. **Term time work:** College's policy to allow term time work for full-time first degree students – external concert engagements make significant contribution to professional development; 75% believed to work. Term (and vac) work available on campus (bar, front of house) and help finding work in concerts/gigs for suitable students. **Hardship funds:** Government access funds and other funds used to alleviate student hardship especially when students do not qualify for mandatory grants. Some entrance awards for students of outstanding promise.

Duration of first degree equivalent courses: 4 years. **Total first degree students 1995/96:** 430. **Overseas students:** 65. **Male/female ratio:** 2:3. **Teaching staff:** 33 full-time, 113 part-time. **Total full-time students 1995/96:** 578. **Postgraduate students:** 133. **Tuition fees:** Home students, paying their own fees in 1996/97, paid £1,600 (postgraduates £3,310–£3,730); Overseas: £6,750 (non-vocal), £7,350 (vocal).

WHAT IT'S LIKE   It's the youngest of the four British Royal Schools of Music and boasts some of the most up-to-date facilities and opportunities for music students in Britain. Facilities include a fully staffed opera theatre (and own workshop), concert hall, recital room, lecture theatre, comprehensive practice room facilities and its own hall of residence. Most students live in the Didsbury/Chorlton/Fallowfield area. Good reputation leads to high proportion of overseas and mature students; most aim to become professional musicians. Fairly small but able to take advantage of most of the university's facilities for social activities, bars, clubs and health centre. Students actively encouraged to seek external work with local orchestras and music clubs; close links with BBC Philharmonic, Hallé, Liverpool Philharmonic and Camerata Orchestras. In this highly competitive field, RNC is a surprisingly friendly place, perhaps due to its large refectory area where students congregate. Active and enthusiastic SU puts on numerous weekly entertainments, plus endless late-night parties and a New Year Ball.

PAUPER NOTES   **Accommodation:** Cheapest housing in Moss-Side, Hulme and Whalley range. Fair number of squats in Hulme. **Drink:** Many good locals; SU bar (cheap) and university SU. **Eats:** Approx 30 Indian restaurants in Rusholme (most cheap and very good). Good vegetarian. **Ents:** Lots of cinemas (student discount). Student reductions at most theatres. Royal Exchange Theatre very good. Lots of socials at SU. **Sports:** Use of university facilities – Moss-Side Leisure Centre very cheap and convenient. **Hardship funds:** College and SU have limited resources for small loans and scholarships. **Travel:** College fund for studying abroad. **Work:** Gigs and teaching relatively easy to find by the time you've been at college for a couple of years. 20% do bar work etc during term time.

INFORMAL NAME   RNC

MORE INFO?   Enquiries to President SU (0161 273 4017).

ALUMNI (EDITORS' PICK)   Peter Donohoe, Jane Eaglen, Brodsky Quartet, Howard Jones.

ROYAL SCOTTISH ACADEMY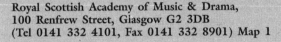

Royal Scottish Academy of Music & Drama,
100 Renfrew Street, Glasgow G2 3DB
(Tel 0141 332 4101, Fax 0141 332 8901) Map 1

STUDENT ENQUIRIES: Registrar
APPLICATIONS: Direct

Broad study areas: Music, drama. (Subject details are in the *Subjects and Places Index*.)

Founded: 1847. **Main undergraduate awards:** BA, BEd, BMus. **Awarding body:** Royal Scottish Academy. **Site:** Central Glasgow. **Special features:** Many top professional concert artists and theatre directors in recitals, productions and masterclasses. **Academic features:** Degrees in acting, Scottish music as well as BMus (performance) and BEd (music). **Europe:** Singing students undertake language studies in German and Italian. Links and exchanges with eg Germany, Russia. **Library:** 80,120 music volumes, 13,750 books, 7,570 sound recordings, 26 study places, 9 listening booths, computer lab. **Welfare:** Counsellor. **Careers:** Information and advice. **Amenities:** Concert hall (360 seats), theatre (340 seats); TV studio; recital room; broadcasting studio; electronic recording studio.

Accommodation: No academy accommodation; 40 places available in halls of residence managed by other institutions, preference given to first years. Most students live in privately owned accommodation: £35–£50 per week for self-catering, £38–£50 B&B. **Hardship funds:** Total available in 1995/96: £11,857 government access funds, 44 students helped. Entrance scholarships of £100–£500 available for approx 25 students.

Duration of first degree courses: 3 or 4 years. **Total first degree students 1995/96:** 392. **BEd students:** 77. **Overseas students:** 7. **Mature students:** 158. **Male/female ratio:** 2:3. **Teaching staff:** 31 full-time, 158 part-time. **Total full-time students 1995/96:** 431. **Postgraduate students:** 71. **First degree tuition fees:** Home students, paying their own fees in 1996/97, paid £1,600; Overseas students £7,350.

WHAT IT'S LIKE   Impressive orange brick building in a good vantage point on corner of Hope and Renfrew Streets in the centre of Glasgow. Full of modern facilities; the public BMus the New Athenaeum and Chandler Studio theatres for performances, and Stevenson Concert Hall for concerts. Extensive library on top, complete with hi-fi, CD players and video equipment. TV studio with cameras, lighting, sound and editing. Large technical dept. Practice rooms for music and drama students. Small canteen and smaller common room. Noticeable lack of SU bar in the building. Plenty of nightclubs and bars; good gay community. Lot of visiting companies and musicians in the Academy and plenty going on locally in the arts. Large shopping centres; Glasgow Central and Queen Street rail stations nearby, also Cowcaddens Subway and Buchanan bus station (buses to most places in city at average prices). Easy access to parts of Scotland eg Loch Lomond only 30 minutes away. Few drop out once they have started the course although people drop out just before they start because of (or for fear of) lack of funds. Minimal interaction between music and drama students (though being addressed). Can feel claustrophobic but few students are unhappy. RSAD is widely respected and opportunities after graduating verge on the excellent.

PAUPER NOTES   **Accommodation:** Some Academy accommodation; office has list of places for rent but mainly up to students. Glasgow can be expensive – southside and West End popular. **Drink:** Pubs everywhere – Art School, Trader Joe's, Brunswick Cellars, Nice and Sleazy. Cheap beer can be found but Glasgow getting very trendy. **Eats:** Academy canteen not subsidised. Cheap local places easily found. **Ents:** Lots of cheap theatre and music. Arthouse cinema at Glasgow Film Theatre. Nightlife good. Generally lots to do – Glasgow is a major cultural centre. **Sports:** Kelvin Hall Sports Centre (easy by tube). **Hardship funds:** Academy loan scheme and various directors' funds. **Travel:** No travel scholarships as such. Hitching good on 8. uses average. Discounts on train with railcard. **Work:** Ushering in college, music teaching, plenty bars and restaurants. A job is often needed in these hard times.

MORE INFO?   Enquiries to SRC President (0141 332 5080).

ALUMNI (EDITORS' PICK)   Hannah Gordon, Moira Anderson, Sheena Easton, Tom Conti, Sir Alexander Gibson, Bill McCue, Fulton Mackay, James Loughran, Margaret Marshall, Isobel Buchanan, Ian Richardson, Bill Paterson, Neil Mackie, Bryden Thomson, Judith Howarth, David Hayman, Mary Marquis, Phyllis Logan, John Cairney, John Grieve, Ruby Wax.

ROYAL VETERINARY COLLEGE

Royal Veterinary College, University of London,
Royal College Street, London NW1 0TU
(Tel 0171 468 5149, Fax 0171 388 2342) Map 5

STUDENT ENQUIRIES: Registry
APPLICATIONS: UCAS

Broad study areas: Veterinary medicine.

Founded: 1791. **Structural features:** College of London University. **Main undergraduate awards:** BVetMed, BSc. **Awarding body:** London University. **Site:** Pre-clinical studies at Camden Town, north London; clinical studies on 230-hectare campus at Hawkshead, near Potters Bar, Hertfordshire. **Access:** Camden Town site, buses and tubes (Camden Town, Euston and King's Cross stations); Hawkshead site, 20 mins by train from King's Cross to Brookmans Park or Potters Bar. **Academic features:** Individual project in final year forms part of degree examination. **Europe:** Students may carry out components of extra-mural study in Europe, attend clinics in Munich University veterinary school (exchange agreement) or undertake study in food hygiene at Royal Veterinary & Agricultural University, Copenhagen. **Library:** Library and reading rooms at both sites; reference copies of standard text. **Other learning facilities:** Computer suites and animal hospitals at both sites. Large animal practice and small animal referral hospital at Hawkshead. **Welfare:** Camden students may register with health services of University College or London University Central Institutes. Physician and occupational health team visit Hawkshead regularly during term. **Amenities:** ULU building in Malet Street, refectory and common room on both campuses. Playing fields and swimming pool at Hawkshead.

Accommodation: *Camden*: No college accommodation, but about 85% of first years live in London University intercollegiate halls (probably all who choose to). *Hawkshead*: 2 halls for clinical students: £70.50–£80 per week for half board plus weekend lunches; £50 per week self-catering. Many prefer to share private accommodation in area; SU keeps database of addresses. **Hardship funds:** Government access funds and limited college funds. Applications before February deadline considered on individual merit (assistance may be given earlier in academic year to students in particular difficulty).

Duration of first degree courses: 5 years. **Total first degree students 1995/96:** 463. **Overseas students:** 31. **Mature students:** 92. **Male/female ratio:** 2:3. **Teaching staff:** 70. **Total full-time students 1995/96:** 556. **Postgraduate students:** 127 (full- and part-time). **First degree tuition fees:** Home students, paying their own fees in 1996/97, paid £1,600 (pre-clinical), £2,800 (clinical); Overseas students £10,980.

WHAT IT'S LIKE   It's on two sites: Camden (Central London) and Potters Bar (semi-rural extreme north London). First two (pre-clinical) years of 5-year course taught at Camden. Final three years, at Potters Bar, is clinically oriented and a more professional and mature attitude expected. Experience real student life in central London for first two years – and can be extended with intercalated BSc from another London University college. Excellent city to be in, apart from the cost of living – perhaps less of a problem for veterinary students who get preferential deals from some banks. Also, the workload is heavier than for most other students leaving less chance to spend money. In first year virtually all students live in London University intercollegiate halls. In last three years a proportion live in two halls at Potters Bar site – almost essential unless you (or a friend) have a car because local public transport poor. About 500 students and a broad range. Social life (and the profession) is stereotyped by the work hard, play even harder mentality. The student community is small and largely self-sufficient. For those wanting to be a vet and who can cope with the work and living in a 'veterinary village' (though London not far away) the RVC is the place.

PAUPER NOTES **Accommodation:** London University intercollegiate halls during 1st year, possibly 2nd. College hall in final 3 years, though living out is reasonably priced. **Drink:** ULU bars and other unions (especially UCL), the Rising Sun (Euston Road) can be happening. **Eats:** Campus/college food OK. UCL/ULU are good when in London. **Ents:** Good and lively college social events. **Sports:** Field station has playing field, squash court, swimming pool. Use of all ULU and Imperial facilities. **Hardship Funds:** Access fund. **Travel:** Variety of scholarships for projects abroad. **Work:** Difficult because of 35-hour week but possible part-time, during first three years; impossible in last two. In final three years lots of minimally paid (mandatory) coursework on farms and in veterinary practice.

MORE INFO? Enquiries to SU, 01707 666310.

INFORMAL NAME RVC.

ST ANDREWS UNIVERSITY

University of St Andrews, College Gate, St Andrews, Fife
KY16 9AJ (Tel 01334 476161, Fax 01334 463330) Map 1

STUDENT ENQUIRIES: Schools Liaison Office
APPLICATIONS: UCAS

Broad study areas: Sciences (including biological, chemical, geological, physical and medical), arts (including modern languages, history, philosophy, psychology and international relations), divinity. (Subject details are in the *Subjects and Places Index*.)

Founded: 1410. **Main undergraduate awards:** BD, MA, BSc, MChem, MSci, MTheol. **Awarding body:** St Andrews University. **Site:** St Andrews town centre, North Haugh site half-mile west of the centre. **Access:** Nearest station is Leuchars (5 miles away) on main London-Aberdeen line, then bus; good road links. **Academic features:** Semester and modular system. Many new single and joint honours courses including MA in modern languages (1, 2 or 3 languages); 4 year honours system gives great flexibility – final choice of subject(s) can be delayed until end of second year. General entrance requirements are relaxed for mature students. **Europe:** 22% first degree students take a language as part of course, and 10% spend 6 months or more abroad. Some 25 formal exchange programmes, many with multiple links, involving 9 other countries. Many subjects can be studied jointly with a language. **Library:** 730,000 volumes, 10,000 periodicals, 680 study areas. Annual expenditure on library materials, £138.08 per FTE student. **Other learning facilities:** Computing laboratory, Gatty marine laboratory, language centre. **Welfare:** Doctor, FPA, chaplain, student counsellor. Limited residential facilities for married and disabled students. **Careers:** Information, advice and placement service. **Amenities:** SU with coffee and snack bars, newspaper, arts and crafts area etc. **Sporting facilities:** Modern physical education centre; excellent playing fields; 6 squash courts; 5 golf courses (including 'Old' course); local leisure complex with indoor swimming pool.

Accommodation: In 1995/96, 66% of all students in university accommodation, 100% first years who want it. 3,117 places available: 2,119 full-board places (1,480 for first years) from £58.17–£77.14 per week (£56.70–£66.22 shared), term time or longer; 950 self-catering places (240 for first years) at £26.74–£47.32 per week. Students may choose to live in privately owned accommodation: rents £40–£55 per week for self-catering, £45–£65 for half-board. 2% first degree students live at home. **Term time work:** University's policy to allow term time work for full-time first degree students. Limited term (and vac) work available on campus as cleaners etc. **Hardship funds:** Total available in 1995/96: £115,765 government access funds, 462 students helped; £15,000 own funds, 70 helped; plus £10,000 other funds, 30 helped. Special help: single parents, mature students, self-financing students; own funds also available for overseas students and others not eligible for access funds; other funds (Wolfson Trust) available for Scottish students.

Duration of first degree courses: 4 years honours; 3 years general. **Total first degree students 1995/96:** 5,135. **Overseas students:** 509. **Mature students:** 408. **Male/female ratio:** 1:1. **Teaching staff:** 353 full-time, 16 part-time. **Total full-time students 1995/96:** 5,997. **Postgraduate students:** 862. **First degree tuition fees:** Home students, paying their own fees in 1996/97, paid £750 (classroom), £1,600 (lab); Overseas students £6,000 (classroom), £8,000 (lab), £10,000 (pre-clinical).

WHAT IT'S LIKE   5,000 students inhabit this historic town on east coast of Scotland, the 'home of golf'; little industry beside university, tourism and RAF Leuchars. Town small, but lots of facilities, with good mix of historic and new. Campus spread over town, sciences on 1960s campus-style North Haugh site. Very friendly close-knit community. Cosmopolitan mix – 13% overseas, 41% Scottish, 41% English, 5% Northern Irish. All first years guaranteed places in hall; university-owned flats and private accommodation for most others. Students' Association (SA) central to university life as only club/venue in town. It also provides welfare advisers, resource centre, regular films, oldest debating society in Europe and secondhand bookshop. 100 societies, from serious (One World) to bizarre (Tunnocks Caramel Wafer Appreciation Society) to serious (Amnesty International). Successful charity campaign (rag); athletic union provides excellent facilities for almost all sports. Strong dramatic tradition; many theatre groups and musical societies. Balls for everything: halls, union, debates, societies. Traditions include red gowns, raisin weekend, academic families and May morning dip in the North Sea! Modular course structures, entry by faculty, requires no honours specialisation before third year. Psychology, medieval, modern and Scottish history, art history, international relations and maths have excellent reputation. Good graduate employment record. You might never leave St Andrews for good, but find yourself drawn back again and again.

PAUPER NOTES   **Accommodation:** Mix of university accommodation and private. Cheap flats can be hard to find but nowhere is more than 20 minutes away. **Drink:** SA cheapest. **Eats:** Lots of coffee shops; Indians and Chinese expensive; 'memorabilia' style places (eg

Ziggies) popular. SA runs late night cafe. **Ents:** One cinema, Byre theatre, Crawford Arts centre. Union for small-scale ents and large-scale bands, discos etc. **Sports:** Athletic union free. Cheap deal on golf and leisure centre. **Hardship funds:** Through Hebdomadar. **Travel:** Good student travel service, but nearest BR station is 5 miles away on East Coast line; limited coaches (need to go to Dundee). **Work:** Mostly bars and waitress service, but jobs go fast. Many have regular term time work; more get occasional jobs, eg phonathons during Dunhill Cup. Small amount of vacation work in local tourism.

MORE INFO?   Enquiries to Students' Association (01334 462700/1).

ALUMNI (EDITORS' PICK)   Sir Hugh Cortazzi, Colin Young, Fay Weldon, Alastair Reid, Eric Anderson, James Michener, Siobhan Redmond, Zoe Fairbairns, Michael Forsyth, Allan Stewart, Alex Salmond.

ST BARTHOLOMEW'S & ROYAL LONDON

St Bartholomew's and the Royal London School of Medicine and Dentistry, University of London, Turner Street, London E1 2AD (Tel 0171 377 7000, Fax 0171 377 7677) Map 6

STUDENT ENQUIRIES: Admissions Officer
APPLICATIONS: UCAS

Broad study areas: Medicine, dentistry. (Subject details are in the *Subjects and Places Index*.)

Founded: 1995 as new school of Queen Mary and Westfield College, incorporating St Bartholomew's (founded 1123), London Hospital Medical College (1785) and Dental Teaching Hospital (1911). **Structural features:** Part of Queen Mary and Westfield College, London University. **Main undergraduate awards:** MBBS, BDS, BSc. **Awarding body:** London University. **Site:** City and East London: Whitechapel, West Smithfield and Mile End. **Access:** Whitechapel, St Paul's, Barbican and Mile End underground stations. **Academic features:** Pre-clinical teaching (2 years; 3 if student interclates a BSc) centred at Mile End campus with innovative curriculum, including project work, integrated teaching, and self-directed learning. Clinical teaching at hospital sites. 50–60 students p.a. join clinical course after pre-clinical at eg Oxbridge. Intercalated BMedSci course open to students who have completed 4th year of MBBS. **Europe:** Erasmus programme. **Library:** Three main collections: Whitechapel, West Smithfield and Mile End. All have audio-visual learning aids, computer resources and study places. **Welfare:** Health centre, in-house dental treatment, nursery, 'nightline', counsellors, chaplains. **Amenities:** Association of Medical and Dental Students plus QMW SU: book shops, travel centre, bank, snackbars, billiards room, common rooms, nightclub, bars. **Sporting facilities:** Numerous sports clubs, multigym, squash courts, gymnasium, swimming pool, athletics grounds, rowing club with boats at Chiswick. Sailing club with own cottage at Burnham-on-Crouch.

Accommodation and hardship funds: See Queen Mary and Westfield College.

Duration of first degree courses: 5 years; **others:** 6 years (with intercalated BSc or BMedSci). **Total first degree students 1995/96:** 1,525. **Overseas students:** 138. **Mature students:** 277. **Male/female ratio:** 7:5. **Teaching staff:** 405. **Total full-time students 1995/96:** 1,741. **Postgraduate students:** 549. **First degree tuition fees:** Home students, paying their own fees in 1996/97, paid £1,600 (pre-clinical) £2,800 (clinical); Overseas students £8,600–£10,867 (pre-clinical), £15,400 (clinical).

WHAT IT'S LIKE It's a new medical school, a faculty within QMW formed from the merger of two of Britain's oldest schools – Barts and Royal London. The hospitals serve the City and East End communities, providing an enormous variety of patients and diseases for clinical students. Applicants with interests and achievements outside medicine are favoured and over 30% students intercalate a BSc in the 3rd/4th year. School is noted for its friendly, informal atmosphere among the students and with the staff. Medical and dental students mix with doctors, nurses, radiographers and physios at social events (usually weekly). Rag Week raises more than £120,000 by entertaining and shocking the London public – essential for 1st years. SU encompasses 39 vibrant clubs from bridge to water-polo; DramaSoc performs 6–7 productions a year; sailing club has own cottage in Burnham; boat club has own boathouse on the river Lea. The sports clubs compete independently from QMW in tournaments (eg National Association of Medical Schools). Grounds at Chislehurst (SE London) and Hale End (East London) well-equipped for field sports and have own bars. Ents committee frequently organise post-exam cocktail parties. The new school is based on 3 sites. *QMW at Mile End*, where preclinical students are taught; medics and dentists don't spend much time here other than for lectures. Good library and excellent computer facilities. New Globe pub just up the road for post-exam celebrations. *Barts at Charterhouse Square*. St Bartholomew's Hospital serves the people of the City and oncology patients from all over the UK. Barts SU is in The Square (5 minutes from hospital, 2 mins from Barbican tube), as is BMedSci course building, library, clinical lecture theatre, research institute; also College Hall which houses over 200 first year and clinical students and has well-equipped kitchens, showers and bathrooms on every floor. Refectory is open for lunch. Multigym and squash courts. theatre for DramaSoc productions. College life revolves around the bar (open to 11 pm every night and a disco every Friday); run by a group of students (the Wine Committee). The Square has a large picturesque lawn which offers a haven from the hub-bub of the City; it is also the site of the massive Barbican Ball in June. Theatres and cinemas of the Barbican Centre just round the corner and all-night greasy spoons for Smithfield market workers; restaurants and pubs of Smithfield, the Strand and Islington within walking distance; a stone's throw from the West End. *The Royal London at Whitechapel* serves the East End community and is the major trauma centre for south east England; it's also the site of the Dental Institute. The Clubs Union is open all day and has a snack bar, common room and bar, open for lunch and in the evenings until 11 pm. Also contains the SU offices and College Hostel, which houses some first year students (meals provided for residents). 2 gyms which also serve as theatres and house discos (4 a term); a swimming pool in hospital grounds. Whitechapel tube across the road, there-fore good for transport. Traditional East End pubs with friendly atmosphere, picturesque water-front pubs and numerous eateries of all sorts. *Gareth Bashir*

PAUPER NOTES **Accommodation:** College accommodation at all three sites and inter-collegiate halls. After first year, most students live out in Mile End, Bow, Hackney and Whitechapel; £45/week (college housing cheaper). **Drink:** College bars (beer £1 at Barts, £1.40 at Royal London). Many good pubs near all sites, including Blind Beggar (of Kray Brothers fame) near Whitechapel. **Eats:** *Charterhouse Square*: Pierre Victoire, Café du Marché, Dome; several sandwich shops and greasy spoons incl infamous Dallas (open 11pm–5am for market workers; excellent for post-bar food). *Whitechapel*: Numerous cheap

Chinese and Indian restaurants (Brick Lane); also greasy spoons and pizza joints. **Ents:** College discos; Barbican close. **Hardship funds:** Access funds. College helps. **Travel:** Elective scholarships. STA Travel at Mile End. **Work:** Bar work popular; portering, agency nursing, drug and research trials, library attendants.
MORE INFO?   Get students alternative prospectus. Contact SU on 0171 982 5839 or 0171 377 7641.
ALUMNI (EDITORS' PICK)   *London*: Frederick Treaves (physician to John Merrick 'the Elephant Man'), Dr Barnado. *Barts*: William Harvey, John Abernethian, James Paget, Richard Gordon, Graham Chapman, Percival Pott, Thomas Vicary, W G Grace, Graham Gardner, Penfolds (as Australian wine).

ST GEORGE'S

St George's Hospital Medical School, University of London, Cranmer Terrace, London SW17 0RE (Tel 0181 672 9944) Map 5

STUDENT ENQUIRIES: Registry
APPLICATIONS: UCAS; direct for nursing.

Broad study areas: Medicine, nursing. (Subject details are in the *Subjects and Places Index*.)

Founded: 1751. **Structural features:** Part of London University. **Main undergraduate awards:** MBBS, BSc. **Awarding body:** London University. **Site:** Single site in Tooting, for pre-clinical and clinical studies. **Access:** Tooting Broadway underground station; buses. **Special features:** Free-standing medical school. **Academic features:** New curriculum allows students to combine compulsory core with own choice of special study modules; much teaching in body-system modules, with emphasis on clinical relevance of basic sciences. **Europe:** No students learn a language or spend time abroad. **Library:** 30,000 monographs, 90,000 journal volumes, 800 periodicals, 400 study places. Annual expenditure on library materials, £175 per FTE student. **Welfare:** Student counsellor, student health service, chaplains. **Careers:** Help available for newly-qualified doctors. **Amenities:** Hospital chapel; bookshop managed by school club; bar and common rooms, banks. **Sporting facilities:** 6 squash courts, aerobics room and gymnasium; Olympic standard public swimming pool just off site; playing fields, tennis courts.

Accommodation: In 1995/96, 25% of all students in school accommodation, 100% of first years. 256 self-catering places available (172 for first years) at £41 per week, term time only. Students live in privately owned accommodation for 3–4 years: rents £40–£50 per week for self-catering. 1% first degree students live at home. **Term time work:** No school policy to allow term time work for full-time first degree students. **Hardship funds:** Total available in 1995/96: £40,918 government access funds, 133 students helped.

Duration of first degree courses: MB BS 5 years; 6 years (with intercalated BSc); 4 years part-time, nursing studies and midwifery. **Total first degree students 1995/96:** 894. **Overseas**

students: 34. **Mature students:** 78. **Male/female ratio:** 4:3. **Teaching staff:** 215 full-time, 300 part-time. **Total full-time students 1995/96:** 1,085. **Postgraduate students:** 261. **First degree tuition fees:** Home students, paying their own fees in 1996/97, paid £1,600 (pre-clinical), £2,800 (clinical); Overseas students £8,130 (pre-clinical), £14,970 (clinical).

WHAT IT'S LIKE   Large modern complex of buildings in Tooting, south west London; all pre-clinical and approximately half clinical teaching on site. Mixed self-catering halls of residence are ten minutes' walk from the medical school, with room for 256 students (first years are guaranteed places). Halls life is good (socially) and easy (financially and domestically). Central London is easily accessible by tube (about 20 minutes' ride). Tooting is good for eating and drinking; theatre, film and cabaret require a short five-minute bus journey. SU has fortnightly discos held in the medical school (longest student bar in London) with many events in between (plays, films, happy hours, quiz nights) and special events (Christmas revue, rag week, freshers fortnight). The bar serves the usual plus hot and cold food, with guest beers, wines and malts on constant promotion. Most sports and leisure interests are catered for and new clubs are constantly becoming active, inactive and reactive (depending on demand). Sports ground is at Cobham (Surrey) but a sports hall on site with 6 squash courts and 2 multigyms and free use of Tooting swimming pool. Successful clubs include hockey, football, basketball, cricket, tennis and rowing; all clubs are remarkably active socially! Work load is relatively light in the first year compared to the rest of the course. Failures are not by a set rate (although the chances of a second retake are dwindling) and once through the first year you're unlikely to be thrown out. About a third of students do an intercalated BSc at the end of the pre-clinical course; also a clinical BSc offered. Student-staff relations are relaxed and friendly. If you want to become a capable and caring physician, and still enjoy every moment of your five years, come to St George's.

PAUPER NOTES   **Accommodation:** Halls for 1st years, about £35 week, local housing £45-ish and plentiful. **Drink:** SU bar – prices slashed! Tooting Tavern, Selkirk, JJ Moons. Young's beer, brewed nearby in Wandsworth. **Eats:** Curry! Tooting is the curry centre of SW London. **Ents:** SU events, v well equipped; comedy nights, quizzes, live bands – plenty of local clubs. **Sports:** Cheap good on-site sports centre; free entry to local pool; 45-acre sports ground. **Hardship funds:** Access funds and grovelling sometimes gets med school loan; very few financial dropouts (mature students more likely). Banks very reasonable to medics. **Travel:** School scholarships for electives. **Work:** Student bar (£3 per hour); nursing temp easy (£6 per hour) and lab work during vacs.

MORE INFO?   Enquiries to President SU (0181 725 2709).

INFORMAL NAME   George's.

ALUMNI (EDITORS' PICK)   Henry Gray, Edward Wilson, Edward Jenner, Thomas Young, John Hunter, Mike Stroud, Harry Hill.

HOW TO START? *SEE SHORTLISTING*, PAGE 535

ST MARK & ST JOHN

College of St Mark & St John, Derriford Road, Plymouth
PL6 8BH (Tel 01752 777188) Map 3

STUDENT ENQUIRIES: Admissions Officer
APPLICATIONS: UCAS

Broad study areas: Education, humanities, information technology, religious studies, social studies. (Subject details are in the *Subjects and Places Index.*)

Founded: 1923, from St John's Battersea (1840) and St Mark's Chelsea (1841); moved from London to Plymouth in 1973. **Structural features:** A Church of England college, affiliated to Exeter University. **Main undergraduate awards:** BA, BEd. **Awarding body:** Exeter University. **Site:** 5 miles Plymouth city centre. 53-acre site overlooking Dartmoor, Plymouth and Plymouth Sound. **Access:** Good bus services. **Academic features:** Modular framework for all BA courses, allowing full and part-time study. Teaching practice and community work opportunities in east London. BA students may spend 1 semester in USA. **Europe:** BA students may study a language as part of their course; some spend a semester abroad. Formal exchange links with some European institutions. **Library:** Over 120,000 volumes, 700 periodicals, plus extensive microfilm and audio-visual materials; CD-Rom facilities. 250 study places. **Welfare:** Careers office, chaplain, nurse, student welfare centre, counsellors. Christian Fellowship and study groups. **Careers:** Specialist careers adviser and information room. **Amenities:** Joint common room with bar and snack bar, games and TV rooms, SU shop, launderette, minibus, printing service, specialist bookshop, part-time banking service, chapel, drama theatre; art centre, theatre, orchestras etc in Plymouth. **Sporting facilities:** Floodlit all-weather sports arena and pitches; sports centre including sports halls, gym, fitness suite, weight training room, squash courts, climbing wall, indoor 25-metre pool. Also Dartmoor and the coast for walking, climbing, water sports.

Accommodation: In 1995/96, almost 100% of first year students in accommodation arranged by college. 526 places available (for first, final and overseas students): £38–£46 per week, either self-catering or, in hall, must buy £175 termly meal ticket. Students live in privately owned accommodation for 2–3 years: £38–£45 per week for self-catering, £56 per week for half-board. **Term time work:** College's policy to allow part time work for full time first degree students. Some vacation work available in college. **Hardship funds:** Total available in 1995/96: £58,232 government access funds, 254 students helped.

Duration of first degree courses: 3 years; **other:** 4 years (BEd); **Total first degree students 1995/96:** 2,198. **BEd students:** 986. **Overseas students:** 175. **Mature students:** 1,504. **Male/female ratio:** 1:2. **Teaching staff:** 134 full-time, 20 part-time. **Total full-time students 1995/96:** 2,438. **Postgraduates:** 175. **First degree tuition fees:** Home students, paying their own fees in 1996/97, paid £750; Overseas students £6,020–£7,080.

WHAT IT'S LIKE   It's situated in rural, picturesque position 5 miles from the centre of Plymouth, within easy reach of the moors, sea and Cornwall. Public transport to and from campus improving. Reasonable accommodation on campus, including 34 houses in student village and 8 halls of residences; total of around 600 campus places, priority given to first and final year students. Small but active SU and developing fast; runs 'corner shop', launderette, games room, transport services and 52 clubs and societies. Sports centre on campus for related courses eg PE and sports science; sports halls, fitness suite, sauna, squash courts and swimming pool and is available to students at restricted times for a yearly subscription. Extensive sports ground; full-sized astro-turf pitch. High proportion of mature and overseas students on some courses. Expanding library and IT facilities. Confidential students services and college provides medical, careers, finance, accommodation and counselling staff. Good shopping in city, lots of hypermarkets for bargains; plus theatres, cinemas, pubs and Arts Centre.

PAUPER NOTES **Accommodation:** Good campus accommodation. Approved lodging system off-campus. **Drink:** JCR bar – cheapest in Plymouth; more variety in city centre. **Eats:** Adequate campus dining-in scheme; snack food through SU shop. **Ents:** Very good on-campus entertainment. Off campus, variety of clubs and pubs with live entertainment. **Sports:** Good training and fixture facilities on campus. **Hardship funds:** Access fund. **Travel:** SU minibus for events. **Work:** SU and JCR bar employs 40+ students part-time; plenty of work in city centre.

MORE INFO?   Enquiries to Jon Smith, SU President (01752 636700 ext 3071); Jo Caswell, Deputy President (ext 4536) or Mick Davies, General Manager (ext 6511).

INFORMAL NAME   Marjons.

ALUMNI (EDITORS' PICK)   Cat Stevens, Peter Duncan, Ron Pickering, Kate Bush, David Icke.

ST MARTIN'S UNIVERSITY COLLEGE

University College of St Martin, Lancaster LA1 3JD
(Tel 01524 63446, Fax 01524 68943) Map 2

STUDENT ENQUIRIES: Academic Registrar
APPLICATIONS: UCAS

Broad study areas: Education, professions allied to medicine.
(Subject details are in the *Subjects and Places Index*.)

Founded: 1963, as Church of England college of education. **Structural features:** Associate College of Lancaster University. **Main undergraduate awards:** BA, BSc, BA/BSc(QTS). **Awarding body:** Lancaster University. **Site:** Pleasant, single open campus 5 minutes from city centre and at Ambleside and Kelsick in the Lake District. **Access:** InterCity rail (London-Glasgow) or motorway (M6); frequent local bus service. **Academic features:** Professional courses in eg Christian ministry, performing arts, youth and community work; range of combined degrees. **Europe:** 5% spend 6 months or more abroad. Extra-curricular languages-for-all programme. European university links. **Library:** 160,000 volumes, 550 periodicals, 250 study places. Wide range of non-book materials. Students can use Lancaster University library. **Other learning facilities:** Computer laboratories, art and ceramic studios, dance studio, music recital and rehearsal rooms. Paramedical building for OT, radiography, sports and imaging science. **Welfare:** Welfare officer, doctor, resident nurse, chaplain, SU solicitor; chapel, medical centre, counselling service. **Careers:** Information and advice service on site. **Amenities:** Campus bookshop, SU bar and social club; shop; new drama studio; separate SU building; chapel; medical centre. **Sporting facilities:** Floodlit all-weather pitch, tennis and squash courts, gymnasia, multi-gym with equipment for aerobic exercise.

Accommodation: In 1995/96, 91% of first year students in college accommodation. 572 places available (538 for first years): 466 full-board places (432 for first years) at £61.30 per week (£54.90 shared) term time only, and 106 self-catering places (88 for first years) at £42 per week, 42-week lease. Students in privately owned accommodation pay £35–£40 per week for self-catering (+ bills). **Term time work:** College's policy to allow term time work for full-time first degree students. Term (and vac) work available on campus in bar; also careers guidance publishes details of jobs off campus. **Hardship funds:** Small bursaries may be awarded from college trust funds.

Duration of first degree courses: 3 years; **others:** 4 years, some BA/BSc(QTS) and nursing studies; 2 years (accelerated BSc(QTS)). **Total first degree students 1995/96:** 3,012. **BA/BSc(QTS) students:** 1,011. **Mature students:** 938. **Male/female ratio:** 1:3. **Teaching staff:** 192 full-time, 32 part-time. **Total full-time students 1995/96:** 3,242. **Postgraduate students:** 451. **First degree tuition fees:** Home students, paying their own fees in 1996/97, paid £2,040 (classroom), £2,940 (lab/studio); Overseas students £5,920 (classroom), £7,830 (lab/studio).

WHAT IT'S LIKE *Lancaster* It's a C of E college, ½ mile from Lancaster, with a very pleasant and friendly campus and has numerous associate satellite colleges, from Carlisle to Whitehaven. Close links with the community and much involvement with local projects. Lancaster has usual high street stores, pubs for all tastes, restaurants for all palates, and a good range of theatre, music and films. Well situated for coastal and countryside activities. Most first years can live in one of 7 warm halls (meals included in hall fees); all have irons, kettles etc for communal use and laundry facilities. Self-catering residence in town centre for 90 students. Other campus facilities include medical centre, laundry, TV lounges, games room with pool table etc, coffee bar, book shop and general shop. Two bars (alcoholic and non-alcoholic drinks); SU responsible for the discos, quiz and games nights and visiting bands, and for major events like the Easter Ball, Autumn Ball, Christmas Cracker and Going Down Ball. Active SU (affiliated to NUS) strives to meet student needs in all areas, eg welfare, entertainments, clubs and societies, magazine, needs of women and minority groups. Range of sports clubs and subject related societies; others include community action group, Labour club, video/film. Strong links with SCAN (Student Cancer Appeal Nationwide); many students participate in a variety of associated events. Access to university facilities, including library, sports centre, theatre, clubs and societies. A place of opportunities where people can be themselves and participate in or initiate those activities which interest them.

PAUPER NOTES   **Accommodation:** Above average on campus. **Drink:** JCR bar extremely cheap and recently refurbished. Vast range of pubs in town. 3 coffee bars on campus open weekdays. **Eats:** Refectory – full meals with vegetarian provision. Coffee bars have range of snack meals. Chinese, Italian, French, burgers – all there. **Ents:** Discos, local bands, films, society organised evenings. **Sports:** Adequate sports facilities plus multi-gym. Access to university facilities and town sports centre. **Hardship funds:** Emergency loan fund. **Travel:** Trust funds and travel scholarships through the chaplaincy. **Work:** Lots of students get term-time work eg social club, JCR discos, JCR bar, plus minibus shuttle service home from evening events. Some local vacation work.

MORE INFO?   Enquiries to SU President, Calum Sabey or SU Vice President, Sally Gordon (01524 65827).
ALUMNI (EDITORS' PICK)   David Coates, Elizabeth Dent, Nicholas Rigby.

WHAT IT'S LIKE   *Charlotte Mason*   Now part of S Martin's College but still known locally as Charlotte Mason. It's on two sites: a large country house at Ambleside in the Lake District; the other in Kelsick, about a mile away past Stock Ghyll Waterfall. The college is a close knit and friendly community. Students spend four years working towards a BA (QTS). Most first years live in halls of residence and others in hostels and rented accommodation around Ambleside. Nearest supermarket is 4 miles away in Windermere, but the SU takes a minibus to Asda in Kendal for those interested in cheaper food bills. SU shop aims to provide for the everyday needs of college life, at a reasonable price. It's a tourist area with many pubs, hotels and restaurants. Most students drink in the SU bar, The Overdraught, with a weekly event eg karaoke, live bands and drink promotions. Not much local entertainment. SU trips to various nightclubs around the north west and for the sporting facilities at Lancaster. The possibilities for outdoor recreation are endless with kit available from college, friends and the SU; some local outdoor shops offer a 10% discount. Public transport in the Lakes is expensive.
PAUPER NOTES   **Accommodation:** College halls £60–£63 inc bills and 3 meals/day; private rents £35–£45 a week plus bills. **Drink:** Cheap booze at SU bar, the Overdraught; number of unusual beers (eg banana beer) at Masons Arms, Strawberry Bank. **Eats:** Cafés cheap eg Pippins, Stock Ghyll. **Ents:** Cheap plays at college; Kendall Brewery Arts Centre; SU ents. **Sports:** Kendal Leisure Centre: good student rates (swimming, step classes etc). **Hardship funds:** Difficult to get. **Travel:** Hitching good, otherwise travelling expensive. **Work:** 70% work part time. Plenty of jobs in tourist hotels, restaurants etc.

ST MARY'S UNIVERSITY COLLEGE

St Mary's University College, Strawberry Hill, Twickenham TW1 4SX (Tel 0181 240 4000, Fax 0181 240 4255) Map 5

STUDENT ENQUIRIES: The Registrar
APPLICATIONS: UCAS

Broad study areas: Education, humanities, science. (Subject details are in the *Subjects and Places Index*.)

Founded: 1850 as a Roman Catholic college; moved to present site 1925. **Structural features:** Accredited college of Surrey University. **Main undergraduate awards:** BA, BSc, BA(QTS). **Awarding body:** Surrey University. **Site:** 18th-century Gothic house built by Horace Walpole in Strawberry Hill just outside Twickenham town centre. **Access:** Bus and BR (Strawberry Hill station). **Europe:** Languages as supplementary courses. Some students (including QTS) can exchange through Erasmus scheme. **Library:** 150,000 volumes, 700 periodicals,

234 study places, reference copies of course books. **Other learning facilities:** TV studio, CCTV, computer centre, theatre, learning resources centre. **Welfare:** Medical centre, 2 nurses, visiting doctors; student services, counsellors, personal tutors, chaplains, wardens. **Careers:** Information and advice. **Amenities:** New student union, campus bookshop, SU shop, bar, coffee lounge, refectory open to resident and non-resident students. **Sporting facilities:** Gymnasium, dance studio, exercise physiology laboratory, sports hall, sport rehabilitation studio.

Accommodation: In 1995/96, 25% of all students in college accommodation, 99% of first years (and all overseas students). 620+ places available: half-board at £65–£85 per week (includes 9 meals pw), term time only. Students live in privately owned accommodation for 2 years: £45–£50 per week for self-catering. **Term time work**: College's policy to allow term time work for full-time first degree students. Term (and vac) work available on campus in bar, library and registry. **Hardship funds:** Total available in 1995/96: £61,000 government access funds, 1,205 students helped; £6,000 own funds, 15 helped; plus £2,000 other funds for 1 student. Special help: single parents, mature students, late grants and those with extra course costs, childcare or exceptionally high accommodation costs; own funds also available for tuition fees and accommodation for refugee students.

Duration of first degree courses: 3 years; **others:** 4 years. **Total first degree students 1995/96:** 1,950; **Total BA(QTS):** 673. **Overseas students:** 150. **Mature students:** approx 200. **Male/female ratio:** 2:3. **Teaching staff:** 130 full-time. **Total full-time students 1995/96:** 2,222. **Postgraduate students:** 272. **First degree tuition fees:** Home students, paying their own fees in 1996/97, paid £750 (classroom), £1,600 (lab/studio); Overseas students £4,500 (classroom), £5,500 (lab/studio). In addition, first year students pay £340 validation fee.

WHAT IT'S LIKE   Steeped in history and tradition (a beautiful 18th-century mansion is still part of the college), it is a classic setting in the south west suburbs of London only half an hour from the West End. Spacious college grounds are home for a year for vast majority of first years who choose to live in; 3 new halls of residence. All halls are mixed and all college accommodation within five minutes' walk of heart of campus. Opportunities for fruitful interactions between individuals abound, nowhere more so than at the thrice-weekly disco. Other SU events include Christmas and Going-Down balls. Sporting facilities excellent. Sports science, drama and RS the most significant disciplines at St Mary's. Any attempt to define typical St Mary's student is bound to end in disappointment. They could be of British/Irish/Malaysian origin, and of any religious background (the Catholic tradition of the college being far from oppressive); they may or may not intend becoming a teacher and could be studying virtually any combination of subjects. SU role is to ensure a fair deal for all students as well as encouraging a friendly atmosphere and creating superb social life. College caters for those preferring the cosy ambience of a smaller college to larger, more anonymous institutions.

PAUPER NOTES   **Accommodation:** Many live on campus; others in local area. Housing is good value – £45–£50 per week. **Drink:** St Mary's is famous for its ale appreciation. 3 bars cater for teetotallers. Atmospheric bar with animated drinking and japes galore. **Eats:** Cheap on campus. Curry houses galore. **Ents:** Campus bands and discos, good local nightclubs with cheap beer. Good theatre in college. Party scene in college amazing. London is just around the corner with kicking nightclubs. **Sports:** Sporting college, good grounds, women's rugby team. **Hardship funds:** College access fund. **Travel** ISIC cards handy; close to Heathrow. **Work:** Work on campus, evening work in supermarkets etc. 50% students work in term time; students without grants have to work very hard. Further 25% work in vacation – shops etc.

MORE INFO?   Enquiries to SU President (0181 892 0051).
ALUMNI (EDITORS' PICK)   Robert Ackerman, Patricia Mordecai, Tom O'Connor, David
Bedford, John Callander (President of Commonwealth Institute), Julian 'Corkey' Kelly (Irish
reggae star), Geoffrey (from Rainbow), Pete Postlewaite, Robert Beck (actors).

ST MARY'S HOSPITAL

St Mary's Hospital Medical School, University of London,
Paddington, London W2 1PG
(Tel 0171 723 1252, Fax 0171 724 7349) Map 6

STUDENT ENQUIRIES: The Admissions Secretary
APPLICATIONS: UCAS

Broad study areas: Medicine.

Founded: 1854, becoming part of London University in 1900; merged with Imperial College
1988. **Main undergraduate awards:** BSc, MBBS. **Awarding body:** London University. **Site:**
Near Paddington station. **Access:** Paddington and Edgware Road underground stations.
Academic features: Offers both pre-clinical and clinical studies and courses for intercalated BSc. Small number of clinical students admitted after pre-clinical studies at Oxford
or Cambridge. **Europe:** No students learn a language or spend time abroad. **Library:** 30,000
volumes, 245 periodicals, 168 study places, departmental libraries. **Welfare:** Student health
service, university chaplains. **Careers:** Postgraduate office assists graduate students to find
first 2 house officer posts and offers advice on subsequent career development. **Amenities:**
SU bookshop (second-hand), nearby local bookshop specialising in medical textbooks.
Sporting facilities: Excellent cricket, rugby, soccer and hockey at the sports ground
in Teddington; swimming pool; 2 squash courts; multi-purpose recreation hall. Mountain
hut in Snowdonia. Access to Imperial College and University of London union facilities, eg
rowing and sailing.

Accommodation: In 1995/96, 45% of all students in college accommodation, 75% first years.
270 self-catering places: 95 for first year pre-clinical students at £50.05 per week (34 week
contracts) and 175 for clinical students at £49 (year-long contracts). Students live in privately
owned accommodation for 3 years: £45–£85 per week for self-catering (+ bills), £60–£125
for B&B, £75–£130 for half-board (up to £150 with weekend meals). 1–2% of first degree
students live at home. **Term time work:** Policy to allow term time work. Term (and vac)
work in hospital bars and exceptionally in labs. **Hardship funds:** Total available in 1995/96:
£19,000 government access funds, grants of up to £500 awarded.

Duration of first degree courses: 5 years; **others:** 6 years (with intercalated BSc). **Total first
degree students 1995/96:** 632. **Overseas students:** 29. **Mature students:** 30. **Male/female
ratio:** 5:6. **Teaching staff:** 74 full-time, 150 part-time. **Total full-time students 1995/96:** 699.
Postgraduate students: 165 (inc 98 p-t). **First degree tuition fees:** Home students, paying
their own fees in 1996/97, paid £750; Overseas students £9,450 (pre-clinical), £15,000
(clinical).

WHAT IT'S LIKE   Centred in Paddington, close to Hyde Park and central London attractions. Renowned for friendliness, one immediately feels welcome. Course leads to degrees of Bachelor of Medicine and Bachelor of Surgery (MB, BS), also clinical medicine courses for students from Oxbridge. Many students encouraged to take an additional intercalated or clinical BSc course. Pre-clinical teaching, lasting 2 years, on basis of lectures, practicals and tutorials studying basic medical sciences including anatomy (fun dissection classes), physiology, biochemistry and pharmacology. Course is intensive, a lot of work is expected. On the whole teaching is very good and most cope (sometimes organisation would help!). Clinical teaching, lasting 3 years, is ward-based; it's up to the individual to gain the maximum from what is offered on your firm of medical staff. SU very active. Many facilities, including swimming pool, weights room, squash courts, recreation centre and a sports ground at Teddington. Formidable all-round sporting record, notably in United Hospitals' competitions – especially in rugby, rowing and hockey. Music and drama has an impressive reputation. About 50 clubs and societies, for a diversity of activities, ensures never a dull moment. Clubs vary from rugby, waterpolo, rifle shooting, rowing to music, photography, aerobics, wine tasting, mountaineering; if there isn't one to suit your tastes you can easily set one up. Community at St Mary's is small, comprises students, doctors, nurses and staff involved in research. Students can use extensive facilities offered by Imperial College union and ULU. Majority of medical students have overdrafts of £5k–£10k on qualification; none drop out solely on financial grounds because of mix of part-time work, access funds, top-up loans and very friendly bank managers.

PAUPER NOTES   **Accommodation:** Guaranteed for first year students; most 4th and 5th years housed. First class hall – Wilson House – reasonable cost, self-catering 5 minutes walk from medical school. **Drink:** Mainly SU bar (beer £1.20; wide variety). Also The Heron, The Exchange, The Marquis, The Flem. **Eats:** The Canal (hospital canteen), Glady's (med school canteen), Micky's, Toula's, Wong Kei, The Connoisseurs, Sandwich Time, McDonald's, Burger King etc. **Ents:** Film Soc, fringe and pub theatres, West End etc, discos and Balls in Med School; band nites featuring Mary's All Stars and small outside bands. Reduced rates into ents in London and SU run ents, eg freshers week, balls, discos. Sky TV in Wilson House and med school. **Sports:** Swimming pool, squash courts, sports hall and sports ground. ULU and Imperial facilities. **Hardship funds:** Numerous entrance scholarships and mature student scholarships. Funding available for those wanting to study for additional BSc. Hardship (access) fund. Local banks very helpful. **Travel:** Extensive elective scholarships. **Work:** Not advised as too much study and playing to do! Some work in SU bar, SU shop and in local area (eg auxillary nursing). Also clinical trials (a bit dodgy). But about 10% work part-time during term; common in pre-clinical holidays.

MORE INFO?   Get students' Alternative Prospectus. Enquiries to SU President (Sami Ansari) or Vice President (Deepa Rangarajan), 0171 594 3696. Feel free to phone up and arrange informal tour – Tues and Wed lunchtimes during autumn term.

INFORMAL NAME   Mary's.

ALUMNI (EDITORS' PICK)   J P R Williams, Sir Roger Bannister, Sir Almroth Wright, Sir Alexander Fleming, Dr David Bell, Sir Rodney Porter.

SALFORD UNIVERSITY

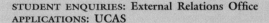

University of Salford, Salford, Greater Manchester M5 4WT
(Tel 0161 745 5000, Fax 0161 745 5999) Map 2

STUDENT ENQUIRIES: External Relations Office
APPLICATIONS: UCAS

Broad study areas: Art and design technology; engineering; science; information technology; business, management and consumer studies; environment; health, care and social work; media, music and performance; social sciences, languages and humanities. (Subject details are in the *Subjects and Places Index*.)

Founded: 1896 as The Royal Salford Technical Institute. University charter in 1967. **Main undergraduate awards:** BA, BSc, BEng, MEng. **Awarding body:** Salford University. **Site:** Different sites within walking distance from each other, 1½ miles from Manchester city centre. **Access:** Motorway links (M602), buses and trains from Manchester. Main line railway station on main campus. Manchester airport in easy reach. **Academic features:** New courses in economics with gambling studies, health sciences and social policy. 4-year degree programmes run jointly by university and local HE/FE colleges (students spend 2 years at each). Over 40% of students take courses which include industrial or professional training; 'student capability schemes' improve skills in teamwork, verbal and written communication and presentation. **Special features:** Integrated chairs where professors work part-time in university and part-time in senior positions in their company eg British Aerospace (aeronautical engineering), Unilever (applied chemistry), British Telecom (information technology), Granada TV (media). **Europe:** All students have the chance to study a language outside their degree, most can take one within a degree (eg physics with Russian) and spend 6–12 months working/studying abroad. Exchange links with some 30 universities/colleges. **Library:** Combined library and computing service: 381,000 volumes in total, 1,220 periodicals, 1,340 study places plus 750 computer workstations. Information includes recommended student texts, HMSO and British Standards material, specialist music collections and access to CD-Rom and networked databases. Annual expenditure on library materials, £65.19 per FTE student. **Welfare:** Health centre, psychotherapist, professional welfare officers, overseas students' adviser, equal opportunities officer, chaplaincy; access to nursery (for children aged 1–5 years). Some residential facilities for married and disabled students. **Careers:** Information (excellent library of employers' material, videos and reference books), advice and placement through 'milk round'. **Amenities:** Restaurants, snackbars, bookshop, union shop and bank on campus; SU building with bar, insurance and travel bureau. Salford city art gallery and Lowry collection near campus. **Sporting facilities:** Leisure centre with 6 squash courts, climbing wall, gym, tennis courts, all-weather pitches, fitness room, indoor swimming pool under construction. Outdoor playing fields at student village.

Accommodation: In 1995/96, 68% of all students (95% of first years) in university accommodation. 4,877 places available (1,989 for first years): some in halls of residence £62.85

per week full-board; self-catering and half-board, £33.80–£47.80 per week. Direct leasing scheme operates to help those renting privately, £37.50–£41 per week. **Hardship funds:** Total available in 1995/96: £94,252 government access funds, 191 students helped.

Duration of first degree courses: 3 or 4 years. **Total first degree students 1995/96:** 13,000. **Overseas students:** 6%. **Male/female ratio:** 3:2. **Teaching staff:** 734 (full and part-time). **Total full-time students 1995/96:** 18,336. **Postgraduate students:** 2,536. **First degree tuition fees:** Home students, paying their own fees in 1996/97, paid £750 (classroom), £1,600 (lab); Overseas students £6,100 (classroom), £7,820 (lab).

WHAT IT'S LIKE   The single modern – but green – campus, is closer to the centre of Manchester than Manchester University. All the university accommodation is within two miles. First years are guaranteed accommodation and 65% of all students are housed; good selection, including catered if required. Recently merged with the old University College Salford, the 'new university' is thriving and facilities growing. Strong links with industry and opportunity for industrial sandwich years (home or abroad) on many courses. Specialising in engineering, modern languages, technology and sociology, graduates have a fine employment record, among the best in the country. Media and communications are also growing rapidly; own media centre (The Adelphi) and strong links with Granada TV. Two student advice centres where students can get help with any problem at all: financial, legal, accommodation, visa, personal or academic; also provide a legal adviser, overseas counsellor, student counsellor and run various health campaigns, eg Aids awareness, safe sex, women's health etc. Union runs campus shops, launderette, hairdresser, optician and print shop and produces monthly magazine, *Salford Scoop*, and weekly newsletter Profile. SU very active with emphasis on clubs and societies (more than 90), entertainments and other student services. Massive participation in outdoor pursuits. Very active community services section – includes Christmas parties for senior citizens, children; English lessons for partners of overseas students; work with ex-offenders; work with the disabled. Sports policy is to provide for as many as possible to participate, then to achieve excellence. Over 15 different overseas societies. About 10% of students from overseas, from all over the globe, contribute greatly to university life. SU international secretary gives advice and organises a Welcome Week and various international events. Financial difficulties increasing although easier for the many who are on sandwich/placement course or sponsored by industry. University large but has very friendly atmosphere and the community spirit is overwhelming.

PAUPER NOTES   **Accommodation:** University accommodation; some married quarters. SU has list of private accommodation (cheap in this part of Manchester). **Drink:** 4 main bars, 2 smaller lounges, 1 pub. Late bar till 2 am, 3 nights/week, at the Pavilion (recently refurbished) and Sub Club; cheaper than local pubs; John Smith's, Coors, Stella, Theakstons – lots of promotion nights. Local pubs a bit rough. **Eats:** The Cage at the Pavilion (run by union) open every night, range of cheap meals. Lots of takeaways and restaurants in Manchester. **Ents:** Two main venues: The Pav mainly plays house on Thursdays and Saturdays, 70s/80s disco on Tuesdays. Sub Club (smaller) has eg regular band nights. In town, excellent nightlife – lots of cheap cinemas, concerts, theatres and nightclubs and loads of students. **Sports:** Union runs leisure centre – weights room, sports hall, fitness centre, climbing wall, snooker room, sunbed, sports shop, video library, squash courts, outdoor play area, all very cheap. New swimming pool. **Hardship funds:** Access funds. Some interest-free loans from university. **Travel:** Union travel bureau on campus; cheap air, train and coach fares. **Work:** Minimal amount of work in bars, ents and library; difficult to get (high demand, low supply). Main local vac work with exam boards, checking marks add up. Limited work in local industry.

MORE INFO? Union handbooks and survival guides. Enquiries to Karl Dayson, President SU (0161 736 7811).
ALUMNI (EDITORS' PICK) John Howard, Sarah Greene. *Salford College*: John Cooper Clarke (poet), Albert Finney, Bill Beaumont, Paul Fryer, Paula Dunne-Thomas (athletics), Peter Williams, C S Lowry.

SANDHURST

Royal Military Academy Sandhurst, Camberley, Surrey GU15 4PQ (Tel 01276 63344, Fax 0171 824 3356) Map 4

STUDENT ENQUIRIES: (Officers' Enquiries) Army Officer Entry, Freepost 4335, Department 0439, Bristol, Avon BS1 3YX.

Broad study areas: Strategic studies, war studies, leadership and management skills. (Subject details are in the *Subjects and Places Index.*)

Founded: 1802 as Royal Military College, Sandhurst. Women's Royal Army Corps College incorporated in 1984. **Special features:** Provides training for British Army officers (male/female, graduate/non-graduate). The principle course is 3-term commissioning course for officer cadets. Female officer cadets are administered separately but complete the same training with men. **Aim:** To develop qualities of leadership, character and intellect through military training and education. **Course objectives:** To develop commanders of courage and willpower with the temperament for decisive action in difficult and dangerous circumstances; to foster attitudes of integrity, selflessness and loyalty which set the soldier apart; to teach cadets how to think and communicate as commanders and to foster interest and care for the individual; to achieve a grounding in British military doctrine; to encourage the analysis of strategic and war studies; and to train cadets in basic skills and battlefield discipline. **Library:** 100,000 books, 350 periodicals. **Specialist collection:** Military history. **Other learning facilities:** Audio-visual equipment; closed circuit TV recording and playback studios. **Sporting facilities:** Squash, badminton and rackets courts; playing fields; indoor swimming pool; gymnasium; physical and recreational training; adventurous training pursuits; skiing; rowing and sailing (own canoes, dinghies and sailing boats); facilities for golf, boxing, field sports; many indoor sports clubs, parachuting, caving and climbing, fencing, judo and equitation.

Accommodation: 100% of students in academy accommodation (single rooms, occasionally share for first few weeks), at £134 per month, full board. **Hardship funds:** All officer cadets are salaried, from £9,774 to £13,932 on commissioning. Pre-Sandhurst undergraduates may apply for sponsorship through university. Bursaries of £1,500 pa for 230 individuals.

Total full-time students 1996: 760 approx of which 80% are expected to be graduate entrants, 10% are from overseas. **Male/female ratio:** 7:1 **Staff:** 531 military; 263 civilian.

WHAT IT'S LIKE   It is set in one of the most beautiful estates in the south of England. A young officer who recently left had this to say: 'Sandhurst dismantles you bit by bit, kicks you around for a couple of weeks, and then reassembles you in a more officer-like fashion. It teaches you a great deal: you are given the widest opportunities and the chance to tackle things you never even thought of! You learn a lot about working with other people and most especially you learn about yourself. In retrospect, of course, it was tremendous fun but very hard. You can experience frustrations as well as enjoyment and real satisfaction when you've made it.' Sandhurst is not for the faint-hearted. You will almost certainly become fitter through physical pursuits like military and adventurous training exercises. The physical is, however, counter-balanced by study. You will learn about military history, current affairs, organisation and military tactics, and presentation skills both via the media and instructional methods. You will become proficient in handling weapons, signals communications, cross country navigation – as well as learning how to behave as an officer. 'Behave like an officer' has often been made fun of: in reality it means that you will be courteous, caring and will always put the welfare of your soldiers before yourself. If you successfully negotiate Sandhurst and gain your commission you will then go on a Special to Arm course with the Regiment or Corps of your choice. It is designed to give you a general appreciation of the more specialist technical aspects of your Regiment or Corps, after which you will take up your first command appointment.

ALUMNI (EDITORS' PICK)   Winston Churchill, General Haig, General Montgomery, King Hussein of Jordan, David Niven.

SCHOOL OF PHARMACY

The School of Pharmacy, University of London,
29/39 Brunswick Square, London WC1N 1AX
(Tel 0171 735 5800, Fax 0171 753 5829) Map 6

STUDENT ENQUIRIES: The Registrar
APPLICATIONS: UCAS

Broad study areas: Pharmacology, pharmacy, toxicology.
(Subject details are in the *Subjects and Places Index*.)

Founded: 1842, joining London University in 1926. **Structural features:** A school of London University. **Main undergraduate awards:** MPharm, BSc. **Awarding body:** London University. **Site:** Central London (between Russell Square and Grays Inn Road). **Access:** Russell Square underground station. **Special features:** BPharm become 4 year MPharm in 1997, to bring it in line with Europe; 4-year BSc course in toxicology and pharmacology includes 1 year industrial experience. **Europe:** No students learn a language. European exchanges have taken place in many European countries. **Library:** 30,000 volumes, 200+ periodicals, 74 study places; recommended books in reserve collection. **Other learning facilities:** Computer and multimedia unit. **Welfare:** London University health service. **Careers:** Information, advice and placement. **Amenities:** SU with shop; ULU nearby; also British Museum etc. **Employment:** Pharmacists in general practice, hospitals and industrial organisations; toxicologists in industrial and government laboratories, or with environmental, regulatory and law enforcement authorities.

Accommodation: In 1995/96, 50% first years in university accommodation. Approx 120 catered places (60 for first years) at £71–£80 per week term time only; and 12 self-catering places at £58 per week. Students live in privately owned accommodation for 1 year: £60–£80 per week for self-catering. **Hardship funds:** Total available in 1995/96: £14,100 government access funds, 40 students helped.

Duration of first degree courses: 4 years. **Total first degree students 1995/96:** 380. **Overseas students:** 45. **Mature students:** 30. **Male/female ratio:** 1:2. **Teaching staff:** 40 full-time. **Total full-time students 1995/96:** 480. **Postgraduate students:** 110 full-time, 90 part-time. **First degree tuition fees:** Home students, paying their own fees in 1996/97, paid £1,600; Overseas students £8,400.

WHAT IT'S LIKE   It's in central London, just off Russell Square. Its academic excellence is respected throughout the world but, just as importantly, it's a very friendly college where virtually everyone knows everyone else by the end of first year. All staff are internal and on hand if students experience any work problems. Social functions very popular with internal and external students, which enables one to meet people from other institutions. SU apolitical but active both socially and looking after its members' interests. Many different events: Ball, at a prestigious location (eg Hyde Park Hotel); garden party and bonfire party, at the school's sports ground (shared with the Royal Free Hospital) at Myddleton House – always superb fun; Christmas panto and party produce many a laugh both for students and lecturers alike; and, of course, excellent freshers and rag weeks. Rag week is highlight of the second term and includes a bed push down Oxford Street and a three-legged pub crawl. Regular Friday night bop-till-u-drop disco held in student common room which has its own bar (some of the cheapest prices in London), pool table etc. Many clubs and societies within the union: football, hockey, rugby, film, kabadi, Islamic, Afro-Caribbean, netball, Asian, Chinese, Jewish and Christian Union. Successful sporty teams and the highlight of the year is when everyone travels to the BPSA sports weekend. All societies hold their own functions (meals, pub crawls, trips to Paris or Alton Towers!); also affiliated to ULU which offers many varied activities. Students have a happy and enjoyable time whilst in The Square, making lifelong friends.
PAUPER NOTES   **Accommodation:** 6 intercollegiate halls within 5 minutes' walk; most 2nd and some 3rd years live out. **Drink:** Cheap student bar; ULU bar; numerous good pubs. **Eats:** Good quality cheap refectory in college – many restaurants within 5 minutes' walk (Chinese, Indian, Greek, Italian, hamburgers etc). **Ents:** Crowded, noisy, lively, discos every Friday night, frequent theme nights. Numerous other events including pantomime, rag week, midsession ball etc. **Sports:** Football, netball, rugby, hockey, kabadi, cricket in college; ULU nearby with multitude of societies and sports facilities. **Hardship funds:** Some. **Travel:** No travel scholarships. **Work:** Jobs in pharmacies (usually Boots) during vacations, but not much time otherwise for work during term due to intensive nature of course.
INFORMAL NAME   SOP or The Square.

WANT TO HELP WITH THE NEXT EDITION? SEE PAGE 66

SCOTTISH AGRICULTURAL COLLEGE

Scottish Agricultural College, Auchincruive, Ayr, Scotland
KA6 5HW (Tel 01292 525350, Fax 01292 525349) Map 1

STUDENT ENQUIRIES: Academic Registrar
APPLICATIONS: UCAS

Broad study areas: Agriculture; food science; environmental studies; rural business and resources, plant and animal science; horticulture; leisure & recreation. (Subject details are in the *Subjects and Places Index.*)

Founded: 1990, from amalgamation of North of Scotland, West of Scotland and East of Scotland agricultural colleges. **Main undergraduate awards:** BSc, BTechnol. **Awarding bodies:** Strathclyde, Aberdeen, Glasgow universities. **Site:** 3 sites: Aberdeen and Edinburgh (both urban on university campuses) and Auchincruive (rural, 3 miles from Ayr). **Access:** Rail, road and air links at each centre. **Academic features:** Communication, numeracy and business/computing literacy emphasised; project and industry-based links. Links with Glasgow, Strathclyde, Edinburgh, Robert Gordon and Aberdeen universities. **Europe:** Under 10% first degree students take a language as part of course (while at Strathclyde University); some students (BTechnol and a few others) spend 6 months or more abroad. Many formal links with European universities/colleges but not for exchanges. **Library:** 45,000 books, 500 periodicals, 200 study places. **Other learning facilities:** Laboratories, several farms including poultry farm, 2 countryside interpretation centres, food processing plant, glasshouse units, arboretum. **Careers:** Library-based information and advice service. **Welfare:** Student services manager, welfare officers at each site. **Amenities:** Range of clubs and societies at each centre; use of all university facilities at Aberdeen and Edinburgh. **Sporting facilities:** Full range of sports facilities plus access to golf courses, water sports, hill-walking and climbing.

Accommodation: In 1995/96, 20% of all students in college accommodation, 40% first years. 200 half-board places at £55 per week, term time only; and 25 self-catering places at £28 per week, Sept–June. 200 new self-catering places planned. Privately owned accommodation: rents £30–£40 per week for self-catering, £50–£80 for half-board. 40% first degree students live at home. **Term time work:** College's policy to allow term time work for full-time first degree students. Term (and vac) work available on campus. **Hardship funds:** Access funds; local trusts, usually with residential qualifications.

Duration of first degree courses: Standard: 4 years; **other:** 3 years. **Total first degree students 1995/96:** 402. **Overseas students:** 5%. **Mature students:** 10%. **Male/female ratio:** 2:1. **Teaching staff:** 100 full-time. **Total full-time students 1995/96:** 1,200. **Postgraduate students:** 121. **First degree tuition fees:** Home students, paying their own fees in 1996/97, paid £1,350; Overseas students £8,370.

WHAT IT'S LIKE   Small college based on three sites in Aberdeen and Edinburgh, both urban; and Auchincruive, a rural site near Ayr. Each centre is a strong community. Mixture of colours, creeds and nationalities. Staff friendly and approachable. Good, informal working relations.

WHAT IT'S LIKE *Aberdeen* It's 10 minutes from the centre of Aberdeen, at the Craibstone Estate in Bucksburn. This is an experimental farm, so allows a mix of practical and classroom activities. Courses include food marketing, conservation and science based courses. Staff/student relations good and relaxed working atmosphere. Library not the best but access to Aberdeen Uni library. This is in the Agri Building on King Street, where some lectures held, and there are computing facilities and a great canteen. Regular minibus connection. Good sporting facilities and access to uni swimming pool, badminton courts and sports clubs. Active campus sports clubs; also gym and table tennis to quicken the pulse rates and a bar to slow them down again. Halls of residence varied but all functional and comfortable. The Bobbin (aka The King Street Mill) popular start for social scene – many promotions and handy for quick lunch time pint or monumental night. Ice skating, beach leisure centre, ten pin bowling, cinemas and shopping centre in city centre, all easy to get to.

PAUPER NOTES **Accommodation:** Halls expensive; good deals can be found in private accommodation. **Drink:** The Bobbin, Ma Cameron's (cheapish); Smart Alex (very cheap at certain times); Zuu (the Agris' bar). **Eats:** Cheap food in union. **Ents:** Ceilidhs, annual ball, live bans in union and pubs, pub quizzes and crawls. **Sports:** University facilities; city centre sports clubs.

FURTHER INFO? Contact Morag Reid 01224 711189

WHAT IT'S LIKE *Edinburgh* 4 miles from the city centre, at the furthest and most inaccessible corner of King's Buildings which bear an uncanny resemblance to a 1970s industrial estate and also houses the scientific branch of Edinburgh University. Diversified from traditional agriculture students, courses now include rural resource management, environmental protection and management and horticulture with plantsmanship. No accommodation on site but help and information from nice ladies in the education office. Known as the Athens of the north for its cultural amenities, Edinburgh's clubs and pubs are legendary in their own right. New students find their own watering hole – have to, as there is no SAC bar on campus (but can infiltrate Edinburgh Uni's with SAC card).

WHAT IT'S LIKE *Auchincruive* About 3 miles inland from the centre of Ayr, on the west coast of Scotland and offers a range of courses (conservation, leisure and tourism, food manufacture, and science and technology), in addition to the long-established agricultural and horticultural courses. Small but expanding rapidly (finding your way around doesn't take long); improving facilities and reasonable library and computing services. Those on degree courses registered with Glasgow University can use its more extensive library. Some accommodation on campus in two halls of residence; others in private rented accommodation nearby. The Cronin Building is the home of the active Auchincruive Students' Society, which represents students to the college authorities, provides entertainment, financially supports sports and societies, and attempts to provide other services to students. The building also contains a TV room (with satellite television), and bar – a popular gathering place in the evenings. Central Ayr has a swimming pool, ten-pin bowling, and many pubs; bus service into Ayr regular. Sport is high on the list of priorities for many students – lots on Wednesday afternoons which are generally free, including football, hockey, rugby (both women's and men's) and Gaelic football (Irish and non-Irish students); also facilities for badminton, volleyball, snooker/pool, table tennis and tennis. Other societies include Christian Union, conservation society, kayaking club and outdoor pursuits club for the Chris Bonnington types.

PAUPER NOTES   Accommodation: Nothing cheap. **Drink:** Student bar. **Eats:** College food; refectory sells vegetarian lunch and dinner. **Ents:** College bar, student quiz, live bands, dances, summer ball and the disco is on every week. **Sports:** Swimming pool in Ayr; numerous sports on and off campus. **Hardship funds:** Access funds. **Travel:** Bus, ferry, train discounts.

MORE INFO?   Contact SU President on 01292 525170 or fax 525176.

ALUMNI (EDITORS' PICK)   'Doddy' Weir – Scottish rugby international.

SCOTTISH COLLEGE OF TEXTILES

The Scottish College of Textiles, Galashiels, Selkirkshire
TD1 3HF (Tel 01896 755511, Fax 01896 758965) Map 1

STUDENT ENQUIRIES: Admissions Office
APPLICATIONS: UCAS

Broad study areas: Textile design, clothing and technology.
(Subject details are in the *Subjects and Places Index*.)

Founded: 1883; part of Heriot-Watt University since 1990. **Main undergraduate awards:** BA, BSc. **Awarding body:** Heriot-Watt University. **Site:** Outskirts of Galashiels. **Access:** Bus from Edinburgh (34 miles). **Special features:** Close links with industry. **Europe:** French offered with some courses. **Library:** New library housing 18,000 volumes, 300 periodicals, 80 study places. Annual expenditure on library materials, £50 per FTE student. **Specialist collections:** Fabric samples and shawls. **Other learning facilities:** Outstanding handloom weaving workshop, studios, textile and clothing workshops, IBM 4331 computer, micro-computing labs, computer-aided textile design centre, lecture theatres with video-conferencing. **Welfare:** Welfare and careers officers; college chaplaincy; other services with local practitioners. **Careers:** Information and advice. **Amenities:** Student/staff social club, shop. **Sporting facilities:** Sports hall for aerobics, badminton, netball, basketball and football training.

Accommodation: In 1995/96, college accommodation on campus guaranteed for all first years. 450 places available: 128 full-board places (all first years) at £53 per week; and 322 self-catering places (72 on campus for first years) at £37 per week, and 250 off-campus at £33, term time only. Students live in privately owned accommodation for 2 years: £30–£35 per week for self-catering, £45 for B&B. **Term time work:** College policy to allow term time work for first degree students (55% believed to work). Little work on campus; careers service helps find outside work. **Hardship funds:** Small trust fund.

Duration of first degree courses: 4 years. **Total first degree students 1995/96:** 538. **Overseas students:** 11. **Mature students:** 100. **Male/female ratio:** 1:2. **Teaching staff:** 52 full-time, 14 part-time. **Total full-time students 1995/96:** 715. **Postgraduate students:** 39. **First degree tuition fees:** Home students, paying their own fees in 1996/97, paid £750 (classroom), £1,600 (lab/studio); Overseas students £5,500 (classroom), £7,000 (lab/studio).

WHAT IT'S LIKE   It's modern, purpose-built, on outskirts of Galashiels, a small country town, 33 miles south-east of Edinburgh (1½ hours by bus). Now faculty of Heriot-Watt University; excellent facilities for recreation and study with specially designed laboratories and design studios. Very well equipped textile technology and colour chemistry departments; design and technology departments have vast hand weaving shed (Europe's biggest), complemented by extensive modern high-speed weaving and knitting looms allowing students first-hand experience of designing commercial fabrics; printing facilities are some of the best in Europe. Pleasant library, lecture theatre, recreation hall, refectory, licensed club room. Halls of residence (full board or self-catering) on hillside near college; students may have visitors of either sex on Friday and Saturday evenings. Plenty of student flats in Galashiels, and the college owns flats for 2nd and 4th years. Student body international – from 11 different countries; high ratio of women to men. Non-political SRC provides welfare, social and cultural facilities. Social and sporting links with Heriot-Watt; inter-site visits by bus and mini-bus. Usual sports and activities including football, rugby (men's and women's), hockey, netball, basketball, camera, squash, badminton, tennis, pool. Regular discos and visiting DJs (eg Alistair Whitehead and Gareth Somerville) – acclaimed 'house' night on Thursdays. Annual charities week. Excellent employment record for SCOT graduates in textile industry. Most courses now industrially orientated with industrial placement in 2 BSc and clothing courses.

PAUPER NOTES   **Accommodation:** Halls and college-owned flats plus privately rented accommodation. A few large married quarters. **Drink:** Student/staff club – cheap, good beer and food. Good local pubs. **Eats:** Halls and refectory food cheap with a good choice and vegetarian option. Bistro food sold in union. Hall dining room open to non-resident students (£2 per meal). **Ents:** Regular clubnight and alternative night, regular visits to Heriot-Watt University for social ents. Multiscreen cinema in town. **Sports:** Badminton, netball, basketball, aerobics, 5-a-side football etc in college sports hall. Local swimming pool. Active football/rugby teams. **Hardship funds:** Good access and hardship funds – well distributed and easily accessible. Short to medium term loans available from SRC. **Travel:** Regular local bus to Edinburgh. Many travel scholarships for textile designers. **Work:** Locally restaurants, supermarkets; lots of flexible bar work (£3.20/hour). Student/staff club also employs students. Some vacation work in local mills.

MORE INFO?   Enquiries to SRC (01896 751869).

INFORMAL NAME   SCOT.

ALUMNI (EDITORS' PICK)   Sir Russell Fairgrieve MP, Lord Sanderson of Bowden, Sir Alan Smith.

CAN'T FIND WHAT YOU'RE LOOKING FOR? USE THE INDEX!

SHEFFIELD HALLAM UNIVERSITY

Sheffield Hallam University, City Campus, Pond Street,
Sheffield S1 1WB (Tel 0114 272 0911, Fax 0114 253 4023)
Map 2

STUDENT ENQUIRIES: Admissions office
APPLICATIONS: UCAS

Broad study areas: Technology, applied science, engineering, computing, construction & property development, education, professions allied to medicine, leisure & food management, financial studies & law, business studies, urban studies. (Subject details are in the *Subjects and Places Index*.)

Founded: 1969 as Sheffield City Poly, from colleges of technology, art and education. University status in 1992. **Main undergraduate awards:** BA, BEd, BEng, MEng, BSc. **Awarding body:** Sheffield Hallam University. **Site:** 5 sites in or near Sheffield city centre. **Access:** City centre site, opposite central rail and bus stations. Good public transport and free internal inter-site transport available. **Academic features:** Emphasis on applied and vocational courses; high proportion of sandwich courses. Access and credit accumulation and transfer schemes in operation. **Europe:** 5% first degree students take a language as part of course, most spending a period abroad. All students have the option of learning a language and spending time abroad. Formal exchange links with a number of universities/colleges. **Library:** Major new learning centre on main city campus (1,600 workstations) plus conventional libraries on other campuses: 500,000 volumes in total, 2,200 periodicals; multi-site catalogue on microfiche. Extensive short loan and reference collection. Annual expenditure on library materials, £64.15 per FTE student. **Other learning facilities:** TV and media resources centres. Microcomputing and over 250 terminals to mainframe throughout university. **Welfare:** 3 doctors, FPA, solicitor, 2 chaplains, 2 counsellors. Day nursery (1–5 year-olds). **Careers:** Information, advice and placement. Also sandwich training placement support. **Amenities:** Purpose-built SU in town centre; union facilities on each site; theatre, film studios, national exhibitions. **Sporting facilities:** Tennis courts, hockey pitches, running tracks, climbing wall.

Accommodation: In 1995/96, 2,170 places available (1,500 for first years): half-board places (10 meals per week) at £47.48–£59.36 per week, term time only, and self-catering places at £40.78–£43.80 per week, Sept–July. Students live in privately owned accommodation for 2–3 years: recommended lodgings rates, £45 per week. **Term time work:** University's policy to allow term time work for full-time first degree students; advisory limit of 15 hours per week (62% believed to work). Term (and vac) work available on campus in SU bars, sports attendants, halls of residence, catering, clerical, library; student part time employment service helps find work off campus. **Hardship funds:** Total available in 1995/96: £311,392 government access funds, 634 students helped (58% applicants). Special help: students with children, high accommodation or travel costs, students with disabilities or self-financing students; own funds also available for part time, unemployed, local students.

Duration of first degree courses: 3 years full-time, 4 years sandwich, up to 5 years part-time. **Total first degree students 1995/96:** 16,128. **BEd students:** 1,988. **Overseas students:** 1,087. **Mature students:** 11,064. **Male/female ratio:** 3:2. **Teaching staff:** 877 full-time, 104 part-time. **Total full-time/sandwich students 1995/96:** 14,419. **Postgraduate students:** 3,216. **First degree tuition fees:** Home students, paying their own fees in 1996/97, paid £1,300 (class-room), £2,770 (lab/studio); Overseas students £5,780–£7,660.

WHAT IT'S LIKE   To many people, Sheffield means knives and forks; still being made, but not so much now. New air of prosperity to the city. Millions of pounds of development in the city centre and the lower Don Valley. Industrial city; more than compensated by its greenness; the Peaks and the Dales are a short drive away. Sheffield has nightclubs and pubs galore – the famous 'Sheff 1' has to be sampled to be believed. Recently refurbished Works offers a variety of brilliant nights out. Clubs, pubs and plenty of curries and kebab places, as well as the ubiquitous chippie. There are cultural delights too – the Crucible Theatre does not exist solely for the snooker tournament! Four cinemas as well as multi-plex cinema, Crystal Peaks outside the city.
PAUPER NOTES   **Accommodation:** Lack of private accommodation. **Drink:** Union bars cheapest bitter/lager; Bankers Draft – cheap. Good pubs – Slug & Fiddle, Lescor, Porters Cottage, The Broadfield. **Eats:** Curry. Bean Beanies. **Ents:** Student nights in most discos; Stardust, Sheff 1, Vaselene, all at union. **Sports:** Most sports on sites, clubs etc well funded by union. **Hardship funds:** Access funds. Hardship funds available over summer. **Travel:** Sheffield Union Travel Shop. Near M1, good for hitching. **Work:** Mainly in pubs in evening and Union bar. SU part-time employment bureau. Approx 60% work during term.
ALUMNI (EDITORS' PICK)   Bruce Oldfield, David Mellor.

SHEFFIELD UNIVERSITY

University of Sheffield, Western Bank, Sheffield S10 2TN
(Tel 0114 222 2000, Fax 0114 272 8014) Map 2

STUDENT ENQUIRIES: Undergraduate Admissions Office
APPLICATIONS: UCAS

Broad study areas: Arts, pure science, medicine, dentistry, law, engineering, social sciences, architecture. (Subject details are in the *Subjects and Places Index*.)

Founded: 1897, as University College from three existing colleges. University Charter in 1905. **Main undergraduate awards:** BA, BMus, BSc, MChem, MMath, MPhys, MBChB, BDS, BMedSci, LLB, BEng, MEng. **Site:** Campus falf mile from city centre. **Access:** Sheffield super-tram. **Academic features:** New courses in biological chemistry, material science and engineering with a modern language, medical materials science and engineering. **Europe:** 5% first degree students take a language as part of course and 2% spend 6 months or more abroad. Formal exchange links with 20 European universities/colleges plus Erasmus links. Increase in language options in all disciplines and joint qualifications with European partners. **Library:** Major branch network and most departments have their own (duplicate) libraries; over 1 million books and periodicals. Annual expenditure on library materials, £76.98 per FTE student. **Other learning facilities:** Audiovisual and television centre, computing centre, centre for English cultural tradition and language, drama studio, English language teaching centre, language labs, computer-aided design lab. **Amenities:** Bars, food outlets, shops, travel agency, printing service, launderette, bank, insurance office. **Sporting facilities:** Sports complex with playing fields, 2 sports halls, 2 artificial turf floodlit pitches, large heated indoor swimming pool, 8 squash courts; additional 38 acres of playing fields 5 miles away; sailing at Ogston reservoir (20 miles from campus).

Accommodation: In 1995/96, 30% of all students in university accommodation, 99% of first years. 4,776 places available (3,552 for first years): 2,544 half-board places (1,959 for first years) at £61.45 per week, term time only; and 2,232 self-catering (1,606 for first years) at £31.12–£51.18 per week, Sept–June. Most students live in privately owned accommodation for 2 years: £32–£38 per week for self-catering (+ bills), approx £55 for half-board and weekend meals. 9% first degree students live at home. **Term time work:** University's policy to allow term time work for full-time first degree students, to a limit of 15 hours per week (40% believed to work). Term (and vac) work available on campus in bars, offices, etc; also student employment service (Tempus) helps students find jobs locally. **Hardship funds:** Government access funds and university's own schemes to help students in financial hardship.

Duration of first degree courses: 3 or 4 years; **others:** dentistry 5 or 6 years; medicine 5 or 6 years; architecture 6 years. **Total first degree students 1995/96:** 15,628 (incl 2,122 part-time). **Overseas students:** 2,588. **Mature students:** 8,479. **Male/female ratio:** 1:1. **Teaching staff:** 1,891 full-time, 207 part-time. **Total full-time students 1995/96:** 14,183. **Postgraduate students:** 4,820. **First degree tuition fees:** Home students, paying their own fees in 1996/97, paid £912; Overseas students £6,198–£8,208, £15,102 (clinical).

WHAT IT'S LIKE   Sheffield is a lively and growing city, which boasts more park space within its boundaries than any other major European city. The much heralded Super Tram makes access to the city centre much better. Culturally it's very active; sports facilities second to none. It's a non-campus university. Like Rome, it's built on seven hills; impressive Pennine peaks are a mere 30 minutes' bus ride away. Main academic buildings just 10 minutes' walk from city centre and within 15 minutes' walk of each other, including halls of residence, in pleasant leafy suburbs. University is still expanding. Good bus services link sites and accommodation. SU has excellent community links involving student community action, Sheffield student charities appeal, conservation volunteers and an innovative student development unit. Sheffielders are especially friendly and welcoming. One of the largest nurseries in the country; women's minibus service and safety information. Excellent SU advice centre, staffed by 4 full-time professionals specialising in finance, housing and international student matters (open 9–5 Mon-Fri terms and vacations). SU produces an *Essential Guide to Student Finance*. Also plays a big social role; up to 20 events each week in range of venues, including multi-purpose Octagon Centre, and the Foundry. Regular programme of major bands. Relations between university and SU generally good. Major new development at SU recently completed: new 400-seat cinema/lecture theatre, meeting and training rooms, student activity space and computer suite.
PAUPER NOTES   **Accommodation:** Six good halls; flats and university houses high standard, rents average to slightly expensive for north. **Drink:** SU has excellent bars (cheapest in city) and its own two pubs, the Fox and Duck (Broomhill, a main student area) and The Rising Sun (Fulwood, a quieter area). Friendly local pubs including several Jazz and Irish pubs. Very strong beer brewed on site at The Frog and Parrot; local brewery, Ward's,

supplies many pubs, beer OK. **Eats:** Growing Asian, African and Latin American scene, excellent Italian and American Diners, many cheap takeaways. Some good veggie restaurants and very cheap Castle Market in town centre. **Ents:** SU gigs sell over 140,000 tickets a year on campus. Lots of clubs, jazz and comedy. Cinema at Crystal Peaks; SU has its own purpose-built cinema showing arts, house and mainstream films four nights a week. Crucible and Lyceum Theatres very active, as is University Drama Studio at the SU. **Sports:** 55 clubs, well funded and expanding. University facilities free, good and expanding. Excellent pool. **Hardship funds:** University loans. Access funds. **Travel:** Excellent travel shop, ferry, coach, rail and flights, very cheap. Well-connected rail network and buses out to the Peaks. Good national rail links. **Work:** Some casual and part time work in SU. Employment agency on campus. 10% undertake paid work in term-time, 60% during long vac.

ALUMNI (EDITORS' PICK) David Blunkett, Amy Johnson, Jane Irving, Tony Miles, Willy Hamilton MP, Tim Robinson, Sir Peter Middleton, Jack Rosenthal, Carol Barnes, Roger Humm.

SHRIVENHAM

Royal Military College of Science Shrivenham, Swindon
SN6 8LA (Tel 01793 785435, Fax 01793 783966) Map 3

STUDENT ENQUIRIES: Undergraduate Admissions Office,
Academic Registry (Tel 01793 785400)
APPLICATIONS: UCAS

Broad study areas: Engineering, science, radiography, information systems. (Subject details are in the *Subjects and Places Index*.)

Founded: 1946; a faculty of Cranfield University since 1984. **Main undergraduate awards:** BEng, BSc. **Awarding body:** Cranfield University. **Site:** 265 hectare country campus at Shrivenham. **Access:** A420; bus to Oxford, train from Swindon. **Special features:** LEA places and Shrivenham scholarships for civilian students. 48% of students are RAF or army officers. **Academic features:** Leading centre for specialised defence education, also offering broader range of multi-disciplinary technical topics. **Europe:** Languages form part of a degree course. **Library:** 100,000 books, 65,000 reports, 850 periodicals. **Welfare:** Resident nurse in medical centre; doctor in Shrivenham village. Student counsellor; churches (C of E and RC) on site. Each student has own academic adviser. **Amenities:** Heated outdoor swimming pool, stables, small theatre. **Sporting facilities:** Squash courts and golf course in large grounds.

Accommodation: In 1995/96, 67% of all students in college accommodation, 95% of first years. 260 places available (138 for first years): 189 full-board places (87 for first years) at £79.52 per week, term time only; and 71 self-catering places (51 for first years) at £37 per week, term time only or students' choice; plus married quarters for serving officers. Students live in privately owned accommodation for 2 years: £40–£50 per week for self-catering, £55–£60 for B&B, £65–£75 for half-board. 3% first degree students live at home.

Hardship funds: Total available in 1995/96: £15,000 own funds, 4 helped; plus £40,000 other funds, 15 helped; government access funds paid to Cranfield, 8 Shrivenham students helped. Special help: own funds available for self-financing postgraduate and overseas students; other funds available for well-qualified, academically able students.

Duration of first degree courses: 3 years; **others:** 4 years. **Total first degree students 1995/96:** 490. **Overseas students:** 25. **Male/female ratio:** 20:1. **Teaching staff:** 104. **Total full-time students 1995/96:** 854. **Postgraduate students:** 364. **First degree tuition fees:** Home students, paying their own fees in 1996/97, paid £1,600; Overseas students £5,900 (BSc), £6,900 (engineering).

WHAT IT'S LIKE   Situated in the beautiful Wiltshire countryside of the Vale of White Horse, this campus college runs undergraduate courses for military and civilian students in equal proportion. RMCS has most of the facilities enjoyed by other colleges and universities – library (only radiographers need to buy books), some free stationery, tutoring and counselling etc. On-site full-board accommodation available for the majority of students; limited self-catering places. Some students live out. Swindon (7 miles) and Oxford (23 miles) are the nearest towns for cinemas, nightclubs, fitness centres, main shops, etc.

PAUPER NOTES   **Accommodation:** College accommodation relatively cheap, convenient for lectures. **Drink:** Cheap bars on campus. Several local, friendly pubs within walking distance. **Eats:** Very good Indian restaurant in village, also Chinese takeaway. Good cheap food in local pubs. **Ents:** Wednesday night parties, balls every term. Multi-screen cinemas, ice rink, and other leisure facilities at West Swindon. Reading and Oxford within easy evening travelling distance. **Hardship funds:** Available. **Travel:** Close to M4 and M5. **Sports:** On campus swimming pool, golf course and stables. Nearly every sport and activity represented and subsidised. **Work:** Mainly pub work.

INFORMAL NAME   Shrivenham or RMCS

SILSOE COLLEGE

Silsoe College, Cranfield University, Silsoe, Bedford
MK45 4DT (Tel 01525 863318, Fax 01525 863316) Map 4

STUDENT ENQUIRIES: Student Recruitment Executive
APPLICATIONS: UCAS

Broad study areas: Agriculture, engineering, geography, environmental and food marketing. (Subject details are in the *Subjects and Places Index.*)

Founded: 1962; became part of Cranfield University 1975. **Structural features:** School of Agriculture, Food and Environment of Cranfield University. **Main undergraduate awards:** BEng, BSc. **Awarding body:** Cranfield University. **Site:** Silsoe, midway between Luton and Bedford (20 km south of Cranfield). **Access:** A6 and M1. **Europe:** All first degree students take a language as part of course (compulsory part of first year); 20% spend 6 months or more abroad. Formal exchange links with 3 EU universities/colleges. **Library:** 60,000 books and pamphlets, 300 periodicals, 49 study places. Annual expenditure on library materials, £230 per FTE student. **Other learning facilities:** Language centre, college farm, computer facilities, workshop areas, teaching laboratories. **Welfare:** Doctor, dentist, nurses, student services adviser. **Careers:** Careers information and advice. **Amenities:** Restaurant; shop; SU with bar; vehicle repair shop; sports hall. **Sporting facilities:** Wide range on campus (eg soccer, cricket, rugby, tennis and squash).

Accommodation: In 1995/96, almost 100% of students in college accommodation (all first years); full-board places at £1,665 pa, term time only. **Term time work:** No college policy on students' term time work. Term (and vac) work available on campus in bar and restaurant; help given in finding work off campus in vacations and for sandwich students. **Hardship funds:** Government access funds and own funds.

Duration of first degree courses: 3 or 4 years. **Total first degree students 1995/96:** 297. **Overseas students:** 9. **Mature students:** 130. **Male/female ratio:** 3:1. **Teaching staff:** 60 full-time, 4 part-time. **Total full-time students 1995/96:** 565. **Postgraduate students:** 268. **First degree tuition fees:** Home students, paying their own fees in 1996/97, paid £750–£1,600; Overseas students £5,000–£7,300.

WHAT IT'S LIKE   The campus is set amongst 30 acres of landscaped lawns and wooded areas in the pleasant mid-Bedfordshire village of Silsoe. Bedford and Luton both 10–12 miles away with bus access. Buildings modern low-level; college farm adjacent. One third of students are undergraduates reading for agricultural/environment engineering, rural resources management and marketing. Courses made up of study units, seminars, visits and practical work. Study facilities good: computerised library, good computing facilities, labs, glasshouses, workshops. Acres of trial and project land. Social life good and varied with discos, live bands and bar. Sporting facilities include new sports hall; many clubs and societies, different religions and cultures provided for. Undergraduates guaranteed accommodation (self-catering at weekends). College food good and varied, but can be expensive. Many students have transport. Major bus and railway stations within easy access.

PAUPER NOTES   **Accommodation:** Reasonably priced; limited married quarters. Some cheap farm cottages. **Drink:** College bar; good cheap bar, Star and Garter in village, students always welcome. Need cars for most others: Crosskeys (Pulloxhill), jazz on Sunday nights; Jolly Coopers (Flitton), good food. **Eats:** Good varied food on campus (incl veggie and ethnic) but expensive. Nearest chip shop 4 miles. Chinese and Indian 5 miles at Flitwick. **Ents:** Weekly films and other ents in college. Cheap cinema in Bedford, Mondays. Ten-screen at Milton Keynes, student reductions. **Sports:** Sports centre with wide range of facilities including: weights, badminton and squash courts. Good selection of outdoor pitches. **Hardship funds:** Available. **Travel:** M1 close, good hitching. Hourly bus links, no student fares. Nearest train station Flitwick 5 miles, direct to London. **Work:** Few students work during term – college bar and canteen work available (£3.50 per hour). Otherwise need own transport to find work in Bedford, Luton or Flitwick. UK students return home to work in vacs.

MORE INFO?   Enquiries to Union President (01525 863355).

CAN'T FIND WHAT YOU'RE LOOKING FOR? USE THE INDEX!

SLADE

Slade School of Fine Art, University College London,
Gower Street, London WC1E 6BT
(Tel 0171 387 7050 ext 2313, Fax 0171 380 7801) Map 6

STUDENT ENQUIRIES: The Slade Administrator
APPLICATIONS: UCAS

Broad study areas: Fine art. (Subject details are in the *Subjects and Places Index.*)

Founded: 1871. **Structural features:** Part of University College London. **Main undergraduate award:** BA. **Awarding body:** London University. **Site:** Gower Street, Bloomsbury. **Access:** Warren Street or Euston Square underground stations; buses. **Special features:** All staff are practising artists. **Academic features:** 4-year degree courses composed mainly of studio work plus history of art, theoretical studies and one other subject from another UCL department. **Europe:** 10% first degree students take a language as part of course and 20% spend 3 months or more abroad. Erasmus exchange programme with Helsinki, Frankfurt, Paris. **Library:** Donaldson Library of University College; 4,500 periodicals and 60 study places; Slade/Duveen fine art reference library; slide collection of University College. **Welfare:** Professional welfare officer; all other facilities from student health association. **Careers:** Information and advice service. **Amenities:** Automatic membership of University College SU, with bar, television, music rooms etc; also central collegiate building with theatre, indoor sports facilities; Slade itself maintains a close relationship with all major galleries in London.

Accommodation: See *University College London.* 5% first degree students live at home. **Term time work:** School's policy to allow term time work for full-time first degree students, limit of 12 hours per week (50% believed to work). Term (and vac) work available both in UCL (bars, library, cleaning) and the Slade (studio clearing, preparation for degree shows, admin, portering); also UCL careers office helps with vacation jobs. **Hardship funds:** See *University College London.*

Duration of first degree courses: 4 years. **Total first degree students 1995/96:** 132. **Overseas students:** 26. **Mature students:** 17. **Male/female ratio:** 1:1. **Teaching staff:** 16 full-time, 25 part-time. **Total full-time students 1995/96:** 132. **Postgraduate students:** 111. **First degree tuition fees:** Home students, paying their own fees in 1996/97, paid £860; Overseas students £9,445.

WHAT IT'S LIKE   Small art college within a large university. Reputation on international level; all tutors/lecturers are practising artists, working alongside rather than teaching their students. Separate first year studios; other years' studios arranged into painting and life, sculpture, and media. Postgraduate studios for painting, sculpture, printing, theatre design and media. Facilities for sound recording and general workshops. New department of art history and theoretical studies. Access increasingly dependent on which department you are in. In spite of traditional reputation there are few constraints. Tutors very willing to discuss problems. The setting within the quadrangle of University College and the West End more than make up for any of the college's disadvantages. Extensive building programme of new and better studio and workshop spaces.

PAUPER NOTES   **Accommodation:** Extremely difficult if you aren't in halls. Halls epitome of studentdom, but don't be put off. **Drink:** UCL union and ULU cheap for London. **Eats:** UCL union is best. Otherwise the whole of London is open to you – some very cheap places. **Ents:** You'd have to be boring to be bored in London. **Sports:** Very good sporting societies; bit expensive outside college; swimming pool at ULU. **Hardship funds:** Don't count on them, but there is money available if you really need it. **Travel:** Annual scholarship abroad. Opportunities for exchange half-yearly trips in third year.

ALUMNI (EDITORS' PICK)   Augustus John, Stanley Spencer, Gwen John, Derek Jarman, Mona Hatoum, Christopher le Brun, Rachel Whiteread.

SOAS

School of Oriental & African Studies, University of London, Thornhaugh Street, Russell Square, London WC1H 0XG (Tel 0171 637 2388, Fax 0171 436 4211, E-mail registrar@soas.ac.uk) Map 6

STUDENT ENQUIRIES: Registrar
APPLICATIONS: UCAS

Broad study areas: African, Asian, Near East and Islamic languages/studies, anthropology, art and archaeology, economics, geography, history, law, music, politics, religious studies. (Subject details are in the *Subjects and Places Index.*)

Founded: 1916. **Structural features:** Part of London University. **Main undergraduate awards:** BA, BSc, LLB. **Awarding body:** London University. **Site:** University precinct in Bloomsbury. **Access:** Russell Square, Goodge Street underground stations; buses. **Academic features:** Unique range of African, Asian and Middle Eastern languages from Amharic to Vietnamese. Degree courses may be single subject or two-subject. **Europe:** French (taught at University College London) may be combined with a number of Asian or African languages. Undergraduates may study for a year at certain European universities. **Library:** 850,000 items, 4,500 periodicals, 600 study places; reserve and short loan collections. Annual expenditure on library materials, £170.52 per FTE student. **Specialist collections:** Regional libraries on Africa, Far East, South and South-East Asia, Near and Middle East; subject collections on law, geography, social sciences. Percival David Foundation of Chinese art. **Welfare:** Welfare officer; access to doctors, dentists, FPA, psychiatrist, chaplains, counsellor, optician, behavioural psychologist; free legal advice centre. **Careers:** Information and advice service. **Amenities:** Refectory, bar; also all facilities of ULU. **Sporting facilities:** Sports ground at Greenford; boat house at Chiswick and sailing club; squash courts, gymnasium. All ULU facilities (including swimming pool).

Accommodation: 25% of all students in school accommodation, 20% in university intercollegiate halls; others in self-catering flats. 500 ensuite rooms in school residence on Pentonville Road (15 minutes walk).

Duration of first degree courses: 3 years; 4 years for some languages. **Total first degree students 1995/96:** 1,475. **Overseas students:** 20%. **Mature students:** c25%. **Male/female ratio:** 3:4. **Teaching staff:** 200. **Total full-time students 1995/96:** 2,000. **Postgraduate students:** 350. **First degree tuition fees:** Home students, paying their own fees in 1996/97, paid £750; Overseas students £7,100.

WHAT IT'S LIKE   SOAS has an international reputation in its field – though little known in the rest of the country. Founded in 1916 to train administrators for the empire, it is unique in the western world in combining fields of Asian and African studies; some feel it has not completely thrown off its past and that courses and departments can be Eurocentric in their approach. Student population is a mixture. Students come from all over the world, many pursuing postgraduate courses, and there is a large proportion of overseas and mature students. Foreign Office and Ministry of Defence staff take crash courses in languages and politics, and business types do diploma in Japanese and Japanese economy. The original building is attached to a late '70s building (lecture rooms and staff offices) which surrounds the college's five-storey library (open six days a week). It's located in a surprisingly pleasant area of central London, off Russell Square, where students laze and the rugby team train. All handy for the British Museum and Library and a short walk from Oxford Street and Tottenham Court Road. Work mainly assessed by end-of-year exams, though some courses are graded on essays and/or dissertations. Teaching is by a combination of lectures and seminars with regular tutorials. Staff are quite approachable for help. SU small but active – and has a radical reputation. There is very little of the faction fighting and bureaucracy which can dog some unions. If you're willing to get involved there's a chance for individuals to shine. Largest societies are the Africa Society, Palestine Society, Women's Group and the Lesbian and Gay Society. Understandably, the union has a reputation for supporting liberation campaigns in Asia and Africa, though it's also active in national and local campaigns. SOAS ents are improving and cover a wide range from Thrash Indie bands through to jazz and world music; frequent African and Asian bands and discos. Film society shows many films from Africa and Asia not seen anywhere else. It is easy for students to meet each other – through the societies to meet those with the same interests, the larger ents events for those with differing interests. SOAS degrees have both a national and international standing.

PAUPER NOTES   **Accommodation:** In SOAS or intercollegiate halls – get booked up early so think ahead. **Drink:** SOAS bar very cheap; lots of other SU bars near by. ULU has annual beer festival, SOAS a real ale society. **Eats:** SOAS food cheap but not very good. Locally – Greenhouse vegetarian restaurant and Eternal Teapot Café (Tavistock Place). First Out is lesbian and gay vegetarian café, good but not cheap. **Ents:** Improving. Locally – Scala cinema, cheap deals for students. Asia nightclub in Islington (world music, Thursday nights) recommended. **Sports:** Small gym at SOAS. Squash courts. ULU facilities nearby – pool, weights, badminton and squash courts. **Hardship funds:** Some – but very hard to get hold of. **Travel:** Research scholarships available for Easter holidays. Cycling popular (helmets a must). **Work:** SOAS bar, cloakroom, shop. Outside – bar and shop work is easy to come by but may pretty bad. Avoid agencies – they get you work but rip you off.

MORE INFO?   Enquiries to SU President (0171 580 0916).

ALUMNI (EDITORS' PICK)   Paul Robeson, Walter Rodney.

HOW TO START? *SEE SHORTLISTING*, PAGE 535

SOUTH BANK UNIVERSITY

South Bank University, Borough Road, London SE1 0AA
(Tel 0171 928 8989, Fax 0171 815 6199) Map 6

STUDENT ENQUIRIES: Central Registry (Admissions Office)
APPLICATIONS: UCAS

Broad study areas: Business, science, education, professions allied to medicine, engineering, computing, built environment, law, social sciences and health. (Subject details are in the *Subjects and Places Index.*)

Founded: 1970 as South Bank Poly, from 6 colleges of further education; university status 1992. **Main undergraduate awards:** BA, BEd, BEng, BSc, LLB. **Awarding body:** South Bank University. **Site:** 2 main locations in central South London (Elephant & Castle and Wandsworth Road, Vauxhall). **Access:** Elephant & Castle, Stockwell, London Bridge and Waterloo stations. **Europe:** 500 first degree students take a language as part of course (an option on many courses); those on language degrees with international studies/business spend 6 months or more abroad. Some formal exchange links with EU universities/colleges, many open to non-language students. European studies available with various engineering specialisms. **Library:** 2 main libraries, 280,000 volumes and other catalogued items; 29,500 bound volumes of periodicals and some 2,225 subscriptions to periodicals; 1,370 study places. Specialist collections in education, law, computing and the built environment. OYNIX software system on MIPS computer for cross referencing. Annual expenditure on library materials, £50.96 per FTE student. **Other learning facilities:** Language lab. Microcomputers in departmental computing labs. Learning resource centre. **Welfare:** Housing service, professional counsellors, chaplain, visiting medical officers, nursery. **Careers:** Information and counselling. **Amenities:** Shops, bars, food outlets. **Sporting facilities:** Sports complex at London Road with sports hall, gymnasium and fitness suites; 21-acre sports ground at Dulwich.

Accommodation: In 1995/96, 30% of first year undergraduates in university accommodation. Approx 1,200 places in halls, £55–£66 per week. Some students live in privately owned accommodation for whole course; rent £45+ per week. 60% first degree students live at home. **Term time work:** University's policy to allow term time work for full-time first degree students (some 25% believed to work). Summer vac work (admissions) available on campus. **Hardship funds:** Government access funds plus limited university hardship funds available.

Duration of first degree courses: 3 or 4 years. **Total first degree students 1995/96:** 12,000. **Number of BEd students:** 400. **Overseas students:** 800. **Male/female ratio:** 1:1. **Teaching staff:** 600 full-time, 500–700 part-time. **Total full-time students 1995/96:** 11,500. **Postgraduate students:** 4,200. **First degree tuition fees:** Home students, paying their own fees in 1996/97, paid £1,000 (classroom), £1,500 (lab/studio); Overseas students £6,250 (classroom), £6,600 (lab/studio).

WHAT IT'S LIKE Variety of sites: three main ones are Borough Road (science, engineering, school of bakery), London Road (social studies, languages, law, business), and Wandsworth Road (built environment). Public transport provides easy access except to

Wandsworth Road which is a bit more isolated. London Road business school is externally in the style of the Technopark but internally looks like an H-block; Borough Road has town hall cakey appearance; Wandsworth is more of an architectural oddity. Limited university accommodation available at present, though some being built. Otherwise it's digs or bedsits which vary in quality and can be pricey. SU facilities improved tenfold in new building; increased space incorporates new club venue. Usual range of sports activities and numerous culturally based societies. Sports at both main sites, playing fields at Dulwich (quite a trek away). Courses are practical, including industrial placements and studies abroad. Lots of access courses; many mature students. Library services are improved by the new Learning Resource Centre, but be prepared to queue.

PAUPER NOTES **Accommodation:** Students share cheap houses. **Drink:** SU is cheapest , Goose and Firkin popular but pricey (brews own potent beer, live ents most nights). **Eats:** Uni food just adequate. SU outlets cheaper and becoming more popular due to wider variety. **Ents:** Society socials, bands, comedy, discos, live screenings at least six days a week. Films most Wednesday afternoons. Drama society active at local fringe theatre. **Hardship fund:** Arranged by SU. **Travel:** No travel grants. **Work:** Part-time jobs in town and also in SU in bars and ents.

SOUTHAMPTON INSTITUTE

Southampton Institute, East Park Terrace, Southampton, Hampshire SO14 0YN
(Tel 01703 319000, Fax 01703 222259) Map 3

STUDENT ENQUIRIES: Registrar (Marketing Services for prospectus). APPLICATIONS: UCAS

Broad study areas: Business, art & design, maritime studies, technology, environment studies, built environment. (Subject details are in the *Subjects and Places Index*.)

Founded: 1968. **Main undergraduate awards:** BA, BSc, BEng, LLB. **Awarding body:** Nottingham Trent University. **Site:** 2 sites: main campus in Southampton city centre; maritime centre at Warsash. **Access:** Near BR station; buses. **Special features:** Courses in yacht and small craft design, media policy, and fine arts valuation. **Europe:** 25% first degree students take a language as part of course and 5% spend 6 months or more abroad. Languages involved in most degrees and part time courses available. **Library:** 2 libraries; 110,000 books, 1,500 periodicals, 1,100 study places. Annual expenditure on library materials, £64.73 per FTE student. **Specialist collections:** Godden Collection (antiques, ceramics). **Other learning facilities:** Test tank, computer suite, 1 manned model ship, metrology lab, language labs, advanced manufacturing technology centre, CD-Roms. **Careers:** Information, advice and placement service. **Welfare:** Student development, Jobshop, community services, including health centre and chaplain; SU welfare officer. **Amenities:** SU block with bank, book shop, bars, coffee lounge, games rooms. **Sporting facilities:** Sports hall, fitness suite, sports field (12 acres) 3 miles from campus, facilities for water sports on Solent (own jetty and facilities).

Accommodation: In 1996/96, 2,350 rooms in halls of residence (most for first years), £66–£68 without meals. Privately owned accommodation rents: £40–£45 per week for self-catering, £57 B&B, £76 half-board and weekend meals. **Term time work:** Institute's policy to allow term time work for full-time first degree students. Term (and vac) work available on campus through job pool, helping in faculty or services; also outside jobs posted on noticeboards. **Hardship funds:** Total available in 1995/96: £152,839 government access funds, 818 students helped (average award £186). Special help: single parents, self-financing students, mature students; own funds used for those with cash flow problems, late grant arrival etc.

Duration of first degree courses: 3 years; others: 4 or 5 years. **Total first degree students 1995/96:** 8,500. **Overseas students:** 220. **Mature students:** 30%. **Male/female ratio:** 3:2. **Teaching staff,** 400 full and part time. **Total full-time students 1995/96:** 9,504. **Postgraduate students:** 250. **First degree tuition fees:** Home students, paying their own fees in 1996/97, paid £750 (classroom); £1,600 (lab/studio); Overseas students £4,900.

WHAT IT'S LIKE   It's on 2 campuses – one in city centre (split site across park); the other at Warsash 10 miles away. Halls of residence at city site (all new, generally ensuite) for first years; flats for second and third years. Otherwise students live in private rented sector. Library and IT facilities open until 9.00 pm and at weekends. Good student scene, cheap restaurants and student nights at clubs. Lots of students from Hampshire area. Good graduate employment rate due to type of course offered eg business studies, law, social science. Many courses have year abroad or in industry; many media courses.

PAUPER NOTES   **Accommodation:** Halls for nearly 2,500 in city centre; private rents £35–£45. **Drink:** Bilbos, Brass Tap and Biffas Bars at SU; very cheap (average pint £1.25). Real ale bar. **Eats:** Bilbos Bar, new food bar, excellent cheap hot food. Loads of foreign and vegetarian eateries. **Ents:** Discos, nightclubs in town; also Harbour Lights, cinema in Ocean Village – cheap with great range. 5 balls a year; comedy nights and hypnotists in SU. **Sports:** All usual sports spread over city. 40 sports clubs including rugby, football and hockey. Gym on campus; cheap and well equipped. **Hardship funds:** Access fund and emergency loan scheme (max £150). **Travel:** Cheap travel on city buses. Good rail links. **Work:** Bar and shop work available on and off campus. Temping work during vacations.
ALUMNI (EDITORS' PICK)   R Parkes (HCC wicket keeper).

SOUTHAMPTON UNIVERSITY

University of Southampton, Highfield, Southampton
SO17 1BJ (Tel 01703 595000, Fax 01703 593037,
Web http://www.soton.ac.uk) Map 3

STUDENT ENQUIRIES: Academic Registrar
APPLICATIONS: UCAS

Broad study areas: Arts, engineering and applied science, law, maths, medicine, health and biological sciences, social sciences. (Subject details are in the *Subjects and Places Index.*)

Founded: 1862; received Royal Charter 1952. **Structural features:** Includes Winchester School of Art; you can look it up separately. **Main undergraduate awards:** BA, BEng, BM, BMid, BN, BSc, LLB, MEng. **Awarding body:** Southampton University. **Site:** Campus 2 miles from Southampton city centre. **Europe:** Languages may be combined with many subjects. Most faculties have exchange links with European institutions. Courses in contemporary Europe, MEng with European studies, European law. **Library:** Main library with 5 subsidiary specialist libraries; 900,000+ volumes, 1,300 study places; short-loan collection, computerised catalogue on network; CD-Roms and on-line information. Annual expenditure on library materials, £105 per FTE student. **Specialist collections:** Agriculture to 1900, local history, parliamentary papers, history of relations between Jewish and non-Jewish peoples, Wellington papers, Mountbatten papers. **Other learning facilities:** Over 500 PCs and Unix workstations, access to specialist computation and information servers, internet and e-mail. Language centre. **Welfare:** Student advice and health centres on campus; doctor, psychiatrist, 3 chaplains, counsellors, legal advice centre; adviser for students with disabilities. Residential facilities for married and disabled students. 50-place nursery (must apply early). **Careers:** Information, advice and placement service. **Amenities:** SU shop, bookshop, travel agency, launderette, banks, concert hall, theatre and art gallery. **Sporting facilities:** Excellent playing fields and sailing facilities, 6 squash courts and sports hall, multi-gym, table-tennis room, fitness studio and martial arts centre.

Accommodation: In 1995/96, 40% of all students in university accommodation; guaranteed for all first years unless they live locally or are accepted through clearing. 3,500 places: 2,485 self-catering £33.80–£47.50, Sept–June or longer; 1,015 half-board, £64.35–£78.70 per week, term-time only. Students usually live in private rented accommodation 1–2 years: £38 per week self-catering, c £60 B&B/half board. **Hardship fund:** Government access funds and own fund.

Duration of first degree courses: 3 years; **others:** 4 years (language courses, MEng, double honours courses, nursing, sociology); 5 years (medicine). **Total first degree students 1995/96:** 8,974. **Overseas students:** 727. **Mature students:** 590. **Male/female ratio:** 1:1. **Teaching staff:** 835 full-time, 43 part-time. **Total full-time students 1995/96:** 10,728. **Postgraduate students:** 1,754. **First degree tuition fees:** Home students, paying their own fees in 1996/97, paid £800; Overseas students £6,300 (classroom), £8,280 (lab/studio), £15,450 (clinical).

WHAT IT'S LIKE   Grassy and attractive campus contains a mixture of traditional red brick buildings and modernistic high-rise boxes. Split across four sites; medical sciences and arts students about 8 minutes walk from the main campus; oceanography and geology students on a waterside campus in the city centre. New building projects include new chemistry building. All halls are off campus but within walking distance, most of high quality with good facilities. Nearly all first years with unconditional offers are offered a place in halls with a choice of self or fully catered. Most are single study bedrooms with shared cooking and bath facilities, although some are ensuite. Students are represented on all faculty boards and most university committees. The SU provides an excellent range of services including the travel centre, sports shop, video shop and retail centre; also catering and bar facilities. Student advice and information centre provides representation and advice for all students. Events department puts on a range of excellent entertainments including live bands, comedy and cabaret. Rag is particularly strong (raised £23,000+ in 1996). Politics present but not overwhelming – pushing towards right of centre.

PAUPER NOTES   **Accommodation:** Halls for most 1st years and some finalists; specialised accommodation for disabled students; some married quarters. Private housing reasonable; accommodation office helps with digs. **Drink:** 2 SU bars, incl Sports and Games bar. Numerous hall bars (members only); good prices for the south. **Eats:** Wide range of food at SU coffee bar and Gordon's Bistro. Many takeaways near campus and halls; plenty of good restaurants to take the parents to. **Ents:** Excellent SU ents: bands, discos, balls, comedy, films, quiz nights, karaoke and even bingo! Town variable; seems quiet to those from big cities. **Sports:** SU has use of good sports grounds; also 6 squash courts, sports hall and multi-gym. No swimming pool. Loads of sports clubs. **Hardship funds:** SU/university hardship fund for loan if grant late. Also access fund for disabled, single parents, etc. **Work:** SU has info on part time work available; Job Shop in careers centre. Seasonal work, eg boat show in summer; bar and shop work always available.

MORE INFO? Enquiries to Simon Coningsby, President (01703 595200, ext 217), Dan Stock, Student Affairs (ext 212), Paddy Lynch, Communications (ext 211) or any of SU officers.

ALUMNI (EDITORS' PICK) Jon Potter, T G Thomas, John Nettles, Baroness Hooper, Lord Tonypandy, Jenny Murray, Chris Packham, Kathy Tayler, John Sopel, John Denham MP, Alan Whitehead, Roger Black, Stuart Maister.

SPURGEON'S COLLEGE

Spurgeon's College, South Norwood Hill, London SE25 6DJ
(Tel 0181 653 0850, Fax 0181 771 0959) Map 5

STUDENT ENQUIRIES: Admissions Administrator
APPLICATIONS: Direct

Broad study areas: Theology. (Subject details are in the *Subjects and Places Index.*)

Founded: 1856. **Structural features:** Private college. **Main undergraduate award:** BD. **Awarding body:** Wales University. **Site:** 8-acre campus in south London. **Access:** By train to Norwood Junction; local buses. **Special features:** Theological college; a denominational college training men and women for various forms of Christian service, especially as ordained Baptist ministers. Strong vocational bias. Ministerial applicants not accepted straight from school. **Academic features:** Postgraduate research, taught masters courses, part-time and open learning courses and awards in counselling. **Europe:** No languages excepting New Testament Greek and Hebrew. **Library:** 40,000 volumes, over 90 periodical series. Annual expenditure on library materials, £120 per FTE student. **Other learning facilities:** Audio-visual equipment.

Accommodation: In 1995/96, 13 full-board rooms in college, £2,187 pa, term time only; 16 self-catering flats/flatlets, including some for married students, £106–£216 per month, year-long contracts. Other students may live in vacant church-owned property. **Term time work:** College's policy to allow term time work for full-time first degree students, limit of 10 hours per week (2% believed to work). **Hardship fund:** In 1995/96, some 40 students helped (approx £710 each). Special help: overseas students particularly from Eastern Europe.

Duration of first degree courses: 3 years; others: 5–6 years, part-time. **Total first degree students 1995/96:** 73. **Overseas students:** 8. **Mature students:** 73. **Male/female ratio:** 7:1.

Teaching staff: 10 full-time, 5 part-time. **Total full-time students 1995/96:** 48. **Postgraduate students:** 73 (part-time). **First degree tuition fees:** Home and overseas students, paying their own fees in 1996/97, paid £5,140.

WHAT IT'S LIKE   A theological college for the training of Baptist ministers and other Christian workers, as well as providing many part-time training and correspondence courses. It's in south London so all the facilities of central London are close. Crystal Palace National Sports Complex is five minutes away by car. 30 students in hall of residence, another 40 live locally; unmarried students live in. Food and living expenses included in fees. All students are mature: school leavers not generally accepted. Some overseas students and few female students. Social activities are organised for students and their spouses. There is a well-stocked computer-catalogued library and a bookshop on site. Sports facilities include tennis, snooker and table-tennis. Football, cricket and rugby matches are arranged against other colleges.

PAUPER NOTES   **Accommodation:** College tries to assist in finding accommodation. Rooms automatically available on campus for single students. **Drink:** Not on campus. **Eats:** Available on site, included in maintenance fee. The economically/gastronomically astute may be able to provide for themselves more cheaply. **Ents:** Student rates at Fairfield Halls/Warehouse Theatre in Croydon. **Sports:** Tennis court and croquet lawn on site. Crystal Palace sports stadium. **Hardship funds:** Students operate their own fellowship fund. **Travel:** Buy student railcard. **Work:** Some vacation work available on campus, otherwise local shop work.

SSEES

School of Slavonic & East European Studies, University of London, Senate House, Malet Street, London WC1E 7HU (Tel 0171 637 4934, Fax 0171 436 8916) Map 6

STUDENT ENQUIRIES: The Registry
APPLICATIONS: UCAS

Broad study areas: Slavonic and Eastern European studies and languages, social sciences, humanities. (Subject details are in the *Subjects and Places Index*.)

Founded: 1915 as part of King's College; became an institute of London University in 1932. **Structural features:** Part of London University. **Main undergraduate award:** BA. **Awarding body:** London University. **Site:** Heart of London University area, Bloomsbury. **Access:** Goodge Street, Tottenham Court Road, Russell Square underground stations; buses. **Special features:** Visiting lecturers teach each language; Russian television by satellite. **Academic features:** All degrees by course units. 4-year courses for students without an A- or AS-level in particular language (first year intensive language year). Language and social sciences students spend a period of study abroad. Joint degrees in Russian with French/German. Students can take course units in north/west European languages, as offered by other London University colleges. **Library:** 325,000 volumes, 1,100 periodicals,

70 study places; reference facilities for course books. Annual expenditure on library materials, £258.32 per FTE student. **Specialist collections:** Romanian and Hungarian literature; pre-1800 Russian and Church Slavonic books. **Other learning facilities:** Language laboratory. **Welfare:** London University health service. **Careers:** Information, advice and placement; careers computer. **Amenities:** Student common room, bar and canteen. All facilities of ULU in Malet Street.

Accommodation: No school accommodation. 50% first year students in London University intercollegiate halls. 25% of first degree students live at home. **Term time work:** University policy to allow term time work (30% believed to work). Occasional term (and vac) work available in university in library, assisting with conferences. **Hardship funds:** Total available in 1995/96: £10,500 government access funds, 60 students helped. Special help: students in private accommodation, mature students with children or housing commitments, students whose parents won't pay their share, studying abroad, self-financing.

Duration of first degree courses: 4 years (languages); **others:** 3 years (history and contemporary East European studies). **Total first degree students 1995/96:** 350. **Overseas students:** 3. **Mature students:** 110. **Male/female ratio:** 1:1. **Teaching staff:** 50 full-time, 9 part-time. **Total full-time students 1995/96:** 500. **Postgraduate students:** 150. **First degree tuition fees:** Home students, paying their own fees in 1996/97, paid £750; Overseas: £.6,950

WHAT IT'S LIKE   Yes, one of the smallest colleges within London University, right in the heart of the university area behind the British Museum. However, its smallness (c.500 students) means that it's very easy to get to know everyone and its camaraderie is infamous. It can also have advantages in lectures; students of Bulgarian or Hungarian often find themselves with very little company apart from the tutor. But being part of London University means that you are neither academically nor socially isolated. Academically, it is possible to choose courses from other colleges and many students from other colleges come to SSEES. It has an excellent reputation for sending students abroad to experience their subject at first hand. Socially, ULU offers a limitless supply of entertainments and sports facilities, as do many of the other larger colleges. In SSEES itself the social life centres around the bar and the free pool room which is the place to meet students from other colleges. This is especially true during Rag Week, which no one manages to escape. The highlight of the year though is the May Ball held at one of London's top Russian or East European restaurants. There are also many societies including mountaineering, debating and a growing Masaryk society, for all those interested in the Czeck and Slovak republics. Easy to find out about events in the college's weekly info-sheet, appropriately named *Samizdat*. Few other colleges have such a unique combination which stuns enquirers into silence.

PAUPER NOTES   **Accommodation:** No college accommodation, but good intercollegiate halls near by can be used for up to 2 years of a course. University accommodation office helpful. **Drink:** SSEES bar, run by students, has short hours but good parties and promotions. Many college and hall bars near by; bars in ULU building. Good pubs in the vicinity; Lord John Russell has authentic Slav lager on tap. **Eats:** SSEES canteen for tea, coffee, sandwiches and a limited selection of hot meals, including vegetarian dishes. Wider selection at ULU or other nearby college canteens. **Ents:** Near the West End and best selection of clubs, theatres, cinemas, concerts in the country; cheap standby tickets often available. **Sports:** Teamed up with SOAS to provide wider variety. Recent successes in football, rugby and netball. **Societies:** Drama, aerobics, south Slav, kid care, Christian Union, Masary, Polish film, Roumanian, mountaineering. **Work:** Available in ULU and well-paid part-time work can be found in the major chain stores. Always possible to find part-time work.
ALUMNI (EDITORS' PICK)   Jonathan Ross.

STAFFORDSHIRE UNIVERSITY

Staffordshire University, College Road, Stoke-on-Trent ST4 2DE
(Tel 01782 294000, Fax 01782 745422) Map 2

STUDENT ENQUIRIES: Head of Student Recruitment
APPLICATIONS: UCAS

Broad study areas: Art & design (including ceramics), humanities, business, engineering, computing, law, nursing, science, social sciences. (Subject details are in the *Subjects and Places Index*.)

Founded: 1970 as Staffordshire Poly from Stoke-on-Trent colleges of art and technology and Stafford College of Technology. University status in 1992. **Main undergraduate awards:** BA, BSc, BEng, LLB. **Awarding body:** Staffordshire University. **Site:** 2 campuses: Stafford Campus, 1½ miles from town centre; Stoke Campus, between Hanley and Stoke. **Access:** Easy access to both sites by road (M6) and rail (Stoke-on-Trent and Stafford stations on main line routes to London). **Academic features:** Extended engineering degrees for students with A-levels in subjects other than maths and physics. All first degrees in modular framework. **Europe:** Language options, including Russian, available for most programmes; opportunities to study or undertake a work placement abroad. Links with universities across Europe, in many subjects. **Library:** Libraries on each site; total of 310,000 books, 2,200 periodicals, CD-Rom, 900+ study places. **Other learning facilities:** Extensive computing facilities, language, science and engineering laboratories, design and fine art studios. Study skills support. **Welfare:** Counsellors, health and chaplaincy service, childcare provision and support for disabled students. **Amenities:** SU with office on each site, snack bars, shops, minibus service, travel company; banking facilities on Stafford site; cinema and art gallery on Stoke campus. **Sporting facilities:** Sports hall on Stoke site, together with playing fields and all weather football pitch. Stafford students have concessionary access to local leisure complex.

Accommodation: In 1995/96, 50% of first year students in university accommodation. 2,000 self-catering places available in halls, flats, shared houses or head tenancies at £30–£40 per week, 40-week contract. Students live in privately owned accommodation for 2+ years: £30–£40 per week for self-catering (plus fuel). 25% first degree students live at home. **Term time work:** University's policy to allow term time work for full-time first degree students (35% believed to work). Term (and vac) work available on campus in SU bar, library etc. **Hardship funds:** Total available in 1995/96: £234,621 government access funds, 400 students helped. Special help: students with dependants (childcare), additional needs, travel costs, exceptional or unforeseen circumstances or summer vacation hardship.

Duration of first degree courses: 3 years; **others:** 4 years (sandwich courses; extended engineering degrees); 5 years (sandwich extended engineering degrees). **Total first degree students 1995/96:** 10,635. **Overseas students:** 405. **Mature students:** 3,501. **Male/female ratio:** 3:2. **Teaching staff:** 432 full-time, 88 part-time. **Total full-time students 1995/96:** 11,569. **Postgraduate students:** 621. **First degree tuition fees:** Home students, paying their own fees in 1996/97, paid £750 (classroom) £1,600 (lab/studio); Overseas students £5,501 (classroom), £5,930 (lab/studio).

WHAT IT'S LIKE Based both in Stoke and Stafford, 17 miles apart. Stoke is the larger site both in student numbers and size of the premises. An industrial town based around the Potteries and what's left of mining and steel industries. Easy to get out into Peak District countryside and to major cities, particularly if you can afford a car; railway station is part of the university. Stafford is a pleasant market town south of Stoke; more up-market than surrounding areas. Stafford student body principally (male-dominated) computing and engineering and (female-dominated) business enterprise modular course. Humanities taught at Stoke. Much accommodation in Stoke is in long, terraced streets in urban renewal area. Stafford is better but costs more. Some halls in Stoke are a long way from uni, though there is a limited bus service between sites and halls. Union offers facilities ranging from shops and travel to 4 bars and 3 venues. Excellent variety of ents; regular comedy, gigs and a disco. Also athletics union and many societies. Students come from all over the UK and overseas. Staffordshire can be a good place to see the world from – it's cheap, and the university is really holding its own.

PAUPER NOTES **Accommodation:** Halls. Some good, some hideous. Local accommodation is OK in Stoke; more expensive in Stafford. **Drink:** Union. Good, cheap bars and local pubs. Banks, Marstons Pedigree. **Eats:** Campus food not brilliant but getting better. Many discounts in local places; vegetarian and vegan foods as well as good Italian, Indian, balti, kebab shops galore. **Ents:** Regular live music at all 3 unions; venue at Stafford used occasionally, most notably at all-night May Ball. Thriving local music scene in Stoke. Plenty of theatres and cinemas. **Sports:** University sports centre (with 3 astroturf pitches), swimming pool nearby. Local authority has students 'recreation key', allowing cheap/free use of local facilities. **Hardship funds:** Government access funds and a few loans from the union. **Travel:** Good access: London 1 hr 40 mins, Manchester and Birmingham less than 1 hr, so possible for nights out. Union coaches to places of interest; Alton Towers very close. **Work:** 10–15% students work in pubs, cinemas, nightclubs and local zoo, during term time; 40% work in vacation. Union has a job-board on all main sites.

MORE INFO? Enquiries to President SU at Stafford (01785 353311) or Stoke (01782 294629).

STIRLING UNIVERSITY

The University of Stirling, Stirling FK9 4LA
(Tel 01786 473171) Map 1

STUDENT ENQUIRIES: Director, Schools and Colleges Liaison
(Tel 01786 467046, Fax 01786 466800)
APPLICATIONS: UCAS

Broad study areas: Natural sciences, management/finance, education, arts, languages, social sciences. (Subject details are in the *Subjects and Places Index*.)

Founded: 1967. **Main undergraduate awards:** BA, BSc, BAcc. **Awarding body:** Stirling University. **Site:** 360-acre site 2 miles north-east of Stirling. **Access:** A9; buses from Stirling direct to campus. **Special features:** Semester system (2 semesters of 15 weeks each);

concurrent education (teacher training) courses; continuous assessment policy. **Europe:** 30% first degree students take a language as part of course and up to 20% spend a period abroad in their third year. Formal exchange links with well over 100 universities/colleges across Europe. Wide and increasing number of European-orientated course options. **Library:** 500,000 volumes, 2,400 periodicals, 1,000 study places; reference collection. Computerised catalogue and issue system. Annual expenditure on library materials, £106 per FTE student. **Specialist collections:** Rare books (19th century); government publications. **Welfare:** Doctor, chaplains, counsellors and academic advisers on site; other services available locally. Limited residential facilities for married and disabled students. **Careers:** Information and advice. 4 careers advisers. **Amenities:** Bookshop on campus, chaplaincy centre, students' association with shop and travel service; bank, supermarket, chemist, post office; MacRobert Arts Centre (including cinema/theatre); good facilities for disabled students (wheelchair routes, paraplegic toilets). **Sporting facilities:** Gannochy sports centre with wide range of indoor and outdoor sports; swimming pool, golf course and indoor tennis centre all on campus.

Accommodation: In 1995/96, 60% of all students in university accommodation, 100% first years. 2,150 self-catering places on campus at £35–£40 per week; contracts term time, Sept–June or year long. More accommodation available off campus. Students typically live in privately owned accommodation for 1–2 years: average rents £150–£160 per month. 15% of first degree students live at home. **Term time work:** University does not prevent term time work. Term (and vac) work available on campus in catering, bars, arts centre, SA bars; Careers Service advertises outside part-time jobs and SA has Jobsboard. **Hardship funds:** Government access funds.

Duration of first degree courses: 4 years (honours); **others:** 3 years (general). **Total first degree students 1995/96:** 5,000. **Male/female ratio:** 1:1. **Teaching staff:** 370, 95 research. **Total full-time students 1995/96:** 5,500. **Postgraduate students:** 680. **First degree tuition fees:** Home students, paying their own fees in 1996/97, paid £750; Overseas students £5,800 (classroom), £7,650 (lab/studio).

WHAT IT'S LIKE   On the Airthrey Estate, it's backed by a massive hill, surrounded by woods and has a lake (sorry, loch) in the middle; easy to see why it's called one of Europe's most beautiful campuses. It has an extremely active union with a wide variety of clubs and societies to cater for the 90 nationalities that form the university's population; also houses the campus radio station. Sports facilities were excellent even before the new Scottish National Tennis Centre was opened. Nationally renowned for allowing students a flexibility in course choice hard to better elsewhere. Students tend to buy necessities on campus and leave weekly shopping until they visit the town centre. Plenty of pubs and restaurants, and if you're bored with the town you can easily travel to Glasgow or Edinburgh for the day.

PAUPER NOTES   **Accommodation:** Breezeblock/wooden chalets; moving towards market rents. **Drink:** 5 bars, including a new ale house. Good selection lagers and beers. Plenty of promos. **Eats:** Food excellent value in SA eateries, especially bistro; veggie food available. **Ents:** Active ents scene, good enough to keep most students on campus. **Sports:** Excellent sports facilities on campus. Plenty sports clubs. **Hardship Funds:** Access fund available to off-campus students. **Travel:** Exchange programme 3rd year; otherwise it's the travel shop. **Work:** Union bars; vacation work on campus/town. Shops tend not to employ students unless they can guarantee availability for long period.

ALUMNI (EDITORS' PICK)   Tommy Sheridan, Dr John Reid MP, Stewart Hepburn, Mike Connarty MP.

STRATHCLYDE UNIVERSITY

The University of Strathclyde, Glasgow G1 1XQ
(Tel 0141 552 4400, Fax 0141 552 7362) Map 1

STUDENT ENQUIRIES: Registry
APPLICATIONS: UCAS

Broad study areas: Arts, social sciences, education, engineering, science, business. (Subject details are in the *Subjects and Places Index.*)

Founded: 1964 from merger of Royal College of Science & Technology (founded as Anderson's Institution, 1796) and Scottish College of Commerce; merged with Jordanhill Education College, 1993. **Main undergraduate awards:** BA, BArch, BSc, BEng, MEng, BEd, LLB. **Awarding body:** Strathclyde University. **Site:** Glasgow city centre (John Anderson campus) and west end (Jordanhill campus). **Academic features:** Flexible credit-based system for all courses. Assessment by course work as well as final examination; practical training and experience are features of many degree courses. **Europe:** 20% first degree students learn a language as part of their course, 15% spend 6 months or more abroad. Languages may be combined with a range of subjects; 7 languages may be studied by any student on self-serve basis in language laboratory. Exchange links with 150+ universities/colleges across Europe, all open to non-language specialists. Approx 225 students went to Europe on Erasmus programmes in 1995/96. **Library:** *Anderson campus –* 650,000 volumes, 1,468 study places, short loan collection. *Jordanhill campus –* 200,000 volumes, 502 study places. Annual expenditure on library materials, £86.56 per FTE student. **Specialist collections:** Business information centre, Fleck chemistry library, law library, electrical engineering library, rare books and manuscripts in Andersonian Library. **Welfare:** Health clinics on site; consultant psychiatrist; chaplaincy centre; student advisers. Limited number of flats for married students; playgroup run by students' association. **Careers:** Information and advice service. **Amenities:** 10-storey Students' Association building with entertainment, sport, catering and support facilities. **Sporting facilities:** Sports centre with large twin-court games hall; gymnasium, swimming pool; 7 football pitches; astroturf pitch (American football and hockey); soccer and club training; 41 sections of Sports Union, for most indoor and outdoor sports.

Accommodation: In 1995/96, 19% of all students in university accommodation, 26% of first years. 2,442 places available (1,370 for first years): 313 full-board places (258 for first years) at £54.15, term time only; and 2,129 self-catering places (1,112 for first years) at £39.10 per week, term-time or longer. Students live in privately owned accommodation for 2 years: rents £35–£50 per week for self-catering, £45–£60 for B&B. 57% first degree students live at home. **Term time work**: University's policy to allow term time work for full-time first degree students (50% believed to work). Term (and vac) work available on campus in SU, registries, accommodation; some help given by careers service finding off-campus jobs. **Hardship funds:** Total available in 1995/96: £363,000 government access funds, 1,220 students helped; plus various other funds including £20,000 for childcare (over 130 students helped). Special help: single parents, those with dependants, disabilities.

Duration of first degree courses: 4 years (honours); **others:** 5 years (MEng); 3 years (ordinary). **Total first degree students 1995/96:** 10,184. **Overseas students:** 417. **Mature students:** 30%. **Male/female ratio:** 11:9. **Teaching staff:** 843 full-time, 60 part-time. **Total full-time students 1995/96:** 12,627. **Postgraduate students:** 2,443. **First degree tuition fees:** Home students, paying their own fees in 1996/97, paid £750 (classroom), £1,600 (lab/studio); Overseas students £6,100–£7,990.

WHAT IT'S LIKE   Main campus, John Anderson campus is in the city centre; the education faculty is to the west at Jordanhill. *John Anderson* is an attractively landscaped city centre campus between George Square and magnificent Glasgow cathedral. Modern, sought after residences on campus; further university accommodation off campus including married quarters. University located on a series of hills – not all buildings accessible by wheelchair. Well served by all forms of public transport. SA has purpose-built union building with 10 levels: 5 bars/lounges selling wide variety of snacks and meals; games room; major band venue capable of holding 800 people; film society; debating chamber; suites available for hire; bank and shopping mall in building; launderette and child care facility organised by SA. Over 200 different sports and non-sports clubs boasting over 6,000 members. Students from west of Scotland mix well with high proportion of overseas students from 107 nations. Very high numbers of mature students add character to student mix. Elective classes available; university is proud of its technological eminence though arts and other faculties also strong. New graduate business school. *Jordanhill campus* houses the education faculty on an attractive green-field site in the west of the city. Accommodation in campus halls is sought after. SA runs a shop, bar, games room and discos, and has a welfare service and offices too. Also a bank and bookshop on campus. Excellent sporting facilities. Large proportion of mature and postgraduate students. All Strathclyde students can use the facilities on both campuses. On the whole, Jordanhill is less impersonal than the larger John Anderson campus.

PAUPER NOTES   **Accommodation:** Halls competitively priced; but luxury accommodation means high price. **Drink:** SU bars; various trendy yuppie bars in city. Cheapest drink in the union. Most popular beer is Tennents or McEwan's; soft drink, Irn Bru. **Eats:** All types of food in union, including vegetarian or vegan. **Ents:** Glasgow has a thriving music scene, mirrored in the union. Glasgow Film Theatre (student discount) and Citizens Theatre/ Trongate. **Sports:** Massive sports union with full facilities. Sports centres in central Glasgow tend to be private. **Hardship funds:** University-run funds. **Travel:** Bus, train and underground transcards are fairly economical. **Work:** Bars, shops and many new tourist-orientated businesses. Union employs some students. Some city-centre work but scarce.

ALUMNI (EDITORS' PICK)   John Logie Baird, Sir Monty Finniston, Bobby McGregor, Frank Clement, David Livingstone, John Reith, Sir Ian McGregor, Sir Adam Thompson; Malcolm Bruce, Douglas Henderson, Dick Douglas, Maria Fyfe, Clive Soley (MPs); James Kelman (writer), Douglas Trainer (NUS president), Craig Brown (Scotland Manager), Dougie Donnley (BBC).

GET HOLD OF THE PROSPECTUSES

SUNDERLAND UNIVERSITY

University of Sunderland, Langham Tower, Ryhope Road,
Sunderland SR2 7EE
(Tel 0191 515 2000, Fax 0191 515 2423) Map 2

STUDENT ENQUIRIES: Student Recruitment Office
(Unit 4C, Technology Park, Chester Road, Sunderland
SR2 7PS; Tel 0191 515 3000, Fax 0191 515 3805,
E-mail student helpline@sunderland.ac.uk)
APPLICATIONS: UCAS (SWAS for social work)

Broad study areas: Art, design & communication, computing & information systems, education, engineering & technology, environment, health sciences, social and international studies, business. (Subject details are in the *Subjects and Places Index*.)

Founded: 1969 as Sunderland Poly, from colleges founded in 1860 onwards. University status 1992. **Main undergraduate awards:** BA, BSc, BEng. **Awarding body:** Sunderland University. **Site:** 4 town centre sites within 10 min walk. New campus on banks of River Wear, housing schools of business, computing and information systems. **Special features:** Students from over 50 countries. UK students have chance to study abroad on a number of courses in universities/colleges in America, Japan and Russia, as well as western Europe. Many building are accessible to mobility-impaired students. **Academic features:** Franchise scheme; modular credit scheme. **Europe:** 800+ first degree students take a language and spend 6 months or more abroad. Links with over 60 universities/colleges across Europe – including student exchanges. Approved Erasmus programme. **Library:** 4 libraries at different sites: total of 350,000 volumes, 2,000 periodicals, 100,0000 slides and photographs and 1,900 study places. On-line catalogue, large CD-Rom networks, access to 70 databases etc. Annual expenditure on library materials, £105 per FTE student. **Other learning facilities:** Art gallery; language centre; media resources unit; journalism suite; computer network with access to mini-computers and main computer. All students have e-mail accounts and access to internet. **Welfare:** Counselling service, professional welfare officer, solicitor through SU, chaplain, nursing sister on call for first aid, 2 day nurseries. **Careers:** Information, advice and placement. **Amenities:** SU with numerous societies (including ski club), travel centre and shop; 2 bookshops on site. **Sporting facilities:** Sports centre with fitness suite, swimming pool and sports hall. Special access to local leisure centre and sports facilities.

Accommodation: In 1995/96, 43% of all students in university accommodation; 80% of first years (all who want it). 3,153 places available: average rents for catered places £39–£49 per week, £27–£38 self-catering, Sept–June. Students live in privately owned accommodation for 2 years: rents £32–£38 per week for self-catering. 14% first degree students live at home. **Term time work:** University's policy to allow term time work for full-time first degree students. Term (and vac) work available on campus in SU, library, student bars, clubs, societies, administration; also off-campus jobs advertised on noticeboards. **Hardship funds:** Total available in 1995/96: £198,000 government access funds, 1,267 helped. Special help: self-financing students and those with dependants.

Duration of first degree courses: 2 or 3 years full time; 4 years sandwich; 3–5 years part-time. **Total first degree students 1995/96:** 10 017 full-time, 4,467 part-time. **Overseas students:** 6%. **Male/female ratio:** 1:1. **Teaching staff:** 466 full-time, 34 part-time. **Total full-time students 1995/96:** 10,546. **Postgraduate students:** 1,402. **First degree tuition fees:** Home students, paying their own fees in 1996/97, paid £750 (classroom), £1,600 (lab/studio); Overseas students £5,250 (classroom), £6,250 (lab).

WHAT IT'S LIKE   An expanding city centre university, split over three campuses – Chester Road, Langham and St Peter's. All the buildings are within 20 minutes walk of each other but university provides free campus bus service which runs continuously between the sites. Cosmopolitan mix of students; large number of mature and local people as well as foreign students from over 50 different countries. 2,300 places in hall of residence-style accommodation and a further 700 available in university-managed property; privately owned accommodation in plentiful supply. Strong lecturing staff in most areas, particularly pharmacy, technology, engineering, fine arts, business studies, environment and media studies. Computer resources have recently been updated; 24 hour access. 4 libraries and plans to extend its main site. St Peter's campus recently opened; also a Sunday cinema project and the only biosphere in the north! SU is active and has representation on all three sites; two popular bars, night club, shop and a travel service, all extremely cheap. Union also supplies professional advice services for welfare and academic problems and its own Nightline. It also provides a free shuttle bus service between the halls and the union bars; during the day the buses are available for use by any of the 100+ clubs and societies (sporting, political, cultural) which the union supports. The cheaper cost of living in the north east is a definite bonus. Also many local shops have student discounts.

PAUPER NOTES   **Accommodation:** Halls of residence. Head tenancy scheme (university sublet private property to ensure standards). Some lodgings available for families. **Drink:** Union's three bars are the cheapest. Many good local pubs. Local brewery is Vaux. Samson and Double Maxim recommended. **Eats:** Lots of pizza, kebab, Chinese, Indian and chip-shop takeaways. Some good cheap local restaurants, predominantly Italian. Lack of specialist veggie restaurants. **Sports:** Limited university sports facilities but good local provision. **Ents:** Good SU ents. **Hardship funds:** Access fund, strict criteria. Financial pressures are grounds for academic appeal. **Travel:** All sites in walking distance. Campus bus and SU evening shuttle bus provided free. **Work:** Difficult to find work in any area other than bar/waiting. Union provides work in bars, as shuttle bus drivers, stewards and distribution.

MORE INFO?   Enquiries to Julie Carolan, Student Services secretary (0191 514 5512).
ALUMNI   Steve Cram.

SURREY INSTITUTE

The Surrey Institute of Art & Design, Farnham Campus,
Falkner Road, Farnham, Surrey GU9 7DS
(Tel 01252 722441, Fax 01252 733869) Map 4

STUDENT ENQUIRIES: The Registry (01252 732232/3,
Fax 01252 718313). APPLICATIONS: UCAS

Broad study areas: Art & design, media, fashion, communication. (Subject details are in the *Subjects and Places Index.*)

Founded: 1994 from amalgamation of two existing art colleges, both founded in 1890s. **Main undergraduate award:** BA. **Awarding body:** Surrey Institute. **Site:** Two sites: Farnham and Epsom town centres. **Special features:** Academic staff are practising artists, designers, film makers, media and crafts people. Many students major award winners, participate in festivals, trade fairs and receive external commissions. **Academic features:** Unique degree in animation. **Europe:** Option to study a language and a small number spend time abroad. Exchange links with EU universities/colleges. **Library:** *Farnham:* 50,000 volumes, 250,000 slides, 8,000 videos, 250 periodicals. *Epsom:* 22,000 volumes, 50,000 slides, 900 videos, 145 periodicals. **Other learning facilities:** IT centres on each campus, TV and photographic studios. **Welfare:** Doctor, welfare officers, counsellors, accommodation officer, chaplains. **Careers:** Information, advice and informal placement. **Amenities:** Shop on each site. **Sporting facilities:** Games hall; local sports centres in each town.

Accommodation: In 1995/96, 17% of all students in college accommodation, 45% of first years. 830 places: 480 self-catering places (400 for first years) at £35 on average per week for term time only; 350 hall places (Farnham). Students live in privately owned accommodation for 2+ years: £40–£45 per week self-catering; £45–£50 B&B. **Term time work:** Institute's policy to allow term time work for first degree students. Term (and vac) work available on campus. **Hardship funds:** Total available in 1995/96: £74,312 government access funds (274 students helped; 14 given loans). Special help to students with children, disabled students.

Duration of first degree courses: 3 years; others: 5 years (part-time). **Total first degree students 1995/96:** 2,301. **Overseas students:** 76. **Mature students:** 690. **Male/female ratio:** 2:3. **Teaching staff:** 76 full-time, 300 part-time. **Total full-time students 1995/96:** 2,728. **Postgraduate students:** 15. **First degree tuition fees:** Home students, paying their own fees in 1996/97, paid £750 (classroom), £1,600 (studio); Overseas students £2,964 (classroom), £6,484 (studio).

WHAT IT'S LIKE   Based both in Farnham and in Epsom. The Farnham campus is within a couple of minutes from the town centre (50 mins by train from London); the Epsom campus is even closer to the town centre (30 mins by train to London). Good reputation, especially in arts and media; animation students and graduates have won many awards (eg Oscar nomination for animation 1994). Faculty of design has a good reputation and offers one of the few degree courses for the study of glass, plus degree courses in design management and packaging. Most degree courses offer limitless expression within your work and a chance to experiment. Due to its size there's a good community feeling. Farnham's a small market town in pleasant surroundings. It has a good selection of pubs, wine bars and restaurants, as does the leafy town of Epsom (home of the famous racecourse). SU organises bands, discos, parties, films, cabarets, sports clubs and societies. Accommodation availability has improved. There is a new student village at Farnham and the accommodation office helps; all accommodation at the Epsom campus is in privately rented. Specialist libraries are well stocked and a new library/learning resource centre is planned for the Farnham campus.

PAUPER NOTES   **Accommodation:** Halls/shared rooms for 1st years. Overseas students automatically allocated place in hall. Student houses, bedsits and B&B lodgings. **Drink:** SU bar (Grapes Club) – cheap. Large selection of spirits, beers, real ales and lagers. **Eats:** Lots of restaurants around town – Indian, Chinese, Italian, Nepalese. College refectory. **Ents:** SU bops, discos, bands, cabarets, films etc. **Sports:** Farnham has well-equipped sports centre. Epsom's leisure centre offers concessions to students. Sports clubs organised by SU. **Hardship funds:** Access funds. SU welfare fund lends money to tide over. **Work:** Vacation work in restaurants, supermarkets and cleaning.

ALUMNI (EDITORS' PICK)   Annabelle Jankel (cucumber animation – Max Headroom), Dave Banks (editorial photographer – *Face*, etc), Mark Bauer (Grand Prix, Annely), Mark Baker (Oscar nomination 1994), Dan Greaves (Oscar winner 1992), Hugh Miles (director, BAFTA winner), Mike Edwards (camera CBS, Emmy award winner), Stephen Dodd (TV director), Kate Broom (director BBC2), Nick Sinclair (portrait photographer).

SURREY UNIVERSITY

The University of Surrey, Guildford, Surrey GU2 5XH
(Tel 01483 300800, Fax 01483 300803,
Web http://www.surrey.ac.uk) Map 4

STUDENT ENQUIRIES: Undergraduate Admissions Office
APPLICATIONS: UCAS

Broad study areas: Science, engineering, human studies (including dance and sound recording), social science, languages, business and management. (Subject details are in the *Subjects and Places Index*.)

Founded: Royal Charter 1966, previously Battersea College of Technology. **Main undergraduate awards:** BMus, BSc, BA, BEng, MEng, MSci. **Awarding body:** Surrey University. **Site:** Single campus, 1 mile outside Guildford. **Access:** 10 mins' walk from station, bus from Guildford, A3. **Special features:** Most first degree courses offer periods of industrial/professional training in UK or abroad. Applications from mature students are welcomed. **Academic features:** BSc/BEng incorporate foundation year for those without subject qualifications. BSc chemistry for Europe (France/Germany). **Europe:** 10% first degree students take a language as integral part of course and spend 6 months or more abroad (includes engineering/science students); opportunities for other students to take professional training abroad. Aims to provide language teaching to all students; 6 languages available. Formal exchange links with 30 universities/colleges in EU. **Library:** 350, volumes, 2,600 current periodicals, 560 study places, CD-Rom and networked databases. Annual expenditure on library materials, £144 per FTE student. **Other learning facilities:** Computing facilities include UNIX-based servers, large number of PCs and Apple-Macs available to students 24 hours a day; these connected together and to over 1,000 work-stations across campus; access to SuperJanet and high performance computers. High ratio of PCs/students. **Welfare:** 2 student counsellors, doctor, FPA, psychiatrist, welfare officer, chaplains. Limited residential facilities for married and disabled students. **Careers:** Information, advice and counselling. **Amenities:** SU house with print-room, games-room, restaurants, bars, canteen; bookshop, grocer, post office, launderette, bank, restaurants, hairdresser on campus.

Accommodation: In 1995/96, 60% of all students in university accommodation, 90% first years. 2,800 self-catering places (1,350 for first years) at £32–£52 per week, some semester time, some Sept–May. Students live in privately owned accommodation for 1–2 years: rents £43–£55 per week for self-catering. 10% first degree students live at home. **Term time work:** University's policy to allow term time work for full-time first degree students (30% believed to work). Term (and vac) work available on campus; help finding work off campus through SU Job Shop. **Hardship funds:** Total available in 1995/96: £141,868 government access funds, 661 helped (average undergraduate award, £159); limited own funds. Special help for hardship due to either exceptional and unexpected circumstances, or to additional costs incurred by non-traditional students.

Duration of first degree courses: 3 years; **others:** 4 years (including MEng, MSci, professional training or integrated foundation year); 4½ years (MEng); 5 years (professional training and foundation year). **Total first degree students 1995/96:** 5,151. **Overseas students:** 771. **Mature students:** 823. **Male/female ratio:** 1:1. **Teaching staff:** 368 full-time, 35 part-time. **Total full-time students 1995/96:** 7,369. **Postgraduate students:** 3,255. **First degree tuition fees:** Home students, paying their own fees in 1996/97, paid £750 (classroom), £1,600 (lab); Overseas students £6,070 (arts), £8,050 (science).

WHAT IT'S LIKE It's a medium-sized campus on the grassy Cathedral hillside, over-looking Guildford – 10 minutes' walk to the railway (35 minutes' to London) and 15 to the bus station. Being on a hill, it is not ideal for disabled students. First year, overseas and many final year students are housed in university accommodation. Standard ranges from okay to very good; most rooms have a basin, some have ensuite facilities. Between 7–14 share a kitchen with single and mixed floors; a good community exists on campus. There is also a residence site 3 miles from university. Students living within a 3 mile radius are normally unable to have a car on campus. Campus has a launderette, small shop, plus bookshop, hairdresser, post office and bank. Large library, open until 10pm, as is the sports hall. The Union has excellent entertainments (some free), and weekly Friday night discos. It produces a weekly student magazine, and there is a campus radio station. The university gives social advice and support, plus university health centre with family planning advice, confidential counselling service and a student-run night help line. The Union also houses a full-time welfare officer. Guildford is expensive but three nightclubs offer student discounts, there is a good number of pubs, a theatre, cinema, concert hall and lovely coun-tryside. The university is a social centre – an easy place to make friends. Basically a technological university but thriving language, law and European studies departments. Courses are generally up to date, many now modular, and most have a period of place-ment in industry (some abroad) offering valuable experience. Workload varies from okay to hard – generally combining yearly exams with assessed course work; semester system.

Accommodation: University accommodation is affordable (c.£38.84 pw ...; £51.46 for ensuite). Few married/family flats. Practically no provision for ... ut nursery on site (long waiting list). Off-campus accommodation expen- ...**rink:** 4 union bars provide a range of drinking environments (quiet to disco) an... ...e of beers and spirits. Most pubs are expensive. Good local brews – Gales HSB. **Eats:** Un...ersity and union run various catering outlets; vegetarian catered for; campus pizza parlour. Town – good choice and variety of prices. **Ents:** Very good on site, with cabaret, free Sunday night band, lunchtime concerts, discos, balls and annual festivals. Town offers theatre, cinema and concert hall. **Sports:** Good cheap facilities; friendly and competitive events. Floodlight astro-turf pitch. **Hardship funds:** University and access fund. SU has own hardship fund. **Travel:** Travel office in SU offers student fares. **Work:** Some available on site in the bars and catering outlets; shop work and telephone sales in town at reasonable rates; large proportion take part-time jobs.

MORE INFO?   Enquiries to President SU (01483 259227).

ALUMNI (EDITORS' PICK)   Alan Wells (sprinter).

SUSSEX UNIVERSITY

University of Sussex, Falmer, Brighton, Sussex BN1 9RH
(Tel 01273 678416, Fax 01273 678545) Map 4

STUDENT ENQUIRIES: Undergraduate Admissions Office, Sussex
House. APPLICATIONS: UCAS

Broad study areas: Arts, social sciences, science, engineering.
(Subject details are in the *Subjects and Places Index*.)

Founded: 1961. **Main undergraduate awards:** BA, BSc, BEng, LLB, MChem, MPhys, MEng, MMath. **Awarding body:** Sussex University. **Site:** Single campus, 4 miles from Brighton town centre. **Access:** Bus, train. **Academic features:** 20% of students take a year abroad; possible with most subjects, usually in 3rd year of 4 year course. Possible to combine science and engineering with a language, management studies or North American studies. **Europe:** 20% first degree students take a language as part of course and spend a year abroad (normally 3rd year of 4-year course). Almost all subjects can be taken with a language, European studies and a period abroad. Formal exchange links with universities in all EU and EFTA countries. **Library:** 750,000 volumes, 3,500 periodicals, 850 study places, short loan collection, audio-visual section, CD-Rom databases. Annual expenditure on library materials, £150 per FTE student. **Welfare:** Health service, dentist, sick bay on campus, personal counselling and psychotherapy unit. Residential facilities for disabled students; crèche and nursery. **Careers:** Information and advice (also for vacation work). **Amenities:** SU with concert hall, bar, vegetarian restaurant, shops, television studio, campus student radio station; Gardner Arts Centre, banks, chemist, opticians, launderette. **Sporting facilities:** Sports centre for most indoor sports; playing fields, tennis courts, etc, adjoining campus, sports injury clinic. **Employment:** Local and central government; health; social, community and legal; finance; information technology, communications and media industries; overseas development; teaching.

Accommodation: In 1995/96, 42% of all students in university accommodation, 88% first years (remainder chose not to). 2,838 self-catering places available (2,186 for first years), including some family accommodation: £39–£43.50 per week (£32–£39 shared), most academic year conracts but some term time only or students' choice. Some students in university-managed accommodation beyond the first year (self-selecting groups); remainder live in privately owned accommodation: £40–£48 per week for self-catering, £45–£63 for full-board. 15% students live at home. **Term time work**: University's policy to allow term time work for full-time first degree students (70% believed to work); advisory limit of 15 hours per week. Term (and vac) work available on campus in bar, catering, retail, admin, research, translation (none allowed in medical or academic records); also help in finding work off campus through well-established university Job Centre and Employment Agency. **Hardship funds:** Total available in 1995/96: £190,291 government access funds, 949 students helped. Also loans from Vice-Chancellor's fund for students experiencing short-term difficulties.

Duration of first degree courses: 3 or 4 years. **Total first degree students 1995/96:** 6,667. **Overseas students** 407. **Mature students:** 27%. **Male/female ratio:** 1:1. **Teaching staff:** 430 full-time, 95 part-time. **Total full-time students 1995/96:** 8,245. **Postgraduate students:** 2,598. **First degree tuition fees:** Home students, paying their own fees in 1996/97, paid £750; Overseas students £6,100 (classroom), £8,100 (lab/studio).

WHAT IT'S LIKE   Award-winning red-brick architecture amidst trees and beautiful South Downs, 3 miles from Brighton centre. Many arts taught with open-minded attitude, challenging established ideas. Interdisciplinary system means varied (if sometimes superficial) education which can be a rewarding distraction from your major. Emphasis on independent research. Students on Euro and American studies have third year abroad. Science and engineering more formal, structured and conservative; excellent reputation for attracting research grants. Still has reputation as one of Britain's more radical universities. Active SU encourages student involvement; very active campaigning societies (eg women's group and lesbian and gay). Cosmopolitan, anti-racist, anti-sexist and anti-homophobic atmosphere predominates. Union societies represent wide range of interests, political and non-political. Many mature and overseas students but large majority from the home counties. Facilities for disabled students somewhat lacking but constantly under review. Brighton is excellent student town, with lively social scene. Loads of pubs, clubs and the beach combine to fill all your non-study time. Major problems for average student: money and finding somewhere to live.
PAUPER NOTES **Accommodation:** Campus: mainly single self-catering, but some doubles and family flats. No petty regulations on visitors. Housing shortage in Brighton area; rents expensive. **Drink:** 6 main campus bars. Many and varied watering holes in Brighton. **Eats:** Plenty of choice in all price ranges; refectory, coffee shop, canteen and snack bars on campus; many good cheap places in Brighton. **Ents:** Good 'alternative' pubs and clubs. Campus has regular club nights, bands, films and own Gardner Arts Centre and cinema. **Sports:** Plenty of facilities, wide range of activities for all levels of participation. Competitive and non-competitive sports. **Hardship funds:** Access funds (hopelessly inadequate); union has little money and some funds from academic schools. **Travel:** Good public transport; trains and buses from campus but quite expensive. Hitching on and off campus OK in pairs. **Work:** Good opportunities in town during summer but wages low. Student employment office on campus. Union employs casual staff in shops and bars.
ALUMNI (EDITORS' PICK) Ian McEwan, Bernard Coard, Howard Brenton, Brendan Foster, Neil from 'The Young Ones', Virginia Wade, Kathy Foster, Howard Barker, Julia Somerville, Peter Jones, Brian Behan, Peter Hain, Thabo Mbeki (Deputy President, South Africa), Simon Fanshaw (That's Life etc).

SWANSEA INSTITUTE

Swansea Institute of Higher Education,
Townhill Road, Swansea SA2 0UT
(Tel 01792 481000, Fax 01792 481263) Map 3

STUDENT ENQUIRIES: Registry
APPLICATIONS: UCAS

Broad study areas: Art & design, humanities, business, computing, education, engineering, built environment, tourism, law, transport. (Subject details are in the *Subjects and Places Index.*)

Founded: 1976 from colleges of art, technology and education. **Structural features:** An associated college of Wales University. **Main undergraduate awards:** BA, BSc, BEd, BEng, BNursing, LLB. **Awarding bodies:** Wales University; Bristol UWE; London University. **Site:** 3 main campuses: 2 in town centre, 1 outside. **Access:** Public transport. **Europe:** 2% first degree students take a language as part of course and spend a period abroad. Some European exchange links. **Library:** 3 libraries (Mount Pleasant and Townhill sites); 125,000 volumes in total, 1,100 periodicals, 565 study places. **Other learning facilities:** Visual aid centre, print room and resources centre. **Welfare:** Student counsellor, doctor, chaplains. **Careers:** Careers counsellor. **Amenities:** Student centre, SU bar, gymnasia.

Accommodation: In 1995/96, 15% of all students in institute accommodation, 18% of first years. 250 self-catering places available (227 for first years), £36 per week, term time only. Students live in privately owned accommodation for 1–4 years: £35–£40 per week for self-catering or B&B, £45–£55 for half-board. 40% of first degree students live at home. **Term time work:** Institute's policy to allow term time work for first degree students; no work available on campus. **Hardship funds:** Total available in 1995/96: £54,000 government access funds, 60 students helped; plus emergency loan fund. Special help: single parents, mature students, disabled, self-financing students.

Duration of first degree courses: 3 years **Other:** 4 years. **Total first degree students 1995/96:** 2,339. **BEd students:** 445. **Overseas students:** 82. **Mature students:** 1,158. **Male/female ratio:** 2:3. **Teaching staff:** 218 full-time, 86 part-time. **Total full-time students 1995/96:** 2,791. **Postgraduate students:** 261. **First degree tuition fees:** Home students, paying their own fees in 1996/97, paid £750 (classroom), £1,600 (lab/studio); Overseas students £5,658.

WHAT IT'S LIKE   On three sites, all close to each other: main campuses at Townhill and Mount Pleasant, annexe at Alexandra Road. Wide range of courses – business studies, education, stained glass, ceramics and technology most popular. Extensive range of diploma courses. Recreational facilities improving; Townhill campus has a fitness centre but few other facilities. Compensated for by free use of Swansea Leisure centre for students during the day and 'passport to leisure' scheme all round Swansea with SU card. Halls only cater for c250 students so apply really early; private accommodation difficult because of proximity of university. SU very active and developing (now has 3 sabbatical officers), provides many facilities including two coffee bars, materials and stationery shops. About 35 societies including many sports; expanding athletic union with clubs to cater for all tastes.

Confidential counselling services. Libraries at Townhill and Mount Pleasant open 9am – 9pm, closed at weekends, limited vacation hours. All sites close to town centre and the famous Gower Peninsula is only a 25-minute bus ride away. Relationship with town is good; those between staff and students a priority. Students from all over UK, Europe, China, Nigeria, America, etc (overseas and ethnic minorities encouraged). Drop-out rate is relatively low. A close-knit atmosphere as students tend to live in the same area. Many students visit Ireland (Cork and Dublin) a couple of times in the year.

PAUPER NOTES **Accommodation:** Halls relatively cheap but definitely not the Ritz. Bedsits, flats etc, moderate but very scarce; grab places before the uni does. **Drink:** Bar at Townhill; juke box, pool tables, quite cheap. Loads of local pubs – majority are student dominated. **Eats:** College refectories not bad. SU coffee bars for snacks and drinks. Lots of Chinese, Indian, Cantonese and Greek food. Local chippies very good, cheap and everywhere. Some health food shops and restaurants; few veggies. **Ents:** Wide variety to cater for all. Cinema discount with SU card. Lots of good pubs and clubs; student night every night somewhere in Swansea. **Sports:** Free use of Swansea Leisure Centre with SU card and passport to leisure scheme. **Hardship funds:** Institute emergency fund and access funds but need extenuating circumstances to get anything. **Travel:** M4 express hitch route to the east. Good coach and train services. Shared lifts always advertised. **Work:** Local department stores, bar/restaurant work. Summer jobs not bad but pay poor.

ALUMNI (EDITORS' PICK) Mervyn Davies, Wayne Proctor (Wales rugby internationalist).

SWANSEA UNIVERSITY

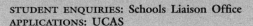

**University of Wales Swansea, Singleton Park, Swansea
SA2 8PP (Tel 01792 205678, Fax 01792 295613) Map 3**

STUDENT ENQUIRIES: Schools Liaison Office
APPLICATIONS: UCAS

Broad study areas: Science; health care studies; arts and social sciences; engineering; business, economics and law. (Subject details are in the *Subjects and Places Index*.)

Founded: 1920. **Structural features:** Part of Wales University. **Main undergraduate awards:** BA, BSc, BEng, BScEcon, LLB, MEng, MPhys. **Awarding body:** Wales University. **Site:** Campus 2 miles west of Swansea, by the sea near Gower Peninsula. **Access:** Bus onto campus from Swansea city centre and station. **Academic features:** Modular degree scheme. 4-year BEng/BSc with foundation year and 4 year undergraduate masters courses. Opportunity to study abroad (eg USA, Japan, Finland, Mexico) in many departments. **Europe:** Many students take a language and spend 6 months or more abroad as part of their course. Formal exchange links with over 100 universities/colleges in east and west Europe. **Library:** Main library plus departmental collections; over 600,000 volumes in total, 4,000 periodicals, 11,000 study places in library complex plus 150 in maths/physics/applied science buildings. Annual expenditure on library materials, £125.15 per FTE student. **Welfare:** Doctor, dentist, chaplains, counsellors; legal and financial advice through SU. Resident welfare facilities for students with families. Facilities for sight-impaired (eg broadcast quality recording centre), the hearing-impaired and for students in wheelchairs (ramps, lifts, toilets); specialist accommodation for disabled students and their helpers. **Careers:** Information, advice and placement service. **Amenities:** SU building with shop, travel centre, copy shop, launderette, radio station, bar; CCTV unit; large arts centre on campus. City has new museum of Egyptology, large leisure centre, clubs, pubs, art gallery, theatres etc. **Sporting facilities:** Modern indoor sports centre with gym, swimming pool, squash courts. Outdoor pitches (including all-weather) catering for range of sports especially soccer, rugby and cricket. Surfing and other sea sports eg canoeing. Sports scholarships available worth £700 pa.

Accommodation: In 1995/96, 40% of all students in university accommodation, 98% of first years. Some 3,000 places available (1,800 for first years): 525 half-board places (475 for first years) at £62.50 per week and 637 B&B at £45 (£52 en suite), term time only; 1,700+ self-catering places (900 for first years) at £32.50 per week, Sept–June. Students live in privately owned accommodation for 1–2 years: £32–£38 per week for self-catering, £42–£45 for B&B, £50–£57 for half-board (to £65 with weekend meals). 5+% first degree students live at home. **Term time work**: University's policy to allow term time work for full-time first degree students (20% believed to work). Term (and vac) work available on campus in catering, SU bars, cleaning; SU job finding service. **Hardship funds:** Total available in 1995/96: £187,483 government access funds, 815 students helped. University has sports and cultural scholarships (£700 pa each).

Duration of first degree courses: 3 years; **others:** 4 years (eg philosophy, languages, courses with foundation years and undergraduate masters). **Total first degree students 1995/96:** 6,943. **Overseas students:** 3%. **Mature students:** 15%. **Male/female ratio:** 6:5. **Teaching staff:** 650. **Total full-time students 1995/96:** 8,476. **Postgraduate students:** 1,433. **First degree tuition fees:** Home students, paying their own fees in 1996/97, paid £820; Overseas students £5,765 (classroom), £7,645 (lab).

WHAT IT'S LIKE   Located in Singleton Park and can be very picturesque. All facilities on campus except teacher training centre and some nursing courses (20 minutes' walk). Six halls of residence: three on campus (breakfast only), three off (20 minutes' walk and meals provided). Hendrefolan student village is 30 minutes' walk from campus, regular bus service plus SU minibus; it's a self-catering complex housing 1,750 with facilities including a union-run shop, bar, diner, launderette, tennis courts and car park. Rented accommodation reasonable and most quite close to campus. Many overseas and mature students – the very mixed backgrounds reflected in a relaxed atmosphere at college. SU very active, including excellent welfare service, nursery, counselling service, sabbatical women's officer and overseas officer. Union services include two shops, two bars, two diners, launderettes, coffee bar, copy shop, travel office and large ents department. Over 100 societies, various political groups, green action, community action, women's group, macabre etc, as well as rag and a huge athletics union. Ents programme wide and varied. Semi-student city, very friendly – plenty of pubs, clubs, cinemas and theatres. Gower Peninsula and good beaches nearby for walks, surfing, rock climbing etc. Quite easy to change course in first year as often made up of three subjects. Language and American studies get a year abroad but no sponsored or sandwich course students. Easy to take a year out (Wales University has five-year rule). Work assessed differently from course to course (course work modules, single or split finals). Work rate reasonable. Quality of degree generally excellent.

PAUPER NOTES   **Accommodation:** Some pressure on accommodation. Student areas in Uplands, Brymill, Mumbles. Generally OK – average rent £35 and rising. Student village best all-round value for money. **Drink:** SU bars for cheapest beer in Swansea (open till

1 am at weekends). Several student pubs. **Eats:** College refectory could be better. 2 SU-run diners (on campus and in village) – tasty, fast food. Locally, over 40 Indian/Chinese restaurants; plenty for all tastes, vegetarian, vegan, ethnic. **Ents:** Union ents good and diverse. Also range of cheap clubs – student nights in most of the big ones. Multi-screen cinema complex, 10 pin bowling and lazerquest. Blues, jazz, folk, rock/pop scene in town, but requires investigation. Variety of theatre productions. Outdoor and indoor markets. Most tastes and interests catered for. **Sports:** Leisure centre good and cheap. Very cheap campus sports centre. All easy to get to. **Hardship funds:** Little joy from college. **Travel:** SU travel shop with good reductions. **Work:** SU employs some students for bar, security and catering work. Casual/seasonal work, but in these times very hard to get, and low paid in Swansea. MORE INFO? Enquiries to Paul Edwards, SU president (01792 295466).
INFORMAL NAME UWS, Swansea University.
ALUMNI (EDITORS' PICK) Donald Anderson MP, John Morgan, Lamin Mybe, Mark Wyatt, Paul Thorburn, Gwynne Howell, Mavis Nicholson, Alun Richards, Ian Bone (Head of Class War), Nigel Evans MP, Half of Manic Street Preachers.

TEESSIDE UNIVERSITY

University of Teesside, Middlesbrough, TS1 3BA
(Tel 01642 218121, Fax 01642 342067) Map 2

STUDENT ENQUIRIES: Admissions Officer
APPLICATIONS: UCAS

Broad study areas: Design, computing, mathematics, technology, humanities, social and health studies, engineering, science, business and management. (Subject details are in the *Subjects and Places Index*.)

Founded: 1970 as Teesside Poly from college founded in 1930. University status in 1992. **Main undergraduate awards:** BA, BSc, BEng, MEng, LLB. **Awarding body:** Teesside University. **Site:** Main site (most undergraduate facilities) near Middlesbrough town centre; postgraduate site at Flatts Lane, Normanby (4 miles away). **Access:** Nearby bus and railway stations; A19 road; Teesside international airport. **Academic features:** New courses in creative visualisation, information society, business entrepreneurship and development. **Europe:** 5% first degree students take a language as part of course and 2% spend up to a year abroad. Languages built into some degrees, an option in many others and all students have open access courses to the language centre. Formal exchange links with universities/colleges across the EU, most open to all students. Internationally orientated courses. **Library:** New learning resource centre: 250,000 books and journals, 1,000 study places, 400 electronic workstations linked to internet, video machines, CD-Roms etc. Smaller library at Flatts Lane. Annual expenditure on library materials, £69.07 per FTE student. **Welfare:** Occupational nurse, accommodation officer, student financial adviser, adviser for special needs, counsellor, chaplains. Limited residential facilities for the disabled; 66-place nursery (enquire when applying). **Careers:** Information and guidance on vocations, jobs and further courses. **Amenities:** Recreation unit, amenities block with SU bars, coffee bar, shop, refectory, welfare unit. **Sporting facilities:** Sports hall, fitness centre, playing fields.

Accommodation: 1,014 places available, all 33 week contracts; some self-catering some B&B at £32.12–£43.66 per week (plus electricity in some cases). 300 places in university head tenancy scheme. Students live in privately owned accommodaiton for 2+ years, £27 per week for self-catering; £30–£37 for B&B; £40–£51 for full board. **Term time work:** No university policy on part time work for students. Term time work available on campus in library and SU. **Hardship Funds:** Total available in 1995/96 £145,000 government access funds (400 students helped) with special help for local and mature students.

Duration of first degree courses: 3 years; 4 years sandwich. **Total first degree students 1995/96:** 5,744 (f-t), 643 (p-t). **Overseas students:** 400. **Male/female ratio:** 1:1. **Teaching staff:** 619. **Total full-time students 1995/96:** 8,439. **Postgraduate students:** 1,337. **First degree tuition fees:** Home students, paying their own fees in 1996/97, paid £1,300 (classsroom), £2,770 (lab/studio); Overseas students £5,000.

WHAT IT'S LIKE   Main campus in Middlesborough town centre; business school 5 miles out at Flatts Lane; also 6 health school sites dotted around the region and a growing number of franchised courses at 8 external colleges. Over 1000 students in halls of residence; many others live in reasonably priced university head tenancy accommodation. Number of mature students is increasing, partly because of the diversity of courses and availability of franchised courses. Multi-million pound learning resource centre, adjacent to SU building contains library and computer facilities; to blend with it, SU had new entrance built which not only looks good but tremendously improves disabled access. Union prides itself on sports clubs. Lively SU bar, the Union Central, holds 600 students and sells the cheapest beer in Middlesborough. Facilities include big-screen TV, pizzeria, and a brand new arcade with 4 pool tables and various arcade games. Upstairs is The Zoo (nightclub venue, with a capacity of 1000), large new bottle-bar and DJ booth, to cope with increasing number of students. Ents good; acts include Meanswear, Space, Chunbawamba, and club nights such as Cream, Ministry of Sound and Up Yer Ronson appearing regularly – even Danny Rampling from Radio 1. Teesside Park, just outside town, has 10-screen cinemas, bowling alleys, laser quest, restaurants and bars. Finances always a problem, but Teesside one of the cheapest areas in the country to live.

PAUPER NOTES   **Accommodation:** Often problems at start of year. **Drink:** SU cheapest in town. **Eats:** Great variety of fast foods and restaurants. **Ents:** SU ents are cheap and varied. Cheap films on campus. **Sports:** SU sports clubs. Sports pavilion. **Hardship funds:** Access funds. **Travel:** Coach travel from London (5 hours) and BR ever more expensive. Middlesborough on some direct routes. **Work:** Can be a problem (Teesside has high unemployment rates). SU employs about 70 students casually (bar, pizzeria, security); approx £3.30/hour.

ALUMNI (EDITORS' PICK)   David Bowe MEP, Stephen Hughes MEP.

THAMES VALLEY UNIVERSITY

Thames Valley University
- Ealing Campus, St Mary's Road, Ealing, London W5 5RF (Tel 0181 579 5000, Fax 0181 231 2900) Map 5
- Slough Campus, Wellington Street, Slough, Berkshire SL1 1YG (Tel 01753 534585, Fax 01753 574264) Map 4

STUDENT ENQUIRIES: Guidance centres on either campus
APPLICATIONS: UCAS

Broad study areas: Accountancy, business, languages, leisure & hospitality, law, technology, humanities, music, information management. (Subject details are in the *Subjects and Places Index.*)

Founded: 1991 as West London Poly, incorporating London College of Music (you can look this up separately), Ealing College, Queen Charlotte's College of Health Care Studies, Thames Valley College. University status 1992. **Main undergraduate awards:** BA, BMus, BSc. **Awarding body:** Thames Valley University. **Site:** 2 sites, at Ealing and Slough, 15 miles apart. **Access:** A4, M4 and A40; Slough campus close to bus and rail stations; Ealing campus near rail, tube and buses. **Academic features:** Modular scheme gives flexibility to all degree courses: specialist, major/minor and 3 subject combinations available. **Europe:** Approx 55% first degree students take a language as part of course and 30% spend 6 months or more abroad. Formal exchange links with 64 universities/colleges in western Europe, many open to non-language specialists. Also franchise programmes in Poland and Bulgaria. **Library:** 215,600 volumes, 1,500+ periodical titles, 570 study places. Learning resource centres at both sites. **Welfare:** Student services provides medical, counselling and welfare services. **Careers:** Information and advice service. **Amenities:** Well-equipped students union on both sites. Free mini-bus between sites. **Sporting facilities:** State-of-the-art fitness centre at Slough, small fitness suite at Ealing.

Accommodation: No university accommodation at present. Accommodation officer helps find local flats and lodgings. Many students live locally. **Term time work:** University policy to allow term time work for first degree students; limit of 15 hours per week. University employs students (term and vac) where possible eg library, admin, design, telemarketing etc; also university temp agency helps find work locally. **Hardship funds:** Total available 1995/96: £149,438 government access funds, plus £18,150 own funds, 241 students helped; £16,500 other funds, 11 students helped. Special help for single parents, self-funded students, disabled students and those experiencing exceptional hardship; other funds also for childcare, overseas students. Some funds assigned before the start of the course.

Duration of first degree courses: 3 or 4 years. **Total first degree students 1995/96:** 4,239 f-t; 1,219 p-t. **Overseas students:** 800. **Mature students:** 35%. **Male/female ratio:** 1:1. **Teaching staff:** 442 full-time, 407 part-time. **Total full-time students 1995/96:** 11,500. **Postgraduate students:** 1,748. **First degree tuition fees:** Home students, paying their own fees in 1996/97, paid £1,040 (classroom), £1,500 (lab/studio); Overseas students £5,547.

WHAT IT'S LIKE A two campus university based in Ealing, on the western side of London, and Slough, 18 miles to the west along the M4. Ealing campus is 30 minutes from central London by tube (easy walking distance to Ealing Broadway and South Ealing stations). Slough campus is 2 minutes walk from the station and right next to the town centre. It caters for many non-degree as well as degree courses. Good train and bus links and free inter-site minibus. Both sites have friendly atmosphere, avoiding the impersonality of larger institutions. Lively, effective SU. Slough campus has entertainments hall (named after Chancellor, Paul Hamlyn), café (Diner Mite, serving variety of meals all day, including vegetarian) and an excellent college gym. Ealing has two bars (one named Freddie's after Freddie Mercury, a former student at the Ealing School of Art), both with a capacity of 150–200 and serve a wide selection of beverages; the main venue hall, Artwoods Hall holds about 800 people with permanent lighting and PA system; also a shop and cashpoint. SU runs a wide range of social events and activities and supports a number of clubs: standard sporting, cultural and political groups, ethnic groups (Afro-Caribbean, Asian etc). SU deals with wide range of problems (financial, accommodation and academic). University targets the local community so many students live at home (80% of students are local, over half are mature). No halls of residence yet; rents are high locally. Improving facilities for students with disabilities. SU has non-sexist and non-racist policy. Confidential counselling service available in SU and student services. Low drop-out rate. Courses are student driven/orientated and innovative (eg design and media management). Good relationship between SU and college. Free handbooks to all students on enrolment and free in-house magazine – *The Undergrad* – published 4 times a year.

PAUPER NOTES **Accommodation:** Uni help finding accommodation. **Drink:** Student bar cheaper than local pubs. Firkin pubs popular – lively, drink-inducing atmosphere, eg Photographer & Firkin. **Eats:** Cheap food (including vegetarian) in student cafés, SU shop and bar. Some restaurants give student discounts, eg Bella Pasta (Ealing Broadway). **Ents:** Wide and increasing range of SU-based events – discos, Bhangra, cabaret, live bands. Waterman Centre, Zenith nightclub – cheap student night Tuesdays. Plenty of local cinemas; local arts centre (Watermans); easy access to central London for theatre, films etc. **Sports:** Student discounts at some centres, eg Gurnell swimming pool and Ealing squash courts. **Hardship fund:** Access funds – limited; financial advice shop. **Travel:** Good foreign placements on various courses, eg USA, Russia, Mexico and Europe. Young Persons Railcard a must. STA travel shop on site. **Work:** SU and university employ students (eg in SU bar). Uni job agency (TVU Temps) helps find work locally, part-time and in Christmas/summer vacation.

INFORMAL NAME TVU.
MORE INFO? Ring SU executive on (0181 231 2276).
ALUMNI (EDITORS' PICK) Freddie Mercury

CAN'T FIND WHAT YOU'RE LOOKING FOR? USE THE INDEX!

TRINITY & ALL SAINTS

Trinity & All Saints University College, Brownberrie Lane,
Horsforth, Leeds LS18 5HD
(Tel 0113 283 7123, Fax 0113 283 7200) Map 2

STUDENT ENQUIRIES: Admissions Officer
APPLICATIONS: UCAS

Broad study areas: Media, management, education. (Subject details are in the *Subjects and Places Index*.)

Founded: 1966. **Structural features:** A college of Leeds University. **Main undergraduate awards:** BA, BSc, BA/BSc(QTS). **Awarding body:** Leeds University. **Site:** Single campus in semi-rural surroundings, 6 miles from central Leeds. **Access:** Bus stop at gate (direct services Leeds and Bradford); rail station 10 minutes' walk (Leeds to Harrogate line). **Academic features:** All courses are modular and designed to lead to specific career outcomes – most students combine an academic and a professional subject. Two six-week attachments for non-initial teacher training students. **Special features:** Originally an independent Catholic foundation, it continues to maintain an active Catholic Christian life but entry not restricted to Catholics. **Europe:** 10% first degree students take a language as part of course and spend a year abroad. Exchange links with 21 universities/colleges in the EU. **Library:** 100,000 volumes, 800 periodicals, 200 study places. Annual expenditure on library materials, £68 per FTE student. **Other learning facilities:** Computer labs, sound radio studio, video editing suite, TV studio, photography dark rooms, science labs, primary and secondary education bases. **Welfare:** 2 part-time counsellors; health centre, local GP visits. Special co-ordinator for mature/access students. Nursery (run for students as part of early years education course). **Careers:** Information and advice available. **Amenities:** SU building with performance centre, 2 bars and coffee bar. Recreational and cultural activities, including performing arts, golf, karate, keep fit etc. **Sporting facilities:** Double gym, 5 squash courts, all-weather pitch, rugby, soccer and cricket pitches, fitness centre.

Accommodation: In 1995/96, 25% of all students in college accommodation, 75% of first years. 495 full board places, 100 with ensuite facilities (455 for first years) at £58–£66 per week, term time only. Students live in privately owned accommodation for 2+ years: £35–£46 per week for self-catering, £40–£45 for B&B, £45–£50 for half board. Accommodation best in Yeadon and Horsforth. 15% first degree students live at home. **Term time work:** No university policy on part time work for students. Some term (and vac) work available on campus in bars, kitchens, conference support. **Hardship funds:** Total available in 1995/96: £42,871 government access funds (300 students helped), £31,000 own funds (75 helped). Special help: students with pre-school/nursery age children.

Duration of first degree courses: 3 years; 4 years (BA/BSc with QTS or languages). **Total first degree students 1995/96:** 2,000. **QTS students:** 615. **Overseas students:** 15. **Mature students:** 200. **Male/female ratio:** 1:2. **Teaching staff:** 85 full-time, 15 part-time. **Total full-time students 1995/96:** 2,030. **Postgraduate students:** 210. **First degree tuition fees:** Home students, paying their own fees in 1996/97, paid £750 (classroom), £1,600 (lab/studio); Overseas students £5,500.

WHAT IT'S LIKE   It was built in the sixties and is a pretty fine place. 43 acres of land to play on and get away from the hustle and bustle; only 20 mins bus ride to Leeds. Nearly all first years are housed on campus but as numbers increase, more are living out. Nine halls of residence, fully catered, all mixed. College is famed for its friendliness and good atmosphere on campus – you get to know everyone and their business! Social life on campus is good with plenty to do. Leeds and Bradford are only stone throws away, both are geared towards students. Travel is easy with buses outside the college and a BR station only 10 mins walk. Leeds/Bradford airport is just 2 miles away, so excellent for plane spotters!

PAUPER NOTES   **Accommodation:** Plenty of housing in Horsforth, Headingly, Burley and Kirkstall; average £36–£42 per week. **Drink:** College bar, good selection and reasonably priced. Local pubs and good ale houses: The Observatory, Planet Earth, Europa, Nato. **Eats:** Cheap eats: The Outside Inn, Moghul, Burger King. **Ents:** Clubs, pubs, cinemas, bars, bops, theatre all geared to students. NUS card a must for ace discounts. **Sports:** 22 clubs and societies. **Hardship funds:** Some available (through Dean of Students). **Travel:** Metro cards for local bus and train; £9 a week, £31 a month. **Work:** Pubs, restaurants, pizza places, fast food.

INFORMAL NAME   TASC.

TRINITY COLLEGE CARMARTHEN

Trinity College, Carmarthen SA31 3EP
(Tel 01267 676767, Fax 01267 676766) Map 3

STUDENT ENQUIRIES: **Registrar**
APPLICATIONS: **UCAS**

Broad study areas: Education, humanities, sciences.
(Subject details are in the *Subjects and Places Index*.)

Founded: 1848, Church voluntary college. **Structural features:** An associated college of Wales University. **Main undergraduate awards:** BA(Ed), BA, BSc. **Awarding body:** Wales University. **Site:** On outskirts of market town of Carmarthen, within easy reach of the Pembrokeshire and Brecon Beacons national parks. **Special features:** Bilingual college (most courses can be followed in English or Welsh). 30 USA students in college. **Europe:** Formal exchange links with Eire, Italy and France. **Other learning resources:** Micro-computers; film cameras and closed circuit TV; 130-acre farm. Modernised language lab; modern theatre. **Careers:** Guidance given. **Amenities:** Self-service restaurant. **Sporting facilities:** Indoor swimming pool, gymnasia, weights room; multi-purpose floodlit all-weather playing surfaces; strong rugby tradition.

Accommodation: Most first and third year students in college accommodation on campus; £49–£63 per week. Second year students live in privately owned accommodation. **Term time work:** No college policy to allow term time work for first degree students. **Hardship funds:** Access funds £25,000.

Duration of first degree courses: 3 years. **Total first degree students 1996/97:** 1,400. **BA(Ed) students:** 660. **Overseas students:** 20. **Mature students:** 310. **Male/female ratio:** 1:3. **Teaching staff:** 105 full-time. **Postgraduate students:** 220. **First degree tuition fees:** Home students, paying their own fees in 1996/97, paid £750 (classroom), £1,600 (lab/studio); Overseas students £5,500.

WHAT IT'S LIKE Not the sprawling metropolis you may expect but it was a city in Roman times and is in legend the birth place of Merlin. Carmarthen is the largest town in south west Wales. It is surrounded by beautiful rolling hills, countryside and castles of old – all bringing a touch of enchantment on frosty, misty, autumn mornings. The college is bilingual (courses taught in English and Welsh) and most students are Welsh, English or Irish. Accommodation on the whole good, though you may be unlucky and end up sharing a tiny room. It's a good place for sport and entertainment. Excellent facilities on campus and off for sport, everything is just a 15 minutes walk. The sports teams are of a good standard (although the hockey team recently suffered a historic defeat, 14–0). Active drama societies, choir, contemporary music societies and a host of others. Small college, so you get to know lots of people. Freshers week is always excellent, pulling in good bands and comedy acts. Wednesday and Friday nights are main disco nights; lots of cheap booze. Town can be a bit rough at night but still a good laugh! Food on campus is good quality and nutritious. Food provided during the week for first years on campus; sandwiches and cold snacks at weekends (or ring-ripping curries if you can afford it). College offers a few jobs on campus but town centre is best place for work (police offer £10 to star in a line up – have a cup of tea, play pool and appear next to a suspect).

PAUPER NOTES **Accommodation:** Expensive on the whole. Campus hostels; some good digs in town. **Drink:** Cheap SU bar (£1.20/pint, beer or cider). Reasonable town prices. Welsh Felinfoel is local brew (a few pints and you're 'feeling foul'). **Eats:** Few vegetarian restaurants in town; some Balti and curry houses. **Ents:** Cheap ents in union. Small cinema in town; Swansea nearest for good up-to-date film. **Sports:** Good gyms, weight training facilities, astro-turf; large local leisure centre. **Travel:** Railway station and buses, excellent hitching due to trucks from the Irish ferries and the M4 link. **Hardship funds:** Ever popular access fund – get your claim in early. **Work:** Always work in campus restaurant. Lots in town, but beware of low pay (local employers tell SU of vacancies). Not much vacation work.

MORE INFO? Contact Robin Rowlands on 01267 676834.

ALUMNI (EDITORS' PICK) Barry John, Carwyn James.

TRINITY COLLEGE OF MUSIC

Trinity College of Music, Mandeville Place, London W1M 6AQ
(Tel 0171 935 5773, Fax 0171 224 6278, E-mail info@tcm.ac.uk)
Map 6

STUDENT ENQUIRIES: Registrar
APPLICATIONS: Direct.

Broad study areas: Music performance.

Founded: 1872. **Special features:** A conservatoire for training performers for a variety of careers in music. **Main undergraduate awards:** BMus. **Awarding body:** Trinity College, Westminster and London universities. **Site:** Just off Oxford Street, central London. **Access:** Bond Street underground station; buses. **Academic features:** Professional studies, musicianship, communication and teaching skills, contextual studies. BMus for (music plus); MMus (performance and related studies); MA (music education); specialist short courses for overseas students. **Europe:** Language classes in French, German and Italian for singing students as well as French and Italian song and German lieder. **Library:** 40,000 volumes, 60 periodicals, 50 study places. Annual expenditure on library materials, £116 per FTE student. **Other learning facilities:** Recording studio. **Specialist collections:** CYM collection; Barbirolli collection of scores. **Welfare:** Doctor, FPA, psychiatrist, physiotherapist, welfare officer. **Careers:** Information, advice and placement.

Accommodation: No college accommodation. 40+ places in mixed hall run by Music Students' Trust, £550–£800 per term (priority to those outside London area). Warden's office helps first years. **Term time work:** College policy to allow part time work. Some term (and vac) work in college eg helping with auditions/examinations, library, setting up equipment. **Hardship funds:** Limited funds available.

Duration of first degree courses: 4 years; **others:** 3 years. **Total first degree students 1995/96:** 343. **Overseas students:** 33 + 18 EU. **Male/female ratio:** 2:3. **Teaching staff:** 8 full-time, 137 part-time. **Total full-time students 1995/96:** 463. **Postgraduate students:** 95. **First degree tuition fees:** Home students, paying their own fees in 1996/97, paid £3,100; Overseas students £7,300.

WHAT IT'S LIKE Trinity is a small but perfectly-formed, friendly college with around 500 students studying all aspects of music. Although most students are British nationals, there is a strong overseas contingent from countries as diverse as Brazil and Bosnia. Trinity has long history of music education: it started as a conservatoire for church music in 1872 and has expanded ever since; it pioneered practical music exams (1879) and introduced the first junior department to a conservatoire. The college itself consists of three buildings a couple of minutes' walk from each other in heart of the West End. The symphony orchestra, sinfonia and chamber groups give regular public concerts at various venues in and around London. Student facilities recently much improved: new purpose-built library and e-mail for all students. Now the leading edge in music research and IT. Newly refurbished common room and new student cafe strengthened the unique community spirit that Trinity students relish. Students have use of a local bar from midday–11 pm, 5 days a week, where there are various entertainments. Active student union carries a powerful voice in all committee meetings.

PAUPER NOTES **Accommodation:** Some places in Henry Wood House, which houses music students; most in flatshares on outer limits of London. **Drink:** 14 pubs and bars within 5 mins of college; all used at some time. **Eats:** No college canteen; lots of local sandwich shops. Overwhelming choice of cuisine nearby. **Ents:** SU regularly puts on social events. **Sports:** 5-a-side football team regularly competes against other music colleges. Use of ULU facilities; local gym and fitness centre. **Hardship funds:** Access funds for extreme cases. **Travel:** 5 mins from Bond Street tube station; masses of buses in Oxford Street; London travel expensive. **Work:** Some part time work in college; also private teaching, gigs etc.

INFORMAL NAME Trinity or TCM.

ALUMNI (EDITORS' PICK) Heather Harper, Margaret Price, John Hancorn, Manoug Parikian, Gilbert Biberian (composer/guitarist), Steve Sidwell (Wham), Winston Rollins (Aswad), Mark Nightingale (Harry Connick Jnr), Joe Loss.

ULSTER UNIVERSITY

University of Ulster, Cromore Road, Coleraine,
County Londonderry, Northern Ireland BT52 1SA
(Tel 01265 44141, Fax 01265 40908) Map 1

STUDENT ENQUIRIES: Admissions Officer
APPLICATIONS: UCAS; direct for some nursing courses.

Broad study areas: Art & design, business and management, engineering, humanitites, informatics, science, social and health sciences. (Subject details are in the *Subjects and Places Index*.)

Founded: 1984, from merger of New University of Ulster and Ulster Polytechnic. **Main undergraduate awards:** BA, BSc, BMus, BEng, MEng, BTech. **Awarding body:** Ulster University. **Site:** 4 campuses: Main campuses at Jordanstown (7 miles NE of Belfast) and Coleraine (on north coast, 55 miles north of Belfast). Also campus in heart of Belfast, and Magee College in Londonderry. **Access:** All campuses have road and rail connections. Air and sea routes from UK. **Academic features:** New courses in biotechnology, engineering with business, textile technology. **Europe:** 12% first degree students take a language as part of course and 2% spend a period abroad. Formal exchange links with 22 EU universities/colleges and in 20 Erasmus/Lingua exchange programmes, most open to non-language specialists; some dual awards available. **Library:** Library on each site; main libraries at Coleraine and Jordanstown; 556,000 volumes in total; 5,100 periodicals. Annual expenditure on library materials, £78.99 per FTE student. **Other learning facilities:** Education technology unit; computer services; social skills training centre. **Welfare:** Counsellors; doctors, chaplains. Residential facilities for married and disabled students (Jordanstown); crèche and day nursery (Coleraine, Jordanstown and Magee College). **Careers:** Information, advice and placement. **Amenities:** SU with extensive leisure facilities. **Sporting facilities:** Sports centres on Coleraine and Jordanstown sites with full facilities including swimming and diving pools at Jordanstown.

Accommodation: 1,416 campus places available (80% for first years) and 851 head-leased places: 411 campus places and 630 head leased at Coleraine; 733 campus and 221 head leased at Jordanstown; 272 campus at Magee. Rents for single room £26.65–£33.25 per week. Students live in privately rented accommodation for 2 years: rents from £25 per week for self-catering, £30 per week for B&B. **Hardship funds:** Total available 1995/96: £191,500 government access funds, 1,554 awards made; £5,575 other funds (48 loans of £10–£50 and 28 awards of £50–£150). Special help from access funds to single parents, students with children and disabled students; other funds help Ulster students experiencing hardship.

Duration of first degree courses: 3 years; **others:** 4 years (eg sandwich; courses including period abroad); 5 years (MEng). **Total first degree students 1995/96:** 12,974; **Overseas students:** 102. **Mature students:** 27%. **Male/female ratio:** 6:7. **Teaching staff:** 870. **Total full-time students 1995/96:** 13,548. **Postgraduate students:** 1,151 (f-t), 3,186 (p-t). **First degree tuition fees:** Home students, paying their own fees in 1996/97, paid £785 (classroom), £1,635 (lab/studio); Overseas students £6,000 (classroom), £7,850 (lab/studio).

WHAT IT'S LIKE   4 campuses in Belfast , Londonderry and on the north coast. Belfast campus has all the advantages of the city's wide-ranging services. Students work in bright, airy buildings of ex-art college (art and design subjects dominant – some 20% of students on foundation programmes). Atmosphere relaxed, facilities adequate. Jordanstown, 7 miles north, is the largest campus and has good facilities. Business management, science, technology and engineering are major courses. Very high proportion of part-time students; good reputation for industry. Student village with 900 places attractive. Campus well integrated with European, American/Canadian and Far East students. Coleraine houses humanities and university headquarters. 60s campus, close to two of N Ireland's main holiday resorts, Portstewart and Portrush – much favoured by students for accommodation outside the summer months. Cosmopolitan atmosphere; facilities are excellent and a high reputation in sports. All major faculties present at Coleraine. Academic courses strongly favour continuous assessment. Magee campus in Londonderry recently transformed. New buildings surround the 19th-century college, and more planned. Been a major success in attracting mature students to foundation, degree and postgraduate courses. The student union has strong links with the Student Housing Association Co-operative.

PAUPER NOTES   **Accommodation:** Halls of residence (3 campuses only). South side of Belfast has large student population with good services but rents high for only fair accommodation. Reasonable amount of accommodation at Coleraine, reasonable prices. More students living at home. **Drink:** Univ bar cheapest (Guinness £1.45). Good bars in the city. **Eats:** Okay if you like meat and 2 veg – bad for vegetarians. **Ents:** Good social life on campus. Wide range univ ents. Film club at Coleraine. **Sports:** Swimming pool at Jordanstown, new sports centre at Magee; expanded fitness suite at Coleraine; nothing at Belfast site. **Hardship funds:** Minimal access funds; SU hardship fund. **Travel:** Many offers and deals with Ulsterbus/NIR. Cheap taxis from city to Jordanstown site. Advise against hitching alone. **Work:** Union students part-time. Seasonal holiday work available in Coleraine; usual city work in Belfast and Londonderry – rates not brilliant. SU-run job shop on 4 campuses.

MORE INFO?   Ring William Cooper (01265 56321 or 01232 365121

INFORMAL NAME   UU; The Poly (Jordanstown).

ALUMNI (EDITORS' PICK)   Mark Robson (commentator), Kate Hoey MP.

UMDS

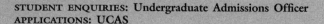

United Medical & Dental Schools of Guy's & St Thomas's Hospitals, Lambeth Palace Road, London SE1 7EH (Tel 0171 922 8013, Fax 0171 928 0069) Map 6

STUDENT ENQUIRIES: Undergraduate Admissions Officer
APPLICATIONS: UCAS

Broad study areas: Medicine, dentistry.

Founded: 1982 from merger of medical schools of Guy's (founded 1726) and St Thomas's (12th century). **Structural features:** School of London University. Merger with King's Medical & Dental School under discussion. **Main undergraduate awards:** MBBS, BDS. **Awarding**

body: London University. **Site:** St Thomas's Hospital (south of Westminster Bridge) and Guy's Hospital (south of London Bridge). **Special features:** Students admitted for both pre-clinical and clinical studies (some places for students who have completed pre-clinical studies at other UK medical schools). Revised integrated, systems-based courses. Dental students taught mainly at Guy's, medical students on both sites. **Europe:** Formal exchange links with University of Lille and Charles University (Prague). As an alternative to the intercalated BSc course, students can opt in the third year to learn a language and develop knowledge of health care delivery in another European country. **Library:** Substantial libraries on both sites together with computer-assisted and audio-visual learning facilities. **Welfare:** Doctor, dentist, counsellors, welfare officer, chaplain, student advisers and tutors. **Careers:** Various pre-registration posts reserved for UMDS students at hospitals in or near London. **Sporting facilities:** Swimming pools, gymnasium, squash courts and 2 sports grounds. Playing fields, 10 mins and 40 mins by train from London Bridge/Waterloo.

Accommodation: In 1995/96, 30% of students in school accommodation, 100% of first years. 435 self-catering places available (290 first years), average rent £45 per week, term time only (pre-clinicals), year-long contracts (clinicals). Students live in privately owned accommodation for 3 or 4 years. **Hardship funds:** Total available in 1995/96: £53,000 government access funds, plus trust fund. Special help to mature and self-financed students; trust fund also helps students in financial hardship. £3,000 pa for first 2 years assigned to 2 mature, self-financed students.

Duration of first degree courses: 5 years. **Total first degree students 1995/96:** 1,565. **Overseas students:** 65. **Mature students:** 120. **Male/female ratio:** 1:1. **Teaching staff:** 200 full-time, 400 part-time. **Total full-time students 1995/96:** 1,645. **Postgraduate students:** 600. **First degree tuition fees:** Home students, paying their own fees in 1996/97, paid £840; Overseas students £8,580 (pre-clinical), £16,500 (clinical).

WHAT IT'S LIKE   Formed in the late eighties from two of London's most prestigious medical schools: Guy's and St Thomas's. St Thomas's has stunning site opposite Houses of Parliament, and only 10 minutes walk away from the West End. Guy's is a short bus journey away at London Bridge and has peaceful gardens and courtyards. Teaching for medics is evenly spread between campuses; for dentists it is almost exclusively at Guy's. The dental school is unique in that it supplies you with an engraved dental kit (worth £3,000) for free. There are 4 libraries, 2 student bars, shops, laundries and canteens; also 2 sports grounds, 2 snooker rooms, swimming pool, multi-gym, 4 squash courts and photography room. Teaching is by systems (eg cardio-vascular system); large amount of clinical experience in pre-clinical years (including GP and nursing attachments and introductory pre-clinical firm). Pastoral guidance throughout the course by a tutor/guidance scheme. Sport is strong and successes at university level are matched by the variety on offer (including sub-aqua). Rowing, soccer, hockey and cricket all successful; rugby club is oldest in the world (153 years). Very active drama society with regular shows and has appeared at Edinburgh Festival. Music is strong and are rehearsal rooms and PA system for college bands and concert groups. Large summer ball (2,500 in 1996) and Hallowe'en ball. Social events on at least one campus every week and if that doesn't keep you happy, then London also has plenty to offer in entertainment. Places in halls on campus for all first year students and for final years if they wish – all self-catering.

PAUPER NOTES   **Accommodation:** Student halls at both campuses. **Drink:** Campus bars are some of cheapest in London (Guy's £1.20 a pint, Tommies, £1.10). **Eats:** Two subsidised restaurants, cheap hospital canteens (if you dare!) and first hospital McDonald's in Europe.

Lots of kebab and curry houses nearby. **Ents:** Very active SU. Hops every week, regular balls (2–4 per year), Christmas review. West End in easy reach. **Sports:** On site: two gyms with weights, swimming pool, 4 squash courts; mountaineering hut in Snowdonia; sailing club at Burnham-on-Crouch; 2 sports grounds (south London and Cobham). **Hardship funds:** Some scholarships available and access funds. **Travel:** Biking between campuses quick, easy and cheap; free inter-campus bus service every 20 mins; both campuses next to tube and rail. Anywhere in London in easy reach by bus. **Work:** Holiday work sometimes available from hospital as auxiliary nurse or porter. Evening work in the many local pubs/bars or weekend work (eg WH Smith – £8/hour on Sundays).

INFORMAL NAME   Guy's and Tommies.

ALUMNI (EDITORS' PICK)   David Owen, Somerset Maugham, John Keats, Lord Butterfield, Thomas Addison (as in disease), Sir Astley Cooper, Florence Nightingale, Sir William Gull (possibly Jack the Ripper).

UMIST

The University of Manchester Institute of Science & Technology, PO Box 88, Sackville Street, Manchester M60 1QD (Tel 0161 236 3311, Fax 0161 228 7040) Map 2

STUDENT ENQUIRIES: Undergraduate Admissions Officer
APPLICATIONS: UCAS

Broad study areas: Science, engineering, technology, optometry, languages, management, maths, computation. (Subject details are in the *Subjects and Places Index.*)

Founded: 1824, charter awarded 1956. **Structural features:** An independent university, still retaining some links with Manchester University. **Main undergraduate awards:** BSc, BEng, BScMEng, MChem, MChemPST, MEng, MMath, MPhys. **Awarding body:** Manchester University. **Site:** Compact site in centre of Manchester. **Access:** Bus, train and metrolink; 25 mins from Manchester Airport. **Academic features:** BEng and MEng courses in major engineering disciplines. Flexible pure sciences programme with undergraduate masters options available. Unique degree course in paper science. Many joint courses including languages, environmental studies and management. Large and prestigious school of management. **Europe:** 8% first degree students take a language as part of course and 4% spend 6 months or more abroad. Formal exchange links with 67 EU and EFTA universities/colleges. Languages may be combined with many subjects. **Library:** Over 231,000 volumes; also resources of main university library. Annual expenditure on library materials, £98.52 per FTE student. **Centres of excellence:** John Rylands University Library at Manchester, Joule Library (UMIST). **Welfare:** Dentists, psychiatric adviser, clinical psychologist, counsellors and nurses. Purpose-built chapel for all denominations. Overseas student adviser. **Careers:** Information, advice and placement. **Amenities:** SU building with bar, shop, travel bureau, nightclub, halls, lounges; wide range of clubs and societies; sports centre; students may also join Manchester University SU.

Accommodation: Halls of Residence jointly run with Manchester University. *See Manchester University*. 10% first degree students live at home. **Term time work**: No institutional policy on part time work. Term time work available in SU and some vacation admin work; Skills Exchange helps finding vac work. **Hardship funds:** Total available 1995/96, £119,000 government access fund. Also hardship fund.

Duration of first degree courses: 3 years; **others:** 4 years. **Total first degree students 1995/96:** 4,405. **Overseas students:** 787. **Mature undergraduate students:** 19%. **Male/female ratio:** 7:3. **Teaching staff:** 467 full-time, 29 part-time. **Total full-time students 1995/96:** 5,840. **Postgraduate students:** 1,435. **First degree tuition fees:** Home students, paying their own fees in 1996/97, paid £750 (classroom), £1,600 (lab) or in certain circumstances £864; Overseas students £6,100 (classroom), £8,100 (lab).

WHAT IT'S LIKE   It's a campus university, in the heart of Manchester, 2 minutes' walk from the city centre with all the clothes stores, record stores, fast food shops you'll ever need. Manchester University and UMIST have a variety of halls – catered, self-catering, married quarters, postgraduate only – the standard varies from standard room to those with ensuite facilities and satellite TV (all UMIST halls have a phone in each room with free internal calls). Pubs such as The Old Garratt, Lass O'Gowrie and Harry's (the SU bars) all no more than 60 seconds away from campus. SU facilities range from café, bar etc to the shop and copyshop with computer typesetting facilities and photocopying (including colour). Campus travel bureau in SU building is among the most popular in Manchester, offering special student discounts. SU advice centre includes international student adviser, welfare and financial advisers, solicitor and counsellors, to deal with any problems students may have on or off campus. SU fortnightly newspaper, *Grip*, written, composed, typeset and arranged by students. SU nightclub (Club Underground) has a wide selection of music night to night – from rave, hip hop, hard core techno, soul, pop, funk, to heavy metal and indie, including the ever popular Friday night Scandalous. Regular bar promotions ensure that UMIST SU has cheapest bars in Manchester. Most entertainment organised by students who DJ, act as roadies for bands, set up lighting rigs, mix and publicise. About 60 societies and very active community action and rag groups (who run the infamous annual real ale festival). International students' society caters for many cultures through international societies and events. Athletic union caters for nearly every sport you can think of – usual tennis, rugby, netball but also skating, windsurfing, lacrosse, rock climbing. One of the few universities that is still on the main employers' milkround for careers. World-wide reputation for science research and winner of the Queen's Award for Export Achievement. A separate university with its own campus and union but students can also take full advantage of Manchester University facilities, societies, social events, sports facilities and halls. About 55% students have to work in term time; sponsorship and careers offices advertise both termtime and vacation work.

PAUPER NOTES   **Accommodation:** UMIST and university halls. **Drink:** Harry's, Lass O'Gowrie, Jabez Clegg, The Clarence and O'Sheas (Irish pubs), Mantos (gay/mixed wine bar), King's Arms. **Eats:** Loads of Chinese; massive Asian quarter in Rusholme, all manner of dishes at wildly varying prices; Est! Est! Est! (Didsbury) reasonably priced Italian food; Chicago Diner (East Didsbury); standard range in centre. **Ents:** Free concert and movie tickets if reviewing for SU newspaper. 7 theatres, 8 cinemas, 5 art galleries, SU discos most nights, loads of clubs. Loads of student discounts. **Sports:** McDougall Sports Centre, Armitage centre, Sugden centre featuring squash, pool, gym etc. **Hardship funds:** Institute access funds, hardship and international students fund. SU welfare loans. **Travel:** Campus Travel in SU. **Work:** SU take on students as minibus drivers, bar staff and for security work, DJs and technicians. Casual work in shops, restaurants, factories, offices and bars locally

MORE INFO?   Ring Ruby Sheera, UMIST Union, PO Box 88, Sackville Street, Mancester M60 1QD (tel 0161 200 3290, fax 0161 200 3268; e-mail president@umist.ac.uk; web site www.un.umist.ac.uk).
ALUMNI (EDITORS' PICK)   Sir John Cockroft, Sir Alan Veale, Gary Bailey, Sir William Barlow, David Clark MP, Keith Oates.

UNIVERSITY COLLEGE LONDON

University College London, Gower Street, London WC1E 6BT
(Tel 0171 387 7050, Fax 0171 387 8057) Map 6

STUDENT ENQUIRIES: Admissions and General Enquiries Office
(Tel 0171 380 7365, Fax 0171 380 7380, E-mail degree-info@ucl.ac.uk). APPLICATIONS: UCAS

You can look up *Institute of Archaeology* and *Slade* separately.

Broad study areas: Mathematics and physical sciences, social and historical sciences, engineering, life science, medicine, arts and languages, built environment, law, speech sciences.
(Subject details are in the *Subjects and Places Index*.)

Founded: 1826. **Structural features:** Part of London University. **Main undergraduate awards:** BA, BSc, MBBS, LLB, BEng, MEng, MSci. **Awarding body:** London University. **Site:** Heart of London University area in Bloomsbury. **Access:** Warren Street, Euston Square, Goodge Street underground stations, buses. **Academic features:** 3 or 4 year LLB course available; MEng in chemical engineering, biochemical engineering, electronic and electrical engineering. **Europe:** BA modern European studies; many courses can include a European language. Sophisticated language centre. Formal exchange links with numerous European universities/colleges. **Special features:** School of medicine offers clinical studies to students who have completed pre-clinical studies at Oxbridge. **Library:** Main library in ten departments – 1,300,000 volumes, 7,000 periodicals, 1,162 study places; special reference facilities for some course books; extensive specialist collections. Annual expenditure on library materials, £139.32 per FTE student. **Welfare:** Doctor, dentist, psychiatrist, solicitor, student counselling service. **Careers:** Information, advice and placement service. **Amenities:** Own theatre (Bloomsbury) and TV station. **Sporting facilities:** 60-acre athletic ground at Shenley; fitness centre.

Accommodation: 3,750 places in UCL and London University managed residences (all first years accommodated). Rents: halls £61–£65 per week; UCL self-catering house £38–£44. Most students live out for part of their course; local rents approx £55 per week self-catering, £62 B&B. **Term time work:** University's policy to allow term time work for full-time first degree students provided that it does not have an adverse effect on academic work. Term (and vac) work available on campus in library, refectory, SU; also careers service helps with vacation work. **Hardship Funds:** Available but not for first-year students.

Duration of first degree courses: 3 years; **others:** 4 years. **Total first degree students 1995/96:** 9,217. **Overseas students:** 3,500. **Male/female ratio:** 1:1. **Teaching staff:** 2,150. **Total full-time students 1995/96:** 13,000. **Postgraduate students:** 4,270. **First degree tuition fees:** Home students, paying their own fees in 1996/97, paid £750 (classroom), £1,600 (lab, studio, pre-clinical), £2,800 (clinical); Overseas students £7,050 (classroom), £9,020 (lab/studio), £10,120 (pre-clinical), £16,030 (clinical).

WHAT IT'S LIKE   Catering for almost 13,000 students in the centre of London, UCL can appear daunting at first. However the union has plenty to offer, including over 100 clubs and societies – one devoted to building a human-powered flight machine! – and a TV station; recently built specialised clubs and societies centre encompassing everything from state-of-the-art desktop publishing to leadership training workshops. UCL has its own theatre, The Bloomsbury, which is a successful fringe theatre, home to the world-famous UCL Opera and houses student drama and dance productions; also a cinema-sized screen where film soc shows latest films. Regular student productions shown in the studio Garage Theatre. There are many sports clubs (between UCL union and ULU, almost every sport is covered); new sports hall in nearby south Camden. Two UCL sports grounds: at Chislehurst in Kent; and a professional-standard ground in Shenley, Hertfordshire (part leased to Arsenal FC). Two main disco venues, Easy J's and the Windeyer and wide range of ents: Friday club nights at the Windeyer feature famous DJs (eg C J Mackintosh); Thursday is infamous Cocktails night; regular Tuesday comedy nights; three black tie balls (Freshers, Christmas and Summer) always sell out early. Many students from London and the home counties but the number of overseas students is rising every year. About a quarter of all students are postgraduates. College is continually building new halls of residence and student houses; aims to accommodate every first year applying before a given date. Library hours are long (8.45 am till 10.00 pm on typical weekday); open on Sundays during exams. Student welfare a top priority: union runs a rights and advice centre; college runs counselling service. UCL is a traditional college and work is demanding although not impossible. Over 50% of students can expect to leave with a first or upper second degree and are among the most likely in the country to get jobs when they graduate. UCL is consistently ranked in the top five institutions nationwide and the opportunity to study in this friendly place, within shouting distance of the sights and sounds of London, shouldn't be passed up.

PAUPER NOTES   **Accommodation:** Good student halls, situated centrally. Blocks of flats for couples, and two bungalows for students with families. Union housing booklet. **Drink:** UCL union has 6 bars, ULU has 2. London pubs are expensive. **Eats:** Number of SU food outlets, cheap and varied; a lot of veggie. Good Indian/vegetarian food in nearby Drummond St. **Ents:** Great college ents; London at your feet. **Sports:** Fitness centre with cheap rates for students. ULU pool 5 mins walk away. **Hardship funds:** Access funds (allocated in first and second terms). Union loans in cases of severe hardship. Union runs budgeting workshops and money management guide. Rights & advice office gives advice on a drop in basis. **Travel:** Some departments award travel scholarships for the long vacation. Travel agent in union. Most students use the tube or walk/cycle in London. **Work:** Union-run employment agency for part time and temp work in union and college and outside (min £3.25/hour).

INFORMAL NAMEs   UCL, UC.

ALUMNI (EDITORS' PICK)   David Lodge, Jonathan Miller, Jonathan Dimbleby, David Gower, Margaret Hodge, Fiona Armstrong.

WALES COLLEGE OF MEDICINE

University of Wales College of Medicine, Heath Park, Cardiff
CF4 4XN (Tel 01222 747747, Fax 01222 742914) Map 3

STUDENT ENQUIRIES: Undergraduate Admissions Officer
APPLICATIONS: UCAS

Broad study areas: Medicine; dentistry; nursing; professions allied to medicine including occupational therapy, physiotherapy, radiography. (Subject details are in the *Subjects and Places Index.*)

Founded: 1931 as Welsh National School of Medicine. Royal Charter and new name in 1984. **Structural features:** Part of Wales University. **Main undergraduate awards:** MBBCh, BDS, BN, BSc. **Awarding body:** University of Wales. **Site:** Part of complex shared with University Hospital of Wales, 2 miles from Cardiff city centre. **Access:** By road. **Special features:** Students from a wide variety of health care disciplines train and socialise together. Offers 6-year medical and dental courses (students usually admitted direct to second year; early stages studied at Cardiff University). 2- and 4-year courses in nursing. Clinical teaching provided in hospitals and the community throughout Wales for all courses. **Europe:** Exchange programme in Europe for students with appropriate linguistic abilities. **Library:** 7 libraries: total 150,000 volumes, 1,300 current periodicals, 378 study places, seminar room, IT services, audio-visual facilities, 24-hour reading rooms. Annual expenditure on library materials, £159.20 per FTE student. **Centres of excellence:** Cancer research, nephrology, medical genetics, cardiovascular biology, wound healing unit. **Welfare:** Occupational health service, chaplain, student counsellor, international development officer. **Special categories:** Some residential facilities for married students; crèche at Cardiff University. **Careers:** Information and advice (pre-registration house officer posts in Welsh University virtually automatic). **Amenities:** Medical bookshop on campus, music and drama societies. Staff and students' social club. **Sporting facilities:** Athletics facilities of Cardiff University. UWCM campus – swimming pool, sauna/jacuzzi, squash and badminton courts, multigym.

Accommodation: In 1995/96, all first year students guaranteed accommodation (dental and medical students at Cardiff University). 24% of all clinical students in college accommodation. 208 self catering places at £29 per week; 96 self-catering places at £70 per month. Students live in privately owned accommodation for 2–3 years; £30–£45 per week self-catering, £35–£50 B&B, £50–£60 half board. **Term time work:** Students are not encouraged to undertake term time work. **Hardship funds:** Total available in 1995/96: £36,805 government access funds (95 students helped); £8,000 emergency loan fund (£250 average award). Special help to self-financing students, and those students experiencing severe financial difficulties.

Duration of first degree courses: 5–6 years BDS, MB, BCh; 2–4 years BN; 3 years BSc. **Total first degree students 1995/96:** 1,155. **Overseas students:** 53. **Mature students:** 232. **Male/female ratio:** 1:3. **Teaching staff:** 439 full-time, 128 part-time. **Total full-time students**

1995/96: 1,791. **Postgraduate students:** 387. **First degree tuition fees:** Home students, paying their own fees in 1996/97, paid £834; Overseas students £7,740 (BN, BSc and pre-clinical), £14,550 (clinical).

WHAT IT'S LIKE   It's on a 53-acre campus, purpose-built in the 1970s, some two and a half miles north of the city centre. It is easily accessible, on most main bus routes. UWCM provides teaching facilities for students in medicine, dentistry, as well as nursing, occupational therapy, physiotherapy, and radiography; the emphasis is on developing well-rounded individuals, rather than academics who cannot communicate. The dental pre-clinical and early stages of the medical course are taught at nearby Cardiff University (UWC) and first years are guaranteed accommodation in UWC halls of residence (self-catering or full board). First years on most other courses are guaranteed accommodation on campus (single study bedrooms, shared catering and laundry facilities) as are some 2nd year dental and 3rd year medical students. Small number of places for married students. Other students find lodgings – plentiful in area. SU and bar (Med Club) are in hall on site. Apolitical SU but active socially; fields teams in most major sports (not just rugby!). Good relations with college authorities; it's an autonomous body within the NUS (unlike many other medical student associations). Students can make full use of the UWC facilities. It is a highly regarded medical school, an excellent teaching record and high pass rate. Teaching by lectures, seminars and tutorials; emphasis on clinical skills. Free transport for students is provided to hospitals around the Cardiff area. Most students can study in hospitals throughout Wales, as well as an elective period either abroad or in UK. Students are assessed by course work and exams (traditional, multiple choice papers as well as vivas). Resits are possible, but there is no fixed failure rate. Medically trained staff act as student counsellors. Large student population in Cardiff, which has much to offer: cultural and sporting centre of Wales, boasting the National Museum of Wales and Welsh National Opera, fine castle, superb civic buildings as well as seven cinemas and four theatres (including the 2,000-seat St. David's Hall). Excellent shopping centre and numerous pubs, clubs and restaurants. Students come here from a wide variety of backgrounds: 40% Welsh students, 50% from other UK countries and 10% overseas students with a male/female ratio of nearly 1:1. There is no discrimination of any description.

PAUPER NOTES   **Accommodation:** Campus hall relatively cheap, generally high standard; rented houses cost a lot more. Small number of houses/flats for married students. **Drink:** Med Club cheapest prices in Cardiff. Brains is local brew, but many other excellent local beers. **Eats:** Excellent variety of restaurants in town, now with many vegetarian and ethnic eateries. Many offer 10% student discount. **Ents:** Sherman Theatre; 9-screen cinema. Students go half-price Wed afternoons at most cinemas; cheap stand-by tickets at most theatres. **Sports:** All SU sports club free; National Sports Centre reasonable. Sports and social club on campus has reasonable membership fee. **Hardship funds:** Access funds. Also interest-free emergency loans. **Travel:** Free transport to hospitals in Cardiff area. Scholarships available to help fund electives. **Work:** Some students work in Medical Club Bar. In the early stages of the medical and dental courses students have similar holidays to other students; in later stages students have little/no time to work due to long academic terms.

MORE INFO?   Get students' Alternative Prospectus (Freshers Handbook).
Enquiries to General Secretary UWCMSC (01222 742125/743619).
INFORMAL NAME   UWCM.
ALUMNI (EDITORS' PICK)   Dr Gareth Crompton, J N Parry, John Peters, Doreen Vermeulencranch, Professor B Knight.

WALES UNIVERSITY

The University of Wales, University Registry, Cathays Park, Cardiff CF1 3NS. (Tel 01222 382656, Fax 01222 396040)

STUDENT ENQUIRIES: To each of the institutions listed below; each has an individual profile in the book.
APPLICATIONS: To the constitutent colleges, usually via UCAS

Founded: 1893, originally bringing together three existing colleges at Aberystwyth, Bangor and Cardiff. **Structural features:** A federal university. It consists of six constituent institutions which incorporate University of Wales into their titles: the original three colleges at *Aberystwyth*, *Bangor* and *Cardiff*, later joined by *Swansea* (1920), *Lampeter* (1971), and *Wales College of Medicine* (1931). In addition, two new university colleges joined in 1996: University of Wales Institute, Cardiff (look it up under *Cardiff Institute*) and University of Wales College, Newport (*Newport College*). Teaching, academic appointments and the selection of students are all left to the colleges and institutions. You can look each up separately.

Three independent Welsh colleges have associated college status: *North East Wales Institute*, *Swansea Institute* and *Trinity College Carmarthen*. Their University of Wales examinations and certificates are administered in the same way as those of the constituent institutions. Each of these can be looked up separately too.

Duration of first degree courses: 3 or 4 years. **Total first degree students 1995/96:** 36,100.
Tuition fees 1996/97 (self-financing students on first degrees): *See individual institutions*.

WARRINGTON UNIVERSITY COLLEGE

University College Warrington, Padgate Campus, Crab Lane, Fearnhead, Warrington WA2 0DB
(Tel 01925 494494, Fax 01925 816077) Map 2

STUDENT ENQUIRIES: Academic Registrar
APPLICATIONS: UCAS

Broad study areas: Business, media, leisure, performing arts, sports studies. (Subject details are in the *Subjects and Places Index*.)

Founded: 1993, incorporating various local colleges. **Structural features:** A college of Manchester University. **Main undergraduate award:** BA. **Awarding body:** Manchester University. **Site:** Extensive landscaped site, close to town centre. **Access:** Within easy reach of M6, M56 and M62 motorways. **Special features:** Flagship institution chosen by Granada

TV in Education and Media Partnership. **Academic features:** Modular degree courses for mature students (joint and combined honours), with range of modules and a work-based assignment. **Europe:** 5% first degree students take a language as part of course and spend 3 months or more abroad on work-based assignments. No formal exchange links with EU universities/colleges. **Library:** Several libraries; 95,000+ books, range of periodicals, reading rights at Manchester University library. **Other learning facilities:** Computer facilities; TV and sound studios, darkroom etc; desktop publishing; fully equipped theatre for use by students and touring companies; study skills centre. **Welfare:** Careers guidance, counselling and welfare services. **Amenities:** Good sporting facilities, fitness centre; own SU complex.

Accommodation: In 1995/96, 70% of all students in college accommodation, 90% of first years. 482 self-catering places available (247 for first years), at £26–£34.50 per week, term time only. Students living in privately owned accommodation pay £35–£40 per week for self-catering, £45 for B&B, £50 for half-board. **Term time work:** College policy to allow term time work for first degree students. Term (and vac) work available on campus in SU bar. **Hardship funds:** Total available in 1995/96: £42,906 government access funds, 500 students helped; also loans. Special help: those needing help with childcare.

Duration of first degree courses: 3 years. **Total first degree students 1995/96:** 710. **Mature students:** 29%. **Male/female ratio:** 1:1. **Teaching staff:** 65 full-time, 6 part-time. **Total full-time students 1995/96:** 876. **First degree tuition fees:** Home students, paying their own fees in 1996/97, paid £750 (classroom), £1,600 (lab/studio); Overseas students £5,979.

WHAT IT'S LIKE Small yet extremely friendly college in Warrington – midway between Manchester and Liverpool. The degree courses include sports studies, leisure, media and performing arts – all including business management. Accommodation provided for first and third years in mixed halls of residence; most first years share but can be the opportunity to meet your first new friends. Always students around on campus and, being slightly out of town, most activities are in SU bar. SU provide a range of clubs and societies, activities and entertainments throughout the year; together with the athletics union, it supports sports clubs and provides sports facilities. All in all, the college is an extremely friendly and pleasant place to be for three years and, if you can survive your lectures, finances and friends, you will thoroughly enjoy your time. *Jo Wragg*

PAUPER NOTES **Accommodation:** Halls comparatively cheap; limited off campus. **Drink:** SU bar cheapest (£1.40 most expensive pint); some student nights in town. **Eats:** SU bar has pub grub (cheap and tasty) lunchtimes and evenings. Range of ethnic restaurants in Warrington; various delivery places. **Ents:** SU bar and venue. Close to Manchester and Liverpool. **Sports:** Sports hall and fitness centre on campus. **Hardship funds:** Limited, but available from college. **Travel:** Two main stations in Warrington for access across the country; close to M6; Manchester airport reasonably close. **Work:** Mainly bar work, on and off campus; little retail opportunities.

MORE INFO? Enquiries to SU (tel 01925 821336 or 01925 494494 ext 2275; fax 01925 816077).

ALUMNI (EDITORS' PICK) Alan Bleasdale, Mike Hall MP, Diane Modahl (Olympic athlete)

HOW TO START? *SEE SHORTLISTING*, PAGE 535

WARWICK UNIVERSITY

The University of Warwick, Coventry CV4 7AL
(Tel 01203 523523, Fax 01203 461606) Map 3

STUDENT ENQUIRIES: Academic Registrar
APPLICATIONS: UCAS

Broad study areas: Arts, education, science, social studies.
(Subject details are in the *Subjects and Places Index*.)

Founded: 1964. **Main undergraduate awards:** BA, BA(QTS), BSc, LLB, BEng, MEng.
Awarding body: Warwick University. **Site:** Single campus 2½ miles south west of Coventry
city centre. **Access:** Buses from Coventry and Leamington Spa. **Academic features:** Degrees
in chemistry with business studies, European engineering, international business. Degrees
with local FE colleges (2 years in college, 2 at university) in eg environmental studies,
European studies, labour studies, social studies, technology with business. **Special
features:** University provides adult and continuing education courses locally and validates
an open access scheme; range of part-time degrees by day and/or evening study. Many
visiting professors. Arts centre and music centre; string quartet in residence. Successful
science park; business school; close links with industry and local community. **Europe:** 9%
first degree students take a language as part of course and 5% spend 6 months or more
abroad. 80% of students have a language option. Formal exchange links and Erasmus partnerships with 150+ universitites in Europe and the Americas, many open to non-language
specialists. **Library:** 2 main libraries; nearly 870,000 volumes in total, 5,000 periodicals; 1,440
study places (1,150 in central library); short-term loan period for books in heaviest demand.
Annual expenditure on library materials, £131.76 per FTE student. **Specialist collections:**
Modern records centre; BP archive centre. **Other learning facilities:** Computing centre;
language centre. **Welfare:** Doctors, dentists, opticians, psychiatrist, chaplains, law centre
(in school of law), 5 student counsellors and personal/residential tutor system. **Special
categories:** Crèche with 25 places. **Careers:** Careers library, individual counselling, sponsorship officer, employers' recruitment visits. **Amenities:** Modern SU building, student
newspaper, travel and insurance offices; refectory; university arts centre (theatres, concert
hall, music centre, cinema, art gallery, sculpture court, bookshop, restaurant and bars);
shops, banks, post office on campus. Close to Coventry (swimming pool, theatre, museums
and galleries) and Stratford (RSC). **Sporting facilities:** Extensive playing fields, tennis courts,
dri-play floodlit area, running track, trim track, sports centre (two 25m pools, squash courts,
well-equipped fitness room, indoor climbing centre).

Accommodation: In 1995/96, 56% of all students in university accommodation, 95% of first
years (all who apply). 4,000+ self-catering places, £30.70–£33.85 per week (£45 ensuite) for
30–39 weeks. 50% of final year students return to campus (decided by ballot). 2,000 places
in university managed properties (in Coventry, Kenilworth and Leamington Spa), £30–£35
per week self-catering. Some students live in privately owned accommodation, £35–£45
per week. **Term time work:** University's policy to allow term time work for full-time first
degree students; advise no more than 10–15 hours per week. Term (and vac) work available on campus in admin, SU etc; careers library and SU have info on work off campus.
Hardship funds: Total available in 1995/96: £189,655 government access funds (232 students
helped); £5,000 other funds (5 students helped) plus other postgraduate awards. Special

help to those suffering financial hardship, eg self-financing students, disabled students. Some scholarships intended for particular groups (eg *The Voice* scholarship), some available to students prior to starting course.

Duration of first degree courses: 3 years; **others:** 4 years (incl BEng/MEng, BA(QTS), languages). **Total first degree students 1995/96:** 8,042; **Total QTS students:** 774. **Overseas students:** 2,136 (u/g and p/g). **Mature students:** 19%. **Male/female ratio:** 1:1. **Teaching staff:** 706. **Total full-time students:** 11,560. **Postgraduate students:** 5,409. **First degree tuition fees:** Home students, paying their own fees in 1996/97, paid £750 (classroom), £1,600 (lab/studio); Overseas students £6,210 (classroom), £7,905 (lab/studio).

WHAT IT'S LIKE   Large campus university just outside Coventry, it boasts a fine academic record, excellent facilities and one of the largest student unions in the country – the focal point of most student activity. The campus is pleasant with a balance between buildings and lakes, fields and woods. On-campus accommodation for all first years except clearing – all good quality self-catering, sheets laundered regularly; rooms usually with washbasin, many with ensuite bathrooms. Off-campus, students usually live in Leamington Spa (8 miles) or Coventry (3 miles); travel links good, frequent and cheap public transport. University encouraging use of public transport by charging for car parking (mostly prohibited for on-campus students) and funding the buses to keep fares low. The SU provides professional advice and welfare service, a shop, Endsleigh Insurance, travel shop, opticians, launderette, 7 bars, 3 catering outlets, take-away pizza, an academic affairs unit and, most recently, an employment centre. 230 clubs and societies (70 of which are sporting); band, music, rag and film societies most active. Also has the award-winning radio station (W963) and newspaper (the *Warwick Boar*). An event every night of the week; comedy, discos, clubs, cabaret, quizzes and drama. Live bands on Saturday nights (you pay what you think the band is worth) recently include Echnobelly, KulaShaker, Ocean Colour Scene, Cream and Megadog. Union tends to be independent; it has prominent and powerful voice in NUS and student politics generally. Top courses include maths, history, politics, law and business studies. Assessment based on long essays and examination. Changing courses reasonably easy. Students come from all over the country and from varying social backgrounds; neither the university nor SU allow discrimination on the grounds of gender, sexual preference, race or disability.

PAUPER NOTES   **Accommodation:** £30–£45 per week on campus; £25–£38/week off campus, plus bills and transport. Very few married places. **Drink:** Cheap bars on campus. Whitbread, S&N. Local: M+B, Ansells. **Eats:** Large selection of vegetarian/vegan food in union. Hot meals, sandwich bars, pizza restaurant and take-away. Newly revamped diner. **Ents:** Student discount at Warwick Arts Centre on campus. Cheap ents programme in all-new Cooler Club. **Sports:** 2 university-run sports centres free, including pools and tracks. **Hardship funds:** Limited access funds (controlled by Senior Tutor). **Travel:** Bus – 60p to Coventry, £1.10 to Leamington – uni subsidised, £52 per term pass. **Work:** Union employs 300 students across all its outlets; £2.75/hour for stewards, £3.50 bar staff. Limit of 16 hours per week in term time. Some vacation work through union and university, eg conference work.

MORE INFO?   Enquiries to Jon Norburn, President (01203 417220 ext 170).

ALUMNI (EDITORS' PICK)   Sting (for 1 term), Dave Nellist (Militant MP), David Davis MP, Jeff Rooker MP, Stephen Pile (journalist), Simon Mayo (DJ), Timmy Mallett, Frank Skinner (TV personalities).

WELSH COLLEGE OF MUSIC AND DRAMA

Welsh College of Music and Drama, Castle Grounds,
Cathays Park, Cardiff CF1 3ER
(Tel 01222 342854/6, Fax 01222 237639) Map 3

STUDENT ENQUIRIES: School of Music (Tel 01222 640054) or
School of Drama (Tel 01222 371440).
APPLICATIONS: Direct

Broad study areas: Music, drama, theatre design, stage management. (Subject details are in the *Subjects and Places Index*.)

Founded: 1949, as Cardiff College of Music; present title since 1971. **Main awards:** BA, Performers Diploma Music, Advanced Diploma, MA. **Awarding body:** Wales University. **Site:** Cardiff city centre. **Access:** Site close to main bus and railway stations. **Special features:** Visiting artists: Brodsky Quartet, Victor Morris, Balász Szokolay. **Academic features:** Emphasis on practical studies; degrees in music and in theatre studies (acting, stage design or stage management). **Europe:** Languages taught to singing students (11%). No students spend time abroad. **Library:** 10,000 volumes, 35 periodicals, 34 study places. **Welfare:** Counsellor, chaplain. **Careers:** Information, advice and placement service. **Amenities:** Theatre on site; studios and workshops, Studio Theatre, refectory. Concert and opera ticket concessions; strong practical association with BBC and WNO.

Accommodation: No college accommodation available; all students live in privately owned accommodation; £25–£45 per week for self-catering. SU holds list of reputable landlords, housing agencies etc (tel 01222 372700). **Term time work:** College policy to allow part time work. Some available in college, ushers, front of house, bars. **Hardship funds:** Access funds available.

Duration of first degree courses: 3 years. **Total first degree students 1995/96:** 401. **Male/female ratio:** 1:1. **Teaching staff:** 24 full-time, 300 part-time. **Total full-time students 1995/96:** 439. **Postgraduate students:** 73. **First degree tuition fees:** Home students, paying their own fees in 1996/97, paid £1,600; Overseas students £5,750.

WHAT IT'S LIKE   It's situated in the picturesque surroundings of Cathays Park, just behind Cardiff Castle (built on Roman remains). Access is good, only ten minutes from the city centre, bus station and railway station. Most students live within easy walking distance in Cathays, Roath, or Canton. No halls of residence, but finding accommodation is not hard thanks to a comprehensive housing list compiled by the SU and the many housing bureaux. Variety of ages and nationalities, students from Europe and further afield. SU is enthusiastic, organising successful Graduands' and Freshers' balls, and a freshers' week packed full of entertainment of which any union would be proud. Small number of student means there are not many societies (though the football club and Christian Union are very active). However, the intimate nature of the college ensures that you will soon discover the fellow students who have similar interests to you. As a capital city, Cardiff has a plethora of pubs, restaurants and take-aways to suit all tastes, and of course, markets, cinemas, art houses and theatres. St David's Hall houses the stars – pop and classical as well as comedians. Cardiff Arms Park is a popular venue (eg REM, Bon Jovi, the Rolling Stones, U2, Simple Minds . . .) as well as being the spiritual home of Welsh rugby; Cardiff has a brilliant ice-hockey team and Glamorgan County Cricket Club. Staff/student relationships are good as much of the teaching is done in small seminar groups. The atmosphere for both music and drama is not as cut throat as some London colleges and the drop-out rate is low. Courses are varied with the many options. A buzzing micro-technology department and a harmoniously humming early music department. As well as numerous concerts, there is an annual full-scale opera and four drama department productions a term (musicals to Jacobean tragedy); the annual must is the stage management pantomime, which mercilessly mocks the college actors! Whatever the course, the emphasis is firmly on performance. There is some part time work available at the college, box office and ushering for performances; large numbers work in theatre, concert halls, pubs and bars.

PAUPER NOTES   **Accommodation:** No halls. Average local rent £40 pw. **Drink:** College bar cheap. Lots of studenty pubs around. Brains is the local brewer, you'll either love or hate it. **Eats:** College canteen cheap prices. Outside college there's an abundance of good (and bad!) curry houses, Chinese, pizza parlours, chippies etc. Try a Clark's pie, a local delicacy! **Ents:** Regular in college, and Cardiff full of things to do. **Sports:** Union sports societies; access to university sports centre; cheap student membership at the Welsh Institute of Sport. **Hardship funds:** Bursary funds and access funds. College helpful to self-funding students. **Travel:** Main BR and bus stations within walking distance. Student accommodation areas near college. **Work:** During term time relatively easy to find part-time work. Casual work available from college and union. Town theatres employ a lot of WCMD students. Full-time temporary work not so easy to come by unless you apply early.

INFORMAL NAME   WCMD.

ALUMNI (EDITORS' PICK)   Anthony Hopkins, Victor Spinetti, Peter Gill, Caryl Thomas, Sioned Thomas, David Gwesyn Smith, Kenneth Smith, Iris Williams, Anthony Stuart Lloyd, Rakie Ayooha.

WELSH INSTITUTE OF RURAL STUDIES

Welsh Institute of Rural Studies, University of Wales Aberystwyth, Llanbadarn Fawr, Aberystwyth, Ceredigion SY23 3AL
(Tel 01970 624471, Fax 01970 611264) Map 3

STUDENT ENQUIRIES: Admissions Office
APPLICATIONS: UCAS

Broad study areas: Agriculture, agribusiness, rural economy, countryside management, equine science. (Subject details are in the *Subjects and Places Index.*)

Founded: 1971. **Structural features:** Part of Aberystwyth, and so part of Wales University. **Main undergraduate award:** BSc. **Awarding body:** Wales University. **Site:** Single site on an Aberystwyth University campus, overlooking Cardigan Bay. **Access:** A44, A487; BR link to

Shrewsbury; Holyhead and Fishguard ferries to Ireland. **Europe:** Languages available to equine students. Formal exchange links with Friesland College of Agriculture in Netherlands. **Library:** Use of Aberystwyth University library. Specialist collections in agriculture, countryside management and equine studies. **Other learning facilities:** Specialist science labs, computer labs (24 hour access), mechanisation and rural craft workshops, riding school, outdoor manège, over 560 acres of mixed farm and woodland, glasshouse complex. **Careers:** Information, advice and placement service. **Welfare:** Welfare officer, counsellors, childcare, nightline, local GPs; tutorial service for students. **Special facilities:** Crèche on campus. **Amenities:** Wide range provided by Aberystwyth Guild of Students, including arts centre, student bars, restaurant, bank etc; over 50 societies and clubs. **Sporting facilities:** 50 acres playing fields close by; Snowdonia within easy reach; sports hall provides for all major sports.

Accommodation: In 1992/1993, 40% of all students in college accommodation, 80% of first years (guaranteed for all who want it). Variety of catered, self-catered and pay-as-you-eat, rents £25–£57 per week. See also *Aberystwyth University*. **Hardship funds:** Self-financing students considered for access funding before start of course.

Duration of first degree courses: 3–4 years. **Total first degree students 1995/96:** 650 **Overseas students:** None. **Mature students:** 10. **Male/female ratio:** 3:2. **Teaching staff:** 26 full-time. **Total full-time students 1995/96:** 450. **Postgraduate students:** 60. **First degree tuition fees:** Home students, paying their own fees in 1996/97, paid £1,600; Overseas students £8,020.

WHAT IT'S LIKE   It's at Llanbadarn Fawr village, on the outskirts of Aberystwyth and well positioned for access to open countryside, the Welsh coastline and Snowdonia National Park. A small closely knit campus with a good mix of students. Originally catering for education in agriculture, it's now in the forefront of developing new courses such as countryside management and equine studies. The college itself provides an excellent environment for learning and the young teaching staff are very enthusiastic and have a very open door attitude. College bar is an excellent meeting point with a good juke box and TV. Beer promotions are often on offer and bands and discos arranged. Aberystwyth is a small friendly place with shops catering for all tastes and plenty of pubs. Aber has a nightclub as well as seafront bars/discos which stay open till the early hours. All sports catered for: rugby is the traditional game but good football, netball, hockey, cricket and shooting teams. Many students are involved in outdoor activities. Accommodation on campus is generally good and the college refectory food is just about palatable. There is a good shop on site and holds good stock of essentials like bread, pies, paper, pens. If you prefer to live out then there is plenty of student accommodation in town (approximately 30% of the population of Aberystwyth are students) but can be expensive. Just come and have a look, you might get to like the place.

PAUPER NOTES   **Accommodation:** Plenty of student houses in Aberystwyth; good campus accommodation. **Drink:** Cheap promotions at college and in town. **Eats:** Full range of fast food, variety of cheap restaurants and cafés. Refectory good but basic. **Ents:** Cheap, good bands at the university arts centre, bands and disco on campus. **Sports:** Very good sports facilities, pool in village, good sports grounds. **Hardship funds:** All usual funds available, regular meetings. **Work:** Around 5% students work part-time, mainly in bars, cafés, factories. Agricultural students work on home farm. Not much vacation work – some farm work at Easter.

MORE INFO?   Write to Student President.

WEST HERTS COLLEGE

West Herts College, Watford Campus, Hempstead Road,
Watford, Herts WD1 3EZ (Tel 01923 257500,
Fax 01923 257556) Map 5

STUDENT ENQUIRIES: Marketing department (Tel 01923 257565)
APPLICATIONS: UCAS

Broad study areas: Media and leisure studies, business, graphic arts and packaging technology, publishing, hotel, catering & hospitality management. (Subject details are in the *Subjects and Places Index.*)

Founded: 1874. **Main undergraduate awards:** BSc, BA. **Awarding body:** Hertfordshire University. **Site:** Watford town centre and 3 other sites. **Access:** Watford Junction station (British Rail). **Europe:** 50% of first degree students study a language; 10% spend 6 months or more abroad. No formal exchange links with universities/colleges, although many international links. **Library:** Main library, plus 2 site libraries; 45,000 volumes in total, 350 periodicals, 300 study places. Separate publishing, printing technology and management library. Annual expenditure on library materials, £40 per FTE student. **Other learning facilities:** Computers, CD-Rom. **Welfare:** Medical advisory service, counselling service. **Careers:** Information, advice and informal placement service. **Amenities:** Social centre and bar, bookshop on site. Concert hall, live theatre, cinemas, Division 1 football in Watford.

Accommodation: No college accommodation; welfare officer will assist in finding lodgings in and around Watford. **Hardship funds:** Total available in 1995/96: £40,000 government access funds (350 students helped); £40,000 own funds (200 students helped). Special help to students who are single parents.

Duration of first degree courses: 3 years; 4 years sandwich. **Total first degree students 1995/96:** 400. **Overseas students:** 80. **Mature students:** 80. **Male/female ratio:** 3:2. **Teaching staff (degree):** 50 full-time, 35 part-time (college as a whole: 200 full-time, 200 part-time). **Total full-time students 1995/96:** 4,500. **Postgraduate students:** 150. **First degree tuition fees:** Home students, paying their own fees in 1996/97, paid £750; Overseas students £5,200.

WHAT IT'S LIKE   Made up of seven sites, of which six are in Watford and one is in Hemel Hempstead, about 8 miles away. No halls of residence but student services have a register of local landlords; also there is a YMCA and YWCA. Watford itself is a grey place though it has a good shopping centre, The Harlequin, in the middle of town. Entertainment is pretty standard – one nightclub, Kudos; the Colosseum (owned and run by Town & Country) has a regular '70s disco, The Love Train, holds regular big name concerts and is a major student employer. Watford also has lots of pubs (varying degrees of style) but most college ents take place in the refurbished function room (The Gap) and adjoining bar. Not content with just one freshers week, the SU have one every term. The international friendship society, run by overseas students, holds very popular events on a Friday night. The fact that there is only one bar and function area between seven sites is a bit poor but you will be coming here to work. The print course is world renowned and the rapidly growing areas of media production, image-making and graphic media are also becoming known in industry. Employment after graduation always difficult but helped by the excellent links many courses have with industry.

PAUPER NOTES   Accommodation: None – register of private landlords (prices average). YMCA and YWCA. **Drink:** College bar cheapest in town. Cheap promo nights at Kudos and Chicago's. The Horns is popular. **Eats:** College refectories reasonable for variety and prices. Myriad of fast-food outlets in and around town, catering for every possible taste. Some good priced restaurants. **Ents:** Good events at Hempstead Road site, not much at others. Live bands at college. Pump House Theatre, good. Watford has poor 2-screen cinema; UCI at Hatfield shows arthouse films regularly. **Sports:** Sports facilities at Leggatts campus, free Wednesday afternoons. Swimming pools and golf centres in town. **Hardship Funds:** Access funds plus short-term loans. **Travel:** Good hitching on nearby M1 and M25. London 20 mins by train. **Work:** Part-time jobs available if prepared to look – SU has details.

WESTMINSTER COLLEGE

Westminster College, Oxford OX2 9AT
(Tel 01865 247644, Fax 01865 251847) Map 3

STUDENT ENQUIRIES: The Registrar
APPLICATIONS: UCAS

Broad study areas: Education, theology, humanities. (Subject details are in the *Subjects and Places Index*.)

Founded: 1851 in London, moving to Oxford 1959. **Structural features:** Free-standing Methodist higher education institution. **Main undergraduate awards:** BA, BEd, BTh. **Awarding bodies:** Oxford University (BEd, BTh), Open University (BA). **Site:** Single site with 100 acres overlooking Oxford. **Access:** Just off Oxford ring road (A34); Oxford rail/coach stations. **Special features:** Methodist college but welcomes other faiths, denominations and cultures. Visiting professors/students from USA. **Largest field of study:** Education. **Europe:** Language tuition available (3 languages); some students spend a period abroad, including exchanges in 10 countries. **Library:** 100,000 volumes, 600 periodicals, 100 study places. Annual expenditure on library materials, £50 per FTE student. **Specialist collections:** Archives of Methodist education. **Other learning facilities:** TV studio, drama area, primary classrooms, art block, IT facilities. **Careers:** Information and advice from visiting careers adviser. **Welfare:** Medical centre, student services office. **Special facilities:** Crèche over half term.

Accommodation: All first years accommodated who want to be. In 1995/96, 520 rooms on site (some shared), £60–£70 per week, term time (includes meal allowance of £27 per week). Good supply of privately rented accommodation: £40–£60 per week self-catering; £60–£75 B&B. 5% first degree students live at home. **Term time work:** College's policy to allow term time work for full-time first degree students (40% believed to work). Term (and vac) work available on campus in library, clerical, cleaning, maintenance. **Hardship funds:** Total available in 1995/96: £32,000 government access funds (97 students helped). Special help to students suffering financial hardship through unforeseen circumstances.

Duration of first degree courses: BEd 4 years; BTh and BA 3 years.**Total first degree students 1995/96:** 948. **Total BEd students:** 718. **Mature students:** 287. **Male/female ratio:** 1:5. **Teaching staff:** 65 full-time, 20 part-time. **Total full-time students 1995/96:** 1,191. **Postgraduate students:** 213. **First degree tuition fees:** Home students, paying their own fees in 1996/97, paid £2,700 (BA, BTh), £3,200 (BEd), £4,850 (lab); Overseas students £4,675 (class-room), £6,975 (lab).

WHAT IT'S LIKE Offers a varied menu: the social life of Oxford and the security of a small free-standing college. Between the city centre and Boars Hill, it has its own sports grounds and even a golf course. The majority of first years are offered accommodation and many return for their third and fourth years. There are two new houses and traditional houses contain 12–13 students, single sex and mixed. Resident students take meals in hall (cafeteria style) and there are a number of formal meals during the year. There is a good mix of students, with a strong international presence; around a quarter are mature. Staff/student relations are good – not surprising considering the size and nature of the college and the Union Society reflects this. College sport is strong and students may join the Oxford University clubs; sports include rowing (college boat in regattas and eights week), rugby, football, cricket, hockey, netball, volleyball and swimming. The college has a leisure centre with an indoor swimming pool, squash courts and outdoor tennis courts; various classes, including aerobics, are on offer. Societies and clubs are open to everyone and the seconds sports teams welcome anyone regardless of talent. What the college does not offer Oxford certainly will. College courses are varied: a relatively new BA in contem-porary studies, BTh which is placed in a social context and BEd with increasing school-based experience. The library makes up in technology what it lacks in space and a new IT centre is planned; staff are friendly and assist students whose ideas of cyber-space are limited (now on the Internet). Students also have access to the Bodleian Library.
PAUPER NOTES **Accommodation:** Most mature students live at home; others in the nearby estate. **Drink:** College bar – reasonable prices. Students may join the Oxford Union, and traditionally gather there on Friday nights. Oxford pubs are popular and varied. **Eats:** Superb local pubs. The White Hart at Fyfield is popular for meals; Cumnor village also offers excellent food. **Ents:** Good student rates for theatres. **Sports:** Good facilities on campus. **Hardship funds:** Access fund popular. The Union Society is good at assisting students who get into financial difficulty. **Travel:** Travel bursaries offered by alumni organ-isation. **Work:** Term time work is easy to find: the college employs students in the library and dining hall; many find work in the bars of Oxford colleges and in local shops.
MORE INFO? Enquiries to Union Society President (01865 200067).

GET HOLD OF THE PROSPECTUSES

WESTMINSTER UNIVERSITY

University of Westminster, 309 Regent Street, London
W1R 8AL (Tel 0171 911 5000, Fax 0171 911 5118) Map 6

STUDENT ENQUIRIES: Central Student Administration
APPLICATIONS: UCAS

Broad study areas: Built environment, engineering, science, business management, social sciences, law, languages, communications, media and design. (Subject details are in the *Subjects and Places Index*.)

Founded: 1838 (subsequently Regent Street Poly and Central London Poly). University status in 1992. **Main undergraduate awards:** BA, BSc, BEng. **Awarding body:** Westminster University. **Site:** 12 main sites: most in central London (W1/NW1), 1 in Harrow. **Access:** All major sites within 15 minutes' walk of each other, apart from Harrow site (25 minutes by tube). All on major bus and tube lines. **Academic features:** Modern engineering foundation (1 year); degrees in computer systems technology; housing studies; photographic and electronic imaging sciences; film, video and photographic arts. **Europe:** 20% first degree students take a language as part of course and 10% spend a period abroad. Languages can be included in all degrees and all students can use Polylang (extensive teach-yourself labs). Some links with universities/colleges. **Library:** 7 libraries, 380,000 volumes, 2,500 periodicals, 1,400 study places. On-line catalogue system. Annual expenditure on library materials, £62.03 per FTE student. **Welfare:** Doctor, FPA, psychiatrist, international students officer, student adviser and counsellor, chaplain, accommodation adviser; health and advice services at Harrow. 20 place nursery in central London, playgroup at Harrow. **Careers:** Careers centres in central London and Harrow. **Amenities:** Refectory and/or bars at 3 central London sites and at Harrow. **Sporting facilities:** Gymnasia, squash courts, fitness rooms; sports ground with various pitches, tennis courts and boathouse at Chiswick.

Accommodation: In 1995/96, 11% of all students in university accommodation. 800 places available: £50–£60 per week self-catering. 470 new places in Harrow for 1997. Students live in privately owned accommodation for 2+ years: £45–£60 per week self-catering. **Term time work:** University's policy to allow term time work for full-time first degree students (at discretion of course leader). Term (and vac) work available on campus. **Hardship funds:** Central fund administered by hardship committee. Access fund loans, nursery bursaries and grants may be awarded to students facing unexpected financial hardship.

Duration of first degree courses: 3 years; 4 years (language and sandwich courses). **Total first degree students 1995/96:** 10,000. **Mature students:** 750. **Male/female ratio:** 1:1. **Teaching staff:** 600 full-time, 400 part-time. **Total full-time students 1995/96:** 8,900. **Postgraduate students:** 3,400. **First degree tuition fees:** Home students, paying their own fees in 1996/97, paid £750 (classroom), £1,600 (lab/studio); Overseas students £5,300 (classroom), £5,700 (lab/studio).

WHAT IT'S LIKE   Sites are spread throughout central London and a large faculty in Harrow. Law, languages, computing and most sciences have good reputations, as do photography and media courses run by faculty of communication. Main advantage of studying in London is accessibility of wide range of arts and entertainment venues and cosmopolitan nature of the capital although all are expensive. Main disadvantage is acute housing shortage; the university is near the bottom of the league tables for student accommodation, housing very few students. Finding a decent, affordable place to live can be a full-time job. SU supports a wide range of political and cultural clubs and societies as well as over thirty different sports clubs. It produces a fortnightly magazine, distributed free to students, that gives information on what's on and matters of interest to students. There are two union bars, one at central London site (Bolsover Street) and another at Harrow. Facilities and provisions made for the student union getting better. The Union's main campaigns are concerned with protecting and enhancing facilities, especially the nursery, and campaigning against student poverty.

PAUPER NOTES **Accommodation:** High rents account for more than whole grant. Squatting becoming popular by necessity but obviously more difficult. **Drink:** Union bar has wide selection and is cheap! The Melting Pot, Bolsover Street is popular. **Eats:** Canteens improving, vegetarians and ethnic minorities are catered for. Windeyer Café (Middlesex Hospital). Daley Bread – very cheap, popular full to bursting sandwiches. **Ents:** Union organises club nights, cabarets, bands and discos for every night of the week. **Sports:** Union organises about 30 sports clubs. ULU has pool which students can use. **Hardship Funds:** Some funds (administered by student services) but very difficult to get. **Work:** 25% students work during term time and in vacations.

MORE INFO? Enquiries to SU President (0171 636 6271).

ALUMNI (EDITORS' PICK) Quentin Crisp, Pink Floyd, Pamela Armstrong, Bernard Wiltshire, Fred and Judy Vermorel, Peter Bruinvels, Margaret Harker, Alexander Fleming, Vic Reeves, Paul Gascoigne, The Emmanuels, Eric McGuiness, Vivienne Westwood.

WIMBLEDON SCHOOL OF ART

Wimbledon School of Art, Merton Hall Road, London SW19 3QA (Tel 0181 540 0231, Fax 0181 543 1750) Map 5

STUDENT ENQUIRIES: Registrar
APPLICATIONS: UCAS (Route B)

Broad study areas: Art & design. (Subject details are in the *Subjects and Places Index.*)

Founded: 1890. **Main undergraduate award:** BA. **Awarding body:** Surrey University. **Site:** Main site plus annexe (foundation course) both in Wimbledon, SW London. **Access:** Wimbledon station or bus for main site; South Wimbledon or Merton Park stations or bus (77a) for annexe. **Academic features:** Degrees in fine art (painting or sculpture) and theatre (theatre design, technical arts or costume/design or interpretation): all include mandatory history of art and contextual studies. Normally students must have completed foundation course. **Special features:** Programme of visiting lectures by professional artists and designers. **Europe:** Some exchange programmes with colleges in other European countries. **Library:** 28,000 books, 100 periodicals, 57 study places; slide collection, video tapes. Annual expenditure on library materials, £45 per FTE student. **Welfare:** Trained counsellor; welfare officer; information held on all other services. **Careers:** Departmental advice service. **Amenities:** SU with common rooms, shop, canteen, etc; workshop theatre.

Accommodation: 11 places in student house next to school. Most students live in privately owned accommodation, £48–£58 per week self-catering. 20% first degree students live at home. **Term time work:** School's policy to allow term time work for full-time first degree students (50% believed to work). No work available on campus. **Hardship funds:** Total available in 1995/96: £12,345 government access funds (44 students helped).

Duration of first degree courses: 3 years. **Total first degree students 1995/96:** 373. **Overseas students:** 18. **Mature students:** 210. **Male/female ratio:** 3:7. **Teaching staff:** 28 full-time, 26 part-time. **Total full-time students 1995/96:** 556. **Postgraduate students:** 61. **First degree tuition fees:** Home students, paying their own fees in 1996/97, paid £1,600; Overseas students £6,652.

WHAT IT'S LIKE   It's situated in quiet, leafy suburbia in south west London, 5 minutes' walk from Wimbledon Chase station and 15–20 minutes from Wimbledon or South Wimbledon. Far enough out of the centre for a small town feeling yet close enough for galleries or going out at night (10 minutes by rail to Waterloo). Foundation course in the annexe in Palmerston Road; some facilities are shared. The staff on all courses are very experienced and helpful, some are well known and respected in the art world. One of the largest regular part-time staffs in the country and occasional visiting artists and lecturers with fresh views and a great deal of energy. Facilities generally excellent. Sculpture dept is equipped for large-scale works in stone, steel, wood or plaster and a life room of its own. Large painting studio spaces; film and video room. Preparation and woodwork rooms for making stretchers, stretching canvas, grinding paint etc, a painting seminar room for large-scale works, exhibitions, discussions and a permanent life room with usually three models. Print dept can cater for all major fine art printing methods (can be used by painting students). Theatre dept has own theatre, with up-to-date facilities for lighting and sound. Individual studio spaces for students, workshops for model-making, large props and wardrobe (industrial sewing machines and separate areas for pattern cutting, fitting etc). Ample opportunity to work with designers and directors in the theatre world. Friendly and efficient staff in well-stocked library (plus slide library, video collection). Space in the foyer for exhibitions and a well-stocked school shop with good discounts. Materials are not free but many of them are covered by a levy which is paid once a year. Canteen not bad; a bit plain but friendly. Student common room small and a bit grubby but due to be redesigned soon. Common room contains a pool table, darts board and a video game but no tea or food machines and no bar. Social life very much up to the students. SU social evenings popular; 2 or 3 parties a term in the theatre, often with bands; touring theatre and ballet companies perform there at the start of tours (often free if design and wardrobe depts been involved). Theatre can be used for performance-based projects. Film and video club tries to put on a film every week. Essentially a place for working. However, atmosphere is very friendly; large number of private parties which all students are usually invited to. Almost no student housing provided, but housing officer helps and generally people have no problem getting somewhere reasonable. But look as soon as you get the housing list and if you're using a housing agency find out just what you'll get for your money.

PAUPER NOTES   **Accommodation:** Ask housing officer. **Drink:** Leather Bottle and Prince of Wales. **Eats:** Vegetarian café; Greek, Italian, Chinese, Indian and McDonalds. **Ents:**

Theatre, cinema and central London 10 min; SU film soc, and parties. **Sports:** YMCA.
Work: Restaurants and summer bar work in Wimbledon if you can get it.
ALUMNI (EDITORS' PICK) Louise Belson (freelance designer with RSC), Rolf
Langenfass (designer, Vienna Opera), Iona McLeish (freelance designer, Pal Joey), John
Pascoe, James Acheson (Oscar winner 1988), Raymond Briggs, Raymona Brooks.

WINCHESTER SCHOOL OF ART

Winchester School of Art, Park Avenue, Winchester SO23 8DL
(Tel 01962 842500, Fax 01962 842496) Map 3

STUDENT ENQUIRIES: Marketing Assistant
APPLICATIONS: UCAS

Broad study areas: Fine arts, textiles/fashion, history of art &
design. (Subject details are in the *Subjects and Places Index*.)

Founded: 1870; merged with Southampton University 1996. **Structural features:** A school
within Southampton University's faculty of arts. **Main undergraduate award:** BA. **Awarding
body:** Southampton University. **Site:** Winchester town centre; also centre in Barcelona.
Access: M3 or 1 hour by train to London; 20 minutes to coast. **Special features:** Teaching
staff are practising painters, sculptors, designers or historians. Two-semester system.
Academic features: Normally entrants must have completed a foundation course (or
BTEC/GNVQ equivalent) for full-time BA studio courses; applications welcomed from
mature/overseas candidates without standard UK qualifications. New joint honours courses
planned within Southampton University (eg design and management studies; Spanish with
fine art). **Europe:** All full-time first degree students can take a language and most go on
exchanges (1–3 months) as part of course. Formal exchange links with universities/colleges
across Europe. Own studios in Barcelona, currently housing MA courses; possibility of new
centre in northern Italy. **Library:** 25,000 volumes, 100,000 slides, 4,000 videos, 160 periodicals, 80 study places; automated link with Hartley Library, Southampton University. **Other
learning facilities:** CD-Rom, internet, Janet, CAD/CAM equipment. **Careers:** Information
service by careers adviser/academic staff. **Amenities:** New SU, own public gallery. **Sporting
facilities:** Recreation centre and park adjacent to college.

Accommodation: 100% first years accommodated in new student village: 386 self-catering
study bedrooms, £51.50 per week, Sept–June (places for couples, wheelchair users). Most
students live in privately owned accommodation for 2 years: £40–£60 per week self-catering.
Term time work: School's policy to allow term time work for full-time first degree students.
Term time work available on campus, office cleaning, SU bars; careers advisors give help
finding vac work. **Hardship funds:** Government access funds are available.

Duration of first degree courses: 3 years (4 years including foundation course). **Total first
degree students 1995/96:** 716. **Overseas students:** 46. **Mature students:** 570. **Male/female
ratio:** 1:3. **Teaching staff:** 55 full-time, 235 part-time. **Total full-time students 1995/96:** 824.

Postgraduate students: 119. **First degree tuition fees:** Home students, paying their own fees in 1996/97, paid £2,950; Overseas students £6,450.

WHAT IT'S LIKE   Small but expanding and forward-looking college. Set in beautiful surroundings on the banks of the River Itchen, very close to the centre of Winchester. A '60s-style building with '80s additions and new extensions provide space for textiles, fine art, sculpture and MA students. Car parking is an increasing problem, with no places for students and very expensive local car parks. New college hostel, Erasmus Park, is some 5 minutes' walk from the college, and has places for 400 students in shared houses of 10–15 people (with ensuite bathrooms). Otherwise accommodation is expensive – and limited due to lage student population in Winchester; students mainly live in self-catering flats, houses and lodgings. Launderettes are few and far between, but the SU provides washing facilities (Erasmus Park has machines). Many part-time tutors have good links with London studios and are working artists. Good work placements and foreign college exchanges for students on many courses; College has its own studio at the Barcelona Art School and access to a cottage in Cornwall for drawing excursions. Although the library is small at the moment, it includes slide and video facilities. Separate SU building planned, with bar and dance floor downstairs and lounge/chill out room and offices upstairs. SU provides regular entertainments in form of live bands, guest DJs, parties, pool, darts, cheap beer and definitely the place to be! A friendly and fun atmosphere, open to suggestions and comments but remember – Winchester School of Art is relatively small and everyone knows everything on the grapevine.

PAUPER NOTES   **Accommodation:** New hostel; town expensive. **Drink:** City full of pubs, many of distinctive individual character. Local brew, Marstons. Good places – The Willow Tree, The Bush, The Mash Tun (student discounts), Railway Inn (live music), The Vine, Greens Wine Bar (live jazz bands). **Eats:** Refectory with good, slightly overpriced meals – good veggie food. Various places in town from cafés to pizza, Chinese, Indian, kebab and chip shops. **Ents:** SU puts on bands, video and dance nights. In Winchester; 3 theatres plus Tower Arts Centre; Theatre Royal shows films and productions regularly with good reductions for students, no main cinema; one nightclub – and an early closing club/pub called The Porthouse. Guildhall displays variety of exhibitions; craft, book and antique fairs. Southampton bigger and better. **Sports:** Very good recreation centre situated close to college with excellent leisure pool and fitness complex (with a student package). Competitive/fun football team. Group and individual sport available; cheapest on day-user ticket or with SU card. **Hardship funds:** Access fund. **Travel:** Close to London. **Work:** Jobs available but becoming more difficult to obtain – mainly barwork, cleaning, shopwork and waiter/waitressing.

INFORMAL NAME   WSASU.

WANT TO HELP WITH THE NEXT EDITION? SEE PAGE 66

WOLVERHAMPTON UNIVERSITY

The University of Wolverhampton, Wulfruna Street,
Wolverhampton WV1 1SB
(Tel 01902 321000, Fax 01902 322680) Map 3

STUDENT ENQUIRIES: Admissions Unit
APPLICATIONS: UCAS

Broad study areas: Art & design, humanities, social sciences, engineering, business, languages and European studies, law, education, science and technology, built environment, nursing and midwifery. (Subject details are in the *Subjects and Places Index*.)

Founded: 1969 as Wolverhampton Poly, incorporating colleges of technology and art, and 4 teacher training institutions. University status in 1992. **Main undergraduate awards:** BA, BEd, BSc, BEng, LLB. **Awarding body:** Wolverhampton University. **Site:** Main Wolverhampton site plus 4 other sites. **Access:** Free shuttle service; public transport. **Academic features:** Degrees in interactive multimedia communication and licensed retail management. Credit accumulation and transfer and modular degree schemes enable students to select individually tailored programmes of study. Work placements encouraged. Strong emphasis on continuing education and the development of international links. **Europe:** 6% first degree students take a language as part of course and 1% spend a period abroad. Language tuition available to all undergraduates. Formal exchange links with over 50 universities/colleges in EU, open to students on most courses. Two courses with simultaneous awards and equal time spent in UK and abroad. **Library:** Libraries on each site; over 440,000 books and 5,000 journals in total; 1,200+ study places, computerised databases. Annual expenditure on library materials, £70.85 per FTE student. **Specialist collections:** Regional history of West Midlands, company and legal reports, European Documentation Centre. **Other learning facilities:** Computer centre; resource-based learning provision. **Welfare:** Advice, networked with other agencies and health consultancy service; access to dentist, FPA, psychiatrist, professional welfare officer, overseas student counsellor, chaplains; financial adviser; academic counselling based on Higher Education Shop (also advises applicants). **Careers:** Information and advice. **Amenities:** SU premises on each site (coffee bar, TV rooms, bank, shops, bars). **Sporting facilities:** *Wolverhampton*: sports hall, fitness suite; *Dudley*: sports hall, tennis courts, playing fields; *Walsall*: sports hall, tennis courts, playing fields, running track, swimming pool, dance studio.

Accommodation: In 1995/96, 40% of all non-local students in university accommodation, 95% first years. 2,394 places (2,100 for first years): 2,233 self-catering (2,063 for first years) at £34.46 per week (£39.90 ensuite) for 38 weeks; 100 part board places (70 for first years), £40,26 per week, Sept–June. Most students live in privately owned accommodation for 2 years: £16–£35 per week self-catering; £35–£40 B&B; £45–£50 half board. 40% first degree students live at home. **Term time work:** University's policy to allow term time work for full-time first degree students (45% believed to work); limit of 15 hours per week. Term (and vac) work available on campus in market research, clerical, library, catering, IT, marketing, admin etc; also student employment bureau helps find wok off campus. **Hardship funds:** Total available in 1995/96: £166,525 government access funds (£717 average award, 232 students helped). Discretionary fee reduction facility for overseas students in financial difficulties. Occasional advance awards from access fund given to students prior to starting course.

Duration of first degree courses: 3 years; **others:** 4 years. **Total first degree students 1995/96:** 16,069. **BEd/BA(QTS) students:** 1,261. **Overseas students:** 3,178. **Male/female ratio:** 1:1. **Teaching staff:** 690 full-time. **Total full-time students 1995/96:** 15,161. **Postgraduate students:** 2,945. **First degree tuition fees:** Home students, paying their own fees in 1996/97, paid £750 (classroom), £1,600 (lab/studio); Overseas students £5,250

WHAT IT'S LIKE   It's on 5 sites but the largest one is in the centre of Wolverhampton. Others are Dudley (7 miles), Walsall (9 miles), and Telford, the newest and smallest (15 miles). Travel between sites should be provided by the university – not always reliable. Accommodation provided for majority of freshers, all sites self-catering; halls service basic and expensive. Rented accommodation varied yet plentiful. Highly innovative combined studies allows combination of almost every course; modular scheme works well, allowing students to pick and choose. Workloads realistic and can be quite low if year's work carefully planned; continuous assessment and examinations. Large number of European and overseas students, particularly on law course. Minimal numbers from independent schools. Low drop-out rate speaks volumes for the quality of the courses and the social life provided. SU very active socially: top bands and seven bars, some of the busiest in town. Redeveloped SU facilities. Comedy circuit rivals none eg Lee Evans, Jack Dee and Nicholas Parsons. Politically it's fairly quiet but strong anti-racist stance.
PAUPER NOTES   **Accommodation:** Expensive halls, some ensuite. Plenty private but varied quality. **Drink:** Good union bar, fairly cheap; Whitbread, Scottish Courage, S & N. Local pubs – Banks. **Eats:** Campus food unexciting and expensive. Union supply snacks from bars. **Ents:** Excellent, varied comedy, major venue. Cheap, plentiful. **Sports:** Newly formed athletics union. Facilities on all sites; many sporting successes in football, hockey, basketball, cricket, rugby. **Hardship funds:** Excellent welfare service both uni and SU. **Travel:** Computer networked campus travel. **Work:** Well-paid work at union bars. Some available in town. Student employment bureau.
INFORMAL NAME   Wolves Uni.

WORCESTER COLLEGE

Worcester College of HE, Henwick Grove, Worcester
WR2 6AJ (Tel 01905 855000, Fax 01905 855132) Map 3

STUDENT ENQUIRIES: Registry
APPLICATIONS: UCAS

Broad study areas: Education, biological sciences, humanities, horticulture. (Subject details are in the *Subjects and Places Index*.)

Founded: 1946. **Structural features: Main undergraduate awards:** BA, BSc, BA/BSc(QTS). **Awarding body:** Coventry University. **Site:** 55-acre campus, 2 miles from Worcester city centre. **Access:** Bus service from city centre. **Special features:** Primary teaching centre. Opportunity for 2nd year students to spend term in USA. Sponsorship/bursary scheme for BA/BSc students. **Academic features:** Welcomes mature students and overseas students. **Europe:** No students learn a language or spend 6 months or more abroad, but some exchange visits. **Library:** Over 100,000 volumes, 550 periodicals, 280 study places. Annual expenditure on library materials, £47 per FTE student. **Other learning facilities:** Media services, primary centre. **Welfare:** Medical and health centre (doctor, FPA), chaplain, counselling service, advisory tutor system. **Careers:** Information and advice service. **Amenities:** SU bar, shops, newspaper, dance studios, drama studio, computer centres. **Sporting facilities:** Playing fields, tennis courts, gymnasia, floodlit hard playing area on site.

Accommodation: 24% students in college accommodation (70% first years). 679 places (409 for first years), at £42 per week self-catering, £46 with 5 meals/week, term time only. Students live in private accommodation for 2+ years: £30–£50 per week self-catering or B&B. 7% students live at home. **Term time work:** College policy to allow part time work for students. Some vac work available in college; ads for jobs off campus displayed. **Hardship funds:** Access fund available.

Duration of first degree courses: 3 years; 4 years horticulture and BA/BSc(QTS). **Total first degree students 1995/96:** 2,453; **BA/BSc(QTS) students:** 576. **Mature students:** 2,090. **Male/female ratio:** 2:3. **Teaching staff:** 177 full-time, 15 part-time. **Total full-time students 1995/96:** 2,854. **Postgraduate students:** 274. **First degree tuition fees:** Home students, paying their own fees in 1996/97, paid £750 (classroom), £1,600 (lab/studio) plus registration £175 in first year; Overseas students £5,150 (classroom), £6,150 (lab/studio).

WHAT IT'S LIKE   Worcester is set on the banks of the river Severn, against the scenic backdrop of the Malvern Hills. Its rich built heritage combines with a modern, commercial centre containing all the usual high street regulars, many friendly pubs and good, cheap places to eat. The city also provides good entertainment – from theatres, cinema, bowling, sports centres, county cricket ground and race course right through to balloon trips, river boat cruises and Victorian Christmas Fayre. The college is a single site campus about five minutes walk from the river, ten from the city centre. There's a large buzz around the college as it aims to gain university status. There have been many recent developments: new halls for first years and PGCE students, astroturf, sports fields, library and students union; and planned are new sports centre and nurse and midwifery block on campus. A wide variety of courses catering for a wide range of students. You'll find no typical student: everybody is an individual and treated as such, evident in the excellent student/tutor relations. The number of mature students is increasing. Sports science is growing rapidly and the QTS courses have good reputation. SU has had a half million refit, the complex now contains two bars, nightclub, large shop, union offices, non-smoking lounge with canteen area and a new student advice bureau. Active SU runs a number of sporting and non-sporting clubs; on the social side, the union bar has a proud record of consuming more drinks per head then any other union because of great events in freshers' week and throughout the year. *Nick Mills*

PAUPER NOTES   **Accommodation:** Good halls (most new); 6 single bedroom self-catered flats with a living room and kitchen. Hall fees competitive and match rents for local houses. Plenty of accommodation around; £30–£40 (inclusive of bills). College runs effective housing list. **Drink:** SU bars have cheap beer. **Eats:** College refectory good: full meal around £2.80. Snack area in SU complex. Plenty of reasonably priced restaurants in town. **Ents:** Cheap

SU entertainments; weekly ents programme; excellent rag and freshers weeks; vali and grad balls. **Sports:** Good local facilities (cheap with city card). Teams active in university leagues and most have sponsorship and professional coaching. **Hardship funds:** Available through college for those with real problems; also college loans and financial advice. **Travel:** Good train and bus services, one hour from Birmingham. **Work:** Plenty locally, term and vac: telesales, pub and bar work, casual factory/packing work. Firms regularly contact SU to advertise in daily campus mailings.

MORE INFO?　Ring SU President or Deputy Prez (01905 748522).

WRITTLE COLLEGE

Writtle College, Chelmsford, Essex CM1 3RR
(Tel 01245 420705, Fax 01245 420456,
E-mail postmaster@writtle.ac.uk) Map 4

STUDENT ENQUIRIES: Student Registration Officer
APPLICATIONS: UCAS

Broad study areas: Agriculture; horticulture; leisure, amenity and rural management; agricultural engineering; environmental science; landscape construction; equine studies, garden design. (Subject details are in the *Subjects and Places Index.*)

Founded: 1893. **Structural features:** A regional college of Anglia Poly University and partner with Essex University (BSc Ag). **Main undergraduate award:** BSc, BEng. **Awarding bodies:** Anglia Poly University, Essex University. **Site:** Single campus on edge of Writtle village. **Access:** Just off A414 at Writtle. Chelmsford railway station 2 miles. **Academic features:** Modular courses; flexible learning methods. **Europe:** 10% students take a language as part of course, 5% spend 6 months or more abroad. Formal exchange links with 6 European colleges and some work experience for horticulture students. **Library:** 50,000 volumes, 400 periodicals, 100 study places. **Other learning facilities:** 500-acre estate including 3 farms; separate fruit farm, commercial glass, equestrian centre, new amenity landscape centre, farm shop, garden centre, engineering workshops, design centre, computer suite, science centre. **Careers:** Information, advice and placement service. **Welfare:** Counselling service, chaplains. **Amenities:** Recreation centre. Bar/disco/social centre. Adequate parking and motor bike storage space. **Sports:** Sports hall, squash, tennis, fitness centre.

Accommodation: In 1995/96, 30% of all students in college accommodation, 50% of first years. 330 full board places (320 for first years) at £55 per week (shared) to £78 (single, ensuite), term time only. Students live in privately owned accommodation for 2+ years: £35–£50 per week self-catering; £55–£70 B&B; £70–£80 half board. 15% first degree students live at home. **Term time work:** College's policy to allow term time work for full-time first degree students (50% believed to work). Term (and vac) work available on campus in farms and bars; also farm work placement officer helps find work off campus. **Hardship funds:**

Total available in 1995/96: £40,000 government access funds (£200 average award, 200 students helped); £10,000 own funds (50 students helped). Special help from own funds to overseas students and other students not eligible for access funds.

Duration of first degree courses: 3 years. **Total first degree students 1995/96:** 600. **Overseas students:** 150. **Mature students:** 250. **Male/female ratio:** 3:2. **Teaching staff:** 90 full-time, 10 part-time. **Total full-time students 1995/96:** 1,250. **Postgraduate students:** 30. **First degree tuition fees:** Home students, paying their own fees in 1996/97, paid £2,825; Overseas students £5,800.

WHAT IT'S LIKE   Although in Essex and all the myths that are associated with the county, Writtle breaks the mould. Located just outside Chelmsford (A12 just minutes away and the M11 20 minutes) it has an extensive campus covering three farms. A great deal of building work has been undertaken in the last three years to include a modern CAD system in purpose built facilities, science block, a unique amenity horticulture building, library and a halls of residence. The main teaching block is close to the residences, so getting out of bed 5 minutes before lectures is not unheard of! As there are practical teaching areas throughout the farms eg equine unit, a car is advisable; however many students have cars, so getting a lift is not difficult. The residences are well maintained, clean, and well equipped with showers, laundry, self-catering facilities and pay phones; ensuite bathrooms in the new block and other halls are constantly upgraded. There is a great atmosphere in all blocks. Apply early for accommodation as there is always demand; however, there is plenty in the area. The village itself provides the students with a fair amount of entertainment with four quality pubs; also the basics (newsagent, chemist, co-op store and a friendly and approachable doctors' surgery). Chelmsford is 7 mins away, with all the facilities of a large town and the social scene: two main nightclubs (Zeus the most popular), Moulsham St with 11 pubs (a regular challenge), theatre and multiplex cinema. The standard student diet from McDonald's and Burger King. Everyone gathers in the union bar, usually every Thursday, for SU social events but campus does tend to empty out at weekends. Sport is popular and there are active clubs including rugby (men and women's), football and hockey teams. Work is generally self-dictated with a few lectures thrown in for good measure; projects involve working with other students, so be friendly. Most courses offer a year out or sandwich year. The college lecturing staff are friendly, approachable and are keen to see you succeed. The typical Writtle student is a fun-loving, active minded, well managed individual. Many have a background in either agriculture or horticulture but this is steadily decreasing.

PAUPER NOTES   **Accommodation:** 350+ rooms available. **Drink:** The Inn on the Green – OK, The Victoria – best Guinness anywhere. **Eats:** Campus facilities good and quite cheap. All kinds of junk food in town. **Ents:** Disco, group, comedy every Thursday, films weekends. **Sports:** Good facilities on campus. Good quality teams. **Hardship funds:** Access fund. **Travel:** Old students' scholarship annually. Good rail and road network. **Work:** Hard to find locally; college has some jobs, also local farms at peak times. Most students work in vacations. MORE INFO?   Ring Claire Whitaker (01245 422752).

CAN'T FIND WHAT YOU'RE LOOKING FOR? USE THE INDEX!

WYE COLLEGE

Wye College, University of London, Ashford, Kent
TN25 5AH (Tel 01233 812401, Fax 01233 813320) Map 4

STUDENT ENQUIRIES: Academic Registrar
APPLICATIONS: UCAS

Broad study areas: Natural sciences, business and management related to agriculture, horticulture and the environment. (Subject details are in the *Subjects and Places Index*.)

Founded: 1894; joined London University 1900. **Structural features:** A college of London University. **Main undergraduate award:** BSc. **Awarding body:** London University. **Site:** Combination of medieval and modern buildings in Wye town centre, plus a 400 hectare estate. **Access:** Wye station; M20 from London, A28 from Ashford. **Special features:** Research includes the impact of human activity in the environment eg recycling organic waste, Channel Tunnel, sustainable agriculture; and into aspects of food production in developed and developing countries. **Europe:** French (non-examined) available to all undergraduates; some students have option of course (agriculture, food and environment in Europe), taught in French. Business studies students may go abroad in their sandwich year. Formal exchange links with 20 European universities; ad hoc links with a number of others. **Library:** 39,000 books, 600 periodical titles, 120 study places. Annual expenditure on library materials, £151 per FTE student. **Specialist collections:** European Documentation Centre, historical collection of agricultural and horticultural books. **Other learning facilities:** Labs, glasshouses, field laboratories; 400 hectares of arable and grassland including sites for amenity and conservation, 5 hectares horticultural crops and orchards. **Welfare:** College medical officer, resident nursing sister, counselling service, college chaplain, wardens (halls of residence and hostels). **Special categories:** Limited accommodation for married students; 2 undergraduate rooms with wheelchair access. **Careers:** Information and advice service through both college and university careers services. **Amenities:** SU building with bar, music room, photographic facilities and many active clubs and societies; cultural facilities of Canterbury 11 miles away. **Sporting facilities:** Tennis courts, playing fields, swimming pool, squash courts. **Employment:** Agricultural and horticultural industries; civil service; local government; scientific research establishments; conservation and resource management.

Accommodation: In 1995/96, 49% of all students in college accommodation, 75% of first years. 194 full board places (all for first years), £65 per week, term time only. Students live in privately owned accommodation for 2 years: £38–£48 per week self-catering; £40–£80 B&B. 17% of first degree students live at home. **Term time work:** Part time work not officially sanctioned (10% of students believed to work). Work available on campus for postgraduate students; careers and placement offices help find outside vac work. **Hardship funds:** Total available in 1995/96: £21,700 government access funds, £6,000 own funds; 80 students helped. Special help to students with dependants, mature students, disabled students.

Duration of first degree courses: 3 years; 4 years sandwich. **Total first degree students 1995/96:** 523. **Overseas students:** 13. **Mature students:** 151. **Male/female ratio:** 6:5. **Teaching**

staff: 64 full-time, 6 part-time, 48 research. **Total full-time students 1995/96:** 851. **Post-graduate students:** 328. **First degree tuition fees:** Home students, paying their own fees in 1996/97, paid £750 (classroom), £1,600 (lab); Overseas students £6,930 (classroom), £8,520 (lab).

WHAT IT'S LIKE   It's a London University college, unique in its situation and lifestyle; Wye provides students with London University qualifications while being in a very beautiful part of the Kent countryside. Students from a wide geographical area and varied social backgrounds but generally all in some way involved with the countryside. The result is a very harmonious community (almost equal mix of male:female). Courses run on a unit system, with some assessment on course work during the year, and exams in the summer. Failure rates low. Wye has its own farm estate to give students real practical knowledge, plus many well-equipped lecture rooms. Most staff have worked in their field of study in the private sector. All students have a director of studies to help them if they run into trouble. First years accommodated in halls of residence all within easy walking distance from lectures, SU, village shops, and local BR station. In the second and third years, students tend to live further away in large number of rented houses available; useful to own a car then. SU very active, but not politically aligned, mainly due to the rather easy-going nature of the students. Any group of students who wish to form a society can be sponsored by the union (currently over 50); NUS and ULU facilities available but not close. SU particularly successful at fund raising for charity in rag week, usually by fairly unconventional means; this is one of the highlights of first year, as is freshers week and cricket week (after exams in the summer). There are approximately 5 black tie balls in the year (a good idea to lay your hands on appropriate clothes!), and a live band or a disco in the union most weeks in term. First years quickly feel at home in Wye's relaxed and easy-going atmosphere. It remains at the top of its class in teaching, facilities, the student participation in the union and the enjoyment students get out of Wye. Wellies and a generally laid back attitude essential.

PAUPER NOTES   **Accommodation:** 3 halls of residence. Most are single rooms, with cleaners, kitchens, bathrooms, and breakfast on week days. Price reasonable and includes weekday evening meals at the canteen. **Drink:** Union bar – good standard bitters and lagers (well run by students). Local pubs – plenty of them, friendly atmospheres and more varied types of beer. **Eats:** At the canteen (OK but not spectacular). 3 formal meals per term. Local pubs – excellent and reasonably priced. Restaurants in Wye (including Indian), Canterbury (12 miles) and Ashford (4 miles). **Ents:** Very active SU – discos, live bands, theme nights and official balls. Also cinema and theatre in Canterbury. **Sports:** Rugby (men's and women's), hockey, cricket, football, squash, tennis, swimming pool, gymnasium, riding, clay shooting, rowing all available on campus. There are also annual ski trips, paintball games – in fact anything is possible! Stow centre, Ashford, excellent sports facilities, some student discounts. **Hardship funds:** For exceptional financial problems. **Travel:** 60 miles from London. Road – M25, M11, M20. Rail to Ashford or Wye. Louis Dreyfuss award for study in Europe. Cheap fares through ULU's STA travel. **Work:** Some farm and canteen work available on campus. College connections provide opportunities for harvest work.

ALUMNI (EDITORS' PICK)   Sir Peter Mills, MP; Professor Chris Baines; Professor Bill Hill FRS, Rebecca Stephens (first woman to climb Everest).

HOW TO START? *SEE SHORTLISTING*, PAGE 535

YORK UNIVERSITY

University of York, Heslington, York YO1 5DD (Tel 01904 430000, Fax 01904 433433) Map 2

STUDENT ENQUIRIES: Undergraduate Admissions Office (Tel 01904 433539, Fax 01904 433538)
APPLICATIONS: UCAS

Broad study areas: Arts, science and technology, social sciences. (Subject details are in the *Subjects and Places Index*.)

Founded: Early sixties. **Main undergraduate awards:** BA, BEng, BSc, MEng, MMath, MPhys, MSci. **Awarding body:** York University. **Site:** Main campus (86 hectares) at Heslington, about 2 miles from city centre; also historic buildings in city centre for history of art and archaeology. **Access:** Bus from York station (London King's Cross 1¾ hours); sign-posted turnings off A64. **Special features:** College system. Resident quartet. Institute for Applied Biology, Centre for Women's Studies. **Academic features:** Modular course structure. Languages-for-all programme gives free first-year tuition in a range of languages including Russian, Japanese, Chinese. IT courses for students without science or maths A-level. **Europe:** All first degree students can take a language as part of course; 8% spend 6 months or more abroad. Formal exchange links with 10 universities/colleges in a range of subjects. Formal combined courses include language with history, IT/business management. Maths, biology and chemistry can be taken with a year in Europe. **Library:** 560,000 volumes, 2,800 periodicals; 725 reading places (university library) + 390 (college libraries); multiple copies of course books; reserve collection. Annual expenditure on library materials, £113.54 per FTE student. **Other learning facilities:** Audio-visual centre, computing service, language teaching centre. **Amenities:** Over 100 student societies; social functions, discos, community action projects; student newspaper, television and radio; 3 studios for pottery, printmaking and painting for use of all students; drama studio, open-air chess board and boules terrain; children's nursery; all colleges have rooms adapted for disabled students. **Sporting facilities:** 40 acres of playing fields on site; 400-metre 7-lane athletics track; boathouse on the River Ouse for rowing; York's 3 swimming pools ½ mile away.

Accommodation: In 1995/96, 62% of all students in university accommodation, 100% of first years and non-EU overseas students. 3,562 places (1,622 for first years): 416 self-catering (277 for first years); 477 with property rental scheme, Sept–June; 2,117 college places (1,206 for first years), mostly term time – all at £32 per week. Most students live in privately owned accommodation for 1 year: £35–£41 per week self-catering and B&B; £44–£50 half board. 1% of first degree students live at home. **Term time work:** University policy to allow limited term time work for first degree students provided it doesn't interfere with full-time study (growing number work). Term (and vac) work available on campus in catering, grounds, cleaning; also limited help from careers service to find outside jobs. **Hardship funds:** Total available in 1995/96: £138,239 government access funds (487 students helped). Special help to students with children, students with financial difficulties from medical/compassionate reasons or withdrawal of financial support. Own funds also help overseas students. £12,000 assigned to 15–20 self-financing students prior to starting course.

Duration of first degree courses: 3 years; **others:** 4 years. **Total first degree students 1995/96:** 4,538. **Overseas students:** 399. **Mature students:** 11%. **Male/female ratio:** 7:6. **Teaching staff:**

375 full-time. **Total full-time students 1995/96:** 4,230. **Postgradua**
377 (p-t). **First degree tuition fees:** Home students, paying their own
£750 (classroom), £1,600 (lab/studio); Overseas students £6,150 (c
(lab/studio).

WHAT IT'S LIKE   York is one of the nicest cities in Britain, second only to ⌐   n
the tourist trail. At one stage, it had 365 pubs and 52 churches; it still boasts vintag ales,
the Minster and a plentiful selection of tea rooms. The university itself is college-based,
although there is not the strong college identification seen at the older universities. Social
life, sports and entertainments are provided by the junior college room committees, which
are in turn co-ordinated by the Students' Union. Accommodation levels are excellent on
campus; virtually 70% of students are guaranteed a room, that is all first years and the
vast majority of third year students. Rooms vary in size and quality from glorified broom
cupboards to capacious ensuite conference rooms, all costing the same. Canteen food is
unexciting but relatively cheap; self catering is always the most tasty and economical
option. Teaching is excellent and high staff student ratio. Courses are becoming increasingly flexible with course transfers and modularisation. There are also foreign exchange
schemes to US, free language-for-all programmes and computer literacy courses. Extensive
university welfare system, together with the college system and SU, provides a comprehensive safety net for any problems or queries. SU, one of the most active in the country,
runs a number of welfare and political campaigns, fights for the rights of its students and
provides support where and when it can. Over 80 societies from debating to the Rocky
Horror, along with 50+ sports clubs; very strong media base, including 2 newspapers, TV
and radio station and very distinguished media alumni. Basically it is a very friendly place
to study with an excellent academic reputation. Although stereotypical York students is an
Oxbridge reject, white middle class southerner, the composition is slowly changing and
there is little overt discrimination. The provision of extra curricular facilities is strong and
the students don't work themselves to oblivion or take themselves too seriously. You won't
be disappointed.   *Fergus Drake*

PAUPER NOTES   **Accommodation:** Campus cheap, all rooms same price; some family
flats in new complex. Town rents £38/week on average. New housing complex, including
family houses. **Drink:** Excellent pubs; cheap Theakston's country. **Eats:** Campus food bland
but cheap. Good variety of restaurants in town. **Ents:** Good cinemas (art house and popular);
4 clubs suit most tastes. **Sports:** New state-of-the-art astroturf pitch, mediocre sports
centre. No swimming pool but 4 close. **Hardship funds:** Union and university helpful. **Travel:**
STA shop on campus. US exchanges. **Work:** 60% of students work in term time, good
opportunities in pubs/clubs; vacation work available in tourist season.

MORE INFO?   Get students' Alternative Prospectus. Enquiries to Jago Parker (01904
433723/4).

ALUMNI (EDITORS' PICK)   Tony Banks, Michael Brown and Harriet Harman (MPs),
Harry Enfield and Victor Lewis-Smith (comedians), Moray Welsh (cellist), Paul Roberts
(pianist), Genista McIntosh (Director of the National Theatre), Trevor Jones and Dominic
Muldowney (composers), Tom Gutteridge and Sebastian Cody (TV producers).

SHORTLISTING

You can't apply to them all. There's a mind-boggling range of choices, so you've got to begin by shortlisting.

Your own ideas matter most – perhaps the subject(s) you want to study; or the cities or the part of the country you prefer; the distance from home (no more than 30 miles for some; not less than 200 for others); the environment (campus or city centre, north or south); top university or somewhere less academically aspiring; term time work (can you have a term time job); or size (thousands of students or just a few hundred); social life, hardship funds. You'll need your own personal shortlisting strategy.

Here are four shortcuts to help you start:

MAPS   537

GEOGRAPHICAL SEARCH INDEX   548

Where do you fancy spending the next three or four years of your life – and how would you get there and home again? This search index lists the universities and colleges in selected places eg Brighton, South Wales, Hertfordshire, Manchester or Northern Ireland.

SUBJECT AND PLACES INDEX   555

This tells you where your subject(s) are taught. So if you want to know where you can concentrate on aerodynamics, anthropology, Arabic or art; war studies, wildlife management or wood technology – this will give you a list of the prospectuses worth looking at.

RESEARCH QUALITY SEARCH INDEX   627

This gives our selection of the top research institutions and top departments (selected from the 1996 HEFC Research Assessment Exercise).

You can look up all these universities and colleges in *Where To Study*.

MAPS

To help you find out what's on offer in any region of the country.

Map 1   Northern Ireland and Scotland.
Map 2   Northern England, Northern Wales and the Midlands.
Map 3   Southern Wales and South West England (including Birmingham, Oxford, and the Isle of Wight).
Map 4   South East England.
Map 5   Greater London up to a border of the M25 motorway.
Map 6   Inner/Central London.

Map A   Motorways – Major Roads

MAP 1 – SCOTLAND AND NORTHERN IRELAND

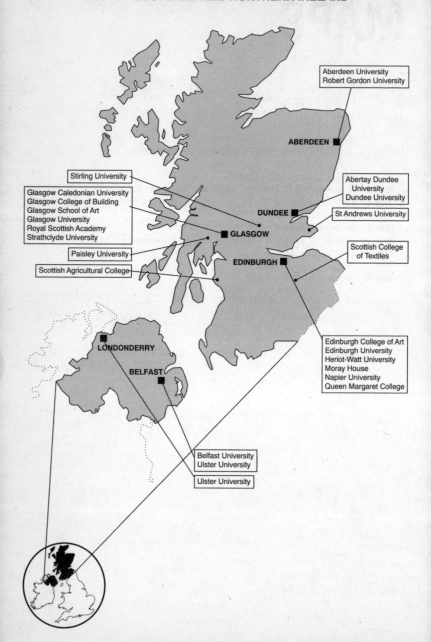

MAP 2 – NORTHERN ENGLAND, NORTHERN WALES AND THE MIDLANDS

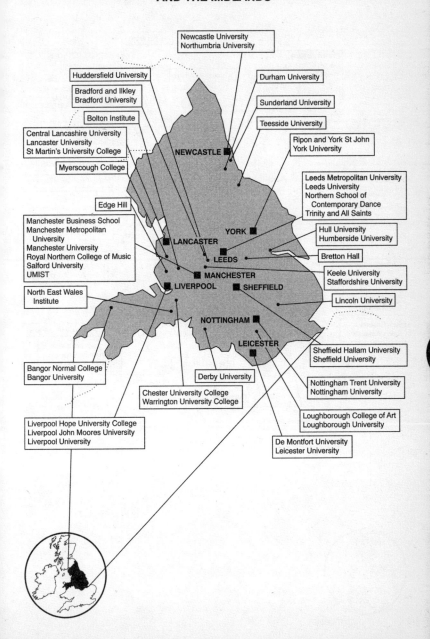

Newcastle University
Northumbria University

Huddersfield University

Durham University

Bradford and Ilkley
Bradford University

Sunderland University

Bolton Institute

Teesside University

Central Lancashire University
Lancaster University
St Martin's University College

Ripon and York St John
York University

Myerscough College

Leeds Metropolitan University
Leeds University
Northern School of
   Contemporary Dance
Trinity and All Saints

Edge Hill

Manchester Business School
Manchester Metropolitan
   University
Manchester University
Royal Northern College of Music
Salford University
UMIST

Hull University
Humberside University

Bretton Hall

Keele University
Staffordshire University

North East Wales
Institute

Lincoln University

Bangor Normal College
Bangor University

Sheffield Hallam University
Sheffield University

Derby University

Nottingham Trent University
Nottingham University

Chester University College
Warrington University College

Loughborough College of Art
Loughborough University

Liverpool Hope University College
Liverpool John Moores University
Liverpool University

De Montfort University
Leicester University

NEWCASTLE

YORK

LANCASTER

LEEDS

MANCHESTER

LIVERPOOL

SHEFFIELD

NOTTINGHAM

LEICESTER

MAP 3 – SOUTHERN WALES AND SOUTH WEST ENGLAND

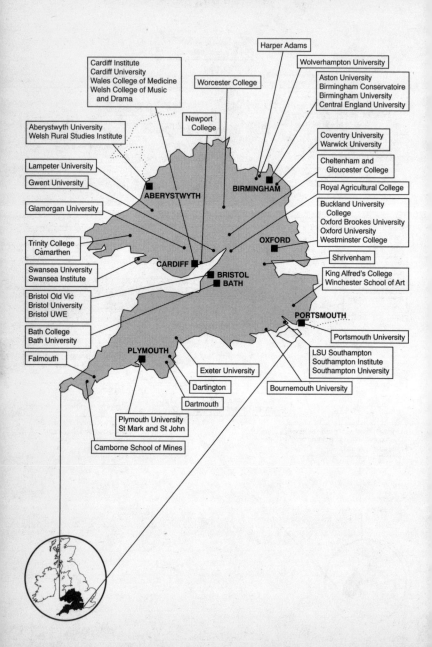

Harper Adams

Wolverhampton University

Cardiff Institute
Cardiff University
Wales College of Medicine
Welsh College of Music
and Drama

Worcester College

Aston University
Birmingham Conservatoire
Birmingham University
Central England University

Newport
College

Aberystwyth University
Welsh Rural Studies Institute

Coventry University
Warwick University

Lampeter University

Cheltenham and
Gloucester College

BIRMINGHAM

Gwent University

Royal Agricultural College

Glamorgan University

ABERYSTWYTH

Buckland University
College
Oxford Brookes University
Oxford University
Westminster College

Trinity College
Camarthen

OXFORD

Swansea University
Swansea Institute

CARDIFF

Shrivenham

Bristol Old Vic
Bristol University
Bristol UWE

BRISTOL
BATH

King Alfred's College
Winchester School of Art

Bath College
Bath University

PORTSMOUTH

Falmouth

Portsmouth University

PLYMOUTH

LSU Southampton
Southampton Institute
Southampton University

Exeter University

Dartington

Bournemouth University

Dartmouth

Plymouth University
St Mark and St John

Camborne School of Mines

MAP 4 – SOUTH EAST ENGLAND

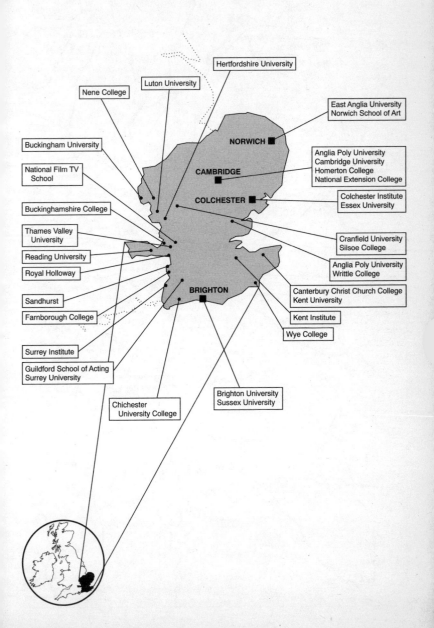

Hertfordshire University

Luton University

Nene College

East Anglia University
Norwich School of Art

Buckingham University

NORWICH

Anglia Poly University
Cambridge University
Homerton College
National Extension College

CAMBRIDGE

National Film TV
School

COLCHESTER

Colchester Institute
Essex University

Buckinghamshire College

Thames Valley
University

Cranfield University
Silsoe College

Reading University

Royal Holloway

Anglia Poly University
Writtle College

BRIGHTON

Sandhurst

Canterbury Christ Church College
Kent University

Farnborough College

Kent Institute

Wye College

Surrey Institute

Guildford School of Acting
Surrey University

Chichester
University College

Brighton University
Sussex University

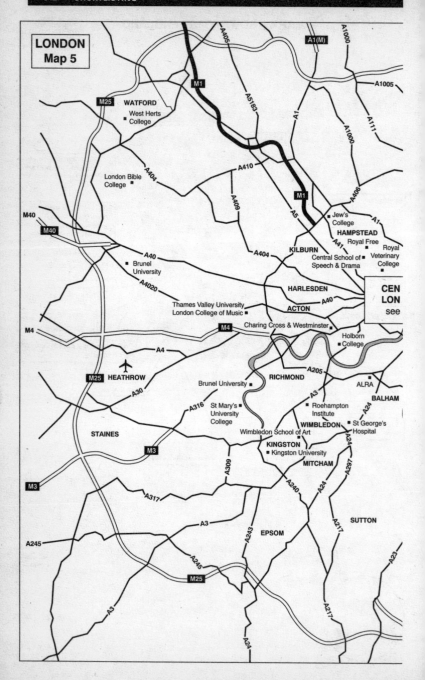

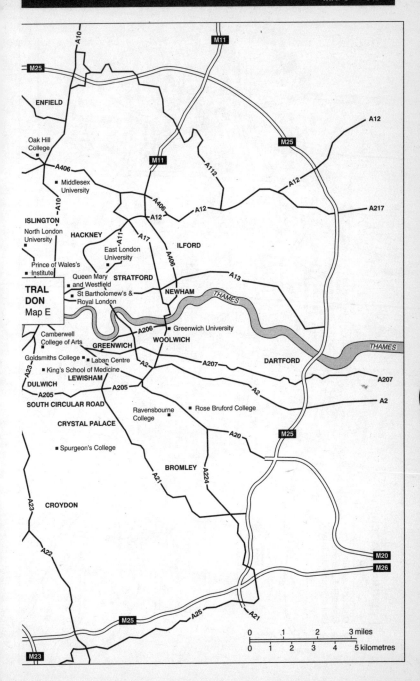

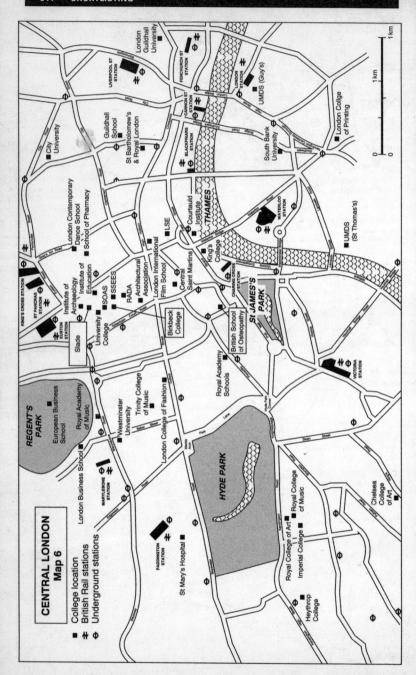

CENTRAL LONDON
Map 6

- ■ College location
- ⇌ British Rail stations
- ⊖ Underground stations

REGENT'S PARK

European Business School

Royal Academy of Music

London Business School

Westminster University

MARYLEBONE STATION

Trinity College of Music

London College of Fashion

PADDINGTON STATION

St Mary's Hospital

HYDE PARK

Park Lane

Mile End

Marble Arch

Hyde Park Corner

Knightsbridge

Royal College of Art

Imperial College

Royal College of Music

Chelsea College of Art

Heythrop College

Sloane Street

KING'S CROSS STATION

ST PANCRAS STATION

EUSTON STATION

City University

Guildhall School

St Bartholomew's & Royal London

London Contemporary Dance School

School of Pharmacy

Institute of Archaeology

Institute of Education

University College

Slade

Birkbeck College

SOAS

SSEES

RADA

Architectural Association

London International Film School

Central Saint Martins

Royal Academy Schools

British School of Osteopathy

LIVERPOOL ST STATION

London Guildhall University

FENCHURCH ST STATION

CANNON ST STATION

BLACKFRIARS STATION

LSE

Courtauld Institute

King's College

CHARING CROSS STATION

St JAMES'S PARK

VICTORIA STATION

THAMES

WATERLOO STATION

LONDON BRIDGE STATION

UMDS (Guy's)

London College of Printing

South Bank University

UMDS (St Thomas's)

1 km

1 km

0

0

MOTORWAYS AND MAJOR ROADS
Map A

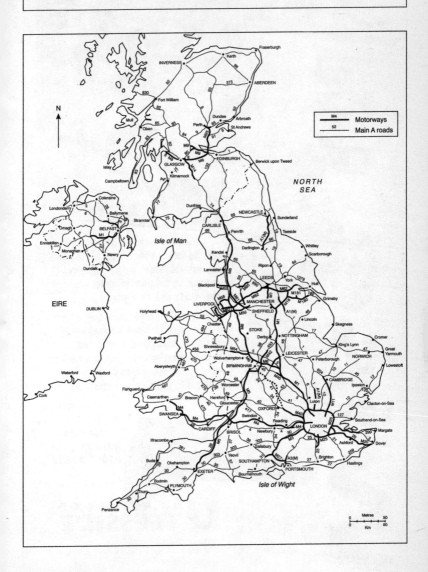

GEOGRAPHICAL SEARCH INDEX

In this Geographical Search Index, all *The Student Book* universities and colleges are listed under key cities, towns and counties so that you can see which universities and colleges are in your favourite place.

It is arranged in the following ten regions. We have chopped up the UK into nine regions with big overlaps — so your geography doesn't need to be very good — and also added Paris.

North of England
Midlands
East Anglia
Greater London (within M25)
South and South East of England
South West of England

Northern Ireland
Scotland
Wales
Paris

NORTH OF ENGLAND

BRADFORD
Bradford & Ilkley
Bradford University

CHESHIRE
Chester University College
Warrington University College

DERBY
Derby University

DURHAM
Durham University

HULL
Hull University
Humberside University

LANCASHIRE
Central Lancashire University
Edge Hill University College
Lancaster University
Myerscough College
St Martin's University College

LANCASTER
Central Lancashire University
St Martin's College

LEEDS
Leeds Metropolitan University
Leeds University
Northern School of Contemporary
    Dance
Trinity & All Saints

LINCOLN
Lincoln University

LIVERPOOL
Liverpool Hope University College
Liverpool John Moores University
Liverpool University

MANCHESTER CITY
Manchester Business School
Manchester Metropolitan University
Manchester University
Royal Northern College of Music
Salford University
UMIST

MANCHESTER – GREATER
Bolton Institute
Manchester Business School
Manchester Metropolitan University
Manchester University
Royal Northern College of Music
Salford University
UMIST

NEWCASTLE
Newcastle University
Northumbria University, Newcastle

SHEFFIELD
Sheffield Hallam University
Sheffield University

SHROPSHIRE
Harper Adams

STAFFORDSHIRE
Keele University
Staffordshire University

TEESSIDE
Teesside University

TYNE & WEAR
Newcastle University
Northumbria University, Newcastle
Sunderland University

YORK
Ripon & York St John
York University

YORKSHIRE
Bradford & Ilkley
Bradford University
Bretton Hall
Huddersfield University
Leeds Metropolitan University
Leeds University
Northern School of Contemporary
    Dance
Ripon & York St John
Sheffield Hallam University
Sheffield University
Trinity & All Saints
York University

MIDLANDS

BEDFORDSHIRE
Cranfield University
Luton University
Silsoe College

BIRMINGHAM
Aston University
Birmingham Conservatoire
Birmingham University
Central England University

BUCKINGHAMSHIRE
Buckingham University
Buckinghamshire College

COVENTRY
Coventry University

DERBY
Derby University

GLOUCESTERSHIRE
Cheltenham & Gloucester College
Royal Agricultural College

HERTFORDSHIRE
Hertfordshire University
Royal Veterinary College
West Herts College

LEICESTER
De Montfort University
Leicester University

LEICESTERSHIRE
De Montfort University
Leicester University
Loughborough College of Art
Loughborough University

LINCOLN
Lincoln University

LOUGHBOROUGH
Loughborough College of Art
Loughborough University

NORTHAMPTONSHIRE
Nene College

NOTTINGHAM
Nottingham Trent University
Nottingham University

OXFORD
Buckland University College
Oxford Brookes University
Oxford University
Westminster College

STAFFORDSHIRE
Keele University
Staffordshire University

WARWICKSHIRE
Coventry University
Warwick University

WEST MIDLANDS
Aston University
Birmingham Conservatoire
Birmingham University
Central England University
Coventry University
Wolverhampton University

WOLVERHAMPTON
Wolverhampton University

WORCESTER
Worcester College

EAST ANGLIA

CAMBRIDGE
Anglia Polytechnic University
Cambridge University
Homerton College

NORWICH
East Anglia University
Norwich School of Art

GREATER LONDON – WITHIN M25

CENTRAL LONDON – WITHIN CIRCLE LINE
Architectural Association
Birkbeck College
British School of Osteopathy
Central Saint Martins
Chelsea College of Art
City University
Courtauld Institute
European Business School
Guildhall
Heythrop College
Imperial College
Institute of Archaeology
Institute of Education
King's College London
London Business School
London College of Fashion
London Contemporary Dance School
London Guildhall University
London International Film School
LSE
Prince of Wales's Institute
RADA
Royal Academy of Music
Royal Academy Schools
Royal College of Art
Royal College of Music
St Bartholomew's & Royal London
St Mary's Hospital
School of Pharmacy
Slade
SOAS
SSEES
Trinity College of Music
UMDS
University College London
Westminster University

INNER LONDON
ALRA
Camberwell College of Arts
Central School of Speech and Drama
Charing Cross and Westminster
Chelsea College of Art
European Business School, London

Goldsmiths College
Greenwich University
Holborn College
King's School of Medicine & Dentistry
Laban Centre
London Business School
London College of Printing
London Guildhall University
North London University
Prince of Wales's Institute
Queen Mary & Westfield
Royal Free
Royal Veterinary College
St Bartholomew's & Royal London
St George's
South Bank University
UMDS
Wimbledon School of Art

OUTER LONDON – SOUTH WEST
Kingston University
Roehampton Institute
St George's
St Mary's University College
Wimbledon College of Art

OUTER LONDON – SOUTH EAST
Ravensbourne College
Rose Bruford
Spurgeon's College

OUTER LONDON – NORTH WEST
Brunel University
Jews' College
London Bible College
London College of Music
Middlesex University
Oak Hill College
Royal Veterinary College
Thames Valley University
West Herts College

OUTER LONDON – NORTH EAST
East London University
North London University

SOUTH AND SOUTH EAST ENGLAND

BEDFORDSHIRE
Cranfield University
Luton University
Silsoe College

BERKSHIRE
Reading University
Thames Valley University

BRIGHTON
Brighton University
Sussex University

BUCKINGHAMSHIRE
Buckingham University
Buckinghamshire College
National Film School

CANTERBURY
Canterbury Christ Church College
Kent Institute
Kent University

DORSET
Bournemouth University

ESSEX
Anglia Poly University
Colchester Institute
East London University
Essex University
Writtle College

GUILDFORD
Guildford School of Acting
Surrey University

HAMPSHIRE
Farnborough College
King Alfred's College
LSU Southampton
Portsmouth University
Southampton Institute
Southampton University
Winchester School of Art

HERTFORDSHIRE
Hertfordshire University
Royal Veterinary College
West Herts College

KENT
Canterbury Christ Church College
Kent Institute
Kent University
Ravensbourne College
Rose Bruford College
Wye College

MIDDLESEX
Brunel University
London Bible College
Middlesex University

NORTHAMPTONSHIRE
Nene College

OXFORD
Buckland University College
Oxford Brookes University
Oxford University
Westminster College

READING
Reading University

SOUTHAMPTON
LSU Southampton
Southampton Institute
Southampton University

SURREY
Guildford School of Acting
Kingston University
Royal Holloway
St Mary's University College
Sandhurst
Surrey Institute
Surrey University

SUSSEX
Brighton University
Chichester University College
Sussex University

WILTSHIRE
Shrivenham

SOUTH WEST OF ENGLAND

AVON
Bath College
Bath University
Bristol Old Vic
Bristol University
Bristol UWE

BATH
Bath College
Bath University

BRISTOL
Bristol Old Vic
Bristol University
Bristol UWE

CORNWALL
Cambourne School of Mines
Falmouth

DEVON
Dartington College of Arts
Dartmouth
Exeter University
Plymouth University
St Mark & St John

DORSET
Bournemouth University

GLOUCESTERSHIRE
Cheltenham & Gloucester College
Royal Agricultural College

NORTHERN IRELAND

Belfast University
Ulster University

SCOTLAND

ABERDEEN
Aberdeen University
Robert Gordon University

CENTRAL SCOTLAND
Abertay Dundee University
Dundee University
Edinburgh College of Art
Edinburgh University
Glasgow Caledonian University
Glasgow College of Building
Glasgow School of Art
Glasgow University
Heriot-Watt University
Moray House
Napier University
Paisley University
Queen Margaret College
Royal Scottish Academy
St Andrews University
Scottish Agricultural College
Stirling University
Strathclyde University

DUNDEE
Abertay Dundee University
Dundee University

EDINBURGH
Edinburgh College of Art
Edinburgh University
Heriot-Watt University
Moray House
Napier University
Queen Margaret College

GLASGOW
Glasgow Caledonian University
Glasgow College of Building
Glasgow School of Art
Glasgow University
Paisley University
Royal Scottish Academy
Strathclyde University

NORTH SCOTLAND
Aberdeen University
Robert Gordon University
Scottish Agricultural College

SCOTTISH BORDERS
Scottish College of Textiles

WALES

NORTH WALES
Aberystwyth University
Bangor University
North East Wales Institute
Welsh Institute of Rural Studies

SOUTH WALES
Aberystwyth University
Cardiff Institute
Cardiff University
Glamorgan University
Lampeter University
Newport College
Swansea Institute
Swansea University

Trinity College Carmarthen
Wales College of Medicine
Welsh Institute of Rural Studies
Welsh College of Music and Drama

CARDIFF
Cardiff Institute
Cardiff University
Wales College of Medicine
Welsh College of Music and Drama

SWANSEA
Swansea Institute
Swansea University

PARIS

British Institute in Paris

SUBJECT AND PLACES INDEX

This search index helps you identify where you can study in depth some 500 different subjects. The aim is to help you select the prospectuses worth getting hold of if you want to study a particular subject for the whole (or major part) of a first degree.

Beware: Once the prospectuses have crashed through your letter box, you may not be able to find the subject you want – usually because they have got some other whizzo name for it (some are obvious – life sciences rather than biology – others less so). Persevere and you should eventually find it.

GET HOLD OF THE PROSPECTUSES

A

ACCOUNTANCY

Possible prospectuses: Aberdeen Univ, Abertay Dundee Univ, Aberystwyth Univ, Anglia Poly Univ, Aston Univ, Bangor Univ, Belfast Univ, Birmingham Univ, Bolton Inst, Bournemouth Univ, Bradford & Ilkley, Bradford Univ, Brighton Univ, Bristol Univ, Bristol UWE, Buckingham Univ, Cardiff Univ, Central England Univ, Central Lancashire Univ, City Univ, De Montfort Univ, Derby Univ, Dundee Univ, East Anglia Univ, East London Univ, Edinburgh Univ, Essex Univ, European Business Sch, Exeter Univ, Farnborough Coll, Glamorgan Univ, Glasgow Caledonian Univ, Glasgow Univ, Greenwich Univ, Heriot-Watt Univ, Hertfordshire Univ, Huddersfield Univ, Hull Univ, Humberside Univ, Kent Univ, Kingston Univ, Lancaster Univ, Leeds Metro Univ, Leeds Univ, Liverpool John Moores Univ, Liverpool Univ, London Guildhall Univ, Loughborough Univ, LSE, Luton Univ, Manchester Metro Univ, Manchester Univ, Middlesex Univ, Napier Univ, Nene Coll, Newcastle Univ, Newport Coll, North London Univ, Northumbria Univ, Nottingham Trent Univ, Nottingham Univ, Oxford Brookes Univ, Paisley Univ, Plymouth Univ, Portsmouth Univ, Reading Univ, Robert Gordon Univ, Royal Agricultural Coll, Salford Univ, Sheffield Hallam Univ, Sheffield Univ, South Bank Univ, Southampton Inst, Southampton Univ, Staffordshire Univ, Stirling Univ, Strathclyde Univ, Sunderland Univ, Swansea Inst, Teesside Univ, Thames Valley Univ, Ulster Univ, Warwick Univ, Wolverhampton Univ.
See also: Business studies.

ACOUSTIC ENGINEERING

Possible prospectuses: Cambridge Univ, Salford Univ, Southampton Univ.
See also: Electrical engineering.

ACOUSTICS

See: Acoustic engineering; electronic engineering; music; physics; speech sciences.

ACTING

Possible prospectuses: ALRA, Bretton Hall, Bristol Old Vic, Central Sch Speech/Drama, City Univ, Exeter Univ, Guildford Sch Acting, Guildhall, Manchester Metro Univ, Middlesex Univ, Queen Margaret Coll, RADA, Rose Bruford Coll, Royal Scottish Academy, Welsh Coll Music/Drama.
See also: Drama

ACTUARIAL STUDIES

Possible prospectuses: City Univ, Heriot-Watt Univ, Kent Univ, London Guildhall Univ, LSE, Southampton Univ, Swansea Univ.
See also: Mathematics; social science; statistics.

ADMINISTRATION

See: Business administration; estate management; housing administration; personnel administration; public administration; social administration.

ADVERTISING

Possible prospectuses: Bournemouth Univ, Buckinghamshire Coll, Lancaster Univ, London Coll Printing, Queen Margaret Coll, Ulster Univ.

ADVERTISING DESIGN
See: Graphic design.

AERODYNAMICS
Possible prospectuses: Cambridge Univ, Cranfield Univ (p/g only), Dartmouth, Imperial Coll, Kingston Univ, Manchester Univ, Strathclyde Univ.

AERONAUTICAL ENGINEERING
Possible prospectuses: Bath Univ, Belfast Univ, Bristol Univ, Bristol UWE, Brunel Univ, Cambridge Univ, City Univ, Coventry Univ, Cranfield Univ (p/g only), Dartmouth, Farnborough Coll, Glasgow Univ, Hertfordshire Univ, Humberside Univ, Imperial Coll, Kingston Univ, Liverpool Univ, Loughborough Univ, Manchester Univ, North East Wales Inst, Queen Mary & Westfield, Salford Univ, Shrivenham, Southampton Univ, Surrey Univ, UMIST.

AESTHETICS
See: Art history; philosophy.

AFRICAN STUDIES
Possible prospectuses: Birmingham Univ, Edge Hill Univ Coll, SOAS, Sussex Univ.
See also: Archaeology; Asian studies; Near East studies.

AFRO-ASIAN STUDIES
See: African studies; Asian studies.

AGRICULTURAL BOTANY
Possible prospectuses: Aberystwyth Univ, Belfast Univ, Glasgow Univ, Greenwich Univ, Imperial Coll, Leeds Univ, Newcastle Univ, Reading Univ, Royal Agricultural Coll, Scottish Agricultural Coll, Wye Coll.
See also: Agriculture; botany.

AGRICULTURAL CHEMISTRY
See: Chemistry; agriculture.

AGRICULTURAL ECONOMICS
Possible prospectuses: Aberdeen Univ, Aberystwyth Univ, Bangor Univ, Belfast Univ, Edinburgh Univ, Exeter Univ, Glasgow Univ, Newcastle Univ, Nottingham Univ, Reading Univ, Royal Agricultural Coll, Scottish Agricultural Coll, Silsoe Coll, Wye Coll.
See also: Economics; agriculture.

AGRICULTURAL ENGINEERING
Possible prospectuses: Anglia Poly Univ, De Montfort Univ, Harper Adams, Newcastle Univ, Silsoe Coll, Writtle Coll.

AGRICULTURE
Possible prospectuses: Aberdeen Univ, Aberystwyth Univ, Anglia Poly Univ, Bangor Univ, Belfast Univ, Bournemouth Univ, De Montfort Univ, Edinburgh Univ, Glasgow Univ, Greenwich Univ, Harper Adams, Humberside Univ, Myerscough Coll, Newcastle Univ, Nottingham Univ, Plymouth Univ, Reading Univ, Royal Agricultural Coll, Scottish Agricultural Coll, Silsoe Coll, Welsh Inst Rural Studies, Writtle Coll, Wye Coll.

AGRONOMY
See: Agriculture.

AIRCRAFT ENGINEERING
See: Aeronautical engineering; air transport engineering.

AIR TRANSPORT ENGINEERING
Possible prospectuses: City Univ, Cranfield Univ (p/g only), Imperial Coll, Loughborough Univ.

AKKADIAN
Possible prospectuses: Cambridge Univ, Liverpool Univ, University Coll London.
See also: Near East studies.

AMERICAN STUDIES
Possible prospectuses: Aberystwyth Univ, Belfast Univ, Birmingham Univ, Brunel Univ, Canterbury Christ Church Coll, Central Lancashire Univ, De Montfort Univ, Derby Univ, Dundee Univ, East Anglia Univ, Edinburgh Univ, Essex Univ, Exeter Univ, Glamorgan Univ, Glasgow Univ, Greenwich Univ, Hull Univ, Keele Univ, Kent Univ, King Alfred's Coll, King's Coll London, Lancaster Univ, Leeds Univ, Leicester Univ, Liverpool Hope Univ Coll, Liverpool John Moores Univ, Manchester Metro Univ, Manchester Univ, Middlesex Univ, Nene Coll, Nottingham Univ, Reading Univ, Ripon & York St John, Sheffield Univ, Staffordshire Univ, Sunderland Univ, Sussex Univ, Swansea Univ, Thames Valley Univ, Ulster Univ, Warwick Univ, Wolverhampton Univ.

AMHARIC
See: Asian studies; oriental studies.

ANALOGUES
See: Computing; electrical engineering; electronic engineering.

ANALYTICAL
See: individual subjects, eg chemistry.

ANATOLIA
See: Archaeology.

ANATOMY
Possible prospectuses: Belfast Univ, Birmingham Univ, Bristol Univ, Cambridge Univ, Cardiff Univ, Dundee Univ, Edinburgh Univ, Glasgow Univ, King's Coll London, Leeds Univ, Liverpool Univ, Manchester Univ, Queen Mary & Westfield, Sheffield Univ, University Coll London.
See also: Medicine; human biology.   •

ANCIENT HISTORY
Possible prospectuses: Belfast Univ, Birmingham Univ, Bristol Univ, Cambridge Univ, Cardiff Univ, Durham Univ, Edinburgh Univ, Exeter Univ, Keele Univ, King's Coll London, Lampeter Univ, Leicester Univ, Liverpool Univ, Manchester Univ, Newcastle Univ, Nottingham Univ, Oxford Univ, Reading Univ, Royal Holloway, St Andrews Univ, Swansea Univ, University Coll London, Warwick Univ.
See also: Classics; history; classical studies.

ANGLO SAXON
Possible prospectuses: Cambridge Univ.

ANIMAL SCIENCE
Possible prospectuses: Aberdeen Univ, Aberystwyth Univ, Anglia Poly Univ, Bangor Univ, Birmingham Univ, Cambridge Univ, De Montfort Univ, East London Univ, Edinburgh Univ, Glasgow Univ, Harper Adams, Imperial Coll, Leeds Univ, Leicester Univ, Newcastle Univ, Nottingham Univ, Open Univ, Reading Univ, Royal Agricultural Coll, Royal Vet Coll, St Andrews Univ, Scottish Agricultural Coll, Sheffield Univ, Southampton Univ, Welsh Inst Rural Studies, Wolverhampton Univ, Writtle Coll, Wye Coll, York Univ.

ANIMALS
See: Agriculture; animal science; veterinary studies; wildlife management; zoology.

ANIMATION
Possible prospectuses: Bournemouth Univ, Dundee Univ, Edinburgh Coll Art, Humberside Univ, Kingston Univ, Lincoln Univ, Manchester Metro Univ, National Film Sch (p/g only), Newport Coll, Ravensbourne Coll, Royal Coll Art (p/g only), Surrey Inst.
See also: Film studies.

ANTHROPOLOGY
Possible prospectuses: Brunel Univ, Cambridge Univ, Durham Univ, East Anglia Univ, East London Univ, Goldsmiths Coll, Hull Univ, Keele Univ, Kent Univ, Lampeter Univ, LSE, Oxford Brookes Univ, Oxford Univ, St Andrews Univ, SOAS, Sussex Univ, Swansea Univ, University Coll London.
See also: Social anthropology.

APPLIED
See: individual subjects, eg biology.

AQUACULTURE
Possible prospectuses: Aberdeen Univ, Glasgow Univ, Scottish Agricultural Coll, Stirling Univ.

ARABIC
Possible prospectuses: Aberdeen Univ, Cambridge Univ, Durham Univ, Edinburgh Univ, Exeter Univ, Leeds Univ, Oxford Univ, St Andrews Univ, Salford Univ, SOAS, Westminster Univ.

ARAMAIC
See: Near East studies.

ARCHAEOLOGY
Possible prospectuses: Bangor Univ, Belfast Univ, Birmingham Univ, Bournemouth Univ, Bradford Univ, Bristol Univ, Cambridge Univ, Cardiff Univ, Durham Univ, East Anglia Univ, East London Univ, Edinburgh Univ, Exeter Univ, Glasgow Univ, Inst Archaeology, King Alfred's Coll, King's Coll London, Lampeter Univ, Leicester Univ, Liverpool Univ, Manchester Univ, Newcastle Univ, Newport Coll, Nottingham Univ, Oxford Univ, Reading Univ, St Andrews Univ, Sheffield Univ, SOAS, Southampton Univ, Trinity Coll Carmarthen, University Coll London, Warwick Univ, York Univ.

ARCHITECTURE
Possible prospectuses: Architectural Association, Bath Univ, Belfast Univ, Bournemouth Univ, Brighton Univ, Bristol UWE, Cambridge Univ, Cardiff Univ, Central England Univ, De Montfort Univ, Derby Univ, Dundee Univ, East London Univ, Edinburgh Coll Art, Edinburgh Univ, Glasgow Sch Art, Glasgow Univ, Greenwich Univ, Heriot-Watt Univ, Huddersfield Univ, Humberside Univ, Kent Inst, Kingston Univ, Leeds Metro Univ, Leeds Univ, Liverpool John Moores Univ, Liverpool Univ, Luton Univ, Manchester Metro Univ, Manchester Univ, Middlesex Univ, Newcastle Univ, North London Univ, Nottingham Univ, Oxford Brookes Univ, Plymouth Univ, Portsmouth Univ, Prince of Wales's Inst, Robert Gordon Univ, Royal Coll Art (p/g only), Sheffield Univ, South Bank Univ, Southampton Inst, Strathclyde Univ, Teesside Univ, University Coll London, Westminster Univ.

ARMY
Possible prospectuses: Sandhurst.

ART
Possible prospectuses: Aberystwyth Univ, Anglia Poly Univ, Bangor Univ, Bath Coll, Bradford & Ilkley, Bretton Hall, Brighton Univ, Bristol UWE, Brunel Univ, Buckinghamshire Coll, Camberwell Coll, Canterbury Christ Church Coll, Cardiff Inst, Central England Univ, Central Lancashire Univ, Central Saint Martins, Chelsea Coll Art, Cheltenham & Gloucester Coll, Chester Univ Coll, Chichester Univ Coll, Colchester Inst, Coventry Univ, Dartington Coll Arts, Derby Univ, Dundee Univ, East London Univ, Edge Hill Univ Coll, Edinburgh Coll Art, Falmouth Coll Arts, Glamorgan Univ, Glasgow Univ, Goldsmiths Coll, Heriot-Watt Univ, Hertfordshire Univ, Humberside Univ, Kent Inst, King Alfred's Coll, Kingston Univ, Lancaster Univ, Leeds Metro Univ, Leeds Univ, Liverpool Hope Univ Coll, Liverpool John Moores Univ, London Guildhall Univ, Loughborough Coll, LSU Southampton, Manchester Metro Univ, Middlesex Univ, Nene Coll, Newcastle Univ, Newport Coll, North East Wales Inst, Northumbria Univ, Nottingham Trent Univ, Oxford Brookes Univ, Oxford Univ, Plymouth Univ, Portsmouth Univ, Prince of Wales's Inst, Reading Univ, Ripon & York St John, Robert Gordon Univ, Roehampton Inst, Royal Academy Sch (p/g only), St Mark & St John, S Martin's Univ Coll, Sheffield Hallam Univ, Slade, Southampton Inst, Southampton Univ, Staffordshire Univ, Sunderland Univ, Surrey Inst, Swansea Inst, Teesside Univ, Ulster Univ, University Coll London, Wimbledon Sch Art, Winchester Sch Art, Wolverhampton Univ, Worcester Coll.
See also: Graphic design; photography; silversmithing; textiles; three-dimensional design.

ART HISTORY
Possible prospectuses: Aberdeen Univ, Aberystwyth Univ, Anglia Poly Univ, Birkbeck, Birmingham Univ, Bolton Inst, Brighton Univ, Bristol Univ, British Institute in Paris, Buckingham Univ, Buckinghamshire Coll, Camberwell Coll, Cambridge Univ, Cardiff Inst, Central England Univ, Central Lancashire Univ, Chester Univ Coll, Courtauld Institute, Coventry Univ, De Montfort Univ, Derby Univ, East Anglia Univ, East London Univ, Edinburgh Coll Art, Edinburgh Univ, Essex Univ, Exeter Univ, Falmouth Coll Arts, Glamorgan Univ, Glasgow Univ, Goldsmiths Coll, Hull Univ, Kent Univ, Kingston Univ, Lancaster Univ, Leeds Metro Univ, Leeds Univ, Leicester Univ, Liverpool John Moores Univ, Loughborough Coll, Manchester Metro Univ, Manchester Univ, Middlesex Univ, Newcastle Univ, Northumbria Univ, Nottingham Trent Univ, Nottingham Univ, Open Univ, Oxford Brookes Univ, Oxford Univ, Plymouth Univ, Portsmouth Univ, Reading Univ, Robert Gordon Univ, St Andrews Univ, Sheffield Hallam Univ, Slade, SOAS, Southampton Inst, Southampton Univ, Staffordshire Univ, Sunderland Univ, Sussex Univ, Swansea Inst, Ulster Univ, University Coll London, Warwick Univ, Winchester Sch Art, Wolverhampton Univ, York Univ.

ARTIFICIAL INTELLIGENCE
Possible prospectuses: Aberdeen Univ, Birmingham Univ, Cranfield Univ (p/g only), Derby Univ, Durham Univ, Edinburgh Univ, Essex Univ, Imperial Coll, Leeds Univ, Manchester Univ, Middlesex Univ, Nottingham Trent Univ, Nottingham Univ, Open Univ, Reading Univ, Sussex Univ, UMIST, Westminster Univ.

ARTS ADMINISTRATION
Possible prospectuses: Greenwich Univ, Queen Margaret Coll, Royal Coll Art (p/g only), South Bank Univ, Warrington Univ Coll.

ASIAN STUDIES
Possible prospectuses: Cambridge Univ, De Montfort Univ, Edge Hill Univ Coll, Edinburgh Univ, Newcastle Univ, North London Univ, Oxford Univ, Portsmouth Univ, Sheffield Univ, SOAS, Sussex Univ, Ulster Univ, Westminster Univ.
See also: Near East studies; South East Asian studies; oriental studies.

ASSYRIOLOGY
See: Archaeology; Near East studies.

ASTRONAUTICS
See: Aerodynamics; space.

ASTRONOMY
Possible prospectuses: Cardiff Univ, Central Lancashire Univ, Edinburgh Univ, Glasgow Univ, Hertfordshire Univ, Leicester Univ, Manchester Univ, Newcastle Univ, Northumbria Univ, Open Univ, Queen Mary & Westfield, St Andrews Univ, Sheffield Univ, Southampton Univ, University Coll London.

ASTROPHYSICS
Possible prospectuses: Aberystwyth Univ, Belfast Univ, Birmingham Univ, Bristol Univ, Cambridge Univ, Cardiff Univ, Central Lancashire Univ, Cranfield Univ (p/g only), Edinburgh Univ, Glasgow Univ, Hertfordshire Univ, Imperial Coll, Keele Univ, Kent Univ, King's Coll London, Leeds Univ, Leicester Univ, Liverpool John Moores Univ, Manchester Univ, Newcastle Univ, Northumbria Univ, Queen Mary & Westfield, Royal Holloway, St Andrews Univ, Southampton Univ, Surrey Univ, Sussex Univ, UMIST, University Coll London, York Univ.

AUDIO-VISUAL COMMUNICATION
See: Communication studies; electronic engineering; art.

AUTOMOTIVE ENGINEERING
Possible prospectuses: Bath Univ, Birmingham Univ, Brunel Univ, Central England Univ, Coventry Univ, Cranfield Univ (p/g only), Hertfordshire Univ, Kingston Univ, Leeds Univ, Loughborough Univ, Newcastle Univ, Oxford Brookes Univ, Sheffield Hallam Univ, Southampton Univ, Sunderland Univ, Swansea Inst.

AVIONICS
Possible prospectuses: Bristol Univ, Coventry Univ, Cranfield Univ (p/g only), Glasgow Univ, Humberside Univ, Imperial Coll, Loughborough Univ, Queen Mary & Westfield, Salford Univ, York Univ.
See also: Aeronautical engineering.

B

BACTERIOLOGY
Possible prospectuses: Birmingham Univ, Brunel Univ, Edinburgh Univ, Imperial Coll, King's Coll London, Reading Univ, Surrey Univ.

BANKING
Possible prospectuses: Bangor Univ, Birmingham Univ, Buckingham Univ, Cardiff Univ, Central England Univ, City Univ, Glasgow Caledonian Univ, London Guildhall Univ, Loughborough Univ, Middlesex Univ, Portsmouth Univ, Reading Univ, Stirling Univ, Ulster Univ.
See also: Business studies; economics; financial services.

BEHAVIOURAL SCIENCE
Possible prospectuses: Abertay Dundee Univ, Anglia Poly Univ, Brunel Univ, De Montfort Univ, Glamorgan Univ, Huddersfield Univ, Nene Coll, Nottingham Univ, Paisley Univ, Portsmouth Univ, Reading Univ, St Andrews Univ, Ulster Univ, Westminster Univ.
See also: Psychology; zoology.

BENGALI
Possible prospectuses: SOAS.
See also: Asian studies; oriental studies.

BERBER
See: African studies.

BIBLICAL STUDIES
Possible prospectuses: Aberdeen Univ, Bangor Univ, Belfast Univ, Birmingham Univ, Edinburgh Univ, Glasgow Univ, Heythrop Coll, Jews' Coll, King's Coll London, London Bible, Manchester Univ, National Extension Coll, Newcastle Univ, Oak Hill Coll, St Andrews Univ, St Mary's Univ Coll, Sheffield Univ, Spurgeon's Coll, Stirling Univ, Trinity Coll Carmarthen.
See also: Religious studies; theology.

BIOCHEMICAL ENGINEERING
Possible prospectuses: Birmingham Univ, Bradford Univ, Cranfield Univ (p/g only), Heriot-Watt Univ, Imperial Coll, King's Coll London, Luton Univ, Surrey Univ, Swansea Univ, UMIST, University Coll London.
See also: Biochemistry; biotechnology; chemical engineering.

BIOCHEMISTRY
Possible prospectuses: Aberdeen Univ, Aberystwyth Univ, Anglia Poly Univ, Bangor Univ, Bath Univ, Belfast Univ, Birkbeck, Birmingham Univ, Bradford Univ, Bristol Univ, Bristol UWE, Brunel Univ, Cambridge Univ, Cardiff Univ, Central Lancashire Univ, Coventry Univ, Dundee Univ, Durham Univ, East Anglia Univ, East London Univ, Edinburgh Univ, Essex Univ, Glasgow Caledonian Univ, Glasgow Univ, Greenwich Univ, Heriot-Watt Univ, Hertfordshire Univ, Huddersfield Univ, Imperial Coll, Keele Univ, Kent Univ, King's Coll London, Kingston Univ, Lancaster Univ, Leeds Univ, Leicester Univ, Liverpool John Moores Univ, Liverpool Univ, Luton Univ, Manchester Metro Univ, Manchester Univ, Newcastle Univ, North East

Wales Inst, North London Univ, Northumbria Univ, Nottingham Trent Univ, Nottingham Univ, Open Univ, Oxford Univ, Paisley Univ, Portsmouth Univ, Queen Mary & Westfield, Reading Univ, Royal Holloway, St Andrews Univ, Salford Univ, Sheffield Univ, South Bank Univ, Southampton Univ, Staffordshire Univ, Stirling Univ, Strathclyde Univ, Sunderland Univ, Surrey Univ, Sussex Univ, Swansea Univ, Ulster Univ, UMIST, University Coll London, Warwick Univ, Westminster Univ, Wolverhampton Univ, Wye Coll, York Univ.

BIOLOGICAL CHEMISTRY
Possible prospectuses: Anglia Poly Univ, Central Lancashire Univ, Dundee Univ, East Anglia Univ, Essex Univ, Exeter Univ, Glasgow Caledonian Univ, Heriot-Watt Univ, Hertfordshire Univ, Imperial Coll, Kent Univ, King's Coll London, Leicester Univ, North East Wales Inst, North London Univ, Nottingham Univ, Oxford Brookes Univ, Queen Mary & Westfield, Salford Univ, Sheffield Univ, Stirling Univ, Warwick Univ.
See also: Biotechnology.

BIOLOGY
Possible prospectuses: Aberdeen Univ, Abertay Dundee Univ, Aberystwyth Univ, Anglia Poly Univ, Aston Univ, Bangor Univ, Bath Univ, Belfast Univ, Birkbeck, Birmingham Univ, Bolton Inst, Brighton Univ, Bristol Univ, Bristol UWE, Brunel Univ, Cambridge Univ, Canterbury Christ Church Coll, Cardiff Inst, Cardiff Univ, Central Lancashire Univ, Chester Univ Coll, Coventry Univ, De Montfort Univ, Derby Univ, Dundee Univ, Durham Univ, East Anglia Univ, East London Univ, Edge Hill Univ Coll, Edinburgh Univ, Essex Univ, Exeter Univ, Glamorgan Univ, Glasgow Caledonian Univ, Glasgow Univ, Greenwich Univ, Heriot-Watt Univ, Hertfordshire Univ, Homerton Coll, Huddersfield Univ, Hull Univ, Imperial Coll, Keele Univ, Kent Univ, King's Coll London, Kingston Univ, Lancaster Univ, Leeds Univ, Leicester Univ, Liverpool John Moores Univ, Liverpool Univ, LSU Southampton, Luton Univ, Manchester Metro Univ, Manchester Univ, Middlesex Univ, Napier Univ, Newcastle Univ, North East Wales Inst, North London Univ, Nottingham Trent Univ, Nottingham Univ, Open Univ, Oxford Brookes Univ, Oxford Univ, Paisley Univ, Plymouth Univ, Portsmouth Univ, Queen Mary & Westfield, Reading Univ, Roehampton Inst, Royal Holloway, St Andrews Univ, S Martin's Univ Coll, St Mary's Univ Coll, Salford Univ, Sheffield Hallam Univ, Sheffield Univ, South Bank Univ, Southampton Univ, Staffordshire Univ, Stirling Univ, Strathclyde Univ, Sunderland Univ, Sussex Univ, Swansea Univ, Ulster Univ, University Coll London, Warwick Univ, Westminster Univ, Wolverhampton Univ, Worcester Coll, Wye Coll, York Univ.
See also: Botany; microbiology; zoology.

BIOMEDICAL ELECTRONICS
Possible prospectuses: Anglia Poly Univ, Brunel Univ, Imperial Coll, Kent Univ, Northumbria Univ, Salford Univ, Staffordshire Univ, Ulster Univ.

BIOMEDICAL SCIENCE
Possible prospectuses: Aberdeen Univ, Anglia Poly Univ, Belfast Univ, Birmingham Univ, Bradford Univ, Brighton Univ, Bristol UWE, Cardiff Inst, Central Lancashire Univ, De Montfort Univ, Durham Univ, East London Univ, Exeter Univ, Glasgow Caledonian Univ, Glasgow Univ, Greenwich Univ, Hull Univ, Imperial Coll, Keele Univ, Kent Univ, King's Coll London, Kingston Univ, Leicester Univ, Liverpool John Moores Univ, Manchester Metro Univ, Napier Univ, North London Univ, Northumbria Univ, Nottingham Trent Univ, Paisley Univ, Portsmouth Univ, Queen Mary & Westfield, Royal Holloway, Salford Univ, Sheffield Hallam Univ, Sheffield Univ, Southampton Univ, Sunderland Univ, Ulster Univ, UMIST, Westminster Univ, Wolverhampton Univ.

BIOPHYSICS
Possible prospectuses: Aberdeen Univ, Anglia Poly Univ, Birmingham Univ, East London Univ, Imperial Coll, King's Coll London, Leeds Univ, Liverpool John Moores Univ, Newcastle Univ, Portsmouth Univ.

BIOSOCIAL SCIENCE
Possible prospectuses: Anglia Poly Univ, King Alfred's Coll, Sussex Univ.
See also: Human sciences.

BIOTECHNOLOGY
Possible prospectuses: Aberdeen Univ, Abertay Dundee Univ, Anglia Poly Univ, Birmingham Univ, Bristol Univ, Bristol UWE, Cardiff Univ, Cranfield Univ (p/g only), De Montfort Univ, East London Univ, Glamorgan Univ, Heriot-Watt Univ, Hertfordshire Univ, Huddersfield Univ, Hull Univ, Imperial Coll, Kent Univ, King's Coll London, Leeds Univ, Leicester Univ, Liverpool John Moores Univ, Liverpool Univ, Luton Univ, Manchester Metro Univ, Nottingham Univ, Paisley Univ, Plymouth Univ, Reading Univ, Royal Holloway, St Andrews Univ, Scottish Agricultural Coll, Sheffield Hallam Univ, Sheffield Univ, Silsoe Coll, South Bank Univ, Strathclyde Univ, Sunderland Univ, Surrey Univ, Sussex Univ, Teesside Univ, Ulster Univ, UMIST, University Coll London, Westminster Univ, Wolverhampton Univ, Wye Coll.
See also: Biochemical engineering; biochemistry.

BOTANY
Possible prospectuses: Aberdeen Univ, Aberystwyth Univ, Bangor Univ, Belfast Univ, Birmingham Univ, Bristol Univ, Cambridge Univ, Cardiff Univ, Dundee Univ, Durham Univ, East London Univ, Edinburgh Univ, Exeter Univ, Glasgow Univ, Greenwich Univ, Imperial Coll, Leeds Univ, Leicester Univ, Liverpool Univ, Manchester Univ, Newcastle Univ, Nottingham Univ, Oxford Univ, Plymouth Univ, Reading Univ, Royal Holloway, St Andrews Univ, Sheffield Univ, Southampton Univ, Stirling Univ, University Coll London, Wye Coll.
See also: Agriculture; biology; horticulture.

BREWING
Possible prospectuses: Heriot-Watt Univ.
See also: Microbiology.

BROADCASTING
Possible prospectuses: Leeds Univ, London Coll Fashion, Ravensbourne Coll, Warrington Univ Coll.
See also: Communication studies; film studies; journalism; media studies.

BUILDING AND CONSTRUCTION
Possible prospectuses: Abertay Dundee Univ, Bath Univ, Bournemouth Univ, Bradford & Ilkley, Brighton Univ, Bristol UWE, Buckinghamshire Coll, Central Lancashire Univ, Coventry Univ, Cranfield Univ (p/g only), De Montfort Univ, Glamorgan Univ, Glasgow Caledonian Univ, Glasgow Coll Building, Greenwich Univ, Heriot-Watt Univ, Huddersfield Univ, Imperial Coll, Kingston Univ, Leeds Metro Univ, Liverpool John Moores Univ, Loughborough Univ, Luton Univ, Middlesex Univ, Napier Univ, Nene Coll, North East Wales Inst, Northumbria Univ, Nottingham Trent Univ, Oxford Brookes Univ, Paisley Univ, Portsmouth Univ, Reading Univ, Robert Gordon Univ, Salford Univ, Sheffield Hallam Univ, South Bank Univ, Southampton Inst, Swansea Inst, Teesside Univ, Ulster Univ, UMIST, University Coll London, Westminster Univ, Wolverhampton Univ.
See also: Architecture; building surveying; building technology; civil engineering.

BUILDING STUDIES

Possible prospectuses: Anglia Poly Univ, Bradford & Ilkley, Brighton Univ, Brunel Univ, Buckinghamshire Coll, Central Lancashire Univ, Coventry Univ, De Montfort Univ, Dundee Univ, Glamorgan Univ, Glasgow Caledonian Univ, Glasgow Coll Building, Greenwich Univ, Heriot-Watt Univ, Kingston Univ, Liverpool John Moores Univ, Luton Univ, Napier Univ, North East Wales Inst, Northumbria Univ, Nottingham Trent Univ, Oxford Brookes Univ, Plymouth Univ, Reading Univ, Robert Gordon Univ, Royal Agricultural Coll, Sheffield Hallam Univ, South Bank Univ, Southampton Inst, Teesside Univ, Ulster Univ, UMIST, University Coll London, Westminster Univ, Wolverhampton Univ.
See also: Architecture; building surveying; building technology; civil engineering.

BUILDING SURVEYING

Possible prospectuses: Abertay Dundee Univ, Anglia Poly Univ, Bolton Inst, Brighton Univ, Bristol UWE, Buckinghamshire Coll, Central England Univ, Central Lancashire Univ, Coventry Univ, De Montfort Univ, Glamorgan Univ, Glasgow Caledonian Univ, Glasgow Coll Building, Greenwich Univ, Heriot-Watt Univ, Kingston Univ, Leeds Metro Univ, Liverpool John Moores Univ, Loughborough Univ, Luton Univ, Napier Univ, North East Wales Inst, Northumbria Univ, Nottingham Trent Univ, Plymouth Univ, Portsmouth Univ, Reading Univ, Robert Gordon Univ, Royal Agricultural Coll, Salford Univ, Sheffield Hallam Univ, South Bank Univ, Staffordshire Univ, Ulster Univ, UMIST, Westminster Univ, Wolverhampton Univ.
See also: Quantity surveying.

BUILDING TECHNOLOGY

Possible prospectuses: Anglia Poly Univ, Bournemouth Univ, Brighton Univ, Bristol UWE, Coventry Univ, Cranfield Univ (p/g only), Glamorgan Univ, Glasgow Caledonian Univ, Glasgow Coll Building, Heriot-Watt Univ, Liverpool Univ, Loughborough Univ, Luton Univ, Napier Univ, Nene Coll, Nottingham Trent Univ, Nottingham Univ, Reading Univ, Robert Gordon Univ, South Bank Univ, Strathclyde Univ, Ulster Univ, UMIST, Wolverhampton Univ.

BULGARIAN

Possible prospectuses: Sheffield Univ, SSEES.

BURMESE STUDIES

Possible prospectuses: SOAS.
See also: Asian studies; oriental studies.

BUSINESS

See: Accountancy; business administration; business studies; economics; law; management.

BUSINESS ADMINISTRATION

Possible prospectuses: Abertay Dundee Univ, Aberystwyth Univ, Anglia Poly Univ, Aston Univ, Bath Univ, Birmingham Univ, Bolton Inst, Bradford & Ilkley, Bradford Univ, Brighton Univ, Bristol UWE, Brunel Univ, Buckinghamshire Coll, Cardiff Inst, Cardiff Univ, Central England Univ, Central Lancashire Univ, Coventry Univ, De Montfort Univ, Derby Univ, East Anglia Univ, European Business Sch, Farnborough Coll, Glamorgan Univ, Glasgow Caledonian Univ, Greenwich Univ, Harper Adams, Heriot-Watt Univ, Hertfordshire Univ, Huddersfield Univ, Keele Univ, Kent Univ, King Alfred's Coll, Kingston Univ, Lancaster Univ, Leeds Metro Univ, Liverpool John Moores Univ, London Business Sch (p/g only), London Guildhall Univ, Loughborough Univ, Luton Univ, Manchester Business Sch (p/g only), Manchester Metro Univ, Middlesex Univ, Napier Univ, Nene Coll, Newcastle Univ, Newport

Coll, North East Wales Inst, North London Univ, Northumbria Univ, Nottingham Trent Univ, Nottingham Univ, Oxford Brookes Univ, Paisley Univ, Plymouth Univ, Portsmouth Univ, Reading Univ, Robert Gordon Univ, Royal Agricultural Coll, Salford Univ, Scottish Coll Textiles, Sheffield Hallam Univ, Silsoe Coll, South Bank Univ, Southampton Inst, Staffordshire Univ, Stirling Univ, Strathclyde Univ, Sunderland Univ, Swansea Inst, Teesside Univ, Thames Valley Univ, Trinity & All Saints, Warrington Univ Coll, West Herts Coll, Westminster Univ, Wolverhampton Univ.

BUSINESS ECONOMICS
Possible prospectuses: Abertay Dundee Univ, Aberystwyth Univ, Anglia Poly Univ, Birmingham Univ, Bradford Univ, Brunel Univ, Buckingham Univ, Cardiff Univ, Central England Univ, Coventry Univ, Durham Univ, East Anglia Univ, East London Univ, European Business Sch, Exeter Univ, Glasgow Caledonian Univ, Heriot-Watt Univ, Hertfordshire Univ, Hull Univ, Leicester Univ, Liverpool Univ, London Guildhall Univ, Loughborough Univ, Luton Univ, Middlesex Univ, North London Univ, Nottingham Trent Univ, Paisley Univ, Plymouth Univ, Portsmouth Univ, Queen Mary & Westfield, Reading Univ, Robert Gordon Univ, Royal Agricultural Coll, Royal Holloway, Salford Univ, Scottish Coll Textiles, Southampton Univ, Staffordshire Univ, Stirling Univ, Sunderland Univ, Surrey Univ, Swansea Inst, Swansea Univ, Teesside Univ, Thames Valley Univ, Westminster Univ, Wolverhampton Univ.

BUSINESS STUDIES
Possible prospectuses: Abertay Dundee Univ, Aberystwyth Univ, Anglia Poly Univ, Aston Univ, Bangor Univ, Birmingham Univ, Bolton Inst, Bournemouth Univ, Bradford & Ilkley, Bradford Univ, Brighton Univ, Bristol UWE, Brunel Univ, Buckingham Univ, Buckinghamshire Coll, Canterbury Christ Church Coll, Cardiff Inst, Cardiff Univ, Central England Univ, Central Lancashire Univ, Cheltenham & Gloucester Coll, City Univ, Colchester Inst, Coventry Univ, De Montfort Univ, Derby Univ, East Anglia Univ, East London Univ, Edge Hill Univ Coll, European Business Sch, Exeter Univ, Glamorgan Univ, Glasgow Caledonian Univ, Greenwich Univ, Heriot-Watt Univ, Hertfordshire Univ, Huddersfield Univ, Hull Univ, Humberside Univ, Kent Univ, King Alfred's Coll, Kingston Univ, Leeds Metro Univ, Leeds Univ, Liverpool John Moores Univ, London Coll Printing, London Guildhall Univ, Loughborough Univ, Luton Univ, Manchester Business Sch (p/g only), Manchester Metro Univ, Middlesex Univ, Napier Univ, Nene Coll, Newport Coll, North East Wales Inst, North London Univ, Northumbria Univ, Nottingham Trent Univ, Oxford Brookes Univ, Paisley Univ, Plymouth Univ, Portsmouth Univ, Queen Margaret Coll, Queen Mary & Westfield, Reading Univ, Robert Gordon Univ, Roehampton Inst, Royal Agricultural Coll, Royal Holloway, Salford Univ, Scottish Coll Textiles, Sheffield Hallam Univ, Sheffield Univ, Silsoe Coll, South Bank Univ, Southampton Inst, Southampton Univ, Staffordshire Univ, Stirling Univ, Strathclyde Univ, Sunderland Univ, Sussex Univ, Swansea Inst, Swansea Univ, Teesside Univ, Thames Valley Univ, Trinity & All Saints, Ulster Univ, UMIST, Warrington Univ Coll, Warwick Univ, Westminster Univ, Wolverhampton Univ, Worcester Coll, Wye Coll.

BYZANTINE STUDIES
See: Classics; history.

C

CANADIAN STUDIES
See: American studies.

CARBON DATING
See: Archaeology.

CARIBBEAN STUDIES
Possible prospectuses: North London Univ, Warwick Univ.

CARING
See: Education; medicine; nursing; social administration; social work; youth and community work.

CARPET DESIGN
Possible prospectuses: Heriot-Watt Univ, Wolverhampton Univ.
See also: Textiles.

CATALAN
Possible prospectuses: Cambridge Univ, Cardiff Univ, Liverpool Univ, Queen Mary & Westfield, Salford Univ, Sheffield Univ, Swansea Univ.
See also: Spanish.

CATERING
Possible prospectuses: Bournemouth Univ, Cardiff Inst, Central England Univ, Colchester Inst, Glasgow Caledonian Univ, Huddersfield Univ, Manchester Metro Univ, Middlesex Univ, Napier Univ, North London Univ, Oxford Brookes Univ, Queen Margaret Coll, Robert Gordon Univ, Sheffield Hallam Univ, South Bank Univ, Thames Valley Univ, Ulster Univ, Wolverhampton Univ.
See also: Dietetics; hotel and catering management.

CELL BIOLOGY
Possible prospectuses: Aberdeen Univ, Abertay Dundee Univ, Aberystwyth Univ, Anglia Poly Univ, Birmingham Univ, Bradford Univ, Brunel Univ, Cambridge Univ, Durham Univ, East Anglia Univ, Essex Univ, Glasgow Caledonian Univ, Glasgow Univ, Huddersfield Univ, Imperial Coll, Kent Univ, King's Coll London, Leicester Univ, Liverpool Univ, Manchester Univ, Oxford Brookes Univ, Plymouth Univ, Portsmouth Univ, Royal Holloway, St Andrews Univ, Sheffield Univ, Southampton Univ, Stirling Univ, Surrey Univ, UMIST, University Coll London, Westminster Univ, Wolverhampton Univ, York Univ.
See also: Microbiology.

CELLULAR PATHOLOGY
Possible prospectuses: Bradford Univ, Bristol Univ, Bristol UWE, Imperial Coll, Reading Univ, St Andrews Univ.
See also: Pathology.

CELTIC STUDIES
Possible prospectuses: Aberdeen Univ, Aberystwyth Univ, Belfast Univ, Cambridge Univ, Edinburgh Univ, Glasgow Univ, Manchester Univ, Swansea Univ.
See also: Irish studies, Scottish studies; Welsh studies.

CENTRAL EUROPEAN STUDIES
See: European studies.

CERAMIC SCIENCE
See: Chemistry.

CERAMICS
Possible prospectuses: Bath Coll, Bradford & Ilkley, Bretton Hall, Bristol UWE, Buckinghamshire Coll, Camberwell Coll, Canterbury Christ Church Coll, Cardiff Inst, Central England Univ, Central Saint Martins, De Montfort Univ, Dundee Univ, Edinburgh Coll Art, Falmouth Coll Arts, Glasgow Sch Art, Heriot-Watt Univ, Kent Inst, Leeds Univ, Liverpool Hope Univ Coll, Loughborough Coll, Manchester Metro Univ, Middlesex Univ, North East Wales Inst, Portsmouth Univ, Robert Gordon Univ, Royal Coll Art (p/g only), Sheffield Univ, Staffordshire Univ, Sunderland Univ, Surrey Inst, Swansea Inst, Ulster Univ, Westminster Univ, Wolverhampton Univ.
See also: Three-dimensional design.

CHEMICAL ENGINEERING
Possible prospectuses: Aston Univ, Bath Univ, Belfast Univ, Birmingham Univ, Bradford Univ, Cambridge Univ, Edinburgh Univ, Exeter Univ, Glamorgan Univ, Heriot-Watt Univ, Huddersfield Univ, Imperial Coll, Leeds Univ, Loughborough Univ, Newcastle Univ, Nottingham Univ, Oxford Univ, Paisley Univ, Sheffield Univ, South Bank Univ, Strathclyde Univ, Surrey Univ, Swansea Univ, Teesside Univ, UMIST, University Coll London.

CHEMICAL PHYSICS
Possible prospectuses: Anglia Poly Univ, Bristol Univ, East Anglia Univ, Edinburgh Univ, Glasgow Univ, Imperial Coll, Kent Univ, Liverpool Univ, Manchester Univ, Open Univ, Queen Mary & Westfield, Sheffield Univ, Southampton Univ, Sussex Univ, UMIST, University Coll London.

CHEMISTRY
Possible prospectuses: Aberdeen Univ, Abertay Dundee Univ, Anglia Poly Univ, Aston Univ, Bangor Univ, Bath Univ, Belfast Univ, Birkbeck, Birmingham Univ, Bradford Univ, Brighton Univ, Bristol Univ, Bristol UWE, Brunel Univ, Cambridge Univ, Cardiff Univ, Central Lancashire Univ, Coventry Univ, De Montfort Univ, Derby Univ, Dundee Univ, Durham Univ, East Anglia Univ, Edinburgh Univ, Essex Univ, Exeter Univ, Glamorgan Univ, Glasgow Caledonian Univ, Glasgow Univ, Greenwich Univ, Heriot-Watt Univ, Hertfordshire Univ, Huddersfield Univ, Hull Univ, Imperial Coll, Keele Univ, Kent Univ, King's Coll London, Kingston Univ, Lancaster Univ, Leeds Metro Univ, Leeds Univ, Leicester Univ, Liverpool John Moores Univ, Liverpool Univ, Loughborough Univ, Manchester Metro Univ, Manchester Univ, Napier Univ, Newcastle Univ, North East Wales Inst, North London Univ, Northumbria Univ, Nottingham Trent Univ, Nottingham Univ, Open Univ, Oxford Brookes Univ, Oxford Univ, Paisley Univ, Plymouth Univ, Portsmouth Univ, Queen Mary & Westfield, Reading Univ, Robert Gordon Univ, St Andrews Univ, St Mary's Univ Coll, Salford Univ, Scottish Coll Textiles, Sheffield Hallam Univ, Sheffield Univ, South Bank Univ, Southampton Univ, Staffordshire Univ, Stirling Univ, Strathclyde Univ, Sunderland Univ, Surrey Univ, Sussex

Univ, Swansea Univ, Teesside Univ, UMIST, University Coll London, Warwick Univ, Wolverhampton Univ, York Univ.

CHINESE
Possible prospectuses: Cambridge Univ, Durham Univ, Edinburgh Univ, Leeds Univ, Newcastle Univ, Oxford Univ, Sheffield Univ, SOAS, Westminster Univ, York Univ.
See also: Asian studies; oriental studies.

CHIROPODY
See: Podiatry.

CHOREOGRAPHY
Possible prospectuses: Chichester Univ Coll, Laban Centre, London Contemp Dance Sch, Middlesex Univ.

CHURCH HISTORY
Possible prospectuses: Aberdeen Univ, Glasgow Univ, Lampeter Univ, London Bible, Oak Hill Coll, St Andrews Univ, Spurgeon's Coll, Wolverhampton Univ.
See also: Religious studies.

CIVIL ENGINEERING
Possible prospectuses: Aberdeen Univ, Abertay Dundee Univ, Aston Univ, Bath Univ, Belfast Univ, Birmingham Univ, Bolton Inst, Bradford Univ, Brighton Univ, Bristol Univ, Bristol UWE, Cambridge Univ, Cardiff Univ, City Univ, Coventry Univ, Cranfield Univ (p/g only), Dundee Univ, Durham Univ, East London Univ, Edinburgh Univ, Exeter Univ, Glamorgan Univ, Glasgow Caledonian Univ, Glasgow Univ, Greenwich Univ, Heriot-Watt Univ, Hertfordshire Univ, Imperial Coll, Kingston Univ, Leeds Univ, Liverpool John Moores Univ, Liverpool Univ, Loughborough Univ, Manchester Univ, Middlesex Univ, Napier Univ, Newcastle Univ, North East Wales Inst, Nottingham Trent Univ, Nottingham Univ, Oxford Brookes Univ, Oxford Univ, Paisley Univ, Plymouth Univ, Portsmouth Univ, Queen Mary & Westfield, Salford Univ, Sheffield Hallam Univ, Sheffield Univ, Shrivenham, South Bank Univ, Southampton Univ, Strathclyde Univ, Sunderland Univ, Surrey Univ, Swansea Univ, Teesside Univ, Ulster Univ, UMIST, University Coll London, Warwick Univ, Westminster Univ, Wolverhampton Univ.
See also: Engineering (general).

CLASSICAL STUDIES
Possible prospectuses: Belfast Univ, Birkbeck, Birmingham Univ, Bristol Univ, Durham Univ, Edinburgh Univ, Exeter Univ, Glasgow Univ, Inst Archaeology, Keele Univ, Kent Univ, King's Coll London, Lampeter Univ, Liverpool Univ, Manchester Univ, Newcastle Univ, North London Univ, Nottingham Univ, Open Univ, Reading Univ, Royal Holloway, St Andrews Univ, St Mary's Univ Coll, Swansea Univ, Warwick Univ.
See also: Ancient history; classics.

CLASSICS
Possible prospectuses: Belfast Univ, Birkbeck, Birmingham Univ, Bristol Univ, Cambridge Univ, Durham Univ, Edinburgh Univ, Exeter Univ, Glasgow Univ, Kent Univ, King's Coll London, Lampeter Univ, Leeds Univ, Liverpool Univ, Manchester Univ, Newcastle Univ, North London Univ, Nottingham Univ, Oxford Univ, Reading Univ, Royal Holloway, St Andrews Univ, Swansea Univ, University Coll London, Warwick Univ.
See also: Classical studies; Greek; Latin.

CLIMATE
See: Geography; meteorology.

CLOTHING
See: Fashion; textiles.

COASTAL ENGINEERING
See: Civil engineering.

COGNITIVE SCIENCE
Possible prospectuses: Dundee Univ, Essex Univ, Exeter Univ, Hertfordshire Univ, Imperial Coll, King Alfred's Coll, Leeds Univ, Oxford Brookes Univ, Portsmouth Univ, Sheffield Univ, Sussex Univ, Westminster Univ.
See also: Psychology.

COMMERCE
Possible prospectuses: Abertay Dundee Univ, Birmingham Univ, European Business Sch, Glasgow Caledonian Univ, Heriot-Watt Univ, Napier Univ, North East Wales Inst, Robert Gordon Univ, Scottish Coll Textiles, Thames Valley Univ.
See also: Business studies.

COMMUNICATION ENGINEERING
Possible prospectuses: Anglia Poly Univ, Aston Univ, Bath Univ, Birmingham Univ, Bradford Univ, Brighton Univ, Bristol Univ, Cardiff Inst, Central England Univ, Coventry Univ, De Montfort Univ, Edinburgh Univ, Essex Univ, Glamorgan Univ, Greenwich Univ, Heriot-Watt Univ, Huddersfield Univ, Humberside Univ, Imperial Coll, Kent Univ, Leeds Metro Univ, Liverpool John Moores Univ, Liverpool Univ, Luton Univ, Middlesex Univ, Napier Univ, Newport Coll, North London Univ, Northumbria Univ, Paisley Univ, Plymouth Univ, Portsmouth Univ, Queen Mary & Westfield, Ravensbourne Coll, Robert Gordon Univ, Salford Univ, Sheffield Univ, Shrivenham, Southampton Univ, Staffordshire Univ, Strathclyde Univ, Sunderland Univ, Swansea Univ, Teesside Univ, UMIST.

COMMUNICATION STUDIES
Possible prospectuses: Anglia Poly Univ, Bangor Univ, Bournemouth Univ, Bradford Univ, Bristol UWE, Brunel Univ, Cardiff Inst, Cardiff Univ, Central England Univ, Coventry Univ, East London Univ, Edge Hill Univ Coll, Glamorgan Univ, Glasgow Caledonian Univ, Goldsmiths Coll, Greenwich Univ, Huddersfield Univ, Kent Inst, Kent Univ, King Alfred's Coll, Lancaster Univ, Leeds Univ, Leicester Univ, Lincoln Univ, Liverpool Univ, London Coll Printing, London Guildhall Univ, Loughborough Univ, Middlesex Univ, Napier Univ, North London Univ, Nottingham Trent Univ, Queen Margaret Coll, Ravensbourne Coll, Ripon & York St John, Robert Gordon Univ, Sheffield Hallam Univ, Southampton Inst, Stirling Univ, Sunderland Univ, Teesside Univ, Thames Valley Univ, Trinity & All Saints, Ulster Univ, Warrington Univ Coll, Wolverhampton Univ.
See also: Media studies.

COMMUNITY ARTS
Possible prospectuses: Bretton Hall, Dartington Coll Arts, Heriot-Watt Univ, Laban Centre, Middlesex Univ, Roehampton Inst, Strathclyde Univ.

COMMUNITY STUDIES
See: Public administration; social work; sociology; town planning; urban studies; youth and community work.

COMPARATIVE LITERATURE
Possible prospectuses: Anglia Poly Univ, Bradford Univ, Buckingham Univ, East Anglia Univ, Essex Univ, Greenwich Univ, Kent Univ, Middlesex Univ, Ripon & York St John, Staffordshire Univ, Sunderland Univ, Warwick Univ.

COMPUTER ENGINEERING
Possible prospectuses: Abertay Dundee Univ, Anglia Poly Univ, Aston Univ, Bangor Univ, Belfast Univ, Birmingham Univ, Bournemouth Univ, Bradford Univ, Brighton Univ, Bristol Univ, Bristol UWE, Brunel Univ, Buckinghamshire Coll, Cardiff Inst, Central England Univ, City Univ, Coventry Univ, Cranfield Univ (p/g only), Dartmouth, Derby Univ, East Anglia Univ, East London Univ, Essex Univ, Glasgow Caledonian Univ, Greenwich Univ, Heriot-Watt Univ, Hertfordshire Univ, Huddersfield Univ, Hull Univ, Imperial Coll, Kent Univ, Lancaster Univ, Leicester Univ, Liverpool John Moores Univ, Loughborough Univ, Luton Univ, Manchester Univ, Middlesex Univ, Napier Univ, Nene Coll, Newcastle Univ, North London Univ, Northumbria Univ, Nottingham Trent Univ, Nottingham Univ, Paisley Univ, Portsmouth Univ, Queen Mary & Westfield, Robert Gordon Univ, Salford Univ, Sheffield Hallam Univ, Sheffield Univ, Shrivenham, South Bank Univ, Southampton Univ, Staffordshire Univ, Strathclyde Univ, Sunderland Univ, Surrey Univ, Sussex Univ, Swansea Inst, Teesside Univ, UMIST, Warwick Univ, Westminster Univ, York Univ.
See also: Computer technology.

COMPUTER SCIENCE
Possible prospectuses: Aberdeen Univ, Abertay Dundee Univ, Aberystwyth Univ, Anglia Poly Univ, Aston Univ, Belfast Univ, Birmingham Univ, Bournemouth Univ, Bradford Univ, Brighton Univ, Bristol Univ, Bristol UWE, Brunel Univ, Buckingham Univ, Cambridge Univ, Cardiff Univ, Central England Univ, Chester Univ Coll, City Univ, Coventry Univ, Cranfield Univ (p/g only), Dartmouth, De Montfort Univ, Derby Univ, Dundee Univ, Durham Univ, East Anglia Univ, Edinburgh Univ, Essex Univ, Exeter Univ, Glamorgan Univ, Glasgow Caledonian Univ, Glasgow Univ, Goldsmiths Coll, Greenwich Univ, Heriot-Watt Univ, Hertfordshire Univ, Hull Univ, Imperial Coll, Keele Univ, Kent Univ, King's Coll London, Kingston Univ, Lancaster Univ, Leeds Univ, Leicester Univ, Liverpool John Moores Univ, Liverpool Univ, Loughborough Univ, Luton Univ, Manchester Metro Univ, Manchester Univ, Napier Univ, Newcastle Univ, North East Wales Inst, North London Univ, Nottingham Trent Univ, Nottingham Univ, Open Univ, Oxford Brookes Univ, Paisley Univ, Portsmouth Univ, Queen Mary & Westfield, Reading Univ, Robert Gordon Univ, Royal Holloway, St Andrews Univ, Salford Univ, Scottish Coll Textiles, Sheffield Hallam Univ, Sheffield Univ, Shrivenham, South Bank Univ, Southampton Inst, Southampton Univ, Staffordshire Univ, Stirling Univ, Strathclyde Univ, Sunderland Univ, Surrey Univ, Sussex Univ, Swansea Inst, Swansea Univ, Teesside Univ, Ulster Univ, UMIST, University Coll London, Warwick Univ, Westminster Univ, Wolverhampton Univ, York Univ.
See also: Computing.

COMPUTER TECHNOLOGY
Possible prospectuses: Abertay Dundee Univ, Aberystwyth Univ, Anglia Poly Univ, Aston Univ, Bath Univ, Birmingham Univ, Bournemouth Univ, Bradford Univ, Bristol Univ, Bristol UWE, Brunel Univ, Cardiff Inst, Central England Univ, Coventry Univ, Cranfield Univ (p/g only), Dartmouth, De Montfort Univ, Derby Univ, Essex Univ, Glasgow Caledonian Univ, Heriot-Watt Univ, Imperial Coll, Kingston Univ, Liverpool Univ, Loughborough Univ, Luton

Univ, Manchester Metro Univ, Manchester Univ, Middlesex Univ, Napier Univ, Nene Coll, Nottingham Trent Univ, Open Univ, Oxford Brookes Univ, Paisley Univ, Portsmouth Univ, Robert Gordon Univ, Salford Univ, Scottish Coll Textiles, Sheffield Hallam Univ, Sheffield Univ, South Bank Univ, Southampton Inst, Southampton Univ, Staffordshire Univ, Sunderland Univ, Surrey Univ, Swansea Inst, Teesside Univ, Thames Valley Univ, UMIST, Warwick Univ, Westminster Univ, Wolverhampton Univ.
See also: Computer science.

COMPUTING
Possible prospectuses: Aberdeen Univ, Abertay Dundee Univ, Aberystwyth Univ, Anglia Poly Univ, Aston Univ, Bangor Univ, Bath Univ, Belfast Univ, Birkbeck, Birmingham Univ, Bolton Inst, Bournemouth Univ, Bradford Univ, Brighton Univ, Bristol UWE, Brunel Univ, Buckinghamshire Coll, Canterbury Christ Church Coll, Cardiff Inst, Cardiff Univ, Central England Univ, Central Lancashire Univ, Cheltenham & Gloucester Coll, City Univ, Coventry Univ, Dartmouth, De Montfort Univ, Derby Univ, Dundee Univ, East Anglia Univ, East London Univ, Essex Univ, Exeter Univ, Farnborough Coll, Glamorgan Univ, Glasgow Caledonian Univ, Glasgow Univ, Goldsmiths Coll, Greenwich Univ, Heriot-Watt Univ, Hertfordshire Univ, Huddersfield Univ, Hull Univ, Humberside Univ, Imperial Coll, Kent Univ, King Alfred's Coll, Kingston Univ, Leeds Metro Univ, Leeds Univ, Leicester Univ, Liverpool John Moores Univ, Liverpool Univ, London Guildhall Univ, Loughborough Univ, LSU Southampton, Luton Univ, Manchester Metro Univ, Manchester Univ, Middlesex Univ, Napier Univ, Nene Coll, Newcastle Univ, Newport Coll, North East Wales Inst, North London Univ, Northumbria Univ, Nottingham Trent Univ, Open Univ, Oxford Brookes Univ, Oxford Univ, Paisley Univ, Plymouth Univ, Portsmouth Univ, Queen Mary & Westfield, Reading Univ, Robert Gordon Univ, Roehampton Inst, St Andrews Univ, Salford Univ, Scottish Coll Textiles, Sheffield Hallam Univ, South Bank Univ, Southampton Inst, Staffordshire Univ, Stirling Univ, Sunderland Univ, Surrey Univ, Sussex Univ, Swansea Inst, Teesside Univ, Thames Valley Univ, Ulster Univ, UMIST, University Coll London, Warwick Univ, Westminster Univ, Wolverhampton Univ.
See also: Computer science; information technology.

CONFLICT
See: War studies.

CONSERVATION
Possible prospectuses: Anglia Poly Univ, Bolton Inst, Bournemouth Univ, Camberwell Coll, Cardiff Univ, Cheltenham & Gloucester Coll, De Montfort Univ, East Anglia Univ, Edinburgh Coll Art, Hertfordshire Univ, Huddersfield Univ, Inst Archaeology, London Guildhall Univ, Northumbria Univ, Roehampton Inst, Royal Agricultural Coll, Royal Coll Art (p/g only), Silsoe Coll, South Bank Univ, Stirling Univ, Sussex Univ, Trinity Coll Carmarthen, Welsh Inst Rural Studies, Writtle Coll, Wye Coll.
See also: Archaeology; biology; ecology; environmental studies.

CONSTRUCTION
See: Building and construction.

CONSUMER STUDIES
Possible prospectuses: Abertay Dundee Univ, Bradford & Ilkley, Cardiff Inst, Dundee Univ, Glasgow Caledonian Univ, Leeds Metro Univ, Liverpool John Moores Univ, Manchester Metro Univ, North London Univ, Northumbria Univ, Queen Margaret Coll, Robert Gordon Univ, Roehampton Inst, Salford Univ, South Bank Univ, Teesside Univ, Ulster Univ.

CONTROL ENGINEERING
Possible prospectuses: Aberdeen Univ, Birmingham Univ, Bolton Inst, Bradford Univ, Brunel Univ, Central England Univ, City Univ, Coventry Univ, Cranfield Univ (p/g only), Dartmouth, East London Univ, Glasgow Caledonian Univ, Heriot-Watt Univ, Huddersfield Univ, Hull Univ, Humberside Univ, Imperial Coll, Leicester Univ, Loughborough Univ, Middlesex Univ, Napier Univ, North East Wales Inst, Open Univ, Reading Univ, Robert Gordon Univ, Salford Univ, Sheffield Hallam Univ, Sheffield Univ, South Bank Univ, Staffordshire Univ, Strathclyde Univ, Sunderland Univ, Teesside Univ, UMIST, Westminster Univ.

CORROSION
See: Materials science.

COSMETIC TECHNOLOGY
See: Chemistry.

COUNSELLING
See: Social work.

COUNTRY PLANNING
See: Town and country planning.

CRIMINOLOGY
Possible prospectuses: Bangor Univ, Buckinghamshire Coll, Central England Univ, Coventry Univ, Glamorgan Univ, Hull Univ, Humberside Univ, Keele Univ, Kingston Univ, Lincoln Univ, Liverpool John Moores Univ, Middlesex Univ, Nottingham Trent Univ, Sheffield Univ, Southampton Inst, Teesside Univ, Thames Valley Univ, Westminster Univ.

CROAT
See: Serbo-Croat.

CROP TECHNOLOGY
Possible prospectuses: Bangor Univ, Bath Univ, De Montfort Univ, Harper Adams, Nottingham Univ, Reading Univ, Royal Agricultural Coll, Scottish Agricultural Coll, Wolverhampton Univ, Writtle Coll, Wye Coll.

CULTURAL STUDIES
Possible prospectuses: Aberdeen Univ, Birmingham Univ, Bristol UWE, Buckinghamshire Coll, Central Lancashire Univ, De Montfort Univ, East Anglia Univ, East London Univ, Falmouth Coll Arts, Greenwich Univ, King Alfred's Coll, Lampeter Univ, Lancaster Univ, Liverpool John Moores Univ, Manchester Metro Univ, Middlesex Univ, Nene Coll, North London Univ, Norwich Sch Art, Nottingham Trent Univ, Portsmouth Univ, Queen Margaret Coll, Ripon & York St John, Salford Univ, Sheffield Hallam Univ, Southampton Inst, Staffordshire Univ, Sussex Univ, Teesside Univ, Trinity & All Saints, Warrington Univ Coll, Warwick Univ, Wolverhampton Univ.

CUNEIFORM STUDIES
See: Near East studies.

CYBERNETICS
Possible prospectuses: Loughborough Univ, Reading Univ.
See also: Computing; control engineering.

CZECH/SLOVAK
Possible prospectuses: Cambridge Univ, Glasgow Univ, Oxford Univ, Sheffield Univ, SSEES.

D

DANCE
Possible prospectuses: ALRA, Birmingham Univ, Bretton Hall, Brighton Univ, Chester Univ Coll, Chichester Univ Coll, City Univ, Coventry Univ, De Montfort Univ, Hertfordshire Univ, King Alfred's Coll, Laban Centre, Liverpool John Moores Univ, London Contemp Dance Sch, Manchester Metro Univ, Middlesex Univ, Northern Sch Cont Dance, Nottingham Trent Univ, Ripon & York St John, Roehampton Inst, S Martin's Univ Coll, Surrey Univ, Wolverhampton Univ.
See also: Drama; movement studies; performance arts.

DANISH
Possible prospectuses: East Anglia Univ, Edinburgh Univ, Hull Univ, University Coll London.
See also: Scandinavian studies.

DATA PROCESSING
Possible prospectuses: Aberdeen Univ, Abertay Dundee Univ, Anglia Poly Univ, Bradford Univ, Bristol UWE, Cranfield Univ (p/g only), Dartmouth, Imperial Coll, Leeds Univ, Middlesex Univ, Napier Univ, Open Univ, Sheffield Univ, Thames Valley Univ, Ulster Univ.
See also: Computing.

DECISION THEORY
Possible prospectuses: Coventry Univ, Hertfordshire Univ, North London Univ, Wolverhampton Univ.
See also: Business studies; economics; politics.

DEMOGRAPHY
See: Geography; sociology; statistics.

DENTISTRY
Possible prospectuses: Belfast Univ, Birmingham Univ, Bristol Univ, Dundee Univ, Glasgow Univ, King's Coll London, King's Coll Sch of Medicine, Leeds Univ, Liverpool Univ, Manchester Univ, Newcastle Univ, Queen Mary & Westfield, St Bartholomew's & Royal London, Sheffield Univ, UMDS, Wales Coll Medicine.

DESIGN
See: individual subjects, eg interior design, industrial design.

DEVELOPMENTAL BIOLOGY
Possible prospectuses: Glasgow Univ, University Coll London.
See also: Biology.

DEVIANCE
See: Psychology; sociology, statistics.

DIETETICS
Possible prospectuses: Cardiff Inst, Glasgow Caledonian Univ, King's Coll London, Leeds Metro Univ, North London Univ, Queen Margaret Coll, Robert Gordon Univ, Surrey Univ, Ulster Univ.
See also: Nutrition.

DIGITAL MICROELECTRONICS
Possible prospectuses: Abertay Dundee Univ, Anglia Poly Univ, Birmingham Univ, Bradford Univ, Bristol UWE, Dundee Univ, Glasgow Caledonian Univ, Heriot-Watt Univ, Imperial Coll, Kent Univ, Liverpool John Moores Univ, Middlesex Univ, Open Univ, UMIST, Westminster Univ.
See also: Computing; electronic engineering.

DIVINITY
See: Theology; religious studies.

DRAMA
Possible prospectuses: Aberystwyth Univ, ALRA, Birmingham Univ, Bretton Hall, Bristol Old Vic, Bristol Univ, Brunel Univ, Central Sch Speech/Drama, Chester Univ Coll, De Montfort Univ, Derby Univ, East Anglia Univ, Edge Hill Univ Coll, Exeter Univ, Glamorgan Univ, Glasgow Univ, Goldsmiths Coll, Guildford Sch Acting, Guildhall, Hertfordshire Univ, Homerton Coll, Huddersfield Univ, Hull Univ, Kent Univ, King Alfred's Coll, Kingston Univ, Lancaster Univ, Leeds Univ, Liverpool Hope Univ Coll, Liverpool John Moores Univ, Loughborough Univ, Manchester Metro Univ, Manchester Univ, Middlesex Univ, Nene Coll, Northumbria Univ, Nottingham Trent Univ, Plymouth Univ, Queen Margaret Coll, Queen Mary & Westfield, RADA, Reading Univ, Ripon & York St John, Roehampton Inst, Rose Bruford Coll, Royal Holloway, Royal Scottish Academy, S Martin's Univ Coll, St Mary's Univ Coll, Sussex Univ, Ulster Univ, Warrington Univ Coll, Welsh Coll Music/Drama, Wolverhampton Univ, Worcester Coll.
See also: Dance; performance arts.

DUTCH
Possible prospectuses: Cambridge Univ, Hull Univ, Sheffield Univ, University Coll London.

E

EARTH SCIENCES
Possible prospectuses: Aberdeen Univ, Aberystwyth Univ, Anglia Poly Univ, Birmingham Univ, Brunel Univ, Camborne Sch Mines, Cambridge Univ, Cheltenham & Gloucester Coll, Derby Univ, Durham Univ, Edinburgh Univ, Exeter Univ, Glasgow Univ, Greenwich Univ, Hull Univ, Imperial Coll, Kingston Univ, Leeds Univ, Liverpool John Moores Univ, Liverpool Univ, Manchester Univ, Middlesex Univ, Nene Coll, Open Univ, Oxford Brookes Univ, Oxford Univ, Plymouth Univ, Portsmouth Univ, Reading Univ, Royal Holloway, St Andrews Univ, Sheffield Univ, Southampton Univ, Staffordshire Univ, Stirling Univ, University Coll London, Wolverhampton Univ.
See also: Geology.

ECOLOGY
Possible prospectuses: Aberdeen Univ, Abertay Dundee Univ, Anglia Poly Univ, Bangor Univ, Cambridge Univ, Cardiff Univ, Derby Univ, Dundee Univ, Durham Univ, East Anglia Univ, East London Univ, Edinburgh Univ, Essex Univ, Harper Adams, Huddersfield Univ, Hull Univ, Imperial Coll, Lancaster Univ, Leeds Univ, Liverpool John Moores Univ, Loughborough Univ, LSU Southampton, Luton Univ, Manchester Univ, Middlesex Univ, North London Univ, Open Univ, Plymouth Univ, Queen Mary & Westfield, Roehampton Inst, Royal Agricultural Coll, Royal Holloway, St Andrews Univ, Sheffield Univ, South Bank Univ, Stirling Univ, Sussex Univ, Ulster Univ, University Coll London, Westminster Univ, Wolverhampton Univ, Worcester Coll, Writtle Coll, York Univ.
See also: Biology; botany; zoology.

ECONOMETRICS
Possible prospectuses: Aberdeen Univ, Birmingham Univ, Brunel Univ, Essex Univ, Heriot-Watt Univ, Kent Univ, Leeds Univ, Liverpool Univ, Loughborough Univ, LSE, Manchester Univ, Nottingham Univ, Reading Univ, Sheffield Univ, Southampton Univ, Staffordshire Univ, Surrey Univ, Warwick Univ, York Univ.
See also: Economics; mathematics.

ECONOMIC HISTORY
Possible prospectuses: Aberdeen Univ, Aberystwyth Univ, Anglia Poly Univ, Belfast Univ, Birmingham Univ, Bristol Univ, Bristol UWE, Cambridge Univ, East Anglia Univ, Edinburgh Univ, Essex Univ, Exeter Univ, Glasgow Caledonian Univ, Glasgow Univ, Hull Univ, Leeds Univ, Leicester Univ, Liverpool Univ, LSE, Manchester Metro Univ, Manchester Univ, Nottingham Univ, Open Univ, Portsmouth Univ, Queen Mary & Westfield, Reading Univ, Royal Holloway, St Andrews Univ, Salford Univ, Sheffield Univ, Southampton Univ, Staffordshire Univ, Stirling Univ, Strathclyde Univ, Sussex Univ, Swansea Univ, University Coll London, Warwick Univ, Westminster Univ, York Univ.
See also: History.

ECONOMICS
Possible prospectuses: Aberdeen Univ, Abertay Dundee Univ, Aberystwyth Univ, Anglia Poly Univ, Bangor Univ, Bath Univ, Belfast Univ, Birkbeck, Birmingham Univ, Bradford Univ, Brighton Univ, Bristol Univ, Bristol UWE, Brunel Univ, Buckingham Univ, Cambridge Univ, Cardiff Univ, Central England Univ, Central Lancashire Univ, City Univ, Coventry Univ, De Montfort Univ, Derby Univ, Dundee Univ, Durham Univ, East Anglia Univ, East London Univ, Edinburgh Univ, Essex Univ, European Business Sch, Exeter Univ, Glasgow Caledonian Univ, Glasgow Univ, Goldsmiths Coll, Greenwich Univ, Heriot-Watt Univ, Hertfordshire Univ, Huddersfield Univ, Hull Univ, Keele Univ, Kent Univ, Kingston Univ, Lancaster Univ, Leeds Metro Univ, Leeds Univ, Leicester Univ, Lincoln Univ, Liverpool John Moores Univ, Liverpool Univ, London Guildhall Univ, Loughborough Univ, LSE, Luton Univ, Manchester Metro Univ, Manchester Univ, Middlesex Univ, National Extension Coll, Nene Coll, Newcastle Univ, North London Univ, Northumbria Univ, Nottingham Trent Univ, Nottingham Univ, Open Univ, Oxford Brookes Univ, Oxford Univ, Paisley Univ, Plymouth Univ, Portsmouth Univ, Queen Mary & Westfield, Reading Univ, Robert Gordon Univ, Royal Holloway, St Andrews Univ, Salford Univ, Sheffield Univ, SOAS, South Bank Univ, Southampton Univ, Staffordshire Univ, Stirling Univ, Strathclyde Univ, Sunderland Univ, Surrey Univ, Sussex Univ, Swansea Inst, Swansea Univ, Thames Valley Univ, Ulster Univ, University Coll London, Warwick Univ, Westminster Univ, Wolverhampton Univ, Wye Coll, York Univ.

EDUCATION

Possible prospectuses: Aberystwyth Univ, Anglia Poly Univ, Bangor Univ, Bath Coll, Belfast Univ, Birmingham Univ, Bolton Inst, Bradford & Ilkley, Bretton Hall, Brighton Univ, Bristol UWE, Brunel Univ, Cambridge Univ, Canterbury Christ Church Coll, Cardiff Inst, Cardiff Univ, Central England Univ, Central Lancashire Univ, Central Sch Speech/Drama, Cheltenham & Gloucester Coll, Chester Univ Coll, Chichester Univ Coll, De Montfort Univ, Derby Univ, Dundee Univ, Durham Univ, East Anglia Univ, East London Univ, Edge Hill Univ Coll, Exeter Univ, Glasgow Univ, Goldsmiths Coll, Greenwich Univ, Heriot-Watt Univ, Hertfordshire Univ, Homerton Coll, Huddersfield Univ, Hull Univ, Inst Education, Keele Univ, King Alfred's Coll, King's Coll London, Kingston Univ, Lancaster Univ, Leeds Metro Univ, Liverpool Hope Univ Coll, Liverpool John Moores Univ, Liverpool Univ, Loughborough Univ, LSU Southampton, Manchester Metro Univ, Middlesex Univ, Moray House, National Extension Coll, Nene Coll, Newport Coll, North East Wales Inst, North London Univ, Northumbria Univ, Nottingham Trent Univ, Open Univ, Oxford Brookes Univ, Paisley Univ, Plymouth Univ, Portsmouth Univ, Reading Univ, Ripon & York St John, Roehampton Inst, St Mark & St John, S Martin's Univ Coll, St Mary's Univ Coll, Sheffield Hallam Univ, South Bank Univ, Stirling Univ, Strathclyde Univ, Sunderland Univ, Swansea Inst, Trinity & All Saints, Trinity Coll Carmarthen, Ulster Univ, Warwick Univ, Westminster Coll, Wolverhampton Univ, Worcester Coll, York Univ.

EGYPTOLOGY

Possible prospectuses: Cambridge Univ, Inst Archaeology, Liverpool Univ, Oxford Univ, University Coll London.
See also: Archaeology; history; Near East studies.

ELECTRICAL ENGINEERING

Possible prospectuses: Aberdeen Univ, Abertay Dundee Univ, Aston Univ, Bangor Univ, Bath Univ, Belfast Univ, Birmingham Univ, Bradford Univ, Brighton Univ, Bristol Univ, Bristol UWE, Brunel Univ, Cambridge Univ, Cardiff Inst, Cardiff Univ, Central England Univ, Central Lancashire Univ, City Univ, Coventry Univ, Dartmouth, De Montfort Univ, Derby Univ, Dundee Univ, Durham Univ, East London Univ, Edinburgh Univ, Exeter Univ, Glamorgan Univ, Glasgow Caledonian Univ, Glasgow Univ, Greenwich Univ, Heriot-Watt Univ, Hertfordshire Univ, Huddersfield Univ, Humberside Univ, Imperial Coll, King's Coll London, Leeds Metro Univ, Leeds Univ, Leicester Univ, Liverpool John Moores Univ, Liverpool Univ, Loughborough Univ, Luton Univ, Manchester Metro Univ, Manchester Univ, Middlesex Univ, Napier Univ, Newcastle Univ, Newport Coll, North East Wales Inst, Northumbria Univ, Nottingham Trent Univ, Nottingham Univ, Oxford Univ, Paisley Univ, Plymouth Univ, Portsmouth Univ, Queen Mary & Westfield, Robert Gordon Univ, Salford Univ, Sheffield Hallam Univ, Sheffield Univ, Shrivenham, South Bank Univ, Southampton Univ, Staffordshire Univ, Strathclyde Univ, Sunderland Univ, Surrey Univ, Sussex Univ, Swansea Univ, Teesside Univ, Ulster Univ, UMIST, University Coll London, Warwick Univ.
See also: Electronic engineering; engineering (general).

ELECTROMECHANICAL ENGINEERING

Possible prospectuses: Abertay Dundee Univ, Aston Univ, Brunel Univ, Dartmouth, De Montfort Univ, Glamorgan Univ, Glasgow Caledonian Univ, Heriot-Watt Univ, Imperial Coll, Lancaster Univ, Leeds Univ, Loughborough Univ, Manchester Metro Univ, Middlesex Univ, Robert Gordon Univ, Southampton Univ, Strathclyde Univ, Sussex Univ, UMIST.
See also: Engineering (general).

ELECTRONIC ENGINEERING
Possible prospectuses: Aberdeen Univ, Abertay Dundee Univ, Aston Univ, Bangor Univ, Bath Univ, Belfast Univ, Birmingham Univ, Bolton Inst, Bournemouth Univ, Bradford Univ, Brighton Univ, Bristol Univ, Bristol UWE, Brunel Univ, Cambridge Univ, Cardiff Inst, Cardiff Univ, Central England Univ, Central Lancashire Univ, City Univ, Coventry Univ, De Montfort Univ, Derby Univ, Dundee Univ, Durham Univ, East Anglia Univ, East London Univ, Edinburgh Univ, Essex Univ, Exeter Univ, Glamorgan Univ, Glasgow Caledonian Univ, Glasgow Univ, Greenwich Univ, Heriot-Watt Univ, Hertfordshire Univ, Huddersfield Univ, Hull Univ, Humberside Univ, Imperial Coll, Kent Univ, King's Coll London, Kingston Univ, Lancaster Univ, Leeds Metro Univ, Leeds Univ, Leicester Univ, Liverpool John Moores Univ, Liverpool Univ, Loughborough Univ, Luton Univ, Manchester Metro Univ, Manchester Univ, Middlesex Univ, Napier Univ, Newcastle Univ, Newport Coll, North East Wales Inst, North London Univ, Northumbria Univ, Nottingham Trent Univ, Nottingham Univ, Oxford Brookes Univ, Oxford Univ, Paisley Univ, Plymouth Univ, Portsmouth Univ, Queen Mary & Westfield, Ravensbourne Coll, Reading Univ, Robert Gordon Univ, Salford Univ, Sheffield Hallam Univ, Sheffield Univ, Shrivenham, South Bank Univ, Southampton Inst, Southampton Univ, Staffordshire Univ, Strathclyde Univ, Sunderland Univ, Surrey Univ, Sussex Univ, Swansea Inst, Swansea Univ, Teesside Univ, Ulster Univ, UMIST, University Coll London, Warwick Univ, Westminster Univ, York Univ.
See also: Electrical engineering; engineering (general).

ELECTRONIC MECHANICS
Possible prospectuses: Abertay Dundee Univ, Bristol Univ, Brunel Univ, Coventry Univ, East London Univ, Glamorgan Univ, Glasgow Caledonian Univ, Heriot-Watt Univ, Imperial Coll, King's Coll London, Middlesex Univ, Salford Univ, Swansea Inst.
See also: Electronic engineering.

ELECTRONICS
Possible prospectuses: Abertay Dundee Univ, Anglia Poly Univ, Aston Univ, Bangor Univ, Belfast Univ, Birmingham Univ, Bournemouth Univ, Bradford Univ, Brighton Univ, Bristol UWE, Brunel Univ, Cardiff Inst, Cardiff Univ, Central England Univ, Central Lancashire Univ, Coventry Univ, Cranfield Univ (p/g only), Dartmouth, De Montfort Univ, Dundee Univ, East Anglia Univ, Edinburgh Univ, Essex Univ, Glamorgan Univ, Glasgow Caledonian Univ, Glasgow Univ, Greenwich Univ, Heriot-Watt Univ, Hertfordshire Univ, Huddersfield Univ, Humberside Univ, Imperial Coll, Keele Univ, Kent Univ, Lancaster Univ, Leeds Metro Univ, Leeds Univ, Leicester Univ, Liverpool John Moores Univ, Liverpool Univ, Loughborough Univ, Manchester Metro Univ, Middlesex Univ, Napier Univ, Newport Coll, North East Wales Inst, North London Univ, Northumbria Univ, Nottingham Trent Univ, Nottingham Univ, Open Univ, Oxford Brookes Univ, Paisley Univ, Plymouth Univ, Portsmouth Univ, Queen Mary & Westfield, Reading Univ, Robert Gordon Univ, Royal Holloway, St Andrews Univ, Salford Univ, Sheffield Hallam Univ, Sheffield Univ, Southampton Inst, Southampton Univ, Staffordshire Univ, Sussex Univ, Swansea Inst, Swansea Univ, Teesside Univ, Ulster Univ, UMIST, Warwick Univ, Wolverhampton Univ, York Univ.

EMBROIDERY
Possible prospectuses: Glasgow Sch Art, Manchester Metro Univ, Ulster Univ.

EMBRYOLOGY
See: Developmental biology; medicine.

ENERGY ENGINEERING
Possible prospectuses: City Univ, Cranfield Univ (p/g only), Glamorgan Univ, Glasgow Caledonian Univ, Heriot-Watt Univ, Imperial Coll, Leeds Univ, Middlesex Univ, Napier Univ, Robert Gordon Univ, South Bank Univ, Strathclyde Univ.

ENERGY STUDIES
Possible prospectuses: Brighton Univ, Brunel Univ, Coventry Univ, Cranfield Univ (p/g only), Glamorgan Univ, Glasgow Caledonian Univ, Heriot-Watt Univ, Leeds Univ, Middlesex Univ, Nene Coll, South Bank Univ, Southampton Inst.

ENGINEERING (GENERAL)
Possible prospectuses: Aberdeen Univ, Abertay Dundee Univ, Anglia Poly Univ, Bournemouth Univ, Bradford & Ilkley, Brighton Univ, Bristol UWE, Brunel Univ, Camborne Sch Mines, Cambridge Univ, Cardiff Inst, Cardiff Univ, Central England Univ, City Univ, Coventry Univ, Cranfield Univ (p/g only), Dartmouth, De Montfort Univ, Durham Univ, East London Univ, Edinburgh Univ, Exeter Univ, Glamorgan Univ, Glasgow Caledonian Univ, Greenwich Univ, Heriot-Watt Univ, Hertfordshire Univ, Hull Univ, Humberside Univ, Imperial Coll, Lancaster Univ, Leeds Metro Univ, Leicester Univ, Liverpool John Moores Univ, Liverpool Univ, Loughborough Univ, Luton Univ, Manchester Metro Univ, Middlesex Univ, Napier Univ, Newcastle Univ, North East Wales Inst, Nottingham Trent Univ, Oxford Brookes Univ, Oxford Univ, Paisley Univ, Portsmouth Univ, Queen Mary & Westfield, Reading Univ, Robert Gordon Univ, Salford Univ, Sheffield Hallam Univ, Shrivenham, Silsoe Coll, South Bank Univ, Southampton Inst, Southampton Univ, Staffordshire Univ, Sunderland Univ, Surrey Univ, Sussex Univ, Ulster Univ, UMIST, Warwick Univ, Westminster Univ, Wolverhampton Univ.
See also: Electrical engineering; mechanical engineering.

ENGINEERING MATHEMATICS
Possible prospectuses: Aberdeen Univ, Bristol Univ, Brunel Univ, Coventry Univ, Cranfield Univ (p/g only), Dartmouth, Glasgow Caledonian Univ, Heriot-Watt Univ, Imperial Coll, Leeds Univ, Loughborough Univ, Middlesex Univ, Napier Univ, Nottingham Univ, Open Univ, Queen Mary & Westfield.
See also: Mathematics.

ENGLISH
Possible prospectuses: Aberdeen Univ, Aberystwyth Univ, Anglia Poly Univ, Bangor Univ, Bath Coll, Belfast Univ, Birkbeck, Birmingham Univ, Bretton Hall, Bristol Univ, Bristol UWE, Buckingham Univ, Cambridge Univ, Canterbury Christ Church Coll, Cardiff Univ, Central England Univ, Central Lancashire Univ, Cheltenham & Gloucester Coll, Chester Univ Coll, Chichester Univ Coll, Colchester Inst, De Montfort Univ, Derby Univ, Dundee Univ, Durham Univ, East Anglia Univ, Edge Hill Univ Coll, Edinburgh Univ, Essex Univ, Exeter Univ, Glamorgan Univ, Glasgow Univ, Goldsmiths Coll, Hertfordshire Univ, Homerton Coll, Huddersfield Univ, Hull Univ, Keele Univ, Kent Univ, King Alfred's Coll, King's Coll London, Kingston Univ, Lampeter Univ, Lancaster Univ, Leeds Univ, Leicester Univ, Liverpool Hope Univ Coll, Liverpool John Moores Univ, Liverpool Univ, Loughborough Univ, LSU Southampton, Luton Univ, Manchester Metro Univ, Manchester Univ, Middlesex Univ, National Extension Coll, Nene Coll, Newcastle Univ, Newport Coll, North East Wales Inst, North London Univ, Northumbria Univ, Nottingham Trent Univ, Nottingham Univ, Open Univ, Oxford Brookes Univ, Oxford Univ, Plymouth Univ, Portsmouth Univ, Queen Mary & Westfield, Reading Univ, Ripon & York St John, Roehampton Inst, Royal Holloway, St Andrews Univ, St Mark & St John, S Martin's Univ Coll, St Mary's Univ Coll, Salford Univ,

Sheffield Hallam Univ, Sheffield Univ, South Bank Univ, Southampton Univ, Staffordshire Univ, Stirling Univ, Strathclyde Univ, Sunderland Univ, Sussex Univ, Swansea Inst, Swansea Univ, Teesside Univ, Thames Valley Univ, Trinity & All Saints, Trinity Coll Carmarthen, Ulster Univ, University Coll London, Warwick Univ, Westminster Coll, Westminster Univ, Wolverhampton Univ, Worcester Coll, York Univ.

ENGLISH AS A FOREIGN LANGUAGE
Possible prospectuses: Buckingham Univ, Chichester Univ Coll, East Anglia Univ, Glamorgan Univ, Hertfordshire Univ, Hull Univ, Humberside Univ, Liverpool John Moores Univ, Middlesex Univ, Stirling Univ, Thames Valley Univ, Wolverhampton Univ.

ENTOMOLOGY
See: Biology; zoology.

ENVIRONMENTAL ARCHAEOLOGY
Possible prospectuses: Bradford Univ, Edinburgh Univ, Inst Archaeology, Lampeter Univ, Luton Univ, Nene Coll, Sheffield Univ, Trinity Coll Carmarthen.

ENVIRONMENTAL BIOLOGY
Possible prospectuses: Abertay Dundee Univ, Aberystwyth Univ, Anglia Poly Univ, Bangor Univ, Bath Coll, Belfast Univ, Birmingham Univ, Colchester Inst, Essex Univ, Greenwich Univ, Hull Univ, Imperial Coll, Leicester Univ, Liverpool Univ, Manchester Univ, Middlesex Univ, Napier Univ, Nene Coll, Newcastle Univ, North East Wales Inst, Nottingham Trent Univ, Oxford Brookes Univ, Paisley Univ, Reading Univ, Salford Univ, South Bank Univ, Staffordshire Univ, Sunderland Univ, Swansea Univ, Wye Coll.
See also: Biology; environmental science.

ENVIRONMENTAL CHEMISTRY
Possible prospectuses: Aberdeen Univ, Abertay Dundee Univ, Anglia Poly Univ, Bangor Univ, Belfast Univ, Birmingham Univ, Bristol Univ, Brunel Univ, Camborne Sch Mines, Coventry Univ, East Anglia Univ, Edinburgh Univ, Essex Univ, Glasgow Caledonian Univ, Glasgow Univ, Greenwich Univ, Hertfordshire Univ, Lancaster Univ, Leeds Univ, Liverpool John Moores Univ, Northumbria Univ, Plymouth Univ, Portsmouth Univ, Reading Univ, Salford Univ, Sheffield Hallam Univ, Staffordshire Univ, Stirling Univ, Surrey Univ, Swansea Univ, UMIST, Warwick Univ, York Univ.
See also: Chemistry; environmental science.

ENVIRONMENTAL ENGINEERING
Possible prospectuses: Abertay Dundee Univ, Bath Univ, Bradford Univ, Brighton Univ, Brunel Univ, Cardiff Inst, Cardiff Univ, Central England Univ, Coventry Univ, Edinburgh Univ, Exeter Univ, Glamorgan Univ, Glasgow Caledonian Univ, Harper Adams, Heriot-Watt Univ, Hertfordshire Univ, Imperial Coll, Kent Univ, Kingston Univ, Lancaster Univ, Leeds Univ, Liverpool John Moores Univ, Liverpool Univ, Loughborough Univ, Luton Univ, Middlesex Univ, Newcastle Univ, Northumbria Univ, Nottingham Univ, Paisley Univ, Portsmouth Univ, Salford Univ, Sheffield Hallam Univ, Sheffield Univ, Silsoe Coll, Southampton Univ, Staffordshire Univ, Strathclyde Univ, Sunderland Univ, Surrey Univ, Ulster Univ, UMIST, Univ Coll London.

ENVIRONMENTAL HEALTH
Possible prospectuses: Bristol UWE, Cardiff Inst, Edinburgh Univ, Greenwich Univ, King's Coll London, Leeds Metro Univ, Luton Univ, Manchester Metro Univ, Middlesex Univ, Nottingham Trent Univ, Open Univ, Salford Univ, South Bank Univ, Strathclyde Univ, Trinity Coll Carmarthen, Ulster Univ.

ENVIRONMENTAL SCIENCE
Possible prospectuses: Aberdeen Univ, Abertay Dundee Univ, Aberystwyth Univ, Anglia Poly Univ, Aston Univ, Bangor Univ, Bath Coll, Belfast Univ, Birkbeck, Birmingham Univ, Bournemouth Univ, Bradford Univ, Brighton Univ, Bristol UWE, Brunel Univ, Camborne Sch Mines, Canterbury Christ Church Coll, Chester Univ Coll, Chichester Univ Coll, Colchester Inst, Coventry Univ, De Montfort Univ, Dundee Univ, Durham Univ, East Anglia Univ, East London Univ, Edge Hill Univ Coll, Edinburgh Univ, Essex Univ, Exeter Univ, Farnborough Coll, Glamorgan Univ, Glasgow Caledonian Univ, Glasgow Univ, Greenwich Univ, Heriot-Watt Univ, Hertfordshire Univ, Huddersfield Univ, Hull Univ, King's Coll London, Kingston Univ, Lancaster Univ, Leeds Univ, Liverpool John Moores Univ, Liverpool Univ, London Guildhall Univ, Loughborough Univ, Luton Univ, Manchester Metro Univ, Manchester Univ, Middlesex Univ, Napier Univ, Nene Coll, Newcastle Univ, North East Wales Inst, North London Univ, Northumbria Univ, Nottingham Univ, Open Univ, Oxford Brookes Univ, Paisley Univ, Plymouth Univ, Portsmouth Univ, Queen Mary & Westfield, Reading Univ, Ripon & York St John, Robert Gordon Univ, Roehampton Inst, Royal Holloway, St Andrews Univ, St Mary's Univ Coll, Salford Univ, Scottish Agricultural Coll, Sheffield Hallam Univ, Sheffield Univ, South Bank Univ, Southampton Inst, Southampton Univ, Staffordshire Univ, Stirling Univ, Strathclyde Univ, Sussex Univ, Ulster Univ, UMIST, Warwick Univ, Welsh Inst Rural Studies, Westminster Univ, Wolverhampton Univ, Worcester Coll, Writtle Coll, Wye Coll, York Univ.

ENVIRONMENTAL STUDIES
Possible prospectuses: Aberdeen Univ, Abertay Dundee Univ, Anglia Poly Univ, Bangor Univ, Birkbeck, Bolton Inst, Bradford Univ, Bretton Hall, Bristol UWE, Brunel Univ, Cardiff Univ, Central Lancashire Univ, Cheltenham & Gloucester Coll, De Montfort Univ, Derby Univ, Dundee Univ, Durham Univ, East Anglia Univ, East London Univ, Edinburgh Coll Art, Exeter Univ, Farnborough Coll, Glamorgan Univ, Greenwich Univ, Harper Adams, Hertfordshire Univ, Keele Univ, Lampeter Univ, Leeds Univ, Lincoln Univ, Liverpool Hope Univ Coll, London Guildhall Univ, Luton Univ, Manchester Metro Univ, Manchester Univ, Middlesex Univ, Newport Coll, North East Wales Inst, North London Univ, Nottingham Trent Univ, Open Univ, Portsmouth Univ, Reading Univ, Ripon & York St John, Roehampton Inst, Royal Agricultural Coll, Royal Holloway, St Mary's Univ Coll, Salford Univ, Scottish Agricultural Coll, Sheffield Univ, Silsoe Coll, South Bank Univ, Southampton Inst, Southampton Univ, Staffordshire Univ, Stirling Univ, Sunderland Univ, Sussex Univ, Thames Valley Univ, Trinity Coll Carmarthen, UMIST, Univ Coll London, Welsh Inst Rural Studies, Westminster Univ, Wolverhampton Univ, Wye Coll, York Univ.
See also: Environmental archaeology; environmental science.

EQUINE STUDIES
Possible prospectuses: Aberystwyth Univ, Bristol Univ, Central Lancashire Univ, Cheltenham & Gloucester Coll, Coventry Univ, De Montfort Univ, Humberside Univ, Myerscough Coll, Royal Agricultural Coll, Welsh Inst Rural Studies, Writtle Coll, Wye Coll.

ERGONOMICS
Possible prospectuses: Aston Univ, Glasgow Caledonian Univ, Loughborough Univ.

ESTATE MANAGEMENT
Possible prospectuses: Aberdeen Univ, Anglia Poly Univ, Bristol UWE, Central England Univ, City Univ, De Montfort Univ, Glamorgan Univ, Glasgow Caledonian Univ, Greenwich Univ, Harper Adams, Heriot-Watt Univ, Kingston Univ, Liverpool John Moores Univ, Luton Univ, Napier Univ, Newcastle Univ, North East Wales Inst, Northumbria Univ, Nottingham Trent Univ, Oxford Brookes Univ, Plymouth Univ, Portsmouth Univ, Reading Univ, Royal Agricultural Coll, Sheffield Hallam Univ, Silsoe Coll, South Bank Univ, Staffordshire Univ, Ulster Univ, Westminster Univ, Writtle Coll, Wye Coll.
See also: Urban estate management.

ETHICS
See: Philosophy; theology.

EUROPEAN BUSINESS STUDIES
Possible prospectuses: Aberdeen Univ, Abertay Dundee Univ, Anglia Poly Univ, Aston Univ, Bangor Univ, Birmingham Univ, Bournemouth Univ, Brighton Univ, Bristol UWE, Buckinghamshire Coll, Cardiff Inst, Central England Univ, Central Lancashire Univ, Coventry Univ, De Montfort Univ, Derby Univ, East Anglia Univ, European Business Sch, Farnborough Coll, Glamorgan Univ, Glasgow Caledonian Univ, Greenwich Univ, Heriot-Watt Univ, Hull Univ, Humberside Univ, Kent Univ, Kingston Univ, Lancaster Univ, Leeds Metro Univ, Liverpool John Moores Univ, London Guildhall Univ, Loughborough Univ, Luton Univ, Manchester Metro Univ, Middlesex Univ, Nene Coll, Newcastle Univ, North East Wales Inst, North London Univ, Northumbria Univ, Nottingham Trent Univ, Oxford Brookes Univ, Paisley Univ, Plymouth Univ, Portsmouth Univ, Reading Univ, Robert Gordon Univ, Royal Agricultural Coll, Salford Univ, Scottish Agricultural Coll, Sheffield Hallam Univ, South Bank Univ, Staffordshire Univ, Strathclyde Univ, Surrey Univ, Swansea Inst, Swansea Univ, Ulster Univ, Westminster Univ, Wolverhampton Univ, Wye Coll.

EUROPEAN STUDIES
Possible prospectuses: Aberdeen Univ, Abertay Dundee Univ, Aberystwyth Univ, Anglia Poly Univ, Aston Univ, Bath Univ, Belfast Univ, Bolton Inst, Bradford & Ilkley, Bradford Univ, Bristol Univ, Bristol UWE, Brunel Univ, Buckingham Univ, Cardiff Univ, Central Lancashire Univ, Coventry Univ, Derby Univ, Dundee Univ, Durham Univ, East Anglia Univ, East London Univ, Edge Hill Univ Coll, Edinburgh Univ, Essex Univ, Exeter Univ, Goldsmiths Coll, Hertfordshire Univ, Hull Univ, Keele Univ, Kent Univ, King's Coll London, Leeds Univ, Leicester Univ, Liverpool Hope Univ Coll, Liverpool John Moores Univ, Loughborough Univ, LSE, LSU Southampton, Manchester Metro Univ, Manchester Univ, Middlesex Univ, Newcastle Univ, Newport Coll, North East Wales Inst, North London Univ, Northumbria Univ, Nottingham Trent Univ, Nottingham Univ, Open Univ, Plymouth Univ, Portsmouth Univ, Queen Mary & Westfield, Reading Univ, Ripon & York St John, Royal Holloway, St Andrews Univ, Salford Univ, Sheffield Hallam Univ, South Bank Univ, Southampton Inst, Southampton Univ, SSEES, Staffordshire Univ, Stirling Univ, Strathclyde Univ, Sunderland Univ, Surrey Univ, Sussex Univ, Thames Valley Univ, Ulster Univ, Univ Coll London, Warwick Univ, Westminster Univ, Wolverhampton Univ.
See also: Iberian studies; Scandinavian studies.

EXPLORATION
Possible prospectuses: Camborne Sch Mines, Cardiff Univ, Univ Coll London.
See also: Mining; geology.

F

FASHION
Possible prospectuses: Bradford & Ilkley, Bretton Hall, Brighton Univ, Bristol UWE, Central England Univ, Central Lancashire Univ, Central Saint Martins, Cheltenham & Gloucester Coll, De Montfort Univ, Derby Univ, East London Univ, Edinburgh Coll Art, Glasgow Caledonian Univ, Heriot-Watt Univ, Huddersfield Univ, Kent Inst, Kingston Univ, Liverpool John Moores Univ, London Coll Fashion, Manchester Metro Univ, Middlesex Univ, Nene Coll, Newport Coll, Northumbria Univ, Nottingham Trent Univ, Ravensbourne Coll, Salford Univ, Scottish Coll Textiles, Southampton Inst, Surrey Inst, Ulster Univ, Westminster Univ, Winchester Sch Art.
See also: Textiles.

FERMENTATION
See: Biochemistry; brewing; microbiology.

FILM MUSIC
Possible prospectuses: London Int Film Sch, National Film Sch (p/g only).

FILM STUDIES
Possible prospectuses: Aberdeen Univ, Aberystwyth Univ, Bolton Inst, Bournemouth Univ, Brunel Univ, Buckinghamshire Coll, Canterbury Christ Church Coll, Cardiff Univ, Central Lancashire Univ, Central Saint Martins, Derby Univ, Dundee Univ, East Anglia Univ, Edinburgh Coll Art, Glasgow Univ, Goldsmiths Coll, Kent Inst, Kent Univ, King Alfred's Coll, Lincoln Univ, Liverpool John Moores Univ, London Coll Printing, London Int Film Sch, Manchester Metro Univ, Middlesex Univ, Napier Univ, National Film Sch (p/g only), Newcastle Univ, Newport Coll, North London Univ, Northumbria Univ, Portsmouth Univ, Reading Univ, Ripon & York St John, Roehampton Inst, Royal Coll Art (p/g only), Royal Holloway, Sheffield Hallam Univ, Southampton Inst, Staffordshire Univ, Stirling Univ, Surrey Inst, Swansea Inst, Warrington Univ Coll, Warwick Univ, Westminster Univ, Wolverhampton Univ.
See also: Media studies; video.

FINANCE
Possible prospectuses: Abertay Dundee Univ, Aberystwyth Univ, Aston Univ, Bangor Univ, Belfast Univ, Birmingham Univ, Bournemouth Univ, Bradford Univ, Brighton Univ, Bristol UWE, Brunel Univ, Buckingham Univ, Cardiff Univ, Central England Univ, Central Lancashire Univ, Cheltenham & Gloucester Coll, City Univ, Coventry Univ, Dundee Univ, East Anglia Univ, East London Univ, Essex Univ, European Business Sch, Glamorgan Univ, Glasgow Caledonian Univ, Greenwich Univ, Heriot-Watt Univ, Huddersfield Univ, Humberside Univ, Keele Univ, Kingston Univ, Lancaster Univ, Leeds Metro Univ, Leeds Univ, Liverpool John Moores Univ, London Guildhall Univ, Loughborough Univ, LSE, Luton Univ, Manchester Metro Univ, Manchester Univ, Middlesex Univ, Nene Coll, North London Univ, Northumbria Univ, Nottingham Trent Univ, Paisley Univ, Plymouth Univ, Portsmouth Univ, Reading Univ, Robert Gordon Univ, Royal Agricultural Coll, Salford Univ, Sheffield Hallam Univ, South Bank Univ, Staffordshire Univ, Stirling Univ, Strathclyde Univ, Swansea Inst, Teesside Univ, Thames Valley Univ, Ulster Univ, Warwick Univ, Westminster Univ, Wolverhampton Univ, York Univ.
See also: Banking, financial services.

FINANCIAL SERVICES
Possible prospectuses: Abertay Dundee Univ, Bournemouth Univ, Bristol UWE, Buckingham Univ, Central England Univ, Central Lancashire Univ, Cheltenham & Gloucester Coll, Derby Univ, Glasgow Caledonian Univ, London Guildhall Univ, Manchester Metro Univ, Napier Univ, Northumbria Univ, Nottingham Trent Univ, Portsmouth Univ, Sheffield Hallam Univ.
See also: Banking.

FINE ART
See: Art; painting; photography; printmaking; sculpture.

FINE ARTS
See: Art history.

FINNISH STUDIES
Possible prospectuses: SSEES.
See also: Scandinavian studies.

FIRE SAFETY ENGINEERING
Possible prospectuses: Central Lancashire Univ, Leeds Univ, South Bank Univ.

FISHERIES MANAGEMENT
See: Wildlife management.

FISHERY SCIENCE
Possible prospectuses: Aberdeen Univ, Heriot-Watt Univ, Plymouth Univ, Scottish Agricultural Coll, Stirling Univ.

FOOD SCIENCE
Possible prospectuses: Bath Coll, Belfast Univ, Bournemouth Univ, Bradford Univ, Cardiff Inst, Chester Univ Coll, Dundee Univ, Glasgow Caledonian Univ, Harper Adams, Huddersfield Univ, Leeds Univ, Lincoln Univ, Liverpool John Moores Univ, Loughborough Univ, Manchester Metro Univ, North London Univ, Northumbria Univ, Nottingham Univ, Oxford Brookes Univ, Plymouth Univ, Queen Margaret Coll, Reading Univ, Robert Gordon Univ, Scottish Agricultural Coll, Sheffield Hallam Univ, Silsoe Coll, South Bank Univ, Strathclyde Univ, Surrey Univ, Teesside Univ, Trinity & All Saints, Ulster Univ.
See also: Nutrition.

FOOTWEAR
Possible prospectuses: De Montfort Univ.
See also: Textiles.

FORENSIC SCIENCE
See: Chemistry.

FORESTRY
Possible prospectuses: Aberdeen Univ, Bangor Univ, Bournemouth Univ, Central Lancashire Univ, De Montfort Univ, Edinburgh Univ, Myerscough Coll, Royal Agricultural Coll.

FRENCH
Possible prospectuses: Aberdeen Univ, Aberystwyth Univ, Anglia Poly Univ, Aston Univ, Bangor Univ, Bath Univ, Belfast Univ, Birkbeck, Birmingham Univ, Bolton Inst, Bradford Univ, Brighton Univ, Bristol Univ, Bristol UWE, British Institute in Paris, Brunel Univ,

Buckingham Univ, Cambridge Univ, Cardiff Univ, Central Lancashire Univ, Cheltenham & Gloucester Coll, Coventry Univ, De Montfort Univ, Derby Univ, Durham Univ, East Anglia Univ, East London Univ, Edge Hill Univ Coll, Edinburgh Univ, Essex Univ, European Business Sch, Exeter Univ, Glasgow Caledonian Univ, Glasgow Univ, Goldsmiths Coll, Heriot-Watt Univ, Huddersfield Univ, Hull Univ, Humberside Univ, Keele Univ, Kent Univ, King's Coll London, Kingston Univ, Lampeter Univ, Lancaster Univ, Leeds Univ, Leicester Univ, Lincoln Univ, Liverpool Hope Univ Coll, Liverpool John Moores Univ, Liverpool Univ, London Guildhall Univ, Loughborough Univ, LSU Southampton, Luton Univ, Manchester Metro Univ, Manchester Univ, Middlesex Univ, Napier Univ, National Extension Coll, Nene Coll, Newcastle Univ, North London Univ, Northumbria Univ, Nottingham Trent Univ, Nottingham Univ, Oxford Brookes Univ, Oxford Univ, Plymouth Univ, Portsmouth Univ, Queen Mary & Westfield, Reading Univ, Ripon & York St John, Robert Gordon Univ, Roehampton Inst, Royal Holloway, St Andrews Univ, Salford Univ, Sheffield Hallam Univ, Sheffield Univ, South Bank Univ, Southampton Univ, SSEES, Staffordshire Univ, Stirling Univ, Strathclyde Univ, Sunderland Univ, Surrey Univ, Sussex Univ, Swansea Univ, Thames Valley Univ, Trinity & All Saints, Ulster Univ, UMIST, Univ Coll London, Warwick Univ, Westminster Coll, Westminster Univ, Wolverhampton Univ, York Univ.

FRESHWATER BIOLOGY
See: Marine biology.

FUEL SCIENCE
See: Chemistry; energy studies.

FURNITURE DESIGN
Possible prospectuses: Bournemouth Univ, Buckinghamshire Coll, Central England Univ, Central Saint Martins, De Montfort Univ, Edinburgh Coll Art, Heriot-Watt Univ, Kent Inst, Kingston Univ, Leeds Metro Univ, London Guildhall Univ, Loughborough Coll, Middlesex Univ, Newport Coll, Northumbria Univ, Nottingham Trent Univ, Ravensbourne Coll, Royal Coll Art (p/g only), Ulster Univ, Wolverhampton Univ.

FURNITURE PRODUCTION
Possible prospectuses: Buckinghamshire Coll, Edinburgh Coll Art, London Guildhall Univ, Newport Coll.

G

GENDER STUDIES
Possible prospectuses: Anglia Poly Univ, Bolton Inst, Bradford Univ, Bristol UWE, Buckinghamshire Coll, Edinburgh Univ, Hull Univ, North London Univ, Roehampton Inst, Staffordshire Univ, Sunderland Univ.
See also: Women's studies.

GENETICS
Possible prospectuses: Aberdeen Univ, Aberystwyth Univ, Belfast Univ, Birmingham Univ, Cambridge Univ, Cardiff Univ, Dundee Univ, East Anglia Univ, Edinburgh Univ, Essex Univ, Glasgow Univ, Leeds Univ, Leicester Univ, Liverpool Univ, Manchester Univ, Newcastle Univ, Nottingham Univ, Queen Mary & Westfield, St Andrews Univ, Sheffield Univ, Sussex Univ,

Swansea Univ, Univ Coll London, York Univ.
See also: Biology.

GEOCHEMISTRY
Possible prospectuses: Anglia Poly Univ, Glasgow Univ, Greenwich Univ, Imperial Coll, Manchester Univ, Reading Univ, St Andrews Univ.
See also: Geology; chemistry.

GEOGRAPHY
Possible prospectuses: Aberdeen Univ, Aberystwyth Univ, Anglia Poly Univ, Bangor Univ, Bath Coll, Belfast Univ, Birkbeck, Birmingham Univ, Bradford Univ, Brighton Univ, Bristol Univ, Bristol UWE, Brunel Univ, Cambridge Univ, Canterbury Christ Church Coll, Central Lancashire Univ, Cheltenham & Gloucester Coll, Chester Univ Coll, Chichester Univ Coll, Coventry Univ, Derby Univ, Dundee Univ, Durham Univ, Edge Hill Univ Coll, Edinburgh Univ, Exeter Univ, Glamorgan Univ, Glasgow Caledonian Univ, Glasgow Univ, Greenwich Univ, Homerton Coll, Huddersfield Univ, Hull Univ, Keele Univ, Kent Univ, King Alfred's Coll, King's Coll London, Kingston Univ, Lampeter Univ, Lancaster Univ, Leeds Univ, Leicester Univ, Liverpool Hope Univ Coll, Liverpool John Moores Univ, Liverpool Univ, London Guildhall Univ, Loughborough Univ, LSE, LSU Southampton, Luton Univ, Manchester Metro Univ, Manchester Univ, Middlesex Univ, National Extension Coll, Nene Coll, Newcastle Univ, Newport Coll, North London Univ, Northumbria Univ, Nottingham Trent Univ, Nottingham Univ, Open Univ, Oxford Brookes Univ, Oxford Univ, Plymouth Univ, Portsmouth Univ, Queen Mary & Westfield, Reading Univ, Ripon & York St John, Roehampton Inst, Royal Holloway, St Andrews Univ, St Mark & St John, S Martin's Univ Coll, St Mary's Univ Coll, Salford Univ, Sheffield Hallam Univ, Sheffield Univ, Silsoe Coll, SOAS, South Bank Univ, Southampton Univ, Staffordshire Univ, Strathclyde Univ, Sunderland Univ, Sussex Univ, Swansea Univ, Trinity & All Saints, Ulster Univ, Univ Coll London, Westminster Coll, Westminster Univ, Wolverhampton Univ, Worcester Coll.

GEOLOGY
Possible prospectuses: Aberdeen Univ, Aberystwyth Univ, Anglia Poly Univ, Belfast Univ, Birkbeck, Birmingham Univ, Bristol Univ, Brunel Univ, Camborne Sch Mines, Cambridge Univ, Cardiff Univ, Cheltenham & Gloucester Coll, Derby Univ, Durham Univ, East Anglia Univ, Edinburgh Univ, Exeter Univ, Glamorgan Univ, Glasgow Univ, Greenwich Univ, Hertfordshire Univ, Imperial Coll, Keele Univ, Kingston Univ, Leeds Univ, Leicester Univ, Liverpool John Moores Univ, Liverpool Univ, Luton Univ, Manchester Univ, Middlesex Univ, Open Univ, Oxford Brookes Univ, Oxford Univ, Plymouth Univ, Portsmouth Univ, Queen Mary & Westfield, Royal Holloway, St Andrews Univ, Sheffield Hallam Univ, Sheffield Univ, Southampton Univ, Staffordshire Univ, Sunderland Univ, Univ Coll London.

GEOPHYSICS
Possible prospectuses: Birmingham Univ, Camborne Sch Mines, Durham Univ, East Anglia Univ, Edinburgh Univ, Glasgow Univ, Greenwich Univ, Imperial Coll, Lancaster Univ, Leeds Univ, Leicester Univ, Liverpool Univ, Open Univ, Southampton Univ, Univ Coll London.
See also: Geology; physics.

GERMAN
Possible prospectuses: Aberdeen Univ, Aberystwyth Univ, Anglia Poly Univ, Aston Univ, Bangor Univ, Bath Univ, Belfast Univ, Birkbeck, Birmingham Univ, Bolton Inst, Bradford Univ, Brighton Univ, Bristol Univ, Bristol UWE, Brunel Univ, Cambridge Univ, Cardiff Univ, Central Lancashire Univ, Coventry Univ, De Montfort Univ, Derby Univ, Durham Univ, East

Anglia Univ, East London Univ, Edinburgh Univ, Essex Univ, European Business Sch, Exeter Univ, Glasgow Caledonian Univ, Glasgow Univ, Goldsmiths Coll, Heriot-Watt Univ, Huddersfield Univ, Hull Univ, Humberside Univ, Keele Univ, Kent Univ, King's Coll London, Kingston Univ, Lampeter Univ, Lancaster Univ, Leeds Univ, Leicester Univ, Lincoln Univ, Liverpool John Moores Univ, Liverpool Univ, London Guildhall Univ, Loughborough Univ, LSU Southampton, Luton Univ, Manchester Metro Univ, Manchester Univ, Middlesex Univ, Napier Univ, National Extension Coll, Nene Coll, Newcastle Univ, North London Univ, Northumbria Univ, Nottingham Trent Univ, Nottingham Univ, Open Univ, Oxford Brookes Univ, Oxford Univ, Plymouth Univ, Portsmouth Univ, Queen Mary & Westfield, Reading Univ, Robert Gordon Univ, Royal Holloway, St Andrews Univ, Salford Univ, Sheffield Hallam Univ, Sheffield Univ, South Bank Univ, Southampton Univ, SSEES, Staffordshire Univ, Stirling Univ, Strathclyde Univ, Sunderland Univ, Surrey Univ, Sussex Univ, Swansea Univ, Thames Valley Univ, Ulster Univ, UMIST, Univ Coll London, Warwick Univ, Westminster Univ, Wolverhampton Univ, York Univ.

GLASS
Possible prospectuses: Buckinghamshire Coll, Central England Univ, Edinburgh Coll Art, Heriot-Watt Univ, Manchester Metro Univ, North East Wales Inst, Royal Coll Art (p/g only), Sheffield Univ, Staffordshire Univ, Sunderland Univ, Surrey Inst, Swansea Inst, Wolverhampton Univ.
See also: Three-dimensional design.

GOLDSMITHING
See: Silversmithing.

GOVERNMENT
See: Politics.

GRAPHIC DESIGN
Possible prospectuses: Anglia Poly Univ, Bath Coll, Bournemouth Univ, Bradford & Ilkley, Bretton Hall, Brighton Univ, Bristol UWE, Buckinghamshire Coll, Camberwell Coll, Cardiff Inst, Central England Univ, Central Lancashire Univ, Central Saint Martins, Cheltenham & Gloucester Coll, Colchester Inst, Coventry Univ, De Montfort Univ, Derby Univ, Dundee Univ, East London Univ, Edinburgh Coll Art, Falmouth Coll Arts, Glasgow Sch Art, Goldsmiths Coll, Heriot-Watt Univ, Hertfordshire Univ, Humberside Univ, Kent Inst, Kingston Univ, Leeds Metro Univ, Liverpool John Moores Univ, London Coll Printing, Loughborough Coll, Luton Univ, Manchester Metro Univ, Middlesex Univ, Nene Coll, Newport Coll, North East Wales Inst, Northumbria Univ, Norwich Sch Art, Nottingham Trent Univ, Portsmouth Univ, Ravensbourne Coll, Reading Univ, Robert Gordon Univ, Royal Coll Art (p/g only), Salford Univ, Southampton Inst, Staffordshire Univ, Surrey Inst, Swansea Inst, Teesside Univ, Ulster Univ, West Herts Coll, Westminster Univ, Wolverhampton Univ.

GREEK, ANCIENT/CLASSICAL
Possible prospectuses: Belfast Univ, Birmingham Univ, Bristol Univ, Cambridge Univ, Durham Univ, Edinburgh Univ, Exeter Univ, Glasgow Univ, Kent Univ, King's Coll London, Lampeter Univ, Leeds Univ, Manchester Univ, Newcastle Univ, Nottingham Univ, Oxford Univ, Reading Univ, Royal Holloway, St Andrews Univ, Swansea Univ, Univ Coll London.
See also: Classics; classical studies.

GREEK, MODERN
Possible prospectuses: Birmingham Univ, Cambridge Univ, Edinburgh Univ, King's Coll London, Oxford Univ.

GUJARATI
Possible prospectuses: SOAS.
See also: Asian studies.

H

HARBOURS
See: Civil engineering.

HAUSA
Possible prospectuses: SOAS.
See also: African studies.

HEALTH
Possible prospectuses: Aberdeen Univ, Anglia Poly Univ, Bangor Univ, Bath Coll, Bournemouth Univ, Bradford & Ilkley, Bradford Univ, Bristol UWE, Brunel Univ, Central England Univ, Central Lancashire Univ, Chester Univ Coll, Chichester Univ Coll, City Univ, Coventry Univ, De Montfort Univ, Derby Univ, Dundee Univ, Durham Univ, East London Univ, Glasgow Caledonian Univ, Greenwich Univ, Huddersfield Univ, Hull Univ, Leeds Metro Univ, Lincoln Univ, Liverpool Hope Univ Coll, Liverpool John Moores Univ, Luton Univ, Manchester Metro Univ, Middlesex Univ, Napier Univ, Nene Coll, Newport Coll, North East Wales Inst, North London Univ, Northumbria Univ, Open Univ, Oxford Brookes Univ, Paisley Univ, Queen Margaret Coll, Ripon & York St John, Robert Gordon Univ, Roehampton Inst, S Martin's Univ Coll, Salford Univ, Sheffield Hallam Univ, South Bank Univ, Staffordshire Univ, Sunderland Univ, Teesside Univ, Trinity Coll Carmarthen, Wolverhampton Univ, Worcester Coll.

HEBREW
Possible prospectuses: Aberdeen Univ, Cambridge Univ, Cardiff Univ, Edinburgh Univ, Glasgow Univ, Jews' Coll, Liverpool Univ, London Bible, Oxford Univ, St Andrews Univ, SOAS, Univ Coll London.
See also: Near East studies; religious studies.

HELLENISTIC STUDIES
See: Classics; Greek, ancient/classical.

HIGHWAY/TRAFFIC
See: Civil engineering; town planning; transport studies.

HINDI
Possible prospectuses: Cambridge Univ, SOAS, York Univ.
See also: Asian studies.

HINDUSTANI
See: Asian studies.

HISPANIC STUDIES
Possible prospectuses: Aberdeen Univ, Belfast Univ, Birkbeck, Birmingham Univ, Bristol Univ, Cardiff Univ, De Montfort Univ, Edinburgh Univ, Glasgow Univ, Hull Univ, King's Coll London, Leeds Univ, Liverpool Univ, Manchester Univ, North London Univ, Nottingham Univ, Portsmouth Univ, Queen Mary & Westfield, Salford Univ, Sheffield Univ, Southampton Univ, Stirling Univ, Swansea Univ, Thames Valley Univ, Trinity & All Saints, Wolverhampton Univ.
See also: Iberian studies; Portuguese; Latin American studies; Spanish.

HISTORY
Possible prospectuses: Aberdeen Univ, Aberystwyth Univ, Anglia Poly Univ, Bangor Univ, Bath Coll, Belfast Univ, Birkbeck, Birmingham Univ, Bolton Inst, Bradford Univ, Bristol Univ, Bristol UWE, Brunel Univ, Buckingham Univ, Cambridge Univ, Canterbury Christ Church Coll, Cardiff Univ, Central Lancashire Univ, Cheltenham & Gloucester Coll, Chester Univ Coll, Chichester Univ Coll, Colchester Inst, Coventry Univ, De Montfort Univ, Derby Univ, Dundee Univ, Durham Univ, East Anglia Univ, East London Univ, Edge Hill Univ Coll, Edinburgh Univ, Essex Univ, Exeter Univ, Glamorgan Univ, Glasgow Caledonian Univ, Glasgow Univ, Goldsmiths Coll, Greenwich Univ, Hertfordshire Univ, Homerton Coll, Huddersfield Univ, Hull Univ, Keele Univ, Kent Univ, King Alfred's Coll, King's Coll London, Kingston Univ, Lampeter Univ, Lancaster Univ, Leeds Univ, Leicester Univ, Liverpool Hope Univ Coll, Liverpool John Moores Univ, Liverpool Univ, London Guildhall Univ, LSE, LSU Southampton, Luton Univ, Manchester Metro Univ, Manchester Univ, Middlesex Univ, Nene Coll, Newcastle Univ, Newport Coll, North East Wales Inst, North London Univ, Northumbria Univ, Nottingham Trent Univ, Nottingham Univ, Open Univ, Oxford Brookes Univ, Oxford Univ, Plymouth Univ, Portsmouth Univ, Queen Mary & Westfield, Reading Univ, Ripon & York St John, Roehampton Inst, Royal Holloway, St Andrews Univ, St Mark & St John, S Martin's Univ Coll, St Mary's Univ Coll, Salford Univ, Sheffield Hallam Univ, Sheffield Univ, SOAS, Southampton Univ, SSEES, Staffordshire Univ, Stirling Univ, Strathclyde Univ, Sunderland Univ, Sussex Univ, Swansea Univ, Teesside Univ, Thames Valley Univ, Trinity & All Saints, Trinity Coll Carmarthen, Ulster Univ, Univ Coll London, Warwick Univ, Westminster Univ, Wolverhampton Univ, Worcester Coll, York Univ.
See also: Economic history; social history.

HISTORY OF ART
See: Art history.

HISTORY/PHILOSOPHY OF SCIENCE
Possible prospectuses: Aberdeen Univ, Belfast Univ, Cambridge Univ, Kent Univ, King's Coll London, Kingston Univ, Lancaster Univ, Leeds Univ, Leicester Univ, Manchester Univ, Open Univ, St Andrews Univ, Univ Coll London.

HORTICULTURE
Possible prospectuses: Central Lancashire Univ, De Montfort Univ, Greenwich Univ, Hertfordshire Univ, Nottingham Univ, Reading Univ, Scottish Agricultural Coll, Strathclyde Univ, Worcester Coll, Writtle Coll, Wye Coll.

HOTEL AND CATERING MANAGEMENT
Possible prospectuses: Bournemouth Univ, Brighton Univ, Buckingham Univ, Cardiff Inst, Central England Univ, Central Lancashire Univ, Cheltenham & Gloucester Coll, Colchester Inst, Dundee Univ, Glasgow Caledonian Univ, Huddersfield Univ, Leeds Metro Univ, Manchester Metro Univ, Middlesex Univ, Napier Univ, North London Univ, Nottingham Trent Univ, Oxford Brookes Univ, Plymouth Univ, Portsmouth Univ, Queen Margaret Coll, Robert

Gordon Univ, Salford Univ, Sheffield Hallam Univ, South Bank Univ, Strathclyde Univ, Surrey Univ, Thames Valley Univ, Ulster Univ, Wolverhampton Univ.
See also: Catering.

HOUSING ADMINISTRATION
Possible prospectuses: Anglia Poly Univ, Bristol UWE, Cardiff Inst, Central England Univ, Edinburgh Coll Art, Heriot-Watt Univ, Luton Univ, Northumbria Univ, Salford Univ, Sheffield Hallam Univ, Stirling Univ, Ulster Univ, Westminster Univ.
See also: Urban estate management.

HUMAN BIOLOGY
Possible prospectuses: Aberdeen Univ, Aston Univ, Cambridge Univ, East London Univ, Hertfordshire Univ, King's Coll London, Kingston Univ, Leeds Metro Univ, Leeds Univ, Liverpool Hope Univ Coll, Liverpool Univ, Loughborough Univ, Luton Univ, Nene Coll, Nottingham Trent Univ, Oxford Brookes Univ, Plymouth Univ, Queen Mary & Westfield, Roehampton Inst, S Martin's Univ Coll, South Bank Univ, Wolverhampton Univ.
See also: Anatomy; physiology.

HUMAN COMMUNICATION
Possible prospectuses: Central England Univ, Central Sch Speech/Drama, Coventry Univ, De Montfort Univ, Exeter Univ, Glasgow Caledonian Univ, Lancaster Univ, Leicester Univ, Manchester Metro Univ, Manchester Univ, Queen Margaret Coll, Robert Gordon Univ, St Mark & St John, Sheffield Univ, Ulster Univ.
See also: Communication studies; psychology.

HUMAN MOVEMENT
See: Movement studies.

HUMAN RESOURCE MANAGEMENT
Possible prospectuses: Anglia Poly Univ, Aston Univ, Bolton Inst, Bradford & Ilkley, Bradford Univ, Cheltenham & Gloucester Coll, Glamorgan Univ, Keele Univ, Kent Univ, Liverpool John Moores Univ, London Guildhall Univ, Luton Univ, North London Univ, Northumbria Univ, Paisley Univ, Plymouth Univ, Robert Gordon Univ, Salford Univ, Scottish Coll Textiles, Southampton Inst, Staffordshire Univ, Stirling Univ, Strathclyde Univ, Sunderland Univ, Thames Valley Univ, Wolverhampton Univ.

HUMAN SCIENCES
Possible prospectuses: Bournemouth Univ, Bradford Univ, Brunel Univ, Durham Univ, Kingston Univ, Loughborough Univ, Nottingham Trent Univ, Nottingham Univ, Open Univ, Oxford Univ, Queen Margaret Coll, Queen Mary & Westfield, Roehampton Inst, Stirling Univ, Surrey Univ, Sussex Univ, Univ Coll London.
See also: Biosocial science.

HUMANITIES
Possible prospectuses: Belfast Univ, Birkbeck, Bolton Inst, Bradford Univ, Bretton Hall, Brighton Univ, Bristol UWE, Brunel Univ, Colchester Inst, De Montfort Univ, Derby Univ, Edge Hill Univ Coll, Edinburgh Univ, Exeter Univ, Glamorgan Univ, Glasgow Univ, Greenwich Univ, Hertfordshire Univ, Hull Univ, Kent Univ, Kingston Univ, Lancaster Univ, Lincoln Univ, Liverpool John Moores Univ, Luton Univ, Manchester Metro Univ, Newport Coll, North

London Univ, Northumbria Univ, Nottingham Trent Univ, Open Univ, Plymouth Univ, Roehampton Inst, St Andrews Univ, Staffordshire Univ, Stirling Univ, Sussex Univ, Swansea Inst, Teesside Univ, Thames Valley Univ, Trinity Coll Carmarthen, Ulster Univ, Wolverhampton Univ.

HUNGARIAN
Possible prospectuses: Cambridge Univ, SSEES, Westminster Univ.

HYDRAULIC ENGINEERING
See: Civil engineering.

I

IBERIAN STUDIES
Possible prospectuses: Leeds Univ, Manchester Univ, Portsmouth Univ, Southampton Univ, Univ Coll London.
See also: Hispanic studies; Portuguese; Spanish.

ICELANDIC
Possible prospectuses: Univ Coll London.
See also: Scandinavian studies.

ILLUSTRATION
See: Graphic design.

IMMUNOLOGY
Possible prospectuses: Aberdeen Univ, Bristol UWE, Brunel Univ, East London Univ, Edinburgh Univ, Glasgow Univ, Imperial Coll, King's Coll London, Kingston Univ, Plymouth Univ, Strathclyde Univ, Univ Coll London.
See also: Bacteriology; microbiology.

INDIAN STUDIES
See: Asian studies.

INDONESIAN STUDIES
Possible prospectuses: SOAS.

INDUSTRIAL DESIGN
Possible prospectuses: Bolton Inst, Bournemouth Univ, Brunel Univ, Cardiff Inst, Central England Univ, Central Lancashire Univ, Central Saint Martins, Colchester Inst, Coventry Univ, Cranfield Univ (p/g only), De Montfort Univ, Heriot-Watt Univ, Imperial Coll, Loughborough Univ, Luton Univ, Manchester Metro Univ, Napier Univ, Northumbria Univ, Open Univ, Ravensbourne Coll, Robert Gordon Univ, Royal Coll Art (p/g only), Scottish Coll Textiles, Sheffield Hallam Univ, South Bank Univ, Staffordshire Univ, Teesside Univ, Thames Valley Univ, Westminster Univ, Wolverhampton Univ.
See also: Three-dimensional design.

INDUSTRIAL ENGINEERING
Possible prospectuses: Bournemouth Univ, Bradford Univ, Cranfield Univ (p/g only), Exeter Univ, Heriot-Watt Univ, Imperial Coll, Middlesex Univ, Napier Univ, Nottingham Trent Univ, Royal Coll Art (p/g only), South Bank Univ, Staffordshire Univ, Surrey Univ, Teesside Univ, Westminster Univ, Wolverhampton Univ.

INDUSTRIAL RELATIONS
Possible prospectuses: Brunel Univ, Cardiff Univ, Coventry Univ, Kent Univ, Lancaster Univ, Leeds Univ, LSE, Middlesex Univ, Scottish Coll Textiles, Southampton Univ, Stirling Univ.
See also: Business studies; economics; law; sociology.

INDUSTRIAL STUDIES
Possible prospectuses: Central England Univ, East London Univ, Leeds Univ, Loughborough Univ, Nene Coll, Nottingham Trent Univ, Nottingham Univ, Sheffield Hallam Univ.

INFORMATICS
Possible prospectuses: Brighton Univ, City Univ, Heriot-Watt Univ, Hertfordshire Univ, Lampeter Univ, Leeds Metro Univ, Manchester Univ, Plymouth Univ, Portsmouth Univ, Queen Mary & Westfield, Sheffield Hallam Univ, Teesside Univ, Ulster Univ.

INFORMATION DESIGN
See: Graphic design.

INFORMATION SCIENCE
Possible prospectuses: Aberystwyth Univ, Anglia Poly Univ, Belfast Univ, Bristol UWE, Coventry Univ, Cranfield Univ (p/g only), De Montfort Univ, Hull Univ, Humberside Univ, Imperial Coll, Luton Univ, Nene Coll, North London Univ, Open Univ, Paisley Univ, Portsmouth Univ, Queen Margaret Coll, Robert Gordon Univ, South Bank Univ, Staffordshire Univ, Strathclyde Univ, Teesside Univ, Thames Valley Univ, UMIST, Univ Coll London, Westminster Univ.

INFORMATION STUDIES
Possible prospectuses: Aberystwyth Univ, Belfast Univ, Bournemouth Univ, Brighton Univ, Brunel Univ, Central England Univ, East London Univ, Falmouth Coll Arts, Leeds Metro Univ, Liverpool Univ, London Coll Printing, Loughborough Univ, Luton Univ, Manchester Metro Univ, Nene Coll, North London Univ, Northumbria Univ, Queen Margaret Coll, Robert Gordon Univ, Scottish Coll Textiles, Sheffield Univ, Shrivenham, Southampton Inst, Thames Valley Univ, Ulster Univ, Univ Coll London, Westminster Univ.
See also: Library studies.

INFORMATION TECHNOLOGY
Possible prospectuses: Aberdeen Univ, Abertay Dundee Univ, Aberystwyth Univ, Anglia Poly Univ, Aston Univ, Belfast Univ, Bournemouth Univ, Bradford Univ, Brighton Univ, Bristol UWE, Brunel Univ, Buckinghamshire Coll, Canterbury Christ Church Coll, Cardiff Inst, Central England Univ, Central Lancashire Univ, Cheltenham & Gloucester Coll, Chester Univ Coll, City Univ, Coventry Univ, Cranfield Univ (p/g only), Dartmouth, De Montfort Univ, Derby Univ, East London Univ, Edge Hill Univ Coll, Edinburgh Univ, Essex Univ, European Business Sch, Exeter Univ, Glamorgan Univ, Glasgow Caledonian Univ, Goldsmiths Coll, Greenwich Univ, Heriot-Watt Univ, Huddersfield Univ, Humberside Univ, Imperial Coll, Kingston Univ, Lancaster Univ, Leeds Univ, Liverpool Hope Univ Coll, London Guildhall Univ, Loughborough Univ, Luton Univ, Manchester Metro Univ, Manchester Univ, Middlesex Univ, Napier Univ,

Newport Coll, North East Wales Inst, North London Univ, Northumbria Univ, Nottingham Trent Univ, Open Univ, Oxford Brookes Univ, Paisley Univ, Portsmouth Univ, Queen Margaret Coll, Reading Univ, Robert Gordon Univ, St Mark & St John, Salford Univ, Scottish Coll Textiles, Sheffield Hallam Univ, Sheffield Univ, Shrivenham, South Bank Univ, Southampton Inst, Staffordshire Univ, Strathclyde Univ, Sunderland Univ, Surrey Univ, Swansea Inst, Teesside Univ, Thames Valley Univ, Trinity Coll Carmarthen, UMIST, Warrington Univ Coll, Westminster Univ, Wolverhampton Univ, Worcester Coll, York Univ.

INSTRUMENTATION
Possible prospectuses: Anglia Poly Univ, Brunel Univ, Cranfield Univ (p/g only), Glasgow Caledonian Univ, Heriot-Watt Univ, Luton Univ, Manchester Metro Univ, Middlesex Univ, Newport Coll, Open Univ, Robert Gordon Univ, Sheffield Hallam Univ, Teesside Univ.

INSURANCE
See: Actuarial studies; business studies; financial services.

INTERIOR DESIGN
Possible prospectuses: Bournemouth Univ, Brighton Univ, Buckinghamshire Coll, Cardiff Inst, Central England Univ, Chelsea Coll Art, De Montfort Univ, Dundee Univ, Edinburgh Coll Art, Glasgow Caledonian Univ, Glasgow Coll Building, Glasgow Sch Art, Heriot-Watt Univ, Huddersfield Univ, Humberside Univ, Kent Inst, Kingston Univ, Leeds Metro Univ, London Guildhall Univ, Luton Univ, Manchester Metro Univ, Middlesex Univ, Napier Univ, North London Univ, Northumbria Univ, Nottingham Trent Univ, Ravensbourne Coll, Robert Gordon Univ, Royal Coll Art (p/g only), Salford Univ, Surrey Inst, Teesside Univ.

INTERNATIONAL BUSINESS
Possible prospectuses: Anglia Poly Univ, Aston Univ, Birmingham Univ, Bournemouth Univ, Bradford Univ, Brighton Univ, Bristol UWE, Buckinghamshire Coll, Central Lancashire Univ, Coventry Univ, European Business Sch, Greenwich Univ, Heriot-Watt Univ, Hertfordshire Univ, Humberside Univ, Lancaster Univ, Liverpool John Moores Univ, Luton Univ, Manchester Metro Univ, Newcastle Univ, North London Univ, Northumbria Univ, Paisley Univ, Plymouth Univ, Portsmouth Univ, Reading Univ, Royal Agricultural Coll, Sheffield Hallam Univ, South Bank Univ, Southampton Inst, Staffordshire Univ, Strathclyde Univ, Sunderland Univ, Surrey Univ, Teesside Univ, Ulster Univ, UMIST, Warwick Univ, Westminster Univ, Wolverhampton Univ.
See also: Business studies; European business studies.

INTERNATIONAL RELATIONS
Possible prospectuses: Aberdeen Univ, Aberystwyth Univ, Birmingham Univ, Bradford Univ, Coventry Univ, Hull Univ, Keele Univ, Kent Univ, Lancaster Univ, Lincoln Univ, London Guildhall Univ, LSE, Nottingham Trent Univ, Open Univ, Plymouth Univ, Reading Univ, St Andrews Univ, Scottish Coll Textiles, South Bank Univ, Southampton Univ, Staffordshire Univ, Surrey Univ, Sussex Univ, Swansea Univ, Thames Valley Univ, Ulster Univ, Warwick Univ, Westminster Univ.
See also: Politics; war studies.

INTERPRETING AND TRANSLATING
Possible prospectuses: British Institute in Paris, East Anglia Univ, Heriot-Watt Univ, Luton Univ, Salford Univ, Thames Valley Univ, Westminster Univ.

INVESTMENT
See: Business studies.

IRANIAN STUDIES
See: Near East studies.

IRISH STUDIES
Possible prospectuses: Aberystwyth Univ, Belfast Univ, Liverpool Univ, North London Univ, St Mary's Univ Coll, Ulster Univ.
See also: Celtic studies.

ISLAMIC STUDIES
Possible prospectuses: Durham Univ, Edinburgh Univ, Exeter Univ, Lampeter Univ, Leeds Univ, Oxford Univ, St Andrews Univ, SOAS.

ITALIAN
Possible prospectuses: Aberystwyth Univ, Anglia Poly Univ, Bath Univ, Belfast Univ, Birmingham Univ, Bristol Univ, Cambridge Univ, Cardiff Univ, Central Lancashire Univ, Coventry Univ, East London Univ, Edinburgh Univ, European Business Sch, Exeter Univ, Glasgow Univ, Hull Univ, Kent Univ, Lancaster Univ, Leeds Univ, Leicester Univ, Luton Univ, Manchester Metro Univ, Manchester Univ, National Extension Coll, Nene Coll, Oxford Brookes Univ, Oxford Univ, Plymouth Univ, Portsmouth Univ, Reading Univ, Royal Holloway, St Andrews Univ, Salford Univ, Sheffield Hallam Univ, Strathclyde Univ, Sussex Univ, Swansea Univ, Univ Coll London, Warwick Univ, Westminster Univ.

J

JAPANESE
Possible prospectuses: Cambridge Univ, Cardiff Univ, Central Lancashire Univ, Durham Univ, Edinburgh Univ, European Business Sch, King Alfred's Coll, Leeds Univ, Liverpool John Moores Univ, Luton Univ, Manchester Metro Univ, Newcastle Univ, Oxford Univ, Royal Holloway, Sheffield Hallam Univ, Sheffield Univ, SOAS, Stirling Univ, Sussex Univ, Ulster Univ, Westminster Univ.
See also: Asian studies; oriental studies.

JEWELLERY
Possible prospectuses: Buckinghamshire Coll, Central England Univ, Central Saint Martins, Dundee Univ, Edinburgh Coll Art, Glasgow Sch Art, Heriot-Watt Univ, Kent Inst, London Guildhall Univ, Loughborough Coll, Middlesex Univ, North East Wales Inst, Northumbria Univ, Robert Gordon Univ, Royal Coll Art (p/g only), Sheffield Hallam Univ, Ulster Univ.
See also: Silversmithing; three-dimensional design.

JEWISH STUDIES
Possible prospectuses: Jews' Coll, Oxford Univ, SOAS, SSEES, Univ Coll London.
See also: Hebrew.

JOURNALISM
Possible prospectuses: Bournemouth Univ, Cardiff Univ, Central Lancashire Univ, City Univ, Falmouth Coll Arts, Goldsmiths Coll, Liverpool John Moores Univ, London Coll Printing, London Coll Fashion, Luton Univ, Middlesex Univ, Napier Univ, Nottingham Trent Univ, Sheffield Univ, Southampton Inst, Surrey Inst, Teesside Univ, Warrington Univ Coll, Westminster Univ.
See also: Broadcasting; media studies.

JURISPRUDENCE
See: Law

L

LABOUR
See: Business studies; economics; industrial relations; law; politics; sociology.

LAND ADMINISTRATION
See: Estate management.

LAND ECONOMY
Possible prospectuses: Aberdeen Univ, Anglia Poly Univ, Bournemouth Univ, Cambridge Univ, East London Univ, Harper Adams, Luton Univ, Paisley Univ, Royal Agricultural Coll, Scottish Agricultural Coll, Sheffield Hallam Univ, Wye Coll.

LAND SURVEYING
See: Quantity surveying.

LANDSCAPE ARCHITECTURE
Possible prospectuses: Central England Univ, Cheltenham & Gloucester Coll, Edinburgh Coll Art, Greenwich Univ, Heriot-Watt Univ, Kingston Univ, Leeds Metro Univ, Manchester Metro Univ, Manchester Univ, Sheffield Univ, Southampton Inst.

LANDSCAPE STUDIES
Possible prospectuses: Edinburgh Coll Art, Heriot-Watt Univ, King Alfred's Coll, Manchester Metro Univ, Middlesex Univ, Plymouth Univ, Reading Univ, Sheffield Univ, Writtle Coll.
See also: Architecture; geography; horticulture.

LANGUAGES
See: individual languages (eg French) or regional studies (eg African studies).

LASER
See: Physics.

LATIN
Possible prospectuses: Belfast Univ, Birmingham Univ, Bristol Univ, Cambridge Univ, Durham Univ, Edinburgh Univ, Exeter Univ, Glasgow Univ, King's Coll London, Lampeter Univ, Leeds Univ, Manchester Univ, Newcastle Univ, Nottingham Univ, Oxford Univ, Reading Univ, Royal Holloway, St Andrews Univ, Swansea Univ, Univ Coll London, Warwick Univ.
See also: Classics; classical studies.

LATIN AMERICAN STUDIES
Possible prospectuses: Aberdeen Univ, Bristol Univ, Essex Univ, Goldsmiths Coll, King's Coll London, Leeds Univ, Liverpool Univ, Manchester Univ, Middlesex Univ, Newcastle Univ, North London Univ, Portsmouth Univ, St Andrews Univ, Southampton Univ, Swansea Univ, Univ Coll London, Warwick Univ.
See also: Hispanic studies; Iberian studies; Portuguese; Spanish.

LAW
Possible prospectuses: Aberdeen Univ, Abertay Dundee Univ, Aberystwyth Univ, Anglia Poly Univ, Aston Univ, Belfast Univ, Birkbeck, Birmingham Univ, Bournemouth Univ, Bradford & Ilkley, Bristol Univ, Bristol UWE, Brunel Univ, Buckingham Univ, Buckland Univ Coll, Cambridge Univ, Cardiff Univ, Central England Univ, Central Lancashire Univ, City Univ, Coventry Univ, De Montfort Univ, Derby Univ, Dundee Univ, Durham Univ, East Anglia Univ, East London Univ, Edinburgh Univ, Essex Univ, Exeter Univ, Glamorgan Univ, Glasgow Caledonian Univ, Glasgow Univ, Greenwich Univ, Hertfordshire Univ, Holborn Coll, Huddersfield Univ, Hull Univ, Keele Univ, Kent Univ, King's Coll London, Kingston Univ, Lancaster Univ, Leeds Metro Univ, Leeds Univ, Leicester Univ, Lincoln Univ, Liverpool John Moores Univ, Liverpool Univ, London Guildhall Univ, LSE, Luton Univ, Manchester Metro Univ, Manchester Univ, Middlesex Univ, Napier Univ, National Extension Coll, Nene Coll, Newcastle Univ, Newport Coll, North London Univ, Northumbria Univ, Nottingham Trent Univ, Nottingham Univ, Open Univ, Oxford Brookes Univ, Oxford Univ, Plymouth Univ, Queen Mary & Westfield, Reading Univ, Robert Gordon Univ, Sheffield Hallam Univ, Sheffield Univ, SOAS, South Bank Univ, Southampton Inst, Southampton Univ, Staffordshire Univ, Strathclyde Univ, Surrey Univ, Sussex Univ, Swansea Inst, Swansea Univ, Teesside Univ, Thames Valley Univ, Ulster Univ, Univ Coll London, Warwick Univ, Westminster Univ, Wolverhampton Univ.

LEATHER TECHNOLOGY
Possible prospectuses: City Univ, Nene Coll.

LEISURE STUDIES
Possible prospectuses: Anglia Poly Univ, Bangor Univ, Bolton Inst, Bournemouth Univ, Bradford & Ilkley, Brighton Univ, Brunel Univ, Buckinghamshire Coll, Canterbury Christ Church Coll, Cardiff Inst, Cheltenham & Gloucester Coll, Colchester Inst, Coventry Univ, Farnborough Coll, Glamorgan Univ, Glasgow Caledonian Univ, Glasgow Univ, Heriot-Watt Univ, Huddersfield Univ, Leeds Metro Univ, Luton Univ, Manchester Metro Univ, Manchester Univ, Moray House, Myerscough Coll, North London Univ, Portsmouth Univ, Ripon & York St John, Salford Univ, Scottish Agricultural Coll, Sheffield Hallam Univ, South Bank Univ, Southampton Inst, Staffordshire Univ, Swansea Inst, Thames Valley Univ, Ulster Univ, Warrington Univ Coll, Wolverhampton Univ, Writtle Coll.
See also: Recreation studies.

LEVANT
See: Archaeology.

LIBRARY STUDIES
Possible prospectuses: Aberystwyth Univ, Brighton Univ, Central England Univ, Leeds Metro Univ, Liverpool John Moores Univ, Loughborough Univ, Manchester Metro Univ, North London Univ, Northumbria Univ, Robert Gordon Univ, Thames Valley Univ.
See also: Information studies.

LIFE SCIENCE
See: Biology.

LINGUISTICS
Possible prospectuses: Bangor Univ, Birkbeck, Brighton Univ, Central Lancashire Univ, Durham Univ, East Anglia Univ, East London Univ, Edinburgh Univ, Essex Univ, Exeter Univ, Greenwich Univ, Hertfordshire Univ, Kent Univ, Lancaster Univ, Leeds Univ, Luton Univ, Manchester Univ, Newcastle Univ, Queen Mary & Westfield, Reading Univ, Ripon & York St John, St Mark & St John, Sheffield Univ, SOAS, Southampton Univ, Surrey Univ, Sussex Univ, Ulster Univ, UMIST, Univ Coll London, Westminster Univ, Wolverhampton Univ, York Univ.
See also: individual languages, eg French.

LITERATURE
See: individual languages, eg Chinese.

LOGIC
See: Mathematics; philosophy.

M

MALAY
Possible prospectuses: SOAS.
See also: South East Asian studies.

MANAGEMENT
Possible prospectuses: Aberdeen Univ, Abertay Dundee Univ, Aston Univ, Bangor Univ, Belfast Univ, Birkbeck, Birmingham Univ, Bournemouth Univ, Bradford & Ilkley, Bradford Univ, Brighton Univ, Bristol UWE, Brunel Univ, Buckinghamshire Coll, Buckland Univ Coll, Cambridge Univ, Cardiff Univ, Central England Univ, Central Lancashire Univ, Cheltenham & Gloucester Coll, City Univ, Coventry Univ, Cranfield Univ (p/g only), Derby Univ, East Anglia Univ, East London Univ, Edge Hill Univ Coll, European Business Sch, Glamorgan Univ, Glasgow Caledonian Univ, Glasgow Univ, Greenwich Univ, Heriot-Watt Univ, Hertfordshire Univ, Huddersfield Univ, Hull Univ, Humberside Univ, Keele Univ, Kent Univ, King's Coll London, Kingston Univ, Lampeter Univ, Lancaster Univ, Leeds Metro Univ, Leeds Univ, Lincoln Univ, Liverpool John Moores Univ, Liverpool Univ, London Business Sch (p/g only), London Guildhall Univ, Loughborough Univ, LSE, Luton Univ, Manchester Business Sch (p/g only), Manchester Metro Univ, Napier Univ, National Extension Coll, Nene Coll, Newcastle Univ, North East Wales Inst, North London Univ, Nottingham Trent Univ, Nottingham Univ, Oxford Brookes Univ, Oxford Univ, Paisley Univ, Plymouth Univ, Queen Margaret Coll, Reading Univ, Ripon & York St John, Robert Gordon Univ, Royal Agricultural Coll, Royal Holloway, St Andrews Univ, Salford Univ, Scottish Coll Textiles, Sheffield Hallam Univ, Sheffield Univ, Shrivenham, Silsoe Coll, South Bank Univ, Southampton Univ, Staffordshire Univ, Stirling Univ, Strathclyde Univ, Sunderland Univ, Sussex Univ, Swansea Univ, Teesside Univ, Thames Valley Univ, Trinity & All Saints, Ulster Univ, UMIST, Warwick Univ, Westminster Univ, Wolverhampton Univ, Writtle Coll, Wye Coll.
See also: Business studies; economics; estate management; European business studies; hotel and catering management; leisure studies; public administration; recreation studies.

MANUFACTURING ENGINEERING
Possible prospectuses: Aberdeen Univ, Anglia Poly Univ, Aston Univ, Bath Univ, Belfast Univ, Birmingham Univ, Bolton Inst, Bradford Univ, Brighton Univ, Bristol Univ, Bristol UWE, Brunel Univ, Cambridge Univ, Cardiff Inst, Cardiff Univ, Central England Univ, Central Lancashire Univ, Coventry Univ, Cranfield Univ (p/g only), Derby Univ, Dundee Univ, Durham Univ, East London Univ, Exeter Univ, Glamorgan Univ, Glasgow Caledonian Univ, Greenwich Univ, Heriot-Watt Univ, Hertfordshire Univ, Huddersfield Univ, Hull Univ, Humberside Univ, Imperial Coll, Kingston Univ, Leeds Metro Univ, Leeds Univ, Liverpool John Moores Univ, Liverpool Univ, Loughborough Univ, Luton Univ, Manchester Metro Univ, Middlesex Univ, Newcastle Univ, Newport Coll, North East Wales Inst, Northumbria Univ, Nottingham Trent Univ, Nottingham Univ, Paisley Univ, Plymouth Univ, Portsmouth Univ, Salford Univ, Sheffield Hallam Univ, South Bank Univ, Staffordshire Univ, Strathclyde Univ, Sunderland Univ, Teesside Univ, Ulster Univ, UMIST, Warwick Univ, Westminster Univ, Wolverhampton Univ.
See also: Production engineering.

MARINE ARCHITECTURE
Possible prospectuses: Heriot-Watt Univ, Newcastle Univ, Southampton Univ, Strathclyde Univ, Univ Coll London.
See also: Naval architecture; naval engineering.

MARINE BIOLOGY
Possible prospectuses: Aberdeen Univ, Aberystwyth Univ, Bangor Univ, Colchester Inst, Essex Univ, Heriot-Watt Univ, Hull Univ, Liverpool Univ, Newcastle Univ, Plymouth Univ, Portsmouth Univ, Queen Mary & Westfield, St Andrews Univ, Southampton Univ, Stirling Univ, Swansea Univ.
See also: Maritime studies.

MARINE ENGINEERING
Possible prospectuses: Cranfield Univ (p/g only), Dartmouth, Heriot-Watt Univ, Liverpool John Moores Univ, Liverpool Univ, Newcastle Univ, Surrey Univ.

MARITIME STUDIES
Possible prospectuses: Bangor Univ, Cardiff Univ, Dartmouth, Liverpool John Moores Univ, Plymouth Univ, Southampton Inst.

MARKETING
Possible prospectuses: Abertay Dundee Univ, Aberystwyth Univ, Aston Univ, Bolton Inst, Bournemouth Univ, Bradford & Ilkley, Bradford Univ, Buckinghamshire Coll, Canterbury Christ Church Coll, Central England Univ, Central Lancashire Univ, Cheltenham & Gloucester Coll, Coventry Univ, De Montfort Univ, Derby Univ, Dundee Univ, East London Univ, European Business Sch, Farnborough Coll, Glamorgan Univ, Glasgow Caledonian Univ, Greenwich Univ, Harper Adams, Huddersfield Univ, Humberside Univ, Lancaster Univ, Leeds Metro Univ, Liverpool John Moores Univ, London Coll Printing, London Guildhall Univ, Loughborough Univ, Luton Univ, Manchester Metro Univ, Middlesex Univ, Napier Univ, North London Univ, Northumbria Univ, Oxford Brookes Univ, Paisley Univ, Plymouth Univ, Queen Margaret Coll, Robert Gordon Univ, Roehampton Inst, Royal Agricultural Coll, Salford Univ, Scottish Coll Textiles, Silsoe Coll, South Bank Univ, Southampton Inst, Staffordshire Univ, Stirling Univ, Strathclyde Univ, Sunderland Univ, Teesside Univ, Thames Valley Univ, Ulster Univ, UMIST, Westminster Univ, Wolverhampton Univ, Writtle Coll.
See also: Business studies.

MATERIALS SCIENCE
Possible prospectuses: Aberdeen Univ, Abertay Dundee Univ, Bath Univ, Birmingham Univ, Brunel Univ, Cambridge Univ, Coventry Univ, Cranfield Univ (p/g only), Durham Univ, Greenwich Univ, Heriot-Watt Univ, Imperial Coll, Leeds Univ, Liverpool Univ, Loughborough Univ, Manchester Metro Univ, Manchester Univ, North East Wales Inst, North London Univ, Nottingham Univ, Open Univ, Oxford Univ, Queen Mary & Westfield, Robert Gordon Univ, Sheffield Hallam Univ, Sheffield Univ, Shrivenham, Strathclyde Univ, Surrey Univ, Swansea Univ, UMIST, Wolverhampton Univ.
See also: Chemistry; engineering; metallurgy.

MATERIALS TECHNOLOGY
Possible prospectuses: Aberdeen Univ, Abertay Dundee Univ, Birmingham Univ, Bradford Univ, Brunel Univ, Coventry Univ, Cranfield Univ (p/g only), Durham Univ, Heriot-Watt Univ, Imperial Coll, Leeds Univ, Loughborough Univ, Manchester Metro Univ, North East Wales Inst, Northumbria Univ, Nottingham Univ, Open Univ, Plymouth Univ, Robert Gordon Univ, Sheffield Hallam Univ, Sheffield Univ, Surrey Univ, Swansea Univ, UMIST, Wolverhampton Univ.

MATHEMATICS
Possible prospectuses: Aberdeen Univ, Abertay Dundee Univ, Aberystwyth Univ, Anglia Poly Univ, Aston Univ, Bangor Univ, Bath Univ, Belfast Univ, Birmingham Univ, Bolton Inst, Bradford Univ, Brighton Univ, Bristol Univ, Bristol UWE, Brunel Univ, Cambridge Univ, Canterbury Christ Church Coll, Cardiff Univ, Central Lancashire Univ, Chester Univ Coll, Chichester Univ Coll, City Univ, Coventry Univ, De Montfort Univ, Derby Univ, Dundee Univ, Durham Univ, East Anglia Univ, East London Univ, Edge Hill Univ Coll, Edinburgh Univ, Essex Univ, Exeter Univ, Glamorgan Univ, Glasgow Caledonian Univ, Glasgow Univ, Goldsmiths Coll, Greenwich Univ, Heriot-Watt Univ, Hertfordshire Univ, Homerton Coll, Hull Univ, Imperial Coll, Keele Univ, Kent Univ, King's Coll London, Kingston Univ, Lancaster Univ, Leeds Univ, Leicester Univ, Liverpool Hope Univ Coll, Liverpool John Moores Univ, Liverpool Univ, London Guildhall Univ, Loughborough Univ, LSE, LSU Southampton, Luton Univ, Manchester Metro Univ, Manchester Univ, Middlesex Univ, Napier Univ, Nene Coll, Newcastle Univ, North London Univ, Northumbria Univ, Nottingham Trent Univ, Nottingham Univ, Open Univ, Oxford Brookes Univ, Oxford Univ, Paisley Univ, Plymouth Univ, Portsmouth Univ, Queen Mary & Westfield, Reading Univ, Ripon & York St John, Robert Gordon Univ, Royal Holloway, St Andrews Univ, St Mark & St John, S Martin's Univ Coll, St Mary's Univ Coll, Salford Univ, Sheffield Hallam Univ, Sheffield Univ, Shrivenham, South Bank Univ, Southampton Univ, Staffordshire Univ, Stirling Univ, Strathclyde Univ, Sunderland Univ, Surrey Univ, Sussex Univ, Swansea Univ, Teesside Univ, Trinity & All Saints, Ulster Univ, UMIST, Univ Coll London, Warwick Univ, Westminster Univ, Wolverhampton Univ, York Univ.

MECHANICAL ENGINEERING
Possible prospectuses: Aberdeen Univ, Abertay Dundee Univ, Aston Univ, Bath Univ, Belfast Univ, Birmingham Univ, Bolton Inst, Bradford Univ, Brighton Univ, Bristol Univ, Bristol UWE, Brunel Univ, Cambridge Univ, Cardiff Inst, Cardiff Univ, Central England Univ, Central Lancashire Univ, City Univ, Coventry Univ, Cranfield Univ (p/g only), Dartmouth, De Montfort Univ, Derby Univ, Dundee Univ, Durham Univ, Edinburgh Univ, Exeter Univ, Glamorgan Univ, Glasgow Caledonian Univ, Glasgow Univ, Greenwich Univ, Heriot-Watt Univ, Hertfordshire Univ, Huddersfield Univ, Hull Univ, Humberside Univ, Imperial Coll, King's Coll London, Kingston Univ, Lancaster Univ, Leeds Univ, Leicester Univ, Liverpool John Moores Univ, Liverpool Univ, Loughborough Univ, Luton Univ, Manchester Metro Univ, Manchester Univ,

Middlesex Univ, Newcastle Univ, North East Wales Inst, Northumbria Univ, Nottingham Trent Univ, Nottingham Univ, Oxford Brookes Univ, Oxford Univ, Paisley Univ, Plymouth Univ, Portsmouth Univ, Queen Mary & Westfield, Reading Univ, Robert Gordon Univ, Salford Univ, Sheffield Hallam Univ, Sheffield Univ, Shrivenham, South Bank Univ, Southampton Univ, Staffordshire Univ, Strathclyde Univ, Sunderland Univ, Surrey Univ, Sussex Univ, Swansea Univ, Teesside Univ, Ulster Univ, UMIST, Univ Coll London, Warwick Univ, Westminster Univ.
See also: Engineering.

MEDIA AND PRODUCTION
See: Graphic design.

MEDIA STUDIES
Possible prospectuses: Birmingham Univ, Bournemouth Univ, Bradford Univ, Brighton Univ, Bristol UWE, Brunel Univ, Buckinghamshire Coll, Canterbury Christ Church Coll, Central England Univ, Central Lancashire Univ, Cheltenham & Gloucester Coll, Chichester Univ Coll, City Univ, Colchester Inst, De Montfort Univ, East Anglia Univ, East London Univ, Edge Hill Univ Coll, Exeter Univ, Falmouth Coll Arts, Farnborough Coll, Glamorgan Univ, Glasgow Caledonian Univ, Goldsmiths Coll, Greenwich Univ, Hertfordshire Univ, Huddersfield Univ, Kent Inst, King Alfred's Coll, Lincoln Univ, Liverpool John Moores Univ, London Coll Printing, London Guildhall Univ, Loughborough Univ, Luton Univ, Manchester Metro Univ, Middlesex Univ, Napier Univ, Newport Coll, Northumbria Univ, Nottingham Trent Univ, Paisley Univ, Plymouth Univ, Portsmouth Univ, Queen Margaret Coll, Roehampton Inst, Royal Holloway, St Mark & St John, Salford Univ, Sheffield Hallam Univ, Slade, South Bank Univ, Southampton Inst, Staffordshire Univ, Stirling Univ, Sunderland Univ, Surrey Inst, Sussex Univ, Swansea Inst, Teesside Univ, Thames Valley Univ, Trinity & All Saints, Ulster Univ, Warrington Univ Coll, Westminster Univ, Wolverhampton Univ.
See also: Broadcasting; communication studies; film studies.

MEDICAL LABORATORY SCIENCE
Possible prospectuses: Birmingham Univ, Bournemouth Univ, Bradford Univ, Bristol UWE, Cardiff Inst, Coventry Univ, De Montfort Univ, Leeds Metro Univ, Portsmouth Univ, Ulster Univ, Westminster Univ.

MEDICAL MICROBIOLOGY
Possible prospectuses: Newcastle Univ, Surrey Univ.
See also: Microbiology.

MEDICINAL CHEMISTRY
Possible prospectuses: Anglia Poly Univ, Aston Univ, Brunel Univ, Dundee Univ, East Anglia Univ, Essex Univ, Exeter Univ, Glasgow Univ, Greenwich Univ, Hertfordshire Univ, Huddersfield Univ, Hull Univ, Imperial Coll, Keele Univ, Kingston Univ, Leeds Univ, Leicester Univ, Loughborough Univ, Manchester Univ, Newcastle Univ, Portsmouth Univ, Salford Univ, Sussex Univ, Swansea Univ, UMIST, Univ Coll London, Warwick Univ.
See also: Chemistry; biomedical science; biochemistry.

MEDICINAL PHYSICS
Possible prospectuses: East Anglia Univ, Hull Univ, King's Coll London, Leicester Univ, Newcastle Univ, Nottingham Univ, Salford Univ, Surrey Univ, Univ Coll London.
See also: Physics.

MEDICINE
Possible prospectuses: Aberdeen Univ, Belfast Univ, Birmingham Univ, Bristol Univ, Cambridge Univ, Charing Cross & Westminster, Dundee Univ, Edinburgh Univ, Glasgow Univ, Imperial Coll, King's Coll London, King's Coll Sch of Medicine, Leeds Univ, Leicester Univ, Liverpool Univ, Manchester Univ, Newcastle Univ, Nottingham Univ, Oxford Univ, Queen Mary & Westfield, Royal Free, St Andrews Univ, St Bartholomew's & Royal London, St George's, St Mary's Hospital, Sheffield Univ, Southampton Univ, UMDS, Univ Coll London, Wales Coll Medicine.

MEDIEVAL STUDIES
Possible prospectuses: Birmingham Univ, Cardiff Univ, Durham Univ, Edinburgh Univ, Glasgow Univ, Lampeter Univ, Lancaster Univ, Manchester Univ, Oxford Univ, Queen Mary & Westfield, Reading Univ, St Andrews Univ, Sheffield Univ, Swansea Univ.
See also: History.

MEDITERRANEAN STUDIES
Possible prospectuses: Birmingham Univ, Bristol Univ.
See also: Archaeology.

MESOPOTAMIA
See: Archaeology.

METALLURGY
Possible prospectuses: Birmingham Univ, Brunel Univ, Camborne Sch Mines, Cranfield Univ (p/g only), Greenwich Univ, Imperial Coll, Leeds Univ, Liverpool Univ, Loughborough Univ, Manchester Univ, Oxford Univ, Sheffield Hallam Univ, Sheffield Univ, Strathclyde Univ, Surrey Univ, UMIST.
See also: Materials science.

METAPHYSICS
See: Philosophy.

METEOROLOGY
Possible prospectuses: Dartmouth, Edinburgh Univ, Reading Univ.
See also: Geography.

MICROBIOLOGY
Possible prospectuses: Aberdeen Univ, Abertay Dundee Univ, Aberystwyth Univ, Anglia Poly Univ, Belfast Univ, Birmingham Univ, Bradford Univ, Bristol Univ, Bristol UWE, Brunel Univ, Cambridge Univ, Cardiff Univ, Dundee Univ, East Anglia Univ, East London Univ, Edinburgh Univ, Glasgow Caledonian Univ, Glasgow Univ, Heriot-Watt Univ, Hertfordshire Univ, Huddersfield Univ, Imperial Coll, Kent Univ, King's Coll London, Leeds Univ, Leicester Univ, Liverpool John Moores Univ, Liverpool Univ, Manchester Metro Univ, Manchester Univ, Napier Univ, Newcastle Univ, North London Univ, Nottingham Trent Univ, Nottingham Univ, Paisley Univ, Plymouth Univ, Portsmouth Univ, Queen Mary & Westfield, Reading Univ, Royal Holloway, St Andrews Univ, Sheffield Univ, South Bank Univ, Staffordshire Univ, Strathclyde Univ, Sunderland Univ, Surrey Univ, UMIST, Univ Coll London, Warwick Univ, Westminster Univ, Wolverhampton Univ.
See also: Bacteriology; biochemistry; biology; genetics; medical microbiology; virology.

MICROELECTRONICS
Possible prospectuses: Aberdeen Univ, Abertay Dundee Univ, Anglia Poly Univ, Bolton Inst, Bournemouth Univ, Bradford Univ, Brunel Univ, Cardiff Univ, Derby Univ, Dundee Univ, Edinburgh Univ, Glasgow Caledonian Univ, Glasgow Univ, Heriot-Watt Univ, Imperial Coll, Kingston Univ, Liverpool Univ, Middlesex Univ, Newcastle Univ, Northumbria Univ, Nottingham Trent Univ, Open Univ, Oxford Brookes Univ, Paisley Univ, Robert Gordon Univ, Salford Univ, Swansea Inst, Swansea Univ, UMIST.
See also: Electronics; computer science.

MIDDLE EAST STUDIES
See: Near East studies; Asian studies.

MIDWIFERY
Possible prospectuses: Anglia Poly Univ, Bournemouth Univ, Bradford Univ, Bristol UWE, Canterbury Christ Church Coll, Central England Univ, Central Lancashire Univ, City Univ, Coventry Univ, De Montfort Univ, Derby Univ, East Anglia Univ, Edge Hill Univ Coll, Glamorgan Univ, Greenwich Univ, Hertfordshire Univ, Huddersfield Univ, King Alfred's Coll, King's Coll London, Leeds Metro Univ, Leeds Univ, Liverpool John Moores Univ, Luton Univ, Middlesex Univ, Napier Univ, North East Wales Inst, Northumbria Univ, Oxford Brookes Univ, Portsmouth Univ, Queen Margaret Coll, S Martin's Univ Coll, South Bank Univ, Southampton Univ, Stirling Univ, Surrey Univ, Teesside Univ, Thames Valley Univ, Wolverhampton Univ, York Univ.

MINERAL PROCESSING TECHNOLOGY
Possible prospectuses: Birmingham Univ, Camborne Sch Mines, Exeter Univ, Glamorgan Univ, Heriot-Watt Univ, Imperial Coll, Leeds Univ, Leicester Univ, Nottingham Univ.
See also: Geology; mining.

MINERALOGY
See: Geology.

MINING
Possible prospectuses: Camborne Sch Mines, Exeter Univ, Imperial Coll, Leeds Univ, Leicester Univ, Nottingham Univ.
See also: Exploration; geology.

MODERN LANGUAGES
See: individual languages (eg French) or regional studies (eg Scandinavian studies).

MOLECULAR BIOLOGY
Possible prospectuses: Aberdeen Univ, Abertay Dundee Univ, Anglia Poly Univ, Belfast Univ, Birkbeck, Birmingham Univ, Bradford Univ, Bristol Univ, Bristol UWE, Cambridge Univ, Cardiff Univ, Dundee Univ, Durham Univ, East Anglia Univ, Edinburgh Univ, Essex Univ, Glasgow Univ, Hertfordshire Univ, Huddersfield Univ, Hull Univ, Imperial Coll, Kent Univ, King's Coll London, Leeds Univ, Leicester Univ, Liverpool John Moores Univ, Liverpool Univ, Manchester Univ, Newcastle Univ, Nottingham Univ, Oxford Brookes Univ, Portsmouth Univ, Queen Mary & Westfield, Reading Univ, Royal Holloway, St Andrews Univ, Sheffield Univ, Southampton Univ, Stirling Univ, Surrey Univ, UMIST, Univ Coll London, York Univ.

MORAL PHILOSOPHY
See: Philosophy.

MOVEMENT STUDIES
Possible prospectuses: Brighton Univ, Bristol Old Vic, Cardiff Inst, Central Sch Speech/Drama, Greenwich Univ, Heriot-Watt Univ, King Alfred's Coll, Laban Centre, Leeds Metro Univ, Liverpool Univ, Moray House, Ripon & York St John.
See also: Dance; drama; physical education.

MUSIC
Possible prospectuses: Anglia Poly Univ, Bangor Univ, Bath Coll, Belfast Univ, Birmingham Conservatoire, Birmingham Univ, Bournemouth Univ, Bretton Hall, Brighton Univ, Bristol Univ, Brunel Univ, Cambridge Univ, Canterbury Christ Church Coll, Cardiff Univ, Central England Univ, Chichester Univ Coll, City Univ, Colchester Inst, Coventry Univ, Dartington Coll Arts, De Montfort Univ, Derby Univ, Durham Univ, East Anglia Univ, Edge Hill Univ Coll, Edinburgh Univ, Essex Univ, Exeter Univ, Glasgow Univ, Goldsmiths Coll, Guildhall, Homerton Coll, Huddersfield Univ, Hull Univ, Keele Univ, King Alfred's Coll, King's Coll London, Kingston Univ, Lancaster Univ, Leeds Univ, Liverpool Hope Univ Coll, Liverpool Univ, London Coll Music, Manchester Metro Univ, Manchester Univ, Middlesex Univ, Napier Univ, Nene Coll, Newcastle Univ, Northumbria Univ, Nottingham Trent Univ, Nottingham Univ, Open Univ, Oxford Brookes Univ, Oxford Univ, Reading Univ, Ripon & York St John, Roehampton Inst, Royal Academy Music, Royal Coll Music, Royal Holloway, Royal Northern Coll Music, Royal Scottish Academy, S Martin's Univ Coll, Salford Univ, Sheffield Univ, SOAS, Southampton Univ, Strathclyde Univ, Sunderland Univ, Surrey Univ, Sussex Univ, Thames Valley Univ, Trinity Coll Carmarthen, Trinity Coll Music, Ulster Univ, Welsh Coll Music, Westminster Univ, Wolverhampton Univ, York Univ.
See also: Film music; popular music.

MUSIC TECHNOLOGY
Possible prospectuses: Anglia Poly Univ, Bretton Hall, Buckinghamshire Coll, Edinburgh Univ, Glasgow Univ, Huddersfield Univ, Imperial Coll, Leeds Metro Univ, London Guildhall Univ, Rose Bruford Coll, Salford Univ, Surrey Univ, Welsh Coll Music, York Univ.

MYCOLOGY
See: Botany.

MYTHOLOGY
See: Anthropology; classics; psychology.

N

NAUTICAL STUDIES
See: Maritime studies.

NAVAL ARCHITECTURE
Possible prospectuses: Glasgow Univ, Newcastle Univ, Southampton Univ, Strathclyde Univ, Univ Coll London.
See also: Marine architecture; naval engineering.

NAVAL ENGINEERING
Possible prospectuses: Dartmouth, Glasgow Univ, Newcastle Univ, Univ Coll London.
See also: Marine engineering.

NAVY
Possible prospectuses: Dartmouth.

NEAR EAST STUDIES
Possible prospectuses: Cambridge Univ, Durham Univ, Manchester Univ, Oxford Univ, St Andrews Univ, SOAS.
See also: Asian studies.

NEUROBIOLOGY
See: Biology; physiology; psychology.

NEUROSCIENCE
Possible prospectuses: Aberdeen Univ, Cardiff Univ, Central Lancashire Univ, Edinburgh Univ, Glasgow Univ, Keele Univ, Kent Univ, Manchester Univ, Nottingham Univ, Sheffield Univ, Sussex Univ, University Coll London.

NORSE
See: Anglo Saxon.

NORWEGIAN
Possible prospectuses: East Anglia Univ, Edinburgh Univ, Hull Univ, University Coll London.

NUCLEAR SCIENCE
Possible prospectuses: Imperial Coll, Surrey Univ, Westminster Univ.

NUCLEAR TECHNOLOGY
Possible prospectuses: Imperial Coll.

NURSING
Possible prospectuses: Abertay Dundee Univ, Anglia Poly Univ, Bangor Univ, Birmingham Univ, Bournemouth Univ, Brighton Univ, Bristol UWE, Buckinghamshire Coll, Canterbury Christ Church Coll, Central England Univ, Chester Univ Coll, City Univ, Coventry Univ, De Montfort Univ, Derby Univ, East Anglia Univ, East London Univ, Edge Hill Univ Coll, Edinburgh Univ, Glamorgan Univ, Glasgow Caledonian Univ, Glasgow Univ, Greenwich Univ, Hertfordshire Univ, Hull Univ, King Alfred's Coll, King's Coll London, Kingston Univ, Leeds Metro Univ, Liverpool John Moores Univ, Liverpool Univ, Luton Univ, Manchester Metro Univ, Manchester Univ, Middlesex Univ, Napier Univ, Nene Coll, North East Wales Inst, Northumbria Univ, Nottingham Univ, Oxford Brookes Univ, Portsmouth Univ, Queen Margaret Coll, Robert Gordon Univ, St George's, S Martin's Univ Coll, Salford Univ, Sheffield Hallam Univ, South Bank Univ, Southampton Univ, Stirling Univ, Sunderland Univ, Surrey Univ, Swansea Inst, Swansea Univ, Thames Valley Univ, Ulster Univ, Wales Coll Medicine, Wolverhampton Univ.
See also: Midwifery.

NUTRITION
Possible prospectuses: Bradford Univ, Cardiff Inst, Central Lancashire Univ, Chester Univ Coll, Dundee Univ, Glasgow Caledonian Univ, Greenwich Univ, Huddersfield Univ, King's Coll

London, Leeds Metro Univ, Lincoln Univ, Liverpool John Moores Univ, Newcastle Univ, North London Univ, Nottingham Univ, Oxford Brookes Univ, Queen Margaret Coll, Robert Gordon Univ, South Bank Univ, Southampton Univ, Surrey Univ, Teesside Univ, Trinity & All Saints, Ulster Univ.

O

OCCUPATIONAL PSYCHOLOGY
See: Psychology.

OCCUPATIONAL THERAPY
Possible prospectuses: Brunel Univ, Canterbury Christ Church Coll, Colchester Inst, Coventry Univ, Derby Univ, East Anglia Univ, East London Univ, Exeter Univ, Glasgow Caledonian Univ, Liverpool Univ, Nene Coll, Northumbria Univ, Oxford Brookes Univ, Portsmouth Univ, Queen Margaret Coll, Ripon & York St John, Robert Gordon Univ, S Martin's Univ Coll, Salford Univ, Sheffield Hallam Univ, South Bank Univ, Southampton Univ, Teesside Univ, Ulster Univ, Wales Coll Medicine, Westminster Univ.

OCEANOGRAPHY
Possible prospectuses: Aberdeen Univ, Bangor Univ, Dartmouth, Liverpool Univ, Plymouth Univ, Southampton Univ.

OFFICE ORGANISATION
Possible prospectuses: Buckinghamshire Coll, Glasgow Caledonian Univ, Humberside Univ, Northumbria Univ, Thames Valley Univ.
See also: Business studies.

OFFSHORE ENGINEERING
Possible prospectuses: Cranfield Univ (p/g only), Glasgow Univ, Heriot-Watt Univ, Imperial Coll, Liverpool John Moores Univ, Liverpool Univ, Newcastle Univ, Robert Gordon Univ, Strathclyde Univ, Surrey Univ.

OPERATIONAL RESEARCH
Possible prospectuses: Aston Univ, Belfast Univ, Birmingham Univ, Brighton Univ, Brunel Univ, Cardiff Univ, Central Lancashire Univ, Coventry Univ, Dundee Univ, Essex Univ, Exeter Univ, Hertfordshire Univ, Lancaster Univ, Leeds Univ, Loughborough Univ, North London Univ, Nottingham Trent Univ, Paisley Univ, Royal Holloway, Salford Univ, Southampton Univ, Staffordshire Univ, Strathclyde Univ, Swansea Univ, Teesside Univ, UMIST, Warwick Univ, Westminster Univ.

OPTHALMIC OPTICS
Possible prospectuses: Anglia Poly Univ, Aston Univ, Bradford Univ, Cardiff Univ, City Univ, Glasgow Caledonian Univ, UMIST.

ORGANISATIONAL BEHAVIOUR
Possible prospectuses: Aston Univ, Bradford Univ, European Business Sch, Hull Univ, Luton Univ, Queen Margaret Coll, Teesside Univ, Thames Valley Univ.

ORGANISATIONAL STUDIES
Possible prospectuses: Aston Univ, Bradford & Ilkley, Central Lancashire Univ, Heriot-Watt Univ, Lancaster Univ, Queen Margaret Coll, Reading Univ, Scottish Coll Textiles, Thames Valley Univ, Ulster Univ.

ORIENTAL LANGUAGES
See: individual languages, eg Japanese.

ORIENTAL STUDIES
Possible prospectuses: Cambridge Univ, Edinburgh Univ, Oxford Univ, SOAS.
See: Asian studies; South East Asian studies.

ORNITHOLOGY
See: Zoology.

ORTHOPTICS
Possible prospectuses: Coventry Univ, East London Univ, Glasgow Caledonian Univ, Liverpool Univ, Sheffield Univ.

OSTEOPATHY
Possible prospectuses: British Sch Osteopathy, East London Univ, Manchester Metro Univ, Westminster Univ.

P

PACKAGING TECHNOLOGY
Possible prospectuses: Sheffield Hallam Univ, West Herts Coll.

PAINTING
Possible prospectuses: Anglia Poly Univ, Bath Coll, Bradford & Ilkley, Bretton Hall, Brighton Univ, Bristol UWE, Camberwell Coll, Canterbury Christ Church Coll, Central England Univ, Central Saint Martins, Chelsea Coll Art, Cheltenham & Gloucester Coll, Coventry Univ, De Montfort Univ, Dundee Univ, East London Univ, Edinburgh Coll Art, Falmouth Coll Arts, Glasgow Sch Art, Goldsmiths Coll, Heriot-Watt Univ, Humberside Univ, Kent Inst, Kingston Univ, Lancaster Univ, Liverpool Hope Univ Coll, Liverpool John Moores Univ, Loughborough Coll, Manchester Metro Univ, Middlesex Univ, Northumbria Univ, Norwich Sch Art, Nottingham Trent Univ, Portsmouth Univ, Reading Univ, Ripon & York St John, Robert Gordon Univ, Royal Academy Sch (p/g only), Royal Coll Art (p/g only), Sheffield Hallam Univ, Slade, Staffordshire Univ, Surrey Inst, Swansea Inst, Ulster Univ, Wimbledon Sch Art, Winchester Sch Art, Wolverhampton Univ.

PAMS (PROFESSIONS ALLIED TO MEDICINE)
See: individual subjects, eg podiatry.

PAPER SCIENCE
Possible prospectuses: UMIST.

PARASITOLOGY
Possible prospectuses: Aberdeen Univ, East London Univ, Glasgow Univ, Imperial Coll, King's Coll London.

PATHOLOGY
Possible prospectuses: Aberdeen Univ, Bradford Univ, Bristol Univ, Cambridge Univ, Edinburgh Univ, Glasgow Univ, Imperial Coll, Leeds Univ, Reading Univ, St Andrews Univ.

PEACE STUDIES
See: War studies.

PERFORMANCE ARTS
Possible prospectuses: ALRA, Birmingham Univ, Bretton Hall, Brighton Univ, Bristol Old Vic, Central Sch Speech/Drama, Chichester Univ Coll, Coventry Univ, Dartington Coll Arts, De Montfort Univ, Derby Univ, Exeter Univ, Glasgow Univ, Goldsmiths Coll, Hertfordshire Univ, Kent Univ, King Alfred's Coll, Laban Centre, Liverpool John Moores Univ, Loughborough Univ, Manchester Metro Univ, Middlesex Univ, Nene Coll, North London Univ, Northumbria Univ, Nottingham Trent Univ, Plymouth Univ, Queen Margaret Coll, RADA, Ripon & York St John, Rose Bruford Coll, Royal Northern Coll Music, S Martin's Univ Coll, St Mary's Univ Coll, Salford Univ, Sunderland Univ, Trinity Coll Carmarthen, Trinity Coll Music, Ulster Univ, Warrington Univ Coll, Welsh Coll Music/Drama.
See also: Dance; drama.

PERSIAN
Possible prospectuses: Cambridge Univ, Edinburgh Univ, Oxford Univ, SOAS.
See also: Near East studies.

PETROLEUM ENGINEERING
Possible prospectuses: Aberdeen Univ, Heriot-Watt Univ, Imperial Coll, Robert Gordon Univ, Strathclyde Univ.
See also: Energy studies.

PETROLOGY
See: Geology.

PHARMACOLOGY
Possible prospectuses: Aberdeen Univ, Aston Univ, Bath Univ, Bradford Univ, Bristol Univ, Bristol UWE, Cambridge Univ, Cardiff Univ, Central Lancashire Univ, Coventry Univ, Dundee Univ, East London Univ, Edinburgh Univ, Glasgow Univ, Greenwich Univ, Hertfordshire Univ, King's Coll London, Leeds Univ, Liverpool Univ, Luton Univ, Manchester Univ, North London Univ, Nottingham Univ, Portsmouth Univ, Queen Mary & Westfield, St Andrews Univ, Sch Pharmacy, Sheffield Univ, Southampton Univ, Strathclyde Univ, Sunderland Univ, University Coll London.
See also: Pharmacy.

PHARMACY
Possible prospectuses: Aston Univ, Bath Univ, Belfast Univ, Bradford Univ, Brighton Univ, Cardiff Univ, De Montfort Univ, King's Coll London, Kingston Univ, Liverpool John Moores Univ, Manchester Univ, Nottingham Univ, Portsmouth Univ, Robert Gordon Univ, Sch Pharmacy, Strathclyde Univ, Sunderland Univ.
See also: Pharmacology.

PHILOSOPHY

Possible prospectuses: Aberdeen Univ, Anglia Poly Univ, Belfast Univ, Birkbeck, Birmingham Univ, Bolton Inst, Bradford Univ, Bristol Univ, Brunel Univ, Cambridge Univ, Cardiff Univ, Central Lancashire Univ, City Univ, Dundee Univ, Durham Univ, East Anglia Univ, Edinburgh Univ, Essex Univ, Glamorgan Univ, Glasgow Univ, Greenwich Univ, Hertfordshire Univ, Heythrop Coll, Hull Univ, Jews' Coll, Keele Univ, Kent Univ, King Alfred's Coll, King's Coll London, Kingston Univ, Lampeter Univ, Lancaster Univ, Leeds Univ, Liverpool John Moores Univ, Liverpool Univ, London Bible, LSE, Manchester Metro Univ, Manchester Univ, Middlesex Univ, National Extension Coll, North London Univ, Nottingham Univ, Open Univ, Oxford Univ, Reading Univ, St Andrews Univ, St Mark & St John, Sheffield Univ, Southampton Univ, Staffordshire Univ, Stirling Univ, Sunderland Univ, Sussex Univ, Swansea Univ, Ulster Univ, University Coll London, Warwick Univ, Wolverhampton Univ, York Univ.

PHILOSOPHY OF SCIENCE

See: History/philosophy of science.

PHONETICS

See: Linguistics.

PHOTOGRAPHY

Possible prospectuses: Bradford & Ilkley, Brighton Univ, Central Saint Martins, Cheltenham & Gloucester Coll, Derby Univ, Edinburgh Coll Art, Falmouth Coll Arts, Glasgow Sch Art, Goldsmiths Coll, Heriot-Watt Univ, Humberside Univ, Kent Inst, Kingston Univ, London Coll Printing, Manchester Metro Univ, Middlesex Univ, Napier Univ, Newport Coll, Northumbria Univ, Nottingham Trent Univ, Plymouth Univ, Royal Coll Art (p/g only), Sheffield Hallam Univ, Slade, Staffordshire Univ, Sunderland Univ, Surrey Inst, Swansea Inst, Teesside Univ, Thames Valley Univ, Westminster Univ, Wolverhampton Univ.

PHYSICAL EDUCATION

Possible prospectuses: Bangor Univ, Birmingham Univ, Brighton Univ, Canterbury Christ Church Coll, Cardiff Inst, Cheltenham & Gloucester Coll, Chester Univ Coll, Chichester Univ Coll, De Montfort Univ, Edge Hill Univ Coll, Exeter Univ, Goldsmiths Coll, Greenwich Univ, Heriot-Watt Univ, King Alfred's Coll, Lancaster Univ, Leeds Metro Univ, Leeds Univ, Liverpool Hope Univ Coll, Liverpool John Moores Univ, Loughborough Univ, Manchester Metro Univ, Moray House, Newport Coll, Nottingham Trent Univ, Plymouth Univ, Reading Univ, Ripon & York St John, St Mark & St John, St Mary's Univ Coll, Sheffield Hallam Univ, Strathclyde Univ, Trinity & All Saints, Trinity Coll Carmarthen, Warwick Univ, Wolverhampton Univ, Worcester Coll.

See also: Sports studies.

PHYSICAL SCIENCE

See: individual sciences, eg chemistry.

PHYSICS

Possible prospectuses: Aberdeen Univ, Abertay Dundee Univ, Aberystwyth Univ, Anglia Poly Univ, Bath Univ, Belfast Univ, Birkbeck, Birmingham Univ, Brighton Univ, Bristol Univ, Bristol UWE, Brunel Univ, Cambridge Univ, Cardiff Univ, Central Lancashire Univ, Coventry Univ, De Montfort Univ, Derby Univ, Dundee Univ, Durham Univ, East Anglia Univ, Edinburgh Univ, Essex Univ, Exeter Univ, Glasgow Caledonian Univ, Glasgow Univ, Greenwich Univ, Heriot-Watt Univ, Hertfordshire Univ, Hull Univ, Imperial Coll, Keele Univ, Kent Univ, King's Coll London, Kingston Univ, Lancaster Univ, Leeds Univ, Leicester Univ, Liverpool John Moores

Univ, Liverpool Univ, Loughborough Univ, Manchester Metro Univ, Manchester Univ, Napier Univ, Newcastle Univ, North East Wales Inst, North London Univ, Northumbria Univ, Nottingham Trent Univ, Nottingham Univ, Open Univ, Oxford Univ, Paisley Univ, Portsmouth Univ, Queen Mary & Westfield, Reading Univ, Robert Gordon Univ, Royal Holloway, St Andrews Univ, Salford Univ, Sheffield Hallam Univ, Sheffield Univ, Shrivenham, Southampton Univ, Staffordshire Univ, Strathclyde Univ, Surrey Univ, Sussex Univ, Swansea Univ, UMIST, University Coll London, Warwick Univ, York Univ.

PHYSIOLOGY
Possible prospectuses: Aberdeen Univ, Belfast Univ, Birmingham Univ, Bristol Univ, Cambridge Univ, Cardiff Univ, Central Lancashire Univ, Dundee Univ, East London Univ, Edinburgh Univ, Glasgow Univ, Greenwich Univ, King's Coll London, Leeds Univ, Leicester Univ, Liverpool Univ, Loughborough Univ, Manchester Metro Univ, Manchester Univ, Newcastle Univ, Oxford Univ, Queen Mary & Westfield, Reading Univ, Royal Holloway, St Andrews Univ, Sheffield Univ, South Bank Univ, Southampton Univ, Sunderland Univ, University Coll London, Westminster Univ, York Univ.

PHYSIOTHERAPY
Possible prospectuses: Birmingham Univ, Bradford Univ, Brighton Univ, Bristol UWE, Brunel Univ, Coventry Univ, East Anglia Univ, East London Univ, Glasgow Caledonian Univ, Hertfordshire Univ, Huddersfield Univ, Keele Univ, King's Coll London, Leeds Metro Univ, Liverpool John Moores Univ, Liverpool Univ, Manchester Univ, Northumbria Univ, Nottingham Univ, Oxford Brookes Univ, Queen Margaret Coll, Robert Gordon Univ, Salford Univ, Sheffield Hallam Univ, Southampton Univ, Teesside Univ, Ulster Univ, Wales Coll Medicine.

PLANETARY PHYSICS
See: Astrophysics.

PLANT SCIENCE
See: Botany.

PLASTICS
See: Polymers.

PODIATRY
Possible prospectuses: Belfast Univ, Brighton Univ, Cardiff Inst, Central England Univ, Derby Univ, Glasgow Caledonian Univ, Huddersfield Univ, LSU Southampton, Nene Coll, Plymouth Univ, Queen Margaret Coll, Salford Univ, Sunderland Univ, University Coll London, Westminster Univ.

POLISH
Possible prospectuses: Cambridge Univ, Glasgow Univ, Sheffield Univ, Southampton Inst, SSEES.

POLITICAL ECONOMY
See: Economics.

POLITICS
Possible prospectuses: Aberdeen Univ, Aberystwyth Univ, Anglia Poly Univ, Bath Univ, Belfast Univ, Birkbeck, Birmingham Univ, Bradford Univ, Bristol Univ, Bristol UWE, Brunel

Univ, Buckingham Univ, Cambridge Univ, Cardiff Univ, Central England Univ, Central Lancashire Univ, Coventry Univ, De Montfort Univ, Dundee Univ, Durham Univ, East Anglia Univ, East London Univ, Edge Hill Univ Coll, Edinburgh Univ, Essex Univ, Exeter Univ, Glamorgan Univ, Glasgow Caledonian Univ, Glasgow Univ, Goldsmiths Coll, Greenwich Univ, Huddersfield Univ, Hull Univ, Keele Univ, Kent Univ, Kingston Univ, Lancaster Univ, Leeds Univ, Leicester Univ, Liverpool John Moores Univ, Liverpool Univ, London Guildhall Univ, Loughborough Univ, LSE, LSU Southampton, Luton Univ, Manchester Metro Univ, Manchester Univ, Middlesex Univ, Nene Coll, Newcastle Univ, North London Univ, Northumbria Univ, Nottingham Trent Univ, Nottingham Univ, Open Univ, Oxford Brookes Univ, Oxford Univ, Plymouth Univ, Portsmouth Univ, Queen Mary & Westfield, Reading Univ, Royal Holloway, Salford Univ, Sheffield Hallam Univ, Sheffield Univ, SOAS, South Bank Univ, Southampton Univ, Staffordshire Univ, Stirling Univ, Strathclyde Univ, Sunderland Univ, Sussex Univ, Swansea Univ, Teesside Univ, Thames Valley Univ, Ulster Univ, Warwick Univ, Westminster Univ, Wolverhampton Univ, York Univ.

POLLUTION
Possible prospectuses: Bradford Univ, Cranfield Univ (p/g only), Glamorgan Univ, Luton Univ, South Bank Univ.
See also: Ecology; environmental science; environmental studies.

POLYMERS
Possible prospectuses: Aberdeen Univ, Birmingham Univ, Brunel Univ, Coventry Univ, Cranfield Univ (p/g only), Heriot-Watt Univ, Imperial Coll, Lancaster Univ, Loughborough Univ, Manchester Metro Univ, Manchester Univ, Napier Univ, North London Univ, Queen Mary & Westfield, Scottish Coll Textiles, Sheffield Univ, Sussex Univ, UMIST.
See also: Chemistry; materials science.

POPULAR MUSIC
Possible prospectuses: Anglia Poly Univ, Bretton Hall, Dartington Coll Arts, Derby Univ, Liverpool Univ, Salford Univ, Thames Valley Univ, Westminster Univ, Wolverhampton Univ.
See also: Film music; music.

PORTUGUESE
Possible prospectuses: Birmingham Univ, Cambridge Univ, Cardiff Univ, Edinburgh Univ, Essex Univ, Glasgow Univ, King's Coll London, Leeds Univ, Liverpool Univ, Manchester Univ, Newcastle Univ, Nottingham Univ, Oxford Univ, Portsmouth Univ, Salford Univ, Sheffield Univ, Southampton Univ.
See also: Hispanic studies; Iberian studies; Latin American studies.

PRINTING AND TYPOGRAPHY
Possible prospectuses: Camberwell Coll, Kent Inst, Liverpool Hope Univ Coll, London Coll Printing, Manchester Metro Univ, Napier Univ, Reading Univ, Swansea Inst, West Herts Coll.

PRINTMAKING
Possible prospectuses: Anglia Poly Univ, Bradford & Ilkley, Bretton Hall, Brighton Univ, Bristol UWE, Camberwell Coll, Central Lancashire Univ, Central Saint Martins, Chelsea Coll Art, Cheltenham & Gloucester Coll, Derby Univ, Dundee Univ, Edinburgh Coll Art, Falmouth Coll Arts, Glasgow Sch Art, Goldsmiths Coll, Heriot-Watt Univ, Humberside Univ, Kent Inst, Leeds Metro Univ, London Coll Printing, Loughborough Coll, Manchester Metro Univ, Middlesex Univ, Newcastle Univ, Northumbria Univ, Norwich Sch Art, Portsmouth Univ,

Reading Univ, Robert Gordon Univ, Royal Coll Art (p/g only), Sheffield Hallam Univ, Slade, Staffordshire Univ, Surrey Inst, West Herts Coll, Westminster Univ, Winchester Sch Art, Wolverhampton Univ.

PROBATION
See: Social work.

PRODUCT DESIGN
Possible prospectuses: Abertay Dundee Univ, Bournemouth Univ, Brighton Univ, Brunel Univ, Buckinghamshire Coll, Cardiff Inst, Central England Univ, Central Lancashire Univ, Central Saint Martins, City Univ, Coventry Univ, De Montfort Univ, Derby Univ, East London Univ, Glamorgan Univ, Glasgow Sch Art, Goldsmiths Coll, Heriot-Watt Univ, Hertfordshire Univ, Huddersfield Univ, Kent Inst, Kingston Univ, Leeds Metro Univ, Liverpool John Moores Univ, Loughborough Univ, Luton Univ, Middlesex Univ, Nene Coll, Newport Coll, Northumbria Univ, Nottingham Trent Univ, Ravensbourne Coll, Ripon & York St John, Robert Gordon Univ, Salford Univ, Sheffield Hallam Univ, South Bank Univ, Southampton Inst, Staffordshire Univ, Strathclyde Univ, Sunderland Univ, Swansea Inst, Swansea Univ, Teesside Univ, Thames Valley Univ, Westminster Univ, Wolverhampton Univ.

PRODUCTION ENGINEERING
Possible prospectuses: Aston Univ, Birmingham Univ, Bradford Univ, Brighton Univ, Bristol UWE, Brunel Univ, Cambridge Univ, Cardiff Inst, Central England Univ, Central Lancashire Univ, Coventry Univ, Cranfield Univ (p/g only), De Montfort Univ, Glamorgan Univ, Glasgow Caledonian Univ, Heriot-Watt Univ, Hertfordshire Univ, Imperial Coll, Kingston Univ, Liverpool John Moores Univ, Loughborough Univ, Luton Univ, Middlesex Univ, Newcastle Univ, Newport Coll, North East Wales Inst, Nottingham Trent Univ, Nottingham Univ, Paisley Univ, Portsmouth Univ, Robert Gordon Univ, South Bank Univ, Staffordshire Univ, Strathclyde Univ, Sunderland Univ, Teesside Univ, UMIST, Warwick Univ, Westminster Univ, Wolverhampton Univ.

PROFESSIONS ALLIED TO MEDICINE (PAMS)
See: individual subjects, eg speech therapy.

PROGRAMMING
See: Computing; computer science.

PSYCHOLOGY
Possible prospectuses: Aberdeen Univ, Abertay Dundee Univ, Anglia Poly Univ, Aston Univ, Bangor Univ, Bath Coll, Bath Univ, Belfast Univ, Birkbeck, Birmingham Univ, Bolton Inst, Bradford Univ, Bristol Univ, Bristol UWE, Brunel Univ, Buckingham Univ, Cambridge Univ, Canterbury Christ Church Coll, Cardiff Inst, Cardiff Univ, Central Lancashire Univ, Central Sch Speech/Drama, Cheltenham & Gloucester Coll, Chester Univ Coll, City Univ, Coventry Univ, Cranfield Univ (p/g only), De Montfort Univ, Derby Univ, Dundee Univ, Durham Univ, East London Univ, Edinburgh Univ, Essex Univ, Exeter Univ, Glamorgan Univ, Glasgow Caledonian Univ, Glasgow Univ, Goldsmiths Coll, Greenwich Univ, Hertfordshire Univ, Huddersfield Univ, Hull Univ, Humberside Univ, Keele Univ, Kent Univ, King Alfred's Coll, Kingston Univ, Lancaster Univ, Leeds Metro Univ, Leeds Univ, Leicester Univ, Lincoln Univ, Liverpool Hope Univ Coll, Liverpool John Moores Univ, Liverpool Univ, London Guildhall Univ, Loughborough Univ, LSE, LSU Southampton, Luton Univ, Manchester Metro Univ, Manchester Univ, Middlesex Univ, Nene Coll, Newcastle Univ, North East Wales Inst, North London Univ, Northumbria Univ, Nottingham Trent Univ, Nottingham Univ, Open Univ, Oxford

Brookes Univ, Oxford Univ, Paisley Univ, Plymouth Univ, Portsmouth Univ, Queen Margaret Coll, Reading Univ, Ripon & York St John, Roehampton Inst, Royal Holloway, St Andrews Univ, Sheffield Hallam Univ, Sheffield Univ, South Bank Univ, Southampton Inst, Southampton Univ, Staffordshire Univ, Stirling Univ, Strathclyde Univ, Sunderland Univ, Surrey Univ, Sussex Univ, Swansea Univ, Teesside Univ, Thames Valley Univ, Trinity & All Saints, Ulster Univ, University Coll London, Warwick Univ, Westminster Univ, Wolverhampton Univ, Worcester Coll, York Univ.

PUBLIC ADMINISTRATION
Possible prospectuses: Anglia Poly Univ, Aston Univ, Birmingham Univ, Brighton Univ, Brunel Univ, De Montfort Univ, Glamorgan Univ, Glasgow Caledonian Univ, Goldsmiths Coll, Hull Univ, Kent Univ, Leeds Univ, LSE, Luton Univ, Manchester Metro Univ, Northumbria Univ, Open Univ, Robert Gordon Univ, Royal Holloway, Sheffield Hallam Univ, Southampton Inst, Southampton Univ, Staffordshire Univ, Teesside Univ, Trinity & All Saints.
See also: Social administration.

PUBLIC HEALTH
Possible prospectuses: Anglia Poly Univ, Glasgow Caledonian Univ, Greenwich Univ, Open Univ, Queen Margaret Coll, South Bank Univ.
See also: Environmental health.

PUBLIC RELATIONS
Possible prospectuses: Bournemouth Univ, Central Lancashire Univ, European Business Sch, Leeds Metro Univ, London Coll Fashion, Queen Margaret Coll, St Mark & St John, Southampton Inst, Ulster Univ, Westminster Univ.

PUBLISHING
Possible prospectuses: Bournemouth Univ, London Coll Printing, Middlesex Univ, Napier Univ, Oxford Brookes Univ, Robert Gordon Univ, Thames Valley Univ, West Herts Coll.

Q

QUALITY CONTROL
See: Production engineering.

QUANTITY SURVEYING
Possible prospectuses: Abertay Dundee Univ, Anglia Poly Univ, Bolton Inst, Bristol UWE, Central England Univ, Central Lancashire Univ, Glamorgan Univ, Glasgow Caledonian Univ, Glasgow Coll Building, Greenwich Univ, Heriot-Watt Univ, Kingston Univ, Leeds Metro Univ, Liverpool John Moores Univ, Loughborough Univ, Luton Univ, Napier Univ, Nene Coll, North East Wales Inst, Northumbria Univ, Nottingham Trent Univ, Plymouth Univ, Portsmouth Univ, Reading Univ, Robert Gordon Univ, Salford Univ, Sheffield Hallam Univ, South Bank Univ, Staffordshire Univ, Ulster Univ, UMIST, Westminster Univ, Wolverhampton Univ.
See also: Surveying.

R

RADAR
See: Electronic engineering.

RADIO
See: Electronic engineering.

RADIOGRAPHY
Possible prospectuses: Anglia Poly Univ, Bangor Univ, Bradford Univ, Bristol UWE, Canterbury Christ Church Coll, Central England Univ, City Univ, Derby Univ, East London Univ, Glasgow Caledonian Univ, Hertfordshire Univ, King's Coll London, Kingston Univ, Liverpool Univ, Portsmouth Univ, Queen Margaret Coll, Robert Gordon Univ, S Martin's Univ Coll, Salford Univ, Sheffield Hallam Univ, Shrivenham, South Bank Univ, Teesside Univ, Ulster Univ, Wales Coll Medicine.

RECREATION STUDIES
Possible prospectuses: Birmingham Univ, Bournemouth Univ, Bradford & Ilkley, Cardiff Inst, Cheltenham & Gloucester Coll, Coventry Univ, Glamorgan Univ, Glasgow Univ, Heriot-Watt Univ, Leeds Metro Univ, Liverpool Hope Univ Coll, Loughborough Univ, Moray House, North London Univ, Portsmouth Univ, St Mark & St John, Scottish Agricultural Coll, Sheffield Hallam Univ, Staffordshire Univ, Swansea Inst, Thames Valley Univ, Trinity & All Saints, Warrington Univ Coll, Writtle Coll.
See also: Leisure studies; sports studies; tourism; town planning.

RELIGIOUS STUDIES
Possible prospectuses: Aberdeen Univ, Aberystwyth Univ, Bangor Univ, Bath Coll, Birmingham Univ, Bristol Univ, Brunel Univ, Cambridge Univ, Canterbury Christ Church Coll, Cardiff Univ, Cheltenham & Gloucester Coll, Chester Univ Coll, Chichester Univ Coll, Derby Univ, Edge Hill Univ Coll, Edinburgh Univ, Exeter Univ, Glamorgan Univ, Glasgow Univ, Greenwich Univ, Homerton Coll, Kent Univ, King Alfred's Coll, King's Coll London, Lampeter Univ, Lancaster Univ, Leeds Univ, Liverpool Hope Univ Coll, London Bible, LSU Southampton, Manchester Metro Univ, Manchester Univ, Middlesex Univ, National Extension Coll, Newcastle Univ, Newport Coll, Oak Hill Coll, Oxford Univ, Ripon & York St John, Roehampton Inst, St Andrews Univ, St Mark & St John, S Martin's Univ Coll, St Mary's Univ Coll, SOAS, Spurgeon's Coll, Stirling Univ, Sunderland Univ, Trinity & All Saints, Trinity Coll Carmarthen, Wolverhampton Univ.
See also: Biblical studies; theology.

RENAISSANCE STUDIES
See: History.

RETAIL MANAGEMENT
Possible prospectuses: Abertay Dundee Univ, Bournemouth Univ, Glasgow Caledonian Univ, Huddersfield Univ, London Coll Printing, Loughborough Univ, Manchester Metro Univ, North London Univ, Oxford Brookes Univ, Queen Margaret Coll, Robert Gordon Univ, Roehampton Inst, Silsoe Coll, Surrey Univ, Ulster Univ.

RISK
See: Actuarial studies.

RUMANIAN
Possible prospectuses: SSEES, University Coll London.

RURAL ENVIRONMENT STUDIES
Possible prospectuses: Aberdeen Univ, Aberystwyth Univ, Anglia Poly Univ, Bangor Univ, Cheltenham & Gloucester Coll, Coventry Univ, Dundee Univ, Harper Adams, Newcastle Univ, North East Wales Inst, Plymouth Univ, Reading Univ, Royal Agricultural Coll, Scottish Agricultural Coll, Silsoe Coll, Trinity Coll Carmarthen, Welsh Inst Rural Studies, Writtle Coll, Wye Coll.

RUSSIAN
Possible prospectuses: Bangor Univ, Bath Univ, Birmingham Univ, Bradford Univ, Bristol Univ, Cambridge Univ, Coventry Univ, Durham Univ, Essex Univ, European Business Sch, Exeter Univ, Glasgow Univ, Heriot-Watt Univ, Keele Univ, Leeds Univ, Liverpool John Moores Univ, LSU Southampton, Manchester Univ, Northumbria Univ, Nottingham Univ, Oxford Univ, Portsmouth Univ, Queen Mary & Westfield, St Andrews Univ, Sheffield Univ, SSEES, Strathclyde Univ, Surrey Univ, Sussex Univ, Swansea Univ, Thames Valley Univ, Westminster Univ, Wolverhampton Univ.
See also: Russian studies; Slavonic studies.

RUSSIAN STUDIES
Possible prospectuses: Birmingham Univ, Essex Univ, Glasgow Univ, Keele Univ, Leeds Univ, Liverpool Univ, LSE, Manchester Univ, Nottingham Univ, Portsmouth Univ, St Andrews Univ, Sheffield Univ, SSEES, Surrey Univ, Sussex Univ, Swansea Univ, Westminster Univ, Wolverhampton Univ.
See also: Russian; Slavonic studies.

S

SAFETY
See: Environmental health.

SANSKRIT
Possible prospectuses: Cambridge Univ, Edinburgh Univ, Oxford Univ, SOAS.
See also: Near East studies.

SCANDINAVIAN STUDIES
Possible prospectuses: East Anglia Univ, Edinburgh Univ, Hull Univ, University Coll London.
See also: individual languages, eg Danish.

SCIENTIFIC/TECHNICAL GRAPHICS
Possible prospectuses: Falmouth Coll Arts, Middlesex Univ.
See also: Graphic design.

SCOTTISH STUDIES
Possible prospectuses: Aberdeen Univ, Edinburgh Univ, Glasgow Univ, St Andrews Univ, Stirling Univ, Strathclyde Univ.
See also: Celtic studies.

SCULPTURE
Possible prospectuses: Anglia Poly Univ, Bath Coll, Bretton Hall, Brighton Univ, Bristol UWE, Camberwell Coll, Central England Univ, Central Lancashire Univ, Central Saint Martins, Chelsea Coll Art, Cheltenham & Gloucester Coll, Coventry Univ, De Montfort Univ, Dundee Univ, East London Univ, Edinburgh Coll Art, Falmouth Coll Arts, Glasgow Sch Art, Goldsmiths Coll, Heriot-Watt Univ, Humberside Univ, Kent Inst, Kingston Univ, Liverpool Hope Univ Coll, Liverpool John Moores Univ, Loughborough Coll, Manchester Metro Univ, Middlesex Univ, Newport Coll, Northumbria Univ, Norwich Sch Art, Portsmouth Univ, Reading Univ, Robert Gordon Univ, Royal Academy Sch (p/g only), Royal Coll Art (p/g only), Sheffield Hallam Univ, Slade, Staffordshire Univ, Sunderland Univ, Surrey Inst, Ulster Univ, Westminster Univ, Wimbledon Sch Art, Winchester Sch Art, Wolverhampton Univ.

SECRETARIAL STUDIES
See: Office organisation.

SEISMOLOGY
See: Geology.

SEMICONDUCTORS
See: Electronic engineering.

SEMITIC LANGUAGES
Possible prospectuses: Aberdeen Univ, Cambridge Univ, SOAS.
See also: individual languages, eg Arabic.

SERBO-CROAT
Possible prospectuses: Nottingham Univ, SSEES.
See also: Slavonic studies.

SHIPBUILDING
See: Naval architecture; marine architecture.

SILVERSMITHING
Possible prospectuses: Buckinghamshire Coll, Camberwell Coll, Central England Univ, Central Saint Martins, De Montfort Univ, Dundee Univ, Edinburgh Coll Art, Glasgow Sch Art, Heriot-Watt Univ, Kent Inst, Liverpool Hope Univ Coll, London Guildhall Univ, Loughborough Coll, Robert Gordon Univ, Royal Coll Art (p/g only), Sheffield Hallam Univ, Ulster Univ.
See also: Jewellery; three-dimensional design.

SLAVONIC STUDIES
Possible prospectuses: Glasgow Univ, Leeds Univ, Nottingham Univ, Sheffield Univ, SSEES.

SLOVAK
See: Czech/Slovak.

SOCIAL ADMINISTRATION
Possible prospectuses: Anglia Poly Univ, Birkbeck, Birmingham Univ, Brighton Univ, Bristol Univ, Cardiff Univ, Central Lancashire Univ, Essex Univ, Glasgow Caledonian Univ, Goldsmiths Coll, Hull Univ, Kent Univ, Lancaster Univ, Leeds Metro Univ, LSE, Middlesex Univ, Nottingham Trent Univ, Nottingham Univ, Open Univ, Paisley Univ, Plymouth Univ, Portsmouth Univ, Robert Gordon Univ, Roehampton Inst, Sheffield Hallam Univ, Sheffield Univ, Southampton Univ, Stirling Univ, Ulster Univ, Warwick Univ, Westminster Univ, Wolverhampton Univ, York Univ.

SOCIAL ANTHROPOLOGY
Possible prospectuses: Belfast Univ, Brunel Univ, Cambridge Univ, Edinburgh Univ, Goldsmiths Coll, Hull Univ, Keele Univ, Kent Univ, Lampeter Univ, LSE, Manchester Univ, St Andrews Univ, SOAS, Sussex Univ, Swansea Univ, Ulster Univ, University Coll London.
See also: Anthropology.

SOCIAL BIOLOGY
Possible prospectuses: King Alfred's Coll, Roehampton Inst.
See also: Biosocial science; human sciences.

SOCIAL HISTORY
Possible prospectuses: Aberdeen Univ, Aberystwyth Univ, Belfast Univ, Brighton Univ, Bristol Univ, Bristol UWE, East Anglia Univ, Edinburgh Univ, Exeter Univ, Glasgow Caledonian Univ, Glasgow Univ, Hull Univ, Kent Univ, Kingston Univ, Lancaster Univ, Leicester Univ, Liverpool Univ, Manchester Metro Univ, Manchester Univ, Newcastle Univ, Nottingham Univ, Open Univ, Portsmouth Univ, Reading Univ, Robert Gordon Univ, St Andrews Univ, Sheffield Univ, Staffordshire Univ, Strathclyde Univ, Sussex Univ, Swansea Univ, Warwick Univ, Wolverhampton Univ, York Univ.
See also: Economic history; history.

SOCIAL POLICY
Possible prospectuses: Anglia Poly Univ, Bangor Univ, Bath Univ, Birmingham Univ, Bradford & Ilkley, Bradford Univ, Brighton Univ, Bristol Univ, Cardiff Univ, Central Lancashire Univ, Coventry Univ, Derby Univ, Durham Univ, East Anglia Univ, East London Univ, Edinburgh Univ, Essex Univ, Exeter Univ, Glasgow Univ, Goldsmiths Coll, Hertfordshire Univ, Hull Univ, Leeds Metro Univ, Leeds Univ, Lincoln Univ, London Guildhall Univ, Luton Univ, Manchester Metro Univ, Manchester Univ, Middlesex Univ, Newcastle Univ, North London Univ, Nottingham Univ, Open Univ, Paisley Univ, Plymouth Univ, Portsmouth Univ, Robert Gordon Univ, Roehampton Inst, Royal Holloway, Sheffield Hallam Univ, Sheffield Univ, Stirling Univ, Sussex Univ, Swansea Univ, Teesside Univ, Ulster Univ, Wolverhampton Univ, York Univ.
See also: Social administration; social work.

SOCIAL PSYCHOLOGY
See: Psychology.

SOCIAL SCIENCE
Possible prospectuses: Aberdeen Univ, Abertay Dundee Univ, Anglia Poly Univ, Bath Coll, Belfast Univ, Birmingham Univ, Bradford & Ilkley, Bradford Univ, Bristol Univ, Bristol UWE, Brunel Univ, Cambridge Univ, Canterbury Christ Church Coll, City Univ, Coventry Univ, Derby Univ, East Anglia Univ, East London Univ, Edge Hill Univ Coll, Edinburgh Univ, Essex Univ, Exeter Univ, Glamorgan Univ, Glasgow Caledonian Univ, Glasgow Univ, Goldsmiths Coll, Hertfordshire Univ, Hull Univ, Humberside Univ, Keele Univ, Kent Univ, Lancaster Univ, Leeds

Metro Univ, Liverpool John Moores Univ, Liverpool Univ, Loughborough Univ, Manchester Metro Univ, Manchester Univ, Middlesex Univ, Napier Univ, Newcastle Univ, North London Univ, Nottingham Trent Univ, Open Univ, Paisley Univ, Plymouth Univ, Queen Margaret Coll, Ripon & York St John, Robert Gordon Univ, Royal Holloway, Salford Univ, Sheffield Hallam Univ, South Bank Univ, Southampton Inst, Southampton Univ, Staffordshire Univ, Stirling Univ, Sunderland Univ, Surrey Univ, Sussex Univ, Swansea Univ, Thames Valley Univ, Ulster Univ, Westminster Univ, Wolverhampton Univ, York Univ.
See also: individual subjects (eg economics, politics, sociology).

SOCIAL STATISTICS
See: Statistics; sociology.

SOCIAL STUDIES
Possible prospectuses: Anglia Poly Univ, Aston Univ, Birmingham Univ, Bradford Univ, Bretton Hall, Bristol Univ, Bristol UWE, Central Lancashire Univ, Chichester Univ Coll, Coventry Univ, East Anglia Univ, East London Univ, Exeter Univ, Huddersfield Univ, Keele Univ, Lancaster Univ, Liverpool John Moores Univ, Liverpool Univ, Luton Univ, Manchester Metro Univ, Manchester Univ, Nene Coll, Newcastle Univ, Nottingham Trent Univ, Nottingham Univ, Open Univ, Paisley Univ, Robert Gordon Univ, Sheffield Hallam Univ, South Bank Univ, Southampton Inst, Southampton Univ, Staffordshire Univ, Stirling Univ, Strathclyde Univ, Sussex Univ, Swansea Univ, Teesside Univ, Warwick Univ, York Univ.
See also: Social science.

SOCIAL WORK
Possible prospectuses: Anglia Poly Univ, Bath Univ, Bradford & Ilkley, Bradford Univ, Bristol Univ, Brunel Univ, Buckinghamshire Coll, Cardiff Inst, Cardiff Univ, Central England Univ, Central Lancashire Univ, Cheltenham & Gloucester Coll, Chichester Univ Coll, Coventry Univ, Derby Univ, Dundee Univ, East Anglia Univ, East London Univ, Exeter Univ, Glasgow Caledonian Univ, Glasgow Univ, Heriot-Watt Univ, Hertfordshire Univ, Huddersfield Univ, Hull Univ, Humberside Univ, Kingston Univ, Lancaster Univ, Leeds Metro Univ, Liverpool John Moores Univ, Liverpool Univ, Luton Univ, Manchester Metro Univ, Middlesex Univ, Moray House, Nene Coll, North East Wales Inst, North London Univ, Northumbria Univ, Nottingham Trent Univ, Oxford Brookes Univ, Paisley Univ, Plymouth Univ, Portsmouth Univ, Robert Gordon Univ, Salford Univ, Sheffield Hallam Univ, South Bank Univ, Southampton Univ, Staffordshire Univ, Stirling Univ, Strathclyde Univ, Sunderland Univ, Sussex Univ, Teesside Univ, Ulster Univ, Warrington Univ Coll, York Univ.

SOCIOLOGY
Possible prospectuses: Aberdeen Univ, Anglia Poly Univ, Aston Univ, Bangor Univ, Bath Coll, Bath Univ, Belfast Univ, Birmingham Univ, Bradford Univ, Bristol Univ, Bristol UWE, Brunel Univ, Buckinghamshire Coll, Cambridge Univ, Cardiff Univ, Central England Univ, Central Lancashire Univ, Cheltenham & Gloucester Coll, City Univ, Colchester Inst, Coventry Univ, Derby Univ, Durham Univ, East Anglia Univ, East London Univ, Edinburgh Univ, Essex Univ, Exeter Univ, Glamorgan Univ, Glasgow Caledonian Univ, Glasgow Univ, Goldsmiths Coll, Greenwich Univ, Hertfordshire Univ, Huddersfield Univ, Hull Univ, Humberside Univ, Keele Univ, Kent Univ, Kingston Univ, Lancaster Univ, Leeds Metro Univ, Leeds Univ, Leicester Univ, Liverpool Hope Univ Coll, Liverpool John Moores Univ, Liverpool Univ, London Guildhall Univ, Loughborough Univ, LSE, LSU Southampton, Manchester Metro Univ, Manchester Univ, Middlesex Univ, Nene Coll, Newcastle Univ, North London Univ, Northumbria Univ, Nottingham Trent Univ, Nottingham Univ, Open Univ, Oxford Brookes Univ, Plymouth Univ, Portsmouth Univ, Queen Margaret Coll, Reading Univ, Robert Gordon

Univ, Roehampton Inst, Royal Holloway, St Mark & St John, St Mary's Univ Coll, Salford Univ, Sheffield Hallam Univ, Sheffield Univ, South Bank Univ, Southampton Univ, Staffordshire Univ, Stirling Univ, Strathclyde Univ, Sunderland Univ, Surrey Univ, Sussex Univ, Swansea Univ, Teesside Univ, Thames Valley Univ, Trinity & All Saints, Ulster Univ, Warwick Univ, Westminster Univ, Wolverhampton Univ, Worcester Coll, York Univ.

SOFTWARE ENGINEERING
Possible prospectuses: Aberdeen Univ, Aberystwyth Univ, Anglia Poly Univ, Belfast Univ, Birmingham Univ, Bournemouth Univ, Bradford Univ, Brighton Univ, Bristol UWE, Central England Univ, Central Lancashire Univ, City Univ, Coventry Univ, Cranfield Univ (p/g only), De Montfort Univ, Derby Univ, Durham Univ, East London Univ, Edinburgh Univ, Essex Univ, Glamorgan Univ, Glasgow Univ, Goldsmiths Coll, Greenwich Univ, Heriot-Watt Univ, Hertfordshire Univ, Huddersfield Univ, Hull Univ, Imperial Coll, Kingston Univ, Lancaster Univ, Leicester Univ, Liverpool John Moores Univ, Luton Univ, Manchester Metro Univ, Napier Univ, Newcastle Univ, North London Univ, Nottingham Trent Univ, Oxford Brookes Univ, Paisley Univ, Portsmouth Univ, Robert Gordon Univ, Salford Univ, Sheffield Hallam Univ, Sheffield Univ, Shrivenham, South Bank Univ, Southampton Inst, Staffordshire Univ, Stirling Univ, Swansea Inst, Teesside Univ, Ulster Univ, UMIST, Westminster Univ, Wolverhampton Univ, York Univ.
See also: Computing.

SOIL SCIENCE
Possible prospectuses: Aberdeen Univ, Aberystwyth Univ, Anglia Poly Univ, East Anglia Univ, Edinburgh Univ, Greenwich Univ, Newcastle Univ, Reading Univ, Royal Agricultural Coll, Writtle Coll.
See also: Geology.

SOLID STATE ELECTRONICS
See: Electronics.

SOLID STATE PHYSICS
See: Physics.

SOUTH AMERICA
See: Latin American studies.

SOUTH EAST ASIAN STUDIES
Possible prospectuses: Edinburgh Univ, Hull Univ, Leeds Univ, North London Univ, SOAS.
See also: Asian studies; oriental studies.

SPACE
Possible prospectuses: Aberystwyth Univ, Birmingham Univ, Kent Univ, Leicester Univ, Southampton Univ.
See also: Astronomy.

SPANISH
Possible prospectuses: Aberdeen Univ, Aberystwyth Univ, Anglia Poly Univ, Belfast Univ, Birkbeck, Birmingham Univ, Bradford Univ, Bristol Univ, Bristol UWE, Buckingham Univ, Cambridge Univ, Cardiff Univ, Central Lancashire Univ, Coventry Univ, Derby Univ, Durham Univ, East London Univ, Edinburgh Univ, Essex Univ, European Business Sch, Exeter Univ, Glasgow Caledonian Univ, Glasgow Univ, Goldsmiths Coll, Heriot-Watt Univ, Huddersfield

Univ, Hull Univ, Humberside Univ, Kent Univ, King's Coll London, Kingston Univ, Lancaster Univ, Leeds Univ, Lincoln Univ, Liverpool John Moores Univ, Liverpool Univ, London Guildhall Univ, Loughborough Univ, Luton Univ, Manchester Metro Univ, Manchester Univ, Middlesex Univ, Napier Univ, National Extension Coll, Nene Coll, Newcastle Univ, North London Univ, Northumbria Univ, Nottingham Trent Univ, Nottingham Univ, Oxford Brookes Univ, Oxford Univ, Plymouth Univ, Portsmouth Univ, Queen Mary & Westfield, Roehampton Inst, Royal Holloway, St Andrews Univ, Salford Univ, Sheffield Hallam Univ, Sheffield Univ, South Bank Univ, Southampton Univ, Staffordshire Univ, Stirling Univ, Strathclyde Univ, Surrey Univ, Sussex Univ, Swansea Univ, Thames Valley Univ, Trinity & All Saints, Ulster Univ, University Coll London, Westminster Univ, Wolverhampton Univ.
See also: Hispanic studies; Iberian studies; Latin American studies.

SPANISH STUDIES
See: Hispanic studies; Iberian studies; Latin American studies; Spanish.

SPEECH SCIENCES
Possible prospectuses: Central Sch Speech/Drama, City Univ, Manchester Metro Univ, Queen Margaret Coll, Reading Univ, Sheffield Univ, Strathclyde Univ, University Coll London.

SPEECH THERAPY
Possible prospectuses: Cardiff Inst, Central England Univ, Central Sch Speech/Drama, City Univ, De Montfort Univ, Leeds Metro Univ, Manchester Metro Univ, Manchester Univ, Newcastle Univ, Queen Margaret Coll, Reading Univ, St Mark & St John, Sheffield Univ, Strathclyde Univ, Ulster Univ.
See also: Speech sciences

SPORTS STUDIES
Possible prospectuses: Bangor Univ, Birmingham Univ, Brighton Univ, Brunel Univ, Canterbury Christ Church Coll, Cardiff Inst, Cheltenham & Gloucester Coll, Chester Univ Coll, Chichester Univ Coll, Colchester Inst, Coventry Univ, De Montfort Univ, Edge Hill Univ Coll, Exeter Univ, Farnborough Coll, Glamorgan Univ, Glasgow Univ, Greenwich Univ, Heriot-Watt Univ, Huddersfield Univ, Hull Univ, King Alfred's Coll, Kingston Univ, Leeds Metro Univ, Leeds Univ, Liverpool Hope Univ Coll, Liverpool John Moores Univ, Liverpool Univ, Loughborough Univ, LSU Southampton, Luton Univ, Manchester Metro Univ, Moray House, Nene Coll, Newport Coll, North London Univ, Northumbria Univ, Nottingham Trent Univ, Portsmouth Univ, Roehampton Inst, S Martin's Univ Coll, St Mary's Univ Coll, South Bank Univ, Southampton Inst, Staffordshire Univ, Stirling Univ, Strathclyde Univ, Sunderland Univ, Teesside Univ, Trinity & All Saints, Ulster Univ, Warrington Univ Coll, Wolverhampton Univ, Worcester Coll.
See also: Physical education.

STAGE MANAGEMENT
Possible prospectuses: ALRA, Bretton Hall, Bristol Old Vic, Central Sch Speech/Drama, Guildford Sch Acting, Guildhall, Queen Margaret Coll, RADA, Rose Bruford Coll, Royal Scottish Academy, Salford Univ, Trinity Coll Carmarthen, Welsh Coll Music/Drama.

STATISTICS
Possible prospectuses: Aberdeen Univ, Abertay Dundee Univ, Aberystwyth Univ, Anglia Poly Univ, Bath Univ, Belfast Univ, Birkbeck, Birmingham Univ, Bradford Univ, Brighton Univ, Bristol Univ, Bristol UWE, Brunel Univ, Cardiff Univ, Central Lancashire Univ, City Univ, Coventry Univ, Derby Univ, Dundee Univ, East Anglia Univ, East London Univ, Edinburgh

Univ, Essex Univ, Exeter Univ, Glasgow Caledonian Univ, Glasgow Univ, Goldsmiths Coll, Greenwich Univ, Heriot-Watt Univ, Huddersfield Univ, Hull Univ, Imperial Coll, Keele Univ, Kent Univ, Kingston Univ, Lancaster Univ, Leeds Univ, Leicester Univ, Liverpool John Moores Univ, Liverpool Univ, Loughborough Univ, LSE, Luton Univ, Manchester Univ, Middlesex Univ, Newcastle Univ, North London Univ, Northumbria Univ, Nottingham Trent Univ, Nottingham Univ, Open Univ, Oxford Brookes Univ, Paisley Univ, Plymouth Univ, Portsmouth Univ, Queen Mary & Westfield, Reading Univ, Robert Gordon Univ, Royal Holloway, St Andrews Univ, Salford Univ, Sheffield Hallam Univ, Sheffield Univ, South Bank Univ, Southampton Univ, Staffordshire Univ, Strathclyde Univ, Surrey Univ, Sussex Univ, Swansea Univ, Teesside Univ, Ulster Univ, UMIST, University Coll London, Warwick Univ, Westminster Univ, Wolverhampton Univ, York Univ.
See also: Mathematics.

STRATEGIC STUDIES
See: War studies.

STRUCTURAL ENGINEERING
Possible prospectuses: Bath Univ, Birmingham Univ, Bradford Univ, Bristol UWE, Coventry Univ, Cranfield Univ (p/g only), Edinburgh Univ, Glasgow Caledonian Univ, Heriot-Watt Univ, Hertfordshire Univ, Imperial Coll, Liverpool Univ, Manchester Univ, Newcastle Univ, North East Wales Inst, Paisley Univ, Sheffield Univ, South Bank Univ, UMIST, University Coll London, Westminster Univ.

SURVEYING
Possible prospectuses: Aberdeen Univ, Anglia Poly Univ, Brighton Univ, Bristol UWE, Camborne Sch Mines, Central England Univ, Central Lancashire Univ, City Univ, East London Univ, Glamorgan Univ, Glasgow Caledonian Univ, Greenwich Univ, Harper Adams, Heriot-Watt Univ, Hertfordshire Univ, Kingston Univ, Liverpool John Moores Univ, Loughborough Univ, Luton Univ, Napier Univ, Newcastle Univ, North East Wales Inst, Nottingham Trent Univ, Paisley Univ, Plymouth Univ, Portsmouth Univ, Reading Univ, Robert Gordon Univ, Royal Agricultural Coll, Salford Univ, Sheffield Hallam Univ, South Bank Univ, Staffordshire Univ, Ulster Univ, UMIST, University Coll London, Westminster Univ, Wolverhampton Univ.
See also: Quantity surveying.

SWAHILI
Possible prospectuses: SOAS
See also: African studies.

SWEDISH
Possible prospectuses: East Anglia Univ, Edinburgh Univ, Hull Univ, Lampeter Univ, Sheffield Univ, Surrey Univ, University Coll London.
See also: Scandinavian studies.

SYSTEMS ANALYSIS
Possible prospectuses: Aberdeen Univ, Anglia Poly Univ, Bournemouth Univ, Bristol UWE, Cardiff Univ, City Univ, Cranfield Univ (p/g only), Imperial Coll, Kent Univ, Luton Univ, Manchester Univ, Middlesex Univ, North London Univ, Sheffield Hallam Univ, South Bank Univ, Staffordshire Univ, UMIST, Westminster Univ.
See also: Computer science; computing.

T

TALMUD
See: Jewish studies.

TAMIL
Possible prospectuses: SOAS.
See also: Asian studies; oriental studies.

TEACHING
See: Education.

TECHNICAL GRAPHICS
See: Scientific/technical graphics.

TELECOMMUNICATIONS ENGINEERING
Possible prospectuses: Anglia Poly Univ, Aston Univ, Birmingham Univ, Bradford Univ, Coventry Univ, East London Univ, Essex Univ, Heriot-Watt Univ, Hull Univ, Imperial Coll, King's Coll London, Lancaster Univ, Luton Univ, Open Univ, Oxford Brookes Univ, Portsmouth Univ, Queen Mary & Westfield, Salford Univ, South Bank Univ.

TELEVISION
See: Broadcasting; communication studies; film studies; media studies.

TEXTILE TECHNOLOGY
Possible prospectuses: Bolton Inst, De Montfort Univ, Heriot-Watt Univ, Huddersfield Univ, Leeds Univ, Nottingham Trent Univ, Scottish Coll Textiles, Ulster Univ, UMIST, Wolverhampton Univ.

TEXTILES
Possible prospectuses: Bath Coll, Bolton Inst, Bradford & Ilkley, Bretton Hall, Brighton Univ, Bristol UWE, Buckinghamshire Coll, Central England Univ, Central Saint Martins, Chelsea Coll Art, Cheltenham & Gloucester Coll, De Montfort Univ, Derby Univ, Dundee Univ, East London Univ, Edinburgh Coll Art, Glasgow Sch Art, Goldsmiths Coll, Heriot-Watt Univ, Huddersfield Univ, Leeds Univ, Liverpool Hope Univ Coll, Liverpool John Moores Univ, London Coll Fashion, London Guildhall Univ, Loughborough Coll, Manchester Metro Univ, Middlesex Univ, Nene Coll, Newport Coll, Norwich Sch Art, Nottingham Trent Univ, Robert Gordon Univ, Royal Coll Art (p/g only), Scottish Coll Textiles, Surrey Inst, Teesside Univ, Ulster Univ, UMIST, Winchester Sch Art, Wolverhampton Univ.

THAI STUDIES
Possible prospectuses: North London Univ, SOAS.
See also: Oriental studies.

THEATRE DESIGN
Possible prospectuses: Bretton Hall, Bristol Old Vic, Central England Univ, Central Saint Martins, Central Sch Speech/Drama, Edinburgh Coll Art, Heriot-Watt Univ, Laban Centre, Nottingham Trent Univ, Queen Margaret Coll, RADA, Rose Bruford Coll, Royal Scottish

Academy, Salford Univ, Slade, Trinity Coll Carmarthen, Welsh Coll Music/Drama, Wimbledon Sch Art.

THEATRE STUDIES
Possible prospectuses: Aberystwyth Univ, Birmingham Univ, Bristol Old Vic, Coventry Univ, Dartington Coll Arts, Derby Univ, Glamorgan Univ, Glasgow Univ, Goldsmiths Coll, Huddersfield Univ, Kent Univ, Laban Centre, Lancaster Univ, Leeds Univ, Liverpool John Moores Univ, Manchester Metro Univ, Middlesex Univ, Queen Margaret Coll, Reading Univ, Ripon & York St John, Rose Bruford Coll, Trinity Coll Carmarthen, Ulster Univ.
See also: Drama; acting.

THEOLOGY
Possible prospectuses: Aberdeen Univ, Bangor Univ, Belfast Univ, Birmingham Univ, Bristol Univ, Cambridge Univ, Cardiff Univ, Cheltenham & Gloucester Coll, Chester Univ Coll, Chichester Univ Coll, Derby Univ, Durham Univ, Edinburgh Univ, Exeter Univ, Glasgow Univ, Greenwich Univ, Heythrop Coll, Hull Univ, Kent Univ, King's Coll London, Lampeter Univ, Lancaster Univ, Leeds Univ, Liverpool Hope Univ Coll, London Bible, LSU Southampton, Manchester Univ, Newcastle Univ, Nottingham Univ, Oak Hill Coll, Oxford Univ, Ripon & York St John, Roehampton Inst, St Andrews Univ, St Mark & St John, St Mary's Univ Coll, Spurgeon's Coll, Trinity & All Saints, Westminster Coll.
See also: Religious studies

THIRD WORLD STUDIES
Possible prospectuses: Coventry Univ, Derby Univ, East Anglia Univ, East London Univ, Leeds Univ, Middlesex Univ, Open Univ, St Mark & St John, Staffordshire Univ, Swansea Univ, Westminster Univ.

THREE-DIMENSIONAL DESIGN
Possible prospectuses: Brighton Univ, Bristol UWE, Buckinghamshire Coll, Cardiff Inst, Central England Univ, Central Lancashire Univ, Central Saint Martins, Central Sch Speech/Drama, Coventry Univ, De Montfort Univ, Dundee Univ, Edinburgh Coll Art, Heriot-Watt Univ, Humberside Univ, Kent Inst, Kingston Univ, Leeds Metro Univ, Liverpool Hope Univ Coll, Loughborough Coll, Loughborough Univ, Manchester Metro Univ, Middlesex Univ, Northumbria Univ, Open Univ, Plymouth Univ, Portsmouth Univ, Ravensbourne Coll, Reading Univ, Ripon & York St John, St Mark & St John, Salford Univ, Sheffield Hallam Univ, Staffordshire Univ, Sunderland Univ, Surrey Inst, Westminster Univ, Wolverhampton Univ.

TOPOGRAPHICAL SCIENCE
Possible prospectuses: Glasgow Univ, Swansea Univ.

TOURISM
Possible prospectuses: Abertay Dundee Univ, Bangor Univ, Bolton Inst, Bournemouth Univ, Brighton Univ, Bristol UWE, Buckingham Univ, Buckinghamshire Coll, Canterbury Christ Church Coll, Cardiff Inst, Central Lancashire Univ, Cheltenham & Gloucester Coll, Derby Univ, Glamorgan Univ, Glasgow Caledonian Univ, Hertfordshire Univ, Huddersfield Univ, Leeds Metro Univ, Lincoln Univ, Luton Univ, Manchester Metro Univ, Napier Univ, North London Univ, Northumbria Univ, Oxford Brookes Univ, Plymouth Univ, Queen Margaret Coll, Scottish Agricultural Coll, Sheffield Hallam Univ, South Bank Univ, Staffordshire Univ, Strathclyde Univ, Sunderland Univ, Surrey Univ, Swansea Inst, Thames Valley Univ, Ulster Univ, Warrington Univ Coll, Westminster Univ, Wolverhampton Univ, Writtle Coll.
See also: Recreation studies.

TOWN AND COUNTRY PLANNING
Possible prospectuses: Aberdeen Univ, Belfast Univ, Birmingham Univ, Bristol UWE, Cardiff Univ, Central England Univ, Cheltenham & Gloucester Coll, Coventry Univ, Dundee Univ, Edinburgh Coll Art, Heriot-Watt Univ, Liverpool John Moores Univ, Liverpool Univ, Luton Univ, Manchester Univ, Newcastle Univ, North East Wales Inst, Northumbria Univ, Nottingham Univ, Oxford Brookes Univ, Portsmouth Univ, Reading Univ, Royal Agricultural Coll, Sheffield Hallam Univ, Sheffield Univ, South Bank Univ, Strathclyde Univ, University Coll London, Westminster Univ.
See also: Environmental studies.

TOXICOLOGY
Possible prospectuses: Aberdeen Univ, Anglia Poly Univ, Bradford Univ, Glasgow Caledonian Univ, Hull Univ, Luton Univ, Sch Pharmacy, Surrey Univ.

TRAFFIC
See: Civil engineering; town and country planning; transport studies.

TRANSLATION
See: Interpreting and translating.

TRANSPORT STUDIES
Possible prospectuses: Aston Univ, Cardiff Univ, Coventry Univ, Cranfield Univ (p/g only), Huddersfield Univ, Liverpool John Moores Univ, Loughborough Univ, Middlesex Univ, Napier Univ, Oxford Brookes Univ, Plymouth Univ, Salford Univ, Southampton Inst, Staffordshire Univ, Swansea Inst, Ulster Univ.

TURKISH
Possible prospectuses: Cambridge Univ, Edinburgh Univ, Oxford Univ, SOAS, Westminster Univ.
See also: Near East studies.

TYPOGRAPHY
See: Printing and typography.

U

UNITED STATES
See: American studies.

URBAN ESTATE MANAGEMENT
Possible prospectuses: Aberdeen Univ, Anglia Poly Univ, Bristol UWE, Central England Univ, De Montfort Univ, Heriot-Watt Univ, Kingston Univ, Liverpool John Moores Univ, Luton Univ, North East Wales Inst, Northumbria Univ, Nottingham Trent Univ, Oxford Brookes Univ, Portsmouth Univ, Reading Univ, Sheffield Hallam Univ, South Bank Univ, Westminster Univ, Writtle Coll.

URBAN STUDIES
Possible prospectuses: Aberdeen Univ, Anglia Poly Univ, Aston Univ, Birmingham Univ, Bolton Inst, Bristol UWE, Central England Univ, Coventry Univ, Durham Univ, Edge Hill Univ Coll, Edinburgh Coll Art, Greenwich Univ, Kent Univ, Leeds Metro Univ, Liverpool John Moores Univ, Middlesex Univ, North East Wales Inst, North London Univ, Open Univ, Portsmouth Univ, Reading Univ, Sheffield Hallam Univ, Sheffield Univ, Worcester Coll.

URDU
Possible prospectuses: SOAS.
See also: Asian studies; oriental studies.

V

VALUATION
See: Estate management; quantity surveying; surveying.

VETERINARY STUDIES
Possible prospectuses: Bristol Univ, Cambridge Univ, Edinburgh Univ, Glasgow Univ, Liverpool Univ, Royal Vet Coll.

VICTORIAN STUDIES
Possible prospectuses: Lampeter Univ, Open Univ.

VIDEO
Possible prospectuses: Cheltenham & Gloucester Coll, Derby Univ, Goldsmiths Coll, Kent Inst, Newport Coll.
See also: Communication studies; film studies; media studies.

VIETNAMESE STUDIES
Possible prospectuses: SOAS.
See also: Asian studies.

VIROLOGY
Possible prospectuses: Reading Univ, Warwick Univ.

VISUAL COMMUNICATION
See: Graphic design.

W

WAR STUDIES
Possible prospectuses: Aberystwyth Univ, Bolton Inst, Bradford Univ, Dartmouth, King's Coll London, Sandhurst, Ulster Univ, Wolverhampton Univ.
See also: History; international relations; politics.

WATER RESOURCES
Possible prospectuses: Cranfield Univ (p/g only), Heriot-Watt Univ, Middlesex Univ, Oxford Brookes Univ, Silsoe Coll, South Bank Univ, Writtle Coll.

WELFARE STUDIES
See: Social administration; social work; youth and community work.

WELSH STUDIES
Possible prospectuses: Aberystwyth Univ, Bangor Univ, Cardiff Univ, Glamorgan Univ, Glasgow Univ, Lampeter Univ, North East Wales Inst, Swansea Univ, Trinity Coll Carmarthen. *See also:* Celtic studies.

WILDLIFE MANAGEMENT
Possible prospectuses: East London Univ, Edinburgh Univ, Silsoe Coll, Welsh Inst Rural Studies, Writtle Coll.

WOMEN'S STUDIES
Possible prospectuses: Aberdeen Univ, Anglia Poly Univ, Bangor Univ, Belfast Univ, Bolton Inst, Bradford & Ilkley, Bradford Univ, Bristol UWE, Central Lancashire Univ, Cheltenham & Gloucester Coll, Chichester Univ Coll, Coventry Univ, De Montfort Univ, East London Univ, Edge Hill Univ Coll, Glamorgan Univ, Hull Univ, Kingston Univ, Lampeter Univ, Lancaster Univ, Leeds Univ, Liverpool John Moores Univ, Liverpool Univ, Luton Univ, Manchester Univ, Middlesex Univ, North London Univ, Northumbria Univ, Ripon & York St John, Roehampton Inst, Sheffield Hallam Univ, Staffordshire Univ, Westminster Univ, Wolverhampton Univ, Worcester Coll.
See also: Gender studies.

WOOD TECHNOLOGY
Possible prospectuses: Abertay Dundee Univ, Bangor Univ, Buckinghamshire Coll.

Y

YOUTH AND COMMUNITY WORK
Possible prospectuses: Bradford & Ilkley, Canterbury Christ Church Coll, De Montfort Univ, Derby Univ, Durham Univ, Goldsmiths Coll, Heriot-Watt Univ, Huddersfield Univ, Leeds Metro Univ, Manchester Metro Univ, Moray House, North East Wales Inst, Reading Univ, St Mark & St John, S Martin's Univ Coll, Sunderland Univ, Ulster Univ.

Z

ZOOLOGY
Possible prospectuses: Aberdeen Univ, Aberystwyth Univ, Bangor Univ, Belfast Univ, Birmingham Univ, Bristol Univ, Cambridge Univ, Cardiff Univ, Dundee Univ, Durham Univ, East Anglia Univ, East London Univ, Edinburgh Univ, Exeter Univ, Glasgow Univ, Imperial Coll, Leeds Univ, Leicester Univ, Liverpool John Moores Univ, Liverpool Univ, Manchester

Univ, Newcastle Univ, Nottingham Univ, Oxford Univ, Portsmouth Univ, Queen Mary & Westfield, Reading Univ, Roehampton Inst, Royal Holloway, St Andrews Univ, Sheffield Univ, Southampton Univ, Stirling Univ, Swansea Univ, University Coll London, Westminster Univ, Wye Coll.

See also: Animal science.

ZULU
See: African studies.

RESEARCH QUALITY SEARCH INDEX

The Student Book selection of top UK research institutions and top departments – those undertaking world class research, or at least research of national excellence – is taken from the 1996 Research Assessment Exercise undertaken by the Higher Education Funding Councils.[1]

The top 50 research institutions in the *Student Book* selection all have high level research across all departments. They are listed alphabetically under **Super league** and **First division**.

We also provide search inde.xes for each of 67 subjects. We list universities with top departments in any of the following subject areas:

Accountancy
Agriculture (incl rural resources)
American studies
Anatomy
Anthropology
Archaeology
Art and design
Asian studies
Biochemistry
Biological sciences
Built environment
Business and management studies
Celtic studies
Chemical engineering
Chemistry
Civil engineering
Classics, ancient history, Byzantine and
    modern Greek studies
Clinical laboratory sciences (eg pathology,
    microbiology, virology)
Communication, cultural and media
    studies
Computer science

Dentistry
Drama, dance and performing arts
Earth sciences
Economics and econometrics
Education
Electrical and electronic engineering
Engineering – general
English language and literature
Environmental sciences
European studies
Food science and technology
French
Geography
German, Dutch and Scandinavian
    languages
History
History of art, architecture and design
Iberian and Latin American languages
Italian
Law
Linguistics
Library and information management
Mathematics – pure

1: Source: *1996 Research Assessment Exercise: The Outcome* published by HEFCE, £15 from External Relations, HEFCE, Northavon House, Coldharbour Lane, Bristol BS16 1QD. Tel 0117 931 7438; fax 0117 931 7463. Ref RAE 96 1/96

Mathematics – applied
Mechanical, aeronautic and
  manufacturing engineering
Medicine
Metallurgy and materials
Middle Eastern and African studies
Mineral and mining engineering
Music
Nursing (including midwifery)
Pharmacology
Pharmacy
Philosophy
Physics
Physiology
Politics and international studies

Professions allied to medicine
  (incl biomedical sciences,
  optometry)
Psychology
Russian, Slavonic and East European
  languages
Social policy and administration
Social work
Sociology
Sport-related subjects
Statistics and operational research
Theology, divinity and religious
  studies
Town and country planning
Veterinary science

TOP 50 RESEARCH INSTITUTIONS

Super league

Bath University
Cambridge University
Courtauld Institute
Imperial College
Institute of Education
London Business School

LSE
Oxford University
School of Pharmacy
UMIST
University College London
Warwick University

First division

Birkbeck College
Birmingham University
Bristol University
Cardiff University
Cranfield University
Durham University
East Anglia University
Edinburgh University
Essex University
Exeter University
Goldsmiths College
King's College London
Lancaster University
Leeds University
Leicester University
Liverpool University
Loughborough University
Manchester University
Newcastle University

Nottingham University
Queen Mary & Westfield
Reading University
Royal Academy of Music
Royal College of Art
Royal College of Music
Royal Free
Royal Holloway
Royal Northern College of Music
Royal Veterinary College
St Andrews University
Sheffield University
SOAS
Southampton University
SSEES
Sussex University
UMDS
Wimbledon School of Art
York University

ACCOUNTANCY

Super league   Manchester University

First division   Aberystwyth University, Brunel University, Dundee University, Edinburgh University, Essex University, Exeter University, Glasgow University, LSE, Stirling University, Strathclyde University

AGRICULTURE
(incl rural resources)

Super league   Reading University

First division   Aberdeen University, Bangor University, Belfast University, Edinburgh University, Leeds University, Newcastle University, Nottingham University, Stirling University

AMERICAN STUDIES

First division   East Anglia University, Keele University, Liverpool University, Nottingham University, Sussex University

ANATOMY

Super league   Birmingham University, Royal Free, University College London

First division   Cambridge University, Dundee University, Liverpool University, Oxford University

ANTHROPOLOGY

Super league   Cambridge University

First division   Belfast University, Brunel University, Durham University, Edinburgh University, Goldsmith's College, LSE, Manchester University, Oxford University, St Andrews University, SOAS, Sussex University, University College London

ARCHAEOLOGY

Super league   Cambridge University, Oxford University, Sheffield University

First division   Belfast University, Birmingham University, Bradford University, Bristol University, Cardiff University, Durham University, Edinburgh University, Glasgow University, Leicester University, Liverpool University, Reading University, Southampton University, University College London, York University

ART AND DESIGN

Super league   Brunel University, Goldsmiths College, University College London (inc Slade)

First division   Bournemouth University, Brighton University, Coventry University, Dundee University, Middlesex University, Open University, Oxford University, Reading University, Royal College of Art, Sheffield Hallam University, Southampton University, Ulster University, Westminster University, Wimbledon School of Art

ASIAN STUDIES

Super league   Oxford University

First division   Cambridge University, Durham University, Edinburgh University, Hull University, Leeds University, SOAS

BIOCHEMISTRY

Super league   Cambridge University, Dundee University, Oxford University

First division   Birmingham University, Bristol University, Glasgow University, Imperial College, Leeds University, Leicester University, Manchester University, Newcastle University, Royal Free, University College London

BIOLOGICAL SCIENCES

Super league   Cambridge University, Nottingham University

First division   Bath University, Birmingham University, Bristol University, Cranfield University, East Anglia University, Edinburgh University, Essex University, Glasgow University, Imperial University, Kent University, Lancaster University, Leeds University, Leicester University, Liverpool University, Manchester University, Oxford University, Queen Mary & Westfield, St Andrews University, Sheffield University, Southampton University, Sussex University, UMIST, University College London, Warwick University, York University

BUILT ENVIRONMENT

Super league   Reading University, Salford University

First division   Cambridge University, Cardiff University, Heriot-Watt University, Liverpool University, Loughborough University, Newcastle University, Nottingham University, Sheffield University, Strathclyde University, Ulster University, University College London

BUSINESS AND MANAGEMENT STUDIES

Super league   Lancaster University, London Business School, UMIST

First division   Aston University, Bath University, Birmingham University, Bradford University, Cambridge University, Cardiff University, City University, Cranfield University, Edinburgh University, Glasgow University, Imperial College, Keele University, Leeds University, LSE, Manchester University, Nottingham University, Oxford University, Reading University, St Andrews University, Sheffield University, Southampton University, Strathclyde University, Warwick University

CELTIC STUDIES

First division   Aberystwyth University, Belfast University, Cardiff University, Edinburgh University, Glasgow University, Oxford University, Swansea University, Ulster University

CHEMICAL ENGINEERING

Super league   Imperial College

First division   Bath University, Birmingham University, Cambridge University, Leeds University, Loughborough University, UMIST, University College London

CHEMISTRY

Super league   Cambridge University, Oxford University

First division   Bath University, Birmingham University, Bristol University, Durham University, Edinburgh University, Exeter University, Hull University, Imperial College, Leeds University, Leicester University, Liverpool University, Manchester University, Nottingham University, Reading University, St Andrews University, Sheffield University, Southampton University, Strathclyde University, Sussex University, University College London, UMIST, York University

CIVIL ENGINEERING

Super league   Imperial College, Newcastle University, Swansea University

First division   Belfast University, Bradford University, Bristol University, Cardiff University, City University, Dundee University, Edinburgh University, Glasgow University, Heriot-Watt University, Liverpool University, Loughborough University, Manchester University, Nottingham University, Sheffield University, Southampton University, University College London

CLASSICS, ANCIENT HISTORY, BYZANTINE AND MODERN GREEK STUDIES

Super league   Cambridge University, King's College London, Oxford University, University College London

First division   Birmingham University, Bristol University, Durham University, Edinburgh University, Exeter University, Glasgow University, Leeds University, Liverpool University, Manchester University, Newcastle University, Reading University, Royal Holloway, St Andrews University, Swansea University, Warwick University

CLINICAL LABORATORY SCIENCES
(eg pathology, microbiology, virology)

Super league   Oxford University

First division   Birmingham University, Bristol University, Cambridge University, Dundee University, Edinburgh University, Glasgow University, Imperial College, Royal Free, Southampton University, University College London, Wales College of Medicine

COMMUNICATION, CULTURAL AND MEDIA STUDIES

First division   Birmingham University, Bristol UWE, East Anglia University, East London University, Goldsmiths College, Stirling University, Sussex University, Warwick University, Westminster University

COMPUTER SCIENCE

Super league   Cambridge University, Glasgow University, Imperial College, Oxford University, Warwick University, York University

First division   Aberdeen University, Aberystwyth University, Aston University, Bath University, Belfast University, Birmingham University, Bristol University, Cardiff University, Dundee University, Durham University, East Anglia University, Edinburgh University, Essex University, Exeter University, Heriot-Watt University, Hertfordshire University, Kent University, Lancaster University, Leeds University, Loughborough University, Manchester University, Newcastle University, Nottingham University, Queen Mary & Westfield, Reading University, Royal Holloway, St Andrews University, Sheffield University, Southampton University, Sussex University, Swansea University, UMIST, University College London

DENTISTRY

Super league UMDS

First division Bristol University, King's College London, Leeds University, Manchester University, Queen Mary & Westfield, University College London

DRAMA, DANCE AND PERFORMING ARTS

Super league Royal Holloway

First division Birmingham University, Bristol University, Exeter University, Glasgow University, Goldsmiths College, Hull University, Kent University, Lancaster University, Manchester University, Reading University, Roehampton Institute, Surrey University, Warwick University

EARTH SCIENCES

Super league Cambridge University, Oxford University

First division Birkbeck College, Bristol University, Cardiff University, Durham University, Edinburgh University, Imperial College, Leeds University, Leicester University, Liverpool University, Manchester University, Newcastle University, Open University, Reading University, Royal Holloway, University College London

ECONOMICS AND ECONOMETRICS

Super league LSE, Oxford University, University College London

First division Aberdeen University, Birmingham University, Birkbeck College, Bristol University, Cambridge University, Dundee University, East Anglia University, Edinburgh University, Essex University, Exeter University, Glasgow University, Keele University, Kent University, Liverpool University, Loughborough University, Manchester University, Newcastle University, Nottingham University, Queen Mary & Westfield, Reading University, St Andrews University, Southampton University, Stirling University, Strathclyde University, Surrey University, Sussex University, Swansea University, Warwick University, York University

EDUCATION

Super league Institute of Education, King's College London

First division Aberdeen University, Bath University, Belfast University, Birmingham University, Bristol University, Cambridge University, Cardiff University, Durham University, East Anglia University, Edinburgh University, Exeter University, Goldsmiths College, Lancaster University, Leeds University, Manchester University, Newcastle University, Nottingham University, Open University, Oxford University, Sheffield University, Southampton University, Stirling University, Surrey University, Sussex University, Ulster University, Warwick University, York University

ELECTRICAL AND ELECTRONIC ENGINEERING

Super league Edinburgh University, Sheffield University, Southampton University, Surrey University, University College London

First division Aston University, Bath University, Belfast University, Birmingham University, Bristol University, Cardiff University, Essex University, Glasgow University, Heriot-Watt University, Imperial College, Kent University, King's College London, Liverpool University, Loughborough University, Newcastle University, Queen Mary & Westfield, Strathclyde University, Swansea University, UMIST, York University

ENGINEERING – GENERAL

Super league Cambridge University, Keele University, Oxford University

First division Aston University, Cranfield University, Dundee University, Durham University, Imperial College, Lancaster University, Leicester University, Liverpool John Moores University, Strathclyde University, Sussex University, Warwick University

ENGLISH LANGUAGE AND LITERATURE

Super league Cambridge University, Oxford University, University College London

First division Birmingham University, Birkbeck College, Bristol University, Cardiff University, Durham University, East Anglia University, Edinburgh University, Essex University, King's College London, Lancaster University, Leeds University, Leicester University, Liverpool University, Manchester University, Nottingham University, Queen Mary & Westfield, Reading University, Royal Holloway, St Andrews University, Sheffield University, Southampton University, Sussex University, Warwick University, York University

ENVIRONMENTAL SCIENCES

Super league East Anglia University, Reading University

First division Bangor University, Edinburgh University, Imperial College, Lancaster University, Southampton University

EUROPEAN STUDIES

Super league Birmingham University

First division Aston University, Bath University, Belfast University, Bradford University, Cardiff University, Glasgow University, Heriot-Watt University, Hull University, Loughborough University, Portsmouth University, Salford University, Strathclyde University, Surrey University

FOOD SCIENCE AND TECHNOLOGY

Super league Leeds University, Nottingham University

First division Belfast University, Heriot-Watt University, Reading University, Surrey University

FRENCH

Super league Cambridge University, Nottingham University, Oxford University, University College London

First division Aberdeen University, Belfast University, Birmingham University, Birkbeck College, Bristol University, Durham University, Edinburgh University, Exeter University, Glasgow University, Hull University, Keele University, King's College London, Leeds University, Leicester University, Liverpool University, Manchester University, Newcastle University, Queen Mary & Westfield, Reading University, Royal Holloway, St Andrews University, Sheffield University, Southampaton University, Stirling University, Sussex University, Warwick University

GEOGRAPHY

Super league Bristol University, Cambridge University, Durham University, Edinburgh University, University College London

First division Aberystwyth University, Birmingham University, East Anglia University, Exeter University, Hull University, Lancaster University, Leeds University, Liverpool University, LSE, Loughborough University, Manchester University, Newcastle University, Nottingham University, Open University, Oxford University, Queen Mary & Westfield, Royal Holloway, Sheffield University, Southampton University, Swansea University

GERMAN, DUTCH AND SCANDINAVIAN LANGUAGES

Super league   Cambridge University, Kings College London, Nottingham University, Oxford University

First division   Birmingham University, Birkbeck College, East Anglia University, Edinburgh University, Exeter University, Lancaster University, Leicester University, Liverpool University, Manchester University, Queen Mary & Westfield, St Andrews University, Sheffield University, Southampton University, Sussex University, Swansea University, University College London, Warwick University

HISTORY

Super league   Cambridge University, King's College London, LSE, Oxford University, SOAS, University College London, Warwick University

First division   Aberystwyth University, Belfast University, Birmingham University, Birkbeck College, Bristol University, Cardiff University, Durham University, East Anglia University, Edinburgh University, Essex University, Exeter University, Glasgow University, Goldsmiths College, Hull University, Imperial College, Keele University, Kent University, Lancaster University, Leeds University, Leicester University, Liverpool University, London Guildhall University, Manchester University, Newcastle University, Nottingham University, Open University, Oxford Brookes University, Queen Mary & Westfield, Reading University, Royal Holloway, St Andrews University, Sheffield University, Sheffield Hallam University, Southampton University, SSEES, Stirling University, Strathclyde University, Sussex University, Ulster University, York University

HISTORY OF ART, ARCHITECTURE AND DESIGN

Super league   Cambridge University, Courtauld Institute, Sussex University

First division   Birkbeck College, East Anglia University, Edinburgh University, Essex University, Kent University, Leeds University, Manchester University, Newcastle University, Open University, Oxford Brookes University, Reading University, Royal College of Art, St Andrews University, SOAS, Southampton Institute, University College London, Warwick University

IBERIAN AND LATIN AMERICAN LANGUAGES

Super league Cambridge University

First division Aberdeen University, Aberystwyth University, Belfast University, Birmingham University, Birkbeck College, Bristol University, Exeter University, Hull University, Kings College London, Leeds University, Liverpool University, Manchester University, Nottingham University, Oxford University, Queen Mary & Westfield, Sheffield University, Southampton University, Swansea University, University College London

ITALIAN

Super league Cambridge University, Leeds University, University College London

First division Lancaster University, Oxford University, Reading University, Royal Holloway, Sussex University, Westminster University

LAW

Super league Cambridge University, Oxford University

First division Aberdeen University, Birmingham University, Birkbeck College, Bristol University, Brunel University, Cardiff University, Dundee University, Durham University, Edinburgh University, Essex University, Glasgow University, Keele University, Kent University, Kings College London, Leeds University, Leicester University, Manchester University, Nottingham University, Queen Mary & Westfield, Sheffield University, Southampton University, Strathclyde University, University College London, Warwick University

LINGUISTICS

First division Cambridge University, Edinburgh University, Essex University, Lancaster University, Manchester University, Newcastle University, Oxford University, Queen Mary & Westfield, SOAS, Thames Valley University, University College London, York University

LIBRARY AND INFORMATION MANAGEMENT

Super league City University, Sheffield University

First division Loughborough University, Salford University, Strathclyde University

MATHEMATICS – PURE

Super league   Imperial College, Oxford University, Warwick University

First division   Bath University, Birmingham University, Bristol University, Cambridge University, Cardiff University, Durham University, East Anglia University, Edinburgh University, Glasgow University, Hull University, Kings College London, Lancaster University, Leeds University, Liverpool University, Manchester University, Nottingham University, Queen Mary & Westfield, Royal Holloway, St Andrews University, Sussex University, Swansea University, UMIST, University College London, York University

MATHEMATICS – APPLIED

Super league   Cambridge University, Oxford University

First division   Aberystwyth University, Bath University, Birmingham University, Bristol University, Brunel University, Dundee University, Durham University, East Anglia University, Edinburgh University, Exeter University, Glasgow University, Heriot-Watt University, Imperial College, Keele University, Kings College London, Leeds University, Liverpool University, Loughborough University, Manchester University, Newcastle University, Notttingham University, Queen Mary & Westfield, St Andrews University, Sheffield University, Southampton University, Strathclyde University, Sussex University, UMIST, University College London

MECHANICAL, AERONAUTIC AND MANUFACTURING ENGINEERING

Super league   Bath University, Belfast University, Imperial College, Kings College London, Leeds University

First division   Bradford University, Bristol University, Brunel University, Cardiff University, Cranfield University, Glasgow University, Liverpool University, Loughborough University, Manchester University, Nottingham University, Queen Mary & Westfield, Sheffield University, Southampton University, Strathclyde University, Swansea University, UMIST, University College London

MEDICINE

Super league   Cambridge University, Oxford University, Imperial College, King's College London, University College London

First division   Birmingham University, Edinburgh University, Glasgow University, Manchester University, Queen Mary & Westfield, Royal Free, St George's, Sheffield University, Southampton University, UMDS, Wales College of Medicine

METALLURGY AND MATERIALS

Super league Birmingham University, Cambridge University, Liverpool University, Manchester University, Oxford University, Sheffield University, Swansea University, UMIST

First division Bath University, Brunel University, Imperial College, Leeds University, Loughborough University, Nottingham University, Queen Mary & Westfield, Surrey University

MIDDLE EASTERN AND AFRICAN STUDIES

Super league Birmingham University

First division Cambridge University, Durham University, Edinburgh University, Manchester University, Oxford University, SOAS, University College London

MINERAL AND MINING ENGINEERING

Super league Heriot-Watt University

First division Exeter University (incl Camborne School of Mines), Imperial College, Leeds University, Nottingham University

MUSIC

Super league Kings College London, Liverpool University, Manchester University, Oxford University, Royal Holloway, SOAS

First division Belfast University, Birmingham University, Bristol University, Cambridge University, Cardiff University, City University, De Montfort University, Durham University, Edinburgh University, Exeter University, Goldsmiths College, Huddersfield University, Hull University, Keele University, Lancaster University, Leeds University, Nottingham University, Open University, Reading University, Royal Academy of Music, Royal College of Music, Royal Northern College of Music, Sheffield University, Southampton University, Surrey University, Sussex University, York University

NURSING
(including midwifery)

First division King's College London, Manchester University, Surrey University

PHARMACOLOGY

Super league Leicester University, Royal Free, University College London

First division Bristol University, Cambridge University, Dundee University, Edinburgh University, Liverpool University, Nottingham University, Oxford University, Queen Mary & Westfield

PHARMACY

Super league Nottingham University

First division Bath University, Cardiff University, King's College London, Manchester University, School of Pharmacy, Strathclyde University

PHILOSOPHY

Super league Cambridge University, Oxford University

First division Birmingham University, Birkbeck College, Bradford University, Bristol University, Durham University, Essex University, Hull University, King's College London, Leeds University, LSE, Reading University, St Andrews University, Sheffield University, Stirling University, Sussex University, University College London

PHYSICS

Super league Cambridge University, Oxford University

First division Aberystwyth University, Bath University, Belfast University, Birmingham University, Bristol University, Cardiff University, Durham University, East Anglia University, Edinburgh University, Essex University, Exeter University, Glasgow University, Heriot-Watt University, Hertfordshire University, Imperial University, King's College London, Leeds University, Leicester University, Liverpool University, Liverpool John Moores University, Manchester University, Newcastle University, Nottingham University, Queen Mary & Westfield, Reading University, Royal Holloway, St Andrews University, Sheffield University, Southampton University, Strathclyde University, Surrey University, Swansea University, UMIST, University College London, Warwick University, York University

PHYSIOLOGY

Super league Liverpool University

First division Birmingham University, Bristol University, Cambridge University, Royal Free, Newcastle University, Oxford University, University College London

POLITICS AND INTERNATIONAL STUDIES

Super league Essex University, King's College London, LSE, Oxford University

First division Aberdeen University, Aberystwyth University, Belfast University, Birkbeck College, Bradford University, Bristol University, Edinburgh University, Exeter University, Glasgow University, Hull University, Keele University, Leicester University, Manchester University, Newcastle University, Queen Mary & Westfield, Sheffield University, Southampton University, SSEES, Strathclyde University, Sussex University, Swansea University, York University

PROFESSIONS ALLIED TO MEDICINE (including biomedical sciences, optometry)

Super league Southampton University, Strathclyde University, Ulster University

First division Aston University, Bradford University, Cardiff University, Glasgow University, Greenwich University, King's College London, Loughborough University, Napier University, Portsmouth University, Sheffield Hallam University, Surrey University, UMIST

PSYCHOLOGY

Super league Cambridge University, Oxford University, St Andrews University, York University

First division Aberdeen University, Bangor University, Birmingham University, Birkbeck College, Bristol University, Cardiff University, City University, Dundee University, Durham University, Essex University, Exeter University, Glasgow University, Goldsmiths College, Lancaster University, Leeds University, Manchester University, Newcastle University, Nottingham University, Reading University, Royal Holloway, Sheffield University, Stirling University, Surrey University, Swansea University, University College London, Warwick University

RUSSIAN, SLAVONIC AND EAST EUROPEAN LANGUAGES

Super league   Nottingham University, Queen Mary & Westfield

First division   Bangor University, Bristol University, Cambridge University, Keele University, Leeds University, Oxford University, Portsmouth University, St Andrews University, Sheffield University, SSEES, Swansea University

SOCIAL POLICY AND ADMINISTRATION

Super league   LSE

First division   Bangor University, Bath University, Birmingham University, Bristol University, Brunel University, Edinburgh University, Glasgow University, Hull University, Keele University, Kent University, Manchester University, Middlesex University, Open University, Sheffield University, South Bank University, Ulster University, York University

SOCIAL WORK

Super league   Stirling University

First division   Bristol University, East Anglia University, Edinburgh University, Huddersfield University, Keele University, Lancaster University, Leicester University, Swansea University, Warwick University, York University

SOCIOLOGY

Super league   Essex University, Lancaster University

First division   Belfast University, Brunel University, Cambridge University, Cardiff University, City University, Edinburgh University, Glasgow University, Goldsmiths College, Leeds University, Leicester University, LSE, Loughborough University, Manchester University, North London University, Open University, Oxford University, Salford University, Southampton University, Surrey University, Sussex University, Warwick University, York University

SPORT-RELATED SUBJECTS

First division   Bangor University, Birmingham University, Glasgow University, Liverpool John Moores University, Loughborough University, Manchester Metropolitan University

STATISTICS AND OPERATIONAL RESEARCH

Super league Cambridge University

First division Bath University, Birmingham University, Bristol University, Brunel University, Edinburgh University, Glasgow University, Imperial College, Kent University, Lancaster University, LSE, Newcastle University, Nottingham University, Open University, Queen Mary & Westfield, St Andrews University, Salford University, Sheffield University, Southampton University, Strathclyde University, Surrey University, University College London, Warwick University

THEOLOGY, DIVINITY AND RELIGIOUS STUDIES

Super league Lancaster University, Manchester University, Sheffield University

First division Aberdeen University, Bath University, Birmingham University, Bristol University, Cambridge University, Cardiff University, Durham University, Edinburgh University, Glasgow University, Goldsmiths College, Hull University, King's College London, Lampeter University, Leeds University, Nottingham University, Oxford University, Roehampton Institute, St Andrews University, SOAS

TOWN AND COUNTRY PLANNING

Super league Cardiff University, Glasgow University, Leeds University

First division Aberdeen University, Cheltenham & Gloucester College, Liverpool University, Loughborough University, Newcastle University, Reading University, Sheffield University

VETERINARY SCIENCE

First division Bristol University, Cambridge University, Edinburgh University, Glasgow University, Liverpool University, Royal Veterinary College

INDEX